# Avoiding the Terrorist Trap

Why Respect for Human Rights
is the Key to Defeating Terrorism

# Insurgency and Terrorism Series

(Print)   ISSN: 2399-7443
(Online)  ISSN: 2399-7451

(*formerly known as Imperial College Press Insurgency and Terrorism Series —* ISSN: 2335-6847)

**Series Editor:** Rohan Gunaratna *(Nanyang Technological University, Singapore)*

Terrorism and insurgency present a tier-one threat to the national security of governments and societies. New threats are always emerging, either due to strategic shifts in policies that give rise to new opportunities for insurgents to rear their heads, or due to changes in the political climates of societies. For example, the withdrawal of U.S.-led forces from Iraq and Afghanistan and the strategic defeat of the West in the Middle Eastern and Asian campaigns have emboldened threat groups worldwide. The U.S. withdrawal will recreate the conditions in Afghanistan for the return of al Qaeda, the Taliban and their associated groups. Will this threat spread to India and China, the emerging superpowers?

While the Arab Spring seems to have marginalized al-Qaeda and their associated groups, their infiltrators and ideologies are challenging the emergence of a stable Middle East. From this turmoil, a new epicentre of terrorism and insurgency is emerging in Africa. Ideological extremism and its vicious by-products of terrorism and insurgency will threaten the world in the foreseeable future. These recent regional and functional developments have renewed our interest in the study of terrorism and insurgency.

This series on Insurgency and Terrorism delineates extant and emerging threats and identifies governmental and societal responses. It focuses on threats and challenges confronting our globalizing world, informing policy and academic communities.

*Published*

Vol. 12   *Avoiding the Terrorist Trap: Why Respect for Human Rights is the Key to Defeating Terrorism*
by Tom Parker

Vol. 11   *Understanding the Lord's Resistance Army Insurgency*
by Adam Dolnik and Herman Butime

*Forthcoming*

*The Rohingya Crisis*
by Rohan Gunaratna, Jolene Jerard and Iftekharul Bashar

For the complete list of titles in this series, please visit
http://www.worldscientific.com/series/icpits

*(Continued at the end of the book)*

Insurgency & Terrorism Series

Volume

12

# Avoiding the Terrorist Trap

## Why Respect for Human Rights is the Key to Defeating Terrorism

Tom Parker

**World Scientific**

NEW JERSEY · LONDON · SINGAPORE · BEIJING · SHANGHAI · HONG KONG · TAIPEI · CHENNAI · TOKYO

*Published by*

World Scientific Publishing Europe Ltd.

57 Shelton Street, Covent Garden, London WC2H 9HE

*Head office:* 5 Toh Tuck Link, Singapore 596224

*USA office:* 27 Warren Street, Suite 401-402, Hackensack, NJ 07601

**Library of Congress Cataloging-in-Publication Data**

Names: Parker, Tom, 1968–   author.

Title: Avoiding the terrorist trap : why respect for human rights is the key to defeating terrorism /
    Tom Parker (United Nations Counter Terrorism Implementation Task Force (CTITF)).

Description: New Jersey : World Scientific, [2018] |
    Series: Insurgency and terrorism series ; volume 12

Identifiers: LCCN 2017060416 | ISBN 9781783266548 (hc : alk. paper)

Subjects: LCSH: Terrorism--Prevention. | Human rights.

Classification: LCC HV6431 .P3635 2018 | DDC 363.325/17--dc23

LC record available at https://lccn.loc.gov/2017060416

**British Library Cataloguing-in-Publication Data**

A catalogue record for this book is available from the British Library.

For any available supplementary material, please visit
http://www.worldscientific.com/worldscibooks/10.1142/P995#t=suppl

Desk Editors: Dipasri Sardar/Jennifer Brough/Shi Ying Koe

Typeset by Stallion Press
Email: enquiries@stallionpress.com

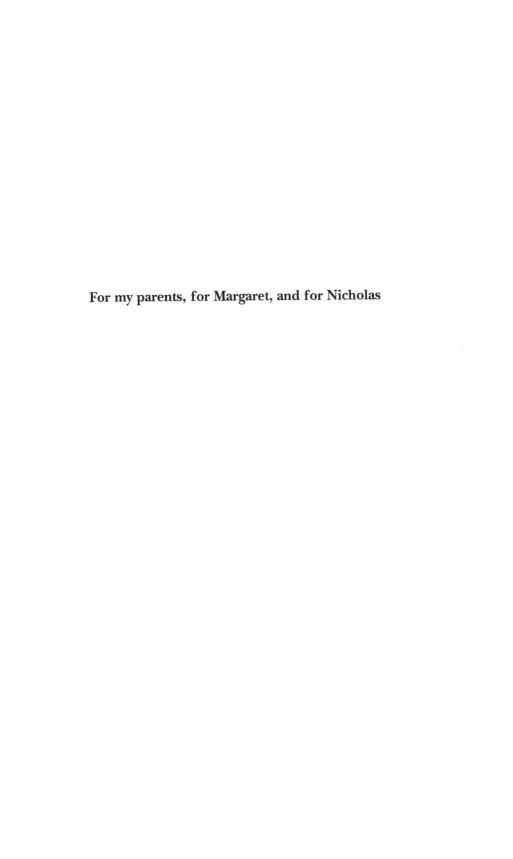

For my parents, for Margaret, and for Nicholas

# About the Author

*Credit:* Amy Stern
Photography

**Tom Parker** has spent the past three years as a European Union-sponsored adviser to the Office of the National Security Adviser (ONSA) in Baghdad, Iraq, prior to which he served as a Counter-Terrorism Strategist at the United Nations Counter-Terrorism Centre (UNCCT) and as the Adviser on Human Rights and Counter-Terrorism to the United Nations Counter-Terrorism Implementation Task Force (CTITF), where he co-authored the Secretary-General's Plan of Action to Prevent Violent Extremism. Over the past decade Tom has worked extensively as a consultant on post-conflict justice, security sector reform, and counter-terrorism projects around the world, including assignments in Chad, Colombia, Georgia, Guatemala, Kyrgyzstan, Lebanon, Mexico, Nepal, Peru, Rwanda, Sri Lanka, Tajikistan, Thailand, Uganda and Ukraine. He has also served as the Policy Director for Terrorism, Counter-terrorism and Human Rights for Amnesty International USA, as the Special Adviser on Transitional Justice to the Coalition Provisional Authority, as a war crimes investigator with the International Criminal Tribunal for the former Yugoslavia (ICTY) in both Bosnia and Kosovo, and as an Intelligence Officer in the British Security Service (MI5).

Tom has taught courses on international terrorism as an adjunct professor at Bard College, the National Defense University at Fort Bragg, Yale University, and John Jay College of Criminal Justice. He is also a member of the adjunct faculty of the Defense Institute for International Legal Studies (DIILS) and has been an occasional lecturer at the Joint Special Operations University (JSOU). He is a graduate of the London School of Economics, the University of Leiden, and Brown, and has held research fellowships at Yale and Duke universities.

# Acknowledgments

I would particularly like to thank a number of colleagues without whom this book would never have been written: Philip Heymann and Juliette Kayyem at Harvard Law School and the Belfer Center for Science and International Affairs who launched me on this path way back in 2003 by inviting me to participate in their ground-breaking Long-Term Legal Strategy Project for Preserving Security and Democratic Norms in the War on Terrorism; Ted Bromund, Minh Luong and International Security Studies at Yale who offered me a fellowship to start researching this subject; Dr. Alex Schmid, a trailblazer for so many of us in this field, who first pressed me to write about this topic for his journal *Perspectives on Terrorism*; Professor Jim Morone of the Political Science Department at Brown who never stopped believing in me, although I gave him every reason to; Rohan Gunaratna of the International Centre for Political Violence and Terrorism Research in Singapore who pitched me the idea of writing this book and found a publishing house for the project; Richard Barrett, Peter Bergen, Richard English, Mike German, John Horgan, Peter Neumann, Gary Schmitt, and Patricia Steinhoff for their inspirational support and advice; Professor Nick Sitter at the Central European University who has been my friend, occasional writing partner, and sounding-board since we first met during Fresher's Week at the London School of Economics, more years ago than I care to remember; Geneve Mantri, my onetime partner-in-advocacy at Amnesty International USA, whose unflagging encouragement ultimately gave me the confidence to believe that writing this book was even possible; Mr. Jehangir Khan, Director of the UN Counter-Terrorism

Implementation Task Force, who has been my public policy mentor; and finally, Jonny Cristol, Mia McCully, Rachel Meyer, Stephanie Szitanyi, Anna Seidner, and the students of the Bard Globalization International Affairs program (especially Lysan Boshuijzen, Anya Degtyarenko, Tareian King, Evie McCorkle, Winta Mehari, Srilekha Murthy, Stephanie Presch, Zoe Rohrich and Omurkan Sabyrzhan) who have hunted down articles, provided feedback, and occasionally pushback, for so many aspects of this book. That said, despite their generous encouragement and support, none of the above should be considered in any way responsible for any errors of fact or judgment that have crept into the final text — these are entirely my own.

Tom Parker
Baghdad, 2018

# Contents

# Glossary of Organizations

*Ação Libertadora Nacional* (ALN) — National Liberation Action, Brazil

*Action Directe* (AD) — Direct Action, France

*Action Française* (AF) — French Action, France

*Ad-Dawlah al-Islāmiyah fī 'l-ʿIrāq wa-sh-Shām* (ISIL) — Islamic State of Iraq and the Levant, Syria and Iraq

African Union Mission to Somalia (AMISOM), Somalia

*Afwaj al-Muqawama al-Lubnaniyya (Amal)* — Lebanese Resistance Regiments, Lebanon

*Ansar al-Jihad* — Defenders of the Jihad, Egypt

*Antiimperialistische Zelle* (AIZ) — Anti-Imperialist Cell, Germany

*Asbat al-Ansar* — League of the Partisans, Lebanon

*Ashbal al-Khilafah* — Cubs of the Caliphate, Iraq and Syria

Association of Chief Police Officers (ACPO), United Kingdom

*Aum Shinrikyo,* Japan

*Bagong Hukbong Bayan* (NPA) — New People's Army, Philippines

*Berit Trumpeldor* (BETAR) — Trumpeldor Alliance, British Mandate of Palestine

*Bewegung 2. Juni* — Movement 2nd June, West Germany

*Bráithreachas Phoblacht na hÉireann* (IRB) — Irish Republican Brotherhood, United Kingdom

*Brigate Comuniste* — Communist Brigades, Italy

*Brigate Rosse* (BR) — Red Brigades, Italy

*Brit Hashmonaim* — The Alliance of the Hasmonean, British Mandate of Palestine

*Bundeskriminalamt* (BKA) — Federal Criminal Investigation Office, Germany

Canadian Security and Intelligence Service (CSIS), Canada

*Cellules Communistes Combattantes* (CCC) — Communist Combatant Cells, Belgium

Central Intelligence Agency (CIA), United States

*Centro Superior de Información de la Defensa* (CESID) — Superior Center for Defense Information, Spain

*Chernoe znamia* — Black Banner, Russia

*Clan na Gael* — Family of the Gaels, United States

*Coiste na n-Iarchimí* — Ex-Prisoners Association, United Kingdom

*Collettivo Politico Metropolitano* (CPM) — Metropolitan Political Collective, Italy

Combat 18 (C18), United Kingdom

*Conseil National de la Résistance* (CNR) — Council of National Resistance, France

*Coordinadora Gesto por la Paz de Euskal Herria* (Gesto) — Co-ordination for a Gesture for Peace in the Basque Country, Spain

*Corriente de Renovación Socialista* (CRS) — Current of Socialist Renovation, Colombia

*Cumann na mBan* — Irish Women's Council, Ireland

*Detasemen Khusus 88* (Densus 88) — Special Detachment 88, Indonesia

*Devrimci Halk Kurtuluş Partisi-Cephesi* (DHKP-C) — Revolutionary People's Liberation Party-Front, Turkey

*Direction de la surveillance du territoire* (DST) — Directorate of Territorial Surveillance, France

*Ejército de Liberación Nacional* (ELN) — Army of National Liberation, Colombia

*Ejército Popular de Liberación* (EPL) — Popular Liberation Army, Colombia

*Ejército Revolucionario del Pueblo* (ERP) — People's Revolutionary Army, Argentina

*Epanastatikos Agonas* (EA) — Revolutionary Struggle, Greece

*Epanastatikos Laikos Agonas* (ELA) — Revolutionary Popular Struggle, Greece

*Ertzaintza* — People's Guard, Spain

*Ethniki Organosis Kyprion Agoniston* (EOKA) — National Organization of Cypriot Fighters, Cyprus

*Euskadi Ta Askatasuna* (ETA) — Basque Homeland and Freedom, Spain

*Fadaiyan-e-Khalq* — Organization of the People's Fedayeen Guerillas, Iran

*al-Fasael al-Musallaha al-Thawriyya al-Lubnaniyya* (LARF) — Lebanese Armed Revolutionary Factions, Lebanon

*Fatah* — Conquest, Palestinian diaspora

*Fatah al-Islam* — Conquest of Islam, Lebanon

Federal Bureau of Investigation (FBI), United States

*Frente Farabundo Marti para la Liberación Nacional* (FMLN) — Farabundo Martí National Liberation Front, El Salvador

*Front de Libération du Québec* (FLQ) — Quebec Liberation Front, Canada

*Front de Libération Nationale* (FLN) — National Liberation Front, Algeria

*Front Islamique du Salut* (FIS) — Islamic Salvation Front, Algeria

*Fuerzas Armadas Revolucionarias de Colombia — Ejército del Pueblo* (FARC-EP)-Revolutionary Armed Forces of Colombia — People's Army, Colombia

*al-Gama'a al-Islamiyya* (GI) — Islamic Group, Egypt

*Geheime Staatspolizei* (Gestapo) — Secret State Police, Germany

*Glavnoye razvedyvatel'noye upravleniye* (GRU) — Main Intelligence Directorate, Russia

*Grenzschutzgruppe 9* (GSG9) — Border Protection Group 9, Germany

*Groupe d'intervention de la Gendarmerie nationale* (GIGN) — National Gendarmerie Intervention Group, France

*Groupe Islamique Armé* (GIA) — Armed Islamic Group, Algeria

*Grupo Colina* — Colina Group, Peru

*Grupos Antiterroristas de Liberación* (GAL) — Anti-terrorist Liberation Group, Spain

*Gruppi di Azione Partigiani* (GAP) — Partisan Action Groups, Italy

*Guardia Civil* — Civil Guard, Spain

*Haganah* — The Defense, British Mandate of Palestine

*HaMakhteret HaYehudit* (*Makhteret*) — Jewish Underground, Israel

*HaMossad leModi'in uleTafkidim Meyuhadim* (*Mossad*) — Institute for Intelligence and Special Operations, Israel *al-Haraka Salafiya* — The Salafi Movement, Spain

*Harakat al-Jihād al-Islāmi fi Filastīn* (PIJ) — Palestinian Islamic Jihad, Palestinian National Authority

*Harakat al-Muqawama al-Islamiyya* (*Hamas*) — Islamic Resistance Movement, Palestinian National Authority

*Harakat ash-Shabāb al-Mujāhidīn* (*al-Shabaab*) — Movement of Striving Youth, Somalia

*Harakat-ul-Jihad al-Islami* (HuJI) — Islamic Jihad Movement, South East Asia

*Harkat ul-Mujahideen* (HuM) — Movement of the Holy Warriors, Pakistan

*Hayasdani Azadakrut'ean Hay Kaghtni Panag* (ASALA) — Armenian Secret Army for the Liberation of Armenia, Turkey and Lebanon

*Herri Batasuna* (HB) — Popular Unity, Spain

*Hezbollah* — Party of God, Lebanon

*Hizb al-Dawa* — Islamic Call Party, Iraq

*Hizb al-Tahrir al-Islami* — Party of Islamic Liberation, pan-national

*Hizb-i Islami* — Islamic Party, Afghanistan

*Hukbong Bayan Laban sa mga Hapones* (*Hukbalahap* or *Huk*) — The Nation's Army Against the Japanese Soldiers, Philippines

International Security Assistance Force (ISAF), Afghanistan

*Irgun Zvai Leumi* (*Irgun*) — National Military Organization, British Mandate of Palestine

*Ittihād al-mahākim al-islāmiyya* (ICU) — Islamic Courts Union, Somalia

*al-Jabhah al-Islamiyya li-l-Inqadh* (FIS) — Islamic Salvation Front, Algeria

*al-Jabhah al-Sha`biyyah li-Taḥrīr Filasṭīn* (PFLP) — Popular Front for the Liberation of Palestine, Palestinian diaspora

*Jabhat al-Nusra li Ahl al-Sham* (JN) — The Support Front for the People of Al-Sham, Syria

*Jabhat Taḥrīr Moro al-ʿIslāmiyyah* (MILF) — Moro Islamic Liberation Front, Philippines

*Jamaʾat Ahl as-Sunnah lid-Daʾwah waʾl-Jihad* (*Boko Haram*) — Group of the People of Sunnah for Preaching and Jihad, Nigeria

*Jamaat Islamiyya* — Islamic Groups, Egypt

*Jamiʾah al-Ikhwān al-Muslimūn* (MB) — Society of the Muslim Brothers (more popularly known as the Muslim Brotherhood), Egypt

*Jammat al-Muslimin* — Society of Muslims, Egypt

*Janatha Vimukthi Peramuna* (JVP) — The People's Liberation Front, Sri Lanka

*Jemaah Islamiyah* (JI) — Islamic Congregation, South East Asia (especially Indonesia and Malaysia)

*Jihaz al-Mukhabarat al-Amma* (DGI) — Directorate of General Intelligence, Iraq

*al-Jihaz al-Sirri* — the Secret Apparatus, Egypt

Ku Klux Klan (KKK), United States

*Kyōsanshugisha Dōmei Sekigunha* — Communist League Red Army Faction, Japan

*Lashkar-e-Tayiba* (LeT) — Army of the Righteous, Pakistan

*Lohamei Herut Israel* (LEHI) — Fighters for the Freedom of Israel, British Mandate of Palestine

*Lotta Continua* (LC) — Ongoing Struggle, Italy

*Mojahedin-e-Khalq* (MEK) — People's Mujahedin, Iran

*Mouvement national algérien* (MNA) — National Algerian Movement, Algeria

*Mouvement pour le Triomphe des Libertés Démocratiques* (MTLD) — Movement for the Triumph of Democratic Liberties, Algeria

*Movimento Comunista Rivoluzionario* (MCR) — Revolutionary Communist Movement, Italy

*Movimiento 19 de Abril* (M-19) — Movement of the 19th April, Colombia

*Movimiento de Liberación Nacional — Tupamaros* (MLN-T) — National Liberation Movement — Tupamaros, Uruguay

*Movimiento Peronista Montonero* (MPM) — Montoneros, Argentina

*Movimento Revolucionário 8 de Outubro* (MR8) — Revolutionary Movement of the 8th October, Brazil

*Movimiento Revolucionario Túpac Amaru* (MRTA) — Tupac Amaru Revolutionary Movement, Peru

*Movimiento Todos por la Patria* (MTP) — All for the Fatherland Movement, Argentina

*al-Muhajiroun* — The Immigrants, United Kingdom

*Munazzamat Aylūl al-aswad* — Black September Organization, Palestinian diaspora

Muslim Janbat Force (MJF), Kashmir

*Narodnaya Rasprava* (NR) — People's Justice, Russia

*Narodnaya Volya* (NV) — People's Will, Russia

National Consortium for the Study of Terrorism and Responses to Terrorism (START), United States

National Security Agency (NSA), United States

*Nationalsozialistischer Untergrund* (NSU) — National Socialist Underground, Germany

New York Police Department (NYPD), United States

*Nihon Kyōsantō Kakumei Saha* (*Kakusa*) — Japan Communist Party Revolutionary Left Wing, Japan

*Nihon Sekigun* (NS) — Japanese Red Army, Lebanon

Official Irish Republican Army (OIRA), United Kingdom and Republic of Ireland

*Okhrannoye otdelenie* (Okhrana) — Department for Protecting the Public Security and Order, Russia

*Ordine Nuovo* (ON) — New Order, Italy

*Organisation de l'armée secrète* (OAS) — Organization of the Secret Army, France

Organization for Security and Cooperation in Europe (OSCE)

*Orthodoxos Christianiki Enosis Neon* (OHEN) — Union of Greek Orthodox Youth, Cyprus

*Otdeleniye po Okhraneniyu Obshchestvennoy Bezopasnosti i Poryadka* (Okhrana) — The Department for the Protection of Public Security and Order, Russia

*Panagrotiki Enosis Kyprou* (PEK) — Pan-Agrarian Union of Cyprus, Cyprus

*Pankyprios Ethniki Organosis Neolaisas* (PEON) — Pan-Cyprian National Youth Organization, Cyprus

*Partido Socialista Popular* (PSP) — Popular Socialist Party, Cuba

*Partiya Karkerên Kurdistan* (PKK) — Kurdistan Workers' Party, Turkey

*Politiets Efterretningstjeneste* (PET) — Security and Intelligence Service, Denmark

*Politiki Epitropi Kypriakou Agonos* (PEKA) — Political Committee of the Cyprus Struggle, Cyprus

Popular Front for the Liberation of Palestine — External Operations (PFLP-EO), Palestinian diaspora

Popular Front for the Liberation of Palestine — General Command (PFLP-GC), Palestinian diaspora

*Potere Operaio* (PO) — Workers' Power, Italy

*Prima Linea* (PL) — Front Line, Italy

Provisional Irish Republican Army (PIRA), United Kingdom and Republic of Ireland

*al-Qaeda* — The Foundation, Afghanistan and Pakistan

*al-Qaeda* in the Arabian Peninsula (AQAP), Saudi Arabia and Yemen

Real Irish Republican Army (RIRA), United Kingdom and Republic of Ireland

*Rengō Sekigun* (RS) — United Red Army, Japan

*Revolutionäre Zellen* (RZ) — Revolutionary Cells, West Germany

Revolutionary United Front (RUF), Sierra Leone

*Rossiyskaya Sotsial-Demokraticheskaya Rabochaya Partiya* (RSDWP) — Russian Social-Democratic Workers' Party, Russia

*Rote Armee Fraktion* (RAF) — Red Army Faction, West Germany

Royal Air Force (RAF), United Kingdom

Royal Canadian Mounted Police (RCMP), Canada

*Sayeret Matkal* — General Staff Reconnaissance Unit, Israel

Secret Intelligence Service (SIS), United Kingdom

Security Service (MI5), United Kingdom

*Sekigun* — Red Army, Japan

*Sendero Luminoso* (SL) — Shining Path, Peru

*Sendero Rojo* (SR) — Red Path, Peru

*Šerut ha-Bitaḫon haKlali* (Shin Bet) — General Security Service, Israel

*Servizio Informazioni Difesa* (SID) — Defense Intelligence Service, Italy

*Servizio per le Informazioni e la Sicurezza Militare* (SISMI) — Military Intelligence and Security Service, Italy

*Shayetet 13* — Flotilla 13, Israel

*Sinn Féin* — We Ourselves, United Kingdom and Republic of Ireland

*Soiuz sotsialistov-revoliutsionerov maksimalistov* (Maximalists) — Union of Maximalist Socialist-Revolutionaries, Russia

*Sotsialisty Revolyutsionery — Boyevaya Organizatsiya* (SR-CO) — Socialist Revolutionaries — Combat Organization, Russia

*Sozialistisches Patientenkollektiv* (SPK) — The Socialist Patients' Collective, West Germany

Special Air Service (SAS) — United Kingdom

*Spetsnaz* — Special Purpose Forces, Russia

Stern Gang (subsequently LEHI), British Mandate of Palestine

Symbionese Liberation Army (SLA), United States

*Synomosía Pyrínon Tis Fotiás* (SPF) — Conspiracy of the Cells of Fire, Greece

*al-Tali'ah al-Muqatilah* — The Combatant Vanguard, Syria

*Taliban* — The Students, Afghanistan

*Tamilīla viṭutalaip pulikaḻ* (LTTE) — Liberation Tigers of Tamil Eelam, Sri Lanka

*Tanzim al-Jihad* (EIJ) — Egyptian Islamic Jihad, Egypt

*Tanzim Qaidat al-Jihad fi Bilad al-Rafidayn* (AQI) — al-Qaeda in Iraq, Iraq

*Tehrik-i-Taliban Pakistan* (TTP) — Taliban Movement of Pakistan, Pakistan

The Covenant, the Sword, and the Arm of the Lord (CSA), United States

Transportation Security Administration (TSA), United States

*Tsva ha-Hagana le-Yisra'el* (IDF) — Israeli Defense Forces, Israel

Ulster Volunteer Force (UVF), United Kingdom

*Umkhonto we Sizwe* (MK) — Spear of the Nation, South Africa

*Union Française Nord-Africaine* — French Union of North Africa, Algeria

*Vatreshna Makedonska Revolyutsionna Organizatsiya* (IMRO) — Internal Macedonian Revolutionary Organization, Bulgaria

*Vezarat-e Ettela'at va Amniat-e Keshvar* (MOIS) — Ministry of Intelligence and Security, Iran

Weathermen, United States

*Zemlya i Volya* — Land and Freedom, Russia

*Zentralrat der umherschweifenden Haschrebellen* — Central Council of Rambling Hash Rebels, West Germany

"Terrorism is a psychological weapon, even though it uses physical means. It stops you from claiming the world as your own. It stops you from relating to other people. It creates fear and hatred. The only way to fight terrorists, as a citizen, is to deny them those emotions. That is the only thing terrorists don't expect. Everything else they expect: retaliation, bombing, attacks. All of that is exactly what they want. Deny them fear, and they lose."

Mariane Pearl

"We will never give up on our values. Our answer is more democracy, more openness and more humanity."

Jens Stoltenberg

# Introduction

"The Ogre does what ogres can."[1]

This is a book about terrorism and human rights. Or, more specifically, it is a book about why human rights matter fundamentally in the fight against terrorism. So, let me start by stating very plainly that I had only one motive in mind as I embarked on this project — and it is probably not the motive you suspect — I want to see terrorism defeated. I spent six years as an officer in the British Security Service (MI5), I have been blown up twice in attacks by armed groups, once in London and once in Baghdad, and I have spent countless hours taking statements from victims of politically-motivated violence. I understand better than most the seriousness of the threat posed by terrorism, and its human cost. So, please understand in turn that this is not so much a book about the importance of human rights, as it is a book about defeating, or at least containing, terrorism.

Terrorism is a modern phenomenon. Certainly, there are examples of small clandestine groups that have used violence for political ends dating back centuries, even millennia. Typically, in this context, reference is made to such groups as the *Sicarii*, the ancient Jewish "dagger-men" who murdered Roman administrators in occupied biblical Judea, or the Order of the Assassins established by Hassan-i Sabbah in the eleventh century to strike against both Muslim political rivals and the incursions of Crusader warlords into Muslim

---

[1] W. H. Auden, *August 1968.*

1

lands.[2] But these organizations and others like them did not carry out acts of terror against the wider public in the manner we typically ascribe to terrorist groups today. Similarly, attempts to tease relevance out of the etymology of the word "terrorism" in the Great Terror of the French Revolution are equally forced.

It is practically axiomatic that terrorism eludes precise definition — or at least a definition that can attract universal acceptance. However, the reality is, like great art or pornography, individually we all feel that we know terrorism when we see it — although we don't always see it from the same perspective — and analogues such as the *Sicarii*, the Assassins, or the French Revolution's Committee of Public Safety don't measure up.

Most analysts agree that terrorists share certain characteristics.[3] They tend to act clandestinely and with a political purpose. Attacks are conceived and designed in such a way as to advance this political purpose. This distinguishes them from what British counter-terrorism officials in Northern Ireland used to refer to as ordinary decent criminals. In the words of Carlos Marighella, author of the influential 1970s underground publication *Minimanual of the Urban Guerrilla*: "The urban guerrilla ... differs radically from the criminal. The criminal benefits personally from his actions, and attacks indiscriminately without distinguishing between the exploiters and the exploited ... The urban guerrilla follows a political goal and only attacks the government, the big businesses and the foreign imperialists."[4]

As groups, terrorist organizations tend to be small in number — at least in terms of active membership — and they operate from the shadows, holding little or no territory. When they grow in size and influence, we tend to graduate to terms such as guerrilla or insurgent to describe them — and indeed such labels are not necessarily

---

[2] See Bruce Hoffman, *Inside Terrorism* (New York, NY: Columbia University Press; 2006); Walter Laqueur, *Terrorism* (London: Widenfeld and Nicholson; 1977); and Bernard Lewis, *The Assassins* (Basic Books; 2002).

[3] See Bruce Hoffman, *Inside Terrorism* (New York, NY: Columbia University Press; 2006) and Louise Richardson, *What Terrorists Want: Understanding the Enemy, Containing the Threat* (USA: Random House; 2006).

[4] Carlos Marighella, *Minimanual of the Urban Guerilla* (Havana; Tricontinental; 1970).

mutually exclusive. Violence is the terrorist's principal tool and it is used in such a way as to impact an audience far beyond the target of any individual attack — the choice of target therefore tends to have a universal, quotidian, quality. It is also likely to have symbolic value and is intended to terrify a wider audience than those immediately affected. Repetition, the promise of further attacks to come, is another important quality — as is the popular perception that such attacks will be consequential in scope, even if this perception, strategically at least, may be somewhat flawed. Terrorists may or may not receive state support, but when a state directly indulges in similar acts of political violence, the labels we use to describe such events tend to be somewhat different. After all, sovereignty has consequences.

The term "terrorism" is problematic precisely because it is not merely descriptive, it is a value-laden term with wholly negative connotations that has only rarely been embraced by those who use political violence — and only then somewhat ironically, as when Osama bin Laden told the *Al Jazeera* correspondent Taysir Allouni in October 2001: "We practice the good terrorism."[5] That the term is damaging to the militant cause was immediately obvious to those who were among the first to endorse such methods. Mikhail Bakunin, one of the most influential early anarchist theorists on the use of revolutionary violence, observed dismissively: "They will call it terrorism! They will give it some resounding nickname! All right, it's all the same to us. We don't care for their opinion."[6] Nonetheless, as Bakunin knew all too well, in the struggle for legitimacy labels matter, and "terrorism" is one of the most potent and potentially consequential political labels there is. A Sikh separatist leader once told the researcher Mark Juergensmeyer that he believed that the label "terrorist" had replaced the term "witch" as the ultimate mark of public disapproval and concomitant persecution.[7]

---

[5] Quoted in Peter Bergen, *The Longest War: The Enduring Conflict between America and Al-Qaeda* (New York, NY: Free Press; 2011), p. 61.
[6] Walter Laqueur (ed.), Mikhail Bakunin, Revolution, Terrorism, Banditry (1869), *Voices of Terror* (New York, NY: Reed Press; 2004), p. 70.
[7] Mark Juergensmeyer, *Terror in the Mind of God: The Global Rise of Religious Violence* (CA, USA: University of California Press; 2003), p. 9.

Narratives are powerful. Framing both grievances and actions for public consumption is a central preoccupation of political life, and terrorism, to paraphrase the celebrated Prussian military strategist Carl Von Clausewitz, is simply the continuation of politics by other means. Those who use terrorist violence and their supporters prefer to embrace more neutral terms such as "revolutionary", "volunteer", "armed struggle" or, as with Carlos Marighella above, "urban guerrilla warfare". In a hugely influential political speech delivered to the General Assembly of the United Nations in November 1974, Yasir Arafat offered perhaps the classic situational rejection of the "terrorist" label telling delegates: "The difference between the revolutionary and the terrorist lies in the reason for which each fights."

Advocates of violent opposition typically seek to create a moral equivalency between their actions and those of the state, as in this elegant formulation by the Irish playwright, and convicted member of the Irish Republican Army, Brendan Behan: "The man with a big bomb is a statesman, while the man with a small bomb is a terrorist." Some, like the right-wing American white supremacist leader David Lane, argue that negative labels simply illustrate the marginalization of "revolutionary" thinkers: "The difference between a terrorist and a patriot is control of the press."[8]

However, in my view, the key element that makes an act of violence "terrorism", and every bit as heinous as the label is intended to imply, is the willingness, and perhaps even the desire, to deliberately target members of the general public. In many ways, this is the ultimate taboo. Even in war, it is unlawful in any and all circumstances to deliberately target civilians — in the law of armed conflict, this is known as the doctrine of distinction. To intentionally set out to kill civilians is a war crime. Alex Schmid, who has repeatedly attempted to distil a definition of terrorism that will attract consensus support, offered this short definition for consideration: "An act of terrorism [equals] the peacetime equivalent of a war crime."[9]

---

[8] David Lane, *88 Precepts of Natural Law.*

[9] Short Legal Definition Proposed by A. P. Schmid to the United Nations Crime Branch (1992). See also Mike German, *Thinking Like a Terrorist: Insights of a Former FBI Undercover Agent* (Lincoln, Nebraska: Potomac Books; 2007), p. 34.

While this formulation is somewhat problematic from a legal perspective, I nevertheless find it a useful conceptual prism through which to view political violence.

For the purposes of this book, the reductive, descriptive definition of terrorism that I will be using encompasses repetitive violent acts committed by clandestine non-state actors that deliberately target civilians for political ends. This is not a legal definition — I will explore the various unsuccessful international attempts to reach a universally accepted definition in Part III and the compromise that has resulted — it is simply my bottom line for determining consistently whether or not a political event or group can appropriately be characterized as belonging to the genus "terrorist". By excluding state actors from this definition, I am not suggesting that states can commit similar acts of brutality with impunity, only that when they do so we can call it something else — the unlawful use of force, human rights abuse, a war crime, a crime against humanity, or even genocide. These are all serious charges in their own right and, I think, sufficiently equal "terrorist" in the opprobrium they attract.

For terrorism to become a viable political strategy for marginalized or disenchanted groups, a number of structural changes had to occur in the make up of modern society — mostly driven by the development of new technologies — changes that occurred more or less simultaneously in the middle of the nineteenth century.

The first was a revolution in military technology that concentrated the destructive power previously associated with mass military formations into the hands of a few individuals. Gunpowder had been the primary explosive in use for about 1,000 years when in 1847 an Italian chemist called Ascanio Sobrero created nitroglycerine — a liquid compound that is eight times more powerful by weight than gunpowder. In its liquid form, nitroglycerine proved immensely unstable and difficult to transport, but, after his brother Emil was killed in an industrial accident while working with nitroglycerine, Alfred Nobel began to experiment with methods of stabilizing the explosive and this led to his invention of dynamite, which he patented in 1867. Rather ominously, the name dynamite was derived

from the Greek word for power, *dýnamis*.[10] Other key developments
in weapons technology were the introduction of the revolver by
Samuel Colt in 1835, the Orsini bomb (a hand-thrown contact grenade) designed and used by Felice Orsini for an assassination
attempt on Emperor Napoleon III in 1858, the repeating rifle first
manufactured by Christopher Spencer in 1860, and the so-called
"horological torpedo", a time delay bomb first deployed by the
Confederate spies in an attack on the headquarters of Union General
Ulysses S. Grant in City Point, Virginia, which killed more than fifty
people in August 1864.[11] Indeed, the Confederacy had been one of
the first governments to grasp the potential that this revolution in
military capabilities represented. In 1863, the Louisiana planter and
lawyer, Bernard Janin Sage, shared a pamphlet with local lawmarkers
titled *Organization of Private Warfare* promoting the use of irregular
bands of "destructionists", which he conceived as operating under
loose official direction on land much as privateers operated at sea, in
such a way that the Confederacy could "do the most harm with the
least expense to ourselves."[12] The pamphlet influenced the creation
of the Confederate Bureau of Special and Secret Service, which was
behind the attack on Grant's headquarters. The sudden availability
of powerful, affordable, portable and concealable weapons — which
could also be easily acquired or manufactured by private citizens —
would prove to be a significant force multiplier for states and
non-state actors alike.

The second was the development of new mass communication
technologies that allowed knowledge of ideas and events to be rapidly distributed across thousands of miles, and enabled individuals
to travel easily across borders, and even across oceans, in larger

---

[10] Dynamite made Nobel's fortune and profits from its sale today support the activities of the
Norwegian Nobel Committee, which awards the annual Nobel Peace Prize. It is worth noting
in passing that the Peace Prize has been awarded to four individuals who had previously held
leadership positions with what are commonly considered to be terrorist organizations: Seán
MacBride (Irish Republican Army), Menachem Begin (*Irgun Zvai Leumi*), Nelson Mandela
(*Umkhonto we Sizwe*) and Yasir Arafat (*Fatah*).

[11] John Grady, The Confederate Torpedo, Opinionator, *The New York Times*, 15 August 2014.

[12] William A. Tidwell, *April '65: Confederate Covert Action in the American Civil War* (Kent, OH:
Kent State University Press; 1995), pp. 206–212.

numbers than ever before, opening up an era of mass migration and commensurate dislocation. The first working telegraph was built between Washington DC and Baltimore by Samuel Morse (who also developed Morse code to aid the transmission of messages) becoming operational in 1844. The laying of the first transatlantic telegraph cable was completed in 1858,[13] and the use of the telegraph by the print media really took off in the 1860s when British newspaper offices like *The Scotsman* and *The Times* began to install telegraph lines in their newsrooms to receive news rapidly from national capitals and overseas correspondents.[14] The steam-powered rotary printing press invented in the United States in 1843 allowed for the reproduction of millions of pages of text in a single day.[15] Improvements in paper production, such as the introduction of much cheaper printing stock made from wood pulp in the 1880s, and the invention of the linotype typesetting machine in 1884 further boosted newspaper circulation, as did the move towards universal education in more developed countries, which produced a new generation of literate consumers for these publications. The 1880s saw the circulation of newspapers in Britain, France and the United States surpass 100,000 copies.[16] On land, the world's first commercial railway, the Stockton and Darlington Railway in England, began operation in 1825, the first railway in continental Europe opened in Belgium in 1835, and Russia got its first railway line in 1837, but the great expansion of railway networks occurred in the 1850s and 1860s as the individual national railway networks began to link up, offering passengers the possibility of traveling across Europe by rail. The United States completed its first transcontinental railway in 1869. On sea, the construction of the iron-hulled SS Great Western by Isambard Kingdom Brunel in 1838 inaugurated the age of the transatlantic passenger steamer, but it took the adoption of the screw propeller, iron hulls, and compound and triple

---

[13] The first cable only functioned for three weeks and was not successfully replaced until 1866.

[14] Andrew Marr, *My Trade: A Short History of British Journalism* (London, UK: Pan Books; 2005), p. 15.

[15] Philip Meggs, *A History of Graphic Design* (New York: John Wiley & Sons; 1998), p. 147.

[16] Richard Bach Jensen, Daggers, Rifles and Dynamite: Anarchist Terrorism in Nineteenth Century Europe, *Terrorism and Political Violence*, Vol. 16, No. 1 (Spring 2004), p. 141.

expansion engines, which all combined to increase the size, fuel efficiency and range of commercial vessels, to make trans-oceanic shipping economically viable on a large scale by 1870. Accordingly, some of the earliest modern terrorists — European anarchists and Irish nationalists — can be said to have posed a transnational threat almost from their inception.

The third and final revolution took place in the realm of ideas. Prior to the nineteenth century, political activity had been to all intents and purposes the exclusive province of social elites. New technologies brought access to educational opportunities that had not previously existed, agricultural laborers and artisans flocked to urban centers attracted by new employment opportunities and creating a new social class — the industrial proletariat. Karl Marx, Friedrich Engels, Mikhail Bakunin, Pierre-Joseph Proudhon and a host of others developed political theories that put the common man at the center of societal progress and created a language of working class empowerment.

The German revolutionary Karl Heinzen was the first to articulate the use of violence, even mass murder, by private individuals to effect political change in his influential 1853 pamphlet, *Mord und Freiheit*, coining the term *freiheitskämpfer* or freedom fighter in the process.[17]

The European-wide popular unrest of 1848 and the example set by the short-lived Paris Commune of 1871 held out hope to the disenfranchised that popular government by the masses was not beyond reach and that meaningful social change was possible. The mutiny of the Paris National Guard in March 1871 and the decision by the mutineers to hold an election, which led to the creation of a socialist government that ruled Paris for three months implementing a radical political agenda, would become a beacon of promise for social revolutionaries. The fact that the Paris Commune ended in a reactionary bloodbath that claimed at least ten thousand lives as the French government reasserted control only strengthened their

---

[17] Karl Heinzen, *Murder and Freedom* (New York; 1853) reproduced in Daniel Bessner and Michael Stauch, Karl Heinzen and the Intellectual Origins of Modern Terror, *Terrorism and Political Violence*, Vol. 22 (2010).

resolve, drawing the battle lines even more clearly.[18] As the Swiss anarchist Paul Brousse observed in an article published by the radical journal *Bulletin de la Fédération Jurassienne*: "Prior to the Paris Commune, who in France was conversant with the principle of communal autonomy? No one."[19] Afterwards it was an idea that resonated with the dispossessed and marginalized across the Western world.

Heinzen had dedicated *Mord und Freiheit* to the Hungarian nationalist Libényi János who attempted to assassinate the Austrian Emperor Franz Joseph I in February 1853, and populist nationalism was also beginning to play an important role in international politics. In 1848, Mikhail Bakunin had penned *The Appeal to the Slavs* calling on the Slavic peoples of central and southern Europe to rise up against the Austro-Hungarian empire, and in the Balkans the "national sympathies" to which he appealed would eventually give rise to one of the most active and enduring early terrorist organizations, the Internal Macedonian Revolutionary Organization (IMRO), as well as one of the most consequential terrorist attacks of all time — the assassination of the Austrian Archduke Franz Ferdinand by the Bosnian Serb Gavrilo Princep in June 1914, which precipitated the outbreak of World War I. Princep was explicit about his motivation, declaring at his trial: "I am a Yugoslav nationalist, aiming for the unification of all Yugoslavs, and I do not care what form of state, but it must be freed from Austria."[20] The cause of Italian reunification was also the motivating force behind Felice Orsini's assassination attempt on Napoleon III, and the pivotal role played by Giuseppe Garibaldi and his 1,000 redshirts in the Italian *Risorgimento* was hugely influential on other revolutionary movements, as it demonstrated that a small group of determined men could have a decisive impact on the affairs of great powers.

The nineteenth century brought together the means, the motive, and the opportunity for small bands of committed radicals to take the fight to the established order, and the men who had first

---

[18] Jacques Rougerie, *La Commune de 1871* (Paris, France: Presses Universitaires de France; 2014), p. 118.

[19] Paul Brousse, Propaganda by the Deed, *Bulletin de la Fédération Jurassienne*, August 1877.

[20] Noel Malcolm, *Bosnia: A Short History* (NY: New York University Press; 1996), p. 153.

articulated alternate political utopias were quick to realize the game-changing tools that the march of science had placed in the hands of their followers. Karl Marx wrote that the very force of an explosion had a "therapeutic quality" capable of "psychologically renovating" the working class. Karl Heinzen admonished comrades that dreamt of conquering their enemies on the field of battle that "physics and chemistry can be more important for the revolution than your entire chivalry and science of war."[21] The German anarchist Johann Most published *The Science of Revolutionary Warfare: A Handbook of Instruction Regarding the Use and Manufacture of Nitroglycerine, Dynamite, Gun-Cotton, Fulminating Mercury, Bombs, Arsons, Poisons, etc.,* in 1885 to spread knowledge of these new weapons amongst socialist and anarchist revolutionaries, and earned himself the derisory nickname General Boom Boom amongst his rivals on the German left.[22] The Russian anarchist Prince Peter Kropotkin urged anarchists to develop their bomb-making skills noting, "I have said that when a party is put in the position of having to use dynamite, it ought to use it."[23]

Although there were earlier isolated incidents of political violence perhaps worthy of the label — the three bombs thrown by Felice Orsini and his accomplices at Napoleon III's carriage left eight bystanders dead and 140 injured[24] — terrorism truly came of age in the 1870s and 1880s. In the former Confederate States of America the

---

[21] Karl Heinzen, *Murder and Freedom* (New York; 1853) reproduced in Daniel Bessner and Michael Stauch, Karl Heinzen and the Intellectual Origins of Modern Terror, *Terrorism and Political Violence,* Vol. 22 (2010), p. 164.

[22] Michael Burleigh, *Blood and Rage: A Cultural History of Terrorism* (New York, NY: Harper; 2009), p. 72.

[23] Marie Fleming, Propaganda by the Deed: Terrorism and Anarchist Theory in Late Nineteenth-Century Europe, *Terrorism: An International Journal,* Vol. 4 (1980), p. 12.

[24] Felice Orsini was an associate of the Italian statesman Giuseppe Mazzini and a supporter of Italian unification, to which Napoleon III was perceived as an obstacle. In a transnational conspiracy, which saw Orsini build and test a contact bomb of his own devising in England before traveling to Paris, Orsini and his Italian co-conspirators planned to bomb the Emperor's coach as he drove to the opera on the evening of 14 January 1858. Three "Orsini" bombs, employing fulminate of mercury as an explosive, detonated killing and injuring a number of onlookers in the crowd but leaving Napoleon and his entourage essentially unharmed. Injured in the blasts, Orsini was detained before he could make good his escape and was ultimately sent to the guillotine.

Ku Klux Klan, a secret society of loosely affiliated "dens" with little central direction, was founded by veterans of the civil war to resist the Unionist reconstruction of the South and northern attempts to integrate former slaves into the political institutions of the southern states.[25] During the eleven years of reconstruction from 1865 to 1876, the Klan and its supporters killed an estimated 3,000 freed former slaves and brutally intimidated black communities from realizing any semblance of equality. Seven black legislators elected during the 1867–1868 constitutional conventions were murdered. The failure of the federal government to intervene to secure the 1875 election in Mississippi, with predictable consequences for black voters, led its Republican Governor, Adelbert Ames, to proclaim in disgust: "A revolution has taken place (by force of arms) and a race are disenfranchised — they are to be returned to a condition of serfdom."[26] The Ku Klux Klan had snatched no small measure of victory from the jaws of defeat. Although reconstruction was abandoned in 1876, the Klan's racially motivated violence would continue for decades spawning beatings, lynchings, bombings and even assassination. This violence attracted little attention outside the southern United States until the 1960s and, as such, it exerted little influence on political developments further afield, but the Klan might nevertheless be reasonably described as the first modern terrorist organization.

In 1880, the Russian populist revolutionary Nikolai Morozov published *The Terrorist Struggle* — it is a prescient document with remarkable contemporary resonance. In it, Morozov argues that terrorism can be used incrementally to force a government to make concessions and suggests that a collection of small independent terrorist groups, rather than one coherent organization, would be more difficult for the police to counter. *The Terrorist Struggle* was written in part to explain to the public the logic of a series of attacks on Russian political figures by the Russian underground movement *Narodnaya Volya* such as the murder of the head of the Tsarist secret

---

[25] See David Rapoport, Before the Bombs There Were the Mobs: American Experiences with Terror, in Jean Rosenfeld (ed.), *Terrorism, Identity and Legitimacy: The Four Waves Theory and Political Violence* (Abingdon, UK: Routledge; 2011).

[26] ibid., p. 151.

police, Nikolai Mezentsev, stabbed to death on a St. Petersburg street in August 1878. Morozov wrote *The Terrorist Struggle* in exile in Switzerland after breaking with *Narodnaya Volya* because he feared the political ambition of its leader Lev Tikhomirov, although he remained sympathetic to the group's objectives. He returned to Russia in order to distribute his pamphlet but was arrested in November 1880. Found guilty in 1882, he served seventeen years in St. Petersburg's notorious Peter and Paul Fortress until being released following the first Russian Revolution in 1905. You can still visit his old cell in the Trubetskoy Bastion today.

The assassination of Tsar Alexander II by *Narodnaya Volya* in March 1881 announced the arrival of this violent new form of political expression on the world stage. Although *Narodnaya Volya* focused its efforts on targeting senior figures of the Tsarist regime, rather than members of the general public, it was quite prepared to sacrifice royal attendants or innocent bystanders in pursuit of its objectives. One of the two handheld bombs thrown during the assassination of the Tsar also took the life of a young child who had been watching the royal entourage go past.[27] Previous attempts on the Tsar's life had sought to derail the royal train and blow up the Winter Palace in St. Petersburg, the latter attack killed eleven members of his household staff, and injured fifty-six.[28] *Narodnaya Volya*'s example inspired similar efforts elsewhere in Europe. In September 1883, a ring of conspirators, led by the self-described anarchist-socialist Friedrich August Reinsdorf, only narrowly failed to blow up Kaiser Wilhelm I, the "Iron Chancellor" Otto von Bismarck, and the Imperial German court, as they traveled to attend the inauguration of a giant statue of "Germania" on the summit of Niederwald above the Rhine.[29] The Imperial party was saved because the dynamite, concealed in a culvert along the route, failed to detonate. Reinsdorf and two of his accomplices were subsequently executed.

---

[27] Ronald Seth, *The Russian Terrorists: The Story of Narodriki* (London: Barrie and Rockliff; 1966), p. 100.

[28] Max Boot, *Invisible Armies: An Epic History of Guerrilla Warfare from Ancient Times to the Present* (New York: Liveright Publishing Corporation; 2013), p. 237.

[29] See Ernest Alfred Vizetelly, The Advent of Dynamite, *The Anarchists: Their Faith and Their Record* (Edinburgh: Turnbull and Spears; Printers; 1911).

At the same time that the *Narodnaya Volya* campaign was gathering momentum in Russia, and attracting emulators in Europe, a secret society of Irish nationalists based in the United States known as *Clan na Gael* launched an equally violent assault on the major cities of the British mainland. The campaign was eight years in the making. In the autumn of 1875, Patrick Ford, the editor of the Brooklyn-based newspaper *Irish World*, and his brother Augustine, both passionate supporters of Irish independence, developed the idea of dispatching what they termed "skirmishers" from the United States to undermine British rule in Ireland.[30] Patrick explained: "The Irish cause requires skirmishers. It requires a little band of heroes who will initiate and keep up without intermission a guerilla warfare — men who will fly over the land and sea like invisible beings — now striking the enemy in Ireland, now in India, now in England itself, as occasion may present."[31] Using their newspaper as a platform, the Fords joined with the Irish nationalist leader Jeremiah O'Donovan Rossa to establish a Skirmishing Fund to raise money for their plan, and it was the revenue from this fund (renamed the National Fund in 1878) that would be used to *Clan na Gael*'s operations, as well as additional attacks by "skirmishers" working directly for Rossa. Between 1881 and 1887, the so-called Dynamite Campaign saw high-profile targets in London like Tower Bridge, Scotland Yard, the Palace of Westminster and the new Underground rail system come under attack — one bomb that detonated on the Metropolitan line injured seventy-two people, mostly third class passengers.[32] There were further bombings in Manchester, Liverpool, and Glasgow. Terrorist suspects in the United Kingdom are still often charged under the Explosive Substances Act of 1883, a legacy of the campaign.[33]

The familiar architecture of counter-terrorism had also begun to take shape by the end of the 1880s. Tsarist Russia established the

---

[30] Niall Whelehan, *The Dynamiters: Irish Nationalism and Political Violence in the Wider World 1867–1900* (Cambridge: Cambridge University Press; 2012), p. 77.

[31] K. R. M. Short, *The Dynamite War: Irish-American Bombers in Victorian Britain* (Dublin: Gill and Macmillan; 1979), p. 38.

[32] ibid., p. 162 and 229.

[33] Lord Lloyd of Berwick, *Inquiry into Legislation against Terrorism* (London: Stationary Office; 1996), p. ix.

Department of State Police to coordinate the response to the *Narodniks* in August 1880 after three failed attempts on Tsar Alexander II's life.[34] The Department would fail to prevent the fourth, successful, attempt. The Special Irish Branch of the Metropolitan Police, which in time would evolve into Britain's modern day Counter Terrorist Command, was created in March 1883 specifically in response to the threat posed by *Clan na Gael*.[35] Both Italy and Russia sent agents overseas to spy on, and intrigue against, anarchist émigrés now living elsewhere in Europe, and in both North and South America — a development satirized insightfully by Joseph Conrad in his novel *The Secret Agent*.[36] European states came together at the Anti-Anarchist Conference convened in Rome in 1898 to lay the foundation for international police cooperation in such areas as the definition of criminal offenses, common extradition standards, and forensic exchanges. This international cooperation would lead directly to the establishment of the international police organization Interpol in 1923.[37]

Although neither *Narodnaya Volya* nor *Clan na Gael* achieved their political goals, their example inspired plenty of imitators. Anarchist violence spread throughout the Western world. Between 1894 and 1901, anarchists killed President Sadi Carnot of France, Prime Minister Antonio Cánovas of Spain, Empress Elizabeth of Austria, King Umberto I of Italy and US President William McKinley. The 1890s would become known as the decade of the regicide. The general public, albeit the better off amongst them, also increasingly

---

[34] Charles Ruud and Sergei Stepanov, *Fontanka 16: The Tsar's Secret Police* (Gloucestershire: Sutton Publishing; 1999), p. 49.

[35] Rupert Allason, *The Branch: History of the Metropolitan Police Special Branch, 1883–1983* (London: Secker and Warburg; 1983).

[36] Richard Bach Jensen, *The Battle against Anarchist Terrorism: An International History, 1878–1934* (Cambridge: Cambridge University Press; 2014), p. 219 and Alex Butterworth, *The World That Never Was: A True Story of Dreamers, Schemers, Anarchists and Secret Agents* (New York, NY: Pantheon Books; 2010), p. 333.

[37] See Peter Romaniuk, *Multilateral Counter-Terrorism: The Global Politics of Cooperation and Contestation* (UK: Routledge; 2010) and Richard Bach Jensen, The International Anti-Anarchist Conference of 1898 and the Origins of Interpol, *Journal of Contemporary History*, Vol. 16 (1981), pp. 323–347.

found themselves the target of anarchist bombs. Perhaps, the three best known examples are the bombing of the Liceu Theater in Barcelona in November 1893 by Santiago Salvador which killed twenty audience members,[38] the bombing of the Café Terminus in Paris in February 1894 by Émile Henry, which killed one diner and injured twenty,[39] and the bombing of a Catholic religious procession in Barcelona during the festival of Corpus Christi, most likely by Jean Girault, in June 1896, which killed twelve people (including a six-year-old child) and injured sixty.[40] French journalist and anarchist sympathizer Félix Fénéon offered an insight into the evolution of the militant mind-set when he observed that Henry's targeting of the Café Terminus was entirely appropriate "being directed toward the voting public, more guilty in the long run, perhaps, than the representatives they elected."[41] Over the course of the 1890s, terrorist incidents attributed to anarchists in Europe, the United States, and even Australia, killed more than sixty people and injured at least 200.[42]

That many of the perpetrators of these attacks had been inspired by the actions of their peers elsewhere is made explicit by both their public statements and their actions. Émile Henry referenced the example of comrades who had died for the anarchist cause in Spain, Germany, and the United States at his trial.[43] Leon Czolgosz, the assassin of President McKinley, slept with a newspaper cutting about King Umberto I of Italy's assassination under his pillow and even purchased the same model of Iver Johnson .32

---

[38] Marie Fleming, Propaganda by the Deed: Terrorism and Anarchist Theory in Late Nineteenth-Century Europe, *Terrorism: An International Journal*, Vol. 4 (1980), p. 15.

[39] See John Merriman, *The Dynamite Club: How a Bombing in Fin-de-Siécle Paris Ignited the Modern Age of Terror* (USA: Houghton Mifflin Harcourt; 2009).

[40] Richard Bach Jensen, The Pre-1914 Anarchist "Lone Wolf" Terrorist and Government Responses, *Journal of Terrorism and Political Violence*, Vol. 26, No. 1 (2014), p. 88.

[41] Alex Butterworth, *The World That Never Was: A True Story of Dreamers, Schemers, Anarchists and Secret Agents* (New York, NY: Pantheon Books; 2010), p. 348.

[42] Richard Bach Jensen, *The Battle against Anarchist Terrorism: An International History, 1878–1934* (Cambridge: Cambridge University Press; 2014), p. 36.

[43] John Merriman, *The Dynamite Club: How a Bombing in Fin-de-Siécle Paris Ignited the Modern Age of Terror* (USA: Houghton Mifflin Harcourt; 2009), p. 187.

revolver used by Umberto's assassin, Gaetano Bresci.[44] The Irish nationalist leader Michael Collins, who perhaps more than any other single man crystallized the concept of modern urban terrorism, admitted to being inspired in part by the murder in 1904 of the Russian Governor General of Finland, Nikolai Bobrikov, by the Finnish nationalist Eugen Schauman, which prompted Tsar Nicholas II to introduce free elections and establish a national parliament in an attempt to head off revolution in this restive corner of the Russian Empire. Collins described the positive impact of Bobrikov's murder as being like a "fairy tale".[45]

The political scientist David Rapoport has famously posited that there have been four distinct waves of terrorist violence in the modern era: an anti-authoritarian wave driven by would-be anarchist and socialist revolutionaries such as those described above and loosely dating from the 1870s to the 1920s; an anti-colonial wave waged mostly within the borders of the British and French Empires between the 1910s and the 1960s; a Marxist-Leninist-Maoist wave that peaked globally in the 1970s and 1980s; and a religious wave that started in the 1970s and is still active today.[46] With a concept as slippery and heterogeneous as terrorism, it should come as no surprise that historical events do not quite fit as neatly into this simple typology. Two key nineteenth century terrorist groups *Clan na Gael* and the Ku Klux Klan had little in common with their anarchist contemporaries. Many of the nationalist terrorist groups of the past thirty or forty years such as the Provisional Irish Republican Army (PIRA), Popular Front for the Liberation of Palestine (PFLP), the Armenian Secret Army for the Liberation of Armenia (ASALA), or the Basque separatist group *Euskadi Ta Askatasuna* (ETA) mixed nationalist sentiment with a Marxist sensibility. Egypt's *Jami'ah al-Ikhwān al-Muslimūn* (Society of the Muslim Brothers or,

---

[44] Scott Miller, *The President and the Assassin: McKinley, Terror, and Empire at the Dawn of the American Century* (New York, NY: Random House; 2011), p. 6.

[45] T. Ryle Dwyer, *The Squad and the Intelligence Operations of Michael Collins* (Cork: Mercier; 2005), p. 65.

[46] See David C. Rapoport, The Four Waves of Modern Terrorism, in Audrey Kurth Cronin and James Ludes (eds.), *Attacking Terrorism: Elements of a Grand Strategy* (Washington, D.C.: Georgetown University Press; 2004).

more popularly, Muslim Brotherhood) predates the religious wave to which it helped give rise by almost half a century. From a theological perspective, there is also a robust debate about the degree to which groups like *al-Qaeda* can be said to be accurately interpreting religious tenets, and the same point could be made about the religious cast of much of the modern white supremacist movement in the United States. In fairness to Rapoport, these are problems that he has freely acknowledged but while wave theory undoubtedly provides a simple and conceptually clean narrative to help students and researchers alike to organize their thoughts, it is hard to get past the fact that there are just too many anomalies — nationalists, populists, nativists, and religious extremists all begin to explore the use of terrorism as a means to effect change as early as the 1850s and 1860s, and all four political strains coexist to a greater or lesser extent at the same time, increasing and decreasing in prominence over the ensuing decades.

I find the concept of a "contagion effect" a significantly more compelling explanation of how terrorism has spread as political tool than wave theory.[47] There is a rich sociological literature on how and under what context organizations learn from their peers and rivals, associated with scholars such as Barbara Levitt and James G. March.[48] Non-state organizations learn both from direct experience and from the stories they develop to make sense of that experience, as well as from experiences and stories generated by their peers. Organizations that interact regularly with direct competitors learn from both their own and their rivals' successes. The fields of anthropology and communication studies have generated similar theories about the contagiousness of ideas to explain the diffusion of innovative

---

[47] See Peter Waldmann, Social-revolutionary Terrorism in Latin America and Europe, in Tore Bjørgo (ed.), *Root Causes of Terrorism: Myth, Reality and Ways Forward* (Abingdon, UK: Routledge; 2005). See also Manus Midlarsky, Martha Crenshaw and Fumihiko Yoshida, Why Violence Spreads: The Contagion of International Terrorism, *International Studies Quarterly*, Vol. 24, No. 2 (June 1980) and Tom Parker and Nick Sitter, The Four Horsemen of Terrorism: It's Not Waves, It's Strains, *Journal of Terrorism and Political Violence*, Vol. 28, No. 2 (2016).

[48] Barbara Levitt and James. G. March, Organizational Learning, *Annual Review of Sociology*, Vol. 14 (1988), pp. 319–340; James. G. March, Exploration and Exploitation in Organizational Learning, *Organization Science*, Vol. 2, No. 1 (1991), pp. 71–87. (*Special Issue: Organizational Learning: Papers in Honor of (and by) James G. March*).

practices across societies.[49] Political scientists have used contagion
theory to explain how political parties have learnt from more successful opponents how to revitalize their own electoral programs,
party organizations, and electoral strategy.[50] The German academic
Peter Waldmann was one of the first working in the field of terrorism studies to reference this kind of "contagion effect" for terrorist
groups, arguing that the perceived success of some groups attracted
others to emulate aspects of their approach, and perhaps also
aspects of their ideology.[51] Indeed, several early modern terrorists
actually expressed the hope that they would set an example for others to follow, with the Russian populist Nikolai Morozov observing
that "when a handful of people appears to represent the struggle of
a whole nation and is triumphant over millions of enemies, then the
idea of terroristic struggle will not die once it is clarified for the people and proven it can be practical."[52] The beauty of contagion theory
is that it accounts for both temporal clusters of likeminded terrorist
organizations and for isolated outbreaks that do not go viral.

There is a great deal of empirical evidence to support the existence
of such a process — for example, think of Michael Collins' admiration
of Eugen Schauman, and Leon Czolgosz's self-conscious emulation of
Gaetano Bresci cited above. Johann Most reprinted the works of Karl
Heinzen decades after they first appeared and praised the 1882 Phoenix
Park murders, committed by Irish nationalists, in the pages of *Freiheit,*

---

[49] See Robert Winthrop, *Dictionary of Concepts in Cultural Anthropology* (New York: Greenwood;
1991) and Everett Rogers, *Diffusion of Innovations* (New York: Free Press; 2003).

[50] See Maurice Duverger, *Political Parties: Their Organization and Activity in the Modern State*
(London: Methuen; 1954) and Richard S. Katz and Peter Mair (eds.), *How Parties
Organize: Change and Adaptation in Party Organizations in Western Democracies* (London:
Sage; 1995).

[51] See Peter Waldmann, Social-revolutionary terrorism in Latin America and Europe, in Tore
Bjørgo (ed.), *Root Causes of Terrorism: Myth, Reality and Ways Forward* (London: Routledge;
2005). See also Manus Midlarsky, Martha Crenshaw and Fumihiko Yoshida, Why Violence
Spreads: The Contagion of International Terrorism, *International Studies Quarterly*, Vol. 24,
No. 2 (June 1980), 262–298.

[52] Nikolai Morozov, The Terrorist Struggle (1880), republished in Walter Laqueur (ed.), *Voices
of Terror: Manifestos, Writings and Manuals of Al Qaeda, Hamas, and other Terrorists from Around the
World and Throughout the Ages* (Naperville Ill.: Reed Press; 2004), p. 81.

the radical newspaper he edited in America.[53] The Marxist Weather Underground Organization, which operated in the United States from 1969 to 1977, is one of many terrorist groups that was happy to publicly declare the debt it owed to comrades elsewhere: "Now we are adapting the classic guerrilla strategy of the *Viet Cong* and the urban guerrilla strategy of the *Tupamaros* to our own situation here in the most technically advanced country in the world."[54] The Symbionese Liberation Army's 1974 kidnapping of newspaper heiress Patty Hearst was directly inspired by the *Tupamaros*' 1971 kidnapping of Homero Fariña, the editor of the conservative Uruguayan newspaper *Accion*.[55] Dimitris Koufodinas, Operations Chief of the Greek terror group November 17, taught himself Spanish in his prison cell so he could translate the prison memoirs of two *Tupamaros* leaders, Mauricio Rosencof and Eleuterio Fernández Huidobro.[56] We know from O'Donovan Rossa's private correspondence that he was well aware of the attempt by *Narodnaya Volya* to assassinate Tsar Alexander II by bombing the Winter Palace in February 1880.[57] Eldridge Cleaver, one of the early leaders of the Black Panthers, adopted Sergei Nechaev's nineteenth century *Catechism of the Revolutionist* as his "revolutionary bible".[58] The Norwegian white supremacist Anders Behring Breivik quoted extensively from the Unabomber, Theodore Kaczynski, in his own political manifesto, *2083 — A European Declaration of Independence,* and told his court-appointed psychiatrists that he had learned much from studying *al-Qaeda*.[59]

---

[53] Benjamin Grob-Fitzgibbon, From the Dagger to the Bomb: Karl Heinzen and the Evolution of Political Terror, *Terrorism and Political Violence*, Vol. 16, No. 1 (Spring 2004), p. 109, and Michael Burleigh, *Blood and Rage: A Cultural History of Terrorism* (London: Harper; 2009), p. 72.

[54] Bernardine Dohrn, *Declaration of a State of War*, The Berkeley Tribe, 31 July 1970 at http://www.lib.berkeley.edu/MRC/pacificaviet/scheertranscript.html.

[55] Jeffrey Toobin, *American Heiress: The Wild Saga of the Kidnapping, Crimes and Trial of Patty Hearst* (London: Doubleday; 2016), p. 42.

[56] George Kassimeris, *Inside Greek Terrorism* (Oxford University Press; 2013), p. 33.

[57] K. R. M. Short, *The Dynamite War: Irish-American Bombers in Victorian Britain* (Gill and Macmillan; 1979), p. 47.

[58] Paul Avrich, *Anarchist Portraits* (Princeton University Press; 1988), p. 13.

[59] Åsne Seierstad, *One of Us: The Story of Anders Breivik and the Massacres in Norway* (Farrar, Straus and Giroux; 2013), p. 366 and 425 and Benjamin Ramm, The Unabomber and the Norwegian mass murderer, *BBC Magazine*, 28 May 2016 at http://www.bbc.com/news/magazine-36399515 (viewed on 30 May 2016).

The German Marxist Horst Mahler suggested the name *Rote Armee Fraktion* in conscious homage to a Japanese precursor, *Sekigun-ha*, and other German groups of the period adopted the names like *Tupamaros* West Berlin and *Tupamaros* Munich.[60] Andreas Baader quoted the Brazilian Carlos Marighella in a letter addressed to the press, and appears to have identified closely with the *Front de Libération Nationale* (FLN) hitman Ali La Pointe, or at least the cinematic incarnation of La Pointe featured in Gillo Pontecorvo's influential film, *The Battle of Algiers*.[61] Another prominent German urban guerrilla, Michael Baumann, cited Eldridge Cleaver's *Soul on Ice*, as well as Mikhail Bakunin, as influences.[62] The Chechen Islamist militant Shamil Basayev carried a photograph of Che Guevara in the breast pocket of his battledress, and the Chechen group responsible for the bombing of two Russian passenger aircraft in August 2004 named itself after Khaled al Islambouli, leader of the *Tanzim al-Jihad* cell that killed President Anwar Sadat in October 1981.[63] The Indian nationalist Barin Ghose, jailed for his role in a 1909 conspiracy to assassinate a member of the British government administration in Bengal, wrote that his "cult of violence" was "learnt from the Irish Seinfeinners [sic] and Russian secret societies".[64] The August 1909 execution of fellow Indian nationalist Madan Lal Dhingra, murderer of Sir William Curzon Wyllie, was marked by the mysterious appearance of placards across Ireland declaring: "Ireland honours Mada Lal Dhingra [sic], who was proud to lay down his life for the cause of his country."[65]

---

[60] Otto Billig, The Lawyer Terrorist and His Comrades, *Political Psychology*, Vol. 6, No. 1 (March 1985), p. 32 and Michael Baumann, *Terror or Love?* (New York, NY: Grove Press; 1977), p. 63.

[61] Michael Burleigh, *Blood and Rage: A Cultural History of Terrorism* (Harper; 2009), p. 229.

[62] Stefan Aust, *Baader-Meinhof: The Inside Story of the RAF* (Oxford: Oxford University Press; 2009), p. 150 and Michael Baumann, *Terror or Love?* (New York, NY: Grove Press; 1977), pp. 65–66.

[63] Charles Kurzman, *The Missing Martyrs: Why There Are So Few Muslim Terrorists* (Oxford: Oxford University Press; 2011) p. 30 and Stephen Ulph, The Islambouli Enigma, *Terrorism Focus*, Vol. 1, No. 3 (May 2005).

[64] Peter Heehs, Terrorism in India during the Freedom Struggle, *The Historian* (Spring 1993), p. 474.

[65] Ireland: A Scandalous Placard, *The Times*, 18 August 1909 at http://www.executedtoday. com/2009/08/17/1909-madanlal-dhingra-indian-revolutionary/. Viewed 29 Ocotber 2016.

Hocine Aït Ahmed, the head of the Algerian *Mouvement pour le Triomphe des Libertés Démocratiques,* analyzed the Irish struggle for independence, as well as the triumph of communism in China and the tactics of the *Viet Minh* in Indochina.[66] Although he mourned the creation of the state of Israel, the Egyptian theocrat Sayyid Qutb urged his fellow Islamists to learn from the success that the Jewish terrorist groups *Lohamei Herut Israel* (LEHI) and *Irgun Zvai Leumi* (*Irgun*) had enjoyed influencing the British policy in Palestine.[67] LEHI's Avigad Landau in turn studied the operational practices of the Irish nationalist movement, *Narodnaya Volya* and the Serbian Black Hand, and Avraham Stern, out of whose eponymous militant group LEHI evolved, translated excerpts of P. S. O'Hegarty's book *The Victory of Sinn Féin* into Hebrew.[68] Yasir Arafat's intelligence chief Salah Khalaf, better known to posterity by his *nom de guerre* Abu Iyad, noted in his memoirs: "The guerrilla war in Algeria, launched five years before the creation of *Fateh,* had a profound influence on us ... [It] symbolized the success we dreamed of."[69] Nelson Mandela also acknowledged the influence that the Algerian independence struggle had on the thinking of the African National Congress (ANC), as well as the inspiration he had drawn personally from the memoirs of the Philippine *Hukbong Bayan Laban sa mga Hapon* leader Luis Taruc and *Irgun*'s Menachem Begin.[70] According to the Provisional IRA volunteer Maria McGuire, it was not the indiscriminate use of force by the

---

[66] Christopher Cradock and M.L.R. Smith, No Fixed Values: A Reinterpretation of the Influence of the Theory of Guerre Révolutionnaire and the Battle of Algiers 1956–1957, *Journal of Cold War Studies,* Vol. 9, No. 4 (Fall 2007), pp. 80–81.

[67] John Calvert, *Sayyid Qutb and the Origins of Radical Islamism* (New York: Columbia University Press; 2010), p. 122.

[68] Gerold Frank, *The Deed* (Simon and Schuster; 1963), p. 131 and Bruce Hoffman, *Anonymous Soldiers: The Struggle for Israel, 1917–1947* (New York: Knopf; 2015), p. 105.

[69] Abu Iyad and Eric Rouleau, *My Home, My Land: A Narrative of the Palestinian Struggle* (New York: Times Books; 1981), p. 34.

[70] Nelson Mandela, *Long Walk to Freedom* (New York: Abacus; 1994), p. 326 and p. 355, Michael Burleigh, *Blood and Rage: A Cultural History of Terrorism* (New York: Harper; 2009), p. 137, and Boying Pimentel, *Mandela the rebel and his Filipino counterparts,* Inquirer.net, 10 December 2013 at http://globalnation.inquirer.net/93825/mandela-the-rebel-and-his-filipino-counterparts. Viewed on 18 June 2016.

FLN in Algeria but the much more measured application of violence favored by EOKA in its campaign to force the British out of Cyprus that was one of the organization's main inspirations.[71] In the early 1970s, Provisional *Sinn Féin* President and veteran IRA man Ruairí Ó Brádaigh distributed seven copies of Robert Taber's classic study of guerrilla warfare, *The War of the Flea*, to each member of the Provisional IRA's Army Council.[72] The *al-Qaeda* ideologue Mustafa Setmarian Nasar — perhaps best known by his alias Abu Mus'ab al-Suri — employed the *nom de plume* "Castro,"[73] and the current leader of *al-Qaeda*, Ayman al-Zawahiri, published a critique of the "shortcomings" of the Society of the Muslim Brothers in 1991 entitled *The Bitter Harvest*.[74]

Mia Bloom has similarly written of a "demonstration effect" by which effective tactics spread from one conflict to another. She describes how the adoption of suicide bombing by the Palestinian terrorist group *Hamas* can be traced back to the December 1992 expulsion of 415 senior Palestinian Islamic Jihad (PIJ) activists from the Occupied Territories to Marj al-Zahour in Southern Lebanon.[75] Despite *Hamas* and PIJ both being *Sunni* organizations, the activists were taken in by the *Shia* Lebanese terrorist group *Hezbollah* who provided both aid and operational training, including in the use of explosives, to the expellees. Although many of those expelled from Israeli-controlled territory had been intellectuals rather than frontline fighters, on their return to the Occupied Territories in September 1993, many took a more active part in hostilities and several were linked to suicide bombings by the Israeli authorities — a tactic that had not previously been used by Palestinian groups.[76] On 19 October 1994, Saleh al-Souwi

---

[71] Maria McGuire, *To Take Arms: A Year in the Provisional IRA* (London: MacMillan; 1973), p. 74.

[72] ibid.

[73] Jarret Brachman and William McCants, *Stealing Al Qaeda's Playbook, Studies in Conflict and Terrorism*, Vol. 29, No. 4 (June 2006).

[74] John Calvert, *Sayyid Qutb and the Origins of Radical Islamism* (New York: Columbia University Press; 2010), p. 223.

[75] Mia Bloom, *Dying to Kill: The Allure of Suicide Terror* (New York: Columbia University Press; 2005), p. 122.

[76] ibid., p. 123.

boarded a bus in Tel Aviv carrying a bomb concealed in a brown bag that he then detonated taking twenty-two civilian lives along with his own, and injuring fifty others, making it the worst bomb attack in Israeli history up until that point. The following day a public announcement was read out in mosques across Gaza in which *Hamas* boasted that the attack had been carried out using knowledge and techniques learned directly from *Hezbollah*.[77]

There are plenty of other related examples in the literature. In January 1966, the Cuban government hosted a two-week Tricontinental Conference attended by representatives from eighty-two aspirant National Liberation Movements drawn from Africa, Asia, and Latin America. In his closing address, Fidel Castro told the conference: "We have had the opportunity of seeing how the solidarity of the peoples has been growing; how the strength of the revolutionary movement grows on a world scale, and how the mutual assistance of the peoples grows and can grow in times to come."[78] His words were prophetic — peer-to-peer engagement blossomed in the following decade. In June 1970, the founders of the *Rote Armee Fraktion*, including Andreas Baader, Gudrun Ensslin, Ulrike Meinhof and Horst Mahler, travelled to Jordan to receive training in guerrilla warfare from Yasir Arafat's *Fateh* organization.[79] Many other Marxist cadres from around the world would soon make similar journeys to camps run by the Popular Front for the Liberation of Palestine in South Yemen.[80] By its own admission, the PFLP also dispatched instructors to Turkey "to train Turkish youth in urban guerrilla fighting, kidnappings, plane hijackings, and other matters."[81] Basque separatists visiting Ireland in the early 1970s traded fifty revolvers to the Provisional IRA

---

[77] Jeffrey William Lewis, *The Business of Martyrdom: A History of Suicide Bombing* (Maryland, USA: Naval Institute Press; 2012), p. 158.

[78] Fidel Castro, *At the Closing Session of the Tricontinental Conference*, 15 January 1966, at https://www.marxists.org/history/cuba/archive/castro/1966/01/15.htm, accessed in the University of Texas Fidel Castro Speech Database on 10 August 2015.

[79] Stefan Aust, *Baader-Meinhof: The Inside Story of the R.A.F.* (London: Oxford University Press; 2009), pp. 65–72.

[80] Claire Sterling, *The Terror Network: The Secret War of International Terrorism* (Holt, Rinehart and Winston; 1981), pp. 90–91.

[81] ibid., p. 240.

in return for receiving instruction in the use of explosives[82] and in 1975 ETA sent members to Algeria to receive training in clandestine warfare from veterans of the FLN's struggle for independence.[83] Indeed, the interchange between different terrorist groups was so great during the 1970s that by 1976 the US Central Intelligence Agency estimated that more than 140 groups from fifty countries and territories were in some form of contact with each other.[84]

The transfer of technical knowledge continues to be feature of terrorism today. In 2000, an *al-Qaeda* member called Abu Hudhayfa sent a detailed letter to Osama bin Laden suggesting improvements to the organization's communications strategy: "How nice it would be if in the future the executor of an operation is video-taped while he is giving an inciting speech to the nation and then his speech is published after the operation is carried out successfully similar to what *Hamas* is doing."[85] *Al-Qaeda* took this advice to heart and a number of the 9/11 hijackers recorded martyrdom videos. In December 2004, three Irish nationals associated with a dissident republican group who had been arrested in Colombia were convicted *in absentia* for providing paramilitary training to members of the Marxist terrorist organization *Fuerzas Armadas Revolucionarias de Colombia — Ejército del Pueblo* (FARC-EP).[86] In 2005, the Colombian General Carlos Ospina told reporters that FARC-EP had been using homemade mortars and grenades copied from models developed by the Provisional IRA.[87] In 2010, the online English-language magazine *Inspire*, produced by *al-Qaeda* in the Arabian Peninsula, published an article entitled *Make a Bomb in the Kitchen of your Mom*. The article was downloaded in the United States by Dzhokhar

---

[82] Maria McGuire, *To Take Arms: A Year in the Provisional IRA* (London: MacMillan; 1973), p. 110.

[83] Claire Sterling, *The Terror Network: The Secret War of International Terrorism* (Holt, Rinehart and Winston; 1981), p. 195.

[84] ibid., p. 10.

[85] Charles Kurzman, *The Missing Martyrs: Why There Are So Few Muslim Terrorists* (Oxford, UK: Oxford University Press; 2011), p. 76.

[86] Sibylla Brodzinsky, Irishmen in hiding jailed for 17 years, *The Guardian*, 16 December 2004 at http://www.theguardian.com/world/2004/dec/17/colombia.sibyllabrodzinsky (accessed 18 July 2015).

[87] Jeremy McDermott, IRA influence in Farc attacks, *BBC News*, 9 May 2005 at http://news.bbc.co.uk/2/hi/americas/4528109.stm (accessed 18 July 2015).

Tsarnaev, as he and his brother, Tamerlan, planned their attack on the Boston Marathon in April 2013, which killed three people and injured 264 more.[88] In many ways, *Inspire* is little more than the modern equivalent of Johann Most's *The Science of Revolutionary Warfare* — there really is little new under the sun.

The simple truth is that terrorist groups come in many shapes and sizes, and they evolve and mutate. Jessica Stern coined the phrase "the Protean enemy" — a term derived from a shape-shifting character featured in Greek mythology — to describe the challenge posed by terrorism because of the constantly changing nature of the groups involved and the changing nature of the threat itself.[89] This too is a useful analogy. Terrorism is not, and will never be, a conceptually clean label. Terrorists are complex actors who may at times simultaneously inhabit multiple identities — terrorist and drug trafficker, terrorist and freedom fighter, terrorist and revolutionary, Marxist and nationalist — but at their core all the groups featured in this book have one thing in common: They are prepared to indiscriminately and violently target civilians for political gain.

In the chapters ahead, I will be drawing on examples from the broadest geographical and temporal spread of terrorist organizations that I can find, from the latter half of the nineteenth century to the present day, to support my arguments, but the reader should bear in mind that just as there are points of similarity between some groups there are also great differences between others — this is not a cohesive data set by any stretch of the imagination. As a result, when we find trends that are common across different temporal and geographical clusters, this is significant and worth remarking upon. Inevitably, some terrorist groups will feature more heavily than others — some like *al-Qaeda* and the Provisional IRA will no doubt be familiar to even the most casual reader, others like *Narodnaya Volya* or the militant wing of the African National Congress, *Umkhonto we Sizwe* (MK), will be less so.

---

[88] Richard Serrano, Boston Bombing Indictment: Dzhokar Tsarnaev inspired by Al Qaeda, *Los Angeles Times*, 27 June 2013 at http://articles.latimes.com/2013/jun/27/nation/la-na-nn-boston-marathon-bombing-suspect-indictment-20130627 (accessed 18 July 2015).

[89] Jessica Stern, The Protean Enemy, *Foreign Affairs*, July/August 2003.

As each new group is introduced, I will try to set it in context but this will not be a linear narrative.

The whole point of this book is that there is a lot of information available about terrorism, terrorist groups, and individual terrorists. Yet, despite a well-documented history of terrorist violence stretching back 150 years or so that has afflicted almost every corner of the globe; despite in-depth case studies and analyses of terrorist campaigns churned out by think tanks and universities by the dozen; despite shelves of published memoirs, articles, and statements written by terrorists of all stripes; despite all this data, state after state confronting terrorist violence for the first time seems to treat it as an unknown quantity and to replicate the same mistakes made by so many guardians of law and order before them. Indeed, so inevitable do such missteps seem to be that the Irish academic and terrorism expert Louise Richardson has even posited the existence of a predictable pathology of state overreaction, which equally inevitably plays right into the terrorists' hands.[90]

In the aftermath of the May 1886 Haymarket bombing in Chicago, State's Attorney Julius Grinnell urged police investigators to "make the raids first, and look up the law afterwards".[91] Confronting the disorder created by Michael Collins and his men in post-World War I Ireland, the Liberal British Prime Minister David Lloyd George confided to the Chief of the Imperial General Staff, Field Marshal Sir Henry Wilson, his belief that "a counter murder association was the best answer to *Sinn Féin* murders."[92] The French Interior Minister (and future President) François Mitterrand responded to the attacks across French colonial Algeria on 1 November 1954, which heralded the beginning of the FLN's campaign of national liberation, by telling the Chamber of Deputies: "I will not agree to negotiate with the enemies of the

---

[90] Louise Richardson, *What Terrorists Want: Understanding the Enemy, Containing the Threat* (USA: Random House; 2006), p. 234.

[91] Michael Burleigh, *Blood and Rage: A Cultural History of Terrorism* (New York: Harper; 2009), p. 76.

[92] T. Ryle Dwyer, *The Squad and the Intelligence Operations of Michael Collins* (Cork: Mercier; 2005), p. 136.

homeland. The only negotiation is war!"[93] And so it was again in the immediate aftermath of the 11 September 2001 attacks on New York and Washington. US Vice-President Dick Cheney gave an interview to the NBC news program *Meet The Press* in which he said that the US was going to have to embrace what he termed "the dark side" if it was to triumph against *al-Qaeda*.[94] It was a remark that came to encapsulate the approach to counter-terrorism adopted by the Bush administration and it still exerts a powerful gravitational pull over the national security debate in the United States more than a decade-and-a-half later.

To those accustomed to the exercise of power there seems to be something both reassuring and seductive in the notion that the unrestrained use of that power can meet any challenge. Following the bombing of Pan Am 103 over Lockerbie, Scotland, in December 1988 with the loss of 270 lives, US President George H. W. Bush established the President's Commission on Aviation Security and Terrorism to investigate the incident and draw up policy recommendations to prevent any future reoccurrence. The Commission concluded in its final report: "National will and the moral courage to exercise it are the ultimate means for defeating terrorism."[95] For many of the "hard men" in the national security community, this seems to be a consistent article of faith. The same cry went up after the September 11th attacks — as the former Head of the CIA's Clandestine Service, Jose Rodriguez, put it to reporter Lesley Stahl: "We needed to get everybody in government to put their big boy pants on and provide the authorities that we needed [to go after the terrorists]."[96] But is this sound public policy? Empirical historical research and accepted social science theory suggest that it is not, at least not for democracies. As Nikolai Morozov noted in his essay

---

[93] Gilles Kepel, *Terror in France: The Rise of Jihad in the West* (Princeton University Press; 2017), p. 7 and Paul Aussaresses, *The Battle of the Casbah: Terrorism and Counterterrorism in Algeria 1955–1957* (Enigma Books; 2002), p. 2.

[94] Vice-President Dick Cheney interviewed by Tim Russert on NBC's *Meet The Press*, 16 September 2001, at http://afpakwar.com/blog/archives/576.

[95] Report of the President's Commission on Aviation Security and Terrorism, Washington DC, 15 May 1990, p. i.

[96] Lesley Stahl, Hard Measures: Ex-CIA head defends post-9/11 tactics, 60 Minutes, 29 April 2012.

*The Terrorist Struggle*: "Force is only dreadful to the obvious enemy. Against the secret one it is completely useless."[97] There is a wealth of evidence to suggest that Morozov's analysis is spot on.

Terrorism is often described as the weapon of the weak, and in terms of the strategic threat that it poses to most states this is a pretty apt description.[98] One of the central contentions of this book is that terrorism is an essentially contingent political tactic — any success depends in large part on the manner in which the target state chooses to respond to terrorist activity. Mike German, the author of *Thinking Like a Terrorist*, has observed: "Our failure to understand [terrorists] is peculiar, because terrorism is all about the message and terrorists are vocal about who they are, what they want, and how they intend to get it. They are prolific writers and enthusiastic public speakers, but we rarely pay enough attention to what they write or to what they say."[99] German gained his insights the hard way — as an FBI Special Agent, he completed two undercover assignments infiltrating right-wing terrorist groups.

This book is organized into three constituent parts. Part I takes German's critique to heart and explores the phenomenon of terrorism from the terrorists' perspective and, drawing on the wealth of published material authored by the architects of terrorist violence over the years, unpacks how terrorists seek to use violence as a tactic to force political change. In particular, it identifies six core concepts underpinning the use of violence by terrorist groups that are common to all four strains of terrorist activity — asymmetrical warfare, attrition, propaganda by deed, the construction of revolutionary prototypes and martyrs, seeking to provoke an overreaction, and challenging for legitimacy — and illustrates how each concept has been used by such groups in practice. By carefully analyzing the processes by which terrorists seek to achieve their goals, we will be better placed to understand which state responses are likely to have

---

[97] Nikolai Morozov, The Terrorist Struggle, in Walter Laqueur (ed.), *Voices of Terror* (Sourcebooks Inc.; 2004), p. 77.

[98] Martha Crenshaw, The Causes of Terrorism, *Comparative Politics*, Vol. 13, No. 4 (1981), p. 387.

[99] Mike German, *Thinking Like a Terrorist: Insights of a Former FBI Undercover Agent* (Potomac Books; 2007), p. viii.

a positive impact and which are more likely to play straight into the terrorists' hands.

Part II explores why individual terrorists turn to violence in the first place by reviewing the most influential social science research conducted on violent extremism and radicalization that leads to terrorism, and what conclusions we can draw from this research about the optimum state response to these processes. In particular, it considers five broad explanatory frameworks which have been widely credited within both the academic and practitioner communities as offering meaningful insights into the motivations of individuals who join terrorist organizations — empathy, self-actualization, social networks, poverty, and government aggression. The literature associated with this research suggests that the use of unrestrained force may not just be relatively ineffective but might actually be counterproductive, and this has important public policy implications, further suggesting that a more measured response guided by established international human rights principles might be far better suited to countering extremist threats. It is my contention that a close reading of the literature addressing both processes of radicalization, and terrorist group formation and longevity, offers plenty of qualitative evidence to support this conclusion.

Indeed, terror groups seem to instinctively grasp and exploit the very factors that the social science suggests motivates young men and women to turn to violence, while governments seem, almost just as instinctively, to exacerbate them. Even the most powerful terrorist groups are minority actors with relatively insignificant resources when compared to the weakest states. Governments would appear to have substantial advantages at their disposal in terms of men, material and treasure, and yet history is replete with examples of states failing to deal effectively with terrorist violence.

Having established what political actors are hoping to achieve by adopting some or all of the violent tactics associated with terrorism, and having considered the processes that social science suggests drive people to embrace violent opposition, Part III lays out the international legal regime governing state responses to terrorist violence. These are the rules that should — but often don't — bind state responses to terrorist threats. It is the central argument of this book that these rules — when followed — can actively prevent states from falling into the kinds of tactical and strategic traps deliberately set by terrorist groups as outlined in Part I, or from actively radicalizing alienated individuals by their actions as outlined in Part II, but that when these rules are ignored the long-term consequences are typically dire.

Part III also explores in detail the range of coercive and noncoercive tools that states have adopted to meet the terrorist threat. Some of these tools are unique to counter-terrorism, others were first developed in response to serious criminal activity or severe civil disturbance, and have subsequently been adapted for a counterterrorism role. For each tool, I will review the existing international jurisprudence that applies to their use, some of the challenges involved in using such tools, and existing examples of both good and poor practice. This section focuses on five core tools in the counter-terrorism arsenal — community engagement, special investigation techniques, investigative interviewing, detention regimes, and the use of force. Traditional human rights discourse tends to focus on condemnation and prohibition — so I will also seek to proactively identify human rights-compliant counter-terrorism tools of proven effectiveness that can be deployed to prevent terrorist violence. There is little point condemning states' missteps unless one can actually propose an effective alternative. There is a role for force within such an approach but, knowing that force poorly applied is only likely to fan the flames of violent opposition, it must be carefully controlled. After all, fire is best fought, not with fire, but with water.[100]

The former President of Israel's Supreme Court, Aharon Barak, once observed that although a democracy was often forced to fight with "one hand tied behind its back", its values nevertheless ensured that it had the upper hand.[101] While well intentioned, the metaphor hardly helped support the sentiment. I would argue that a more

---

[100] See Tom Parker and Nick Sitter, Fighting Fire with Water: NGO and Counter-Terrorism Policy Tools, *Global Policy*, Vol. 5, No. 2 (May 2014).

[101] H.C. 5100/94, Pub. Comm. Against Torture in Isr. v. Gov't of Israel, 53(4) P.D. 817–845.

accurate characterization would be that these same values, when observed, actually ensure that, rather than swinging wildly, the state acts with greater control and precision — in fact, to carry an unwieldy metaphor through to its conclusion, the application of these values, much like good coaching and hard training, frees up the fighter to set about his or her task with both hands, and with much greater effectiveness. In summary, the purpose of this book is to suggest that might is not necessarily right, and that in fighting ogres it is not necessary to become one in the process to defeat them. No matter how well intentioned, an ogre is still an ogre, and, if fairy tales have anything to teach us, it must surely be that the story never ends well for the ogre.

# Part I

# A Not-So-Secret Formula

> "By pen and gun
> By word and bullet
> By tongue and teeth."[1]

Terrorists and their supporters are surprisingly prolific authors. From the first, the theorists and practitioners of terrorism have been keen to explain their motivation for adopting such violent tactics. This need to explain has generated a rich universe of commentary: Public speeches by prominent users of political violence like the Irish revolutionary Michael Collins, *Sendero Luminoso*'s Abimael Guzmán, and *Hezbollah*'s Hassan Nasrallah; Operational manuals like Johann Most's *The Science of Revolutionary Warfare*, Carlos Marighella's *Minimanual of the Urban Guerrilla*, or the *Handbook for Volunteers of the Irish Republican Army*; Theoretical treatises like Abu Mus'ab al-Suri's *The Call to Global Islamic Resistance*, or Nikolai Morozov's *The Terrorist Struggle*; Public communiqués such as those issued by the *Rote Armee Fraktion*, and the Weather Underground; Captured internal documents like *Umkhonto we Sizwe*'s Operation Mayibuye strategy paper, or the *al-Qaeda* hard drives recovered during the raid on Osama bin Laden's Abbottabad hideout; Periodicals like the nineteenth century anarchist paper *L'En-dehors*,[2] the underground newspaper of *Euskadi Ta Askatasuna*, *Zutik*,[3] or *al-Qaeda* in the Arabian Peninsula's

---

[1] *Al Qaeda Training Manual*, released by the United States Department of Justice on 7 December 2001.
[2] The Outside.
[3] Stand Up!

33

online English language magazine *Inspire*; Countless interviews given by key terrorist actors like the Algerian *Front de Libération Nationale's* Saadi Yacef, the Popular Front for the Liberation of Palestine's Leila Khaled or Susanna Ronconi, a veteran of Italy's *Brigate Rosse* and *Prima Linea*; Courtroom statements like those by the French anarchist Émile Henry, 9/11 mastermind Khalid Sheikh Mohammed at the Military Commission hearings in Guantanamo Bay, or November 17's Dimitris Koufodinas; And, finally, detailed memoirs such as those written by *Narodnaya Volya's* Vera Figner, *Irgun's* Menachem Begin, EOKA's Georgios Grivas, and *Fateh's* Abu Iyad.

Michael Scheuer, the former Chief of the CIA's Bin Laden Issue Station, observed in his insightful biography of Osama bin Laden that a good rule of thumb when analyzing an individual's thoughts and actions is to balance the comments and insights made by observers, rivals and opponents, with the actual statements made by the individual him or herself.[4] Clearly, such statements can frequently be disingenuous, deceitful and self-serving, as academic researchers Mary Beth Altier, John Horgan and Christian Thoroughgood have pointed out, but even in this regard, careful reading and analysis can provide important insights.[5] In this spirit, our purpose in Part I will be to review a representative geographic and temporal sample of primary sources like those described above to identify the common strategies employed by terrorist groups, the core objectives sought through these strategies, and the thought processes underpinning their use. While the tools available to terrorist groups have changed considerably in the shift from the industrial to the information age, the strategic use of terrorism has actually evolved very little since terrorists first appeared on the world stage in the nineteenth century. As a result, a number of key strategic principles common to most, if not all, terrorist groups can be identified. Once we have a better understanding of what terrorists are trying to achieve, and

---

[4] Michael Scheuer, *Osama bin Laden* (Oxford University Press; 2011), p. 19.
[5] See Mary Beth Altier, John Horgan and Christian Thoroughgood, In Their Own Words? Methodological Considerations in the Analysis of Terrorist Autobiographies, *Journal of Strategic Security*, Vol. 5, No. 4 (2012).

how they trying to achieve it, we can have a much better sense of which counter-terrorism responses are best suited to thwarting their ambitions.

## Asymmetrical Warfare

Former FBI Special Agent Mike German observed in *Thinking Like a Terrorist* that "a true picture of terrorists would show poorly selected, poorly trained, and poorly equipped soldiers in a poorly organized army."[6] This state of affairs is not lost on terrorists themselves. Terrorist groups over the past 150 years have all understood the unequal nature of the struggle on which they have embarked and as a result have embraced the comparative advantage of weakness. As Bruce Hoffman, one of the trailblazers of terrorism research, famously put it: "Terrorism is designed to create power where there is none or to consolidate power where there is very little."[7]

No matter how sophisticated modern weapons systems get, conventional land-based warfare still adheres to the same basic tactical framework elucidated by Carl von Clausewitz in his classic work on military strategy, *On War*. Retain the initiative, seek to fix the enemy in a single point in space and time, then mass one's forces — ideally in greater numbers than the enemy possesses — and maneuver these forces into a position where they can annihilate the enemy. This approach can be boiled down to the aphorism often attributed to the Confederate cavalry general and early leader of the Ku Klux Klan, Nathan Bedford Forrest, as "getting there firstest with the mostest".

The strategic element is pretty conceptually straightforward too — identify a military objective for a campaign, identify the physical or military factors that have to be attained to achieve that objective, and then devise a plan of consecutive actions that lead inexorably to this conclusion. The plan formed, you advance to

---

[6] Mike German, *Thinking Like a Terrorist: Insights of a Former FBI Undercover Agent* (Potomac Books; 2007), p. 53.

[7] Bruce Hoffman, *Inside Terrorism* (Columbia University Press; 1998), p. 44.

contact with the enemy, seek to gain the initiative, press your advantage by maintaining constant physical pressure on the enemy, and then maneuver or degrade the enemy to the point of defeat, thus bringing the campaign to a decisive conclusion. Modern militaries have a number of buzzwords for these concepts, such as locating the enemy's "center of gravity", maintaining "continuity of operations", and reaching the "culminating point of victory".[8] The difference between tactics and strategy is, in essence, simply that between short- and long-term planning. Unsurprisingly, military strategy favors large, mobile, well-supplied armies equipped with the most advanced weaponry and it finds its ultimate expression in the Powell Doctrine of "overwhelming force", named after the former US Secretary of State and Chairman of the Joint Chiefs of Staff, Colin Powell, and its popular attendant colloquialism "shock and awe".

Traditional military doctrine is thus both well established and well known. The power differential between even the most modest military establishment and its terrorist counterpart is likely to be such that few terrorist groups will be foolish enough to engage the security forces of a state directly with any confidence of success. Karl Heinzen, a veteran of the failed popular uprisings that swept through western and central Europe in 1848, was one of the first of a new breed of political activist to suggest an alternative approach in his 1853 pamphlet *Mord und Freiheit*. Noting that it was their virtual monopoly of military power that kept despots in power, and inspired by the recent invention of nitroglycerin, Heinzen offered an alternative program of political action which amounted to terrorism in all but name: "The most important thing, above all, is to abrogate the preponderance of means of destruction that is and could not be at our disposal through the homeopathic application, as it were, of radical materials of destruction, whose provision or preparation is not too expensive and carries with it little danger of discovery."[9]

---

[8] See Timothy Hoyt, Attacking Terrorism: Elements of a Grand Strategy, in Audrey Kurth Cronin and James Ludes (eds.), *Military Force* (Georgetown University Press; 2004).

[9] Karl Heinzen, *Murder and Freedom* (New York; 1853) reproduced in Daniel Bessner and Michael Stauch, Karl Heinzen and the Intellectual Origins of Modern Terror, *Terrorism and Political Violence*, Vol. 22 (2010), p. 165.

The early populists, socialists, and anarchists learned the value of Heinzen's insight with the defeat of the short-lived Paris Commune in 1871.[10] The brutal suppression of the Communards at the hands of the French army cost at least ten thousand working class men and women their lives. For militants like Nikolai Morozov, this was a turning point in the history of revolutionary struggle, the dawn of a new era in which revolutionaries sought not to seize power in a single throw of the dice but to slowly chip away at the ruling establishment over time — a strategy Morozov labeled "terroristic revolution".[11] As Morozov's comrade Sergei Kravshinski (also known as Stepniak) put it in his memoirs, *Underground Russia*: "It being absolutely impossible to overcome [the government] by force ... a flank movement was necessary."[12] In *The Terrorist Struggle*, Morozov described how this "flank movement" would work in practice: "Justice is done here, but those who carry out it remain alive. They disappear without a trace and thus they are able to fight again against the enemy, to live and to work for the cause."[13] He added that adopting this strategic approach would neutralize the government's superior force of arms: "The revolutionary group is not afraid of bayonets and the government's army because it does not have to clash, in its struggle, with this blind and insensible force, which strikes down those whom it is ordered to strike. This force is only dreadful to the obvious enemy. Against the secret one it is completely useless."[14]

---

[10] A lesson that was still being cited more than 100 years later by Marxist groups like the Red Army Faction. See Ulrike Meinhof, *On the Liberation of Andreas Baader*, 13 September 1974, in J. Smith and André Moncourt, *The Red Army Faction A Documentary History: Volume 1 — Projectiles for the People* (PM Press; 2009), p. 360. See also Lawrence Freedman, *Strategy: A History* (Oxford University Press; 2013), p. 271.

[11] Nikolai Morozov, The Terrorist Struggle (1880), in Walter Laqueur (ed.), *Voices of Terror: Manifestos, Writings and Manuals of Al Qaeda, Hamas, and other Terrorists from Around the World and Throughout the Ages* (Sourcebooks; 2004), p. 76.

[12] S. Stepniak, *Underground Russia: Revolutionary Profiles and Sketches From Life* (Charles Scribner's Sons; 1883), p. 38.

[13] Nikolai Morozov, The Terrorist Struggle (1880), in Walter Laqueur (ed.), *Voices of Terror: Manifestos, Writings and Manuals of Al Qaeda, Hamas, and other Terrorists from Around the World and Throughout the Ages* (Sourcebooks; 2004), p. 78.

[14] ibid., pp. 76–77.

The members of the Irish nationalist movement in the United States that made up the ranks of *Clan na Gael* included many veterans from both sides of the American Civil War. Like the popular movement in Europe, Irish nationalists had seen more conventional revolutionary action, like John O'Neill's repeated cross-border Fenian incursions into Canada between 1866–1871 and the 1867 uprising organized in Ireland by the Irish Republican Brotherhood, fail, and so they developed a new concept of operations inspired by the emerging military practice of sending out skirmishers in advance of the main army to probe the enemy's dispositions for weaknesses and to harass the enemy's forces as they maneuvered. The use of skirmishers had attracted significant attention during the Civil War as a result of a series of influential articles written by General John Watts de Peyster under the title *New American Tactics,* which advocated considering the skirmish line as a distinct line of battle in its own right, and brought a new fluidity to the conventional battlefield and the practice of mobile warfare.[15] In October 1874, the Brooklyn-based nationalist newspaper *Irish World* wrote that the cause of Irish Independence was in need of "some band of men to pioneer the way — sometimes to skirmish, sometimes to act as a forlorn hope, sometimes to give martyrs and confessors; always acting, always showing that we still have amongst us brave men ready to do or dare all that brave men ever did and dared for the salvation of a fallen land."[16] Within a year, the idea of sending "skirmishers" from a base of operations in America across the Atlantic to strike at the heart of the British Empire had begun to take shape, driven in large part by the editor of the *Irish World,* Patrick Ford.

Early proponents of the use of violence for political ends, like Mikhail Bakunin, Sergei Kravshinski and Michael Collins, also studied the lessons to be learned from impactful guerrilla

---

[15] Lewis Hamersly Randolph, *Biographical Sketches of Distinguished Officers of the Army and Navy* (Henry E. Huntington Library; 1905).

[16] K. R. M. Short, *Dynamite War: Irish American Bombers in Victorian Britain* (Gill and Macmillan; 1979), p. 34.

campaigns, including Imam Shamil's fierce resistance to Tsarist Russian expansion into the Caucasus, the rebellion of Dutch South African settlers (known as the Boers) against the British Empire, and the exploits of the Confederate "bush-whackers" like William Quantrill who engaged Unionist troops along the Missouri–Kansas border and helped inspire the formation of the Ku Klux Klan. Bakunin coined the dictum that "popular revolution is born from the merging of the revolt of the brigand with that of the peasant."[17] Kravshinski wrote a manual on guerrilla warfare after fighting alongside Herzegovinian insurgents in their revolt against Ottoman rule in the mid-1870s.[18] Collins would even write an appreciative letter to the Boer commander Christiaan de Wet, thanking him for being his "earliest inspiration".[19] The Boer *Kommando*, a light mobile guerrilla force, was especially influential being adopted by the Irish nationalists in their struggle for independence from Britain after World War I as the "flying column". From these modest beginnings, terrorists have evolved their own concepts of operation that owe much to guerrilla warfare and essentially amount to a negative image of conventional military tactics — driven by one cardinal operational principle above all: hit and run. As Collins put it, "It is never possible for us to be militarily strong, but we could be strong enough to make England uncomfortable (and strong enough to make England too uncomfortable)."[20]

One of the most successful and influential twentieth century exponents of guerrilla warfare is the Chinese communist leader Mao Tse-tung whose classic treatise *On Guerrilla Warfare* has served as an inspiration to generations of terrorists all over the world. Mao's first law of guerrilla warfare was "preserve ourselves and destroy the enemy". His strategy was simple: "When guerrillas

---

[17] Alex Butterworth, *The World That Never Was: A True Story of Dreamers, Schemers, Anarchists and Secret Agents* (Pantheon Books; 2010), p. 116.

[18] See ibid., p. 115.

[19] Max Boot, *Invisible Armies: An Epic History of Guerrilla Warfare from Ancient Times to the Present* (Liveright; 2013), p. 250.

[20] Michael Collins, *The Path to Freedom* (Roberts Rinehart; 2000), p. 53.

engage a stronger enemy, they withdraw when he advances; harass him when he stops; strike him when he is weary; pursue him when he withdraws. In guerrilla strategy, the enemy's rear, flanks, and other vulnerable spots are his vital points, and there he must be harassed, attacked, dispersed, exhausted and annihilated."[21] He once remarked that guerrillas must be experts at running away since they must do it so often, and guerrillas and terrorists alike have taken his advice very much to heart.[22]

*On Guerrilla Warfare* was written in 1937 while Chinese communists were fighting both the invading Imperial Japanese Army and Chinese Nationalist Army of Chiang Kai-shek, with the outcome of both struggles very much in doubt. In it, Mao advanced a three-phase approach to revolutionary warfare: (1) earn the population's support through propaganda and by attacking the organs of government; (2) escalate attacks against the government's military forces and vital institutions; (3) conventional warfare and fighting to seize cities, overthrow the government, and assume control of the country. Significantly, Mao believed that guerrilla operations alone were "incapable of providing a solution to the struggle"[23] and that the third phase of conventional warfare and mass revolutionary activity was simply the goal to which guerrilla operations helped build: "Experience shows that if … regular hostilities are not conducted with tenacity, guerrilla operations alone cannot produce final victory."[24]

Not every terrorist movement is revolutionary in aspiration — some come to realize that societal transformation is too great an ask, so set their sights on concessions and negotiated settlements instead. It is therefore not the totality of Mao's theory of guerrilla warfare that is so influential but rather the applicability of his general insights. One can find echoes of Mao's advice — especially relating to phases one and two of his model — littered through the manuals

---

[21] Mao Tse-tung, *On Guerrilla Warfare* translated by Brigadier General Samuel B. Griffith II (University of Illinois Press; 1961), p. 46.

[22] ibid., p. 24.

[23] ibid., p. 42.

[24] ibid., p. 62.

and memoirs produced by many modern terrorist movements, and not just those of an avowedly Maoist character like Peru's *Sendero Luminoso.* Michael Ryan, author of *Decoding Al-Qaeda's Strategy,* wryly notes: "*al-Qaeda* strategic writings may begin and end with Islamic references and prayers but their core arguments have less to do with Islam than with the texts of communist insurgents and idealogues."[25]

The *Handbook for Volunteers of the Irish Republican Army,* distributed to members of the IRA during the 1956–1962 cross-border campaign against British and pro-British loyalist targets in Northern Ireland, describes the organization's operational approach entirely in terms that Mao would instantly recognize: "The guerrilla strikes not one large blow but many little ones; he hits suddenly, gnaws at the enemy's strength, disengages himself, withdraws, disperses and hits again … Since the guerrilla's main task is to drain the enemy it follows that he hits the enemy in his most vulnerable area and fights for the initiative — never ground."[26]

Similarly, Menachem Begin described the basic operating principles of the Assault Force (AF) of *Irgun Zvai Leumi* in its struggle against the British authorities in the League of Nations Mandate of Palestine during the mid-1940s: "The battle tactics of the AF were based on the maximum exploitation of the factor of surprise and the employment of small forces for big blows."[27] He added: "We did not have to attack 20 British camps simultaneously in order to develop acute apprehension amongst all. It was enough to attack one in order that all should be afflicted with fear by night and with uneasy expectation by day."[28] Begin likened the overall effect to a broken-down piano: "You press one note and the whole piano emits a cacophony of noise."[29] The random nature of surprise

---

[25] Michael Ryan, *Decoding Al Qaeda's Strategy: The Deep Battle Against America* (Columbia University Press; 2013), pp. 4–5.

[26] *Handbook for Volunteers of the Irish Republican Army: Notes on Guerrilla Warfare,* 1956 Edition (Paladin Press; 1985), pp. 6–10.

[27] Menachem Begin, *The Revolt: Story of the Irgun* (Steimatzky's Agency Ltd.; 1977), p. 95.

[28] ibid.

[29] ibid.

attack after surprise attack serves to amplify the impact of relatively minor kinetic operations.

You find the same approach again in *apartheid* South Africa. In July 1963, police raided a small farmhouse in the suburbs of Johannesburg that was being used as a safe house by the leadership of militant wing of the anti-*apartheid* African National Congress, *Umkhonto we Sizwe*. In the course of the raid, police discovered a short six-page draft strategy document titled Operation Mayibuye, which had been developed by Arthur Goldreich, a Jewish painter and member of the *Umkhonto we Sizwe* High Command.[30] Like Menachem Begin, before moving to South Africa, Goldreich had fought in the Jewish independence movement in Palestine in the 1940s and his experience helped shape *Umkhonto we Sizwe* in its formative years. Although Operation Mayibuye was never formally adopted by the organization's leadership, the document nevertheless offers useful insights into their thinking during this period, most notably in this context: "The cornerstone of guerrilla operations is 'shamelessly attack the weak and shamelessly flee from the strong.'"[31] Regular military forces think in terms of discrete sequential operational steps, terrorists pursue instead a cumulative approach in which sequence matters for very little and everything hinges on the mounting burden of their attacks being too great for a state to absorb.[32]

Terrorists and guerrillas alike understand that great undertakings start from small beginnings. As US Brigadier General Samuel B. Griffith observes in the introduction to his classic translation of Mao's manual, the "base" of Fidel Castro's revolution in Cuba was just twelve men.[33] Numbers simply aren't that important. Georgios

---

[30] Douglas O. Linder, *The Nelson Mandela (Rivonia) Trial: An Account*, 2010, at http://law2.umkc.edu/faculty/projects/ftrials/mandela/mandelaaccount.html.

[31] http://www.historicalpapers.wits.ac.za/inventories/inv_pdft/AD1844-Aa5-text.pdf.

[32] Rear Admiral J. C. Wylie, *Military Strategy: A General Theory of Power Control* (Rutgers University Press; 1967), p. 24.

[33] Mao Tse-tung, *On Guerrilla Warfare* translated by Brigadier General Samuel B. Griffith II (University of Illinois Press; 1961). See also Jac Weller, Irregular But Effective: Partizan Weapons Tactics in the American Revolution, Southern Theatre, *Military Affairs*, Vol. 21, No. 3 (Autumn 1957).

Grivas, the leader of the anti-colonial Greek Cypriot *Ethniki Organosis Kyprion Agoniston* (EOKA) movement that from 1955 to 1959 fought against British control of Cyprus and for *Enosis,* or union, with Greece, certainly had no intention of engaging the British on equal terms, observing: "All war is cruel and the only way to win against superior forces is by ruse and trickery; you can no more make a difference between striking in front or behind than you can between employing rifles and howitzers."[34] Grivas was an experienced former Greek Army officer who had fought in two World Wars, a Civil War, and had served in the Greek Underground during the German occupation of Greece.[35] This made him a formidable opponent as one senior British intelligence officer, W. T. Magan, acknowledged: "He is undismayed by the hazards that fate and the day may bring forth, confident in his own strength and resourcefulness to cope with them ... clear-headed in exceptional degree, invested in large measure with the power to command, trained and practiced as a soldier for 30 years, and brutalized by the barbarities that he has shared."[36] Grivas' strategy in Cyprus was simple — stay in the fight and keep landing significant blows until international political pressure forced a British capitulation. This was considerably easier to achieve with a tight disciplined force than with a sprawling coalition of fractious supporters. He therefore set out to keep the number of operational cells taking the fight to the British to a minimum, writing to supporters: "I do not believe the number of strike groups should be increased at present, for a higher number would find it harder to find hiding places and their chance of escape under attack would be lessened."[37]

The Marxist terror groups of the late 1960s and 1970s were based primarily in urban areas and were often constituted around a core of activists that had come together on university campuses. Carlos

---

[34] Matthew Carr, *The Infernal Machine: A History of Terrorism* (The New Press; 2007), p. 70.

[35] David French, *Fighting EOKA: The British Counter-Insurgency Campaign on Cyprus, 1955–1959* (Oxford University Press; 2015), pp. 46–47.

[36] ibid., p. 47.

[37] George Grivas-Dighenis and Charles Foley, *The Memoirs of General Grivas* (Longmans; 1964), p. 204.

Marighella wrote the *Minimanual of the Urban Guerrilla* as a practical guide for these comrades, adapting the lessons in Mao's handbook for the industrialized cities of the developed and developing world. Marighella was the founder of the Brazilian Marxist terrorist group *Ação Libertadora Nacional* (ALN), best known for working in alliance with the *Movimento Revolucionário 8 de Outubro* (MR-8) to kidnap the United States Ambassador to Brazil, Charles Burke Elbrick, in September 1969. Ambassador Elbrick was released after 78 hours in captivity in exchange for fifteen imprisoned leftists. The two groups issued a joint declaration explaining the reasoning behind their action in classic guerrilla terms: "By kidnapping the US Ambassador we wish to demonstrate that it is possible to triumph over dictatorship and exploitation if we are properly armed and organized. We act where the enemy expects it least and we disappear immediately, weakening the dictatorship, terrorizing the exploiters and bringing hopes of victory to the oppressed."[38] The great embarrassment that Elbrick's kidnapping caused the ruling military *junta* sealed Marighella's fate — he was shot and killed in an ambush by Brazilian police in November 1969.

Marighella's *Minimanual* was immensely influential amongst Marxist-inspired terrorist organizations such as the *Rote Armee Fraktion* and the *Brigate Rosse*. November 17 foot soldier Patroklos Tselentis recalled participating in a raid on a branch of the National Bank of Greece which was dutifully executed following the instructions in the *Minimanual*'s chapter on "expropriations".[39] Marighella, who visited Communist China in 1953–1954, was familiar with Mao's work and adapted his insights on asymmetrical warfare for combat in the urban environment, but they remained eminently recognizable: "With the arrogance typical of the police and the military fascist authorities, the enemy will come to fight us with heavy guns and equipment and with elaborate maneuvers by men armed to the teeth. The urban guerrilla must respond to this with light weapons easily transported, so he can always escape with

---

[38] Carlos Marighela, *For the Liberation of Brazil* (Pelican Books; 1971), p. 25.
[39] George Kassimeris, *Inside Greek Terrorism* (Oxford University Press; 2013), p. 41.

maximum speed, without ever accepting open fighting. The urban guerrilla has no mission other than to attack or retreat."[40]

One trait that asymmetrical warfare does share with conventional military operations is the emphasis on seizing and retaining the initiative. However, unlike conventional military practice, this is rarely done within the broader framework of continuity of operations. Terrorists typically seek to keep their opponents perpetually off-balance by varying the geographic focus of their actions, the tempo of their attacks, and the type of target selected. This purposefully makes it difficult for the authorities to develop an effective counter-strategy. For terrorists, the cumulative point of victory lies in the political realm not the physical one, their goal, as EOKA's General Grivas put it, is "to bring about a moral defeat".[41] General Stanley McChrystal summed up the frustration of regular military officers facing such tactics when he described the situation he encountered taking command of US Special Forces operations in Iraq in 2004 in the fight against a variety of hostile insurgent and terrorist groups: "Our *people* weren't losing: They won all their fights. Our *units* weren't losing: They could point to their progress. Every element of my several-thousand-strong task force was effectively and steadily *winning* when it came to their area and their problem set. Yet, collectively, we were still losing."[42]

*Al-Qaeda* has explicitly built on the insights gained by previous guerrilla and terrorist organizations. One can find references to authors like Mao and Marighella, as well as to the terrorist campaigns of the Provisional IRA, the *Brigate Rosse*, and ETA in the work of influential *al-Qaeda* military theorists, such as Abu Ubayd al-Qurashi,[43] Abu Bakr Naji, Abd al-Aziz al-Muqrin, and Abu Mus'ab

---

[40] Carlos Marighella, *Minimanual of the Urban Guerrilla* (Havana; Tricontinental 1970).

[41] George Grivas-Dighenis and Charles Foley, *The Memoirs of General Grivas* (Longmans; 1964), p. 204.

[42] Stanley McChrystal, *The Courage to Change*, LinkedIn, 14 May 2013 at http://www.linkedin.com/today/post/article/20130514223634-86145090-the-courage-to-change?trk=NUS_UNIU_PEOPLE_FOLLOW-megaphone-fllw.

[43] Abu Ubayd al-Qurashi is a pseudonym, at the time of writing the author's real name has still not been definitively established.

al-Suri. Lectures were given in *al-Qaeda* training camps in Afghanistan and Pakistan on Robert Taber's seminal book on guerrilla warfare, *The War of the Flea.*[44] American troops searching the caves of Tora Bora after the rout of *al-Qaeda* forces in late 2001 even found among detritus left behind a copy of William S. Lind's equally influential 1989 article on asymmetrical warfare, *The Changing Face of War. Into the Fourth Generation,* originally published in the *Marine Corps Gazette.*[45] It is a truism of warfare that the enemy gets a vote in what happens — the enemy also gets to study, to learn from others' mistakes, and to evolve.

Osama bin Laden understood asymmetrical warfare all too well. In his August 1996 *Declaration of War Against the Americans Occupying the Land of the Two Holy Places,* published in the London-based newspaper *Al Quds al Arabi,* bin Laden laid out the strategy that he would pursue as *al-Qaeda* took its war to the United States: "It must be obvious to you that, due to the imbalance of power between our armed forces and the enemy forces a suitable means of fighting must be adopted, such as using fast moving forces operating in total secrecy. In other words to initiate guerrilla warfare, where the sons of the nation, and not the military forces, take part in it."[46] He also cautioned his Western foes in one taped statement: "Do not be deluded by your power and modern weapons. Although they win some battles, they lose the war. Patience and steadfastness are better than them."[47] Abu Mus'ab al-Suri, a respected veteran of several Islamic extremist movements who taught recruits in *al-Qaeda*'s Derunta and Al-Ghuraba training camps prior to the 9/11 attacks, even went so far as to argue that the ubiquity of America's international presence was in itself a

---

[44] Michael Ryan, *Decoding Al Qaeda's Strategy: The Deep Battle Against America* (Columbia University Press; 2013), p. 235. See also Robert Taber, *The War of the Flea: How Guerrilla Fighters Could Win the World!* (Citadel Press; 1970).

[45] Michael Ryan, *Decoding Al Qaeda's Strategy: The Deep Battle Against America* (Columbia University Press; 2013), p. 7.

[46] Osama bin Laden, Declaration of War Against the Americans Occupying the Land of the Two Holy Places, *Al Quds al Arabi,* 31 August 1996.

[47] Osama bin Laden, Text: Bin Laden Tape, *BBC,* January 19, 2006.

weakness since it afforded *al-Qaeda*, and like-minded affiliates and supporters, an almost unlimited supply of targets.[48]

Asymmetry is not confined solely to the military sphere. Abu Ubayd al-Qurashi identified five major asymmetries between *al-Qaeda* and its principle foe, the United States: Military power — the US is an overwhelming land, sea, and air power, while *al-Qaeda* has only a small determined force; information — the US has access to any information it needs and the ability to transmit its narrative all over the world, while *al-Qaeda* did not, at least in al-Qurashi's opinion, until the 9/11 attacks demonstrated once and for all the power of *al-Qaeda*'s message; institutions — the United States speaks for democracy, states and international organizations, while *al-Qaeda* speaks for the masses and for religious faith; space — the United States thinks in terms of regions, while *al-Qaeda* has a global outlook that does not recognize borders; and time — the United States lives in the present, while *al-Qaeda* is focused on the future.[49]

Asymmetry can even extend to the manner in which terrorist groups organize themselves. While some terrorist groups do mirror the military structures of their opponents, organizing their forces into battalions or columns, other groups have evolved a decentralized approach that is the very antithesis of the command and control systems of modern militaries. The evolution of the Internet and mobile communications technology has liberated terrorist groups to recruit and empower isolated actors with a high degree of autonomy, which in turn makes the emergence of new threats difficult for states to anticipate or interdict. As early as 1983, a neo-Nazi in the United States had created a "computerized bulletin board system", which connected far-right activists across the country.[50] The American white supremacist Louis Beam was quick to see the potential of this new technology creating the Aryan Nations Liberty Net

---

[48] Michael Ryan, *Decoding Al Qaeda's Strategy: The Deep Battle Against America* (Columbia University Press; 2013), p. 237.

[49] Michael Ryan, *Decoding Al Qaeda's Strategy: The Deep Battle Against America* (Columbia University Press; 2013), p. 107.

[50] Bipartisan Policy Center, *Countering Online Radicalization in America*, December 2012, p. 15.

the following year and developing his theory of "leaderless resistance" which, to combat sophisticated state surveillance, advocated
the use of "virtual networks" where leaders do not issue orders but
inspire small cells or individuals to take action on their own initiative. The racist author Dr. William Pierce, the founder of the
National Alliance white supremacist group and author of *The Turner
Diaries* (of which more below), described this scenario in his 1989
novel *Hunter*, in which the protagonist Oscar Yeager is inspired to
carry out a string of racist murders. A copy of *Hunter* was found in
the possession of Terry Nichols, who, along with Timothy McVeigh,
was convicted in connection with the April 1995 bombing of the
Alfred P. Murrah Federal Building in Oklahoma City, which took
168 lives, including those of nineteen children attending a daycare
center in the building.

American white supremacists are not the only movement to
adopt this approach. *Front de Libération du Québec* (FLQ) member
and propagandist Pierre Vallières, whose *Nègres Blanc d'Amérique*
had been extremely influential in separatist circles, described the
French–Canadian separatist movement in very similar terms:
"There has never been an FLQ organization as such but rather a
collection of groups or cells with little or no contact between them,
with no guiding nucleus and no real strategy."[51] Indeed, political
violence researchers Jeffrey Ross and Ted Gurr concluded that the
FLQ "was as much a state of mind as an organization".[52] *Al-Qaeda*
has also developed a very similar concept of operations, and
indeed at least one researcher, Michael Reynolds, has reported
that Islamic groups have explicitly recommended Beam's theory
of leaderless resistance to their supporters.[53] In 2004, Abu Mus'ab
al-Suri published the *Call to Global Islamic Resistance*, a comprehensive study of the modern jihadist movement covering the
period 1920 to 2001, from which he drew a number of strategic
lessons for *al-Qaeda*'s future, including a new concept for jihadist

---

[51] Jeffrey Ross and Ted Gurr, Why Terrorism Subsides: A Comparative Study of Canada and the
United States, *Comparative Politics*, Vol. 21, No. 4 (July 1989), p. 414.

[52] ibid.

[53] Jessica Stern, The Protean Enemy, *Foreign Affairs*, July/August 2003.

operations that he called *nizam la tanzim* — a system, not an organization. The *Call to Global Islamic Resistance* initially appeared online, but excerpts have been widely republished — most notably in the *al-Qaeda* in the Arabian Peninsula publication *Inspire* in 2010.

Al-Suri had begun his career as a militant in 1980 as a member of a Syrian offshoot of the Muslim Brotherhood known as *al-Tali'ah al-Muqatilah*, and by 1982 he was one of the military leaders of the Muslim Brotherhood uprising in the City of Hama, which was brutally suppressed by the forces of President Hafez al-Assad. Al-Suri fought against the Soviet invasion of Afghanistan from 1988 to 1992, participated in the media operations of *Ansar al-Jihad* during the Algerian Civil War, and then returned to Afghanistan to fight alongside the *Taliban* during their rise to power.[54] Al-Suri is a naturalized Spanish citizen through marriage and he was indicted in connection with the March 2004 Madrid train bombings, which claimed 191 lives. Al-Suri's extensive career on the frontline of global *jihad* has leant his voice a unique authority.

*Call to Global Islamic Resistance* was written in the aftermath of the rout of *Taliban* and *al-Qaeda* forces from Afghanistan following the 9/11 attacks, during which period al-Suri was moving from safe house to safe house, trying to stay one step ahead of the US and its allies, and it was the product of a decade of research and reflection. Having just experienced the raw power of the US military first hand, al-Suri was convinced that the United States was too strong to confront on the battlefield. He also believed that US technical capabilities were too adept at identifying conspiracies, and hierarchical organizations too vulnerable to surveillance and infiltration, for a traditional clandestine movement to have much expectation of success in opposing it. He therefore believed that actions carried out by independent cells or individuals would be more effective than those planned by larger organizations. He called this concept "individual resistance" — by breaking the connection between cells

---

[54] Michael Ryan, *Decoding Al Qaeda's Strategy: The Deep Battle Against America* (Columbia University Press; 2013), p. 195.

and the center, greater operational security was achieved, overall direction would come from the center, but it would only come in the form of public commentary — inspirational speeches, analysis, and propaganda — and not clandestine communications.[55] As al-Suri put it: "There [would be] no organizational binds of any kind between the members of the Global Islamic Resistance Units, except the binds of a program of beliefs, a system of action, a common name, and a common goal."[56]

Al-Suri was finally detained by the Pakistani authorities in Quetta in 2005 and was handed over to the Syrian government, where he was reportedly still being held in prison at the time of writing, but his influence on the jihadist movement is, if anything, stronger today than ever. Indeed, the influence of *Call to Global Islamic Resistance* on *al-Qaeda*, and particularly on its current leader, Ayman al-Zawahiri, whom al-Suri has referred to as "my Shaykh", is readily apparent. Writing in *Knights Under the Prophet's Banner*, al-Zawahiri echoed al-Suri's key insight: "The role of the leadership is to inspire young men by making them aware of their obligations to the faith and setting an example to follow."[57]

Most terrorist groups do not fixate on trying to hold territory but rather follow the injunction in the IRA's *Handbook for Volunteers* that "it is not [the guerrilla's] job to hold a line or take a city or maintain a strategically vital area."[58] Abu Mus'ab al-Suri notes in *Call to Global Islamic Resistance* that attempting to defend a fixed position before the time is ripe is one of the greatest traps that a guerrilla force can fall into.[59] When groups ignore this advice — as the *Tehrik-i-Taliban Pakistan* (TTP) did trying to seize and hold the Swat Valley in 2009 — they present a tangible target for conventional military

---

[55] ibid., p. 210.

[56] Jeffrey William Lewis, *The Business of Martyrdom: A History of Suicide Bombing* (Naval Institute Press; 2012), p. 239.

[57] ibid., p. 238 and Laura Mansfield, *Ayman al-Zawahiri, His Own Words: Translation and Analysis of the Writings of Dr. Ayman al-Zawahiri* (TLG Publications; 2006), p. 207.

[58] *Handbook for Volunteers of the Irish Republican Army: Notes on Guerrilla Warfare*, 1956 Edition (Paladin Press; 1985), p. 7.

[59] Michael Ryan, *Decoding Al Qaeda's Strategy: The Deep Battle Against America* (Columbia University Press; 2013), p. 233.

forces and their true military weakness is exposed. The British novelist John Masters described his experience of counterinsurgency operations against the Pashtun hill tribes of the Afghan–Pakistan (then Indian) border region as a young British Gurkha officer in the 1930s: "We had light automatic guns, howitzers, armored cars, tanks and aircraft. The Pathan had none of those things … And when he stayed and defended something, whether a gun or a village, we trapped him and pulverized him. When he flitted and sniped, rushed and ran away, we felt as if we were using a crowbar to swat wasps."[60] Eighty-five years later, little has changed on the Northwest Frontier. The Islamic State of Iraq and the Levant has also learned this lesson the hard way, relinquishing its last territorial gains on Iraqi soil in 2017.

There are of course some notable exceptions to this rule. Terrain can be a key factor — remote mountainous regions or thick jungle can negate many of the advantages enjoyed by conventional military forces, such as armored vehicles and air support. Groups like the *Partiya Karkerên Kurdistan* (PKK) in Turkey, *Fuerzas Armadas Revolucionarias de Colombia — Ejército del Pueblo* (FARC) in Colombia and the Liberation Tigers of Tamil Eelam (LTTE) in Sri Lanka were all able to hold rural areas in which they enjoyed strong local support for many years. Ernesto "Che" Guevara, the Argentine Marxist revolutionary who helped Fidel Castro seize power in Cuba, developed a theory of guerrilla warfare based on his own experience during the Cuban revolution that recommended the establishment of a "rural fortress" to create a "revolutionary situation" that can attract and build support for the overthrow of an oppressive state. But this approach ultimately did not work out well for Che himself who was cornered in the Bolivian jungle, captured, and then executed by US-trained Special Forces in October 1967. It also didn't work out much better for the other groups that followed this strategy. The Sri Lankan military eventually overran the Tamil Tigers, and Latin American rebel groups like FARC and *Sendero*

---

[60] Quoted in Max Boot, *Invisible Armies: An Epic History of Guerrilla Warfare from Ancient Times to the Present* (Liveright; 2013), p. 175.

*Luminoso* found that it proved difficult to overthrow a state from a remote jungle camp or highland redoubt. For that, aspirant revolutionaries have to move into the cities, where seizing and holding territory is a much less viable proposition — as Chechen separatists fighting the Russian military discovered in Grozny in 1999–2000. Those that opt to remain in their rural hideaways tend either to dwindle into irrelevance or turn their attention more and more to lucrative criminal activities, such as drug trafficking.

## Summary

The vast majority of terrorist organizations, even those with revolutionary aspirations, never progress to the second and third stages of Mao's model of guerrilla warfare. They operate in the first stage of hit-and-run operations hoping to force political concessions from their opponents through the cumulative pressure of successful attacks. Because such attacks are delivered precisely where government forces are not, threat cascades from one unprotected target to the next, even as other potential terrorist targets are secured from harm.[61] The key takeaway for counter-terrorist practitioners is that modern terrorists have no intention of meeting them on the field of battle or of fighting fair. Force is only a viable response if it can be brought to bear effectively on the threat. Unfortunately for states, terrorists, like guerrillas, have evolved a concept of operations that is wholly designed to ensure that this encounter never happens.

## Attrition

Sun-Tzu wrote in *The Art of War* that there had never been a protracted war from which a country has benefited, and this observation remains as valid today as it was 2,500 years ago. Closely allied to the concept of asymmetrical warfare in terrorist operations is the idea that the cumulative effect of consecutive attacks will wear down the

---

[61] Benjamin Friedman, Leap Before You Look, *Breakthroughs* (Spring 2004) at http://web.mit.edu/ssp/Publications/breakthroughs/Breakthroughs04.pdf.

enemy, both as a consequence of the attacks themselves and by forc-ing the state to adopt a defensive posture. In an 1849 essay titled *Der Mord*, which anticipated many of the ideas that he later expanded on in *Mord und Freiheit*, Karl Heinzen set the scene theatrically: "The revolutionaries must try to bring about a situation where the barbar-ians are afraid for their lives every hour of the day and night. They must think that every drink of water, every mouthful of food, every bed, every bush, every paving stone, every path and footpath, every hole in the wall, every slate, every bundle of straw, every pipe bowl, every stick, every pin may be a killer."[62] Terrorists seek to wage a war of attrition against the state and their targets are manpower, treas-ure, and social capital. As Nikolai Morozov explained in *The Terrorist Struggle*, the objective is to "bring about the final disorganization, demoralization, and weakening of government ... through a consist-ent, punishing system."[63]

Terrorists typically appreciate that they lack the firepower to deal their opponent a knockout blow. Aside from the occasional spectacular operation like the 9/11 attacks, most terrorist strikes are more the kind of short jabs that a boxer uses to wear down his opponent. As Mao Tse-tung put it: "They may be compared to innu-merable gnats, which, by biting a giant both in front and in rear, ultimately exhaust him. They make themselves as unendurable as a group of cruel and hateful devils."[64] The former *al-Qaeda* in the Arabian Peninsula commander Abd al-Aziz al-Muqrin echoed Mao in a manual he produced for the volunteers under his command, describing his concept of operations as the war of the flea and the dog: "The flea continually bites the dog, wounds it, and escapes; whereupon the dog begins to bite itself and scratch its skin. Then the flea returns and bites the dog again and so forth until [the dog]

---

[62] Benjamin Grob-Fitzgibbon, From the Dagger to the Bomb: Karl Heinzen and the Evolution of Political Terror, *Terrorism and Political Violence*, Vol. 16, No. 1, Spring 2004, pp. 101–102.

[63] Nikolai Morozov, The Terrorist Struggle (1880), in Walter Laqueur (ed.), *Voices of Terror: Manifestos, Writings and Manuals of Al Qaeda, Hamas, and other Terrorists from Around the World and Throughout the Ages* (Sourcebooks; 2004), p. 81.

[64] Mao Tse-tung, *On Guerrilla Warfare* translated by Brigadier General Samuel B. Griffith II (University of Illinois Press; 1961), p. 54.

loses its equilibrium and [the flea] exhausts and kills it."[65] Al Muqrin was killed in a gun battle with Saudi police in Riyadh on 18 June 2004 trying to put this strategy into action.

Adopting "the war of the flea" does not mean landing blows without purpose. Some targets will inevitably be attacked simply because they are targets of opportunity — the bar attended by off-duty police officers or the unguarded bridge — but others are chosen because of their strategic value. Speaking with an American journalist reporting on the Anglo-Irish conflict, Michael Collins explained that he perfectly understood that the British military could easily replace every soldier it lost to fighting in Ireland, but he also knew that were a small number of key assets without whom the military could not hope to function effectively: "To paralyze the British machine it was necessary to strike at individuals. Without her spies England was helpless. It was only by means of their accumulated knowledge that the British machine could operate."[66] In one crippling operation on 21 November 1920, Michael Collins' men killed fourteen British intelligence officers in coordinated raids across Dublin, effectively, in Collins' famous phrase, "putting out the eyes of the British" in Ireland. A war of attrition also means targeting resources that are not easily replaced.

But, in general, terrorist campaigns, like guerrilla warfare, are about the depletion of enemy resources. More often than not — particularly where the object is to end outside occupation — it will be sufficient to make the cost to the state of holding the territory in question outweigh the material benefits of doing so. The *Handbook for Volunteers of the Irish Republican Army* numbered draining "the enemy's manpower and resources" as one of the campaign's three principal objectives.[67] Osama bin Laden similarly echoed this insight in a 2004 video broadcast: "[It] is easy for us to provoke and bait ...

---

[65] Michael Ryan, *Decoding Al Qaeda's Strategy: The Deep Battle Against America* (Columbia University Press; 2013), pp. 132–133.

[66] Ulick O'Connor, *Michael Collins and the Troubles: The Struggle for Irish Freedom 1912–1922* (W. W. Norton & Company; 1996), p. 138.

[67] *Handbook for Volunteers of the Irish Republican Army: Notes on Guerrilla Warfare*, 1956 Edition (Paladin Press; 1985), p. 9.

All we have to do is to send two *Mujahedin* … to raise a piece of cloth on which is written *al-Qaeda* in order to make the generals race there to cause America to suffer human, economic and political losses."[68]

Defense is not, as it might seem, a passive act. Mounting an effective defense against attack requires continual vigilance and constant readiness — it is both exhausting and expensive. Terrorist groups have understood this from their earliest incarnations and explicitly aim to exhaust the state through, what *Narodnaya Volya* activist Sergei Kravshinski termed, "the continuous tension of its own strength".[69] Kravshinski's terrorist credentials are impeccable — he stabbed the head of the Tsarist secret police, Nikolai Mezentsov, to death on a St. Petersburg street in 1878. In the 1960s, Carlos Marighella emphasized the same point in his book *Minimanual of the Urban Guerrilla*, urging his readers to "weaken the local guards or the security system of the dictatorship … [by] catching the government in a defensive position with its troops mobilized in defense of the entire complex of national maintenance."[70]

Similarly, for the terrorist group, survival, and better yet longevity, can be an end in itself. Menachem Begin, military commander of *Irgun* and future Prime Minister of Israel, made precisely this point in his memoirs: "The very existence of an underground, which oppression … fail[s] to crush or to weaken must, in the end, undermine the prestige of a colonial regime that lives by the legend of its omnipotence. Every attack which it fails to prevent is a blow to its standing."[71] A *Rote Armee Fraktion* pamphlet, *The Urban Guerrilla Concept,* picked up on the same theme: "The Red Army Faction intends to temporarily put specific parts of the state's government and security apparatus out of action. This will destroy the myth of the

---

[68] Osama bin Laden, video message broadcast in November 2004, Messages to the World: The Statements of Osama bin Laden (Verso; 2005), pp. 241–242.

[69] Audrey Kurth Cronin, *How Terrorism Ends: Understanding the Decline and Demise of Terrorist Campaigns* (Princeton University Press; 2009), p. 73.

[70] Carlos Marighella, *Minimanual of the Urban Guerrilla* (Havana; Tricontinental 1970).

[71] Matthew Carr, *The Infernal Machine: A History of Terrorism* (The New Press; 2007), p. 71.

overwhelming nature and invincibility of the system."[72] A communiqué issued by the Greek Marxist group *Epanastatikos Agonas* in May 2004 justifying bomb attacks on an Athens courthouse and a local bank also made a similar point, declaiming, "we all have two choices: either through our inactivity to strengthen the existing barbarity, or through action to cancel the system's 'omnipotence', to rupture acquiescence, to dissipate social fear which today is the basic component of modern hegemony."[73] Naim Qassem, the Deputy Secretary-General of *Hezbollah*, has written of the importance of persistence: "Resistance activity is a cumulative effort that cannot be achieved through a limited number of rounds, for it is the persistence of such activity that achieves future results."[74] The Palestinian *Hamas* commander Ahmed Ishtawi echoed Qassem's observation in conversation with the *Time* reporter Johanna McGeary: "It's not a hobby to kill, you know; when we attack, the voice of the Palestinians is heard. We are sending a message to say, 'We are here.' If we stop, no one will care about us."[75] This commitment to the long haul has become known as the "long war doctrine" and it is an essential feature of most terrorist campaigns.

The Provisional IRA adopted an explicit long war strategy in 1977 that was perhaps best articulated in an editorial published in the republican newspaper *An Phoblacht*[76] the following year: "The war to liberate and unify this country will be a bitter and long drawn out struggle. There is no quick solution to our British problem ... We are committed to and more importantly geared to a long term war."[77] The so-called Manchester Manual seized by British police during a raid on an apartment used by suspected *al-Qaeda* member Nazih Abdul Hamed al-Raghie in May 2000 likewise warns recruits: "[The member] should have plenty of patience for [enduring]

---

[72] Red Army Faction, *The Urban Guerrilla Concept* (Kersplebedeb Publishing; 2005), p. 27.

[73] George Kassimeris, *Inside Greek Terrorism* (Oxford University Press; 2013), p. 126.

[74] Naim Qassem, *Hizbullah: The Story from Within* (Saqi; 2007), p. 148.

[75] Johanna McGeary, Inside Hamas, *Time Magazine*, 6 April 2004.

[76] Republican News.

[77] M. L. R. Smith, *Fighting for Ireland: The Military Strategy of the Irish Republican Movement* (Routledge; 1997), p. 153.

afflictions if he is overcome by the enemies. He should not abandon this great path and sell himself and his religion to the enemies for his freedom. He should be patient in performing the work, even if it lasts a long time."[78] The current leader of *al-Qaeda*, Ayman al-Zawahiri, emphasized the same point in his monograph *Knights Under the Prophet's Banner*, penned to rally the faithful in the aftermath of America's successful post-9/11 campaign to overthrow the *Taliban* regime in Afghanistan: "After every blow, we must build anew, even if we are compelled to begin from zero. But in reality we never begin from zero; victory is gained through an accumulation of the efforts of generations. What may appear to be a disaster in one phase can be a spark to light the torch of guidance in a following phase."[79] Having suffered a series of equally calamitous reversals, the leader of the Islamic State of Iraq and the Levant, Abu Bakr al-Baghdadi, adopted a similar tone to encourage his demoralized supporters in an August 2018 speech entitled *Give Glad Tidings to the Patient*: "The scale of victory or defeat with the *Mujahedin*, the people of faith and piety, is not tied to a city or a village that was taken … the land of God is wide and the tides of war change."[80] M. L. R. Smith has noted that the "long war doctrine" serves two vital purposes — it is a tonic for flagging terrorist morale when times are hard and, more importantly, it establishes an extended but flexible framework within which adjustments can be made in terrorist tactics and strategy without any admission of desperation or failure.[81]

---

[78] *The Al Qaeda Manual*, Second Lesson, UK/BM-15 Translation at http://www.justice.gov/ag/manualpart1_1.pdf. See also John Rosenthal, Is Libi's *Al-Qaeda* Manual a Blueprint for Arab Spring, *Al-Monitor*, 20 October 2013. There is some suggestion that the manual actually originated with one of the Egyptian terrorist groups, such as Egyptian Islamic Jihad, active in the 1980s, but it has been adopted by *al-Qaeda* and was introduced as evidence at the trial of *al-Qaeda* members involved in the simultaneous August 1998 bombings of the US Embassies in Nairobi and Dar Es Salaam in 2001.

[79] Michael Ryan, *Decoding Al Qaeda's Strategy: The Deep Battle Against America* (Columbia University Press; 2013), p. 77.

[80] Michael Munoz, *Selling the Long War: Islamic State Propaganda after the Caliphate*, CTC Sentinel, November 2018, at 31–32.

[81] M. L. R. Smith, *Fighting for Ireland: The Military Strategy of the Irish Republican Movement* (Routledge; 1997), p. 154.

Conventional military strategy places great stress on the economy of force — using just enough force to get the job done and not wasting resources unnecessarily. As John Mueller and Benjamin Friedman have both persuasively demonstrated, this concept seems to be jettisoned completely in counter-terrorism operations where huge quantities of men and material are routinely deployed to counter relatively minor strategic threats.[82] In 2011, Mueller calculated the overall odds of an American being killed in a terrorist attack as 1 in 3,500,000.[83] Charles Kurzman, author of *The Missing Martyrs*, notes that of approximately 190,000 murders committed in the United States between the 9/11 attacks and the end of 2013, only 37 were committed by Islamic terrorists[84] and that Americans are statistically more likely to kill themselves than they are to be murdered by someone else, regardless of motive.[85] Yet, terrorism seems to hold a disproportionate grip on the imagination, distorting the security landscape, and terrorists actively seek to exploit this. As the Harvard law professor Philip Heymann has observed: "A little terrorism goes a long way."[86]

Even the wealthiest countries have finite financial resources and national economic life, on which these resources are dependent, is especially vulnerable to disruption by terrorist activity — offering terrorists two strategic goals for the price of one. Carlos Marighella advised his readers to exploit this opportunity: "The urban guerrilla should endanger the economy of the country, particularly its economic and financial aspects, such as its domestic and foreign

---

[82] John Mueller, *Overblown: How Politicians and the Terrorism Industry Inflate National Security Threats, and Why We Believe Them* (Free Press; 2006) and Benjamin Friedman, Leap Before You Look, *Breakthroughs*, Spring 2004.

[83] John Mueller, The Truth about Al Qaeda, *Foreign Affairs*, 2 August 2011.

[84] Charles Kurzman, *Muslim American Terrorism in 2013*, Triangle Center on Terrorism and Homeland Security, 5 February 2014 at http://sites.duke.edu/tcths/files/2013/06/Kurzman_ Muslim-American_Terrorism_in_2013.pdf.

[85] Center for Disease Control, Deaths: Preliminary Data for 2011, *National Vital Statistics Reports*, Vol. 61, No. 6, 10 October 2012 at http://www.cdc.gov/nchs/data/nvsr/nvsr61/ nvsr61_06.pdf.

[86] Philip B. Heymann, *Terrorism, Freedom, and Security: Winning Without War* (Belfer Center Studies in International Security; 2004) at 3.

commercial network, its exchange and banking systems, its tax collection system, and others."[87] Seeking to bleed a government treasury dry has become a common terrorist tactic because it plays so strongly to terrorist groups' asymmetrical strength. EOKA's Georgios Grivas understood this advantage all too well, calling on Greek Cypriots in February 1958 to embrace what he called Total War: "We shall fight the occupant wherever we find him — in his economy and in his administration."[88] Documents recovered by the British security forces during a raid in Nicosia revealed that in 1956, EOKA was spending just £1,540 a month to fund its terrorist campaign on Cyprus, from which the historian David French has extrapolated that the entire conflict may have cost EOKA just £71,000, or in today's figures less than $2,000,000.[89] By contrast, in the financial year 1957–1958 alone, the British government spent £7,300,000 on emergency measures, or more than $190,000,000 in today's terms.[90]

From the outset of The Troubles in Northern Ireland, the Provisional IRA mixed a policy of hit-and-run strikes on the British security forces with a deliberate policy of economic warfare designed to degrade the Province's economic base by bombing commercial centers, driving away business investment, and forcing the British government to take on the burden of paying compensation to bombed out business owners.[91] Early Provisional IRA volunteer Maria McGuire recalled: "The campaign was aimed at economic targets ... It was intended to bring life in the Six Counties to a halt, drive out international investors, and make it so costly for the British to repair the damage we were causing that they would have to meet our demands."[92] As the Officer Commanding PIRA's Derry Brigade in the early 1970s, Martin McGuinness likewise told the Daily

---

[87] Carlos Marighella, *Minimanual of the Urban Guerrilla* (Havana; Tricontinental 1970).

[88] David French, *Fighting EOKA: The British Counter-Insurgency Campaign on Cyprus, 1955–1959* (Oxford University Press; 2015), p. 248.

[89] ibid., p. 59.

[90] ibid., p. 185.

[91] Sean MacStiofain, *Memoirs of a Revolutionary* (Gordon & Cremonesi; 1975), p. 243.

[92] Maria McGuire, *To Take Arms: A Year in the Provisional IRA* (MacMillan; 1973), p. 35.

Telegraph: "We are prepared to bomb any building that will cause economic devastation and put more pressure on the Government."[93] In the 1990s, the Provisional IRA took this strategy to the British mainland detonating four massive truck bombs in the City of London and Manchester between 1992 and 1996. The cost of repairing the damage caused by the 1993 Bishopsgate bombing alone, which destroyed several hundred thousand square meters of office space in London's financial district, has been estimated at anything between £350,000,000 and £1,000,000,000. The former Head of the British Security Service, Eliza Manningham-Buller, noted that these sophisticated attacks "were designed to drive away foreign investment and hurt the UK economically."[94] With the City of London fighting off a challenge from Frankfurt in the mid-1990s to supplant London as the pre-eminent European financial center, they came very close to succeeding. Republican dissidents still hold to a version of this economic strategy today — as one Real IRA activist told the *Irish Sunday Tribune* in 2008: "Don't ridicule planting incendiaries in shops. They cause millions of pounds in damage, present little risk to civilians and volunteers, and cost the movement minimal expense. A few incendiaries can have the same impact as a 500 lb bomb without the risks."[95]

Osama bin Laden also seems to have been remarkably consistent about his strategic intentions in this regard. In a video message broadcast in November 2004, he explained: "We have gained experience in guerrilla and attritional warfare in our *jihad* against that great and wicked superpower, Russia, which we, alongside the *mujahedin*, fought for ten years until, bankrupt, it was forced to withdraw — all praise be to *Allah*! And so we are continuing the same policy: to make America bleed till it becomes bankrupt — *Allah* willing."[96] In an unsigned letter addressed to the leader of *al-Qaeda*

---

[93] Kevin Toolis, *Rebel Hearts* (St. Martin's Griffin; 1997), p. 305.

[94] Eliza Manningham-Buller, *Securing Freedom* (Profile Books; 2012), p. 17.

[95] Suzanne Breen, War Back On – Real IRA, *Sunday Tribune*, 3 February 2008 at http://www.nuzhound.com/articles/Sunday_Tribune/arts2008/feb3_RIRA_interview__SBreen.php.

[96] Osama bin Laden, video message broadcast in November 2004, in Bruce Lawrence (ed.), *Messages to the World: The Statements of Osama bin Laden* (Verso; 2005), p. 241.

in the Arabian Peninsula, Nasir al-Wuhayshi, recovered during the May 2011 raid on bin Laden's compound in Abbotabad, he returned to the same theme: "Anyone following up with the latest events should know that our work and messages concentrate on exhausting and straining the American [sic], especially after September 11. We will continue to pressure the Americans until there is a balance in terror, where the expense of war, occupation, and the influence on our countries becomes a disadvantage for them and they become tired of it, and finally withdraw from our countries and stop supporting the Jews."[97]

Bin Laden's successor as leader of *al-Qaeda*, Ayman al-Zawahiri, has stayed the course. In an audio message to mark the 12th anniversary of the 9/11 attacks, al-Zawahiri told his listeners: "We must bleed America economically by provoking it, so that it continues its massive expenditures on security. America's weak spot is its economy, which begins to totter from the drain of its military and security expenditure."[98] He added that *al-Qaeda* would continue to force "the drain of military and security expenditures so that we keep America in a state of tension and anticipation, [wondering] when and where the next blow will come ... Keeping America in a state of tension and anticipation does not cost us anything but [organizing] dispersed strikes here and there."[99]

In an article in *Al Ansar* entitled *America and the Crusader Campaign: Where To?* published in June 2002, *al-Qaeda* strategist Abu Ubayd al-Qurashi noted that the US security response to 9/11 had already cost tens of billions of dollars and told his readers that it would be possible to defeat America if it could be forced to overspend and over-extend.[100] By October 2003, the US Secretary of Defense Donald Rumsfeld seemed to realize the trap the United

---

[97] SOCOM-2012-0000016-HT, *The Osama bin Laden Files: Letters and Documents Discovered by SEAL Team Six During Their Raid on bin Laden's Compound* (Skyhorse Publishing; 2012), p. 124.

[98] Osama bin Laden, video message broadcast in November 2004, *Messages to the World: The Statements of Osama bin Laden* (Verso; 2005), pp. 241–242.

[99] Gordon Corera, Al Qaeda chief Zawahiri urges "lone wolf" attacks on US, 13 September 2013, *BBC News* at http://www.bbc.co.uk/news/world-middle-east-24083314.

[100] Michael Ryan, *Decoding Al Qaeda's Strategy: The Deep Battle Against America* (Columbia University Press; 2013), p. 114.

States had fallen into, writing in a memo to his staff: "The cost–benefit ratio is against us! Our cost is billions against the terrorists' costs of millions ... Is our current situation such that 'the harder we work, the behinder [sic] we get'?"[101] If anything, Rumsfeld underestimated the vast degree of this economic asymmetry, but his opponents certainly had not. In his November 2004 videotape, bin Laden noted that "*al-Qaeda* spent $500,000 on the September 11 attacks, while America lost more than $500 billion ... that makes a million American dollars for every *al-Qaeda* dollar."[102] When *al-Qaeda* in the Arabian Peninsula secreted bombs in printer toner cartridges on UPS and FedEx jets leaving Yemen in October 2010, the group claimed that the attack had only cost $1,000 to put into effect but caused millions in losses to the air haulage industry, boasting: "That's what we call leverage."[103]

Over the past decade, America has spent astronomical sums on its security programs. According to an analysis by the budget expert Linda Bilmes and the economist Joseph Stiglitz, in the decade after 9/11, the combined direct and indirect costs of the US intervention in Iraq alone was likely to exceed more than $3 trillion.[104] In July 2011, Admiral Dennis Blair, Director of National Intelligence under both Presidents Bush and Obama, told the Aspen Security Forum that the US spent about $80 billion a year on counterterrorism programs, not including its expenditures in Iraq and Afghanistan. Generous estimates of the strength of *al-Qaeda* and its affiliates, Blair added, put them at between 3,000 and 5,000 men. This meant that the US was spending between $16 million and $27 million per year on each potential terrorist.[105] It is hard to

---

[101] Rumsfeld's Long Hard Slog, *Air Force Magazine*, December 2003, Vol. 86, No. 12 at www.airforcemag.com/MagazineArchive/Pages/2003/December%202003/1203keeper.aspx.

[102] Osama bin Laden, video message broadcast in November 2004, in Bruce Lawrence (ed.), *Messages to the World: The Statements of Osama bin Laden* (Verso; 2005), p. 242.

[103] Shiraz Maher and Samar Batrawi, What Jihadists Thought About Boston: "Allah Akbar. Let's Move On", *Foreign Affairs*, 7 May 2013.

[104] Joseph Stiglitz and Linda Bilmes, The true cost of the Iraq war: $3 trillion and beyond, *Washington Post*, 5 September 2010.

[105] "Threat vs. Response with Adm. (Ret.) Dennis Blair," a video from the Aspen Security Forum, July 2011, available at aspensecurityforum.org/2011-video.

imagine that such a financial burden would be sustainable over the long run, and, even if it were, that such disproportionate spending would be sound public policy.

As Carlos Marighella noted, the concept of attrition even operates at the psychological level obliging "the army and the police, with the commanders and their assistants, to change the relative comfort and tranquility of their barracks and their usual rest, for a state of alarm and growing tension in the expectation of attack or in search for tracks that vanish without trace."[106] *Hezbollah* capitalized on this effect by running a sophisticated propaganda campaign against Israel broadcasting images of dead or wounded Israeli soldiers under the tagline "Who's Next?".[107] This was another insight that was also shared by Osama bin Laden — in an interview given just weeks after the 9/11 attacks, he told the Karachi newspaper *Ummat*: "Terror is the most dreaded weapon in [the] modern age and Western media is mercilessly using it against its own people. It can add fear and helplessness in the psyche of the people of Europe and the United States. It means that what the enemies of the United States cannot do, its media is doing that."[108] In his audio message to mark the 12th anniversary of the 9/11 attacks, al-Zawahiri echoed his former chief, demonstrating little had changed in *al-Qaeda*'s outlook in the intervening period: "Just as we defeated [America] in a war of nerves in Somalia, Yemen, Iraq and Afghanistan, we must afflict it with a similar war in its own home."[109] In light of the disproportionate level of public spending on countering the threat posed by *al-Qaeda*, which in Western democracies at least can be said to reflect the importance placed on counter-terrorism by the electorate, it is hard to dispute that a strategy of attrition can be a powerful and impactful weapon. In the words of the legendary American

---

[106] Carlos Marighella, *Minimanual of the Urban Guerrilla* (Havana; Tricontinental 1970).

[107] Max Boot, *Invisible Armies: An Epic History of Guerrilla Warfare from Ancient Times to the Present* (Liveright; 2013), p. 510.

[108] Michael Scheuer, *Osama bin Laden* (Oxford, NY: Oxford University Press, 2011), p. 134 and Faisal Devji, *Landscapes of the Jihad: Militancy, Morality, Modernity* (London: Hurst; 2005), p. 160.

[109] Gordon Corera, Al Qaeda chief Zawahiri urges 'lone wolf' attacks on US, 13 September 2013, *BBC News* at http://www.bbc.co.uk/news/world-middle-east-24083314.

newsman Ted Koppel: "We have created an economy of fear, an industry of fear, a national psychology of fear. *Al-Qaeda* could never have achieved that on its own. We have inflicted it on ourselves."[110]

## Summary

Speaking at the National Defense University in May 2013, President Barack Obama offered a vision to the American people of what he believed the successful conclusion of the War on Terror would look like: "Our victory against terrorism won't be measured in a surrender ceremony on a battleship, or a statue being pulled to the ground. Victory will be measured in parents taking their kids to school; immigrants coming to our shores; fans taking in a ballgame; a veteran starting a business; a bustling city street. The quiet determination; that strength of character and bond of fellowship; that refutation of fear — that is both our sword and our shield."[111] This desire to return to the way things were before, to restore a degree of normalcy to every day life, is one of the principal strategic goals of most counter-terrorism campaigns. The constant detrition of this sense of stability and security is one of the core goals of most terrorist groups. Trained men, material, treasure, morale, and even prestige are all potentially finite government resources.[112] The tipping point at which a government may be prepared to cut its losses and negotiate may differ according to context — some governments are more robust than others, and a government may be more willing to reach accommodation with a separatist or anti-colonial movement than with a revolutionary one seeking its overthrow — but such a point exists in most conflicts. Fully understanding that they are unlikely to be able to defeat their enemies by force of arms

---

[110] Ted Koppel, America's Chronic Overreaction to Terrorism, *Wall Street Journal*, 6 August 2013.

[111] Ezra Klein, President Obama's speech on the future of the war on terror, *Washington Post*, 23 May 2013 at https://www.washingtonpost.com/news/wonk/wp/2013/05/23/read-president-obamas-speech-on-the-future-of-the-war-on-terror/?utm_term=.51a75e82c2ab. Viewed on 3 November 2017.

[112] Edward L. Katzenbach, Time, Space, and Will: The Politico-Military Views of Mao Tse-Tung, in Lt. Col. T. N. Greene (ed.), *The Guerrilla and How to Fight Him: Selections from the Marine Corps Gazette* (US Marine Corps, FMFRP-12-25; 1962), pp. 12–13.

alone, terrorist groups therefore explicitly set out to exhaust their opponent's physical, political, and psychological resources to the point that they become resigned to making significant concessions.

## Propaganda by Deed

The idea that the medium is the message is hardwired into terrorism. The nineteenth century anarchist revolutionaries, like Johann Most and Luigi Galleani, who first promoted the use of terrorist violence also married it to the concept of propaganda by deed, which still drives terrorist violence today. The French anarchist Paul Brousse is usually credited with first coining the term, observing, in an article entitled *La propaganda par le fait*, which appeared in the *Bulletin de la Fédération Jurassienne* in August 1877, that while the anarchist philosopher Pierre-Joseph Proudhon had written "magnificent books", it was the example of the Paris Commune that introduced the principle of communal autonomy to "peasants and workers alike".[113] Brousse urged his readers to take up the challenge: "Just once take over a commune ... if attacked, fight back, defend oneself, and if one loses, what matter? The idea will have been launched, not on paper, not in a newspaper, not on a chart; no longer will it be sculpted in marble, carved in stone nor cast in bronze: having sprung to life, it will march, in flesh and blood, at the head of the people."[114]

In actual fact, the concept, if not the phrasing, significantly predated Brousse's article. Mikhail Bakunin had produced what is perhaps the best known formulation of the concept seven years earlier: "We must spread our principles, not with words but with deeds, for this is the most popular, the most potent, and the most irresistible form of propaganda."[115] It was also another Russian anarchist and revolutionary, Prince Peter Kropotkin, who produced the most definitive exposition of how the concept worked in practice in his 1880 pamphlet, *The Spirit of Revolt*, in which he praised "the lonely

---

[113] Paul Brousse, La propaganda par le fait, *Bulletin de la Fédération Jurassienne*, August 1877.
[114] ibid.
[115] Mikhail Bakunin, Letters to a Frenchman on the Present Crisis (1870).

sentinels who enter the battle long before the masses are sufficiently roused to raise openly the banner of insurrection" whose actions compel general attention, thus ensuring that revolutionary ideas seep into people's minds and win over converts to the cause. Kropotkin concluded with a flourish: "One such act may, in a few days, make more propaganda than thousands of pamphlets."[116] By 1881, the concept had become so ubiquitous in the literature of the revolutionary left that, under Kropotkin's watchful gaze, the first International Congress of Anarchists held in London that July formally adopted a policy of propaganda by deed as a tool to mobilize working class opinion without seeking to exert centralized control. As the French anarchist Auguste Valliant declared at his trial in 1894 for throwing a bomb into the French Chamber of Deputies — a near definitive act of propaganda by deed: "It takes a loud voice to make the deaf hear."[117]

Grant Wardlaw argued in his classic work *Political Terrorism: Theory, Tactics and Counter-Measures* that terrorists "consciously script" attacks[118] and acts of terrorism have been variously likened to theater, a live-action spectacular, performance art, and even sermons.[119] The assassination of kings, presidents, and prime ministers in Bulgaria, France, Italy, Russia (both Alexander II in 1881 and Pyotr Stolypin in 1911), Spain (both Antonio Cánovas in 1897 and José Canalejas in 1912), the United States, and (possibly) Greece by anarchist militants over a period of more than thirty years made a profound statement about the anarchist movement's opposition to

---

[116] Peter Kropotkin, The Spirit of Revolt, in Roger Baldwin (ed.), *Kropotkin's Revolutionary Pamphlets,* (Dover, 1970), p. 40.

[117] August Valliant, Assassination, in Upton Sinclair (ed.), *The Cry for Justice: An Anthology of the Literature of Protest* (The John C. Winston Co.; 1915).

[118] Grant Wardlaw, *Political Terrorism: Theory, Tactics and Counter-Measures* (Cambridge University Press; 1989), p. 76.

[119] Brian Jenkins, *Will Terrorists Go Nuclear?* (Prometheus Books; 2008), p. 101; Strobe Talbot, Nyan Chanda and John Lewis Gaddis, *The Age of Terror: America and the World After September 11* (Basic Books; 202), p. xiii; J. B. Bell, Terrorist Scripts and Live-Action Spectaculars, *Columbia Journalism Review*, May–June 1978 at 50; and Fawaz Gerges, *Journey of the Jihadist: Inside Muslim Militancy* (2006), p. 207. At his trial, the Norwegian white supremacist Anders Behring Breivik went so far as to describe his July 2011 attacks on Oslo and Utøya as his "book launch", telling the court that he had even estimated how many people he would have to kill — he thought probably around a dozen — to make sure people would actually read the political manifesto he had posted online.

authoritarian government and the vulnerability of the old order in the industrial age.[120] The assassination of French President Carnot in particular, stabbed to death by an Italian anarchist called Sante Geronimo Caserio in June 1894 in part for his refusal to pardon Auguste Valliant, put politicians on notice that they would be held personally responsible for their actions.

The Italian radical Luigi Galleani, one of the most vociferous apostles of violence of the anarchist era, argued that by its very example, every single violent act made a significant contribution to the anarchist cause, writing: "No act of rebellion is useless; no act of rebellion is harmful … Every one of them … has deep echoes and lasting gains, which compensate abundantly for them … All, all of them scourge cowardice, rebel against submission, engrave a lesson; they do the work of revolution."[121] In the same vein, Johann Most cataloged anarchist *attentats* in his US-based newspaper, *Freiheit,* to inspire his readership to action, observing in one editorial that "once an action has been carried out, the important thing is that the world learns of it from the revolutionaries, so that everyone knows what the position is."[122] Two days after President McKinley was assassinated by Leon Czolgosz, Most reprinted Karl Heinzen's essay *Der Mord* to provide political context to the incident — a gesture that earned him a conviction in the New York courts for willfully and wrongfully endangering the public peace.[123]

Attacks like the bombing of Barcelona's Liceu Theater in November 1893 by Santiago Salvador and Émile Henry's assault on the Café Terminus in Paris in February 1894 served to highlight the division between rich and poor, as well as the individual culpability of the well-to-do. In a statement to the court during his trial, Henry

---

[120] Peter Romaniuk, *Multilateral Counter-Terrorism: The Global Politics of Cooperation and Contestation* (Routledge; 2010), p. 21.

[121] Nunzio Pernicone, Luigi Galleani and Italian Anarchist Terrorism in the United States, *Studi Emigrazione*, Vol. 30 (September 1993), p. 481.

[122] Johann Most, Action as Propaganda, *Freiheit,* 25 July 1885. See also Benjamin Grob-Fitzgibbon, From the Dagger to the Bomb: Karl Heinzen and the Evolution of Political Terror, *Terrorism and Political Violence*, Vol. 16, No. 1, Spring 2004, p. 111.

[123] Daniel Bessner and Michael Stauch, Karl Heinzen and the Intellectual Origins of Modern Terror, *Terrorism and Political Violence*, Vol. 22 (2010), p. 152.

explained the logic of his actions: "I wanted to show the bourgeoisie that henceforward their pleasures would not be untouched, that their insolent triumphs would be disturbed, that their golden calf would rock violently on its pedestal until the final shock that would cast it down among filth and blood. At the same time I wanted to make the miners understand that there is only one category of men, the anarchists, who sincerely resent their sufferings and are willing to avenge them."[124] And people paid attention. The lurid story of the attack on the Liceu Theater, in which twenty opera-goers died, sold more copies of the New York City newspaper *World* — half way round the globe — than any edition in the history of American journalism to that point.[125] Santiago Salvador was even immortalized as one of the gargoyles adorning the interior of Antoni Gaudí's *Basílica de la Sagrada Família*, where a demon can be seen handing an Orsini bomb to a figure dressed as a laborer.

The anti-authoritarian movements of the nineteenth century also bequeathed us a second related concept that serves to magnify the impact of propaganda by deed — an almost mystical fascination with both the actual and symbolic potency of explosives, which is often described as "the philosophy of the bomb". Karl Marx wrote of the "therapeutic quality" of explosions and Émile Henry of "the voice of dynamite".[126] The anarchist paper *L'En-dehors* noted enthusiastically that when dynamite spoke, people listened, and the conspiracy of silence ended. Johann Most relished the symmetry of using an industrial tool to punish the captains of industry: "A bomb that can blow a hole in a rock face is bound to do a fair bit of damage at court or at a monopolists' ball."[127] Albert Parsons, the Chicago-based anarchist leader and newspaper editor executed in the witch-hunt that followed the 1886 Haymarket bombing,

---

[124] Émile Henry, *Defense* (1894).

[125] Richard Bach Jensen, Daggers, Rifles and Dynamite: Anarchist Terrorism in Nineteenth Century Europe, *Terrorism and Political Violence*, Vol. 16, No. 1 (Spring 2004), p. 141.

[126] Émile Henry, *Defense* (1894).

[127] Johann Most, The Case for Dynamite, in Walter Laqueur (ed.), *Voices of Terror: Manifestos, Writings and Manuals of Al Qaeda, Hamas, and other Terrorists from Around the World and Throughout the Ages* (Sourcebooks; 2004), p. 340.

declared: "Dynamite comes as the emancipator of man from the domination and enslavement of his fellow men ... it is democratic, it makes everyone equal ... it is a peacemaker."[128] A Spanish periodical, *Prologo*,[129] went even further waxing hyperbolically of the impact of Alfred Nobel's game-changing invention, "it seems that the spirit of Shiva, the god of destruction, eternal destroyer of life, resides in the depths of its strange composition ... it creates and it destroys, it annihilates and it gives life; it is chained Prometheus and angry Jupiter; it illuminates and darkens. From civilization's necessity, it becomes its chastiser."[130]

*Narodnaya Volya* activists favored the use of gelatin dynamite over firearms for its operations because they believed bombings would demonstrate "a new stage in the revolutionary movement" rather than being interpreted as "ordinary murder".[131] Nikolai Morozov emphasized the symbolic narrative of such acts in *The Terrorist Struggle*: "The tsars and despots who oppress the nation cannot live peacefully any longer in their palaces. The unseen ravager will let them know by a deafening explosion that their time has come and the despots will feel the earth is collapsing under their feet among the sounds of music, the frightened screams of the innumerable crowds, during dessert at a refined dinner."[132] Vera Figner, who served on the Executive Committee of *Narodnaya Volya*, took care to stress in her memoirs that such violent actions were always carried out in service of the political message the Committee sought to communicate: "The work of propaganda and organization always went hand in hand with that of destruction; it was less evident, but

---

[128] Ze'ev Iviansky, Individual Terror: Concept and Typology, *Journal of Contemporary History*, Vol. 12 (1977), p. 48.

[129] Prologue.

[130] Richard Bach Jensen, Daggers, Rifles and Dynamite: Anarchist Terrorism in Nineteenth Century Europe, *Terrorism and Political Violence*, Vol. 16, No. 1 (Spring 2004), pp. 116–117.

[131] ibid., pp. 129–130 and Ze'ev Iviansky, Individual Terror: Concept and Typology, *Journal of Contemporary History*, Vol. 12 (1977), p. 47.

[132] Nikolai Morozov, The Terrorist Struggle (1880), in Walter Laqueur (ed.), *Voices of Terror: Manifestos, Writings and Manuals of Al Qaeda, Hamas, and other Terrorists from Around the World and Throughout the Ages* (Sourcebooks; 2004), p. 79.

it was nevertheless destined to bear its fruits."[133] Even some government agents embraced the philosophy of the bomb — T. E. Lawrence, better known to posterity as Lawrence of Arabia, while reporting on the progress of his Arabian guerrilla campaign against the Ottoman Turks in July 1917, told his superiors: "The noise of dynamite explosions we find everywhere the most effective propagandist measure possible."[134]

This effect has been exponentially enhanced in the modern media age. J. B. Bell likened modern terrorists to "television producers constructing a package so spectacular, so violent, so compelling that the networks, acting as executives, supplying the cameramen and the audience, cannot refuse the offer."[135] A study of terrorist methodology by the Breakthrough Institute noted that the drama of an explosion creates a spectacle for the senses: "Within split seconds victims and bystanders see an incredible flash, hear a boom of thunder, feel a bursting shockwave of heat and fire, and smell the acrid stench of burning fuel and flesh."[136] It even has an almost atavistic impact — loud noises have been proposed by some behavioral scientists as one of humanity's three innate fears, along with pain and a sudden loss of support.[137] All in all, an explosion makes for compelling viewing — footage of such incidents are often played over and over again by media outlets and this subliminally reinforces the message that the perpetrators are seeking to convey. The modern phenomenon of suicide bombing adds yet a further dimension to the message communicated, emphasizing in the most primal manner imaginable

---

[133] Vera Figner, *Memoirs of a Revolutionist* (Northern Illinois University Press; 1991), p. 75.

[134] James Barr, *Setting the Desert on Fire: T. E. Lawrence and Britain's Secret War in Arabia 1916–1918* (W. W. Norton and Co., 2008), p. 153.

[135] J. B. Bell, Terrorist Scripts and Live-Action Spectaculars, *Columbia Journalism Review*, May–June 1978 at 50. See also Jeffrey D. Simon, *The Terrorist Trap: America's Experience with Terrorism* (Indiana University Press; 2001), p. 10.

[136] Nick Adams, Ted Nordhaus and Michael Shellenberger, Planes, Trains and Car Bombs: The Method Behind the Madness of Terrorism, *The Science of Security* (Breakthrough Institute; January 2012), p. 39.

[137] See J. B. Watson, *Psychological Care of Infant and Child* (W. W. Norton and Co.; 1928).

the self-sacrificing ideological commitment of the perpetrator and the implacable determination of those engaged in the struggle.

The concept of propaganda by deed can be found as a theme, at times implicit at others explicit, in the writings of groups from all four strains of terrorist activity. It is referenced from the outset by nationalist groups. As early as 1876, Jeremiah O'Donovan Rossa, writing in the *Irish World*, had noted both the propaganda value and the practical value to the Irish republican movement of conducting a high profile attack on British soil: "A successful strike that will do [England] half a million dollars worth of damage will bring us enough funds to carry on the work."[138] The coalition of socialist and nationalist radicals that made up the Irish Republican Brotherhood (IRB), and who were behind the failed 1916 Easter Uprising, sought in large part to reverse a process of Irish assimilation into British culture that was already far advanced. In his essay, *The Proof of Success: What the Rising of 1916 Did*, Michael Collins wrote that the goal of British rule was to "blot out" Irish civilization and turn the island of Ireland into an English province, commenting wryly, "the Gael was to go."[139] He added that the rebels of 1916 knew that the odds were against the uprising's success from the start: "During the rising the leaders of Easter Week 'declared a Republic.' But not as a fact. We knew it was not a fact. It was a wonderful gesture — throwing down the gauntlet of defiance to the enemy, expressing to ourselves the complete freedom we aimed at, and for that reason was an inspiration to us."[140] This "wonderful gesture" succeeded beyond the IRB's wildest dreams in rekindling a sense of Irish national identity. In the British general election of 1918, seventy-five nationalist candidates were elected to Parliament and broke away from London to establish their own national assembly,

---

[138] Irish World cited in Lindsay Clutterbuck, The Progenitors of Terrorism: Russian Revolutionaries or Extreme Irish Republicans?, *Journal of Terrorism and Political Violence*, Vol. 16, No. 1 (2004), p. 163.

[139] Michael Collins, The Proof of Success: What the Rising of 1916 Did, *The Path to Freedom* (Welsh Academic Press; 1996), p. 46.

[140] ibid., pp. 53–54.

the *Dáil*, in Dublin.[141] By 1922, the Irish Republic was "a fact" in all but name — under the Anglo-Irish Treaty, which ended the war of independence waged by Michael Collins and the original Irish Republican Army, the United Kingdom had recognized the establishment of the Irish Free State in the twenty-six southern counties of Ireland.

Bhagat Singh, one of the leaders of the Hindustan Socialist Republican Association (HSRA) opposing British colonial rule in India, was heavily influenced by the thinking of Mikhail Bakunin,[142] and he explained his group's decision to adopt terrorist tactics in familiar terms in a manifesto entitled *The Philosophy of the Bomb*: "Terrorism instills fear in the hearts of the oppressors, it brings hopes of revenge and redemption to the oppressed masses."[143] In December 1928, Singh and an accomplice, Shivaram Rajguru, gunned down Assistant Superintendent John Saunders as a reprisal for the violent suppression of a demonstration by the colonial police, which had resulted in the death of the prominent Punjabi leader Lala Lajpat Rai. After killing Saunders, the HSRA put up posters and pamphlets around Lahore that declared: "The assassination of Lala Lajpat Rai has been avenged ... Today the world has seen that the people of India are not lifeless; their blood has not become cold. They can lay down their lives for the country's honour."

While still in hiding, Singh proposed to the leadership of the HSRA a dramatic act that would generate great publicity for their cause.[144] In deliberate emulation of the French anarchist Auguste Valliant, Singh followed the attack on Saunders by hurling two small bombs onto the floor of the Central Legislative Assembly in

---

[141] Ethan Bueno de Mesquita and Eric Dickson, The Propaganda of the Deed: Terrorism, Counterterrorism, and Mobilization, *American Journal of Political Science*, Vol. 51, No. 2 (April 2007), p. 364.

[142] From May to September 1928 Bhagat Singh published a series of articles he had written on anarchist thought in Kirti, the journal of the Kirti Kisan Party.

[143] See Gerard Chaliand and Arnaud Blin (eds.), *The History of Terrorism: From Antiquity to Al Qaeda* (University of California Press; 2007), p. 188.

[144] Ishwar Dayal Gaur, *Martyr as Bridegroom: A Folk Representation of Bhagat Singh* (Anthem Press India; 2008), pp. 99–100.

New Delhi while the chamber was in session.[145] After the attack, Singh and another HSRA militant, Batukeshwar Dutt, waited calmly in the public gallery to be taken into custody intending to use their trial as platform to promote their cause. Singh's trial, which he described himself as a "drama", and his subsequent execution had the effect he desired, helping to further inflame nationalist sentiment on the Indian subcontinent. Riots broke out in northern India at the news of his hanging. The first Prime Minster of an independent India, Jawaharlal Nehru, later wrote that "Bhaghat Singh did not become popular because of his act of terrorism but because he seemed to vindicate, for the moment, the honour of Lala Lajpat Rai, and through him of the nation. He became a symbol, the act was forgotten, the symbol remained, and within a few months each town and village of the Punjab, and to a lesser extent in the rest of northern India, resounded with his name."[146] Today, Bhaghat Singh is regarded as a hero of India's struggle for independence and in 2008, an eighteen-foot-tall bronze statue of him was installed outside the Indian parliament building he had once tried to bomb.

Menachem Begin of *Irgun* was also no stranger to the concept of propaganda by deed. When *Irgun* recommenced operations against the British authorities in Palestine in February 1944, Begin symbolically selected the Immigration Department offices in Jerusalem, Tel Aviv and Haifa as its first targets in a carefully coordinated attack intended both to telegraph the organization's martial capabilities and to protest the continued British enforcement of restrictions on Jewish immigration to Palestine.[147] A press release delivered the following morning by an *Irgun* operative to the office of the US Consul General in Jerusalem, Lowell Pinkerton, further illustrated the sophistication with which *Irgun* married its use of violence to its propaganda efforts, by evoking both American values and the catastrophe that had befallen the Jewish population of occupied

---

[145] Kuldip Nayar, *The Martyr: Bhagat Singh Experiments in Revolution* (Haranand Publications; 2000), pp. 70–73.

[146] S. K. Mittal and Irfan Habib, The Congress and the Revolutionaries in the 1920s, *Social Scientist*, Vol. 10, No. 6 (June 1982), pp. 20–37.

[147] Bruce Hoffman, *Anonymous Soldiers: The Struggle for Israel, 1917–1947* (Knopf; 2015), p. 127.

Europe: "The Jewish fighting youth is convinced that the government and the pubic opinion of your great country faithful to the
best traditions of freedom and justice, will understand and appreciate our struggle for the life and future of an ancient nation — our
people — suffering extermination by the Nazi Barbarians."[148] Begin
fully appreciated that *Irgun* carried out its operations on a public
stage and thus that its use of violence had to be carefully calibrated,
writing: "We never believed that our struggle would cause the total
destruction of our people. We knew that *Eretz* Israel, in consequence
of the revolt, resembled a glass house. The world was looking into it
with ever-increasing interest and could see most of what was happening inside ... Arms were our weapons of attack; the transparency of
the 'glass' was our shield of defence."[149]

In his memoir, *The Revolt*, Begin also demonstrated a sophisticated understanding of the different messages communicated to
different audiences by each of the group's attacks. For his fellow
Jews, each successful attack attracted support for the nationalist
cause: "We of the *Irgun Zvai Leumi* arose therefore to rebel and
fight, not in order to instill fear but to eradicate it."[150] But he noted
that his comrades were acutely aware of the psychological effect
that successful Jewish attacks on British government buildings were
having, not only on the British Mandate authorities, but also on the
Arab population of the Mandate of Palestine whom the Jewish
population would confront directly in the event of a British withdrawal. Begin recalled: "We studied them closely. They were
dumbfounded ... Their talk was a confused mixture of amazement,
fear and admiration. And so it was with all the later attacks the
results of which they were able to see ... The fact that the mighty
British government not only failed to put an end to our struggle
but, on the contrary, continued to be subjected to blows of ever-
increasing severity, exercised a very healthy influence on the
Arabs."[151] Avraham Stern, who split from *Irgun* to form his own

---

[148] Bruce Hoffman, *Anonymous Soldiers: The Struggle for Israel, 1917–1947* (Knopf; 2015), p. 127.
[149] Menachem Begin, *The Revolt: Story of the Irgun* (Steimatzky's Agency Ltd.; 1977), p. 56.
[150] ibid., p. 60.
[151] ibid., pp. 49–50.

terrorist organization, known to *Irgun* loyalists as the Stern Group and to the British authorities as the Stern Gang, liked to remind his men: "Actions educate."[152]

The Algerian *Front de Libération Nationale* (FLN) demonstrated an equally keen appreciation of the propaganda dimension of its struggle with France, developing a strategy that was tailored in part to engage international public opinion and influence the United Nations General Assembly. The FLN formally adopted a plan for the "internationalization" of the Algerian conflict at its Soummam conference in August–September 1956, and the organization would go on to establish a permanent office in New York to engage the United Nations, as well as international bureaus in seven major cities across the Muslim world, including Cairo, Karachi, and Jakarta.[153] Delegations were dispatched to raise the FLN's profile at international cultural, student and trade union events.[154] Ramdane Abane, perhaps the most influential member of the FLN's *Comité de Coordination et d'Exécution*[155] and the prime mover behind the Soummam conference, also developed a military strategy to compliment the organization's political agenda which designated the City of Algiers as the central battleground for the independence movement. Abane explained this decision to the FLN's supporters in Directive Number 9: "Is it preferable for our cause to kill ten enemies in an *oued* of Telergma or a single man in Algiers which will be noted the next day by the American press? Though we are taking some risks, we must make our struggle known."[156] A general strike and a wave of terrorist operations — at least 100 individual attacks in Algiers and more than 4,000 across the entire country — were deliberately timed to coincide with the lead up to the UN

---

[152] Gerold Frank, *The Deed* (Simon and Schuster; 1963), p. 131.

[153] Michael Connelly, Rethinking the Cold War and Decolonization: The Grand Strategy of the Algerian War of Independence, *International Journal of Middle Eastern Studies*, Vol. 33, No. 2 (2001), p. 227.

[154] ibid.

[155] Committee for Coordination and Execution.

[156] Matthew Connelly, Rethinking the Cold War and Decolonization: The Grand Strategy of the Algerian War of Independence, *International Journal of Middle East Studies*, Vol. 33, No. 2 (May 2001), p. 228.

General Assembly's annual session on 27 January 1957 and thus raise the profile of the FLN's struggle.[157] Abane also showed a preference for attacks on civilian targets, which he knew would attract more attention, coining the cynical aphorism: "One corpse in a jacket is always worth more than twenty in uniform."[158]

*Umkhonto we Sizwe*, the armed wing of the African National Congress, whose own leadership was greatly influenced by the example of the FLN,[159] ominously chose to mark its arrival on the public stage by mounting its first series of bombings on 16 December 1961 — a public holiday known as The Day of the Vow, which commemorates the Battle of Blood River fought between the Zulu king Dingane kaSenzangakhona and Dutch *Voortrekkers* encroaching on Zulu territory in 1838. The choice of 16 December was already heavy with symbolic meaning, but to drive the point home, *Umkhonto we Sizwe*'s leadership, led by the future Nobel laureate and President of South Africa Nelson Mandela, also distributed a manifesto in leaflet form, which contained a stark warning for the *apartheid* authorities: "We hope — even at this late hour — that our first actions will awaken everyone to a realization of the disastrous situation to which the Nationalist policy is leading. We hope that we will bring the government and its supporters to their senses before it is too late, so that both the government and its policies can be changed before matters reach the desperate state of civil war."[160] Between December 1961 and July 1963, the South African government recorded 235 separate acts of sabotage targeting government buildings, power facilities, and even deliberate crop burning — although at this early stage of operations, *Umkhonto we Sizwe* was careful to avoid human casualties.

---

[157] Bruce Hoffman, *Inside Terrorism* (Columbia University Press; 2013) at 59 and Christopher Cradock and M. L. R. Smith, "No Fixed Values" — A Reinterpretation of the Influence of the Theory of the Guerre Révolutionnaire and the Battle of Algiers, *Journal of Cold War Studies*, Vol. 9, No. 4 (Fall 2007), p. 82.

[158] Alistair Horne, *A Savage War of Peace: Algeria 1954–1962* (New York Review Books Classics; 2006), p. 132.

[159] Bruce Hoffman, *Inside Terrorism* (Columbia University Press; 2013), p. 57.

[160] Command of *Umkhonto we Sizwe*, Manifesto of *Umkhonto we Sizwe* Leaflet, 16 December 1961.

Propaganda by deed tended to play an explicit role in the ideological narrative of Marxist terrorist groups, as befits a concept born on the political left. In 1965, the French philosopher and activist Régius Debray published an article in *New Left Review* entitled *Latin America: The Long March* which proposed that the great lesson of Fidel Castro's successful revolution was that the creation of a revolutionary *foco* or situation was a viable alternative to the traditional Leninist focus on building the party, and party orthodoxy, as the necessary vanguard of any revolutionary movement.[161] Although Castro's ragtag band of guerrillas had managed against the odds to seize power from the dictatorial regime of Fulgencio Batista, for Debray, this was the exception to the rule: "The *foco* does not by any means attempt to seize power on its own, by one audacious stroke. Nor even does it aim to conquer power by means of war or through a military defeat of the enemy: it only aspires to enable the masses themselves to overthrow the established power."[162] In a phrase that could have almost been lifted direct from the writings of Kropotkin or Brousse, he noted: "The conquest from the enemy of a small area of fertile land belonging to the *latifundist* is better propaganda for agrarian reform than a hundred illustrated pamphlets."[163] Debray's idea was that aspirant revolutionaries would establish themselves at the most vulnerable zone of the national territory and then slowly spread out from this location, "like an oil patch", to the smaller towns, and finally to the capital, raising political awareness and attracting mass support through their actions.[164] Despite his belief in the galvanizing effect of this approach, Debray also acknowledged that "the *foco* cannot constitute a strategy in itself without condemning itself to failure: it is a moment of struggle

---

[161] Régius Debray, Latin America: The Long March, *New Left Review*, No. 33 (September–October 1965), pp. 33–58. Debray had taught philosophy at the University of Havana in post-revolutionary Cuba and joined Che Guevara's ill-fated Guerrilla campaign in Bolivia where he was arrested and imprisoned for several years by the Bolivian authorities until an international campaign secured his release.

[162] Régius Debray, Latin America: The Long March, *New Left Review*, No. 33 (September–October 1965), p. 27.

[163] ibid., p. 41.

[164] ibid., p. 27.

whose place can only be defined within an overall integrating strategy."[165] Debray was no mere armchair strategist — in 1967, he joined Che Guevara's ill-fated attempt to foment revolution in Bolivia. He spent three years incarcerated in a Bolivian prison until an international campaign led by prominent intellectuals such as Jean-Paul Sartre and André Malraux secured his freedom.

The Uruguayan union organizer Raúl Sendic, founder of the influential Marxist urban guerrilla group *Movimiento de Liberación Nacional — Tupamaros*, was one of the first of a new generation of urban guerrillas to translate Debray's theory of revolutionary action into practice — an approach the *Tupamaros* christened "armed propaganda".[166] In June 1968, an interview with Sendic entitled *30 Questions for a Tupamaro* was published in the Chilean review *Punto Final*, in which he laid out the nascent group's strategy in some detail.[167] Guevara and Debray had argued that, based on the Cuban model, a *foco* had to be created in the countryside, not the city — the *Tupamaros*, operating in a small state with no remote rural areas, believed the concept could also be adapted to the urban landscape. Sendic's *30 Questions* would exert tremendous influence on the emerging wave of Latin American and Western European revolutionary movements. Particularly influential was Sendic's declaration that "revolutionary action in itself, the very act of taking up arms, preparing for and engaging in actions which are against the basis of bourgeois law, creates a revolutionary consciousness, organization and conditions ... revolutionary situations are created by revolutionary actions."[168]

The *Tupamaros* were born out of an informal committee known as the *Coordinador* that had been established by a number of Uruguayan Marxist parties to develop training regimens for their

---

[165] ibid., p. 35.

[166] The name *Tupamaros* was derived from the Incan ruler Tupac Amaru II who had resisted Spanish expansion into the Andes in the eighteenth century and had been first used by Spanish troops to describe his followers. The term had become a local synonym for "rebels'.

[167] Alain Labrousse (trans. Dinah Livingstone), *The Tupamaros: Urban Guerrillas in Uruguay* (Penguin Books; 1973), pp. 133–145.

[168] ibid., p. 133.

party militias, and the group's leaders were all too familiar with various doctrinal disputes that bedeviled cooperation between the Maoist and Leninist wings of the communist movement. For this reason, the *Tupamaros* deliberately chose an approach that placed an emphasis on revolutionary action, rather than political theory or the consolidation of party influence, adopting the slogan "Action Unites Us, Words Divide Us".[169] Sendic told *Punto Final*: "Revolution is not made by carefully constructing political platforms. The basic principles of a socialist revolution have been illustrated in a country like Cuba. It is enough to accept these principles and to prove by the facts of armed struggle that it will be successful."[170]

The *Tupamaros*' definitive act of armed propaganda was the takeover of the Radio Sarandí transmitter in Montevideo on 15 May 1969. The operation was timed to coincide with the first leg of the final of the *Copa Libertadores* between the Uruguayan side *Nacional* and the Argentinian side *Estudiantes*, and, having seized control of the transmitter with the whole of the country already glued to their radios, the *Tupamaros* broadcast a pre-recorded political address on a loop for more than 40 minutes with a simple message for their audience: "Uruguayans, those of you who suffer from penury and hardship because of a bad government should not lose hope."[171] Another celebrated attack targeted the trendy Montevideo nightclub Zum-Zum, which was torched in an arson attack. The *Tupamaros* responsible left behind the immortal graffito: "Either everyone dances or nobody does."[172] Other such symbolic targets included the San Rafael casino, Carrasco Bowling Club, and Montevideo's Club de Golf.

The Brazilian Carlos Marighella was also influenced by Debray, whose insights he incorporated into his *Minimanual of the Urban*

---

[169] Pablo Brum, *The Robin Hood Guerrillas: The Epic Journey of Uruguay's Tupamaros* (CreateSpace; 2014), p. 51.

[170] Alain Labrousse (trans. Dinah Livingstone), *The Tupamaros: Urban Guerrillas in Uruguay* (Penguin Books; 1973), p. 135.

[171] Pablo Brum, *The Robin Hood Guerrillas: The Epic Journey of Uruguay's Tupamaros* (CreateSpace; 2014), pp. 92–93.

[172] ibid., p. 177.

*Guerrilla*: "The coordination of urban guerrilla actions, including each armed action, is the principal way of making armed propaganda. These actions, carried out with specific and determined objectives, inevitably become propaganda material for the mass communication system."[173] In a 1980 address to the Central Committee of the Peruvian Maoist *Sendero Luminoso*, the group's leader Abimael Guzmán told his audience that ideological education alone would not be enough to radicalize the rural poor: "They will need overwhelming deeds ... that hammer their hard heads, that break their speculations to pieces, in order for the reality of this, our fatherland, to take root in their souls."[174] His message was internalized by *Sendero Luminoso*'s revolutionary cadres, one young recruit told the journalist Tina Rosenberg: "People don't want words; they want deeds. You talk to the masses in simple language, and the simplest and clearest is with bullets and dynamite."[175] True to form, *Sendero Luminoso* chose to announce its arrival on the political stage on 17 May 1980 by raiding a polling station in the small Ayacucho village of Chuschi and burning the voting lists and ballot boxes needed for the following day's general election in the town square in a symbolic rejection of the democratic process.[176]

The Colombian Marxist terrorist group *Movimiento 19 de Abril* (M-19) launched its campaign against the right-wing National Front government of Misael Pastrana Borrero in 1974 by stealing Simón Bolívar's sword from the Quinta de Bolívar Museum in Bogota.

---

[173] Carlos Marighella, *Minimanual of the Urban Guerrilla* (Havana; Tricontinental 1970).

[174] Carlos Iván Degregori, The Maturation of a Cosmocrat and the Building of a Discourse Community: The Case of Shining Path, in David Apter (ed.), *The Legitimization of Violence* (New York University Press; 1997), p. 65.

[175] Quoted in Jeffrey D. Simon, *The Terrorist Trap: America's Experience with Terrorism* (Indiana University Press; 2001), p. 351.

[176] Carlos Iván Degregori, The Maturation of a Cosmocrat and the Building of a Discourse Community: The Case of Shining Path, in David Apter (ed.), *The Legitimization of Violence* (New York University Press; 1997), p. 35; Cyrus Zirakzadeh, From Revolutionary Dreams to Organizational Fragmentation: Disputes over Violence within ETA and Sendero Luminoso. *Terrorism and Political Violence*, Vol. 14, No. 4 (2002), p. 79; and El Diario, *Interview with Chairman Gonzalo* (Committee to Support the Revolution in Peru; 1991), p. 41.

Simón Bolívar is known throughout Latin America as "The Liberator" for the central role he played in freeing Latin American from Spanish colonial rule — many on the left believed that the National Front had stolen the 1970 election through widespread fraud and storming into Bolívar's former residence and quite literally taking up his sword was a powerful act of political symbolism.[177] Another signature operation of M-19 was to seize a truck loaded with groceries, or rob a supermarket, and then take the food to a poor neighborhood in the city where they would give the food away to the local population knowing that the story would also be more easily picked up by the media in an urban setting.[178]

Patroklos Tselentis, testifying against his former comrades from November 17 in court, said that the Greek terrorist group's "military" actions had been "intended as armed propaganda, used to demonstrate to the populace and movement, new possibilities of political action and armed intervention. It was a way to persuade society that change could only be achieved through violent revolutionary action. As such, the selection of targets had to be easily understood and widely accepted by the populace."[179] The group's Chief of Operations, Dimitris Koufodinas, known by the nickname "poison hand" because of his exploits with a handgun, echoed this observation stating that armed action only advanced the organization's cause if the target chosen "spoke for itself and [was] also one that ordinary people immediately understood and identified with".[180] He added that November 17 selected as targets "symbols of power and authority in every political, economic and social sphere — representatives of institutional mechanisms and of imperialistic hegemony and capitalist exploitation, corrupted politicians and civil servants, thieves of social wealth and public property".[181] Marxist groups had a bias for

---

[177] Mauricio Florez-Morris, Joining Guerrilla Groups in Colombia: Individual Motivations and Processes for Entering a Violent Organization, *Studies in Conflict and Terrorism*, Vol. 30, No. 7 (2007), p. 616.

[178] ibid., p. 623.

[179] George Kassimeris, *Inside Greek Terrorism* (Oxford University Press; 2013), pp. 42–43.

[180] ibid., p. 29.

[181] ibid.

targeting successful businessmen, such as the banker Jürgen Ponto murdered by the *Rote Armee Fraktion* in 1977, the General Director of Renault, George Besse, killed by the French group *Action Directe* (Direct Action) in 1987, or the Greek newspaper publisher Nikos Momferatos shot dead by November 17 in 1985. When the *Brigate Rosse* briefly kidnapped Idalgo Macchiarini, Director of the company Sit Siemens, in March 1972, they released a photograph of him with a placard hanging around his neck which proclaimed, amongst other slogans, "strike one to educate a hundred".[182]

Another compelling example of the power of propaganda by deed, or perhaps in this instance more accurately propaganda after the deed, is the defense mounted by Yasir Arafat against Israeli forces in the Palestinian refugee camp of Al Karameh in Jordan on 21 March 1968. A *Fateh* unit from Al Karameh had planted a mine on a road inside Israel which had detonated under a school bus killing two children and injuring twenty-eight. In response, the Israeli Defense Force (IDF) mounted a punitive cross-border raid against the refugee camp. Forewarned of the attack, the local Jordanian commander, General Amer Khammash, advised Arafat to pull his forces out of the camp but Arafat refused, reportedly telling the general: "We want to persuade the world that there are those in the Arab nation who will not withdraw or flee."[183] *Fateh* fighters, led by Arafat who had briefly served as a reserve officer in the Egyptian Army, held off the Israeli assault long enough that the IDF was forced to withdraw before the Jordan military could respond in force. The IDF lost thirty-three men, while the Palestinian side suffered 156 fatalities. Before the battle, Arafat had told his men: "We will make Karameh the second Leningrad."[184] In the aftermath of the clash, it soon became clear that he had in part succeeded. The engagement at Al Karameh quickly became a central totem of *Fateh*'s identity and more important still, the myth

---

[182] Michael Burleigh, *Blood and Rage: A Cultural History of Terrorism* (Harper; 2009), p. 199.

[183] Yezid Sayigh, *Armed Struggle and the Search for State, the Palestinian National Movement 1949–1993* (Oxford University Press; 1997), p. 178.

[184] Tony Walker and Andrew Gowers, *Arafat: The Biography* (Virgin Books; 2003), p. 50.

of Israeli invincibility had been dented.[185] As Leila Khaled of the rival Popular Front for the Liberation of Palestine (PFLP) recalled with more than a hint of asperity: "*Fateh* became a folksong, a fashion, a fetish. Its leaders, cadres, office clerks were regarded as saviours, saints and seraphim."[186]

This minor triumph also came at a crucial moment when Palestinian spirits were at a desperately low ebb in the aftermath of the disastrous reversals of the Six Day War only nine months earlier, and the subsequent failure of attempts to sustain resistance to the Israeli military occupation of the West Bank. The name Al Karameh was prophetic — it means "dignity" in Arabic and this was precisely what the battle gave young Palestinians. Jamal al-Gashey, one of the three Black September terrorists who survived the organization's 1972 Munich Olympics hostage operation, told a reporter it was the victory of Al Karameh that had first inspired him to join Arafat's *Fateh* movement: "I joined *Fateh* immediately."[187] Similarly inspired, thousands of other young Arabs flocked to *Fateh*'s banner. Al Karameh was also a turning point for Arafat personally, boosting his political profile and launching him onto the world stage — he appeared on the cover of *Time Magazine* for the first time later that year and in 1969 was elected Chairman of the Palestine Liberation Organization (PLO), a position he then held until his death in 2004.

The lesson of *Fateh*'s perceived success at Al Karameh was well learned, and armed propaganda became an integral part of operations conducted by all the disparate Palestinian nationalist groups. Leila Khaled admitted that the PFLP was well aware that its operations generally had a more political than military impact on Israeli interests: "Generally, we act not with a view to crippling the enemy — because we lack the power to do so — but with a view

---

[185] Max Boot, *Invisible Armies: An Epic History of Guerrilla Warfare from Ancient Times to the Present* (Liveright; 2013), p. 463.

[186] Leila Khaled and George Hajjar, *My People Shall Live: The Autobiography of a Revolutionary* (Hodder and Stoughton; 1973), p. 107.

[187] Simon Reeve, *One Day in September: The Full Story of the 1972 Munich Olympics Massacre and the Israeli Revenge Operation "Wrath of God"* (Arcade Publishing; 2000), pp. 29–30.

to disseminating revolutionary propaganda, sowing terror in the heart of the enemy, mobilizing our masses, making our cause international, rallying the forces of progress on our side, and underscoring our grievances before an unresponsive Zionist-inspired and Zionist-informed Western public opinion... We act heroically in a cowardly world to prove the enemy is not invincible."[188] Jamal al-Gashey and his Black September comrades prepared a political testament to explain their actions in Munch, which also acknowledged the wider symbolic purpose behind their action: "Only the strong enjoy the respect of the world. We shall not be strong by words, announcements and information. We shall be strong only when we regard death as we regard life, and turn the honor commitment into an honor of practice, thus giving our slogans a content of practical struggle, that would make our enemies doubt their ability to confront us, and make them eventually believe that they have no alternative but to meet our just demands."[189]

The world's monotheistic religions had demonstrated an instinctive grasp of the power of propaganda by deed many, many centuries before the term was coined by Paul Brousse — Christ's death on the cross to "expiate man's sins" or the Prophet Mohammed's conquest of Mecca could both be regarded as exemplars of the basic concept — and so it is little surprise that religious terrorism offers many fresh examples of the practice. However, one example clearly dwarfs all the others — *al-Qaeda's* attacks on New York and Washington on 11 September 2001. Osama bin Laden told the Pakistani journalist Hamid Mir in the last interview he would give before going into hiding, that *al-Qaeda* deliberately chose the World Trade Center and the Pentagon as targets because they were "America's icons of military and economic power".[190] Their collective destruction demonstrated American vulnerability

---

[188] Leila Khaled and George Hajjar, *My People Shall Live: The Autobiography of a Revolutionary* (Hodder and Stoughton; 1973), p. 126.

[189] Will of the Munich Guerrillas, *Palestine News Agency* (WAFA), 11 September 1972.

[190] Tim Weiner, A Nation Challenged: Al Qaeda; Bin Laden Asserts He Has Nuclear Arms, *The New York Times*, 10 November 2001.

for all to see, leading bin Laden to boast in startlingly similar terms to the language used in Kropotkin's *The Spirit of Revolt* 120 years earlier: "The sermons they gave in New York and Washington, made the whole world hear — the Arabs, the non-Arabs, the Indians, the Chinese — and are worth much more than millions of books and cassettes and pamphlets."[191] Anxious to ensure that his message was interpreted correctly, bin Laden even sat down for interviews with international media networks including CNN, ABC and *Al-Jazeera* prior to the 9/11 attacks to explain his grievances against the West.[192] Similarly, a video commemorating the first anniversary of the 2005 London Transport bombings produced by *al-Qaeda*'s media wing *As-Sahab*[193] took pains to establish that "the knights of London ... determined the targets with precision. The names of the stations that were targeted have significance, both symbolically and in terms of morale, for the Crusader West."[194]

The Islamic State of Iraq and the Levant (ISIL) has described its claims of responsibility for attacks in Britain and France as "media projectiles".[195] In April 2016, ISIL circulated a manual entitled *Media Operative, You Are a Mujahid Too* on the social media platform Telegraph, which celebrated the role played by its propagandists, proclaiming: "It is no exaggeration to say that the media operative is a martyrdom-seeker without a belt."[196] The manual set out the group's media strategy in some detail, a key component of which is the careful coordination of its terrorist operations with its propaganda messaging to magnify the impact of

---

[191] Fawaz Gerges, *Journey of the Jihadist: Inside Muslim Militancy* (2006), p. 207.

[192] Max Boot, *Invisible Armies: An Epic History of Guerrilla Warfare from Ancient Times to the Present* (Liveright; 2013), p. 523.

[193] The Clouds.

[194] *American Al-Qaeda Operative Adam Gadahn, Al-Qaeda Deputy Al-Zawahiri, and London Bomber Shehzad Tanweer in New Al[sic]-Sahab/Al-Qaeda Film Marking the First Anniversary of the 7/7 London Bombings*, The Middle East Media Research Institute, Special Dispatch No. 1201, 11 July 2006.

[195] Charlie Winter and Haroro Ingram, Why ISIS Is So Good at Branding Its Failures as Successes, *The Atlantic*, 19 September 2017.

[196] Charlie Winter, Media Jihad: The Islamic State's Doctrine for Information Warfare, *International Centre for the Study of Radicalisation and Terrorist Violence* (2017), p. 8 and p. 13.

each attack and to ensure that the group's intended message is properly understood by its audience. The researcher Charlie Winter has described ISIL's integrated approach as "turbocharged narrative-led terrorism".[197] The manual also explained in detail how Western media outlets can be manipulated as an important psychological tool with the "far-reaching potential to change the balance in respect to the war between the Muslims and their enemies" and concluded that "media weapons [can] actually be more potent than atomic bombs".[198]

## Summary

The American political scientist David Apter, who wrote extensively on the topic of political violence, once noted that "people do not commit to political violence without discourse."[199] By their own admission, terrorists use violence as a means of communication and so it makes sense that those involved in countering terrorist threats should make decoding these communications a high priority. And yet, more often than not, both terrorists and counter-terrorism officials are talking past each other in a dialogue of the deaf that would be absurd if its consequences weren't so tragic. Terrorists use violence in large part discursively to promote narratives that attract support and undermine opponents' claims of legitimacy. We ignore these narratives at our peril.

## The Revolutionary Prototype

Closely related to the concept of propaganda by deed is the importance to the terrorist cause of charismatic leadership. In 1869, Sergei Nechaev, the Russian anarchist and founder of *Narodnaya Rasprava*, authored *The Catechism of the Revolutionist*, in

---

[197] ibid., p. 18.

[198] ibid.

[199] David Apter, Political Violence in Analytical Perspective, in David Apter (ed.), *The Legitimization of Violence* (New York University Press; 1997), p. 2.

which, and with himself very much in mind, he sketched out the central role he believed would be played in an underground struggle by what he termed a "revolutionary prototype". In Nechaev's somewhat melodramatic vision, this revolutionary prototype is a romantic figure whom inspires others through his single-minded dedication to the cause: "The revolutionary is a doomed man. He has no personal interests, no affairs, no sentiments, attachments, property, not even a name of his own. Everything in him is absorbed by one exclusive interest, one thought, one passion — the revolution."[200]

Nechaev had already sought to personally transform himself into just such a figure by promoting a heroic personal mythos that included a daring escape from the notorious Tsarist political prison in St. Petersburg's Peter and Paul fortress.[201] The escape was a carefully constructed fabrication. Nechaev sent a note to a known member of St. Petersburg's radical underground, stating that he had been arrested and taken to the prison. For added dramatic effect and apparent authenticity, he also concocted a covering letter from an anonymous student who claimed to have recovered the note after seeing a scrap of paper dropped surreptitiously from the window of a prisoners' carriage. A short time later, Nechaev began spreading the rumor that he had escaped from the fortress and was making his way to exile in Switzerland. In one fell swoop, Nechaev established his revolutionary credentials and his reckless daring without ever setting foot inside prison, and, with his legend

---

[200] Sergei Nechaev, *The Catechism of the Revolutionist*. The authorship of the Catechism is disputed. The document was written in cipher and carried back to Russia by Nechaev where it was recovered by the Tsarist authorities when they detained some of his followers. It was drafted during a period that Nechaev and Mikhail Bakunin were in close collaboration, and Bakunin's associate Michael Sazhin claimed of have seen a copy of the manuscript in Bakunin's handwriting. However, Bakunin also referred to the Catechism in a letter to Nechaev as "your Catechism" and "the Catechism of *abreks* (bandits)." See Michaël Confino, Bakunin et Nečaev, *Cahiers du monde russe et soviétique*, Vol. 7, No. 4 (1966), p. 581–699. On balance, the Catechism is usually attributed to Nechaev, not least because it seems more in keeping with his, rather than his mentor's, contemporary public statements.

[201] Clark McCauley and Sophia Moskalenko, *Friction: How Radicalization Happens to Them and Us* (Oxford University Press; 2011), p. 150.

established, he was able to gain the trust of some of Russia's leading radical exiles, including Mikhail Bakunin, who saw much of himself in the young firebrand.

The revolutionary prototype soon became part of the anarchist canon. Writing in 1880, the influential anarchist theorist Prince Peter Kropotkin described the archetype that the anarchist movement was hoping to attract to its ranks: "Men of courage, not satisfied with words, but ever searching for means to transform them into action — men of integrity for whom the act is one with the idea, for whom, prison, exile, and death are preferable to a life contrary to their principles — intrepid souls who know that it is necessary to *dare* in order to succeed — there are the lonely sentinels who enter the battle long before the masses are sufficiently aroused to raise openly the banner of insurrection and to march, arms in hand, to the conquest of their rights."[202] This was certainly how anarchist revolutionaries tended to see themselves. In his self-referential memoir, *Underground Russia,* Sergei Kravshinski described "the terrorist" in terms very similar to those used by Nechaev: "He is noble, terrible, irresistibly fascinating, for he combines in himself the two sublimities of human grandeur: the martyr and the hero ... He has no other object than to overthrow this abhorred despotism, and to give to his country, what all civilized nations possess, political liberty."[203] Kravshinski, a dashing former Russian army officer who besides fighting against the Ottoman Turks had also participated in the short-lived 1877 anarchist uprising led by Errico Malatesta in Benevento, Italy, which helped inspire Brousse's article in the *Bulletin de la Fédération Jurassienne,*[204] before ultimately joining *Narodnaya Volya,* was

---

[202] Peter Kropotkin, The Spirit of Revolt, in Roger Baldwin (ed.), *Kropotkin's Revolutionary Pamphlets,* (Dover, 1971), p. 39 and Marie Fleming, Propaganda by the Deed: Terrorism and Anarchist Theory in Late Nineteenth-Century Europe, *Terrorism: An International Journal,* Vol. 4 (1980), p. 7.

[203] S. Stepniak, *Underground Russia: Revolutionary Profiles and Sketches From Life* (Charles Scribner's Sons; 1883), pp. 42–45.

[204] Marie Fleming, Propaganda by the Deed: Terrorism and Anarchist Theory in Late Nineteenth-Century Europe, *Terrorism: An International Journal,* Vol. 4 (1980), p. 4.

denied a martyr's death — he was rather prosaically hit and killed by train while crossing a railway line in London in 1895.

Another early revolutionary prototype (although it was not a term he would have used himself) was the Irish nationalist leader Michael Collins. The Head of British Intelligence operations in Ireland, General Sir Ormonde Winter, said of Collins: "He combined the characteristics of Robin Hood with those of an elusive Pimpernel. His many narrow escapes, when he managed to elude almost certain arrest, shrouded him in a cloak of historical romance."[205] It was an image that Collins appears to have cultivated. Irish historian John Regan has written that he had a sophisticated understanding of the power of still and moving images — he rarely posed for press photographs instead forcing reporters to capture his image as he strode past the camera ensuring that the image conveyed to the public was that of a dynamic man of action and in June 1922 shortly after the outbreak of the Irish Civil War, Collins reached out to the new Irish Minister of Propaganda, Desmond FitzGerald, to urge him to consider using cinema as a means to get the government's message out to a wider audience.[206] And it certainly seems to have worked — Collins is a rare political figure whose image has not greatly tarnished over the years, and he certainly seems to have acted as an inspiration to others. One notable admirer was future Israeli Prime Minster Yitzhak Shamir who, while he was the leader of the Zionist terrorist group *Lohamei Herut Israel* (LEHI), adopted "Michael" as his *nom de guerre* during the struggle against the British Mandate authorities — in explicit homage to Collins.[207] Shamir recorded in his memoirs: "I was stirred in some special manner by what I had read about Collins ... The spirit and

---

[205] T. Ryle Dwyer, *The Squad and the Intelligence Operations of Michael Collins* (Mercier; 2005), p. 223.

[206] See John Regan, Looking at Mick Again; Demilitarising Michael Collins, *History Ireland*, Vol. 3, No. 3 (Autumn 1995).

[207] Colin Shindler, *The Land Beyond Promise: Israel, Likud and the Zionist Dream* (I.B.Tauris; 2001) at 177 and Patrick Bishop, *The Reckoning: How the Killing of One Man Changed the Fate of the Promised Land* (William Collins; 2014), p. 166.

circumstances of his struggle against the British came to life for me in faraway Poland and remained with me."[208]

Mao Tse-tung, whose influence on generations of terrorist actors is almost unrivaled, understood the concept of a revolutionary prototype intimately, writing in *On Guerrilla Warfare*: "Leaders must be models for the people."[209] As a leader, Mao was an accomplished storyteller adept at using his own experiences — and particularly the dramatic epic of the Long March — as a vehicle to transmit ideas and create a powerful shared identity for Chinese communists. For this reason, Mao has been described as a cosmocrat, the leader and personification of an entire belief system, so bound up was his personal story with that of the triumph of Chinese communism.[210] Like Collins, Mao was careful also to burnish his international image allowing the American reporter (and dedicated communist) Edgar Snow extensive access so that he could produce the hagiographic biography, *Red Star Over China*, which introduced Mao to the wider world. Mao later commented that the book "had merit no less than Great Yu [a legendary dynastic Chinese leader] controlling the floods" in terms of the influence it had on shaping international opinion.

Perhaps unsurprisingly, *Sendero Luminoso*'s Abimael Guzmán closely modeled his leadership style on that of Mao, successfully establishing himself as his movement's cosmocratic leader in the process. Guzmán created a revolutionary alter ego, Presidente Gonzalo, whom he described variously as the "greatest living Marxist–Leninist–Maoist", "the fourth sword of Marxism", and, in one overblown but illuminating peroration in his manifesto *For The New Flag*, the voice of the soloist in the final movement of Beethoven's Ninth Symphony soaring above the tumult.[211] Other

---

[208] Yitzhak Shamir, *Summing Up: An Autobiography* (Weidenfeld and Nicolson; 1994), p. 8.

[209] Mao Tse-tung, *On Guerrilla Warfare* translated by Brigadier General Samuel B. Griffith II (University of Illinois Press; 1961), p. 45.

[210] David Apter and Tony Saich, *Revolutionary Discourse in Mao's Republic* (Harvard University Press; 1994), p. 73.

[211] Carlos Iván Degregori, The Maturation of a Cosmocrat and the Building of a Discourse Community: The Case of Shining Path, in David Apter (ed.), *The Legitimization of Violence* (New York University Press; 1997), p. 73.

communist icons like Ernesto "Che" Guevara, Fidel Castro and the Vietnamese General Võ Nguyên Giáp also helped inspire successive generations to emulate their example. Guevara, author of *Guerrilla Warfare, Guerrilla Warfare: A Method,* and *A Message to the Tricontinental,* was quite literally the poster child of European Marxist groups like the *Rote Armee Fraktion* and the *Brigate Rosse,* but his influence spread to every corner of the globe. LTTE leader Vellupillai Prabhakaran told an interviewer in 1986 that "Che Guevara is the guerrilla leader who inspires me the most"[212] and the notorious PFLP double hijacker Leila Khaled wrote in her memoirs that it was news of her hero Che's "assassination" at the hands of US-trained Bolivian Rangers that pricked her conscience and finally inspired her to "join the revolution".[213] Khaled took a copy of Ricardo Rojo's *My Friend Che* along on her first hijacking.[214] General Giáp features heavily in the works of *al-Qaeda* theorists like Abu Ubayd al-Qurashi and Abu Mus'ab al-Suri.[215]

Yasir Arafat took deep care to cultivate his image in such a way as to appeal to, and inspire, the disenfranchised Palestinian diaspora. He quite shamelessly promoted the legend of the battle of Karameh and was careful to gloss over aspects of his biography that could dent his appeal — like the fact he was actually born in Cairo and not Jerusalem. He would also talk up his participation in the fighting in Jerusalem in the 1948 Arab–Israeli war despite the fact that his most memorable engagement in the conflict began and ended with him accidentally shooting himself in the leg as he drew his pistol — Arafat rarely let the truth get in the way of a good story.[216] *Fateh* even launched itself on the world stage with an unintentional falsehood — *Fateh*'s first attack on Israeli territory was intended to be on a section of the Israeli National Water Carrier in

---

[212] Stephen Hopgood, Tamil Tigers 1987–2002, in Diego Gambetta (ed.), *Making Sense of Suicide Missions* (Oxford University Press; 2005), p. 48.

[213] Leila Khaled and George Hajjar, *My People Shall Live: The Autobiography of a Revolutionary* (Hodder and Stoughton; 1973), p. 94.

[214] ibid., p. 134.

[215] Michael Ryan, *Decoding Al Qaeda's Strategy: The Deep Battle Against America* (Columbia University Press; 2013), p. 95 and p. 234.

[216] Thomas Kiernan, *Arafat: The Man and the Myth* (W. W. Norton & Co.; 1976), p. 139.

Beit Netopha Valley in December 1964, the assault was called off at the last moment, but *Fateh* had already issued its Military Communiqué No. 1 claiming responsibility for the operation and its claim was picked up by news agencies and printed as fact.[217] Inflated and exaggerated claims would become a hallmark of *Fateh*'s media strategy. A political chameleon, Arafat was also careful to position himself to appeal to the widest possible constituency flirting with Arab nationalists, communists, and Islamic radicals as need dictated, as he put it in an interview with the Lebanese newspaper *Al-Sayyad* in January 1969: "What meaning does the left or the right have in the struggle for the liberation of my homeland? I want that homeland even if the devil is the one to liberate it for me."[218] Arafat was born Mohammed Abdel Rahman Abdel Raouf Al-Qudwa but he took the name Yasir, and his *nom de guerre* Abu Ammar, in tribute to the legendary Arab warrior and companion of the Prophet Mohammed, Ammar ibn Yasir.

When Arafat first assumed the role of *Fateh*'s official spokesman in April 1968, he would meet Western media representatives in isolated caves in the hills around Amman when he could just as easily have met them in a comfortable downtown hotel — simply to heighten the drama.[219] He was rarely ever photographed in public without his trademark black and white *keffiyeh*, carefully folded so that it hung down in such a way as to match the shape of the Palestinian homeland, and he typically wore a simple khaki military uniform unadorned with badges or medals, except for a Palestinian flag shoulder patch, to emphasize that he was a soldier and a man of the people — "a general in a private's uniform".[220] Arafat's stage management perhaps reached its apogee with his speech before the General Assembly of the United Nations in November 1974. At the climax of a speech layered in meaning and historical references, Arafat declared dramatically: "Today I have come bearing an olive branch

---

[217] ibid., pp. 240–242.

[218] ibid., p. 57.

[219] ibid., p. 53 and Barry Rubin and Judith Colp Rubin, *Yasir Arafat: A Political Biography* (Oxford University Press; 2005), p. 227.

[220] Tony Walker and Andrew Gowers, *Arafat: The Biography* (Virgin Books; 2003), p. 14.

and a freedom fighter's gun. Do not let the olive branch fall from my hand. I repeat: Do not let the olive branch fall from my hand." As he raised his arms above his head at the end of the speech, sharp-eyed observers caught a glimpse of a [empty] holster under his jacket, underscoring his message in the most dramatic way possible.[221]

Another contemporary example of a revolutionary prototype, in this instance an example purposefully manufactured by a political party, is Nelson Mandela. Mandela first rose to prominence as a leading light of the anti-*apartheid* African National Congress and as the public face of the ANC's armed wing *Umkhonto we Sizwe*. Indeed, the ANC's transition to armed struggle was actually presaged in June 1961 by a letter from Mandela to various South African newspapers threatening violence unless the government heeded calls to convene a national constitutional convention. Convicted in 1963 of his role in helping to plan *Umkhonto we Sizwe*'s early attacks, Mandela was sentenced to life in prison — he was already serving a five-year sentence for leaving the country without a passport and inciting a strike at the time. In the late 1960s, the ANC took a deliberate decision to promote Mandela as the face of the anti-*apartheid* movement, and in 1980, the Johannesburg *Sunday Post* launched a "Free Mandela" campaign that caught the imagination of the global public. The white South African regime recognized the danger of allowing Mandela to become a figurehead and banned the reproduction of any image bearing his features (and that of other jailed ANC leaders). The South African writer William Gumede recalled being *sjambokked* — whipped — by a police officer simply for drawing a crude image of Mandela along with the slogan "Liberation before Education" on his school bag.[222] When Mandela was finally released from prison on 11 February 1990, no one had been able to publish a contemporary photograph of him since 1964,[223] but his

---

[221] ibid., p. 128.

[222] William Gumede, How a Prisoner Became a Legend, *BBC News Magazine*, 6 December 2013 at http://www.bbc.co.uk/news/magazine-25256818.

[223] Nelson Mandela Obituary, *The Economist*, 14 December 2013 at http://www.economist.com/news/obituary/21591539-nelson-mandela-man-who-freed-south-africa-apartheid-died-december-5th-aged?fsrc=scn%2Ffb%2Fwl%2Fmdla%2Fob%2Fmandela.

status as the pre-eminent hero of the anti-*apartheid* movement, the ANC's artfully constructed revolutionary prototype, gave him the authority to sell the South African peace process to his people.

The Palestinian scholar and Afghan veteran Abdullah Azzam produced a series of works in the 1980s that helped inspire a generation of Islamist extremists to volunteer their services to *al-Qaeda* and its affiliates. His most influential work, *Join the Caravan*, was an impassioned appeal to his fellow Muslims to join the *jihad* against the Soviet Union in Afghanistan. Azzam believed that the practice of *jihad* would restore the Muslim community to its "rightful place" in the world and that warrior-scholars (not unlike himself) would play a critical role in rousing Muslims to action. In *Martyrs: The Building Blocks of Nations*, Azzam expounded on his theory: "History does not write its lines except with blood. Glory does not build its lofty edifices except with skulls. Honor and respect cannot be established except on a foundation of cripples and corpses. Empires, distinguished peoples, states, and societies cannot be established except with examples."[224] David Cook noted that through his own actions, Azzam provided the Muslim world "with an obvious example of a capable man who did not spend his life in the pursuit of wealth or status, but lived for the sake of Islam and *jihad*".[225] That Azzam was martyred in a car bombing in Peshawar in November 1989 only served to add to his allure.[226] However, Azzam's most significant contribution to Islamist cause was probably as the spiritual guide and mentor of Osama bin Laden who surpassed his teacher as the embodiment of the warrior-scholar archetype that the older man had expounded.

As Michael Scheuer observes, bin Laden's biography — the billionaire's son who gave up a life of luxury to fight in one of the harshest environments on earth for his faith — "is the stuff legends are made of in all cultures".[227] Bin Laden's conspicuously aesthetic and abstemious lifestyle, famously abjuring such modern

---

[224] David Cook, *Understanding Jihad* (University of California Press; 2015), p. 129.

[225] ibid., p. 130.

[226] Azzam's killers have never been satisfactorily identified.

[227] Michael Scheuer, *Osama bin Laden* (Oxford University Press; 2011), p. 167.

conveniences as air conditioning and Coca Cola, helped situate him firmly in the Salafist narrative. As his bodyguard, Abu Jandal, recalled: "The man was very simple in all his dealings and in everything in his life ... I used to hear him telling sons, 'sons, your father's millions about which you hear are not for your father to use. This money is for the Muslims and I hold it as a trust for the cause of God.'"[228] Bin Laden's widely reported piety and his use of poetry — both classical works and pieces of his own composition[229] — consciously invited comparisons with the early followers of the Prophet Mohammed and Islamic knights like Nur al-Din who made use of poetry both to rally the faithful and to publicize their achievements. Bin Laden often invoked the exploits of Saladin, the medieval Muslim general who recaptured Jerusalem from the Crusaders, in his rhetoric, drawing parallels between episodes in Saladin's life and the challenges facing *al-Qaeda* in his statements: "For the path to honor, glory, happiness, and regaining Palestine is clear and manifest in the religion of Almighty God and that path was taken by the heroic leader Salah-al-Din Ayyubi."[230] Bin Laden is even filmed on one *al-Qaeda* propaganda video reading a poem about Saladin's victories over the Crusader armies.[231]

Bin Laden's long track record of staying one step ahead of his enemies echoed another powerful trope of Islamic history, the devout servant of God struggling against overwhelming odds to defeat a stronger and better-armed foe — an outcome seen as evidence of divine favor. Bin Laden survived firefights with the Soviets, rivals' assassination attempts in Afghanistan and Sudan, US cruise missile strikes after the 1998 Embassy bombings in Kenya and Tanzania, and the encirclement of Tora Bora by the US

---

[228] Peter Bergen, *The Osama bin Laden I Know: An Oral History of Al Qaeda's Leader* (Free Press; 2006), p. 267–268.

[229] Many Arabic scholars regard Bin Laden to have been a capable poet in his own right — he published a collection of his poetry in March 2001 titled *Qasida* [Epic].

[230] Michael Scheuer, *Osama bin Laden* (Oxford University Press; 2011), p. 214–215.

[231] Peter Bergen, *The Osama bin Laden I Know: An Oral History of Al Qaeda's Leader* (Free Press; 2006), p. 291 and Michael Scheuer, *Osama bin Laden* (Oxford University Press; 2011), pp. 214–215.

and its Afghan allies in December 2001.[232] Each time he cheated death, his legend grew. Echoing Sir Ormonde Winter's description of Michael Collins, Professor Liaquat Ali Khan described the potency of this mythmaking in the Bangladeshi newspaper *The Daily Star* in 2004: "One can build a legend around Osama, even a bigger legend than that of Robin [Hood]."[233] Bin Laden's leadership style traded heavily on his status as a revolutionary prototype, as his childhood friend Khalid al-Batarfi describes: "He was a natural leader ... he leads by example and by hints more than direct orders. He just sets an example and then expects you to follow, and somehow you follow even if you are not 100% convinced."[234] Like Arafat, bin Laden also displayed a fondness for imposing props, such as the AK74 assault rifle taken as a trophy from a dead Soviet *Spetsnaz* officer and given to him by his military adviser, Abu Ubaidah al-Banshiri, after the Battle of the Lion's Den in 1987, bin Laden's most intense personal experience of combat.[235] In his videotaped statements, this weapon, along with an Afghan *pakol* hat and camouflage jacket, often served as a visual reminder to his audience of his *Mujahedin* pedigree. Bin Laden's successor as leader of *al-Qaeda*, Ayman al-Zawahiri, once wrote: "The role of the leadership is to inspire young men by making them aware of their obligations to the faith and setting an example to follow."[236] Bin Laden is an exemplar of how terrorist leaders can accomplish this.

Bin Laden is certainly not alone among the pantheon of terrorist leaders in trying to draw parallels between himself and consequential historical figures — terrorists often seek to boost their appeal by forging a link between themselves and more established national

---

[232] Michael Scheuer, *Osama bin Laden* (Oxford University Press; 2011), pp. 131–132.

[233] Liaquat Ali Khan, Who is Feeding the Bin Laden Legend, *The Daily Star*, 28 December 2004.

[234] Peter Bergen, *The Osama bin Laden I Know: An Oral History of Al Qaeda's Leader* (Free Press; 2006), p. 14.

[235] Lawrence Wright, *The Looming Tower: Al Qaeda and the Road to 9/11* (Knopf; 2007), p. 119.

[236] Jeffrey William Lewis, *The Business of Martyrdom: A History of Suicide Bombing* (Naval Institute Press; 2012), p. 238 and Laura Mansfield, *Ayman al-Zawahiri, His Own Words: Translation and Analysis of the Writings of Dr. Ayman al-Zawahiri* (TLG Publications; 2006), p. 207.

heroes.[237] EOKA's General Grivas took the *nom de guerre* "Digenis", after Digenis Akritas, the hero of a Byzantine epic and a series of folk ballads derived from the tenth century.[238] In his first revolutionary proclamation, Grivas also summoned imagery drawn from heroic Hellenic legend to call his fellow islanders to his banner: "Brother Cypriots, from the depths of past centuries all those who have glorified Greek history while preserving their freedom are looking at us: the warriors of Marathon, the warriors of Salamis; the 300 of Leonides and those who, in more recent times, fought in the epic Albanian war. The fighters of 1821 are looking to us — those fighters who showed us that liberation from the yoke of a ruler is always won by bloodshed. All Hellenism is looking to us, and following us anxiously, but with national pride."[239] The militant Zionist Avraham Stern chose the *nom de guerre* Yair in deliberate reference to the ancient Jewish hero Elazar ben Yair who had inspired the rebel garrison of the hilltop fortress of Masada to commit suicide rather than surrender to the Roman army besieging them.[240] The German political scientist Peter Merkl has neatly characterized the invocation of such historical narratives as "taking up the rifle" of earlier struggles.[241]

Although I have focused on leadership figures, revolutionary prototypes can come in all shapes and sizes and it is worth noting that not all of them become famous and that almost anyone can be a hero to someone. Colombian M-19 recruit "Fanny" told the researcher Mauricio Florez-Morris that she had joined M-19 because she had been inspired by her cousin, an M-19 fighter who was killed in a bomb explosion: "When he was alive I did not know that he was

---

[237] Margaret MacMillan, *Dangerous Games: The Uses and Abuses of History* (Modern Library; 2009), p. 17.

[238] George Grivas-Dighenis and Charles Foley, *The Memoirs of General Grivas* (Longmans; 1964), p. 32.

[239] EOKA's First Revolutionary Leaflet, 1 April 1955, in George Grivas-Dighenis and Charles Foley, *The Memoirs of General Grivas* (Longmans; 1964), p. 208.

[240] Patrick Bishop, *The Reckoning: How the Killing of One Man Changed the Fate of the Promised Land* (William Collins; 2014), p. 48 and p. 69.

[241] Peter Merkl, Conclusion: Collective Purposes and Individual Motives, *Political Violence and Terror: Motifs and Motivations* (University of California Press; 1986).

with the M-19, but when he died, in the way he died, we learned
about it. Then, I started to look up to him as a role model, an ideal;
I wanted to be like him, I wanted to have his courage and strength."[242]
Fifteen of the forty-three Colombian left-wing guerrillas interviewed
by Mauricio Florez-Morris told him that one of their reasons for
joining their respective groups was the example of someone they
already knew in the group who they had come to admire as a role
model.[243]

An influential revolutionary prototype can even be fictional —
perhaps the best example of this is Earl Turner, the eponymous
hero of *The Turner Diaries*, a white supremacist fantasy thriller from
the poisonous pen of Dr. William Pierce.[244] Turner is a member of
a racist organization seeking to overthrow the United States
government in the near future who, after helping to ethnically
cleanse Southern California, volunteers to detonate a plane carrying a nuclear warhead over the Pentagon, sacrificing himself for
the future of the white race.[245] Pierce has claimed that more than
200,000 copies of his book are in circulation and it has been
reported to have inspired the actions of a number of far-right terrorists in the United States.[246] Timothy McVeigh, the former US
Army veteran behind the Oklahoma City bombing, had distributed
copies of *The Turner Diaries* to his army buddies and had sold the
book at gun shows.[247] At the time of McVeigh's arrest, police found
photocopied pages from *The Turner Diaries* in an envelope in his
car, he had even highlighted one passage in particular that

---

[242] Mauricio Florez-Morris, Joining Guerrilla Groups in Colombia: Individual Motivations and
Processes for Entering a Violent Organization, *Studies in Conflict and Terrorism*, Vol. 30, No. 7
(2007), pp. 626–627.

[243] ibid., p. 630.

[244] *The Turner Diaries* was first published by William Pierce in 1980 under the pseudonym
Andrew MacDonald.

[245] Michael Barkun, Appropriated Martyrs: The Branch Davidians and the Radical Right,
*Terrorism and Political Violence*, Vol. 19, No. 1 (2007), p. 122.

[246] ibid.

[247] George Michael, *Confronting Right-Wing Extremism and Terrorism in the USA* (Routledge;
2003), p. 107.

discussed the psychological impact of mass casualty attacks.[248] The manner of the Oklahoma City bombing also bore a striking similarity to an episode in *The Turner Diaries* in which Turner detonates a truck bomb outside the headquarters of the FBI in Washington DC. Later in prison, McVeigh read another right-wing thriller called *Unintended Consequences* by the author John Ross. In this book, the protagonist, firearms activist Henry Bowman, hunts down and kills government agents one by one — McVeigh commented: "If people say *The Turner Diaries* was my Bible, *Unintended Consequences* would be my New Testament. I [thought it] was a better book. It might have changed my whole plan of operations if I'd read that one first."[249]

## The concept of martyrdom

Closely allied to the concept of a revolutionary prototype is the concept of martyrdom, which is common to religious and secular terrorist organizations alike. Celebrating heroic deaths and noble self-sacrifice turns, in David Apter's memorable phrase, martyrdom into testimony, further reinforcing the concept of propaganda by deed. [250] There are few discourses more powerful than the epic tales of courage and self-sacrifice woven about martyrs, which also serve to further cement group solidarity and legitimize a cause.[251] Such narratives are rarely left to chance. Michael Barkun notes the critical role played by "martyrologists", go-betweens who lend carefully scripted meaning to individual events: "A martyr is not ... simply a creation of an individual who decides to die in a particular way. It is, rather, a persona that needs to be constructed, and at least requires the cooperation of martyrologists who present the death in the

---

[248] ibid., p. 108.

[249] Lou Michel and Dan Herbeck, *American Terrorist: Timothy McVeigh and the Oklahoma City Bombing* (Harper; 2001), p. 304.

[250] David Apter, Political Violence in Analytical Perspective, in David Apter (ed.), *The Legitimization of Violence* (New York University Press; 1997), p. 2.

[251] Jeffrey William Lewis, *The Business of Martyrdom: A History of Suicide Bombing* (Naval Institute Press; 2012), p. 37.

desired way."[252] In *The Business of Martyrdom*, Jeffrey William Lewis shares another important insight — that martyrdom is a reciprocal process. He writes: "Martyrdom gives meaning simultaneously to individual deaths and to general causes; the individual dies for a cause, and the cause is legitimized thought the blood sacrifice of the individual in a process of mutual feedback."[253] The protagonist gains something important from the transaction too: paradise, renown, revenge, and, perhaps, vindication. This makes for a heady and arresting combination.

An apprehension of the potential power of martyrdom can be traced almost all the way back to the birth of modern terrorism. In September 1867, a gang of several dozen Irish Republican Brotherhood supporters ambushed a British prison transport carrying two detained leaders of their movement, both incidentally veterans of the American Civil War, Thomas Kelly and Timothy Deasy, to Belle Vue Gaol in Manchester. One of the prisoners' escorts, Police Sergeant Charles Brett, was shot and killed during the escape. Three of those involved in the prison break — William Philips, Michael Larkin and Michael O'Brien — were subsequently arrested by the British authorities and sentenced to hang. The execution itself turned into a macabre spectacle when the hangman, William Calcraft, botched his job so badly that he was forced to jump on Larkin's back until his neck broke. The British then refused to return the bodies to Ireland for burial, compounding Irish outrage. Friedrich Engels wrote to Karl Marx with remarkable perspicacity after the execution: "The only thing that the Fenians still lacked were martyrs. They have now been provided with these by [Prime Minister] Derby and [Home Secretary] G. Hardy. Only the execution of the three has made the liberation of Kelly and Deasy the heroic deed as which it will now be sung to every Irish

---

[252] Michael Barkun, Appropriated Martyrs: The Branch Davidians and the Radical Right, *Terrorism and Political Violence*, Vol. 19, No. 1 (2007), p. 120.

[253] Jeffrey William Lewis, *The Business of Martyrdom: A History of Suicide Bombing* (Naval Institute Press; 2012), p. 35.

babe in the cradle in Ireland, England, and America."[254] The deaths of the Manchester Martyrs were marked for decades afterward by large demonstrations in Ireland providing a rallying point for opponents of British rule and are still referenced by Irish nationalists to the present day.[255]

In Switzerland, Mikhail Bakunin meeting Sergei Nechaev for the first time wrote breathlessly to a friend: "I have here one of those young fanatics who know no doubts, who fear nothing and who have decided quite definitely that many, many of them will have to perish at the hands of government but who will not let this stop them until the Russian people arise. They are magnificent, these young fanatics, believers without God, heroes without rhetoric."[256] Indeed, young men (and women) like Alexander Solovyov, who failed in his attempt to gun down Tsar Alexander II with a revolver in April 1879, were explicitly inspired by the self-sacrifice of their peers. After his arrest, Solovyov told police investigators: "Like ghosts, the martyrs for the people, who figured in many major political trials and who perished prematurely, pass through my imagination."[257] In an early example of martyrology, Prince Peter Kropotkin's description of the execution of Sophie Perovskaya, who was sentenced to death for the part she played in *Narodnaya Volya*'s successful assassination of Tsar Alexander II, makes David Apter's point perfectly: "She read in the sad looks which were directed sympathetically towards her that by her death she was dealing an even more terrible blow from which the autocracy will never recover."[258] The drama of Perovskaya's story was difficult to resist. Ivan Turgenev dedicated his novel *On The Eve* to *Perovskaya* and the Australian politician Sir Henry Parkes

---

[254] Donal Fallon, Friedrich Engels, Letters to Marx, *John MacBride: 16 Lives* (O'Brien Press; 2015), p. 200.

[255] ibid., p. 201.

[256] Mia Bloom, *Dying to Kill: The Allure of Suicide Terror* (Columbia University Press; 2005), p. 4.

[257] Jeffrey William Lewis, *The Business of Martyrdom: A History of Suicide Bombing* (Naval Institute Press; 2012) p. 50 and Edvard Radzinsky, *Alexander II: The Last Great Tsar* (Free Press; 2005), p. 295.

[258] Marie Fleming, Propaganda by the Deed: Terrorism and Anarchist Theory in Late Nineteenth-Century Europe, *Terrorism: An International Journal*, Volume 4 (1980), p. 9.

composed his poem *The Beauteous Terrorist* in tribute.[259] Perovskaya's *Narodnaya Volya* comrade Vera Figner wrote a letter to the new Tsar, Alexander III, in which she struck a defiant note: "Whole dozens of our leaders have been seized and hanged. They have died with the courage and calmness of martyrs, but the movement has not been suppressed, it has grown and gained strength."[260]

The British decision in May 1916 to execute fifteen leading figures of the Easter Uprising against British rule in Ireland after perfunctory military court martials gave fresh impetus to the Irish struggle for independence, as Michael Collins himself acknowledged: "That valiant effort and the martyrdoms which followed it finally awoke the sleeping spirit of Ireland."[261] The manner of the executions attracted widespread condemnation. The socialist leader and founder of the Irish Citizen Army James Connolly's ankle had been shattered in the siege of Dublin's General Post Office (GPO) building and he was unable to stand unaided. The British tied him to a chair in front of a firing squad so that his execution would not be delayed. Another of those executed was the school teacher and barrister Pádraic Pearse who had been chosen to read the *Proclamation of the Irish Republic* on the steps of the GPO at the start of the Uprising. Eight months earlier, Pearse had delivered a famous oration at the funeral of Jeremiah O'Donovan Rossa, the leading light of the nineteenth century Fenian and Skirmisher movement, in which he had declared: "Life springs from death; and from the graves of patriot men and women spring living nations ... the fools, the fools, the fools! They have left us our Fenian dead, and while Ireland holds these graves, Ireland unfree shall never be at peace." Well aware of the likely destination of the path he was embarked on, Pearse returned to the same theme in a pamphlet simply entitled *Ghosts*: "There is only one way to appease a ghost,

---

[259] Ze'ev Iviansky, Individual Terror: Concept and Typology, *Journal of Contemporary History*, Vol. 12 (1977), p. 56.

[260] Jeffrey William Lewis, *The Business of Martyrdom: A History of Suicide Bombing* (Naval Institute Press; 2012), p. 51.

[261] Michael Collins, The Proof of Success: What the Rising of 1916 did, *The Path to Freedom* (Welsh Academic Press; 1996), p. 53.

you must do the thing it asks you. The ghosts of a nation sometimes ask very big things; and they must be appeased whatever the cost."[262] With the Easter Uprising, Pearse and his confederates explicitly set out to establish what he termed "a theology of insurrection" and the choice of Easter Monday for the rising was also deliberate in this regard, with its connotations of sacrifice and resurrection.[263] The action of the British authorities only served to amplify this effect. The Provisional IRA intelligence officer Eamon Collins would write more than eighty years later: "In my mind, Pearse and Connolly were all linked together. They were martyrs for our Catholic faith, the true religion: Religion and politics fused together by the blood of the martyrs. I was prepared to be martyr, to die for this Catholic faith."[264]

The British made much the same mistake again during their administration of the League of Nations Mandate in Palestine. When in February 1942 Palestinian Police Force officers cornered the leader of the Stern Gang, Avraham Stern, he was shot dead "trying to escape". The controversial circumstances surrounding his death reenergized his moribund organization, which was relaunched in August 1943 as *Lohamei Herut Israel* (LEHI). One LEHI pamphlet declared of Stern: "With his death his doctrine did not die but will be continued by his faithful servants and soldiers. His body has been taken from us but no one can take from us that doctrine which he taught us and for which he died."[265] Another pamphlet promised that LEHI would honor his memory with "a tombstone of blood and fire",[266] a promise that the organization would make good on in the following years assassinating, among others, the British Resident Minister in the Middle East, Lord Moyne, in November 1944 and

---

[262] Michael Burleigh, *Blood and Rage: A Cultural History of Terrorism* (Harper; 2009), p. 19.

[263] Jeffrey William Lewis, *The Business of Martyrdom: A History of Suicide Bombing* (Naval Institute Press; 2012), p. 125.

[264] Mia Bloom and John Horgan, Missing Their Mark: The IRA's Proxy Bomb Campaign, in Michael A. Innes and William Banks (eds.), *Making Sense of Proxy Wars: States, Surrogates & the Use of Force* (Potomac Books; 2012), p. 39.

[265] Patrick Bishop, *The Reckoning: How the Killing of One Man Changed the Fate of the Promised Land* (William Collins; 2014), p. 218.

[266] ibid.

the United Nations mediator Count Folke Bernadotte in September 1948. LEHI member David Shomron, who gunned down the British detective Tom Wilkin in September 1944, told the author Patrick Bishop: "The fact that Yair [Stern] was murdered turned him into a symbol for us."[267] Twenty-five years after his death, Stern, who in his lifetime had been a marginal and unpopular figure even within the Zionist community, was being hailed as a founding father of the State of Israel and a national hero. Streets were named after him in Jerusalem, Tel Aviv and Beersheba, a postage stamp was issued bearing his portrait in 1978, and in 1981, a town in central Israel was even named in his honor, Kochav Yair (Yair's Star).[268]

Time and time again, national liberation movements have been able to mobilize sympathetic public opinion around the death or execution of their members by elevating the status of these individuals into martyrs for the cause. The Jewish leader and future Prime Minister of Israel David Ben Gurion noted the impact that the example of Sheikh Izz al-Din al-Qassam, the founder of the Arab terror group The Black Hand, had on the attitude of Palestinian Arabs, stating: "This time they really have national heroes, and this educates a movement, especially the youth."[269] The Black Hand carried out a number of attacks against Jewish settlements between 1930 and 1935 before al-Qassam was finally cornered and killed in a firefight with British security forces after murdering a British police officer near Jenin. Ben Gurion reacted to the news of al-Qassam's death in a meeting of his party's Political Committee by observing that his self-sacrifice had set a new standard for Palestinian youths to emulate. Ben Gurion was more prescient than even he imagined — more than fifty years after al-Qassam's death, Palestine's Islamic Resistance Movement, better known by its Arabic acronym *Hamas*, would name its militant wing in his honor and it would be volunteers

---

[267] ibid., p. 224.

[268] ibid., p. 256.

[269] Charles Townshend, The Defence of Palestine: Insurrection and Public Security 1936–1939, *The English Historical Review*, Vol. 103, No. 409 (October 1988), p. 919.

from the Izz al-Din al-Qassam Brigades who would carry out the first suicide bombing campaign inside Israel.

In May 1956, British forces in Cyprus executed the first of a series of convicted EOKA fighters, Michalis Karaolis and Andreas Dimitriou. More executions followed and the bodies were buried on prison grounds with the intention that the Greek Cypriot movement would be deprived of a site of pilgrimage around which to organize. As General Grivas later wrote in his memoirs, the plan backfired: "Instead they created a national shrine, and found their enemies were as dangerous in death as they were in life."[270] Realizing the propaganda opportunity presented to them by the actions of the British authorities, the political wing of EOKA, *Politiki Epitropi Kypriakou Agonos* (PEKA), churned out leaflets celebrating the lives and heroism of the martyred fighters.[271]

The Liberation Tigers of Tamil Eelam (LTTE), who along with *Hezbollah* pioneered the tactic of using suicide bombers to strike at well-defended targets, built a cult of martyrdom around the fighters who sacrificed their lives for the cause of Tamil nationhood. The LTTE celebrated an annual Heroes' Day on 27 November, the date on which the movement's first "martyr", Lieutenant Shankar, was killed trying to elude a Sri Lankan military patrol in Jaffna.[272] The organization later added a Black Tiger Day to specifically commemorate the sacrifice of the LTTE's elite cadre of suicide bombers, the so-called Black Tigers. Black Tigers were invited to have a last supper with the LTTE leader Velupillai Prabhakaran before embarking on their mission, and the relatives of dead Black Tigers were celebrated as *Maha Viru* (Great Hero) families.[273] Prabhakaran was quoted as saying that the death of a "Liberation hero" is a miraculous event that is actually life-affirming: "The truth is that a liberation

---

[270] George Grivas-Dighenis and Charles Foley, *The Memoirs of General Grivas* (Longmans; 1964), p. 71.

[271] David French, *Fighting EOKA: The British Counter-Insurgency Campaign on Cyprus, 1955–1959* (Oxford University Press; 2015), p. 8.

[272] Stephen Hopgood, Tamil Tigers 1987–2002, in Diego Gambetta (ed.), *Making Sense of Suicide Missions* (Oxford University Press; 2005), p. 48.

[273] Brigadier Dr S. P. Sinha, Unmasking of Prabhakaran, *Indian Defence Review*, Vol. 17, No. 2 (April–June 2002).

fighter does not die … What is called the 'flame of his aim' which has shone for his life will not be extinguished. This aim is like a fire, like a force in history and it takes hold of others. The national soul of the people has been touched and awakened."[274] With the Tamil population inspired by the celebrated deeds of Black Tiger commandos, the LTTE had little difficulty finding fresh volunteers to fill their depleted ranks.

The Marxist terror groups of the 1960s and 1970s also instinctively understood the power of martyrdom, which was already a well-established theme in communist propaganda. Mao Tse-tung observed in a much quoted memorial address extolling the life and achievements of Chang Szu-the, a party member and veteran of The Long March, "everyone dies, but death can vary in its significance". This would become an article of faith for many Marxist militant groups.[275] Mao's China would become known for its promotion of everyday martyrs to the communist cause — such as the Red Army soldiers Lei Feng, killed directing traffic, and Ouyang Hai, killed pushing a packhorse out of the way of an oncoming train — relatable heroes whose reported exploits inspired "hundreds of millions of revolutionary people" to emulate them.[276] Mao well understood the power of a compelling human narrative to move the masses and it was a lesson his admirers around the world took up, even as government after government confronting terrorist violence often seemed to ignore his insight.

The *Rote Armee Fraktion* embraced the concept of martyrdom in its pamphlet *The Urban Guerrilla Concept* quoting the nineteenth century French socialist Louis Auguste Blanqui with approval: "The duty of all revolutionaries is to fight, to carry on fighting, to fight to the death."[277] The RAF named most of its operational "commando

---

[274] Stephen Hopgood, Tamil Tigers 1987–2002, in Diego Gambetta (ed.), *Making Sense of Suicide Missions* (Oxford University Press; 2005), p. 63.

[275] Mao Tse-tung, *Serve the People*, 8 September 1944 — speech delivered at a memorial meeting for Comrade Chang Szu-teh held by departments directly under the Central Committee of the Communist Party of China.

[276] Study "Serve the People", *Peking Review*, Vol. 10, No. 2, 6 January 1967, pp. 9–13.

[277] Red Army Faction, *The Urban Guerrilla Concept* (Kersplebedeb Publishing; 2005), p. 29. Blanqui also believed that power should be seized by a small group of revolutionaries

units" after fallen comrades. The Holger Meins Commando, for example, which took over the West German Embassy in Stockholm in April 1975 killing two German diplomats, was named after a member of the Baader-Meinhof group who had died in prison while on hunger strike. In all, more than twenty different RAF commandos adopted the names of deceased German terrorists including those of such RAF luminaries as Andreas Baader, Gudrun Ensslin, Petra Schelm, and Jan-Carl Raspe, as well appropriating the names of various foreign fighters including the American Black Panther George Jackson, the Spanish Maoist José Manuel Sevillano and the Popular Front for the Liberation of Palestine – General Command's Khaled Aker. This memorialization of fallen "heroes" is a common terrorist trope. *Hamas* has its Izz ad-Din al-Qassam Brigades and Yahya Ayyash Units,[278] the latter named after the *Hamas* bomb maker known as "The Engineer" who was assassinated by the Israeli General Security Service, *Shin Bet*, in Gaza in January 1996.[279] *Fateh's* elite commando unit, Force 17, was named after a group of seventeen *Fateh* fighters killed defending a trench against Israeli tanks in the Battle of Karameh.[280] The modern Greek anarchist group *Synomosía Pyrínon Tis Fotiás* named one of its units the Commando Horst Fantazzini, after an Italian anarchist famed for robbing banks with toy weapons.[281]

Self-sacrifice was also a staple theme of the rhetoric of the *Sendero Luminoso* leader Abimael Guzmán who would tell his followers they needed to pay a "quota of blood" to water the revolution. *Sendero Luminoso* recruits were required to pledge "to

---

who would consolidate control during a period of transitional tyranny before handing power over to the masses. He is perhaps best known today for the slogan "He who has iron, has bread", which was appropriated by Mussolini for the masthead of his fascist newspaper *Il Popolo d'Italia*.

[278] US Department of State, Office of the Coordinator for Counterterrorism, *Country Reports on Terrorism 2011*, 31 July 2012, at http://www.state.gov/j/ct/rls/crt/2011/195553.htm.

[279] Ami Pedahzur, *The Israeli Secret Services and the Struggle Against Terrorism* (Columbia University Press; 2009), pp. 104–106.

[280] Max Boot, *Invisible Armies: An Epic History of Guerrilla Warfare from Ancient Times to the Present* (Liveright; 2013), p. 463.

[281] George Kassimeris, *Inside Greek Terrorism* (Oxford University Press; 2013), p. 104.

struggle and give one's life for the worldwide revolution",[282] with Guzmán extolling: "If our blood and life are demanded, let us have a posture — to carry them in our hands to surrender them ... our death for the good cause would be the seal on our revolutionary action."[283] In a similar vein, Mauricio Florez-Morris noted that in his interviews with former Colombian fighters active in three different underground Marxist groups that "the idea of dying for the group, and for the common cause, was a central part of the group culture. This idea was reinforced by cultural tools used in the movement, such as songs and stories of past heroic acts."[284]

Martyrdom is an especially powerful trope in the context of Islamic extremism and was an integral part of the rhetoric of the first modern Islamist revival movement, The Society of the Muslim Brothers Founded in Egypt in March 1928, the central virtues of the Muslim Brotherhood's philosophy were militancy (within the context of *jihad*) and martyrdom.[285] The group's clandestine and semi-autonomous military wing, known as the *al-jihaz al-sirri* (Secret Apparatus), which was likely established in 1940, carried out terrorist attacks against Egyptian government figures, British military targets in the Suez Canal Zone, and businesses considered emblematic of unwelcome Western influence, such as cinemas and nightclubs.[286] The Brotherhood even sent volunteers to fight in the Arab–Israeli War of 1948. For the Society's founder, a former school teacher called Hasan al-Banna, martyrdom was the apogee of political struggle: "The supreme martyrdom is only conferred on those who

---

[282] Carlos Iván Degregori, The Maturation of a Cosmocrat and the Building of a Discourse Community: The Case of Shining Path, in David Apter (ed.), *The Legitimization of Violence* (New York University Press; 1997), p. 71.

[283] ibid., p. 67.

[284] Mauricio Florez-Morris, Joining Guerrilla Groups in Colombia: Individual Motivations and Processes for Entering a Violent Organization, *Studies in Conflict and Terrorism*, Vol. 30, No. 7 (2007), p. 629.

[285] Richard Mitchell, *The Society of the Muslim Brothers* (Oxford University Press; 1969), pp. 206–207.

[286] John Calvert, *Sayyid Qutb and the Origins of Radical Islamism* (Columbia University Press; 2010), p. 119 and Richard Mitchell, *The Society of the Muslim Brothers* (Oxford University Press; 1969), pp. 58–62.

slay or are slain in the way of God. As death is inevitable and can happen only once, partaking in *jihad* is profitable in this world and the next."[287] Al-Banna believed that the Brotherhood could not hope to triumph unless its followers embraced the possibility of martyrdom, coining the aphorism: "Victory can only come with the mastery of 'the art of death'."[288] The Society of the Muslim Brothers was forcibly disbanded by the Egyptian Prime Minister Mahmoud an-Nukrashi Pasha in early December 1948, and many of its senior figures were taken immediately into custody and its assets seized, although Hasan al-Banna himself was left at liberty. However, when an-Nukrashi was assassinated by a student member of the Brotherhood just three weeks later, the regime's response was not long in coming — al-Banna was gunned down on a street in Cairo by the Egyptian Secret Police in February 1949.[289] He had finally attained the martyrdom he had extolled so many others to seek out, thus securing his place on the Islamist roll of honor, and the Muslim Brotherhood would re-emerge on the Egyptian stage (albeit briefly) after the overthrow of the Egyptian monarchy by the Free Officers led by Muhammad Naguib and Gamal Abdel Nasser in July 1952.

A former school inspector and public intellectual, Sayyid Qutb, would build on al-Banna's legacy. A charismatic polemical author, Qutb joined the Muslim Brotherhood in February 1953 after a brief and unsatisfactory flirtation with the Revolutionary Command Council established by the Free Officers.[290] The respect he was accorded as a leading voice of the Islamist movement meant Qutb was immediately inducted into the Brotherhood's Guidance Council and, when the Free Officers moved against the Brotherhood in January 1954, Qutb was one of 450 members of the movement arrested. He was briefly released and then rearrested after a failed

---

[287] Hasan Banna and Charles Wendell, *Five Tracts of Hasan Al-Bannā (1906–1949): A Selection from the Majmū'at Rasā'il al-Imām al-Shahīd, 1978.*

[288] Richard Mitchell, *The Society of the Muslim Brothers* (Oxford University Press; 1969), p. 207.

[289] ibid., p. 67 and pp. 70–71.

[290] John Calvert, *Sayyid Qutb and the Origins of Radical Islamism* (Columbia University Press; 2010), pp. 182–186.

assassination attempt on Nasser by a member of the Secret Apparatus in October 1954. It was in prison, where Qutb suffered torture and humiliation at the hands of the Egyptian authorities, that the political dimension of his Islamism hardened and he authored perhaps his most enduring work, *Milestones*, which maps out an uncompromising program for advancing the Islamist cause: "Preaching alone is not enough to establish the dominion of *Allah* on earth ... Those who have usurped the authority of *Allah* and are oppressing *Allah*'s creatures are not going to give up their power merely through preaching."[291] While he was still languishing in prison, Qutb was approached by a group of former Muslim Brotherhood activists, a "righteous remnant", seeking to reactivate the organization on a clandestine basis who petitioned him to act as their spiritual guide. *Milestones* was written with this role in mind although it was also published for a more general readership — Qutb's biographer John Calvert compares *Milestones* to Lenin's similarly influential *What is to be Done?*[292]

In May 1964, Qutb was finally released from prison after the President of Iraq, Abd al-Salam Arif, personally intervened on his behalf during a state visit to Egypt, but he was rearrested little over a year later after Nasser's regime became aware of the existence of the Brotherhood's new clandestine vanguard and its embryonic plans to acquire weapons and mount attacks against leading government figures. Qutb understood that his role within the clandestine movement, and the publication of *Milestones*, had made him a particular target for the regime. He also knew that he was not a well man and a return to prison could be fatal for him. The "art of death" was much on his mind and he told a visiting journalist shortly before his arrest: "Sometimes the departure of the righteous is more beneficial. I do not intend to hasten my own end, but we must be firm in our stance, knowing that this firmness can hasten destruction."[293]

---

[291] Sayyid Qutb, *Milestones* (Dar al-Ilm; 2007), pp. 47–48. John Calvert, *Sayyid Qutb and the Origins of Radical Islamism* (Columbia University Press; 2010), p. 225.

[292] John Calvert, *Sayyid Qutb and the Origins of Radical Islamism* (Columbia University Press; 2010), p. 225.

[293] ibid., p. 246.

Qutb also foresaw that his martyrdom at Nasser's hands would only strengthen the power of his message — excerpts of his writings were already being broadcast by Saudi radio. In August 1966, Qutb was sentenced to death along with six companions, although four of the sentences were later commuted. He reportedly greeted the sentence with the words: "Praise be to God, I performed *jihad* for fifteen years until I earned this martyrdom."[294] Qutb was offered clemency the night before his execution if he would only publicly admit that the Muslim Brotherhood had been conspiring with other subversive political forces inside Egypt, but he rejected the offer telling his sister Hamida: "My words will be stronger if they kill me."[295] A second offer of clemency was reportedly extended to him on the scaffold to which he replied: "Never! I would not exchange this temporary life for a life which will never disappear!"[296]

In February 1946, four British armored cars had run down several Egyptian protestors outside Qasr al-Nil Barracks in Cairo provoking a riot, which left twenty-three people dead.[297] In a newspaper editorial written to mark "Martyrs Day" — a day of protest called by the National Committee of Workers and Students to commemorate these deaths — Qutb had written: "Blood is the pledge of freedom in every time and place, and martyrdom is always the price of respect, both today and tomorrow."[298] The nationalist upheavals of the immediate post-war period and the example of those militants who had lost their lives fighting against continued British interference in Egyptian affairs had marked an important stage in Qutb's political evolution. Now, twenty years later, it would be the example set by his own martyrdom that would inspire the next generation of Islamist militants to take up the fight. Future *al-Qaeda*

---

[294] ibid., p. 261.

[295] Clark McCauley and Sophia Moskalenko, *Friction: How Radicalization Happens to Them and Us* (Oxford University Press; 2011), p. 188.

[296] John Calvert, *Sayyid Qutb and the Origins of Radical Islamism* (Columbia University Press; 2010), p. 263.

[297] Joel Beinin and Zachary Lockman, *Workers on the Nile: Nationalism, Communism, Islam, and the Egyptian Working Class 1882–1954* (American University in Cairo Press; 1998), pp. 341–342.

[298] John Calvert, *Sayyid Qutb and the Origins of Radical Islamism* (Columbia University Press; 2010), p. 118.

leader Ayman al-Zawahiri formed his first underground cell in response to Qutb's execution and offered the following comment on his significance in *Knights under the Prophet's Banner.* "Sayyid Qutb became an example of sincerity and adherence to justice. He spoke justice in the face of the tyrant and paid his life as a price for this. The value of his words increased when he refused to ask for a pardon from Jamal Abd al-Nasir [sic]."[299] Both Gulbuddin Hekmatyar, who led the political movement *Hizb-i Islami* against the Soviet occupation of Afghanistan in the late 1970s and 1980s, and Shaykh Salamat Hashim, former leader of the Moro Islamic Liberation Front in the Philippines, publicly credited Qutb as their inspiration.[300] Osama bin Laden attended public lectures given by Qutb's brother, Muhammad, at King Abdul-Aziz University in Jeddah. In John Calvert's sober assessment: "Not only did [Qutb's] death communicate that Islam was an ideal worth dying for, it also highlighted the essential illegitimacy of the powers that rule over Muslims in Egypt and elsewhere."[301]

In the past three decades, the term "martyrdom" has become almost synonymous with suicide bombings, a tactic that Hugh Barlow has perhaps more accurately described as "predatory martyrdom" since the term "suicide" has somewhat misleading pathological connotations.[302] Islamist terrorist groups have themselves displayed a marked preference for the term "martyrdom operations" since in most cultures the act of suicide is condemned by both religion and society alike. In 2005, there were more than 300 bombings in which the perpetrator deliberately sacrificed him or herself to press home the attack and these claimed a total of 3,171 lives. In 2007, there were 658 such attacks recorded — mostly, but not exclusively, in the Middle East.[303] It is important to note

---

[299] ibid., pp. 264–265.

[300] ibid., p. 3 and p. 265.

[301] ibid., p. 265.

[302] Hugh Barlow, *Dead for Good: Martyrdom and the Rise of the Suicide Bombers* (Paradigm Publishers; 2007), Part IV.

[303] Jeffrey William Lewis, *The Business of Martyrdom: A History of Suicide Bombing* (Naval Institute Press; 2012), pp. 4–5.

that "predatory martyrdom" is not a tactic exclusively associated with religiously motivated terrorist groups — nationalist groups like the Tamil LTTE and Kurdish PKK have also carried out such operations.[304] Indeed, the LTTE successfully dispatched operatives wearing explosive vests to assassinate two heads of state: Prime Minister Rajiv Gandhi of India in 1991 and President Ranasinghe Premadasa of Sri Lanka in 1993.

The first recorded "martyrdom operation" was a car bomb attack carried out on the Iraqi Embassy in Beirut on 15 December 1981 by a volunteer from the Iraqi *Shia* opposition *al-Dawa* party. Sixty-one people were killed. Other Lebanese groups adopted the tactic and similar assaults on an Israeli military headquarters in Tyre and on the US Embassy in Beirut followed in November 1982 and April 1983. However, it was only on 23 October 1983, when *Hezbollah* volunteers simultaneously drove trucks laden with explosives into the barracks of the United States and French contingents of the multi-national peacekeeping force in Beirut killing themselves and 241 US Marines and 58 French paratroopers, that the international community truly began to take notice. The multi-national peacekeeping force withdrew from Lebanon five months later, a decision that only served to embolden future generations of terrorists. Writing in his 1996 *Declaration of War Against the Americans Occupying the Land of the Two Holy Places*, Osama bin Laden dismissed declarations of American resolve to standup to terrorist violence by referencing the withdrawal from Beirut: "Where was this supposed bravery in Beirut, after the attack of 1403 [1983], which turned your 241 Marines into scattered fragments and torn limbs?"[305] Speaking at a memorial service in October 2013 marking the thirtieth anniversary of the bombing, Marine Corps Commandant General James Amos commented that the Beirut attack had "defined the beginning of what has become known today as the war on terror."[306]

---

[304] Ehud Sprinzak, Rational Fanatics, *Foreign Affairs*, 1 September 2000.

[305] Osama bin Laden, Declaration of War Against the Americans Occupying the Land of the Two Holy Places, *Al Quds al Arabi*, 23 August 1996.

[306] Justin Fishel, Is Iran Thumbing Nose at US 30 years after Beirut Bombing?, *Fox News*, 23 October 2013, at http://www.foxnews.com/politics/2013/10/23/is-iran-thumbing-nose-at-us-30-years-after-beirut-bombing/.

The practice of "predatory martyrdom" meshes seamlessly with the concept of asymmetrical warfare, as this statement by the Secretary-General of Palestinian Islamic Jihad, Dr. Ramadan Shalah, makes quite clear: "Our enemy possesses the most sophisticated weapons in the world and its army is trained to a very high standard ... We have nothing with which to repel killing and thuggery against us except the weapon of martyrdom. It is easy and costs us only our lives ... human bombs cannot be defeated, not even by nuclear bombs."[307] The Chechen separatist leader (and former Soviet Major-General) Dzokhar Dudaev made the same point about the mismatch between Chechen irregular forces and the Russian military in the 1990s: "We do not have armaments, military vehicles, military equipment, a military-industrial complex. We were left naked, and therefore we have been forced to establish suicide battalions."[308] That human bombs can act as a force multiplier, enabling terrorist groups to punch above their weight, has now become something of an article of faith. As Naim Qassem, the Deputy Secretary General of *Hezbollah*, acknowledges: "The weapon of martyrdom is the main and pivotal weapon on which we can rely, one that has proven its effectiveness and that prompts the enemy to reconsider its objectives."[309] Qassem also notes that: "Martyrdom renders the military power threatening death ineffective, for such a menace acts only upon those who fear it, and is powerless in front of those who seek it."[310]

Another senior *Hezbollah* official has written that a further purpose of martyrdom operations is to make a clear and inspirational distinction between the fearless *Hezbollah* operative and the Israeli soldier who "hides in the safety of his military machines, afraid of direct military conflict."[311] This theme crops

---

[307] Ehud Sprinzak, Rational Fanatics, *Foreign Affairs*, 1 September 2000.

[308] Jeffrey William Lewis, *The Business of Martyrdom: A History of Suicide Bombing* (Naval Institute Press; 2012), pp. 200–201.

[309] Naim Qassem, *Hizbullah: The Story from Within* (Saqi Books; 2005), p. 49.

[310] ibid. (Saqi; 2007), p. 149.

[311] Jeffrey William Lewis, *The Business of Martyrdom: A History of Suicide Bombing* (Naval Institute Press; 2012), p. 10.

up with great frequency in Islamist propaganda. The self-avowed mastermind of the 9/11 attacks, Khaled Sheikh Mohammed, made a similar point in a statement to a United States Military Commission hearing in Guantanamo Bay: "You do not fight us face-to-face, man-to-man. But rather, you fight us from behind roadblocks, trenches, and warplanes, which are thousands of feet in the air."[312] Shehzad Tanweer, one of the four *al-Qaeda* affiliated suicide bombers that attacked the London Transport system in July 2005 killing fifty-two members of the public, left behind a video message in which he contrasted the depth of his commitment to Islam with what he saw as the shallowness of the Western way of life, proclaiming: "We love death as you love life."[313] Martyrologists are adept at presenting relative weakness as moral strength.

Menachem Begin wrote that his years leading the Zionist terrorist organization *Irgun* had taught him that "in all history there is no greater force than the readiness for self-sacrifice."[314] The willingness to sacrifice one's life for a cause is an incredibly powerful statement of intent and commitment. In August 1920, the nationalist Lord Mayor of Cork and commander of the 1st Cork Brigade of the Irish Republican Army, Terence MacSwiney, was sentenced to two years in jail by a British military court in August 1920 for being caught in possession of a police cipher that had been stolen by Michael Collins' intelligence apparatus. He immediately went on hunger strike demanding to be treated as a political prisoner.[315] Because MacSwiney was also an elected member of the British parliament (although he hadn't taken his seat), his action attracted a great deal of attention. He survived seventy-four days before finally passing away, along with two other

---

[312] The 9/11 Shura Council, *The Islamic Response to the Government's Nine Accusations*, United States of America vs. Khalid Sheikh Mohammed *et al.*, 1 March 2008, p. 5.

[313] *American Al-Qaeda Operative Adam Gadahn, Al-Qaeda Deputy Al-Zawahiri, and London Bomber Shehzad Tanweer in New Al-Sahab[sic]/Al-Qaeda Film Marking the First Anniversary of the 7/7 London Bombings*, The Middle East Media Research Institute, Special Dispatch No. 1201, 11 July 2006.

[314] Menachem Begin, *The Revolt: Story of the Irgun* (Steimatzky's Agency Ltd.; 1977), p. 41.

[315] T. Ryle Dwyer, *The Squad and the Intelligence Operations of Michael Collins* (Mercier; 2005), p. 137.

hunger strikers. Speaking at a rally called to commemorate the death of MacSwiney and his comrades, the future leader of the Irish Free State, Eamon De Valera, quoted the celebrated Irish poet W. B. Yeats:[316]

> "They shall be remembered forever,
> They shall be alive forever,
> They shall be speaking forever,
> The people will hear them forever."

If there is a better encapsulation of the power of martyrdom, I have yet to hear it.

## Summary

The terrorism researcher Bryan Price has argued that because terrorist leaders head organizations with no legal standing, and thus have no basis for their legal authority, they depend more on their charisma to attract, control, and retain followers than other leaders.[317] As we will discuss in Part II, the identification of role models worthy of emulation by the members of a wider community can also have a significant developmental impact on maturing minds. Terrorist organizations of all political and religious persuasions have long intuited the potential influence that idealized versions of their best selves can exert over young men and women still seeking direction in their lives. The carefully curated role models and archetypes promoted by terrorist groups tend to emphasize purity, steadfast commitment, and sacrifice, along with a healthy dash of what the author Tom Wolfe dismissively termed "radical chic" — the glamor of a life lived outside mundane, quotidian constraints.[318] Religious groups also tend to include an additional mystical element, such as the accounts of visions or perfumed corpses that feature

---

[316] ibid., pp. 154–155.

[317] Bryan Price, Targeting Top Terrorists: How Leadership Decapitation Contributes to Counterterrorism, *International Security*, Vol. 36, No. 4 (Spring 2012), p. 17.

[318] Tom Wolfe, *Radical Chic: That Party at Lenny's*, New York Magazine, 8 June 1970.

prominently in the biographies of Islamist martyrs.[319] In essence, revolutionary prototypes perform an important soft power function for the groups that promote them by providing an emotional point of connection for potential recruits which cuts through more complex political or religious narratives, and by modeling behavioral cues for neophyte militants to follow. From Sergei Nechaev to Osama bin Laden, the evidence suggests that the outsider appeal of the revolutionary anti-hero remains just as strong as ever.

## Provoking an Overreaction

In his influential work on military strategy, *A General Theory of Power Control*, Rear-Admiral Joseph C. Wylie wrote that "the primary aim of the strategist in the conduct of war is some selected degree of control of the enemy for the strategist's own purpose."[320] The same holds true for terrorist campaigns. Terrorist groups don't stop at trying to neutralize the coercive organs of a state, they actively seek to put them to work on their behalf — as Louise Richardson has observed, "part of the genius of terrorism is that it elicits a reaction that furthers the interests of the terrorists more often than their victims."[321] By crafting attacks designed to provoke a draconian state response, terrorists hope to exploit the inevitable societal polarization that results to attract new recruits to their banner while undermining the state's own claim to be acting legitimately. It is a strategy that has been described as "political jujitsu"[322] and we can

---

[319] See Thomas Hegghammer, *The Soft Power of Militant Jihad*, New York Times, 18 December 2015.

[320] Rear Admiral J. C. Wylie, *Military Strategy: A General Theory of Power Control* (Rutgers University Press; 1967), p. 91. An earlier version of this section first appeared in Tom Parker, It's A Trap: Provoking an Overreaction is Terrorism 101, *RUSI Journal*, Vol. 160, No. 3, June/July 2015. The paragraphs reproduced here are reprinted by the kind permission of Taylor & Francis Ltd, http://www.tandfonline.com on behalf of *RUSI Journal*. Copyright © RUSI Journal.

[321] Louise Richardson, *What Terrorists Want: Understanding the Enemy and Containing the Threat*, (Random House; 2007), p. 103.

[322] See Clark McCauley, Jujitsu Politics: Terrorism and Responses to Terrorism, in Paul Kimmel and Chris Stout (eds.), *Collateral Damage: The Psychological Consequences of America's War on Terrorism* (Praeger Publishers; 2006). See also David Fromkin, The Strategy of Terrorism, *Foreign Affairs*, Vol. 53, No. 4 (July 1975), p. 688.

find clear statements of this intent present in terrorist writings from the mid-nineteenth century to the present day.

In a series of articles written between January and October 1850 for the *Neue Rheinische Zeitung's Politisch-ökonomische Revue* (and republished by Friedrich Engels in 1895 under the title *The Class Struggles in France 1848–1850*), Karl Marx reflected on the lessons the revolutionary left could learn from the failure of the widespread uprisings that occurred across Europe in 1848, concluding that the socialist cause "made headway not by its immediate tragi-comic achievements, but on the contrary by the creation of a powerful, united counter-revolution, by the creation of an opponent, by fighting which the party of revolt first ripened into a real revolutionary party."[323] Marx's insight would develop over time into doctrine on the revolutionary left as underground groups sought to provoke states into acts that would further polarize society and radicalize their base of support.

One of the first apostles of terrorist violence to articulate this strategy was the Russian anarchist Sergei Nechaev whose *Catechism of the Revolutionist* advises readers that violent officials should be "granted temporary respite to live, solely in order that their bestial behavior shall drive the people to inevitable revolt."[324] Nechaev also notes in his catechism that once the government in power begins to realize the inevitability of a popular revolt it will use "all its resources and energy toward increasing and intensifying the evils and miseries of the people until at last their patience is exhausted and they are driven to a general uprising."[325] Nechaev developed a theory of political provocation in which he aimed to push young radicals into direct confrontation with the authorities resulting in "the traceless death of the majority and a real revolutionary formation of the few."[326] As he told one public meeting in

---

[323] Marx and Engels, *Selected Works II*, V. Adoretsky (ed.), (London: Lawrence and Wishart; 1942), p. 192.

[324] Sergey Nechaev, Catechism of the Revolutionist, in Walter Laqueur (ed.), *Voices of Terror: Manifestos, Writings and Manuals of Al Qaeda, Hamas, and Other Terrorists from Around the World and Throughout the Ages* (Sourcebooks; 2004), p. 74.

[325] Sergey Nechaev, Catechism of the Revolutionist, at https://www.marxists.org/subject/anarchism/nechayev/catechism.htm and Max Nomad, *Apostles of Revolution* (Collier Books; 1961), p. 234.

[326] https://www.marxists.org/subject/anarchism/nechayev/catechism.htm.

Russia: "I have only one, though strong, hope in the government ... Let it imprison more students, let students be expelled from universities forever, let them be sent to Siberia, thrown out of their tracks, be stunned by the persecution, brutality, unfairness and stupidity. Only then will they harden in their hatred to the foul government, to the society which heartlessly watches all the atrocities of the government."[327]

Prince Peter Kropotkin picked up on the same theme in *The Spirit of Revolt*. Having extolled the power of propaganda by deed, Kropotkin went on to consider the state's response to such actions: "The government resists; it is savage in its repressions. But, though formerly persecution killed the energy of the oppressed, now, in periods of excitement it produces the opposite result. It provokes new acts of revolt, individual and collective, it drives the rebels to heroism; and in rapid succession these acts spread, become general, develop. The revolutionary party is strengthened by elements which up to this time were hostile or indifferent to it."[328]

The celebrated Irish republican Dan Breen recalled the deliberations that took place amongst the leadership of the 3rd Tipperary Brigade of the IRA as they debated ambushing a shipment of commercial explosives in Soloheadbeg in January 1919. The IRA action resulted in the murder of Constables Patrick MacDonnell and James O'Connell of Royal Irish Constabulary and is commonly considered to have precipitated the outbreak of the Anglo-Irish War. Breen claimed that this was his intention, and that of his confederates, all along: "We took the action deliberately, having thought over the matter and talked it over between us. [Seán] Treacy had stated to me that the only way of starting a war was to kill someone, and we wanted to start a war, so we intended to kill some of the police whom we looked upon as the foremost and most important branch of the enemy forces... The only regret that we had following the ambush was that there were only two

---

[327] Clark McCauley and Sophia Moskalenko, *Friction: How Radicalization Happens to Them and Us* (Oxford University Press; 2011), p. 152.

[328] Peter Kropotkin, The Spirit of Revolt, in Roger Baldwin (ed.), (Dover, 1971), p. 39.

policemen in it, instead of the six we had expected."[329] The IRA gunmen got the war they wanted and it unfolded much in the way that they had hoped.

In March 1920, the British began to deploy police auxiliaries hastily recruited from the ranks of demobilized World War I veterans who became known as the Black and Tans because of the mixture of military and police uniforms they were deployed in. The uniform serves as a metaphor for the auxiliaries' mission as a whole — neither fully police nor soldier. The Black and Tans became associated with a series of atrocities in rural towns like Tubbercurry, Templemore, Balbriggan, and Limerick in the summer and autumn of 1920 alienating the Irish citizenry, something that was deftly exploited by the IRA.[330] *The London Daily News* lamented: "Three months ago, the word 'reprisals' merely recalled the latter stages of the Great War. Today, to the whole of the English-speaking world it means one thing and one thing only — the method by which Great Britain is waging war upon Ireland."[331] One incident in particular that neatly summed up the IRA's approach took place in December 1920 when a company of Royal Irish Constabulary Auxiliaries responded to an IRA ambush that killed one officer and wounded eleven others by sacking the center of Cork in an orgy of looting and violence. An IRA man who witnessed the destruction told the reporter James Gleeson: "We could have shot most of them that night if we had wanted to ... but it would have ruined the whole show. They were doing all they could to help us."[332] Dan Breen would later write in his memoirs: "The frightfulness of the Tans proved a boomerang against those who had cast it, for the people were finally goaded into such fury that they made up their minds, 'come hell or high water', never to give way before such tyranny."[333]

---

[329] Quoted in Kevin Haddick Flynn, Review: Dan Breen and the IRA by Joe Ambrose, *History Ireland*, Vol. 15, No. 3, May 2007, p. 56.

[330] Charles Townshend, *The Republic: The Fight for Irish Independence* (Allen Lane; 2013), pp. 162–169.

[331] ibid., p. 168.

[332] J. B. E. Hittle, *Michael Collins and the Anglo-Irish War: Britain's Counterinsurgency Failure* (Potomac Books; 2011), pp. 179–180.

[333] Dan Breen, *My Fight for Irish Freedom* (Anvil Books; 1981), p. 104. First published by the Talbot Press in 1924.

The IRA integrated the lessons of the 1919–1921 Anglo-Irish War into its operational doctrine. The *Handbook for Volunteers of the Irish Republican Army* issued during the 1956–1962 cross-border campaign established three main strategic goals for the nationalist movement: "(1) Drain the enemy's manpower and resources; (2) Lead the resistance of the people to enemy occupation; (3) Break down the enemy's administration ... [The volunteer] achieves the second by remembering that the people will bear the brunt of the enemy's reprisal tactics and inspiring them with the aims of the movement."[334]

In his analysis of the potential weaknesses of the Japanese army of occupation in *On Guerrilla Warfare*, Mao Tse-tung identified Japan's "cruelty to the inhabitants of conquered areas" as a major area of vulnerability.[335] Mao noted that because the Japanese soldier was both "a foreigner and a barbarian" Chinese guerrillas could "gain the confidence of millions of their countrymen".[336] He urged guerrilla commanders to intensify this effect by conducting "intensive guerrilla warfare" in areas controlled by the Japanese so that "in order to subdue the occupied territory, the enemy will have to become increasingly severe and oppressive", ensuring that the gulf between occupied and occupier widened still further.[337] Mao understood both the strategic importance of winning and maintaining public support, and also how easily security force personnel could be provoked into abusing the local population and so undermining their own position: "It is only undisciplined troops who make the people their enemies and who, like the fish out of its native element, cannot live."[338]

In Palestine, Irgun had independently begun to evolve a similar concept of operations. The American author and historian David Fromkin recalled attending a meeting in New York City in 1945

---

[334] *Handbook for Volunteers of the Irish Republican Army: Notes on Guerrilla Warfare*, 1956 Edition (Paladin Press; 1985), p. 9.

[335] Mao Tse-tung, *On Guerrilla Warfare* translated by Brigadier General Samuel B. Griffith II (University of Illinois Press; 1961), p. 99.

[336] ibid., p. 100.

[337] ibid., p. 107.

[338] ibid., p. 93.

where he heard "one of the founders of the *Irgun*" explain how the organization expected to defeat the British: "To do so ... his organization would attack property interests ... This, he said, would lead the British to overreact by garrisoning the country with an immense army drawn from stations in other parts of the world. But postwar Britain could not afford financially to maintain so great an army either there or anywhere else for an extended period of time. Britain urgently needed to demobilize its armed forces. The strain would tell; and eventually economic pressure would drive the Attlee-Bevin government either to withdraw from Palestine or else to try some reckless and possibly losing gamble in an effort to retrieve the situation."[339] This strategy, with the concomitant challenges intuited by Mao, was not lost on the British themselves. The Joint Planning Staff of the British War Office concluded in a March 1947 assessment of security options for confronting Zionist terrorism in the British Mandate of Palestine that both *Irgun* and LEHI "wish to force us to employ sterner measures which can be represented as punitive against [the] community, thereby swinging moderate opinion against us and obtaining more recruits for themselves."[340] Yet, despite some apparent awareness of the trap they faced, the increasing tempo of attacks nevertheless still propelled the British headlong into it.

EOKA commander Georgios Grivas was also quick to understand how the strength of the British forces on Cyprus could be turned to his advantage as he sought to bring British colonial rule to an end: "The 'security forces' set about their work in a manner which might have been deliberately designed to drive the population into our arms. On the pretext of searching they burst into people's homes by day and night, made them stand for hours with their hands up, abused and insulted them ... Anyone who protested had scant hope of getting justice."[341] In his primer on

---

[339] David Fromkin, The Strategy of Terrorism, *Foreign Affairs*, Vol. 53, No. 4 (July 1975), pp. 687–688.

[340] Bruce Hoffman, *Anonymous Soldiers: The Struggle for Israel, 1917–1947* (Knopf; 2015), pp. 601/1042.

[341] George Grivas-Dighenis and Charles Foley, *The Memoirs of General Grivas* (Longmans; 1964), p. 53.

guerrilla tactics, *Guerrilla Warfare and EOKA's Struggle*, Grivas stressed the importance of mobilizing the youth — as "a testing ground and nursery from which I selected fighters for my groups of guerrillas and saboteurs" — describing in detail the effect of the so-called "Battle of the Flags" waged by Greek Cypriot schoolboys against the British authorities. When the British banned any public display of the Greek national flag, Grivas issued an order designed to bring schoolchildren into the struggle for *Enosis*: "See that the Greek flag is flown from all elementary schools and is kept flying."[342] The British responded by closing schools, detaining those responsible, and sometimes their teachers, as well as by doling out beatings on the spot, which, Grivas noted, "failed in their purpose and merely fanned the pupils' fanaticism".[343]

During the Algerian war of independence, the FLN's Ramdane Abane promoted an approach to the conflict that actively sought to provoke the French authorities to "accelerate repression" arguing that harsh French counter-terrorism measures would force the Algerian population to turn to the FLN for protection. Abane believed that only the way to separate the Algerian population from the French colonial system, with all its cultural baggage, was to precipitate, in Martha Crenshaw's words, a "sharp and brutal break".[344] Abane, shared the analysis that another veteran of the Algerian conflict, Frantz Fanon, would later make famous in his classic work on psychopathology, *The Wretched of the Earth*: "If the last shall be first, this will only come to pass after a murderous and decisive struggle between the two protagonists."[345] Fanon believed that violence was a cleansing force: "It frees the native from his inferiority complex and from his despair and inaction; it makes him fearless and restores his self-respect."[346] We know from the

---

[342] ibid., p. 62.

[343] George Grivas, *Guerrilla Warfare and EOKA's Struggle* (Longmans; 1964), pp. 15–16, and George Grivas and Charles Foley, *The Memoirs of General Grivas* (Longmans; 1964), p. 62.

[344] Martha Crenshaw, The Effectiveness of Terrorism in the Algerian War, in Martha Crenshaw (ed.), *Terrorism in Context* (Pennsylvania State University Press; 1995), p. 487.

[345] Frantz Fanon, *The Wretched of the Earth* (Grove Press; 1963), p. 37.

[346] ibid., p. 94.

testimony of Abane's nephew that the FLN leader was interested in Fanon's ideas.[347] Indeed, the two men met briefly and clandestinely, at Abane's request, in December 1956, leading Fanon to declare afterward: "I am assured that the Algerian revolution is in good hands."[348] Abane was assassinated by rivals within the FLN the following year.

The historian Alastair Horne has described the "Philippeville massacre" of 20 August 1955 (actually a series of brutal attacks on European settlers that took place in both Philippeville and the surrounding area) as a textbook example of a terrorist group deliberately setting out to provoke an overreaction from the authorities.[349] This was especially true of the murders that took place in the small pyrite mining settlement of El-Halia where thirty-seven French nationals, including ten children, were butchered in bestial fashion. El-Halia had enjoyed a reputation for excellent relations between the local French and Muslim residents and was deliberately targeted for this reason — to create a climate of distrust between the two communities. The viciousness of the killings, with bodies dismembered and desecrated, was intended to provoke a furious response from the French authorities and further polarize the population. The French response did not disappoint and the FLN later claimed almost 12,000 local Arabs had been killed in reprisal.[350] This in turn had the anticipated effect of boosting the FLN's recruitment efforts.

By October 1955, the FLN's strength in the North Constantine region where the atrocities had occurred had increased from 500 to 1,400 regular volunteers.[351] Youssef Zighout, the commander of the local FLN network and the prime instigator of the Philippeville massacre, justified the targeting of defenseless civilians by equating his

---

[347] Beläid Abane, Frantz Fanon and Abane Ramdane: Brief Encounter in the Algerian Revolution, in Nigel Gibson (ed.), *Living Fanon: Global Perspectives* (Palgrave MacMillan; 2011), pp. 31–32.

[348] ibid., p. 32.

[349] Alistair Horne, *A Savage War of Peace: Algeria 1954–1962* (New York Review Books Classics; 2006), p. 118 and p. 123.

[350] ibid., p. 122.

[351] ibid., p. 123.

actions to those of the French forces: "To colonialism's policy of collective repression we must reply with collective reprisals against Europeans, military and civil, who are united behind the crimes committed upon our people. For them, no pity, no quarter!"[352] The Governor-General of Algeria, Jacques Soustelle, lamented: "It was not only the sacked houses or poor mutilated corpses that the *fellagha* left in their passage — it was confidence, hope, peace ... There had been well and truly dug an abyss through which flowed a river of blood."[353] The future French President François Mitterrand, then Interior Minister, put it more simply still describing Algeria's descent into bloodshed as a *"cercle infernale"*. However, these comments fail to truly capture the strategic failure that doomed French Algeria. As David Fromkin observed in his influential 1975 article *The Strategy of Terrorism*, the French had profoundly misunderstood the nature of the conflict that they were engaged in, and by doing so they ended up playing right into the FLN's hands: "Even though the FLN had written the script, the French, with suicidal logic, went ahead to play the role for which they had been cast."[354]

Che Guevara was initially more ambivalent about such tactics acknowledging in *Guerrilla Warfare* that one drawback of using "terrorism" was that it provoked police oppression making the task of organizing the masses and other clandestine activity more difficult.[355] He also criticized terrorism — as distinct from "sabotage" — as a "generally ineffective and indiscriminate" method that often "makes victims of innocent people and destroys a large number of lives that would be valuable to the revolution".[356] However, by the time Che penned *Message to the Tricontinental* in 1967, his views had evolved considerably, he still favored the revolutionary method of Cuban-style guerrilla warfare fought from rural strongholds that he described in *Guerrilla Warfare* and *Guerrilla Warfare: A Method*, but he now acknowledged the need to "carry the war into every corner the

---

[352] ibid., p. 119.

[353] ibid., p. 123.

[354] David Fromkin, The Strategy of Terrorism, *Foreign Affairs*, Vol. 53, No. 4 (July 1975), p. 690.

[355] Che Guevara, Guerrilla Warfare (1960), *Guerrilla Warfare* (Souvenir Press; 2003), p. 22.

[356] ibid., p. 21.

enemy happens to carry it: to his home, to his centers of entertainment; a total war." He wrote: "It is necessary to prevent [the enemy] from having a moment of peace, a quiet moment outside his barracks or even inside; we must attack him wherever he may be; make him feel like a cornered beast wherever he may move. Then his moral fiber shall begin to decline. He will even become more beastly, but we shall notice how the signs of decadence begin to appear."[357] Che had come to see value in provoking repressive action as it served to galvanize and stiffen resistance to authoritarian rule, and bred "hatred as an element of the struggle; a relentless hatred of the enemy, impelling us over and beyond the natural limitations that man is heir to and transforming him into an effective, violent, selective and cold killing machine." He concluded somberly: "Our soldiers must be thus; a people without hatred cannot vanquish a brutal enemy."[358]

The American reporter Robert Taber, who got to know both Che and Fidel Castro well in their Sierra Maestra stronghold during the Cuban revolution, described how government repression was exploited in practice by revolutionary movements: "If there are atrocities in the way of reprisal on the part of the authorities, they must be well publicized. If there are martyrs, there must be big funerals, protests led by the mothers of the slain, outcries of popular indignation. Ideally there will be a general strike. With it will come further repression, a curfew, beatings, arrests, creating further alienation of the populace from the regime, perhaps creating new martyrs, new incidents."[359]

Another key theorist of provocation was the Basque nationalist Federico Krutwig. In 1963, Krutwig published *Vasconia*, a treatise on Basque nationhood that would become a key text for the Basque separatist group ETA, despite the fact that Krutwig himself was not

---

[357] Che Guevara, Message to the Tricontinental (1967), *Guerrilla Warfare* (Souvenir Press; 2003), p. 173.

[358] ibid.

[359] Robert Taber, *The War of the Flea: How Guerrilla Fighters Could Win the World* (Citadel Press; 1970), p. 36.

a member of the movement.[360] José Luis Álvarez Enparantza, one of the original founders of ETA who was better known by his pseudonym Txillardegi, called *Vasconia*, "the most important book on *Euskadi* [the Basque homeland] published in this century"[361] and it was endorsed by ETA's Second Assembly. Krutwig placed great emphasis on popular action and, directly inspired by the revolutions in Cuba and Algeria, he saw guerrilla warfare as the most suitable strategy to help Basques to attain independence. In particular, Krutwig outlined what he termed the "Action–Repression–Action" theory of violence. In stage one, "the guerrillas" carry out a provocative violent action against the state; in stage two, the state responds in a heavy-handed fashion with repression against "the masses"; and in stage three, "the masses" respond in turn with a mixture of panic and rebellion, at which point "the guerrillas" carry out a new attack to begin the cycle again and push "the masses" into further acts of insurrection.[362] José Luís Zalbide synthesized the passages on armed struggle in *Vasconia*, along with liberal contributions from Mao and Guevara, into an operational manual entitled *Insurrección en Euskadi* that was also formally adopted by ETA. Hardliners within ETA began to argue in favor of attacking senior regime figures in the hope of provoking Franco's government into "excessive and non-discriminatory retaliation against all Basque residents".[363] The hardliners finally got their wish with the successful assassination of the Spanish Prime Minister Admiral Luis Carrero Blanco by a car bomb in December 1973. However, unusually, the Spanish state didn't react quite as Krutwig predicted — Carrero

---

[360] Daniele Conversi, *The Basques, the Catalans, and Spain: Alternative Routes to Nationalist Mobilisation* (University of Nevada Press; September 2000), pp. 92–93.

[361] ibid., p. 93.

[362] Paddy Woodworth, Why Do They Kill? The Basque Conflict in Spain, *World Policy Journal* (Spring 2001), p. 5.

[363] Cyrus Zirakzadeh, From Revolutionary Dreams to Organizational Fragmentation: Disputes over Violence within ETA and Sendero Luminoso. *Terrorism and Political Violence*, Vol. 14, No. 4 (2002), pp. 73–76. See also Michel Wieviorka, ETA and Basque Political Violence, in David Apter (ed.), *The Legitimization of Violence* (New York University Press; 1997), p. 300 and Claire Sterling, *The Terror Network: The Secret War of International Terrorism* (Holt, Rinehart and Winston; 1981), p. 178.

Blanco's successor as Prime Minister, Carlos Arias Navarro, actually ushered in a series of liberalizing reforms.

In the *Minimanual of the Urban Guerrilla*, the Brazilian communist Carlos Marighella explicitly encouraged terrorist groups to mount attacks designed to provoke state authorities into overreaction, writing: "The government has no alternative except to intensify its repression ... The people refuse to collaborate with the government, and the general sentiment is that this government is unjust [and] incapable of solving problems."[364] Marighella theorized that a repressive state response would alienate the government from its population generating support for the terrorists, and that declining governmental legitimacy would strengthen the terrorist cause, as "the political situation in the country is transformed into a military situation in which the [government] appear more and more to be the ones responsible for the violence, while the lives of the people grow worse."[365] Practicing precisely what he preached, the Brazilian leftist group *Ação Libertadora Nacional*, established by Marighella in 1967, actually went so far as to spell out its intention to create a crisis that would provoke a military response in its founding manifesto.[366] In Uruguay, the *Tupamaros* also set out deliberately to provoke a repressive response from the state and thus achieve the "transformation of a political situation into a military one".[367] The *Tupamaros* succeeded in achieving this goal, but subsequent events did not then turn out in their favor — in 1973, the Uruguayan military deposed the democratically elected civilian government and established a military *junta* that remained in power until 1985.

In a *Rote Armee Fraktion* pamphlet entitled *Serve the People: The Urban Guerrilla and Class Struggle*, that first appeared in April 1972, the authors outlined the group's commitment to the Marxist concept

---

[364] Carlos Marighella, *Minimanual of the Urban Guerrilla* (Havana; Tricontinental 1970), pp. 35–36.

[365] ibid.

[366] Louise Richardson, *What Terrorists Want: Understanding the Enemy and Containing the Threat* (Random House; 2007), p. 199.

[367] Claire Sterling, *The Terror Network: The Secret War of International Terrorism* (Holt, Rinehart and Winston; 1981), p. 163.

of the dialectic of revolution and counterrevolution, quoting the North Korean communist leader Kim Il Sung: "It isn't a question of whether we want the reactionary militarization or not; it is a question of whether we have the conditions necessary to transform the fascist militarization into a revolutionary mobilization, whether we can transform the reactionary militarization into a revolutionary one."[368] The pamphlet argued that the Federal Republic of Germany's reaction to the RAF's activities was playing straight into the group's hands as those in power "are obliged to violate their own system, and in so doing they show their true colors as enemies of the people — and the left creates accurate propaganda at a high dialectical level, as ought to be the case, when they say: 'this terror is not directed against the RAF, but rather against the working class.'"[369] Ulrike Meinhof returned to the same theme in a statement she made at her trial in September 1974 alongside Hans-Jürgen Bäcker and Horst Mahler: "The enemy unmasks itself by its defensive maneuvers, by the system's reaction, by the counterrevolutionary escalation, by the transformation of the political state of emergency into a military state of emergency. This is how it shows its true face — and by its terrorism it provokes the masses to rise up against it, reinforcing the contradictions and making revolution inevitable."[370] The idea that West Germany had never truly broken with its national-socialist past, and, that by engaging the security apparatus of the state, the RAF would force this hidden reality into public view, was one of the central operational principles underpinning the organization's almost three-decade long campaign.[371]

Giangiacomo Feltrinelli, one of the founders of the *Gruppi di Azione Partigiani* (GAP), a precursor of Italy's *Brigate Rosse*, circulated

---

[368] J. Smith and André Moncourt, Serve the People: The Urban Guerrilla and Class Struggle, April 1972, *The Red Army Faction A Documentary History: Volume 1 — Projectiles for the People* (PM Press; 2009), pp. 141–142.

[369] ibid.

[370] Ulrike Meinhof, On the Liberation of Andreas Baader, 13 September 1974, in J. Smith and André Moncourt, *The Red Army Faction A Documentary History: Volume 1 — Projectiles for the People* (PM Press; 2009), p. 368.

[371] *The Urban Guerrilla Is History*, The Final Communiqué From The Red Army Faction, 1 March 1998 at http://germanGuerrilla.com/1998/03/01/the-urban-guerrilla-is-history/.

a paper entitled *Italy 1968: Political Guerrilla Warfare* in which he urged leftist militants to "violate the law openly … [by] challenging and outraging institutions and public order in every way."[372] He added: "When the state intervenes as a result, with police and the courts, it will be easy to denounce its harshness and repressive dictatorial tendencies."[373] Renato Curcio, one of the early leaders of the *Brigate Rosse,* later echoed Feltrinelli's insight in a public communiqué, explaining: "Faced with working-class terror, the bourgeoisie by now has an obligatory course — to reestablish control by intensified repression and progressive militarization of the state."[374] The Italian left labeled this concept of advancing revolutionary change "*tanto peggio, tanto meglio*", literally "the worse, the better".[375] Amir Parviz Puyan, a prominent member of the *Fadaiyan-e-Khalq,* a Marxist–Leninist guerrilla group established in Iran in 1971, advanced much the same argument, and his work was also referenced in *Rote Armee Fraktion* publications: "By extending the violence against the resistance fighters, creating an unanticipated reaction, the repression inevitably hits all other oppressed milieus and classes in an even more massive way. As a result, the ruling class augments the contradictions between the oppressed classes and itself and creates a climate which leads of necessity to a great leap forward in the consciousness of the masses."[376]

Deeply influenced by Maoist People's War theory — Palestinian cadres even received military training in China[377] — Yasir Arafat's *Fateh* evolved an explicit concept of operations that came to be known as *al-taffir al-mutasalsil* or "consecutive detonation".[378] Khalid al-Hasan,

---

[372] Claire Sterling, *The Terror Network: The Secret War of International Terrorism* (Holt, Rinehart and Winston; 1981), p. 38.

[373] ibid.

[374] ibid., p. 163.

[375] ibid., p. 162.

[376] Ulrike Meinhof, On the Liberation of Andreas Baader, 13 September 1974, in J. Smith and André Moncourt, *The Red Army Faction A Documentary History: Volume 1 — Projectiles for the People* (PM Press; 2009), p. 369.

[377] Abu Iyad and Eric Rouleau, *My Home, My Land: A Narrative of the Palestinian Struggle* (Times Books; 1981), p. 66.

[378] Yezid Sayigh, *Armed Struggle and the Search for State: The Palestinian National Movement, 1949–1993* (Oxford University Press; 2011), p. 120, and Daniel Byman, *A High Price: The Triumphs and Failures of Israeli Counterterrorism* (Oxford University Press; 2011), p. 32.

who had been with *Fateh* more or less since its foundation, explained the logic of this strategy: "Our military action provokes an Israeli action against our people, who then become involved and are supported by the Arab masses. This extends the circle of conflict and compels the Arab governments either to join us or stand against us."[379] As one early *Fateh* publication, entitled *A Statement on Timing*, noted: "Any act of liberation that does not take conscious entanglement of the masses into account will fail at the outset because it has overlooked the strongest active force in the battle."[380] The Popular Front for the Liberation of Palestine (PFLP) took a similar view — when the Israeli air force raided Beirut International Airport in December 1968 destroying thirteen Middle East Airlines passenger jets in reprisal for the attack on El Al Flight 253 in Athens two days earlier, the PFLP "thanked the Israelis for enlisting Lebanese support for the revolution", concluding they "had helped the cause more than we dared contemplate by their prompt and decisive 'reprisal'."[381] Harsh Israeli counter-terrorism measures also served to bolster the "narratives of brutality and injustice" that psychologically enable individuals to embrace violent opposition and endure the privations of clandestine warfare.[382] Many Israeli security officials have come to appreciate the dilemma they face — Ami Ayalon, who served as the Head of *Shin Bet* in the late 1990s, has implicitly acknowledged the effectiveness of consecutive detonation as a strategy: "War against terrorism is part of a vicious cycle. The fight itself creates ... even more frustration and despair, more terrorism and increased violence."[383]

Shaul Mishal, Avraham Sela and Andrea Nüsse have similarly argued that part of the motivation for *Hamas* in mounting attacks against Israeli targets during the First *Intifada* was to provoke a

---

[379] Yezid Sayigh, *Armed Struggle and the Search for State: The Palestinian National Movement, 1949–1993* (Oxford University Press; 2011), p. 120.

[380] ibid., p. 119.

[381] Leila Khaled and George Hajjar, *My People Shall Live: The Autobiography of a Revolutionary* (Hodder and Stoughton; 1973), p. 112.

[382] Jeffrey William Lewis, *The Business of Martyrdom: A History of Suicide Bombing* (Naval Institute Press; 2012), p. 199.

[383] Daniel Byman, *A High Price: The Triumphs and Failures of Israeli Counterterrorism* (Oxford University Press; 2011), p. 365.

repressive response, thus further radicalizing the Palestinian population and boosting international support for the Palestinian cause.[384] Beverley Milton-Edwards and Stephen Farrell have also described how *Hamas* exploits Israeli reprisals carried out in response to its operations — such as home demolitions — to stoke community anger and build its base.[385] In August 2014, the Israeli Defense Forces published excerpts from a *Hamas* manual on urban warfare reportedly recovered during an offensive conducted against the Shuja'iya Brigade of the Al-Qassam Brigades. While the authenticity of the manual has been questioned in some quarters, it does seem to tally closely with the reported behavior of *Hamas* units on the ground in Gaza. A section of the manual notes that the destruction of civilian homes "increases the hatred of the citizens towards the attackers [the IDF] and increases their gathering [support] around the city defenders (resistance forces)".[386] *Hamas'* well-documented use of locations typically protected from being targeted under the laws of armed conflict, such as schools and hospitals, would also seem to fit this strategy — hostile fire originating from such a location can void its protection under international law, but the public relations fallout from shelling or bombing a school or hospital typically overshadows the potential legitimacy of a decision to retaliate against an enemy firing position.[387]

When the Provisional IRA split from the Official IRA in December 1969, its newly constituted Army Council, led by Seán MacStiofáin, adopted a plan of action built around a three-stage approach to ending British rule in Northern Ireland: first, the defense of Catholic communities; second, a combination of defense and retaliation against the loyalist community and the British authorities; and third, a sustained offensive engagement with the

---

[384] Shaul Mishal and Avraham Sela, *The Palestinian Hamas: Vision, Violence, and Coexistence* (Columbia University Press; 2006), p. 62 and Andrea Nüsse, *Muslim Palestine: The Ideology of Hamas* (Harwood Academic; 1998), p. 166.

[385] Beverley Milton-Edwards and Stephen Farrell, *Hamas* (Polity Press; 2010), p. 113.

[386] IDF Blog, Captured Hamas Combat Manual Explains Benefits of Human Shields, 4 August 2014, at www.idfblog.com/blog/2014/08/04/captured-hamas-combat-manual-explains-benefits-human-shields/.

[387] Beverley Milton-Edwards and Stephen Farrell, *Hamas* (Polity Press; 2010), pp. 150–152.

British in a guerrilla campaign.[388] However, the situation PIRA faced in January 1970 was complex. The British Army had been deployed to Northern Ireland in August 1969 by the Labour government of Prime Minister Harold Wilson, following a summer of rioting and sectarian violence in which the local police force, the Royal Ulster Constabulary (RUC), had abandoned any pretense of impartiality and had sided wholeheartedly with the loyalist community. Ten people had been killed and nearly 900 injured; 200 houses and sixteen factories had been destroyed beyond repair, and many more had been damaged; 1,820 families had been forced from their homes.[389] The British Army initially found itself interposed between the two warring communities striving under London's direction to at least appear, in the Prime Minister's words, "firm, cool and fair".[390] Soldiers were advised to employ the "MIDAS touch" — Minimum force, Impartiality, Discipline, Alertness and Security.[391] Even Joe Cahill, the Officer Commanding the PIRA's Belfast Brigade and a member of the ruling Army Council, admitted, that when the British Army first deployed to Northern Ireland, "people were glad to see them because the [Official] IRA had betrayed them [by failing to protect Catholic neighborhoods]."[392]

Given that expelling the British presence from island of Ireland was the organization's main *raison d'être*, this presented the Provisional IRA leadership with a dilemma and they responded by staging provocations aimed at eroding the "neutrality" of the British Army and exposing British partisanship.[393] In the words of Tommy Gorman, a member of PIRA's 1st Battalion in Andersonstown: "We were creating this idea that the British state is not your friend ... and at every twist in the road they were compounding

---

[388] Richard English, *Armed Struggle: The History of the IRA* (Oxford University Press; 2004), p. 125.

[389] John Newsinger, *supra* note 10, p. 157.

[390] Prime Minister Harold Wilson quoted in Peter Neumann, *Britain's Long War: British Strategy in the Northern Ireland Conflict 1969–1998* (Palgrave; 2003), p. 52.

[391] Peter Neumann, *supra* note 15, p. 52.

[392] M. L. R. Smith, *Fighting for Ireland: The Military Strategy of the Irish Republican Movement* (Routledge; 1995), p. 85.

[393] J. Bowyer Bell, *The Irish Troubles Since 1916*, (Columbia International Affairs Online; 2002) available from http://www.isn.ch/pubs/ph/details.cfm?lng=en&v33=60242&id=6828, p. 13.

what we were saying, they were doing what we were saying, fulfilling all the propaganda ... The British Army, the British government, were our best recruiting agents."[394] In June 1970, a Conservative government led by Edward Heath took power in London and the role of the British Army began to change from somewhat neutral arbiter to security partner of the loyalist establishment, playing right into the Provisional IRA's hands.[395]

The shift in policy from peacekeeping to counterinsurgency was soon cemented by an aggressive Army house-to-house search through the Catholic Lower Falls area of Belfast from 3–5 July 1970, which left five locals dead.[396] The Belfast Social Democratic and Labour Party (SDLP) politician Paddy Devlin noted that in one fell swoop the Army had succeeded in turning the Catholic working class "from neutral or even sympathetic support for the military to outright hatred".[397] From July 1970 onwards, the battle lines were drawn and the British Army increasingly began to employ the same tactics it had used in counter-insurgency operations overseas. In the face of escalating violence, and the first British military casualties,[398] the government introduced internment — open-ended detention without charge for suspected terrorists — in August 1971, which only served to further alienate the Catholic population, as did the news that some of the internees had been subjected to coercive interrogation techniques imported by the military such as hooding, wall-standing, the use of "white noise", with-holding food and water, and sleep deprivation.[399] This alienation was made complete on 30 January 1972 when British paratroopers fired on an anti-internment protest in Londonderry ultimately killing fourteen

---

[394] Richard English, *Armed Struggle: The History of the IRA* (Oxford University Press; 2004), p. 122.

[395] John Newsinger, *British Counter-Insurgency: From Palestine to Northern Ireland* (Palgrave; 2002), p. 161.

[396] Peter Neumann, *Britain's Long War: British Strategy in the Northern Ireland Conflict 1969–1998* (Palgrave; 2003), p. 51.

[397] John Newsinger, *British Counter-Insurgency: From Palestine to Northern Ireland* (Palgrave; 2002), p. 162.

[398] The first British soldier was killed in Northern Ireland in February 1971.

[399] Donald Jackson, Prevention of Terrorism: The United Kingdom Confronts the European Convention on Human Rights, *Journal of Terrorism and Political Violence*, Vol. 6, No. 4 (Winter 1994), p. 509.

demonstrators and wounding twenty-eight, an event immortalized in the public consciousness as Bloody Sunday.[400] The Provisional IRA's tactic had worked like a charm and Gerry Adams, who commanded PIRA's 2nd Battalion in Belfast during this period, would later acknowledge that the attitude and presence of British troops had resulted in a "resurgence of national consciousness and an almost immediate politicization of the local populace".[401] The operational manual first distributed to volunteers by the Provisional leadership in 1977, known colloquially as the *Green Book*, drew a similar lesson: "We exploit the enemy's mistakes by propagating facts. So it was with their murderous mistakes of the Falls Road curfew, Bloody Sunday and internment."[402]

Ironically enough, this same strategic concept is still driving the actions of dissident Irish republican groups who reject the Northern Ireland Peace Process — a process that Adams himself ultimately played such a key role in promoting — as well as some fringe British nationalist groups. A member of the rejectionist Real IRA told the reporter Suzanne Breen in 2008: "With more attacks on the RUC/PSNI [the Royal Ulster Constabulary and its successor the Police Service of Northern Ireland] we believe the stage will be reached where British soldiers are brought back on the streets to bolster the cops. This will shatter the facade that the British presence has gone and normality reigns. People will once again be made visibly aware that we remain occupied."[403] A similar logic underpins the strategy espoused by Combat 18, a British far-right extremist group with terrorist aspirations (1 and 8 represent the first and eighth letters of the alphabet, A and H, Adolf

---

[400] John Newsinger, *British Counter-Insurgency: From Palestine to Northern Ireland* (Palgrave; 2002), p. 166.

[401] ibid., p. 169. Since entering party politics Adams has consistently denied that he was an active member of the Provisional IRA but his role as a prominent early leader of the organization has been well documented, perhaps most notably by one of his closest allies during this period, former Belfast Brigade stalwart and senior republican Brendan Hughes. See Ed Moloney, *Voices from the Grave: Two Men's War in Ireland* (Public Affairs; 2010).

[402] Provisional IRA, *Green Book*, 1977 ed. quoted in Mike German, *Thinking Like a Terrorist: Insights of a Former FBI Undercover Agent* (Washington, DC: Potomac Books, 2007), p. 167.

[403] Suzanne Breen, War Back On — Real IRA, *Sunday Tribune*, 3 February 2008 at http://www.nuzhound.com/articles/Sunday_Tribune/arts2008/feb3_RIRA_interview__SBreen.php.

Hitler's initials). For the most part, Combat 18 targets ethnic minorities and leftist political figures, although it is also associated with the slogan "no surrender to the IRA" and has reported links to loyalist paramilitaries in Northern Ireland. In one publication, the group urges its supporters to carry out attacks on minorities to drive polarization in British society: "If this is done regularly, effectively and brutally, the aliens will respond by attacking the whites at random, forcing them off the fence and into self-defence."[404]

But perhaps the most successful example of a terror group deliberately setting out to provoke a counterproductive state response is also one of the most recent. The US journalist Alan Cullison scored a major scoop when he purchased two abandoned *al-Qaeda* computers from a "semiliterate jewelry salesman" who had looted them from *al-Qaeda*'s central office in Kabul. Reviewing the contents, Cullison came across internal communications discussing the likely outcome of the 9/11 attacks which made it clear that the strike was intended to have a unifying effect on the many disparate *Mujahedin* factions and that, recalling the war in Afghanistan against the Soviet invaders, *al-Qaeda* leaders hoped 9/11 would have a galvanizing effect on the Arab world.[405] In this respect at least, the attacks were profoundly successful. In a broadcast in November 2004, Osama bin Laden gleefully compared President George Bush to the cantankerous goat who according to an ancient parable willfully dug up a lost knife buried in the ground that was later used to slaughter it.[406] Ayman al-Zawahiri had also long believed that drawing America's Muslim allies into a wider conflict would be an effective strategy for mobilizing domestic resistance to their rule, writing in *Knights under the Prophet's Banner*: "We win ... by exposing the regime to the Muslim people when it attacks us in defense of its masters, the Americans and the

---

[404] Audrey Kurth Cronin, *How Terrorism Ends: Understanding the Decline and Demise of Terrorist Campaigns* (Princeton University Press, 2009), p. 99.

[405] Alan Cullison, Inside Al Qaeda's Hard Drive, *The Atlantic*, 1 September 2004.

[406] Raymond Ibrahim, *The Al Qaeda Reader, The Essential Texts of Osama Bin Laden's Terrorist Organization* (Broadway Books; 2007), p. 218.

Jews, showing thereby the ugly face, the face of the policeman, the faithful hireling in the service of the occupier, the enemies of the Muslim *umma* (the community of the [Muslim] faithful)."[407]

In 2005, the *al-Qaeda* insider Abu Bakr Naji published *The Administration of Savagery*, serialized in seven installments in the online *Sawt al-Jihad*[408] magazine, to explain *al-Qaeda's* strategy in detail to its supporters around the world. Naji wrote that *al-Qaeda* set "a trap" for the United States in Afghanistan, which it then fell into — by seeking revenge for the 9/11 attacks, Naji asserted, the United States had committed itself to operations that would inevitably intensify over time, provoking a backlash from the Muslim community.[409] Naji further argued that what had worked against the Soviet Union would work against the United States — indeed, he went on to suggest that it would actually be easier to defeat the "soft" United States because the Soviets had been much tougher opponents. Naji cited the Yale historian Paul Kennedy's influential study *The Rise and Fall of the Great Powers* in support of his central thesis: "If America expands its employment of military power and extends strategically more than necessary, this will lead to its downfall."[410] He also noted that *al-Qaeda* would be able to attract more recruits as a consequence of being able to demonstrate America's direct interference in the Islamic world.[411] In much the same spirit, one *al-Qaeda* publication actually heralded the US invasion of Iraq with an article entitled *Thank You, Oh Zio-Crusaders.*[412]

Abu Mus'ab al-Zarqawi, the Jordanian-born leader of *Tanzim Qaidat al-Jihad fi Bilad al-Rafidayn* (better known as *al-Qaeda* in Iraq

---

[407] Michael Ryan, *Decoding Al Qaeda's Strategy: The Deep Battle Against America* (Columbia University Press; 2013), p. 77.

[408] Voice of *Jihad*, published online by Al Qaeda in the Arabian Peninsula between 2004–2007.

[409] Michael Ryan, *Decoding Al Qaeda's Strategy: The Deep Battle Against America* (Columbia University Press; 2013), p. 175.

[410] ibid., p. 159. Copy of Paul Kennedy's *The Rise and Fall of the Great Powers* was also found in bin Laden's hideout in Abbottabad.

[411] Michael Ryan, *Decoding Al Qaeda's Strategy: The Deep Battle Against America* (Columbia University Press; 2013), p. 163.

[412] Charles Kurzman, *The Missing Martyrs: Why There Are So Few Muslim Terrorists* (Oxford University Press; 2011), p. 144.

or AQI) from 2004 to 2006, also pursued a strategy of deliberate provocation in his fight against US-led Coalition forces and the Coalition-backed interim Iraqi administration. Al-Zarqawi believed the key to driving the US out of Iraq was to provoke a civil war between the *Sunni* and *Shia* communities.[413] He outlined his intentions in a letter to *al-Qaeda*'s leadership intercepted by US forces in January 2004: "[The *Shia*] in our opinion are the key to change. I mean that targeting and hitting them in [their] religious, political, and military depth will provoke them to show the *Sunnis* their rabies and bare the teeth of the hidden rancor working in their breasts. If we succeed in dragging them into the arena of sectarian war, it will become possible to awaken the inattentive *Sunnis* as they feel imminent danger and annihilating death at the hands of these Sabeans [presumably intended as a reference to the *Shia* although the Sabeans are a distinct religious tradition]."[414] To this end, under al-Zarqawi's direction, AQI bombed *Shia* shrines in Karbala and Baghdad in March 2004, the cities of Najaf and Karbala in December 2004, and most likely the al-Askari Mosque in Samarra in February 2006, as well as conducting a host of other deliberately lurid and vicious attacks. Al-Zarqawi believed that Iraq's descent into civil war would also incite "the wrath of the people against the Americans, who brought destruction and were the reason for this miasma".[415]

Echoes of this strategy of provocation have even percolated down to so-called "lone wolf" actors, individuals inspired to emulate the example of *al-Qaeda* and the Islamic State in Iraq and the Levant (ISIL), like the killers of the British soldier Lee Rigby, Michael Adebowale and Michael Adebolajo. In May 2013, the two men deliberately ran down Fusilier Rigby on a street near Woolwich Barracks in Southeast London and then jumped out of their car armed with a knife and a meat cleaver to finish him off. The lurid and shocking nature of the attack was deliberate. As he waited near

---

[413] Coalition Provisional Authority English Translation of Terrorist Musab al-Zarqawi Letter Obtained by United States Government in Iraq, February 2004, at http://2001-2009.state.gov/p/nea/rls/31694.htm.
[414] ibid.
[415] ibid.

Rigby's body for the police to arrive, Adebowale told eyewitness Ingrid Loyau-Kennett: "We want to start a war in London tonight."[416]

In December 2014, Ilich Ramírez Sánchez, better known as the notorious PFLP terrorist Carlos the Jackal who had been incarcerated in France since August 1994, sent the French academic and prominent terrorism expert, Gilles Kepel, a manuscript entitled *La guerre psychologique*, in which he cast a professional eye over the tactics adopted by *al-Qaeda*, ISIL and their affiliates: "The jihadists have followed this line of psychological warfare with great success in the media. The decapitations now carried out openly by citizens of countries that are members of NATO, transmitted over the Internet, are a magisterial media coup with immense, unparalleled benefits ... Now the imperialist states will be subjected to reprisal attacks within their borders against which they cannot defend themselves, leading to indiscriminate repression which will multiply the recruitment of volunteers for *jihad*."[417] ISIL itself, in *Media Operative, You Are a Mujahid Too*, acknowledged that part of the intent behind its terrorist operations was to provoke hostile governments into knee-jerk policy responses that would only further alienate their Muslim populations.[418]

## Polarization

The American political scientist David Apter has noted that "political violence not only divides people, it polarizes them around affiliations of race, ethnicity, religion, language, class."[419] Provoking an overreaction from the authorities helps accelerate that polarization by

---

[416] Arthur Martin, Sam Greenhill, Chris Greenwood and Rob Cooper, You and Your Children will be Next, *The Daily Mail*, 22 May 2013 at http://www.dailymail.co.uk/news/article-2329089/Woolwich-attack-Two-men-hack-soldier-wearing-Help-Heroes-T-shirt-death-machetes-suspected-terror-attack.html.

[417] Gilles Kepel, *Terror in France: The Rise of Jihad in the West* (Princeton University Press; 2017), p. 133.

[418] Charlie Winter, *Media Jihad: The Islamic State's Doctrine for Information Warfare*, International Centre for the Study of Radicalisation and Terrorist Violence (2017), p. 18.

[419] David Apter, Political Violence in Analytical Perspective, in David Apter (ed.), *The Legitimization of Violence* (New York University Press; 1997), p. 1.

alienating potential security partners, like moderate members of a minority community, and providing powerful support to terrorist narratives of victimhood and injustice. In *The Administration of Savagery*, *al-Qaeda* theorist Abu Bakr Naji discussed the importance of drawing ordinary people into the jihadist camp by polarizing the conflict.[420] He wrote that conflict splits the Muslim population into three groups: (1) those that join the jihadists, (2) those that oppose them, and (3) those waiting to see which group is in the ascendant. It is the third group that Naji believes *al-Qaeda* needs to influence "because this faction might have a decisive role in the last stages of the present battle."[421] He therefore argues that jihadist operations must be made as violent as possible so that the middle ground is chipped away and people have to choose between the two warring sides.

Quoting Osama bin Laden, ISIL articulated a similar strategy in an article entitled *The Extinction of the Grayzone*, published in the January/February 2015 issue of ISIL's glossy English-language magazine *Dabiq*: "The world today is divided into two camps. Bush spoke the truth when he said, 'either you are with us or you are with the terrorists.' Meaning, either you are with the crusade or you are with Islam."[422] To this end, ISIL has deliberately set out to "bring division to the world" and reduce the space for compromise, moderation and multicultural exchange — the "grayzone" of the article's title — which it dismisses as the hideout of hypocrites.[423] The article is explicit about ISIL's intention to provoke through its actions a draconian crackdown on the Muslim communities living in Western countries: "Muslims in the Crusader countries will find themselves driven to abandon their homes for a place to live in the *Khilāfah*, as the Crusaders increase persecution against Muslims living in

---

[420] Michael Ryan, *Decoding Al Qaeda's Strategy: The Deep Battle Against America* (Columbia University Press; 2013), p. 187.

[421] ibid.

[422] *Dabiq*, Issue No. 7, January/February 2015 [1436 Rabi' Al-Akhir], p. 54; accessed on 17 November 2015 at http://media.clarionproject.org/files/islamic-state/islamic-state-dabiq-magazine-issue-7-from-hypocrisy-to-apostasy.pdf.

[423] ibid.

Western lands."[424] The group's ultimate objective is to manufacture a clash of civilizations in which no middle ground remains: "Eventually, the grayzone will become extinct and there will be no place for grayish calls and movements. There will only be the camp of *īmān* versus the camp of *kufr*."[425]

Many terrorist groups are not above accelerating the process of polarization with the deliberate application of violence against their own communities. For example, in September 1955, a series of communiqués from Ahmed Ben Bella, a leading member of the *Front de Libération Nationale*'s governing committee and a future President of Algeria, to the FLN field commander, Bachir Chihani, were recovered by the French Deuxième Bureau when Chihani's headquarters in Djeurf was overrun. There was little surprising about the orders to kill collaborators and burn down the homes of native Algerian volunteers serving in the French military. However, the list of targets did not end there — to complete the polarization of Algerian society, Ben Bella was determined to eliminate moderate voices as well. One instruction read: "Liquidate all personalities who want to play the role of *interlocuteur valable*."[426] Ben Bella would ultimately sit out most of the Algerian conflict in a French prison after a Moroccan Airlines flight bound for Tunis that he was traveling on was forced to land in Algiers by French fighter planes in October 1956, but, by then, his instructions had already helped set the tone for the ruthlessness with which the Algerian campaign for independence would be waged. The military wing of the FLN had warned "the people of Algeria" in a short statement issued in late 1954 that "not to involve

---

[424] ibid.

[425] ibid.

[426] Alistair Horne, *A Savage War of Peace: Algeria 1954–1962* (New York Review Books Classics; 2006), p. 135, and Obituary: Ahmed Ben Bella, *Daily Telegraph*, 12 April 2012. Like Frantz Fanon, Ben Bella was a veteran of the French Army who had received the *Croix de Guerre* and the *Médaille Militaire* for his service during World War II. General De Gaulle had presented the latter medal, which he won for pulling his wounded Commanding Officer into cover during the Battle of Monte Cassino, to Ben Bella personally. He had refused to accept an officer's commission after the brutal suppression of a Muslim uprising in the small Algerian town of Sétif in May 1945 by French forces and local French colonists that claimed at least 5,000 lives.

yourself in the struggle is a crime ... to hinder our actions is treason", and the FLN's Communiqué Number 1, issued on 30 October
1955, sought to draw a line between "good Algerians" and the pro-
French population by effectively prohibiting Western habits under
the slogan: "Drink no more, Smoke no more, Play no more."[427] It is
instructive to note that the FLN killed considerably more native
Algerians than French settlers or French troops in the course of its
independence struggle,[428] just as the great preponderance of the
violence unleashed by *al-Qaeda*, ISIL and their affiliates has claimed
vastly more Muslim lives than Western ones.

## Summary

A government confronting terrorism is caught on the horns of a
dilemma: It cannot realistically ignore the threat posed by a terrorist group — its authority is being challenged in the most
primal, Weberian, fashion. Moreover, its citizens expect to be
protected. They want to see expeditious action taken to end
terrorist attacks — raids, arrests, and an increased police presence — all measures that can be repressive in the extreme,
especially if concentrated on a small segment of the population.
But the government will also suffer the consequences of any
repressive action that it takes. Any additional hardship imposed
on communities potentially sympathetic to the aims of the terrorist group is only likely to increase support for terrorist violence as
the opportunity costs of violence decrease and the community
concludes that the government is hostile to their welfare.[429]
The genius of terrorism is that it turns us into our own worst
enemies. Democratic societies are particularly vulnerable as politicians

---

[427] David Macey, *Frantz Fanon: A Biography* (Picador; 2001), pp. 251–253 and Martha Crenshaw,
The Effectiveness of Terrorism in the Algerian War, in Martha Crenshaw (ed.), *Terrorism in
Context* (Pennsylvania State University Press; 1995), p. 484.

[428] Martha Crenshaw, The Causes of Terrorism, *Comparative Politics*, Vol. 13, No. 4 (1981), p. 387.

[429] Ethan Bueno de Mesquita and Eric Dickson, The Propaganda of the Deed: Terrorism,
Counter-terrorism, and Mobilization, *American Journal of Political Science*, Vol. 51, No. 2 (April
2007), p. 365.

frequently succumb to popular prejudices as a simple shortcut to boosting their own popularity. It is a vulnerability that terrorist groups have long known how to exploit.

## Building Legitimacy

Terrorist groups are simultaneously engaged in dialogue with multiple audiences: they seek to engage governments, they seek to engage publics, and they seek to engage the communities that they believe make up their constituents. The messages they seek to communicate to each of these audiences may differ in specifics, but the core narrative tends to revolve around one key concept: legitimacy.[430] Legitimacy is a multifaceted, mutable and deeply contested value — what seems legitimate to one individual may not seem legitimate to another, and, furthermore, a given individual's idea of what is or is not legitimate may also change over time with the accumulation of more information. This makes legitimacy a very elusive variable to get to grips with, but in essence, in the realm of terrorism and counter-terrorism, there are only two legitimizing narratives that really matter: the first is a narrative that promotes the practicality of a given course of action — to attract significant support, a terrorist group must be able to make a persuasive case that it can achieve its declared objectives and that the strategy it is pursuing is viable; the second narrative is more philosophical in nature — the terrorist group must be able to demonstrate persuasively that it is morally right to take the action it is taking, and that by doing so it will be able to offer a more attractive future to its supporters.[431]

The construction and dissemination of a narrative that legitimizes their conduct is a core concern of those who embrace the use

---

[430] See Richard Barrett, Legitimacy, Credibility and Relevance, in Alex P. Schmid and Garry F. Hindle (eds.), *After the War on Terror: Regional and Multilateral Perspectives on Counter-Terrorism Strategy* (Royal United Services Institute; 2009).

[431] In much the same manner, Ralf Dahrendorf identified legitimacy and effectiveness as the two key variables contributing to a state's stability. See Ralf Dahrendorf, On the Governability of Democracies, in Roy C. Macridis and Bernard Brown, (eds.), *Comparative Politics: Notes and Readings* (Harcourt Brace College Publishers; 1996), p. 332.

of political violence, and terrorist groups are no exception. The Harvard political scientist Joseph Nye argued in his seminal work *Soft Power* that terrorism "depends on its ability to attract support from the crowd at least as much as its ability to destroy the enemy's will to fight" and we can see narratives designed to do precisely this promoted by terrorist groups of every stamp.[432] As the Provisional IRA's *Green Book* notes: "It is not an easy thing to take up a gun and go out to kill some person without strong convictions or justification. The [Irish Republican] Army, its motivating force, is based upon strong convictions which bonds the Army into one force and before any potential volunteer decides to join the Army he must have these strong convictions."[433] Terrorist propaganda seeks to develop a narrative that identifies a "law beyond law" and "places justice at the core of criminality" so that acts that might otherwise seem unlawful and criminal — for example, the murder of a judge or policeman — appear righteous and just when viewed through the prism of this legitimizing narrative.[434] In constructing such narratives, terrorist groups tend to exploit certain popular totems — historical parallels, the exhaustion of restraint, perceived injustice, religious faith — to justify their actions and create a sense of solidarity and shared identity amongst their supporters. As difficult as it might be to acknowledge, terrorist groups seek to establish a moral foundation for their actions, and their long-term cohesion and survival depends heavily on the creation of a clear moral identity that their supporters can rally around.[435]

For nineteenth century anarchist and socialist revolutionaries, the task of establishing a moral framework for a violent assault on the existing social order was relatively straightforward given the manifest inequalities apparent in societies across Europe and

---

[432] Joseph Nye, *Soft Power: The Means to Succeed in World Politics* (Public Affairs; 2004), p. 22.

[433] *Handbook for Volunteers of the Irish Republican Army: Notes on Guerrilla Warfare,* 1977 Edition (Paladin Press; 1985). See also Tim Pat Coogan, *The I.R.A.* (1993).

[434] Liaquat Ali Khan, Who is Feeding the Bin Laden Legend, *The Daily Star,* December 28, 2004 quoted in Michael Scheuer, *Osama bin Laden,* p. 167.

[435] Alison Jamieson, Identity and Morality in the Italian Red Brigades, *Terrorism and Political Violence,* Vol. 2, No. 4 (1990), p. 508.

North America. Amongst the advocates of terrorism, Karl Heinzen was the first to make the case: "A revolutionary, in whose power it were to destroy the collected bearers of the system of violence and murder that rules and ravages the earth, earns a thousand-fold the death of a traitor if he hesitates only for a blink of an eye ... If we desire the end, we must also desire the means; if we desire the life of the people; so we must desire the death of their enemies; if we desire humanitarianism, then we must desire — murder."[436] Others soon took up the same theme — Prince Peter Kropotkin wrote in *The Spirit of Revolt*: "The popular conscience rises up against the scandals which breed amidst the privileged and the leisured, against the crimes committed in the name of the *law of the stronger*, or in order to maintain these privileges. Those who long for the triumph of justice ... perceive the necessity of a revolutionary whirlwind which will sweep away all this rottenness."[437] The US-based anarchist Emma Goldman, whose lover Alexander Berkman had been jailed following his failed 1892 attempt on the life of the industrialist Henry Clay Frick, was even blunter, writing in her widely circulated essay on *The Psychology of Political Violence* that "compared with the wholesale violence of capital and government, political acts of violence are but a drop in the ocean."[438]

The influential Italian anarchist Errico Malatesta, who had led the failed 1877 anarchist uprising in the province of Benevento, expressed similar sentiments, writing: "Violence is justifiable only when it is necessary to defend oneself and others from violence. It is where necessity ceases that crime begins. The slave is always in a state of legitimate violence against the boss, against the oppressor, is always morally justifiable ... a transitional, revolutionary, violence is the only way to put an end to the far greater, and permanent,

---

[436] Karl Heinzen, *Murder and Freedom* (New York; 1853) reproduced in Daniel Bessner and Michael Stauch, Karl Heinzen and the Intellectual Origins of Modern Terror, *Terrorism and Political Violence*, Vol. 22 (2010), p. 159 and p. 163.

[437] Peter Kropotkin, The Spirit of Revolt, in Roger Baldwin (ed.), (Dover, 1971), p. 36.

[438] Emma Goldman, *The Psychology of Political Violence* (1917), p. 74.

violence which keeps the majority of mankind in servitude."[439]
While Malatesta himself disapproved of terrorism, warning "hate
does not produce love, and with hate the world cannot be renewed",
many of his followers graduated to more violent methods within the
moral framework he constructed.[440]

The power of a strong legitimizing narrative was also well demonstrated by the case of Vera Zasulich, a disciple of both Bakunin and
Nechaev, who in January 1878 shot and wounded the Governor of
St. Petersberg, Colonel Fyodor Trepov, in retaliation for his having
ordered the flogging of the political prisoner Alexei Bogolyubov.
Zasulich's lawyer, Peter Alexandrov, turned the tables on the authorities by making Trepov's vicious treatment of Bogolyubov the focus of
the trial. By the time Zasulich took the witness stand to explain her
motives, she received a sympathetic audience: "I could ... picture to
myself the hellish impression which this torture must have made on
all political prisoners ... It is terrible to aim at a man's life, but I had
to do it."[441] When the jury ultimately acquitted Zasulich of all charges,
the verdict was greeted with applause and she was escorted out of the
courtroom by an ecstatic crowd of supporters.[442] Oscar Wilde's first
publicly performed play — *Vera or, The Nihilists* — was inspired by her
story.

Establishing individual culpability on the part of those targeted by anarchist *attentats* was another important theme in
anarchist propaganda, and it was a lesson that was well learned.
The young shoemaker Léon-Jules Léauthier, who in November
1893 stabbed the Serbian Ambassador to France in a random
attack on diners in a Paris restaurant, wrote to the anarchist
Sébastien Faure the night before: "I shall not strike an innocent if

---

[439] Errico Malatesta, *Anarchism and Violence* (Zabalaza Books), pp. 2–3, first published as
*Anarchia e violenza*, Pensiero e Volontà, 1 September 1924.

[440] Nunzio Pernicone, Luigi Galleani and Italian Anarchist Terrorism in the United States,
*Studi Emigrazione*, Vol. 30 (September 1993), p. 481.

[441] Adam Ulam, *In the Name of the People: Prophets and Conspirators in Prerevolutionary Russia* (The
Viking Press; 1977), p. 272.

[442] ibid., p. 273 and David Rapoport, The Four Waves of Modern Terrorism, in Audrey Kurth
Cronin and James Ludes (eds.), *Attacking Terrorism: Elements of a Grand Strategy* (Georgetown
University Press; 2004), p. 51.

I strike the first bourgeois I meet."[443] Auguste Valliant, the French anarchist who attacked the Chamber of Deputies in December 1893, warned the French bourgeoisie in his last public statement: "Woe be to those who remain deaf to the cries of the starving, woe to those who, believing themselves of superior essence, assume the right to exploit those beneath them! There comes a time when the people no longer reason; they rise like a hurricane, and rush onward like a torrent."[444] The Café Terminus bomber Émile Henry similarly told the court during his trial: "Those good bourgeois who hold no office but who reap their dividends and live idly on the profits of the workers' toil, they also must take their share in the reprisals."[445]

The nineteenth century Russian radical Gerasim Tarnovsky, author of *Terrorism and Routine*, argued that the use of terrorism was a moral alternative to "the blood-drenched revolution of the masses" because it spared unnecessary widespread suffering for "many thousands of innocent victims".[446] Similarly, Lev Shternberg in *Political Terror and Russia* presented terrorism as "the way of realizing the aims with the least number of victims and in the shortest possible time".[447] *Narodnaya Volya*'s Nikolai Morozov injected a note of heroism and nobility into the narrative of violent resistance to injustice: "This is the struggle of force against force, of equal against equal; the struggle of heroism against oppression, knowledge and education against bayonets and gallows."[448] He also praised the efficacy of terrorist attacks noting that such acts tell the people: "Do not be

---

[443] Marie Fleming, Propaganda by the Deed: Terrorism and Anarchist Theory in Late Nineteenth-Century Europe, *Terrorism: An International Journal*, Vol. 4 (1980), p. 14 and John Merriman, *The Dynamite Club: How a Bombing in Fin-de-Siécle Paris Ignited the Modern Age of Terror* (Houghton Mifflin Harcourt; 2009), p. 134.

[444] August Valliant, Assassination, in Upton Sinclair (ed.), *The Cry for Justice: An Anthology of the Literature of Protest* (The John C. Winston Co.; 1915).

[445] Émile Henry, *Defense* (1894).

[446] Ze'ev Iviansky, Individual Terror: Concept and Typology, *Journal of Contemporary History*, Vol. 12 (1977), p. 55.

[447] ibid.

[448] Nikolai Morozov, Voices of Terror: Manifestos, Writings and Manuals of Al Qaeda, Hamas, and other Terrorists from around the world and Throughout the Ages (1880), in Walter Laqueur (ed.), *The Terrorist Struggle*, (Sourcebooks; 2004), p. 78.

afraid of the tsar, do not be afraid of despotic rulers because all of them are weak and helpless against secret, sudden assassinations."[449] But it was Morozov's comrade-in-arms, Vera Figner, who made the most crucial point by emphasizing that the key legitimizing aspect of an act of terrorism was not the act itself but the larger purpose which it served: "Terror for its own sake was never the aim of the party. It was a weapon of protection, of self-defence, regarded as a powerful instrument for agitation, and employed only for the purpose of attaining the ends for which the organization was working."[450] That the end justifies the means is perhaps the most enduring theme of legitimizing narratives.

For Irish nationalists seeking to drive the British government out of Ireland in the late nineteenth and early twentieth centuries, the challenge was slightly different. Since the Tudor king Henry VIII had unilaterally asserted his sovereignty over Ireland in 1541 — "united, annexed and knit for ever to the Imperial Crown of the Realm of England"[451] — there had been periodic Irish uprisings against British rule, and plenty of Irishmen remained committed to this cause. The greater challenge was that these uprisings had failed and the mismatch between the forces of Irish nationalism and the might of the British Empire at the apogee of its strength was clear for anyone to see. To attract support, Irish nationalists needed to demonstrate that violent opposition to British rule was capable of achieving results — proof that this was possible came about almost by accident. On 13 December 1867, a large cart bomb exploded outside London's Clerkenwell prison. The incident had actually been an ill-conceived attempt to break the prominent Irish rebel Colonel Ricard O'Sullivan Burke out of jail — the conspirators used too much gunpowder and, instead of just breaching the prison walls, the blast flattened a number of private houses opposite the prison, killing twelve people and injuring more than one hundred. However, Irish nationalists noted how, as the British intelligence official Sir Robert Anderson put it, "terror took possession of [Victorian]

---

[449] ibid., p. 77.

[450] Vera Figner, *Memoirs of a Revolutionist* (Northern Illinois University Press; 1991), p. 75.

[451] Robert Kee, *The Green Flag: A History of Irish Nationalism* (Penguin, London; 2000), p. 11.

society."[452] Prime Minister William Ewart Gladstone publicly admitted that the Clerkenwell explosion had convinced him that he needed to give the Irish question a prominent position on his government's agenda. This was all that was needed to persuade radicals like Patrick Tynan that "terror and panic" could be used to induce further concessions.[453] Tynan was one of the founders of the so-called Invincibles, a nationalist group that would be responsible for the May 1882 Phoenix Park Murders, in which the Chief Secretary for Ireland Lord Frederick Cavendish and Permanent Under Secretary Thomas Burke were stabbed to death while promenading in a Dublin park.

Michael Collins, in particular, demonstrated a sophisticated understanding of the need to create an aura of inevitability about the triumph of the Irish republican movement and the importance of building a strong sense of identity and community among the supporters of independence. In *Collapse of the Terror*, written in 1922, Collins noted that previous uprisings had failed because they did not "go the root of the problem", which was that the people of Ireland first needed to "recover belief in their own ways and ideas and put them into practice" before the English could be tackled and defeated.[454] The republican movement set out to accomplish this by establishing a shadow state to offer an Irish alternative to British institutions: "We would take the government out of the hands of the foreigners, who had no right to it, and who could exercise it only by force ... The National Government was set up in the face of great difficulties. *Dáil Éireann* came into being. British law was gradually superseded. *Sinn Féin* courts were set up ... Volunteer police were enrolled ... The local governing bodies of the country were directed, inspected, and controlled by *Dáil Éireann*. We established a bank to finance societies which wished to acquire land."[455]

---

[452] Sir Robert Anderson, *Sidelights on the Home Rule Movement* (London, 1906), p. 77.

[453] Patrick Tynan, *The Irish National Invincibles and Their Times* (London, 1894), p. 26.

[454] Michael Collins, Collapse of the Terror: British Rule's Last Stages, in *The Path to Freedom* (Welsh Academic Press; 1996), p. 63.

[455] Michael Collins, Collapse of the Terror: British Rule's Last Stages, *The Path to Freedom* (Welsh Academic Press; 1996), pp. 64–65.

Collins, with his genius for asymmetrical warfare, also used Britain's conception of itself, and of the values it stood for, against it: "England had put a weapon into our hands against herself. The observation of the world was focused upon the mighty European War. We could call attention to the difference between England's principles as expounded to the world and practice as against ourselves. We were put into the position of being able to force her to recognize our freedom or to oppress us for proclaiming that simple right."[456] Like many of the urban guerrillas that would come after him, Collins went to great lengths to fix the blame for bloodshed on the government side. Railing against Prime Minister David Lloyd George's description of the IRA as "a real murder gang", Collins retorted: "The 'murders' were the legitimate acts of self-defence which had been forced upon the Irish people by English aggression … For all the acts of violence committed in Ireland from 1916 to 1921 England, and England alone, is responsible. She willed the conflict and fixed the form it was to take."[457] He also added that Irish side had "conducted the conflict, difficult as it was, with the unequal terms imposed by the enemy, as far as possible, according to the rules of war."[458] Of course, Collins was not above stretching the truth to support his narrative — his claim, in *Collapse of the Terror*, that no police were killed by the Republican forces in 1918 and 1919 conveniently ignored, for example, the killing of the two constables in Soloheadbeg in January 1919 by Dan Breen and his cohorts, and the April 1919 murder of Resident Magistrate John Milling in Westport, County Mayo, as well as several other fatal attacks in May and June.[459] Collins himself authorized the murder of Dublin-based Detective Sergeant Patrick Smith at the hands of the elite group of gunman he commanded known as "The Squad" in July 1919, and The Squad would gun down three more G Division detectives on Collins' orders before the end of the year.

---

[456] ibid., p. 57–58.

[457] ibid., p. 68.

[458] ibid., p. 70.

[459] ibid., p. 66.

By Hassan al-Banna's own account, the Society of the Muslim Brothers was founded in 1928 when, following one of his public talks, he was approached by a group of laborers working for the British-owned Suez Canal Company who asked him to deliver them from the humiliation of foreign domination and guide them to the glory of Islam.[460] Al-Banna placed religious education and community service at the heart of the Muslim Brothers' program: "The solution is the education and molding of the souls of the nation in order to create a strong moral immunity, firm and superior principles, and steadfast ideology. This is the best and fastest way to achieve the nation's goals and aspirations, and it is therefore our aim and the reason for our existence ... it is the 'founding' of souls."[461] The Brotherhood built a compelling narrative for revolutionary change around a vision of Islam that placed faith at the heart of politics, as exemplified by the slogan: "God is our objective; the *Koran* is our constitution; the Prophet is our leader; Struggle is our way; and death for the sake of God is the highest of our aspirations." Al-Banna also drew heavily on Islam's rich history to give weight to his arguments, noting in *Toward The Light*: "The Islamic way has been tried before and ... history has testified to its soundness."[462] Initially a non-violent social movement that sought to influence rather than lead political life, the Muslim Brothers became increasingly more militant in the late 1930s. The Society offered support to the Arab Revolt in the British Mandate of Palestine, and al-Banna also ratcheted up his rhetoric against the British and their supporters in Egypt declaring in May 1938: "We are at war with every leader, every party and every organization that does not work for the victory of Islam."[463] During the Second World

---

[460] Roxanne Euben and Muhammad Qasim Zaman (eds.), *Princeton Readings in Islamist Thought: Texts and Contexts from al-Banna to Bin Laden* (Princeton University Press; 2009), pp. 50–51.

[461] Brynjar Lia, *The Society of the Muslim Brothers in Egypt: The Rise of an Islamic Mass Movement 1928–1942* (Ithaca Press; 1998), p. 67.

[462] Roxanne Euben and Muhammad Qasim Zaman (eds.), *Princeton Readings in Islamist Thought: Texts and Contexts from al-Banna to Bin Laden* (Princeton University Press; 2009), p. 58.

[463] Brynjar Lia, *The Society of the Muslim Brothers in Egypt: The Rise of an Islamic Mass Movement 1928–1942* (Ithaca Press; 1998), p. 251.

War, the political environment for dissenters of all stripes became considerably more difficult and the Muslim Brotherhood's responded by establishing the Secret Apparatus to protect the organization from external threats. Firmly convinced that his cause was both just and sacred, al-Banna was not opposed to violence in pursuit of the Brotherhood's agenda, but he was careful to ensure the organization did not adopt such methods prematurely believing that the successful "execution" of the Brotherhood's program could only follow social transformation and the completion of preparatory phases of "propaganda, education, and preaching" and "selection, formation, and mobilization".[464] By the late 1940s, the movement felt strong enough to shift to the "execution" phase of its program, the Secret Apparatus stepped up its activities, but in doing so, it provoked the government clampdown that ultimately cost al-Banna his life.

Sayyid Qutb, who ultimately picked up the baton of leadership from Hassan al-Banna, went further still by defining governments in the Muslim world that did not operate by Islamic principles alone as *jahili* or illegitimate: "Although they believe in the one of God, still they have relegated the legislative attributes to others and submit to this authority."[465] In his Koranic commentary, *Milestones*, Qutb argued for the formation of a vanguard of believers to imbue the people with an Islamic consciousness and lead them to eventual victory against the forces of the *jahili*. Qutb also believed, much in the manner of Frantz Fanon, that the struggle to create a just Islamic society was itself ennobling, declaring "horizons are opened to him in the faith which would never be opened to him if he were to sit immobile and at rest."[466] For Qutb, such action took place firmly within the traditionally defensive Islamic tradition of *jihad*, although he was quite prepared to expand the

---

[464] Roxanne Euben and Muhammad Qasim Zaman (eds.), *Princeton Readings in Islamist Thought: Texts and Contexts from al-Banna to Bin Laden* (Princeton University Press; 2009), p. 54.

[465] Milestones 67–8, 101 at John Calvert, *Sayyid Qutb and the Origins of Radical Islamism* (Columbia University Press; 2010), p. 218.

[466] John Calvert, *Sayyid Qutb and the Origins of Radical Islamism* (Columbia University Press; 2010), p. 226.

definition of what could be considered defensive action. Writing in *In The Shade of the Koran*, Qutb urged his readers: "When we understand the nature of Islam ... we realize the inevitability of *jihad* ... If we must describe *jihad* as defensive, then we need to amend the meaning of the term "defense" so that it means defending mankind against all factors that hinder their liberation and restrict their freedom."[467] Qutb also believed the situation was critical, his own visit to America in the late 1940s had convinced him of the cultural and moral threat "primitive" Western values posed to Muslim life,[468] and he firmly believed the time had come to assert the supremacy of Islamic values: "Everything around us is *jahiliyya* — people's ideas, their beliefs, their habits, their traditions, the sources of their culture, their art, their literature, rules, and laws ... We must rid ourselves of the oppression of *jahili* society, *jahili* ideas, *jahili* traditions, and *jahili* leadership ... *jahili* coercion and oppression prohibit us from living in the way ordained by God."[469] Qutb would apply his analysis to the pan-Arabist regime of Gamal Abdel Nasser working with the Secret Apparatus to develop a provisional plan to strike at Nasser's government, thus setting the stage for his fatal confrontation with the Egyptian leader.[470] Qutb's lasting legacy was a vocabulary of Islamic resistance revolving around the nobility of *jihad* and the illegitimacy of secular authority, which built on the foundations of al-Banna's ministry to create an empowering narrative frame within which young Egyptians, and soon young Muslims from across the Arab and Muslim worlds, could find the inspiration and authority to engage in acts of violent opposition against their states.

---

[467] Roxanne Euben and Muhammad Qasim Zaman (eds.), *Princeton Readings in Islamist Thought: Texts and Contexts from al-Banna to Bin Laden* (Princeton University Press; 2009), p. 149.

[468] John Calvert, *Sayyid Qutb and the Origins of Radical Islamism* (Columbia University Press; 2010), p. 152.

[469] Roxanne Euben and Muhammad Qasim Zaman (eds.), *Princeton Readings in Islamist Thought: Texts and Contexts from al-Banna to Bin Laden* (Princeton University Press; 2009), p. 143.

[470] John Calvert, *Sayyid Qutb and the Origins of Radical Islamism* (Columbia University Press; 2010), pp. 242–243.

For the militant Zionist groups seeking to force a British withdrawal from Mandatory Palestine, similarly powerful legitimizing narratives could be found in Jewish scripture and the tragedies of Jewish history. One of the first editions of the underground newspaper circulated by LEHI, *He Khazit* (The Front), featured an article entitled *Terror*, which sought to justify the use of terrorist violence by the group: "Neither Jewish ethics nor Jewish tradition can disqualify terrorism as a means of combat. We are very far from having any moral qualms as far as our national war goes. We have before us the command of the *Torah*, whose morality surpasses that of any other body of laws in the world: 'Ye shall blot them out to the last man.' But first and foremost, terrorism is for us a part of the political battle being conducted under the present circumstances, and it has a great part to play: speaking in a clear voice to the whole world, as well as to our wretched brethren outside this land, it proclaims our war against the occupier." *Irgun's* Menachem Begin also invoked "the law of just retribution"[471] and acknowledged the powerful connection that returning Jews felt with their Biblical homeland in his memoirs: "The revolt sprang from the earth. The ancient Greek story of Antaeus and the strength he drew from contact with Mother Earth, is a legend. The renewed strength which came to us, and especially to our youth, from contact with the soil of our ancient land, is no legend but a fact."[472] He further reflected: "We used physical force because we were faced by physical force. But physical force was neither our aim nor our creed. We believed in the supremacy of moral forces. It was our enemy who mocked them. That is why, notwithstanding the enemy's tremendous preponderance in physical strength, he it was who was defeated, and not we. That is the law of history."[473] When reports reached Begin that Orthodox Jews were praying for his safety in Tel Aviv synagogues, he later recalled that he had never

---

[471] Menachem Begin, *The Revolt: Story of the Irgun* (Steimatzky's Agency Ltd.; 1977), pp. 231–236.
[472] ibid., p. 40.
[473] ibid., p. 60.

been moved more deeply in his life, even though he was not a conventionally religious man.[474]

However, for both *Irgun* and LEHI, the most powerful narrative of all was the dark shadow cast by the Holocaust, and it was given added urgency by the British decision to limit Jewish immigration into Palestine even after the genocidal intentions of the Nazi regime had become quite clear. This decision led to a number of tragic incidents of which perhaps the most notable was the February 1942 sinking of the tramp steamer Struma with the loss of 767 Jewish refugees fleeing the persecution of the Iron Guard in Romania.[475] LEHI didn't hesitate to draw parallels between the Nazis and the Mandate authorities, commenting in one communiqué: "Whilst Hitler conceived the idea of imprisoning Jews in compounds, it is England who has established just such a compound in our land."[476] Begin also framed the struggle for a Jewish homeland in existential terms: "Blood too brought the revolt to life. The blood of our people cried out to us from the foreign soil on which it had been shed, fired revolt in our hearts and gave the rebels strength . . . Had we anything to lose? This was no rhetorical question . . . we were convinced that our people truly had nothing to lose except the prospect of extermination."[477] Another *Irgun* member, Meir Feinstein, on trial for the part he played in the bombing of Jerusalem railway station in October 1946, which claimed the life of a police explosives expert, told the presiding judge: "We were not spared in order to live in slavery and oppression and to await some new Trebinki [sic]. We were spared in order to ensure life and freedom and honour for ourselves, for our people, for our children and for our children's children. We were spared in order that there should be no repetition of what happened there and of what has happened and is still

---

[474] ibid., p. 230.

[475] Patrick Bishop, *The Reckoning: How the Killing of One Man Changed the Fate of the Promised Land* (William Collins; 2014), p. 190.

[476] Joseph Heller, *The Stern Gang: Ideology, Politics and Terror 1940–1949* (Frank Cass; 1995), p. 122.

[477] Menachem Begin, *The Revolt: Story of the Irgun* (Steimatzky's Agency Ltd.; 1977), pp. 40–41.

likely to happen here, under your rule."[478] Feinstein remained defiant to the end — hours before their scheduled execution, he and fellow prisoner Moshe Barazani, a veteran of LEHI, blew themselves up in their cell with two improvised grenades smuggled into Jerusalem's Central Prison inside hollowed-out oranges. Begin was so affected by their sacrifice that he asked to be buried next to them on the Mount of Olives, which he finally was in 1992.[479]

For EOKA, a passionate commitment to the Greek Orthodox Church was an integral component of the struggle for *Enosis*, which in turn lent a legitimacy to EOKA's actions. This reality was further underlined by the fact that the parallel political campaign for *Enosis* was led by Archbishop Makarios III (Michael Mouskos), a charismatic preacher born of humble Cypriot peasant stock who had been elected to the Archbishopric of Nova Justiniana and All Cyprus in 1950. Makarios III would go on to become the first President of the Republic of Cyprus in 1960, a position he held until 1974. New EOKA members were inducted into the organization by an Orthodox priest and swore a religious oath to serve it faithfully. In a neat phrase, the historian David French noted that the centrality of faith helped EOKA to "develop its own moral economy to justify terrorism" and served to reinforce commanders' authority in the field, which is why EOKA's commander, General Grivas, tasked his subordinate Archimandrite Constantinos Lefkosiatis with creating a "spiritual supply service" to spread religious propaganda through the group's ranks.[480] British security personnel remarked on the religiosity of EOKA members, noting after the detention of one cell in May 1957: "A notable feature of the mentality of these gangsters is the religious fervor with which they had sustained their morale. Even their capture on Good Friday lent itself to a suitable interpretation in their minds."[481]

---

[478] ibid., p. 42.

[479] 60 Years Later: Feinstein's Bible Returned to Family, *Begin Center Bulletin*, Vol. 3, No. 28, 26 April 2007.

[480] David French, *Fighting EOKA: The British Counter-Insurgency Campaign on Cyprus, 1955–1959* (Oxford University Press; 2015), pp. 66–67.

[481] ibid., p. 67.

Like LEHI, EOKA also invested heavily in promoting a narrative that compared British counter-terrorism tactics with those used by the Nazis, with Grivas describing Governor Harding in one leaflet as the "*Gauleiter* of Cyprus".[482] In spring 1956, Grivas began actively collecting reports of the ill treatment of local people and circulated a leaflet calling on loyal Cypriots to report all such incidents to EOKA.[483] When two British Captains, Robin Linzee and Gerald O'Driscoll, were court martialed in April 1956 on charges of attempting to pervert the course of justice and assaulting EOKA suspect Christo Constantinou (and in Linzee's case, a second suspect, Andreas Koronides), EOKA took great advantage of the scandal. Linzee and O'Driscoll were both dismissed from the British Army, but this did not stop supporters of *Enosis* alleging — with apparent credibility — that Britain was routinely torturing the prisoners held in its custody.[484] Human Rights Committees sprang up across the island coordinated by the Nicosia Bar Association, and the Greek government lodged two complaints against the British government before the European Court of Human Rights, the second listing forty-nine cases in which British security forces had allegedly employed torture.[485] By 1958, EOKA was issuing pro-forma surveys to villages that had been subjected to British searches for them to comment on the misbehavior of the troops. The propaganda push never let up with one senior EOKA figure, Kyriacos Matsis, telling his subordinates in autumn 1958: "Propaganda should be directed against cultivating hatred against the English through their acts of vandalism, their searches, [and]

---

[482] ibid., p. 198.

[483] ibid.

[484] ibid., and Charlie Standley, The British Army, Violence, Interrogation and Shortcomings in Intelligence Gathering During the Cyprus Emergency, 1955–59, in Christopher Andrew and Simona Tobia (eds.), *Interrogation in War and Conflict: Comparative and Interdisciplinary Analysis* (Routledge; 2014), pp. 161–163.

[485] David French, *Fighting EOKA: The British Counter-Insurgency Campaign on Cyprus, 1955–1959* (Oxford University Press; 2015) p. 198 and A. W. Brian Simpson, *Human Rights and the End of Empire: Britain and the Genesis of the European Convention* (Oxford University Press; 2004), pp. 924–1052.

their partiality towards the Turks."[486] The British were all too well aware of the damage such activity was having on their position, with the Director of Operations on Cyprus, Major-General Douglas Kendrew, issuing a directive to his forces in September 1958 that warned: "Indiscriminate roughness, unnecessary destruction of property, discourtesy and collective punitive measures ... have no place in internal security operations and merely make the task of the Security Forces harder by playing into the hands of the other side."[487]

The Algerian *Front de Libération Nationale* was extremely adept at shaping the narrative around its independence struggle. The FLN announced its arrival on the political stage in November 1954 with a proclamation that both set out its program and offered a place "equal both as to rights and as to duties" for French settlers in an independent Algeria if its demands were met. In the following twelve months, the FLN's leading strategist, Ramdane Abane, shaped an ideology for the organization that sought to embrace both Marxism–Leninism and Islamism without becoming beholden to either, while still being able to leverage the symbolic language of both creeds in the service of forging genuine unity of purpose.[488] Abane was also behind the creation of the FLN's underground newspaper *El Moudjahid* in June 1956 to spread "the truth on the War of Independence, of its goal for peace".[489] The choice of title was deliberate, evoking the religious obligation of *jihad*, but in an apposite illustration of the juggling act Abane was seeking to perform, the paper's first editorial cautioned readers not to read too much into the name: "Some will doubtless be surprised by the choice of title, which they might believe inspired by a form of political sectarianism or religious fundamentalism, when our goal is to liberate

---

[486] David French, *Fighting EOKA: The British Counter-Insurgency Campaign on Cyprus, 1955–1959* (Oxford University Press; 2015), p. 198.

[487] ibid., p. 203.

[488] Alistair Horne, *A Savage War of Peace: Algeria 1954–1962* (New York Review Books Classics; 2006), p. 133.

[489] Editorial of the First Issue of *El Moudjahid* at https://www.marxists.org/history/algeria/1956/elmoudjahid-01.htm.

ourselves of de-nationalizing colonialist restraints, and for democracy and equality among all Algerians, regardless of race or religion ... It just so happens that Islam was in Algeria the last refuge of [superior and indispensable] values hounded and profaned by an outrageous colonialism. Is there any reason then to be surprised that, in recovering a national consciousness, it contributes to the victory of a just cause?"[490] Abane also invited the nationalist poet Moufdi Zakaria to write the FLN anthem, *Le Kassaman* (We Pledge), which would become the national anthem after independence, and established the clandestine radio station *Voix de l'Algérie* (Voice of Algeria), which by the end of 1956 was broadcasting FLN propaganda to a wider and wider audience. Indeed, the broadcasts proved so popular that the country's entire supply of transistor radios sold out.[491] The FLN's leadership proved to be very skilled at turning criticism of the FLN's tactics back on the French government in press interviews. When asked by a reporter whether he thought hiding bombs in women's baskets was cowardly, FLN commander Larbi Ben M'Hidi replied: "Doesn't it seem to you even more cowardly to drop napalm bombs on defenseless villages, so that there are a 1,000 times more innocent victims? Of course, if we had your airplanes it would be a lot easier for us. Give us your bombers, and you can have our baskets."[492] Creating a sense of moral equivalency between both sides of the conflict is another vital tool in a terror group's propaganda armory. Ironically enough, Ben M'Hidi would become part of that narrative himself when he was murdered in French custody in March 1957.

Examples of both individual terrorists and militant groups asserting an equivalency between their actions and those of the state abound in the literature. Michele Angiolillo, the anarchist who assassinated the Spanish Prime Minister Antonio Cánovas in August 1897, posed the rhetorical question: "Is it wrong to kill a

---

[490] ibid.

[491] Alistair Horne, *A Savage War of Peace: Algeria 1954–1962* (New York Review Books Classics; 2006), p. 133.

[492] Louis Proyect, *Looking Back At The Battle Of Algiers,* Swans Commentary, 11 April 2011, at http://www.swans.com/library/art17/lproy67.html.

bloodthirsty tiger, who splits chests open with its claws and tears people's heads off with its jaws? Is it a crime to crush a poisonous reptile?"[493] After it hung two captured British sergeants, Clifford Martin and Mervyn Paice, in July 1947, *Irgun* issued a defiant statement justifying its action in the face of widespread condemnation: "We recognize no one-sided laws of war. If the British are determined that their way out of the country should be lined by an avenue of gallows and of weeping fathers, mothers, wives, and sweethearts, we shall see to it that in this there is no racial discrimination. The gallows will not be all of one color ... Their price will be paid in full."[494] *Brigate Rosse* member Mario Moretti, who admitted to the kidnapping and murder of Aldo Moro, offered a classic framing comparison: "If a partisan pumped half a kilo of lead into the belly of a German soldier, do you think you could ask him, 'didn't you think that perhaps Fritz has a wife and five children, raises cows, and doesn't want anything else?' 'Yes, but I am defending my country', he would have replied."[495] One of the founders of the *Brigate Rosse*, Margherita Cagol made a similar observation in a letter to her mother: "I am doing the right thing and History will show that I am right as it did for the Resistance in 1945 ... there are no other means. This police state is based on the use of force and it can only be fought on the same level."[496] Cagol was killed in a shoot-out with Italian *Carabinieri* in June 1975. The "declaration of war" that announced the formation of the Japanese militant group *Kyōsanshugisha Dōmei Sekigunha* (Communist League Red Army Faction) in September 1969 framed the issue succinctly: "If you killed our Black Panther comrades and have the right to oppress the ghetto with police cars, we have the right to kill Nixon, Sato, Kissinger, and de Gaulle, and to blow up the

[493] Anna Geifman, *Death Orders: The Vanguard of Modern Terrorism in Revolutionary Russia* (Praeger Security International; 2010), p. 148.

[494] John Bowyer Bell, *Terror out of Zion: Irgun Zvai Leumi, LEHI, and the Palestine Underground, 1929–1949* (Academy Press; 1977), p. 236.

[495] Michael Burleigh, *Blood and Rage: A Cultural History of Terrorism* (Harper; 2009), p. 198.

[496] ibid., p. 200.

Pentagon, Japanese Defense Headquarters, and your homes [the symbols of power in the imperialist nations]."[497]

On 20 April 1964, Nelson Mandela, who was a keen student of the FLN's struggle in Algeria, stood in the dock of a South African courtroom on trial for three counts of sabotage and he delivered one of his most famous orations, defending the African National Congress' decision to take up arms against the *apartheid* regime. Mandela admitted to the role he had played in the creation of the ANC's armed wing, *Umkhonto we Sizwe,* and his role in planning a series of attacks on infrastructure targets: "I do not, however, deny that I planned sabotage. I did not plan it in a spirit of recklessness, nor because I have any love of violence. I planned it as a result of a calm and sober assessment of the political situation that had arisen after many years of tyranny, exploitation, and oppression of my people by the Whites."[498] He also noted that the ANC's use of violence had been constrained and measured: "Four forms of violence were possible. There is sabotage, there is guerrilla warfare, there is terrorism, and there is open revolution. We chose to adopt the first method and to exhaust it before taking any other decision."[499]

Mandela carefully explained the logic that had led the ANC's leadership to the reluctant adoption of violent methods to his courtroom audience: "I, and the others who started the organization [*Umkhonto we Sizwe*], did so for two reasons. Firstly, we believed that as a result of Government policy, violence by the African people had become inevitable, and that unless responsible leadership was given to canalize and control the feelings of our people, there would be outbreaks of terrorism which would produce an intensity of bitterness and hostility between the various races of this country which is not

---

[497] Patricia Steinhoff, Ideology, Identity, Political Violence in Four Linked Japanese Groups, Paper presented at European Consortium on Political Research 2015 General Conference session on "The Role of Ideology in Violent Politics: Mobilization, Strategy, and Targeting," Political Violence Section, European Consortium for Political Research General Conference, Montreal, August 28, 2015, p. 8.

[498] http://www.washingtonpost.com/blogs/worldviews/wp/2013/12/05/read-the-most-important-speech-nelson-mandela-ever-gave.

[499] ibid.

produced even by war. Secondly, we felt that without violence there would be no way open to the African people to succeed in their struggle against the principle of white supremacy. All lawful modes of expressing opposition to this principle had been closed by legislation, and we were placed in a position in which we had either to accept a permanent state of inferiority, or to defy the Government. We chose to defy the law. We first broke the law in a way which avoided any recourse to violence; when this form was legislated against, and then the Government resorted to a show of force to crush opposition to its policies, only then did we decide to answer violence with violence."[500]

In May 1961, following a whites-only referendum the previous year, the government of South Africa had declared a Republic, taking the country out of the British Commonwealth. Deeply apprehensive of what the establishment of a "White Republic" might mean for the majority of non-white residents of South Africa the multi-party All-in Africa Conference, of which Mandela had been appointed Secretary, called for a general strike — a national stay-at-home — to coincide with the declaration of the Republic. Mandela reminded the court: "The stay-at-home, in accordance with ANC policy, was to be a peaceful demonstration. Careful instructions were given to organizers and members to avoid any recourse to violence. The Government's answer was to introduce new and harsher laws, to mobilize its armed forces, and to send Saracens, armed vehicles, and soldiers into the townships in a massive show of force designed to intimidate the people. This was an indication that the Government had decided to rule by force alone, and this decision was a milestone on the road to *Umkhonto*."[501] In his work on mechanisms of moral disengagement, the psychologist Albert Bandura noted that "the task of making violence morally defensible is facilitated when non-violent options are judged to have been ineffective and utilitarian justifications portray the suffering caused by violent counterattacks as greatly outweighed by the human suffering inflicted by the foe."[502]

---

[500] ibid.

[501] ibid.

[502] Albert Bandura, Mechanisms of Moral Disengagement, in Walter Reich (ed.), *Origins of Terrorism: Psychologies, Ideologies, Theologies, States of Mind* (Johns Hopkins University Press; 1998), p. 164.

When the United Nations General Assembly invited the PLO Chairman Yasir Arafat to address the body on 13 November 1974, he also delivered a classic grievance framing speech that in this instance sought to brand the PLO as a national liberation movement fighting against imperialism, colonialism, and racism.[503] In doing so, Arafat set out to redefine the narrative of the Arab–Israeli conflict in the aftermath of the Six Day and Yom Kippur Wars, in which Israel had typically been portrayed in the international media as a plucky David facing off against the Goliath of the Arab world. Instead, Arafat presented Israel as a "racist entity" founded on what he termed "the imperialist–colonialist concept" and formed into a base of imperialism and an arsenal of aggression. Arafat knew that his audience in the General Assembly included the representatives of many newly independent states that had either successfully thrown off the shackles of colonial rule or saw themselves as being threatened by what they perceived as the neo-colonial power of the United States and its Western allies, and so he deliberately shaped his arguments in language that he knew would resonate with them deeply, noting: "Many of you in this assembly hall were considered terrorists ... Many of you present here today once stood in exactly the same resistance position as I now occupy and from which I must fight."[504] Arafat cast the Palestinians in the role of colonized victim and aligned Palestine's struggle for national self-determination with that of the native populations of Zimbabwe, Namibia, South Africa, and other "oppressed peoples compelled by intolerable circumstances into a confrontation with such oppression", while also condemning Western "aggression" against Laos, Cambodia, Vietnam and North Korea.[505] He also appealed to the American people to see his movement as belonging to the same tradition as the "heroic" George Washington, the "champion of the destitute and the wretched" Abraham Lincoln, and Woodrow Wilson supposedly "venerated" by Palestinians for his support for national self-determination.

---

[503] Speech of Yasir Arafat before the UN General Assembly, 13 November 1974.

[504] ibid.

[505] ibid.

In addition to weaving an argument articulating the legitimacy of the Palestinian cause, Arafat took great pains to undermine the legitimacy of Israeli actions by painting Zionism in the most negative possible terms as "reactionary and discriminatory", and the "chief form" of racism, comparing the father of Zionism, Theodor Herzl, with the rapacious nineteenth century British imperialist Cecil Rhodes, characterizing Jewish emigration to Ottoman and Mandatory Palestine as an "invasion", describing the United Nations partition of Palestine as unlawful, and accusing Israel of supporting reactionary causes around the world, such as the *Organisation de l'armée secrète* active during the Algerian war of independence, the *apartheid* regime in South Africa, and the US-backed government of South Vietnam. In one of the most egregious passages of the speech, Arafat claimed: "While we [were] vociferously condemning the massacres of Jews under Nazi rule, the Zionist leadership appeared more interested at that time in exploiting them as best it could in order to realize its goal of immigration to Palestine." In reality, the most prominent Palestinian leader during World War II, the Grand Mufti of Jerusalem Haj Mohammed Effendi Amin el-Husseini, actually met with Adolf Hitler seeking his support and helped the Germans recruit Bosnian Muslims for the Waffen-SS, declaring in a speech delivered in Sarajevo in July 1943: "You, my Bosnian Muslims, are the first Islamic division [and] serve as an example of the active collaboration ... My enemy's enemy is my friend."[506]

Arafat forcefully rejected the idea that one could describe the violent actions of Palestinian militants as terrorism, commenting scornfully: "Those who call us terrorists wish to prevent world public opinion from discovering the truth about us and from seeing the justice on our faces. They seek to bide the terrorism and tyranny of their own acts, and our own posture of self-defence."[507] In the previous five years, such acts of Palestinian "self-defence" had included detonating a barometric bomb on Swissair Flight SR330 killing all forty-seven passengers and crew, the massacre of twenty-six travelers

---

[506] George Lepre, *Himmler's Bosnian Division: The Waffen-SS Handschar Division 1943–1945* (Schiffer Military History; 1997), p. 75.

[507] Speech of Yasir Arafat before the UN General Assembly, 13 November 1974.

at Lod Airport, the majority Christian pilgrims from Puerto Rico, and the assault on the Munich Olympics which claimed the lives of eleven Israeli athletes and a West German policeman. But for Arafat, the justice of the cause determined the right to struggle: "For whoever stands by a just cause and fights for freedom and liberation of his land from the invaders, the settlers and the colonists, cannot possibly be called terrorist."[508] His formulation was — ironically — remarkably similar to Menachem Begin's own admonition to those who had described *Irgun* and LEHI militants as terrorists: "What has a struggle for the dignity of man, against oppression and subjugation, to do with 'terrorism'?"[509]

Mindful of the importance of stressing his preference for a peaceful solution to the conflict, Arafat concluded his speech in a manner that was intended to shift the blame for any continued violence onto the Israeli side: "I announce here that we do not wish one drop of either Arab or Jewish blood to be shed; neither do we delight in the continuation of killing, which would end once a just peace, based on our people's rights, hopes and aspirations had been [agreed]."[510] He finished with the dramatic rhetorical flourish in which he offered Israelis a choice between an olive branch and the freedom fighter's gun — it had been a master class on the art of public relations. Arafat's speech proved to be a game-changer — nine days after the speech the General Assembly adopted by overwhelming majority vote Resolution 3236, which recognized the right to self-determination and national independence of the Palestinian people, and Resolution 3237, which invited the PLO to participate in the sessions and the work of the General Assembly and international conferences organized by the United Nations in the capacity of an observer.[511]

The power of the kind of legitimizing historical narratives constructed in Arafat's speech to spur terrorist recruitment is well

---

[508] ibid.

[509] Menachem Begin, *The Revolt: Story of the Irgun* (Steimatzky's Agency Ltd.; 1977), p. 60.

[510] Speech of Yasir Arafat before the UN General Assembly, 13 November 1974.

[511] United Nations General Assembly Resolutions A/RES/3236 and A/RES/3237, 22 November 1974.

illustrated by a story told by the PFLP hijacker Leila Khaled in *My People Shall Live*. Khaled describes getting into trouble with her mother as a young child for skipping a demonstration against "the Zionist occupation of Palestine" to focus on her schoolwork: "I agreed that the demonstration was desirable, but insisted that school work was more important. Mother was surprised by my treasonous talk, and lectured me on the three historical days of betrayal that every Palestinian should remember: the Balfour Declaration of 2 November 1917; the partition of Palestine, 29 November 1947; and the proclamation of the state of Israel, 15 May 1948. Ever since, these dates have become a vital and integral part of my life."[512] Khaled herself also harnessed historical narratives in her memoir to justify the PFLP's tactic of hijacking American and European airliners arguing that hijacking international aircraft was justified because "the list of the sins of the West is overwhelming."[513] Khaled criticized West Germany for paying war reparations to Israel; France for supplying the Israeli Air Force with Mystère, Super Mystère and Mirage jets, and for providing the technological know-how to help the Israelis manufacture an atomic bomb; Switzerland for detaining "Arab revolutionaries"; Britain for being guilty of "every imaginable crime against my people"; and the United States for perpetuating Britain's crimes, supplying Israel with Hawk missiles and Phantom aircraft, and acting as Israel's "defender, apologist and financier". She concludes with the crushing indictment: "Israel is America and Europe combined in Palestine."[514]

For the left-wing urban terrorist groups operating in Italy in the 1970s, factory workers in Milan and Turin became the representative proxy of the proletariat and hence the popular arbiter of legitimacy. The first kidnapping the *Brigate Rosse* undertook was of Fiat's Personnel Director Ettore Amerio and he was released unharmed when the company agreed to rescind 400 redundancy notices. This success also served to bolster the militants' arguments

---

[512] Leila Khaled and George Hajjar, *My People Shall Live: The Autobiography of a Revolutionary* (Hodder and Stoughton; 1973), pp. 31–32.
[513] ibid., p. 127.
[514] ibid., p. 128.

in favor of violent direct action over the more traditional trade union approach of negotiations and strike threats. Fulltime members of the *Brigate Rosse* operating underground were paid a wage based on the salary of a Fiat metal mechanic.[515] The *Brigate Rosse* even deliberately avoided robbing post offices or payroll offices so as not to inconvenience workers, the unemployed or pensioners.[516]

Exposing the "fascist reality" of the state was one of the key stated objectives of many far-left terrorist groups, such as the *Rote Armee Fraktion, Brigate Rosse* and the Greek *Epanastatikos Laikos Agonas* (ELA). In an interview with *Le Monde Diplomatique*, representatives of the *Rote Armee Fraktion* detained in German prisons told reporters: "The legal attacks on anti-imperialist politics in the [Federal Republic of Germany] have political relevance, because they completely unmask social democracy. The RAF was clear that this was how it would unfold and that the [Social Democratic Party] was the transmission belt of the new fascism."[517] An amnesty in 1946 had allowed many of Mussolini's supporters to reenter public life in Italy and, as in Germany, former fascists continued to be a significant presence in the police and judiciary.[518] The *Movimento Sociale Italiano* (MSI), a political party founded by surviving members of Mussolini's regime in 1946, had begun to play an increasingly prominent role in Italian political life and, by 1960, a pact forged between the MSI and the mainstream conservative Christian Democratic Party helped to keep the latter in power. Renato Curcio wrote to his mother that in joining the *Brigate Rosse*, he felt he had "picked up" the gun of his uncle who had been killed fighting against Mussolini with the partisans during World War II.[519] Christos Tsigarides of the ELA similarly

---

[515] Alison Jamieson, Identity and Morality in the Italian Red Brigades, *Terrorism and Political Violence*, Vol. 2, No. 4 (1990), p. 512.

[516] ibid., p. 513.

[517] Interview with Le Monde Diplomatique, 10 June 1976, in J. Smith and André Moncourt, *The Red Army Faction A Documentary History: Volume 1 — Projectiles for the People* (PM Press; 2009), pp. 426–427.

[518] Alison Jamieson, Identity and Morality in the Italian Red Brigades, *Terrorism and Political Violence*, Vol. 2, No. 4 (1990), p. 511.

[519] ibid., p. 512.

dismissed the attempts at "dejuntafication" which followed the collapse of the so-called Regime of the Colonels in 1974 as a farce: "Apart from the *junta* leaders, all the key people that made up the *junta* state apparatus remained unpunished ... all the appointees of, and collaborators with, the *junta* in state bureaucracy, the police apparatus, education and the judiciary remained untouched."[520]

However, in Western Europe Marxist terrorist groups ultimately failed to develop a narrative that was sufficiently compelling to attract significant popular support. Reflecting from prison on the failure of the *Rote Armee Fraktion* to attract a greater following in a 1997 interview, the former RAF member Stefan Wisniewski commented that he and his comrades had failed to explain their actions effectively in a way the general public could relate to. He dwelt particularly on the 1977 kidnapping and subsequent murder of the German industrialist and former Nazi SS officer, Hanns Martin Schleyer, in which he had played a key role: "It was only much later, during my trial, that I began to see ... that we should have made it much clearer why we had decided to take Schleyer prisoner. We should have presented our demands in a totally different way. It's clear that we should have demanded that Daimler-Benz open its archives about the use of slave labor, that the corporation should pay compensation for the use of slave labor. We could have said that the question of the prisoners was simply a matter of a deadly confrontation, while explaining that there was another terrain on which there were significant issues to be addressed."[521] Hans-Joachim Klein, a member of the *Revolutionäre Zellen* who took part in the assault on the headquarters of the Organization of the Petroleum Exporting Countries (OPEC) led by Carlos the Jackal in December 1975, later observed of his comrades' actions: "The connection between the objective and the means gets screwed up ... From [their] humanity to [their] political ideals, [they] sink deeper and deeper into shit."[522]

The RAF survived, albeit in much diminished form, into the late 1990s when the few remaining members still at large sent an

---

[520] George Kassimeris, *Inside Greek Terrorism* (Oxford University Press; 2013), p. 64.

[521] André Moncourt and J. Smith, *We Were so Terribly Consistent: A Conversation About the History of the RAF*, Stefan Wisniewski interviewed by TAZ (Kersplebedeb; 2009), p. 29.

[522] Klaus Croissant, Defender of German Terrorists, *The New York Times*, 28 October 1977.

eight-page statement to the Reuters News Agency announcing portentously: "The urban guerrilla in the form of the RAF is now history."[523] However, it is apposite to note that in this, its final collective act, the rump membership of the RAF was still consumed by its failure to attract popular support and devoted much of its last communiqué to a lengthy assertion of the legitimacy of its previous actions: "The RAF was the revolutionary attempt by a minority of people to resist the tendencies in this society and contribute to the overthrow of capitalist conditions ... The end of this project shows that we were not able to succeed on this path. But this does not speak against the necessity and legitimacy of revolt."[524] Describing its campaign as the historic flash of decisive opposition, the statement predictably highlighted the career of Hanns Martin Schleyer, murdered now some twenty years earlier but still the organization's most high-profile action, as evidence of a persistent fascist taint to German society that had demanded a response: "Nazis built careers in the West German state in government positions, the courts, the police apparatus, the armed forces, the media, and in major corporations. These anti-Semites, racists, and genocidal murderers were often times the same people responsible for crimes against humanity under the Nazis, and now they were back among the powerful elite."[525]

Casting one's opponents in the worst possible light is an enduring staple of legitimizing narratives, but negative comparisons have to strike their intended audience as plausible to have any real impact, and, while many Nazis did thrive in the Federal Republic, it was equally apparent to most Germans that the booming consumer society of the 1970s and 1980s bore little relation to Adolf Hitler's Third Reich. RAF member Horst Mahler acknowledged as much in an interview published in the German magazine *Der Spiegel* in 1980: "[The RAF] were mistaken if they expected to find a decayed population looking at their government as a burden. Instead, they met people who were prepared to defend the

---

[523] The Urban Guerrilla is History, *The Final Communiqué From The Red Army Faction*, 1 March 1998 at http://germanGuerrilla.com/1998/03/01/the-urban-guerrilla-is-history/.
[524] ibid.
[525] ibid.

existing social order and its laws in spite of their discontent and their loud complaints."[526] Of course, equally damaging to the RAF's narrative — and indeed those of other European Marxist groups like the *Brigate Rosse* and November 17 — was the collapse of what the RAF termed "real existing socialism" across the Soviet Bloc from late 1989 onwards. The "anti-emancipatory experiences with the authoritarian and state bureaucratic concepts of real existing socialism" had discredited the model the RAF had hitherto aspired to promote and while the authors of the RAF's final communiqué suggested that "future paths to liberation" might soon emerge, they were unable to offer any substantial guidance on what these might be.[527]

For the *Tupamaros* in Uruguay, establishing legitimacy in a conflict with a democratically elected regime that provided a decent level of social service provision to its citizens meant exposing corruption amongst the ruling class. Many of the operations conducted by the *Tupamaros* targeted the assets of the most wealthy and privileged members of Uruguayan society, but, in addition to expropriating funds, the group often added a twist — as in the robbery of the private banking house Financiera Monty or the bullion vault of the Mailhos family — stealing private ledgers containing evidence of illegal foreign currency transactions or the failure to pay taxes, which they then passed on through intermediaries to the authorities and the media in order to expose the hypocrisy and criminality of the country's traditional elites.[528] Raúl Sendic explained in *30 Questions to a Tupamaro* that such actions not only served to attract new volunteers to the *Tupamaros'* colors, but they also discredited the state in the eyes of its own agents and potential supporters: "It is a fundamental fact that the majority of the population, even if they are not prepared to engage in the armed struggle,

---

[526] *Der Minister und der Terrorist: Gespräche zwischen Gerhart Baum und Horst Mahler* (Spiegel Buch; 1980).

[527] The Urban Guerrilla Is History, *The Final Communiqué From The Red Army Faction*, 1 March 1998 at http://germanGuerrilla.com/1998/03/01/the-urban-guerrilla-is-history/.

[528] Pablo Brum, *The Robin Hood Guerrillas: The Epic Journey of Uruguay's Tupamaros* (CreateSpace; 2014), pp. 83–85 and 124–126.

are not going to be themselves killed in defence of a government which oppresses them."[529]

*Sinn Féin* President Gerry Adams published *The Politics of Irish Freedom* in 1986 as a personal statement of his republicanism, and the volume is an extended examination of the legitimacy of the Provisional IRA struggle to "liberate" Northern Ireland from British rule: "By its very nature British rule cannot be just or peaceful and, while this is so, revolutionary struggle will continue to strive to overthrow it in pursuit of true justice, peace and happiness. Violence in Ireland has its roots in the conquest of Ireland by Britain. This conquest has lasted through several stages for many centuries and, whether economic, political, territorial or cultural, it has used violence, coercion, sectarianism and terrorism as its methods and has had power as its objective."[530] Adams also made the point that a group's longevity speaks to the legitimacy of the cause it represents, noting: "Despite British propaganda stories it is obvious that the IRA exists and operates with the active consent of a sufficient number of people to finance, arm, clothe, feed, accommodate and transport IRA volunteers and in every way build up around them a voluntary political infrastructure."[531]

Speaking at a *Sinn Féin* party conference in 1983, Adams had declared: "There are those who tell us that the British Government will not be moved by armed struggle. As has been said before, the history of Ireland, and of British colonial involvement throughout the world, tell us that they will not be moved by anything else."[532] He expanded on this argument in *The Politics of Irish Freedom*, making the case for the necessity of armed struggle, writing: "The tactic of armed struggle is of primary importance because it provides a vital cutting edge. Without it the issue of Ireland would not even be an issue. So, in effect, the armed struggle becomes armed

---

[529] Alain Labrousse (trans. Dinah Livingstone), *The Tupamaros: Urban Guerrillas in Uruguay* (Penguin Books; 1973), p. 140.

[530] Gerry Adams, *The Politics of Irish Freedom* (Brandon Book Publishers; 1986), p. 62.

[531] ibid., p. 63.

[532] Brendan O'Brien, *The Long War: The IRA and Sinn Féin* (Syracuse University Press, New York; 1999), pp. 116–117.

propaganda."[533] *Sinn Féin* and the IRA were not the only political
actors in Northern Ireland representing the Catholic community
and Adams was careful to acknowledge the legitimacy of dissenting
views up to a point: "Very many people who disagree absolutely with
the IRA nevertheless see it as a very important part of the political
equation. They might deplore it, dislike it, have moral objections to
it, but still have the feeling that if it did not exist there would be no
hope of getting change."[534] Adams also addressed concerns that if it
was successful in driving the British out of Ireland, the Provisional
IRA might then turn its weapons on its fellow countrymen, including the government of the Republic of Ireland in the south. This was
a real concern. The Irish War of Independence had been followed
in 1922 by a vicious twelve-month internecine civil war in the Irish
Free State and the IRA had played a major role in the conflict, fighting on the losing side. Several thousand Irish lives had been lost,
including that of one of the great heroes of the independence struggle, Michael Collins. The 1970s had also been marked by a violent
feud between the Official IRA (OIRA) and the Irish National
Liberation Army (INLA) that had left a number of prominent
republicans dead on both sides, including the founder of INLA,
Seamus Costello. Adams assured his readers that if the British pulled
out of Northern Ireland, there would be no appetite for further
fighting: "Following the restoration of Irish national independence
there would be no popular support for armed struggle. The handful
of people who make up [the IRA] could not hope to win anything
by pursuing armed struggle without popular support."[535]

Like Arafat, Adams stressed his own personal distaste for violence: "I wish that physical force had never been part of the political
struggle in my lifetime in Ireland. But a statelet which was born in
violence has maintained itself throughout its more than sixty years
of existence by violence and has been supported in so doing by the
British army and government."[536] In moving the blame for the

---

[533] Gerry Adams, *The Politics of Irish Freedom* (Brandon Book Publishers; 1986), p. 64.
[534] ibid.
[535] ibid., p. 67.
[536] ibid., p. 51.

violence onto the British and loyalist side, he also characterizes the Provisional IRA's use of violence in purely defensive terms: "The IRA's armed struggle ... originated as a defensive response to the combined attacks of the RUC, loyalists and the British Army, and it has always been massively outgunned."[537] Adams lays great stress on the power mismatch between the IRA and British forces, and emphasizes that Provisional IRA volunteers are at heart civilians, operating against professional soldiers representing a vastly numerically and technologically superior force, who feel they "are using the only means at their disposal to bring home the message in terms that will be understood and taken seriously enough to result in action and movement ... The IRA is ordinary people facing up against the monster of imperial power."[538]

Staking a claim to combatant status for its fighters is an important mainstay of most terrorist organizations' narratives. The reason for this is quite simple — in law, as in logic, killing an enemy in war is a legitimate act, within certain parameters. Recognition as a soldier places the terrorist on an equal conceptual footing with government forces, it also removes the taint of criminality from the terrorist's actions. In 1981, the Provisional IRA (and INLA) called a hunger strike by republican prisoners in an effort to assert the status of convicted members as "political" rather than "criminal" detainees. In all, ten prisoners starved themselves to death before the strike was called off. One hunger striker, Bobby Sands, who had been convicted of the illegal possession of a handgun, was elected to the British Parliament during the strike but died shortly afterward. More than 100,000 mourners attended his funeral. Sands had written in his prison diary: "They will not criminalise us, rob us of our true identity, steal our individualism, depoliticize us ... they will never label our liberation struggle as criminal."[539] However, British Prime Minister Margaret Thatcher refused to back down because she also well understood the principle at stake: "There can be no

---

[537] ibid.

[538] ibid., pp. 68–69.

[539] Denis O'Hearn, *Nothing But An Unfinished Song: Bobby Sands, The Irish Hunger Striker Who Ignited a Generation* (Nation Book; 2006) and http://www.bobbysandstrust.com/writings/prison-diary.

question of political status for someone who is serving a sentence for crime. Crime is crime is crime. It is not political, it is crime, and there can be no question of granting political status."[540] The Provisionals may not have won the battle of wills with Mrs. Thatcher, but the courage and commitment demonstrated by the hunger strikers, as well as the perceived callousness of the British government, radicalized nationalist opinion and eventually helped to make *Sinn Féin* a mainstream political party. Sixty-one people were killed in the seven months of violence accompanying the hunger strikes.[541] The former *Sinn Féin* Director of Publicity Danny Morrison, who acted as a spokesman for the hunger strikers, recalled: "Recruits flocked to the IRA. Its support multiplied. Its operations intensified."[542] Bobby Sands remains an icon of the republican struggle to this day, immortalized in songs, murals, books, and even film. Gerry Adams opened *The Politics of Irish Freedom* with a powerful poem written by Sands in prison entitled *The Rhythm of Time*.

The construction of powerful legitimizing narratives has probably reached its apogee in the media operations run by *Hezbollah, Hamas, al-Qaeda*, and ISIL. *Hezbollah*'s legitimizing narrative rests on theological foundations found in the teachings of three immensely influential contemporary *Shia* clerics — Imam Mussa al-Sadr, Ayatullah Muhammad Mahdi Shamseddine, and Ayatullah al-Sayyed Muhammad Hussein Fadlallah — and is underpinned by the inspirational example of the Islamic revolution in Iran led by Ayatollah Ruhollah Musavi Khomeini in 1979. Naim Qassem, the Deputy Secretary-General of *Hezbollah*, has summarized the "three pillars" of *Hezbollah*'s world view as being: the belief in Islam ("it is a conviction and a code of law"[543]); commitment to *jihad* ("*jihad* is a door towards life, not death. For uprightness is a concern of life, as are pride, freeing the land and overcoming oneself"[544]); and recognition of the

---

[540] Witness: IRA Hunger Strikers, *BBC World Service*, May 6, 2013.

[541] Peter Taylor, *Provos: The IRA & Sinn Féin* (Bloomsbury Publishing; 1997), p. 237.

[542] Danny Morrison, Thirty Years on, Bobby Sands's Stature Has Only Grown, *The Guardian*, 5 May 2011.

[543] Naim Qassem, *Hizbullah: The Story from Within* (Saqi; 2007), p. 67.

[544] ibid., p. 93.

jurisdiction of the Jurist–Theologian Ayatollah Khomeini, and subsequently his successor Ayatollah Khamenei ("it is a duty to obey the orders of the custodian of all Muslims on all general matters, of which defending Islam and Muslims against aggressors, tyrants and the blasphemous"[545]). The third pillar is key, *Hezbollah*'s program is carefully built around the religious guidance of clerics — the organization only adopted the tactic of suicide bombing after an extensive internal theological debate about whether or not the perpetrators of such attacks were indeed committing suicide, which is forbidden in Islam. The clerics ultimately concluded they were not and sanctioned the practice, which as previously discussed is typically referred to as the conduct of "martyrdom operations" in *Hezbollah* communications: "Martyrdom for the sake of liberation goes beyond its material aspect, representing a form of obedience to God's ordained duty of defending the land. It is thus a death for the sake of God."[546]

*Hezbollah* pioneered the terrorist use of visual media with the launch of its television station *Al Manar*[547] in June 1991, which the organization has used to promote *Hezbollah*'s role as "the spearhead of the Islamic resistance" and to showcase its opposition to US hegemony and its support for the Palestinian cause.[548] The station began broadcasting via satellite in 2000, and the station's chairman, Nayyaf Krayyem, described this as an important weapon for *Hezbollah*, observing: "It's a political weapon, social weapon, and cultural weapon."[549] As demonstrating that the political goals of an organization are both practical and achievable is an essential element of establishing widespread legitimacy and support, in addition to acting as a platform from which its leaders can address a global audience, *Hezbollah* has used *Al Manar* to magnify the military successes it has

---

[545] Ayatollah Khomenei quoted in Naim Qassem, *Hizbullah: The Story from Within* (Saqi; 2007), p. 95.

[546] Naim Qassem, *Hizbullah: The Story from Within* (Saqi; 2007), p. 106.

[547] The Beacon, or Lighthouse.

[548] Judith Palmer Harik, *Hezbollah: The Changing Face of Terrorism* (I. B. Taurus; 2004), p. 189.

[549] Nicholas Blanford, *Warriors of God: Inside Hezbollah's Thirty-Year Struggle Against Israel* (Random House; 2011), p. 135.

enjoyed against the Israeli military. *Al Manar* reporters are often embedded with *Hezbollah* fighters[550] and the channel places an emphasis on airing footage taken fresh from the battlefield — when *Hezbollah* fighters briefly overran an Israeli Defense Force outpost in Rousset al-Alam, Southern Lebanon, in April 2000, the video footage of *Hezbollah*'s flag being raised over the Israeli position was broadcast on *Al Manar* TV the same evening and became part of the channel's iconography.[551] *Al Manar* routinely memorializes *Hezbollah* or Palestinian fighters "martyred" in clashes with the Israelis, and displays images of Israeli casualties often accompanied by provocative slogans — such as "who will be next?" — aimed at demoralizing the Israeli public and boosting supporters' morale.[552] In July 2006, when eyewitness footage of a *Hezbollah* engagement in which an Israeli tank was destroyed was not available, unwilling to miss an opportunity to celebrate their fighters' success, the channel prepared a video animation of the battle instead.[553] According to *Al Manar* officials, more than ten million viewers watched the station's coverage of the July 2006 conflict with Israel making it one of the top five most watched channels in the Arab world.[554] The Israeli Air Force deliberately targeted *Al Manar* in air strikes during the conflict, but station managers had anticipated this eventually and switched seamlessly to a second hidden broadcast facility to remain on the air.[555] In doing so, *Al Manar* became part of the story itself emerging from the conflict, as one commentator put it, as "an icon of steadfastness against Western hegemony and aggression".[556]

---

[550] Assem Nasr, An Historical Perspective on Fundamentalist Media: The Case of Al-Manar Television, *Global Media Journal*, Vol. 6, No. 11 (Fall 2007).

[551] Judith Palmer Harik, *Hezbollah: The Changing Face of Terrorism* (I. B. Taurus; 2004) at 189

[552] ibid., p. 134 and p. 161.

[553] Matthias Gebauer, *Hezbollah's Al-Manar: Broadcasting from the Bunker*, Spiegel Online, 10 August 2006.

[554] Assem Nasr, An Historical Perspective on Fundamentalist Media: The Case of Al-Manar Television, *Global Media Journal*, Vol. 6, No. 11 (Fall 2007).

[555] Matthias Gebauer, *Hezbollah's Al-Manar: Broadcasting from the Bunker*, Spiegel Online, 10 August 2006.

[556] Assem Nasr, An Historical Perspective on Fundamentalist Media: The Case of Al-Manar Television, *Global Media Journal*, Vol. 6, No. 11 (Fall 2007).

For *Hamas*, the key goal was to construct a legitimizing narrative that was distinct from that of its rivals in *Fateh* and the PLO, which meant displacing familiar secular, nationalist tropes with a liberation narrative built around religion.[557] This was no small undertaking and the *Hamas* Charter emphasized the importance of recruiting "educators and teachers, information and media people" to lead the spiritual reawakening of the Palestinian people, and stressed the need to enlist "the book, the article, the bulletin, the sermon, the thesis, the popular poem, the poetic ode, the song, the play and others" to spread the organization's message.[558] To this end, *Hamas* has inserted both itself, and its messaging, into every public space it can find. Children have been a particular target of *Hamas* propaganda — a deliberate policy that the organization calls "training the Muslim generation" and "Islamization from below".[559] *Hamas* runs summer camps for Palestinian youths offering a mix of religious and political indoctrination, parade ground drill, sports, computer skills, and even in some cases small arms training.[560] One camp instructor, "Abdullah", interviewed in 2008 described the goals of the movement's summer camps as "to continue the education of the children and to teach them about the movement, and religion, and how to be a good Muslim. It also goes with the general goals of *Hamas* to create a new generation which is able to face the problems and the hard life we face."[561] Imam Jasser al-Mashoukhi elaborated further: "We hire professional captains and teachers to polish up the physical and mental skills of our children, who, God willing, will liberate Palestine."[562] In 2009, *Hamas* said it expected 100,000 young people would attend its summer camps in Gaza and

---

[557] Matthew Levitt, *Hamas: Politics, Charity and Terrorism in the Service of Jihad* (Yale University Press; 2006), p. 107.

[558] ibid., p. 140.

[559] Michael Arena and Bruce Arrigo, *The Terrorist Identity: Explaining The Terrorist Threat* (New York University; 2006), p. 142.

[560] Matthew Levitt, *Hamas: Politics, Charity and Terrorism in the Service of Jihad* (Yale University Press; 2006), p. 126.

[561] Beverley Milton-Edwards and Stephen Farrell, *Hamas* (Polity Press; 2010), p. 159.

[562] Matthew Levitt, *Hamas: Politics, Charity and Terrorism in the Service of Jihad* (Yale University Press; 2006), p. 126.

introduced Koranic recitation camps for a further 10,000 students.[563]
Groups like the *Hamas* Islamic Student Movement in the Bethlehem
area have handed out Instruction Cards featuring pictures of "martyred" suicide bombers, and other *Hamas* committees have distributed
collectable trading cards of prominent "martyrs" emblazoned with
slogans like: "There is nothing more certain other than that Glory
bows down before [the Izz al-Din al Qassam Brigades], and only
before them."[564]

In January 2006, *Hamas* launched *al-Aqsa* Television to compliment the radio station it had already established. *Al-Aqsa* Television
broadcast a mixture of Koranic readings, Islamist discussion
programs, and the children's show, *Tomorrow's Pioneers*, to Arabic-
speaking viewers around the world. *Tomorrow's Pioneers*, which played
between April 2007 and October 2009, attained a special degree of
global notoriety. Prior to the show's launch, its creator Hazim
Sharawi told *The New York Times*: "Our television show will have a
message, but without getting into the tanks, the guns, the killing and
the blood ... I will show [the children] our rights through the
history."[565] In the event, the show did not flinch from showing the
darker side of the Palestinian condition featuring a cast of child-
friendly anthropomorphic characters, most of whom met a series of
grisly deaths at the hands of the Israeli authorities — Farfour the
Mouse was beaten to death by an Israeli interrogator, Nahoul the
Bee died when the Israelis refused to allow him to leave Gaza for a
life-saving operation, and Assoud the Rabbit was injured fatally in
an Israeli raid. The only animal character to survive the series,
Nassur the Bear, claimed to have come to Gaza to join the
*Mujahedin*. The show featured episodes such as "Farfour and the
AK47", "Assoud vs Denmark" which condemned the publication of
cartoons of the prophet Mohammed in the Danish newspaper
*Jyllands-Posten*, "Nassur and the Expulsion of the Jews", and

---

[563] Beverley Milton-Edwards and Stephen Farrell, *Hamas* (Polity Press; 2010), p. 157.

[564] Matthew Levitt, *Hamas: Politics, Charity and Terrorism in the Service of Jihad* (Yale University Press; 2006), p. 125.

[565] Craig Smith, Warm and Fuzzy TV, Brought to You by Hamas, *The New York Times*, 18 January 2006.

"Nassur and the Children of Reem Riyashi", in which Nassur visited the children of *Hamas*'s first female suicide bomber. While it is difficult to assess the long-term impact of *Tomorrow's Pioneers* on its youthful audience, it is worth noting that when Sharawi, who played Uncle Hazim on the show, appeared at *Hamas*-sponsored festivals during the show's run, his appearance would attract as many as 10,000 children at a time.[566]

Both Osama bin Laden and Ayman al-Zawahiri have certainly demonstrated a deep commitment to information operations. In 2002, bin Laden wrote to the *Taliban* spiritual leader Mullah Muhammad Omar: "It is obvious that the media war in this century is one of the strongest methods; in fact, its ratio may reach 90% of the total preparation for the battles."[567] In July 2005, Ayman al-Zawahiri offered similar advice in a letter to *al-Qaeda* in Iraq's leader Abu Mus'ab al-Zarqawi: "We are in battle, and ... more than half of this battle is taking place in the battlefield of the media."[568] Drawing on Joseph Nye's influential concept of soft power, the *al-Qaeda* strategist Abu Bakr Naji described superpower resources as falling into two categories: "almighty military power" and a "deceptive media halo".[569] Writing in *The Administration of Savagery*, Naji argued that the "deceptive media halo" surrounding the United States sought to portray the superpower as a supporter of freedom, justice, and equality but that this was a false front designed to make people submit to the superpower out of "love".[570] He also argued that communist propaganda formerly performed a similar function for the Soviet Union. Naji asserted that a successful campaign against the United States must address American power on three axes — military power, propaganda, and social cohesion — and so exposing the falsehoods of America's "deceptive media halo" should

---

[566] ibid.

[567] Audrey Kurth Cronin, *How Terrorism Ends: Understanding the Decline and Demise of Terrorist Campaigns* (Princeton University Press; 2009), p. 176.

[568] Letter from Ayman Al Zawahiri to Abu Musab al-Zarqawi, released by the United States Office of the Director of National Intelligence, 11 October 2005.

[569] Michae l Ryan, *Decoding Al Qaeda's Strategy: The Deep Battle Against America* (Columbia University Press; 2013), p. 158.

[570] ibid., p. 159.

be a key strategic goal, which when achieved would both undermine American social cohesion at home and the attractiveness of American values overseas.[571]

The close attention Osama bin Laden paid to building legitimacy in core constituencies for *al-Qaeda*'s operations can be clearly seen in the October 2002 letter he addressed to the American people, which laid out in detail *al-Qaeda*'s *casus belli* for striking out at the United States — posted online for anyone to read, it is a message carefully designed to resonate with multiple audiences. Like so many other terrorist actors before him, bin Laden was careful to coach *al-Qaeda*'s actions in defensive terms, unconsciously echoing Émile Henry's powerful courtroom jeremiad of more than a century earlier, he wrote: "You attacked us in Somalia; you supported the Russian atrocities against us in Chechnya, the Indian oppression against us in Kashmir, and the Jewish aggression against us in Lebanon."[572] Although *al-Qaeda* had not intervened directly in the Palestinian–Israeli conflict, bin Laden identified the subjugation of Palestine as one of the principle grievances driving its operations: "The creation and continuation of Israel is one of the greatest crimes, and you are the leaders of its criminals... The blood pouring out of Palestine must be equally avenged."[573] Bin Laden cited the UN sanctions regime imposed on Iraq as another act of Western aggression: "It is a wonder that more than 1.5 million Iraqi children have died as a result of your sanctions, and that you have not shown concern."[574] He also excoriated Western support for authoritarian rulers in the region, the presence of US military bases in the Middle East, and the theft of Muslim oil. Bin Laden was remarkably consistent in his complaints — these were all grievances that also appeared in his 1996 *Declaration of War against the Americans Occupying*

---

[571] ibid., pp. 160–163.

[572] Osama bin Laden, To the Americans, 6 October 2002, in Bruce Lawrence (ed.), *Messages to the World: The Statements of Osama bin Laden* (Verso; 2005), p. 163. Henry had told the court: "You have hanged us in Chicago, decapitated us in Germany, garroted us in Jerez, shot us in Barcelona, guillotined us in Montbrison and Paris, but what you will never destroy is anarchy."

[573] ibid., p. 162.

[574] ibid., p. 164.

*the Land of the Two Holy Places. The Betrayal of Palestine* had been the subject of his first public statement, an open letter to the Chief Mufti of Saudi Arabia Abdul Aziz bin Abdullah bin Baz, published in December 1994.[575]

Another key component of bin Laden's messaging was his argument that the West was not merely targeting *al-Qaeda* but all Muslims, and that the current conflict was merely a continuation of the age-old struggle between Islam and the unfaithful. When President George Bush made a casual reference to "this crusade, this war on terrorism" in a Q&A with the press on the White House lawn five days after the September 11 attacks, bin Laden was quick to exploit the reference. In a statement given to the news channel *Al-Jazeera* on 24 September 2001, bin Laden made reference to the "neo-Crusader-Jewish campaign led by Bush, the biggest Crusader, under the banner of the cross."[576] He returned to the same theme in another statement issued in November 2001: "Bush left no room for doubts or media opinion. He stated clearly that this war is a Crusader war. He said this in front of the whole world so as to emphasize this fact. Those who maintain that this is a war against terrorism, what is this terrorism that they talk about when the people of the *umma* have been slaughtered for decades?"[577] And then again in December 2001: "It has become all too clear that the West in general, with America at its head, carries an unspeakable Crusader hatred for Islam."[578] Bin Laden hoped that by raising the specter of historical incursions into Muslim lands, he would be able to spark a spiritual reawakening and attract volunteers from across the Muslim world to oppose the US intervention in Afghanistan that followed the September 11 attacks. Bin Laden was well aware of the scale of the undertaking he had embarked on and, in seeking to convince his audience that victory was a realistic goal,

---

[575] Osama bin Laden, The Betrayal of Palestine, 29 December 1994, in Bruce Lawrence (ed.), *Messages to the World: The Statements of Osama bin Laden* (Verso; 2005), pp. 3–14.

[576] Osama bin Laden, To Our Brothers in Pakistan, 24 September 2002, in Bruce Lawrence (ed.), *Messages to the World: The Statements of Osama bin Laden* (Verso; 2005), p. 101.

[577] Osama bin Laden, Crusader Wars, 3 November 2001, in Bruce Lawrence (ed.), *Messages to the World: The Statements of Osama bin Laden* (Verso; 2005), p. 135.

[578] Osama bin Laden, Nineteen Students, 26 December 2001, in Bruce Lawrence (ed.), *Messages to the World: The Statements of Osama bin Laden* (Verso; 2005), p. 146.

he took pains to evoke both the Soviet defeat in Afghanistan and the American retreat from Vietnam as evidence that the United States could be successfully engaged and defeated. The investigative journalist Lawrence Wright reported that in the early 1990s bin Laden liked to tell supporters who visited his Soba Farm facility in Sudan that America was weak and cowardly: "Look at Vietnam, look at Lebanon, whenever soldiers start coming home in body bags, Americans panic and retreat. Such a country needs only to be confronted with two or three sharp blows, then it will flee in panic, as it always has ... America lacks conviction. It cannot stand against warriors of faith who do not fear death."[579]

We also know that bin Laden took the concept of branding very seriously. In a letter seized by US Special Forces during the 2011 raid on his compound in Abbottabad, he ruminated on the potential benefits of rebranding *al-Qaeda*. He expressed concern that the name of an entity "carries its message and represents it" and that the name "*al-Qaeda* described a military base with fighters without reference to our broader mission to unify the nation."[580] He felt that over time this had allowed his enemies — and notably President Obama — to effectively make the case that the West is at war with *al-Qaeda* and not with Islam or the Muslim world. In seeking suggestions on possible alternate names from his correspondent, bin Laden commented: "It would help if the name is a method of delivery of our message to reach the sons of the *umma*." He went on to suggest ten possible alternative names he has considered including the *Al-Aqsa* Liberation Group, the Restoration of the Caliphate Group, and the Muslim Unity Group.

Bin Laden also sought to address criticism of *al-Qaeda*'s attacks on civilian targets by offering a justification for the organization's actions grounded in the democratic character of Western life: "The American people are the ones who chose their government by way of their own free will ... The American people are the ones who pay the taxes which fund the planes that bomb us in Afghanistan, the

---

[579] Lawrence Wright, *The Looming Tower: Al Qaeda and the Road to 9/11* (Knopf; 2006), p. 187.
[580] SOCOM-2012-0000009-HT, *The Osama bin Laden Files: Letters and Documents Discovered by SEAL Team Six During Their Raid on bin Laden's Compound* (Skyhorse Publishing; 2012), p. 65.

tanks that strike and destroy our homes in Palestine, the armies which occupy our lands in the Arabian Gulf, and the fleets which ensure the blockade of Iraq ... This is why the American people cannot be innocent of all the crimes committed by the Americans and Jews against us."[581] Such reasoning is not uncommon — in September 1970, a PFLP spokesman justified the embrace of international terrorism by the group in a statement reprinted in *The Times*: "In today's world nobody is 'innocent', nobody 'neutral'. A man is either oppressed or he is with the oppressors. He who takes no interest in politics gives his blessing to the prevailing order, that of the ruling classes and exploiting forces."[582] Gerasimos Tsakalos, a member of the modern Greek anarchist group *Synomosía Pyrínon Tis Fotiás,* similarly argued that the civilian population deserved to be targeted every bit as much as the politicians governing Greece: "Who votes them in? Who respects them by bowing their heads? Who admires them and wants to be like them? Who keeps quiet in front of the gross injustices they commit? The answer is easy: Society. Society selected them in the first place and it gave them power to take decisions on its behalf. And if we were to accept that everyone is entitled to a mistake, making the same mistake over and over again, seems to me deliberate."[583]

Finally, bin Laden consistently sought to repudiate other Western values beyond democracy in his public statements, calling on America to abandon its "lies, immorality and debauchery" and to embrace Islam.[584] As early as his August 1996 *Declaration of War against the Americans Occupying the Land of the Two Holy Places,* bin Laden rejected international human rights law as a meaningless Western construct: "All false claims and propaganda about 'human rights' were hammered down and exposed by the

---

[581] Osama bin Laden, To the Americans, 6 October 2002, in Bruce Lawrence (ed.), *Messages to the World: The Statements of Osama bin Laden* (Verso; 2005), p. 165.

[582] Yezid Sayigh, *Armed Struggle and the Search for State, the Palestinian National Movement 1949–1993* (Oxford University Press; 1997), p. 214.

[583] George Kassimeris, *Inside Greek Terrorism* (Oxford University Press; 2013), p. 107.

[584] Osama bin Laden, To the Americans, 6 October 2002, in Bruce Lawrence (ed.), *Messages to the World: The Statements of Osama bin Laden* (Verso; 2005), p. 166.

massacres that took place against the Muslims in every part of the world."[585] In his 2002 *Letter To The Americans*, he returned to this theme, "let us not forget one of your major characteristics: your duality in both manners and values; your hypocrisy in manners and principles. All manners, principles, and values have two scales: one for you and one for everybody else ... You have claimed to be the vanguards of human rights, and your Ministry of Foreign Affairs issues annual reports containing statistics of those countries that violate any human rights. However, all these things vanished when the *Mujahedin* hit you, and you then implemented the methods of the same documented governments that you used to curse. In America, you captured thousands of Muslims and Arabs, took them into custody with neither reason, court trial, nor even disclosing their names."[586] This was a consistent theme in *al-Qaeda* propaganda — the US detention facility in Guantanamo Bay, Cuba, was alone mentioned thirty-two times in public statements disseminated by *al-Qaeda* between 2003 and 2010.[587] The American commander of the International Security Assistance Force (ISAF) in Afghanistan, General David Petraeus, ruefully acknowledged the power of bin Laden's critique, observing in an interview in 2010: "Abu Ghraib and other situations like that are non-biodegradable. They don't go away. The enemy continues to beat you with them like a stick."[588]

Bin Laden's deputy Ayman al-Zawahiri similarly attacked Western hypocrisy in his political testament, *Knights Under the Prophet's Banner*. "The West is not only an infidel but also a hypocrite and a liar. The principles that it brags about are exclusive to, and the personal property of, its people alone. They are not to be shared by the peoples

---

[585] Osama bin Laden, *Declaration of War against the Americans Occupying the Land of the Two Holy Places*, August 1996.

[586] Osama bin Laden, To the Americans, 6 October 2002, in Bruce Lawrence (ed.), *Messages to the World: The Statements of Osama bin Laden* (Verso; 2005), pp. 169–170.

[587] James Gordon Meek, Gitmo Fades As "Recruiting Tool for Al Qaeda", *New York Daily News*, 25 January 2010.

[588] Joseph Berger, U.S. Commander Describes Marja Battle as First Salvo in Campaign, *New York Times*, 21 February 2010.

of Islam."[589] In February 2005, al-Zawahiri released an audio address on the subject of freedom in which he contrasted *al-Qaeda*'s aspirations with those of the Western world: "The freedom we want is not the freedom of lowly rascal America ... It is not the freedom of AIDS and the industry of atrocities and same-sex marriage ... It is not the freedom of two-faced principles and the division of the people into looters and looted. It is not the freedom of Hiroshima and Nagasaki ... It is not the freedom trading torture systems, and of supporting the systems used to defeat and suppress others at the hands of America's friends ... It is not the freedom of Guantanamo and Abu Ghraib. It is not the freedom of the bombing of Al Sagadi, with seven-ton bombs and cluster bombs ... Our freedom is the freedom of unity and manners and chastity and fairness and justice."[590]

However, it is important to note that by engaging on this issue both bin Laden and al-Zawahiri also opened up linguistic ground for a conversation about universal rights and abuses with their sympathizers.[591] As the British political scientist Rodney Barker has observed, "legitimacy ... cannot ... be seen as a simple language instrument of those who claim or express it. As a language it provides both opportunities and constraints for those who employ it."[592] In December 2007 when al-Zawahiri ventured into cyberspace to take questions from members of an online militant forum, he was repeatedly questioned about *al-Qaeda*'s indiscriminate use of violence. One participant pointedly asked him: "Excuse me, Mr. Zawahiri, but who is it who is killing with your blessing the innocents in Baghdad, Morocco, and Algeria? Do you consider the killing of women and

---

[589] Ayman Al Zawahiri, Knights Under the Prophet's Banner, Excerpted in Walter Laqueur (ed.), *Voices of Terror* (Sourcebooks; 2004), p. 428.

[590] Laura Mansfield, *Ayman al-Zawahiri, His Own Words: Translation and Analysis of the Writings of Dr. Ayman al-Zawahiri* (TLG Publications; 2006), pp. 240–241.

[591] See Wiktor Osiantynski, Are Human Rights Universal in an Age of Terrorism? in Richard Ashby Wilson (ed.), *Human Rights in the "War on Terror"* (Cambridge University Press; 2005).

[592] Rodney Barker, *Political Legitimacy and the State* (Clarendon Press; 1990), p. 139. See also Richard Barrett, Legitimacy, Credibility and Relevance: The Tools of Terrorists and "Counter-Terrorists", in Alex Schmid and Garry Hindle (eds.), *After the War on Terror: Regional and Multilateral Perspectives* (2009).

children to be *jihad?*"[593] The experiment went so badly for *al-Qaeda* that it has not been repeated. There is plenty of evidence in the literature that terrorists take the opinion of their constituents extremely seriously and modify their behavior to fit within the limits that their constituents place on what they consider to be legitimate opposition to authority.[594] These limits vary from conflict to conflict, and they fluctuate continually within each given conflict in response to events on the ground, but they are always there.

## The centrality of popular support

French military theorists, like Roger Trinquier and David Galula, involved in fighting Ho Chi Minh's communist insurgents in Indochina in the 1950s noted that the writings of Lenin and Mao Tse-tung placed a great deal of emphasis on securing base areas from which to support the revolution and came to the conclusion that this referred primarily not to physical strongholds but to the moral support of the population.[595] Communist guerrillas did not have to control the physical battle space if they could move invisibly through the population surrounded by supporters and exerting social control through the operation of a virtual shadow state. Trinquier summed up this insight in his influential military treatise *La Guerre Moderne*: "We know that the *sine qua non* of modern warfare is the unconditional support of the population."[596] The key theorists of irregular warfare and urban guerrilla combat — Mao, Régius Debray, Che Guevara and Carlos Marighella — all emphasized the centrality of popular support to the effective use of political violence.

---

[593] Peter Bergen and Katherine Tiedemann, The Almanac of Al Qaeda, *Foreign Policy*, May/June 2010. See also http://www.washingtonpost.com/wp-srv/world/OpenMeetingZawahiri_Part1.pdf for a full transcript of al Zawahiri's remarks.

[594] See Richard English, *Terrorism: How to Respond* (Oxford University Press; 2009), p. 115.

[595] Christopher Cradock and M. L. R. Smith, "No Fixed Values" — A Reinterpretation of the Influence of the Theory of the Guerre Révolutionnaire and the Battle of Algiers, *Journal of Cold War Studies*, Vol. 9, No. 4 (Fall 2007), p. 76. See also David Galula, *Counterinsurgency Warfare: Theory and Practice* (Frederick A. Praeger; 2005).

[596] Roger Trinquier, *Modern Warfare: A French View of Counterinsurgency* (Psi Classics of the Counterinsurgency Era; 2006), p. 4.

In *On Guerrilla Warfare,* Mao warned "because guerrilla warfare basically derives from the masses and is supported by them, it can neither exist nor flourish if it separates itself from their sympathies and cooperation."[597] He also cautioned that "vagabonds and vicious people" should not be accepted for service in a guerrilla force for fear that their depravations might alienate the surrounding population.[598] Mao even recommended treating captured enemy soldiers with compassion, albeit with an ulterior political motive: "We further our mission of destroying the enemy by propagandizing his troops, by treating his captured soldiers with consideration, and by caring for those of his wounded who fall into our hands. If we fail in these respects, we strengthen the solidarity of our enemy."[599] Debray echoed Mao's insights and applied them to the situation in Latin America in the 1960s: "The *foco* [the nucleus of resistance], at the beginning, can only survive to the extent to which it obtains the support of the peasantry."[600] In rural guerrilla movements, this was quite literally the case as guerrilla bands depended on being able to obtain food and shelter from those around them. Debray's old comrade Guevara similarly advised in his primer on guerrilla warfare: "The guerrillas cannot forget their function as vanguard of the people — their mandate — and as such they must create the necessary political conditions for the establishment of a revolutionary power based on the masses' support. The peasants' aspirations or demands must be satisfied to the degree and form which circumstances permit so as to bring about the decisive support and solidarity of the whole population."[601]

Carlos Marighella was the only one of the four to focus on operations conducted primarily in the urban environment but the principles he espoused would be immediately recognizable to his peers: "One of the permanent concerns of the urban guerrilla is his

---

[597] ibid., p. 44.

[598] ibid., p. 87.

[599] ibid., p. 93.

[600] Régius Debray, Latin America: The Long March, *New Left Review,* No. 33 (September–October 1965), p. 48.

[601] Ernesto "Che" Guevara, Guerrilla Warfare: A Method, *Guerrilla Warfare* (Souvenir Press; 2003), p. 155.

identification with popular causes to win public support. Where government actions become inept and corrupt, the urban guerrilla should not hesitate to step in to show that he opposes the government and to gain mass sympathy."[602] Marighella expanded on the point: "The urban guerrilla's arms are inferior to the enemy's, but from a moral point of view, the urban guerrilla has an undeniable superiority. This moral superiority is what sustains the urban guerrilla."[603] He observed that the logic of polarization ensured that, as popular support increased for the urban guerrillas, there would inevitably be a commensurate decline in support for the government forces, noting "as soon as a reasonable portion of the population begins to take seriously the actions of the urban guerrilla, his success is guaranteed."[604] Marighella demonstrated a particularly sophisticated understanding of public relations, writing that urban guerrillas should exploit by every possible means "the mistakes and the failures of the government and its representatives, forcing them into demoralizing explanations and justifications."[605] He also suggested making use of civil society organizations to put pressure on authoritarian rulers by "presenting denunciations to foreign embassies, the United Nations, the papal nunciature [sic], and the international judicial commissions defending human rights or freedom of the press, exposing each concrete violation and use of violence by the military dictatorship."[606]

There is plenty of documentary and anecdotal evidence that the leaders of armed groups have long understood the importance of not alienating potential supporters either through their actions or their public statements. As Louise Richardson has noted, "terrorism, to survive and thrive, needs a complicit society, a societal surround sympathetic to its aspirations."[607] The loyalty of their constituents is

---

[602] Carlos Marighella, *Minimanual of the Urban Guerrilla* (Havana; Tricontinental 1970).
[603] ibid.
[604] ibid.
[605] ibid.
[606] ibid.
[607] Louise Richardson, *What Terrorists Want: Understanding the Enemy, Containing the Threat* (Random House; 2006), p. 69. See also Leonard Weinberg, The Red Brigades, in Robert Art and Louise Richardson (eds.), *Democracy and Counterterrorism: Lessons from the Past* (United States Institute of Peace; 2007), pp. 41–42.

an important guarantor of terrorists' physical safety, their operational capabilities, and even their long-term viability.[608] Terrorist groups therefore typically monitor constituents' reaction to their activities and recalibrate their behavior when it appears that they are out of step with their base.

EOKA's General Grivas laid out his military strategy in a *Preparatory General Plan* drawn up two years before the start of the conflict in Cyprus. He did not aim to inflict "a total material defeat" on British forces, instead he hoped to achieve a "moral" victory that would bring pressure on Great Britain through the United Nations to acquiesce to Greek Cypriot demands. He also believed that popular support was the key to sustaining that pressure, writing later: "Who wins over the people, has won half the battle... Throughout the struggle I never ceased for a single moment to strive to hold the people's moral support."[609] EOKA's sensitivity to maintaining the moral high ground extended to its potential international supporters, when EOKA operatives threw a bomb into a Nicosia restaurant accidentally killing the US Vice-Consul and undercover CIA officer William Boteler in June 1956, Grivas immediately issued an apology: "We state categorically that it was a tragic mistake. No Greek bears hatred for the American people, whose liberal feelings must, we feel sure, place the majority of them on our side in the righteous struggle."[610]

The post-war IRA learnt also this lesson well, advising its volunteers: "Co-operation of the people is also vital to the guerrillas. Because it has to be stressed that support for the aims of the guerrillas must come from the population. Cut loose from the people, a guerrilla formation can neither develop nor survive ... Successful guerrilla operations involve the people. It is the quality of their resistance to the enemy and support for the guerrillas which in the end

---

[608] See Richard English, *Terrorism: How to Respond* (Oxford University Press; 2009), p. 115.

[609] General Grivas, *Guerrilla Warfare and Eoka's Struggle* (Longmans, Green and Co. Ltd; 1964), p. 12.

[610] George Grivas-Dighenis and Charles Foley, *The Memoirs of General Grivas* (Longmans; 1964), p. 72.

will be the decisive factor."[611] Like most of its peers, the IRA of this period placed great emphasis on the importance of effective information operations, noting in the handbook it distributed to volunteers: "The guerrilla education campaign must be continuous, must beat the enemy at his propaganda game and must expose his lies to the people and indeed to the whole world. This end of the guerrilla operations is no less important than the destruction of enemy resources and bases."[612] However, during the cross-border campaign in the 1950s and 1960s, the IRA never succeeded in putting this strategy into action and failed to ignite much nationalist excitement around its efforts, with the result that the offensive soon petered out. When in February 1962 the IRA's Army Council bowed to the inevitable and gave the now traditional instruction to its active volunteers to stand down and dump arms, an IRA statement published in the Irish News tacitly acknowledged this shortcoming by blaming the failure of the campaign on "the attitude of the general public whose minds had been deliberately distracted from the supreme issue facing the Irish people — the unity and freedom of Ireland."[613]

The Society of the Muslim Brothers explicitly set out to build sympathetic community support by marrying its political program to charitable works such as free clinics, schools, and other social services.[614] Hasan Al-Banna wrote in his memoirs: "The Islamic call is like a hospital where patients come for treatment. Never close the door in their face. If you can attract them by any means, do it!"[615] The FLN also developed parallel institutions aimed at displacing the French administration in Algeria — trade unions

---

[611] *Handbook for Volunteers of the Irish Republican Army: Notes on Guerrilla Warfare*, 1956 Edition (Paladin Press; 1985), p. 12 and p. 17.

[612] ibid., p. 18.

[613] Ian Wood, The IRA's Border Campaign 1956–1962, in Malcolm Anderson and Eberhard Bort (eds.), *The Irish Border: History, Politics, Culture* (Liverpool University Press; 1999), p. 122 and Richard English, *Armed Struggle: The History of the IRA* (Oxford University Press, 2003), p. 75.

[614] Richard P. Mitchell, *The Society of the Muslim Brothers* (Oxford University Press; 1969), p. 9 and p. 291.

[615] Brynjar Lia, *The Society of the Muslim Brothers in Egypt: The Rise of an Islamic Mass Movement 1928–1942* (Ithaca Press; 1998), p. 108.

and committees devoted to the local provision of judicial, financial, and health services.[616] Franz Fanon himself served the FLN in this capacity as a medical doctor, offering medical and psychiatric support to FLN cadres. This is a model adopted today by many Islamist groups such as *Hezbollah* and *Hamas*. Service provision creates its own dynamic strengthening bonds between armed groups and their constituents, but creates obligations also. As *Hezbollah* spokesman Ghassan Darwish noted to reporters in 2006: "*Hezbollah* is not just about rockets and fighting, otherwise people would have left us long ago."[617] *Hezbollah*'s Naim Qassem elaborated further: "Social work serves to enrich supporters' confidence in the viability of the Party's causes and course, as it cooperates, collaborates and joins forces to remain strong and tenacious in its political and resistance roles."[618] The practice has also spread to secular terrorist groups. The Naxalites, a Maoist terrorist group active in southern and eastern India, has sought to create a so-called Compact Revolutionary Zone where they provide public services, such as roads, schools, and clinics, to the local population.[619]

Raúl Sendic, the founding father of the *Tupamaros* movement, emphasized how the group sought to orientate its revolutionary activities by carefully monitoring the national mood: "We tried to act in consideration of the Uruguayan mentality, keeping violence to a minimum. It was then that we conducted those actions that were celebrated internationally due to the imagination we applied to avoid violence … At a later moment we escalated our violence. We called it the Guatemalization of the guerrilla, and it was exactly what we had

---

[616] Christopher Cradock and M. L. R. Smith, "No Fixed Values" — A Reinterpretation of the Influence of the Theory of the Guerre Révolutionnaire and the Battle of Algiers, *Journal of Cold War Studies*, Vol. 9, No. 4 (Fall 2007), p. 81.

[617] Jerrold M. Post, *The Mind of the Terrorist: The Psychology of Terrorism from the IRA to Al Qaeda* (Palgrave MacMillan; 2007), p. 173.

[618] Naim Qassem, *Hizbullah: The Story from Within* (Saqi; 2007), p. 165.

[619] Naureen Chowdhury Fink and Rafia Barakat, *Strengthening Community Resilience Against Violence and Extremism: The Roles of Women in South Asia*, Center on Global Counterterrorism Cooperation (2013), p. 10. See also Rajat Kumar Kujur, From CRZ to SEZ: Naxal Reins of Terror, Institute of Peace and Conflict Studies, No. 2271, 21 April 2007.

originally tried to avoid."[620] The increased use of violence by the *Tupamaros* — and in particular the deliberate cold-blooded murder of Pascasio Báez an innocent ranch-hand, husband and father who had the misfortune to stumble across a rural *Tupa tatucera* or hideout — badly tarnished the image of the group that Time Magazine had once dubbed *The Robin Hood Guerrillas* and rallied support behind the government.[621] Reflecting decades later on the fatal missteps made by the organization, the former *Tupamaros* leader Eleuterio Fernández Huidobro, who completed his political journey as a democratically-elected Senator and in 2010 became Uruguay's Minister of National Defense, commented wistfully: "Power does not lie where we thought it did in the 1960s — in the barracks, in guns. It lies in the heart and conscience of the people."[622]

In a letter he addressed to the media in 1972, Andreas Baader took time to explain the intent behind his comrades' recent operations, and the goals he expressed are similarly illuminating: "The RAF's current activities are directed towards the formation of politico-military cadre, acquiring better arms and training for revolutionaries, and the anchoring of the group in a sympathetic scene that is ready to support armed resistance."[623] In the event, the RAF singularly failed to develop this sympathetic scene beyond an inner core of "legal" supporters. Michael Baumann of *Bewegung 2. Juni* blamed this failure on the secretive demands of a clandestine lifestyle: "Because you're illegal, you can't keep your contact with the people at the base. You no longer take part directly in any further development of the whole scene ... Consequently, the group becomes increasingly closed. The greater the pressure from outside, the more you stick together, the more mistakes you make, the more pressure is turned inward."[624] Baumann argued that one consequence of this

---

[620] Pablo Brum, *The Robin Hood Guerrillas: The Epic Journey of Uruguay's Tupamaros* (CreateSpace; 2014), p. 341.

[621] ibid., p. 280, and Uruguay: The Robin Hood Guerrillas, *Time Magazine*, 16 May 1969.

[622] Pablo Brum, *The Robin Hood Guerrillas: The Epic Journey of Uruguay's Tupamaros* (CreateSpace; 2014), p. 344.

[623] J. Smith and André Moncourt, *The Red Army Faction A Documentary History: Volume 1 — Projectiles for the People* (PM Press; 2009), p. 120.

[624] Michael Baumann, *Terror or Love?* (Grove Press; 1977), p. 108.

isolation was that his comrades in the RAF failed to explain their actions effectively to the wider population and ended up alienating vital supporters: "[The RAF] threw bombs suddenly, not against a specific target, but against God and the world — police, Americans, judges, Springer. In the process, of course, they made large mistakes, and blew up workers at Springer. And that's when the real turnabout happened, a total falling away, people really started to withhold their support."[625] In its final communiqué, the RAF also acknowledged that it had failed to sufficiently engage with the issues that were of most concern to its potential constituents, while focusing instead on the Palestinian conflict with Israel, and the confrontation between NATO and the Soviet Union. The communiqué noted: "The social revolutionary outlook disappeared from the theory and praxis of the RAF. The orientation became reduced to the anti-imperialist line, and the result of this was the anti-imperialist front. The RAF was not a factor in social questions. This was a fundamental mistake."[626]

A communiqué issued by the California-based Symbionese Liberation Army (SLA) after six of its members, including the group's leader Donald DeFreeze, were killed in a shoot-out with the Los Angeles Police Department in May 1974, similarly acknowledged that the group had failed to sufficiently engage the public: "We have learned from our criticism … And will work harder to have our actions understood. The assault on the people's enemy is a difficult objective to make clear to all at once. And no military can exist without the people's need."[627] The SLA was a short-lived leftist group that had announced its arrival on the American political scene with the murder of the superintendent of the Oakland public school system, Dr. Marcus Foster, in November 1973, and attracted national notoriety by kidnapping, and then coopting into its ranks, the newspaper heiress Patty Hearst in February 1974. The group never really succeeded in articulating a coherent political message.

---

[625] ibid., p. 110.

[626] The Urban Guerrilla Is History, *The Final Communiqué From The Red Army Faction*, 1 March 1998 at http://germanGuerrilla.com/1998/03/01/the-urban-guerrilla-is-history/.

[627] Communiqué II, Acting Secretary of the General Staff of Region II, Symbionese Liberation Army, May 1974.

November 17 showed rather more operational sensitivity to the good opinion of its core constituents than the leaders of the SLA or the RAF. November 17's Chief of Operations, Dimitris Koufodinas, testified in court that the organization's actions were designed to have a delegitimizing impact on the Greek government without having any repercussions for the group's working class base of support.[628] Targeting decisions were, he said, "inextricably linked to the wide popular masses and their everyday problems and therefore strikes were directed against targets like the tax system of the swindler state or against the regime of public hospital doctors whose lack of ethos and humanity forced patients into bug doctors and private clinics spending huge sums."[629] Greek terror groups also demonstrated a solid appreciation for the importance of legitimizing narratives, with November 17 recruit Sotiris Kondylis observing: "Guns need hands but they also need ideas. If the ideas are not there, the guns won't work."[630] And in an eleven-page statement entitled *We Respond to Bullets with Bullets*, released after Greek police shot dead 15-year-old Alexandros Grigoropoulos in December 2008, *Epanastatikos Agonas* adopted an efficacy-based narrative to explain the rationale behind its decision to target police officers in retaliatory actions: "If a few fighters managed in the most policed area of Athens to come face-to-face with the regime's guards and humiliated them operationally, then we can imagine what could be achieved by a mass armed revolutionary movement."[631]

In August 1982, the French terrorist group *Action Directe* mounted a combined operation with the Lebanese Armed Revolutionary Factions (LARF) to place a bomb under a car belonging to Roderick Grant, a Commercial Attaché at the US Embassy in Paris. When the bomb was discovered prematurely, *Action Directe* immediately claimed responsibility for its role in the attack. However, when the device subsequently detonated killing one member of the Paris bomb

---

[628] Helena Smith, Leaders of Greek Terrorist Group Jailed for Life, *The Guardian*, 17 December 2003.

[629] George Kassimeris, *Inside Greek Terrorism* (Oxford University Press; 2013), p. 29.

[630] ibid., p. 56.

[631] ibid., p. 85.

squad and maiming another, *Action Directe*, likely mindful of the negative publicity that might result, immediately contacted the authorities to retract its statement of involvement.[632] Similarly, when a bomb planted outside the Federation of Belgian Enterprises on 1 May 1985, by the *Cellules Communistes Combattantes* exploded killing two firemen sent to the scene, and wounding 13 others, the Belgian group issued a communiqué expressing deep regret for the loss of the firemen's lives and seeking to fix the blame unconvincingly on the Brussels Gendarmerie: "The deaths of these two men shock us deeply and arouse our rage at those responsible ... The deaths of these public servants has destroyed and obviated the power of our initiative [and] has concealed the correctness of the attack ... The police campaign which is being carried out in the media concerning our so-called 'contempt for human life' is a despicable falsification of our political texts."[633]

In his memoir *Killing Rage*, former Provisional IRA enforcer Eamon Collins explained the constraints he and his associates operated under in Northern Ireland as they planned their operations: "The IRA ... tried to act in a way that would avoid severe censure from within the nationalist community; they knew they were operating within a sophisticated set of informal restrictions on their behavior, no less powerful for being largely unspoken."[634] Provisional IRA volunteer Maria McGuire described experiencing these informal restrictions when she met with worried nationalist sympathizers following an attack in August 1971 on an Electricity Board office in South Belfast which had resulted in the death of one of the staff members and the injury many others: "It seemed a clear enough warning that civilian casualties would cost us support."[635] Collins further noted that PIRA typically "sought to avoid any operations which had obviously

[632] Bonnie Cordes, When Terrorists do the Talking: Reflections on Terrorist Literature, *The Rand Corporation*, August 1987, p. 24. See also Carolyn Lesh, *Paris Bomb Attack Directed Against U.S. Embassy Official* (Associated Press; 1982).

[633] ibid., p. 25–26.

[634] Eamon Collins, *Killing Rage* (Granta; 1998), p. 295.

[635] Maria McGuire, *To Take Arms: A Year in the Provisional IRA* (Macmillan; 1973), p. 35.

sectarian overtones — a policeman could be justified as a legitimate target, his non-combatant Protestant family could not."[636]

Writing in the nationalist newspaper *An Phoblacht* under the byline "Brownie" in 1982, Gerry Adams also emphasized to his fellow republicans the importance of winning support from the wider nationalist community: "While it may be possible to struggle on without mass support, to be successful we must strive towards mobilizing the maximum amount of people and enlisting their support, in a structured manner based on their needs and geared towards republican people's objectives. We cannot gain the republic without the people. We cannot do it on our own."[637] Adams returned to the theme as President of *Sinn Féin* in 1984, publicly warning his supporters in the Provisional IRA that "there are varying degrees of tolerance within the nationalist electorate for aspects of the armed struggle."[638] In his book, *The Politics of Irish Freedom*, Adams elaborated still further: "IRA members do not go to people who provide support without being receptive to their thoughts. They do not constantly ask people to do things for them without being responsive to their needs, being careful about how they deal with them, and taking on board some of the criticisms they might have of aspects of the armed struggle. Not only is that receptiveness and responsiveness correct in political terms, it is also a practical necessity in everyday circumstances."[639]

On 8 November 1987, the Provisional IRA planted a 40 lb bomb near a war memorial in the Northern Irish town of Enniskillen timed to detonate during a Remembrance Day ceremony at the site. The resulting explosion killed ten civilians and a police officer, and injured sixty-three others. A twelfth victim died after thirteen years

---

[636] Eamon Collins, *Killing Rage* (Granta; 1998), p. 295. In January 1999 Collins became the most high-profile Republican to be killed by former colleagues when he was stabbed to death in his hometown of Dorans Hill, Newry. Despite death threats, Collins had chosen not to spend his life on the run. He had renounced violence, turned informer and written a memoir detailing the violence of the Provisional IRA. His colleagues were not forgiving.

[637] M. L. R. Smith, *Fighting for Ireland: The Military Strategy of the Irish Republican Movement* (Routledge; 1997), p. 163.

[638] Rogelio Alonso, *The IRA and the Armed Struggle* (Routledge; 2007), p. 149.

[639] Gerry Adams, *The Politics of Irish Freedom* (Brandon Book Publishers; 1986), p. 63.

in a coma. The Enniskillen bombing did profound damage to the Provisional IRA's reputation both within its own community and in the wider world at large, leading the organization to publicly admit that the attack had been a mistake. *An Phoblacht* described the bombing as a "monumental error" that would strengthen the Provisional IRA's opponents.[640] The fallout did significant electoral damage to PIRA's political wing, *Sinn Féin*, whose overall share of the Northern Ireland vote fell 2.2% (from 13.6% to 11.4%) in the 1987 General Election.[641] In January 1989, the Provisional IRA actually disbanded the West Fermanagh Brigade, which had been responsible for the Enniskillen attack, after it murdered a former police officer who had retired to Donegal, south of the border.[642] Later the same month, Gerry Adams told the annual party conference of *Sinn Féin*: "IRA mistakes are welcomed by the British state [as] it seeks to demoralize and confuse the wider nationalist support base."[643] A spokesman for the Real IRA, the splinter group that opposes the Northern Ireland Peace Process the Provisional IRA supports, acknowledged a similar sentiment in a rare media interview: "Targets aren't chosen always on legitimacy but on whether hitting them would be politically expedient or counter-productive, and on the likely effect on public support. The IRA never attacked the British Army in Scotland because of its support base there and what was seen as solidarity with a fellow Celtic nation."[644]

Islamist terrorist organizations operate within the same restrictions as their secular peers. On 17 November 1997, *al-Gama'a al-Islamiyya* attacked the Temple of Queen Hatshepsut in Luxor murdering fifty-eight tourists and four local Egyptians. The majority of the victims were from Switzerland and Japan, a number of bodies were mutilated, and the youngest victim was a five-year-old

---

[640] Howell Raines, Terrorism; With latest Bomb, I.R.A. Injures Its Own Cause, *The New York Times*, 15 November 1987.

[641] John Newsinger, *British Counter-insurgency from Palestine to Northern Ireland* (Palgrave; 2002), p. 190.

[642] Harry Patterson, *The Politics of Illusion: A Political History of the IRA* (Serif, London; 1997), p. 211.

[643] ibid., p. 212.

[644] Suzanne Breen, War Back On — Real IRA, *Sunday Tribune*, 3 February 2008 at http://www.nuzhound.com/articles/Sunday_Tribune/arts2008/feb3_RIRA_interview__SBreen.php.

British child. The group immediately issued a communiqué taking responsibility for the attack but the public backlash — driven partly by its extreme brutality and partly by the threat it posed to tourism as the lifeblood of the Egyptian economy — was so vociferous that three days later the group issued a second communiqué claiming that it would never deliberately attack foreigners and blaming the government for the incident.[645] Further communiqués followed stating that the group would not target tourists or the tourism trade. While these public statements stopped short of an apology, they amounted to a clear admission that the group had lost touch with its base and was actively seeking realignment.

The fact that the vast majority of those killed by *al-Qaeda* and its affiliate groups have been Muslims has not been lost on many observers in the Islamic world, and *al-Qaeda*'s support has diminished significantly over time as a result.[646] In one of the documents recovered during the Abbottabad raid, Osama bin Laden noted the negative impact that the indiscriminate use of violence by his followers had had on *al-Qaeda*'s relations with the local population in the Iraqi province of Anbar: "The killing of a greater number of tribesmen often boosts tribes' vengeful attitudes. The *Mujahedin*, hence, must be extremely careful about initiating operations to which they know little about the consequences."[647] In 2010, bin Laden also sent a message via an associate, Shaykh Mahmud, addressed to "the brothers in Somalia" urging them to be more "compassionate" and take greater care to reduce casualties among local residents when attacking African Union Mission to Somalia (AMISOM) forces deployed as peacekeepers in the country. Bin Laden instructed his correspondent: "Please talk to the Somali brothers about reducing the harm to Muslims at

---

[645] David Cook, *Understanding Jihad* (University of California Press; 2015), p. 133.

[646] The favorable ratings enjoyed by Al Qaeda leader Osama bin Laden fell by half in the two most populous Islamic countries, Indonesia and Pakistan, between 2002 and 2009. See Peter Bergen and Katherine Tiedemann, The Almanac of Al Qaeda, *Foreign Policy*, May/June 2010.

[647] SOCOM-2012-0000017-HT, *The Osama bin Laden Files: Letters and Documents Discovered by SEAL Team Six During Their Raid on bin Laden's Compound* (Skyhorse Publishing; 2012), p. 136.

Bakarah Market [in Mogadishu] as result of attacking the head-quarters of the African forces."[648]

Ayman al-Zawahiri, has demonstrated a similarly nuanced view of the use of violence, writing in *Knights under the Prophet's Banner* that "we must not leave any space available without filling it; we must gain the peoples' trust, love, and respect. The people will not love us unless they feel our love for them, our concern, and our [willingness] to defend them."[649] He added that the jihadist movement "must take every precaution to avoid separating itself from its community." This was no mere sophistry, in his intercepted July 2005 communication with the then leader of *al-Qaeda* in Iraq, Abu Mus'ab al-Zarqawi, al-Zawahiri cautioned the Jordanian to scale back the viciousness of his attacks on civilian targets: "The strongest weapon which the *Mujahedin* enjoy — after the help and granting of success by God — is popular support from the Muslim masses in Iraq, and the surrounding Muslim countries ... Therefore, the *Mujahed* movement must avoid any action that masses do not understand or approve."[650]

In his 2004 work *The Administration of Savagery*, al-Qaeda strategist Abu Bakr Naji made a similar point about the failure of *al-Gama'a al-Islamiyya* to explain the logic and necessity behind its attacks on the Egyptian tourist industry in the 1990s, including that on Luxor.[651] He noted that, as a result, the Egyptian government was easily able to paint the attacks as impacting ordinary hardworking Egyptians most of all thus undermining support for the group. Abu Mus'ab al-Suri also stressed the importance of gaining and retaining the support of the wider Muslim community.[652] In *A Practical Course for Guerrilla War*, Abd al-Aziz al-Muqrin offered *al-Qaeda*

---

[648] Elias Groll and David Francis, Osama bin Laden Would Not Have Taken Ramadi, *Foreign Policy*, 20 May 2015 and Letter dated 07 August 2010, Office of the Director of National Intelligence at http://www.dni.gov/files/documents/ubl/english/Letter%20dtd%2007%20August%202010.pdf [viewed on 24 May 2015].

[649] Michael Ryan, *Decoding Al Qaeda's Strategy: The Deep Battle Against America* (Columbia University Press; 2013), p. 67.

[650] Intercepted letter from Ayman al-Zawahiri to Abu Mus'ab al-Zarqawi, July 2005.

[651] Jarret Brachman and William McCants, Stealing Al Qaeda's Playbook, *Studies in Conflict and Terrorism*, Vol. 29, No. 4 (June 2006).

[652] ibid.

recruits the "important observation" that fighters should not target "the agents of the Crusaders", by which he meant the local Saudi security forces, but only the "Jews and Crusaders" themselves, for fear of alienating the local population.[653]

Al-Muqrin emphasized the critical importance that securing and retaining local support would play in *al-Qaeda* in the Arabian Peninsula's eventual success, but in the event he ignored his own advice carrying out a series of attacks inside the Kingdom that claimed Saudi lives and turned the Saudi public against AQAP. However, the Yemeni branch of AQAP seemed to have learned this lesson rather better. On 5 December 2013, AQAP mounted an attack on a military hospital in Sana'a that left fifty-two people dead, including medical personnel from Germany, India, the Philippines and Vietnam. CCTV footage of an AQAP gunman walking through hospital wards tossing grenades and gunning down unarmed staff and patients outraged the local population. Indeed, the backlash was so damaging to AQAP in Yemen that the group's military leader Qassim al-Raimi posted a video on Islamist websites in which he apologized for the attack stating: "Now we acknowledge our mistake and our guilt. We offer our apology and condolences to the victims' families. We accept full responsibility for what happened in the hospital and will pay blood money for the victims' families."[654] Al-Raimi added that the group had given strict instructions to the assault team not to attack hospital buildings on the military compound but that one fighter ignored this instruction: "We rid ourselves of what our brother did, we did not order him to do so, and we are not pleased with what he did."[655]

Max Abrahms and Philip Potter have offered further contemporary examples of this phenomenon: The *Taliban* leader Mullah Mohammad Omar reportedly admonished his fighters not to attack

---

[653] Michael Ryan, *Decoding Al Qaeda's Strategy: The Deep Battle Against America* (Columbia University Press; 2013), p. 144.

[654] Associated Press, *Al-Qaeda Branch in Yemen Regrets Hospital Attack*, 22 December 2013 at www.nytimes.com/2013/12/23/world/middleeast/al-qaeda-branch-in-yemen-apologizes-for-attack-on-hospital-at-defense-ministry.html?_r=0.

[655] ibid.

the Afghan population indiscriminately but rather to focus their fire on "foreign invaders, their advisors, their contractors and members of all associated military, intelligence and auxiliary departments" while protecting "the lives and wealth of ordinary people";[656] Doku Umarov, leader of the *al-Qaeda*-linked Caucasus Emirate, cautioned his followers "to focus their efforts on attacking law enforcement agencies, the military, the security services, state officials" but "to protect the civilian population";[657] Murat Karayilan, who became *de facto* leader of the Kurdistan Workers' Party (PKK) after the capture of Abdullah Öcalan in 1999, instructed his forces to engage "military targets" and "not harm civilians";[658] And Hafiz Muhammad Saeed of the Pakistan militant group *Lashkar-e-Taiba* distanced himself from the November 2008 attacks on civilian targets in Mumbai, ascribing them to "rogue elements within the group".[659] In short, most terrorist groups well understand that their ability to command loyalty and support is intimately tied to the legitimacy with which they can successfully invest their operations.

## Summary

Propaganda by deed is a demonstrably effective mechanism for spreading a message, but unless it is a message that strikes a chord with its audience then that effort is wasted. Ultimately, the appeal of any message is grounded in the perceived legitimacy of the sentiments expressed. Most terrorist organizations have demonstrated a sophisticated understanding over time that unless they can persuade potential followers that their cause is just, and that their actions, as difficult as they may be to embrace, are necessary, they will fail. We will see in Part II how legitimizing narratives can play an important role in recruiting, socializing, and retaining supporters. However, there are some terrorist groups that go too far, who

---

[656] Max Abrahms and Philip Potter, Explaining Terrorism: Leadership Deficits and Militant Group Tactics, *International Organization* (Vol. 69, No. 2 (Spring 2015), pp. 311–342).
[657] ibid.
[658] ibid.
[659] ibid.

lose touch with their base, and whose legitimacy is called into question by the very communities to whom they are hoping to appeal. Sometimes, this leads to a recalibration within the group and a change of strategy, sometimes it leads to the group's extinction. In late 2005, the *al-Qaeda* insider Atiyah Abd al-Rahman wrote to Abu Mus'ab al-Zarqawi in a second attempt by *al-Qaeda* in Iraq's parent organization to rein in its brutal offshoot. Speaking from his own personal experience, Al-Rahman drew an explicit parallel between AQI and the *Groupe Islamique Armé* (GIA) in Algeria, which had ultimately failed to prevail in its struggle with the Algerian state during the 1990s, despite the savagery with which it had fought. He cautioned al-Zarqawi: "They destroyed themselves with their own hands, with their lack of reason, delusions, their ignoring of people, their alienation of them through oppression, deviance, and severity, coupled with a lack of kindness, sympathy, and friendliness. Their enemy did not defeat them, but rather they defeated themselves, were consumed and fell."[660] Al-Zarqawi ignored al-Rahman's warning and in September 2006 thirty tribes in Iraq's Anbar Province — AQI's *Sunni* heartland and safe haven — came together to form the Awakening movement and force AQI out of the region. Al-Rahman's prediction had come true, although al-Zarqawi himself did not live to see it. The Islamic State of Iraq and the Levant (ISIL) has recently traversed a very similar trajectory.

## Conclusion

The Israeli Prime Minister Benjamin Netanyahu, is a former elite *Sayeret Matkal* commando who took part in the successful storming of Sabena Flight 571 after it was hijacked by Black September in May 1972.[661] He was wounded in the course of the action, which saved the lives of all but one of the passengers on board the aircraft. Netanyahu's brother, Yonatan, was killed leading the daring Israeli rescue operation that freed 102 passengers held hostage in Entebbe Airport in

---

[660] https://ctc.usma.edu/wp-content/uploads/2013/10/Atiyahs-Letter-to-Zarqawi-Translation.pdf. Viewed on 5 November 2017.
[661] Now Ben Gurion International Airport.

July 1976. He has a great deal of personal experience of terrorist violence, the sum of which he sought to distil in his 2001 book *Fighting Terrorism*. In one memorable passage, Netanyahu dismissed the "amateur practitioners" of terrorism as being no match for professional soldiers.[662] It is a common observation in military circles and, in a fair fight, Netanyahu is probably right. But this completely misses the point. It's not a fair fight. Terrorists aren't trying to be professional soldiers, they are trying to be professional terrorists, and the evidence suggests most terrorist groups devote a great deal of energy to honing their craft. As one discussion paper produced by Italian leftists in the late 1960s noted: "You can't be a part-time revolutionary, nor is there a short working week for militants."[663] A veteran of the Uruguayan *Tupamaros* movement echoed the same point: "The armed struggle is a technical issue and therefore requires technical knowledge: training, morale and, last of all, practice."[664]

Terrorism has been around as a viable political strategy for more than 150 years, and over this entire period, across diverse temporal and geographic boundaries, this strategy has consisted of six core tactics: asymmetrical warfare, waging a war of attrition, propaganda by deed, charismatic leadership, provoking an overreaction, and establishing legitimacy. These are the basic building blocks of terrorism. To be clear, I am not suggesting that these are the only behavioral characteristics shared by terrorist groups, nor even that they are common to every terrorist campaign without exception, my point is simply that these are the terrorist tactics that are adopted with greatest frequency and consistency, and that an effective counter-terrorism strategy must likely take these tactics into account if it is to have any realistic chance of success. There is nothing secret about any of these tactics, generation after generation of terrorists

---

[662] Benjamin Nethanyahu, *Fighting Terrorism: How Democracies Can Defeat Domestic and International Terrorists* (Farrar, Straus and Giroux; 2001), p. 29.

[663] The paper was written by members of the *Collettivo Politico Metropolitano* (Metropolitan Political Collective), a forerunner of the *Brigate Rosse*. See Alison Jamieson, Entry, Discipline and Exit in the Italian Red Brigades, *Terrorism and Political Violence*, Vol. 2, No. 1 (1990), p. 2.

[664] 30 Questions *to a Tupamaro* in J. Smith and André Moncourt (eds.), *The Red Army Faction A Documentary History: Volume 1 — Projectiles for the People* (PM Press; 2009), p. 360. See also Lawrence Freedman, *Strategy: A History* (Oxford University Press; 2013), p. 122.

have written about them, talked about them, and used them, and yet government after government responds to terrorist threats in a manner that almost seems designed to exacerbate the impact of such tactics — aggressive displays of force, kinetic military action, house-to-house searches, arbitrary detention, collective reprisals, and even torture. And yes, of course, there is double standard at work here. Terrorists get to excoriate the state for tactics and actions that mirror their own behavior. But that's the rub, states — especially liberal, democratic states — are held to a higher standard.

It is also important to note at this juncture that success is a relative concept. Terrorist tactics have proved profoundly successful in prolonging or even widening conflicts, and sometimes they have even forced major policy reversals on governments, as in the case of the 2004 Madrid train bombings which convinced a new Spanish government to withdraw its troops from Coalition Forces in Iraq,[665] and on rarer occasions still they have helped to accumulate sufficient political capital for a group, or at least its political representatives, to be included in government, as in the case of the Provisional IRA and *Sinn Féin*. However, there is a difference between tactical success and strategic success. As scholars such as Walter Laqueur, Martha Crenshaw, Thomas Schelling, and Max Abrahms have all forcefully demonstrated over the past 150 years, terrorist groups have typically failed to achieve their stated end goals and actually win conflicts outright.[666] In fact, while terrorism has proved to be a powerful driver of change, it has rarely produced the change that those behind it were aiming for. Furthermore, terrorism alone has never presented an existential threat to any state — except in the most abstract of terms.

---

[665] William Rose and Rysia Murphy, Does Terrorism Ever Work? The 2004 Madrid Train Bombings, Correspondence, *International Security*, Vol. 32, No. 1 (Summer 2007).

[666] See Walter Laqueur, The Futility of Terrorism, *Harper's Magazine*, March 1976, pp. 99–105; Martha Crenshaw, Theories of Terrorism: Instrumental and Organizational Approaches, *Journal of Strategic Studies*, Vol. 10, No. 4 (1987); Thomas Schelling, What Purposes Can International Terrorism Serve? in R. G. Frey and Christopher Morris (eds.), *Violence, Terrorism, and Justice* (Cambridge University Press; 1991); and Max Abrahms, Does Terrorism Really Work? Evolution in the Conventional Wisdom Since 9/11, *Defence and Peace Economics*, Vol. 22, No. 6 (2011).

One of the central images in Jean Larteguy's seminal novel of French counter-insurgency efforts in Indochina and Algeria, *The Centurions*, is that the French military establishment thinks it is engaged in a game of cards with the *Viet Minh*, while in reality the two protagonists are playing different games with different decks of cards. One of the novel's central characters, the wily young Lieutenant Yves Marindelle, explains to a colleague: "When we make war, we play *belote* with thirty-two cards in the pack. But the *Viet Minh*'s game is bridge, and they have fifty-two cards, twenty more than we do. Those twenty cards short will always prevent us from getting the better of them."[667] The analogy is a powerful one, and one that works equally well to describe the shortcomings of most counter-terrorism campaigns — with the additional irony that where terrorism is concerned both protagonists — terrorists and governments — appear to be wedded to strategies that have little demonstrable track record of ultimate success. The purpose of Part I of this book has been to distil the essence of the terrorist playbook from the vast body of terrorist literature readily available for review. In Part II, we will explore the ever-expanding universe of social science research that seeks to explain the processes by which ordinary men and women turn to violence, and take up arms on behalf of terrorist organizations. If we can establish both the how and the why of terrorist violence, we can then set about establishing with a greater degree of confidence which tools in the public policy tool box available to democratic states are most likely to have a positive — and a negative — impact on terrorist actors, rather than simply reaching for the first blunt instrument to hand.

In a speech delivered in September 2003 at an event sponsored by the Norwegian government and the International Peace Academy entitled *Fighting Terrorism for Humanity — A Conference on the Roots of Evil*, the then Secretary General of the United Nations, Kofi Annan, noted the UN's own recent losses at the hands of *al-Qaeda* in Iraq, but told the assembled delegates, including twenty-two Heads

---

[667]Jean Larteguy, *The Centurions* (Penguin Classics; 2015), p. 188. See also Fred Kaplan, *The Insurgents: David Petraeus and the Plot to Change the American War* (Simon and Schuster; 2013), p. 16.

of State: "While terrorism is an evil with which there can be no compromise, we must use our heads, not our hearts, in deciding our response. The rage we feel at terrorist attacks must not remove our ability to reason. If we are to defeat terrorism, it is our duty, and indeed our interest, to try to understand this deadly phenomenon, and carefully to examine what works, and what does not, in fighting it."[668] Few wiser words addressing the threat of terrorist violence have ever been uttered.

---

[668] Kofi Annan, *Ability to Reason Vital in Fighting Terrorism, Secretary-General Tells Conference*, Press Release SG/SM/8885, 22 September 2003 at http://www.un.org/News/Press/docs/2003/sgsm8885.doc.htm.

# Part II

# Social Science and Violent Extremism

"He was born to a wretched fate.
And was taught in a hard school"[1]

As the Chief Commissioner of the *Bundeskriminalamt* (BKA) between 1971 and 1981, Horst Herold effectively led the West German government's fight against the *Rote Armee Fraktion*. Herold was a thoughtful and successful counter-terrorism practitioner who pioneered the use of computers and big data in the hunt for terrorist suspects. He also devoted a great deal of his time to trying to understand the phenomenon of terrorism, summarizing his insights in a speech delivered during the trial of the founders of the RAF: "The first question is to decide whether terrorism, in its manifestations in Germany or indeed all over the world, is a product of the brains of its perpetrators, of the Baaders and the Meinhofs — of their sick brains, as many would say — or whether terrorism is a reflection of certain social situations in the Western and indeed in the Eastern world, so that its superstructure only mirrors problems which have an objective existence. In so doing, we would have to consider who, in that case, should be primarily engaged in the struggle against terrorism: the police or the

---

[1] Peter Julicher, *Renegades, Rebels and Rogues Under the Tsars* (McFarland and Co.; 2003), p. 192. These lines are taken from the poem "A Student" by the Russian poet Nikolai Ogarev, which was dedicated by the author to his "young friend" Sergei Nechaev.

politicians."[2] The answer to this question has profound public policy implications, and, in the years since, considerable effort has been devoted by practitioners and social scientists alike to identifying the root causes of terrorism and to constructing a working profile of the typical terrorist, efforts that have only redoubled since the September 11 attacks. Yet, despite the considerable effort expended, nothing approaching a professional or scholarly consensus has emerged.

The problem, quite simply, is that terrorists are an eclectic bunch — some are dissolute, others abstemious; some are well-educated, others barely attended school; some start out as healers, others as violent criminals; and some come from lives of great suffering, while others are born with every advantage life can offer. Take, for example, brothers Mohamed Merah and Abdelghani Merah who grew up in the same household in Toulouse, France. Mohamed embraced *al-Qaeda*'s message and murdered seven people, including three Jewish schoolchildren, the oldest only eight-years-old, in a killing spree in 2012. Abdelghani, by contrast, married outside his faith and became a youth worker trying to combat the spread of violent extremism on predominantly Muslim housing estates, assisting the French police in their investigation of Mohamed.[3] As the founder of the CIA's Center for the Analysis of Personality and Political Behavior, psychologist Jerrold Post, concluded after a lifetime spent studying terrorist profiles: "There are nearly as many variants of personality who become involved in terrorist pursuits as there are variants of personality ... Yet, no matter how justified the cause, no matter how repressive the society, there are some who join and some who don't. Not every son of a Basque joins ETA."[4]

This is an important observation. Researcher Bonnie Cordes of the RAND Corporation reached a very similar conclusion after

---

[2] Stefan Aust, *Baader-Meinhof: The Inside Story of the RAF* (Oxford University Press; 2009), p. 138.

[3] Henri Astier, Attack on Nice: My brother the jihadist Mohamed Merah, *BBC News*, 21 July 2016 at http://www.bbc.com/news/world-europe-36838216. Viewed 21 July 2016.

[4] Jerrold Post, Notes on a Psychodynamic Theory of Terrorist Behavior, *Terrorism*, Vol. 7, No. 3 (1984), pp. 242–243.

completing a review of terrorist literature in the 1980s noting that "part of the complexity of terrorism is the fact that it is conducted by a variety of idiosyncratic individuals with widely divergent national and sociocultural backgrounds."[5] More recently, a 2011 review of radicalization studies conducted under the auspices of the Australian Ministry of Defence found that little tangible progress had been made towards a universal theory of radicalization in the intervening years, commenting: "About the only thing that radicalisation experts agree on is that radicalisation is a process. Beyond that there is considerable variation as to make existing research incomparable."[6] In an article written after the 2016 Pulse Nightclub shooting in Florida by self-identified ISIL supporter Omar Mateen, Peter Bergen, a journalist who has spent more than twenty years writing about terrorism, including a recent study of the personal journeys of American ISIL volunteers, reflected: "Why would someone take the lives of innocent civilians who are total strangers? That is a question to which I have long sought an answer. But my search has led me instead to another question: Is an answer even possible?"[7]

To complicate matters still further, terrorists do not merely come from widely divergent backgrounds, they have also taken up arms in the service of a range of diverse and often counterposed causes: authoritarian government and populism, the empowerment of the proletariat and the maintenance of elite privilege, white supremacy and black liberation, and national self-determination and universal brotherhood. As the researcher Aaron Mannes, channeling the Russian novelist Leo Tolstoy, has observed: "Like unhappy families, terrorist groups differ from each other and finding universally applicable rules to understand them may not be realistic."[8] If one examines the personal histories of terrorists and

---

[5] Bonnie Cordes, *When Terrorists do the Talking: Reflections on Terrorist Literature*, The Rand Corporation, August 1987, p. 5.

[6] Minerva Nasser-Eddine, Bridget Garnham, Katerina Agostino and Gilbert Caluya, *Countering Violent Extremism (CVE) Literature Review* (Australian Government, Department of Defence; March 2011), p. 13.

[7] Peter Bergen, Why Do Terrorists Commit Terrorism? *The New York Times*, 14 June 2016.

[8] Aaron Mannes, Testing The Snake Head Strategy: Does Killing or Capturing its Leaders Reduce a Terrorist Group's Activity? *Journal of International Policy Solutions*, Vol. 9 (Spring 2008), p. 44.

aspirant terrorists from across the political spectrum, the only observation that one can make with any real confidence about what drives an individual to embrace terrorist violence is that it is unique and personal to them and is probably reflective in some way of the world around them.

The Italian anarchist Luigi Galleani, whose followers in the United States perpetrated a number of terrorist outrages in the 1910s and 1920s, recognized this essential truth, writing that individual acts of rebellion were driven forward by "the intricate convergence of the causes, which demand [action] at a certain time, in a certain way and not otherwise" and also by the personal experiences of "the instrument called upon to accomplish it".[9] A century later, former *al-Qaeda* member Aimen Dean reached much the same conclusion: "There is no single process of radicalisation. Some people, it took them years to be convinced of coming to the *jihad* and some people it took them minutes. Some people were studying in religious seminaries … and some people basically just came straight out of a night club … [So] you see immediately that you know there isn't one single classical journey there, that there are so many journeys."[10] Reductive academic theories have proved utterly inadequate to explain such a complex phenomenon. Radicalization may indeed be, as Dean suggests, and as most researchers now agree, a process, but it is not an easily predictable one, nor does it necessarily follow a simple linear progression. Trying to establish a universal theory of radicalization is too ambitious a goal, perhaps even an unobtainable one, but that does not mean that social science is devoid of useful insights that can serve to illuminate policy decisions and help counter-terrorist officials avoid courses of action that are only likely to add fuel to the fire.

There does appear to be general agreement among both scholars and practitioners that radicalization is typically driven by a combination of factors, tempered by a widespread acknowledgement that each person responds to these factors differently, making

---

[9] Luigi Galleani, *The End of Anarchism?* (Elephant Editions; 2012), p. 84.

[10] Peter Marshall, The spy who came in from Al-Qaeda, *BBC News Magazine*, 2 March 2015.

it very difficult, if not impossible, to predict who will and will not be radicalized, and which combination of factors will be important. The founder of the German Institute on Radicalization and De-Radicalization Studies, Daniel Koehler, has explained the process he and his colleagues have adopted in their work with both far-right and Islamist extremists: "I try to figure out the individual driving factors, what I call the radicalization recipe. It's a combination of positive and negative aspects. Positive aspects like quest for significance, justice, help, poor, defend, women and children, Syria, delivering humanitarian aid [sic]. So this is a very strong positive urge. The negative aspects — lack of perspective, problems in family, problems in school, and their employment, whatever — they have not felt that they are part of a society. And these positive and negative aspects are bound together by radical ideology."[11] In her groundbreaking 1981 article, *The Causes of Terrorism*, the doyenne of counter-terrorism researchers, Martha Crenshaw, made a similarly useful distinction between the "reasons" — the underlying "preconditions" and more immediate "precipitants" — that give rise to terrorist activity, and the "opportunities" — the "enabling" and "permissive" factors — that allow terrorism to flourish.[12]

In an influential 2011 study, the United States Agency for International Development (USAID) suggested a binary classification system for the drivers of radicalization, which it divided into "Push and Pull factors" — an approach that was also adopted by the *Preventing Violent Extremism Plan of Action* proposed by UN Secretary-General Ban Ki Moon in 2015.[13] The Royal United Services Institute (RUSI) in the United Kingdom expanded USAID's typology to suggest three levels of analysis: structural motivations,

---

[11] All Things Considered, German Program Helps Families De-Radicalize Members Prone To Extremism, *National Public Radio*, 13 March 2015, at http://www.npr.org/2015/03/13/392845800/german-program-helps-families-de-radicalize-members-prone-to-extremism.

[12] Martha Crenshaw, The Causes of Terrorism, *Comparative Politics*, Vol. 13, No. 4 (1981), pp. 381–383.

[13] USAID Policy, *The Development Response to Violent Extremism and Insurgency*, United States Agency for International Development (September 2011).

individual incentives, and enabling factors.[14] In *What Terrorists Want,* the Irish academic Louise Richardson also identified three core factors, which she christened "the lethal triple cocktail of personal disaffection, an enabling society and a legitimizing ideology".[15] Other theories that have attracted particular attention in recent years include Fathali Moghaddam's "staircase to terrorism" which conceptualizes radicalization as a series of narrowing choices,[16] the some what derivative "pyramid model of radicalization" developed by the Association of Chief Police Officers (ACPO) as part of the United Kingdom's Prevent strategy,[17] and Clark McCauley and Sophia Moskalenko's "twelve mechanisms of political radicalization", which posits twelve dimensions of radicalization operating at the individual, group, and societal levels.[18]

As with David Rapoport's four waves of terrorism theory, such typologies, metaphors, and models are useful for providing a framework within which to process tremendous amounts of data and to begin to develop policy responses, but they also all suffer from the inevitable shortcomings and compromises that result from any attempt to impose coherence on a process that is essentially chaotic and inchoate. My purpose in this section is rather more modest. I have identified five core themes in the radicalization literature that I believe have crucial implications for the development of successful counter-terrorism measures. Taken collectively, these themes do not necessarily form a coherent whole, nor are they intended too; they are neither universally applicable nor necessarily mutually reinforcing. They are, however, themes that are echoed over and over again in social science research and

---

[14]James Khalil and Martine Zeuthen, *Countering Violent Extremism and Risk Reduction,* Royal United Services Institute Whitehall Report 2–16, June 2016, p. 9.

[15]Louise Richardson, *What Terrorists Want: Understanding the Enemy, Containing the Threat* (Random House; 2006), p. 70.

[16]Fathali Moghaddam, The Staircase to Terrorism: A Psychological Exploration, *American Psychologist,* Vol. 60, No. 2, February–March 2005.

[17]Kris Christmann, *Preventing Religious Radicalisation and Violent Extremism: A Systematic Review of the Research Evidence,* Youth Justice Board for England and Wales (2012).

[18]Clark McCauley and Sophia Moskalenko, Mechanisms of Political Radicalization: Pathways Toward Terrorism, *Journal of Terrorism and Political Violence,* Vol. 20, No. 3, July 2008.

in the personal narratives of individual terrorists. They are comprised of insights that are understood and exploited by terrorist groups, both in the construction of legitimizing narratives and in their day-to-day operations, and as such, they are tremendously important for counter-terrorism practitioners to understand and take into account as they respond to terrorist threats. Taken collectively, they also support the central contention of this book that human rights-compliant counter-terrorism strategies represent the most effective response to terrorism, in this instance because such strategies do not further fuel many of the social processes that have been well documented to drive terrorist recruitment.

Finally, a word about the term "radicalization" itself, I have used it because it is the term in common usage in the literature, but it is more than a little problematic. "Radical" is not a synonym for "terrorist".[19] In most democracies, taking a radical viewpoint is not, in and of itself unlawful, and international human rights law guarantees freedom of conscience and belief. Indeed, historically, radicalism has been an important motor for positive social change — human rights advocates described as radicals by their contemporaries pushed for the abolition of slavery, for universal and female suffrage, and for an end to racial discrimination.[20] For this reason, international institutions prefer to employ rather more precise terms, focusing on violent extremism in the case of the United Nations or violent extremism and radicalization leading to terrorism in the case of the Organization for Security and Cooperation in Europe (OSCE), to distinguish between radical but lawful activity, and, violent, and consequently unlawful, activism. Many of the processes driving radicalization, however, would essentially appear to apply to individuals

---

[19] See Jamie Bartlett and Carl Miller, The Edge of Violence: Towards Telling the Difference Between Violent and Non-Violent Radicalization, *Terrorism and Political Violence*, Vol. 24, No. 1 (2012).

[20] Office for Democratic Institutions and Human Rights and the OSCE Secretariat Transnational Threats Department, *Preventing Terrorism and Countering Violent Extremism and Radicalization that Lead to Terrorism: A Community Policing Approach* (Organization for Security and Cooperation in Europe; 2014), p. 19.

embarked on both violent and non-violent trajectories. Indeed, to a large extent, the embrace of violent extremism can be said to nest within the larger social phenomenon of radicalization, and so it is not really possible to examine the former without also considering the latter. I will therefore be using both terms in the pages ahead while also bearing this critical distinction in mind, which is so important when it comes to developing potential policy responses to terrorist threats.

## Empathy

It may seem counter-intuitive, but the evidence suggests that a surfeit of empathy can play an important role in radicalizing an individual to the point that he or she is prepared to embrace violence to effect change. In his influential primer, *Inside Terrorism*, Bruce Hoffman suggests that a terrorist is fundamentally an altruist who "believes in serving a 'good' cause designed to achieve a greater good for a wider constituency".[21] As with almost any other categorical statement about terrorism, this is easy enough to falsify — it is not difficult to identify individuals whose involvement in terrorist groups is entirely self-serving, David Kilcullen, for instance, labels such individuals "conflict entrepreneurs"[22] — but there is nevertheless still a great deal of merit in this statement, although perhaps it would be more accurate to say that most terrorists aspire to be seen as altruists. Empathy for those suffering, albeit clearly rather selective empathy, is both a staple of terrorist propaganda and of individual narratives of radicalization. The operations chief of the Greek terrorist group November 17, Dimitris Koufodinas, tried to explain the logic of this perspective to the court during his trial in 2003: "An armed revolutionary ... chooses violence as a direct response through political analyses ... [his] life choices are actually made against his personal interests."[23] He added that a revolutionary

---

[21] Bruce Hoffman, *Inside Terrorism* (Columbia University Press; 2006), p. 43.

[22] David Kilcullen, *Blood Year: The Unraveling of Western Counterterrorism* (Oxford University Press; 2016), p. 28.

[23] George Kassimeris, *Inside Greek Terrorism* (Oxford University Press; 2013), p. 30.

"takes up arms because he cherishes life, not the contrary."[24] For men and women like Koufodinas, terrorism is simply the lesser of two evils. This is a persistent theme in terrorist literature and in the personal biographies of individual terrorists.

Terrorists are often individuals who in other circumstances might be making a positive contribution to their community. While it is certainly true that one finds plenty of petty criminals like Andreas Baader and Abu Mus'ab al-Zarqawi moving in terrorist circles, there are also plenty of more public-minded souls amongst their ranks too, like the journalist Ulrike Meinhof, or the former British National Health Service doctor Issam Abuanza who volunteered his services to ISIL in 2014.[25] Indeed, it is striking that medicine is a professional calling that correlates surprisingly highly with terrorism. For instance, the current *al-Qaeda* leader Ayman al-Zawahiri, *Hamas* co-founder Abdel Aziz al-Rantisi, and Popular Front for the Liberation of Palestine (PFLP) founders George Habash and Wadie Haddad all began their careers as medical doctors. Habash, Haddad, and Rantisi were pediatricians by training, as was the leader of Palestinian Islamic Jihad, Fathi Shaqaqi. The Jewish religious extremist Baruch Goldstein, who killed twenty-nine Muslim worshippers at the Tomb of the Patriarchs in the West Bank town of Hebron in February 1994, was a doctor who had graduated from Albert Einstein College of Medicine in New York City.[26] Pavel Pechenkin, a Russian convert to Islam, who detonated a suicide vest in Volgograd railway station in December 2013 killing seventeen and wounding at least fifty more, had worked for five years as a paramedic in the Kazan emergency services.[27]

---

[24] ibid., p. 34.

[25] Danny Boyle, NHS doctor leaves family in Sheffield to "join Islamic State in Syria", *The Daily Telegraph*, 24 May 2016.

[26] Mark Juergensmeyer, *Terror in the Mind of God: The Global Rise of Religious Violence* (University of California Press; 2003), p. 8.

[27] Interfax-Ukraine, *Suspected perpetrator of Volgograd railway station attack went missing a year ago*, *Kyiv Post*, 2 January 2014, at http://www.kyivpost.com/content/russia-and-former-soviet-union/suspected-perpetrator-of-volgograd-railway-station-attack-went-missing-a-year-ago-334571.html.

Che Guevara was famously radicalized while traveling around Latin America by motorcycle as a young medical student dedicated to finding a treatment to alleviate the affliction of leprosy. As he traveled from Argentina to Chile and on to Peru and Colombia, Che became more and more sensitive to the plight of the rural and urban poor that made up the greater part of the population of the southern cone, and his empathy for their suffering slowly awakened his political consciousness. In an interview recorded in a rebel camp in Cuba's Sierra Maistra in the spring of 1958, Che explained his eventual decision to join Fidel Castro's nascent guerrilla army in the following terms: "The truth is that after the experience of my wanderings across all of Latin America and, to top it off, in Guatemala [where he had personally witnessed the CIA backed ouster of the leftist regime of Jacobo Arbenz] it didn't take much to incite me to join any revolution against a tyrant ... It was time to stop crying and fight."[28] Humam al-Balawi, a Jordanian intelligence asset turned by the *Tehrik-i-Taliban Pakistan* (TTP) who detonated a suicide vest while meeting with CIA personnel on a US base in Khost, Afghanistan, in December 2009 killing nine, worked as a doctor at the United Nations' Center for Motherhood and Children in Marka refugee camp, which was established outside Amman for Palestinian refugees displaced by the 1967 Arab–Israeli War. Even one of the *Aum Shinrikyo* cult members who left sarin nerve gas on the Tokyo subway, killing twelve and incapacitating more than 5,500, the only successfully prosecuted WMD terrorist attack to date, had been a cardiovascular surgeon.[29] One doesn't typically think of doctors as dangerous revolutionaries, but a surprising number have made the transition from healer to killer in the name of a higher cause than medicine.

Equally, there are many examples of individuals from privileged backgrounds turning their backs on their birthright to take up arms on behalf of a marginalized or persecuted out-group. The social scientists Alan Krueger, David Laitin and Jitka Malečková have

---

[28] Jon Lee Anderson, *Che Guevara: A Revolutionary Life* (Grove Press; 1997), p. 309.

[29] Mark Juergensmeyer, *Terror in the Mind of God: The Global Rise of Religious Violence* (University of California Press; 2003), p. 104.

described this phenomenon as the "Robin Hood" model of terrorism.[30] Such individuals appear to be acting out of sympathy for those less fortunate than themselves rather than as a result of direct personal suffering. *Narodnaya Volya* counted many sons and daughters of the Russian elite amongst its members, including women like Vera Figner, Anna Korba, and Sophia Perovskaya.[31] Indeed, Perovskaya was actually the daughter of a former Governor-General of St. Petersburg and the granddaughter of an Interior Minister. She was also the first woman to be hanged in Russia for a political crime. LEHI member Eliahu Hakim, who took part in the murder of the British minister of state in the Middle East, Lord Moyne, in November 1944, was from one of the wealthiest Jewish families in Mandate Palestine.[32]

The founding member of the Italian *Gruppi d'Azione Partigiana*, Giangiacomo Feltrinelli, was one of the richest men in Europe. A convert to revolutionary communism, Feltrinelli's publishing house had translated Marighella's *Minimanual of the Urban Guerrilla* into French and Italian. Feltrinelli killed himself by accident in March 1972, while trying to dynamite a high-tension electricity pylon on the outskirts of Milan.[33] *Prima Linea* founding member Marco Donat-Cattin was the son of senior Christian Democrat politician.[34] Ulrich Wessel, a member of the *Rote Armee Fraktion*

---

[30] Alan Krueger and David Laitin, Kto Kogo? A Cross-Country Study of the Origins and Targets of Terrorism, in Philip Keefer and Norman Loayza (eds.), *Terrorism, Economic Development, and Political Openness* (Cambridge University Press; 2008) p. 149 and Alan Krueger and Jitka Malečková, Education, Poverty, Political Violence, and Terrorism: Is There a Causal Connection? *Journal of Economic Perspectives*, Vol. 17, No. 4 (Fall 2003), p. 137.

[31] See Vera Figner, *Memoirs of a Revolutionist* (Northern Illinois University Press; 1991) and Matthew Carr, *The Infernal Machine* (The New Press; 2007), pp. 21–22. Curiously enough, in addition to all serving on Narodnaya Volya's Executive Committee, Figner, Korba and Perovskaya also all had medical backgrounds to some degree. Figner studied medicine as a student in Zurich, Korba served as a nurse in a Russian field hospital during the Russo-Turkish War, and Perovskaya inoculated peasants against smallpox in the Russian countryside.

[32] Gerrold Frank, *The Deed* (Simon and Schuster; 1963), p. 37.

[33] Claire Sterling, *The Terror Network: The Secret War of International Terrorism* (Holt, Rinehart and Winston; 1981), pp. 25–48.

[34] Jerrold Post, Notes on a Psychodynamic Theory of Terrorist Behavior, *Terrorism*, Vol. 7, No. 3 (1984), p. 246.

commando that seized control of the West German Embassy in Stockholm in April 1975, was the son of a well-known Hamburg millionaire.[35] Wessel was killed when the explosives the commando had deployed around the Embassy suddenly exploded. Two other RAF members killed in separate police shoot-outs, Georg von Rauch and Thomas Weisbecker, were both sons of successful university professors.[36] William Powell, the author of *The Anarchist's Cookbook*, the American counterculture weapons manual frequently referenced by terrorist groups, was the son of a United Nations Press Officer.[37] Aspirant Times Square bomber Faisal Shahzad was the youngest child of a Vice Air Marshal in the Pakistani Air Force.[38] The underwear bomber Umar Farouk Abdulmutallab was the son of a prominent Nigerian banker and had been educated at an English boarding school.[39] Ayman al-Zawahiri's father was a professor of pharmacology at Cairo's Ein Shams University, one grandfather was a former Ambassador, and a great uncle, Abdul Rahman Hassan Azzam, was the founding Secretary-General of the Arab League. And of course, perhaps most famously of all, Osama bin Laden was the son of one of the Middle East's leading construction magnates.[40]

So, why would a doctor dedicated to preserving human life or the scion of a wealthy family turn his or her back on family and professional accomplishment, and take up arms on behalf of those less fortunate than themselves? The Islamist ideologue Sayyid Qutb saw a similarity between the mindset the revolutionary and that of the

---

[35] Stefan Aust, *Baader-Meinhof: The Inside Story of the R.A.F.* (Oxford University Press; 2009), p. 224.

[36] Michael Burleigh, *Blood and Rage: A Cultural History of Terrorism* (Harper; 2009), p. 242.

[37] Richard Sandomir, William Powell, 'Anarchist Cookbook' Writer, Dies at 66, *New York Times*, 29 March 2017. See also William Powell's extended interview with the director Charlie Siskel in the documentary film *American Anarchist* (2017).

[38] Peter Bergen, *United States of Jihad: Investigating America's Homegrown Terrorists* (Crown; 2016), p. 124.

[39] Anna Geifman, *Death Orders: The Vanguard of Modern Terrorism in Revolutionary Russia* (Praeger Security International; 2010), p. 22.

[40] See Steve Coll, *The Bin Ladens: An Arabian Family in the American Century* (The Penguin Press; 2008).

medical practitioner, likening the role of the "Islamist vanguard" to that of a doctor treating a patient, noting: "We often see the patient refuse medicine, shrink away from the doctor and claim to be fit and healthy when medicine and the doctor's treatment are needed most."[41] Che's biographer, Jon Lee Anderson, reached a similar conclusion about his subject, noting: "Like the medical researcher he was on his way to becoming, Ernesto searched for a cause when he saw a symptom. And, having found what he thought was the cause, he searched for its antidote."[42] The American anarchist Emma Goldman argued in *The Psychology of Political Violence* that *attentaters* (a French synonym for terrorist), like her longtime lover Alexander Berkman who tried to assassinate the Operating Manager of Carnegie Steel, Henry Clay Frick, because of the role he had played in violently putting down the labor strike at the Homestead Steel Plant in Pennsylvania, or Russian noblewoman Vera Zazulich who shot and wounded the governor of St. Petersburg, Fyodor Trepov, for ordering the flogging of an incarcerated student she had never met, were "high strung, like a violin string" attuned to the suffering of others and that it was this compassion for those less fortunate than themselves which moved them to take action.[43] All three writers essentially make the same case — that empathy for others can play an important role in the decision to embrace armed struggle.

Certainly, there is no shortage of terrorists who seek to present or explain their actions in an altruistic light. The German deradicalization specialist Daniel Koehler noted that one key commonality he had observed in his work with both neo-Nazi and Islamic extremists was that "they talk a lot about justice. They talk a lot about freedom. They want to change the society into a positive direction. They believe that they're doing something good for

---

[41] John Calvert, *Sayyid Qutb and the Origins of Radical Islamism* (Columbia University Press; 2010), p. 185.

[42] Jon Lee Anderson, *Che Guevara: A Revolutionary Life* (Grove Press; 1997), p. 82.

[43] Emma Goldman, *Anarchism and Other Essays* (Mother Earth Publishing Association; 1911), pp. 113–144. See also Clark McCauley and Sophia Moskalenko, *Friction: How Radicalization Happens to Them and Us* (Oxford University Press; 2011), pp. 21–22.

humanity."[44] Even the most cursory review of terrorist literature and the personal statements of individual terrorists suggests Koehler's experience is not unusual and that the expression of such sentiments can be traced all the way back to the origins of terrorism as a political strategy. If one examines the *Revised and Amended Prescript of Ku Klux Klan*, which was adopted in 1868, one finds within a description of the Klan as "an institution of Chivalry, Humanity, Mercy, and Patriotism" established "to protect the weak, the innocent, and the defenceless" and "relieve and assist the injured, oppressed, suffering, and unfortunate, especially widows and orphans of Confederate soldiers".[45] At its inception, the Klan professed an agenda so high-minded that the historian Allen Trelease commented that it was "hard to imagine a greater parody than this on the Ku Klux Klan as it actually operated."[46]

It was no different on the political left, in his seminal essay *Mord und Freiheit*, Karl Heinzen wrote "the path to humanity leads over the summit of barbarism" and his roadmap was enthusiastically embraced by successive generations of populist and anarchist terrorists.[47] The French anarchist Émile Henry, responsible for the attempted bombing of the offices of the Carmaux Mining Company and the successful bombing of the Café Terminus in Paris, initially took up arms to support coal miners in Carmaux who had gone on strike to protest their working conditions in the autumn of 1892. The mine's owner, Baron René Reille, was able to draw on his reserves of coal to outlast the strikers and force them back to work. Henry had visited the mine out of solidarity during the strike and had witnessed the dire situation of the miners first hand. Henry's father, Fortuné, had been forced into exile in Spain after the suppression of the

---

[44] All Things Considered, *German Program Helps Families De-Radicalize Members Prone To Extremism*, National Public Radio, 13 March 2015, at http://www.npr.org/2015/03/13/392845800/german-program-helps-families-de-radicalize-members-prone-to-extremism.

[45] Allen Trelease, *White Terror: The Ku Klux Klan Conspiracy and Southern Reconstruction* (Louisiana State University Press; 1971), pp. 16–17.

[46] ibid., p. 17.

[47] Karl Heinzen, *Murder and Freedom* (New York; 1853) reproduced in Daniel Bessner and Michael Stauch, Karl Heinzen and the Intellectual Origins of Modern Terror, *Terrorism and Political Violence*, Vol. 22 (2010), p. 163.

Paris Commune and he had found work in a copper mine. He died of mercury poisoning — most likely contracted in the mine — when Émile was only ten-years-old. In such circumstances, it was unsurprising that Henry should empathize so strongly with the miners' plight. As he told the audience at his trial: "To those who say that hate does not give birth to love, I say that it is love, human love, that often engenders hate."[48] Similarly, the anarchist assassin of US President McKinley, Leon Czolgosz, told an associate that he was concerned about the harsh treatment of workers, "things were getting worse and worse — more strikes and they were getting more brutal against the strikers … something must be done."[49]

The generation of Marxist urban guerrillas who terrorized Latin America and European societies in the 1960s and 1970s tended to see their role in very similar terms to their anarchist predecessors. In a 1965 essay entitled *Socialism and the New Man*, Che Guevara wrote: "Let me say, at the risk of appearing ridiculous, that the true revolutionary is guided by strong feelings of love … Our vanguard revolutionaries must idealize their love for the people, for the most scared causes, and make it one and indivisible … Every day we must struggle so that this love of living humanity is transformed into concrete facts, into acts that will serve as an example, as a mobilizing factor."[50] The leading *Tupamaro* cadre Henry Engler deeply mourned the emotional distance he developed as an inevitable side effect of violent action: "In the toughest periods I increasingly hardened myself as a person, and lost much of that humane tenderness that had once been the most important thing, and which drove me to the [*Tupamaros*]. It is very difficult to harden oneself without losing one's tenderness."[51] Engler's comrade-in-arms, José Mujica, who, in one of the most remarkable political second acts in history, would go

---

[48] John Merriman, *The Dynamite Club: How a Bombing in Fin-de-Siècle Paris Ignited the Modern Age of Terror* (Houghton Mifflin Harcourt; 2009), p. 60.

[49] Richard Bach Jensen, The Pre-1914 Anarchist "Lone Wolf" Terrorist and Government Responses, *Journal of Terrorism and Political Violence*, Vol. 26, No. 1 (2014), p. 89.

[50] Jon Lee Anderson, *Che Guevara: A Revolutionary Life* (Grove Press; 1997), pp. 636–637.

[51] Pablo Brum, *The Robin Hood Guerrillas: The Epic Journey of Uruguay's Tupamaros* (CreateSpace; 2014), p. 339.

on to become President of Uruguay in March 2010, reflected in a speech delivered during his term in office that his generation had "filled itself with Quixote. We dreamed that in fifteen or twenty years it was possible to create an entirely different society — and we crashed into history."[52]

Other Latin American terrorist movements attracted similarly quixotic volunteers. 'Ema', a member of the Colombian terrorist group M-19, explained to the researcher Mauricio Florez-Morris that she had joined the group as a student at a private university because she was horrified by the condition of those in Colombian society less fortunate than herself: "I had always been very sensitive to social issues. I was moved by the existence of street urchins, poverty, and begging. I asked myself why these things were happening, why people were in this situation. And when I learned that I could do something about it, I did."[53] 'Gladis', a former member of *Corriente de Renovación Socialista* (CRS), also shared with Florez-Morris what had motivated her and her comrades to join the armed struggle: "We joined the guerrilla movement the same way that monks entered [a religious order]. I mean, forsaking everything and devoting yourself to a cause. It was the same. The person's attitude was the same; it was to relinquish all personal things and all personal ambitions in order to advance a common cause, and even sacrifice oneself for it."[54]

In Western Europe, Marxist terrorists clung to an equally altruistic narrative. *Rote Armee Fraktion* cadre Beate Sturm was appalled by the living conditions of many families in West Berlin when she arrived there to study at the Free University, particularly the sight of young children playing in the filth and garbage: "It simply makes you feel furious. You don't just feel sorry, no, you feel real blind rage. That was the feeling in Berlin then: smash the thing that's

---

[52] ibid., p. 350.

[53] Mauricio Florez-Morris, Joining Guerrilla Groups in Colombia: Individual Motivations and Processes for Entering a Violent Organization, *Studies in Conflict and Terrorism*, Vol. 30, No. 7 (2007), p. 620.

[54] ibid., p. 629.

smashing you."[55] Another RAF volunteer, Klaus Jünschke, was a former conscientious objector who had avoided military service because he had told the authorities that he couldn't kill another human being: "I must have thought about it a 1,000 times, like anyone who gets life. You have plenty of time to torment yourself puzzling it all out. There was a kind of atmosphere that makes you very ready to sacrifice yourself. Rational thought, in the sense of a calculation, didn't enter in to it at all. Life imprisonment? So what? That may seem very frivolous to an outsider, but the willingness people felt to give their own lives was serious enough."[56] The one-time conscientious objector was sentenced to life in prison for his part in the murder of police officer Herbert Schoner in December 1971. Brigitte Kuhlmann, a member of the West German terrorist group *Revolutionäre Zellen* who took part in the hijacking of Air France 139 in June 1976 and was killed during the rescue mission mounted at Entebbe Airport by Israeli commandos, had been a teacher working with handicapped students.[57] Her comrade Gerd Schnepel described her as a "friendly, caring person with social commitment".[58]

When the *Rote Armee Fraktion* issued its last communiqué in 1998 announcing that it was finally abandoning three decades of conflict with the *Bundesrepublik*, the authors took the opportunity to reflect on the organization's contribution to German society: "Putting the system in question was and still is legitimate as long as there is dominance and oppression instead of freedom, emancipation, and dignity for everyone in the world."[59] Rather than apologize to its victims, the RAF instead stood behind its actions and regretted only that it had not been successful in overthrowing capitalism: "The global wave of revolt, which the RAF arose from as well, did not

---

[55] Stefan Aust, *Baader-Meinhof: The Inside Story of the RAF* (Oxford University Press; 2009), p. 89.

[56] ibid., pp. 120–121.

[57] Saul David, *Operation Thunderbolt: Flight 139 and the raid on Entebbe Airport, the Most Audacious Hostage Rescue in History* (Little, Brown and Company; 2015), p. 48.

[58] ibid., p. 48.

[59] The Urban Guerrilla Is History, *The Final Communiqué From The Red Army Faction*, 1 March 1998, at http://germanguerilla.com/1998/03/01/the-urban-guerrilla-is-history/.

succeed, which does not mean that the destructive and unjust developments up until today can't still be turned around. The fact that we still don't see sufficient answers to these developments weighs more heavily upon us than the mistakes which we made."[60] Even in defeat, the surviving members of the RAF continued to believe that the sincerity of their intent to make the world a better place justified the means they had employed to achieve it. *Brigate Rosse* leader Renato Curcio called the kidnapping of the former Italian Prime Minister Aldo Moro "the highest act of humanity possible in a class-divided society".[61]

Although nationalist terrorist organizations by their very nature tend to have a less universal, more exclusionary, outlook than those devoted to socialist revolution, they too attract individuals who often seem to feel deep compassion for fellow members of their community. LEHI volunteer Eliahu Hakim recorded in his diary how deeply affected he was by the February 1942 sinking of the refugee ship Struma, with the loss of 767 Jewish lives: "I was dumbfounded by that disaster ... How can a man sit contentedly in a café, how can he drink and be merry when he knows that only yesterday his brothers were on a rotting ship, living under impossible conditions, on the edge of death?"[62] For a period in the early 1970s, ETA was led by a Benedictine seminarian, Eustaquio Mendiábal Benito, known as 'Txikia'. 'Thamilini', a senior female LTTE official, told *New York Times* reporter Amy Waldman that applications to join the LTTE's elite cadre of Black Tigers were only accepted if the application demonstrated "a clear conception of why and for what we are fighting. A deep humanitarianism is very necessary — a love of others, for the people."[63] In a speech delivered in 1993, the leader of the LTTE, Vellupillai Prabhakaran, described the Black Tigers in

---

[60] ibid.

[61] Robin Wagner-Pacifici, *The Moro Morality Play: Terrorism as Social Drama* (University of Chicago; 1986), p. 187.

[62] Gerold Frank, *The Deed* (Simon and Schuster; 1963), p. 176.

[63] Stephen Hopgood, Tamil Tigers 1987–2002, in Diego Gambetta (ed.), *Making Sense of Suicide Missions* (Oxford University Press; 2005), p. 60.

similar terms, noting: "They possess an iron will, yet their hearts are so very soft."[64]

The writer Ghassan Kanafani, who acted as a spokesman for the PFLP and was a close confidant of George Habash, wrote in the organization's newspaper, *Al Hadaf*,[65] that "it is not enough to hate and believe in the past to make a revolution. Hatred and belief in the past are sufficient prods for the rebellion phase. We must love and be future-oriented if we wish to carry out the revolution."[66] Kanafani, who had been photographed in the company of one of the *Nihon Sekigun* operatives responsible for the Lod Airport Massacre, was assassinated by *Mossad* in July 1972.[67] Some nationalist terrorists have even allowed their compassion to extend, albeit temporarily, to their enemies. The *Front de Libération Nationale* commander in Algiers, Saadi Yacef, actually called off attacks on French civilians in June 1956 after an old *pied noir* friend of his was among those killed, and his fiancé maimed, by a bomb planted in Algiers' Casino nightclub on Yacef's orders.[68]

As Mark Juergensmeyer noted in his excellent study of religious terrorism, *Terror in the Mind of God*, every major religion has spawned terrorist groups — even Buddhism, as the activities of *Janatha Vimukthi Peramuna* (JVP) in Sri Lanka and *Aum Shinrikyo* in Japan so ably attest. Juergensmeyer also observed that religious terrorism is carried out by "pious people dedicated to a moral vision of the world" who might otherwise appear to the neutral observer to be "good".[69] It is not surprising then that religious terrorists should also tend to think of themselves in such terms and to justify their actions in altruistic language. The 1993 World Trade Center bomber Mahmud Abouhalima summed up the attitude of many would-be

---

[64] ibid., p. 64.

[65] The Target.

[66] Leila Khaled and George Hajjar, *My People Shall Live: The Autobiography of a Revolutionary* (Hodder and Stoughton; 1973), Frontispiece.

[67] Ami Pedahzur, *The Israeli Secret Services and the Struggle Against Terrorism* (Columbia University Press; 2009), pp. 39–40.

[68] Michael Burleigh, *Blood and Rage: A Cultural History of Terrorism* (Harper; 2009), p. 124.

[69] Mark Juergensmeyer, *Terror in the Mind of God: The Global Rise of Religious Violence* (University of California Press; 2003), p. 7.

*jihadists* when he declared: "It is my job as a Muslim ... to go wherever there is oppression and injustice and fight it."[70] In his 2002 *Letter to the American People*, Osama bin Laden shared his vision of the true character of Islam in terms that were both utopian and altruistic: "It is to this religion that we call you; the seal of all the previous religions. It is the religion of Unification of God, sincerity, the best of manners, righteousness, mercy, honor, purity, and piety. It is the religion of showing kindness to others, establishing justice between them, granting them their rights, and defending the oppressed and the persecuted. It is the religion of enjoining the good and forbidding the evil with the hand, tongue and heart ... And it is the religion of unity and agreement on the obedience to *Allah*, and total equality between all people, without regarding their color, sex, or language."[71] The American reporter Jeffrey Goldberg described interviewing Rehman Khalil, the leader of *Harkat ul-Mujahideen* in Pakistan, as a discombobulating experience: "I was appalled by his message, and I wanted readers to understand the horror of it. But Khalil believed he was doing good works, and he wanted the world to celebrate his philosophy."[72]

A former ISIL *imam* who had been involved in processing foreign recruits for the organization told the anthropologist Scott Atran: "The young who came to us were not to be lectured at like witless children; they are for the most part understanding and compassionate, but misguided."[73] Hanif Qadir traveled to Afghanistan in 2002 because he wanted to help the local Afghan population and he found himself pulled into the orbit of *al-Qaeda*: "I wanted to help the innocent women and children of Afghanistan ... I felt I had role to play as a human, but also as a Muslim. This was not fair, I wanted

---

[70] ibid., p. 67.

[71] Bruce Lawrence (ed.), *Messages to the World: The Statements of Osama bin Laden* (Verso; 2005), p. 166.

[72] Jeffrey Goldberg, Before the Beheadings: Remembering a Time When Islamist Extremists Wanted to Persuade Reporters, Not Kill Them, *The Atlantic*, December 2014.

[73] Scott Atran, Mindless Terrorists? The Truth About Isis Is Much Worse, *The Guardian*, 15 November 2015.

to do something ... Over eight to nine months in 2002 I was engaging with a network of individuals that I didn't really understand were from *al-Qaeda* and we started to support the victims over there. I was supporting its efforts in Afghanistan financially and by sending over clothes but I wanted to do more. I wanted to be there and see the effects of our work. The internet images I was seeing and being shown made me more and more angry. I wanted to do something aggressive to the people who were doing this, like any human being would do."[74] Qadir ultimately turned his back on Islamist extremism and went on to found the Active Change Foundation.

This emotional thirst for justice and burning desire to help those co-religionists less fortunate than themselves can be found in the biographies of many Islamist terrorists. One foreign recruit described to Scott Atran being so eager to get to Syria that: "I walked in blind with two brothers I was with ... [to] rid society of its many filths and return the Earth to a state of purity where the law of God is supreme and surpasses everything else."[75] Ahmed Omar Saeed Sheikh, the British-born kidnapper of Wall Street Journal reporter Daniel Pearl, stated in testimony to the Indian police that he had become radicalized while studying at the London School of Economics after watching a film about the Bosnia war, which he said "shook my heart".[76] Chérif Kouachi, one of the two brothers behind the attack on the offices of the French satirical magazine *Charlie Hebdo* in January 2015 in which twelve people were killed, told a reporter who contacted him during his fatal stand-off with French police: "It was everything I saw on the television, the torture at Abu Ghraib prison, all that, which motivated me."[77] Michael Adebolajo, who murdered the British soldier Lee Rigby in a frenzied

---

[74] Alex King, Defusing the Threat from Returning Jihadist Fighters: Fighting Radicalization on the Streets of London, *Huck*, 22 January 2015, at http://www.huckmagazine.com/perspectives/reportage-2/defusing-threat-returning-jihadist-fighters/. Viewed 25 October 2015.

[75] Scott Atran, ISIS is a Revolution, *Aeon*, 15 December 2015, at https://aeon.co/essays/why-isis-has-the-potential-to-be-a-world-altering-revolution. Viewed 22 January 2016.

[76] Dafna Linzer, Islamic Militancy Appealed to Pearl's Killer, *Associated Press*, 15 July 2002.

[77] http://www.juancole.com/2015/01/terrorist-radicalized-torture.html.

attack in South London, told the Court at his subsequent trial: "It was the Iraq war that affected me most."[78] The July 2005 London Transport bomber Mohammad Siddique Khan volunteered his time at a primary school in Beeston where he worked with young students with special needs. The violent former Head of *al-Qaeda* in Iraq, Abu Mus'ab al-Zarqawi, was simultaneously known to his men by two seemingly irreconcilable nicknames: *al-dhabbah* (the slaughterer) and *al-baki* (he who weeps a lot).[79]

To be sure, not every terrorist is a compassionate altruist driven to violence from the purest of motives, and certainly protestations of altruism may be more than a little self-serving, but it is worth considering that many terrorists do see their actions in such terms. To take another's life is not an action most people take lightly or without serious personal and societal consequences. The President of *Sinn Féin* and former Provisional IRA volunteer Gerry Adams pointed out in *The Politics of Irish Freedom* that "IRA volunteers are actually civilians, political people who decide for short periods in their lives to take part in armed action ... There are no careerists in the IRA. Republican volunteers face futures of suffering, imprisonment and death ... The odds are stacked against the IRA volunteers and they operate at great personal risk against forces which are numerically and technologically superior and much better equipped."[80] Seen from the inside, such a life is not, as he notes, an easy calling and requires dedication and determination from its adherents. It is, ultimately, for most who chose this path a life of sacrifice. Believing oneself to be in the right, to be serving a higher purpose, can be crucial to sustaining one's commitment to the fight. In his essay, *L'Homme Révolté*, the French author Albert Camus examined the moral struggles undergone by members of *Narodnaya Volya* and the *Sotsialisty Revolyutsionery — Boyevaya Organizatsiya* (Socialist Revolutionaries — Combat Organization) as they embraced

---

[78] Jason Burke, *The New Threat: The Past, Present and Future of Islamic Militancy* (The New Press; 2015), p. 173.

[79] Thomas Hegghammer, *Why Terrorists Weep: The Socio-Cultural Practices of Jihadi Militants*, Paul Wilkinson Memorial Lecture, University of St. Andrews, 16 April 2015, p. 2.

[80] Gerry Adams, *The Politics of Irish Freedom* (Brandon Book Publishers; 1986), pp. 65–66.

terrorism in an effort to overthrow the autocracy of the Tsars. Camus suggested that the ever-present risk of death acts as a form of absolution for the terrorist, a way of making amends for taking such desperate measures, and he cited Boris Savinkov's memorable description of his co-conspirator Dora Brilliant: "Terror weighed on her like a cross."[81] One can see the same thought process at work in the narratives constructed by the martyrologists we discussed in Part I. Camus concluded his study of the Russian populists by labeling them "*les meurtriers délicats*" (the fastidious assassins). For many of those who embark down this path from what they might consider the best of motives, it is an apt description.

## Dehumanization

In his memoir of fighting for Jewish independence against the British authorities administering Mandate of Palestine as the leader of *Irgun Zvai Leumi*, the future Prime Minster of Israel Menachem Begin wrote: "It is axiomatic that those who fight have to hate — something or somebody."[82] If the decision to take up arms is sometimes driven by humanitarian impulses, the decision to use them involves suppressing those same impulses in relation to the potential targets of any terrorist action. Murder is a near universal societal taboo and many terrorists report feeling great reluctance about crossing this threshold.[83] The Nobel Prize winning behavioral scientist Konrad Lorenz identified "inhibitory mechanisms" that limit intra-species killing, and terrorists, like soldiers, have to overcome these mechanisms to go about their business effectively.[84] Typically, this is done by dehumanizing the

---

[81] Albert Camus, *The Rebel* (Vintage; 1991), p. 168.

[82] Menachem Begin, *The Revolt: Story of the Irgun* (Steimatzky's Agency Ltd.; 1977), p. xii.

[83] Andrea Kohn Maikovich, A New Understanding of Terrorism Using Cognitive Dissonance Principles, *Journal for the Theory of Social Behaviour*, Vol. 35, No. 4 (2005), p. 378 and Arie Kruglanski, Michele Gelfand, Jocelyn Bélanger, Anna Sheveland, Malkanthi Hetiarachchi and Rohan Gunaratna, The Psychology of Radicalization and Deradicalization: How Significance Quest Impacts Violent Extremism, *Advances in Political Psychology*, Vol. 35, Suppl. 1 (2014), p. 77.

[84] Konrad Lorenz, *On Aggression* (Routledge Classics; 2002).

enemy — employing racial epithets or other derogatory terms that emphasize the "otherness" of enemy soldiers and which denigrate their culture and value as human beings.[85] In his seminal work *Faces of the Enemy*, the philosopher Sam Keen coined the term "hostile imagination" to describe the process by which states dehumanize enemy forces by developing caricatured stereotypes that have a transformative impact on public attitudes and create the space for violence and atrocity to unfold.[86] Such systemic attempts to dehumanize one's foes are a well-reported staple of both ancient and modern warfare, and so it should come as no surprise that one finds the same processes at work in the context of both terrorism and counter-terrorism.

The *Soiuz sotsialistov-revoliutsionerov maksimalistov* (Union of Maximalist Socialist-Revolutionaries) theorist Ivan Pavlov believed that mankind was divided into ethical races and explained in a 1907 pamphlet, entitled *The Purification of Mankind*, that those in political, social and economic authority constituted a race that was "morally inferior to our animal predecessors: the vile characteristics of the gorilla and the orangutan progressed and developed in it to proportions unprecedented in the animal kingdom. There is no beast in comparison with which these types do not appear to be monsters."[87] The Maximalists adopted an extreme platform that held "where it is not enough to remove one person, it is necessary to eliminate them by the dozen; where dozens are not enough, they must be got rid of in hundreds."[88] In August 1906, a failed Maximalist attempt to assassinate the Russian Prime Minister, Pyotr Stolypin, in his summer *dacha* took twenty-three other lives.[89] Irish revolutionary Michael Collins likewise offered a similar — if admittedly less expansive — justification in defense of killing British police and intelligence

---

[85] See Ashley Montagu and Floyd Matson, *The Dehumanization of Man* (Mcgraw-Hill; 1984).

[86] See Sam Keen, *Faces of the Enemy: Reflections of the Hostile Imagination* (Harpercollins; 1991) and Philip Zimbardo, *The Lucifer Effect: Understanding How Good People Turn Evil* (Random House; 2007).

[87] Michael Burleigh, *Blood and Rage: A Cultural History of Terrorism* (Harper; 2009), p. 62.

[88] ibid.

[89] Manfred Hildermeier, *The Russian Socialist Revolutionary Party Before the First World War* (Palgrave Macmillan; 2000), p. 123.

officials: "My one intention was the destruction of the undesirables who continued to make miserable the lives of ordinary decent citizens ... If I had a second motive it was no more than a feeling such as I would have for a dangerous reptile. By their destruction the very air is made sweeter."[90] As one might expect, bestial motifs are a common characteristic of dehumanizing narratives.[91]

The German Marxist and *Rote Armee Fraktion* member Ulrike Meinhof offered the French journalist Michéle Ray a classic example of a dehumanizing narrative to justify the targeting of state officials: "Of course we say the cops are pigs. We say the guy in uniform is a pig, not a human being. And that's how we have to deal with him."[92] A female member of *Prima Linea*, who had participated in the 1979 murder of Turin policeman Giuseppe Lorusso, echoed Meinhof in an interview given to Donatella Della Porta: "On one side, there are your friends, and on the other, there are your enemies, and the enemies are in a category, they are functions, they are symbols. They are not human beings."[93] The short-lived Symbionese Liberation Army, best known for the 1974 kidnapping of American heiress Patty Hearst, adopted the slogan: "Death to the Fascist Insect That Preys upon the Life of the People."[94] Like Collins, *Sendero Luminoso* leader Abimael Guzmán described his foes in reptilian terms, railing against "those sinister vipers, those noxious vipers".[95]

American white supremacists seeking to ignite race war through emblematic acts of violence often dismiss more liberal white

---

[90] T. Ryle Dwyer, *The Squad and the Intelligence Operations of Michael Collins* (Mercier; 2005), p. 193.

[91] See Sam Keen, *Faces of the Enemy: Reflections of the Hostile Imagination* (Harpercollins; 1991), Philip Knightly, *The First Casualty* (Deutsch Press; 1975) and Bonnie Cordes, *When Terrorists do the Talking: Reflections on Terrorist Literature*, The Rand Corporation, August 1987, p. 22.

[92] Karin Bauer (ed.), *Everybody Talks About the Weather ... We Don't: The Writings of Ulrike Meinhof* (Seven Stories Press; 2008), p. 65.

[93] Donatella Della Porta, *Social Movements, Political Violence and the State: A Comparative Analysis of Italy and Germany* (Cambridge University Press; 1995), p. 174.

[94] Max Boot, *Invisible Armies: An Epic History of Guerrilla Warfare from Ancient Times to the Present* (Liveright; 2013), p. 457.

[95] Carlos Iván Degregori, The Maturation of a Cosmocrat and the Building of a Discourse Community: The Case of Shining Path, in David Apter (ed.), *The Legitimization of Violence* (New York University Press; 1997), p. 66.

Americans as "sheeple".[96] The World Trade Center bomber Mahmud Abouhalima also dismissed secular US citizens going about their daily lives "looking for jobs, for money to live" — the men and women he tried to kill in February 1993 by bringing down the North Tower with a 1,336 lb truck bomb — as "sheep".[97] The 9/11 hijacker Mohamed Atta carried with him a list of motivational instructions that included the Arabic phrase: "You must make your knife sharp and you must not discomfort your animal during the slaughter."[98] *Al-Qaeda* in Iraq leader Abu Mus'ab al-Zarqawi referred to his Iraqi *Shiite* antagonists as scorpions, snakes and rats.[99] As ISIL ratcheted up tension with the Jordanian government regarding the fate of the downed Royal Jordanian Air Force pilot, Muath Safi Yousef Al-Kasasbeh, the hashtag "suggest ways to kill Jordanian pig" began trending on social media as ISIL appeared to solicit suggestions from its global supporters on how to dispose of him.[100] In January 2015, he was burned alive in a metal cage, with harrowing footage of the execution posted online.

Fathali Moghaddam has suggested that the necessary "psychological distancing" from acts of violence is also achieved in part through the adoption of "terrorist myths".[101] Mark Juergensmeyer describes a process unique to religious terrorist groups that he calls "satanization", the literal demonization of the "other" to create a "cosmic war" mindset amongst adherents of a movement's program: "When an opponent rejects one's moral or spiritual position; when the enemy appears to hold the power to completely annihilate one's community, one's culture, and oneself; when the opponent's victory

---

[96] Mike German, *Thinking Like a Terrorist: Insights of a Former FBI Undercover Agent* (Potomac Books; 2007), p. 107.

[97] Mark Juergensmeyer, *Terror in the Mind of God: The Global Rise of Religious Violence* (University of California Press; 2003), p. 245.

[98] Michael Dorman, Unraveling 9–11 was in the bags, *Newsday*, 17 April 2006.

[99] Max Boot, *Invisible Armies: An Epic History of Guerrilla Warfare from Ancient Times to the Present* (Liveright; 2013), p. 531.

[100] Jason Burke, *The New Threat: The Past, Present and Future of Islamic Militancy* (The New Press; 2015), p. 102.

[101] Fathali Moghaddam, The Staircase to Terrorism: A Psychological Exploration, *American Psychologist*, Vol. 60, No. 2, February–March 2005, p. 166.

would be unthinkable; and when there seems to be no way to defeat the enemy in human terms — all of these conditions increase the likelihood that one will envision one's opponent as a superhuman foe, a cosmic enemy."[102] It follows naturally that to defeat such a foe would require the spiritual warrior to adopt extraordinary, perhaps even deeply distasteful, measures to ensure the ultimate triumph of good over evil. Almost anything can be justified in such circumstances. Thus, we find Osama bin Laden describing the United States as embodying the "forces of evil" and *Hezbollah*'s leader Hassan Nasrallah adopting the language of his Iranian backers to denigrate the United States as "the Great Satan".[103]

Of course, narratives dehumanizing the "other" are typically found on both sides of a violent conflict. Facing what he perceived as a growing homegrown anarchist threat following the end of World War I, US Attorney General A. Mitchell Palmer wrote in an article entitled *The Case Against the Reds*: "As a foe, the anarchist is fearless of his own life, for his creed is a fanaticism that admits no respect of any other creed. Obviously it is a creed of any criminal mind, which reasons always from motives impossible to clean thought."[104] Palmer's response was to organize the unconstitutional mass deportation of more than 500 suspected radicals following raids in November 1919 and January 1920, a decision that backfired spectacularly by putting paid to his own presidential ambitions and provoking the retaliatory bombing of Wall Street in September 1920. The idea that terrorists conform to the popular stereotype of a bestial and remorseless killer with whom there is no reasoning is a powerful trope in governmental responses to terrorism, but it is not a helpful one.

---

[102] Mark Juergensmeyer, *Terror in the Mind of God: The Global Rise of Religious Violence* (University of California Press; 2003), p. 186.

[103] ibid., p. 185, and Nasrallah: U.S. will remain the 'Great Satan', *Al Arabiya*, 25 July 2015, at http://english.alarabiya.net/en/News/middle-east/2015/07/25/Hezbollah-U-S-remains-great-Satan-after-nuke-deal.html. Viewed 22 September 2016.

[104] Mike German, *Thinking Like a Terrorist: Insights of a Former FBI Undercover Agent* (Potomac Books; 2007), pp. 56–57.

US President Ronald Reagan dismissed the Libyan leader Colonel Muammar Gadhafi as the "mad dog of the Middle East" in the aftermath of the 5 April 1986 bombing of the *La Belle Discothèque* in Berlin.[105] Menachem Begin, despite having been a member of a violent terrorist organization himself which had bombed civilian Arab targets such as markets and cinemas as well as attacking British military personnel, frequently characterized the men and women of the Palestine Liberation Organization as "two-legged beasts" without any apparent trace of irony.[106] Similarly, in the immediate aftermath of the September 11 attacks, as American Special Forces and allied local commanders closed in on *al-Qaeda* and *Taliban* redoubts in the cave-riddled Tora Bora region of eastern Afghanistan in December 2001, US Secretary of Defense Donald Rumsfeld warned Pentagon reporters that the final battle was not a foregone conclusion: "We all know that a wounded animal can be dangerous."[107] This process of dehumanization perhaps reached its nadir in the photograph of US Army Specialist Lynndie England dragging a naked Iraqi detainee along the ground by a leash fixed round his neck in the Abu Ghraib prison located outside Baghdad. Alleged 9/11 co-conspirator Mohammed al-Qahtani was reportedly also subjected to similar treatment in the US military's Guantanamo Bay detention facility.[108] This practice, described by the Senate Armed Services Committee as "treating a person like an animal", was adapted from the *Joint Personnel Recovery Agency Instructors' Manual* and had previously been used to put US military personnel under pressure in escape and evasion exercises. Its use on Iraqi security detainees had been specifically authorized by US commanders.[109]

---

[105] The President's News Conference, 9 April 1986, at http://www.presidency.ucsb.edu/ws/index.php?pid=37105.

[106] Matthew Carr, *The Infernal Machine: A History of Terrorism* (The New Press; 2007), p. 72.

[107] Kathleen T. Rhem, Rumsfeld: Taliban, Al-Qaeda Dangerous Like Wounded Animals, *American Forces Press Service*, 11 December 2001, at http://www.defense.gov/News/NewsArticle.aspx?ID=44377.

[108] Senate Armed Services Committee, *Inquiry into the Treatment of Detainees in U.S. Custody*, 20 November 2008, p. xxi.

[109] ibid., p. xiv.

No one seems to be immune from the temptation to frame enemies in such dehumanizing terms. Erin Steuter and Deborah Wills have documented in great detail the use of vermin and disease-based metaphorical language to describe terrorists in the Canadian media in the years following the September 11 attacks, a phenomenon perfectly captured in this May 2004 headline from *The Sudbury Star*: "Terrorists, like rats and cockroaches, skulk in the dark."[110] Steuter and Wills cite article after article in which terrorist organizations are said to "breed" or "spawn" imitators, to control "webs" or "swarms" of willing volunteers, and to operate from "dens", "nests", "lairs" or "holes". A similar process takes place both on the battlefield and in councils of war. For example, in Afghanistan, both American soldiers and policymakers talked of playing "whack-a-mole" with the *Taliban*, of "mowing the grass" and of "squirters". Every army has its equivalent epithets.

However necessary "hostile imagination" may be to liberating societal restraints on the use of violence, it is inevitably inimical to any meaningful understanding of the opposing side of the struggle. Radicalization is a two-way street, violent conflict inevitably has a radicalizing effect on each party involved.[111] The psychological distancing war fighting requires, and the consequent dehumanization of the enemy, can color and cloud policymakers' judgment. Political leaders on both sides of a conflict can quickly become prisoners of their own intemperate rhetoric further fueling violence and making compromise more difficult. Daniel Koehler's experience of working with radicalized youths in Germany led him to conclude that the cultivation of a nuanced world view was a critical defense against the appeal of violent extremism: "There are many, many things that add color to the picture. [The] radicalization process always sucks out color of the picture, it's the typical black-and-white picture because then it's very easy to make

---

[110] Erin Steuter and Deborah Wills, Discourses of Dehumanization: Enemy Construction and Canadian Media Complicity in the Framing of the War on Terror, *Global Media Journal* (Canadian Edition), Vol. 2, No. 2, 2009, p. 15.
[111] Clark McCauley and Sophia Moskalenko, *Friction: How Radicalization Happens to Them and Us* (Oxford University Press; 2011), p. 223.

the decision to leave your family and go ... and kill — potentially kill — other human beings."[112]


## Backlash

In his autobiographical treatise *Knights under the Prophet's Banner*, *al-Qaeda* chief Ayman al-Zawahiri dwelled at length on the unintended death of an innocent twelve-year-old girl called Shayma Abdel-Halim as a consequence of a failed assassination attempt on Egyptian Prime Minister Atif Sidqi in 1993.[113] *Tanzim al-Jihad* (Egyptian Islamic Jihad) detonated a car bomb as Sidqi's motorcade passed by the girl's school — the prime minister escaped serious injury, Shayma was killed by the blast. The Egyptian government was quick to seize on the incident, claiming that Shayma's elementary school was the real target of the bomb and the attack rebounded negatively on Egyptian Islamic Jihad's public support. As Lawrence Wright noted in *The Looming Tower*: "Little Shayma's death captured people's emotions as nothing else had ... when her coffin was borne through the streets of Cairo, people cried, 'Terrorism is the enemy of God!'"[114] Several senior members of Islamic Jihad even resigned from the organization in protest.

If we accept the proposition that most terrorists are motivated in part by a distorted sense of altruism and an empathy for the suffering of at least some fellow human beings with whom they identify, the impact of Shayma's murder should not be too surprising. Her death introduced a note of nuance, or "color", into a conflict that had hitherto been articulated by most of those either inside or supporting Islamic Jihad in strictly Manichaean terms — a young Muslim girl's life had been brutally ended as a direct consequence

---

[112] All Things Considered, German Program Helps Families De-Radicalize Members Prone To Extremism, *National Public Radio*, 13 March 2015, at http://www.npr.org/2015/03/13/392845800/german-program-helps-families-de-radicalize-members-prone-to-extremism.

[113] Jarret Brachman and William McCants, Stealing Al-Qaeda's Playbook, *Studies in Conflict and Terrorism*, Vol. 29, No. 4 (June 2006).

[114] Lawrence Wright, *Looming Tower: Al-Qaeda and the Road to 9/11* (Knopf; 2006), p. 186.

of the callous disregard of an organization that claimed to be fighting to make the world a better and safer place for future generations like her. It humanized the conflict. Cognitive dissonance between words and deeds is difficult for supporters to process and creates an opening for alternate viewpoints to be considered. Despite the fact, as we discussed in Part I, that most terrorist organizations pay close attention to the manner in which their actions are perceived by their supporters, such moments are not uncommon in terrorist campaigns. Attacks sometimes go wrong, which is why the *Tupamaros* leader Raúl Sendic cautioned his followers against the use of explosives: "[They] cannot be controlled. From the moment you leave the bomb in place, a neighbor might choose to walk the dog at three in the morning and you will find yourself hurting innocent people."[115] Sometimes, more extreme elements within a group escalate the level of violence beyond that with which more moderate members are comfortable. There are plenty of examples of individual terrorists abandoning the armed struggle because of a violent incident that they felt devalued, or even betrayed, the cause in which they believed, or sometimes simply because, to borrow a phrase from Daniel Pearl's kidnapper, a particular event, like Shayma's death, shook their heart.

In this respect, as in so many others, actions can speak louder than words. Valerio Morucci, head of the Rome "column" of the *Brigate Rosse*, credited the murders of former Italian Prime Minister Aldo Moro and trade unionist Guido Rossa with hastening his own departure from the movement: "The last straw was the killing of Guido Rossa in Rome ... I wrote that the murder of Rossa had been a serious mistake. All of us in the BR thought so — except the people who killed him. [The BR] just continued killing and we couldn't take it any more."[116] Hans-Joachim Klein publicly resigned from the German *Revolutionäre Zellen* in 1977 — sending his gun, and a letter

---

[115] Pablo Brum, *The Robin Hood Guerrillas: The Epic Journey of Uruguay's Tupamaros* (CreateSpace; 2014), p. 178.

[116] Valerio Morucci quoted in Donatella della Porta, Leaving Underground Organizations: A Sociological Analysis of the Italian Case, in Tore Bjorgo and John Horgan (eds.), *Leaving Terrorism Behind: Individual and Collective Disengagement* (Routledge; 2009), pp. 73–74.

renouncing terrorism, to the news magazine *Der Spiegel* — in large part because he was uncomfortable with the anti-Semitic overtones of the Entebbe hostage crisis in June–July 1976. Wilfried Böse, a *Revolutionäre Zellen* member working with Popular Front for the Liberation of Palestine — External Operations (PFLP-EO), had been reported to have overseen the separation of the Jewish passengers from the other international travellers, and the parallel between his actions and those of Nazi camp guards during the holocaust was quickly drawn in the media.[117]

Maria McGuire, a volunteer in the Provisional IRA, began the long process of disengaging from the group when its members turned their fire away from British soldiers and onto the Protestant community: "My first doubts came in the spring of 1972, when Provisionals began shooting at unarmed Protestants in the streets of Belfast, actions that could only hasten the slide into sectarian civil war in the Six Counties. Then came Bloody Friday, when 11 civilians were killed and over 100 injured by twenty Provisional bombs that exploded in an hour. This was the end for me."[118]

One former ETA gunman told the researcher Fernando Reinares that he had been appalled by the organization's June 1987 attack on the Hipercor department store in central Barcelona, which killed twenty-one shoppers and wounded fifty more – the deadliest attack ever mounted by ETA: "The feeling was that this was just so, well, over the top, that this was not the enemy and that the methods we used had to be targeting the enemy and not … not so, so indiscriminate. Look, don't forget this is also going to make an impact on the state, and you have to hit the state where it hurts. But where it hurts them is also where it hurts a lot of ordinary people and then you are going to end up all alone. But you have to strike at them directly. And keep it clean, as clean as possible. Of course, if you go around getting your hands bloody day after day,

---

[117] Freed Hostages Tell Their Story, *Jewish Telegraphic Agency*, 2 July 1976. It should be noted that some survivors, such as Ilan Hartuv, have since disputed this account, but this does not alter the force of its contemporary impact. Hartuv told the newspaper *Haaretz* in 2011 that it had in fact been the Israeli citizens whom had been separated out, rather than all Jews on the flight.

[118] Maria McGuire, *To Take Arms: A Year in the Provisional IRA* (Macmillan; 1973), pp. 9–10.

you're going to end up being totally isolated … That's not to say I have some problem with the idea of armed struggle. As long as it stays clear that it has to be real armed struggle and… that you play by the rules, if you get my drift. None of this indiscriminate stuff or anything of that sort."[119]

Nazir Abbas, a senior figure in *Jemaah Islamiyah*, broke with the organization because it had begun to focus its attacks on civilian targets. Abbas helped train the *Jemaah Islamiyah* operatives who carried out the 2002 Bali bombings against Western tourists and he has said that he felt "sinful" because of his association with them: "I couldn't understand that exploding bombs against innocent civilians was *jihad*. That was the difference that made me escape from the group."[120] Mosab Hassan Yousef, the son of a senior *Hamas* figure, has written that he turned against *Hamas* while in an Israeli prison when he saw how the organization tortured suspected collaborators among his fellow inmates.[121] Yousef volunteered his services to the Israeli security service, *Shin Bet*, providing valuable intelligence and even assisting the arrest of his own father. The former *al-Qaeda* insider Aimen Dean told the BBC that he turned his back on the group after the bombing of two US embassies in East Africa in 1998, which injured more than two hundred blameless local civilians.[122] Former FBI Special Agent Ali Soufan has described gaining the cooperation of jailed *al-Qaeda* operative Abu Jandal during an interview in Yemen by confronting him in the immediate aftermath of September 11 with photographs and news stories about the attacks, noting that "the scale of the atrocity visibly shook him." The revelation of numerous Yemeni casualties among the dead further undermined Abu Jandal's resolve and,

[119] Fernando Reinares, Exit From Terrorism: A Qualitative Empirical Study on Disengagement and Deradicalization Among members of ETA, *Terrorism and Political Violence*, Vol. 23, No. 5 (2011) p. 794.

[120] Michael Jacobson, Learning Counter-Narrative Lessons from Cases of Terrorist Dropouts, Netherlands National Coordinator for Counterterrorism, *Countering Violent Extremist Narratives*, January 2010, p. 76.

[121] Michael Jacobson, Lessons from Israel's Unlikely Spy, *Jerusalem Post*, March 20, 2010.

[122] Steve Swann, A truly dangerous meeting of minds, *BBC News*, 3 April 2015 in http://www.bbc.com/news/magazine-32065132.

commenting, "I think the Sheikh [bin Laden] went crazy," he began to cooperate with the FBI.[123] We will look at this particular interaction in more detail in Part III.

In September 2007, the influential Saudi cleric Sheikh Salman bin Fahd al-Oadah delivered a powerful *Ramadan* broadcast in which he called on Osama bin Laden to reconsider the path he was on: "How much blood has been spent? How many innocent people, children, elderly and women have been killed, dispersed or evicted in the name *al-Qaeda*? Are you happy to meet *Allah* with this heavy burden on your shoulders? It is a weighty burden indeed — at least hundreds of thousands of innocent people, if not millions ... This religion of ours comes to defense of the life of a sparrow. It can never accept the murder of innocent people, regardless of what supposed justification is given for it."[124] As discussed in Part I, there is evidence to suggest that this critique, and others like it, struck home with the senior leadership of *al-Qaeda* who began to realize that they needed to refine their message or lose support. During the 2011 raid on Osama bin Laden's hideout in Abbottabad, US Navy SEALs recovered an illuminating briefing note prepared for the *al-Qaeda* leader by a leading member of his inner circle, US-born Adam Gadahn. Gadahn's memo contained a powerful critique of the "black reputation" indiscriminate attacks on "innocent Muslims" had earned the *Tehrik-i-Taliban Pakistan* and suggested that *al-Qaeda* issue an unequivocal denunciation of such actions lest it be tainted with the same brush.[125] Gadahn even expressed concern that the "sharp tone" and "bigotry" of Islamic extremist internet forums was alienating potential supporters.

In February 2014, bin Laden's successor Ayman al-Zawahiri went even further, actually expelling the Islamic State of Iraq and the

---

[123] Lawrence Wright, *The Looming Tower* (Alfred A. Knopf; 2006), pp. 365–367.

[124] Shaykh Salman al-Oudah's Ramadan Letter to Osama Bin Laden, 14 September 2007 at http://muslimmatters.org/2007/09/18/shaykh-salman-al-oudahs-ramadan-letter-to-osama-bin-laden-on-nbc/. Viewed 1 October 2016.

[125] Brian Dodwell, The Abbottabad Documents: The Quiet Ascent of Adam Gadahn, *CTC Sentinel*, Vol. 5 No. 5, (2012) at www.ctc.usma.edu/posts/the-abbottabad-documents-the-quiet-ascent-of-adam-gadahn.

Levant from its coalition of like-minded groups, posting the following statement on a sympathetic website: "*al-Qaeda* declares that it has no links to the [ISIL] group. We weren't informed about its creation, nor counseled. Nor were we satisfied with it; rather we ordered it to stop. [ISIL] isn't a branch of *al-Qaeda* and we have no organizational relationship with it. Nor is *al-Qaeda* responsible for its actions and behavior."[126] ISIL had played a major role in the uprising against President Bashar al-Assad in neighboring Syria but in the process had already earned such a bloodcurdling reputation for the manner of its administration of areas under its control, and for its infighting with other rebel groups, that al-Zawahiri was concerned it was harming the Islamist cause. Al-Zawahiri described the infighting as "a catastrophe for *jihad* in Syria" and placed the blame firmly on ISIL and its leader Abu Bakr al-Baghdadi.

When terrorist organizations misread the mood of their constituents, it can unquestionably have major strategic implications for the future success of their operations. On 31 July 1970, the *Tupamaros* launched the inauspiciously named "Plan Satan" to provoke a crisis that they hoped would bring down the Uruguayan government by kidnapping two foreign diplomats — US police adviser Dan Mitrione, who worked at the US Embassy in Montevideo in the Office of Public Safety, and the Brazilian Consul, Aloysio Dias Gomide.[127] The *Tupamaros* believed the Uruguayan authorities would fold in the face of pressure from their two closest allies to secure the release of their nationals and would be forced to release a number of jailed comrades. However, the Uruguayan government responded by launching a massive manhunt to find the two men in the course of which through extraordinary good fortune they managed to capture the bulk of the *Tupamaros* leadership, including Raúl Sendic, in a single raid on one of the group's safe houses in Montevideo.[128] Ironically, this major police coup

---

[126] Ellen Knickmeyer, Al-Qaeda Disavows Rebel Group Fighting Syrian Regime, *The Wall Street Journal*, 3 February 2013.

[127] See David Ronfeldt, *The Mitrione Kidnapping in Uruguay* (RAND Corporation; 1987).

[128] Pablo Brum, *The Robin Hood Guerrillas: The Epic Journey of Uruguay's Tupamaros* (CreateSpace; 2014), pp. 150–154.

had the unintended effect of leaving younger and more radical cadres in charge of the organization and raising the stakes in their confrontation with the state.[129] The group's new leaders threatened to try Mitrione in a People's Court and then execute him if their newly captured comrades were not immediately released. The deadline expired and Mitrione was bound, drugged, and shot to death on 9 August 1970.

Mitrione's murder was callous and brutal in a way that previous operations by "the Robin Hood Guerrillas" had not been, and the public reaction amongst ordinary Uruguayans was one of revulsion. One *Tupamaro* told the reporter Alfonso Lessa: "That was one of the most terrible days I can recall in Montevideo ... It was horrible. Horrible. To me, that day was when terror began to spread in Uruguayan society."[130] Efraín Martínez, one of the senior *Tupamaros* who had been swept up by the police dragnet, told the historian and former *Tupamara* Clara Aldrighi: "In no way did we think of executing someone. It would have been the stupidest thing anyone could conceive ... If [the safe house] had not fallen, Mitrione would be alive. There is no question about it."[131] Even the architect of Plan Satan, Eleuterio Fernández Huidobro, later condemned the execution: "The execution was a very damaging political blow for the [*Tupamaros*], which aborted the current of sympathy it had been enjoying among ample segments of society."[132] Gallup opinion polls taken before and after Mitrione's murder showed a 50% drop in support for the *Tupamaros* and the later poll found that 69% of Uruguayans condemned the murder.[133]

The *Front de Libération du Québec* (FLQ) was a small revolutionary organization inspired by Quebec nationalist sentiment and the international socialist movement,[134] which was also avowedly

---

[129] ibid.

[130] ibid., p. 161.

[131] ibid.

[132] ibid.

[133] ibid.

[134] Jeffrey Ross and Ted Gurr, Why Terrorism Subsides: A Comparative Study of Canada and the United States, *Comparative Politics*, Vol. 21, No. 4 (July 1989), p. 411.

influenced by the writings of Carlos Marighella.[135] From its foundation in February 1963, the FLQ was involved in a low-level terrorist campaign against the Canadian government that averaged about 40 events a year between 1968 and 1971, including 166 violent attacks.[136] The FLQ began by bombing military targets but later extended its campaign to include government buildings and economic targets usually related to industrial disputes. Members of the FLQ trained with the Palestine Liberation Organization.[137] In early October 1970, FLQ cells kidnapped first James Cross, the British Trade Commissioner in Montréal, and then a few days later the Quebec Minister of Labour and Immigration, and Deputy Premier, Pierre Laporte, to put pressure on the authorities to concede to a list of demands that included freedom for twenty-three prisoners held in Canadian jails, the payment of a cash ransom, the publication of the FLQ's political manifesto in the national media, and the revelation of the identity of a police informer. Instead, on 16 October 1970, the Canadian government invoked the War Measures Act characterizing the kidnappings as an "apprehended insurrection" and began rounding up suspected members of the FLQ. The very next day Laporte was killed by his kidnappers — supposedly while trying to escape. His body was callously dumped in the trunk of an abandoned car. The murder of Pierre Laporte, a native Quebecker, turned even separatist sympathizers against the FLQ.[138] The major labor unions in Quebec formed a common front to

---

[135] Raphael Cohen-Almagor, The Terrorists' Best Ally: The Quebec Media Coverage of the FLQ Crisis in October 1970, *Canadian Journal of Communication*, Vol. 25, No. 2 (2000), p. 8.

[136] Jeffrey Ross and Ted Gurr, Why Terrorism Subsides: A Comparative Study of Canada and the United States, *Comparative Politics*, Vol. 21, No. 4 (July 1989), pp. 405–406.

[137] Sean Maloney, A Mere Rustle of Leaves: Canadian Strategy and the 1970 FLQ Crisis, *Canadian Military Journal* (Summer 2000), p. 76.

[138] Raphael Cohen-Almagor, The Terrorists' Best Ally: The Quebec Media Coverage of the FLQ Crisis in October 1970, *Canadian Journal of Communication*, Vol. 25, No. 2 (2000), p. 14; Reg Whitaker, Keeping up with the Neighbours? Canadian Responses to 9/11 in Historical and Comparative Context, *Osgoode Hall Law Journal*, Vol. 41 (Summer/Fall 2003), p. 250; and G. Davidson Smith, Canada's Counter-Terrorism Experience, *Terrorism and Political Violence*, Vol. 5, No. 1 (Spring 1993), p. 87.

denounce the FLQ.[139] The leading separatist *Parti Québecois* condemned political violence as "humanly immoral and politically pointless" and the FLQ soon withered away.[140]

In May 1972, the Official IRA kidnapped and then murdered a young Catholic Private in the Irish Rangers, William Best, while he was visiting his family in Londonderry on leave in May 1972. Northern Irish Catholic soldiers recruited into British regiments like the Irish Rangers and the Irish Guards traditionally did not serve in the Province and thus were usually seen as being outside the conflict. Best was a popular figure in his Catholic neighborhood — he had even attended a wake for a local Catholic youth killed by a British soldier shortly before his abduction. Best's killing provoked such a backlash against the Official IRA from the local Catholic community that they declared a ceasefire, which effectively ended their further involvement in The Troubles.[141]

The kidnapping and subsequent murder of the former Italian Prime Minister Aldo Moro in May 1978 outraged the vast majority of the Italian public[142] and provoked an unequivocal rejection of terrorism from the Italian Communist Party leadership, which had found its public support slipping in the wake of Moro's murder.[143] The radical left began to fragment as a vigorous internal debate erupted over increasingly violent terrorist tactics.[144] The more extremist elements began to alienate comrades and supporters, prompting more moderate members like Valerio Morucci to leave the movement.[145] This exodus was further hastened by two events in

---

[139] Jeffrey Ross and Ted Gurr, Why Terrorism Subsides: A Comparative Study of Canada and the United States, *Comparative Politics*, Vol. 21, No. 4 (July 1989), p. 413.

[140] ibid.

[141] Maria McGuire, *To Take Arms: A Year in the Provisional IRA* (Macmillan; 1973), pp. 117–118.

[142] Eileen MacDonald, *Shoot the Women First* (London; Fourth Estate 1991), p. 191.

[143] Claudio Celani, A Strategy of Tension: The Case of Italy, *Executive Intelligence Review* (March–April 2004).

[144] Alison Jamieson, Entry, Discipline and Exit in the Italian Red Brigades, *Journal of Terrorism and Political Violence* (Spring 1990), pp. 12–14.

[145] Donatella Della Porta, Institutional Responses to Terrorism: The Italian Case, *Terrorism and Political Violence* (Winter 1992), p. 166 and Alison Jamieson, Entry, Discipline and Exit in the Italian Red Brigades, *Journal of Terrorism and Political Violence* (Spring 1990), p. 16.

particular: The murder in January 1979 of the Genoese communist shop steward, Guido Rossa, suspected of informing on the *Brigate Rossa*, and *Prima Linea*'s brutal December 1979 attack on the School of Business Administration in Turin, in which five students and five members of staff were kneecapped by the terrorists in a warning to other aspirant capitalists.[146] 16,000 of Rossa's fellow workers from the Italsider steel works protested his murder by "fascist Brigadists", and an estimated half a million people attended his funeral.[147] The *Brigate Rossa* appeared to be degenerating into little more than a vicious criminal gang intent upon avoiding arrest and evening scores, and many of their supporters had had enough.[148]

On 24 October 1990, the Provisional IRA found itself similarly out of step with its constituents when it mounted a simultaneous attack on three British military targets in the Province using coopted civilians as human or "proxy" bombs. In the cases of two of the victims, Patsy Gillespie and John McEvoy, PIRA gunmen held their families hostage to ensure that they followed through with the attack. The third victim, Gerry Kelly, was actually secured to the vehicle and told he would have time to free himself before the device detonated. PIRA considered the three men, who were all Catholics, to be collaborators because they provided support services to the British security forces — Gillespie was a cook on a British base and McAvoy sold fuel to officers in the Royal Ulster Constabulary. Gillespie was killed along with five British soldiers. Both Kelly and McEvoy were able to escape their vehicles before they exploded, although another British soldier was killed and ten others injured in one of the blasts. The Catholic community was appalled by the callousness of the attacks. The widely respected Social Democratic and Labour Party Member of Parliament John Hume spoke for many when he told reporters: "The one word that is on everybody's lips is the word 'coward'. Let me repeat it. I hope you are listening, you

[146] Eileen MacDonald, *Shoot the Women First* (London; Fourth Estate 1991), p. 176.

[147] Michael Burleigh, *Blood and Rage: A Cultural History of Terrorism* (Harper; 2009), p. 212.

[148] Alison Jamieson, Entry, Discipline and Exit in the Italian Red Brigades, *Journal of Terrorism and Political Violence* (Spring 1990), p. 16.

cowards, using a human being in the way that you did."[149] In unusually powerful language, the Catholic Bishop of Derry, Dr. Edward Daly, described those responsible for the attacks as "Satan's followers" and excoriated the Provisional IRA as "those who try to justify the unjustifiable".[150] PIRA soon abandoned the tactic.

This chilling effect is further magnified if critics within terrorists' own communities begin to organize effectively against them. This began to happen to ETA in the early 1980s and it shook the confidence of many militants within the movement, as one volunteer who left ETA in this period confided to the researcher Fernando Reinares: "You have to comes to terms with the fact that society was really closing ranks against the armed struggle we were carrying out, you know? Even back then it was ordinary people who turned out to protest the actions … people saying: listen, man, this is not, repeat not, the way to go about it. That's when you start thinking things through for yourself until you say: wait a minute, this whole thing is absolutely useless!"[151] In 1986, the *Coordinadora Gesto por la Paz de Euskal Herria* was founded to protest any violent killing committed by either Basque separatists or the Spanish government in communities across the Spanish Basque region.[152] Known more colloquially as *Gesto* (Gesture) from the group's strategy of holding silent fifteen-minute protest demonstrations after each act of political violence, by February 1998 it had organized 15,760 such protests in 150 locations across the Basque country.[153] *Gesto's* core value was an ethics-based rejection of violence in politics and in the aftermath of the abduction of Basque businessman Julio Iglesias Zamora in 1993,

---

[149] Mia Bloom and John Horgan, Missing Their Mark: The IRA's Proxy Bomb Campaign, in Michael A. Innes and William Banks (eds.), *Making Sense of Proxy Wars: States, Surrogates & the Use of Force* (Potomac Books; 2012), p. 50.

[150] ibid., p. 51.

[151] Fernando Reinares, Exit From Terrorism: A Qualitative Empirical Study on Disengagement and Deradicalization Among members of ETA, *Terrorism and Political Violence*, Vol. 23, No. 5 (2011), p. 785.

[152] Paige Whaley Eager, *From Freedom Fighters to Terrorists: Women and Political Violence* (Routledge; 2016), p. 150.

[153] Ludger Mees, The Basque Peace Process, Nationalism and Political Violence, in John Darby and Roger MacGinty (eds.), *The Management of Peace Processes* (Palgrave; 2000), p. 167.

it partnered with several other peace groups to promote the wearing of a blue ribbon to signal an individual's rejection of ETA's policy of kidnapping. *Gesto* was particularly active among Basque youth and by 1997 there were 160 local groups across the region, many of which were linked to schools and universities. In July 1997, ETA kidnapped a well-liked local *Partido Popular* politician from Ermua, Miguel Ángel Blanco, and 6 million people across Spain demonstrated for his release.[154] Their pleas fell on deaf ears and ETA executed Blanco in cold blood — public opinion was outraged and another predominantly Basque anti-ETA protest group *espíritu de Ermua* was founded in protest. Under pressure from its own constituency, ETA announced a ceasefire the following year that lasted until 2000.

Movements like *Gesto* and *espíritu de Ermua* are far from unique and are part of a larger global phenomenon. When a terrorist group stops listening to its base or commits an atrocity that shocks the conscience of potential supporters, opposition frequently coalesces around protest organizations. Other recent examples include the Uganda Muslim Youth Development Forum (UMYDF) and the UK-based Active Change Foundation. UMYDF was founded by Ndugwa Hassan, a survivor of the July 2010 bombing of the Kyadondo Rugby Club in Kampala by the Somali-based Islamic extremist group *al-Shabaab* during the broadcast of a World Cup football match, which killed seventy-four people. When he heard *al-Shabaab* claim to be acting in support of Islamic values, he later recalled, "that is when I became angry."[155] Hassan joined with friends to establish the UMYDF to connect Muslim youth to the political processes that shape their lives. By 2015, he was able to communicate his message of non-violent political engagement to more than 10,000 Ugandan youths through UMYDF's direct training and online platforms. In 2014, the Active Change Foundation organized the #notinmyname campaign to give young Muslims the opportunity to denounce the violent actions of ISIL in their own

---

[154] Michael Burleigh, *Blood and Rage: A Cultural History of Terrorism* (Harper; 2009), pp. 285–286.

[155] Manal Omar, The United States Will Never Win the Propaganda Against the Islamic State, *Foreign Policy*, 9 January 2015.

words by uploading video clips and pictures to YouTube, Instagram, Twitter and other social media sites. The founder of the Active Change Foundation, Hanif Qadir, told one reporter: "Young British Muslims are sick and tired of the hate-filled propaganda the terrorists and their supporters churn out on social media. They are angry that the criminals are using the platforms to radicalize young people and spread their poisonous words of violence in the name of Islam."[156]

## Summary

Most of those who take up arms in the service of a cause believe that they are doing the right thing, maybe also a good thing, and perhaps even a noble thing, but "right", "good", and "noble" are all highly subjective values, which makes belief in the righteousness of one's cause a potential vulnerability if it can be successfully contested. We have seen above that many terrorists are sustained by a belief in the absolute rightness of their cause and that when this belief wavers, they can begin looking for an exit. We have seen how terrorist organizations seek to dehumanize their foes to make violence more palatable to their followers and how the establishment of a human connection can make even hardened terrorists reconsider their actions. We have also considered how violent acts can backfire undermining wider community support for terrorist action. Collectively, these qualities present an opportunity that can be exploited by counter-terrorism practitioners at both the tactical and strategic level. Seamus Finucane, outed in a 1994 House of Commons debate as the Intelligence Officer of the Provisional IRA's Belfast Brigade, acknowledged in an interview with Kevin Toolis: "Certainly, everyone has to reassess their position within the struggle at certain times, when grief comes to your own door or mistakes are

---

[156] Charlotte Meredith, British Muslims Rejecting Islamic State With #NotInMyName Campaign Praised By Barack Obama At UN General Assembly, *Huffington Post UK*, 24 September 2014 at www.huffingtonpost.co.uk/2014/09/24/notinmyname-campaign-obama-un-general-assembly_n_5875206.html.

being made or things are not going well. You have to sit back, think of things, and reassess your position."[157]

At the tactical level, an investigator confronting a terrorist suspect who believes with altruistic passion that they have embarked on a righteous path can seek to chip away at this certainty by challenging the foundations on which this value system rests. The more absolute the value system, the more fragile it is likely to be once an element of doubt is introduced. One of the most effective ways to introduce this element of doubt seems to be to put a human face on the "other" and to make an emotional connection between victim and perpetrator in the same way that FBI Special Agent Ali Soufan was able to reach *al-Qaeda* prisoner Abu Jandal in the aftermath of the 9/11 attacks. It must be acknowledged that this is an approach that will only work with a subset of terrorist actors — perhaps even a minority. Profound faith, profound hatred, or profound disassociation is sometimes impossible to overcome, but the history of the past 150 years teaches that terrorism is most often defeated in increments and not by sweeping victories.

The same logic applies at the strategic level, counter-terrorism practitioners seeking to undermine a terrorist group's relationship with its constituency can chip away at the self-image the group seeks to project, challenging protestations of altruism by highlighting the negative consequences of their actions for their supporters, by exposing evidence of hypocrisy in their ranks, and by putting a human face on the suffering of their victims. As discussed in Part I, terrorist groups explicitly try to manage the flow of information to their constituents and to still discordant voices within their communities, as part of their effort to widen the gulf between their supporters and their opponents, and to further polarize the conflict in which they are engaged. If governments can address this "information asymmetry" by ensuring terrorists' potential constituents gain a more rounded, nuanced, human, picture of what is actually happening, perhaps some middle ground for compromise can be

---

[157] Kevin Toolis, *Rebel Hearts* (St. Martin's Griffin; 1997), p. 183.

secured.[158] By their own account, and by their actions, terrorist groups pay close attention to the opinions and feelings of their constituents, even as they try to shape them. If governments can find a way to effectively influence these constituents, this in turn can influence the terrorist organizations themselves.

## Self-Actualization

Abraham Maslow's influential theory of human developmental psychology posited a hierarchy of needs that shape human endeavors, from basic needs such as sustenance and security to psychological needs such as esteem and fellowship. At the apex of this hierarchy sits the drive for self-actualization, an internal process of self-exploration in which an individual strives to develop his or her full potential as a human being.[159] The personal journey to find meaning in one's existence, and to establish a distinct identity, is perhaps the most universal human rite of passage.[160] Clearly, this search for meaning can take many forms and only very rarely leads to the embrace of violent or extreme positions, but in those rare cases it does seem to be a significant factor, as a June 2008 report on *Understanding Radicalisation and Violent Extremism* prepared by the Behavioral Science Unit of the British Security Service (MI5) recognized, noting "membership of a terrorist group can provide a sense of meaning and purpose. It can lead to enhanced self-esteem, and the individual can feel a sense of control and influence over their lives."[161] The *Rote Armee Fraktion* member Knut Folkerts perhaps summarized this insight best when, reflecting on his own

---

[158] Frank Cilluffo and Daniel Kimmage, How to Beat Al-Qaeda at its Own Game, *Foreign Policy*, April 2009.

[159] Abraham Maslow, A Theory of Human Motivation, *Psychological Review*, Vol. 50, No. 4 (1943), pp. 370–96.

[160] See Arie Kruglanski, Michele Gelfand, Jocelyn Bélanger, Anna Sheveland, Malkanthi Hetiarachchi and Rohan Gunaratna, The Psychology of Radicalization and Deradicalization: How Significance Quest Impacts Violent Extremism, *Advances in Political Psychology*, Vol. 35, Suppl. 1 (2014).

[161] Alan Travis, The making of an extremist, *The Guardian*, 20 August 2008, at www.theguardian.com/uk/2008/aug/20/uksecurity.terrorism. Viewed 5 August 2016.

experience of joining a terrorist group, he concluded that "the choice of armed struggle — when everything is said and done — is first and foremost an existential decision to make."[162] Former *Irgun* commander Menachem Begin put it even more forcefully: "There are times when everything in you cries out: your very self-respect as a human being lies in your resistance to evil. *We fight, therefore we are.*"[163]

Self-actualization is inseparably entwined with identity, and identity has personal, social, and cultural elements that all play an important part in making a person who he or she is.[164] Identity is also sometimes a fluid concept that can undergo major changes throughout a lifetime, or it can stay frozen from an early age. Some men and women spend a lifetime fighting for a cause they believe in, others turn their backs on everything they fought for in a complete *volte face*. The personal odyssey of another former *Rote Armee Fraktion* cadre, Horst Mahler, saw him jailed as a left-wing terrorist for ten years in the 1970s and then again for inciting hatred and holocaust denial in the 2000s after he embraced a variety of neo-Nazi causes. Provisional IRA volunteer Maria McGuire turned her back on Irish nationalism in the early 1970s and resurfaced in the public eye rather more prosiacally decades later as a Conservative Party councillor in the London Borough of Croydon. As with some of the other potential drivers considered in this section, self-actualization is advanced as a process worthy of consideration in plumbing the motives of an individual terrorist, but it should not be considered an exclusive cause nor to act in isolation from other causal factors. Nor should it necessarily be considered to be a reliable predictor of future behavior. However, since we are all human, to a greater or lesser extent a terrorist's internal life will always perforce form some part of the answer to the puzzle of why he or she chose to take up arms and harm others in service of a given

---

[162] George Kassimeris, *Inside Greek Terrorism* (Oxford University Press; 2013), p. 56.

[163] Menachem Begin, *The Revolt: Story of the Irgun* (Steimatzky's Agency Ltd.; 1977), p. 46.

[164] Seth Schwartz, Curtis Dunkel and Alan Waterman, Terrorism: An Identity Theory Perspective, *Studies in Conflict and Terrorism*, Vol. 32, No. 6 (2009), p. 540.

cause. As the British sociologist Richard Jenkins has noted: "Identity is not 'just there', it must always be established."[165]

That membership of a terrorist organization can be empowering for individuals, enhancing their self-esteem and offering a self-perceived opportunity for them to reach their full potential, is well established in the literature. Jamal al-Gashey, who took part in Black September's 1972 Munich Olympics hostage operation, described the moment he joined Yasir Arafat's *Fateh* movement to a reporter: "For the first time, I felt proud and felt that my existence and my life had a meaning, that I was not just a wretched refugee, but a revolutionary figure fighting for a cause."[166] Another Palestinian militant interviewed by Jerrold Post, Ehud Sprinzak and Laurita Denny echoed this sentiment: "My motivation in joining *Fateh* was both ideological and personal. It was a question of self-fulfillment, of honor and a feeling of independence... the goal of every young Palestinian was to be a fighter."[167] The PFLP's Leila Khaled wrote in her memoirs, "I knew that I had a role to play: I realized that my historic mission was as a warrior in the inevitable battle between oppressors and oppressed, exploiters and exploited. I decided to become a revolutionary in order to liberate my people and myself."[168]

Newly installed as Prime Minster of Israel, Menachem Begin considered his elevated position less personally significant than the role he had played in Israel's struggle for nationhood: "I used to say, to friend and opponent alike, that whatever position I may hold, it will never be comparable to the national and human importance of what my friends and I did in the underground during our fight for the liberation of our people ... When a man fights for freedom at the incessant risk of his life, he identifies himself completely with

---

[165] Richard Jenkins, *Social Identity* (Routledge; 1996), p. 4.

[166] Simon Reeve, *One Day in September: The Full Story of the 1972 Munich Olympics Massacre and the Israeli Revenge Operation "Wrath of God"* (Arcade Publishing; 2000).

[167] Jerrold Post, Ehud Sprinzak and Laurita Denny, The Terrorists in Their Own Words: Interviews with 35 Incarcerated Middle Eastern Terrorists, *Terrorism and Political Violence*, Vol. 15, No. 1 (Spring 2003), p. 182.

[168] Leila Khaled and George Hajjar, *My People Shall Live: The Autobiography of a Revolutionary* (Hodder and Stoughton; 1973), p. 22.

the very idea of liberty."[169] Patroklos Tselentis of November 17 testified in court that his decision to join the Greek terrorist group was driven by a sense of destiny that made him feel proud: "I was in the front line, fighting for something I believed was worth fighting for."[170] Former *al-Qaeda* member Aimen Dean described the self-awaking he experienced volunteering to fight with the *Mujahedin* in Bosnia: "I was a bookish nerd from Saudi Arabia just weeks ago and then suddenly I find myself prancing up on the mountains of Bosnia holding an AK-47 feeling a sense of immense empowerment — and the feeling that I was participating in writing history rather than just watching history on the side."[171]

Helmut Ensslin, a socially conscious protestant vicar who was the father of founding *Rote Armee Fraktion* member Gudrun Ensslin, observed at the time of his daughter's first arrest in April 1968 for an arson attack on two Frankfurt department stores: "It has astonished me to find that Gudrun, who has always thought in a very rational, intelligent way, has experienced what is almost a condition of euphoric self-realization, a really holy self-realization such as we find in connection with saints. To me, that is more of a beacon light than the fire of the arson itself — seeing a human being make her way to self-realization through such acts."[172] A court appointed psychiatrist, Reinhard Rethardt, who interviewed Ensslin after her arrest reached a remarkably similar conclusion: "Hers was a heroic impatience. She suffers from the inadequacy of our existence. She was unwilling to wait any longer; she wanted to translate what she had learnt in the parsonage into action, to act on behalf of her neighbor — wholesale and against his will."[173] Ensslin was arrested alongside her lover Andreas Baader and two other friends, Thorwald Proll and Horst Söhnlein. She was initially sentenced to three years in prison but was released pending appeal in June 1969 and

---

[169] Menachem Begin, *The Revolt: Story of the Irgun* (Steimatzky's Agency Ltd.; 1977), foreword.

[170] George Kassimeris, *Inside Greek Terrorism* (Oxford University Press; 2013), pp. 41–42.

[171] Peter Marshall, The spy who came in from Al-Qaeda, *BBC News Magazine*, 2 March 2015.

[172] Stefan Aust, *Baader-Meinhof: The Inside Story of the RAF* (Oxford University Press; 2009), p. 40.

[173] ibid., p. 37.

immediately went underground. She would be recaptured in June 1972 and killed herself in Stammheim prison in October 1977, along with Baader and Jan-Carl Raspe.

Albert Bandura's "social learning theory" posits that young men frustrated with their low status in society will often seek out high status members of their community on whom to model their behavior in the hope and expectation that in this way they may be able to improve their social status.[174] The researcher Muhsin Hassan notes that in patriarchial societies that place a great deal of emphasis on age and achievement, membership of a group like *al-Shabaab* can be a shortcut to status and respect. Former ISIL recruit Abu Ayman told the BBC: "Many brothers joined [ISIL] for new weapons, luxury guns, to drive better jeeps and to show off."[175] Saajid Badat, who was originally paired with failed *al-Qaeda* shoe bomber Richard Reid to attack transatlantic airliners, explained how he had become involved in the plot at the 2012 trial of another *al-Qaeda* operative, Adis Medunjanin, in New York: "It was almost the glamour factor of it, drawing me in."[176] A member of *Fateh* told the former CIA psychologist Jerrold Post: "My motivation in joining *Fateh* was both ideological and personal. It was a question of self-fulfillment, of honor and a feeling of independence ... the goal of every young Palestinian was to be a fighter ... After recruitment, my social status was greatly enhanced. I got a lot of respect from my acquaintances and from the young people in the village."[177] Provisional IRA volunteer Dermot Finucane recalled thinking after he was accepted into the organization: "This is IT! You are with the big boys now."[178] Sometimes laying claim to a militant identity can help outsiders to fit in with a core group. In a 1983 study of ETA members, Robert Clark found that

---

[174] See Albert Bandura, *Social Learning Theory* (General Learning Press; 1977).

[175] Paul Wood, Jihadi John: Mohammed Emwazi was a Cold loner, ex-fighter says, *BBC News*, 1 March 2015, at http://www.bbc.com/news/uk-31686582.

[176] Laura Trevelyan, Shoe-bomber supergrass Saajid Badat testifies in US, *BBC News*, 23 April 2012, at http://www.bbc.co.uk/news/world-us-canada-17820810.

[177] Jerrold Post, The New Face of Terrorism: Socio-Cultural Foundations of Contemporary Terrorism, *Behavioral Sciences and the Law*, Vol. 23, No. 4 (July/August 2005), p. 454.

[178] Kevin Toolis, *Rebel Hearts* (St. Martin's Griffin; 1997), p. 125.

40% of the ETA members he was able to interview actually came from mixed Spanish and Basque families in a fiercely parochial region where such families only formed 8% of the population.[179] He posited that because they felt that they didn't fully belong these mixed-ethnicity youths exaggerated their "political identity" to achieve a "psycho-social identity".[180]

Field research undertaken by Scott Atran in North Africa and David Kilcullen in Afghanistan has identified boredom and a latent thirst for adventure as a powerful causal factor in youthful radicalization.[181] In *The Accidental Guerrilla*, Kilcullen describes an ambush in Afghanistan in which a US unit was attacked first by *Taliban* forces and then by unaffiliated local youths. The local youths later told Kilcullen that their intervention in the firefight was not motivated by any personal animosity towards the United States: "When the battle was right there in front of them, how could they not join in? Did we understand just how boring it was to be a teenager in a valley in central Afghanistan? This was the most exciting thing to happen in their valley for years."[182] Abu Bakr Naji advises would-be Islamist recruiters in *The Administration of Savagery*: "Capture the rebelliousness of youth, their energy and idealism, and their readiness for self-sacrifice, while fools preach 'moderation', security and avoidance of risk."[183] He knew his audience well. Moner Mohammad Abu-Salha was a twenty-two-year-old Florida native who carried out a sixteen-ton suicide truck bombing against a restaurant popular with pro-government Syrian Army soldiers in Idlib Province for *Jabhat al-Nusra*, *al-Qaeda*'s local subsidiary in Syria, in May 2014.[184] In his

---

[179] Robert Clark, Patterns in the Lives of ETA Members, *Terrorism*, Vol. 6, No. 3 (1983).

[180] Jerrold Post, Notes on a Psychodynamic Theory of Terrorist Behavior, *Terrorism*, Vol. 7, No. 3 (1984), p. 247.

[181] Scott Atran, *Talking to the Enemy: Faith, Brotherhood and the (Un)making of Terrorists* (Ecco; 2010), p. 40.

[182] David Kilcullen, *The Accidental Guerrilla: Fighting Small Wars in the Midst of a Big One* (Oxford University Press; 2009), p. 40.

[183] Scott Atran, Mindless terrorists? The truth about ISIS is much worse, *The Guardian*, 15 November 2015.

[184] Frances Robles, Seeking Clues in Man's Arc from Life in Florida to Fatal Blast in Syria, *The New York Times*, 3 June 2014.

martyrdom video, he said; "Just sitting down [for] five minutes drinking a cup of tea with a *mujahedin* is better than anything I've ever experienced in my whole life. I lived in America! I know how it is. You have all the fancy amusement parks, and the restaurants, and the food, and all this crap and the cars and you think you're happy. I was never happy. I was always sad and depressed. Life sucked … All you do is work forty, fifty, sixty hours a week."[185] In a paper on terrorist recruitment written for the United States Institute of Peace (USIP), Colonel John Venhaus singled out "thrill seekers" as one of the four types of "seeker" he had identified amongst terrorist volunteers (the others being revenge seekers, status seekers, and identity seekers).[186] The Norwegian researcher Thomas Hegghammer has also noted anecdotal evidence of some foreign terrorist fighters in Syria and Iraq being motivated by a search for adventure, which he has colorfully dubbed the "Hemingway effect".[187]

Escaping from the mundane routines of daily life seems a common motivation for would-be terrorists of every social class. The Russian anarchist Dmitry Bogrov, who murdered the Russian Prime Minister Pyotr Stolypin in September 1911, famously claimed to have become involved in radical circles because he was tired of a life that had become "nothing but an endless number of cutlets".[188] Although generations apart, when asked by a friend why someone with her privileged background would become a terrorist, Suzanne Albrecht, who as a member of the *Rote Armee Fraktion* assisted in the failed 1977 kidnap-turned-murder of Jürgen Ponto, Chairman of the Dresdener Bank, and the failed assassination attempt on Alexander Haig, NATO Commander-in-Chief, gave an almost identical response: "I was tired of all that caviar."[189] Her colleague Beate

---

[185] Peter Bergen, *United States of Jihad: Investigating America's Homegrown Terrorists* (Crown; 2016), pp. 244–245.

[186] Col. John Venhaus, *Why Youth Join Al-Qaeda*, United States Institute of Peace: Special Report No. 236 (May 2010), p. 1.

[187] Thomas Hegghammer, Should I stay or Should I Go? Explaining Variation in Western Jihadists' Choice between Domestic and Foreign Fighting, *American Political Science Review*, Vol. 107, No. 1 (February 2013), p. 6.

[188] Michael Burleigh, *Blood and Rage: A Cultural History of Terrorism* (Harper; 2009), p. 58.

[189] Matthew Carr, *The Infernal Machine: A History of Terrorism*, (The New Press; 2007), p. 141.

Sturm also admitted: "We thought we knew we'd got into all this for the correct political reasons [but] we liked the thrill of it too."[190] Two decades after her brief career as a PFLP hijacker, Leila Khaled recalled almost wistfully in an interview with the author Eileen MacDonald: "There was something exciting in what we did. There was a heroic dimension to our lives."[191] MacDonald left convinced that this period had clearly been the highlight of Khaled's life. LEHI recruit Eliahu Bet Zouri, arrested for his part in the November 1944 assassination of the British minister of state in the Middle East, Lord Moyne, told his attorney: "Some people live short lives in which nothing significant occurs. That is a tragedy. But to live a short life that includes a deed for one's homeland — that is a triumph. Isn't it better, Mr. Advocate, to lead a brief but significant life than a long but meaningless one?"[192]

Some lives, of course, have false starts. An individual may make life choices they come to regret, or even feel ashamed of, and then decide to make a conscious effort to change. The American academic Mia Bloom identified the search for "redemption" as one of four primary motivations that she repeatedly encountered in her case studies of women terrorists (along with revenge, relationships, and a thirst for respect).[193] MI5's Behavioral Science Unit reached a very similar conclusion in its report on *Understanding Radicalisation and Violent Extremism*, which noted: "Some [volunteers] appeared to have turned to violent extremist groups in the misguided belief that participation in *jihad* might help atone for previous wrongdoing."[194] The report adds: "We have noticed that terrorist groups are remarkably tolerant of individuals with serious criminal histories. This is the case even when those individuals continue to be involved in very serious non-terrorist crimes, including drug-trafficking, assault and

---

[190] Stefan Aust, *Baader-Meinhof: The Inside Story of the RAF* (Oxford University Press; 2009), p. 90.

[191] Eileen MacDonald, *Shoot the Women First* (Random House; 1992), pp. 100–101.

[192] Gerold Frank, *The Deed* (Simon and Schuster; 1963), p. 253.

[193] Mia Bloom, *Bombshell: Women and Terrorism* (University of Pennsylvania Press; 2011), pp. 33–249.

[194] Alan Travis, The making of an extremist, *The Guardian*, 20 August 2008, at www.theguardian.com/uk/2008/aug/20/uksecurity.terrorism. Viewed 5 August 2016.

even rape." Further support for this insight also comes from the French researcher Olivier Roy who compiled a database of 100 people who had been involved in terrorism in France or had left France and Belgium to fight alongside militant groups in the past twenty years, and, while he found no standard terrorist profile, he noted that there was a high preponderance of what he termed "born again" Muslims, second-generation immigrants who had turned their back on a secular Western lifestyle, and in almost half the cases on a life of petty crime, to reacquaint themselves with the faith of their forefathers, repudiating their parents' attempts to assimilate in the process.[195]

The search for redemption is not unique to religious terrorism, but it is inevitably accentuated by religious narratives in which redemption typically features as a central theme.[196] Huthaifa Azzam, the son of Osama bin Laden's mentor Abdullah Azzam, recalled that it had been *Sunni* missionaries who had convinced the founder of *al-Qaeda* in Iraq, Abu Mus'ab al-Zarqawi, to re-embrace his childhood faith: "It was the *Tablighi Jamaat* who convinced him — he had thirty-seven criminal cases against him by then — that it was time to cleanse himself."[197] Azzam added: "I was struck by the way [al-Zarqawi's] past seemed to affect him, as he always struggled with a sense of guilt ... He would say, 'Because of the things I did in my past, nothing could bring *Allah* to forgive me unless I become a *Shahid*'."[198] It is surely no coincidence that, as Roy identifies, prison recruitment has been a particular feature of the Islamist terrorism of the past two decades. The search for redemption is not the only reason for a convict to join an Islamist gang in prison — pre-existing social networks and the need for protection are also potential motivations — but in many cases, it reportedly plays a role. Noting that revolutionary enthusiasm can often serve as a refuge from a guilty conscience, the philosopher Eric Hoffer thoughtfully observed

---

[195] Olivier Roy, Who are the new Jihadis?, *The Guardian*, 13 April 2017.

[196] ibid.

[197] Mary Anne Weaver, The Short, Violent Life of Abu Musab al-Zarqawi, *The Atlantic*, July/August 2006.

[198] Joby Warrick, *Black Flags: The Rise of ISIS* (Doubleday; 2015), p. 53.

in his classic study of mass movements, *The True Believer,* that such groups can derive significant benefits from the skills experienced lawbreakers possess: "It sometimes seems that mass movements are custom-made to fit the needs of the criminal — not only for the catharsis of his soul but also for the exercise of his inclinations and talents."[199]

One of the early pioneers of the theoretical study of identity, Erik Erikson, considered the impact on the sense of self of both positive and negative identities.[200] *Rote Armee Fraktion* member Ulrich Scholze experienced an almost perverse sense of pride in the negative identity placed on the RAF by the West German state: "You have to be emotionally convinced that all attempts at reform simply stabilize the present system of society and consolidate capitalism... Then the prosecuting authorities put pressure on you, and that confirms all you thought. And the sensational press reports and descriptions such as 'Public Enemy Number 1' from government sources create a feeling of success that gives you the strength to carry on."[201] Mark Juergensmeyer has suggested that the "personal loss of power" — accompanied by a deep sense of humiliation — can be a key factor in radicalization.[202] Consider this comment from the former Head of the Provisional IRA Army Council who became the deputy First Minister of Northern Ireland in 2007, Martin McGuinness, explaining why he fought for his community: "The Unionists want power, power they have abused in the past, power they have used to humiliate me, humiliate my father, my forefathers before."[203] The Palestinian scholar Sari Nusseibeh wrote of the First *Intifada* that it "exorcised demons of

---

[199] Eric Hoffer, *The True Believer: Thoughts on the Nature of Mass Movements* (Harper Perennial Modern Classics; 2010), pp. 53–54.

[200] Michael Arena and Bruce Arrigo, *The Terrorist Identity: Explaining The Terrorist Threat* (New York University; 2006), p. 16.

[201] Stefan Aust, *Baader-Meinhof: The Inside Story of the RAF* (Oxford University Press; 2009), p. 91.

[202] Mark Juergensmeyer, *Terror in the Mind of God: The Global Rise of Religious Violence* (University of California Press; 2003), pp. 190–191.

[203] Kevin Toolis, *Rebel Hearts* (St. Martin's Griffin; 1997), p. 330.

humiliation, inferiority, and self-contempt".[204] The *Hamas* leader Dr. Abdul Aziz al-Rantisi also echoed Juergensmeyer's observation when explaining the allure of martyrdom for would-be suicide bombers: "To die in this way is better than to die daily in frustration and humiliation."[205] In a June 2014 *Ramadan* message to his followers, ISIL leader Abu Bakr al-Baghdadi declared: "Terrorism is to refuse humiliation, subjugation and subordination. Terrorism is for the Muslim to live as a Muslim, honorably with might and freedom. Terrorism is to insist upon your rights and not give them up."[206] The ISIL magazine *Dabiq* refers to the volunteers rallying to its banner as "the brothers who have refused to live a life of humiliation".[207]

Juergensmeyer has argued that violence is attractive because it offers "the illusion of power" and it appeals to people who want to make dramatic statements and stake their claim to public space — an attitude perhaps typified by Andreas Baader's proposed title for a projected book setting out the basic tenets of the *Rote Armee Fraktion*: "The Gun Speaks".[208] Juergensmeyer describes the processes through which often marginalized individuals seek to gain some control over their lives as "symbolic empowerment" and suggests that this often manifests itself in the act of joining an established gang or organization, and participating in acts of ritualized violence, or some other form of collective action.[209]

[204] Jeffrey William Lewis, *The Business of Martyrdom: A History of Suicide Bombing* (Naval Institute Press; 2012), p. 143.

[205] Mark Juergensmeyer, *Terror in the Mind of God: The Global Rise of Religious Violence* (University of California Press; 2003), p. 190.

[206] Jason Burke, *The New Threat: The Past, Present and Future of Islamic Militancy* (The New Press; 2015), p. 92 and Abu Bakr al-Baghdadi, *A Message to the Mujahedin and the Muslim Ummah in the month of Ramadan*, Middle East Research Institute, 1 July 2014.

[207] Jessica Stern, Radicalization to Extremism and Mobilization to Violence: What Have We Learned and What Can We Do about It?, *The ANNALS of the American Academy of Political and Social Science*, Vol. 668, No. 1, November 2016, p. 108.

[208] Mark Juergensmeyer, *Terror in the Mind of God: The Global Rise of Religious Violence* (University of California Press; 2003), p. 128 and p. 191. See also Stefan Aust, *Baader-Meinhof: The Inside Story of the RAF* (Oxford University Press; 2009), p. 190.

[209] Mark Juergensmeyer, *Terror in the Mind of God: The Global Rise of Religious Violence* (University of California Press; 2000), p. 185, and Michael Arena and Bruce Arrigo, *The Terrorist Identity: Explaining The Terrorist Threat* (New York University; 2006), p. 8.

Juergensmeyer posits that this path to empowerment typically unfolds over four stages: a sense of alienation and disconnection; the absence of conventional options to effect change; the demonization of an "other" and the adoption of a Manichean world view; and the performance of symbolic acts of power.[210] Franco Freda, an *Ordine Nuovo* affiliate and Italian neo-fascist theorist, wrote in his journal *Quex*: "We are not interested in seizing power, not even, *per se*, in establishing a new order ... what interests us is combat, action in itself, the daily struggle to assert our own nature."[211] An unidentified member of *Fateh* told Jerrold Post: "An armed action proclaims that I am here, I exist, I am strong, I am in control, I am in the field, I am on the map."[212] The American novelist Don DeLillo's description of terrorism as "the language of being noticed" seems particularly apposite.[213]

The psychiatrist and philosopher Frantz Fanon famously applied this insight to national liberation movements. In 1961, he published *The Wretched of the Earth* in which he developed his theory of psychopathology, arguing that the act of resistance to colonial rule actually helped these subject peoples to realize their true identity: "At the level of the individual, violence is a cleansing force. It frees the native from his inferiority complex and from his despair and inaction; it makes him fearless and restores his self-respect."[214] Fanon had fought with the Free French forces in World War II and won the *Croix de Guerre*, but in 1954 he joined the Algerian *Front de Libération Nationale* (FLN) supporting its struggle for independence from French colonial rule. Fanon's work was enormously influential for both anti-colonial and Marxist terrorist groups. RAF member Stefan Wisniewski commented in an interview, "we only saw Germany from

---

[210] Mark Juergensmeyer, *Terror in the Mind of God: The Global Rise of Religious Violence* (University of California Press; 2000), p. 185.

[211] *Quex* #3, 1979, quoted in Franco Ferraresi, *Threats to Democracy: The Radical Right in Italy after the War* (1996), p. 158.

[212] Jerrold Post, The New Face of Terrorism: Socio-Cultural Foundations of Contemporary Terrorism, *Behavioral Sciences and the Law*, Vol. 23, No. 4 (July/August 2005), p. 454.

[213] Louise Richardson, *What Terrorists Want: Understanding the Enemy and Containing the Threat*, (Random House; 2007), p. 103 and Don DeLillo, *Mao II* (Penguin Books; 1992), p. 157.

[214] Frantz Fanon, *The Wretched of the Earth* (Grove Press; 1963), p. 94.

the perspective of *The Wretched of the Earth*,"[215] and the Black Panther Eldridge Cleaver that "every brother on a rooftop can quote Fanon."[216] Perhaps, most notable of all, Che Guevara was a great admirer of Fanon's work, echoes of which can be found in his observation that "the [revolutionary] vanguard creates itself."[217]

The Egyptian Islamist Sayyid Qutb similarly advanced the argument in his writings that the struggle to impose Islamic rule was not just about resistance to oppression but was also in itself ennobling, helping the fighter to realize his true potential: "While struggling against other people [the true Muslim] struggles against himself … Horizons are opened to him in the faith which would never be opened to him if he were to sit immobile and at rest … His soul, feelings, his imagination, his habits, his nature, his reactions and responses — all are brought to a point of development which he could not have attained without hard and bitter experience."[218]

Qutb's belief in the spiritual dimension of combat was of course part of a rich Islamic tradition. The concept of *jihad* is intimately linked to both self-actualization and redemption.[219] The term literally means "striving" or "exerting oneself" and in Islam, it has two very different meanings — the personal, internal, struggle waged against one's baser instincts in an effort to live a godly life, and warfare with spiritual significance.[220] These two meanings are sometimes referred to respectively as the "greater" and "lesser" *jihad* — although the authenticity of the *hadith* in which Mohammed is reported to have remarked after the Battle of Tabuk that he had returned from the lesser *jihad* to the greater *jihad*, and thus privileged one over the other, has been hotly disputed by Islamic militants from Taqī ad-Dīn Ahmad ibn Taymiyyah

---

[215] André Moncourt and J. Smith, *We were so terribly consistent: A conversation about the history of the RAF*, Stefan Wisniewski interviewed by TAZ (Kersplebedeb; 2009), p. 28.

[216] Adam Shatz, The Doctor Prescribed Violence, *The New York Times*, 2 September 2001.

[217] Joanne Wright, *Terrorist Propaganda: The Red Army Faction and the Provisional IRA 1968–1986* (Palgrave MacMillan; 1991), p. 145.

[218] John Calvert, *Sayyid Qutb and the Origins of Radical Islamism* (Columbia University Press; 2010), p. 226.

[219] David Cook, *Understanding Jihad* (University of California Press; 2015), pp. 1–2 and p. 15.

[220] ibid., pp. 1–2.

to Abdullah Azzam. What is not in dispute is the importance for each individual of realizing their full potential through their obedience to, and relationship with, God. For Ayatollah Khomeini, personal revelation — the battle against ego — was a crucial precursor to militant activity: "Without the inner *jihad*, the outer *jihad* is impossible. *Jihad* is inconceivable unless a person turns his back on his own desires and the world."[221] David Cook notes that the 9/11 hijackers similarly referenced the importance of the inner *jihad* in the testament they prepared before setting the New York and Washington attacks in motion.[222] The redemptive aspect of *jihad* is also crucial to understanding its appeal to individual fighters. As a frequently cited *hadith* from the celebrated Medieval warrior-ascetic Abdallah bin al-Mubarak's *Katib al-jihad* elucidates: "Being killed in the path of *Allah* washes away impurity; killing is two things: atonement and rank [in heaven]."[223] As we have seen, it is not uncommon for Islamist terrorists — for example, Abu Mus'ab al-Zarqawi or the shoe bomber Richard Reid — to have had criminal backgrounds before reinventing themselves as "holy warriors". A study of seventy-nine European jihadists conducted by Rajan Basra and Peter Neumann at the International Centre for the Study of Radicalisation in 2016 found that they often admitted that they had been seeking redemption from their past sins.[224]

Another closely associated but rather less elevated benefit of membership of a terrorist group seems to be the sense of empowerment that simply results from the close proximity to firearms. The young LEHI recruit Eliahu Bet Zouri confided to his diary after seeing a LEHI comrade, Joshua Cohen, disarm three British policemen at gunpoint: "The gun, oh the gun. From now on it is my best friend. It equalizes all — the strong and the weak, the oppressor and the

---

[221] ibid., p. 39.

[222] ibid., p. 48.

[223] ibid., p. 15.

[224] Rajan Basra and Peter Neumann, *How Crime and Terror Have Merged: European Jihadists and the New Crime-Terror Nexus*, at https://medium.com/shaping-the-future/how-crime-and-terror-have-merged-european-jihadists-and-the-new-crime-terror-nexus-5a60d13fea85#.36fdam87q.

oppressed."[225] Michael Baumann reflected on his experience as a gun-wielding member of *Bewegung 2. Juni*: "Having a pistol in your belt gives you a feeling of superiority at the beginning. Even the greatest weakling feels stronger than [the boxer] Muhammad Ali. All you have to be able to do is crook your finger. Any idiot can do that. It has a fascination to which many succumb."[226] The leader of the Turin column of the *Brigate Rosse*, Patrizio Peci, who murdered at least eight people, described his relationship with the pistol he was issued with as giving him "a feeling of power and security. It was my good friend. I was more jealous towards it than towards a woman."[227] Another *Brigate Rosse* member described the sense of empowerment he felt carrying a gun in strikingly similar terms: "Arms have a fascination of their own, it is a fascination that makes you feel in some way more ... more virile ... this sensation of feeling stronger, more manly ... I found myself ... showing them to women to impress them."[228]

An *al-Shabaab* recruit told Muhsin Hassan that he found that "walking the city with a gun as a member of *al-Shabaab* ensured everybody feared and respected you. Girls also liked you."[229] The Provisional IRA volunteer Dermot Finucane further echoed this sentiment: "We got a big buzz out of the arms training. I came back with my chest sticking out — "big man!" I should have had a sticker printed on my forehead — "TOP MAN NOW!" It gave you a lift and a sense of achievement."[230] A laboratory experiment conducted by psychologists Jennifer Klinesmith, Tim Kasser and Frank McAndrew found that interaction with a firearm actually boosted testosterone and aggression in male students.[231] While young males certainly

---

[225] Gerold Frank, *The Deed* (Simon and Schuster; 1963), p. 142.

[226] Claire Sterling, *The Terror Network: The Secret War of International Terrorism* (Holt, Rinehart and Winston; 1981), p. 299.

[227] Michael Burleigh, *Blood and Rage: A Cultural History of Terrorism* (Harper; 2009), p. 215.

[228] ibid., p. 194.

[229] Muhsin Hassan, Understanding Drivers of Violent Extremism: The Case of Al-Shabaab and Somali Youth, *CTC Sentinel*, 23 August 2012, p. 19.

[230] Kevin Toolis, *Rebel Hearts* (St. Martin's Griffin; 1997), p. 125.

[231] Jennifer Klinesmith, Tim Kasser and Francis McAndrew, Guns, Testosterone, and Aggression: An Experimental Test of a Mediational Hypothesis, *Psychological Science*, Vol. 17, No. 7 (August 2006).

seem especially susceptible, it should also be noted that this sense of empowerment is not an exclusively masculine phenomenon, as the *Tupamaros*' Mauricio Rosencof famously observed, "women are never more equal to men than when they have a .45 in their hand."[232] The hijacker Leila Khaled certainly thought so, writing in her autobiography: "As a Palestinian, I had to believe in the gun as an embodiment of my humanity and my determination to liberate myself."[233]

The authors of the MI5 report on *Understanding Radicalisation and Violent Extremism* noted that some individuals find "psychological security" in the belief that their sacrifice will be one day be celebrated in the collective memory of their movement, and, in the case of faith-based actors, rewarded in the spiritual realm. Terrorism researcher Louise Richardson also listed "renown" as one of the core goals sought by individual terrorists, and again, we see this motivation repeatedly referenced in the literature. An EOKA volunteer called Levendis told his parents: "I say to you that you must be proud and have clean faces because our struggle, our holy struggle, is going forward to victory, do you think anyone could forget our heroes. 'No'. Because they are not dead, they will be immortal like the heroes of 1821 [The Greek War of Independence from the Ottoman Empire]."[234] EOKA was quick to reinforce such thoughts, issuing a leaflet in September 1956 after the execution of three EOKA fighters which proclaimed: "Their sacrifice waters the roots of the tree of Cyprus Freedom."[235] Abd al-Fattah Inayat was an Egyptian nationalist who was involved in the murder of three senior British colonial officials in Cairo, including the *Sirdar* of the Egyptian Army, Sir Lee Stack, during the early 1920s. After his release from prison in 1947, Inayat published his memoirs in the Cairo newspaper *al-Hawadith* in

---

[232] Pablo Brum, *The Robin Hood Guerrillas: The Epic Journey of Uruguay's Tupamaros* (CreateSpace; 2014), p. 50.

[233] Leila Khaled and George Hajjar, *My People Shall Live: The Autobiography of a Revolutionary* (Hodder and Stoughton; 1973), p. 87.

[234] David French, *Fighting EOKA: The British Counter-Insurgency Campaign on Cyprus, 1955–1959* (Oxford University Press; 2015), p. 68.

[235] ibid., p. 99.

which he described his motivation for taking up the nationalist struggle. He explained that as a young man, he had been deeply impressed by one of the towering nationalist figures of the previous generation, Mustafa Kamil Pasha, and that he had been particularly inspired by Pasha's aphorism that "reputation is an additional age for man."[236] Inayat wrote that he believed that had attained this "additional age" through his militant activities — in his mind, the measure of immortality he had gained through his actions outweighed the price he had paid for them in prison.

In the aftermath of the July 2016 Nice attack, in which self-proclaimed ISIL volunteer Mohamed Lahouaiej Bouhlel drove a heavy goods vehicle into a crowd of pedestrians celebrating Bastille Day, killing eighty-four people, French psychoanalyst Fethi Benslama suggested in a radio interview that it might be time for "a pact" by the French media not to publish the names and images of terrorist perpetrators: "It's a really big boost to their efforts to make themselves world famous, even while their victims are anonymous and will remain anonymous."[237] Benslama argued that a major motivating factor behind such attacks was for the perpetrators "to gain glory in the eyes of their commanders and their friends" and noted that it was common practice for French ISIL supporters to leave their identity cards where they could be easily recovered by police because "they want to be identified very quickly." Benslama's idea was taken up by segments of the French media with *Le Monde*, *Le Figaro*, and *Nouvel Observateur*, amongst others, all choosing, in the words of a *Le Monde* editorial, to "no longer publish photographs of the perpetrators of killings, to avoid the potential effect of posthumous glorification."[238] It remains to be seen how long such paragons of journalistic virtue will be prepared to voluntarily maintain this position in the face of the inevitable public curiosity that follows such events and the cut-throat competition of less scrupulous rivals.

---

[236] John Calvert, *Sayyid Qutb and the Origins of Radical Islamism* (Columbia University Press; 2010), pp. 23–24.

[237] Julian Borger, French media to stop publishing photos and names of terrorists, *The Guardian*, 27 July 2016.

[238] ibid.

The economist David Harrison has sought to look at the phenomenon of suicide bombing using a rational choice framework, which led him to the argument that a personal identity as a "warrior-martyr" had such value that an individual would seek to protect and invest in this identity and ultimately even be prepared to trade life for it: "In return for the promotion of its terrorist objectives, the organization agrees to affirm the volunteer's identity in the community as a warrior-martyr, and also provides the means of destruction and self-destruction to distinguish this identity through violence. As a result the faction can make an impact, and the volunteer can achieve a distinction that would be beyond their reach without this agreement."[239] Applying economic principles still further, Harrison argued that as the frequency of suicide attacks increases, the supply of potential suicide bombers may decrease as martyrdom becomes more commonplace and the value of such a posthumous reputation diminishes.

None of the foregoing really satisfactorily answers the question of why one person might embrace terrorism while another rejects it despite their similar circumstances, but developmental psychology offers some insights into potential vulnerabilities, or "cognitive openings", that might make one person more susceptible to terrorist messaging than another. Writing in the 1950s and 1960s, the ground-breaking developmental psychologist Erik Erikson conceptualized personal identity as falling into one of four categories: "identity diffusion" (an unfixed and unexplored identity), "moratorium" (an unfixed identity undergoing a period of experimentation), "foreclosure" (a fixed but unexplored identity), and "identity achievement" (a fixed and fully explored identity).[240] Two of these states of mind in particular — "foreclosure" and "diffusion" — seem to correlate more highly with a gravitation towards terrorism than the others. However, it also seems reasonable to

---

[239] Mark Harrison, The Logic of Suicide Terrorism, *Royal United Services Institute Security Monitor*, Vol. 2, No. 1 (2003) and Mark Harrison, An Economist Looks at Suicide Terrorism, *World Economics*, Vol. 7, No. 4 (2006).

[240] James Marcia, Development and Validation of Ego Identity Status, *Journal of Personality and Social Psychology*, Vol. 3, No. 5 (1966), p. 552.

presume, as developmental psychologists Seth Schwartz, Curtis Dunkel and Alan Waterman have observed, that by the time an individual actually undertakes a terrorist act, they are not "searching" for an identity any longer, "they engage in it as an expression of the identity they have already developed or have been assigned."[241]

One aspect of the "foreclosed" personality type is a tendency to leave key elements of the adopted identity unexamined since it was adopted without question, and this often translates into a rather immature understanding of key elements of this identity such as faith, ethnicity, or culture. Typically, this identity is adopted wholesale from one's parents and James Marcia notes that the rigid personality type associated with "foreclosure" is likely to feel "extremely threatened" in circumstances in which "parental values were non-functional".[242] Hence, a foreclosed personality who joins a religious terrorist group out of a sense of solidarity might actually know very little about his or her faith having never really embarked on a spiritual quest of any depth, they tend to interpret scripture more literally, and if recruited to fight on its behalf tend to be single-minded in pursuit of the cause.[243] In August 2016, the Associated Press conducted a review of more than 3,000 induction forms for ISIL volunteers obtained by the Syrian opposition website *Zaman al-Wasl*, that, amongst other details, rated the volunteer's religious knowledge of *Shariah* law. The news agency found that ISIL estimated that 70% of those recruits tested had only a "basic" understanding of *Shariah*'s precepts, 24% were rated as having "intermediate" knowledge, and only around 5% as being "advanced". Only five out of the 3,000 recruits had actually memorized the *Koran*.[244] This characteristic is not confined to religious groups — the uncritical

---

[241] Seth Schwartz, Curtis Dunkel and Alan Waterman, Terrorism: An Identity Theory Perspective, *Studies in Conflict and Terrorism*, Vol. 32, No. 6 (2009), p. 539.

[242] James Marcia, Development and Validation of Ego Identity Status, *Journal of Personality and Social Psychology*, Vol. 3, No. 5 (1966), p. 552.

[243] Seth Schwartz, Curtis Dunkel and Alan Waterman, Terrorism: An Identity Theory Perspective, *Studies in Conflict and Terrorism*, Vol. 32, No. 6 (2009), p. 544.

[244] Aya Batrawy, Paisley Dodds and Lori Hinnant, Leaked ISIS documents reveal recruits have poor grasp of Islamic faith, *The Independent*, 16 August 2016.

embrace of orthodoxy takes many forms, especially once the initial commitment has been made. One of the founders of the *Brigate Rosse*, Alberto Franceschini, recalled: "All of us in the Red Brigades were drug addicts of a particular type, of ideology. A murderous drug, worse than heroin."[245] Foreclosure also lends itself to authoritarian value systems and there is some consistency of evidence that organizations that employ force — lawfully or unlawfully — to ensure compliance with their goals tend to attract individuals who are somewhat more authoritarian than normal, and that, as the Stanford Prison experiment so famously demonstrated, placing an individual in a position of power over others will tend to magnify that trait.[246]

By way of contrast, the "diffuse" personality has not formed any meaningful identity commitments.[247] A good example of such an individual is the *Rote Armee Fraktion* member Stefan Wisniewski who described drifting into militancy almost by chance: "I was barely twenty years old. At any of these points, I could have gone in a completely different direction. The anti-authoritarian movement was decisive for me — the new lifestyles, collective houses, the Rolling Stones, long hair — I found it very attractive. Socialism and revolutionary theories came along with this, particularly the sense of equality that came with revolt."[248] Wisniewski's contemporary in the militant anarchist *Bewegung 2. Juni* movement, Michael Baumann, had suffered from a similar lack of direction and purpose before joining the group: "It all kept coming at me because I wasn't really rooted, and I didn't know what I wanted."[249] He added: "You make the revolution for yourself, too. It has to contain all the facets necessary for you to unfold within in it and somehow get on the right

---

[245] Michael Burleigh, *Blood and Rage: A Cultural History of Terrorism* (Harper; 2009), p. 199.

[246] Ken Heskin, Terrorism in Ireland: The past and future, *Irish Journal of Psychology*, Vol. 15, No. 2–3 (1994), p. 471; Stanley Milgram, *Obedience to Authority* (Harper and Row; 1974); and Philip Zimbardo, *The Lucifer Effect: Understanding How Good People Turn Evil* (Random House; 2007).

[247] Seth Schwartz, Curtis Dunkel and Alan Waterman, Terrorism: An Identity Theory Perspective, *Studies in Conflict and Terrorism*, Vol. 32, No. 6 (2009), p. 545.

[248] André Moncourt and J. Smith, *We were so terribly consistent: A conversation about the history of the RAF*, Stefan Wisniewski interviewed by TAZ (Kersplebedeb; 2009), p. 6.

[249] Michael Baumann, *Terror or Love?* (Pulp Press; 1977), p. 33.

road, so this petit-bourgeois nonsense doesn't keep throwing you back; the more radically you break out the better."[250] Other examples cited by Seth Schwartz and his colleagues Curtis Dunkel and Alan Waterman include the British-born shoe bomber Richard Reid and the American *al-Qaeda* insider Adam Gadahn.[251] Diffuse personality types can be particularly vulnerable to manipulation, especially by unscrupulous and charismatic terrorist leaders whom Schwartz *et al* label "identity entrepreneurs".[252]

Morten Storm, a Danish former member of *al-Qaeda* who subsequently worked as double agent for Western intelligence agencies, observed: "It's been my experience that many converts to radical Islam have troubled childhoods, including people who have been bullied. Being part of a tight-knit community of like-minded zealous believers makes them feel appreciated, important and wanted."[253] A major study of 250 West German terrorists conducted by Herbert Jäger, Gerhard Schmidtchen, and Liselotte Suellwold found that 25% of the left-wing terrorists in their study had lost one or both parents by the age of fourteen, and 33% had a severely difficult relationship with their parents.[254] The US-born *al-Qaeda* recruiter Jesse Morton was abused by his mother as a child and despite reaching out to other adults in the community he grew up in, no one stepped in to help: "I developed a severe mistrust of the society around me and when you can't relate with the fold you are born into, of course you are open to alternative ideas ... What happened was I radicalized at a very young age because of that feeling that I needed to identify with something else. And at sixteen I ran away to avoid the abuse and took off into the streets, and started to engage in criminal

---

[250] Seth Schwartz, Curtis Dunkel and Alan Waterman, Terrorism: An Identity Theory Perspective, *Studies in Conflict and Terrorism*, Vol. 32, No. 6 (2009), p. 550.

[251] ibid., p. 545.

[252] ibid., p. 550.

[253] Milo Yiannopoulos and Jeremy Wilson, *Ginger Jihadis: Why Redheads are Attracted to Radical Islam*, Breitbart.com, 9 September 2014 at http://www.breitbart.com/Breitbart-London/2014/09/09/Ginger-Jihadis-Why-Redheads-are-Attracted-to-Radical-Islam.

[254] Andrew Silke, Cheshire-cat Logic: The Recurring Theme of Terrorist Abnormality in Psychological Research, *Psychology, Crime and the Law*, Vol. 4, No. 1 (January 1998), pp. 18–25.

behavior."[255] Morton's path from being descended from one of the Mayflower pilgrims to converting to Islam and embracing terrorism began when in prison he came across the autobiography of Malcolm X whose troubled childhood and early criminality he immediately identified with and whose life turned around when he embraced Islam. Morton started down the same path, and a Moroccan-born fellow prisoner became his spiritual guide.[256] That major life disappointments or personal crises can create a cognitive opening for terrorist propaganda, especially in diffuse personalities, is seen again and again in terrorist biographies. Florida resident Omar Mateen, who gunned down forty-nine people in a gay nightclub in Orlando in June 2016 after pledging his allegiance to ISIL, tried and failed repeatedly to become a police officer and washed out of a Florida Police Academy in 2007.[257] Mohammed Merah, the *al-Qaeda*-inspired gunman who murdered seven people in the French cities of Toulouse and Montauban, had previously tried unsuccessfully to join the regular French Army and the French Foreign Legion.[258] Both men seem to have turned on identities that rejected them.

In the 1970s and 1980s, there was a provocative trend amongst authors and psychologists like Richard Pearlstein and Jerrold Post to diagnose individual terrorists as suffering from personality disorders such as narcissism, paranoia, or psychopathy, but, while such claims occasionally resurface to this day, most subsequent research has suggested that there is little evidence of a high incidence of psychopathy, or indeed any other personality disorder, among terrorist suspects.[259] The psychiatrist Wilfried Rasch

---

[255] *Countering Radicalism and Extremism: Interview with Dr Lorenzi Vidino and Jesse Morton*, SpyCast, International Spy Museum, 18 October 2016.

[256] ibid.

[257] Peter Bergen, Normandy, Istanbul, Dhaka, Nice, Baghdad, Orlando: Why?, *CNN*, 26 July 2016.

[258] Dan Bilefsky, Toulouse Killer's Path to Radicalism a Bitter Puzzle, *New York Times*, 29 March 2012.

[259] See amongst others Andrew Silke, Cheshire-Cat Logic: The Recurring Theme of Terrorist Abnormality in Psychological Research, *Psychology, Crime and the Law*, Vol. 4, No. 1 (January 1998); Fathali Moghaddam, The Staircase to Terrorism: A Psychological Exploration, *American Psychologist*, Vol. 60, No. 2, February–March 2005, p. 161; Martha Crenshaw, The Causes of

personally examined eleven detained West German terrorists, including Andreas Baader, Ulrike Meinhof and Gudrun Ensslin, and found "nothing ... which could justify their classification as psychotics, neurotics, fanatics or psychopaths".[260] Ken Heskin reported similar findings in a series of studies of Provisional IRA volunteers.[261] In their exploration of how the late 1960s American student protest movement gave birth to a terrorist fringe, Richard and Margaret Braungart concluded that established youth development processes — such as identity formation — explained the emergence of the Weathermen better than the individual psychological attributes of its members.[262] In his study of abnormality in terrorism research, *Cheshire-Cat Logic*, Andrew Silke dismissed academic attempts to ascribe terrorism to personality disorders as a classic case of "attribution error" — just as the Cheshire Cat presumes Alice must be mad simply because she is present in Wonderland, we tend to assume terrorists must be sick because their behavior seems so abnormal to us. Silke concluded that as difficult as it may be to admit to ourselves, the clinical evidence suggests that the vast majority of terrorists have cogent reasons for acting as they do and are just ultimately "normal people" too.[263]

However, it is not unreasonable to acknowledge that personality disorders and mental illnesses are not entirely unknown amongst terrorists and that they occasionally may play a role in an

---

Terrorism, *Comparative Politics*, Vol. 13, No. 4, July 1981, pp. 379–399; Charles Ruby, Are Terrorists Mentally Deranged? *Analysis of Social Issues and Public Policy*, Vol. 2, No. 1, December 2002, pp. 15–26; and Clark McCauley and Mary Segal, Social Psychology of Terrorist Groups, in Clyde Hendrick (ed.), *Group Processes and Intergroup Relations* (Sage; 1987).

[260] See Wilfried Rasch, Psychological Dimensions of Political Terrorism in the Federal Republic of Germany, *International Journal of Law and Psychiatry*, Vol. 2, No. 1 (1979).

[261] See Ken Heskin, *Northern Ireland: A Psychological Analysis* (Gill and Macmillan; 1980); Ken Heskin, The Psychology of Terrorism in Northern Ireland, in Yonah Alexander and Alan O'Day (eds.), *Terrorism in Ireland* (Palgrave Macmillan; 1984); and Ken Heskin, Terrorism in Ireland: The Past and Future, *Irish Journal of Psychology*, Vol. 15, No. 2–3 (1994).

[262] Richard Braungart and Margaret Braungart, From Protest to Terrorism: The Case of the SDS and the Weathermen, in Donatella Della Porta (eds.), *Social Movements and Violence: Participation in Underground Organizations* (JAI Press; 1992).

[263] See Andrew Silke, Cheshire-cat Logic: The Recurring Theme of Terrorist Abnormality in Psychological Research, *Psychology, Crime and the Law*, Vol. 4, No. 1 (January 1998), pp. 20–24.

individual's decision to commit acts of violence. One prominent example, the Unabomber Ted Kaczynski, was diagnosed as suffering from paranoid schizophrenia.[264] Kaczynski's seventeen-year terror campaign encompassed sixteen letter bombings that wounded twenty-three and killed three.[265] A French psychiatrist who examined Mohamed Lahouaiej Bouhlel in 2004 diagnosed him as suffering from "the beginnings of psychosis".[266] Man Haron Monis, another self-declared ISIL supporter who took hostage eighteen customers and staff at the Lindt Café in Sydney in December 2014, killing the manager Tori Johnson, had been committed for psychiatric assessment in 2010 after a psychotic episode.[267] White supremacist Buford Furrow, who killed an Asian-American mailman and wounded five people — including three children — at the North Valley Jewish Community Center in August 1999 had been treated for a variety of mental disorders.[268] Just as personality disorders and mental illness are present but not widespread in the general population, they can be found in the subset of individuals belonging to terrorist organizations, but they are more the exception than the rule, skew towards lone wolf actors rather than cadre militants, and offer little causal insight into the larger phenomenon.

Finally, it is also worth noting that perhaps one of the most explicit examples in the literature of the process of self-actualization driving terrorism comes in the form of the *Sozialistisches Patientenkollektiv* (SPK) — founded in 1970 by Heidelberg psychiatrist Wolfgang

---

[264] Adam Majid, The Unabomber Revisited: Reexamining the Use of Mental Disorder Diagnoses as Evidence of the Mental Condition of Criminal Defendants, *Indiana Law Journal Supplement*, Vol. 84, No. 1 (2009) and Clark McCauley and Sophia Moskalenko, Mechanisms of Political Radicalization: Pathways Toward Terrorism, *Journal of Terrorism and Political Violence*, Vol. 20, No. 3, (July 2008), p. 419.

[265] Mark Juergensmeyer, *Terror in the Mind of God: The Global Rise of Religious Violence* (University of California Press; 2003), p. 144.

[266] David Chazan *et al*, Nice terror attack: "soldier of Islam" Bouhlel "took drugs and used dating sites to pick up men and women", *The Telegraph*, 17 July 2016.

[267] David Kilcullen, *Blood Year: The Unraveling of Western Counterterrorism* (Oxford University Press; 2016), p. 112.

[268] Clark McCauley and Sophia Moskalenko, Mechanisms of Political Radicalization: Pathways Toward Terrorism, *Journal of Terrorism and Political Violence*, Vol. 20, No. 3 (July 2008), p. 419.

Huber. The SPK embraced political violence as therapy for mental illness. The group was made up of patients from Huber's clinic who believed mental illness was a condition created by capitalism and embraced political therapy as a cure, as the group's bulletin *Patient Info Nr. 1* put it: "There can be no therapeutic act, which isn't first and foremost clearly a revolutionary act... The system has made us sick, let's give this sick system the death-thrust!" Four former SPK members participated in the takeover of the West German Embassy in Stockholm by the *Rote Armee Fraktion's Kommando Holger Meins* in April 1975, in which two hostages and two terrorists ultimately lost their lives.

## Youth bulge

The empirical relationship between a disproportionally youthful population — a youth bulge — and political violence has been widely commented on in social science literature.[269] The Yale historian Paul Kennedy observed that revolutions occur more often in countries unable to absorb large populations of energetic young men.[270] The political scientist Jack Goldstone argued that youth bulges were one of the central factors driving two waves of revolutions in the mid-seventeenth and late eighteenth centuries, and Herbert Moeller linked a disproportionate expansion of the youth cohort to the rise of fascism and other extremist ideologies in the 1920s.[271] Samuel Huntington likewise noted that the proportion of youth in the Iranian population rose dramatically in the 1970s before the outbreak of the Iranian Revolution in 1979, and that a similar surge took place in Algeria in the early 1990s coinciding with the rise of the *Front Islamique du Salut* (FIS).[272] Huntington echoed Kennedy, describing young people as "the protagonists of protest,

---

[269] Henrik Urdal, A Clash of Generations? Youth Bulges and Political Violence, *International Studies Quarterly*, Vol. 50, No. 3 (2006), p. 623.

[270] Paul Kennedy, *Preparing for the Twenty-First Century* (Random House; 1993), p. 34.

[271] Jack Goldstone, *Revolution and Rebellion in the Early Modern World* (1991) and Herbert Moeller, Youth as a Force in the Modern World, *Comparative Studies in Society and History*, Vol. 10, No. 3 (April 1968).

[272] Samuel Huntington, *The Clash of Civilizations and the Remaking of World Order* (1996), p. 118.

instability, reform and revolution".[273] Little wonder then that one of the most prominent historians of terrorism, Walter Laqueur, once commented that the only common feature of every terrorist movement he had studied was that the bulk of their members were young.[274]

Case studies cutting across the full temporal and geographic spread of terrorist violence bear out Laqueur's observation. Before 1919, the median age of rank and file Irish Volunteers was twenty-three-years-old, and, of the officers, twenty-five. Less than 5% were over forty.[275] John Horgan and Paul Gill's database of more than a 1,000 former members of the Provisional IRA found that average age of volunteers when they first participated in PIRA-related activity was 24.99-years-old.[276] Mauricio Florez-Morris' study of Colombian paramilitary fighters had a lower average of just twenty-years-old.[277] A sample of 172 global jihadists compiled by Marc Sageman for his groundbreaking study *Understanding Terror Networks* had an average age of 25.69-years-old.[278] Perhaps, one of most detailed insights we have into terrorist recruitment comes from the so-called Sinjar records. In October 2007, US forces operating in Sinjar, Iraq, captured detailed personnel records on nearly 700 foreign volunteers who had come to Iraq to fight against the coalition forces occupying the country. The archive had originally been compiled by the organization that had facilitated their travel: the *al-Qaeda*-affiliated Mujahedin Shura Council and its successor *al-Qaeda* in Iraq.[279]

---

[273] ibid., p. 117.

[274] Walter Laqueur, *A History of Terrorism* (Transaction Publishers, 2001), p. 120.

[275] Charles Townshend, *The Republic: The Fight for Irish Independence* (Allen Lane; 2013), p. 44.

[276] Paul Gill and John Horgan, Who Were the Volunteers? The Shifting Sociological and Operational Profile of 1240 Provisional Irish Republican Army Members, *Terrorism and Political Violence*, Vol. 25, No. 3 (2013), p. 439.

[277] Mauricio Florez-Morris, Joining Guerrilla Groups in Colombia: Individual Motivations and Processes for Entering a Violent Organization, *Studies in Conflict and Terrorism*, Vol. 30, No. 7 (2007), pp. 615–634.

[278] Marc Sageman, *Understanding Terror Networks* (University of Pennsylvania Press; 2004), p. 92.

[279] Joseph Felter and Brian Fishman, *Al-Qa'ida's Foreign Fighters in Iraq: A First Look at the Sinjar Records*, Combating Terrorism Center, US Military Academy West Point, 2007, at http://www.ctc.usma.edu/posts/al-qaidas-foreign-fighters-in-iraq-a-first-look-at-the-sinjar-records.

The average age of the volunteers was 24–25-years-old and the median age was even lower at 22–23-years-old, with twice as many volunteers coming from this age group than any other.[280] Samuel Huntington suggested that societies cross a critical threshold and become more war-prone when the proportion of young people between fifteen and twenty-four passes 20% of the total population.[281] Gary Fuller drew a corresponding correlation between the 15–24-year-old age group exceeding 20% of the Tamil population in Sri Lanka and a surge of Tamil Tiger activity in the late 1980s.[282]

Much of the research into the impact of youth bulges on political violence conducted by academic researchers to date relates to revolutions, rather than terrorism *per se*, but some broad principles may nevertheless be adduced. An increase in youth cohort size typically results in a reduction of income and opportunity for the members of the cohort.[283] Youth bulges often coincide with rapid urbanization and in such circumstances, young people typically constitute a disproportionately high number of rural to urban migrants.[284] The increased demand for opportunities creates "institutional bottlenecks" for young people entering the workforce and thus generates frustration with existing societal structures.[285] Paul Collier has suggested that a youth bulge drives down the recruitment costs for anti-establishment actors, in much the same manner that higher unemployment drives down wages.[286] Marc Sommers argues that, as one might expect, this factor is particularly exacerbated when coupled with either social exclusion or

---

[280] ibid., p. 16.

[281] Samuel Huntington, *The Clash of Civilizations and the Remaking of the World Order* (Simon and Schuster; 1996), pp. 259–261.

[282] Gary Fuller, *The Demographic Backdrop to Ethnic Conflict: A Geographic Overview* (1995). See also Samuel Huntington, *The Clash of Civilizations and the Remaking of World Order* (1996), pp. 259–260.

[283] Henrik Urdal, A Clash of Generations? Youth Bulges and Political Violence, *International Studies Quarterly*, Vol. 50, No. 3 (2006), p. 610.

[284] ibid., p. 613.

[285] ibid., p. 615.

[286] Paul Collier, Doing Well Out of War: An Economic Perspective, in Mats Berdal and David Malone (eds.), *Greed and Governance: Economic Agendas in Civil Wars* (Lynne Reinner; 2000), p. 94.

modernization and rising expectations.[287] Henrik Urdal reports a positive correlation between an increased risk of terrorism and youth bulges associated with both economic decline and expanded access to higher education.[288]

Michael Burleigh also suggests a particular connection between outbreaks of terrorism and a sudden expansion of university education. The number of students attending St. Petersburg University increased threefold between 1855 and 1861,[289] and the outbreak of terrorism in West Germany and Italy in the 1970s coincided with a rapid expansion of higher education in both countries — from 268,000 university students in 1965 to 450,000 students in 1968 in Italy, and from 384,000 university students in 1965 to 510,000 students in 1970 in Germany.[290] Burleigh also points out that a similar increase in Egypt from 200,000 students in 1970 to 500,000 in 1977, coupled with an absence of new jobs for what Burleigh describes in his inimitable fashion as this "demi-educated lumpen intelligentsia", coincided with a rise in Islamic extremism and youthful support for *Jamaat Islamiya*.[291] Of the 157 Sinjar volunteers who actually listed a profession on their induction forms, sixty-seven were students, five teachers, four engineers and three doctors.[292] Polling suggests that support for terrorist attacks on Israeli targets is greater among Palestinians with more extensive education.[293] Although, of course, proximity is not necessarily causation, both Urdal's and Burleigh's insights are persuasive.

Education is not just a potential factor at the university level. David French highlights the precursory role played in the Cyprus

---

[287] See Marc Sommers, Governance, Security and Culture: Assessing Africa's Youth Bulge, *International Journal of Conflict and Violence*, Vol. 5, No. 2 (2011).

[288] Henrik Urdal, A Clash of Generations? Youth Bulges and Political Violence, *International Studies Quarterly*, Vol. 50, No. 3 (2006), p. 607.

[289] Adam Ulam, *In the Name of the People: Prophets and Conspirators in Prerevolutionary Russia* (Viking Press; 1977), p. 95.

[290] Michael Burleigh, *Blood and Rage: A Cultural History of Terrorism* (Harper; 2009), p. 192 and p. 223.

[291] ibid., p. 356.

[292] Joseph Felter and Brian Fishman, *Al-Qa'ida's Foreign Fighters in Iraq: A First Look at the Sinjar Records* (Combating Terrorism Center, US Military Academy West Point, 2007), p. 18.

[293] Alan Krueger and Jitka Malečková, Education, Poverty, Political Violence, and Terrorism: Is there a Causal Connection?, *Journal of Economic Perspectives*, Vol. 17, No. 4 (Fall 2003), p. 125.

conflict by the growth of primary education on the island — an
increase in the number of primary schools from 762 in 1922 to
1,060 in 1932 — which led to more young children being socialized
to think of themselves in sectarian terms as Greeks or Turks as their
education was provided by the two indigenous communities rather
than the British colonial state, the only political actor on the island
with an interest in promoting a common shared identity.[294] By the
time the British realized their error and introduced grants to promote multicultural schools and programs in 1935, the two
communities preferred to forgo this funding and maintain the
mono-cultural integrity of their schools, with the Greek Orthodox
Church playing a particularly important role in the secondary education of Greek islanders. One Greek-Cypriot student educated in
the 1930s recalled: "In school, Greek history, as it was taught to the
students, had the orientation that we are Greeks and Great Britain
should return Cyprus to Greece. That was the constant theme on a
daily basis."[295] Little wonder then that by the 1950s EOKA could
count on widespread popular sympathy from its coreligionists during its campaign for *enosis*. The head of EOKA, General Grivas,
noted in his treatise on guerrilla warfare that "it is among the
young people that one finds audacity, the love of taking risks and
the first great and difficult achievements" and thus recalled that "it
was to the Youth of Cyprus that I made my main appeal and called
on to give all their strength to the struggle."[296] Most active members of EOKA were aged between sixteen and twenty-five, more
than 87% of those brought to trial by the British authorities for
terrorism-related offenses were below the age of twenty-five, and
32% were still in high school. The median age of the nine Greek-
Cypriot men executed by the British for terrorist offenses was
twenty-two.[297]

---

[294] David French, *Fighting EOKA: The British Counter-Insurgency Campaign on Cyprus, 1955–1959*
(Oxford University Press; 2015), pp. 16–17.
[295] ibid., pp. 17–18.
[296] ibid., p. 66.
[297] ibid.

So, what mechanism makes youth such a significant factor? Part of the answer, likely, lies in self-actualization. The developmental psychologist Erik Erikson hypothesized that adolescents pass through a period of psychosocial crisis associated with the quest for self-actualization as they approach adulthood, which requires them to "synthesize" childhood identifications and perhaps choose between possible alternative identities so as to form "reciprocal relationships" with their community and maintain a sense of self in a larger world.[298] Erikson postulated that as they develop a sense of identity, many young people seek meaning, a sense of completeness, and "fidelity". Martha Crenshaw summarized Erikson's insight as "a need to have faith in something or someone outside oneself as well as to be trustworthy in its service".[299] The young adult brain is primed for better learning and adaptation, but it also favors sensory reward and immediacy over long-term thinking. Terrorist organizations instinctively seem to sense an opportunity in this phase of youth development. The glossy English-language ISIL magazine *Dabiq* has noted: "This revival of the *Khilāfah* [Caliphate] gave each individual Muslim a concrete and tangible entity to satisfy his natural desire for belonging to something greater."[300] 'Ali', a Dutch Muslim of Iraqi origin, told researchers from the International Centre for Counter-Terrorism in The Hague that he was planning to move to Syria to join ISIL, explaining: "It may sound weird, but when I watch these videos of Islamic fighters, I get a warrior feeling: I like the idea of truly fighting for your religion."[301]

Youth violence is also largely, but not exclusively, associated with the male of the species.[302] This phenomenon is so widely

---

[298] James Marcia, Development and Validation of Ego-Identity Status, *Journal of Personality and Social Psychology*, Vol. 3, No. 5 (1966), p. 551.

[299] Michael Arena and Bruce Arrigo, *The Terrorist Identity: Explaining The Terrorist Threat* (New York University; 2006), p. 21.

[300] *Dabiq*, Issue No. 7, p. 57; accessed on 17 November 2015, at http://media.clarionproject.org/files/islamic-state/islamic-state-dabiq-magazine-issue-7-from-hypocrisy-to-apostasy.pdf.

[301] Edwin Bakker and Peter Grol, *Motives and Considerations of Potential Foreign Fighters from The Netherlands* (International Centre for Counter-Terrorism Policy Brief; July 2015), p. 4.

[302] Eric Neumayer, Good Policy Can Lower Violent Crime: Evidence from a Cross-National Panel of Homicide Rates, 1980–97, *Journal of Peace Research*, Vol. 40, No. 6 (2003),

reported that evolutionary psychology has thrown up a number of possible explanatory pathologies. Some researchers, like Frank McAndrew, have attributed this aggression to spikes in the level of sex hormones — especially testosterone — in young male adults and their biological imperative to dominate other young males in an attempt to make themselves more attractive to potential mates.[303] Canadian psychologists Margo Wilson and Martin Daly coined the term "young male syndrome" to account for the fact that young males are much more likely to be both the perpetrators and victims of homicide than any other segment of the population. Their research led them to conclude that "many, perhaps most, homicides concern status competition."[304] Jennifer Bosson and Joseph Vandello developed a theory of "precarious manhood" which argues male aggression is designed to effectively "demonstrate manhood and thus quell men's concerns about their gender status" — a display of what 'Ali' above described as that "warrior feeling".[305] The British clinical psychologist Paul Gilbert posited a "social attention holding theory" in which he sought to explain how marginalized individuals sought social status through violent acts.[306] What we can say with some confidence is that for some young men, the quest for self-actualization is expressed largely in aggression and violence.

One final insight from the social science research on youth bulges — separately identified by Henrik Urdal, Herbert Moeller and Helen Ware — is that emigration can act as a safety value in societies struggling to respond to the expanding needs and demands

---

p. 621 and Michael Steinberger, Interview with Samuel P. Huntington, *The Observer*, 21 October 2001.

[303] Frank McAndrew, *If you give a man a gun: the evolutionary psychology of mass shootings*, The Conversation, 5 December 2015 at https://theconversation.com/if-you-give-a-man-a-gun-the-evolutionary-psychology-of-mass-shootings-51782. Viewed 26 November 2016.

[304] Margo Wilson and Martin Daly, Competitiveness, Risk Taking, and Violence: The Young Male Syndrome, *Ethology and Sociobiology*, Vol. 6, No. 1 (1985), p. 59.

[305] Jennifer Bosson and Joseph Vandello, Precarious Manhood and Its Links to Action and Aggression, *Current Directions in Psychological Science*, Vol. 20, No. 2 (April 2011), p. 82.

[306] See Paul Gilbert, *Human Nature and Suffering* (Lawrence Erlbaum Associates; 1989).

of a disproportionately large and growing youth cohort.[307] Moeller notes that the large-scale migration from Europe to North and South America in the nineteenth century likely defused widespread youth discontent in Europe by providing opportunities for advancement for those with the drive and talents to take advantage of them, while also perhaps satisfying other important drives such as the urge for adventure and self-actualization.[308] Urdal warns that if emigration opportunities are restricted — as seems to be the current trend across the Western world — countries with large youth cohorts, who might otherwise have been able to alleviate the pressure on their societies by exporting youthful talent overseas, may face a higher risk of political violence, including terrorism, in consequence.[309]

## Burn out

The life of a terrorist is not an easy option — it is a calling that involves considerable sacrifice, discomfort, isolation, and stress over prolonged periods. The Provisional IRA's *Green Book* warns: "Life in an underground army is extremely harsh and hard, cruel and disillusioning at times. So before any person decides to join the Army he should think seriously about the whole thing."[310] Nelson Mandela said of his short time at the head of *Umkhonto we Sizwe* that going underground required a seismic psychological shift: "One has to plan every action, however small and seemingly insignificant. Nothing is innocent. Everything is questioned. You cannot be yourself; you must fully inhabit whatever role you have

---

[307] Henrik Urdal, A Clash of Generations? Youth Bulges and Political Violence, *International Studies Quarterly*, Vol. 50, No. 3 (2006); Herbert Moeller, Youth as a Force in the Modern World, *Comparative Studies in Society and History*, Vol. 10, No. 3 (April 1968); and Helen Ware, Demography, Migration and Conflict in the Pacific, *Journal of Peace Research*, Vol. 42, No. 4 (July 2005).

[308] Herbert Moeller, Youth as a Force in the Modern World, *Comparative Studies in Society and History*, Vol. 10, No. 3 (April 1968), p. 242.

[309] Henrik Urdal, A Clash of Generations? Youth Bulges and Political Violence, *International Studies Quarterly*, Vol. 50, No. 3 (2006), p. 625.

[310] Provisional IRA, *Green Book*.

assumed."[311] For *Narodnaya Volya* Executive Committee member Lev Tikhomirov, it was like living "the life of a hunted wolf".[312] Yurluey Mendoza, a female fighter who joined the FARC at the tender age of fourteen, painted an even starker picture: "Do you know what it's like to spend 20 years at war? It's hard, really hard ... There are times when you can't walk from so many blisters, or your backpack chafes off your skin. Or you have to step over the bodies of comrades, who you love like family, when they fall ... You do it because you tell yourself the sacrifice is worth it."[313] Pierre Dominique Giacomini described his state of mind after taking part in fifty-two operations for the *Organisation de l'armée secrète* (OAS): "If my parents could see me now, they would be horrified. Only the physical aspect of the human being remains. I haven't opened the blinds of my room for some time. My studio apartment is like a lair. I only go out to kill, to make love, to eat. I have lost all sense of time. At night I sleep with one eye open, my Smith & Wesson within easy reach. The slightest noise is enough to make me leap out of bed. The silence which follows is even more oppressive."[314] Andreas Baader warned the original core members of the RAF that they could not even rely on receiving support from within their own ranks: "If you're not tough enough then you've no business here. Our aggression gets bottled up, with the pressures of living outside the law — it has to come out, we can't take it out on the outside world just because we're living underground, so we have to take it out on the group, and then of course we fight; we have to be able to handle that, we have to be tough enough for that."[315] Not everyone has the reserves of strength to walk such a path, and, over time, faith can prove to be a surprisingly perishable commodity.

[311] Nelson Mandela, *Long Walk to Freedom* (Back Bay Books; 1994), p. 266.

[312] Anna Geifman, *Death Orders: The Vanguard of Modern Terrorism in Revolutionary Russia* (Praeger Security International; 2010), p. 93.

[313] Nick Miroff, Do you know what it's like to spend 20 years at war? *Washington Post*, 30 September 2016.

[314] Alexander Harrison, *Challenging De Gaulle: The O.A.S. and the Counterrevolution in Algeria 1954–1962* (Praeger Publishers; 1989), p. 83.

[315] Stefan Aust, *Baader-Meinhof: The Inside Story of the RAF* (Oxford University Press; 2009), p. 99.

Jeffrey Ross and Ted Gurr coined the term "burnout" to describe one of four principle conditions which they believed contribute to the decline of terrorist movements (the other factors being state preemption, state deterrence, and public backlash).[316] Ross and Gurr described burnout as declining commitment to the group and identified aging and changing life circumstances as the main drivers of this phenomenon, which they believed particularly afflicted ideologically-motivated terrorist organizations. Terrorism is a young persons' game, and for most terrorists there comes a moment when they begin to re-evaluate their life choices and start to look to the future. Major life events such as the desire to marry, the birth of a first child, or something as banal as turning thirty, or forty, can trigger a period of profound personal introspection. A *Brigate Rosse* volunteer cited by Claire Sterling complained rather poignantly: "I want to get married and have children, and play with dogs."[317] A former *Jama'at Ahl as-Sunnah lid-Da'wah wa'l-Jihad* (*Boko Haram*) cadre enrolled in a government-sponsored deradicalization program in Nigeria gave an almost identical explanation for why he had decided to turn his back on the organization: "I shed tears when I realized I had ruined my life. All my younger brothers are married with children but I'm not married and I have no child. So now I'm looking at how to start my life afresh."[318] An ETA member interviewed by Fernando Reinares also shared the same outlook: "You say to yourself shit, man … I better get myself a life, because time is running out … Well, we've all got to live a bit."[319] So did November 17 member Patroklos Tselentis: "I had no private life. I couldn't start a family. I had to be secretive and constantly hiding and it came to

[316] Jeffrey Ian Ross and Ted Robert Gurr, Why Terrorism Subsides: A Comparative Study of Canada and the United States, *Comparative Politics*, Vol. 21, No. 4 (July 1989).

[317] Claire Sterling, *The Terror Network: The Secret War of International Terrorism* (Holt, Rinehart and Winston; 1981), p. 304.

[318] Will Ross, Using football to tackle Nigeria's Boko Haram, *BBC News*, 11 September 2015, at http://www.bbc.com/news/world-africa-34126346. Viewed 17 October 2016.

[319] Fernando Reinares, Exit from Terrorism: A Qualitative Empirical Study on Disengagement and Deradicalization Among Members of ETA, *Journal of Terrorism and Political Violence*, Vol. 23, No. 5 (2011), p. 796.

a point when I realize the whole thing was wrong."[320] Even one of the architects of the Provisional IRA's "long war doctrine", Gerry Adams, once acknowledged: "At some time we are going to have to get on with our lives and pursue our own private ambitions."[321]

The concept of burnout has remained a key explanatory variable in the works of many counter-terrorism researchers, and over time it has been somewhat refined to include not just personal growth but also nervous exhaustion, profound disillusionment, and fracturing social groups. In *The Politics of Irish Freedom*, Gerry Adams conceded that that the "long war" could be "a very draining process".[322] The journal of the *Collettivo Politico Metropolitano* made the same point, emphasizing the all-consuming nature of the underground life: "Public and private life, the interior and external dimensions of one's entire social being, have to be sewn together and harmonized. You can't be a part-time revolutionary, nor is there a short working week for militants."[323] Boris Savinkov, head of the *Sotsialisty Revolyutsionery — Boyevaya Organizatsiya*, recalled in his memoirs: "[T]errorist activity did not consist only of throwing bombs ... it was much more minute, difficult and tedious than might be imagined ... a terrorist is called upon to live a rather dull existence for months at a time, eschewing meeting his own comrades and doing most difficult and unpleasant work."[324]

The constant tedium of clandestine existence has ground down many formerly committed terrorist fighters. ETA member María Dolores Katarain, sought by the Spanish authorities in connection with the 1973 murder of the fascist Prime Minister Luis Carrero Blanco, found life on the run as a wanted woman difficult to cope with, describing her circumstances as "this tomb, this living death that was beginning to suffocate me and in which I was physically

---

[320] George Kassimeris, *Inside Greek Terrorism* (Oxford University Press; 2013), p. 45.

[321] Gerry Adams, *The Politics of Irish Freedom* (Brandon Book Publishers; 1986), p. 66.

[322] ibid.

[323] Alison Jamieson, Entry, Discipline and Exit in the Italian Red Brigades, *Terrorism and Political Violence*, Vol. 2, No. 1 (1990), p. 2 .

[324] Boris Savinkov, *Memoirs of a Terrorist* (A. & C. Boni; 1931), p. 147.

dying."[325] She decided to leave the organization and moved to Mexico in 1980 to start a new life.[326] RAF *cadre* Astrid Proll recalled Ulrike Meinhof complaining: "I'm fed up with this. All this hanging around, acting as a look-out, checking out cars. I don't want to end up in jail for that kind of thing, not any more, not for such petty details."[327] *Prima Linae*'s Roberto Sandalo justified his decision to turn *pentito* by saying: "I didn't feel like going back to earn my bread with "The Firm". It was a liberation to let myself be taken. Let them arrest me, and be done with it."[328] An EOKA fighter hiding out in the wilderness after participating in an ambush on British security forces in November 1958 wrote to friend: "I am in a miserable place. My dear friend, you could not walk round or spit, or speak, or get into the hole. After the date of the ambush not one night have I slept outside this hole. I am not half the man I was. Truthfully, if you saw me you would not recognize me."[329] He gave himself up to the British authorities shortly afterwards. The historian and political scientist Janusz Zawodny, a veteran of the Polish underground during World War II, noted from personal experience that the tensions of underground life create a bias towards action as it both reasserts the group's sense of purpose and serves to discharge tension.[330] Zawodny argued that group dynamics dictate that a leader who fails to provide his group with enough action will likely soon be replaced.

In addition to the stress and often suffocating tedium, as we have already discussed, group members are sometimes alienated by the methods or targets adopted by more violent and extreme comrades.

---

[325] Michael Burleigh, *Blood and Rage: A Cultural History of Terrorism* (Harper; 2009), p. 281.

[326] Katarain returned to Spain in 1985 to take up the Spanish government's offer of amnesty. She was murdered by ETA the following year in front of her 3-year-old son.

[327] Stefan Aust, *Baader-Meinhof: The Inside Story of the RAF* (Oxford University Press; 2009), p. 97.

[328] Claire Sterling, *The Terror Network: The Secret War of International Terrorism* (Holt, Rinehart and Winston; 1981), p. 301.

[329] David French, *Fighting EOKA: The British Counter-Insurgency Campaign on Cyprus, 1955–1959* (Oxford University Press; 2015), p. 283.

[330] Jerrold Post, Notes on a Psychodynamic Theory of Terrorist Behavior, *Terrorism*, Vol. 7, No. 3 (1984), p. 253 and Janusz Zawodny, Internal Organizational Problems and the Sources of Tensions of Terrorist Movements as Catalysts of Violence, *Terrorism*, Vol. 1, No. 3 (1978).

PIRA volunteer Sean O'Callaghan claimed he had been prompted to turn police informer by his revulsion at hearing his fellow volunteers hoping that their murder victim was pregnant so that they would have killed "two [victims] for the price of one".[331] *Prima Linae*'s Fabrizio Giai went through a similar evolution in prison, writing in a plaintive letter to his colleagues still carrying on the fight: "Comrades, it's finished! We must have the humility and political courage to recognize our errors and vices ... We have been unpardonably blind ... We have undervalued our own moral, cultural, and material disintegration."[332] The former *al-Qaeda* recruiter Jesse Morton likewise over time became appalled by the violence done in the name of radical Islam: "I suffer from a tremendous amount of guilt, I have seen things that people have done and to know that I once sympathized and supported that view — it sickens me."[333] Noman Benotman, former leader of the Libyan Islamic Fighting Group, expressed similar disenchantment with *al-Qaeda*'s methods in an open letter addressed to his one-time comrade, Osama bin Laden, in September 2010: "What has 11 September brought to the world except mass killings, occupations, destruction, hatred of Muslims, humiliation of Islam, and a tighter grip on the lives of ordinary Muslims by the authoritarian regimes that control Arab and Muslim states? I warned you then, in summer 2000, of how your actions would bring US forces into the Middle East and into Afghanistan, leading to mass unrest and loss of life. You believed I was wrong. Time has proved me right. Your actions have harmed millions of innocent Muslims and non-Muslims alike."[334] It is not easy to make one's peace with the violence and suffering meted out

---

[331] Audrey Kurth Cronin, *How Terrorism Ends: Understanding the Decline and Demise of Terrorist Campaigns* (Princeton University Press, 2009), p. 100.

[332] Claire Sterling, *The Terror Network: The Secret War of International Terrorism* (Holt, Rinehart and Winston; 1981), p. 303.

[333] Elizabeth Cohen, From terrorist to university expert: GW hires former Islamic extremist, CNN. com, 30 August 2016, at http://edition.cnn.com/2016/08/30/health/gw-hires-former-islamic-extremist/. Viewed 31 August 2016.

[334] Noman Benotman, *Al-Qaeda: Your Armed Struggle is Over*, 10 September 2010, at https://azelin.files.wordpress.com/2010/09/noman-benotman-letter-to-bin-laden.pdf. Viewed 9 December 2016.

in the name of a cause, or to participate in it unaffected, something that the psychotherapist in Frantz Fanon understood all too well. Fanon warned his fellow militants: "There is a point at which methods devour themselves."[335]

Finally, not all political passions survive extended contact with reality. *Rote Armee Fraktion* dropout Sigrid Sternebeck simply came to the realization that the RAF's whole project was not feasible: "We live in Central Europe, not under a Fascist dictatorship with a population living at subsistence levels that is ripe for revolution."[336] Sternebeck was ahead of her time, the surviving members of the RAF would belatedly reach the same conclusion in 1998, admitting in their final communiqué: "We overestimated the support for this continuity of our conception of struggle."[337] The realization that the *zeitgeist* had moved on contributed to Patroklos Tselentis' decision to walk away from his comrades: "I could also see society changing whereas we, myself and the other group members, were stuck in the past."[338] *Brigate Rosse pentito* Antonio Savasta also concurred: "The necessity and the inevitability of the armed struggle represented our bet with history. Well, we lost that bet, and our isolation and defeat are the price for having defined reality by abstract theories which oversimplified it, for having concentrated the social reasons for change in a instrument unable to express it."[339] A sense of frustration at an organization's failure to advance its stated goals is a common complaint amongst former militants.[340] While it is true that nothing succeeds like success, it might equally be said that nothing fails like failure. For the former Provisional IRA intelligence officer Eamon Collins, the absence of meaningful progress in the

---

[335] Frantz Fanon, *Black Skin, White Masks* (Grove Press; 1967), p. 12.

[336] Michael Burleigh, *Blood and Rage: A Cultural History of Terrorism* (Harper; 2009), p. 259.

[337] The Urban Guerrilla Is History, *The Final Communiqué From The Red Army Faction*, 1 March 1998 at http://germanguerilla.com/1998/03/01/the-urban-guerrilla-is-history/.

[338] George Kassimeris, *Inside Greek Terrorism* (Oxford University Press; 2013), p. 45. Incredibly having spent much of his youth fighting the state, once he left November 17 Tselentis decided to join the Greek army.

[339] George Kassimeris, *Inside Greek Terrorism* (Oxford University Press; 2013), p. 48.

[340] Audrey Kurth Cronin, *How Terrorism Ends: Understanding the Decline and Demise of Terrorist Campaigns* (Princeton University Press, 2009), p. 98.

fight against the British government led him to question whether the sacrifices, both psychological and material, he felt he had made had been worth it: "I had fought this so-called just war for six years, and what had I become? A diminished, dehumanized being, incapable of feeling for my victims, only capable of feeling for myself and my family. I thought I could be killed at any time: and so what? Another pointless death to add to all the other pointless deaths I had been responsible for."[341]

## Summary

There is now broad consensus amongst terrorism researchers that terrorists are essentially normal individuals who exhibit ordinary personality features albeit resulting in extraordinary behavior.[342] Psychological studies suggest that terrorists are led to embrace such behavior by much the same inner processes that might lead an individual to embrace an identity as a soldier, a lawyer, a policeman, or a social activist — a need for approval, a need for respect, a need to make a connection, a need to explore facets of one's character, or a need to make one's mark upon the world. Arie Kruglanski and his colleagues at the University of Maryland-based National Consortium for the Study of Terrorism and Responses to Terrorism (START) have labeled this fundamental human impulse "the quest for significance".[343] How an individual pursues this goal is likely determined in large part by the environment in which he or she finds

---

[341] Kevin Toolis, Death Foretold, *The Guardian*, 3 July 1999.

[342] See Andrew Silke, Cheshire-Cat Logic: The Recurring Theme of Terrorist Abnormality in Psychological Research, *Psychology, Crime and the Law*, Vol. 4, No. 1 (January 1998); John Horgan, *The Psychology of Terrorism* (Routledge; 2014); Andrea Kohn Maikovich, A New Understanding of Terrorism Using Cognitive Dissonance Principles, *Journal for the Theory of Social Behaviour*, Vol. 35, No. 4 (2005); and Arie Kruglanski, Michele Gelfand, Jocelyn Bélanger, Anna Sheveland, Malkanthi Hetiarachchi and Rohan Gunaratna, The Psychology of Radicalization and Deradicalization: How Significance Quest Impacts Violent Extremism, *Advances in Political Psychology*, Vol. 35, Suppl. 1 (2014).

[343] Arie Kruglanski, Michele Gelfand, Jocelyn Bélanger, Anna Sheveland, Malkanthi Hetiarachchi and Rohan Gunaratna, The Psychology of Radicalization and Deradicalization: How Significance Quest Impacts Violent Extremism, *Advances in Political Psychology*, Vol. 35, Suppl. 1 (2014), p. 73.

him or herself in. Kruglanski *et al.* identify the 2013 Boston Marathon bomber Tamerlan Tsarnaev as an archetypal case study, a recent immigrant and talented boxer whose dreams of representing his adopted country at the Olympics, and thus gaining social significance, were dashed, leading him to seek significance elsewhere, ultimately by embracing the identity of a *mujahid* and martyr.[344] They also note that this quest for significance can find meaning in both broadly positive qualities such as altruism and group loyalty, as well as more negative ones, like a desire for revenge — a further illustration of why it is so important to think holistically about terrorists' motivations which are rarely unitary in nature.

For the counter-terrorist professional, there are a number of key insights to be gleaned from recent research undertaken into the psychology of terrorism. The first, and perhaps the most important, is that there is no obvious terrorist type and that, furthermore, most terrorists are driven by much the same psychological impulses as the rest of us. If terrorists are neither defective nor abnormal, it logically follows that their actions are likely in some way consequences of their experiences and environment. Second, these same psychological processes can pull individuals into terrorism and also push them away from it. Youthfulness may predispose an individual to more radical pathways, but maturity can also lead them away from them. Behavioral analysis is a valuable tool. Burnout and disenchantment with the terrorist lifestyle can open cognitive windows that counter-terrorism professionals — police interviewers, intelligence officers, or deradicalization case workers — can all potentially take advantage of if they are able to recognize the symptoms. We will look at how counter-terrorism programs can make use of such opportunities in Part III.

Third, and finally, a sense of personal identity and status often appears to be an important factor in an individual's decision to join a terrorist group. This also suggests some important potential policy considerations. Posing a threat to an individual's identity — for example, as a member of an ethnic or religious group, or

---

[344] ibid., p. 74.

political party — often just results in that individual reinforcing his or her commitment to this identity.[345] Martha Crenshaw noted, in this sense, ideologies are "guardians of identity" — so a direct assault on an individual's values may not be the best approach to persuade someone to reconsider his or her actions.[346] Jerrold Post similarly warns that the personal identities of most terrorists — unsurprisingly given the all-consuming nature of the experience — are dominated by their choice to take up arms, and to relinquish them "would be to lose their very reason for being".[347] Hyperbole perhaps, but as any veteran of conflict can attest, such an experience has enduring and life-changing significance. Effective disengagement and deradicalization programs, and even successful peace overtures and political accommodations, have to navigate this challenge.

## Social Networks

World Trade Center bomber Ramzi Yousef, *al-Qaeda* logistics hub Ammar al-Baluchi, and 9/11 mastermind Khalid Sheikh Mohammed were all closely related. The original operational concept that evolved into the 9/11 attacks was developed by Ramzi Yousef's childhood friend Abdul Hakim Murad, who obtained a commercial pilot's license in the United States in 1992.[348] Shortly thereafter, Murad joined Yousef's entrepreneurial terrorist cell and told his friend that while working in the US, he had often dreamed of flying a plane loaded with explosives into the Pentagon or the headquarters of the CIA. At the time Yousef was working on his plan to bomb the World Trade Center in New York, but he introduced Murad to his uncle, Khalid Sheikh Mohammed, who became

---

[345] Andrea Kohn Maikovich, A New Understanding of Terrorism Using Cognitive Dissonance Principles, *Journal for the Theory of Social Behaviour*, Vol. 35, No. 4 (2005), pp. 380–381.

[346] Michael Arena and Bruce Arrigo, *The Terrorist Identity: Explaining The Terrorist Threat* (New York University; 2006), p. 21.

[347] Jerrold Post, The New Face of Terrorism: Socio-Cultural Foundations of Contemporary Terrorism, *Behavioral Sciences and the Law*, Vol. 23, No. 4 (July/August 2005), p. 462.

[348] Marc Sageman, *Understanding Terror Networks* (University of Pennsylvania Press; 2004), p. 164.

fascinated with Murad's vision. After the comparative failure of the February 1993 World Trade Center bombing, Yousef and Murad joined Mohammed in the Philippines where they developed the so-called *Bojinka* plot — an ambitious plan to assassinate Pope John Paul II during a papal visit to Manila in January 1995 and then blow up eleven US airliners with scheduled stops in Southeast Asia. The plot was abandoned less than a week before the Pope's arrival in the Philippines after Murad accidentally set the group's Manila safe house on fire while preparing a batch of explosives and was arrested by local police. Khalid Sheikh Mohammed would recycle and refine the *Bojinka* plot until, with further input from Osama bin Laden who apparently suggested using the planes themselves as weapons, it finally took the form that played out on 9/11.[349]

The group of nineteen men who actually carried out the 9/11 operation were also characterized by dense interpersonal connections, although they were not all known to each other before the attack was set in motion. The core of the team was formed by individuals from an *al-Qaeda* cell in Hamburg, which had coalesced around an Islamic study group at the al-Quds mosque in the city. Mohamed Atta was the operational commander for the 9/11 attacks and flew American Airlines Flight 11 into the North Tower of the World Trade Center. Two other members of the Hamburg cell, Marwan al-Shehhi and Ziad Amir Jarrah, also piloted hijacked planes during the attack.[350] Of the so-called muscle hijackers, Wail and Waleed al-Shehri were brothers. They attended Seqely Mosque in Khamis Mushayt, Saudi Arabia, where they befriended two other future 9/11 hijackers, Ahmed al-Nami and Saeed al-Ghamdi.[351] Ahmed al-Nami attended King Khaled University in Abha with two more hijackers, Fayez Ahemed al-Shehri and Muhammad al-Shahri.[352]

---

[349] ibid. *Bojinka* is most likely a Slavic cognate for "Boeing", the manufacturer of the targeted American airliners. A Philippines Airlines Boeing 747 was chosen by Ramzi Yousef for a test run in December 1994. An IED exploded on board flight 434 killing a Japanese passenger but mercifully failing to bring down the plane.

[350] Marc Sageman, *Understanding Terror Networks* (University of Pennsylvania Press; 2004), pp. 105–107.

[351] ibid., p. 50.

[352] ibid.

Two additional pairs of brothers also took part in the assault: Nawaf and Salem al-Hazmi on American Airlines Flight 77, and Hamza and Ahmed al-Ghamdi on United Flight 175. Hijacker Khalid al-Mihdhar's father-in-law Ahmad Mohammad Ali al-Hada acted as an *al-Qaeda* communications hub in Yemen. Khalid's brother-in-law, Ahmed al-Darbi, ended up in Guantanamo accused of involvement in a plot to attack Western ships transiting the Strait of Hormuz.

As the case of the 9/11 plotters suggests, family ties are not the only links that bind conspirators together. The work of Marc Sageman has popularized the importance played by social networks of all types in the development of terrorist organizations, although, in truth, law enforcement and intelligence professionals, from whose ranks Sageman himself comes, have long understood their significance.[353] Sociologists broadly identify five general areas of commonality around which social groupings tend to form: geography, kinship, organizational affiliation, occupational affiliation, role relationships, and cognitive processes such as a shared worldview.[354] Underpinning them all is the general principle of homophily which suggests that, within social networks, like attracts like. Group members tend to prefer such relationships because commonality promotes understanding and thus predictability, it makes communication easier, and also provides a solid foundation on which to build relationships grounded in trust and reciprocity.[355] In *Understanding Terror Networks*, Sageman describes a tripartite process of radicalization that starts with social affiliation with a like-minded group of friends or family members and then proceeds with the twin intensification of both faith and political militancy

---

[353] See Marc Sageman, *Understanding Terror Networks* (University of Pennsylvania Press; 2004) and also Saad Eddin Ibrahim, Anatomy of Egypt's Militant Groups: Methodological Note and Preliminary Findings, *International Journal of Middle East Studies*, Vol. 12, No. 4 (1980).

[354] Miller McPherson, Lynn Smith-Lovin, and James M. Cook, Birds of a Feather: Homophily in Social Networks, *Annual Review of Sociology*, Vol. 27, No. 1 (2001), pp. 415–444 and Kathleen Carley, A Theory of Group Stability, *American Sociological Review*, Vol. 56, No. 3 (1991), pp. 331–354.

[355] Herminia Ibarra, Personal Networks of Women and Minorities in Management: A Conceptual Framework, *Academy of Management Review*, Vol. 18, No. 1 (1993), pp. 56–87.

within the context of this closed social grouping.[356] Sageman's key point is that the transition from holding radical views to active involvement in terrorist activity is predicated, more often than not, on an actual acquaintance, pre-existing or engineered, with a member of a terrorist group: "The critical and specific element to joining the *jihad* is the accessibility of a link to the *jihad*."[357] In this, he restates the observation of three pioneers of social movement theory, David Snow, Louis Zurcher and Sheldon Ekland-Olson: "Recruitment cannot occur without prior contact with a recruitment agent."[358]

Social networks alleviate the single biggest practical hurdle facing aspiring militants: how to actually join a terrorist group. As clandestine organizations, terrorist movements, especially those with tightly-controlled vertical command structures, are difficult to join — an aspirant terrorist has to know someone already on the inside who can act as a conduit to this clandestine world. In a 2007 study of 516 Guantanamo Bay detainees, researchers from the US Military Academy at West Point's Countering Terrorism Center found that evidence of a prior acquaintance with a member of *al-Qaeda* was a significantly better predictor of whether an individual would become involved in terrorism than a general religious belief in the importance of performing *jihad*.[359] MI5's 2008 report on *Understanding Radicalisation and Violent Extremism* concurred: "What is different about those who ended up involved in terrorism is that they came into contact with existing extremists who recognized their vulnerabilities (and their usefulness to the extremist group)."[360] In his follow-up to *Understanding Terror Networks*, *Leaderless Jihad*, Sageman found evidence of a prior connection to an Islamist

---

[356] Marc Sageman, *Understanding Terror Networks* (University of Pennsylvania Press; 2004), p. 135.

[357] ibid., p. 120.

[358] David Snow, Louis Zurcher and Sheldon Ekland-Olson, Social Networks and Social Movements: A Microstructural Approach to Differential Recruitment, *American Sociological Review*, Vol. 45, No. 5 (1980), p. 789.

[359] Joseph Felter and Jarret Brachman, *An Assessment of 516 Combatant Status Review Tribunal Unclassified Summaries*, Combating Terrorism Center Report (15 July 2007), pp. 24–25 and 34.

[360] Alan Travis, The making of an extremist, *The Guardian*, 20 August 2008, at www.theguardian.com/uk/2008/aug/20/uksecurity.terrorism. Viewed 5 August 2016.

terrorist network in two-thirds of the cases he studied.[361] Scott Atran reports that around 20% of the Islamist terrorist networks he studied were made up of relatives and 70% were composed of friends.[362] Shandon Harris-Hogan, a research analyst at Monash University's Global Terrorism Research Centre who reviewed case histories of Australian nationals involved in Islamist terrorist plots, concluded that the influence of family and friends had repeatedly played "a significant role" in radicalizing individuals and that "each jihadist plot ... has had strong social links to previous operational cells."[363] A November 2015 study conducted by the New America Foundation looked at 474 individuals from twenty-five Western countries who had traveled to join ISIL, or other *Sunni* jihadist groups active in the region, and found that approximately a third had existing familial ties to an individual already involved either in Iraq or Syria, or to an Islamist extremist terrorist group.[364] As in so many other walks of life, for the neophyte militant, who you know is often considerably more important than what you know.

Much of the research into the role of social networks in the development of terrorist threats has focused on the Islamist terrorist groups of the past twenty years. However, this concept is not unique to Islamist terrorism and evidence of the critical enabling role played by social networks can be found in the earliest manifestations of terrorism in the nineteenth century and in all the subsequent strains since. The Ku Klux Klan was founded in May or June 1866 by six young well-to-do friends, all veterans of the Confederate army, as a social society modeled in large part on the university fraternities that were already popular on American college campuses.[365] The founders,

---

[361] Marc Sageman, *Leaderless Jihad: Terror Networks in the Twenty-First Century* (University of Pennsylvania Press; 2008), pp. 66–67.

[362] Scott Atran, The Moral Logic and Growth of Suicide Terrorism, *The Washington Quarterly*, Vol. 29, No. 2 (2006), p. 135.

[363] Shandon Harris-Hogan, The Importance of Family: The Key to Understanding the Evolution of Jihadism in Australia, *Security Challenges*, Vol. 10, No. 1 (2014), pp. 31 and 35.

[364] Peter Bergen, Courtney Schuster and David Sterman, *ISIS in the West: The New Faces of Extremism* (New America Foundation; November 2015), p. 8.

[365] Allen Trelease, *White Terror: The Ku Klux Klan Conspiracy and Southern Reconstruction* (Louisiana State University Press; 1971), p. 4.

who lived in the small Tennessee town of Pulaski, were bored with civilian life, and as one of the founders later put it, "hungering and thirsting" for amusement.[366] There is even persuasive evidence, in the form of a surviving photograph, that they may have first come together to form a musical group called the "Midnight Rangers".[367] The Klan was not initially established with any political intent — one of the founders would subsequently send an anonymous letter to the Richmond Enquirer & Examiner in April 1868, lamenting that the organization had become "so perverted as to become political and pernicious in its demonstrations"[368] — but something in the secrecy, the costumes, and the rituals stuck a cord with disenfranchised former soldiers across the South. An early member of the Pulaski Klan "den" was the Confederate General George W. Gordon, the youngest general officer in the Confederacy at the Civil War's close. Gordon would play a major role in the transformation of the Klan into a political enterprise and is credited with writing the organization's first "prescript" or constitution.[369] Other Confederate officers, most notably Nathan Bedford Forrest and John W. Morton, played an important role in promoting the Klan across the old South and providing something of a superstructure to the organization, though it remained at its heart a locally-driven inchoate movement.[370]

The populist terrorist organization *Narodnaya Volya* active in late nineteenth century Tsarist Russia grew out of an essentially non-violent, if subversive, student movement which encouraged politically engaged students to go, in Alexander Herzen's famous exhortation, "to the people", and work to raise the political consciousness of the rural peasantry. This movement culminated in the summer of 1874 with perhaps as many as 1,500 students heading into the Russian countryside. 770 were arrested by the government (612 men and

---

[366] ibid., p. 3.

[367] Elaine Frantz Parsons, *Klu Klux: The Birth of the Klan during Reconstruction* (University of North Carolina Press; 2016), pp. 32–33.

[368] Allen Trelease, *White Terror: The Ku Klux Klan Conspiracy and Southern Reconstruction* (Louisiana State University Press; 1971), p. 6.

[369] ibid., p. 13.

[370] ibid., pp. 5 and 10.

158 women) of whom 265 were detained for a lengthier period.[371] The so-called Pilgrimage to the People had developed in an impulsive and uncoordinated fashion and many of the students involved did not know each other until the state either imprisoned them or brought them together in 1877 for what became known as The Trial of 193, at which most were acquitted.[372] It was as defendants at this trial that Sophie Perovskaya and Andrei Zhelyabov met for the first time and they would ultimately become lovers and then co-conspirators in the assassination of Alexander II.[373] Sophie Perovskaya and her fellow *Narodnaya Volya* Executive Committee member Anna Korba were school friends. Vera Figner did not participate in the Pilgrimage — she had been studying medicine in Zurich where she developed her own network of like-minded young Russian women that included another future *Narodnaya Volya* member, Olga Liubatovich. Family networks also played a role in the propagation of Russian populism, three of Vera Figner's sisters joined revolutionary groups, as did Sophie Perovskaya's brother, Vassily.[374] The Harvard historian Adam Ulam commented: "As one scans the biographical dictionary of the revolutionaries of the 1870s, one is struck that so many of the leading figures had brothers and sisters who chose the same career."[375]

The political scientist Donatella Della Porta collected data from the trials of some 1,214 Italian left-wing militants active during the *anni di piombo*, supplemented by twenty-eight in-depth interviews.[376] She found 70% of these militants had at least one friend already involved in a terrorist organization at the time they

---

[371] Adam Ulam, *In the Name of the People: Prophets and Conspirators in Prerevolutionary Russia* (Viking Press; 1977), p. 214.

[372] ibid., p. 143.

[373] Clark McCauley and Sophia Moskalenko, *Friction: How Radicalization Happens to Them and Us* (Oxford University Press; 2011), p. 52.

[374] Adam Ulam, *In the Name of the People: Prophets and Conspirators in Prerevolutionary Russia* (Viking Press; 1977), pp. 216–217.

[375] ibid., p. 217.

[376] 1969–1982. See Donatella Della Porta, Recruitment Processes in Clandestine Political Organizations: Italian Left-Wing Terrorism, *International Social Movement Research*, Vol. 1 (1988).

joined, of these 74% had more than one friend involved and a staggering 42% more than seven.[377] 298 militants in the sample had at least one close relative — typically a spouse or sibling — who was also active in the same circles, leading Della Porta to conclude that "participation in clandestine groups is more likely when it is strengthened by previous affective ties."[378] Furthermore, her research showed that in 88% of the cases for which she had the relevant data, the recruiter was not a stranger to the recruit, in 44% the recruiter was a friend, and in 20% a relative.[379] A member of *Prima Linea* told her: "[Recruitment happened] through personal ties. In this way the comrades of the *squadre* contacted people whom they had known for a long time, who would have entertained the idea of joining the *squadre* or at least would not have been shocked by the proposal or have created problems for the security of the comrade who made contact."[380] One unnamed Italian militant interviewed by Della Porta recalled: "A choice [made] in cold blood, such as 'now I will become a terrorist' [did] not exist. It was a step-by-step evolution, which passed through a kind of human relation that I had with Guido, and with the people I worked with."[381] Another anonymous interview subject told her: "There are many things I cannot explain by analyzing the political situation, or the social conditions in a city ... as far as I am concerned it was up to emotional feelings, of passions for the people I shared my life with."[382]

We have access to considerably less comprehensive data on the social networks underpinning other leftist movements of the 1960s and 1970s, but the anecdotal evidence suggests that similar relationships were a factor there as well. Astrid Proll was introduced to Andreas Baader and Gundrun Ensslin by her brother Thorwald, who

---

[377] Donatella Della Porta, Recruitment Processes in Clandestine Political Organizations: Italian Left-Wing Terrorism, *International Social Movement Research*, Vol. 1 (1988), p. 158.
[378] ibid.
[379] ibid., p. 160.
[380] ibid.
[381] ibid., p. 168.
[382] ibid.

had participated in their first act of arson before leaving the group, and thus became one of the founding members of the *Rote Armee Fraktion*.[383] Reviewing the personal histories of 227 German terrorists, mostly veterans of the RAF or *Bewegung 2. Juni*, collected as part of a 1981 research project backed by the West German Ministry of Domestic Affairs, the German political psychologist Klaus Wasmund noted: "The number of couples, and brothers and sisters is astonishingly high."[384] Three members of the small but surprisingly active and long-lived Greek terror group November 17 were brothers, two were cousins, and one was godfather to another's children.[385] The compact Japanese terrorist group *Rengō Sekigun* contained three brothers — the eldest of whom, Yoshitaka Katō, recruited his two younger siblings (both minors) — as well as several romantically-involved couples, including leading members Nagata Hiroko and Sakaguchi Hiroshi.[386] Takeshi Okamoto was a member of a Red Army group that hijacked Japan Airlines Flight 351 in March 1970 and flew to North Korea, while his younger brother, Kōzō Okamoto, joined a different Red Army faction, *Arab Sekigun* based in Lebanon, which coordinated its activities with the PFLP, and was the only survivor of the infamous attack on Lod Airport in May 1972.

The Provisional IRA also drew on a dense network of family members, school friends, and neighbors for its volunteers. Support for the republican cause was passed down through what the historian Richard English has described as the trifecta of "family, locality, tradition."[387] *Sinn Féin* President Gerry Adams' father, Gerry Adams Sr., was an active member of the IRA during the Second World War and in 1942 he was involved in an exchange of fire with an officer from the Royal Ulster Constabulary in which both men were

---

[383] See Tom Vague, *The Televisionaries: The Red Army Faction Story, 1963–1993* (AK Press; 2001).

[384] Klaus Wasmund, The Political Socialization of West German Terrorists, in Peter Merkl (ed.), *Political Violence and Terror: Motifs and Motivations* (University of California Press; 1986), p. 204.

[385] George Kassimeris, *Inside Greek Terrorism* (Oxford University Press; 2013), p. 3.

[386] See Patricia Steinhoff, Death by Defeatism and Other Fables: The Social Dynamics of the Rengō Sekigun Purge, in Takie Sugiyama Lebra (ed.), *Japanese Social Organization* (University of Hawaii Press; 1992) and Michael Burleigh, *Blood and Rage: A Cultural History of Terrorism* (Harper; 2009), p. 161.

[387] Richard English, *Armed Struggle: The History of the IRA* (Oxford University Press; 2004), p. 129.

wounded. Adams Sr. was sentenced to eight years in prison and served five. In 1971, both father and son were interned together by the British authorities. William McGuinness, brother of the former PIRA chief and deputy First Minister of Northern Ireland Martin McGuinness, was identified in court as the Commanding Officer of PIRA's Derry Brigade, and Martin's brother-in-law Marvin Canning was convicted of "managing a meeting in support of a proscribed organization", the dissident republican group known as the Real IRA, in 2013.[388] One not untypical incident that illustrates just how dense these networks could be took place on a country road near Drumnakilly in August 1988. British soldiers ambushed a Provisional IRA active service unit *en route* to murder a part-time member of the Ulster Defence Regiment. All three members of the unit were killed. Two of the dead men were brothers: Gerard and Martin Harte. Both men were active members of Loughmacrory St Theresa's Gaelic Athletic Association Club, Martin had been the club captain and Gerard organized the youth teams, and, for years afterward, the club held an annual commemoration of their deaths.[389] The third PIRA volunteer killed in the ambush was Brian Mullin. Martin Harte was married to Brian's sister. Gerry Adams delivered the grave side eulogy for the Harte brothers whom he described as "good, decent, patriotic freedom fighters driven to fight for justice".[390] Elsewhere, Adams has described such groups with deep roots in the republican movement as "spinal republican families".[391]

And so it goes on, the young Islamist army officer Khaled al-Islambouli led the group responsible for the assassination of Egyptian President Anwar Sadat in October 1981 and was subsequently executed by firing squad. Almost fifteen years later, his younger brother, Ahmed Showqi al-Islambouli, an associate of the future

---

[388] Kevin Toolis, *Rebel Hearts* (St. Martin's Griffin; 1997), p. 205, and McGuinness relative Martin Canning charged over rally, *BBC News*, 9 June 2011.

[389] Micheál MacDonncha, Remembering the Past: The Drumnakilly Martyrs, *An Phoblacht* (Republican News), 28 August 2008, and Maeve Connolly, DUP slams GAA club IRA commemoration, *Irish News*, 27 September 2003.

[390] Micheál MacDonncha, Remembering the Past: The Drumnakilly Martyrs, *An Phoblacht* (Republican News), 28 August 2008.

[391] Gerry Adams, *Hope and History: Making Peace in Ireland* (Routledge; 2004), p. 5.

*al-Qaeda* leader Ayman al-Zawahiri, came close to assassinating Sadat's successor, Hosni Mubarak, ambushing his motorcade out-side Addis Ababa as he traveled to attend a regional summit in June 1995. A study of the personal histories of thirty-three *Hamas* suicide bombers conducted by Ariel Merari and the Center for the Study of Terrorism and Political Violence at Tel Aviv University found that most had been recruited through "friendship networks" related to school, sports, or extended family ties.[392] Canadian reporter Sandro Contenta found that more than half of the twenty-one *Hamas* suicide bombers whose lives he researched were close friends.[393] The nucleus of the *al-Qaeda*-affiliated cell behind the 2004 Spanish train bombings was a group of four friends from Tetuan, Morocco.[394] The so-called Sydney Cell, apprehended in 2005 before it could put in motion an evolving plan to "instil terror and panic in the Australian community" had at its heart an uncle and nephew, Khaled and Mustafa Cheikho.[395] Khaled was married to the daughter of Rabiyah Hutchinson who had herself been variously married to members of both *Jemaah Islamiyah* and *al-Qaeda*.[396] The cell's ringleader, Mohammed Elomar, had strong family connec-tions of his own to the Lebanese Islamist terrorist group, *Fatah al-Islam*.[397] Also involved was Omar Jamal, whose older brother, Saleh Jamal, was a former gang member who was radicalized in an Australian prison, joined *Asbat al-Ansar* in Lebanon in 2004, and took part in an attack on a UN compound in Damascus the same year.[398] Shandon Harris-Hogan concluded from his study of

---

[392] Mark Juergensmeyer, *Terror in the Mind of God: The Global Rise of Religious Violence* (University of California Press; 2003), p. 79.

[393] Michael Arena and Bruce Arrigo, *The Terrorist Identity: Explaining The Terrorist Threat* (New York University; 2006), p. 147.

[394] Michael Burleigh, *Blood and Rage: A Cultural History of Terrorism* (Harper; 2009), p. 468.

[395] Rachel Olding and Louise Hall, Terrorist Conspiracy: Five Sydney Cell Members Lose Conviction, Sentencing Appeals, *Sydney Morning Herald*, 12 December 2014.

[396] Shandon Harris-Hogan, The Importance of Family: The Key to Understanding the Evolution of Jihadism in Australia, *Security Challenges*, Vol. 10, No. 1 (2014), p. 44.

[397] ibid., p. 41.

[398] ibid. and Rachel Olding and Louise Hall, Terrorist conspiracy: Five Sydney Cell Members Lose Conviction, Sentencing Appeals, *The Sydney Morning Herald*, 12 December 2014.

Australian Islamist extremists: "Individuals have been far more susceptible to involvement as a result of close friendship and family influences than any other form of recruitment."[399] Other recent high-profile examples of familial links in Islamist terrorism include the Tsarnaev brothers who carried out the bombing of the Boston Marathon in April 2013; Chérif and Saïd Kouachi who carried out the murderous assault on the offices of the French satirical magazine *Charlie Hebdo* in January 2015; and Ibrahim and Khalid el-Bakraoui who blew themselves up in near-simultaneous suicide bombings of Brussels Airport and the Maelbeek metro station in central Brussels in March 2016.

Group ties are sometimes further reinforced by a deliberate policy of inter-marriage — one of bin Laden's sons married the daughter of *al-Qaeda*'s influential military commander Mohammed Atef, who was killed by a US air strike in November 2001.[400] Noor Huda Ismail, the Director of the Institute of International Peacebuilding in Jakarta, noted that matchmaking had also become an important tool for *Jemaah Islamiyah*: "Once inside these [extremist] groups, individuals cement their mutual bonds by marrying sisters and daughters of other members. Therefore, it is difficult for an individual to move away from the group without betraying their closest friends and family."[401] The Indonesian mastermind of the Bali bombings, Ali Ghufron, married his Malaysian bride, Paridah Abas, in part to securely expand *Jemaah Islamiyah*'s network in South Asia.[402] Paridah's brothers Nasir and Hashim were associated with terrorist activity in Mindanao and Singapore. Like Ghufron, Nasir was also a veteran of the Afghan *jihad* against the Soviet Union.

At the heart of tight non-familial social networks, one typically finds a single formal or informal institution. Bin Laden's successor as the leader of *al-Qaeda*, Ayman al-Zawahiri, first met *al-Qaeda*

---

[399] ibid., p. 36.

[400] Michael Burleigh, *Blood and Rage: A Cultural History of Terrorism* (Harper; 2009), p. 376.

[401] Sulastri Osman, Jemaah Islamiyah: Of Kin and Kind, *Journal of Current Southeast Asian Affairs*, Vol. 29, No. 2 (2010), p. 166.

[402] ibid.

stalwart Sayyid Imam al-Sharif, better known as Dr. Fadl, at university in Cairo. Many years later, Al-Zawahiri and al-Sharif went on to establish *al-Jihad Islamiyya* in Peshawar, Pakistan, where they were drawn into Osama bin Laden's orbit after he approached al-Zawahiri for medical treatment. One group of EOKA volunteers were drawn from a circle of students attending Athens University.[403] The ETA researcher Robert Clark identified the *cuadrilla* — a gang of boys from the same Basque village who grow up together sharing all kinds of exploits — as a critical foundation of a number of ETA cells.[404] Jean-Claude Perez described how he gravitated to the *Organisation de l'armée secrète* during the French colonial conflict in Algeria: "I was involved in artisan-style counter-terrorist operations from the outset with pals of mine. Guys I had played football with, old army buddies, guys who were teachers, shopkeepers, construction workers. It was instinctive, spontaneous."[405] The counterculture scene surrounding two magazines — *Rosso* (Red) and *Senza Tregua* (Without Truce) — played a central role in the radicalization of the second wave of Italian left-wing terrorists in the mid-1970s.[406] The German political psychologist Klaus Wasmund highlighted the role played by student cliques and communes as all-encompassing family substitutes for rootless youths in the 1960s and 1970s.[407] Michael Baumann's journey to founding the *Bewegung 2. Juni* terrorist group, for instance, began in Berlin's Kommune 1 and his association with the anarchistic troublemakers of the *Zentralrat der umherschweifenden Haschrebellen* before he graduated to full-blown terrorism. Another communal house in Oakland, California, provided the nucleus of

---

[403] David French, *Fighting EOKA: The British Counter-Insurgency Campaign on Cyprus, 1955–1959* (Oxford University Press; 2015), p. 50.

[404] Robert Clark, Patterns in the Lives of ETA Members, *Studies in Conflict and Terrorism*, Vol. 6, No. 3 (1983), p. 448.

[405] Alexander Harrison, *Challenging De Gaulle: The O.A.S. and the Counterrevolution in Algeria 1954–1962* (Praeger Publishers; 1989), p. 28.

[406] Donatella Della Porta, Recruitment Processes in Clandestine Political Organizations: Italian Left-Wing Terrorism, *International Social Movement Research*, Vol. 1 (1988), p. 162.

[407] Klaus Wasmund, The Political Socialization of West German Terrorists, in Peter Merkl (ed.), *Political Violence and Terror: Motifs and Motivations* (University of California Press; 1986), p. 205.

the Symbionese Liberation Army, responsible for the murder of Oakland School Superintendent Marcus Foster and the kidnapping of Patty Hearst.[408] The aspirant Millennium bomber Ahmed Ressam, who was arrested *en route* to bomb Los Angeles Airport in December 1999, was drawn into the plot by associates he had met at the Assuna Annabawiyah mosque in Montreal, a haven for dislocated Algerian expatriates involved in low-level criminality. As Sageman notes, places of worship can also offer an opportunity to make new friends, reinforce ideological commitment, and ultimately make contact with other militants.[409]

As the example of *Narodnaya Volya* suggests above, detention facilities are particularly associated with the development of terrorist networks. Prisons and internment camps bring together militants from far-flung places who might never otherwise have met and create bonds that can survive their eventual dispersal. After the failure of the 1916 Easter Uprising the British interned almost 2,000 Irish nationalists in a prison camp in rural Wales. Frongoch would later become known in Ireland as *ollscoil na réabhlóide* or the University of the Revolution. It was there that Michael Collins was elected head of the Frongoch contingent of the Irish Republican Brotherhood and gathered around him the men who would go on to cut a swathe through the British security forces in Ireland as members of "The Squad". In the words of Collins' biographer Tim Pat Coogan: "When the Frongoch gates swung open he was in a position to ensure that the spores of revolutionary violence blasted into the air above the [General Post Office] in Easter Week would be wafted into every corner of Ireland."[410] The historian Michael Burleigh reached the same conclusion about the *centres de regroupement* introduced by the French authorities in Algeria to forcibly resettle rural families from so-called "exposed" communities in barbed-wire encampments: "[The] only effect was to create anti-French solidarities among

---

[408] Jeffrey Toobin, *American Heiress: The Wild Saga of the Kidnapping, Crimes and Trial of Patty Hearst* (Doubleday; 2016), p. 29.

[409] Marc Sageman, *Understanding Terror Networks* (University of Pennsylvania Press; 2004), p. 143.

[410] Tim Pat Coogan, *Michael Collins: The Man Who Made Ireland* (Palgrave; 1990), pp. 54–55.

embittered people who had been arbitrarily lifted out of their traditional communities. They ensured 'the concentrated hatred and frustration of thousands' among the 2 millions so affected."[411] In the mid-1970s, Cages 9 and 11 of the Maze Prison brought together a cadre of Provisional IRA volunteers, including Gerry Adams, who would become the 'Brains Trust' of the organization, and an influential faction within it on their release.[412]

When Israel responded to attacks in December 1992 that killed four members of the security forces by detaining 415 *Hamas* and Palestinian Islamic Jihad (PIJ) leaders and then expelling them across the northern border with Lebanon, the militants responded by setting up a tented camp on a hillside near the border, which came to be known as Camp Ibn Taymiyyah after the medieval theologian beloved of radical Islamists.[413] Not only were the Palestinians able to forge stronger bonds amongst themselves, enabling greater future operational efficiency, they also received help and support from the Lebanese *Shia* terrorist group *Hezbollah*. In addition, *Hezbollah* provided the *Hamas* and PIJ cadres with operational training, including in the use of explosives and suicide vests, which had not thus far been used by Palestinian groups but soon would be to deadly effect.[414] The founder of *Jammat al-Muslimin*, Shukri Mustafa, built the organization around a nucleus of comrades from his prison days and family members, including a brother and nephew.[415]

---

[411] Michael Burleigh, *Blood and Rage: A Cultural History of Terrorism* (Harper; 2009), p. 118 and Alistair Horne, *A Savage War of Peace: Algeria 1954–1962* (New York Review Books Classics; 2006), p. 221.

[412] Rachel Stevenson and Nick Crossley, Change in Covert Social Movement Networks: The "Inner Circle" of the Provisional Irish Republican Army, in Nick Crossley and John Krinsky (eds.), *Social Networks and Social Movements: Contentious Connections* (Routledge; 2015), p. 81.

[413] Patrick Tyler, *Fortress Israel: The Inside Story of the Military Elite Who Run the Country — and Why They Can't Make Peace* (Farrar, Straus and Giroux; 2012), pp. 357–358. The Israelis described their action as a "temporary removal" since the Geneva Conventions protect citizens of occupied territory from expulsion.

[414] Mia Bloom, *Dying to Kill: The Allure of Suicide Terror* (Columbia University Press; 2005), p. 122.

[415] Saad Eddin Ibrahim, Anatomy of Egypt's Militant Groups: Methodological Note and Preliminary Findings, *International Journal of Middle East Studies*, Vol. 12, No. 4 (1980), p. 438.

The Spanish authorities reported that 20% of those imprisoned for Islamist-related terrorist offences between 2005 and 2011 had previously served time in prison.[416] The Dutch terrorism researcher Edwin Bakker found in a 2006 study of 242 European jihadists that approximately 25% had a prior criminal record unrelated to terrorist activities.[417] Della Porta's Italian sample identified sixty-seven cases where terrorists had a documented prior criminal history of non-political violent crime.[418]

Prison life encourages inmates to join tight social networks and commit to group norms. Prisoners have plenty of free time to deepen their understanding of these norms, but in an environment where such groups can also control access to information. Organizations with networks outside prison can help inmates find structure and meaning on their release into an often hostile outside world. In 2014, the Iraqi government estimated that seventeen of the twenty-five most important ISIL leaders directing the war in Iraq and Syria had been detained between 2004 and 2011, and a former ISIL militant going by the *nom de guerre* Abu Ahmed has described how the nucleus of ISIL formed in US-run prisons during the Coalition occupation.[419] He told *The Guardian* journalist Martin Churlov: "In prison, all of the princes were meeting regularly. We became very close to those we were jailed with. We knew their capabilities. We knew what they could and couldn't do, how to use them for whatever reason... We had so much time to sit and plan. It was the perfect environment. We all agreed to get together when we got out. The way to reconnect was easy. We wrote each other's details on the elastic of our boxer shorts. When we got out, we called. Everyone who was important to me was written on white elastic. I had their phone numbers, their villages. By 2009, many of us were back doing what we did before we were caught. But this time we were doing it

---

[416] Diego Gambetta and Steffan Hertog, *Engineers of Jihad: The Curious Connection between Violent Extremism and Education* (Princeton University Press; 2016), pp. 64–65.

[417] ibid., p. 64.

[418] Donatella Della Porta, Recruitment Processes in Clandestine Political Organizations: Italian Left-Wing Terrorism, *International Social Movement Research*, Vol. 1 (1988), p. 164.

[419] Martin Churlov, ISIS: The Inside Story, *The Guardian*, 11 December 2014.

better ... If there was no American prison in Iraq, there would be no IS now. [Camp] Bucca was a factory. It made us all. It built our ideology."[420]

Political scientist Max Abrahms has argued that individuals who join terrorist groups are in essence "solidarity seekers" attracted as much by the intense relationships forged by clandestine life as by any underlying ideological commitment.[421] Abrahms drew upon organization theory and the "natural systems model" developed by Chester Barnard.[422] Barnard warned against simplistically equating the goals of an organization with the personal goals of its members. He suggested instead that most individuals had reasons of their own for joining and remaining active within an organization based on their own cost–benefit analysis of the pros and cons of membership. The benefit that stood out in Barnard's research above any other was the social benefit of fellowship. Further support for this insight comes from Douglas McAdam, one of the pioneers of social movement theory (of which more below), whose influential study of the 1964 Freedom Summer campaign to register African-American voters in segregationist Mississippi found that a supportive network could also exert a "pulling" effect on potential activists encouraging them to seek to join the group.[423]

Again, one can find considerable support for the powerful appeal of fellowship in the literature. Che Guevara described, in a letter to his mother, the transformation he underwent while incarcerated by the Mexican authorities in the summer of 1956, along with Fidel Castro and his small band of Cuban revolutionaries, prior to their departure for Cuba and the guerrilla war in the Sierra Maestra: "In these days of prison and the previous ones of training I identified totally with my comrades in the cause ... The concept

---

[420] ibid.

[421] See Max Abrahms, What Terrorists Really Want: Terrorist Motives and Counterterrorism Strategy, *International Security*, Vol. 32, No. 4 (Spring 2008).

[422] ibid., p. 95 and Chester Barnard, *The Functions of the Executive* (Cambridge, Mass.: Harvard University Press, 1938).

[423] Doug McAdam, Recruitment to High-risk Activism: The Case of Freedom Summer, *American Journal of Sociology*, Vol. 92, No. 1 (1986).

of 'I' disappeared totally to give place to the concept 'us'. It was a communist morale and naturally it may seem a doctrinaire exaggeration, but really it was (and is) beautiful to be able to feel that removal of I."[424] Analyzing the 227 life stories of West German terrorists, Klaus Wasmund observed that "in all the biographies of terrorists we find the strong desire for community, for a group commitment."[425] Ulrike Meinhof, who was a successful left-wing journalist with a burgeoning career and two young children, confided to her diary shortly before she made the life-changing decision to throw in her lot with Andreas Baader and the other founders of the *Rote Armee Fraktion*: "Our house, the parties ... all of that's only partly enjoyable ... I even find it pleasant, but it doesn't satisfy my need for warmth, solidarity, belonging to a group."[426] In her memoir, *Remembering the Armed Struggle: Life in Baader-Meinhof*, former SPK and RAF member Margrit Schiller recalled finding the strong sense of belonging shared by members of the group deeply attractive: "They seemed to share a common feeling, they were all on the same wavelength, they almost shared the same thoughts."[427] For a young woman haunted by feelings of "loneliness and sadness" it was intoxicating.[428]

Adriana Faranda, a member of the national council of the *Brigate Rosse* (BR) who participated in the kidnapping of the Italian Prime Minister Aldo Moro, further echoed this sentiment: "I feel that the choice of the Red Brigades is the last of possible choices ... I'm looking not only for organizational solidity but for a feeling of community, of sharing, of solidarity. Much more important, I think, than pure efficiency."[429] Another BR cadre, Patrizio Peci,

---

[424] Jon Lee Anderson, *Che Guevara: A Revolutionary Life* (Grove Press; 1997), pp. 199–200.

[425] Klaus Wasmund, The Political Socialization of West German Terrorists, in Peter Merkl (ed.), *Political Violence and Terror: Motifs and Motivations* (University of California Press; 1986), p. 225.

[426] Stefan Aust, *Baader-Meinhof: The Inside Story of the R.A.F.* (Oxford University Press; 2009), p. 24.

[427] ibid., p. 115.

[428] ibid., p. 114.

[429] Alessandro Orsini, *Anatomy of the Red Brigades: The Religious Mindset of Modern Terrorists* (Cornell University Press; 2011), p. 105.

was still more effusive: "Thank God there was the Organization. I had an appointment twice a week with the Organization. When you're alone, when you make holes in plastic all day, eat in a trattoria, and sleep with strangers, you either go mad or do something. If you have a goal, an important goal, then it's all more bearable. Some have the soccer team, some have their wives, some their automobiles. I had the Organization, and through the Organization I was convinced I was also working for the good of those who thought only of their wives, their soccer team, or their automobiles."[430]

Max Abrahms cites the example of a Turkish study conducted by Ahmet Yayla that was based on a survey of 1,077 incarcerated terrorists, primarily from the Marxist–Leninist *Devrimci Halk Kurtuluş Partisi-Cephesi*, but also members of twelve other terrorist organizations. Yalya found the survey subjects were ten times more likely to say that they had joined the terrorist organization "because their friends were members" than because they had been attracted to the organization's "ideology".[431] In his study of Egyptian terrorist organizations, such as *Jammat al-Muslimin*, Saad Eddin Ibrahim noted that "militant Islamic groups with their emphasis on brotherhood, mutual sharing, and spiritual support become the functional equivalent of an extended family to the youngster who has left his behind."[432] Indeed, the term *usroh* (family) is often also used to describe small communities of the faithful.[433] Ibrahim describes how such groups can play a critical "de-alienating" role for young men who have left home and are struggling to adapt to an unfamiliar environment.[434] Sulastri

---

[430] ibid., p. 106.

[431] See Max Abrahms, What Terrorists Really Want: Terrorist Motives and Counterterrorism Strategy, *International Security*, Vol. 32, No. 4 (Spring 2008), p. 98.

[432] Saad Eddin Ibrahim, Anatomy of Egypt's Militant Groups: Methodological Note and Preliminary Findings, *International Journal of Middle East Studies*, Vol. 12, No. 4 (1980), p. 448.

[433] Sulastri Osman, Jemaah Islamiyah: Of Kin and Kind, *Journal of Current Southeast Asian Affairs*, Vol. 29, No. 2 (2010), p. 169.

[434] Saad Eddin Ibrahim, Anatomy of Egypt's Militant Groups: Methodological Note and Preliminary Findings, *International Journal of Middle East Studies*, Vol. 12, No. 4 (1980), p. 448.

Osman, a researcher at the Centre of Excellence for National Security Studies at the S. Rajaratnam School of International Studies in Singapore specializing in *Jemaah Islamiyah,* has similarly described the sense of solidarity that permeates radical Islamism appositely as *ikhwan*-ship (brotherhood).[435] Between 2005 and 2007, the underwear bomber Umar Farouk Abdulmutallab is credibly believed to have posted 310 times on an Islamic forum website called Gawaher.com under the user name Farouk 1986.[436] One post dated January 2005 read: "I am in a situation where I do not have a friend, I have no one to speak too [sic], no one to consult, no one to support me and I feel depressed and lonely. I do not know what to do."[437] Readers can follow his online journey into a tighter and tighter circle of like-minded religious cohorts and his blossoming sense of fellowship.

Finally, we should briefly circle back to Louise Richardson's concept of complicit surround discussed in Part I, which noted that terrorist organizations depend heavily on sympathizers outside the group. There is a tactical, as well as strategic, dimension to this relationship. Terrorist groups need trusted supporters, ideally unknown to the authorities, to fulfill a variety of functions without which it would be difficult for the group to operate successfully, as a former *Prima Linea* militant explained to Donatella Della Porta: "A key point for an organization like ours is to maintain a 'friendly' network of people who do not want to belong to the organization, to have specific tasks, or to participate in actions, but provide you with housing, fake documents, or keep your guns."[438] The RAF cadre Hans-Joachim Klein also acknowledged that "the RAF and other

---

[435] Sulastri Osman, Jemaah Islamiyah: Of Kin and Kind, *Journal of Current Southeast Asian Affairs,* Vol. 29, No. 2 (2010), p. 157.

[436] Natshan Hodge, Visualizing the Underwear Bomber's Online Life, *Wired,* 7 January 2010.

[437] Anna Geifman, *Death Orders: The Vanguard of Modern Terrorism in Revolutionary Russia* (Praeger Security International; 2010), p. 100 and Online poster appears to be Christmas Day bomb suspect, *CNN News,* 29 December 2009 at http://edition.cnn.com/2009/CRIME/12/29/terror.suspect.online/. Viewed 9 February 2017.

[438] Gilda Zwerman, Patricia Steinhoff and Donatella Della Porta, Disappearing Social Movements: Clandestinity in the Cycle of New Left Protest in the US, Japan, Germany, and Italy, *Mobilization: An International Journal,* Vol. 5, No. 1 (2000), p. 100.

groupings could and still can only survive and work with the support of comrades who are not wanted by the law."[439] Even though these individuals may not be part of the organization, they are nevertheless still likely to be part of the social networks of its members, more often than not extended family, old friends, or fellow students. Social movement theory would characterize such semi-detached relationships as "low risk/cost activism".[440] Some of these supporters may even over time migrate from providing material support to the organization to active membership. Hans-Joachim Klein's own journey into the RAF began as a "legal comrade" laundering stolen currency and arranging a safe house for active terrorists.[441]

Many proponents of social movement theory would contend that, in Doug McAdam's phrase, "structural availability is more important than attitudinal affinity" in determining who joins and who does not join a particular movement.[442] In the terrorism field, the data would seem to support this contention, but this does not mean that attitudinal affinity is without significance. Not all terrorists come from family or friendship networks, some do find their way into the underground alone and win the trust of their new peers. The proliferation of social media tools has greatly facilitated this process. Nor are all terrorists solidarity seekers, there are lone wolves like Leon Czolgosz or Anders Behring Breivik who self-radicalize and self-execute attacks. But unquestionably many terrorists find themselves involved in terrorism not just because of whom they are and what they believe, but because of the social networks they are part of. Terrorists may not be mad, and from a certain perspective, they may not even be bad, but they are undoubtedly dangerous to know.

---

[439] Klaus Wasmund, The Political Socialization of West German Terrorists, in Peter Merkl (ed.), *Political Violence and Terror: Motifs and Motivations* (University of California Press; 1986), p. 213.

[440] Doug McAdam, Recruitment to High-risk Activism: The Case of Freedom Summer, *American Journal of Sociology*, Vol. 92, No. 1 (1986), p. 68.

[441] Klaus Wasmund, The Political Socialization of West German Terrorists, in Peter Merkl (ed.), *Political Violence and Terror: Motifs and Motivations* (University of California Press; 1986), p. 213.

[442] Doug McAdam, Recruitment to High-risk Activism: The Case of Freedom Summer, *American Journal of Sociology*, Vol. 92, No. 1 (1986), p. 65.

## Socialization

Socialization is the process by which individuals adopt and internalize group norms of behavior and take on particular roles. Individuals may go through a number of socializing experiences in a lifetime, often at age-related transition points such as entering the workforce or attending university, and one experience may either build on or supplant another.[443] Sociologists and developmental psychologists furthermore identify certain "agents of socialization" that guide and shape this process, such as family groups, peer groups, institutions, places of worship, workplaces, or even remote influences such as news or social media.[444] The Stanford psychologist Albert Bandura has also stressed the importance played in social learning by role models, individuals who do not so much teach or instruct but inspire emulation by example because of their societal success.[445] As Waseem Iqbal, a young aid worker from the British city of Birmingham, noted, ISIL attracts young recruits from his community because it is "the biggest, most baddest gang in the world [sic]," and sadly for a consequential minority, this equates to success.[446]

The first, and often most profound, socializing influence on most individuals is the family they are born into, and as we have seen in the previous section, there are plenty of examples in the literature of individuals who have been born into militant families and have then taken on the values of their parents and siblings. Provisional IRA volunteer Marian Price recounted a fairly typical experience: "I was born into a very staunchly republican family. My father was a republican (had been a member of the IRA in the forties) and my mother's family were very staunchly republican (her sisters and herself were members of *Cumann na mBan*) ... So we

---

[443] Albert Bandura, Social-Learning Theory of Identificatory Processes, in David Goslin (ed.), *Handbook of Socialization Theory and Research* (Rand McNally & Co.; 1969), p. 251.

[444] Joan Grusec and Paul Hastings, *Handbook of Socialization: Theory and Research* (Guilford Publications; 2006), p. xi.

[445] Albert Bandura, Social-Learning Theory of Identificatory Processes, in David Goslin (ed.), *Handbook of Socialization Theory and Research* (Rand McNally and Co.; 1969), p. 213.

[446] Roz Laws, Extremely British Muslims: "Why some young Birmingham men join ISIS', *Birmingham Mail*, 9 March 2017.

always grew up with republicanism, and with a deep sense of pride in republicanism."[447] *Jemaah Islamiyah* activist Farihin Ahmad was a third-generation Islamist militant, his grandfather had fought the Dutch and his father, Ahmad Kandai, had been involved in a 1957 plot to assassinate President Sukarno.[448] Two of his brothers were also involved in terrorist attacks. Farihin expressed the hope to an interviewer that his own children would follow the family tradition.[449] Ali Hassan Salameh, Chief of Operations for Black September and the architect of the 1972 Munich Olympics massacre, was also the son of a celebrated Palestinian *Fedayeen* commander, Hassan Salameh. He poignantly wrote that his upbringing was politicized from the first: "When my father fell as a martyr, Palestine was passed to me, so to speak. My mother wanted me to be another Hassan Salameh at a time when the most any Palestinian could hope for was to live a normal life ... I wanted to be myself. The fact that I was required to live up to the image of my father created a problem for me. Even as a child I had to follow a certain pattern of behavior. I could not afford to live my childhood. I was made consciously aware of the fact that I was the son of Hassan Salameh and had to live up to that, even without being told how the son of Hassan Salameh should live."[450]

Schools, universities and social clubs are further potential socialization agents. The Indonesian *al-Qaeda* affiliate *Jemaah Islamiyah* formed around a kernel of activists who were faculty members of a religious boarding school in Malaysia called *Pesentren Luqmanul Hakiem*, most prominent among them, Abu Bakar Baasyir and Abdullah Sungkar.[451] Other faculty members who ascended to leadership positions in *Jemaah Islamiyah* were Riduan Isamuddin and Ali Ghufron. Ghufron recruited three of his brothers to take part in the

---

[447] Richard English, *Armed Struggle: The History of the IRA* (Oxford University Press; 2004), pp. 128–129.

[448] Sulastri Osman, Jemaah Islamiyah: Of Kin and Kind, *Journal of Current Southeast Asian Affairs*, Vol. 29, No. 2 (2010), p. 165.

[449] ibid.

[450] Michael Burleigh, *Blood and Rage: A Cultural History of Terrorism* (Harper; 2009), p. 159.

[451] Marc Sageman, *Understanding Terror Networks* (University of Pennsylvania Press; 2004), p. 44.

Bali bombing operation. *Hamas* has set up youth soccer teams in disadvantaged areas like Hebron's Wad Abu Katila neighborhood.[452] One team from Hebron — Jihad Mosque — provided *Hamas* with eight suicide bombers.[453] Three of the *Hamas* activists behind the bombing of the Park Hotel in Netanya in March 2002, the deadliest attack of the Second *Intifada* which killed thirty people and injured 140, mostly senior citizens attending a Passover *seder*, were members of the same *Hamas* singing troupe.[454] The Basque separatist group ETA similarly looked to recruit new members from youth mountaineering clubs.[455] *Hezbollah* runs its own Boy Scout program known as the Mahdi Scouts.[456]

It has been suggested by both Steve Coll and Lawrence Wright that Osama bin Laden himself became radicalized in part because of his involvement in an extracurricular football and religious study group run by a Syrian gym teacher at the elite Al-Thaghr private school in Jeddah who was a former Muslim Brotherhood activist.[457] A schoolmate of Bin Laden's who also attended the study group told Steve Coll: "[The teacher] promised that if we stayed we could be part of a sports club, play soccer. I very much wanted to play soccer. So we began to stay after school with him from 2 o'clock until 5. When it began, he explained that at the beginning of the session we would spend a little bit of time indoors at first, memorizing a few verses from the *Koran* each day, and then we would go play soccer.

---

[452] Scott Atran, *Talking to the Enemy: Faith, Brotherhood and the (Un)making of Terrorists* (Ecco; 2010), p. 406 and Ami Pedahzur and Arie Perliger, The Changing Nature of Suicide Attacks: A Social Network Perspective, *Social Forces*, Vol. 84, No. 4, June 2006, p. 1995.

[453] Luca Ricolfi, Palestinians 1981–2003, in Diego Gambetta (ed.), *Making Sense of Suicide Missions* (Oxford University Press; 2005), p. 113.

[454] Matthew Levitt, *Hamas: Politics, Charity and Terrorism in the Service of Jihad* (Yale University Press; 2006), p. 140.

[455] Martha Crenshaw, *Explaining Terrorism: Causes, Processes and Consequences* (2011), p. 78 and Robert Clark, Patterns in the Lives of ETA Members, *Studies in Conflict and Terrorism*, Vol. 6, No. 3 (1983), p. 439.

[456] Max Boot, *Invisible Armies: An Epic History of Guerrilla Warfare from Ancient Times to the Present* (Liveright; 2013), p. 508.

[457] Steve Coll, *The Bin Ladens: An Arabian Family in the American Century* (The Penguin Press; 2008), pp. 142–147 and Lawrence Wright, *The Looming Tower: A Qaeda and the Road to 9/11* (Knopf; 2006), p. 75.

The idea was that if we memorized a few verses each day before soccer, by the time we finished high school we would have memorized the entire *Koran*, a special distinction."[458] The schoolmate left the study group after the teacher told a story about a son who had killed his father for trying to stop him from praying, a story which ended with the teacher exclaiming: "Lord be praised — Islam was released in that home."[459]

We have already seen in Part I how *Hamas* has used children's television programming to inculcate a Manichean world view of heroic Palestinians and brutal Israelis in Gaza's children, but an even more extreme example of childhood socialization can be found in the territory controlled by ISIL. A detailed study produced by the former Libyan militant Noman Benotman and Nikita Malik for the UK-based Quilliam Foundation looked at Islamic State's attempts to raise a generation of child soldiers.[460] ISIL began by declaring school attendance mandatory for all children and by taking control of the curriculum taught in local schools. Children who had previously been educated in "the disbelieving curriculum" of Western-oriented schools were required to attend special schools, and teachers who opposed their agenda were executed.[461] Children between the ages of five and ten were enrolled in religious schools and those aged ten to fifteen in military schools.[462] Mothers were given books instructing them how to bring up jihadi children with suggestions like telling them bedtime stories about martyrdom and sensitizing them to the violent content of some jihadi websites.[463] In military school, youths were put through physical training that included both martial arts and physical abuse to toughen them up. They were also separated from their families so that they had to rely on ISIL for their daily

---

[458] Steve Coll, *The Bin Ladens: An Arabian Family in the American Century* (The Penguin Press; 2008), pp. 145–146.

[459] ibid., p. 147.

[460] Noman Benotman and Nikita Malik, *The Children of Islamic State*, Quilliam Foundation (March 2016).

[461] ibid., p. 32.

[462] ibid., p. 34.

[463] ibid., p. 35.

subsistence. Some child soldiers were even forced to participate in executions and ISIL posted numerous videos of such activities online.[464] Indeed, the Quilliam report found that 38% of the images produced by ISIL that featured children, featured them in situations in which they were either participating in violence, or in circumstances that were designed to normalize violence for them (playing with weapons, witnessing executions, etc.).[465] By July 2015, the Syrian Observatory for Human Rights had documented nineteen cases of children being used as suicide bombers.[466] Fifteen-year-old Mohammed Ahmed Ismael was apprehended by Kurdish security forces wearing a suicide belt in Kirkuk in August 2016. He had been indoctrinated by ISIL's armed youth wing *Ashbal al-Khilafah* (Cubs of the Caliphate) and described the experience to *The Times* reporter Anthony Loyd: "I cannot say we were happy, for we were often afraid and beaten. But there was comfort in knowing we could go to heaven as martyrs ... We were chosen for suicide tasks. It was not a matter of [our] choice."[467]

Religious institutions can also act as agents of socialization by creating a "cognitive opening" for more extremist ideas. The Greek Cypriot terrorist group EOKA recruited many of its cadres from two Greek Orthodox-sponsored youth organizations, *Orthodoxos Christianiki Enosis Neon* (OHEN) and the Pancyprian National Youth Organization (PEON), as well as from the right-wing Pan Agrarian Union of Cyprus (PEK).[468] Indeed, the British authorities considered OHEN, in particular, to be "probably one of the most efficient means of subversion employed by the Ethnarchy ... with many of its members becoming fanatic supporters of *enosis*."[469] Ku Klux Klan member Wesley Swift founded the Church of Jesus Christ-Christian

---

[464] ibid., p. 42.

[465] ibid., pp. 18–19.

[466] ibid., p. 44.

[467] Anthony Loyd, The children of Islamic State, *The Times Magazine*, 21 January 2017.

[468] David French, *Fighting EOKA: The British Counter-Insurgency Campaign on Cyprus, 1955–1959* (Oxford University Press; 2015), p. 50.

[469] Yiannos Katsourides, *The Greek Cypriot Nationalist Right in the Era of British Colonialism: Emergence, Mobilisation and Transformations of Right-Wing Party Politics* (Springer; 2017), p. 204.

in 1946 to advance his racist agenda and the Christian Identity movement has been linked to a number of disparate violent extremist groups in the United States such as the anti-abortionist Army of God and the white supremacist Aryan Nations.[470] Mohammed Abd al-Salam Faraj, the author of *The Neglected Duty*, and a critical figure in the *Jamaat Islamiyya* movement, preached in a private mosque in Cairo built for the purpose by his in-laws and sought to recruit followers from among his congregation.[471] Faraj was executed in Egypt in 1982 for the role he played in the conspiracy to assassinate Anwar Sadat. The Ibn Taymiyyah mosque in Maiduguri, Borno State, where Mohammed Yusuf presided as *Imam*, was the birthplace of *Boko Haram*.[472] A number of Western mosques have become associated with Islamist terrorism including the Finsbury Park and Baker Street Mosques in London, while under the stewardship of Abu Hamza al-Masri and Omar Mahmoud Othman (better known as Abu Qatada), respectively, the Islamic Cultural Center in Milan, the Abu Bakr Mosque in Madrid, the al-Dawah Mosque in Roubaix, and the al-Faruq Mosque in Brooklyn at which the blind firebrand Egyptian cleric Omar Abdel-Rahman was briefly a preacher.[473]

Most terrorist organizations disseminate explanatory tracts and organizational manuals designed to socialize recruits to the mindset and values required of their members. Examples of this practice include Sergei Nechaev's *The Catechism of the Revolutionist*, Carlos Marighella's *Minimanual of the Urban Guerrilla*, iterations of the IRA and Provisional IRA's *Green Book*, the *General Guide for the Struggle of Jemaah Islamiyah*, and Abu Bakr Naji's *The Administration of Savagery*. Finding inspiration in such books can be a critical step on the path to violent extremism. For many nineteenth century Russian populist revolutionaries, inspiration came not just from political treatises

---

[470] Mark Juergensmeyer, *Terror in the Mind of God: The Global Rise of Religious Violence* (University of California Press; 2003), pp. 33–34.

[471] Marc Sageman, *Understanding Terror Networks* (University of Pennsylvania Press; 2004), p. 30 and p. 134.

[472] Virginia Comolli, *Boko Haram: Nigeria's Islamist Insurgency* (C. Hurst & Co.; 2015), p. 54.

[473] Marc Sageman, *Understanding Terror Networks* (University of Pennsylvania Press; 2004), p. 114.

and manifestos but also from contemporary novels like Nikolai Chernyshevsky's *What is to be Done?* and poems like Ivan Turgenev's *The Threshold.*[474] An Indian Muslim who joined the *al-Qaeda* affiliate *Jabhat al-Nusra li Ahl al-Sham* and fought in Syria ascribed his political awakening to reading the works of Sayyid Qutb: "Someone referred me to *Milestones* by Sayyid Qutb when I was in my teens ... Read it ... Studied more about *jihad* by *al-Qaeda* ... Seemed legit. Wanted to join some group long ago ... Didn't find any way ... *Allah* brought us a mercy from himself in the form of Syrian civil war [sic]."[475] London Transport bombers Mohammad Siddique Khan and Shehzad Tanweer were both trustees of the Iqra Islamic bookshop in the Beeston suburb of Leeds.[476] William Pierce's racist novel *The Turner Diaries* inspired Timothy McVeigh and provided a model for his 1995 attack on the Alfred P. Murrah Federal Building in Oklahoma City. In recent decades, the socializing power of well-crafted words has been magnified still further, first by the circulation of radical sermons on cassette tape and then by the advent of the internet and social media. The British Security Service's Behavioral Science Unit notes: "People do not generally become radicalized simply through passive browsing of extremist websites, but many such sites create opportunities for the 'virtual' social interaction that drives radicalization in the virtual world."[477]

The final, and perhaps most significant, socialization agent is the community of activists within which the terrorist group itself nests. Quintan Wiktorowicz, who studied the membership of the extremist but non-violent Islamist group, *al-Muhajiroun*, concluded that "individuals do not typically awake with a sudden epiphany that drives them to join radical Islamic groups. Instead,

---

[474] See Martin Miller, Entangled Terrorisms in Late Imperial Russia, in Randall Law (ed.), *The Routledge History of Terrorism* (Routledge; 2015).

[475] Lorne Dawson and Amarnath Amarasingam, Talking to Foreign Fighters: Insights in to the Motivations for Hijrah to Syria and Iraq, *Studies in Conflict and Terrorism*, Vol. 40, No. 3 (2017), p. 9.

[476] Christopher Hope and Duncan Gardham, BBC's Children in Need funded 7/7 terrorist propaganda, says Newsnight, *The Telegraph*, 19 August 2008.

[477] Alan Travis, The making of an extremist, *The Guardian*, 20 August 2008, at www.theguardian.com/uk/2008/aug/20/uksecurity.terrorism. Viewed 5 August 2016.

they experience an often extensive socialization process that includes exposure to movement ideas, debate and deliberation, and even experimentation with alternative groups."[478] The former CIA psychiatrist Jerrold Post concurs with Wiktorowicz's assessment: "The path to joining a terrorist group tends to be slow and gradual, from sympathizer, to passive supporter, to active supporter, and finally joining the group itself."[479] One former Islamist extremist 'Aziz' described his journey into extremism thus: "Islam is like karate and the belts." 'Aziz' explained that when he first became a *Salafi*, he was a white belt, but he was pressured over time to demonstrate his commitment and become more and more extreme.[480] The interviews carried out by Mauricio Florez-Morris with forty-two Colombian former Marxist fighters found that they had on average taken anything from two-and-a-half years to just over four years to make the decision to finally join a violent group.[481] Although there are certainly plenty of case studies in which individuals have turned to violence in a shorter time frame, the key point is that the radicalization process is typically a gradual one and thus can afford plenty of opportunity for effective intervention.

Doug McAdam observed that every positive interaction that an aspirant member of a group has with an existing member is likely to deepen his or her ideological affinity and commitment to the group, and his or her receptivity to more high risk/cost activities.[482] Kinship — actual or fictive — is a powerful binding agent.

---

[478] Quintan Wiktorowicz, *Joining the Cause: Al-Muhajiroun and Radical Islam*, at http://insct.syr.edu/wp-content/uploads/2013/03/Wiktorowicz.Joining-the-Cause.pdf. Viewed 5 March 2017.

[479] Jerrold Post, Notes on a Psychodynamic Theory of Terrorist Behavior, *Terrorism*, Vol. 7, No. 3 (1984), p. 254.

[480] Thomas E. Ricks, U.S. Military Cultural Awareness: I was a Pro-Saddam Protestor, was Called a "Camel Jockey," but I AM and American Soldier, *Foreign Policy*, 30 April 2015.

[481] Mauricio Florez-Morris, Joining Guerrilla Groups in Colombia: Individual Motivations and Processes for Entering a Violent Organization, *Studies in Conflict and Terrorism*, Vol. 30, No. 7 (2007), p. 623.

[482] Doug McAdam, Recruitment to High-risk Activism: The Case of Freedom Summer, *American Journal of Sociology*, Vol. 92, No. 1 (1986), p. 70.

Immersion in the clandestine world of a militant organization is the fourth and penultimate "floor" of Fathali Moghaddam's staircase to terrorism: "Commitment to the terrorist cause strengthens as the new recruit is socialized into the traditions, methods, and goals of the organization."[483] Marc Sageman has noted that to reinforce these bonds, terrorist groups — much like street gangs, secret societies and military units — often create initiation rites or tests: "Participation in rituals builds faith and generates group solidarity and integration."[484] Terrorist organizations consciously or unconsciously repetitively use prayer or political instruction as a socialization tool, bringing the group together — as often as the exigencies of underground life allow — to emphasize shared values and reinforce commitment. Some terrorist groups, like the Weathermen who adopted the slogan "smash monogamy", have even promoted ideas of free love, seeking to bind small groups together by using sex as a means to strengthen ties between members.[485]

The newspaper heiress Patty Hearst represents an unusual, but not unique, example of someone who would likely never have come into the orbit of terrorists without having been abducted by Donald DeFreeze and the Symbionese Liberation Army (SLA), and yet subsequently became an active participant in the group's activities.[486] Hearst was kidnapped in February 1974 and initially held in frightening and oppressive circumstances, but over the course of her first two months of captivity, she gradually became integrated into the group under the *nom de guerre* "Tania". She formed a romantic attachment with one member, Willy Wolfe, and slept with at least one other — the SLA adhered to the same "free love" ethos as the Weathermen. She recorded a communiqué in which she declared her allegiance to

---

[483] Fathali Moghaddam, The Staircase to Terrorism: A Psychological Exploration, *American Psychologist*, Vol. 60, No. 2, (February–March 2005), pp. 165–166.

[484] Marc Sageman, *Understanding Terror Networks* (University of Pennsylvania Press; 2004), p. 117.

[485] Gilda Zwerman, Patricia Steinhoff and Donatella Della Porta, Disappearing Social Movements: Clandestinity in the Cycle of New Left Protest in the US, Japan, Germany, and Italy, *Mobilization: An International Journal*, Vol. 5, No. 1 (2000), p. 96.

[486] See Jeffrey Toobin, *American Heiress: The Wild Saga of the Kidnapping, Crimes and Trial of Patty Hearst* (Doubleday; 2016).

the SLA, explaining: "I have changed — grown. I've become conscious and can never go back to the life we led before ... I have been
given the choice of (one) being released in a safe area, or (two) joining the forces of the Symbionese Liberation Army, and fighting for
my freedom and the freedom of all oppressed people. I have chosen
to stay and fight."[487] Hearst remained part of the SLA until her eventual arrest in September 1975, and during her processing at San
Mateo County Jail she gave her profession as "urban guerrilla".[488] In
the previous eighteen months, she had passed up opportunities to
escape, been trusted by the group to carry around a loaded weapon,
participated in a number of bank robberies and bombings, and on
one occasion opened fire on a San Francisco street to free two members of the group detained for shoplifting. At her trial, she claimed to
have been acting throughout under duress, but her account differed
sharply with that of the surviving members of the SLA. It is impossible to know for sure whose account is more truthful, both parties had
good reasons to lie. Despite a degree of public sympathy, Hearst was
convicted and sentenced to seven years in prison. Her sentence was
commuted after twenty-two months by President Jimmy Carter and
she was finally pardoned by Bill Clinton — the only person in US
history to have a sentence commuted by one President and to receive
a pardon from another.

Perhaps, one of the most extreme examples of a purposeful
socialization process at work within a terrorist organization is the
orgy of intergroup criticism that consumed the Japanese Marxist
group *Rengō Sekigun* in the winter of 1971–1972. *Rengō Sekigun* was
the amalgam of two small pre-existing leftist militant groups *Sekigun*
and *Nihon Kyōsantō Kakumei Saha* (*Kakusa*) and the new head, Mori
Tsuneo, formerly the leader of *Sekigun*, was searching for a method
to fuse the two constituent parts closer together. The method he
settled on he termed "*kyōsanshugika*" (communist transformation or
communization) and he introduced it at a remote mountain training camp in Gumma prefecture which brought the two groups

---

[487] ibid., p. 122.
[488] ibid., p. 262.

together in one place for the first time. *Kyōsanshugika* was intended to be a transformative amalgam of self and group criticism which would enable the individual members of *Rengō Sekigun* to become tougher, more effective, revolutionary soldiers willing to subordinate their personal needs and desires to the collective enterprise.[489] What Tsuneo unleased instead was a potent mix of divided loyalties, petty rivalries and sexual jealousy over which he played the role of increasingly unpredictable arbiter.

Initially, Tsuneo imposed simple physical punishments like extra rifle drill as a re-education tool, but the punishments soon began to escalate to food deprivation, extended physical restraint outside in sub-zero temperatures, and beatings — all intended to instil fighting spirit. Because the group members were sincerely committed to the armed struggle, they submitted to Tsuneo's discipline, and Tsuneo himself insisted that every single group member participate in disciplining their comrades as part of their own journey towards revolutionary enlightenment — to refuse was to demonstrate a lack of ideological commitment and to open oneself up disciplinary measures in turn.[490] The first group member to die in December 1971 was Ozaki Atsuo. He had been subjected to a series of educational beatings, but his comrades had not intended to kill him. However, his death raised the stakes for Tsuneo who deflected blame by pronouncing that Atsuo had suffered "death by defeatism", adding that the cadre had died of shock because of his inability to achieve *kyōsanshugika*, despite the best efforts of his peers to help him through the application of revolutionary discipline.[491] Achieving *kyōsanshugika* had suddenly, and unintentionally, become a matter of life or death for the members of *Rengō Sekigun* and by February 1972, when the group was finally located by the Japanese police, eleven

---

[489] Patricia Steinhoff, Death by Defeatism and Other Fables: The Social Dynamics of the Rengō Sekigun Purge, in Takie Sugiyama Lebra (ed.), *Japanese Social Organization* (University of Hawaii Press; 1992), pp. 197–199.

[490] ibid., p. 207.

[491] Patricia Steinhoff, Death by Defeatism and Other Fables: The Social Dynamics of the Rengō Sekigun Purge, in Takie Sugiyama Lebra (ed.), *Japanese Social Organization* (University of Hawaii Press; 1992), p. 208.

more members of the group had fallen victim to the process, almost half the total strength of the combined organization. Even new group members who joined the training camp after the lethal process was underway quickly fell into line accepting the parameters laid down by Tsuneo and *Rengō Sekigun*'s Central Committee in an effort to demonstrate their loyalty, even escalating the violence in some instances.[492] The researcher Patricia Steinhoff concluded: "The *Rengō Sekigun* purge belongs to a large class of events, occurring throughout the world, in which groups of people inflict terrible brutality on their fellow human beings, masking their behavior through ingenious ideological constructions ... To that extent, the purge could have happened anywhere, and it could have been committed by anybody."[493]

One major consequence of socialization predicted by Chester Barnard's natural systems theory is that the failure of a given organization to achieve its goals may not have much impact on the commitment of the organization's members to that organization, as this may be more deeply grounded in a sense of communal solidarity than in tangible evidence of political progress. This in turn suggests that members of militant groups will find it particularly difficult to individually disengage from their peers, even when the cause is faltering, and especially if those peers continue to operate in an environment in which they are under threat. There is considerable evidence of this effect in the historical record. Volker Speitel became progressively disillusioned with the RAF but persisted out of a sense of "loyalty to the people one still knew from earlier times and whom one didn't want to face as the 'swine' that sneaks off ... In this ambivalence all one can do is 'function'. I still had meetings, and even tried to train new couriers, but I could only do that with a lump in my throat and with a completely confused brain which was unable to pose any alternative to my long devotion to the group or any alternative to its goals."[494] One of the Bali

---

[492] ibid., p. 216.

[493] ibid., p. 222.

[494] Klaus Wasmund, The Political Socialization of West German Terrorists, in Peter Merkl (ed.), *Political Violence and Terror: Motifs and Motivations* (University of California Press; 1986), p. 223.

bombers, Ali Imron, described in a prison interview with Sulastri Osman how he had personally opposed carrying out the attack but nevertheless carried out the role he had been assigned, including surveying the targeted nightclubs and driving the VBIED to the target, because the cell leader, Ali Ghufron, was his brother and as such had a greater claim on his loyalty.[495] Clark McCauley and Sophia Moskalenko recount the personal history of Adrian Michailov sucked into the terrorist campaign unleashed by *Narodnaya Volya* against senior Tsarist officials out of a sense of loyalty to his radical "family", when he would have preferred to return to the country-side and his efforts to raise the political consciousness of the peasantry.[496]

The West German government-sponsored study of left-wing ter-rorists primarily associated with the RAF found that many of these individuals had gone through "a process of social isolation" disas-sociating themselves from their homes and family creating a void that was filled by new experiences and social contacts.[497] Psychologists have long posited that prolonged isolation can strengthen group bonds, creating "totalistic groups" that become all-consuming for their members.[498] Adriana Faranda of the *Brigate Rosse* described the sense of obligation she felt with the group even when she disagreed profoundly with her comrades over the decision to execute the cap-tive former Italian Prime Minister Aldo Moro: "When you get involved in a long-term project which absorbs you totally then you have to accept certain rules. You accept for example that when there are political disagreements you follow the majority line. You support the others, it's a kind of pact of obedience. Even when you don't agree you have to follow things through, bring them to completion."[499] When asked by the FBI agent interviewing him in Guantanamo why

---

[495] Sulastri Osman, Jemaah Islamiyah: Of Kin and Kind, *Journal of Current Southeast Asian Affairs*, Vol. 29, No. 2 (2010), p. 165.

[496] Clark McCauley and Sophia Moskalenko, *supra* note 19, pp. 35–41.

[497] Marc Sageman, *Understanding Terror Networks* (University of Pennsylvania Press; 2004), p. 130.

[498] Clark McCauley and Sophia Moskalenko, *Friction: How Radicalization Happens to Them and Us* (Oxford University Press; 2011), p. 130.

[499] Alison Jamieson, Entry, Discipline and Exit in the Italian Red Brigades, *Terrorism and Political Violence*, Vol. 2, No. 1 (1990), p. 12.

he had remained in *al-Qaeda* even though it had targeted so many innocent people, Osama bin Laden's driver, Salim Hamdan, replied: "When one is part of that home, from the inside it is very difficult to think of what is happening on the outside."[500] The German militant Michael Baumann described how he kept faith with his comrades despite his own deep misgivings: "I saw that it was going to go a hundred percent wrong ... I only participated out of solidarity."[501] A member of the RAF, Astrid Proll, remembered feeling a great unwillingness to go against the group even when she felt the tactics being advocated by Baader and Ensslin were flawed: "We were afraid of discussion; It seemed like treachery."[502]

For many terrorists there also seems to be a sense that they have come too far to entertain thoughts of disengagement. One member of an Italian terrorist organization told Donatella Della Porta: "To go right to the end ... [was] the only chance for redemption I had, from a moral point of view, both for the violence I produced and the violence I suffered."[503] Another Italian militant told her: "After having paid such a price, to quit meant to admit that all we had done had been useless."[504] A Provisional IRA volunteer shared similar reasoning with the researcher Robert White: "There's times I've said it to myself, 'Why? You're mad in the head, like.' But ... I just can't turn my back on it ... there's too many of my friends in jail, there's too many of mates given their lives, and ... I've walked behind too many funerals to turn my back on it now."[505] Sociologist Chester Barnard termed this subordination of the individual to the collective the "condition of

---

[500] Ali Soufan and Daniel Freedman, *The Black Banners: The Inside Story of 9/11 and the War Against* Al-Qaeda (W. W. Norton & Company; 2011), p. 456.

[501] Martha Crenshaw, *Explaining Terrorism: Causes, Processes and Consequences* (2011), p. 130.

[502] Stefan Aust, *Baader-Meinhof: The Inside Story of the RAF* (Oxford University Press; 2009), p. 99.

[503] Gilda Zwerman, Patricia Steinhoff and Donatella Della Porta, Disappearing Social Movements: Clandestinity in the Cycle of New Left Protest in the US, Japan, Germany, and Italy, *Mobilization: An International Journal*, Vol. 5, No. 1 (2000), p. 97.

[504] ibid.

[505] Robert White, Commitment, Efficacy, and Personal Sacrifice Among Irish Republicans, *Journal of Political and Military Sociology*, Vol. 16 (1988), p. 83.

communion".[506] The former CIA psychiatrist Jerrold Post has also reported finding that an overarching sense of the collective consumed many of the incarcerated terrorists he interviewed, noting that this sense of belonging created a "powerful pressure to conform within the group, for to disagree is to be seen as being disloyal and risk losing membership in the group."[507] As Uri Avnery, a member of *Irgun*, recalled: "When you live in the underground it completely absorbs you. The organization was everything, and then suddenly there is this rift. It's terrible! The whole world is breaking apart."[508]

All that said, we know that some terrorists experience burnout and that some organizations do split over questions of policy. Fractures can also develop within clandestine movements driven by mundane personality conflicts and mutual suspicion. RAF cadre Astrid Proll complained about the endless in-fighting, frayed tempers and abuse that she encountered living underground.[509] Sergei Nechaev's embryonic terrorist organization, *Narodnaya Rasprava*, came to an abrupt and premature end in November 1869 when he and his small coterie of supporters murdered I. I. Ivanov, one of their number who had quarreled with Nechaev and sought to leave the group. The British neo-Nazi group Combat 18 was also significantly diminished after its core leadership became embroiled in a dispute in 1997 that ended in the murder of member Christopher Castle.[510] It hardly needs stating that terrorists are not saints and that they fall prey to the same human foibles as the rest of us. However, what we can say with some certainty is that while processes of socialization may not always create unbreakable bonds, they certainly do seem to create ties that bind.

---

[506] Chester Barnard, *The Functions of the Executive* (Harvard University Press; 1938), p. 142.

[507] See Jerrold Post, *The Mind of the Terrorist* (Palgrave Macmillan; 2007) and Jerrold Post, Notes on a Psychodynamic Theory of Terrorist Behavior, *Terrorism*, Vol. 7, No. 3 (1984), p. 254.

[508] Patrick Bishop, *The Reckoning: How the Killing of One Man Changed the Fate of the Promised Land* (William Collins; 2014), p. 92.

[509] Stefan Aust, *Baader-Meinhof: The Inside Story of the RAF* (Oxford University Press; 2009), p. 97.

[510] Audrey Kurth Cronin, *How Terrorism Ends: Understanding the Decline and Demise of Terrorist Campaigns* (Princeton University Press, 2009), p. 101.

## Framing narratives

As a concept, socialization is closely related to the social science theory of social construction which holds that to a certain degree the manner in which societies are organized, and the language they use to explain this, helps to create and shape their reality. The political scientist Benedict Anderson used this process to explain the development of nations and nationhood as "imagined communities", purposefully constructed by political leaders to mobilize, and to a certain extent subjugate, their followers.[511] Symbols, shared historical experience, and other cultural totems all play an important role in shaping the identity of nations, and this is true also of the smaller imagined communities of like-minded individuals who make up other social movements. In Part I, we saw the importance terrorist organizations have consistently placed on developing legitimizing narratives; in this section we will explore how these legitimizing narratives act on the individuals involved, both influencing their decision to join up, and sustaining their determination to kill in the name of their cause.

The Stanford psychologist Albert Bandura's influential social learning theory posited that "social behavior is, in large part, developed through exposure to modeling cues and regulated by reinforcement contingencies, many of which are prescribed by one's organizational affiliations."[512] Framing narratives can fulfill the same socializing function remotely that kinship and friendship networks perform through close proximity. The Italian anarchist Luigi Galleani understood this instinctively, writing that "the first cause of all individual acts of revolt is the psychological climate created by our propaganda among the people ... Our responsibility in all acts of rebellion is more precise, more specific and undeniable, where our propaganda has been energetic, vigorous,

---

[511] Benedict Anderson, *Imagined Communities: Reflections on the Origin and Spread of Nationalism* (Verso; 1983).

[512] Albert Bandura, Social-Learning Theory of Identification Processes, in David Goslin (ed.), *Handbook of Socialization Theory and Research* (Rand McNally & Co.; 1969), p. 250.

and has left a deep impression."[513] Terrorism researcher Col. John Venhaus argued that identity seekers find the rules, structure and coherent vision propounded by extremist groups appealing because "they neatly package identity into the ideology."[514] Adam Deen, a former member of the Islamist extremist organization *Al-Muhajiroun,* who turned his back on extremism and became Head of Outreach at the Quilliam Foundation, validates this proposition: "What attracted me was the simplicity, that I was a Muslim, that I should represent these ideas and I belonged inside an Islamic state and everything else was wrong and evil. This was extremely comforting as a young man immersed in a world where I was seeing complexity and not knowing who was right and wrong ... That polarization creates a type of mindset towards non-Muslims — and then you can start rationalizing acts of violence."[515] A communiqué issued by the Algerian *Groupe Islamique Armé* (GIA) in September 1995 neatly summarized the simplicity of such a divinely ordained mission: "Since our religion and our manner are blameless, everything after that is easy."[516] Terrorism researcher Bonnie Cordes has stressed the importance of repeatedly reinforcing group commitment through public statements — what she has termed "auto-propaganda" designed to persuade members of the group that the enemy is real and the cause is just.[517]

Arie Kruglanski *et al.* argue that a strong terrorism-justifying narrative or ideology must contain three critical elements: a grievance, a culprit and, critically, a "morally warranted and effective method" of reversing the perceived injustice.[518] Martha Crenshaw noted that terrorist justifications "usually focus on past

---

[513] Nunzio Pernicone, Luigi Galleani and Italian Anarchist Terrorism in the United States, *Studi Emigrazione,* Vol. 30 (September 1993), p. 481.

[514] Col. John Venhaus, *Why Youth Join Al-Qaeda,* United States Institute of Peace: Special Report No. 236 (May 2010), p. 10.

[515] Dominic Casciani, How Anjem Choudary's mouth was finally shut, *BBC News,* 16 August 2016.

[516] David Cook, *Understanding Jihad* (University of California Press; 2015), p. 186.

[517] Bonnie Cordes, *When Terrorists do the Talking: Reflections on Terrorist Literature* (The Rand Corporation, 1987), pp. 9 and 13.

[518] Arie Kruglanski, Michele Gelfand, Jocelyn Bélanger, Anna Sheveland, Malkanthi Hetiarachchi and Rohan Gunaratna, The Psychology of Radicalization and

suffering, on the glorious future to be created, and on the regime's illegitimacy and violence, to which terrorism is the only available response."[519] As we saw in Part I, terrorist narratives typically hit these marks, the X-factor is then finding a way to tie these elements to a potential volunteer's personal circumstances. The former *al-Qaeda* recruiter Jesse Morton explained how this might work in practice: "What you have to do is frame their personal grievance, making them think that they can contribute to a broader cause. And you have to do that through ideology."[520] Framing narratives help to put personal experiences into context, create powerful collective identities, and offer a cognitive framework for making sense of the world that provides clear instruction to potential recruits regarding the goals they must attain to achieve "significance".[521] To achieve all this, terrorist narratives tend to make careful use of language to create identity markers and provide political cues. They also typically make creative use of historical reference points to bolster arguments and undermine alternate viewpoints. Klaus Wasmund's study of West German Marxist terrorists led him to conclude that ideological narratives played a crucial role in promoting and cementing relationships: "Group ideology is a decisive factor in group cohesion. It welds the individuals into a tightly knit community."[522]

In *Terror in the Mind of God*, Mark Juergensmeyer noted pointedly that it requires "an enormous amount of moral presumption ... to justify the destruction of property on a massive scale or to condone

---

Deradicalization: How Significance Quest Impacts Violent Extremism, *Advances in Political Psychology*, Vol. 35, Suppl. 1 (2014), p. 77.

[519] Martha Crenshaw, The Causes of Terrorism, *Comparative Politics*, Vol. 13, No. 4 (1981), p. 395.

[520] Rukmini Callimachi, Once a Qaeda Recruiter, Now a Voice Against Jihad, *The New York Times*, 29 August 2016.

[521] Arie Kruglanski, Michele Gelfand, Jocelyn Bélanger, Anna Sheveland, Malkanthi Hetiarachchi and Rohan Gunaratna, The Psychology of Radicalization and Deradicalization: How Significance Quest Impacts Violent Extremism, *Advances in Political Psychology*, Vol. 35, Suppl. 1 (2014), p. 76.

[522] Klaus Wasmund, The Political Socialization of West German Terrorists, in Peter Merkl (ed.), *Political Violence and Terror: Motifs and Motivations* (University of California Press; 1986), p. 219.

a brutal attack on another life, especially the life of someone one scarcely knows and against whom one bears no personal enmity. And it requires a great deal of internal conviction, social acknowledgment, and the stamp of approval from a legitimizing ideology or authority one respects."[523] Terrorist narratives must reassure prospective terrorists that the cause they are about to kill for is a just one and that the sacrifice they themselves are about to make will make a difference. Yitzhak Shamir, who as the leader of LEHI knew precisely what it was like to send men out to kill for a cause, opined that "a man who goes forth to take the life of another whom he does not know must believe one thing only — that by his act he will change history."[524] Provisional IRA volunteer Rory O'Connor, who fired on two RUC officers in 1977, wounding one, noted from personal experience: "You can say war is war and innocents die in war. But that doesn't make it any easier. You put it in the back of your mind, but it does get to you. You always have a wee bit in you, a wee bit that says what you did was right. If you didn't have that wee thing, that 'you were right' — what does that make you then? If you haven't got that thing, it makes you a mass murderer."[525]

One sees this important legitimizing process at work in the conscious reframing of the concept of *jihad* by authors like Sayyid Qutb, Abdullah Azzam, and Abd al-Salam Faraj.[526] All three men made a compelling case for combining faith with action, with Abdullah Azzam proclaiming: "History does not write its lines except with blood. Glory does not build its lofty edifices except with skulls. Honor and respect cannot be established except on a foundation of cripples and corpses. Empires, distinguished peoples, states, and

---

[523] Mark Juergensmeyer, *Terror in the Mind of God: The Global Rise of Religious Violence* (University of California Press; 2003), p. 11.

[524] Gerold Frank, *The Deed* (Simon and Schuster; 1963), p. 35.

[525] Corinne Purtill, Anguish Haunts Northern Ireland's Retired Terrorists, *NBC News*, 15 July 2015, at http://www.nbcnews.com/news/world/anguish-haunts-northern-irelands-retired-terrorists-n392326. Viewed 2 October 2016.

[526] Mark Juergensmeyer, *Terror in the Mind of God: The Global Rise of Religious Violence* (University of California Press; 2003), p. 82.

societies cannot be established except with examples."[527] In his influential work *The Neglected Duty*, Faraj argued that committed religious action could precipitate God's intervention: "This means that a Muslim has first of all the duty to execute the command to fight with his own hands. [Once he has done so] God will then intervene [and change] the laws of nature. In this way victory will be achieved through the hands of the believers by means of God's [intervention]."[528] *The Neglected Duty* also forcefully endorsed the use of the kind of underhand methods associated with terrorism. Faraj's arguments were taken up in a document prepared for the *Shura* Council of *al-Qaeda* under the supervision of his fellow countryman Ayman al-Zawahiri, which specifically made the religious case for the legitimacy of terrorist methods quoting prophet Mohammed's precept that "war is deceit" and noting that bombing "the organizations of the infidels and apostates in this day and age has become an imperative of *jihad* in our war with the idolatrous tyrants, where weakened *mujahedin* battle massive and vigilant armies armed to the teeth — it has become next to impossible to confront them in open warfare."[529] In her analysis of the literature produced by European Marxist terrorist groups in the 1970s and early 1980s, Bonnie Cordes noted the prevalence of such "David and Goliath" themes used to cast the authors as heroic underdogs in their struggle against the state — advantageous comparison is a common device in political rhetoric.[530]

Underpinned by widely shared "sacred values", religion provides such an obviously powerful moralizing frame that it is easy to overlook that socialist, nationalist, and even racist narratives can at times claim a similar moral authority.[531] George Kenan observed in his seminal 1947 Foreign Affairs article *The Sources of Soviet Conduct* that

---

[527] David Cook, *Understanding Jihad* (University of California Press; 2015), p. 129.

[528] ibid., pp. 109–110.

[529] Raymond Ibrahim, *The Al-Qaeda Reader, The Essential Texts of Osama Bin Laden's Terrorist Organization* (Broadway Books; 2007), p. 169.

[530] Bonnie Cordes, *When Terrorists do the Talking: Reflections on Terrorist Literature*, The Rand Corporation, August 1987, p. 21.

[531] Scott Atran, *Talking to the Enemy: Faith, Brotherhood and the (Un)making of Terrorists* (Ecco; 2010).

Marxism offered "a highly convenient rationalization of their own instinctive desires" and "pseudo-scientific justification ... for their yearning for power and revenge and for their inclination to cut corners in the pursuit of it."[532] An Italian militant interviewed by Donatella Della Porta concurred, recalling: "We were supported ... also by famous quotes from Marxist literature, in which violence appeared as absolutely legitimate, as part of the history of the working class. Once it [had been] decided that the historical conditions allow for that kind of organization, the rest is only a technical consequence."[533] Michael Collins also powerfully framed the Irish nationalist quest for independence in moral terms: "It was a struggle between two rival governments, the one an Irish government resting on the will of the people and the other an alien government depending for its existence upon military force — the one gathering more and more authority and the other steadily losing ground and growing ever more desperate and unscrupulous."[534] This narrative still held true for Catholics in Northern Ireland more than fifty years later. In March 1972, the republican newspaper *An Phoblacht* welcomed the introduction of direct rule from London to Northern Ireland in an editorial comment observing that henceforth "the lines of demarcation could be fairly and squarely drawn between those whose wish would be to sell their birthright and nationality and those who would strive to maintain it and defend it."[535]

Such narratives are not necessarily mutually exclusive frames. In his anthropological study of Islamist extremists, Scott Atran highlighted the emphasis that Islamist propaganda placed on often long past historical grievances such as the *Reconquista* and the

---

[532] Jessica Stern, Radicalization to Extremism and Mobilization to Violence: What Have We Learned and What Can We Do about It? *The ANNALS of the American Academy of Political and Social Science*, Vol. 668, No. 1, November 2016, p. 111.

[533] Donatella Della Porta, *Social Movements, Political Violence and the State: A Comparative Analysis of Italy and Germany* (Cambridge University Press; 1995), p. 175.

[534] Michael Collins, *Collapse of the Terror: British Rule's Last Stages*, in Michael Collins, *The Path to Freedom* (Welsh Academic Press; 1996), p. 64.

[535] Adrian Guelke, Loyalist and Republican Perceptions of the Northern Ireland Conflict: The UDA and the Provisional IRA, in Peter Merkl (ed.), *Political Violence and Terror: Motifs and Motivations* (University of California Press; 1986), p. 98.

expulsion of the Moors from Spain: "The historical narrative, however stilted or fictitious, translates personal and local ties within and across small groups into a profound connection with the wider Muslim community."[536] Similarly, in the early 1970s, the Provisional IRA married a nationalist agenda to a socialist sensibility in keeping with the youthful revolutionary spirit of the times as well as a demonstrable commitment to its Catholic roots, by declaring its aim to "establish a 32-county Democratic Socialist Republic, based on the proclamation of 1916, to restore the Irish language and culture to a position of strength, and to promote a social order based on justice and Christian principles which will give everyone a just share of the nation's wealth."[537] American white supremacist groups like The Covenant, the Sword, and the Arm of the Lord (CSA) have been closely associated with the Christian Identity movement combining racist beliefs with a fundamentalist reading of Christian scriptures.

Ken Heskin has noted that terrorist organizations are also, to a certain extent, prisoners of the narratives they create: "The Provisional IRA owes its allegiance to a transcendental authority in the form of history and myth of those in previous generations involved in the struggle for Irish emancipation."[538] When the Provisional IRA acted in a manner that undermined its claim to be acting in defense of the Catholic population, it often provoked censure from its own community. In August 1988, PIRA volunteers in Londonderry/Derry tried to lure the Royal Ulster Constabulary into visiting the home of a notorious local petty criminal, Gerry Laird, in Creggan by leaving a trail of clues linking Laird to a recent robbery. They held Laird offsite, set up an IED that would be triggered by anyone opening the front door of his apartment,

---

[536] Scott Atran, The Moral Logic and Growth of Suicide Terrorism, *The Washington Quarterly*, Vol. 29, No. 2 (2006), p. 136.

[537] Adrian Guelke, Loyalist and Republican Perceptions of the Northern Ireland Conflict: The UDA and the Provisional IRA, in Peter Merkl (ed.), *Political Violence and Terror: Motifs and Motivations* (University of California Press; 1986), p. 96.

[538] Ken Heskin, Terrorism in Ireland: The Past and Future, *Irish Journal of Psychology*, Vol. 15, No. 2–3 (1994), p. 476.

and then stood watch for six days hoping the police would fall into their trap. Unfortunately, boredom set in and on the sixth day, the PIRA sentry did not notice three of Laird's neighbors, concerned for his welfare, head round to his apartment to check in on him. All three were killed when they tried to get inside. Martin Dalton, the son of one of those killed by what would become known as "The Good Neighbor Bomb", angrily denounced those responsible: "I challenged them on television to defend what they did there — put a bomb not only in a nationalist area but in a built-up area. And they are supposed to be fighting for the people?"[539] The well-connected Irish journalist Kevin Toolis reported that the incident alienated the entire Bogside community bringing the Derry Brigade "to their political knees".[540]

The Jewish community in Palestine turned against the Stern Gang in similar fashion in January 1942 after two poorly executed operations launched just weeks apart resulted in the deaths of four local Jews (two members of the Palestinian Police Force and two innocent bystanders).[541] The Jewish Agency pledged to assist the British in hunting down "the murderous gang" and to help free Palestine from "this nightmare of holdups and assassinations", while the Jewish National Council passed a resolution condemning the attacks and denouncing Avraham Stern's men as a "lunatic band" and a "gang of senseless criminals".[542] The posting of a £1000 reward for Stern's capture led to a succession of tips from members of the public that enabled the police to rapidly detain one after another of Stern's accomplices until, on 12 February 1942, Stern himself was cornered in safe house in Tel Aviv where he was shot dead in contentious circumstances by Assistant Superintendent Geoffrey Morton, the Head of the Lydda Criminal Investigation Department who Stern had in turn targeted for assassination only a month earlier.[543] The group

---

[539] Kevin Toolis, *Rebel Hearts* (St. Martin's Griffin; 1997), p. 324.

[540] ibid., p. 218.

[541] Bruce Hoffman, *Anonymous Soldiers: The Struggle for Israel, 1917–1947* (Knopf; 2015), p. 112.

[542] ibid.

[543] ibid., p. 113.

would eventually recover, rebranding itself as LEHI, but the loss of the inspirational leadership of its founder was nevertheless a bitter blow to the organization.

When an accepted terrorist narrative proves false, this can also have a devastating effect on individual group members. Former Italian *Brigate Rosse* member Enrico Fenzi described the shock and disillusionment he felt when the group's leader, Mario Moretti, mastermind of the Aldo Moro kidnapping, was stabbed and seriously injured by a fellow prison inmate: "The entire mythology of the past years was shattered ... destroyed. The incredible, the unacceptable had happened. In the very courtyard of a special prison the leader of the Red Brigades had been knifed. Not only he, but the collective image of superiority and privilege had finished in the dust of that yard, and with it the small but precious store of gratification which had always helped to keep up morale. It had happened in a prison in which every proletarian prisoner should have recognized the Brigadist as a model to be loved and reproduced in himself."[544] The dwindling membership of the *Rote Armee Fraktion* experienced a similar existential crisis when existing internal divisions were exacerbated by the German government's offer in January 1992 of early release to those imprisoned members of the group who renounced terrorism.[545] The authors of the RAF's final communiqué admitted that Minister of Justice Klaus Kinkel's initiative had dealt the ailing organization a fatal blow: "In the end, the very hurtful split of one group of the prisoners from us, who declared us to be enemies, completely erased the very conditions which had given rise to the RAF in the first place — solidarity and the struggle for collectivity."[546]

---

[544] Alison Jamieson, Identity and Morality in the Italian Red Brigades, *Terrorism and Political Violence*, Vol. 2, No. 4 (1990), p. 519.

[545] See Assaf Moghadam, Failure and Disengagement in the Red Army Faction, *Studies in Conflict and Terrorism*, Vol. 35, No. 2 (2012).

[546] The Urban Guerrilla Is History, *The Final Communiqué From The Red Army Faction*, 1 March 1998 and Assaf Moghadam, Failure and Disengagement in the Red Army Faction, *Studies in Conflict and Terrorism*, Vol. 35, No. 2 (2012), p. 171.

The spread of Islam from its early beginnings on the Arabian Peninsula in the Seventh Century is a story of conquest, which sets it apart in narrative terms from the other Abrahamic faiths. As the British historian and orientalist Bernard Lewis observed: "Christ was crucified, Moses died without entering the Promised Land ... Mohamed triumphed during his lifetime and died a sovereign and a conqueror."[547] David Cook, author of *Understanding Jihad*, has noted that this military success has more than simply historical significance — it continues to serve as a "confirmatory miracle" for Islam and is regularly cited as such in contemporary Islamist propaganda.[548] Groups like *al-Qaeda* and ISIL are quick to claim divine providence when things are going well, and Islamist propagandists like Abdullah Azzam explicitly note that Mohammed spread Islam through warfare.[549] Success attracts new volunteers — as Osama bin Laden remarked in one videotaped message: "When people see a strong horse and a weak horse, by nature they will like the strong horse."[550]

However, success-based narratives can set up a considerable narrative challenge should a group suffer significant reverses. When ISIL began to lose territory in 2016, it struggled to reframe its messaging. The ISIL newsletter *al-Naba* reminded readers of God's penchant for "trying the believers with misfortune and hardship ... before God's victory will descend upon them", and another ISIL outlet actually encouraged supporters to "rejoice in God's choice ... to extend the period of preparation, tribulation, and difficulty".[551] ISIL's former spokesman, Abu Muhammad al-Adnani, sought to rally the faithful in one of the final speeches he gave before being killed by a US airstrike in August 2016: "Do you think, America, that victory is in the death of one or more leaders? For that is a false victory. Were you victorious when you killed Abu

---

[547] Bernard Lewis, *The Crisis of Islam* (Modern Library; 2003), p. 10.

[548] David Cook, *Understanding Jihad* (University of California Press; 2015), p. 30.

[549] ibid., p. 129.

[550] ibid., p. 150.

[551] Cole Bunzel, Allah Wants ISIS to Retreat, *Foreign Policy*, 25 October 2016 at http://foreign-policy.com/2016/10/25/allah-wants-isis-to-retreat-iraq-mosul/. Viewed 10 March 2017.

Mus'ab [al-Zarqawi] or Abu Hamza [al-Muhajir]? Or Abu Omar [al-Baghdadi] or Osama [bin Laden]?... No way! Victory is for the adversary to be defeated ... Will we be defeated, and will you be victorious, if you take Mosul, Sirte, Raqqa, and all the cities, and we return to how we were before? No! For defeat is the loss of the will and desire to fight."[552] While the travails faced by the Prophet Mohammed during the earliest years of the faith, such as the *Hijrah* (the Prophet's flight from Mecca) and the siege of Medina, provide something of an analog, al-Adnani's defiant tone struck a false note after all the triumphalist rhetoric and slogans like "Remaining and Expanding" on which ISIL had built its brand. Furthermore, such messaging carries with it the promise of an eventual turnabout in the group's fortunes and the longer this is delayed, the more likely it becomes that supporters will begin to drift away.

The language used by politicians, and other public figures, when condemning terrorism also matters. When in the aftermath of the September 11 attacks, President George W. Bush used the word "crusade" to underscore America's resolve in meeting the challenge posed by *al-Qaeda*,[553] this only served to reinforce *al-Qaeda*'s message that aggressive Western powers were at war with Islam. In February 1998, Osama bin Laden had issued a *fatwa* calling for a *jihad* against Jews and Crusaders precisely because he understood the rhetorical power of drawing a parallel between modern American foreign policy and the age of the crusades for a Muslim audience. French Foreign Minister Hubert Vedrine immediately understood that President Bush had played right into bin Laden's hands commenting to reporters: "We have to avoid a clash of civilizations at all costs. One has to avoid falling into this huge trap, this monstrous trap, conceived by the instigators of the assault."[554] The sociologist Erving Goffman, who pioneered frame analysis, described such instances in which one

---

[552] ibid.

[553] *Remarks by the President Upon Arrival*, The White House, 16 September 2001 at http://georgewbush-whitehouse.archives.gov/news/releases/2001/09/20010916-2.html.

[554] Peter Ford, Europe cringes at Bush "crusade" against terrorists, *Christian Science Monitor*, 19 September 2001.

party speaks or acts in a manner that only serves to confirm the other party's narrative as frame amplification.[555]

The final point I want to make in this section is that narrative frames often contain potential entry points, or cognitive openings, for government voices to challenge terrorist messaging — if these entry points can be identified successfully and sensitively addressed. For example, Petter Nesser reports that there were recurring discussions on radical websites in the 2000s around the Islamic obligation to observe "covenants of security" — the notion that Muslims are obligated to observe local laws if the authority in question permits them to practice their faith peacefully on its soil.[556] In 2009, a Somali group based in Sydney, Australia, planning an attack on Holsworthy Army Barracks even dispatched an emissary, Yacqub Khayre, to Somalia to seek religious guidance on this subject.[557] The covenants concept could be a powerful theme for an effective strategic communications campaign — it might not change radicalized minds, but there is some reason to believe that it might resonate with the communities from which they come. In October 2016, three Syrian refugees discovered that a guest in their home, a fourth Syrian refugee called Jaber al-Bakr, was planning to mount a terrorist attack on a Berlin airport, they restrained him while he slept and turned him into the German authorities. One of the men, Mohamed A., told the German tabloid *Bild*: "I was furious with him, I could not accept something like this — especially here in Germany, the country that opened its doors to us."[558] In sum, narrative frames are a crucial component of the radicalization process, often giving both

---

[555] David Snow, E. Burke Rochford, Steven Worden and Robert Benford, Frame Alignment Processes, Micromobilization, and Movement Participation, *American Sociological Review*, Vol. 51 No. 4 (August 1986), p. 466. See also Erving Goffman, *Frame Analysis: An Essay on the Organization of Experience* (Northeastern; 1986).

[556] Thomas Hegghammer, Should I stay or Should I Go? Explaining Variation in Western Jihadists' Choice between Domestic and Foreign Fighting, *American Political Science Review*, Vol. 107, No. 1 (February 2013), p. 9.

[557] Ian Munro, Terrorist cell sought fatwa, court hears, *The Sydney Morning Herald*, 14 September 2010.

[558] David Charter, Syrian refugees tied up fugitive Isis suspect as he slept on sofa, *The Times*, 12 October 2016.

shape and direction to established social bonds, and as such, they present both challenges and opportunities for attentive counter-terrorist officials to address.

## Summary

As Donatella Della Porta points out, obviously not every member of a militant's social network ends up joining a terrorist organization and this is where the other factors discussed in Part II also have a role to play.[559] The key takeaway from this section is rather that a social connection to a member of a terrorist organization is a critical facilitating element in any individual's decision to join the armed struggle. It is important to understand that these dense social networks don't just represent a potential threat, but also a significant opportunity that can be leveraged by intelligence and law enforcement professionals. Family members of Yacqub Khayre, who was finally arrested on terrorism charges in Melbourne in 2009, repeatedly tried to warn the Australian authorities that he was becoming involved with dangerous associates linked to *al-Shabaab*.[560] A substitute *Imam* at the Takoua mosque in Madrid, known only by the police codename 'Cartagena', warned the Spanish authorities as early as October 2002 that a group of mostly Moroccan friends in the mosque's congregation had formed a radical group called *al-Haraka Salafiya*, members of which would go on to participate in the March 2004 Madrid train bombings.[561] Shandon Harris-Hogan notes, "the impact of family connections is not inherently negative as there are also instances of family members persuading individuals away from extremism."[562] This point was enshrined in the 2010 *United States National Security Strategy*

[559] Donatella Della Porta, Recruitment Processes in Clandestine Political Organizations: Italian Left-Wing Terrorism, *International Social Movement Research*, Vol. 1 (1988), p. 160.

[560] Shandon Harris-Hogan, The Importance of Family: The Key to Understanding the Evolution of Jihadism in Australia, *Security Challenges*, Vol. 10, No. 1 (2014), p. 47.

[561] Scott Atran, The Moral Logic and Growth of Suicide Terrorism, *The Washington Quarterly*, Vol. 29, No. 2 (2006), p. 133.

[562] Shandon Harris-Hogan, The Importance of Family: The Key to Understanding the Evolution of Jihadism in Australia, *Security Challenges*, Vol. 10, No. 1 (2014), p. 31.

which asserted that "our best defenses against [radicalization] are well informed and equipped families."[563]

Small-world networks, to use Marc Sageman's apposite description, have a socializing effect on their members that tends to lead to collective group thinking.[564] Klaus Wasmund has observed that the intense nature of clandestine activity results in a closed feedback loop in which attitudes harden and are reinforced by group interactions.[565] While we have seen above that an exogenous shock may persuade an individual to break ranks with their peers, Wasmund's insight would suggest the importance of seeking to remove committed individuals from this environment before seeking to engage with them, which has implications for agent recruitment, investigative interviewing, detention practices, and deradicalization efforts. Furthermore, the intensely personal nature of many inter-group relationships may mean, as Jerrold Post has noted, that coercive or kinetic government action only serves to strengthen the anti-government animus of the group as political differences take on a personal dimension.[566] Sulastri Osman suggests that this necessitates a nuanced response from the authorities: "A delicate carrot-and-stick balance between punishment and rehabilitation has to be struck when dealing with those captured. On the one hand, justice has to be perceived as being served in the eyes of those adversely affected by terrorism. On the other hand, the judgments passed against the terrorist militants have to be recognized by the latter's immediate families as 'fair enough' for the crimes committed."[567] This, ultimately, is the most important message of social network theory — an effective counter-terrorism

---

[563] *National Security Strategy* (The White House, Washington DC, 2010).

[564] Marc Sageman, *Understanding Terror Networks* (University of Pennsylvania Press; 2004), pp. 139–151 and Klaus Wasmund, The Political Socialization of West German Terrorists, in Peter Merkl (ed.), *Political Violence and Terror: Motifs and Motivations* (University of California Press; 1986), p. 200.

[565] Klaus Wasmund, The Political Socialization of West German Terrorists, in Peter Merkl (ed.), *Political Violence and Terror: Motifs and Motivations* (University of California Press; 1986), p. 214.

[566] Martha Crenshaw, *Explaining Terrorism: Causes, Processes and Consequences* (2011), p. 130.

[567] Sulastri Osman, Jemaah Islamiyah: Of Kin and Kind, *Journal of Current Southeast Asian Affairs*, Vol. 29, No. 2 (2010), p. 171.

strategy must take into account both personal and collective narratives, which in turn requires a degree of granularity and flexibility of approach that most states struggle to achieve.

## Poverty

In December 2001, two months after the September 11 attacks, a gathering of Nobel Peace Prize winners in Oslo, Norway, was asked to craft a joint statement on terrorism. Poverty was cited as a driver of terrorism by many of the laureates, with the former President of South Korea Kim Dae-Jung perhaps going furthest, stating: "At the bottom of terrorism is poverty. That is the main cause."[568] The belief that poverty is a significant driver of terrorism is a persistent one, if not in the academic literature, at least in the popular consciousness and in the minds of public policymakers. Both the US and UK governments have increased aid spending to address global poverty as an explicit public policy response to the threat of terrorism.[569] President George W. Bush told the assembled dignitaries at the 2002 Monterey Development Summit: "We fight poverty because hope is an answer to terror";[570] former US Secretary of State John Kerry has described poverty as being in many cases "the root cause of terrorism";[571] and British Prime Minister Tony Blair linked violent extremism and "acute and appalling forms of poverty".[572] Clearly, this does not appear to be a partisan perspective as both progressive and conservative governments have pursued similar policies. Yet, the social science suggests that poverty *per se* is not actually highly correlated with terrorism — as that inveterate agitator Leon Trotsky noted in his *History of the Russian Revolution*: "The mere existence of privations is not enough to cause an insurrection; if it were, the masses would be always in

---

[568] Janet Jai, Getting at the roots of terrorism, *Christian Science Monitor*, 10 December 2001.

[569] William Easterly, The War on Terror vs. the War on Poverty, *The New York Review of Books*, 24 November 2016.

[570] James Piazza, Poverty is a Weak Causal Link, in Stuart Gottlieb (ed.), *Debating Terrorism and Counterterrorism: Conflicting Perspectives on Causes, Contexts, and Responses* (CQ Press; 2010), p. 38.

[571] William Easterly, *The War on Terror vs. the War on Poverty*, The New York Review of Books, 24 November 2016.

[572] ibid.

revolt."[573] While many commentators intuit that poverty and deprivation are somehow related to radicalization, the available evidence suggests that the actual causal mechanism at work, if one exists at all, is both highly complex and poorly understood.

As social science scholars, and research funding, flooded into the hitherto somewhat peripheral field of terrorism studies after the 9/11 attacks, many researchers seeking to understand the underlying causes of terrorism naturally took as their point of departure pre-existing research on superficially related topics, such as criminal behavior and civil conflict. In the late 1960s, the Nobel prizewinning economist Gary Becker developed an influential rational choice theory of criminal behavior that argued individuals allocated their time between legitimate employment or criminal activity in a manner that maximized their utility.[574] Factoring in risk factors such as potential imprisonment and the social stigma associated with criminality, Becker predicted an individual would turn to crime if they could earn a higher income from crime than from a regular job. Becker's model thus predicted that, as legitimate earning opportunities decreased and the potential rewards from crime increased, an individual would turn to crime, and equally that if the risks associated with criminality, opportunity costs such as the likelihood of getting caught or the imposition of harsher penalties, increased, an individual would eschew criminal activity. While scholars have acknowledged that the political nature of terrorism differentiates it from ordinary criminal behavior, Becker's theory has served as the principle theoretical basis for a number of subsequent macro- and microeconomic studies of the potential connection between poverty and terrorism. The central proposition is that poor people will seek to improve their economic position and, if they cannot achieve this through lawful means, they will turn to unlawful methods, which in certain contingent circumstances, as yet to be determined, may include terrorism. Thus, if poverty and terrorism are positively

---

[573] Leon Trotsky, *The History of the Russian Revolution* (Haymarket Books; 2017), p. 353.

[574] Gary Becker, Crime and Punishment: An Economic Approach, *Journal of Political Economy*, Vol. 76, No. 2 (March/April 1968).

correlated, it would logically follow that at the macro level, terrorism would be more common in poor countries than in wealthy ones, and that at the micro level, terrorists would be more likely to come from disadvantaged backgrounds than privileged ones.

The collapse of the former Yugoslavia and the descent of Algeria into a vicious internal armed conflict in the 1990s also attracted a great deal of scholarly attention, and the increasing availability of extensive datasets helped to fuel large-scale quantitative studies into the causes of civil wars. Two studies published in the early 2000s were especially influential: Paul Collier and Anne Hoeffler's *Greed and Grievance in Civil War,* a report commissioned by the World Bank, and James Fearon and David Laitin's *Ethnicity, Insurgency and Civil War.*[575] Using a dataset encompassing 161 countries and seventy-nine civil wars over a period from 1960 to 1999, Collier and Hoeffler found, *inter alia,* that a lower growth rate of GDP *per capita* corresponded with a higher incidence of civil war. This they explained by reasoning that improved economic performance raised the opportunity costs associated with rebellion making staying within the existing system more attractive than trying to overthrow it. They also noted that the presence of valuable natural resources, such as oil or gas deposits, correlated highly with increased conflict since such national assets are vulnerable to acquisition and exploitation by an insurgent force. They concluded that economic motives (greed) trumped political ones (grievance) as a predictor of civil war. Fearon and Laitin developed their own dataset covering 126 civil wars between 1945 and 1999. They also identified poverty and slow growth as being linked to higher rates of civil war, but identified overall state weakness — financial, organizational and political — as the primary cause because, they argued, it favored "the technology of insurgency". Since civil wars do not always give rise to terrorism, it did not follow that these findings were automatically relevant, but they

---

[575]James Fearon and David Laitin, Ethnicity, Insurgency and Civil War, *American Political Science Review,* Vol. 97, No. 1 (2003) and Paul Collier and Anne Hoeffler, *Greed and Grievance in Civil War,* World Bank, Policy Research Working Paper No. 2355 (2000).

nevertheless provided further support for the perception that there might be a connection between poverty and terrorism.

The past fifteen years have seen a number of macro- and micro-level studies investigating what the American political scientist James Piazza has called the "rooted-in-poverty" hypothesis suggested by the studies above, essentially positing that "impoverished countries teeming with poorly educated, unemployed masses qualified by a widening gap between rich and poor combined with low literacy rates are fermentation tanks for dangerous and violent militants."[576] Yet, no major study has convincingly made the case for a direct causal connection between poverty and terrorism because the quantitative data gathered to date simply does not appear to support such a conclusion. To test the "rooted-in-poverty" hypothesis, Piazza compared data collected from the US State Department's *Chronology of Significant Terrorist Incidents* between 1986 and 2003 with a variety of economic, demographic and political variables.[577] He found that while the percentage of the global population living in poverty declined steadily from approximately 66% in 1981 to approximately 47% in 2006, over the same period, the annual rate of transnational terrorist attacks has fluctuated wildly with peaks in the mid-1980s, 1991, and 2001–2005.[578] Furthermore, the poorest region in the world — sub-Saharan Africa — suffered the fewest number of terrorist attacks and the fewest number of terrorism-related casualties between 2000 and 2006, while it was actually countries classified by the United Nations Development Programme (UNDP) as Medium Human Development countries that experienced the highest number of terrorist incidents and casualties.[579] Piazza also examined economic growth rates and found that of the twenty-nine countries that experienced negative growth between 1990 and 2005, seventeen experienced no terrorism at all, and of the remainder, all but

---

[576] James Piazza, Rooted in Poverty? Terrorism, Poor Economic Development, and Social Cleavages, *Terrorism and Political Violence*, Vol. 18, No. 1 (2006), p. 160.

[577] ibid., pp. 165–166.

[578] James Piazza, Poverty is a Weak Causal Link, in Stuart Gottlieb (ed.), *Debating Terrorism and Counterterrorism: Conflicting Perspectives on Causes, Contexts, and Responses* (CQ Press; 2010), p. 39.

[579] ibid., pp. 39–40.

two had lower than average levels of terrorist activity.[580] Likewise, looking at the rate of global inequality, the income gap between the wealthiest and poorest states as defined by GDP, he found the period in the mid-1990s when the gap widened most dramatically corresponded to the sharpest period of decrease in international terrorist incidents.[581] He concluded: "Poor places do not produce or experience more terrorism than rich places ... There is simply no evidence of a direct relationship between poverty and terrorism."[582]

Another American political scientist, Alexander Lee, argued that if poverty and terrorism had a direct positive correlation, one would expect that economic shocks would correlate with spikes in terrorism, and he found no evidence that this was the case.[583] Lee's conclusions were reinforced by the US economist Alan Krueger and Czech historian Jitka Malečková who observed that the first Palestinian *Intifada,* which began in December 1987, and the Second *Intifada,* which broke out in September 2000, ignited in markedly different economic climates — in 1987, graduate unemployment was high and graduate wages falling, but in 2000, unemployment was falling and the local perception was that the economy was on an upward trajectory.[584] In an influential article, *Kto Kogo?*, written a few years later in collaboration with David Laitin, Krueger noted more broadly that "macroeconomic shifts generally fail to map on to changes in terrorist activity."[585]

Lee also identified an inconvenient data point for proponents of a link between terrorism and poverty in micro-level studies of terrorism, noting most terrorist groups tend to be composed of individuals "wealthier and better educated than the average members of the

---

[580] ibid., p. 46.

[581] ibid., pp. 47 and 50.

[582] ibid.

[583] Alexander Lee, Who Becomes a Terrorist? Poverty, Education, and the Origins of Political Violence, *World Politics*, Vol. 63, No. 2 (April 2011), p. 215.

[584] Alan Krueger and Jitka Malečková, Education, Poverty, Political Violence, and Terrorism: Is there a causal connection? *Journal of Economic Perspectives*, Vol. 17, No. 4 (Fall 2003), p. 128.

[585] Alan Krueger and David Laitin, Kto Kogo? A Cross-Country Study of the Origins and Targets of Terrorism, in Philip Keefer and Norman Loayza (eds.), *Terrorism, Economic Development, and Political Openness* (Cambridge University Press; 2008), p. 148. The title "Kto Kogo" recalls Lenin's dictum "who, to whom."

societies from which they recruit".[586] Lee's study focused on 368 non-violent and 372 violent Bengali nationalists active in the 1910s and known to the Intelligence Branch of the British colonial Bengal Police. He found that the activists, including those involved in bombings and expropriations, were mostly educated and urbanized — 15% of the terrorist sample were teachers, a profession comprising just 0.2% of the general population.[587] Bengali terrorists of the period tended to come from comparatively advantaged backgrounds, but were less well off than the non-violent activists. Lee therefore suggested that it is the "poorest members of the politically aware class" who are mostly likely to join terrorist groups.[588]

A number of studies seem to broadly support Lee's insight. Charles Russell and Bowman Miller's 1978 dataset of 350 mostly Marxist-inspired terrorists active in Europe, Latin America, Japan and Turkey in the 1960s and 1970s found that two-thirds came from middle or upper class backgrounds, although the study has been criticized for selection bias and over-representing individuals in leadership positions.[589] The Israeli public policy professor Claude Berrebi studied 285 Palestinian "martyr biographies" published by online media outlets affiliated with *Hamas* and Palestinian Islamic Jihad, compared their personal particulars against a dataset of 41,762 Palestinian males of between fifteen and fifty-six years of age, and found that the "martyrs" were more likely to have come from comparatively well-off families and to have completed high school and attended college.[590] Berrebi's smaller sample of forty-eight Palestinian suicide bombers active between 1987 and 2002 found that the poverty rate among them was half that of the general

---

[586] Alexander Lee, Who Becomes a Terrorist? Poverty, Education, and the Origins of Political Violence, *World Politics*, Vol. 63, No. 2 (April 2011), p. 203.

[587] ibid., pp. 226 and 229.

[588] ibid., p. 242.

[589] Jitka Malečková, Impoverished Terrorists: Stereotype or Reality? in Tore Bjørgo (eds.), *Root Causes of Terrorism: Myths, Reality and Ways Forward* (Routledge; 2005), p. 34 and Charles Russell and Bowman Miller, Profile of a Terrorist, in Lawrence Freedman and Yonah Alexander (eds.), *Perspectives on Terrorism* (Scholarly Resources; 1983).

[590] Claude Berrebi, Evidence about the Link between Education, Poverty and Terrorism among Palestinians, *Peace Economics, Peace Science and Public Policy*, Vol. 13, No. 1 (2007).

population and that they were likely to be comparatively well educated.[591] Indeed, *Hamas* recruiters have admitted a preference for educated and socially adept candidates for suicide missions believing that these qualities ensure a higher likelihood of success.[592] In a separate study conducted with the Israeli economist Efraim Benmelech, Berrebi noted that if competence could be positively correlated with education and income, then this would further undermine the rooted-in-poverty hypothesis.[593] Using data compiled by *Shin Bet* on 168 Palestinian suicide bombers active between September 2000 and August 2005 who were responsible for 515 Israeli deaths, they found that the individuals in this sample had an above-average education in comparison with the wider Palestinian population, and that, of the five bombers who caused the greatest casualties, two were Master's degree students and a third was a law school graduate.[594]

Alan Krueger and Jitka Malečková examined the personal histories of 129 *Hezbollah* militants killed in the 1980s and early 1990s, and found that while some militants did come from poor backgrounds, statistically, poverty was more likely to discourage than encourage an individual to join the organization: "A 30% point reduction in poverty is associated with a 15% increase in participation."[595] Krueger and Malečková also examined the backgrounds of twenty-seven members of the Israeli right-wing nationalist *HaMakhteret HaYehudit* (Jewish Underground), a group that killed twenty-three Palestinians and injured 191 others between

---

[591] Jitka Malečková, Impoverished Terrorists: Stereotype or Reality?, in Tore Bjørgo (ed.), *Root Causes of Terrorism: Myths, Reality and Ways Forward* (Routledge; 2005), pp. 35–36.

[592] James Piazza, *Poverty is a Weak Causal Link*, in Stuart Gottlieb (ed.), *Debating Terrorism and Counterterrorism: Conflicting Perspectives on Causes, Contexts, and Responses* (CQ Press; 2010), p. 49.

[593] Efraim Benmelech and Claude Berrebi, *Attack Assignments in Terror Organizations and The Productivity of Suicide Bombers*, National Bureau of Economic Research, Working Paper No. 12910, February 2007 and Ethan Bueno de Mesquita, The Political Economy of Terrorism: A Selective Overview of Recent Work, *The Political Economist*, March 2008, p. 3. See http://home.uchicago.edu/bdm/PDF/pe-terror.pdf. Viewed 29 April 2017.

[594] Claude Berrebi, The Economics of Terrorism and Counterterrorism: What Matters and Is Rational-Choice Theory Helpful? in Paul Davis and Kim Cragin (eds.), *Social Science for Counterterrorism: Putting the Pieces Together* (Rand; 2009), pp. 158–159.

[595] Jitka Malečková, Impoverished Terrorists: Stereotype or reality? in Tore Bjørgo (ed.), *Root Causes of Terrorism: Myths, Reality and Ways Forward* (Routledge; 2005), p. 35.

1980 and 1984.[596] The members of the Underground included teachers, writers, university students, engineers and an air force pilot, again, hardly an impoverished pool of volunteers. Additional research undertaken by Krueger alone focused on the backgrounds of sixty-three alleged Islamist terrorists detained in the United States since the 9/11 attacks and again found that on average, they were better educated than the wider Muslim American population and did not come from significantly disadvantaged backgrounds.[597]

As terrorism is a form of political activism for the most part freely entered into, some social science researchers argue it can be compared to non-violent forms of political activism such as voting, canvassing, and running for office, all of which are consistently linked in political science research to wealthier and better educated segments of a given population.[598] Alexander Lee summarized the argument as follows: "Terrorists ... are not drawn from a random sample of the population but, rather, from those who have acquired information about the political process, are connected to politicized social networks, and are able to devote time and energy to political involvement."[599] Alan Krueger and Jitka Malečková suggested a similar causal mechanism couched in the language of economics: "In terms of supply of terrorists ... more educated people from privileged backgrounds are more likely to participate in politics, probably in part because political involvement requires some minimum level of interest, expertise, commitment to issues and effort, all of which are more likely if people have enough education and income to concern themselves with more than minimum economic subsistence ... On the demand side, terrorist organizations may prefer educated, committed individuals."[600]

---

[596] Alan Krueger and Jitka Malečková, Education, Poverty, Political Violence, and Terrorism: Is there a Causal Connection? *Journal of Economic Perspectives*, Vol. 17, No. 4 (Fall 2003), p. 137.

[597] See Alan Krueger, What Makes a Homegrown Terrorist? Human Capital and Participation in Domestic Islamic Terrorist Groups in the USA, *Economics Letters*, Vol. 101, No. 3 (December 2008).

[598] Alexander Lee, Who Becomes a Terrorist? Poverty, Education, and the Origins of Political Violence, *World Politics*, Vol. 63, No. 2 (April 2011), p. 207.

[599] ibid., p. 204.

[600] Alan Krueger and Jitka Malečková, Education, Poverty, Political Violence, and Terrorism: Is there a Causal Connection? *Journal of Economic Perspectives*, Vol. 17, No. 4 (Fall 2003), p. 142.

The political economist Ethan Bueno de Mesquita notes that concerns have been expressed about most of these big data studies on two principal counts — the quality of the data used by the researchers and the persuasiveness of the precise causal mechanism identified by the studies.[601] The problem with the data can be summarized simply as one of selection and approximation. Any quantitative study faces an immediate challenge in terms of the data it chooses to include and that which it chooses to exclude. The vast majority of data-driven studies, even those purporting to investigate the same phenomena, draw upon different datasets. They select different independent and dependent variables to represent the phenomenon under investigation — for example, using data on gross domestic product, unemployment, literacy, education levels, or insurance rates to represent the state of the economy — and they may use different criteria to identify acts of political violence. This makes cross-comparison difficult. Furthermore, some important factors — for example, government legitimacy or individual liberty — are extremely complex but are often captured in quantitative studies by simple numerical devices such as the Freedom House's *Index on Political and Civil Liberty*, which seeks to rate the relative freedom of every country in the world, from most to least free, against a rising seven-point scale. This is also the problem with the causal analysis, which tends to be both rather reductive and too easily falsified. In such circumstances, it is hardly surprising that researchers can often reach contradictory conclusions about similar phenomena. However, over time, as individual research questions have become more and more refined, it has become possible to observe a degree of consensus forming amongst quantitatively-inclined scholars that the "rooted-in-poverty" hypothesis has little merit.[602]

---

[601] Ethan Bueno de Mesquita, The Political Economy of Terrorism: A Selective Overview of Recent Work, *The Political Economist*, March 2008 at http://home.uchicago.edu/bdm/PDF/pe-terror.pdf. Viewed 29 April 2017.

[602] Claude Berrebi, The Economics of Terrorism and Counterterrorism: What Matters and Is Rational-Choice Theory Helpful? in Paul Davis and Kim Cragin (eds.), *Social Science for Counterterrorism: Putting the Pieces Together* (Rand; 2009); Alan Krueger and Jitka Malečková,

This emerging consensus was reflected in the landmark *Final Report of the National Commission on Terrorist Attacks Upon the United States*, which stated unequivocally: "Terrorism is not caused by poverty."[603]

And yet, despite the quantitative consensus, there is too much qualitative evidence to rule out the possibility of a significant relationship between poverty and terrorism entirely in some cases. Despite the "affluent terrorist" thesis advanced by many of the quantitative studies, this insight is somewhat undermined by the post-9/11 narrow focus of these studies on predominantly Islamist terrorist groups. Russell and Miller's 1978 study acknowledged that most of the PKK, LTTE, FARC, Official IRA and Provisional IRA terrorists identified by their research came from rural poor or solidly working class backgrounds.[604] The same has been predominantly true of right-wing terrorists in the United States over the past fifty years.[605] Robert Clark compiled forty-eight detailed personal case histories of ETA members, as well as more limited data on 447 ETA affiliated individuals, and concluded that one couldn't say that ETA had been dominated by one particular social class over the years: "The chances are about even that a typical *etarra* comes from a working class or a

---

Education, Poverty, Political Violence, and Terrorism: Is There a Causal Connection? *Journal of Economic Perspectives*, Vol. 17, No. 4 (Fall 2003); Alan Krueger, *What Makes a Terrorist: Economics and the Roots of Terrorism* (Princeton University Press; 2007); Alan Krueger and David Laitin, Kto Kogo? A Cross-Country Study of the Origins and Targets of Terrorism, in Philip Keefer and Norman Loayza (eds.), *Terrorism, Economic Development, and Political Openness* (Cambridge University Press; 2008); James Piazza, Poverty is a Weak Causal Link, in Stuart Gottlieb (ed.), *Debating Terrorism and Counterterrorism: Conflicting perspectives on Causes, Contexts, and Responses* (CQ Press; 2010); Alexander Lee, Who Becomes a Terrorist? Poverty, Education, and the Origins of Political Violence, *World Politics*, Vol. 63, No. 2 (April 2011); and Tim Krieger and Daniel Meierrieks, What Causes Terrorism? *Public Choice*, Vol. 147, No. 1/2 (April 2011).

[603] Alan Krueger, *What Makes a Terrorist: Economics and the Roots of Terrorism* (Princeton University Press; 2007), p. 3.

[604] Alexander Lee, Who Becomes a Terrorist? Poverty, Education, and the Origins of Political Violence, *World Politics*, Vol. 63, No. 2 (April 2011), p. 211 and Ismail Yilmaz, *Terrorist Profiling: Characteristics and Motivations by Arrest Rate*, in Siddik Ekici, Ahmet Ekici, David McEntire, Richard Ward and Sudha Arlikatti (eds.), *Building Terrorism Resistant Communities: Together Against Terrorism* (IOS Press; 2009), p. 44.

[605] Jeffrey Handler, Socioeconomic Profile of an American Terrorist: 1960s and 1970s, *Terrorism*, Vol. 13, No. 3 (1990).

lower middle class background."[606] Marc Sageman's simple analysis of 102 *al-Qaeda* affiliated fighters, for whom he had sufficient data relating to social status, found that eighteen were upper class, fifty-six middle class, and twenty-eight lower class, demonstrating considerable degree of diversity in *al-Qaeda*'s ranks.[607] Baitullah Mehsud, one-time Head of the *Tehrik-i-Taliban Pakistan* (TTP), came from a poor peasant family — as did the founder of the Afghan *Taliban*, Mullah Mohammad Omar — and Martin McGuinness and Gerry Adams who led the Provisional IRA for a generation came from solidly working class stock.[608] Both McGuinness and Adams left school as teenagers, neither of them completed the British equivalent of high school. So, clearly, poor and comparatively uneducated people join and lead terrorist groups too.

James Piazza identified state failure as an important driver of terrorism noting that Afghanistan, Somalia, Colombia, and the Federally Administered Tribal Areas (FATA) of Pakistan all saw an increase in terrorism as state institutions began to collapse and could no longer project state power effectively.[609] The role played by state failure has also been highlighted by James Fearon and David Laitin, by Stephen Walt, who described them as "breeding grounds of instability, mass migration, and murder",[610] and by Robert Rotberg who, adding Lebanon to the list, labeled them "reservoirs and exporters of terror".[611] The failure of national institutions creates political space for terrorist groups to operate unchecked, of which more below, but also to become an important source of income in a collapsing economy. Money talks in such circumstances,

---

[606] Robert Clark, Patterns in the Lives of ETA Members, *Studies in Conflict and Terrorism*, Vol. 6, No. 3 (1983), pp. 429–430.

[607] Marc Sageman, *Understanding Terror Networks* (University of Pennsylvania Press; 2004), p. 73.

[608] Karen von Hippel, The Role of Poverty in Radicalization and Terrorism, in Stuart Gottlieb (ed.), *Debating Terrorism and Counterterrorism: Conflicting Perspectives on Causes, Contexts, and Responses* (CQ Press; 2010), p. 59.

[609] James Piazza, Incubators of Terror: Do Failed and Failing States Promote Transnational Terrorism? *International Studies Quarterly*, Vol. 52, No. 3 (2008).

[610] Stephen Walt, International Relations: One World, Many Theories, *Foreign Policy* (Spring 1998).

[611] Robert Rotberg, *Failed States in a World of Terror, Foreign Affairs* (July/August 2002).

and it attracts recruits. Ajmal Kasab, the only perpetrator to survive the November 2008 Mumbai attacks, which took the lives of more than 160 people, told the court during his trial that he was broke and tired of his poorly paid job as a decorator and had joined the Pakistani militant group *Lashkar-e-Taiba* (LeT), to learn the skills necessary to become "a bandit" and thus make more money.[612] This was a slightly different story than he had given in his original statement when he told investigators that his father had pressured him to join LeT because he would earn a better salary, live in comfort, and also be able to "give us some of the money, too, and we won't be poor anymore. Your brothers and sisters will be able to get married."[613] Such a financial motivation is not uncommon in the literature and has been recorded, *inter alia,* among volunteers of *al-Shabaab* in Somalia, the *Taliban* in Afghanistan, ISIL in Syria and Iraq, and *Boko Haram* in Nigeria.[614]

Peter Bergen reported in 2007 that one reason for the *Taliban's* resilience and its ability to attract fresh recruits despite aggressive US and NATO military activity was that *Taliban* fighters were earning a salary of approximately $300 a month, an attractive proposition when one considers that this was four times the monthly wage of the average Afghan police officer at the time.[615] The researcher Muhsin Hassan interviewed fifteen former members of *al-Shabaab* now living in Kenya and five of his interview subjects said that the fact that *al-Shabaab* had paid them $50–$150 a month was an important reason why they joined. One man told him: "All one had to do was carry around a gun and patrol the streets, it was an easy job compared to other jobs such as construction work."[616] The

---

[612] Vikas Bajaj and Lydia Polgreen, Suspect Stirs Mumbai Court by Confessing, *New York Times,* 20 July 2009.

[613] Vikas Bajaj and Lydia Polgreen, Suspect Stirs Mumbai Court by Confessing, *New York Times,* 20 July 2009.

[614] Karen von Hippel, The Role of Poverty in Radicalization and Terrorism, in Stuart Gottlieb (ed.), *Debating Terrorism and Counterterrorism: Conflicting Perspectives on Causes, Contexts, and Responses* (CQ Press; 2010), p. 60.

[615] Peter Bergen, Afghan Spring, *New Republic,* 18 June 2007.

[616] Muhsin Hassan, Understanding Drivers of Violent Extremism: The Case of Al-Shabaab and Somali Youth, *CTC Sentinel,* 23 August 2012, p. 18.

Palestinian journalist and author Abdel Bari Atwan reported similar findings regarding ISIL: "In both Iraq and Syria, where unemployment rates are rocketing, the prospect of earning a decent, regular salary is a significant incentive. Islamic State pays its fighters a very generous $500–$650 per month (the average salary in Iraq is $590, while in Syria it is just $243)."[617] A former ISIL fighter using the pseudonym "Abu Khaled" told the reporter Michael Weiss: "This is why a lot of people are joining. I knew a mason who worked construction. He used to get 1,000 lira per day. That's nothing. Now he's joined [ISIL] and gets 35,000 lira — $100 for himself, $50 for his wife, $35 for his kids. He makes $600–$700 per month. He gave up masonry. He's just a fighter now, but he joined for the income."[618]

Suicide bombers are often promised material benefits for their next of kin as an additional incentive to participate in martyrdom operations — such as the substantial financial reward (reportedly $25,000 in 2002) offered to the families of Palestinian suicide bombers by the former Iraqi President, Saddam Hussein.[619] Anecdotally at least, this seems to have attracted some volunteers who might not otherwise be engaged in terrorism. The leader of one Palestinian group sympathetic to Saddam's regime, Mahmoud Safi of the Arab Liberation Front, told CBS News: "Some people stop me on the street, saying if you increase the payment to $50,000 I'll do it immediately."[620] A UN Assistance Mission in Afghanistan (UNAMA) study of suicide attacks carried out in the country between 2001 and 2007 found that "poverty and lack of education" figured as factor in the decision-making of all but one of those interviewed.[621] And, in

---

[617] Abdel Bari Atwan, *Islamic State: The Digital Caliphate* (Saqi Books; 2015), p. 150.

[618] Michael Weiss, *Inside ISIS's Torture Brigade*, The Daily Beast, 17 November 2015, at http://www.thedailybeast.com/articles/2015/11/17/inside-isis-torture-brigades.html. Viewed 19 November 2015.

[619] Jerrold Post, The New Face of Terrorism: Socio-Cultural Foundations of Contemporary Terrorism, *Behavioral Sciences and the Law*, Vol. 23, No. 4 (July/August 2005), p. 457.

[620] John Esterbrook, Salaries for Suicide Bombers, *CBS News*, 3 April 2002, and http://www.cbsnews.com/news/salaries-for-suicide-bombers/. Viewed 7 November 2016.

[621] Karen von Hippel, The Role of Poverty in Radicalization and Terrorism, in Stuart Gottlieb (ed.), *Debating Terrorism and Counterterrorism: Conflicting Perspectives on Causes, Contexts, and Responses* (CQ Press; 2010), p. 58.

an intriguing example of a financial disbursement convincing terrorists to set down their weapons, Bruce Hoffman reported that when Yasir Arafat took the decision to wind up Black September in the late 1970s, he put his intelligence chief Abu Iyad in charge of a novel political exit strategy for its personnel. Abu Iyad found potential wives for the Black September cadres and offered them a cash payment of $3,000, as well as a furnished apartment in Beirut, if they agreed to get married, and, in something of a masterstroke, a bonus of $5,000 if they conceived a child within a year. According to Hoffman's source, one of Abu Iyad's former deputies, without exception the men turned their backs on terrorism and settled into stable married life.[622] Clearly, then, the desire to earn money can also be a factor in some terrorists' decision to join, or leave, terrorist groups.

Karin von Hippel, the current Director-General of the Royal United Services Institute (RUSI), who has deep academic and policymaking experience in the terrorism field, has been one of the most prominent terrorism experts to push back against the contention that poverty is not a significant causal factor, asking: "Is there a chance that the emotion-driven, data-poor poverty defenders may at least be partially correct, while the cold-hearted, data-rich number crunchers may be overlooking critical aspects in the debate?"[623] Von Hippel focused on the issue of complicit surround identified by Louise Richardson and on the constituents whose support terrorists court, and while being careful not to claim that poverty is "*the* primary cause of terrorism", she posited that socioeconomic conditions may nonetheless be a relevant factor when seeking to understand popular support for terrorist actions.[624]

As we noted in Part I, groups like *Hamas*, *Hezbollah* and the Society of the Muslim Brothers have all placed a premium on

---

[622] Bruce Hoffman, All You Need Is Love: How the terrorists stopped terrorism, *The Atlantic*, December 2001.

[623] Karen von Hippel, The Role of Poverty in Radicalization and Terrorism, in Stuart Gottlieb (ed.), *Debating Terrorism and Counterterrorism: Conflicting Perspectives on Causes, Contexts, and Responses* (CQ Press; 2010), p. 50.

[624] ibid., p. 52.

providing social services to their constituents at considerable financial cost to the organizations themselves. Although the leaders of
such groups have typically been careful to cast their actions in terms
of charity and piety, it is also reasonable to presume that they see
some tactical or strategic benefit in doing so.[625] Delivering the
eulogy at Martin McGuinness' funeral in March 2017, former US
President Bill Clinton recalled being told by McGuinness that the
achievement the former Provisional IRA commander was proudest
of was that as education minister in the power-sharing executive
established by the Good Friday Agreement, his first budget had recommended "a more than generous allocation in aid to the poorest
schools in the Protestant neighborhoods because he thought those
children would be just as crippled by ignorance as Catholic children
would and that the only way out of poverty and the only way to give
the people the emotional space to learn to live together, work
together and share the future together was if they could have dignity
of a decent job and the empowerment of knowing they could take
care of their families and give something more to their children."[626]
The fact that an experienced former terrorist like McGuinness
should have placed such a premium on improving the economic lot
and educational opportunities of the most disadvantaged of his
potential political foes offers further evidence of the critical importance those on the terrorist practitioner side of the equation ascribe
to economic factors.

Finally, the conservative historian Daniel Pipes has cogently
observed that ideologically-based movements — both religious and
secular — frequently use "the rhetoric of economic oppression" to
strengthen the appeal of their narratives.[627] Unsurprisingly, this is
a prominent feature of the messaging of anarchist and Marxist
groups from the *Rote Armee Fraktion* and *Brigate Rosse* in Europe

---

[625] ibid., p. 53.

[626] Bill Clinton's speech at Martin McGuinness' funeral in full, *The Guardian*, 23 March 2017
in https://www.theguardian.com/uk-news/video/2017/mar/23/bill-clinton-speech-martin-
mcguinness-funeral-full-video. Viewed 24 March 2017.

[627] Col. John Venhaus, *Why Youth Join Al-Qaeda*, United States Institute of Peace: Special Report
No. 236 (May 2010), p. 5.

to the Argentinian *Ejército Revolucionario del Pueblo* and the Philippine *Bagong Hukbong Bayan*.[628] But economic hardship also surfaces as a *casus belli* in Osama bin Laden's 1996 *Declaration of War Against the Americans Occupying the Land of the Two Holy Places* — "People are fully concerned about their every day livelihood, everyone talks about the deterioration of the economy, inflation, high cost of living, ever-increasing debts, and prisons full of inmates" — and the "theft" of Arab oil by Western governments and multinational companies has been a persistent mainstay of both nationalist and Islamist propaganda in the Middle East. The point may seem an obvious one, but if poverty consistently features in terrorist narratives as persuasive evidence of government injustice, further serving to amplify terrorist grievances or garner support from their potential constituents, then, regardless of whether or not it is a "root cause", it is still, as Von Hippel suggests, part of the radicalization equation.

## Relative deprivation and social exclusion

On the 4th of April 1866, Dmitry Karakozov, a student affiliated with a revolutionary Russian populist cell going by the melodramatic name "Hell", attempted to assassinate Tsar Alexander II at the gates of the Summer Garden in St. Petersburg. The Tsar survived, thanks to the timely intervention of a hatter's apprentice called Osip Komisarov, and Karakozov was arrested. When they searched him, the Russian authorities discovered that Karakozov was carrying a manifesto in which he sought to justify his actions. In a key passage, he blamed the Tsar for the immense gulf that had opened up between the wealthiest and poorest of his subjects, asking with a rhetorical flourish: "Why next to the eternal simple peasant and laborer in his factory and workshop are there people who do nothing — idle nobles, a horde of officials and other

---

[628] Daniel Meierrieks, Economic Determinants of Terrorism, in Raul Caruso and Andrea Locatelli (eds.), *Understanding Terrorism: A Socio-Economics Perspective* (Emerald Group Publishing Ltd; 2014), p. 26.

wealthy people — all living in shining houses?"[629] Karakozov's question suggests an entirely different lens through which to understand the relationship between poverty and terrorism, not in absolute terms, but in relative ones.

In *Why Men Rebel*, the political scientist Ted Gurr took up this challenge, positing that, although poverty was not obviously correlated with political violence, significant income inequality coupled with a sense of injustice about the disposition of wealth and privilege often was — a concept he termed relative deprivation and defined as the "perceived discrepancy between men's value expectations and value capabilities".[630] Gurr argued that it was the tension that developed from "a discrepancy between the 'ought' and the 'is' of collective value satisfaction" that led to political violence.[631] He also linked this concept to psychological theories that suggest profound disenchantment, frustration and marginalization are all related to displays of aggression.[632] Published in the same year as *Why Men Rebel*, Robert Taber's *The War of the Flea* explored the same issue from a reporter's perspective, and his experiences working alongside Fidel Castro's ragbag band of revolutionary guerrillas in Cuba led him to much the same conclusions. Taber wrote: "Poverty does not of itself engender revolution. But poverty side by side with progress creates a new amalgam; the hope of social change stimulated by even a little education produces a new social phenomenon: the ambitious poor, the rebellious poor, the cadres of the revolution, who have

---

[629] Geoffrey Hosking, *Russia: People and Empire, 1552–1917* (Harvard University Press; 1999), p. 347 See also Claudia Verhoeven, *The Odd Man Karakozov, Imperial Russia, Modernity and the Birth of Terrorism* (Cornell University Press; 2009). Karakozov was executed a few months later, Komisarov was first elevated to the peerage and then exiled to the countryside because of his drunken and boorish behavior, and Tsar Alexander survived numerous further assassination attempts until he was finally killed by *Narodnaya Volya* in March 1881.

[630] Ted Gurr, *Why Men Rebel* (Princeton University Press; 1970), p. 21.

[631] ibid., pp. 3–4.

[632] Ken Heskin, Terrorism in Ireland: The Past and Future, *Irish Journal of Psychology*, Vol. 15, No. 2–3 (1994), p. 470.

nothing to lose, and see much to gain around them."[633] He called this the revolution of rising expectations.[634]

The key insight of relative deprivation theory is that people will be more likely to revolt against the *status quo* when they collectively perceive that they are being unjustly deprived of a benefit enjoyed by other groups in their polity.[635] Such benefits may be political, economic, or social in nature. Gurr was writing, at least initially, about revolutionary movements rather terrorist groups, but his theories have been adapted by a number of social scientists studying terrorism, including Fathali Moghaddam, for whom perceptions of fairness and relative deprivation form the ground floor of his staircase to terrorism: "In conditions in which the millions of people who occupy the ground floor perceive injustice and feel relatively deprived, some individuals from among the disgruntled population will climb to the first floor in search of solutions."[636] Critically, both Gurr and Moghaddam stress the role played by perception, rather than absolute values, which circumvents some of the conceptual and operational shortcomings associated with the quantitative studies discussed in the last section and offers a powerful causal explanation for why some individuals adopt terrorist violence as a political strategy while others occupying the same political, economic, and social space do not.[637] Relative deprivation theory also receives support from the discipline of criminology, with social constructivists like Robert Agnew arguing that one of the principal causes of crime is that individuals are conditioned by the culture they inhabit to want, and even expect, certain goods, but are denied

---

[633] Robert Taber, *The War of the Flea: How Guerrilla Fighters Could Win the World* (Citadel Press; 1970), p. 157.

[634] ibid., p. 158.

[635] Ted Gurr, Economic Factors, in Louise Richardson (ed.), *The Roots of Terrorism* (Routledge; 2006), p. 87. See also Walter Garrison Runciman, *Relative Deprivation and Social Justice: A Study of Attitudes to Social Inequality in Twentieth-Century England* (Routledge and Kegan Paul; 1966).

[636] Fathali Moghaddam, The Staircase to Terrorism: A Psychological Exploration, *American Psychologist*, Vol. 60, No. 2, February–March 2005, p. 162.

[637] L. Rowell Huesmann and Graham Huesmann, *No: Poverty and Exclusion are not the Root Causes of Terrorism*, in Richard Jackson and Samuel Sinclair (eds.), Contemporary Debates on Terrorism (Routledge; 2012), p. 115.

the opportunity to attain them through lawful enterprise.[638] Put simply, this theory holds that it is not being a have-not that makes an individual susceptible to radicalization — as Trotsky observed, there are billions of have-nots in the world — it is being a "want-more" that can set an individual on the path to terrorist violence.[639]

Applied to the situation that Dmitry Karakozov and his student peers faced in mid-to-late nineteenth century Russia, relative deprivation theory demonstrates considerable explanatory power at both the individual and societal level. Gurr considered a significant or dramatic adverse alteration in status to have a similar effect on groups and individuals as pre-existing structural disparities in treatment and expectation. Populist violence in Tsarist Russia escalated dramatically after the succession of the reform-minded Alexander II who had raised expectations amongst the burgeoning student population before being forced to temper his liberalizing agenda in the face of a conservative backlash from the Russian elite.[640] As student dissent increased, the tsarist regime curtailed freedoms, reintroduced a tighter degree of political censorship, and stepped up surveillance of radical student groups. Young firebrands in turn became increasingly threatening in their public pronouncements, with one, the leader of the Society of Communists, Petr Zaichnevskii, distributing a proclamation declaring: "Soon, soon the day will come when we will unfurl ... the red banner; and march to the Winter Palace and destroy everyone living there. It may happen that the whole matter will end simply with the elimination of the Tsar's family ... it is more likely that the entire imperial party as one will rise to defend the Tsar ... in this case ... we need only shout 'to the axes'."[641] The tsarist government introduced new rules to constrain student behavior in the

---

[638] Robert Agnew, Foundation for a General Strain Theory of Crime and Delinquency, *Criminology*, Vol. 30, No. 1 (February 1992).

[639] Alan Krueger and Jitka Malečková, Education, Poverty, Political Violence, and Terrorism: Is there a Causal Connection? *Journal of Economic Perspectives*, Vol. 17, No. 4 (Fall 2003), p. 128.

[640] Norman Naimark, Terrorism and the Fall of Imperial Russia, *Terrorism and Political Violence*, Vol. 2, No. 2 (1990), p. 175.

[641] ibid., p. 176.

autumn of 1862 and these provoked a series of demonstrations and riots that forced the authorities to temporarily close the universities. Karakozov's failed assassination attempt prompted further crackdowns; in the early 1870s, the Tsar withdrew university scholarships from poorer students, a decision which effectively pushed more than half of these well-educated young men and women onto the streets and many of them ended up in communes of former students where radical ideas spread like wildfire.[642] Further assassination attempts followed, until *Narodnaya Volya* finally succeeded in killing Alexander II in 1881.

The closure of the avenues for advancement that had briefly existed for many native peoples in European colonies during the desperate years of the Second World War, also appears to have played a significant role in the development of national liberation movements dedicated to overthrowing colonial rule in Asia and Africa. Bruce Hoffman has highlighted the impact that the Allied promotion, at the behest of the United States, of the principle of self-determination in much of the propaganda material directed at territories under Axis occupation had on the subject peoples of the European empires.[643] Perhaps, most notable in this regard was the 1941 Atlantic Charter, which pledged to "respect the right of all peoples to choose the form of government under which they will live".[644] Native peoples from British, Dutch and French colonial possessions — such as Algeria, India, Cyprus, and Malaya — fought alongside their Imperial masters against the Axis powers with an expectation that after the war things might be different, only to discover, once the Axis had finally been defeated, that the colonial powers had no intention of granting them their independence, despite the sacrifices they had made. EOKA's General Grivas recorded in his memoirs that by 1947 his patience at British post-war prevarications over wartime promises of self-determination for Cyprus had been exhausted: "More and more it seemed to me that

---

[642] Clark McCauley and Sophia Moskalenko, *Friction: How Radicalization Happens to Them and Us* (Oxford University Press; 2011), p. 111.

[643] Bruce Hoffman, *Inside Terrorism* (Columbia University Press; 2006), pp. 44–45.

[644] ibid., p. 45.

only a revolution would liberate my homeland."[645] Furthermore, on a personal level, many had been honored during wartime only to be shunted aside again once peace came, no longer needed and thus no longer valued. One of the founder members of the *Front de Libération Nationale*, Belkacem Krim, was similarly frustrated by the return to the *status quo ante* in post-war Algeria: "My brother returned from Europe with medals and frost-bitten feet! There everyone was equal. Why not here?"[646]

During World War II, the French settlers in Algeria had mostly remained loyal to General Pétain's collaborationist Vichy government, and so the Free French Forces appealed to the Arab and Berber natives of Algeria for support in 1942. When representatives from the local Muslim population subsequently approached the French General Henri Giraud, newly installed by the allies as High Commissioner for French North and West Africa, seeking a commitment to reform in tacit return for their assistance they were rebuffed by the General in brusque fashion: "I don't care about reforms, I want soldiers first."[647] The Algerian nationalist leader Ferhat Abbas responded by issuing *The Manifesto of the Algerian People* in February 1943, which, invoking the spirit of the Atlantic Charter, proclaimed angrily that "the French colony only admits equality with Muslim Algeria on one level; sacrifice on the battlefields," and demanded greater concessions towards national autonomy.[648] Abbas was soon confined to house arrest by the Free French authorities, but the political tide was moving in his favor. In January 1944, General De Gaulle made his Brazzaville Declaration promising that France would "lead each of the colonial peoples to a development that will permit them to administer themselves, and later, govern themselves."[649] Algerian Muslims were promised equal

---

[645] George Grivas-Dighenis and Charles Foley, *The Memoirs of General Grivas* (Longmans; 1964), p. 13.

[646] Michael Burleigh, *Blood and Rage: A Cultural History of Terrorism* (Harper; 2009), p. 113.

[647] Alistair Horne, *A Savage War of Peace: Algeria 1954–1962* (New York Review Books Classics; 2006), p. 42.

[648] ibid.

[649] ibid., p. 43.

rights with French citizens and a greater role in local government, and in return, Algerian Muslims flocked to the French colors serving with distinction during the invasion of Italy and the liberation of France. Among the most notable Algerian veterans of the war in Europe was Ahmed Ben Bella, later one of the founders of the FLN and the first President of independent Algeria, who served as a sergeant in the French army and was decorated personally by General de Gaulle for his bravery in the bloody Battle of Monte Cassino.[650]

Veterans like Ben Bella arrived back in Algeria after the war expecting things to be different, yet a rude awakening awaited them at home. On 8 May 1945 — Victory in Europe Day — a nationalist demonstration in the town of Sétif in the north-eastern Algerian province of Constantine devolved first into a riot and then into inter-communal violence which raged sporadically across the surrounding area for five days. One hundred and three European settlers were murdered, and a similar number wounded.[651] The French authorities responded with a *ratissage* — literally a "raking over" — of the local Muslim community. There were summary executions, forty villages were bombed by the French air force, and a French naval cruiser bombarded the area around Kerrata.[652] Estimates of the final Muslim death toll vary wildly from approximately 1,020–1,300, recorded by the official *Tubert Commission Report* into the episode, to 45,000 in the Egyptian press.[653] Many veterans of the Seventh Regiment of the Algerian *Tirailleurs* came from the Constantine area and the scenes that greeted them on their repatriation and demobilization hardly represented the homecoming they had been expecting after all the sacrifices they had made to ensure the liberation of France. Such a violent dislocation of expectation — to borrow a term from

---

[650] Michael Burleigh, *Blood and Rage: A Cultural History of Terrorism* (Harper; 2009), pp. 113–114 and Alex Duval Smith, Ahmed Ben Bella: Anti-French activist who became the first president of free Algeria, *The Independent*, 17 April 2012.

[651] Alistair Horne, *A Savage War of Peace: Algeria 1954–1962* (New York Review Books Classics; 2006), p. 26.

[652] ibid.

[653] ibid., p. 27.

psychology that has much in common with the concept of relative deprivation — drove a significant number of these combat veterans to join the nationalist resistance to French rule and ultimately the FLN.[654] Ben Bella later wrote: "The horrors of the Constantine area in May 1945 succeeded in persuading me of the only path; Algeria for the Algerians."[655]

The Sétif emergency did prompt the French authorities to propose a series of concessions to the Muslim population and to replace direct rule from France with a national *Assemblée Algérienne*, albeit with a bifurcated electoral college in which the votes of half a million French settlers were balanced against those of the far greater native majority. This again raised expectations of positive change. However, a strong showing by the Muslim-backed *Mouvement pour le Triomphe des Libertiés Démocratiques* (MTLD) in the 1947 municipal elections convinced the colonial authorities that even this heavily circumscribed experiment in democratic representation could not be allowed to flourish, and so in the 1948 national elections for the new assembly, French troops and police were deployed to scare Muslim voters away from the polls, MTLD candidates were harassed and detained, and ballot boxes interfered with to ensure that the settlers enjoyed a healthy margin of victory and French colonial dominance was not challenged.[656] As historian Michael Burleigh put it: "Let us be entirely clear that the French were deliberately frustrating the extension of democracy to the Arab and Berber populations."[657] M'hamed Yazid, a future FLN Minister of Information, later wrote in *The New York Times*: "More than thirty of us were arrested during the electoral campaign and put into jail for years. A look at the list of those jailed will give you an approximate list of the actual leadership of the Algerian revolution today."[658] The gulf between the native and settler populations in Algeria was

---

[654] ibid., p. 28.

[655] ibid.

[656] ibid., p. 71.

[657] Michael Burleigh, *Blood and Rage: A Cultural History of Terrorism* (Harper; 2009), p. 113.

[658] Alistair Horne, *A Savage War of Peace: Algeria 1954–1962* (New York Review Books Classics; 2006), p. 71.

further exacerbated by the jarring juxtaposition of the relative wealth of the French settlers with the widespread poverty of the Muslim majority, both in the cities and in rural areas. The FLN's Zohra Drif, responsible for the notorious September 1956 Milk-Bar bombing, was moved to take up arms in large part because of the disparity between the suffering of the Muslim population and the relative comfort of "the European population, in its tranquil quarters ... [which] lived peacefully, went to the beach, to the cinema, to *le dancing*, and prepared for their holidays".[659] Her target was chosen precisely because it was a popular Algiers hangout frequented by carefree and hedonistic young French beachgoers. Three patrons were killed and fifty more injured, many seriously.

Ever since the partition of Ireland in 1921, Catholics north of the border have tended to compare their situation to that of their Protestant neighbors, not to that of Catholics in much poorer Eire who received substantially less social welfare support from the Irish state, and where access to secondary and tertiary education was far inferior.[660] The disparity between the two communities in the North was glaringly obvious — in 1981, the unemployment rate for male Catholics in Northern Ireland was 30.2%, while for Protestant males, it was only 12.4%. In some of the areas of Belfast most closely associated with the Provisional IRA and hard-core support for the republican movement, male unemployment rates fluctuated between 50% and 60%.[661] Access to public services was not divided equally between the two communities. In the Protestant-controlled town of Dungannon in County Tyrone, no Catholic family had been granted a secure tenancy for local authority-owned public housing in almost twenty-five years.[662] In the 1971 census, the three principle Protestant denominations made up 53.4% of the total Northern

---

[659] ibid., p. 185.

[660] Michael Burleigh, *Blood and Rage: A Cultural History of Terrorism* (Harper; 2009), p. 287–288. See also Denis O'Hearn, Catholic Grievances, Catholic Nationalism: A Comment, *British Journal of Sociology*, Vol. 34, No. 3 (September 1983).

[661] Henry Patterson, Gerry Adams and the Modernisation of Republicanism, *Conflict Quarterly* (Summer 1990), p. 20. See also Bob Rowthorn and Naomi Wayne, *Northern Ireland: The Political Economy of the Conflict* (Polity Press, 1988), pp. 116–117.

[662] Michael Burleigh, *Blood and Rage: A Cultural History of Terrorism* (Harper; 2009), p. 288.

Ireland population of 1,536,065 people, and Catholics an estimated 31.4%.[663] Yet, in 1968, sixty-two of Ulster's seventy-three local councils were controlled by unionist Protestants.[664] Significant gerrymandering, and the judicious use of electoral qualifications favoring resident occupiers, ensured that even in many areas where Catholics predominated, Protestants retained control — for example, the flashpoint city of Londonderry/Derry was 60% Catholic, but Protestants maintained a seemingly election-proof 12-to-8 seat majority on the local council.[665] In the professions, Catholics made up only 11% of the strength of the Royal Ulster Constabulary, 6% of the mechanical engineers working in the Province, 8% of the university lecturers, and 9% of the senior civil servants.[666] Only 16% of Protestant males were classified as unskilled manual laborers, as opposed to 32% of male Catholics.[667]

By their own account, Provisional IRA members felt the inequality of Northern Irish society very keenly. Martin McGuinness recalled: "It was blatantly clear to me that the community [from] which I came were effectively being treated as second-class citizens in their own country. The state put in place at the time of partition was a unionist state for a unionist people, and any recognition of Irishness was something to be frowned upon by the authorities ... Catholics did not have the liberties that other sections of the community had and were effectively being ruthlessly discriminated against by the unionist administration."[668] Gerry Adams put it even more succinctly: "Catholics in the north of

---

[663] *The Northern Ireland Census 1991: Religion Report* at http://cain.ulst.ac.uk/ni/religion.htm. Viewed 16 August 2016.

[664] Denis O'Hearn, Catholic Grievances, Catholic Nationalism: A Comment, *British Journal of Sociology*, Vol. 34, No. 3 (September 1983), p. 442.

[665] Michael Burleigh, Blood and Rage: A Cultural History of Terrorism (Harper; 2009), p. 288. See also Denis O'Hearn, Catholic Grievances, Catholic Nationalism: A Comment, *The British Journal of Sociology*, Vol. 34, No. 3 (September 1983).

[666] Michael Burleigh, *Blood and Rage: A Cultural History of Terrorism* (Harper; 2009), p. 288.

[667] Denis O'Hearn, Catholic Grievances, Catholic Nationalism: A Comment, *British Journal of Sociology*, Vol. 34, No. 3 (September 1983), p. 443.

[668] Richard English, *Armed Struggle: The History of the IRA* (Oxford University Press; 2004), p. 125.

Ireland were ghettoized, marginalized, treated as inferior."[669]
Over time, the British authorities came to appreciate the importance of addressing these perceived and very real inequalities,
and were able to do so with a significant degree of success, a process that coincided with the evolution of the Northern Ireland
Peace Process. In a commentary published on The Troubles in
1994, the Irish psychologist Ken Heskin acknowledged: "If relative deprivation was a major factor in providing motivation for the
initial stages of the current conflict and for its continuance for
several years, it probably no longer provides such motivation now.
The determination of the administration in Northern Ireland to
remove, as far as possible, sources of perceived inequity of the
kind which provided the early sparks of discontent, such as housing, jobs, and general facilities, has been as visible as it has been
undeniable."[670]

Unsurprisingly, relative deprivation is also a factor that is particularly referenced in class-based struggles. One propaganda
statement released by the Uruguayan *Tupamaros* towards the end of
1969 encapsulated the concept perfectly in poetic fashion: "We are
inspired by nothing other than the possibility of ending the enormous injustices of this regime, whose limousines and palaces we see
next to malnourished, school-less children, of this regime of bunga-
lows and hovels."[671] Many of the memoirs produced by militants
active in the Marxist terrorist and guerrilla movements of 1960s and
1970s echo this sentiment. Che Guevara's account of traveling
around Latin America as a young medical student is an apposite
example — repeatedly encountering great disparities in wealth
and circumstance, typified in one passage by "blond" American
tourists photographing Peruvian Indians picturesque in their destitution, Guevara concluded: "I knew that when the great guiding
spirit cleaves humanity into two antagonistic halves, I will be with

---

[669] ibid., p. 110.

[670] Ken Heskin, Terrorism in Ireland: The Past and Future, *Irish Journal of Psychology*, Vol. 15,
No. 2–3 (1994), p. 474.

[671] Pablo Brum, *The Robin Hood Guerrillas: The Epic Journey of Uruguay's Tupamaros* (CreateSpace;
2014), p. 114.

the people."[672] Susanna Ronconi, a veteran of the *Brigate Rosse* and co-founder of *Prima Linea*, who was linked directly to three murders and to the notorious mass kneecapping at the School of Business Administration in Turin, justified her actions in terms that Gurr would have recognized: "I did not, and do not see myself as a violent person, but I believed that under certain conditions, when one class held power and the other didn't the use of violence was legitimate."[673] Leila Khaled of the PFLP recounted in her autobiography visiting a refuge camp in Lebanon for the first time as a child: "After a tour of the camp, I realized that I was living in luxury. I knew how fortunate I was and how despicable and arrogant the rich people must be. I suddenly became aware of class differences in that upsetting spring for me. As I grew older, I acquired the necessary intellectual and moral ideology to understand what I had felt in that camp, why class society must be abolished and socialism established in its place."[674] She concluded that her visit to the camp had taught her more "in a few hours than a 1,000 books could have done in a 100 years".[675]

There is evidence of this phenomenon operating on the political far-right as well, where resentment of the opportunities afforded immigrants and minorities but perceived to be denied to established white, Christian communities is a staple of white supremacist and neo-Nazi narratives. The first article of the American white supremacist David Lane's *White Genocide Manifesto*, influential in far-right circles, makes this point explicitly: "All existing governments in the once White political states now deny us hegemony and the exclusive territorial imperatives necessary to our survival as a biological and cultural entity."[676] The *Manifesto*'s ninth article also castigates "the denial of jobs to White men through so-called affirmative action and

---

[672] Ernesto Guevara, *The Motorcycle Diaries: Notes on a Latin American Journey* (Ocean Press; 2003), p. 164.

[673] Eileen MacDonald, *Shoot The Women First* (Random House; 1992), p. 182.

[674] Leila Khaled and George Hajjar, *My People Shall Live: The Autobiography of a Revolutionary* (Hodder and Stoughton; 1973), p. 35.

[675] ibid.

[676] http://www.davidlane1488.com/whitegenocide.html. Viewed 29 May 2017.

other nefarious schemes".[677] As a member of the white supremacist group The Order, Lane was involved in the murder of the Denver-based radio personality Alan Berg in June 1984, and was sentenced to 150 years in prison where he died in 2007. Berg was targeted by the group because he was a prominent Jewish liberal who frequently sparred with callers from the Christian Identity movement on his talk radio show.

One can also trace similar themes woven through Neo-Confederate literature, like Ellen Williams' *Bedford, A World Vision* and James Kibler's *Walking Toward Home*, which paint a picture of a white American South marginalized and under threat, prevented from returning to its rightful place in the world. As Kibler writes in *Walking Toward Home*: "We tried for our new July Fourth with all that we had, but got killed and invaded and burned out for our pains. Now we are still paying the price. From the looks of it, we ... still ain't free. Free to get put out of business. Free to starve maybe, but not free."[678] Such works belong to a literary tradition that stretches back to Thomas Dixon's 1905 novel *The Clansman*, later the basis of D. W. Griffiths' epic film *The Birth of a Nation*, which sustains an image of racist groups, like the Ku Klux Klan, defending a beleaguered white population from the depredations of Northern carpetbaggers, cosmopolitan liberals and upstart minorities, and helping to lay the foundation for the South to rise again.[679]

A 2012 report entitled *Challengers from the Sidelines* prepared by Arie Perliger for the Combating Terrorism Center at West Point suggested that relative deprivation might also explain the apparent rise of right-wing and white supremacist extremist groups in the United States when the Republican Party controls at least one House of Congress, in that such groups have higher expectations that their voices will be heard in such circumstances and thus feel commensurately more

---

[677] ibid.

[678] Euan Hague, Heidi Beirich and Edward Sebesta (Eds.), *Neo-Confederacy: A Critical Introduction* (University of Texas Press; 2010), p. 244.

[679] Camille Jackson, *The Turner Diaries, Other Racist Novels, Inspire Extremist Violence*, Intelligence Report, Southern Poverty Law Center, 14 October 2004.

betrayed and marginalized when they are not.[680] In the period 1990–2011, two Democratic Presidents, Bill Clinton and Barack Obama, and two Republican Presidents, George H. W. Bush and George W. Bush, occupied the White House. Perliger found that the average number of violent far-right incidents per year during the Republican administrations was 243.6, as opposed to 163 during Democratic administrations, and this despite the overheated and often hysterical conspiracy theories that circulated around both Clinton and Obama on the far-right.[681]

Marc Sageman has suggested that relative deprivation has significant potential for explaining the rise of *al-Qaeda*, and other modern militant Islamist groups, like ISIL, arguing that "far from being a product of failing expectations ... [support for] *jihad* was more a result of rising expectations among its members."[682] There is a narrative thread in Islamist propaganda grounded in a sense of relative deprivation that has been consistently exploited by *al-Qaeda* and ISIL to create a sense among their followers that Islam's rightful place in the world, and by extension their rightful place in the world, has been usurped by the "Zionist-Crusader alliance". Osama bin Laden stresses this theme in his 1996 *fatwa* which proclaims: "Today we start talking, working and remembering to search for ways to reform whatever happened to the Islamic world in general, land of the two holiest sites in particular. We want to study all possible ways that can be established to restore the situation back to its origin and the rights to their owners, after what happened to the people from great misfortune and serious harm concerning their religion and worldly existence." The US Government's Open Source Center, published a study in September 2011 that identified "restoring the Caliphate" as one of six "master narratives" that dominate the propaganda output of *al-Qaeda* and its

---

[680] Kurt Eichenwald, Right-Wing Extremists Are a Bigger Threat to America Than ISIS, *Newsweek*, 4 February 2016.

[681] Arie Perliger, *Challengers from the Sidelines: Understanding America's Violent Far-Right* (Combating Terrorism Centre at West Point; November 2012), p. 90.

[682] Marc Sageman, *Understanding Terror Networks* (University of Pennsylvania Press; 2004), pp. 76–78.

affiliates.[683] This was, of course, the torch picked up by ISIL. In July 2014, the group's leader, Abu Bakr al-Baghdadi, struck a similar note in an audio message marking the onset of *Ramadan,* promising his supporters: "The disbelievers were able to weaken and humiliate the Muslims, dominate them in every region, plunder their wealth and resources, and rob them of their rights ... O Muslims everywhere, glad tidings to you and expect good. Raise your head high, for today — by *Allah's* grace — you have a state and Caliphate, which will return your dignity, might, rights, and leadership."[684] Such appeals can be closely linked to potential psychological drivers such as self-actualization and humiliation, and often form just one aspect of a more complex cocktail of emotions and perceptions, but they nevertheless represent a powerful framing device.

Finally, relative deprivation might even be a factor that operates at a professional level marking out some professions, in some circumstances, as being more vulnerable to radicalization than others. Diego Gambetta and Steffen Hertog researched the remarkably high incidence of engineering graduates active in Islamic terrorist groups — engineering graduates are found three to four times more frequently in such groups than any other category of degree holder.[685] Indeed, one need look no further than the September 11 attacks for suggestive evidence of this phenomenon in action — three of the four *al-Qaeda* 'pilots' that seized control of the hijacked aircraft were engineers by training. After considering a range of potential explanatory factors from "an engineering mindset" to the attractiveness to a terrorist cell of an engineer's professional experience, Gambetta and Hertog suggest that the most likely explanation is the relative deprivation Arab engineering graduates often experience on leaving university. In many Middle Eastern countries, entry

---

[683] Open Source Center, *Special Report: Al-Qaeda Master Narratives and Affiliate Case Studies* (September 2011), p. 25. The other "Master Narratives" identified in the report are "War on Islam", "Agents of the West", "The *Nakba*", "Violent Jihad", and "Blood of the Martyrs".

[684] Full text at https://news.siteintelgroup.com/Jihadist-News/islamic-state-leader-abu-bakr-al-baghdadi-encourages-emigration-worldwide-action.html. Viewed 31 May 2017.

[685] See Diego Gambetta and Steffen Hertog, Why are There so Many Engineers Among Islamic Radicals? *European Journal of Sociology*, Vol. 50, No. 2 (August 2009).

into an engineering program is considered (along with studying medicine or the natural sciences) to be the apogee of academic achievement. Engineering graduates leave school with high social standing and a powerful expectation of future success but often then encounter stagnating economies and limited opportunities for advancement. Having been raised to expect great things, these high fliers are brought down to earth with a crash. Only in the one Middle Eastern country where opportunities for engineering graduates abound, Saudi Arabia, are they no more likely to be found in the ranks of extremist groups than graduates of other disciplines.[686]

Gambetta and Hertog argue that in many contexts, it is likely frustrated ambition that makes engineers particularly susceptible to terrorist recruitment. A case in point is Yahya Ayyash, who graduated from Birziet University in the West Bank with a degree in electrical engineering in 1991 and hoped to go on to study for a master's degree in Jordan. He was denied an exit visa by the Israeli authorities, and shortly thereafter, he went to work for *Hamas* as a bomb-maker. Known to Israeli intelligence officers as "The Engineer", Ayyash was responsible for building the bombs used in a series of violent attacks between 1993 and 1995 that claimed, by one estimate, at least a hundred Israeli lives, before he was killed in January 1996.[687] The Head of *Shin Bet* during the period of Ayyash's radicalization, Yaakov Peri, later lamented: "If we had known that he was going to do what he did, we would have given him permission to travel along with a million dollars."[688] Reviewing *Hamas* websites, Gambetta and Hertog found "numerous cases" of martyred fighters who had been forced to abandon their university studies and the futures they had been working towards because of economic hardship or other external pressures.[689]

---

[686] ibid., p. 225.

[687] Shaul Bartal, *Jihad in Palestine: Political Islam and the Israeli-Palestinian Conflict* (Routledge; 2015), p. 42.

[688] Daniel Byman, *A High Price: The Triumphs and Failures of Israeli Counterterrorism* (Oxford University Press 2011), p. 93.

[689] Diego Gambetta and Steffan Hertog, *Engineers of Jihad: The Curious Connection between Violent Extremism and Education* (Princeton University Press; 2016), p. 41.

Closely allied to the concept of relative deprivation is the concept of social exclusion, which can be distinguished from the former in that it implies conscious or unconscious discrimination on the part of those in power, rather than just neglect. Simply put, this is the idea that certain groups are materially, and often deliberately, prevented from participating fully in the social, economic, and political life of a given community and this generates powerful feelings of frustration, anger, and resentment. Marc Sageman has argued that being embedded in society encourages a commitment to intercommunal relations: "It makes people sensitive to local criticism ... Being embedded in a segment of society promotes local collective behavior on behalf of this segment. Social bonds also imply some sort of sensitivity and responsiveness to maintain them. The lack of such bonds frees people from these responsibilities and local concerns."[690] When an individual, or a group, is excluded from full membership in the community, this "disembeddedness" can be extremely destabilizing, especially when external actors such as online recruiters or foreign agents can stoke this sense of alienation and its associated grievances.[691] Fathali Moghaddam noted that one can go back as far as Plato to find warnings of the potentially destabilizing consequences of excluding talent from government.[692] Rather more recently, in a 2011 study based on data from the Minorities at Risk Project, James Piazza found that economic discrimination experienced by minorities was "a significant predictor" of domestic terrorist events.[693] The American sociologist Christopher Hewitt reached much the same conclusion in a 1984 comparative study of terrorism in Uruguay, Cyprus, Northern

---

[690] Marc Sageman, *Understanding Terror Networks* (University of Pennsylvania Press; 2004), p. 146.

[691] ibid., p. 161. The concept of embeddedness was developed by the influential American sociologist Mark Granovetter, a pioneer of social network theory, who stressed the role played by personal relations in both generating trust and discouraging malfeasance. See Mark Granovetter, Economic Action and Social Structure: The Problem of Embeddedness, *American Journal of Sociology*, Vol. 91, No. 3 (November 1985).

[692] Fathali Moghaddam, The Staircase to Terrorism: A Psychological Exploration, *American Psychologist*, Vol. 60, No. 2 (February-March 2005), p. 163.

[693] James Piazza, Poverty, Minority Economic Discrimination, and Domestic Terrorism, *Journal of Peace Research*, Vol. 48, No. 3 (March 2011), p. 349.

Ireland, the Basque region, and Italy.[694] As Hewitt's research suggests, one can find substantial evidence to support the contention that social exclusion is closely associated with terrorism in the historical record.

The institutionalized anti-Semitism embraced by the Tsar's successor, Alexander III, pushed many of his educated Jewish subjects into the populist movement, a process accelerated by the "May Laws" of 1882 which introduced a quota on university places for Jews, the 1891 expulsion of Jews from Moscow, and the brutal pogroms against the Jewish populations of Kishenev in 1903, and Kiev, Minsk, and Odessa in 1905.[695] With the transition from populism, with its latent nativist sympathies, to Marxism, with its more internationalist outlook, Russian Jews became more influential within the revolutionary underground.[696] By 1900, they accounted for almost 30% of the persons arrested for political crimes in Russia, and some Maximalist and anarchist groups were almost entirely dominated by Jews.[697] *Sotsialisty Revolyutsionery — Boyevaya Organizatsiya*, the avowedly terrorist Combat Organization of the Socialist Revolutionaries, was established by a Jew, Grigory Gershuni, and in September 1911, Prime Minister Pyotr Stolypin was assassinated by another Jewish terrorist, Dmitry Bogrov. Norman Naimark, who has studied these movements in great detail, noted that both Gershuni and Bogrov had been comparatively well assimilated into Russian society and argued that they had turned to violence "less from direct oppression than from the disappointed hopes associated with assimilation".[698] Gershuni was arrested by the Tsarist authorities in May 1903 and his defiant words to his captors revealed just how deeply he had felt the

---

[694] Christopher Hewitt, *The Effectiveness of Anti-Terrorism Policies* (University Press of America; 1984).

[695] Norman M. Naimark, Terrorism and the fall of Imperial Russia, *Terrorism and Political Violence*, Vol. 2, No. 2 (1990), p. 184.

[696] Leonard Schapiro, The Role of the Jews in the Russian Revolutionary Movement, in Ellen Dahrendorf (ed.), *Russian Studies* (Elisabeth Sifton Books, Viking; 1987), p. 275.

[697] Norman M. Naimark, Terrorism and the Fall of Imperial Russia, *Terrorism and Political Violence*, Vol. 2, No. 2 (1990), p. 174.

[698] ibid., p. 184.

anti-Semitic slights that marked him out as less than equal to his fellow Russians: "I am a Jew. I am sure that many, including you, are convinced that the Jews are cowardly, that they would avoid death by any means... You say that the Jews are only capable of silly rebellions, and I will show you that they are capable of [an] honorable death."[699]

It should also be noted that another marginalized group within Russian society played a similarly significant role when they found their opportunities for advancement blocked by the mores of the day: women. Well-educated and often noble-born Russian women filled significant leadership roles in *Narodnaya Volya* and made up one-third of the membership of *Sotsialisty Revolyutsionery — Boyevaya Organizatsiya*.[700] *Narodnik* Vera Zasulich described the feeling of empowerment she experienced on joining the underground: "Of course it would have been much easier if I had been a boy; then I could have done what I wanted ... And then, the distant specter of revolution appeared, making me the equal of any boy; I too could dream of 'action', of 'exploits', and of 'the great struggle' ... I too could join those 'who perished for the great cause'."[701]

It should come as little surprise that social exclusion plays a major role in the grievance narratives of national liberation movements. The 1948 Algerian election cast a long shadow, confirming for a generation of native Algerians that they would be denied a voice in their own homeland. As Frantz Fanon noted, "the settler's work is to make even dreams of liberty impossible for the native," and in that the French authorities partially succeeded for almost a decade as the pressure for change grew but found no release.[702] Excluded from power, or any mechanism by which to bring about reform within the system, Algerian nationalists turned to violence, the Manichaeism of

---

[699] Grigory Gershuni, *From My Recent Past: Memoirs of a Revolutionary Terrorist* (Lexington Books; 2015), p. 16.

[700] Norman M. Naimark, Terrorism and the Fall of Imperial Russia, *Terrorism and Political Violence*, Vol. 2, No. 2 (1990), p. 174.

[701] Michael Burleigh, *Blood and Rage: A Cultural History of Terrorism* (Harper; 2009), pp. 30–31.

[702] Frantz Fanon, *The Wretched of the Earth* (Grove Press; 1963), p. 93.

the colonist producing, in Fanon's well-turned phrase, a Manichaeism of the colonized.[703] In a famous dialogue that took place in 1957 between the eminent French academic, resistance fighter, and survivor of Ravensbruck concentration camp, Germaine Tillion, and the FLN commander in Algiers, Saadi Yacef, Tillion accused the FLN of being "assassins". In Tillion's account, taken aback at her bluntness, Yacef tearfully replied: "Yes, Madame Tillion, we are assassins ... It's the only way in which we can express ourselves."[704]

Nelson Mandela powerfully described the sense of total exclusion felt by black South Africans in their own homeland in his memoir, *Long Walk to Freedom*: "To be an African in South Africa means one is politicized from the moment of one's birth, whether one acknowledges it or not. An African child is born in an Africans Only hospital, taken home in an Africans Only bus, lives in an Africans Only area and attends Africans Only schools, if he attends school at all. When he grows up, he can hold Africans Only jobs, rent a house in Africans Only townships, ride Africans Only trains and be stopped at any time of the day or night and be ordered to produce a pass, without which he can be arrested and thrown in jail. His life is circumscribed by racist laws and regulations that cripple his growth, dim his potential and stunt his life."[705] Addressing the court during the Rivonia Trials, he explained his motivation for taking a leadership role in *Umkhonto we Sizwe*, and the organization's reasons for adopting violence as a political weapon, in terms that left little doubt of the role that the extreme degree of social exclusion experienced by black South Africans had played in shaping these decisions: "I have done whatever I did, both as an individual and as a leader of my people, because of my experience in South Africa and my own proudly felt African background ... We were placed in a position in which we had either to accept a permanent state of inferiority, or to defy the Government. We chose to defy the law. We first broke the law in a way which avoided any recourse to violence; when this form was legislated against, and the government resorted to a

---

[703] ibid.

[704] Michael Burleigh, *Blood and Rage: A Cultural History of Terrorism* (Harper Press; 2009), p. 124.

[705] Nelson Mandela, *Long Walk to Freedom* (Back Bay Books; 1994), p. 95.

show of force to crush opposition to its policies, only then did we decide to answer violence with violence."[706]

Established in 1952, *Euskadi Ta Askatasuna* was also founded during a period of systemic repression, as Generalissimo Franco's fascist regime sought to ban the Basque language and forbade parents from giving their children identifiably Basque names. One of ETA's leading members in the 1960s, José María Escubi Larraz, also known by the *nom de guerre* Bruno, recalled entering a state-run elementary school in Pamplona for the first time at the age of seven and being plunged into a completely alien environment where all the lessons were taught in Spanish and he was penalized because of his unfamiliarity with the language: "When I got to the school, I realized that no one talked like me; I felt, then, a feeling of loneliness. I couldn't understand Spanish and the lectures of the teacher. They thought that I didn't want to study my lessons, and they punished me. This marked me deeply. And when I grew up I decided to do something for my Basque country."[707]

Structural inequalities and discriminatory practices were also often entrenched by the regimes that replaced colonial administrations, especially in territories that were occupied by more than one distinct ethnic or religious group. When Ceylon (now Sri Lanka) achieved independence from Great Britain in 1948, the Sinhalese majority on the island moved to redress the somewhat privileged position the Tamil minority had enjoyed under the British, who often elevated local minorities to act in support of their colonial rule. The Sinhalese-dominated government introduced legislation in 1956 making Sinhalese the only official language on the island, which provided an excuse to exclude Tamils from government jobs or educational opportunities. This led to higher unemployment levels for Tamils in the 1970s. In 1972, the government adopted a new constitution, which, in addition to changing the country's name to Sri Lanka and repudiating its dominion status as part of

---

[706] http://www.anc.org.za/content/nelson-mandelas-statement-dock-rivonia-trial. Viewed 3 June 2017.

[707] Robert Clark, Patterns in the Lives of ETA Members, *Studies in Conflict and Terrorism*, Vol. 6, No. 3 (1983), p. 437.

the British Commonwealth, made Buddhism the state religion — most Sinhalese were Buddhists, most Tamils were Hindu. The new constitution also encouraged the various Tamil opposition groups to come together to establish the Tamil United Front (TUF), which in May 1973 formally adopted the platform of Tamil independence.[708] While the TUF essentially remained a traditional political party, the Tamil independence movement became considerably more militant with the foundation of the LTTE by Kadirgamapillai Nallainathan (better known by his *nom de guerre* Uma Maheswaran) and Velupillai Prabhakaran in 1976, and the LTTE's launch of a full-blown insurgent and terrorist campaign against the Sri Lankan government in the early 1980s.

This sense of complete social, economic, and political exclusion is not exclusive to ethnic or religious groups — political outsiders can experience it too. The November 17 member Christos Tsigaridas described what attracted him to extreme left-wing politics: "In the village, I saw the full consequences of monarcho-fascism upon proud, decent people who fought for freedom and national independence. Those labeled as *non-ethnikofrones* [literally 'non-nation minded', or vernacularly, 'unpatriotic'] were not able to get even seasonal work. I saw young people with university degrees languishing in society's margins with no jobs. The prerequisite for a better life was to become an *ethnikofron*, or law-abiding citizen and sign a written statement as confirmation. And it was the gendarmerie that would make or break people's lives."[709] The Weather Underground's first communiqué expressed frustration with the traditional avenues of protest, which had roiled the late 1960s but seemed to many to have changed very little: "Tens of thousands have learned that protests and marches don't do it. Revolutionary violence is the only way."[710] The reality of social exclusion was also an article of faith for the *Rote Armee Fraktion*, and it was referenced directly in the group's

---

[708] Jeffrey William Lewis, *The Business of Martyrdom: A History of Suicide Bombing* (Naval Institute Press; 2012), pp. 89–90.

[709] George Kassimeris, *Inside Greek Terrorism* (Oxford University Press; 2013), p. 61.

[710] Bernardine Dohrn, Declaration of a State of War, *The Berkeley Tribe*, 31 July 1970 at http://www.lib.berkeley.edu/MRC/pacificaviet/scheertranscript.html.

final communiqué: "Exclusion and repression through a lack of social feeling within the society as well is normal both here and elsewhere. Racism from below threatens the lives of millions, which in Germany is the murderous mark of the historical continuity which this society carries with it ... Future outlines for liberation must be measured according to this, and they must find a key to unlocking the closed, reactionary consciousness and awakening the desire for emancipation and liberation."[711] Andreas Baader and Gudrun Ensslin made a conscious effort to recruit from state-run young offender institutions reckoning that those on the fringes of society with no real social or family ties would make ideal underground activists.[712] One of their first recruits was Peter Jürgen Boock, who went on to play key roles in the murder-kidnappings of Hanns-Martin Schleyer and Jürgen Ponto as a fully-fledged member of the RAF, and they were ultimately able to attract around 120 former young offenders into their orbit.[713]

Marc Sageman's study of 172 self-proclaimed jihadists found that 80% were "cultural outcasts living at the margins of society" as unassimilated first- or second-generation immigrants in majority non-Muslim countries.[714] Sageman also found that in a slightly smaller sample of 165 *al-Qaeda* biographies, 70% of the volunteers joined the organization in a country they had not grown up in, another 8% were second-generation immigrants and in this sense also somewhat removed from their extended family and cultural roots.[715] Scott Atran, citing research by both Robert Leiken and Marc Sageman, noted that approximately 80% of identified Islamic terrorists lived "in diaspora communities" and operated within social networks consisting of 70% friends and 20% family.[716] He characterized radicalized Muslim youths as being "culturally uprooted

---

[711] *The Urban Guerrilla Is History*, The Final Communiqué From The Red Army Faction, 1 March 1998 at http://germanguerilla.com/1998/03/01/the-urban-guerrilla-is-history/.

[712] Stefan Aust, *Baader-Meinhof: The Inside Story of the RAF* (Oxford University Press; 2009), p. 46.

[713] ibid., p. 50.

[714] Marc Sageman, *Understanding Terror Networks* (University of Pennsylvania Press; 2004), p. 92.

[715] Scott Atran, The Moral Logic and Growth of Suicide Terrorism, *The Washington Quarterly*, Vol. 29, No. 2 (2006), p. 135.

[716] ibid.

and politically restless".[717] A German federal prosecutor, Kay Nehm, observed of the Hamburg cell who formed the core of the 9/11 operation: "All the members of this cell shared the same religious convictions, an Islamic lifestyle, a feeling of being out of place in unfamiliar cultural surroundings that they weren't used to."[718] An Italian prosecutor, Stefano Dambruoso, who had reviewed weeks and weeks of clandestinely recorded conversations of an *al-Qaeda* cell active in Milan, reported: "These are people with a lot of problems. Adapting to this country is devastating to them. In radical religious activity they found rules, a structure. It's not just religious, it's psychological and personal."[719] Adapting to a foreign culture while also retaining important elements of one's original identity is a difficult journey for anyone to make, some navigate it successfully, others do not. The challenge of fitting in and building a new life is greatly exacerbated if the host community is unwelcoming.

Evidence of entrenched discrimination faced by many Muslim communities in the West, undoubtedly made worse by the tensions created by Islamist terrorist attacks on Western targets, abounds. In 2009, the European Minorities and Discrimination Survey conducted by the European Agency for Fundamental Rights found one in three Muslim respondents reported experiencing discrimination, with the highest reported rates among the 16–25 age group.[720] In May 2013, Londoners were horrified by the brutal murder of off-duty soldier Lee Rigby by *al-Qaeda* sympathizers Michael Adebolajo and Michael Adebowale, it is unlikely coincidental that London's Metropolitan Police Service reported a 58% increase in hate crimes against the local Muslim community between 2013 and 2015.[721] Although Muslims only make up 7% of the French population, they account

---

[717] ibid., p. 128.

[718] Marc Sageman, *Understanding Terror Networks* (University of Pennsylvania Press; 2004), p. 108.

[719] ibid.

[720] Jessica Stern, Radicalization to Extremism and Mobilization to Violence: What Have We Learned and What Can We Do about It? *The ANNALS of the American Academy of Political and Social Science*, Vol. 668, No. 1, November 2016, p. 110.

[721] http://www.parliament.uk/business/committees/committees-a-z/commons-select/women-and-equalities-committee/news-parliament-2015/employment-opportunities-for-muslims-evidence-15-16/. Viewed 4 June 2017.

for 70% of the prison population and a Muslim job applicant is two and a half times less likely to be offered a job interview than a similarly qualified Christian applicant.[722] In Belgium, 59% of Turkish and 56% of Moroccan immigrants live below the poverty line — as compared to just 10% of native-born Belgians.[723] In the United Kingdom, Muslims face some of the lowest employment rates and lowest rates of pay of any group.[724] There is not simply a perception of being excluded from full and active membership of the community, for many Muslims living in the West, it is a tangible reality. The Belgian academic and government insider Rik Coolsaet has described the environment in which young Belgian Muslims have grown up as a "no future subculture", further observing: "Frequently, they express feelings of exclusion and absence of belonging, as if they didn't have a stake in society ... The succession of such estrangements result at a certain age in anger."[725] In 2014 Kamal Habib, one of the co-founders of the Egyptian militant group *Tanzim al-Jihad*, offered his own perspective on the volunteers traveling from across the world to fight for ISIL in Syria and Iraq: "They think the Islamic State will give them the respect they don't get as nationals of their own countries. It gives them structure and a place where they can search for meaning."[726]

Social exclusion is frequently identified as a driver of terrorism by Islamist militants, or by other members of the communities from which they come. Mohamed Merah, the *al-Qaeda*-inspired

---

[722] Peter Bergen, *United States of Jihad: Investigating America's Homegrown Terrorists* (Crown; 2016), pp. 13–14.

[723] Jessica Stern, Radicalization to Extremism and Mobilization to Violence: What Have We Learned and What Can We Do about It? *The ANNALS of the American Academy of Political and Social Science*, Vol. 668, No.1, November 2016, p. 110.

[724] http://www.parliament.uk/business/committees/committees-a-z/commons-select/women-and-equalities-committee/news-parliament-2015/employment-opportunities-for-muslims-evidence-15-16/. Viewed 4 June 2017.

[725] Rik Coolsaet, *Facing the Fourth Foreign Fighter Wave: What Drives Europeans to Syria, and to Islamic State? Insights from the Belgian Case*, Egmont-Royal Institute for International Relations (March 2016), p. 24.

[726] Erin Cunningham, In stark transformation, Egyptian rights activist dies fighting for the Islamic State, *The Washington Post*, 5 November 2014.

gunman who murdered seven people in the French cities of Toulouse and Montauban in 2012, had his earlier offer of service rejected by his adopted country. An old school friend, Faoud, told the *New York Times*: "Our passports may say that we are French, but we don't feel French because we are never accepted here. No one can excuse what he did, but he is a product of French society, of the feeling that he had no hope, and nothing to lose. It was not *al-Qaeda* that created Mohamed Merah, it was France."[727] The French political scientist Gilles Kepel has particularly highlighted the alienating impact of the French Law on Secularity and Conspicuous Religious Symbols in Schools introduced in March 2004, which banned the wearing of hijabs in state-funded schools, as well as the summer of inner-city riots the following year, as provoking "the great shift" in French Islam.[728] The Syrian-Spanish *al-Qaeda*-affiliated theorist and propagandist Abu Mus'ab al-Suri was one of the first *jihadists* to recognize the opportunity this "poorly integrated" younger generation of European Muslims represented in his online manifesto, *The Call to Global Islamic Resistance*, which first appeared in December 2004, but it fell to ISIL to really exploit its potential.[729]

In the Anglophone world, the aunt of British-born *al-Qaeda* shoe bomber Richard Reid also attributed his radicalization to a sense of alienation: "He was so lonely, his life so empty ... he found solace with his Muslim brothers."[730] In his youth, Reid had been abandoned by his father, placed in foster care, convicted of multiple petty crimes, and incarcerated in two different prisons. One former British jihadist told the brother of murdered ISIL hostage David Haines that his journey into terrorism started when someone called him "a sand nigger and a raghead" and the mosque he went

---

[727] Dan Bilefsky, Toulouse Killer's Path to Radicalism a Bitter Puzzle, *New York Times*, 29 March 2012.

[728] Gilles Kepel, *Terror in France: The Rise of Jihad in the West* (Princeton University Press; 2017), p. 20.

[729] ibid., p. 10.

[730] Mitchell Silber, *The Al-Qaeda Factor: Plots Against the West* (University of Pennsylvania Press; 2012), p. 29.

to was attacked by local racists.[731] Commenting on the identification of an ISIL militant known as Jihadi John as Londoner
Mohammed Emwazi, Asim Qureshi, Research Director of the contentious British charity organization Cage (formerly Cage Prisoners)
pointedly asked reporters: "When are we going to finally learn that
when we treat people as if they're outsiders they are going to feel
like outsiders and they will look for belonging elsewhere?"[732]
Kuwaiti-born Mohammad Youssuf Abdulazeez, a lone gunman who
killed five US Marines in Chattanooga, Tennessee, during a shooting rampage in July 2015 summed up the experience of many
young male Muslims living in the United States when he wrote in
his high school yearbook: "My name causes national security alerts.
What does yours do?"[733] A Western *al-Qaeda* volunteer interviewed
by Col. John Venhaus for the United States Institute of Peace
explained that he had joined the group because he felt completely
ignored by his community: "I felt like I could not be heard.
No one heard me when I spoke, so I started to shout. No one
heard me shout, so I started to throw things. Still no one listened,
so I went to a place where my voice could not be ignored. They
will hear me now."[734]

Social exclusion can also operate at the international level. The
internationalization of Palestinian nationalist terrorism in the 1970s
was driven in large part by a sense that the world was ignoring the
plight of a community languishing marginalized and forgotten in
refugee camps scattered around the fringes of their former homeland. PFLP founder George Habash explained to the Italian
journalist Oriana Fallaci the logic behind his group's decision to
target international air travel: "The world has been using us and has

---

[731] Colin Freeman, I'm a peace ambassador for my murdered brother, *The Sunday Times*, 28
August 2016.
[732] Heather Saul, Jihadi John: Mohammed Emwazi was "extremely kind, gentle, beautiful
young man', says Cage director, *The Independent*, 26 February 2015. Emwazi played a public
role in the decapitation of five Western hostages held by the group in 2014.
[733] http://www.bbc.com/news/world-us-canada-33559853.
[734] Col. John Venhaus, *Why Youth Join Al-Qaeda*, United States Institute of Peace: Special Report
No. 236 (May 2010), p. 12.

forgotten us. It is time they realized we exist."[735] At the beginning of 1972, the Palestinian Liberation Organization wrote to the International Olympic Committee (IOC) seeking to field a Palestinian team at the 1972 Munich Olympics.[736] The IOC ignored the letter, setting in motion the chain of events that would lead to the Palestinian group Black September holding hostage members of the Israeli Olympic team in the middle of the competition, and ultimately to the deaths of eleven Israeli athletes and five members of Black September. In a statement released by Black September entitled *The Will of the Munich Guerrillas*, the hostage-takers sought to justify their actions in the following terms: "We apologise to the youth of the world who are taking part in the Olympiad, if our operation would hurt their feelings. But we urge them to remember that there is a people who have been occupied and their honor trampled for the past 24 years, a people who are suffering and in pain. There is no harm then if the youth of the world understand their tragedy for a few hours. There is a people who have been suffering for years under the yoke of an enemy who has his place at this tournament. So, let the games stop for a few hours."[737] Abu Iyad, the PLO's Chief of Intelligence who had participated in the planning of the attack, subsequently observed with some satisfaction that the Munich operation had ensured that "world opinion was forced to take note of the Palestinian drama."[738]

A number of commentators and researchers have identified modernization, or perhaps more accurately a fear of modernization, as a driver of political violence and by extension terrorism. Ted Gurr acknowledged the impact that dramatic socioeconomic change brought on by modernization has had on traditional communities, and tied modernization to his theory of relative deprivation by arguing that violence results from the widening gap between

---

[735] Simon Reeve, *One Day in September: The Full Story of the 1972 Munich Olympics Massacre and the Israeli Revenge Operation "Wrath of God"* (Arcade Publishing; 2000), p. 31.

[736] ibid., p. 39.

[737] Will of the Munich Guerrillas, *Palestine News Agency (WAFA)*, 11 September 1972.

[738] Daniel Byman, *A High Price: The Triumphs and Failures of Israeli Counterterrorism* (Oxford University Press 2011), p. 47.

expectations and social realities.[739] Samuel Huntington noted in his classic work *Political Order in Changing Societies* that modernization involves "a fundamental shift in values, attitudes, and expectations" and tends to produce, as an inevitable byproduct experienced by those excluded from the benefits accompanying this transformation, "alienation and *anomie*, normlessness generated by the conflict of old and new values".[740] British sociologist Anthony Giddens has argued that in modern societies, personal identity is more in flux than in traditional societies where identity is often assigned to an individual from outside rather than generated from within.[741] Albert Bandura takes a similar view: "Under conditions of rapid social and technological change, many parental interests, attitudes, and role behaviors that were serviceable at an earlier period may have little functional value for members of the younger generation. New complex patterns of behavior must therefore be learned from other social agents."[742] Audrey Kurth Cronin has suggested that "globalization, in forms including Westernization, secularization, democratization, consumerism, and the growth of market capitalism, represents an onslaught to less privileged people in conservative cultures repelled by the fundamental changes that these forces are bringing — or angered by the distortions and uneven distributions of benefits that result."[743] Jessica Stern has cited "modernity and globalization" as contributing to terrorism.[744] Mark Juergensmeyer has detected "an anti-modern agenda" in religious terrorist groups and has written that modernization creates the "perception

---

[739] Ted Gurr, Economic Factors, in Louise Richardson (ed.), *The Roots of Terrorism* (Routledge; 2006), p. 85.

[740] Samuel Huntington, *Political Order in Changing Societies* (Yale University Press; 1969), p. 32 and p. 37.

[741] Anthony Giddens, *Runaway World: How Globalization is Reshaping Our Lives* (Routledge; 2000), pp. 59–67.

[742] Albert Bandura, Social-Learning Theory of Identification Processes, in David Goslin (ed.), *Handbook of Socialization Theory and Research* (Rand McNally & Co.; 1969), p. 248.

[743] Audrey Kurth Cronin, Behind the Curve: Globalization and International Terrorism, *International Security*, Vol. 27, No. 3 (Winter 2002–2003), p. 45.

[744] Jessica Stern, *Terror in the Name of God: Why Religious Militants Kill* (HarperCollins; 2003), p. 62.

that their communities are already under attack — are being violated — and that their acts are therefore simply responses to the violence they have experienced."[745] And perhaps one of the most thoughtful explorations of this topic has been undertaken by the RAND Corporation researcher Michael Mazarr in *Unmodern Men in the Modern World.*

Mazarr conceptualizes modernization as encapsulating economic development, industrialization, a scientific outlook, diversity, moral relativism, and a secular worldview hostile to more spiritual outlooks. He acknowledges that when modernization "works", producing consistent improvements in standards of living, reliable institutions, and effective leaders, "it can succeed in defraying the psychological costs of its own progress."[746] However, he warns that modernization can also call into question all those factors that top lists of essential human needs such as security, identity, dignity, and belonging when its potentially more negative side effects result in social decline, institutional failure, and economic crisis.[747] In such circumstances, Mazarr suggests that the alienation of modern life and its related material concerns breathe life into "latent psychological distress".[748] He therefore contends that far from terrorism representing an existential threat, we have got it the wrong way round. It is actually the Western way of life that represents an existential threat to groups who feel threatened or excluded from the modern world with its liberal secular values, and terrorism can, in certain circumstances, be considered a response to that existential crisis. Mazarr writes that "compared to the warm communal embrace of the pre-modern" for many "modernity is one long saga of exile" often disconcertingly experienced in their own homeland.[749] He concludes that one might measure a society's vulnerability to the

---

[745] Mark Juergensmeyer, *Terror in the Mind of God: The Global Rise of Religious Violence* (University of California Press; 2003), pp. 12 and 230.

[746] Michael Mazarr, *Unmodern Men in the Modern World: Radical Islam, Terrorism and the War on Modernity* (Cambridge University Press; 2007), p. 15.

[747] ibid., pp. 16–18.

[748] ibid., pp. 10–11.

[749] ibid., pp. 65 and 193.

"anti-modern virus" by the degree to which modernity has fulfilled its promise in bringing wealth, security, and opportunity to the people of that society and the degree to which those people have fully been able to realize their true potential in return.[750]

Echoes of Mazarr's theory of existential dread can be found in the rejectionist literature that has inspired groups like *Hezbollah*, the Society of the Muslim Brothers, *al-Qaeda*, and ISIL. The early twentieth century Lebanese Islamist reformer Rashid Rida called for Islam to be "purged of impurities and Western influences".[751] In his seminal work *Milestones*, Sayyid Qutb dismissed the Western way of life as greedy, shallow and empty: "Look at this capitalism with its monopolies, its usury, at this individual freedom, devoid of human sympathy ... at this materialistic attitude which deadens the spirit."[752] He decried the Western world as being steeped in *jahiliyya* (religious ignorance or paganism), which he characterized as a rebellion against the sovereignty of God on earth, and he warned his readers that "humanity is standing today at the brink of an abyss ... because humanity is bankrupt in the realm of 'values', those values which foster true human progress and development. This is abundantly clear to the Western world, for the West can no longer provide the values necessary for [the flourishing of] humanity."[753] The Iranian writer Jalal Al-e-Ahmad coined the term *gharbzadegi*, most commonly translated as "westoxification", in the early 1960s to describe what he perceived as the predatory and corrosive expansion of Western cultural norms into Middle Eastern societies: "We're like a nation alienated from itself, in our clothing and our homes, our food and our literature, our publications and, most dangerously of all, our education."[754] His message was enthusiastically picked up by Ayatollah Khomeini who denounced "the poisonous culture of imperialism" in

---

[750] ibid., p. 98.

[751] ibid., p. 168.

[752] ibid., p. 49.

[753] ibid., pp. 7 and 173.

[754] Anna Geifman, *Death Orders: The Vanguard of Modern Terrorism in Revolutionary Russia* (Praeger Security International; 2010), p. 23 and Michael Mazarr, *Unmodern Men in the Modern World: Radical Islam, Terrorism and the War on Modernity* (Cambridge University Press; 2007), p. 7.

his own revolutionary writings.[755] In January 2004, Osama bin Laden dismissed the Iraqi interim constitution introduced under the auspices of the US-led occupation authorities, in terms both Qutb and Rida would have applauded, as "man-made and pagan".[756]

Anti-modernism is not an exclusive characteristic of religious terrorism. Mazarr argues that there is a persistent anti-modern strain to the nineteenth century Russian populist movement and to the socialist revolutionaries who succeeded it. He attributes this to urbanization — a feature of modernity that he regards as especially destabilizing.[757] In this, he receives support from the historian Anna Greifman who suggests that the social reordering resulting from the emancipation of the Russian serfs in 1861 provoked an anxiety-provoking shift from communal to individualistic thinking as ordinary Russians began for the first time to think of themselves in terms of "I" not "we".[758] She argues that this dislocation could provoke a sense of alienation in those whose lives did not improve, especially for those who had left the countryside to find work in the cities and had thus been separated from traditional communal support structures. Greifman suggests that for those alienated members of the urban population, the emerging populist political movements came to replace these traditional rural structures affording some measure of tangible and psychological support. In Russia the urban population grew from 9 million in the mid-nineteenth century to around 25 million in 1913, with many Russian cities quadrupling or quintupling in size.[759] The capital, St. Petersburg, itself doubled in size between 1890 and 1910, and was home to a disproportionately large number of single, unmarried residents.[760]

---

[755] Ruhollah Khomeini, *Message to the Pilgrims*, in *Islam and Revolution: Writings and Declarations of Imam Khomeini* (Mizan Press; 1981), p. 195.

[756] Michael Mazarr, *Unmodern Men in the Modern World: Radical Islam, Terrorism and the War on Modernity* (Cambridge University Press; 2007), p. 170.

[757] ibid., p. 40.

[758] Anna Geifman, *Death Orders: The Vanguard of Modern Terrorism in Revolutionary Russia* (Praeger Security International; 2010), p. 16.

[759] ibid., p. 17.

[760] ibid.

However, the secular exemplar of the anti-modern terrorist must surely be the Unabomber, Ted Kaczynski. A brilliant mathematical prodigy who was accepted into Harvard at age sixteen, completed a PhD at the University of Michigan and secured an assistant professorship at the University of California, Berkeley, Kaczynski killed three people and injured twenty-three others in a long-running bombing campaign that lasted from 1978 to 1995, and which targeted individuals associated with modern technology, such as the computing and airline industries, and, rather less obviously, the public relations profession. In April 1995, Kaczynski wrote anonymously to *The New York Times* offering to end his bombing campaign if the newspaper would undertake to publish a 35,000-word manifesto he had drafted entitled *Industrial Society and its Future*. On advice from the Federal Bureau of Investigation, which had made little headway in its investigation of the Unabomber, the *Times* published his submission in its entirety, hoping it might lead to a break in the case. It did, Kaczynski's brother contacted the FBI and turned him in. The Unabomber's manifesto was uncompromisingly anti-modern in tone and content, opening with the declaration: "The Industrial Revolution and its consequences have been a disaster for the human race... [T]hey have destabilized society, have made life unfulfilling, have subjected human beings to indignities, have led to widespread psychological suffering (in the Third World to physical suffering as well) and have inflicted severe damage on the natural world. The continued development of technology will worsen the situation."[761] For Kaczynski, a back-to-nature survivalist who had abandoned academia in 1969 to live a self-sufficient life off-the-grid in rural Montana, the struggle against the modern world was deeply personal. In a prison interview, he explained that he had been driven to violence after a road was built through a remote natural beauty spot: "That summer there were too many people around my cabin so I decided I needed some peace. I went back

---

[761] Ted Kaczynski, *Industrial Society and its Future* (1995) at http://editions-hache.com/essais/pdf/kaczynski2.pdf.

to the plateau and when I got there I found they had put a road right through the middle of it... You just can't imagine how upset I was. It was from that point on I decided that, rather than trying to acquire further wilderness skills, I would work on getting back at the system. Revenge."[762]

Social psychology experiments have successfully tested the proposition that individuals who are excluded from participation in a simple group activity are likely to react aggressively towards that group.[763] The American psychologist Kipling Williams has conducted considerable research into the impact that ostracism can have on the individuals who experience it. He observes that social exclusion threatens four fundamental human needs — to belong; to maintain a healthy degree of self-esteem; to exert some personal control over one's environment; and to be recognized as existing in a meaningful way — and reports that most people tend to react to ostracism in much the same instinctive four ways that they do to any other potential threat: Flee, tend-and-befriend, freeze, or fight.[764] Furthermore, individuals who have been conditioned to expect rejection often exhibit "rejection sensitivity", and research based on personal relationships indicates that individuals who score highly on a rejection sensitivity index have a tendency to react with hostility towards those they fear may reject them.[765] Williams concludes that there is ample evidence that ostracism, social exclusion, and rejection are causally linked to a reduction in prosocial behaviors, and an increase in antisocial behavior directed at those who may

---

[762] Interview with Ted Kaczynski, Administrative Maximum Facility Prison, Florence, Colorado, USA, *Earth First Journal*, June 1999 at https://web.archive.org/web/20090318135703/ http://www.insurgentdesire.org.uk/tedk.htm. Viewed 4 June 2017.

[763] L. Rowell Huesmann and Graham Huesmann, No: Poverty and Exclusion are not the Root Causes of terrorism, in Richard Jackson and Samuel Sinclair (eds.), *Contemporary Debates on Terrorism* (Routledge; 2012), p. 116 and Kipling Williams, Ostracism, *Annual Review of Psychology*, Vol. 58 (2007), pp. 425–452.

[764] Kipling Williams, Ostracism, *Annual Review of Psychology*, Vol. 58 (2007), pp. 436 and 442–443.

[765] See Geraldine Downey, Scott Feldman and Ozlem Ayduk, Rejection Sensitivity and Male Violence in Romantic Relationships, *Personal Relationships*, Vol. 7 (2000).

or may not have been the source of exclusion.[766] In such a context, a display of aggression amounts to an attempt to reassert control.

None of this would have come as a surprise to the early twentieth century German philosopher Max Scheler, who used the term *ressentiment* (resentment) to describe the effect when emotions such as malice, envy, and a desire for revenge have to be suppressed because an individual feels constrained through weakness or fear from acting upon them.[767] Scheler contended that *ressentiment* gave rise to a particularly powerful brand of hatred, a "self-poisoning" that slowly builds up over time before ultimately erupting in violence. Manfred Frings has applied Scheler's theory of *ressentiment* to the psychopathology of terrorism suggesting that, as marginalized members of society, terrorists experience an "existential envy" of the social groups who possess power, success, and the social and political station denied to them.[768] Frings' summation of *ressentiment* as "incurable impotency coupled with an incurable lack of attainability" is as good a description of the psychological impact of social exclusion as one is likely to find.[769] Social psychology suggests at least some of those individuals placed in this invidious positon will choose to fight.

## Political opportunity

Both relative deprivation and social exclusion also relate to another important social science concept that is frequently referenced in the context of revolutionary action and violent political protest: political opportunity. The American sociologist Charles Tilly posited that the principal driver behind political revolutions, violent protest, and even acts of terror, was the degree to which the political system in

---

[766] Kipling Williams, Ostracism, *Annual Review of Psychology*, Vol. 58 (2007), p. 441.

[767] Michael Mazarr, *Unmodern Men in the Modern World: Radical Islam, Terrorism and the War on Modernity* (Cambridge University Press; 2007), pp. 127–128.

[768] Manfred Frings, Max Scheler and the Psychopathology of the Terrorist, *Modern Age*, Vol. 47, No. 3 (Summer 2005), p. 212.

[769] Michael Mazarr, *Unmodern Men in the Modern World: Radical Islam, Terrorism and the War on Modernity* (Cambridge University Press; 2007), p. 128.

which they occur enables independent organization and collective action.[770] Successful political action must overcome several hurdles, some challenges imposed from without, such as coercive state action, and some from within the group. Employing a similar explanatory framework to that used by the economist Gary Becker to explain criminal activity, Tilly noted that there are potential risks or costs associated with taking action — loss of income, threat of arrest — and there are potential costs associated with not taking action — such as ostracism. Individuals will weigh these costs against the potential gains they might reasonably expect to derive from a given course of action. In theory, armed with this insight, and fortified by the belief that individuals will make such choices in a rational manner, it becomes possible to make predictions about what type of society is more likely to be vulnerable to terrorism and who within that society is more likely to gravitate towards terrorism as a tool with which to address social or political grievances. Some of these predictions perform better against the historical record than others.

Tilly suggested that a population in revolt has to chose from a "repertoire of contention" that it is already familiar with — a given population can only choose from a limited set of options that are known to it and are culturally sanctioned by the society from which it comes.[771] Tilly's theory received significant empirical support from Douglas Hibbs' study of instances of political violence between 1948 and 1967, which found that one of the best predicators of such violence was whether there had been previous outbreaks of political violence within a given society.[772] Aristide Zolberg further refined Tilly's concept by arguing that there are "moment of madness" in which new approaches are forged but that these are few and far between. Seeking to meld these two insights, Sidney Tarrow posited that such moments of madness were actually situated in larger cycles of mobilization in which new forms of protest evolve over time

---

[770] Charles Tilly, *From Mobilization to Revolution* (Addison-Wesley; 1978).

[771] ibid., p. 151.

[772] Douglas Hibbs, *Mass Political Violence* (Wiley; 1973).

or are introduced by external actors.[773] Taking the example of the *anni di piombo* when the *Brigate Rosse* was active in Italy, Tarrow argued that cycles of protest create an experimental context, a creative hothouse environment, in which new forms of collective action can develop, concluding: "Few people dare to break the crust of convention. When they do so during moments of madness, they create the opportunities and provide the models for others."[774] The implication of Tarrow's thesis is that certain points in the cycle of protest may be more conducive to unconventional action than others. *Sinn Féin* leader Gerry Adams conceded as much, noting in *The Politics of Irish Freedom* that for the Catholic population of Northern Ireland in the late 1960s, "Bob Dylan, the Beatles and the Rolling Stones, long hair and beads, the 'alternative society', music and fashion were all markers put down by a new generation against the complacencies of the previous one, and one of the most important messages to come across was that one *could* change the world."[775] When the spirit of change is in the air, great things seem possible, and we often see terrorist groups seeking to tap into this spirit, as this statement issued by ISIL spokesman Abu Muhammad al-Adnani in June 2014 illustrates: "The time has come for those generations that were drowning in oceans of disgrace, being nursed on the milk of humiliation, and being ruled by the vilest of all people ... to rise ... The sun of *jihad* has risen. The glad tidings of good are shining. Triumph looms on the horizon. The signs of victory have appeared."[776]

Another prominent American sociologist, Anthony Oberschall, notes there are essentially four dimensions of collective action —

---

[773] Aristide Zolberg, Moments of Madness, *Politics and Society*, Vol. 2 (Winter 1972), p. 196 and Sidney Tarrow, Cycles of Collective Action: Between Moments of Madness and the Repertoire of Contention, *Social Science History*, Vol. 17, No. 2 (Summer 1993), pp. 284–287.

[774] Sidney Tarrow, Cycles of Collective Action: Between Moments of Madness and the Repertoire of Contention, *Social Science History*, Vol. 17, No. 2 (Summer 1993), p. 302.

[775] Gerry Adams, *The Politics of Irish Freedom* (Brandon Books; 1987), p. 10.

[776] Jessica Stern, Radicalization to Extremism and Mobilization to Violence: What Have We Learned and What Can We Do about It? *The ANNALS of the American Academy of Political and Social Science*, Vol. 668, No. 1, November 2016, p. 107. Translation at https://pietervanostaeyen.com/2014/06/29/the-islamic-state-restores-the-caliphate/.

discontent, ideology-feeding grievances, a capacity to organize, and political opportunity — and where all four exist, collective action is possible.[777] Martha Crenshaw has further observed political space may open up because of both internal and external factors.[778] Domestically, this might involve some form of crisis of legitimacy for the government, such as an economic collapse, a leadership challenge, or a demonstrable lack of competence or capacity.[779] A terrorist group may also be driven to act because they perceive a sudden opportunity or moment of weakness in an external threat — the old saw "England's danger is Ireland's opportunity" illustrates precisely why Irish nationalists felt emboldened to launch an uprising in the middle of the World War I and to forge an alliance with Nazi Germany during World War II. A similar logic also drove the Stern Gang, and later LEHI, to step up its activities against the British Mandate authorities in Palestine during the conflict.[780] Social movement theory places great emphasis on an organizing group's belief in the likelihood of success. Robert Taber labeled this the will to revolt, which he defined as "a newly awaked consciousness, not of 'causes' but of potentiality".[781] The *Rote Armee Fraktion* more or less adopted the slogan "the primacy of the praxis" as a mantra, proclaiming in one document: "Whether it is right to organize armed resistance now depends on whether it is possible."[782]

The political opportunity school also has useful insights to contribute at the micro level. Doug McAdam reported in an article entitled *Recruitment to High-Risk Activism* that he had found that a history of prior social and political activism appeared to be related

---

[777] Anthony Oberschall, Explaining Terrorism: The Contribution of Collective Action Theory, *Sociological Theory*, Vol. 22, No. 1 (March 2004), p. 27.

[778] Martha Crenshaw, The Causes of Terrorism, *Comparative Politics*, Vol. 13, No. 4 (1981), p. 388.

[779] ibid., pp. 382–383.

[780] Brendan O'Leary and John McGarry, *The Politics of Antagonism* (Athlone Press; 1993), p. 65, and Bruce Hoffman, *Anonymous Soldiers: The Struggle for Israel, 1917–1947* (Knopf; 2015), p. 105.

[781] Robert Taber, *The War of the Flea* (The Citadel Press; 1970), pp. 18–19.

[782] Stefan Aust, *Baader-Meinhof: The Inside Story of the RAF* (Oxford University Press; 2009), p. 92.

to a willingness to participate in high risk/cost actions.[783] Oberschall also observed that "the surest, quickest, low-cost way of mobilizing a social, political, or religious movement is to use an already existing infrastructure and to convert it to new uses."[784] Indeed, we find that in an effort to exploit sympathetic social networks from which to draw on for potential recruits, terrorist organizations often seek to infiltrate existing institutions or create new institutions of their own to attract like-minded individuals. For the RAF, sympathetic groups like *Rote Hilfe* (Red Aid) and *Gefangenenräte* (Prisoners' Councils) who sought to provide moral and material support to incarcerated militants became a gateway for potential recruits.[785] Volker Speitel had been volunteering for *Rote Hilfe* at the time of Holger Meins' death on hunger strike and it was this event, coupled with the treatment of the other RAF prisoners, that convinced him to take the next step: "For us [Volker and his wife, Angelika] his death was a key experience." He felt guilty that he had been unable to prevent Meins' death through his peaceful activism.[786] Donatella Della Porta's research also led her to conclude that in the Italian case prior participation in other political organizations was a key indicator of an individual's openness to an approach from more militant activists: "It is still striking in how many cases terrorists had been committed to legal political activity before joining the underground groups. Recruitment to terrorism involved 'political' people, that is people who already had a political identity."[787] Many of the individuals who joined Italian terrorist groups had previously joined public protest groups involved in street clashes with the police or had helped marshal demonstrations for groups like the

---

[783] Doug McAdam, Recruitment to High-risk Activism: The Case of Freedom Summer, *American Journal of Sociology*, Vol. 92, No. 1 (1986), p. 82.

[784] Anthony Oberschall, Explaining Terrorism: The Contribution of Collective Action Theory, *Sociological Theory*, Vol. 22, No. 1 (March 2004), p. 33.

[785] Klaus Wasmund, The Political Socialization of West German Terrorists, in Peter Merkl (ed.), *Political Violence and Terror: Motifs and Motivations* (University of California Press; 1986), p. 204.

[786] ibid., pp. 210–211.

[787] Donatella Della Porta, Recruitment Processes in Clandestine Political Organizations: Italian Left-Wing Terrorism, *International Social Movement Research*, Vol. 1 (1988), p. 161.

*Brigate Comuniste.*[788] However, it is also important to note Della Porta's aside that the proportion of late 1960s leftist activists who chose to escalate their opposition to the state to include terrorism was still quite small.[789]

Robert Taber wrote in *The War of the Flea* that "until people believe that a government can be overthrown ... the attempt will not be made" and it is for this reason that terrorist organizations often take great pains to emphasize the potency of the tactics and weapons at their disposal, as well as the vulnerability of the states they oppose, in their messaging.[790] The declaration made by Carlos Marighella's *Ação Libertadora Nacional* in September 1969 is typical of the genre: "We act where the enemy expects it least and we disappear immediately, weakening the dictatorship, terrorizing the exploiters and bringing hopes of victory to the oppressed."[791] The ALN participated in the kidnapping of the US Ambassador Charles Burke Elbirck "to demonstrate that it is possible to triumph over the dictatorship and exploitation if we are properly armed and organized".[792] Osama bin Laden referenced events such as the Soviet Union's defeat in Afghanistan and the United States' withdrawal from Somalia and Beirut in a 1998 interview with ABC News to dismiss the "myth of superpowers" and make the point that American soldiers were "paper tigers" who would "run away in defeat" when faced with the determination and commitment of God's holy warriors.[793] And the *ne plus ultra* of this type of narrative is probably the May 2000 speech by the Secretary General of *Hezbollah*, Hassan Nasrallah, in which he expounded his so-called spider web theory, a metaphor derived from *Sura* 29:41 of the *Koran*, which warns "the frailest of all houses is the

---

[788] ibid., p. 163.

[789] ibid., p. 162.

[790] Robert Taber, *The War of the Flea: How Guerrilla Fighters Could Win the World* (Citadel Press; 1970), p. 135.

[791] Carlos Marighela, *For the Liberation of Brazil* (The Pelican Latin American Library; 1974), p. 25.

[792] ibid.

[793] Usama bin laden: "American Soldiers are Paper Tigers", *Middle East Quarterly*, Vol. 5, No. 4 (December 1998), pp. 73–79. See http://www.meforum.org/435/usama-bin-ladin-american-soldiers-are-paper-tigers. Viewed 15 June 2017.

spider's house."[794] Addressing Palestinian supporters of *Hamas* directly, Nasrallah assured them: "We offer this noble Lebanese model to our people in Palestine. To free your land, you don't need tanks, a strategic balance, rockets, and cannons; you need to follow the way of the past self-sacrifice martyrs who disrupted and horrified the coercive Zionist entity ... The choice is yours, and the model lies right in front of your eyes ... I tell you: Israel, which owns nuclear weapons and the strongest war aircraft in the region, is feebler than a spider's web — I swear to God."[795]

In a similar vein, the Stanford sociologist Mark Granovetter advanced a theory, derived from studying the progressive escalation of rioting, that collective action is a social process in which different individuals have different thresholds for becoming involved.[796] Granovetter argued that riots start when individuals with a very low threshold for violent behavior decide to act out, and then other individuals in the proximity with slightly higher thresholds for violent action are emboldened to join in, because someone else has assumed the risk of going first. Further individuals liberated by a growing sense of safety in numbers cross their personal thresholds for action and join in too. In essence, Granovetter's theory suggested that acts of violence not only had a demonstration effect — whereby awareness of the act encourages emulation — but that the fact that someone else had crossed the threshold into violent action first made it easier for subsequent adopters to take a similar step.[797]

In terrorist literature, Granovetter's theory chimes neatly with the enduring role accorded to a revolutionary vanguard by a wide range

---

[794] Arie Kruglanski, Michele Gelfand, Jocelyn Bélanger, Anna Sheveland, Malkanthi Hetiarachchi and Rohan Gunaratna, The Psychology of Radicalization and Deradicalization: How Significance Quest Impacts Violent Extremism, *Advances in Political Psychology*, Vol. 35, Suppl. 1 (2014), pp. 78. See also Sayyed Hassan Nasserallah, *Breaking the Spider's Web*, Bint Jbeil City, 26 May 2000 at http://breakingthespidersweb.blogspot.com/2011/05/nasrallahs-spider-web-speech.html.

[795] Sayyed Hassan Nasserallah, *Breaking the Spider's Web*, Bint Jbeil City, 26 May 2000 at http://breakingthespidersweb.blogspot.com/2011/05/nasrallahs-spider-web-speech.html.

[796] See Mark Granovetter, Threshold Models of Collective Behavior, *The American Journal of Sociology*, Vol. 83, No. 6 (May 1978).

[797] James Duesenberry, *Income, Saving and the Theory of Consumer Behavior* (Harvard University Press; 1949), p. 27.

of groups, especially, but not exclusively, those of a Marxist orientation. In a speech delivered at an event in Havana sponsored by the
*Partido Socialista Popular* in January 1959, Che Guevara reflected on
the true importance of Fidel Castro's victory: "The example of our
revolution and the lessons it implies for Latin America have destroyed
all the coffeehouse theories — we have demonstrated that a small
group of men supported by the people, and without fear of dying
were it necessary, can overcome a disciplined regular army and
defeat it. This is a fundamental lesson."[798] It was the same approach
adopted by Marxist terrorists in West Germany, as *Bewegung 2. Juni's*
Michael Baumann confirmed: "We always said, do an action anyone
can do. Always make the bomb so primitive that anyone else can
make one too. Even if we're not around anymore, there are always
people who can continue the style."[799] Likewise, the Black Panther
Party, as Sherwin Forte explained: "We referred to ourselves as The
Vanguard, and we were setting, by example, a new course that we
wanted the entire community to follow."[800] The Islamist ideologue
Sayyid Qutb also promoted the need for an Islamist vanguard in his
influential polemic *Milestones* and the concept was adopted as a central organizing principle by *al-Qaeda*, whose very name can be
variously translated as 'the base' or 'foundation'.[801]

The American economist Mancur Olson identified another
obstacle to successful collective action, which he labeled the "free
rider" problem: why would any rational individual opt to join a risky
enterprise when he or she can potentially share in the benefits of its
success without the risk of participating?[802] This conundrum is typically solved in the political arena by organizing and by the provision
of selective incentives to potential participants.[803] In the context of

---

[798] Jon Lee Anderson, *Che Guevara: A Revolutionary Life* (Grove Press; 1997), p. 393.

[799] Michael Baumann, *Terror or Love* (Pulp Press; 1977), p. 77.

[800] Stanley Nelson (Director), *Black Panthers: Vanguard of the Revolution*, PBS Documentary
(Firelight Films; 2016).

[801] John Calvert, *Sayyid Qutb and the Origins of Radical Islamism* (Columbia University Press; 2010),
p. 185 and Christopher Angevine, The Vanguard: The Genesis and Substance of Al-Qaeda's.
Conception of Itself and its Mission, *Yale Journal of International Affairs*, Vol. 3, No. 1 (Winter 2008).

[802] Mancur Olson, *The Logic of Collective Action: Public Goods and the Theory of Groups* (Harvard
University Press; 1965).

[803] See James Q. Wilson, *Political Organizations* (Princeton University Press; 1974).

political violence, it would be more accurate to say that both sides most often seek to solve this problem through coercion. Regimes seek to raise the costs of supporting terrorist activity by imposing harsher penalties, and perhaps even collective punishments such as house demolitions, internal closures, and curfews such as those imposed by the Israeli military in the Occupied Territories of the West Bank and Gaza since the end of the First *Intifada*, in the hope that potential terrorist constituents disown their would-be champions.[804] Terrorist groups similarly seek to raise the costs of passivity by intimidating or even eliminating moderate community voices.[805] This helps to explain why polarization — the elimination of the "grayzone" to borrow the formulation used by ISIL — is such an enduring and effective terrorist tactic. To build up their forces, terrorist organizations set out to drive free riders off the fence by confronting them with a simple choice wrapped up in an implicit threat: "You are either on one side or the other."[806]

A final insight from the political opportunity school is that democracies are likely to be more vulnerable to terrorism than authoritarian states because there is simply more political space within which to organize.[807] This is worth unpacking in a little more detail. In an influential 1993 article entitled *Terrorism and Democracy*, Alex Schmid enumerated six key vulnerabilities of democracies facing a terrorist threat: freedom of movement, freedom of association, an abundance of targets, legal constraints,

---

[804] Daniel Byman, *A High Price: The Triumphs and Failures of Israeli Counterterrorism* (Oxford University Press; 2011), pp. 84 and 158.

[805] Mark Lichbach, An Evaluation of "Does Economic Inequality Breed Political Conflict?" Studies, *World Politics*, Vol. 41. No. 4, (July 1989), p. 464.

[806] Muhsin Hassan, Understanding Drivers of Violent Extremism: The Case of Al-Shabaab and Somali Youth, *CTC Sentinel*, 23 August 2012, p. 18.

[807] Austin Turk, Social Dynamics of Terrorism, *Annals of the American Academy of Political and Social Science*, Vol. 463, No. 1 (September 1982); William Eubank and Leonard Weinberg, Does Democracy Encourage Terrorism? *Terrorism and Political Violence*, Vol. 6, No. 4 (1994). William Eubank and Leonard Weinberg, Terrorism and Democracy: What Recent Events Disclose? *Terrorism and Political Violence*, Vol. 10, No. 1 (1998). Doug McAdam, Sidney Tarrow and Charles Tilly, *Dynamics of Contention* (Cambridge; Cambridge University Press 2001), p. 14; and Claude Berrebi, The Economics of Terrorism and Counterterrorism: What Matters and Is Rational-Choice Theory Helpful? in Paul Davis and Kim Cragin (eds.), *Social Science for Counterterrorism: Putting the Pieces Together* (Rand; 2009), pp. 188–189.

pervasive media coverage, and amoral capitalism.[808] The Basque separatist group *Euskadi ta Askatasuna* is often cited in this context as an example of a terrorist movement founded and active during a period of fascist dictatorship that did not really flourish until the advent of democratic government. The frequency of ETA attacks spiked after the fall of Francisco Franco's regime following his death in 1975, the institution of democratic government in 1977, and the promulgation of a new constitution in 1978. ETA violence peaked in 1981 and remained comparatively high throughout the following decade, with frequent re-eruptions in the 1990s and 2000s.

There is little doubt that the style of asymmetrical warfare typically adopted by terrorist groups is well placed to exploit democratic vulnerabilities, and for such groups, as Osama bin Laden acknowledged, the comparative advantage this offers represents a promise of success: "America is a great power possessed of tremendous military might and a wide-ranging economy, but all this is built on an unstable foundation which can be targeted, with special attention to its obvious weak spots. If America is hit in one hundredth of these weak spots it will stumble, wither away and relinquish world leadership."[809] But for all the operational advantages liberal democracy would appear to offer the potential terrorist, terrorists targeting democratic regimes have been remarkably unsuccessful at achieving their stated goals.[810] Violent and enduring conflicts such as those in Northern Ireland, Colombia, Peru, and the

---

[808] Alex Schmid, Terrorism and Democracy, in Ronald Crelinsten and Alex Schmid (eds.), *Western Responses to Terrorism* (Frank Cass & Co.; 1993), pp. 18–19.

[809] Arie Kruglanski, Michele Gelfand, Jocelyn Bélanger, Anna Sheveland, Malkanthi Hetiarachchi and Rohan Gunaratna, The Psychology of Radicalization and Deradicalization: How Significance Quest Impacts Violent Extremism, *Advances in Political Psychology*, Vol. 35, Suppl. 1 (2014), p. 78.

[810] See Thomas Schelling, What Purposes Can "International Terrorism" Serve? in Raymond Frey and Christopher Morris (eds.), *Violence, Terrorism and Justice* (Cambridge University Press; 1991); Max Abrahms, Are Terrorists Really Rational? The Palestinian Example, *Orbis*, Vol. 48, No. 3 (Summer 2004); and Max Abrahms, Does Terrorism Really Work? Evolution in the Conventional Wisdom Since 9/11, *Defence and Peace Economics*, Vol. 22, No. 6 (2011).

Basque country, as well as the leftist Western European terrorism of the 1970s, have ultimately all been defused within a democratic context.

Democracies do have structural vulnerabilities, but, as terrorism researchers William Eubank and Leonard Weinberg have cautioned, it is important to remember that "to say that democracies provide settings within which it is relatively easy for terrorists to commit violent acts is not identical to asserting that there is something about democratic politics that promotes terrorist violence."[811] Furthermore, to focus on the vulnerabilities is to ignore the inherent strengths of well-functioning democratic systems — good governance, checks and balances, the rule of law, civil rights, and community engagement. Martha Crenshaw offered an important perspective when she observed that because terrorism was most likely to occur in circumstances in which discontent is neither generalized nor severe enough to provoke the majority of the populace to take action against the government, and because only a small minority is actually seeking radical change, terrorism could perhaps more accurately be considered "a sign of a stable society" rather than "a symptom of fragility and impending collapse".[812] The British political scientist Paul Wilkinson, whose work centered on the tension between freedom and security in liberal societies confronting terrorist threats, broadly concurred with Crenshaw's assessment, noting that the only serious threat to a liberal democracy is "the general withdrawal of popular support from government".[813] A trickle of alienated youths, malcontents, religious zealots, and utopian dreamers may have left their homes in the West to join ISIL, but the flood of refugees in the opposite direction tells the real story of whose values are ultimately more attractive and of where the balance of power really resides.

---

[811] William Eubank and Leonard Weinberg, Does Democracy Encourage Terrorism? *Terrorism and Political Violence*, Vol. 6, No. 4 (1994), p. 419.

[812] Martha Crenshaw, The Causes of Terrorism, *Comparative Politics*, Vol. 13, No. 4 (1981), p. 384.

[813] Paul Wilkinson, Terrorism and Democracy: The Liberal State Response (Routledge; 2011), p. 30.

## Summary

So where does all this leave the advocates of poverty reduction and other social programs? In the aftermath of the 9/11 attacks, a number of US academics and public policy advocates — such as Harvard's Joseph Nye, author of *Soft Power*, Laura Tyson at UC Berkeley, and Richard Sokolsky and Joseph McMillan at the National Defense University — proposed instituting major aid programs as a measure to counter terrorism in the Islamic world.[814] However, a study by Quan Li and Drew Schaub found no evidence to suggest that foreign direct investment or portfolio investment had any impact on reducing terrorism.[815] Jean-Paul Azam and Alexandra Delacroix even suggested evidence that the amount of foreign aid a country receives may increase the number of terrorist attacks that originate from that country — the causal mechanism being that terror groups see aid as an attempt to prop up a hated regime and so target the "far enemy" providing succor to their proximate opponents.[816] This, coupled with the fact that successive big data studies have found no evidence that poverty *per se* correlates with terrorism, has led researchers like Alan Krueger to conclude that "there are many reasons for improving education and reducing poverty around the world, but reducing terrorism is probably not one of them."[817]

And yet, it is impossible to dismiss the role played by economic and social disadvantage altogether. A more nuanced view of how such issues play out is required.[818] It is pretty clear from the

---

[814] Jitka Malečková, Impoverished Terrorists: Stereotype or Reality? in Tore Bjørgo (ed.), *Root Causes of Terrorism: Myths, Reality and Ways Forward* (Routledge; 2005), pp. 33–34 and Alan Krueger and Jitka Malečková, Education, Poverty, Political Violence, and Terrorism: Is There a Causal Connection? *Journal of Economic Perspectives*, Vol. 17, No. 4 (Fall 2003), p. 119.

[815] Quan Li and Drew Schaub, Economic Globalization and Transnational Terrorist Incidents: A Pooled Time Series Cross Sectional Analysis, *Journal of Conflict Resolution*, Vol. 48, No. 2 (2004).

[816] Jean-Paul Azam and Alexandra Delacroix, Aid and the Delegated Fight Against Terrorism, *Review of Development Economics*, Vol. 10, No. 2 (2006).

[817] Alan B. Krueger, *What Makes a Terrorist: Economics and the Roots of Terrorism* (Princeton University Press; 2008), p. 90.

[818] Mark Lichbach, An Evaluation of "Does Economic Inequality Breed Political Conflict?" Studies, *World Politics*, Vol. 41, No. 4 (July 1989), p. 465 and Claude Berrebi, The Economics

personal testimonies and terrorist literature gathered by terrorism researchers that economic and social inequality plays, at the very least, a significant role as an intermediate variable. As the political scientist Mark Lichbach has pointed out, the three great ideologies of nationalism, liberalism, and socialism have all spawned revolutionary movements based on ideas of equality — so the concept clearly has immense mobilizing power.[819] What seems to matter most for the radicalization process is how an individual's experience of social and economic exclusion interacts with the other mechanisms described in Part II. Rather than throwing the baby out with the bathwater, James Piazza has made a strong case for the smarter provision of economic assistance — instead of focusing on broad macro-level goals such as controlling inflation, liberalizing trade, or fiscal responsibility as potential counter-terrorism measures, more targeted micro-level goals such as the equalization of national public health and education expenditures across ethnic, religious or other national cleavages might have a more significant impact, not least because they help undermine terrorist narratives of exclusion and social injustice.[820] Indeed, research conducted by Brian Burgoon at the University of Amsterdam suggests increased welfare provision does correlate positively with a "modest" reduction in incidences of terrorism within the country concerned.[821]

Speaking in September 2015 at a United Nations Summit on Countering ISIL and Violent Extremism, President Barack Obama told the assembled dignitaries: "Poverty does not cause terrorism. But as we've seen across the Middle East and North Africa, when people, especially young people, are impoverished and hopeless and feel

---

of Terrorism and Counterterrorism: What Matters and Is Rational-Choice Theory Helpful? in Paul Davis and Kim Cragin (eds.), *Social Science for Counterterrorism: Putting the Pieces Together* (Rand; 2009), pp. 191–192.

[819] Mark Lichbach, An Evaluation of "Does Economic Inequality Breed Political Conflict?" Studies, *World Politics*, Vol. 41. No. 4, (July 1989), p. 433.

[820] James Piazza, Poverty, Minority Economic Discrimination, and Domestic Terrorism, *Journal of Peace Research*, Vol. 48, No. 3 (March 2011), pp. 350–351.

[821] Brian Burgoon, On Welfare and Terror: Social Welfare Policies and Political-Economic Roots of Terrorism, *Journal of Conflict Resolution*, Vol. 50, No. 2 (April 2006), pp. 176 and 197.

humiliated by injustice and corruption, that can fuel resentments that terrorists exploit. Which is why sustainable development — creating opportunity and dignity, particularly for youth — is part of countering violent extremism."[822] As a summary of the existing social science research into the relationship between poverty and terrorism, this statement is hard to beat.

## Government Aggression

As we discussed in Part I, seeking to provoke an overreaction from their opponents has been one of the key tactics consistently employed by terrorist groups over the past century and a half. Terrorist leaders have long understood that violence begets violence and that aggressive government action against their constituents can be a powerful recruitment tool. Researchers Rui de Figueiredo Jr. and Barry Weingast have described this as "the provocation motive" and even developed a useful game theoretic model to illustrate how it works in practice.[823] Seeking to explain the actual causal mechanism at work, Martha Crenshaw has argued that terrorist campaigns often come to resemble "a modern form of feuding" as action provokes reaction drawing more and more protagonists into the struggle and amplifying the anti-government frame within which militant groups operate.[824] Louise Richardson also identified "revenge" as one of what she described as the "three Rs" of terrorism — the others being "renown" and "reaction" — and this seems a constant theme across the literature. De Figueiredo and Weingast emphasized the interaction of revenge and political motivation.[825]

---

[822] *Remarks by President Obama at the Leaders' Summit on Countering ISIL and Violent Extremism,* United Nations Headquarters, 29 September 2015.

[823] Rui de Figueiredo Jr. and Barry Weingast, *Vicious Cycles: Endogenous Political Extremism and Political Violence,* Working Paper No. 9, Institute of Governmental Studies, University of California Berkeley, 2001, p. 3.

[824] Martha Crenshaw, *Explaining Terrorism: Causes, Processes and Consequences* (Routledge; 2011), p. 130.

[825] Rui de Figueiredo Jr. and Barry Weingast, *Vicious Cycles: Endogenous Political Extremism and Political Violence,* Working Paper No. 9, Institute of Governmental Studies, University of California Berkeley, 2001, p. 28.

Ted Gurr stressed the dangers for the state in being drawn into a "threat–fear–aggression sequence" of the type popularized by the American psychiatrist and anti-nuclear weapons campaigner Jerome Frank. Frank warned that "a perceived physical or psychosocial threat to an individual or group is an especially potent source of rage and fear."[826] The Yale psychologist Irving Janus, most famous for developing the concept of "groupthink", further cautioned: "The more a group feels threatened, the more its members are impelled to maintain group solidarity ... even at the expense of their objective judgment."[827] Time and time again governments fall into the same trap. Under pressure from their citizens to eradicate the threat, governments strike back, often blindly in the first instance since at the outset of a terrorist campaign they typically lack the tactical intelligence to act decisively, exacerbating the situation.

This can have profound and readily identifiable consequences. The desire to avenge a personal loss is a powerful *leitmotif* running through many terrorists' stories, and the stated intent to retaliate directly in response to government action is a commonplace feature of terrorist claims of responsibility. Tales of personal loss and suffering abound in terrorist biographies and the following are just a small selection taken from across the temporal and geographic spread of terrorist activity. Gaetano Bresci was an Italian immigrant living in Patterson, New Jersey, earning a living as a weaver. He was active in local anarchist circles and helped found and support an anarchist newspaper called *La Questione Sociale*. In May 1898, Bresci's sister was one of at least 118 protestors cut down by canon fire in Milan during a protest against high bread prices, an incident that became known in Italy as the Bava-Beccaris massacre after the general who had ordered his troops to fire on the protestors.[828]

---

[826] Jerome Frank, *When fears take over*, Bulletin of the Atomic Scientists, April 1979. See also Ken Heskin, Terrorism in Ireland: The past and future, *Irish Journal of Psychology*, Vol. 15, No. 2–3 (1994), p. 470 and Jerome Frank, *Sanity and Survival in the Nuclear Age: Psychological Aspects of War and Peace* (Vintage Books; 1968).

[827] Jerome Frank, *When fears take over*, Bulletin of the Atomic Scientists, April 1979.

[828] Alex Butterworth, *The World That Never Was: A True Story of Dreamers, Schemers, Anarchists and Secret Agents* (Pantheon Books; 2010), p. 371.

King Umberto I had subsequently awarded General Fiorenzo Bava-Beccaris the Great Cross of the Order of Savoy in recognition of his "brave defense of the royal house" prompting Bresci to mark the King as the target of his revenge. Bresci raised the money for a ticket home and traveled to the Lombard city of Monza where, in July 1900, he shot the King four times with a revolver he had brought with him from the United States, killing him. The leading Italian anarchist Errico Malatesta had long worried that personal motivations were beginning to overwhelm the principled ideological commitment of his comrades, commenting sadly: "It's no longer love for the human race that guides them, but the feeling of vendetta joined to the cult of an abstract idea."[829]

The Spanish anarchist Santiago Salvador bombed the Liceu Opera House in Barcelona in November 1893 in large part to avenge the death of his friend and fellow anarchist Paulino Pallás who had been arrested and subsequently executed for a failed assassination attempt on the Captain-General of Catalonia, Arsenio Martínez Campos, which killed two bystanders.[830] Salvador is reported to have justified his actions in the following terms: "The death of Pallás produced in me a terrible feeling and in order to avenge his death, as a tribute to his memory, I conceived of a plan in which it was possible to terrorize those who had enjoyed killing him and who believed that they had nothing to fear ... I did not ponder over it nor did I vacillate about it ... I only meditated about the form of the deed; it had to be something that would make a great deal of noise."[831]

Aleksander Ulyanov, a bombmaker associated with *Narodnaya Volya*, was arrested and subsequently executed in connection with a plot to assassinate Tsar Alexander III in 1887. Aleksander's execution led his younger brother, Vladimir, to explore the ideas for

---

[829] Richard Bach Jensen, Daggers, Rifles and Dynamite: Anarchist Terrorism in Nineteenth Century Europe, *Terrorism and Political Violence*, Vol. 16, No. 1 (Spring 2004), p. 126.

[830] Marie Fleming, Propaganda by the Deed: Terrorism and Anarchist Theory in Late Nineteenth-Century Europe, *Terrorism: An International Journal*, Vol. 4 (1980), p. 15.

[831] George Richard Esenwein, *Anarchist Ideology and the Working-class Movement in Spain, 1868–1898* (University of California Press; 1990), p. 186.

which his sibling had sacrificed his life, starting with Aleksander's favorite novel, Nikolai Chernyshevsky's *What is to be Done?*. Vladimir later recalled: "After the execution of my brother, knowing that Chernyshevsky's novel was one of his favorite works, I began what was a real reading and poured over the book, not several days but several weeks. Only then did I understand its full depth. It is a work which gives one a charge for a whole life."[832] Inspired by his brother's example, Vladimir immersed himself in radical student politics and his activism led to his expulsion from Kazan University. Vladimir would go on to lead the Bolshevik revolution that overthrew the Romanov Tsars and is better known today by his *nom de guerre*, Lenin.

In April 1919, ten-year-old Udham Singh was among the wounded in the Jallianwala garden in Amritsar, India, when British troops under command of Brigadier Reginald Dyer opened fire on a crowd of protestors killing at least 379, and possibly as many as 1,000. The incident became known around the world as the Amritsar massacre. Dyer had been sent to disperse the crowd by the British Lieutenant-Governor of Punjab, Michael O'Dwyer. Udham Singh embarked on a life of revolutionary activity aimed at overthrowing British colonial rule. He joined the Ghadar Party and became a close associate of the prominent socialist revolutionary Bhagat Singh. The colonial authorities jailed him for four years in the late 1920s for the illegal possession of firearms, but this did not deter him. Finally, on 13 March 1940, Singh walked into a public meeting at Caxton Hall in London where O'Dwyer was speaking and shot him dead. He also wounded the Secretary of State for India, the Marquess of Zetland. Singh was hanged for his crime, but he died content: "For a full twenty-one years, I have been trying to wreak vengeance. I am happy that I have done the job."[833]

And so the cycle of violence rolls on. Che Guevara's younger brother, Roberto, had shown little interest in his sibling's revolutionary activities while he was alive, but was radicalized by Che's execution at the hands of Bolivian troops and became active in

---

[832] Ronald Clark, *Lenin* (Harper & Row, 1988), p. 16.

[833] Ben Macintyre, We can't escape our bloody role in Sikh history, *The Times*, 17 January 2014.

Argentina's "Guevarist" guerrilla movement.[834] Black September mastermind Ali Hassan Salameh's father was killed by Jewish *Haganah* forces while leading an attack on Ras al-Ein in June 1948.[835] His posthumous legacy to his son was the invocation: "If I am killed I want my son to carry on my battle."[836] His son would do that in spades by planning the 1972 Munich Olympics attack, amongst many other Black September operations. Montassir al-Zayyat, Ayman al-Zawahiri's biographer, maintains that it was "the traumatic experience suffered by Zawahiri in prison [that] transformed him from being a relatively moderate force in *al-Jihad* into a violent and implacable extremist."[837] Along similar lines, an analysis by the researcher Thomas Hegghammer of the biographies of militants who joined *al-Qaeda* on the Arabian Peninsula (AQAP) and who participated in the terrorist campaign waged inside the Kingdom of Saudi Arabia from May 2003 to the end of 2005, found that 20% had spent time in prison before 2003, and that "most of [them] said they were subjected to physical and/or psychological torture."[838] *Hamas* co-founder Dr. Abdel Aziz al-Rantisi lost his uncle, grandfather, and three cousins to fighting with the Israelis. He told the terrorism researcher Mark Juergensmeyer that the suicide bombings carried out by *Hamas* were intended to make Israelis feel the same pain they had inflicted on Palestinians: "We want to do the same to Israel as they have done to us... It is important for you to understand that we are the victims in this struggle not the cause of it."[839]

Tony Doherty was just nine-years-old when his father, Patrick, was shot dead by British paratroopers in Londonderry/Derry on

---

[834] Jon Lee Anderson, *Che Guevara: A Revolutionary Life* (Grove Press; 1997), p. 746.

[835] Michael Burleigh, *Blood and Rage: A Cultural History of Terrorism* (Harper; 2009), p. 110.

[836] ibid., p. 109.

[837] Lawrence Wright, *The Looming Tower: Al-Qaeda and the Road to 9/11* (Vintage Books, 2007), p. 61.

[838] Thomas Hegghammer, Terrorist Recruitment and Radicalization in Saudi Arabia, *Middle East Policy*, Vol. 13, No. 4 (Winter 2006), p. 46.

[839] Mark Juergensmeyer, *Terror in the Mind of God: The Global Rise of Religious Violence* (University of California Press; 2003), p. 75.

Bloody Sunday in 1972.[840] Patrick Doherty had been a steward on the march. In 1981, Tony joined the Provisional IRA. When first asked by a PIRA recruiter his motivation for joining, his answer was unequivocal: "I wanted to get revenge for the death of my father."[841] Within a year, he had been arrested in possession of explosives while planning to bomb a British government building. He was sentenced to eight years in prison. This dynamic operated on both sides of the Northern Ireland conflict. Robert Henry, whose father, a building contractor with lucrative contracts working for the British security forces, was murdered by the Provisional IRA in April 1987, conspired in the murder of *Sinn Féin* councilor John Davey in February 1989. The murder was claimed by the loyalist terrorist organization, the Ulster Volunteer Force. Davey had been a veteran of the republican armed struggle with a paramilitary history that reportedly dated back to the 1950s. Robert testified at trial that his mind had "filled with hatred and revenge" after his father's murder outside the family home.[842]

Hanadi Jaradat, a twenty-nine-year-old lawyer from the Palestinian West Bank town of Jenin, blew herself up in a restaurant in Haifa in October 2003 killing twenty-one people and injuring fifty-one others. Her fiancé had been killed by the Israeli Defense Forces in 1997, and in June 2003, both her brother and cousin had also been killed during a raid by an undercover unit from the Israeli Border Police.[843] The cousin had been a senior member of Palestinian Islamic Jihad and was a wanted fugitive, but Israeli sources could not agree on whether her brother was an active member of PIJ or not.

---

[840] Ray Moseley, Ex-IRA Recruit Is Ready To Put Bitterness Aside, *Chicago Tribune*, 20 May 1998 at http://articles.chicagotribune.com/1998-05-20/news/9805200195_1_northern-ireland-protestants-roman-catholics.

[841] *BBC World Service*, Witness: Bloody Sunday, 30 January 2012. Interestingly, Tony's answer was actually not sufficient for the Provisional IRA recruiter since it lacked political consciousness and he didn't get admitted to the organization until his second attempt.

[842] Kevin Toolis, *Rebel Hearts* (St. Martin's Griffin; 1997), p. 65.

[843] Arie Kruglanski, Michele Gelfand, Jocelyn Bélanger, Anna Sheveland, Malkanthi Hetiarachchi and Rohan Gunaratna, The Psychology of radicalization and Deradicalization: How Significance Quest Impacts Violent Extremism, *Advances in Political Psychology*, Vol. 35, Suppl. 1 (2014), p. 75.

The Jordanian newspaper *Al Arab al-Yum* reported that, in her eulogy for the two men, Hanadi vowed that their blood would not be shed in vain: "The murderer will yet pay the price and we will not be the only ones who are crying ... If our nation cannot realize its dream and the goals of the victims, and live in freedom and dignity, then let the whole world be erased."[844] Hanadi's father, Taisir, told the *Al Jazeera* television network: "My daughter's action reflected the anger that every Palestinian feels at the occupation. The occupation did not have mercy on my son Fadi, her brother. They killed him even though he was not a wanted person, they murdered him in cold blood before Hanadi's eyes, I will accept only congratulations for what she did. This was a gift she gave me, the homeland and the Palestinian people. Therefore, I am not crying for her. Even though the most precious thing has been taken from me."[845] PIJ claimed responsibility for the attack in Haifa, and the cycle of violence continued when two weeks afterwards the IDF arrived to demolish the Jaradat family's home. Hanadi was the eldest of nine children.

Scott Atran has highlighted the example of the so-called Chechen "Black Widows", women who lost loved ones during the bloody Russian conflict in Chechnya and then joined local Islamist terrorist groups in search of vengeance. He describes how in November 2001 Elza Gazueva walked into the headquarters of the Russian commander who had ordered the torture and execution of her husband and brother, and detonated a suicide vest killing them both.[846] Similarly, Yulia Yuzik reports the case of Malizha Mutaeva, one of the suicide vest-equipped Chechen terrorists who seized the House of Culture in Dubrovka, Moscow, in October 2002. The siege of the theater ended in the deaths of 133 hostages and all forty terrorists. Yuzik notes: "Russian bombs had blown up everything she owned: her house, her family photographs. She had a grudge to bear."[847] 'Elvira', a Chechen mother whose fifteen-year-old son had

---

[844] ibid., p. 75 and Vered Levy-Barzilai, Ticking Bomb, *Haaretz*, 15 October 2003.

[845] Vered Levy-Barzilai, Ticking Bomb, *Haaretz*, 15 October 2003.

[846] Scott Atran, *Talking to the Enemy: Faith, Brotherhood and the (Un)making of Terrorists* (Ecco; 2010), p. 327.

[847] Yulia Yuzik, Russia's New Black Widows, *Foreign Policy*, 24 October 2013.

been killed by Russian troops who had then demanded a bribe of $500 to surrender the body to the family, likewise told a reporter: "Oh yes, I want to kill them. Kill Russians, kill their children. I want them to know what it is like."[848]

A study conducted for the US-based National Bureau of Economic Research on insurgent recruitment in Afghanistan in 2009–2010 found that revenge for the death of a loved one was often a crucial determining factor in an individual's decision to join the insurgency.[849] Sajida al-Rishawi, an aspirant suicide bomber recruited by Abu Musab al-Zarqawi to take part in the November 2005 Amman hotel bombings, had lost two brothers and a brother-in-law to US forces in Iraq. Al-Rishawi took part in the attack at the Radisson Hotel, but her suicide vest failed to go off and she fled the scene. When she was captured by the Jordanian authorities two days later, she told her interrogator: "They told me I would be killing Americans. All I wanted was to avenge the deaths of my brothers."[850] In the fall of 2017, the British journalist Anthony Loyd had the opportunity to ask a senior member of the *Taliban*'s Quetta *Shura* (leadership council) if he had ever felt guilty about recruiting young men to act as suicide bombers. He replied: "We felt sorry for these boys we ordered to carry out suicide attacks, for they had a right to life as you and I do. But they also had a right to revenge. Most were motivated by that desire. They had lost someone — as I lost my mother and brother — in a night raid or an airstrike. So I knew, even if I felt sorry for them, I was giving them something too."[851]

Mia Bloom notes that there is "an empirical regularity" in Chechnya, Palestine, and Sri Lanka linking the loss of a family member to "unjust" state action and the choice to carry out an act of

---

[848] Mia Bloom, *Dying to Kill: The Allure of Suicide Terrorism* (Columbia University Press; 2005), p. 157.

[849] Luke Condra, Joseph Felter, Radha Iyengar and Jacob Shapiro, *The Effect of Civilian Casualties in Afghanistan and Iraq*, Working Paper 16152, National Bureau of Economic Research, July 2010, DTIC Online (ADA524439).

[850] Joby Warrick, *Black Flags: The Rise of ISIS* (Doubleday; 2015), pp. 195 and 197.

[851] Antony Loyd, The War That Never Ends, *The Times Magazine*, 11 November 2017.

suicide terrorism.[852] There is also support for the cycle of violence theory from the world of psychiatry. Research by Christopher Henrich and Golan Shahar following 362 adolescents from southern Israel from 2008 through 2011 found that subjects exposed to rocket attacks and terrorism weren't significantly more anxious than their peers, but they were likely to be more disposed towards violence — indeed for every point the adolescent scored on a standard index measuring the degree of violence to which he or she had been exposed, he or she was roughly twice as likely to commit acts of violence in the future.[853]

In addition to personal acts of revenge, there are many examples of terrorist attacks carried out by concerned parties not directly affected by the initial event but who are nevertheless moved to strike back in explicit retaliation, sometimes motivated by a sense of empathy, solidarity, or injustice, and sometimes simply out of coldblooded political calculation. In December 1893 when Auguste Vaillant bombed the Chamber of Deputies of the French National Assembly, he was protesting the execution of the anarchist François Claudius Koenigstein, better known as Ravachol. The attack injured twenty deputies. Vaillant was executed in turn, despite the fact his assault had killed no one — the first Frenchman executed in the nineteenth century for a non-fatal crime — provoking outrage in leftist circles. Émile Henry bombed the Café Terminus in Paris in an explicit act of revenge, killing one diner and wounding twenty. He later justified his action thus: "You have hanged us in Chicago, decapitated us in Germany, garroted us in Xerez, shot us in Barcelona, guillotined us in Montbrison and Paris, but what you can never destroy is anarchy."[854] In the aftermath of the June 1896 bombing of a Catholic religious procession

---

[852] Mia Bloom, *Dying to Kill: Motivations for Suicide Terrorism*, in Ami Pedahzur (ed.), *Root Causes of Suicide Terrorism: The Globalization of Martyrdom* (Routledge; 2006), p. 37.

[853] Christopher Henrich and Golan Shahar, Effects of Exposure to Rocket Attacks on Adolescent Distress and Violence, *Journal of the American Academy of Child and Adolescent Psychiatry*, Vol. 52, No. 6 (2013).

[854] John Merriman, *The Dynamite Club: How a Bombing in Fin-de-Siécle Paris Ignited the Modern Age of Terror* (Houghton Mifflin Harcourt; 2009), p. 187.

in Barcelona during the festival of Corpus Christi which took the lives of twelve worshippers, the Spanish authorities, unable to identify the culprit (most likely by a French anarchist called Jean Girault who subsequently fled to Argentina), launched a violent crackdown on the anarchist movement in Spain and other dissenters.[855] The government proclaimed martial law in Barcelona and over a six-month period detained more than 400 suspects, many of whom were brutally tortured by the authorities whose methods included pulling out fingernails and crushing their victims' testicles.[856] Shocked by reports of these atrocities and outraged by a personal encounter with one torture survivor in exile in Italy, the Italian anarchist Michele Angiolillo traveled to Spain and assassinated the Spanish Prime Minister, Antonio Cánovas, in August 1897.[857]

In the United States, Alexander Berkman, a Russian immigrant who also happened to be Emma Goldman's lover and an associate of the German propagandist of terrorism Johann Most, bluffed his way into the Pittsburgh offices of the Operating Manager of Carnegie Steel, Henry Clay Frick, and shot and stabbed him multiple times in July 1892.[858] Berkman had chosen his target, who survived the assault, because of the role Frick had played in putting down the labor strike at Carnegie's Homestead Steel Plant earlier in the month, an action which had resulted in the deaths of nine strikers. Despite serving fourteen years for his attempt on Frick's life, on his release Berkman was involved in another plot to kill John D. Rockefeller whose mining interests in Colorado had been the target of industrial action.[859]

One member of the Zionist Stern Gang detained by the British Mandate authorities in Palestine, Yitzhak Reznitsky, explained to his

---

[855] Richard Bach Jensen, The Pre-1914 Anarchist "Lone Wolf" Terrorist and Government Responses, *Journal of Terrorism and Political Violence*, Vol. 26, No. 1 (2014), p. 88.

[856] ibid.

[857] ibid.

[858] Richard Bach Jensen, Daggers, Rifles and Dynamite: Anarchist Terrorism in Nineteenth Century Europe, *Terrorism and Political Violence*, Vol. 16, No. 1 (Spring 2004), p. 135.

[859] Nunzio Pernicone, Luigi Galleani and Italian Anarchist Terrorism in the United States, *Studi Emigrazione*, Vol. 30 (September 1993), p. 482.

interrogators why the group had mounted a flurry of bomb attacks on the Palestine police in April–May 1942: "The severe methods employed by the police ... including the shooting of Zak, Amper, Sevorai [sic], Levshtein [sic] and Stern himself ... convinced the members of the group of the Government's intention to crush their organization at any cost, and it was decided to fight back."[860] Another leading member of the Stern Gang, Nathan Yellin-Mor, later wrote: "The first goal for a revenge attack was perfectly clear — Geoffrey Morton, the murderer of Yair [Stern]."[861] Morton narrowly escaped an IED explosion along his route to work, and other devices targeted the Inspector General and Deputy Inspector General of the Palestine Police. Similarly, the May 1947 murder of Alexander Rubowitz, a young Jewish *Brit Hashmonaim* activist, snatched off the streets by the British undercover unit led by Major Roy Farran, prompted LEHI to mount a wave of reprisal attacks that included the shooting of four British soldiers on a Tel Aviv beach, the murder of a British officer in a restaurant in Haifa, and the mailing of a parcel bomb to Farran's family home in Staffordshire, which detonated killing his brother Rex.[862]

Israeli Prime Minister Golda Meir authorized Operation Wrath of God to punish the Palestinian terrorists behind the Munich Olympics attack. Black September in turn struck back at Mossad officers working in Europe. Bruch Cohen was gunned down in Madrid after being set up for assassination by a Palestinian informant who was in fact a double agent working for Black September. Cohen was murdered in retaliation for the killing of the Black September Resident in Cyprus, Hussein Abd el Hir.[863] A letter bomb sent to the Israeli Embassy in London by Black September also killed an attaché, Dr. Ami Shechori. The assassination of *Hezbollah* terrorist

---

[860] Patrick Bishop, *The Reckoning: How the Killing of One Man Changed the Fate of the Promised Land* (William Collins; 2014), p. 197.

[861] ibid., p. 198.

[862] David Cesarani, *Major Farran's hat: The Untold Story of the Struggle to Establish the Jewish State* (Da Capo Press, Cambridge, Massachusetts; 2009), pp. 138–139 and 193.

[863] Michael Bar-Zohar and Nissim Mishal, *Mossad: The Greatest Missions of the Israeli Secret Service* (Ecco, HarperCollins; 2012), p. 197.

chief Imad Mughniyeh in Damascus in February 2008 led *Hezbollah* Secretary General Hassan Nasrallah to declare: "You crossed the borders. Zionists, if you want an open war, let it be an open war anywhere."[864] According to the Washington Institute's Matt Levitt, Mughniyeh's death actually led directly to the resurgence of *Hezbollah*'s international operations arm — hardly the outcome Israel would have been been hoping for, but equally, given the history of attack and counterattack in the region, surely not entirely unexpected.[865]

In June 1991, a Provisional IRA Active Service Unit was ambushed by the British Special Air Service on their way to murder an off-duty member of the part-time Ulster Defence Regiment. All three members of the unit were killed. Delivering the funeral oration for one of the slain men, PIRA volunteer Tony Doris, Belfast *Sinn Féin* councilor Mairtin O Muilleoir warned the British authorities: "We will teach them a lesson that no matter how many people they kill, how many of our number they kill — and it is always open season on nationalists, they can kill us in our beds, they can kill us in the streets, they can kill us in the fields, they can come in the dark of night, we have no protection — we will teach them a lesson that no matter how many of our number they do to death we will continue on. The British may be slow learners but we are very, very patient teachers. And no matter how often they cut us down, others will pick up and follow on."[866] The reporter Kevin Toolis saw the incident as one in a chain of tit-for-tat killings that plagued East Tyrone in the late 1980s and early 1990s. Another *Sinn Féin* councilor, Francie McNally, told Toolis: "It's a Mexican stand-off. It's a case of you owe them two lives or three or they owe you two or three. It is who kills who now. They [the loyalists] think they owe us [the republicans] one. This is how I think they would be thinking.

---

[864] Kevin Peraino, The Fox is Hunted Down, *Newsweek*, 25 February 2008.

[865] Matthew Levitt, Why a Hezbollah attack in Bulgaria? Why Now? *New Hampshire Sentinel Source*, 13 February 2013 at http://www.sentinelsource.com/opinion/columnists/guest/why-a-hezbollah-attack-in-bulgaria-why-now-by-matthew/article_30fe0808-04b8-5d45-90dd-6a6b45dc3e75.html.

[866] Kevin Toolis, *Rebel Hearts* (St. Martin's Griffin; 1997), pp. 32–33.

It could be me."[867] Sure enough not long after this interview the Ulster Volunteer Force attacked McNally's home and shot and killed his brother, Phelim.

Dr. Abdel Aziz al-Rantisi of *Hamas* told Mark Juergensmeyer that his group had initially restricted its attacks to Israeli military personnel and had only extended its attacks to encompass civilian targets after the massacre perpetrated at Hebron's Tomb of the Patriarchs by Dr. Baruch Goldstein in February 1994.[868] Another senior *Hamas* figure, Imad Faluji, added: "The Israelis killed our women and children during the holy month of *Ramadan*, we wanted to do the same to Israel, to show them that even their women and children are vulnerable — none are innocent."[869] Al-Rantisi made a similar statement after the killing of senior *Hamas* member Salah Shehada in a July 2002 Israeli air strike that also claimed the lives of thirteen members of his extended family: "There will be no peace initiative after today. We will chase them in their houses and in their apartments, the same way they have destroyed our houses and our apartments."[870] Little over a week later, a *Hamas* operative left a bomb in a cafeteria on the campus of Jerusalem's Hebrew University, which exploded without warning killing nine students and staff, and injuring 100 more. At a *Hamas* rally in Gaza City celebrating the attack, one speaker told the crowd: "We give this gift to the soul of Sheikh Salah Shehada and we say to the al Qassam Brigades we are waiting for more."[871] Commenting on the attack, a senior *Hamas* official, Ismail Haniyeh, told the *Los Angeles Times*: "If [the Israelis] are going to attack our children, then they will have to expect to drink from the same poison."[872] This attitude was not unique to *Hamas*, the killings of Abu Ali Mustafa, the leader of the PFLP, in August 2001,

---

[867] ibid., p. 61.

[868] Mark Juergensmeyer, *Terror in the Mind of God: The Global Rise of Religious Violence* (University of California Press; 2003), p. 74.

[869] ibid., p. 137.

[870] Suzanne Goldenberg, 12 dead in attack on Hamas, *The Guardian*, 23 July 2002.

[871] Ross Dunn, Palestinians celebrate revenge attack, *The Age*, 2 August 2002.

[872] Tracy Wilkinson, Blast Kills 7 at University in Jerusalem, *Los Angeles Times*, 1 August 2002.

and of Raed Karmi, leader of the al-Aqsa Martyrs Brigades, in January 2002 were both followed by similar revenge attacks.[873]

Around the world, it is the same story. The Oklahoma City bomber and right-wing extremist Timothy McVeigh had been the best man at Lori Fortier's wedding and he remained close to her husband Michael. In her testimony at McVeigh's trial, she told the court that McVeigh had been upset with the government over the manner in which it had resolved its standoff with the Branch Davidian cult in Waco, Texas. Six cult members had been shot in a confrontation with federal agents and at least seventy more died when a fire broke out during an assault on the cult's compound after a fifty-one-day siege. Fortier testified: "He thought the government had murdered the people of Waco."[874] McVeigh later wrote to the Fortiers that he planned to bomb the Alfred P. Murrah Federal building in Oklahoma City because "it was an easy target and it was a building that housed some of the people that were in the Waco raid."[875] The *Tehrik-i-Taliban Pakistan* double-agent-turned-suicide-bomber Humam al-Balawi, who killed nine CIA affiliated personnel in Khost, Afghanistan, appeared posthumously in a martyrdom video alongside the leader of the TTP, Hakimullah Mehsud, who explained that he had ordered the attack to avenge the killing of his predecessor, Baitullah Mehsud, in a US drone strike six months before.[876] When fifteen-year-old Alexis Grigoropoulos was shot and killed in a confrontation with a Greek police officer in December 2009, it prompted an outbreak of rioting across the country. The Greek terrorist group *Epanastatikos Agonas* responded by ambushing a police patrol in explicit retaliation, critically injuring a young officer. The title of the communiqué the group issued to explain their action left little doubt as to its motivation: *We Respond to Bullets with Bullets.*[877]

---

[873] The blow to peace, *The Economist*, 24 July 2002.

[874] Nolan Clay and Penny Owen, Lori Fortier Testifies McVeigh Told of Bomb, Witness Says She Could Have Prevented Deaths, *The Oklahoman*, 30 April 1997.

[875] ibid.

[876] Peter Bergen, *United States of Jihad: Investigating America's Homegrown Terrorists* (Crown; 2016), p. 124.

[877] George Kassimeris, *Inside Greek Terrorism* (Oxford University Press; 2013), p. 84.

But perhaps the most telling example of all came in a video-taped speech broadcast by *Al Jazeera* in November 2004 in which Osama bin Laden explained why *al-Qaeda* had launched its operation against New York and Washington on 11 September 2001: "*Allah* knows that it had never occurred to us to strike the towers. But after it became unbearable and we witnessed the oppression and tyranny of the American-Israeli coalition against our people in Palestine and Lebanon, it came to my mind. The events that affected my soul in a direct way started in 1982 when America permitted the Israelis to invade Lebanon and the American Sixth Fleet helped them in that. This bombardment began and many were killed and injured and others were terrorized and displaced. I couldn't forget those moving scenes, blood and severed limbs, women and children sprawled everywhere. Houses destroyed along with their occupants and high rises demolished over their residents, rockets raining down on our home without mercy ... In those difficult moments many hard-to-describe ideas bubbled in my soul, but in the end they produced an intense feeling of rejection of tyranny, and gave birth to a strong resolve to punish the oppressors. And as I looked at those demolished towers in Lebanon, it entered my mind that we should punish the oppressor in kind and that we should destroy towers in America in order that they taste some of what we tasted and so that they be deterred from killing our women and children."[878]

Revenge attacks also often follow the judicially-sanctioned state execution of convicted terrorists. On 2 November 1920, despite widespread appeals for clemency, the British hanged a student member of the IRA, Kevin Barry, for his part in an attack that had resulted in the death of three British soldiers. The General Headquarters of the IRA responded by issuing a general order to all units to launch armed reprisals. Within twenty-four hours, seven Royal Irish Constabulary constables were dead and nine more

---

[878] Full transcript of bin Laden's speech, Aljazeera.com, 1 November 2004, at http://www.aljazeera.com/archive/2004/11/200849163336457223.html. Viewed 21 January 2017.

injured.[879] In April 1938, three young members of the Revisionist Zionist youth movement *Betar* resolved to avenge a series of lethal attacks on Jewish travelers near the settlement of Rosh Pinna by ambushing an Arab bus and killing the passengers. The ambush was a complete failure and as the youths made their escape they were apprehended by a British police patrol. Although no one had actually died in the abortive attack — a grenade thrown by the oldest of the group, twenty-two-year-old Shlomo Ben-Yousef, had failed to explode — the Military Court resolved to make an example of them and Ben-Yousef was sentenced to hang. He would be the first member of the Jewish underground to be executed by the British. The Head of the Jewish Agency, David Ben-Gurion, considered this decision to be a critical turning point in the evolution of Jewish militancy: "This single act contributed more than anything else to the growth of the dissident terrorist organization, *Etzel* [*Irgun*]."[880] It also alienated the influential Zionist leader Ze'ev Jabotinsky who furiously told a rally in London in June 1938: "The Jews are beginning to ask themselves whether Ben-Yosef's way is not the best one. We know from history that martyrs become prophets and bombs become altars."[881]

Ben-Yousef went to the gallows on 29 June 1938 confident that he had ignited a wider struggle for an independent Jewish state, reportedly writing to friends in Poland: "I am going to die tomorrow, despite this I'm happy. Why? Because for a period of ten years I gave all of my strength to *Betar* and I am proud to be the first *Betar* member on the gallows ... I believe that after my death they will not restrain themselves."[882] He was absolutely right. Jabotinsky, under whose auspices *Irgun* had been established, had hitherto reined in the group from striking back at Arab targets, but he now lifted this restriction for the first time in the final days before Ben-Yosef's execution. Jabotinsky's authorization for *Irgun* to go on the offensive

---

[879] J. B. E. Hittle, *Michael Collins and the Anglo-Irish War: Britain's Counterinsurgency Failure* (Potomac Books; 2011), p. 159.

[880] Bruce Hoffman, *Anonymous Soldiers: The Struggle for Israel, 1917–1947* (Knopf; 2015), p. 78.

[881] ibid., p. 79.

[882] ibid., p. 77.

marked the beginning of the end of the Jewish community's official policy of restraint (*havlaga*) in the face of Arab provocations. Within a week, *Irgun*'s new commander, David Raziel, set in motion a wave of attacks on Arab targets, the most serious of which occurred on 25 July when a nail bomb exploded without warning in Haifa Central Market killing 53 people, and injuring 45. By the outbreak of World War II in September 1939, and the suspension of the *Irgun* campaign, its largely indiscriminate attacks had claimed the lives of more than 250 Arab victims, including a number of women and children.[883]

This would not be the last occasion on which the British use of the death penalty in a terrorism-related case would result in violent reprisals. Two kidnapped British Army sergeants, Clifford Martin and Mervyn Paice, were hung by *Irgun* following the execution of Haviv Avshalom, Yaakov Weiss, and Meir Nakar by the British Mandate authorities for the role they played in the Acre prison break in July 1947. In May 1956, EOKA likewise murdered two British soldiers it had captured, Gordon Hill and Ronnie Shilton, in retaliation for the execution of two convicted EOKA members, Andreas Dimitriou and Michalis Karaolis.[884] Karaolis had been convicted of the murder of a Cypriot police officer, and Dimitriou of attempting to murder a British shopkeeper. In a letter written to a supporter just a month earlier, EOKA commander General Grivas had stressed the importance of matching the British authorities blow for blow: "I am afraid that the people's morale will sink by the measures taken by [Governor] Harding if we do not retaliate with similar measures."[885] An EOKA leaflet distributed at the time stated more starkly: "We shall answer hanging with hanging and torture with torture."[886] Perhaps most famously of all, the French decision to execute two *Front de Libération Nationale* members, Zabane and Ferradj, led to the outbreak of the Battle of Algiers in 1956. FLN commander Ramdane

---

[883] ibid., p. 97.

[884] David French, *Fighting EOKA: The British Counter-Insurgency Campaign on Cyprus, 1955–1959* (Oxford University Press; 2015), p. 98 and p. 107.

[885] ibid., p. 107.

[886] Charlotte Heath-Kelly, *Politics of Violence: Militancy, International Politics and Killing in the Name* (Routledge; 2016), p. 42.

Abane ordered his subordinate in Algiers, Saadi Yacef, to "kill any European between the ages of eighteen and fifty-four. But no women, no children, no old people" and within seventy-two hours, forty-nine French civilians had been murdered in retaliation.[887] Crenshaw notes that in the Algerian War of Independence, the term *engrenage* — literally the engaging of gears — was used to emphasize the self-perpetuating nature of the conflict.[888]

Given the potent role that feelings of loss and revenge can play in exacerbating politically-motivated terrorist violence, the fact that targeted killing has emerged in the past decade as an increasingly utilized counter-terrorism tool must surely be a real cause for concern. In recent years, Turkey, Colombia, Russia, Israel, and the United States have all carried out targeted killings of alleged terrorist suspects overseas. Past experience suggests that even if, as the Israeli Defense Force claimed in a 2001 testimony before the *Knesset* Foreign Affairs and Defense Committee, some "useful" tactical benefit is gained by the elimination of a key terrorist figure, at the strategic level operations of this nature are only like to provoke further terrorist attacks.[889] As Gregory Johnsen has noted, pursuing a policy of targeted assassination in a country like Yemen with a deep tribal commitment to *thar* (revenge) or Afghanistan where the strict *Pashtunwali* code of honor requires a wronged party to seek *badal* (variously translated as revenge or justice) is only likely to prolong conflict.[890]

## Micromobilization

At its heart, the concept of feuding is essentially a simple binary process in which one can draw a straight line between a single

---

[887] Alistair Horne, *A Savage War of Peace: Algeria 1954–1962* (New York Review Books Classics; 2006), pp. 183–184.

[888] Martha Crenshaw, The Effectiveness of Terrorism in the Algerian War, in Martha Crenshaw (ed.), *Terrorism in Context* (Pennsylvania State Press; 1995), p. 475.

[889] IDF statement to the Knesset Foreign Affairs and Defence Committee quoted in Ha'aretz, 8 January 2001, and cited in *Israel's Assassination Policy: Extrajudicial Executions*, B'Tselem, 2001.

[890] Gregory Johnsen, How we lost Yemen, *Foreign Policy*, August 6, 2013 at http://www.foreign-policy.com/articles/2013/08/06/how_we_lost_yemen_al_qaeda?print=yes&hidecomments= yes&page=full.

violent action and the reaction it elicits. Yet, grievances sometimes build in a much more incremental fashion with repeated slights and humiliations eventually leading an individual to conclude that circumstances are such that only violent action is sufficient to bring about positive change. In his influential study of micromobilization processes in 1970s Northern Ireland, the sociologist Robert White discovered that personal experience of state repression — albeit in a variety of forms — appeared to be a major determinant of individual decisions to embrace political violence. In a series of interviews with Provisional IRA volunteers, White found that their personal interaction with British troops was cited again and again as they explained their decision to take up arms.[891] Furthermore, he noted that Provisional IRA violence increased significantly in months following incidents in which the security forces harmed civilians or carried out particularly emblematic acts of repression, such as the introduction of internment.[892]

Other individual accounts of republican radicalization seem to bear out his analysis. The hunger striker Bobby Sands wrote that his nationalist sentiments had become aroused after watching a unionist mob ambush a Catholic civil rights march at Burntollet Bridge, with apparent police connivance, commenting: "That imprinted itself in my mind like a scar, and for the first time I took a real interest in what was going on. I became angry."[893] A senior member of Provisional IRA told the psychologist John Horgan: "For me anyway, the sight of the B Specials and the Royal Ulster Constabulary beating nationalist people off the street in Derry was a big factor in joining the republican movement."[894] PIRA veteran Anthony McIntyre similarly explained: "Why did I become involved in the IRA? It was because of a process of British state repression as clearly distinct

---

[891] Robert White, From Peaceful Protest to Guerrilla War: Micromobilization of the Provisional Irish Republican Army, *American Journal of Sociology*, Vol. 94 No. 6 (May 1989), p. 1288.
[892] ibid.
[893] Bobby Sands, From a nationalist ghetto to the battlefield of H-Block, *An Phoblacht*, 16 December 1978.
[894] John Horgan, *The Psychology of Terrorism* (Routledge; 2005), p. 86.

from any sort of attachment to republican ideology."[895] Another former PIRA man told the researcher Richard English that one reason he joined the Provisionals was that he came from a republican family but then added: "Another reason — and this cannot, *cannot* be overestimated — was, when the troubles did break out, the reaction of the security forces within the nationalist areas ... So those are basically the two reasons, and mostly I would say the latter — to strike back at what was going on in those districts."[896]

Once the British Army was deployed to Northern Ireland in August 1969, even though it initially arrived on what was essentially a peacekeeping mission to separate the Protestant and Catholic populations, military foot patrols rapidly became a familiar, and much disliked, presence in Catholic neighborhoods, along with the random stopping and questioning of pedestrians. As the situation deteriorated, military operations inevitably increased in tempo exacerbating republican hostility. In 1972, British soldiers searched more than 36,000 homes, in 1973, this figure rose to 75,000 homes. Between April 1973 and April 1974, 4 million were stopped and searched at military checkpoints.[897] PIRA volunteer Pat McGeown credited the deployment of British troops with pushing him towards joining the armed struggle against British rule: "Probably one of the deciding factors would have been constant harassment of British troops at that time on the streets. It generally created an atmosphere of violence and the desire to fight back and not accept that type of state."[898] The brother of another PIRA volunteer, Dermot Finucane, told the reporter Kevin Toolis that "Dermot got his politics from the streets and even now I don't think that the Brits realize how much harm they did to people, whether it's through a house raid or being stopped in the street, and how that could coerce someone into joining the IRA."[899]

---

[895] Richard English, *Armed Struggle: The History of the IRA* (Oxford University Press; 2004), p. 123.

[896] ibid., pp. 122–123.

[897] John Newsinger, *British Counter-insurgency from Palestine to Northern Ireland* (Palgrave; 2002), p. 168.

[898] Richard English, *Armed Struggle: The History of the IRA* (Oxford University Press; 2004), p. 122.

[899] Kevin Toolis, *Rebel Hearts* (St. Martin's Griffin; 1997), p. 172.

The PIRA intelligence officer Eamon Collins wrote that he was radicalized by the experience of being detained and beaten by British paratroopers, along with his father and brother, after a police sniffer dog wrongly confused the odor of creosote in his father's car with that of explosives. After a terrifying and humiliating spell in Bessborough Barracks, the family was released, but the psychological damage was done: "I would feel a surge of rage whose power unbalanced me; I would sit alone in my room and think with pleasure of blowing off the heads of those Para scum."[900] Collins drifted into nationalist politics and soon gravitated toward PIRA. Kevin Toolis spoke to the friends and family of Tony Doris, the young Provisional IRA volunteer killed in an SAS ambush in June 1991, to try to establish why he had chosen to join PIRA when his brother, Martin, had taken a totally different path going to university and training to be a doctor: "Everyone, his father, his mother, his sisters and his friends, returned again and again to the harassment by soldiers that Tony encountered on the street. Tony did not like being stopped and searched by British troops." Tony's mother recalled one incident in particular that had hardened him: "He was arrested when he was sixteen, when he was still at school. They lifted him up and bent him over the back of a chair, they kicked him and spat on him. He had not done anything at that stage."[901] Six years later the "official" obituary published in *Republican News* identified Tony Doris as the Officer Commanding of the Coalisland unit of PIRA's East Tyrone Brigade.[902]

Former PIRA chief Martin McGuinness summed up the prevailing attitude towards the British soldiers in staunchly republican neighborhoods: "It was plain as daylight that there was an army in our town, in our country, and that they weren't there to give out flowers. Armies should be fought by armies."[903] *Sinn Féin* leader Gerry Adams also saw the arrival of British troops as a key moment in the conflict: "The attitude and presence of British troops was also

---

[900] Michael Burleigh, *Blood and Rage: A Cultural History of Terrorism* (Harper; 2009), p. 310.

[901] Kevin Toolis, *Rebel Hearts* (St. Martin's Griffin; 1997), pp. 41–42.

[902] ibid., p. 49.

[903] Richard English, *Armed Struggle: The History of the IRA* (Oxford University Press; 2004), p. 142.

a reminder that we were Irish, and there was an instant resurgence of national consciousness and an almost immediate politicization of the local populace."[904] Adams concluded: "Instead of defusing the situation the British government copper-fastened popular support for the IRA. In Ballymurphy in West Belfast, for example, there were six semi-active republicans and ten supporters in 1969; today in West Belfast *Sinn Féin* draws its biggest vote from that area. The crucial transformation came about when a British army regiment came into Ballymurphy and attempted to beat its people into submission. If they had come in with kid gloves they would still have been unwelcome but they would not have generated the same phenomenon of implacable resistance."[905]

Other case studies from around the world appear to offer substantial support for White's thesis that state repression — including acts that fall short of state-sanctioned killing or execution — drives terrorist recruitment. The leader of *Narodnaya Volya* and mastermind behind the assassination of Tsar Alexander II, Andrei Zhelyabov, was progressively hardened against the Russian state by the rape of his aunt by their landlord who was able to act with complete impunity because of his status, his expulsion from university for protesting at professorial grading practices, and his imprisonment for writing to a jailed friend.[906] The Russian populist revolutionary Sergei Kravshinski recalled in his memoirs that it was the harsh sentences handed down in the so-called "Trial of the 193" that led him to kill police informers.[907] Vera Figner recorded how some members of the non-violent *Zemlya i volya* movement were prompted to split off and form the terrorist organization *Narodnaya Volya* in response to a crackdown on liberal, populist-minded students by the Tsarist regime: "When the youth turned to the people with peaceful propaganda, the government met them with

---

[904] John Newsinger, *British Counter-insurgency from Palestine to Northern Ireland* (Palgrave; 2002), p. 169.

[905] Gerry Adams, *The Politics of Irish Freedom* (Brandon Book Publishers; 1986), p. 56.

[906] Clark McCauley and Sophia Moskalenko, Mechanisms of Political Radicalization: Pathways Toward Terrorism, *Journal of Terrorism and Political Violence*, Vol. 20, No. 3, July 2008, p. 418.

[907] Martha Crenshaw, The Causes of Terrorism, *Comparative Politics*, Vol. 13, No. 4 (1981), p. 394.

wholesale arrests, exile, penal servitude, and central prisons. When, outraged by violence, these young Russians punished a few servants of the government, the central power replied with military rule and executions."[908] In addition to claiming to avenge the death of anarchist comrades at the hands of various European states, the French anarchist Émile Henry also cited a litany of other less existential grievances during his trial in Paris: "The bomb in the Cafe Terminus is the answer to all your violations of freedom, to your arrests, to your searches, to your laws against the Press, to your mass transportations."[909] Henry was referring to the so-called *lois scélérates* — villainous laws — passed in response to Auguste Valliant's attempted bombing of the Chamber of Deputies, which cracked down on the anarchist press and seditious speech by making the advocacy of any crime a crime in itself and effectively criminalizing the glorification or encouragement of *attentats* (violent attacks).[910]

Inevitably, the routine aggressions, restrictions and humiliations of colonial rule, the feeling of being a second-class citizen in one's own homeland, were among the principle drivers of the national liberation movements that sprang up in opposition to European dominion in Africa and South East Asia. Speaking at his trial in Pretoria in April 1964, Nelson Mandela reminded the court that in 1952, he had helped organize the Defiance Campaign of passive resistance against the *apartheid* laws introduced by the National Party two years earlier and that not a single instance of violence had been reported during the campaign and yet more than 8,500 volunteer activists had been jailed by the South African authorities.[911] He then observed: "A government which uses force to maintain its rule teaches the oppressed to use force to oppose it ... It would be wrong and unrealistic for African leaders to continue preaching peace and non-violence at a time when the government met our peaceful

---

[908] Vera Figner, *Memoirs of a Revolutionist* (Northern Illinois University Press; 1991), p. 73.
[909] Émile Henry, *Defense* (1894).
[910] Reg Carr, *Anarchism in France: The Case of Octave Mirabeau* (McGill — Queen's University Press; 1977), p. 64.
[911] http://www.washingtonpost.com/blogs/worldviews/wp/2013/12/05/read-the-most-important-speech-nelson-mandela-ever-gave.

demands with force. This conclusion was not easily arrived at. It was only when all else had failed, when all channels of peaceful protest had been barred to us, that the decision was made to embark on violent forms of political struggle, and to form *Umkhonto we Sizwe.*"[912] Extirpating the cultural and psychological dislocation of colonial rule through the armed struggle for independence, and regaining one's personal dignity, identity and self-respect in the process, was central to the philosophy of resistance propounded by Frantz Fanon in *The Wretched of the Earth.* Fanon explained: "In reality, the soldier who is engaged in armed combat in a national war deliberately measures from day to day the sum of all the degradation inflicted upon man by colonial oppression. The man of action has sometimes the exhausting impression that he must restore the whole of his people, that he must bring every one of them up out of the pit and out of the shadows ... The period of oppression is painful; but the conflict, by reinstating the downtrodden, sets on foot a process of reintegration which is fertile and decisive in the extreme. A people's victorious fight not only consecrates the triumph of its rights; it also gives to that people consistence, coherence, and homogeneity."[913] Fanon, in turn, had been deeply influenced by his experience fighting alongside the FLN, which had announced its war of national liberation in November 1954 by challenging native Algerians: "Think of your humiliating position as colonized men. Under colonialism, justice, democracy and equality are nothing more than deception and tricks."[914]

Systemic police brutality is often cited as a radicalizing factor. Dieter Kunzelmann, one of the leaders of *Tupamaros West Berlin* who was jailed for five years in the early 1970s for terrorism-related offenses, recalled in an interview with the BBC that it was the experience of routine police violence that pushed him and many of his comrades into taking up arms: "The debate over violence in the anti-authoritarian movement which led to armed resistance in the urban guerrilla movement was a result of us getting beaten up such

---

[912] ibid.

[913] Frantz Fanon, *The Wretched of the Earth* (Grove Press; 1963), p. 293.

[914] David Macey, *Frantz Fanon: A Biography* (Picador; 2001), pp. 256 and 657.

a lot [by the police]. That goes without saying." His observation was echoed by the RAF's Horst Mahler: "We marched in the streets against the genocide in Vietnam with the belief that we were doing the best thing in the world. Then, there was the massive aggression of the state apparatus, and there was one death [of the student Benno Ohnesorg]."[915] An Italian militant active in the *Movimento Comunista Rivoluzionario* also blamed aggressive police tactics for escalating tensions between left-wing protestors and the ruling establishment in same period: "It is first of all a problem of suffered violence. The first images are linked to the police charges. The first strong signs of an unsustainable situation, a situation which really had to be changed, comes those years from Avola and Battipaglia. They came from those demonstrations, by the way not student ones, that were hit and repressed, with the death of people who had demonstrated."[916] Likewise, for November 17 member Patroklos Tselentis, it was the violent suppression by the Greek authorities of a student demonstration in 1980 that made the critical difference: "The events at the Polytechnic had a radicalizing effect on me. I was lucky not to have been hurt in the clashes, but many friends of mine, and many friends of theirs, sustained serious injuries at the hands of the police."[917]

As in Northern Ireland, the experience of being detained, or of seeing a loved one detained, especially if that detention seems unjust, is also a commonly reported radicalizing experience. Nicos Sampson was one of EOKA's leading operatives and by January 1957, he was said to have participated in at least twenty-five murders and attempted murders.[918] However, he didn't start out as a hardened criminal or street thug: "I was the best reporter in Cyprus when the police arrested me in Famagusta. I was innocent. I was sent to prison for three months on a false charge and when I came

---

[915] Donatella Della Porta, *Clandestine Political Violence* (Cambridge University Press; 2013), p. 45.

[916] ibid., p. 42.

[917] George Kassimeris, *Inside Greek Terrorism* (Oxford University Press; 2013), pp. 39–40.

[918] David French, *Fighting EOKA: The British Counter-Insurgency Campaign on Cyprus, 1955–1959* (Oxford University Press; 2015), p. 54.

out I began working for EOKA."[919] FARC cadre Yurluey Mendoza told the reporter Nick Miroff that she had joined the movement after witnessing her father being beaten by Colombian police officers. When she was seven-years-old, she had attended a festival in her local town with her father. He had requested that a band playing in the plaza play a popular folk ballad that referenced one of FARC's founders, Manuel Marulanda Vélez. He was arrested, beaten and locked up in the local jail overnight. Mendoza sat all night outside his cell: "There was a space under the door, and I put my hand under it so he could touch my finger. We sat like that on the floor for a long time. I remember how badly I wanted to be big at that moment when they were beating my father, I think that's when I decided I wanted to be powerful, or to be part of something powerful. To make them know they could never do that to us again."[920] Abubaker Deghayes, a British national of Libyan descent was detained in Pakistan in the aftermath of the 9/11 attacks and handed over to US forces, after which he spent more than five years in the Guantanamo Bay detention facility before being released without charge. In 2013–2014, three of Deghayes' sons, whose childhood had been defined by their father's seemingly arbitrary detention, traveled from Britain to Syria to fight for the *al-Qaeda*-affiliated *Jabhat al-Nusra li Ahl al-Sham*, two were killed, the youngest was just sixteen-years-old.[921]

In 2014, the Institute for Security Studies in South Africa approached ninety-five Kenyan residents associated with the Somali terrorist group *al-Shabaab* in an attempt to find out why they had joined the organization. When asked "the single most important factor" that had pushed them to embrace violence, 65% of those approached referenced the Kenyan government's aggressive counter-terrorism strategy towards Kenyan Muslims and Kenyans of Somali descent, specifically citing the assassination of Muslim leaders, collective punishment, arbitrary arrest, and police beatings

---

[919] ibid., p. 63.

[920] Nick Miroff, 'Do you know what it's like to spend 20 years at war?' *Washington Post*, 30 September 2016.

[921] Mary Anne Weaver, Her Majesty's Jihadists, *New York Times*, 14 April 2015.

among their complaints.[922] Al Amin Kimathi, the Chair of the Nairobi-based Muslim Human Rights Forum, who had himself been imprisoned for a year without trial in Luzira Maximum Security Prison by the Ugandan authorities after the July 2010 Kampala bombings, told the BBC: "A lot of youth who have been arrested in the past look at it as some oppression or injustices, they point to those injustices, and they come out angry. Indeed you will even hear it in the first minutes of release, somebody coming out and saying 'I am going to [get] revenge, I cannot stand these sorts of injustices any more.'"[923] Further support for these findings came from a 2015 United Nations Development Programme study, *Journey to Extremism in Africa*, which interviewed 495 current and former African militants and found that 71% cited government action, including the "killing of a family member or friend" or the "arrest of a family member or friend", as the tipping point that prompted them to join a terrorist group.[924] The authors concluded that state security-actor conduct should therefore be considered "a prominent accelerator of recruitment, rather than the reverse."[925]

In his influential work on suicide terrorism, *Dying to Win*, Robert Pape compiled a dataset of 315 suicide bombings that occurred around the world between 1980 and 2003.[926] He found that 95% of these attacks were avowedly undertaken to eject democratic states from territory viewed by terrorist groups as part of their national homeland.[927] Like its historical analog colonial rule, punitive military occupation generates a constant stream of negative interactions between occupier and occupied. As the cycle of action and reaction builds and expands, military counter-insurgency and counter-terrorism operations impact wider and wider segments of

---

[922] Anneli Botha, *Radicalisation in Kenya: Recruitment to al-Shabaab and the Mobasa Republican Council*, Institute for Security Studies, Paper 265 (September 2014), p. 20.

[923] Will Ross, Kenyan MPs investigate attack, *BBC Newshour*, 30 September 2013.

[924] *Journey to Extremism in Africa: Drivers, Incentives and The Tipping Point for Recruitment*, United Nations Development Programme (2017), p. 5.

[925] ibid.

[926] Robert Pape, *Dying to Win: The Strategic Logic of Suicide Terrorism* (Random House; 2005), p. 3.

[927] Robert Pape and James Feldman, *Cutting the Fuse: The Explosion of Global Suicide Terrorism and How to Stop it* (University of Chicago Press; 2010), p. 22.

the population, and if these operations are poorly targeted — and they are very difficult to execute clinically without incisive leadership, exemplary intelligence, and well-trained, disciplined troops — they end up antagonizing and radicalizing more and more people. As one US veteran of the occupation of Iraq, Adam Stevenson, said of the insurgents he was fighting: "I can totally understand why a lot of them do what they do. If somebody kicked my door in at 2 am and took my dad and put a bag over his head and zip-stripped him, I'd be out there the next night with a rocket too. And if you say you wouldn't, you're a liar. Or a wuss."[928] Former Israeli Prime Minister Ehud Barak, a veteran special forces soldier himself, also experienced first hand the often counterproductive outcome of expeditionary military operations: "When we entered Lebanon ... there was no *Hezbollah*. We were accepted with perfumed rice and flowers by the *Shia* in the south. It was our presence there that created *Hezbollah*."[929] The Australian soldier-scholar David Kilcullen coined the term "accidental guerrilla" to describe the radicalizing impact that foreign military intervention often has on third parties not directly involved in an initial conflict.[930] Critiquing the effect that NATO operations in Afghanistan had on local communities with no particular sympathy for *al-Qaeda* or the *Taliban*, Kilcullen noted that lack of cultural sensitivity, limited political understanding, and clumsy targeting decisions — all inevitable by-products of expeditionary warfare in unfamiliar territory — combined to alienate, and ultimately inflame, hitherto neutral communities.

As two of the principal conflicts referenced in Pape's study were between the Tamils and the ruling Sinhalese majority in Sri Lanka, and between the Israelis and the Palestinians, it is worth passing a micromobilization lens over these conflicts to see if the qualitative evidence supports his quantitative analysis. Miranda Alison interviewed sixteen female members of the Sri Lankan LTTE about their

---

[928] Joshua Philips, *None of Us Were Like This Before: American Soldiers and Torture* (Verso; 2010), p. 63.

[929] Matthew Levitt, *Hezbollah: The Global Footprint of Lebanon's Party of God* (Georgetown University Press; 2013), p. 11.

[930] David Kilcullen, *The Accidental Guerrilla: Fighting Small Wars in the Midst of a Big One* (Hurst & Co.; 2009).

experiences in the organization, four mentioned the death of a family member as a contributing factor in their decision to join, six mentioned forced displacement, and ten referenced general violence by the Sri Lankan military.[931] One woman, 'Thamilvily', who joined the LTTE in 1995, told Alison: "We have witnessed the adverse effects of shelling and military action; we have seen people die and be injured. When we ask why, we see it is that we are not free and are at the mercy of the military." Another militant, 'Sudarvili', added: "Because of the occupation of the army we have been forced to take up arms." An aspirant Tamil Tiger suicide bomber called Samandi interviewed in May 2006 by a reporter from *Time* Magazine said that the death of 125 friends and neighbors after the Sri Lankan government carpet-bombed her village drove her to join the LTTE: "I saw all that, all that blood and all those bodies and I thought, 'Tomorrow, I will die like this too. So I will join the LTTE and die for a reason.'"[932] Stephen Hopgood reported a conversation with an LTTE recruiter who admitted: "Times of massive Sri Lankan violence are the easiest time to sign youth up."[933]

The American historian Rashid Khalidi has written that the quintessential Palestinian experience "takes place at a border, an airport, a checkpoint: in short, at any of those many modern barriers where identities are checked and verified. What happens to Palestinians at these crossing points brings home to them how much they share in common as a people. For it is at these borders and barriers that the 6 million Palestinians are singled out for 'special treatment', and are forcefully reminded of their identity: of who they are, and of why they are different from others."[934] Khalil Shaqaqi, Director of the Palestinian Center for Policy and Survey

[931] Miranda Alison, In War, We Never Think We Are Women: Women, Gender, and the Liberation Tamil Tigers of EELAM, in Laura Sjoberg and Caron Gentry (eds.), *Women, Gender, and Terrorism* (University of Georgia Press; 2011), pp. 135–136.
[932] Alex Perry, How Sri Lanka's Rebels Build a Suicide Bomber, *Time*, 12 May 2006 at http://content.time.com/time/world/article/0,8599,1193862,00.html.
[933] Stephen Hopgood, Tamil Tigers 1987–2002, in Diego Gambetta (ed.), *Making Sense of Suicide Missions* (Oxford University Press; 2005), p. 71.
[934] Rashid Khalidi, *Palestinian Identity: The Construction of Modern National Consciousness* (Columbia University Press; 1997), p. I.

Research in Ramallah and the brother of the founder of Palestinian Islamic Jihad Fathi Shaqaqi, has published research suggesting a positive correlation between support for suicide bombing and the number of Israeli checkpoints Palestinians have to pass through as they go about their daily routine.[935] To put that in some kind of perspective, in June 2009, the Israeli military established an average of seventy flying checkpoints in the West Bank every week.[936] Not for nothing has the Palestinian journalist Zuhair Kurdi observed: "The legal father of the suicide bomber is the Israeli checkpoint, whilst his mother is the house demolition."[937] There is some evidence that this phenomenon is not unique to the Palestinian experience. Several *al-Shabaab* veterans interviewed by Muhsin Hassan said that humiliations suffered at the hands of Transitional Federal Government forces — especially some of the treatment endured by female relatives at government checkpoints — had pushed them to join *al-Shabaab* to protect themselves and their families: "[Soldiers] would touch our women inappropriately at the checkpoints. Imagine when you see this being done to your mother or your sister ... it is humiliating and infuriating."[938]

Finally, foreign occupation, and the quotidian humiliations and abuses that come with it, has been a major theme of *al-Qaeda* and ISIL propaganda. The World Islamic Front *fatwa* calling on Muslims "to kill the Americans and their allies — civilian and military" that preceded the twin bombing of US Embassies in Nairobi and Dar es Salaam in August 1998 cited three grievances as its *casus belli*: the US occupation of the Lands of Islam "in the holiest of places ... plundering its riches, dictating to its rulers, humiliating its people, terrorizing its neighbors"; the "great devastation" and "protracted blockade" inflicted on the Iraqi people; and the "occupation of

---

[935] Scott Atran, *Talking to the Enemy: Faith, Brotherhood and the (Un)making of Terrorists* (Ecco; 2010), p. 359.

[936] Daniel Byman, *A High Price: The Triumphs and Failures of Israeli Counterterrorism* (Oxford University Press; 2011), p. 158.

[937] ibid., p. 168.

[938] Muhsin Hassan, Understanding Drivers of Violent Extremism: The Case of Al-Shabaab and Somali Youth, *CTC Sentinel*, 23 August 2012, pp. 18–19.

Jerusalem and murder of Muslims there".[939] 9/11 hijacker Hamza al-Ghamdi echoed this message in his martyrdom video, addressing his target audience directly: "And I say to America: if it wants its armies and people to be safe, then it must withdraw all of its forces from the Muslim lands and depart from all our countries. If not, then let it await the men, prepare its coffins and dig graves for its citizens."[940] *Al-Qaeda* strategist and veteran Islamist militant Abu Mus'ab Al-Suri also noted in his influential online guide *The Call to Global Islamic Resistance* that foreign invasion is one of the best of all climates in which to attract followers to *jihad.*[941] Despite being well aware of this narrative, Western liberal democracies have proved to be remarkably insensitive to the manner in which their often aggressive and intrusive counter-terrorism policies have been perceived by the communities most directly affected by them. Amaryllis Fox, a former CIA Clandestine Service officer, recalled debriefing an *al-Qaeda* fighter who left her challenging the "just war" narrative she had internalized since the 9/11 attacks: "[He] made a point once during a debriefing. He said, all these movies that America makes, like Independence Day and Hunger Games and Star Wars, they're all about a small, scrappy band of rebels who will do anything in their power with the limited resources available to them to expel an outside, technologically advanced invader. And what you don't realize, he said, is that to us, to the rest of the world, you are the empire, and we are Luke and Han. You are the aliens and we are Will Smith."[942]

## Precipitating incidents

The sociologist Anthony Oberschall observed that at the outset of a terrorist campaign, there is often a specific "precipitating incident"

---

[939] World Islamic Front Statement, Jihad Against Jews and Crusaders, 23 February 1998, at https://fas.org/irp/world/para/docs/980223-fatwa.htm. Viewed 22 January 2017.

[940] Robert Pape and James Feldman, *Cutting the Fuse: The Explosion of Global Suicide Terrorism and How to Stop It* (University of Chicago Press; 2010), p. 23.

[941] Michael Ryan, *Decoding Al-Qaeda's Strategy: The Deep Battle Against America* (Columbia University Press; 2013), p. 232.

[942] Al Jazeera Plus at https://www.youtube.com/watch?v=TnEKEfkdrOU.

that prompts a group to go underground and embrace violence.[943] Perhaps the most often cited example in the literature is the reaction of the British authorities to the 1916 Easter Uprising led by a loose alliance of Irish republican groups, including the Irish Republican Brotherhood, the Irish Volunteers, and the Irish Citizen Army. The rising began on 24 April 1916 with the rebels seizing key buildings across the center of Dublin including the General Post Office (GPO), St. Stephen's Green, the Four Courts building, and Jacob's Biscuit Factory. There were also a few related uprisings in the counties of Fingal, Wexford and Galway that primarily targeted police facilities. The fighting lasted for six days until the British were able to reassert their control and the remaining rebel holdouts surrendered. Twenty-three Irish police officers and 128 British Army soldiers were killed during the uprising, along with 318 civilians. By contrast, only sixty-six rebels died in the fighting.

In 1916, there were approximately 168,000 Irishmen of all denominations fighting for the British Army on the battlefields of World War I. In the *Proclamation of the Irish Republic* distributed by the rebels during the uprising, they openly acknowledged that they had received support from "gallant allies in Europe" — a clear and unambiguous reference to Germany. For the many Irish families with sons fighting against the Kaiser's troops on the Western Front, this seemed like a profound betrayal. A number of Irish Volunteers reported receiving a very hostile reception from Dublin residents as they were marched under guard through the city streets after their surrender.[944] In his statement to the Irish Bureau of Military History, Volunteer Robert Holland recalled: "Men, women and children used filthy expressions at us. F Company, which was mainly made up from Inchicore, heard all their names called out at intervals by the bystanders. They were, "shoot the *Sinn Féin* ****s'. My name was called out at intervals by some boys and girls I had gone to school

---

[943] Anthony Oberschall, Explaining Terrorism: The Contribution of Collective Action Theory, *Sociological Theory*, Vol. 22, No. 1 (March 2004), p. 28.
[944] Tim Pat Coogan, *1916: The Easter Uprising* (Cassell; 2002), p. 142.

with … The British troops saved us from manhandling."[945] Another Volunteer, Con Colbert, complained to some of his fellow prisoners that "the people whom we have tried to emancipate have demonstrated nothing but hate and contempt for us."[946] In his official report, the British military governor, General Sir John Maxwell, went out of his way to single out the Irish regiments under his command for particular praise for the role they had played in putting down the uprising.[947] The Easter Uprising had literally pitted brother against brother — Lieutenant Gerald Neilan of the Royal Dublin Fusiliers was killed by the rebels in fighting near the Mendicity Institute while his younger brother, Arthur, was fighting with the Irish Volunteers in the Four Courts. In the immediate aftermath of the Uprising, it was far from certain what side the bulk of Irish public opinion would ultimately come down on. In the assessment of the situation he provided to the British Prime Minister, Herbert Henry Asquith, the Chief Secretary for Ireland, Augustine Birrell, emphasized: "It is not an *Irish* rebellion. It would be a pity if *ex post facto* it became one."[948] Birrell's warning fell on deaf ears.

General Maxwell had been dispatched to Ireland with instructions to put down the Easter Uprising and he took the view that it was "imperative to inflict the most severe sentences" on the organizers of the uprising and the commanders who took part "to act as a deterrent to intriguers and to bring home to them that the murder of His Majesty's subjects or other acts calculated to imperil the safety of the realm will not be tolerated".[949] Fourteen men were sentenced to death in Dublin, and also two other conspirators, Thomas Kent and Roger Casement, in Cork and London, respectively. On 29 April, Father Columbus Murphy met with General

---

[945] Bureau of Military History, 1913–1921, *Statement by Witness Robert Holland*, Document No. W.S. 280, File No. S.1300, p. 45. Ironically, *Sinn Féin* had not actually participated in the uprising but was nevertheless initially blamed erroneously by British officials for what had taken place.

[946] Bureau of Military History, 1913–1921, *Statement by Witness Robert Holland*, Document No. W.S. 280, File No. S.1300, p. 46.

[947] Robert Kee, *The Green Flag: A History of Irish Nationalism* (Penguin, London; 2000), p. 577.

[948] ibid., p. 573.

[949] Tim Pat Coogan, *1916: The Easter Uprising* (Cassell; 2002), p. 143.

Maxwell to request pastoral access to one of the condemned men, Pádraic Pearse, who had read out the *Proclamation of the Irish Republic* on the steps of the GPO building at the beginning of the Uprising. Murphy was granted the access he sought, but in the course of the conversation, General Maxwell made plain his intention to "make those beggars pay" for their disloyalty to the Crown. In response, Father Murphy paraphrased the early Roman Christian author Tertullian, warning the General: "The blood of martyrs is the seed of martyrs."[950] The long-serving Irish Member of Parliament John Dillon similarly urged the leader of the Irish Parliamentary Party, John Redmond, to impress upon the British government "the extreme unwisdom of any wholesale shooting of prisoners. The wisest course is to execute *no one* for the present. If there were shootings of prisoners on any large scale the effect on public opinion might be disastrous in the extreme. So far the feeling of the population in Dublin is against the *Sinn Féiners*. But a reaction might very easily be created."[951] No one in London deigned to listen and the executions went ahead as scheduled, although in Dublin, General Maxwell seems to have had at least some small, belated apprehension of the risk the government was running, advising the British Prime Minister not to return the bodies of the executed rebel leaders to their families: "Irish sentimentality will turn these graves into martyrs' shrines to which annual processions will be made, which would cause constant irritation in this country."[952] A similar logic resulted in Osama bin Laden's 2011 burial at sea after he was killed during the American raid on his hideout in Abbottabad.

General Maxwell's hope that by secretly disposing of the bodies of the executed men, he would deprive republicans of a symbol to unite their fellow countrymen around was soon dashed. Prime Minister Asquith had himself acknowledged in the House of Commons that the rebels had "conducted themselves with great humanity" and "fought very bravely" during the Uprising, and

---

[950] Benedict Cullen, Echoes of the Rising's final shots, *The Irish Times*, 19 April 2003.

[951] Robert Kee, *The Green Flag: A History of Irish Nationalism* (Penguin, London; 2000), p. 573.

[952] ibid., p. 574.

public opinion quickly began to turn against the government.[953] The celebrated Irish playwright George Bernard Shaw spoke for many when he wrote: "My own view is that the men who were shot in cold blood, after their capture or surrender, were prisoners of war, and that it was therefore, entirely incorrect to slaughter them."[954] Accurate reports that the labor leader James Connolly, who had been badly wounded during the fighting at the GPO and was unable to stand unaided, had been tied to a chair before being shot attracted particular public opprobrium.

The veteran republican Tom Clarke, shot in Kilmainham Gaol on 3 May, had sent a final message to supporters through his wife, Kathleen, assuring them: "My comrades and I believe we have struck the first successful blow for freedom, and so sure as we are going out this morning, so sure will freedom come as a direct result of our action ... With this belief, we die happy."[955] He would be proved right with remarkable swiftness. The powerful symbolism of the enforced sacrifice made by the leaders of the Easter Uprising did not diminish over time and became a rallying cry for the republican movement. One man who answered this call to arms was Liam Deasy who joined the the 3rd Cork Brigade of the IRA and went on to play a leading local role in the Irish War of Independence. He later recalled in his memoirs that "in consequence of the events that occurred in the decisive week of the Easter Uprising in 1916, and more particularly of the events that followed it, thousands of young men all over Ireland, indeed thousands of men of all ages in the country, turned irrevocably against the English government and became uncompromisingly dedicated to the cause of obliterating the last vestiges of English rule in Ireland. I was one of them."[956] It is difficult to fault the conclusion reached by Louis Redmond-Howard in his contemporary account of the Easter Uprising: "There

---

[953] Tim Pat Coogan, *1916: The Easter Uprising* (Cassell; 2002), pp. 145–146.

[954] ibid., p. 146.

[955] Ruth Dudley Edwards, *The Seven: The Lives and Legacies of the Founding Fathers of the Irish Republic* (Oneworld Publications; 2016), p. 341.

[956] Richard English, *Armed Struggle: The History of the IRA* (Oxford University Press; 2004), p. 4.

never was, I believe, an Irish crime — if crime it can be called — which had not its roots in an English folly."[957]

The history of nineteenth and early twentieth century anarchism is also full of precipitating events — the execution of Auguste Vaillant in Paris, the flogging of the student Alexei Bogolyubov in St. Petersburg, and the Bava-Beccaris massacre in Milan could all be said to fall into this category of event. Across the Atlantic, as the US government began to prepare for the country's entry into World War I, federal and state authorities introduced legislation to suppress radical organizations and publications that opposed the war, among them the Galleanist newspaper *Cronaca Sovversiva*[958] which the Department of Justice considered "the most rabid, seditious and anarchistic sheet ever published in this country".[959] Luigi Galleani, the titular leader of the movement, was arrested in June 1917 and the government began preparing a case to deport him. Scores of other Galleanisti were arrested on charges such as failure to register for the draft, obstructing the war effort, and insulting the American flag.[960]

Deportation became the US government's punishment of choice and the politicians behind it, like Senator Thomas Hardwick and Attorney General A. Mitchell Palmer, became the Galleanisti's principal targets, with one anarchist leaflet declaring: "Deportation will not stop the storm from reaching these shores. The storm is within and very soon will leap and crash and annihilate you in blood and fire."[961] Although Galleani himself was careful not to associate himself too closely with the violence that followed, a hardcore group of 50–60 of his supporters launched a counter-offensive against the US authorities in the summer of 1917, which would ultimately culminate in the bombing of Wall Street in September 1920 and the deaths of thirty-eight persons, the worst terrorist incident on US soil until the attack on the Alfred P. Murrah Federal Building by Timothy

---

[957] Tim Pat Coogan, *1916: The Easter Uprising* (Cassell; 2002), p. 1.

[958] Subversive Chronicle.

[959] Nunzio Pernicone, Luigi Galleani and Italian Anarchist Terrorism in the United States, *Studi Emigrazione*, Vol. 30 (September 1993), p. 484.

[960] ibid.

[961] ibid., p. 485.

McVeigh in April 1995.[962] Intriguingly, Galleani himself seems to have instinctively anticipated Oberschall's insight in his own writings, observing in his widely read collection of essays *The End of Anarchism?*: "An episode of unusually cruel ferocity ... the mass slaughter on [sic] an unarmed crowd ... or the legal murder of a rebel, even though no one is known to have died as a consequence of his act ... provoke the same indignation, the same violent shock on a cold, balanced, experienced mind as on pure minds and primitive souls."[963]

Similarly, one can identify important precipitating incidents in the histories of many of the movements struggling to free themselves from colonial rule. For a generation of Algerian patriots, the harsh French reprisals that followed the Sétif disturbances of May 1945 represented a critical turning point. The Algerian writer and nationalist activist Kateb Yacine recalled: "I was sixteen years old. The shock which I felt at the pitiless butchery that caused the deaths of thousands of Muslims, I have never forgotten. From that moment my nationalism took definite form."[964] The future FLN leader Ramdane Abane resigned his position as secretary of the French colonial commune of Chateaudun-du-Rhumel in the immediate aftermath of the Sétif reprisals, telling the Director of the Commune: "Between the system you represent and me there is no other link than this pen. Take it, I give it to you."[965] Abane would go on to become one of the colonial authorities' most dangerous and implacable opponents until his death at the hands of rivals within the FLN in December 1957. Less dramatic perhaps but equally pivotal, the historian David French has argued that the decision by the British authorities to deport Greek Cypriot leader Archbishop Makarios III, and some of his closest political associates, to the Sychelles in March

---

[962] See Nunzio Pernicone, Luigi Galleani and Italian Anarchist Terrorism in the United States, *Studi Emigrazione*, Vol. 30 (September 1993).

[963] Luigi Galleani, *The End of Anarchism?* (Elephant Editions; 2012), pp. 86–87.

[964] Alistair Horne, *A Savage War of Peace: Algeria 1954–1962* (New York Review Books Classics; 2006), p. 27.

[965] Beläid Abane, Frantz Fanon and Abane Ramdane: Brief Encounter in the Algerian Revolution, in Nigel Gibson (ed.), *Living Fanon: Global Perspectives* (Palgrave MacMillan; 2011), p. 28.

1956 created "a deep sense of resentment even amongst people who hitherto had been well-disposed to the British" and boosted support for the nationalist terrorist group EOKA.[966] Makarios' deportation also removed a significant restraint on EOKA's activities and there was a considerable increase in the organization's operational tempo. The British authorities recorded 246 EOKA-related incidents in March 1956 and 395 in May, by some margin the most violent month of the conflict so far.[967]

In Latin America, the US-supported Colombian military assault on the village of Marquetalia, which quixotically declared itself a communist republic in 1964, helped transform a minor and unfocused peasant insurrection into a revolutionary force. About fifty guerrillas and peasants survived the attack and founded a self-defense organization called the "Bloc of the South," which aimed to protect the peasantry and fight on against the Colombian state.[968] Manuel Marulanda Vélez, a survivor of Operation Marquetalia, helped reform the Bloc of the South into the *Fuerzas Armadas Revolucionarias de Colombia* (FARC) at a conference in 1964, telling those present: "In order to face the aggression against Marquetalia, we create ... a new type of General Staff as supreme political and military authority."[969] In Spain, the Basque separatist group ETA carried out its first attack as early as 1961, but its operations were relatively desultory and had caused no fatalities until 7 June 1968 when ETA militants Txabi Etxebarrieta and Iñaki Sarasqueta panicked and shot dead a *Guardia Civil*, José Antonio Pardines Arcay, during a routine traffic stop near the Basque town of Tolosa. The two ETA men fled, but their car was eventually forced to stop at a roadblock and the two men surrendered, at which point Etxebarrieta was dragged to the side of the road by *Guardia Civil* incensed by the

---

[966] David French, *Fighting EOKA: The British Counter-Insurgency Campaign on Cyprus, 1955–1959* (Oxford University Press; 2015), p. 105.

[967] Hansard, Vol. 565, Written Answers, p. 104.

[968] Doug Stokes, *America's Other War* (Zed Books; 2013), p. 73.

[969] *Manuel Vélez quoted in Chronology of Resistance: FARC-EP, A History of Struggle*, 17 February 2009 at https://resistencia-colombia.org/index.php/english/463-chronology-of-resistance-farc-ep-a-history-of-struggle. Viewed by the author on 26 March 2016.

death of their comrade and shot.[970] Etxebarrieta's coldblooded roadside execution was the incident that precipitated a major escalation in the conflict. ETA immediately capitalized on Etxebarrieta's death organizing demonstrations across the Basque region, priests held masses in his memory, and ETA's ranks swelled with new volunteers.[971] ETA's first deliberate assassination, the murder of a notoriously brutal local police commander, Melitón Manzanas, followed soon afterwards on 2 August 1968.[972] The Spanish authorities retaliated by declaring a state of emergency in the Province of Guipúzcoa the following day. Two thousand Basques would be detained over the next twelve months, but ETA survived the onslaught and in December 1973 would go on to assassinate Franco's designated successor, Admiral Luis Carrero Blanco. This in turn would prove to be a mortal blow to the continuation of the Francoist regime after the Generalissimo's death.[973]

For German radicals, the key precipitating incident was the 1967 death of Berlin student Benno Ohnesorg at police hands. Ohnesorg was killed in a confrontation with a plainclothes policeman, Karl-Heinz Kurras, in the aftermath of a violent demonstration held to protest a visit by the Shah of Iran to Berlin. Speaking at a student meeting after Ohnesburg's shooting, *Rote Armee Fraktion* founding member Gudrun Ensslin told the gathering: "This fascist state means to kill us all. We must organize resistance. Violence is the only way to answer violence. This is the Auschwitz generation, and there's no arguing with them!"[974] The *Rote Armee Fraktion* would make explicit reference to Ohnesorg's death as a *casus belli*: "The Urban Guerrilla Concept should be seen as an armed struggle taking place in the light of police shoot-to-kill methods and the class justice that

---

[970] Daniele Conversi, *The Basques, the Catalans, and Spain: Alternative Routes to Nationalist Mobilisation* (University of Nevada Press; September 2000), pp. 98–99.

[971] Robert Clark, *The Basque Insurgents: ETA 1952-1980* (University of Wisconsin Press; 1984), p. 49.

[972] Teresa Whitfield, *Endgame for ETA: Elusive Peace in the Basque Country* (Oxford University Press; 2014), p. 43.

[973] ibid., p. 44.

[974] Stefan Aust, *Baader-Meinhof: The Inside Story of the R.A.F.* (Oxford University Press; 2009), p. 27.

managed to free Kurras. The system would bury our comrades alive if we didn't stop it. We will not be demoralized by the violence of the system."[975] As for Ohnesorg's killer, Kurras was suspended for four years but ultimately acquitted of any wrongdoing and, on rejoining the police force, he was eventually promoted to the relatively senior rank of *kriminaloberkommissar*.[976] In a darkly ironic twist, it emerged in May 2009 that Kurras had actually been an agent of the East German secret police, the *Stasi*, at the time of the incident, although there is no evidence to suggest that he was acting under their instructions at the time.

Michael Baumann also described the impact Ohnesorg's death had on him: "Benno Ohnesorg. It did a crazy thing to me. When his casket went by, it just went ding, something got started there."[977] Baumann joined *Bewegung 2. Juni*, an anarchist terrorist group formed in direct response to Ohnesorg's death that took the date of the incident as its name. The group was best known for the 1972 bombing of the British Yacht Club in West Berlin in support of the Provisional IRA, which killed an employee of the club, and for kidnapping West Berlin mayoral candidate Peter Lorenz in 1975. In his memoir, Baumann described the logic behind the group's decision to take up the armed struggle: "The bullet was just as much against *you*; for the first time, they were really shooting at you. It doesn't make a damn bit of difference who is doing the shooting. Of course it was clear now: *hit them*, no more pardons … If the gallows is smiling at you at the end anyway, then you can fight back beforehand."[978] As we touched on in the previous section, for the second-generation *Rote Armee Fraktion* member Volker Speitel and his wife, Angelika, the precipitating incident was the death of the RAF hunger striker Holger Meins. Volker later recalled: "The death of Holger Meins and the decision to take to the gun were one of the same. Sober

---

[975] *Red Army Faction: The Urban Guerrilla Concept* (Kersplebedeb Publishing; 2005), p. 27.

[976] Detective Chief Inspector.

[977] Michael Baumann, *Terror or Love?* (Pulp Press; 1977), p. 40.

[978] ibid., pp. 40–41. Although it should be noted the bullet Baumann is referring to, in this instance, is the one fired at student leader Rudi Dutschke, not Benno Ohnesorg.

thought was impossible by now; it was simply the emotional drive of the last few months reacting."[979]

For the *Brigate Rosse*, it was the 1969 bombing of the headquarters of the *Banca Nazionale dell'Agricoltura* in Milan's Piazza Fontana, which killed seventeen people and left eighty-eight injured. The event was used by the Italian authorities to justify a clampdown on left-wing activism — an anarchist framed for the attack, Giuseppe Pinelli, died in police custody. Police Commissioner Luigi Calabresi, from whose office Pinelli plunged to his death, was killed in turn by the leftist group *Lotta Continua*. One of *Prima Linea* and the *Brigate Rosse*'s most notorious female members, Susanna Ronconi, later observed: "The massacre of Piazza Fontana ... marked a decisive turning point for me because it closed the circle (which had until then still seemed open) between the institutions, the state and the right."[980] The bombing was most likely carried out by right-wing extremists with the connivance of the Italian *Servizio Informazioni Difesa*, making it perhaps the purest example of the unintended social construction of a terrorist movement by a state.[981] In the United States, the Kent State campus shooting on 4 May 1970 — when Ohio National Guardsmen fired sixty-seven rounds into a crowd of unarmed student anti-war protestors killing four and wounding nine — prompted the Weather Underground to issue its first public communiqué, a declaration of a state of war which fulminated, "the insanity of Amerikan 'justice' has added to its list of atrocities six blacks killed in Augusta, two in Jackson and four white Kent State students making thousands more into revolutionaries", and promised a reprisal attack within fourteen days.[982]

In December 1996, the Peruvian Marxist terror group known as the *Movimiento Revolucionario Túpac Amaru* (MRTA) gained

---

[979] Stefan Aust, *Baader-Meinhof: The Inside Story of the R.A.F.* (Oxford University Press; 2009), p. 219.

[980] Alison Jamieson, Identity and Morality in the Italian Red Brigades, *Terrorism and Political Violence*, Vol. 2, No. 4, (1990), p. 511.

[981] Robert Meade, *Red Brigades: The Story of Italian Terrorism* (Palgrave Macmillan; 1990), p. 57 and Philip Willan, *Puppetmasters: The Political Use of Terrorism in Italy* (Constable; 1991), p. 126.

[982] Bernardine Dohrn, Declaration of a State of War, *The Berkeley Tribe*, 31 July 1970 at http://www.lib.berkeley.edu/MRC/pacificaviet/scheertranscript.html.

global notoriety when fourteen militants led by Néstor Cerpa seized control of the Japanese Ambassador's residence in Lima during a reception to mark the birthday of Emperor Akihito.[983] In addition to members of the local diplomatic corps, the terrorists took hostage the Peruvian foreign and agricultural ministers, the President of the Supreme Court, six Supreme Court justices, five generals of the National Police including the chief of Peru's anti-terrorist police, five congressmen, and President Alberto K. Fujimori's mother, sister and brother. Their plan was to force the release of 465 jailed comrades — including Cerpa's wife, Nancy Gilvonio.[984]

Once the MRTA had consolidated their control of the residence on the first day of the siege, the British journalist Sally Bowen, who had been attending the Ambassador's reception, identified herself and was taken with a second reporter to meet Nestor Cerpa. When the two reporters asked why Cerpa had attacked the Japanese Ambassador's Residence, he presented them with a book from his knapsack, *Compañeros, Toman Nuestro Sangre,*[985] about the takeover of a bankrupt textile factory, Cromotex, by union workers led by Cerpa in 1979. The occupation of the factory had finished with a police assault that claimed the lives of six union protestors. Cerpa told the two reporters: "This is where it all began."[986] Cerpa had himself been arrested for his role in the Cromotex strike and jailed for ten months. When he was released from prison, he went underground later remerging as "Commander Huertas", a leader of the fledgling MRTA. He chose "Huertas" as his *nom de guerre* in honor of his close friend and fellow union leader, Hemigidio Huertas, who had been seriously wounded when the police stormed the

---

[983] Tupac Amaru Revolutionary Movement. The MRTA took its name from Tupac Amaru II, an eighteenth century leader of the Inca people who led an indigenous uprising against Spanish rule in Peru in 1780.

[984] Dirección Nacional del MRTA Communicado No. 1 (17 December 1996).

[985] Comrades, They Take Our Blood.

[986] Diana Jean Schemo, How Peruvian Hostage Crisis Became Trip Into the Surreal, *The New York Times,* 26 April 1997 at http://www.nytimes.com/1997/04/26/world/how-peruvian-hostage-crisis-became-trip-into-the-surreal.html?pagewanted=all&src=pm.

Cromotex factory and died later in police custody.[987] The siege of the Ambassador's Residence lasted for 126 days before Peruvian commandos finally stormed the building killing all the terrorists inside, including Néstor Cerpa. One hostage was also killed during the assault, along with two members of the assault team.

In June 2009, Nigerian police in the north-eastern state of Borno clashed with the members of a local Islamic sect called *Boko Haram* over, of all things, their boycott of new legislation making the wearing of protective helmets compulsory for all motorcycle riders. A confrontation between police and *Boko Haram* members at a funeral procession escalated to the point that perhaps as many as seventeen members were injured.[988] Their leader, Mohammed Yusuf, threatened to retaliate in kind stating publicly: "We will not agree with this kind of humiliation, we are ready to die together with our brothers."[989] Tensions escalated with a series of arrests and the seizure of a number of weapons until, on 26 July 2009, *Boko Haram* members attacked Dutsen police station in Bauchi and an estimated fifty people were killed in the fighting that ensued. Further attacks on police and government buildings followed with more than one hundred casualties reported. The Nigerian government dispatched the army's Third Armored Division to regain control of the situation and the troops seized *Boko Haram*'s stronghold of Maiduguri on 30 July after heavy fighting, detaining Mohammed Yusuf and his deputy Abubaker Shekau, and destroying the Ibn Taymiyyah mosque, which was the spiritual center of the movement.[990] However, it was what happened next that sparked off a full-blown terrorist campaign and insurgency.

Mohammed Yusuf was taken into custody by the army and handed over to the local Maiduguri police. The police had suffered significant casualties during the unrest, including at least one

---

[987] Laurie Goering, Mediation Called Key To Peru Standoff, *Chicago Tribune*, 7 January 1997 at http://articles.chicagotribune.com/1997-01-07/news/9701070277_1_peru-standoff-hostage-crisis-tupac-amaru-revolutionary-movement.

[988] Virginia Comolli, *Boko Haram: Nigeria's Islamist Insurgency* (C. Hurst & Co.; 2015), p. 53.

[989] ibid., p. 54.

[990] ibid.

Mobile Police Commissioner who was killed in the fighting. Accounts differ, but an eyewitness interviewed by the researcher Virginia Comolli said that tempers were running high. At some point after his arrival at the police station, Yusuf was shot dead. A video emerged showing police officers dancing around Yusuf's body with one officer clearly heard to remark that he would have been "let off the hook" if he had gone to trial.[991] A police spokesman later declared with considerable hubris: "This group operates under a charismatic leader. They will no more have any [in]spiration ... The leader who they thought was invincible and immortal has now been proved otherwise."[992] Yusuf's deputy Shekau was able to escape police custody and it was he who led the surviving members of *Boko Haram* underground to avenge their spiritual leader's death. Shekau and his followers first fled abroad where they learned about weapons and explosives from militant groups in Mali, Sudan and Libya, and, when they returned to Nigeria, *Boko Haram* escalated its violent attacks carrying out its first terrorist bombing in Borno in January 2011 and within a year *Boko Haram* operations had claimed more than 900 lives.[993]

Given the above, it should come as no surprise that emblematic incidences of state repression can also foreshadow significant escalations in the level of violence in pre-existing conflicts. In response to a rising tide of Jewish violence in June 1946, that included the bombing of ten of the eleven bridges connecting Palestine to the outside world, the British Mandate authorities launched a series of mass arrests across Palestine codenamed Operation Agatha with the objective of, as Menachem Begin put it in his memoirs, "breaking the backbone" of the Jewish revolt.[994] Although more than 2,700 Zionist leaders and officials were detained, none of the main *Irgun* or LEHI leaders were caught by the operation, and, still at large, these men responded by escalating the conflict. On 22 July

---

[991] ibid.

[992] ibid., p. 59.

[993] Adam Nossiter, In Nigeria, a Deadly Group's Rage Has Local Roots, *The New York Times*, 25 February 2012.

[994] Menachem Begin, *The Revolt: Story of the Irgun* (Steimatzky's Agency Ltd.; 1977), p. 204.

1946, *Irgun* bombed the King David Hotel in Jerusalem, which housed the offices of British officialdom in the Mandate and served as the headquarters of the British Army in Palestine, killing ninety-one people — mostly Jewish and Arab civilians — and wounding forty-six.[995]

Another example of an aggressive state response pouring fuel on the fire comes from Northern Ireland. On 30 January 1972, soldiers from the British Parachute Regiment opened fire on a Londonderry/Derry protest march after protestors threw rocks at the soldiers. Thirteen protestors were killed outright, a fourteenth died a few months later from his injuries. The public coroner assigned the case accused the paratroopers of "sheer unadulterated murder".[996] In Dublin, an enraged mob responded to Bloody Sunday by storming the British Embassy and burning it to the ground.[997] However, of most significance was the dramatic escalation of republican terrorist tactics and the fact that, as Gerry Adams later recorded, the Provisional IRA was "inundated with new recruits".[998] PIRA volunteer Maria McGuire noted that Bloody Sunday "more than any other single event demonstrated the nature of the repressive policies of Stormont and the British government."[999] She also observed that, for the Provisional IRA, the aftermath of Bloody Sunday bought "vastly increasing support and a large amount of money from inside and outside Ireland. We knew that we would be able to take increased action against the British Army in the Six Counties, and that it would be approved in the Twenty-Six [i.e. in the Irish Republic]."[1000] In a further explicit response to the events of Bloody Sunday, the Official IRA left a 280 lb car bomb outside the Officer's Mess of the Parachute Regiment in Aldershot,

---

[995] See Calder Walton, *Empire of Secrets: British Intelligence, the Cold War and the Twilight of Empire* (Overlook Hardcover; 2013).

[996] John Newsinger, *British Counter-insurgency from Palestine to Northern Ireland* (Palgrave; 2002), p. 166.

[997] J. Bowyer Bell, *The Secret Army: The IRA 1916–1979* (Poolbeg Press; 1990), p. 384.

[998] Gerry Adams, *The Politics of Irish Freedom* (Brandon Book Publishers; 1986), p. 56.

[999] Maria McGuire, *To Take Arms: A Year in the Provisional IRA* (MacMillan; 1973), p. 85.

[1000] ibid., p. 90. "Six Counties" refers to Northern Ireland and "the Twenty-Six" are the 26 counties of the Irish Republic.

Hampshire.[1001] The blast killed seven people — five female kitchen staff, a gardener and a Roman Catholic army chaplain — the first deaths on the British mainland as a result of "The Troubles" and a hugely significant milestone in the conflict. The Official IRA also mounted an attack on the Northern Irish Minister for Home Affairs, John Taylor, who was badly wounded.[1002] Deliberate attacks on civilian targets by the Provisional IRA on the British mainland soon followed, including four simultaneous car bombs left in London in March 1973, bombs at mainline London railway stations in September 1973, and in public houses in Guildford and Birmingham in the autumn of 1974.

Although not explicitly state-directed, a series of twenty violent bombings of Arab neighborhoods in Algiers by white French settlers — including most notoriously the detonation on 10 August 1956 of a large explosive device in the *Rue de Thèbes* by former French intelligence officer André Achiary and members of the *Union Française Nord-Africaine*, which killed seventy-three local Arab residents — provoked a response from the FLN that marked a significant evolution in the FLN's operational practice from close quarter assassinations to mass murder. Just ten days after the *Rue de Thèbes* attack, the FLN, urged on by Ramdane Abane, adopted an explicit policy of indiscriminate terrorism at the Soummam Conference.[1003] The FLN's operational commander in Algiers, Saadi Yacef, frankly explained the reasoning behind this decision: "In discussing the whole question of bombs and the placing of bombs, you have to understand that at this time the ultracolonialists, the *pieds noirs*, would often disguise themselves as paratroopers, and, because they were not interested in any mercy, they would place bombs indiscriminately, resulting in the death of

---

[1001] *BBC*, The Troubles Fact File at http://www.bbc.co.uk/history/war/troubles/factfiles/ira.shtml and Maria McGuire, *To Take Arms: A Year in the Provisional IRA* (MacMillan; 1973), p. 91.

[1002] Maria McGuire, *To Take Arms: A Year in the Provisional IRA* (MacMillan; 1973), p. 92.

[1003] Alistair Horne, *A Savage War of Peace: Algeria 1954–1962* (History Book Club; 2002), p. 184.

civilians. So we too began to place our bombs indiscriminately, not really worrying about the consequences."[1004]

Finally, a precipitating incident does not necessarily have to even be intentionally coercive in nature, and not all perceived injury is physical in form. Non-kinetic events can also become a flashpoint — the 2005 controversy surrounding the publication of cartoons of the Prophet Mohammed is an example of an unexpected threat that escalated from a relatively peripheral event that took on deep significance for a marginalized community. On 30 September 2005, the Danish newspaper *Jyllands-Posten* published a page containing twelve editorial cartoons by different cartoonists in an avowed attempt to stimulate a debate on self-censorship under the headline: "The Face of Mohammed". Most of the cartoons depicted the Prophet Mohammed — breaking an Islamic taboo on displaying pictures of the Prophet — and most could be interpreted as being disrespectful in tone. The publication of the cartoons was greeted by strong protests from the Muslim community in Denmark. Denmark does have a rarely used anti-blasphemy law (Section 140 of the Danish Criminal Code) and in October 2005, a group of prominent Danish Muslims who had formed the "Committee for Prophet Honoring" filed a complaint with the Danish Police. However, in early January 2006, the public prosecutor concluded that the newspaper's declared aim in publishing the cartoons amounted to a legitimate public interest justification and the case was dropped. Dissatisfied with the response that had greeted their representations, and most notably with the government's refusal to meet with the Ambassadors of eleven Muslim countries represented in Copenhagen to discuss the crisis, the Committee for Prophet Honoring decided to seek further international support for their cause. Led by two prominent Danish *Imams*, Ahmad Abu Laban and Akhamad Akkari, the Committee compiled a forty-three-page dossier on the cartoons and other purported examples of Danish "Islamophobia". Delegations then traveled with the dossier to Egypt, Turkey, Lebanon, Syria, Morocco,

---

[1004] Gary Crowdus, Terrorism and Torture in "The Battle of Algiers': An Interview with Saadi Yacef, *Cineaste Magazine*, Vol. 29, No. 3 (2004), p. 35.

Sudan, Algeria, and Qatar to raise awareness of the case. The dossier was even discussed at the summit of the Organization of Islamic Cooperation (OIC) at the behest of the Egyptian government, which issued a communiqué expressing "concern at rising hatred against Islam and Muslims" and condemning the practice of "using the freedom of expression as a pretext for defaming religions".[1005]

As awareness of the case spread in the Muslim world in January and February 2006, protests escalated, especially after the Danish government refused to intervene against the *Jyllands-Posten* or meet with diplomats from the Muslim world to discuss the case. Danish and other European diplomatic missions, Christian churches, and Western businesses were attacked and dozens of people (mostly pro-testors) were killed in violent outbursts, most notably in Afghanistan, Nigeria, Lebanon, and Egypt. A Catholic priest, Andrea Santoro, was shot dead in Trabzon, Turkey, on 5 February 2006. The local high school student who killed him told police he had been influenced to act by the cartoon controversy. A Danish soldier was also killed by an IED in Iraq — although it is not clear if the attack was motivated by the cartoons, or was simply part of wider insurgent activity. In March 2006, the then deputy leader of *al-Qaeda*, Ayman al-Zawahiri, issued a statement seeking to capitalize on the crisis. In India, a regional minister, Haji Yaqoob Qureishi, announced a reward for anyone who beheaded "the Danish cartoonist". The visceral reaction apparently even took the Committee for Prophet Honouring by surprise. Mr Akkari told reporters: "We did not expect it to end up in such a situation, and with violence and for people to use it politi-cally. This has now gone further than we had expected."[1006] The OIC also denounced calls for the cartoonists to be put to death and the OIC's Secretary General described the violent protests as "unIs-lamic" and called for calm.

Although the cartoon controversy eventually faded from the wider public consciousness, the threat to *Jyllands-Posten* and the car-toonists persisted. One cartoonist, Kurt Westergaard, who had

---

[1005] Daniel Howden, David Hardaker and Stephen Castle, How a meeting of leaders in Mecca set off the Cartoon Wars Around the World, *The Independent*, 10 February 2006.
[1006] ibid.

worked for *Jyllands-Posten* for twenty years, became a particular target. In January 2010, a Somali refugee who had been living in Denmark since 1995, Mohamed Geele, broke into Westergaard's house and attacked him with an axe. While Westergaard sheltered in a panic room, Danish police were able to subdue his attacker. Geele was a former youth worker who had apparently become involved with a *al-Shabaab*.[1007] The editorial offices of *Jyllands-Posten* in Copenhagen have also been the target of repeated terror plots. David Coleman Headley, a US citizen with ties to Pakistan's *Lashkar-e-Tayiba* who pleaded guilty to helping to plan the November 2008 terror attacks in Mumbai, also admitted traveling to Denmark for the terror group in January 2009 to reconnoiter the newspaper as a potential target.[1008] In September 2010, Lors Doukayev, a Belgian national of Chechen descent, was arrested after a letterbomb he was preparing to send to the newspaper on the ninth anniversary of the 9/11 attacks exploded in his hotel room. He was sentenced to twelve years in prison. In December 2010, the Danish and Swedish authorities foiled a major plot to seize control of the *Jyllands-Posten* building as part of a Mumbai-style attack. Four men were convicted for their roles in the plot in 2012 — three Swedish citizens of Egyptian, Lebanese, and Tunisian descent, and a Tunisian national. The *Jyllands-Posten* controversy put cartoonists all over the world in the firing line and the January 2015 Charlie Hebdo massacre in Paris and the failed May 2015 attack on the "Muhammad Art Exhibit and Cartoon Contest" in Garland, Texas, can also both reasonably be considered to be related incidents.

## Summary

A surprising finding of the big-data quantitative studies into the putative relationship between poverty and terrorism conducted in

---

[1007] *BBC News*, Denmark cartoon trial: Kurt Westergaard Attacker Jailed, 4 February 2011 at http://www.bbc.co.uk/news/world-europe-12366076.

[1008] US Department of Justice Press Release, David Coleman Headley Sentenced to 35 Years in Prison for Role in India and Denmark Terror Plots, 24 January 2013 at http://www.justice.gov/opa/pr/2013/January/13-nsd-104.html.

the decade after the 9/11 attacks was that while poverty did not correlate in absolute terms to an increase in terrorism, human rights abuses and the suppression of civil liberties did. Alan Krueger and Jitka Malečková found that at a given level of income, countries with a low Freedom House Index score for civil liberties were consistently more likely to produce international terrorists.[1009] Similarly, a cross-national empirical study conducted by James Walsh and James Piazza found that countries with a poor human rights record were also more likely to experience both domestic and transnational terrorist attacks.[1010] A third study carried out by Freedom House itself found that between 1999 and 2003, 70% of all deaths from terrorist attacks were caused by terrorist groups originating from countries characterized by the organization as "Not Free".[1011] This has proved to be the one consistent takeaway common to most such studies into the causes of terrorism. A number of influential researchers working in this field have reached similar conclusions, including James Fearon, Douglas Hibbs, David Laitin, Mark Lichbach, Ethan Bueno de Mesquita, and Michael Mazarr.[1012]

---

[1009] Jitka Malečková, Impoverished Terrorists: Stereotype or Reality? in Tore Bjørgo (ed.), *Root Causes of Terrorism: Myths, Reality and Ways Forward* (Routledge; 2005), p. 41.

[1010] James Walsh and James Piazza, Why Respecting Physical Integrity Rights Reduces Terrorism, *Comparative Political Studies*, Vol. 43, No. 5 (2010).

[1011] Adrian Karatnycky, Civic Power and Electoral Politics, *Freedom House* (2005), p. 9.

[1012] Douglas Hibbs, *Mass Political Violence* (Wiley; 1973); Mark Lichbach, Deterrence of Escalation? The Puzzle of Aggregate Studies of Repression and Dissent, *The Journal of Conflict Resolution*, Vol. 31, No. 2 (1987); Rui de Fugueiredo and Barry Weingast, *Vicious Cycles: Endogenous Political Extremism and Political Violence*, Institute of Government Studies Working Paper No. 9 (2001); James Fearon and David Laitin, Ethnicity, Insurgency and Civil War, *American Political Science Review*, Vol. 97, No. 1 (2003); Peter Rosendorff and Todd Sandler, Too Much of a Good Thing? The Proactive Response Dilemma, *Journal of Conflict Resolution*, Vol. 48, No. 4 (2004); Ethan Bueno de Mesquita, The Quality of Terror, *American Journal of Political Science*, Vol. 49, No. 3 (2005); Michael Mazarr, *Unmodern Men in the Modern World: Radical Islam, Terrorism and the War on Modernity* (Cambridge University Press; 2007); Bader Araj, Harsh State Repression as a Cause of Suicide Bombing: The Case of the Palestinian-Israeli Conflict, *Studies in Conflict and Terrorism*, Vol. 31 (2008); Alan Krueger and David Laitin, Kto Kogo? A Cross-country Study of the Origins and Targets of Terrorism, in Philip Keefer and Norman Loayza (eds.), *Terrorism, Economic Development, and Political Openness* (Cambridge University Press; 2008); and Ethan Bueno de Mesquita, The Political Economy of Terrorism: A Selective Overview of Recent Work, *The Political Economist* (March 2008).

The relationship between government repression and terrorism is admittedly more complex than this simple data point suggests. Broader academic analysis of aggregate data on social unrest and political violence has produced inconclusive results regarding the net effect of repression on social movements.[1013] This is because there are clearly some instances in which repression has a deterrent effect and some in which it exacerbates the situation. Ted Gurr suggested the relationship between repression and violent dissent resembles a reversed U-curve with repression initially deterring dissent, then provoking it, before subduing opposition once more in highly coercive societies.[1014] A society's position on this U-curve determines the likely outcome that will result from the use of coercive force. However, one should not underestimate the degree of force required at the far end of the curve to achieve the total pacification of an insurgent movement. Gurr certainly did not, cautioning: "No pattern of coercive control, however intense and consistent, is likely to deter permanently all enraged men from violence, except genocide."[1015]

The resource mobilization model popularized by Doug McAdam also suggests that an extremely repressive closed regime will choke off any opportunity for oppositional groups to engage in collective action by shrinking the political space in which they can act safely.[1016] This was certainly the experience in 1970s Latin America where military leaders in Argentina, Brazil, Chile, and Uruguay swept aside democratically-elected governments in order to bring the maximum coercive force to bear on would-be Marxist revolutionaries.[1017] During Argentina's so-called Dirty War, the Argentine general Luciano Menéndez notoriously declared himself prepared to kill 50,000 people — 25,000 subversives, 20,000 sympathizers and

---

[1013] Karl-Dieter Opp and Wolfgang Roehl, Repression, Micromobilization, and Political Protest, *Social Forces*, Vol. 69, No. 2 (1990), pp. 522–523.

[1014] Ted Gurr, A Comparative Study of Civil Strife, in Hugh Graham and Ted Gurr (eds.), *The History of Violence in America* (Praeger; 1969).

[1015] Ted Gurr, *Why Men Rebel* (Princeton University Press; 1970), p. 358.

[1016] Douglas McAdam, *Political Process and the Development of Black Insurgency 1930–1970* (University of Chicago Press; 1982).

[1017] Louise Richardson, *What Terrorists Want* (New York; Random House 2006), p. 182.

5,000 unfortunate innocents — to defeat the *Ejército Revolucionario del Pueblo* and *Movimiento Peronista Montonero*: "The army can't risk the lives of its men and lay its prestige on the line simply to act as a kind of police force that ends up by turning over X-number of political prisoners to some timorous judge... who will apply lenient punishment which in turn will be canceled out by amnesties granted by ambitious politicians courting popularity. We're at war, and war obeys another law: he who wipes out the other side wins."[1018] The approach adopted by men like Menéndez was crude, and for a short period of time, it was effective, but ultimately the Latin American military juntas of the 1970s and 1980s all eventually went the way of colonial empires, Nazi Germany, and the Soviet Union.

Repression is difficult to sustain and tends to act not as a cure, but rather as an anesthetic, suppressing the symptoms of dissent temporarily but failing to eradicate the impulses behind it. In his study of revolutionary movements after the Second World War, the sociologist Jeff Goodwin expanded on this insight arguing that "certain state structures and practices actively form or "construct" revolutionary movements as effectively as the best professional revolutionaries, by channeling and organizing political dissent along radical lines."[1019] State constructivism emphasizes how the actions of the state make "cognitively plausible and morally justifiable" both grievances and grievance-based responses.[1020] Goodwin does not discount the role of individual human agency nor of wider societal processes but argues instead that it is the nature of the state response to the challenge to its authority that frames the subsequent evolution of the conflict: "Violent, exclusionary regimes tend to foster unintentionally the hegemony or dominance of their most radical social critics."[1021] Or as Leon Trotsky, who knew a thing or two about

---

[1018] Paul Lewis, *Guerrillas and Generals: the "Dirty War" in Argentina* (Praeger; 2001), p. 108 and Louise Richardson, *What Terrorists Want* (New York; Random House 2006), p. 182.

[1019] Jeff Goodwin, *supra* note 3, p. 25.

[1020] ibid., p. 40.

[1021] ibid., p. 48.

regime change, put it: "A revolution takes place only when there is no other way out."[1022]

In liberal democratic regimes, the introduction of such extremely repressive measures is not an option, since by definition, they are characterized by the rule of law, an independent judiciary, and a foundation of basic civil rights. Thus, democratic states seeking to restrict the political opportunities open to terrorist groups often tend to resort to authoritarian half-measures in a crisis, the kind of repression-lite typically found at the bottom of Gurr's U-curve that involves the use of preventative detention, coercive interrogation techniques and the occasional application of lethal force, but merely serves to create an environment in which the regime's legitimacy is damaged in the eyes of supporters and opponents alike, while oppositional social organization is still possible and the cost of collective action is not yet prohibitive.[1023] This creates "a cognitive opening" — a susceptibility — to terrorist propaganda amongst those affected and, as we saw in Part I, terrorist groups set out quite deliberately to exploit this opportunity.[1024] The record shows that the cycle of violence ultimately serves the terrorists' cause far better than it does the government's by attracting fresh recruits, burnishing existing grievances, and deepening the resolve of those already in the fight.[1025]

## Conclusion

In 2016, a heated debate broke out in the French media between two of the leading Francophone experts on the phenomenon of Islamist terrorism, Olivier Roy and Gilles Kepel. Roy argued that the focus should not be on the "radicalization of Islam" but the

---

[1022] Leon Trotsky, *The History of the Russian Revolution* (Haymarket Books; 2017), p. 740.

[1023] Edward Muller, Income Inequality, Regime Repressiveness, and Political Violence, *American Sociological Review*, Vol. 50, No. 1 (1985), p. 48.

[1024] Mitchell Silber and Arvin Bhatt, *Radicalization in the West: The Homegrown Threat*, New York Police Department (Intelligence Division), 2007, p. 6.

[1025] Rui de Figueiredo Jr. and Barry Weingast, *Vicious Cycles: Endogenous Political Extremism and Political Violence*, Working Paper No. 9, Institute of Governmental Studies, University of California Berkeley, 2001, p. 3.

"Islamization of radicalization", contending that those flocking to ISIL's banner were engaged in an act of "generational revolt" similar to those youthful activists who joined the *Brigate Rosse* and *Rote Armee Fraktion* two generations earlier.[1026] Olivier Roy's generational revolt thesis was roundly dismissed by Gilles Kepel who accused him of being "ignorant of social realities". Instead, Kepel identified political, economic, and social exclusion as being the prime driver, and credited extremist religious doctrines as playing a more formative role. In reality, they both had important insights to share with counter-terrorism practitioners, but they also both seemed to discount other important factors. Such a zero-sum approach to understanding terrorism is both intellectually arrogant and unproductive. John Horgan has said it best: "Almost everything associated with terrorism is complex. Serious efforts to explain anything related to terrorism are, unsurprisingly, complicated."[1027] Far better then to follow Scott Atran's sage advice and embrace complexity.[1028]

In a 2016 article, Martha Crenshaw lamented that despite the best efforts of researchers to explain that there is no single terrorist profile, policymakers remain fixated on this "holy grail".[1029] But the reality is that there is no universal theory of terrorism that satisfactorily explains why, facing a similar set of circumstances, one individual chooses to carry out an act of terrorism, and another does not; and there is never likely to be. Almost one hundred years ago, the Italian anarchist Luigi Galleani wrote that "in most cases the individual act of rebellion comes even more as a surprise to the comrades than to the enemies."[1030] Not much has changed in the intervening period. The uncle of Ali Rezgui, the ISIL gunman responsible for the June 2015 massacre of thirty-eight Western

---

[1026] Timothy Peace, Who becomes a terrorist, and why? *Monkey Cage, Washington Post*, 10 May 2016, at https://www.washingtonpost.com/news/monkey-cage/wp/2016/05/10/who-becomes-a-terrorist-and-why/. Viewed 13 May 2016.

[1027] John Horgan, The Psychology of Terrorism (Routledge; 2014), pp. 276/328.

[1028] Scott Atran, The Moral Logic and Growth of Suicide Terrorism, *The Washington Quarterly*, Vol. 29, No. 2 (2006), p. 144.

[1029] Brian Michael Jenkins, Bruce Hoffman and Martha Crenshaw, How Much Really Changed About Terrorism On 9/11? *The Atlantic*, 11 September 2016.

[1030] Luigi Galleani, *The End of Anarchism?* (Elephant Editions; 2012), p. 85.

tourists staying at Tunisia's Imperial Marhaba beach hotel, told reporters: "Who could imagine he would commit such a horror? Maybe he was changed where he studied, maybe it was something on the internet. But we just don't have any answers."[1031] Social science has generated a number of compelling theories that seek to explain why an individual might become radicalized to the point of violence, which, when matched retrospectively against individual case studies appear to demonstrate considerable explanatory power. What none of these theories allow the practitioner to do with any real certainty is predict in advance whether or not a given individual is likely to become a terrorist. The interplay of human and societal factors are simply too complex to make such a prediction. Siblings take divergent paths, survivors respond differently to abuse, and political messaging plays differently from community to community. As the *Brigate Rosse's* Adriana Faranda told the researcher Alison Jamieson: "There were a lot of little steps which led to where I ended up."[1032]

However, the social science is sufficiently developed that we can draw some reasonable conclusions regarding the circumstances that are most likely to give rise to terrorist activity. In Part II, I have set out to delineate, as best I can, what the social science suggests those core circumstances are: selective empathy for those suffering, the quest for self-actualization, supportive like-minded social networks, grievances with at least some social legitimacy, a sense of social or political exclusion, and heavy-handed coercive action by state actors. To be clear, not all of these factors will necessarily be present in every case, and in some cases, one or two factors may significantly outweigh others, but they represent the best attempts made to date to understand how and why often quite decent human beings set out to kill people they have likely never met in order somehow to make the world a better place. Furthermore, where we find a

---

[1031] Patrick Markey and Tarek Amara, Tunisia beach attacker; from rap fan to killer, *Reuters*, 28 June 2015 at http://news.yahoo.com/tunisia-beach-attacker-rap-fan-killer-222829044.html, viewed 29 June 2015.

[1032] John Horgan, *The Psychology of Terrorism* (Routledge; 2005), p. 98.

convergence of these factors, we can state with confidence that there is a high likelihood that terrorist incidents will not be far behind.[1033] It is therefore practically axiomatic that any well-conceptualized counter-terrorism strategy will need to take these issues into account. In Part III, we will consider the various policy tools that states use to respond to terrorist threats, how these tools can be deployed to either reduce terrorist threats or exacerbate them, and the critical role that international human rights law can play in ensuring that states' counter-terrorism efforts are actually most effective.

---

[1033] L. Rowell Huesmann and Graham Huesmann, No: Poverty and Exclusion are not the Root Causes of Terrorism, in Richard Jackson and Samuel Sinclair (eds.), *Contemporary Debates on Terrorism* (Routledge; 2012), p. 119.

# Part III

# Countering Terrorism Within a Human Rights Framework

"Justice is the strongest army, and security is the best way of life..."[1]

Part I set out to establish how terrorist organizations use violence and what, by their own admission, they hope to achieve by doing so; Part II explored the social science of what drives some individuals to join such organizations and embrace violence as a catalyst for change, and the often unintended part that both the state and society can play in shaping this decision; Part III will explore the existing international legal regime governing states' responses to terrorism and how this is applied, and ignored, in practice and the consequences that result.

There is a profound and persistent belief in many national security establishments around the world that international legal regimes and human rights norms prohibit effective action against terrorism. The Israeli Prime Minister Benjamin Netanyahu devoted a chapter of his book *Fighting Terrorism* to "The Question of Civil Liberties" and what he labeled the democratic dilemma: "If [democratic governments] do not fight terrorism with the means available to them, they endanger their citizenry; if they do, they appear to endanger the very freedoms which they are charged to protect."[2]

---

[1] Excerpted from an undated letter intended for a US audience that was seized during the 2011 raid on bin Laden's compound in Abbottabad. David Francis, Here's Osama bin Laden's Letter to the American People, *Foreign Policy*, 20 May 2015.

[2] Benjamin Netanyahu, *Fighting Terrorism: How Democracies Can Defeat Domestic and International Terrorists* (Farrar, Straus and Giroux; 2001), p. 30.

Netanyahu is clear on which path he favors, observing that there is "a moment of truth in the life of many modern democracies when it is clear that the unlimited defense of civil liberties has gone too far and impedes the protection of life and liberty."[3] US Vice President Dick Cheney made much the same argument after the September 11 attacks, telling one interviewer "it's going to be vital for us to use any means at our disposal, basically, to achieve our objective."[4] CIA Executive Director A. B. "Buzzy" Krongard concurred, telling a gathering of Wall Street investors in October 2001 that the War on Terror would "be won in large measure by forces you do not know about, in actions you will not see and in ways you may not want to know about".[5] Following the massacre in the offices of the satirical magazine Charlie Hebdo in Paris in January 2015, the French Prime Minster Manuel Valls promised the introduction of "exceptional measures" and declared that France was now in "a war against terrorism, against jihadism, against radical Islam, against everything that is aimed at breaking fraternity, freedom, solidarity".[6] In November 1988, British Prime Minister Margaret Thatcher justified the introduction of a ban preventing Irish republicans from appearing on British television with the observation: "We do sometimes have to sacrifice a little of the freedom we cherish in order to defend ourselves from those whose aim is to destroy that freedom altogether and that is a decision which we should not be afraid to take."[7]

---

[3] ibid., p. 33.

[4] Vice-President Dick Cheney interviewed by Tim Russert on NBC's *Meet The Press*, 16 September 2001, at http://afpakwar.com/blog/archives/576.

[5] Gary Younge, The CIA has brought darkness to America by fighting in the shadows, Comment is Free, *The Guardian*, 9 March 2014.

[6] Laura Smith-Spark and Sandrine Amiel, *PM Valls sets out sweeping measures to safeguard France from terror*, CNN, 21 January 2015 at http://www.cnn.com/2015/01/21/europe/europe-terror-threat/. Viewed 1 May 2015 and Dan Bilefsky and Maïa de al Baume, French Premier Declares 'War' on Radical Islam as Paris Girds for Rally, *The New York Times*, 10 January 2015.

[7] Margaret Thatcher, *Speech at the Lord Mayor's Banquet*, 14 November 1988 at http://www.margaretthatcher.org/document/107380 (accessed 29 April 2015).

But just how accurate is this perception? Are the lawful tools that states have at their disposal really so ineffective? What happens when states ignore their own laws and international norms to use prohibited techniques to address terrorist threats? Can an empirical argument be made that one approach produces better results than the other? International law — and particularly human rights law and international humanitarian law — provides a framework within which lawful state responses to terrorism should be conducted. This framework makes provision for wide-ranging international cooperation on counter-terrorism, establishes the benchmarks that characterize genuinely democratic societies, and creates an international regime of protection for fundamental human rights — such as the right to life, the right to liberty, the right to freedom of conscience, and the right to privacy — to ensure that individuals enjoy a measure of protection from the unbridled power of the state.

Police powers are limited for the most part by the requirement that due process is observed in their application and that they are used in a manner that is reasonable, necessary and proportionate to the threat posed by criminal activity. International law recognizes that, on rare occasions, grave circumstances may arise which may require the temporary suspension of some protected rights — it simply requires that any such suspension must be done in a lawful manner. At both the individual and the national level, the right to defend oneself in the face of attack is accorded particular prominence. In reality, international law accords states considerable latitude in responding to terrorist threats. However, it does also establish some fundamental redlines that states cannot cross in any circumstances. For example, states cannot detain suspects indefinitely without trial, states cannot torture suspects or render them to be tortured, and states cannot murder suspects with impunity. The question I will seek to answer in Part III is whether or not it is possible to mount an effective response to terrorism without crossing these redlines, and moreover whether crossing any of these redlines has ever proved to be a productive counter-terrorism tactic.

## Terrorism and International Law

### Defining terrorism in international law

In September 1898, Empress Elizabeth of Austria — perhaps the closest analog in nineteenth century royalty to Britain's Princess Diana at the height of her fame — was stabbed to death as she waited to board a pleasure steamer on Lake Geneva. Her assailant was an Italian anarchist called Luigi Lucheni, his weapon was a sharpened industrial needle file, and after his arrest, he was open about his political objectives, proclaiming in custody: "I am an anarchist by conviction ... I came to Geneva to kill a sovereign, with the object of giving an example to those who suffer and those who do nothing to improve their social position; it did not matter to me who the sovereign was whom I should kill ... It was not a woman I struck, but an Empress; it was a crown that I had in view."[8] The murder of Empress Elizabeth, a famed beauty known universally by her childhood nickname Sisi and described by no less an authority than *The Times* as the "incarnation of charity and beneficence", was a truly international event that sent shock waves around the world.[9] It also demonstrated the growing political and legal complexity of the anarchist threat since the crime featured an Austrian victim killed on Swiss soil by an Italian national born in France.

Lucheni was a veteran of the Italian Army who had fought in the first Italo-Ethiopian War and, in the aftermath of the assassination, the Italian government in particular came under a great deal of international pressure to act to curb the substantial anarchist presence within its borders.[10] The government responded by inviting twenty-one European nations to attend the Rome Anti-Anarchist Conference held from 24 November to 21 December 1898, which can be considered the first truly international attempt to address the

---

[8] Edward De Burgh, *Elizabeth, Empress of Austria: A Memoir* (J.B. Lippencott Co., 1899), pp. 326–327.
[9] Richard Bach Jensen, *The Battle Against Anarchist Terrorism: An International History, 1878–1934* (Cambridge University Press; 2014), pp. 133–136.
[10] ibid., p. 133.

phenomenon of terrorism.[11] The conference produced a broad definition of anarchist acts (the term terrorism not yet being in common usage) as "having as [their] aim the destruction through violent means of all social organization".[12] The European powers also agreed to criminalize, *inter alia*, the unlawful use and possession of explosives, membership in anarchist organizations, and the deliberate spreading of anarchist propaganda, although states mostly failed to follow through on these commitments. Finally, a number of technical measures were identified to assist the police in preventing future outrages such as sharing data on expulsions and the standardized adoption of the *portrait parlé* identification system developed by the celebrated French pioneer of forensic science Alphonse Bertillon.[13]

In March 1904, ten European states signed the secret St. Petersburg Anti-Anarchist Protocol developed jointly by Russia and Germany, which established shared procedures for expelling anarchists and made arrangements for the establishment of central anti-anarchist bureaus in the capitals of each signatory.[14] The United States, Italy, Spain, Britain, and France were all approached regarding the Protocol but declined to participate, Switzerland finally signed up in 1907. The network for international police cooperation established by the Rome Conference and the St. Petersburg Protocol would ultimately contribute significantly to the creation of the International Criminal Police Commission (ICPC) in 1923, which in turn would evolve into the international police organization Interpol that still operates today with bureaus in 190 states around the world.[15]

The specter of terrorism continued to haunt the Western world after the end of World War I. The September 1920 bombing of

---

[11] Peter Romaniuk, *Multilateral Counter-Terrorism: The Global Politics of Cooperation and Contestation* (Routledge; 2010), p. 22.

[12] ibid., p. 23.

[13] ibid., p. 24.

[14] ibid., p. 25.

[15] Jensen, 1981; Peter Romaniuk, *Multilateral Counter-Terrorism: The Global Politics of Cooperation and Contestation* (Routledge; 2010).

New York's Wall Street — most likely the handiwork of the anarchist and disciple of Luigi Galleani, Mario Buda — was followed by the equally horrific bombing of Milan's Teatro Diana in March 1921, which claimed twenty-one lives and injured 172.[16] France saw a series of anarchist assassination attempts that left Prime Minister Georges Clemenceau wounded and culminated in the murder of the right-wing *Action Française* newspaper editor Marius Plateau in January 1923.[17] The newly created nations of the Balkans were wracked by nationalist violence, with the Internal Macedonian Revolutionary Organization (IMRO) attaining particular notoriety because of its involvement in a series of violent attacks that included the notorious torture and murder in June 1923 of the Bulgarian politician Aleksandar Stamboliyski. In 1926, Romania raised for the first time a proposal to draft a terrorism convention at the League of Nations.

The assassination of King Alexander I of Yugoslavia, along with the French Foreign Minister Louis Barthou and two other bystanders, in Marseilles on 9 October 1934 by a Macedonian nationalist, Vlada Gheorghieff, working with Croatian separatists, revived the Romanian proposal.[18] The refusal of Italy, which supported Croatian national aspirations, to extradite two members of the conspiracy to France on the grounds that their offense was essentially political in nature, prompted the League of Nations to draft a Convention for the Prevention and Punishment of Terrorism. The text of the convention distinguished between international and domestic terrorism, considering the latter beyond the purview of the international community, and defined terrorism as encompassing "all criminal acts directed against a

---

[16] Nunzio Pernicone, Luigi Galleani and Italian Anarchist Terrorism in the United States, *Studi Emigrazione*, Vol. 30 (September 1993), p. 472 and Richard Bach Jensen, Nineteenth Century Anarchist Terrorism: How Comparable to the Terrorism 1 of Al-Qaeda? *Journal of Terrorism and Political Violence*, Vol. 20, No. 4 (2008), p. 595.

[17] Richard Bach Jensen, *The Battle against Anarchist Terrorism: An International History, 1878–1934* (Cambridge University Press; 2014), p. 361.

[18] Ben Saul, The Legal Response of the League of Nations to Terrorism, Symposium on Contributions to the History of the International Criminal Justice, *Journal of International Criminal Justice*, Vol. 4 (2006), p. 79.

State and intended or calculated to create a state of terror in the minds of particular persons or a group of persons or the general public". Although this convention was adopted at an international conference in November 1937 — along with an ambitious second convention to establish an international court to try such offenses — it never came into force.[19]

To this day, the Member States of the United Nations have found it impossible to reach a universally accepted definition of terrorism. This is in large part because terrorism is such a pejorative term that many states are wary of adopting a definition that can be applied to groups for which they may have some sympathy, such as those struggling for self-determination. It is worth remembering that Adolf Hitler justified his occupation of the Sudetenland in Czechoslovakia as being necessary to disarm "terrorist bands threatening the lives of minorities"[20] and that the Nazis described members of European resistance movements in the territories occupied by Axis forces as terrorists. States are also wary of being saddled with a definition that could be applied to their own activities, such as Special Forces action or intelligence operations. In the 1970s and 1980s, both the Third World Bloc and the Soviet Union promoted the concept of "state terrorism" to counterbalance the application of the term "terrorist" to national liberation movements, another clever piece of Cold War branding coined by the Soviets.[21] Questions of scale complicate things still further — how does one distinguish terrorism from acts of sabotage, guerrilla warfare or insurgency, and indeed other forms of armed conflict,[22] or from organized criminality. In May 1993, the Corleone *cosca*, a Sicilian Mafia clan led by Totó Riina, detonated a car bomb outside the Uffizi Gallery

---

[19] ibid., p. 81.

[20] ibid., p. 102 and Ian Brownlie, *International Law and the Use of Force by States* (Clarendon Press; 1963), p. 340.

[21] Peter Romaniuk, *Multilateral Counter-Terrorism: The Global Politics of Cooperation and Contestation* (Routledge; 2010), pp. 42–44.

[22] Paul Wilkinson, *Terrorism and Democracy: The Liberal State Response* (Routledge; 2006), pp. 13–17.

in Florence, killing six people including a nine-year-old girl,[23] and in November 1989, Pablo Escobar's Medellin cartel bombed a civilian airliner, murdering 110 people in an unsuccessful attempt to kill the Colombian presidential candidate César Gaviria Trujillo,[24] but both organizations were motivated by profit rather than politics or aspirations of social justice.

These dilemmas played out inconclusively on the international stage during the course of an extended debate that took place in a United Nations General Assembly Ad Hoc Committee between 1972 and 1979, against a backdrop of Marxist terrorism in Western Europe and the nationalist terrorism of Irish and Palestine groups.[25] States simply could not arrive at any meaningful consensus. The General Assembly's 1994 Declaration on Measures to Eliminate International Terrorism distinguished terrorism from other forms of violence by the "political purposes" that motivated its execution, but this was a non-binding resolution.[26] Further attempts to reach a universal legal definition were made after the September 11 attacks with a similar lack of success. In 2004, the Secretary-General's High-level Panel on Threats, Challenges and Change called for the adoption of a definition of terrorism which would make it clear that "any action constitutes terrorism if it is intended to cause death or serious bodily harm to civilians and non-combatants, with the purpose of intimidating a population or compelling a Government or an international organization to do or abstain from any act."[27] Former UN Secretary General Kofi Annan urged world leaders to unite behind the recommendation, but his appeal fell on deaf ears.[28]

---

[23] John Tagliabue, Bombings Laid to Mafia War on Italy and Church, *New York Times*, 15 July 1994.

[24] Mark Bowden, *Killing Pablo: The Hunt for the World's Greatest Outlaw* (Atlantic Monthly Press; 2001), p. 80.

[25] Ben Saul, The Legal Response of the League of Nations to Terrorism, Symposium on Contributions to the History of the International Criminal Justice, *Journal of International Criminal Justice*, Vol. 4 (2006), p. 98.

[26] Ben Saul, *Defining Terrorism in International Law* (Oxford University Press; 2006), p. 38.

[27] *A More Secure World: Our Shared Responsibility*, Report of the Secretary General's High-level Panel on Threats, Challenges and Change (2004).

[28] Secretary-General Kofi Annan, *Keynote Address to the Closing Plenary of the International Summit on Democracy, Terrorism and Security*, 10 March 2005 at http://www.un.org/News/Press/docs/2005/sgsm9757.doc.htm.

Most recently, in 2010, the UN Special Rapporteur on the promotion and protection of human rights and fundamental freedoms while countering terrorism, Martin Scheinin, increasingly concerned that in a number of states overly broad counter-terrorism legislation was impacting entirely legitimate political and social activities, proposed a draft model definition of terrorism for states' consideration, but this too attracted little support.[29]

In the absence of a comprehensive, universally accepted definition of terrorism, a well-developed international legal regime aimed at preventing acts of terrorism has evolved. This may seem counter-intuitive, but it reflects how states have come together to bypass philosophical disputes over the nature of terrorism by simply designating a wide range of criminal acts taken either individually or in combination as amounting to terrorist activity. Curiously enough, this was an approach presciently recommended by the government of Czechoslovakia in 1937 during the drafting of the ill-fated Convention for the Prevention and Punishment of Terrorism.[30]

There are, at the time of writing, nineteen international legal instruments relating to acts of terrorism, which cover topics such as aviation and maritime hijacking, violence at airports, terrorist financing, hostage taking, the theft and use of nuclear material, terrorist bombings, and the protection of diplomats and UN employees.[31]

---

[29] *Report of the Special Rapporteur on the promotion and protection of human rights and fundamental freedoms while countering terrorism, Martin Scheinin: Ten areas of best practices in countering-terrorism,* A/HRC/16/51, 22 December 2010, p. 28.

[30] Ben Saul, The Legal Response of the League of Nations to Terrorism, Symposium on Contributions to the History of the International Criminal Justice, *Journal of International Criminal Justice,* Vol. 4 (2006), p. 89.

[31] 1963 Convention on Offence and Certain Other Acts Committed on Board Aircraft (Aircraft Convention); 1970 Convention for the Suppression of Unlawful Seizure of Aircraft (Unlawful Seizure Convention); 1971 Convention for the Suppression of Unlawful Acts against the Safety of Civil Aviation (Civil Aviation Convention); 1973 Convention on the Prevention and Punishment of Crimes Against Internationally Protected Persons (Diplomatic Agents Convention); 1979 International Convention against the Taking of Hostages (Hostages Convention); 1980 Convention on the Physical Protection of Nuclear Material (Nuclear Materials Convention); 1988 Protocol for the Suppression of Unlawful Acts of Violence at Airports Serving International Civil Aviation, supplementary to the Convention for the

Each of these instruments typically creates an obligation for States Parties to criminalize the terrorist offense in question, and thereafter either investigate and, when appropriate, prosecute such acts themselves, or extradite an accused individual to a country claiming legitimate jurisdiction over the alleged offense.

These international legal instruments have been greatly reinforced by measures adopted by the United Nations Security Council since 2001, most notably Security Council Resolution 1373 passed in the aftermath of the September 11 attacks, and Security Council Resolution 1566 which was passed after the Beslan school massacre in September 2004. In the latter incident, approximately thirty Chechen separatist terrorists took over a school in the Russian Republic of North Ossetia-Alania holding more than 1,100 students, teachers and parents hostage for three days. In all, 334 people — 186 of them children — were killed during the siege.[32] Both resolutions called upon every Member State to take measures to incorporate the terrorism conventions into their national law "as soon as possible". As they were passed under Chapter 7 of the UN Charter, they are considered to be legally binding on all Member States.

---

Suppression of Unlawful Acts against the Safety of Civil Aviation (Airport Protocol); 1988 Convention for the Suppression of Unlawful Acts against the Safety of Maritime Navigation (Maritime Convention); 1988 Protocol for the Suppression of Unlawful Acts Against the Safety of Fixed Platforms Located on the Continental Shelf (Fixed Platform Protocol); 1991 Convention on the Marking of Plastic Explosives for the Purpose of Detection (Plastics Explosives Convention); 1997 International Convention for the Suppression of Terrorist Bombing (Terrorist Bombing Convention); 1999 International Convention for the Suppression of the Financing of Terrorism (Terrorist Financing Convention); 2005 Amendment to the Convention on the Physical Protection of Nuclear Material; 2005 Protocol to the Protocol for the Suppression of Unlawful Acts against the Safety of Fixed Platforms located on the Continental Shelf; 2005 International Convention for the Suppression of Acts of Nuclear Terrorism (Nuclear Terrorism Convention); 2005 Protocol to the Convention for the Suppression of Unlawful Acts against the Safety of Maritime Navigation; 2010 Convention on the Suppression of Unlawful Acts Relating to International Civil Aviation (New Civil Aviation Convention); 2010 Protocol Supplementary to the Convention for the Suppression of Unlawful Seizure of Aircraft; 2014 Protocol to Amend the Convention on Offences and Certain Other Acts Committed on Board Aircraft.

[32] Tom Balmforth, *Ten years after Beslan school siege, survivors struggle to make a new life*, Radio Free Europe, 1 September 2014 at http://www.theguardian.com/world/2014/sep/01/beslan-school-massacre-ten-years (accessed 8 June 2015).

The Security Council established the Counter-Terrorism Committee and Counter-Terrorism Executive Directorate (CTED) to assist states to meet this target and monitor international compliance with the Resolution 1373.

In essence, Resolutions 1373 and 1566 come together to create a functional definition of terrorism that encompasses all those acts covered by the nineteen international legal instruments. Resolution 1566 went even further stating:

> "Criminal acts, including against civilians, committed with the intent to cause death or serious bodily injury, or taking of hostages, with the purpose to provoke a state of terror in the general public or in a group of persons or particular persons, intimidate a population or compel a government or an international organization to do or to abstain from doing any act, which constitute offences within the scope of and as defined in the international conventions and protocols relating to terrorism, are under no circumstances justifiable by considerations of a political, philosophical, ideological, racial, ethnic, religious or other similar nature."[33]

The resolution then called upon all states to prevent such acts where possible and to ensure that such acts are punished where and when they occur by penalties appropriate to their "grave nature".[34] And this is where matters stand today. Security Council Resolution 2178, which was adopted in September 2014 to address the phenomenon of foreign terrorist fighters — "individuals who travel to a State other than their States of residence or nationality for the purpose of the perpetration, planning, or preparation of, or participation in, terrorist acts or the providing or receiving of terrorist training" — reaffirmed the view of the international community that "terrorism in all forms and manifestations constitutes

---

[33] Resolution 1566 (2004), adopted by the Security Council at its 5053rd meeting, on 8 October 2004, p. 3.

[34] ibid.

one of the most serious threats to international peace and security."[35] While it remains true that at the United Nations the label of "terrorist" is still only applied in official documents to groups specifically identified as such in Security Council Resolutions — *al-Qaeda* and its affiliates, the *Taliban*, and the Islamic State in Iraq and the Levant — it is also true that there is very clear guidance to Member States as to what acts amount to terrorism, no matter where they occur on the globe or who is behind them, and how those responsible for such acts must be treated by the international community.

## Terrorism and international human rights law

The idea that certain fundamental or natural rights exist that are common to all mankind was given modern form by seventeenth and eighteenth century Enlightenment philosophers like John Locke, Montesquieu, Voltaire, and Jean-Jacques Rousseau, and first found powerful political expression in the Declaration of the Rights of Man and of the Citizen adopted by France's revolutionary National Constituent Assembly in 1789 and the Bill of Rights ratified by the fledgling United States in 1791.[36] However, the modern treaty regime that establishes human rights in international law was born with the creation of the United Nations in 1945. The Preamble to the United Nations Charter enjoins Member States to reaffirm their faith "in fundamental human rights, in the dignity and worth of the human person, in the equal rights of men and women".[37] This sentiment was given further form by the adoption of the Universal Declaration of Human Rights by the United Nations General Assembly in December 1948, and, while the Declaration is not a treaty, it encapsulates the belief of the founding members of the United Nations that human rights reflect the "inherent dignity" of all members of the human family and are the "foundation of

---

[35] Resolution 2178 (2014), adopted by the Security Council 7272nd meeting, on 24 September 2014.

[36] Henry Steiner and Philip Alston, *International Human Rights in Context: Law, Politics, Morals* (Oxford University Press; 2000), pp. 324–325.

[37] Charter of the United Nations, 26 June 1945.

freedom, justice and peace in the world". The Declaration was adopted with just eight Member State abstentions (including from the Soviet Union, Saudi Arabia and South Africa) and no votes cast against; it is the foundation on which the treaty regime enshrining human rights protections in international law is built.

As a matter of international law, human rights are enumerated, protected and enforced by treaties signed between states, which are equally binding on all States Parties to a particular convention or protocol. If a state has ratified a treaty, it is obligated to abide by its terms — a universal legal concept known as *pacta sunt servanda* (agreements must be kept) recognized as a fundamental prerequisite for effective cooperation between nations.[38] The two core international human rights treaties are the International Covenant on Civil and Political Rights (ICCPR) and the International Covenant on Economic, Social and Cultural Rights (ICESCR), which were both adopted in 1966 and entered into force in 1976.[39] The ICCPR in particular establishes a legal basis for many of the rights enumerated in the Universal Declaration such as the right to life, the right to liberty, the right to equality before the law, the right to be presumed innocent until proven guilty, the right to privacy, and the right to redress when rights are violated, as well as protecting freedom of thought, conscience and religion or belief, freedom of opinion and expression, freedom of movement, and freedom of assembly and association. The ICCPR also forbids torture and inhuman or degrading treatment, slavery, arbitrary arrest and detention, and propaganda advocating war or hatred based on race, religion, national origin or language. It prohibits discrimination on a similar basis. The Universal Declaration, the ICCPR (including two Optional Protocols, one creating an independent mechanism for receiving complaints and one prohibiting the death penalty), and the ICESCR have collectively set the standards that have inspired more than 100 international and regional human rights conventions, declarations, and sets of rules or general principles. At the time of writing, 168 states have ratified the

---

[38] Malcolm Shaw, *International Law* (Cambridge University Press; 1997), p. 41.
[39] Henry Steiner and Philip Alston, *International Human Rights in Context: Law, Politics, Morals* (Oxford University Press; 2000), pp. 138–139.

ICCPR and have agreed to be bound by its provisions (barring certain reservations). China, Malaysia, Myanmar and Saudi Arabia are currently the most notable holdouts. Ratification of the ICCPR is practically synonymous with democratic governance, or, at least, with an aspiration to achieve it.

A number of other conventions have given further force to the human rights expounded in the Universal Declaration and the ICCPR and the ICESCR, including the 1948 Convention on the Prevention and Punishment of the Crime of Genocide, the 1951 Convention Relating to the Status of Refugees (and its 1967 Protocol), the 1954 Convention Relating to the Status of Stateless Persons, the 1961 Convention on the Reduction of Statelessness, the 1965 International Convention on the Elimination of All Forms of Racial Discrimination (CERD), and the 1984 Convention Against Torture and Other Cruel, Inhuman or Degrading Treatment or Punishment (CAT). Additional conventions specifically protect the rights of women (1979 Convention on the Elimination of All Forms of Discrimination against Women), children (1989 Convention on the Rights of the Child), and migrant workers (1990 Convention on the Protection of the Rights of All Migrant Workers and Members of Their Families). It should be stressed that not every state has signed all these treaties, many have not, and some states have signed while also registering reservations exempting themselves from certain provisions. The identity of the delinquent states can sometimes be rather surprising, for instance, the United States has a relatively poor track record of ratifying international human rights treaties and is among the handful of states that has not ratified the Convention on the Elimination of Discrimination against Women. In addition to the international treaties, there are a number of regional human rights treaties that further build, and sometimes expand, upon the protections established at the international level, the most notable of which are the European Convention on Human Rights (ECHR) adopted in 1950 and subsequent Protocols, the American Convention on Human Rights adopted in 1967 (ACHR), and the African Charter on Human and Peoples' Rights adopted in 1981 (ACHPR).

There are also some critical exceptions to the general rule that if a state has not signed up to a treaty regime, then it is not covered by it. Some rights and legal obligations have also become so well established that they are considered to amount to peremptory norms of international law — meaning that they are considered to be binding on all states whether or not the individual state concerned has signed and ratified the relevant international legal instruments. The concept of peremptory norms dates back to the legal scholarship of such eighteenth century pioneers of international law as Emmerich de Vattel and Christian Wolff, and derives in large part from the interest shown by Enlightenment philosophers in the concept of natural law. Jurisprudence generated in the twentieth century by international courts and tribunals has upheld the existence of peremptory norms in international law and has identified prohibitions against torture, slavery, genocide, racial discrimination, and crimes against humanity as all having attained this status.

Generally speaking, international human rights treaties impose both negative obligations (not to interfere with rights) and positive obligations (to secure and guarantee rights) on States Parties. Human rights can therefore be violated by a state's action but also by state's failure or omission to act. This positive obligation would include putting in place a legal framework to protect rights and taking proactive steps to prevent human rights breaches, which may in some instances require the state to weigh the relative importance of two or more competing rights. For example, in the United Kingdom, newspapers are not allowed to speculate on the guilt or innocence of a suspect in detention while the case is being adjudicated. In this instance, domestic law seeks to find a balance between the right to freedom of expression and the right to the presumption of innocence. States also have an obligation to intervene to protect the human rights of all those persons found within their jurisdiction. Acts of terrorism are likely to infringe many of the rights states are obligated to protect, indeed as former UN Special Rapporteur Ms. Kalliopi Koufa noted in a report on *Terrorism and Human Rights* submitted to the Economic and Social Council in

June 2001: "There is probably not a single human right exempt from the impact of terrorism."[40] Thus, in working to prevent terrorism, in a very real sense, law enforcement and security officials are themselves human rights defenders.

However, it must be admitted that some rights are more equal than others. Put simply, human rights come in two basic categories — absolute rights and limited rights. There are relatively few absolute rights that cannot be infringed or curtailed in any way. No one may be tortured or subjected to unauthorized medical experimentation. No one can be enslaved or required to perform forced or compulsory labor. No one shall be imprisoned merely on the grounds of an inability to fulfill a contractual obligation. No one can be found guilty of a criminal offence on account of an act (or omission) that did not constitute a criminal offence at the time when it was committed. There is also a well-established prohibition on the imposition of a heavier penalty than the one that was applicable at the time the offence was committed. Finally, while certain ancillary aspects of the constellation of rights that make up the right to a fair trial can be limited — for example, the right of public access to a trial may be limited in the interests of morals, public order, national security, or the privacy of those involved — the prevailing international norm is that "a general reservation to the right to a fair trial would be incompatible with the object and purpose of the [ICCPR]."[41] Thus, any deviation from the "fundamental principles of fair trial" — including the presumption that a suspect is innocent until proven guilty — is completely prohibited.[42]

Freedom from discrimination is also regarded to be an absolute human right. Article 1 of the United Nations Charter describes one of the core purposes of the United Nations as promoting respect for

---

[40] Economic and Social Council, *Terrorism and Human Rights: Progress report prepared by Ms. Kalliopi K. Koufa, Special Rapporteur*, E/CN.4/Sub.2/2001/31, 27 June 2001, para 102. See also Ben Saul, *Defining Terrorism in International Law* (Oxford University Press; 2006), p. 28.

[41] Human Rights Committee, *General Comment No. 32, Article 14: Right to equality before courts and tribunals and to a fair trial*, U.N. Doc. CCPR/C/GC/32 (2007), Sec. I.

[42] ibid.

human rights and fundamental freedoms without distinction as to race, sex, language or religion.[43] The ICCPR enjoins states to refrain from discrimination on the basis of "race, colour, sex, language, religion, political or other opinion, national or social origin, property, birth or other status".[44] This standard is reinforced in a number of other international and regional conventions, most notably the International Covenants on Economic, Social and Cultural Rights and on the Elimination of All Forms of Racial Discrimination. As a general principle, a distinction will be considered discriminatory if there is a difference of treatment between distinct groups, if this difference of treatment has no objective and reasonable justification, and if this distinction is disproportionately applied. The Committee on Economic, Social and Cultural Rights has defined discrimination as "any distinction, exclusion, restriction or preference or other differential treatment that is directly or indirectly based on the prohibited grounds of discrimination and which has the intention or effect of nullifying or impairing the recognition, enjoyment or exercise, on an equal footing, of Covenant rights".[45] States must ensure that no discrimination ensues from legislation, regulations, policies, or practices concerning any of the following security measures or activities: border control checks and other static or mobile search procedures; administrative and pre-trial detention; conditions of detention; criminal procedures; protection of personal data; protection of privacy and family life; expulsion, extradition or deportation; issuance of visas, residency status or work permits; and acquisition or revocation of citizenship. Acts of discrimination can also violate the right to the presumption of innocence, the right to honor and reputation, and the prohibition on incitement to discrimination, hostility, or violence. The United Nations General Assembly has identified "ethnic, national

---

[43] Office of the United Nations High Commissioner for Human Rights, *Fact Sheet 32: Human Rights, Terrorism and Counter Terrorism* (July 2008), p. 37.

[44] See Articles 2 and 26 of the International Covenant of Civil and Political Rights (ICCPR).

[45] UN Committee on Economic, Social and Cultural Rights, *General Comment No. 20: Non-discrimination in economic, social and cultural rights (Article 2, paragraph 2, of the International Covenant on Economic, Social and Cultural Rights)*, E/C.12/GC/20, 2 July 2009.

and religious discrimination" as one of the "conditions conducive to the spread of terrorism".[46]

With the exceptions enumerated above, the majority of human rights are limited or qualified to some degree, and this is reflected in the manner in which individual articles giving substance to the right in question are drafted. Many articles include qualifying language — for example, the rights to liberty and privacy, enshrined in Articles 9 and 17 of the ICCPR respectively, can be curtailed on grounds established by law and so long as lawful procedures are followed and the restriction can be considered "reasonable". It is only the right not to be subjected to "arbitrary" detention or interference that is absolute.[47] Article 6 of the ICCPR recognizes the "inherent" right to life, but it also recognizes that some states still apply the death penalty. Again, the key qualification in the text is that no one should be "arbitrarily" deprived of life. The freedom to manifest one's religion or beliefs enshrined in Article 18 of the ICCPR can be limited by law if such limitations are necessary to protect public safety, order, health, or morals, or the fundamental rights and freedoms of others. The right to freedom of opinion and expression enshrined in Article 19 of the ICCPR involves "special duties and responsibilities" that place limits on that expression, which include respect for the rights and reputations of others, the protection of national security, and public order. The right to free expression is further qualified by a prohibition on the advocacy of war, or of national, racial or religious hatred, enshrined in Article 20.

The ICCPR uses as a test of the essential reasonableness of any restriction or limitation placed on an enumerated right that it would be considered "necessary in a democratic society" to take such a step in the interests of national security or public safety, public order, the protection of public health or morals, or the protection of the rights and freedoms of others.[48] The United Nations

---

[46] United Nations General Assembly, *The United Nations Global Counter Terrorism Strategy*, A/RES/60/288, 20 September 2006, p. I.

[47] Human Rights Committee, *Fact Sheet 15 (Rev. 1): Civil and Political Rights* (May 2005), p. 8.

[48] See Articles 14(1), 21 and 22 of the ICCPR.

Economic and Social Council has offered the following guidance on what is meant by a democratic society: "The burden is upon a state imposing limitations ... to demonstrate that the limitations do not impair the democratic functioning of the society. While there is no single model of a democratic society, a society which recognizes and respects the human rights set forth in the United Nations Charter and the Universal Declaration of Human Rights may be viewed as meeting this definition."[49] The UN Human Rights Committee, which is charged with monitoring the implementation of the ICCPR, has emphasized that the scope for permissible limitations is neither wide nor generous, and States Parties are not permitted to act in such a way as to effectively strip a given right of any practical meaning. The burden of justification in such a case lies with the State Party to show that a certain limitation satisfies the key tests of legality, necessity, reasonableness, and legitimate purpose.[50]

International human rights law acknowledges that states may, very rarely, face dire public emergencies that might require some curtailment of established rights and outlines a comprehensive framework for responding to such situations. A State Party to the ICCPR seeking to suspend one or more of its obligations under the treaty — to derogate from its commitments — must make a formal proclamation that a public emergency exists that threatens the life of the nation in accordance with applicable national laws and international treaty obligations.[51] Similar provisions are contained in regional human rights treaties. The standard set in the ICCPR for legitimate temporary derogation from certain human rights positions is contained in Article 4(1) of the Covenant:

> "In time of public emergency which threatens the life of the nation and the existence of which is officially proclaimed, the States Parties to the present Covenant may take measures derogating

---

[49] United Nations, Economic and Social Council, *Siracusa Principles on the Limitation and Derogation Provisions in the International Covenant on Civil and Political Rights*, U.N. Doc. E/CN.4/1985/4, Annex (1985), paras 19–21.

[50] Human Rights Committee, *Fact Sheet 15 (Rev. 1): Civil and Political Rights* (May 2005), p. 8.

[51] ibid., p. 6.

from their obligations under the present Covenant to the extent strictly required by the exigencies of the situation, provided that such measures are not inconsistent with their other obligations under international law and do not involve discrimination solely on the ground of race, color, sex, language, religion or social origin."

A derogation order may seek a restriction of specific identified rights enshrined in the Covenant with the exception of any absolute rights, which remain inviolable regardless of circumstance. The UN Human Rights Committee has issued a *General Comment on States of Emergency* in which it noted any "measures derogating from the provisions of the Covenant must be of an exceptional and temporary nature."[52] For a derogation to be in line with the ICCPR, the Human Rights Committee stated that two fundamental conditions must be met: The situation must amount to a public emergency which threatens the life of the nation; and the State Party must have officially proclaimed a state of emergency. Furthermore, any restriction introduced must be limited "to the extent strictly required by the exigencies of the situation" and the restoration of the *status quo ante* — full rights observance — at the earliest appropriate opportunity must be the primary objective of any State Party derogating from the Covenant. The Human Rights Committee also noted that even in times of national emergency, all persons deprived of their liberty must be treated with humanity and respect, that abductions, hostage-taking, forced transfer of populations and unacknowledged detentions would be absolutely prohibited regardless of circumstance, and that the general prohibition on propaganda for war or the advocacy of national, racial or religious hatred would remain in force.[53]

Requiring that a public emergency must be of sufficient gravity that it "threatens the life of the nation" sets an intentionally high

---

[52] Human Rights Committee, *General Comment 29, States of Emergency (Article 4)*, U.N. Doc. CCPR/C/21/Rev.1/Add.11 (2001).

[53] ibid., para 13 and United Nations Office on Drugs and Crime, *Handbook on Criminal Justice Responses to Terrorism*, (2009), pp. 22–23.

threshold — not every disturbance or catastrophe qualifies as such. In 1985, the United Nations Economic and Social Council promulgated the *Siracusa Principles on the Limitation and Derogation Provisions in the International Covenant on Civil and Political Rights*, which provide guidance on the derogation procedure noting: "Derogation is an authorized and limited prerogative to respond adequately to a threat to the life of the nation. The derogating state shall have the burden of justifying its actions under law."[54] Any derogation must ultimately be considered temporary in nature and should be withdrawn once the emergency that prompted the restriction is over. The principle of strict necessity must be applied in an objective manner to any derogation. Each measure shall be directed to an actual, clear, present, or imminent danger.[55] It follows also that in a state of emergency, the rule of law must prevail.[56] In no circumstances can derogation from a human rights obligation be invoked to justify a violation of international humanitarian law or of a peremptory norm of international law.

It bears repetition that all counter-terrorism measures, including those related to the design and implementation of security infrastructure, must comply with international human rights law, a position reinforced by Security Council Resolution 1456 and UN General Assembly Resolution 58/187. International human rights law accords every individual the right to an effective remedy should their human rights be violated. This obligation is designed to combat impunity and ensure that rights are practical and effective, and may amount to a norm of customary international law. Any failure to bring perpetrators of human rights violations to justice is thus a denial of a victim's rights to justice and redress. National security is

---

[54] United Nations, Economic and Social Council, *Siracusa Principles on the Limitation and Derogation Provisions in the International Covenant on Civil and Political Rights*, U.N. Doc. E/CN.4/1985/4, Annex (1985), p. 64.

[55] See United Nations Office on Drugs and Crime, *Counter-Terrorism Legal Training Curriculum: Module 4 Human Rights and Criminal Justice Responses to Terrorism*, Terrorism Prevention Branch, (2014), p. 34.

[56] United Nations, Economic and Social Council, *Siracusa Principles on the Limitation and Derogation Provisions in the International Covenant on Civil and Political Rights*, U.N. Doc. E/CN.4/1985/4, Annex (1985), p. 64.

not considered sufficient grounds to restrict this right. The *Basic Principles and Guidelines on the Right to a Remedy and Reparation for Victims of Gross Violations of International Human Rights Law and Serious Violations of International Humanitarian Law* adopted in General Assembly Resolution 60/147 offer guidance on how states can ensure adequate, effective and prompt reparation for abuses and note that meaningful reparation should include the following forms of redress as appropriate: restitution, compensation, rehabilitation, satisfaction, and guarantees of non-repetition. The UN has adopted basic principles on a range of issues, which are valuable guides to international best practice standards.

There are a number of international monitoring bodies with a mandate to receive and investigate complaints of individual human rights violations. The Human Rights Council (created by the General Assembly to replace the United Nations Commission on Human Rights in 2006) is the main inter-governmental body within the UN system for addressing human rights violations and it receives reports from the Office of the High Commissioner for Human Rights (OHCHR), as well as from other sources such as UN Special Rapporteurs with subject matter expertise on specific topics. Several of the key human rights conventions such as the ICCPR, ICESCR, CERD, CTC, CEDAW and CAT also create monitoring bodies of prominent experts to hear complaints that their provisions have been breached, of which the most prominent is probably the ICCPR's aforementioned Human Rights Committee. The regional human rights conventions have also established regional courts — such as the European Court of Human Rights (ECtHR), the African Court on Human and People's Rights (ACtHPR), and the Inter-American Court of Human Rights (IACtHR) — to hear cases brought against States Parties by aggrieved citizens. Collectively, these oversight bodies have generated a rich, varied, and constantly evolving body of jurisprudence to help states understand their human rights obligations. Human rights treaties can therefore be considered, to a certain extent, living instruments to be interpreted in the light of modern-day circumstances.

In addition to treaty-monitoring bodies, there are also enforcement mechanisms for certain human rights protections in the shape of both domestic and international criminal judicial institutions. Some human rights violations may lead to legal sanctions in a local or regional context such as an illegal search, physical assault, or invasion of privacy. Some human rights violations may even amount to international crimes. For example, torture is an international crime for which there is no statute of limitations and for which universal jurisdiction exists for any state to prosecute offenders that come within reach of their authority. Other international crimes include genocide and crimes against humanity, and a range of international judicial bodies exist in which individuals may, subject to jurisdictional constraints, be held to account for such offenses, the most prominent of which is the International Criminal Court (ICC).

## Non-state actors and human rights

That terrorism constitutes a threat to the enjoyment of human rights, not least the right to life, is uncontentious. In the past two decades, UN bodies have repeatedly described "acts, methods, and practices of terrorism" as violations of human rights.[57] However, the precise legal responsibility of non-state actors under international human rights instruments is far from settled. Traditionally, the obligation has fallen on states — as the signatories of human rights treaties — to prevent the infringement of rights as a direct consequence of terrorist activity. This creates a paradigm in which states are held accountable for failing to prevent attacks, while human rights law has little to say about the actual perpetrators of the attacks themselves. As Chris Jochnick has highlighted this obscures the true nature of the rights violation[58] and creates an

---

[57] Karima Bennoune, Terror/Torture, *Berkeley Journal of International Law*, Vol. 26, No. 1 (2008), pp. 42–43 and Helen Duffy, *The "War on Terror" and the Framework of International Law* (Cambridge University Press; 2005), p. 67.

[58] Chris Jochnick, Confronting the Impunity of Non-State Actors: New Fields for the Promotion of Human Rights, *Human Rights Quarterly*, Vol. 21 (1999), p. 58.

unequal playing field on which states appear damned if they respond to terrorist violence and damned if they don't, while terrorist groups continue to act with, at least rhetorical, impunity.[59] I lost count of the number of times while I was working for Amnesty International USA that I was asked why the organization seemed to care so much about the rights of terrorists and so little for the rights of victims. A technical answer concerning the legal mechanisms by which human rights are created and upheld satisfied no one. Nor did the fact that Amnesty consistently condemned acts of terrorism in its public statements.

Like concepts such as liberty and democracy, the human rights narrative has powerful global appeal, but the traditional understanding about where the responsibilities enumerated under international human rights law actually lie has made this appeal difficult for governments and international organizations to utilize in their struggle against violent non-state actors — even as those groups decapitate civilian prisoners, persecute defenseless minorities, and concoct increasingly gruesome spectacles to intimidate their opponents.[60] This does not necessarily need to be the case and reflects as much as anything a failure of imagination on the part of both governments and the human rights community — as well as perhaps uneasiness on the part of some governments of being held to the same standards. However, the concept that human rights law may create some obligations for individuals or groups is gaining ground and has in fact been present since the earliest days of the human rights movement. The Universal Declaration of Human Rights, the ICCPR, and the International Covenant on Economic, Social and Cultural Rights all cite an individual responsibility to promote the rights they enumerate.[61] The Convention on the

---

[59] Joan Fitzpatrick, Speaking Law to Power: The War against Terrorism and Human Rights, *European Journal of International Law*, Vol. 14 (2003), p. 243.

[60] Manfred Nowak, *United Nations Covenant on Civil and Political Rights: CCPR Commentary* (1993), p. 38.

[61] Manfred Nowak, *United Nations Covenant on Civil and Political Rights: CCPR Commentary* (1993), p. 63. See also Liesbeth Zegveld, *The Accountability of Armed Opposition Groups in International Law*, Cambridge Studies in International and Comparative Law (Cambridge

Prevention and Punishment of the Crime of Genocide, the first UN-sponsored human rights treaty, explicitly applies to "private individuals".[62] More recent regional conventions such as the African Charter on Human and People's Rights and the American Declaration on the Rights and Duties of Man expressly reference both individual rights and individual obligations.[63]

In regions where state sovereignty is fragmenting international practice increasingly recognizes that non-state actors may take on some of the obligations that the state itself can no longer fulfill. In 1990, the United Nations helped to broker the San José Agreement on Human Rights between the government of El Salvador and the *Frente Farabundo Marti para la Liberación Nacional* (FMLN).[64] The rights enumerated included many from outside the traditional international humanitarian law universe including freedom of association, worship, expression, and movement.[65] This international agreement explicitly recognized that the FMLN, despite its status as a non-state actor, had human rights obligations and the United Nations established an observer mission in El Salvador (ONUSAL) in part to ensure that these obligations were met.

Similarly, between 1997 and 2003, the Special Representative of the Secretary-General for children and armed conflict negotiated commitments from more than sixty armed groups — including the Liberation Tigers of Tamil Eelam in Sri Lanka and the Revolutionary United Front in Sierra Leone — on issues related to

---

University Press; 2002) and UN Commission on Human Rights, *Analytical Report of the Secretary-General on Minimum Humanitarian Standards*, E/CN.4/1998/31. Viewed 5 January 1998.

[62] Liesbeth Zegveld, *The Accountability of Armed Opposition Groups in International Law*, Cambridge Studies in International and Comparative Law (Cambridge University Press; 2002), p. 44 and UN Commission on Human Rights, *Analytical Report of the Secretary-General on Minimum Humanitarian Standards*, E/CN.4/1998/31. Viewed 5 January 1998, paras 62–63.

[63] Helen Duffy, *The "War on Terror" and the Framework of International Law* (Cambridge University Press; 2005), p. 66.

[64] Andrew Clapham, *Human Rights Obligations of Non-State Actors* (Oxford University Press; 2006), p. 272.

[65] Liesbeth Zegveld, *The Accountability of Armed Opposition Groups in International Law*, Cambridge Studies in International and Comparative Law (Cambridge University Press; 2002), p. 50.

child protection.[66] In 1998, the UN's Committee Against Torture found that armed groups in Somalia that exert effective control over territory may be equated to states in the case of certain human rights obligations.[67] The UN Human Rights Commission has condemned "gross violations of human rights perpetrated by terrorist groups".[68] In his 1998 *Analytical Report on Minimum Humanitarian Standards*, UN Secretary-General Kofi Annan acknowledged that there might indeed be a need to move towards the creation of general human rights obligations for "liberation movements and terrorist organizations."[69] By 2012, there appeared to have been a further shift in favor of this interpretation of international law with the Special Rapporteur on the promotion and protection of human rights and fundamental freedoms while countering terrorism, Ben Emmerson, observing to the Human Rights Council:

> "Some still argue that terrorists, rebels and other belligerents cannot commit violations of international human rights law unless the degree of organization, territorial control and State recognition involved in a conflict situation has escalated to the level of a full-blown insurgency or internal armed conflict. However, it is a central tenet of international human rights law that it must keep pace with a changing world. Some of the gravest violations of human rights are nowadays committed by, or on behalf of, non-State actors operating in conflict situations of one kind or another, including by domestic and international terrorist networks. If international human rights law is to keep pace with these changes, the victims of acts of terrorism must now be recognized as victims of grave violations of international human rights law."[70]

---

[66] Andrew Clapham, *supra* note 14, p. 289. See also *Protection of children affected by armed conflict*, UN Doc. A/58/328. Viewed 29 August 2003.

[67] Helen Duffy, *The 'War on Terror' and the Framework of International Law* (Cambridge University Press; 2005), p. 66.

[68] ibid., p. 67.

[69] UN Commission on Human Rights, *supra* note 12, para 65.

[70] United Nations Human Rights Council, *Report of the Special Rapporteur on the promotion and protection of human rights and fundamental freedoms while countering terrorism, Ben Emmerson: Framework principles for securing the human rights of victims of terrorism*, A/HRC/20/14. Viewed 4 June 2012, para 12.

There are countries — notably the United States and the member states of the European Union — that still oppose the use of such language to maintain a clear distinction between the acts of states and the criminal activity of private individuals and to ensure that terrorist groups are not accorded some kind of special status under international law.[71] It is interesting to note that the United States has departed from such logic in the context of military action, asserting a right to use lethal force against *al-Qaeda* in its global war on terror — wars hitherto being the province of states alone. For human rights defenders, an analogous paradigm can be found in the extensive efforts made during the past decade to hold corporate actors, particularly Transnational Corporations (TNCs) and Private Military Contractors (PMCs), accountable to international human rights standards even though, as August Reinisch notes, the existence of a strict obligation for them to respect human rights is still contested.[72] Non-Governmental Organizations (NGOs) have promoted codes of conduct, organized consumer boycotts, and brought civil suits against companies, targeting a range of human rights abuses, all with the objective of modifying corporate behavior.[73] The Human Rights Watch campaign against Shell Oil's activities in the Niger Delta and the Center for Economic and Social Rights exposure of Texaco's dumping of toxic waste into water supplies in the Ecuadorian Amazon in the 1990s and 2000s offer excellent examples of sustained pressure brought to bear on non-state actors to address human rights violations.[74]

---

[71] Peter Romaniuk, *Multilateral Counter-Terrorism: The Global Politics of Cooperation and Contestation* (Routledge; 2010), p. 62.

[72] August Reinisch, The Changing International Legal Framework for Dealing with Non-State Actors, in Philip Alston (ed.), *Non-State Actors and Human Rights* (Oxford University Press; 2005) and Andrew Clapham, *Human Rights Obligations of Non-State Actors* (Oxford University Press; 2006).

[73] Kenneth Rodman, Think Globally, Punish Locally, *Ethics & International Affairs*, Vol. 12 (1998).

[74] Human Rights Watch, *The Price of Oil: Corporate Responsibility and Human Rights Violations in Nigeria's Oil Producing Communities* (New York; 1999); Human Rights Watch, *The Niger Delta: No Democratic Dividend*, Vol. 14, No. 6 (New York; October 2002); and Center for Economic and Social Rights, *Rights Violations in the Ecuadorian Amazon: The Human Consequences of Oil Development* (New York; 1994).

As with corporations, the argument that an armed group may have a distinct personality as an organization, which is more than simply the sum of the individuals that comprises it, has much merit.[75] In an age of "franchise terrorism" where the brand associated with a given terrorist group can inspire copycat violence that is not directed by a group's leadership cadre, it becomes especially important to engage narratives as well as actions.[76] International criminal law and international humanitarian law can afford powerful punitive sanctions — some terrorist actions may amount to war crimes, crimes against humanity and even, in the case of ISIL and its treatment of the Yazidi, genocide. But, crucially, this is not always the case — abuses have to meet to complex criteria before international criminal culpability can be established. A rights-based narrative allows governments and human rights campaigners alike a more consistent platform from which to promote positive values within vulnerable communities in a way that constant references to criminal sanctions simply do not, and also favors a victim-centered approach which privileges the victim's story over that of the perpetrator.

A Rand Corporation study conducted by Fred Charles Iklé in the 1970s into the challenges faced by the United States when negotiating with communist regimes identified a phenomenon it labeled "semantic infiltration" — US officials were unconsciously adopting the language that their communist interlocutors used to define conflict issues and thus ceding control of the narrative in a given dispute.[77] In Ilké's words: "Our officials spend so much time on the opponents' rhetoric that they eventually use his words — first in quotation marks, later without."[78] J. Michael Waller has posited a similar example of

---

[75] Steve Ratner, Corporations and Human Rights: A Theory of Legal Responsibility, *Yale Law Journal*, Vol. 111 (2001), p. 474.

[76] Katya Leney-Hall, *The Evolution of Franchise Terrorism: Al-Qaeda*, Hellenic Foundation for European and Foreign Policy, Working Paper No. 1 (September 2008).

[77] See Tom Parker, Redressing the Balance: how Human Rights Defenders Can Use Victim Narratives to Confront the Violence of Armed Groups, *Human Rights Quarterly*, Vol. 33, No. 4 (November 2011).

[78] Daniel Patrick Moynihan, Further Thoughts on Words and Foreign Policy, *Policy Review* (Spring 1979).

"semantic infiltration" in the use of the term *jihad* by radical Islamist groups.[79] *Jihad* has entered the English language as a shorthand term for Holy War and "jihadist" is a label commonly applied in the United States to militant Islamic groups. This has occurred despite the fact that the Islamic definition is much more complex embracing both an internal quest for spiritual improvement and armed conflict in defense of Muslim lands. It has happened in large part because radical groups have been allowed to expropriate the term on the world stage. Waller notes that as a result American denunciations of *jihad* — "we're dealing with some foreign terrorists, who are coming in from outside the country to fight what they believe is an extremely important *jihad*"[80] — play differently to different audiences. What plays in Peoria may not go down so well in Amman, Rabat or Padang. To Muslim ears, denunciations of "jihadists" may only serve to support the *al-Qaeda* narrative that the West is at war with Islam.

In strategic (if not human) terms, the kinetic impact of a terrorist attack is often secondary to the message it communicates.[81] It is the "propaganda by deed" element of a terrorist act, communicating an idea through action, which most often carries strategic weight. It therefore makes intuitive sense that an effective communications strategy can be a powerful response. By promoting human rights language and values in communities from which armed groups seek to draw support, these concepts may infiltrate and perhaps ultimately reshape the linguistic and political landscape in which they operate. Some terrorist groups have already explicitly engaged in human rights-based dialogues. At the turn of the millennium, Human Rights Watch succeede Non-Governmental Organizations (NGOs) d in engaging several leading figures of the *Fuerzas Armadas Revolucionarias de Colombia — Ejército del Pueblo* (FARC-EP) in a

---

[79] J. Michael Waller, *Fighting the War of Ideas like a Real War* (IWP Press; 2007), p. 55.

[80] The White House, *Interview of the National Security Advisor by KXAS-TV Dallas, Texas*, 10 November 2003.

[81] See Charles Tilly, Terror, Terrorism and Terrorists, *Sociological Theory*, Vol. 22 No. 1 (March 2004), p. 9.

conversation about the group's use of child soldiers.[82] FARC-EP defended its actions by pointing to an internal 1996 regulation that banned the recruitment of children under fifteen years of age. This regulation was loosely applied until Human Rights Watch began campaigning on the issue and in April 2000 Commander Jorge Briceño was prompted to issue an order making this an obligatory standard.[83] Once groups reference international legal standards, they have entered into a legitimizing narrative that is difficult to depart from without paying a political cost. FARC-EP seems to have internalized Human Rights Watch's criticism even as abuses continued. In 2009, FARC-EP commander Simón Trinidad justified the group's continued use of child soldiers to reporter Garry Leech as being in compliance with Article 38 of the UN Convention on the Rights of the Child[84] — a position that left FARC-EP open to pressure to adopt the more restrictive Optional Protocol on the Involvement of Children in Armed Conflict standard, which raises the age of enlistment to eighteen.[85]

One of the most powerful examples of the value of engaging even hard-line individuals in a human rights dialogue is the conversion of Maajid Nawaz, a British citizen of Pakistani descent who became involved in his youth with the radical *Hizb al-Tahrir al-Islami* (Party of Islamic Liberation) movement, which campaigns for the reestablishment of the caliphate in Muslim lands, into a champion of counter-radicalization efforts. In April 2002, the Egyptian government detained Nawaz along with three other British members of the party. He was interrogated for twelve weeks in Cairo's State Security Intelligence building and then sent for pre-trial detention. He was

---

[82] Human Rights Watch, *You'll Learn not to Cry: Child Combatants in Colombia,* 18 September 2003.

[83] Human Rights Watch, *International Humanitarian Law and its Application to the Conduct of the FARC-EP- VII. Child Soldiers,* August 2001.

[84] Garry Leech, *Beyond Bogota: Diary of a Drug War Journalist in Colombia* (Beacon Press; 2009), p. 57.

[85] Article 4(1) of the Optional Protocol to the Convention of the Rights of the Child on the Involvement of Children in Armed Conflict (2002) states that "armed groups that are distinct from the armed forces of a State should not, under any circumstances, recruit or use in hostilities persons under the age of 18 years".

written off by *Hizb al-Tahrir* as "a fallen solder". *Hizb al-Tahrir* is banned from participating in political activity in Egypt and Amnesty International took up Nawaz's case as a freedom of speech issue. In the fall of 2002, an Amnesty delegation visited Egypt and sought access to him in prison. Abandoned by his former colleagues, Nawaz was stunned to learn that an international human rights group had taken up his case: "I was just amazed, we'd always seen Amnesty as the soft power tool of colonialism. So, when Amnesty, despite knowing that we hated them, adopted us, I felt — maybe these democratic values aren't always hypocritical. Maybe some people take them seriously ... it was the beginning of my serious doubts."[86]

In March 2004, Nawaz was formally adopted as a "Prisoner of Conscience" by Amnesty and its members began to correspond with him in prison. One Amnesty volunteer in particular, an elderly human rights activist and church warden from the home counties of England called John Cornwall, entered into an extended correspondence with Nawaz and a strong friendship developed between the two men. Nawaz credits his relationship with Cornwall as being a pivotal factor in his rejection of extremism. After four years of incarceration, Nawaz was released by the Egyptian authorities. He went on to found the Quilliam Foundation that promotes cross-cultural understanding and aims to counter extremism and radicalization in the Muslim community. The Quilliam Foundation has become an influential actor on the European stage, and in 2015, Nawaz ran unsuccessfully as a Liberal Democrat parliamentary candidate for the London constituency of Hampstead and Kilburn.

Armed groups also often embrace victimhood as a rhetorical device to deflect difficult questions about the use of violence, as in this statement by Dr Abdul Aziz al-Rantisi, one of the founders of *Hamas*: "You think we are the aggressors. That is the number one misunderstanding. We are not: We are the victims."[87] Victimhood

---

[86] Johann Hari, Renouncing Islamism: To the Brink and Back Again, *The Independent*, 16 November 2009 and Amnesty International, Egypt: 26 New Prisoners of Conscience, AI Index MDE12/003/2004. Viewed 25 March 2004.

[87] Mark Juergensmeyer. *Terror in the Mind of God*, (University of California Press; 2000), p. 74.

may be a powerful narrative frame, but it also opens up space for contesting perspectives, including a counter-narrative that focuses on the victims of terrorist violence.[88] Frank Cilluffo has suggested that "information asymmetry" — the one-sided presentation of facts — ensures that the narratives terrorist groups use to attract support go unchallenged in the communities they frequent.[89] The United Nations Working Group on Supporting and Highlighting Victims of Terrorism has proposed that this information gap can be addressed by making those who sympathize with terrorist groups more aware of the human toll that the actions taken by these groups have exacted. At a symposium of victim advocates convened by the UN in September 2008, Ingrid Betancourt, the former Colombian Presidential candidate who was kidnapped by FARC-EP and held hostage for six years in the jungles of Colombia, explained the logic of this initiative: "To speak of the victims, to give them a face, an identity, in turn reduces the population's passivity — their implicit resignation — towards the terrorists' crimes."[90] In other words, terrorism depends on the terrorist's ability to dehumanize his or her victims, put a human face on those victims and the appeal of the terrorist narrative diminishes.[91]

Both governments and human rights organizations ought to have more faith that the devil does not necessarily have all the best tunes. The message of universal human rights is a powerful one that has consistently demonstrated tremendous global appeal over the past seventy years. The human rights narrative has already infiltrated the language used by many terrorist groups and this provides

---

[88] See Erving Goffman, *Frame Analysis: An Essay on the Organization of Experience* (Northeastern University Press; 1974) and David Snow, E. Burke Rochford, Steven Worden and Robert Benford, Frame Alignment Processes, Micromobilization, and Movement Participation, *American Sociological Review*, Vol. 51, No. 4 (August 1986).

[89] Frank Cilluffo and Daniel Kimmage, How to Beat Al Qaeda at its Own Game, *Foreign Policy*, April 2009.

[90] Ingrid Betancourt quoted in Executive Office of the Secretary-General, *Supporting Victims of Terrorism* (United Nations; January 2009).

[91] Report of the Secretary-General, *Uniting against terrorism: recommendations for a global counter-terrorism strategy*, A/60/825, 27 April 2006, p. 5.

a bridgehead that can be exploited to force the supporters of such groups to engage in a value-laden dialogue.

## Putting human rights at the heart of counter-terrorism

We saw in Part I that one of the enduring core tactics of terrorist groups is to provoke governments into overreacting in the expectation that repressive counter-terrorism measures will further polarize society and harden the terrorists' natural constituency against making any accommodation with the state. We also saw how groups seek to exploit fallen comrades through the process of martyrology to attract more recruits to their cause. In Part II, we considered a number of social science concepts that seek to explain why individuals join terrorist groups — precipitating incidents, micromobilization, empathy, feuding, grievance frames, and social networking — all of which suggested that excessive coercion on the part of state organs can fuel violent opposition to the state. The former United Nations Secretary-General Ban Ki-Moon observed at a summit on Countering Violent Extremism in February 2015 that while "missiles may kill terrorists ... good governance kills terrorism."[92] Whether or not good governance alone can defeat terrorism is certainly open to debate, but there can be little doubt that bad governance is a major contributing cause of terrorist violence. It therefore follows that a counter-terrorism approach grounded in the rule of law and respect for human rights is likely to avoid many of the traps and other pitfalls that states have historically stumbled into when responding to terrorist outrages for the first time.

A truly coherent counter-terrorism strategy has to encompass a vast range of government services and agencies to ensure a joined-up, all-of-government response to the terrorist threat. In 2002, the British government of Prime Minister Tony Blair adopted a ground-breaking "core strategy" for countering international terrorism

---

[92] Secretary-General's Remarks at Summit for Countering Violent Extremism, Washington, DC, 19 February 2015 at http://www.un.org/sg/statements/index.asp?nid=8408. Viewed 28 July 2015.

known by the appellation CONTEST.[93] The strategy was divided into four principal strands: Prevention, Pursuit, Protection and Preparedness.[94] Prevention consisted of addressing structural problems considered to contribute to radicalism, such as racial discrimination, inequality, and the promotion of extremist narratives; pursuit took the form of intelligence gathering, law enforcement and international cooperation; protection revolved around target hardening and strengthening border security; and preparedness emphasized forward-planning and first-responder training. CONTEST was explicitly conceived as a holistic strategy that aimed to mobilize all arms of government acting in concert.[95] Of particular note is the fact that the use of military force was scarcely mentioned in the original strategy document — the British government declared itself willing in principle to use military force, in accordance with international law, for counter-terrorism purposes when non-military tools could not achieve its goals, but recognized that there were "considerable challenges" to doing so.[96]

While CONTEST has been updated and refined by subsequent British governments, it has essentially become the basic template for states seeking to develop holistic strategies of their own and has inspired a host of imitators. In 2005, the European Union as a whole adopted a Counter-Terrorism Strategy that was built around the same four slightly repackaged pillars: Prevent, Protect, Pursue and Respond.[97] In addition, the *United Nations Global Counter-Terrorism Strategy*, adopted by Member States in September 2006, outlines a comprehensive approach to countering terrorism that has been unanimously adopted by the UN General Assembly. This approach is also organized in four pillars although these do differ

---

[93] Intelligence and Security Committee, *Report into the London Terrorist Attacks on 7 July 2005* (H.M. Stationary Office, May 2006), p. 5.

[94] HM Government, *Countering International Terrorism: The United Kingdom's Strategy* (H. M. Stationary Office; July 2006), pp. 1–2.

[95] ibid., p. 3.

[96] ibid., p. 29.

[97] The European Union Counter-Terrorism Strategy, 14469/4/05 REV 4, 30 November 2005.

more substantially from the CONTEST model: (1) measures to address the conditions conducive to the spread of terrorism; (2) measures to prevent and combat terrorism; (3) measures to build states' capacity to prevent and combat terrorism and to strengthen the role of the United Nations system in this regard; and (4) measures to ensure respect for human rights for all and the rule of law as the fundamental basis of the fight against terrorism. The UN strategy is unique for the emphasis that it places on the promotion of human rights and the rule of law, elevating this to equal status with protective measures, counter-radicalization efforts and hard counter-terrorism tools, and for affirming that this emphasis "is essential to all components of the Strategy, recognizing that effective counter-terrorism measures and the protection of human rights are not conflicting goals, but complementary and mutually reinforcing."[98] In January 2013, the United Nations Counter Terrorism Centre (UNCCT) sponsored an international conference in Bogota that developed overarching, substantial, and procedural principles for the formulation of regional counter-terrorism strategies.[99] The *UN Global Strategy* has since been used as a template for more localized counter-terrorism strategies adopted by regional organizations in Central Asia, Central Africa and Southern Africa.

In short, there appears to be an emerging global consensus that effective counter-terrorism requires a multi-faceted response from governments that encompasses measures to tackle the most commonly identified causes of violent extremism, proactive intelligence gathering and law enforcement action to identify and apprehend terrorists, protective security measures to make specific targets harder to hit, and capacity-building efforts to

---

[98] The United Nations Global Counter-Terrorism Strategy, A/RES/60/288, 8 September 2006, p. IV.

[99] United Nations Counter-Terrorism Centre, *Summary of Discussions: International Conference on National and Regional Counter-Terrorism Strategies*, Bogota, Colombia, 31 January–1 February 2013 at http://www.un.org/en/terrorism/ctitf/pdfs/Summary%20of%20Discussions_National%20and%20Regional%20CT%20Strategies_Bogota_Jan-Feb2013.pdf. Viewed 28 July 2015.

ensure first responders are prepared to handle mass casualty attacks. However, despite the lip service paid by diplomats and policymakers to these core principles, it is also quite clear that when faced with the reality of terrorist attacks on their own soil, these same policymakers still tend to panic and take refuge in tough talk and draconian counter-measures — as Louise Richardson has noted, this response is practically pathological.[100] Terrorist groups count on this dynamic, and they carefully craft their operations to drive it forward.

This is the central challenge that must be successfully addressed by any effective counter-terrorism strategy: Terrorists have to be confronted, they are after all violent law-breakers intent on destabilizing society, but in doing so, governments must avoid responding in a manner that terrorists can anticipate and exploit. To be sure, countering terrorism will likely require governments at one point or another to use the full range of resources at their disposal — community engagement, intelligence collection and surveillance, investigative interviewing, prosecution and detention, and even the lawful use of force. Yet, these are all legitimate activities when conducted within a legal framework that also protects the human rights of every individual that comes within the state's orbit. The evidence strongly suggests that a well-constituted security establishment, operating in full compliance with international human rights law, is perfectly capable of addressing terrorist activity in a manner that frustrates terrorist operations, while minimizing narrative opportunities for terrorist groups to attract more volunteers to their colors.

In the sections that follow, I will explore in detail the core operational tasks that make up the Prevent and Pursuit pillars of an effective counter-terrorism strategy and will outline the human rights considerations that counter-terrorism practitioners must take into account as they seek to achieve these objectives. I will seek to demonstrate that international human rights law affords

---

[100]Louise Richardson, *What Terrorists Want: Understanding the Enemy, Containing the Threat* (Random House; 2006), p. 234.

states more than sufficient latitude for effective operational activity. And finally, I will also seek to demonstrate that when governments depart from the human rights framework, they accrue little, if any, material advantage and also pay a heavy reputational cost that can encourage further terrorist attacks. It is a simple enough cost–benefit analysis: If questionable short-term tactics undermine long-term strategic goals, the price is not worth paying.

## Community Engagement

The burden of countering terrorist threats typically falls first and foremost to law enforcement agencies, and a wide range of fundamental counter-terrorism tasks — from protecting buildings and public figures to investigating terrorist incidents and arresting and detaining terrorists — clearly fall squarely in their wheelhouse. However, when responding to terrorism, states tend to place an emphasis on the hard tools of policing, and while these certainly have their place, and in their place are indispensible, when they are overused, they tend to exacerbate rather than mitigate threats. Fortunately, there are also a wide variety of softer policing tools that have been developed over the past forty or so years — often in response to social unrest or juvenile gang activity — that have considerable practical utility in the context of counter-terrorism. In the past decade, international institutions such as the United Nations and the Organization for Security and Cooperation in Europe (OSCE) have been working to raise international awareness of good practices in this area, with perhaps the most notable contribution being OSCE's 2014 handbook *Preventing Terrorism and Countering Violent Extremism and Radicalization that Lead to Terrorism: A Community Policing Approach.*[101]

---

[101] Office for Democratic Institutions and Human Rights and the OSCE Secretariat Transnational Threats Department, *Preventing Terrorism and Countering Violent Extremism and Radicalization that Lead to Terrorism: A Community Policing Approach* (Organization for Security and Cooperation in Europe; 2014).

## Community-oriented policing

When the British Home Secretary Sir Robert Peel established the
London Metropolitan Police in 1829, nine principles of policing
were distributed to every officer in the force, one of which advised:
"Police, at all times, should maintain a relationship with the public
that gives reality to the historic tradition that the police are the public and the public are the police; the police being the only members
of the public who are paid to give full-time attention to duties which
are incumbent upon every citizen in the interests of community
welfare and existence."[102] This principle was intended to remind
police officers that they were an intrinsic part of the community they
policed and that the duties they performed were undertaken on
behalf of that community. However, traditional policing functions —
responding to specific incidents, maintaining public order,
conducting routine patrols, undertaking investigations, and making
arrests — are for the most part reactive and tend to create social
distance between police and the communities that they serve. This
social distancing was further reinforced in the latter half of the twentieth century by a series of technological advances such as the
introduction of patrol cars, emergency switchboards, radio dispatch,
and predictive analysis of crime statistics, all of which took officers
away from regular community beats in favor of a more targeted rapid
response model of policing.[103]

The social unrest of the 1960s and 1970s left major metropolitan
police departments in Western Europe and North America looking
for strategies to reduce the widening gap between their officers and
the communities they patrolled. The concept of community-
oriented policing was one response to this alienation that first found
expression in the mid-1970s and started to gain more widespread
acceptance in Western nations in the 1990s. The aim was to reduce

---

[102] Linda Miller *et al.*, *Community Policing: Partnerships for Problem Solving* (Cengage Learning;
2013), p. 60. See also John Dempsey and Linda Forst, *An Introduction to Policing* (Delmar
Cengage Learning; 2015), p. 7.

[103] Bureau of Justice Assistance, *Understanding Community Policing: A Framework for Action*, US
Department of Justice (August 1994), p. 6.

the social distance between the police officers and the communities they worked in by emphasizing the role of the police as a service that works with the citizenry, rather than a force that imposes order upon them, and to shift the objective of policing from responding to incidents to solving local problems in partnership with the community by opening new channels of two-way communication between the police and the public.[104] This often involves organizational decentralization — opening more substations and small local offices — and places an emphasis on empowering frontline officers.[105] Most community-oriented policing programs also feature dedicated community liaison officers, who may be fulltime police officers, civilian support staff, or a hybrid of the two with limited police powers like the Royal Canadian Mounted Police's Community Safety Officers. These officers are assigned to develop a relationship with the community and act as the accessible public face of the police department.

The central idea of community-oriented policing is that the personnel assigned to a community liaison role will in time develop a nuanced understanding of the community they are engaging. Community policing requires officers to adopt an external orientation seeking out and listening to voices from outside police ranks and from different ethnic groups or religious communities. Officers also have to take the time to identify the real community influencers — traditional community leaders may not be the most genuinely influential voices within a community. This can be especially true for younger members of the community who may have turned their backs on more moderate establishment figures. Some so-called community spokespeople — sometimes little more than the loudest voices in the room — don't actually represent anyone at all. It is important that community police officers take the time to

---

[104] See Stephen White and Kieran McEvoy, *Countering Violent Extremism: Community Engagement Programmes in Europe*, Qatar International Academy for Security Studies (February 2012), p. 7 and Robert Trojanowicz and Bonnie Bucqueroux, *Community Policing: A Contemporary Perspective* (Anderson Publishing; 1990), p. 5.

[105] See Wesley Skogan and Susan Hartnett, *Community Policing, Chicago Style* (Oxford University Press; 1997).

really get to understand the different centers of influence within their communities and seek to engage all of them. It can be very hard to reach marginalized communities with a long history of distrust of the police, and it can also be very difficult to persuade police officers to let go of their traditional roles. Community-oriented policing changes the power dynamic between the police and policed so that it moves from a vertical top-down relationship — the police telling the policed what to do — to a more horizontal partnership. It also requires police officers to accept community life in all its aspects and to reach out to every segment of the community and not simply separate it into two halves consisting of law-abiding citizens and criminals.

As the purpose of community-oriented policing is to build bridges with, often alienated, communities, it is important that it is carried out within the framework of international protections against discriminatory practices. Freedom from discrimination is one of the most fundamental of all human rights. States have an obligation not to discriminate and an obligation to protect individuals from discrimination by any other parties. Community policing programs must therefore not stigmatize particular communities. The response of the New York Police Department (NYPD) to the September 11 attacks provides a textbook example of how not to go about policing minority communities. With more than 2,600 fellow New Yorkers killed on September 11, and a drumbeat of intelligence reports suggesting further attacks were on the way, the NYPD established the so-called Demographics Unit in 2003 to gather intelligence on Muslim communities living in the city, including information on places of worship, ethnic restaurants, sports clubs and student associations, regardless of whether or not there was any evidence of any wrongdoing. Plainclothes officers were sent to eavesdrop on patrons in popular local community hangouts and informants were recruited to pass on gossip.

A series of high-profile leaks revealed the existence of the clandestine program to the general public in 2011. In December that year, at least a dozen local Muslim leaders declined invitations to New York mayor Michael Bloomberg's annual year-end interfaith breakfast, citing concerns about the NYPD's heavy-handed efforts to infiltrate mosques and spy on Muslim neighborhoods. In April 2014, the NYPD finally disbanded the unit. Linda Sarsour of the Arab American Association of New York told reporters just how damaging revelations about the programme had been to her community: "The Demographics Unit created psychological warfare in our community. Those documents, they showed where we live. That's the cafe where I eat. That's where I pray. That's where I buy my groceries. They were able to see their entire lives on those maps. And it completely messed with the psyche of the community."[106] A senior NYPD commander testified in court that the intelligence program had never produced any terrorism-related leads.[107] The NYPD ended up alienating a number of key communities and gained absolutely nothing in return.

Unfortunately, the overly aggressive and intrusive approach adopted by the NYPD is not an uncommon response to major terrorist incidents. Writing about the application of the Prevention of Terrorism Act in Northern Ireland in the 1980s and early 1990s, the Belfast-based criminologist Paddy Hillyard coined the term "suspect communities" to describe how the Catholic community had come to be treated very differently from the rest of the population in law, policy, and police practices.[108] Floris Vermeulen, who has studied European attempts to engage Muslim communities over the past decade, has similarly warned that by conflating the threat posed by a small minority of radicalized extremists with entire communities, rather than the select few, local authorities risk prescribing public policy solutions that miss their intended target,

---

[106] Matt Apuzzo and Joseph Goldstein, New York Drops Unit That Spied on Muslims, *The New York Times*. At http://www.nytimes.com/2014/04/16/nyregion/police-unit-that-spied-on-muslims-is-disbanded.html?_r=0. Viewed 15 April 2014.

[107] Office for Democratic Institutions and Human Rights, *Preventing Terrorism and Countering Violent Extremism and Radicalization that Lead to Terrorism*, Organization for Security and Cooperation in Europe (February 2014), p. 97.

[108] Floris Vermeulen, Suspect Communities — Targeting Violent Extremism at the Local Level: Policies of Engagement in Amsterdam, Berlin, and London, *Terrorism and Political Violence*, Vol. 26, No. 2 (2014), p. 288. See Paddy Hillyard, *Suspect Community: People's Experience of the Prevention of Terrorism Acts in Britain* (Pluto Press; 1993).

alienate natural allies, and create suspect communities who, isolated from the authorities, are much less likely to push back against the extremists in their midst.[109] One Somali refugee summed up the disconnect perfectly in a conversation with the counter-extremism researchers Heidi Ellis and Saida Abdi: "They feel I am a threat, but I feel I am a target."[110] If they are to have any chance of success, community engagement programs must be perceived as something that is being done in partnership with communities, rather than imposed on them.[111]

To this end, community policing initiatives should be clearly distinguished from counter-terrorism operations and not be used as a front for intelligence gathering activities. Transparency, trust, and partnership are key components of successful community policing initiatives and will be impossible to achieve if members of the community think that the community police officer's true role is to gather intelligence on their community. This does not mean that there should not be any communication between community police officers and counter-terrorism officers, quite the reverse — there should be effective coordination between both sides. It just means that the public should know whom they are dealing with and what that officer's role is at all times. The public will expect community police officers to pass on pertinent information, but they don't want to be spied on. Counter-terrorism officers can benefit greatly from briefing community police officers about ongoing operations so that they can then explain to the community concerned what is going on and why — within the parameters of operational security.

The United Kingdom has created a number of community engagement tools designed to give community representatives a greater appreciation of the challenges and choices facing police officers as they respond to potential terrorist threats and to

---

[109] Floris Vermeulen, Suspect Communities — Targeting Violent Extremism at the Local Level: Policies of Engagement in Amsterdam, Berlin, and London, *Terrorism and Political Violence*, Vol. 26, No. 2 (2014), pp. 287–288.

[110] Heidi Ellis and Saida Abdi, Building Community Resilience to Violent Extremism Through Genuine Partnerships, *American Psychologists*, Vol. 72, No. 3 (2017), p. 297.

[111] ibid., p. 295.

give police officers a more vivid understanding of community concerns. For example, in Operation Archer, community leaders were invited to participate alongside police officers as they worked through a one-day tabletop counter-terrorism exercise. Designed in 2011, Operation Archer revolved around a fictitious terrorist incident in a British town hosting an Olympic training venue and participants were asked to develop an action plan to contain potentially negative fallout from the incident. The exercise set the participants three sequential challenges: (1) understand community dynamics during a counter-terrorism operation; (2) develop a roadmap that will help the community return to normality; (3) help the community develop a partnership approach for future relations with the police.[112] Other community engagement tools developed by the Association of Chief Police Officers included Act Now, a counter-terrorism scenario that gave the public an opportunity to take on the role of police, with a supporting DVD and workbooks, and Operation Nicole, a DVD tabletop exercise which aimed to break down barriers between police and Muslim communities by providing an understanding of how counter-terrorism operations work.

Social psychologists have long understood that communities can play a critical role in violence prevention of all types, and in the past thirty years this insight has been increasingly integrated into broader public policy responses to domestic violence and criminal activity.[113] Underpinning many such initiatives is the theory of social control pioneered by Travis Hirschi and others, which posits that societal socialization processes reduce the inclination to indulge in behavior recognized by the wider community as antisocial.[114] In a landmark 1995 study that set out to test this theory, Robert Sampson, Stephen Raudenbush, and Felton Earls surveyed 8,782 residents of

---

[112] Association of Chief Police Officers, *Operation Archer Fact Sheet*, 12 April 2011 at http://www. acpo.police.uk/documents/TAM/2011/20110412%20Prevent%20Operation%20 Archer%20Factsheet%20(2).pdf.

[113] Heidi Ellis and Saida Abdi, Building Community Resilience to Violent Extremism Through Genuine Partnerships, *American Psychologists*, Vol. 72, No. 3 (2017), p. 289.

[114] See Travis Hirschi, *Causes of Delinquency* (University of California Press; 1969).

343 neighborhoods in Chicago and found that social cohesion, combined with a willingness to intervene on behalf of the common good, was directly correlated to reduced levels of violence.[115] Heidi Ellis and Saida Abdi, who have worked closely with Somalia immigrant communities in Canada and the United States, have argued that this same logic can be applied to promoting community resilience to stop the spread of violent extremism within "at-risk" communities. They highlight three types of social connection which they believe are critical to building resilient communities — social bonds within communities, social connections that bridge communities with different identities, and social connections that link communities with governing institutions.[116] Where these social ties are strong, alienation and misunderstanding can be addressed, empathy and tolerance for others expanded, and trust between the governing and the governed slowly cultivated. In such circumstances, the negative space that can allow extremist views to flourish unchallenged is likely to be commensurately reduced.

Another productive way to engage communities can be to give them the space to resolve conflict in their communities for themselves without resorting to the criminal justice system. This is not an endorsement of vigilantism but rather of a concept known as restorative justice. Restorative justice approaches put the individuals involved — victim and perpetrator — at the heart of the solution, rather than the state. Offenders are encouraged, through third-party mediation, to take ownership of their offense and to make some form of restitution to the victim in the form of an apology, returning stolen goods, or performing community service. Victims are also consulted to ensure that the restitution offered meets their needs.[117] In the words of one pioneer of restorative

---

[115] Robert Sampson, Stephen Raudenbush, and Felton Earls, Neighborhoods and Violent Crime: A Multilevel Study of Collective Efficacy, *Science*, Vol. 277 (August 1997), p. 918.

[116] Heidi Ellis and Saida Abdi, Building Community Resilience to Violent Extremism Through Genuine Partnerships, *American Psychologists*, Vol. 72, No. 3 (2017), p. 290.

[117] See Stephen White and Kieran McEvoy, *Countering Violent Extremism: Community Engagement Programmes in Europe*, Qatar International Academy for Security Studies (February 2012), pp. 48–49. Auld *et al.*, *"The Blue Book": Designing a System of Restorative Justice in Northern Ireland* (1997) at http://crji.ie/wp-content/uploads/2013/09/The-Blue-Book.pdf.

justice, John Braithwaite, the central idea is that "because crime hurts, justice should heal."[118]

Between 1973 and 2007, more than 5,000 shootings and assaults were attributed to paramilitary organizations in Northern Ireland punishing their own people.[119] Petty criminals, joyriders, and drug dealers would be hauled before paramilitary tribunals and, if found guilty of transgressions, subjected to violent physical abuse that often included kneecapping. In 1996, the Provisional IRA entered into dialogue with human rights and peace activists about the group's use of these so-called "punishment beatings" to discipline the population of republican neighborhoods. This led to the adoption of a non-violent community-based justice system supported by both the Provisional IRA and *Sinn Féin*, and based on the principles of restorative justice, which encourages dialogue between victim and offender. Pilot projects were established in four republican areas and expanded over time to eight further neighborhoods as part of an initiative collectively known as Community Restorative Justice Ireland (CRJI). Many of the project staff involved as mediators were themselves former members of the Provisional IRA. Between 1999 and 2005, an external evaluator reported that CRJI had handled at least 500 cases, which would have previously likely resulted in punishment beatings without its intervention.[120] From 2006 to 2012, CRJI has worked with over 10,000 people and in 2010, it dealt with 1,866 new cases alone.[121] CRJI has also been subject to official government oversight by the Northern Ireland Criminal Justice Inspectorate since 2000 to ensure that it operates justly and fairly. Over time, the CRJI became the "go-to" resource for police officers with non-terrorist-related cases in republican communities. In 2011, the Inspectorate reported that it had been informed by senior

---

[118] John Braithwaite, Restorative Justice and De-Professionalization, *The Good Society*, Vol. 13, No. 1 (2004), pp. 28–31.

[119] Heather Hamill, *The Hoods: Crime and Punishment in Belfast* (Princeton University Press; 2010).

[120] Stephen White and Kiernan McEvoy, *Countering Violent Extremism: Community Engagement Programmes in Europe*, Qatar International Academy for Security Studies (February 2012), p. 50.

[121] ibid., p. 51.

police officers responsible for policing the republican strongholds of West Belfast and Londonderry/Derry that they regarded CRJI as "the single most important relationship they have in reaching out to the previously estranged or hard to reach republican/nationalist communities living in those areas".[122]

A further aspect of community-oriented policing is showing sensitivity to community concerns and acknowledging past grievances by making symbolic concessions such as changing the appearance of police uniforms, demilitarizing police units by dispensing with body armor or heavy weapons, or altering cap badges and unit patches. After the restoration of democratic rule in Spain, the Basque region was allowed to establish its own autonomous police force, the *Ertzaintza*,[123] now about 8,000 officers strong. The Spanish gendarmerie, the *Guardia Civil*, was closely associated with the Spanish dictator Franco's regime, which had clamped down hard on any expression of Basque identity. Allowing the creation of the *Ertzaintza* was a powerful demonstration by the new Spanish government that the political climate had changed for the better, although the national police agencies did continue to maintain a presence in the Basque country. The dress uniform of the *Ertzaintza* even features a traditional red Basque beret and the force has played a significant role in counter-terrorism operations against the Basque separatist group *Euskadi Ta Askatasuna*.

Reform of the Royal Ulster Constabulary (RUC) was a crucial plank of the Northern Ireland Peace Process. An Independent Commission on Policing was established to consider the issue. In the words of Commission Chairman Lord Patten: "[the police] have been identified by one section of the population not primarily as upholders of the law but as defenders of the state."[124] A series of

---

[122] Criminal Justice Inspectorate Northern Ireland, *Community Restorative Justice Ireland: A Follow-Up Review of Community Restorative Justice Ireland* (Belfast; 2011), p. 11.

[123] People's Guard.

[124] Stephen White and Kiernan McEvoy, *Countering Violent Extremism: Community Engagement Programmes in Europe*, Qatar International Academy for Security Studies (February 2012), p. 33 and The Report of the Independent Commission on Policing for Northern Ireland, A New Beginning for Policing in Northern Ireland (HMSO; 1992), p. 2.

reforms were undertaken to make the RUC more representative, including renaming it the Police Service of Northern Ireland (PSNI) and changing the crest of the organization to reflect symbols important to both communities. If you look at the two crests side by side, you can see that in the new crest, the harp, symbolizing Ireland, is now given equal prominence to the crown, symbolizing the United Kingdom, alongside new symbols including the scales of justice, the torch of truth, and the olive branch. Symbolism matters and, in this instance, the changes made in Northern Ireland were sufficient to encourage the nationalist community to consider reengaging with local law enforcement. In 2007, the main republican party, *Sinn Féin*, instructed its followers to support policing structures in Northern Ireland. Two *Sinn Féin* representatives, both convicted former members of the Provisional IRA, subsequently joined the Policing Board.

In the aftermath of The Troubles in North Ireland, an organization called *Coiste na n-Iarchimi*[125] was established to help former Provisional IRA detainees reintegrate into society — at its largest, it employed ninety-five people, represented twenty-four groups, and helped with everything from mental health counseling to job-seeking. *Coiste na n-Iarchimi* now plays an important role in engaging the PSNI, even participating in police training courses. A former Provisional IRA member told researchers Stephen White and Kieran McEvoy: "We were at a training day for new PSNI recruits — a senior police officer gave the address and spoke about partition and a sectarian police force and the equality agenda. That would never happen down south. The RUC have been dragged to this position and it is paying off. They are not perfect but no police force is."[126] Given where both communities started, that is high praise indeed.

The concept of community-oriented policing is certainly not intended to turn law enforcement into a social service — it is important that the integrity of police officers as guardians of law and order

---

[125] Ex-Prisoners Association.

[126] Stephen White and Kiernan McEvoy, *Countering Violent Extremism: Community Engagement Programmes in Europe*, Qatar International Academy for Security Studies (February 2012), p. 43.

remains paramount. Communities need to know they have a partner, and they also need to know that that partner is a police officer. However, every police officer also has an important subsidiary role as a gateway to other government services that are often opaque or inaccessible to marginalized communities. Community-oriented policing requires institutional support from outside the police department to really succeed. Local government resources must be mobilized alongside police resources so that there can be a joined-up approach to problem solving. Many community problems will be outside the control of police officers, but with local government support, a range of social services can be harnessed to address community needs.

The advantages of establishing a successful community-oriented policing program are many and varied, and go far beyond simply addressing security concerns although this can be one benefit. A predisposition to treat members of the public as partners and allies helps to cement a culture of respect for human rights and the rule of law in policing structures. This in turn improves public perceptions of the police force. A great deal of tension between marginalized communities and police officers stems from the fact that there is often a real lack of understanding between them. The improved communication between the police and the public that is a feature of community policing helps to lessen misunderstandings. By spending more time with community members, police officers develop an enhanced understanding and knowledge of what matters to these communities and of the dynamics at play within them. This helps police to identify grievances and critical issues in a timely fashion, allowing an opportunity for these to be addressed before the situation can escalate too far. Finally, by pursuing a holistic approach to community engagement, police officers will ensure that marginalized and neglected groups within society will have an opportunity to raise issues of importance to them and thus feel a bit more connected to the wider national community.

One obvious operational benefit that results from a closer relationship between the police and the communities they serve is that community members are more likely to be prepared to act as their eyes and ears if they genuinely believe that they have a common interest in building a safer and more secure community; or to put it in the language of Sir Robert Peel's Nine Principles, community members become more willing to take on the "duties incumbent upon every citizen in the interests of community welfare and existence". This is a tremendous force multiplier for law enforcement, greatly enhancing the state's passive surveillance capability, generating intelligence leads, and prompting early warning of potential threats as disparate as an abandoned bag on a railway platform or an angry and alienated neighborhood teenager flirting with violent extremist beliefs. Using data from case studies of 119 individuals who engaged in, or planned to engage in, lone-actor terrorism within the US and Europe between 1990 and 2014, Paul Gill, John Hogan and Paige Deckert found that in 63.9% of the cases "family and friends were aware of the individual's intent to engage in terrorism-related activities because the offender verbally told them."[127] It is not unreasonable to assume that this percentage would be broadly similar for those belonging to more organized terrorist groups. The former Commissioner of the London Metropolitan Police Service, Sir Ian Blair, has summarized the goal for law enforcement in simple terms: "The whole deal here is to engender the trust that one afternoon may allow ... [community] leaders to say to the sergeant, 'You know, I'm worried about young so-and-so.'"[128] This is exactly what happened in the case of Andrew Ibrahim, a British national who self-radicalized online and was convicted in July 2009 of planning to bomb a shopping center in Bristol. Ibrahim first came to police notice when a member of the local Muslim community, suspicious of chemical burns on Ibrahim's hands, reached out to a police community engagement officer to share his concerns.[129]

Public awareness programs that heighten a community's vigilance in relation to certain threats, like the French government's *Plan Vigipirate* introduced in 1978 in response to a series of attacks carried

---

[127] Paul Gill, John Horgan and Paige Deckert, Bombing Alone: Tracing the Motivations and Antecedent Behaviors of Lone-Actor Terrorists, *Journal of Forensic Sciences*, Vol. 59 No. 2 (March 2014), p. 429.

[128] Christopher Caldwell, After Londonistan, *The New York Times*, 25 June 2006.

[129] BBC News, *Teenager facing terrorism charges*, 29 April 2008 at http://news.bbc.co.uk/2/hi/uk_news/7373929.stm. Viewed 25 October 2017 and National Counter Terrorism HQ, *Hostile Reconnaissance*, Code: Severe Podcast, 1 March 2017.

out by the left-wing terrorist group *Action Directe*, can be a vital counter-terrorism tool. In particular, well-publicized police telephone hotlines can be a valuable source of tips and information — they provide a non-judgmental and anonymous conduit through which members of the public can engage the police. They can also be a tool for spreading awareness of safety issues and victim services. In Northern Ireland, the number of the confidential Anti-Terrorist Hotline was prominently displayed on the side of military and police vehicles. Similarly, in New York, residents are encouraged to call 1-866-SAFENYS (1-866-723-3697) to report suspicious activity under the slogan, "if you see something, say something." However, such initiatives only work if the public at large trusts the organization on the other end of the telephone.

In addition to working with communities and the public at large, community-oriented policing approaches also stress the importance of building positive relationships with key civil society groupings, such as places of worship, business leaders, NGOs, and the media. While, as acknowledged above, mainstream religious leaders may not have the ear of every member of the community, they are — at least in the context of religious terrorism — in an especially good position to identify potential drivers of radicalization in the community, as well as potential terrorist recruiters. Religious leaders typically have a moral authority unmatched by other civil society groups and so may be in a position to powerfully assist the authorities in countering extremist narratives. This may be true even in the context of Marxist and nationalist terrorist campaigns if they are occurring in areas — for example, Northern Ireland or Latin America — in which religious faith is still an important aspect of a community's identity. In more prosperous countries, places of worship may also be well resourced and able to provide a range of services that could be of assistance to community police officers as they try to address some social challenges. Project Schnittmengen is a good example of a successful collaboration between police officers and religious leaders.[130] In 2011,

---

[130] Office for Democratic Institutions and Human Rights, Organization for Security and Cooperation in Europe, *Preventing Terrorism and Countering Violent Extremism and Radicalization that Lead to Terrorism* (February 2014), p. 148.

district police officers from Gütersloh in Germany came together
with the Gütersloh Islamic Center and the local branch of the Anti-
Violence Villigst Academy to involve local youths between the ages of
fifteen and twenty-five in structured activities to foster tolerant attitudes, a commitment to non-violence, and to offer a positive
experience of interacting with local police officers. Participants meet
weekly to take part in sporting activities and once a month for practical training on de-escalating violent situations — in doing so, the
youths gain in confidence and learn practical social skills.

Collective action theories suggest that the surest, quickest, low-cost
way of mobilizing a social, political, or religious movement is to infiltrate an already-existing infrastructure and then convert it to new uses.
This technique is known as "entryism" and was first pioneered by the
exiled Russian communist Leon Trotsky in an attempt to seize control
of the French Section of the Workers' International in the mid-
1930s — it has since been utilized as a tactic by many violent extremist
groups and clandestine organizations. One of the many advantages of
a community-oriented policing approach is that it creates relationships with local institutions, which can provide an early warning of any
such attempts at infiltration by extremist groups. In 1994, a small
group of donors from India, Pakistan, and Bangladesh opened a new
mosque in London's Finsbury Park. In 1997, the trustees of the
mosque employed Abu Hamza al-Masri to preach the Friday sermon.
Al-Masri was an Egyptian national who had initially come to Britain as
a student in 1979. He had fought alongside other Arab volunteers in
the Bosnian conflict and was badly injured in Afghanistan, losing an
eye and both hands to an explosion in unclear circumstances. Once
installed in the mosque, al-Masri proved to be far more extreme than
the trustees had anticipated, intimidating other members of the community and gathering a raucous group of young radical supporters
around him. He publicly expressed support for Osama bin Laden and
*al-Qaeda*, holding an event at the mosque on the first anniversary of
the 9/11 attacks entitled A Towering Day in History.[131]

---

[131] Robert Lambert, *Countering Al-Qaeda in London: Police and Muslims in Partnership* (Hurst;
2011), p. 98.

The Muslim Contact Unit established by the Metropolitan Police worked with the trustees of the Finsbury Park Mosque to develop a plan of action to remove al-Masri from his position, which ultimately involved using the UK's Charity Commission to force his suspension and then dismissal.[132] The mosque was temporarily closed after it was damaged in a police raid in January 2003 related to a major counter-terrorism operation.[133] Al-Masri continued to preach in the street outside the mosque until he was finally arrested in May 2004 on suspicion of terrorism-related offenses. He was detained for many years in connection with a US extradition request, which he fought all the way to the European Court of Human Rights, before finally being transferred to US custody in October 2012. When the mosque reopened in August 2004, al-Masri's supporters once more took control. The Muslim Contact Unit then worked closely with a locally-based NGO — the Muslim Association of Britain, which had been prominent in the protest movement against the Iraq war — to broker an alliance between the Association and the mosque trustees so that they would have the support they needed to expel al-Masri's clique. As a result of this successful collaboration, the mosque was reclaimed for the local community.

Businesses can often be the target of terrorist attacks — we have seen how an important plank of the Provisional IRA's overall strategy in Northern Ireland was a bombing campaign explicitly designed to impact commercial activity and drive away investment. In 2004, the City of London Police created Project Griffin, a police–public partnership to prevent terrorist attacks intended to reassure local businesses and enlist their help in the fight against terrorism.[134] The project reached out specifically to individuals responsible for the safety and security of buildings and businesses, and created a channel for the two-way flow of information about potential threats.

---

[132] ibid., p. 96.

[133] The so-called ricin plot led by Kamel Bourgass. Bourgass would go on to murder DC Stephen Oake.

[134] Office for Democratic Institutions and Human Rights, Organization for Security and Cooperation in Europe, *Preventing Terrorism and Countering Violent Extremism and Radicalization that Lead to Terrorism* (February 2014), pp. 159–160.

Police held "Awareness Days" to highlight specific threats (for instance, car bombs or how to spot possible reconnaissance activity), set up conference calls to update businesses on potential threats, and worked with businesses to develop emergency response plans.

Businesses can also be an unwitting source of equipment and material for terrorist groups, and as such can be an important source of information. Many countries operate controlled substance regimes, overseen by police liaison officers, that monitor sales of dangerous material, such as radioactive isotopes or ammonium nitrate fertilizers. In 2010, the European Union introduced a ban on the sale of fertilizers containing more than 16% nitrogen — a common component of homemade explosives — to private buyers. In The Netherlands, the government responded to this ban by working with industry and trade associations, including the Association of Traders in Chemical Products and the Confederation of Netherlands Industry, to implement effective and workable controls.[135] A center was established for reporting suspicious activity and a Homemade Explosives Information Line was launched. In the aftermath of the 9/11 attacks, the NYPD established Project Nexus to reach out to shopkeepers in the New York area selling items that could be used to manufacture bombs, such as black powder fireworks or metal piping, with the message: "If you see an anomaly in a purchase, let us know."[136]

NGOs exist in large part because the government cannot do everything, nor can it always be relied upon to do the right thing. Many countries around the world struggle with limited resources, a lack of accountability in government, even corruption, and NGOs are often established to address the shortcomings in government experienced by members of the public. NGOs are also a tangible symbol of the community empowerment that community-oriented

---

[135] Government of the Netherlands, Press Release, *Ban on Selling Ammonium Nitrate Fertilizers Containing More Than 16% of Nitrogen to the Private Sector*, 25 June 2010 at http://www.government.nl/documents-and-publications/press-releases/2010/06/25/ban-on-selling-ammonium-nitrate-fertilizers-containing-more-than-16-of-nitrogen-to-the-private-sector.html.

[136] Peter Bergen, *Paris explosives are a key clue to plot*, CNN.com, 17 November 2015, at http://www.cnn.com/2015/11/17/opinions/bergen-explosives-paris-attacks/. Viewed 7 April 2016.

policing seeks to support, so it makes little sense for community police officers to be working at cross-purposes with local NGOs. In many cases, NGOs will have been working with the local community and thus established a level of trust that community police officers are still working to attain, and as such they can be valuable allies for community engagement efforts. They are also more likely to have experience of interacting with the authorities and may have a more realistic expectation about what community police officers can deliver. It is quite possible that some NGOs — such as those involved in countering extremist messaging or preventing youth violence like EXIT Deutschland in Germany, the Quilliam Foundation in Britain, or People Against Violent Extremism (PAVE) in Australia — already share many of the same objectives as police officers.

One subset of civil society organizations that police officers and security officials can often have an antagonistic relationship with are human rights defenders. Human rights defenders are likely to have been critical of some police actions in the past, or of some ongoing aspects of government policy, or the state's counter-terrorism policy. The challenge for law enforcement officials is to resist the natural temptation to become defensive, and to seek to engage such groups constructively. Typically, human rights defenders are seeking to give a voice to those who cannot advocate for themselves, and in doing so, they can make government actors aware of previously unnoticed problems. Police and security officials are best advised to try to see human rights defenders as "critical friends" — advocacy groups provide a safety valve for discontent, and if the community sees protests being taken seriously by the authorities and genuine attempts being made to address concerns, this can also undermine extremist messaging that no change is possible within the current political system and that violent opposition is the only answer.

Any attempt to silence human rights defenders is likely to rebound very negatively on those involved. The United Nations adopted the Declaration on the Right of Individuals, Groups and Organs of Society to Promote and Protect Universally Recognized Human Rights and Fundamental Freedoms, more commonly known as the Declaration on Human Rights Defenders, in December 1998, and as such human rights defenders can be considered to enjoy a specially protected status under international law. The position of UN Special Rapporteur on human rights defenders was established in 2000 to investigate incidences of abuse, and both the African Commission on Human and Peoples' Rights and the Inter-American Commission on Human Rights have also established similar posts.

Many police forces have actually found that human rights defenders can be a powerful resource for their own training and planning activities. The American-Arab Anti-Discrimination Committee (ADC) is an example of a human rights organization that has established a number of very productive relationships with local police departments. Established in the United States to defend the rights of individuals of Arab descent living in America and to promote Arab culture in the aftermath of the 9/11 attacks, the ADC launched its Diversity Education and Law Enforcement Outreach Program to introduce police officers to Arab culture, help improve police officers' cross-cultural skills, and demystify aspects of Arab culture that some officers might find suspicious. In the past decade, more than 20,000 security professionals including officers from local and state law enforcement, the Department of Homeland Security, and the Federal Bureau of Investigation have received training from the ADC.

A second civil society actor that can often have an antagonistic relationship with law enforcement is the media. Institutionalizing a high degree of openness and transparency in police operations can be a key trust-building measure in community-oriented policing, and this requires counter-terrorism professionals to develop positive relationships with media reporters. Interacting with the media can be a bruising experience for law enforcement officers, but it is an essential element of public accountability. Media outlets fulfill a vital watchdog function in a democratic society and governments have an obligation to respect the role they play if they aspire to uphold democratic values. Freedom of expression is also protected by Article 19 of the International Covenant on Civil and Political Rights and public interest expression — a free press — is considered to be one of the most protected forms of speech in international law.

The media can be a powerful resource for police investigators seeking to communicate important information to the public. The London nail bomber David Copeland — a right-wing former member of both the British National Party and the National Socialist Movement who detonated three bombs in Central London over thirteen days in April 1999, killing three people and injuring 139 — was caught after a work colleague recognized him from CCTV images circulated by the police to the media. However, when sharing information with the media, police officers have an obligation to take privacy issues into account — especially where potential witnesses and victims are concerned. Police officers must also bear in mind that suspects are just that — suspects — and that they too have privacy rights. Suspects have not yet been convicted of any crime and in the investigative phase following an attack, many false leads are pursued and ultimately abandoned. Sharing information that subsequently turns out not to be true can have potentially tragic consequences. In the aftermath of the Boston Marathon bombing in April 2013, photographs of two men, wrongly identified by well-meaning members of the public as potential suspects, were circulated on social media and picked up by major news outlets. One of those pictured was identified online as Sunil Tripathi, an American student of Indian descent. Tripathi, who had been suffering from depression, was found drowned in nearby Providence, Rhode Island, eight days later.[137]

Finally, it must be emphasized that community-oriented policing was never conceived as — and should not be approached as — a security measure alone. It is a much broader concept than that, but it can greatly assist in preventing violent extremism by improving the public perception of police, enhancing police–public communication, increasing public awareness and vigilance, improving police understanding and knowledge of communities, identifying grievances and critical issues, and engaging marginalized and neglected groups. Communities which trust their government to

---

[137]Jess Bidgood, Body of Missing Student at Brown Is Discovered, *The New York Times*, 25 April 2013, at http://www.nytimes.com/2013/04/26/us/sunil-tripathi-student-at-brown-is-found-dead.html?_r=0.

seek to protect them and uphold their interests are far more likely to cooperate with the authorities and far less likely to be vulnerable to violent extremist ideologies.

Community-oriented policing works best as an investment in the future — if community-based programs have been in place long before a threat emerges, then the trust-based relationships that have been established can be leveraged in the service of counter-terrorism — in addition to other issues important to the community. Marginalized communities tend to resent post-incident initiatives because it looks like the authorities are only making an effort because they want something back in return — it also sends the unhelpful message that the best way for the community to get attention is to take violent action. Community-oriented policing can counter such impressions because it makes an effort to build bridges with the community as an end in itself — and not as a means to an end. Community-oriented policing is all about long-term engagement. It takes months, sometimes even years, to win a community's trust — and it can take just seconds to lose it.

## Early intervention programs

Early intervention programs are typically a non-punitive counter-radicalization tool designed to identify individuals who are vulnerable to radicalization and then intervene in such a way as to reorient them away from violence and criminality. Such programs typically adopt a multi-agency approach — both to successfully identify potential individuals in need of assistance and then to deliver meaningful intervention strategies specifically tailored to each individual that may have to address a range of social, economic and political risk factors. The end objective is to develop action plans aimed, as the Danish Ministry of Social Affairs and Integration puts it, at "supporting positive change".[138] This is still a relatively new concept — policymakers have traditionally focused on reactive

---

[138] Danish Ministry of Social Affairs and Integration, *Preventing Extremism: Relational Work and Mentoring* (April 2012), p. 16.

deradicalization and disengagement programs centered on custodial institutions, rather than on preempting the radicalization
process in individuals before any criminal activity occurs. Two countries that have been in the forefront of this shift of emphasis are
Denmark and the United Kingdom.

Denmark's VINK program — VINK is both an acronym for
*Viden, Inklusion, København*[139] and a Danish word that means a small
gesture or hint — grew out of a 2008–2010 municipal campaign
entitled "We Copenhagers" that was designed to celebrate citizenship and diversity and to promote social inclusion. The VINK
program was initially conceived to build on the We Copenhagers
campaign by providing practical support to municipal workers
encountering situations where social inclusion had failed, leaving
individuals vulnerable to radicalization and exploitation. VINK aims
to provide municipal employees with information, training, and
resources that will enable them to engage marginalized youths, as
well as act as a repository of problem-solving expertise that municipal staff can draw upon as needed. The program is staffed by a small
team of ten experienced professionals from a wide range of backgrounds including teaching, social work, job seeking, psychiatry,
and theology. One VINK staff member summarized the group's role
as follows: "As a resource person at VINK, my ambition is to enable
vulnerable youths to develop their preferred self-image through
inclusion in the community."[140] A Danish case worker involved in
the project expressed surprise that offers of assistance had been so
readily accepted by individuals assessed to be vulnerable to radicalization: "We had expected that there would be problems. On what
basis could we, as an authority, suggest to people, who have done
nothing to incriminate themselves as such, that they might need a
mentor? I had foreseen problems, but we have only encountered
few."[141]

The approach adopted by police officers in Denmark's second largest city, Århus, to the phenomenon of young local Muslims

---

[139] Knowledge, Inclusion, Copenhagen.
[140] ibid., p. 28.
[141] ibid., p. 21.

traveling to Syria and Iraq to volunteer their services to ISIL has also attracted a great deal of international attention. Crime Prevention Officers in Århus first became aware of this emerging trend in 2012 when two different families contacted the police to report that their sons had gone missing. The officers had had some experience working with right-wing extremist groups and motorcycle gangs in the city and instead of seeking to criminalize the youths' decision, they let it be known in the Muslim community that if the boys returned home, they would receive psycho-social support and help reintegrating into Danish society. Critical to the success of the Århus model has been the support of the city's social services and youth departments, as well as the pairing of both "at-risk" individuals and returning foreign fighters with an older and experienced mentor from their community. The main message the mentors seek to convey is that with a little effort, these youths can find their place in Danish society and that the city of Århus is there to help them with their educational, welfare, and accommodation needs.

Between 2012 and July 2016, thirty-four local residents left Århus to travel to Syria.[142] Six have been reported killed and ten still remained in the region at the time of writing.[143] However, eighteen former fighters have returned home to Denmark and all eighteen have been in contact with the Crime Prevention Office — as have approximately 330 other "at-risk" individuals.[144] Since the initial surge of enthusiasm in 2012–2013, very few local Muslims have left Århus for Syria, even as the numbers of foreign volunteers increased significantly elsewhere in Europe.[145] The city's mayor, Jacob Bundsgaard, explained the logic behind the Århus model in an interview with The Washington Post in October 2014: "These are young people who have turned to religion at a very

---

[142] Hanna Rosin, *How A Danish Town Helped Young Muslims Turn Away From ISIS*, Invisibilia, National Public Radio, 15 July 2016 at http://www.npr.org/sections/health-shots/2016/07/15/485900076/how-a-danish-town-helped-young-muslims-turn-away-from-isis. Viewed 20 July 2016.
[143] ibid.
[144] ibid.
[145] ibid.

difficult time in their lives, and they are dealing with existential questions about going to fight for what they believe in. We cannot pass legislation that changes the way they think and feel. What we can do is show them we are sincere about integration, about dialogue."[146] Århus Police Commissioner, Jorgen Ilum, added: "In 2013, we had thirty young people go to Syria ... [in 2014] to my knowledge, we have had only one. We believe that the main reason is our contact and dialogue with the Muslim community."[147]

The United Kingdom's Channel Programme was first piloted in 2007 and implemented nationwide in 2012. The Counter-Terrorism and Security Act 2015 established a legal duty for local authorities and their partner organizations to support individuals vulnerable to being drawn in terrorism. The Channel Programme aims to accomplish three basic objectives: (1) to identify individuals at risk of being drawn in to violent extremism; (2) to assess the nature and extent of that risk; and (3) to devise appropriate support measures for the individuals concerned.[148] To accomplish these goals, the program builds on existing collaboration between local authorities, the police, and partners from the education sector, social services, the National Health Service, children's and youth services, the National Probation Service, and the local community.

Local authorities are empowered to create a panel to consider the cases of "at-risk" individuals referred by a senior police officer who has reasonable grounds to believe that the individual in question may be vulnerable to radicalization by violent extremists. A local Channel Coordinator is designated to oversee the planned intervention and is supported by the panel, which is typically made up of representatives from the police, schools, universities, health services, social workers, housing departments, civil society groups, the UK border agency, and the National Probation Service. Membership of the panel is essentially open to anyone who

---

[146] Anthony Faiola and Souad Mekhennet, Denmark tries a soft-handed approach to returned Islamist fighters, *The Washington Post*, 19 October 2014.

[147] ibid.

[148] HMSO, *Channel Duty Guidance: Protecting vulnerable people from being drawn into terrorism*, 2015, p. 5.

can make a useful contribution. As part of a strategy of deliberately not securitizing early intervention efforts, the British government is encouraging local authorities (rather than security agencies) to take on the coordination role.[149] Channel is not a judicial tool — in the words of the British government: "Channel is about early intervention to protect and divert people away from the risk they may face before illegality occurs."[150] The Channel Programme is not open to individuals already in police custody.

Once a referral is received, panels consider three basic criteria as they review the case — the degree of an individual's engagement with a group, cause, or ideology, their intent to commit harm, and their capability to commit harm. To enable each panel to make a nuanced assessment, the Channel model further breaks these three criteria down into twenty-two distinct factors for consideration — thirteen relating to engagement, six relating to intent, and three relating to capability — such as a history of violence, possession of violent extremist literature, or marked behavioral changes. Once a preliminary assessment has been reached that an individual is a suitable candidate for the Channel Programme, the panel then develops an intervention action plan, and associated support package, tailored to the individual's unique circumstances. Support may include moving an individual to a different school or to public housing in a different neighborhood, partnering with families, counseling or mentoring, faith guidance, or "diversionary activity" such as civic engagement or employment assistance. Each case is subject to periodic review by the panel. To ensure government workers are aware of the resources available to tackle violent extremism, the United Kingdom created an introductory Workshop to Raise Awareness of Prevent (WRAP) for government and local government personnel. In 2011 alone, 20,000 youth and social workers were briefed on the Channel Programme as part of the WRAP initiative.[151]

---

[149] Home Office, *Channel: Supporting individuals vulnerable to recruitment by violent extremists*, March 2010, p. 7.

[150] ibid., p. 9.

[151] Sarah Connolly, Acting Head of Prevent Strategy, Office for Security and Counter-Terrorism, *UK CVE Strategy Presentation*, Hedayah Workshop on the Development of National Strategies for Countering Violent Extremism, 27 January 2014, Abu Dhabi.

The federal constraints inherent in governing the United States have prevented the development of a coherent nationwide approach to countering or preventing violent extremism, but there have been some innovative efforts at early intervention programs in cities across the country — perhaps most notably in Minnesota, home to the largest Somali population in North America. In 2007–2008, according to the local FBI Field Office, between 20 and 25 young Somalis left the community in Minnesota to join *al-Shabaab* after Ethiopian forces entered Somalia in an attempt to re-impose order on the failed state in December 2006.[152] In October 2008, one of these volunteers, twenty-six-year-old Shirwa Ahmed, became the first US citizen to carry out a suicide terrorist attack, detonating a car bomb inside a government compound in Puntland. More recently, in 2015, six young Somalis were detained as they tried to travel to Syria to join ISIL. Community leaders in the twin cities of Minneapolis and St. Paul have worked with the local authorities to create community-led intervention teams that seek to identify the early warning signs of radicalization and guide younger members away from extremist recruiters. In addition, this collaboration has brought mentorship programs, scholarships, afterschool programs, and job trainers and placement officers into the Somali community in an attempt to build community resilience. Minneapolis City Council member Abdi Warsame told National Public Radio that his Muslim constituents were keen to help the authorities prevent any further youthful volunteers going down the same path: "Our community is a patriotic, hard working community, we are trying to fit into the American way of life, we have started numerous businesses, members of our community have joined the armed forces and defended this country, others have joined the police force and defended our cities here. And this kind of thing, it really sets us back and it also creates tensions between the broader community and

---

[152] Teresa Walsh, *In Minnesota, ISIS Offers a Different Allure*, US News and World Report, 4 June 2015 and Joining the Fight in Somalia, *New York Times*, 30 October 2011, at http://www. nytimes.com/interactive/2009/07/12/us/20090712-somalia-timeline.html?_r=0. Viewed 31 August 2015.

Somali-American community, which is not something we want or need … We are Americans first."[153]

It must be admitted that early intervention programs do have some significant drawbacks — they are expensive, resource intensive, and time consuming. In May 2015 the United Nations Security Council reported that ISIL, *Jabhat al-Nusra*, and other armed groups operating in Iraq and Syria had to that date been able to recruit over 25,000 foreign terrorist fighters from over 100 different countries, which gives some indication of the size of the problem that states are confronting.[154] To add a little further perspective, between April 2007 and March 2013, there were 2,653 referrals to the United Kingdom's Channel program, of whom only 587 were considered to be sufficiently "at-risk" to receive support services.[155] The majority of those referred were eighteen years or older, 113 of those referred were under twelve-years-old. The majority of cases involved Islamic extremist affiliations, 14% of cases involved far-right extremism.

Furthermore, important questions have been raised about the potentially negative impact of some of these programs if they are poorly implemented. After a visit to the UK in April 2017, the UN Special Rapporteur on the rights to freedom of peaceful assembly and of association, Maina Kiai, expressed concern that, by fostering suspicion and giving little clear direction, the UK's Prevent Strategy was "having the opposite of its intended effect: by dividing, stigmatizing and alienating segments of the population, Prevent could end up promoting extremism, rather than countering it."[156] This concern was further reinforced by the Oxford University political scientist Karma Nabulsi in May 2017 when she reported that a

---

[153] Weekend Edition, *Marginalized Young American-Somalis Look East To Join ISIS*, National Public Radio, 30 August 2015, at http://www.npr.org/2015/08/30/436013246/marginalized-young-american-somalis-look-east-to-join-isis.

[154] Statement by the President of the Security Council, S/PRST/2015/11, 29 May 2015.

[155] Association of Chief Police Officers, Freedom of Information Request No. 000117/13, 24 January 2014 at http://www.npcc.police.uk/documents/FoI%20publication/Disclosure%20 Logs/Uniformed%20Operations%20FOI/2013/117%2013%20ACPO%20Response%20 -%20Channel%20Project%20Referrals.pdf.

[156] Karma Nabulsi, Don't Go to the Doctor, *London Review of Books*, Vol. 39, No. 10 (18 May 2017).

Freedom of Information Act request had revealed more than 80% of the reports to the British authorities on individuals suspected of extremism had been dismissed as unfounded, suggesting that the mechanisms used to identify "at-risk" individuals were profoundly flawed.[157] As described above, the UK's Prevent program initially relies heavily on government and private sector employees with minimal training to identify potential threats, which can result in suspicion being cast quite widely — sweeping up many innocents in the process and wasting considerable police time.[158] There's clearly room for improvement.

The onus therefore falls on states to implement early intervention programs in a manner that takes into account community sensitivities and avoids exacerbating existing fears and prejudices. Done well, the evidence to date suggests that on a case-by-case basis, early intervention programs can be effective in turning individuals away from violent extremism. The question of overall community impact is a more complex one, and clearly there are pitfalls that such programs can fall into if they are not designed and implemented carefully. However, early intervention programs do represent an alternative to more punitive policing responses, and there is little doubt of the approach most "at-risk" communities would prefer. Getting it right requires the authorities to keep firmly in mind what the Brookings Fellow William McCants has called the "prime directive" of countering violent extremism: "First, do no harm."[159]

## Proscribing hate speech and extremist organizations

Another important aspect of community engagement is protecting vulnerable communities from the influence of violent extremist voices. It is important at the outset of this section to once again make

---

[157] ibid.

[158] Patrick Cockburn, Britain refuses to accept how terrorists really work — and that's why prevention strategies are failing, *The Independent*, 8 June 2017.

[159] William McCants, *The Foreign Policy Essay — Special Edition: First, Do No Harm*, Lawfare, 17 February 2015 at https://www.lawfareblog.com/foreign-policy-essay—special-edition-first-do-no-harm#, accessed on 29 August 2015.

a clear distinction between extreme or radical opinion, and violent extremism. The former may be protected, but the latter is not, and so any legislation drafted to curtail violent extremist rhetoric must be very tightly drafted to ensure that legitimate speech is not curtailed in any way. Article 5 of the ICCPR enshrines the principle that the exercise of individual rights cannot be exploited to deny the rights and freedoms of others and this has particular relevance to the exercise of free speech, free association, and freedom of conscience. Furthermore, Article 20 of the ICCPR specifically requires that both "propaganda for war" and the "advocacy of national, racial or religious hatred that constitutes incitement to discrimination, hostility or violence" should be prohibited by law.

The Human Rights Committee considered the question of hate speech in *Ross v. Canada* (HRC; 2000).[160] Malcolm Ross was a Canadian schoolteacher who repeatedly espoused anti-semitic views, both verbally and in print. When parent complaints resulted in his being removed from his teaching position, he complained that he was being discriminated against because of his "religious" views. The case was referred to the Human Rights Committee, which found that the publication of anti-Jewish views could fall within the scope of the ICCPR's ban on advocacy of national, racial and religious hatred that constitutes incitement to discrimination, hostility or violence. The Committee also noted that the right to freedom of expression carries with it special duties and responsibilities, which are especially pertinent in the context of a school system with young students.

The European Court of Human Rights has also explored the issue of hate speech in the case of *Norwood v. United Kingdom* (ECtHR; 2004). Mark Norwood was a regional organizer for the British National Party who placed a poster in his front window in November 2001, showing an image of the 9/11 attack on the World Trade Center in New York and the slogan "Islam out of Britain — Protect the British People." Norwood was charged by local police with an aggravated offence under Section 5 of the Public Order Act 1986 — displaying,

---

[160]Views of the Human Rights Committee, U.N. GAOR Hum. Rts Comm., 70th Sess., U.N. Doc. CCPR/C/70/D/736/1997 (2000).

with hostility towards a racial or religious group, a sign which is threatening, abusive or insulting, within the sight of a person likely to be caused harassment, alarm or distress by it. He complained that his free speech rights had been violated and took his case to the European Court of Human Rights. The Court ruled that his rights had not been violated since the poster "amounted to a public expression of attack on all Muslims in the United Kingdom" and "such a general, vehement attack against a religious group, linking the group as a whole with a grave act of terrorism, is incompatible with the values proclaimed and guaranteed by the Convention, notably tolerance, social peace and non-discrimination."[161]

Finally, mention should also be made of the International Criminal Tribunal for Rwanda (ICTR) case *Prosecutor v. Ferdinand Nahimana, Jean-Bosco Barayagwiza and Hassan Ngeze* (ICTR; 2003), in which the defendants were put on trial because of statements they made on *Radio Télévision Libre des Mille Collines* and in the *Kangura* newspaper promoting the killing of Tutsi civilians. In a landmark judgment, the Tribunal held the men accountable for the effect of their speech on others and found them guilty of conspiracy to commit genocide, genocide, direct and public incitement to commit genocide, and persecution and extermination as crimes against humanity.[162] International law clearly recognizes the potential that words have to do great harm.

What all this means in practice is that while the right to hold certain views is absolute, the right to manifest them is qualified in the same manner as other forms of expression. Neither the UN Human Rights Committee nor the European Court of Human Rights has yet found in a case brought before them that the right to manifest a belief trumps a law applicable to the general population. Preventing and deterring incitement to terrorism in the interest of protecting national security and public order would likely therefore,

---

[161] European Court of Human Rights, *Norwood v. United Kingdom*, Application no. 23131/03, 16 November 2004.

[162] International Criminal Tribunal for Rwanda, *Prosecutor v. Nahimana, Barayagwiza and Ngeze*, ICTR-99-52-T, 3 December 2003, para 6.

in most circumstances, constitute legitimate grounds to limit freedom of expression.

However, the UN Special Rapporteur on the promotion and protection of the right to freedom of opinion and expression, Frank La Rue, has expressed concern at the overbroad interpretation by states of what might amount to incitement to terrorism. [163] He reminded states that any such restrictions introduced on freedom of expression must meet a three-part test: (1) new laws must be restricted to criminalizing incitement to conduct that is "truly terrorist in nature"; (2) freedom of expression must only be restricted to the extent that is absolutely necessary to achieve the legitimate purposes of the restriction; and (3) such laws must be drafted in precise terms, eschewing vague offenses, such as "glorifying" or "promoting" terrorism.[164] To assist states strike the right balance, the Special Rapporteur therefore proposed the following best practice formulation for legislation criminalizing incitement to terrorism: "It is an offence to intentionally and unlawfully distribute or otherwise make available a message to the public with the intent to incite the commission of a terrorist offence, where such conduct, whether or not expressly advocating terrorist offences, causes a danger that one or more such offences may be committed."[165]

Even with suitable legislation in place, it must also be acknowledged that the ability of governments to restrict online activity is extremely limited. Comprehensive content filtering programs have proved to be so indiscriminate that they disproportionately breach both privacy and freedom of expression protections. Promoting voluntary action by major internet companies like YouTube, Twitter and Facebook to take down content that promotes terrorism — such as martyrdom or execution videos — has achieved some success, but these companies have all resisted any prescreening obligation as being too onerous — in 2012, approximately seventy-two hours of

---

[163] Note by the Secretary-General, *Promotion and Protection of the Rights to Freedom of Opinion and Expression*, A/66/290, 10 August 2011, paras 32–34.

[164] ibid., para 34.

[165] ibid., para 33.

content was uploaded on YouTube every minute.[166] YouTube has established an Abuse and Safety Center as a point of contact for users to report "hateful" content and in 2010 created a button that allowed users to flag content that supported terrorism.

Taking legal action against authors or websites can be difficult, even where hate speech is concerned and there is a legal obligation for states to consider intervening. The transnational nature of cyberspace means that websites and chatrooms are often hosted beyond the reach of domestic law. Nevertheless, some countries have introduced legislation to enforce formal takedown regimes. The United Kingdom created the Counter-Terrorism Internet Referral Unit (CTIRU) in 2010 and it was responsible for shutting down 156 websites during its first year of operation.[167] The Dutch government has been operating a similar takedown scheme since 2008 although it relies initially on voluntary enforcement by service providers. Bringing effective prosecutions against individuals can be challenging, the degree of separation between author and reader, who have most likely never met, has meant that courts have been extremely reluctant to accept a direct link of causality between reading something online and carrying out an act of violence. States must also weigh the public interest of intervention against the risk of drawing attention to material that might not have thus far received much attention. For example, Samina Malik, known online as the "lyrical terrorist", was a young woman living in London who posted a number of poems online expressing her wish to become a suicide bomber. When these came to the notice of the British authorities, she was arrested and prosecuted. Prior to her arrest, no more than 100 members of an extremist online forum had read her poems — after her arrest, the publicity her case attracted meant that her poems went viral and can now be read on "several thousand" websites across the globe.[168]

Online strategic communications campaigns promoting counter-narratives may offer a more promising alternative. The

---

[166] Bipartisan Policy Center, *Countering Online Radicalization in America*, December 2012, pp. 27–28.

[167] ibid., p. 25.

[168] ibid., p. 27.

United Nations Office on Drugs and Crime (UNODC) report on *The Use of the Internet for Terrorist Purposes* observed that "online discussions provide an opportunity to present opposing viewpoints or to engage in constructive debate, which may have the effect of discouraging potential supporters. Counter-narratives with a strong factual foundation may be conveyed through online discussion forums, images, and videos. Successful messages may also demonstrate empathy with the underlying issues that contribute to radicalization — such as political, economic and social conditions — and highlight alternatives to violent means of achieving the desired outcomes. Strategic communications that provide counter-narratives to terrorist propaganda may also be disseminated via the internet, in multiple languages, to reach a broad, geographically diverse audience."[169] Non-state actors have already led the way. A Colombian civil engineer called Oscar Morales was one of the first individuals to leverage Facebook as a tool for social activism. In January 2008, he created a Facebook page entitled "A Million Voices Against the FARC" and within a week, it had 100,000 members.[170] Within a month, Morales had taken his campaign on to the streets and on 4 February 2008, hundreds of thousands of Colombians gathered in the centers of the country's major cities in a show of solidarity with FARC's victims — most notably those then still held hostage by FARC, like former Colombian Presidential candidate Ingrid Betancourt and her campaign manager Clara Rojas. London-based poet Munir Zamir has self-funded a web-based animated graphic novel titled *The Adventures of Abdul X: Mind of a Scholar, Heart of a Warrior*, which explores "the coming of age of a young Muslim in a time of mass hysteria and ignorance" under the tagline "Has this façade of extremism and ideology not done enough damage?"[171] The Saudi government supports the *Sakinah* (Tranquility) campaign,

---

[169] United Nations Office on Drugs and Crime, *The Use of the Internet for terrorist purposes* (2012), p. 12.

[170] See David Burstein, *Innovation Agents: Oscar Morales and One Million Voices Against FARC*, Fast Company, 21 May 2012 at www.fastcompany.com/1836318/innovation-agents-oscar-morales-and-one-million-voices-against-farc.

[171] www.cypher7ad.com.

which seeks to connect with individuals who visit extremist Islamic websites with Islamic scholars and other volunteers in an effort to engage them in debate about the tenets of their faith. At a conference held in Riyadh in 2011, Dr Abdulrahman al-Hadlaq, Senior Advisor to the Saudi Ministry of the Interior, claimed that *Sakinah* had achieved close to a 50% success rate in gaining a full or partial retraction of radical views from the 3,000 plus militants so far engaged by the programme.[172]

Like free speech, freedom of association is a fundamental requirement of a functioning democratic society, and it is protected by Article 22 of the ICCPR. Associations from political parties to trade unions, and from pressure groups to social clubs are a vital component of democratic life.[173] As such, it can be said that freedom of association provides a platform which guarantees that other rights can be enjoyed.[174] However, associations dedicated to the overthrow of the state, the intimidation of a section of the population, or providing material support to external conflicts pose governments with a very particular challenge. The need to restrict the activities of such associations to protect, *inter alia*, national security or public safety is provided for in the text of Article 22(2).

The Human Rights Committee has not issued a general comment specifically relating to Article 22 and there is very little case law at the international level on this topic. However, the UN Special Rapporteur on the promotion and protection of human rights and fundamental freedoms while countering terrorism, Martin Scheinin, warned in 2006 that while he recognized the need to control the existence of groups that are involved in acts of terrorism — either through carrying them out, planning them, recruiting for them, or

---

[172] Dr Abdulrahman Al Hadlaq, Senior Advisor to the Saudi Ministry of the Interior, *Saudi Arabia and the Internet*, Conference on Use of the Internet to Counter the Appeal of Extremist Violence, Riyadh, Saudi Arabia, 24–26 January 2011.

[173] As a matter of international human rights law the category of "associations" does not include professional regulatory bodies as the membership of such organizations is non-voluntary.

[174] *Report of the UN Special Rapporteur on the promotion and protection of human rights and fundamental freedoms while countering terrorism, Martin Scheinin*, A/61/267, 16 August 2006, para 11.

funding them — he had observed numerous instances where limitations to the right to freedom of association "clearly went beyond the scope necessary to counter-terrorism and could in actual fact be used to limit the rights of political parties, trade unions or human rights defenders".[175]

The Special Rapporteur offered the following guidance to states on the kind of activities that might amount to grounds for implementing restrictions as part of a counter-terrorism response and the kind of activities that would not: "The fact that an association calls for achieving through peaceful means ends that are contrary to the interest of the state is not sufficient to characterize an association as terrorist. Pursuing minority rights protection or the recognition of the existence of a minority, or even calls for self-determination do not on their own amount to terrorist activities. It is only when the association engages in or calls for the use of deadly or otherwise serious violence against persons, i.e. the tactics of terrorism, that it may be characterized as a terrorist group and its rights or existence limited and possibly subjected to the application of criminal law."[176]

## Summary

Community engagement is ultimately the process of building partnerships between state institutions and local communities. Local authorities, social services, schools, and police officers all have an important role to play, and by creating a culture of service, accountability, and problem-solving in state institutions, governments can begin the process of building trust with vulnerable and marginalized communities. Community-oriented policing can be the glue that holds this approach together. Dedicated community police officers or civilian support staff who invest the time in building relationships in the communities they serve can become an important channel for communication and can serve as an early warning system for

---

[175] ibid.
[176] ibid., para 24.

potential points of contention allowing the state to intervene early and positively to prevent any escalation of tensions.

Community engagement is also about fostering a sense of citizenship, empowerment, and accountability in "at-risk" communities. As we have seen, terrorist organizations need complicit communities that can provide them with cover, logistical support, and shelter if they are to survive and thrive in an otherwise hostile environment. If states can erode this culture of complicity amongst terrorists' potential constituents by helping marginalized communities to integrate into mainstream society — and benefit from this integration — the space in which terrorist groups are free to operate in relative safety becomes greatly circumscribed. In the words of the former Commissioner of the London Metropolitan Police Service, Sir Ian Blair: "National security depends on neighborhood security ... It is not the police and the intelligence agencies who will defeat crime and terror and anti-social behavior; it is communities."[177]

## Special Investigation Techniques

International human rights law recognizes the severity of the threat posed by terrorism and acknowledges that to counter this threat, states may be required to adopt extraordinary investigative measures in order to protect the general public from harm, but it also ascribes limits to how such extraordinary measures — collectively known as Special Investigation Techniques (SITs) — can be used. These Special Investigation Techniques are operational resources that are not normally used in day-to-day policing, they can be deployed both pre-emptively and reactively. Many of these techniques involve a degree of deception, and most are employed clandestinely without the concurrent awareness of the target.

The Council of Europe has developed a useful typology that identifies four distinct categories of Special Investigation Techniques:

---

[177] BBC News Transcript from Sir Ian Blair's, Commissioner of Metropolitan Police, Dimbleby Speech, 16 November 2005.

(1) secret investigations with public interaction and without deception, such as informant or source recruitment operations; (2) secret investigations without public interaction and without deception, such as electronic eavesdropping, covert entries, or interception operations; (3) secret investigations with public interaction and with deception, such as the use of undercover officers; and (4) secret investigations without public interaction but with deception, such as sting operations. [178]

## The right to privacy

All Special Investigation Techniques are, by their very nature, likely to infringe aspects of the right to privacy that all individuals enjoy under international human rights law. This right is derived from Article 17 of the International Covenant of Civil and Political Rights, which states that "no one shall be subjected to arbitrary or unlawful interference with his privacy, family, home or correspondence, nor to unlawful attacks on his honor and reputation" and that "everyone has the right to the protection of the law against such interference or attacks." The right to privacy is also enshrined in the Universal Declaration of Human Rights (Article 12), the Convention on the Rights of the Child (Article 16), and the International Convention on the Protection of All Migrant Workers and Members of Their Families (Article 14). At the regional level, the right to privacy is protected by the European Convention on Human Rights (Article 8) and the American Convention on Human Rights (Article 11). The Arab Charter on Human Rights states that "private life is sacred" (Article 17). [179] The European Court of Human Rights has explored the application of this right in the most depth, providing important

---

[178] This typology was developed for the Council of Europe from the work of Professor G. Marx and Professor de Valkeneer. See Council of Europe, *Terrorism: Special Investigation Techniques* (April 2005), pp. 13–15.

[179] Human Rights Council, *Report of the Special Rapporteur on the Promotion and Protection of the Right to the Freedom of Opinion and Expression, Frank La Rue*, A/HRC/23/40, 17 April 2013, para 21.

guidance on how best to navigate privacy issues within the context of democratic governance.

The right to privacy is well established, but what is actually meant by privacy is not.[180] There is no set international definition of privacy, nor of what a private life actually entails, and international courts have been careful not to define either concept exhaustively, preferring to allow evolving jurisprudence to give color and shape to this right over time. However, some legal commentators have found it conceptually helpful to divide privacy concerns into five categories: personal identity, integrity of person, state surveillance, data protection, and media intrusion.[181] Individuals are entitled to define their personal (gender, sexual, etc.) identity as they see fit and are entitled to protection from interference by other private parties, such as secret filming. However, it is generally accepted that the preservation of public safety may require intrusive investigation by the state, although the state's powers in this regard are not unlimited. It is also generally accepted that holding relevant information on individuals for national security purposes may be necessary, but the retention or sharing of private data by the state can nonetheless infringe privacy rights. Individuals have a certain degree of protection from unwarranted media intrusion, however, this right is balanced against both the public's right to know pertinent information and reasonable expectations of privacy. Of these five categories, our primary focus in this section will be on state surveillance.

Although the concept of a private life has eluded precise definition, it can be thought of as a protected sphere of activity that embraces both personal liberty and interaction with other people. In this protected space, an individual is shielded from unwarranted intrusion or intervention by either state or private entities. Some commentators have described the essence of this right as "the right

---

[180] ibid.

[181] Jonathan Cooper, *Countering Terrorism, Protecting Human Rights: A Manual*, Office for Democratic Institutions and Human Rights, Organization for Security and Cooperation in Europe, 2007, pp. 198–199.

to be left alone" — a phrase first coined by the eminent nineteenth century American jurist Thomas Cooley.[182] The manual on *Countering Terrorism, Protecting Human Rights* produced by the Organization for Security and Cooperation in Europe offers a slightly expanded formula, suggesting that the concept of a private life encapsulates the rights "to be oneself, to live as oneself and to keep to oneself".[183] As such, the concept of a private life in a sense also encompasses established civil liberties such as freedom of expression and freedom of conscience.[184]

The concept of privacy does not apply exclusively to individuals. Collective entities, such as families, places of worship, businesses, political parties, and medical facilities, also need a degree of privacy to function. Privacy allows groups to form and function without undue interference and as such is an essential building block in the creation of vibrant and inclusive communities. However, it is also important to note that there can be significant overlap between the public and private spheres since everyone carries out at least part of their private life in public.[185] Furthermore, there are six accepted grounds in international law under which it may be acceptable to interfere with an individual's or group's privacy: national security, public safety, the economic wellbeing of the country, the prevention of disorder or crime, the protection of public health or morals, and the protection of the rights and freedoms of others.

Any effective counter-terrorism strategy is likely to interfere with the privacy rights of some individuals to a significant extent — from traditional policing methods such as the physical search of a suspect to the use of sophisticated technology like eavesdropping devices. The international legal standard is that there must be a legal basis in domestic law for the use of any particular investigative

---

[182] Thomas Cooley, *A Treatise on the Law of Torts or the Wrongs Which Arise Independently of Contract* (Callaghan & Co.; 1888), p. 29.

[183] Jonathan Cooper, *Countering Terrorism, Protecting Human Rights: A Manual*, Office for Democratic Institutions and Human Rights, Organization for Security and Cooperation in Europe, 2007, p. 197.

[184] ibid.

[185] ibid.

technique and that such legislation must be publicly accessible and its effects foreseeable. A legal provision is foreseeable if it is worded sufficiently clearly that an individual is able to take note of the provision and moderate his or her behavior, without implying that a person should be able to foresee exactly when that power may be used.

In practical terms, this means that counter-terrorism and criminal justice legislation must clearly lay out in advance the powers available to police and other security agencies and the circumstances in which they can use them. The UN Office of the High Commissioner for Human Rights has emphasized that states have an obligation to protect against the arbitrary exercise of SITs. In *Klass v. Germany* (ECtHR; 1978), the European Court of Human Rights stated that any system of secret surveillance conducted by the state must be accompanied by adequate and effective guarantees against abuse,[186] and this should be considered a best practice standard. In the early 1980s, the United Kingdom fell foul of the European Court because of the *ad hoc* nature of the regime governing the use of telephone intercepts by government officials. The Court found in the case of *Malone v. United Kingdom* (ECtHR; 1984) that the mechanisms governing the interception of communications by the police were sufficiently legally ill-defined to place Britain in breach of the European Convention on Human Rights.[187] The British government subsequently passed the Interception of Communications Act (1985) as a first step towards putting the agencies involved in intelligence gathering on a statutory footing.

The UN Human Rights Committee has commented that even interference that is permissible under national law may nonetheless contravene the provisions of the ICCPR in certain circumstances. The Committee noted that the reference in Article 17 to "arbitrary interference" had been introduced intentionally "to guarantee that even interference provided for by law should be in accordance with the provisions, aims and objectives of the Covenant and should be,

---

[186] European Court of Human Rights, *Klass v. Germany*, No. 5029/71, Judgment of 6 September 1978, para 50.

[187] European Court of Human Rights, See *Malone v. United Kingdom*, Case A82, 2 August 1984.

in any event, reasonable in the particular circumstances."[188] In the case of *Toonen v. Australia* (HRC; 1994), the Committee has further educed the concept of reasonableness in this context to indicate "any interference with privacy must be proportional to the end sought and be necessary in the circumstances of any given case."[189] More recently in *Szabó and Vissy v. Hungary* (ECtHR; 2016) the European Court of Human Rights ruled that the 2011 National Security Act introduced by the Hungarian government conferred powers on state agents so overly broad and ill-defined that they could target "virtually anyone", commenting further: "A measure of secret surveillance can be found as being in compliance with the Convention only if it is strictly necessary, as a general consideration, for safeguarding the democratic institutions and, moreover, if it is strictly necessary, as a particular consideration, for the obtaining of vital intelligence in an individual operation."[190] The deliberate use of the words "strict" and "vital" clearly signals the Court's intention to set a very high threshold.

Article 16 of the ICCPR guarantees the right of all people to recognition everywhere as persons before the law. The implication for the use of Special Investigation Techniques is that due process considerations must be observed even in the context of counter-terrorism investigations. Some (but by no means all) regulating instruments may allow for special police powers to be lawfully used without appropriate authorization in emergency or urgent circumstances — typically an imminent threat to national security or public safety. For example, in the Republic of Korea, police may institute electronic surveillance measures in response to a public emergency, contingent on their obtaining subsequent judicial authorization within the following thirty-six hours.

---

[188] Human Rights Committee, General Comment 16: Article 17 (The right to respect of privacy, family, home and correspondence, and protection of honour and reputation), HRI/GEN/1/Rev.9 (Vol. I) p.1, 1988, para 4.

[189] Human Rights Committee, *Toonen v. Australia*, Communication no. 488/1992, U.N. Doc CCPR/C/50/D/488/1992, 1994, para 8.3.

[190] European Court of Human Rights, *Szabó and Vissy v. Hungary*, Application no. 37138/14, 12 January 2016, para 73.

The international legal standard for launching a pro-active investigation is that there must be a reasonable suspicion that an offense will be committed. Whether a reasonable ground for this suspicion exists will depend on the circumstances in each individual case, but there must be some objective basis for it. The decision to deploy Special Investigation Techniques must be based on all the facts that bear on the likelihood that a certain type of criminal activity is underway. Reasonable suspicion can never be supported on the basis of personal factors alone — for example, religion or ethnicity — without supporting intelligence bearing on the choice of target. Freedom from discrimination is a fundamental right. Article 1 of the United Nations Charter describes one of the core purposes of the United Nations as promoting respect for human rights and fundamental freedoms without distinction as to race, sex, language or religion, and the core international and regional human rights treaties all reinforce this principle.[191] Profiling based on stereotypical assumptions that persons of a certain race, national or ethnic origin, or religion are likely to be involved in terrorism may lead to practices that are incompatible with the principle of non-discrimination.[192]

The UN Special Rapporteur on the promotion and protection of human rights and fundamental freedoms while countering terrorism has specifically commented on the negative policy implications of terrorist-profiling practices that single out persons for enhanced law enforcement attention simply because they belong to a certain group, noting that this can exert a profound emotional toll and stigmatize the entire group as a suspect community: "This stigmatization may, in turn, result in a feeling of alienation among the targeted groups... The lack of trust between the police and communities may be especially disastrous in the counter-terrorism context. The gathering of intelligence is the key to success in largely preventive law

---

[191] Office of the United Nations High Commissioner for Human Rights, *Fact Sheet 32: Human Rights, Terrorism and Counter Terrorism* (July 2008), p. 37.
[192] *Report of the Special Rapporteur on the promotion and protection of human rights and fundamental freedoms while countering terrorism, Martin Scheinin,* A/HRC/4/26, 29 January 2007, para 34.

enforcement operations... To be successful, counter-terrorism law enforcement policies would have to strengthen the trust between the police and communities."[193] It should also be noted that predictive profiling has proven ineffective in terms of preventing terrorist attacks. Terrorist groups have demonstrated the operational flexibility to circumvent established profiles by recruiting people who are less likely to attract attention — for example, *al-Qaeda* used the Anglo-Caribbean shoe bomber Richard Reid and the Nigerian-born and British-educated underwear bomber Umar Farouk Abdulmutallab to smuggle bombs onto Western airliners past airport security checks that were fixated on males of Middle Eastern appearance.

Where reasonable grounds for suspicion exist, and there is a clear necessity to use Special Investigation Techniques to learn more, three additional principles come into play: subsidiarity, specificity, and proportionality. Special Investigation Techniques should only be employed if there are no less intrusive techniques available to investigators that can obtain the same result, and the public interest in preventing the offense outweighs the general principle of protecting privacy. These considerations are especially important when employing the kind of intrusive techniques — such as eavesdropping devices — that may not only affect the rights of the person who is suspected of unlawful activity, but also, directly or indirectly, the rights of other persons who are not targets of the investigation. The principle of specificity requires that any information gathered by using Special Investigation Techniques can only be used in support of the charge for which they were introduced. In *The Association for European Integration and Human Rights and Ekimdzhiev v. Bulgaria* (ECtHR; 2007), the European Court of Human Rights considered a challenge to the actual legitimacy of legislation governing the use of surveillance tools by the Bulgarian state, which appeared to fail the test of proportionality (and necessity).[194] Considering the evidence submitted in the case, the Court expressed concern that "the system of secret surveillance in

---

[193] ibid., paras 56–58.

[194] European Court of Human Rights, *Association for European Integration and Human Rights and Ekimdzhiev v Bulgaria*, Application no. 62540/00, Judgment, 28 June 2007.

Bulgaria is, to say the least, overused", noting that of at least 10,000 intercept warrants authorized in a two-year period, product from fewer than 270 had actually been used in court proceedings, suggesting that the safeguards intended to prevent the excessive use of telephone intercepts were inadequate.[195] The Court therefore concluded that there had been a violation of the Convention as the law introduced by the Bulgarian government did not afford sufficient protections against "the risks of abuse inherent in any system of covert surveillance".[196]

Another important due process consideration relevant to the use of Special Investigation Techniques is the protection afforded in international human rights law to every defendant charged with a criminal offense to ensure that they receive a fair trial to determine their guilt or innocence, which crucially includes the ability to effectively challenge any evidence presented as part of the case against them.[197] Fair trial rights require the timely disclosure of material relevant to the prosecution case so that the defence may challenge it in court. The UN Human Rights Committee has further clarified that disclosure must include documents and other evidence that the prosecution plans to offer in court against the accused, or that may be exculpatory.[198] Exculpatory material includes not only material establishing innocence but also other evidence that could assist the defense, such as any indication that a confession was not given voluntarily.[199]

In the counter-terrorism context, the increased use of material gathered for intelligence purposes as evidence can lead to significant conflicts between the rights of the defendant and the operational security considerations that attach to most Special Investigation Techniques — notably the desire to protect an operational advantage afforded by any unfamiliar technical

---

[195] ibid., p. 92.

[196] ibid., p. 93.

[197] Communication No. 289/1988, *Dieter Wolf v. Panama* (Views adopted on 26 March 1992), in UN doc. GAOR, A/47/40, para 6.6.

[198] Human Rights Committee, *General Comment No. 32, Article 14: Right to Equality Before Courts and Tribunals and to a Fair Trial*, U.N. Doc. CCPR/C/GC/32, 2007, para 33.

[199] ibid.

capabilities at the state's disposal, to ensure that an active source of intelligence is not compromised, or to safeguard the identity of a human intelligence asset. As the Special Rapporteur on the promotion and protection of human rights and fundamental freedoms while countering terrorism has noted: "Intelligence services operate on the principle that information should not be disclosed unless for compelling reasons, whereas trials operate on the basis of the need for full disclosure."[200]

There is considerable guidance on how these competing interests can be balanced, both in the rules governing the operation of international criminal tribunals and in international human rights case law. In *Rowe and Davis v. The United Kingdom* (ECtHR; 2000), the European Court of Human Rights ruled that the entitlement to disclosure of case-related evidence was not an absolute right, noting: "In any criminal proceedings there may be competing interests, such as national security or the need to protect witnesses at risk of reprisals or keep secret police methods of investigation of crime, which must be weighed against the rights of the accused ... In some cases it may be necessary to withhold certain evidence from the defense so as to preserve the fundamental rights of another individual or to safeguard an important public interest."[201] The key test that must be met is whether or not the decision to withhold information is both necessary and applied in a manner proportional to issues at stake.[202] An assessment of proportionality requires a balance to be struck between how well non-disclosure protects the legitimate aims being pursued in court and the negative impact this has on the ability of the person to respond to the case in line with the due process guarantees afforded under international human rights law.[203] This means that if a less restrictive measure can achieve

---

[200] *Report of the United Nations High Commissioner for Human Rights on the protection of human rights and fundamental freedoms while countering terrorism*, A/HRC/22/26, 17 December 2012, para 38.

[201] European Court of Human Rights, *Rowe and Davis v. The United Kingdom*, Application no. 28901/95, Judgment (Merits and Just Satisfaction), 16 February 2000, para 61.

[202] ibid., para 63 and European Court of Human Rights, *Dowsett v. United Kingdom*, Application no. 39482/98, Judgment (Merits and Just Satisfaction), 24 September 2003, para 44.

[203] European Court of Human Rights, *Doorson v. Netherlands*, Application no. 20524/92, Judgment (Merits and Just Satisfaction), 26 March 1996, para 70 and European Court of

the same legitimate aim (such as providing redacted summaries of evidence), then that measure should be applied.[204]

Besides the need to ensure that non-disclosure of information is necessary and proportionate, any difficulties caused to a party in the proceedings must be "sufficiently counterbalanced" by the judicial authorities in order to ensure that the person is able to respond to the case and that the trial is still fair overall.[205] This might involve, for example, an *ex parte* evaluation by the trial judge of whether all or part of the information should be withheld and whether a redacted summary of the information should be provided. An accused person must always be provided with sufficient information so as to be adequately prepared for the case.[206] If withholding intelligence material means that this criterion cannot be met the state must choose between disclosing the information, proceeding in the case without relying on the information, or withdrawing the proceedings.[207]

The Rules of Procedure and Evidence adopted by the International Criminal Court and the Special Tribunal for Lebanon, created to investigate the 2005 murder of the former Lebanese Prime Minister Rafik Hariri in an incident that bore many of the characteristics of a terrorist attack, further illustrate how these

---

Human Rights, *Rowe and Davis v. The United Kingdom*, Application no. 28901/95, Judgment (Merits and Just Satisfaction), 16 February 2000, para 61.

[204] European Court of Human Rights, *Van Mechelen and Others v. Netherlands*, Application nos. 21363/93, 21364/93 and 21427/93, Judgment (Merits), 23 April 1997, para 58 and European Court of Human Rights, *Rowe and Davis v. The United Kingdom*, Application no. 28901/95, Judgment (Merits and Just Satisfaction), 16 February 2000, para 61.

[205] European Court of Human Rights, *Doorson v. Netherlands*, Application no. 20524/92, Judgment (Merits and Just Satisfaction), 26 March 1996, para 72, European Court of Human Rights, *Van Mechelen and Others v. Netherlands*, Application nos. 21363/93, 21364/93 and 21427/93, Judgment (Merits), 23 April 1997, para 54; and European Court of Human Rights, *Rowe and Davis v. The United Kingdom*, Application no. 28901/95, Judgment (Merits and Just Satisfaction), 16 February 2000, paras 61 and 64–65.

[206] *Report of the United Nations High Commissioner for Human Rights on the protection of human rights and fundamental freedoms while countering terrorism*, A/HRC/22/26, 17 December 2012, para 38.

[207] See also Counter-Terrorism Implementation Task Force, Working Group on protecting human rights while countering terrorism, *Basic Human Rights Reference Guide: Right to a Fair Trial and Due Process in the Context of Countering Terrorism* (2014).

principles can be applied in practice. The Rules of Procedure adopted by both Courts emphasize the fundamental importance of the disclosure of exculpatory material, but also balance this obligation against the need in certain circumstances to protect sensitive information. The ICC Statute allows the prosecutor to apply to the Trial Chamber for an *ex parte* ruling on whether or not it would lawful to withhold material from the defense if its disclosure could jeopardize ongoing investigations.[208] The Statute of the Special Tribunal for Lebanon also allows for the prosecutor, if he or she believes that the disclosure of information in his or her possession may prejudice ongoing or future investigations, cause grave risk to the security of a witness or the witness's family, or be contrary to the public interest or the rights of third parties, to "apply *ex parte* to the Trial Chamber sitting in camera to be relieved in whole or in part of an obligation under the Rules to disclose that material".[209] However, in making such an application, the prosecutor is also expected to provide proposed counterbalancing measures that might include the identification of new, similar information, provision of the information in summarized or redacted form, or stipulation of the relevant facts. The Lebanon Statute further provides that should the prosecutor receive confidential intelligence material from a third party, he or she shall not disclose this information without the consent of the intelligence provider.[210] However, if such material is exculpatory in nature, the prosecutor has an obligation either to obtain the provider's consent to disclose it or to request the provider to share similar information in a form that can be disclosed.

Even though both international and many domestic courts seek to balance the needs of source protection against the needs to the defendant, it is not uncommon for intelligence agencies to try to game the system. A common practice that has emerged among intelligence providers in the context of counter-terrorism investigations is to ensure that law enforcement officers working in

---

[208] See Rule 81(2) of the Statute of the International Criminal Court.
[209] See Rule 116(a) of the Statute of the Special Tribunal for Lebanon.
[210] See Rule 118(a) of the Statute of the Special Tribunal for Lebanon.

the field do not have access to raw intelligence, on the theory that the prosecution cannot be expected to disclose what it doesn't know. In addition to raising major fair trial concerns, this reluctance to share intelligence with those who can actually make use of it can have severe consequences for public safety. Prior to the 11 September 2001 attacks by *al-Qaeda* on New York and Washington, the Central Intelligence Agency had significant intelligence on two of the hijackers involved in the plot, Khalid al-Mihdhar and Nawaf al-Hazmi. Both men had come to the CIA's attention when they attended a high-level *al-Qaeda* meeting in Malaysia in January 2000. Ten days after the meeting in Malaysia, both men flew to Los Angeles. The CIA knew that one of the men had a visa to enter the US and that the other had actually flown to Los Angeles. Even though it knew that both men were members of *al-Qaeda*, because of the perceived sensitivity of this intelligence, the CIA did not share this information with the lead counter-terrorism agency inside the United States — the Federal Bureau of Investigation. Both men lived in San Diego, California, under their own names (although al-Mihdhar left the US for a period travelling to Yemen and Afghanistan), took flight school lessons (unsuccessfully), and would have been relatively easy for the FBI to locate and interview. This action alone might have been sufficient to disrupt, or at the very least delay, the 9/11 plot.[211] Instead, al-Hamzi and al-Mihdhar were two of the hijackers on American Airlines Flight 77 that crashed into the Pentagon, killing 189 people. The "need to know" principle cuts both ways — intelligence must be shared with those who need to know it, otherwise it has no value.

## Human intelligence operations

A human intelligence asset can be the most valuable of all intelligence sources, and it is the threat that terrorist organizations tend to fear the most. Carlos Marighella took care to warn readers of his

---

[211] See *The 9/11 Commission Report: Final Report of the National Commission on Terrorist Attacks Upon the United States*, Authorized Edition (W. W. Norton and Company; 2004), p. 355.

*Minimanual of the Urban Guerrilla* that "the worst enemy of the urban guerrilla and the major danger we run is infiltration into our organization by a spy or informer."[212] The reason for this concern is pretty self-evident — unlike more passive intelligence collection methods, a human source is dynamic, responsive to direction, and, above all, sentient. Such a source can offer insights other intelligence assets cannot, and, as Marighella noted above, they come in two basic varieties — informants, a private individual already associated with the target, and spies, agents of the state who successfully manage to infiltrate a target group or operation. While infiltrating an undercover officer into an organization can be both more dangerous and more difficult than recruiting an informant who is already inside it, the advantage of maneuvering professional officers into such a position is that they tend to be substantially more reliable assets in the field and to have a great deal more credibility in court.

There is nothing in international human rights law to prevent state agencies from using either informants or spies, indeed it is actively encouraged by international institutions. The United Nations Convention against Transnational Organized Crime (UNTOC) encourages States Party to make use of participating informants in the investigation of organized crime groups, and the same logic can be applied to terrorist organizations.[213] However, human intelligence operations are governed by the same human rights obligations as any other SIT — recruiters cannot commit human rights violations, criminal acts, or either blackmail or threaten suspects to gain their cooperation. In addition, acting as an informant on or inside a terrorist group is inherently dangerous and the state has an obligation under human rights law to protect the life and security of the informant.

It is not uncommon for an informant operating in a criminal milieu to be put in a position where he or she may be expected by

---

[212] Carlos Marighella, *Minimanual of the Urban Guerilla* (Havana: Tricontinental; 1970).

[213] Article 26 of the United Nations Convention against Transnational Organized Crime (UNTOC). See United Nations Office on Drugs and Crime, *Counter-Terrorism Legal Training Curriculum: Module 4 Human Rights and Criminal Justice Responses to Terrorism*, Terrorism Prevention Branch (2014), p. 91.

criminal confederates to commit a criminal act or risk exposure. States may therefore promise an informant immunity from prosecution should they be asked to participate in certain acts. The United Nations Office on Drugs and Crime's *Model Legislative Provisions against Organized Crime*, which are intended to assist states in implementing the UNTOC, offer some guidance on the type of activities that an informant (or for that matter an undercover officer) infiltrated into a criminal group might reasonably undertake without being held criminally responsible, such as making available "legal and financial means, transport, storage, housing and communications needed for the perpetration of [related] offences".[214]

However, there is a limit to which a human intelligence asset can lawfully transgress laws in the public interest. International human rights law also places important restrictions on the activities of an informant acting under the direction of the state or its representatives — even when an informant is working for the authorities, it is completely impermissible for him or her to participate in the abuse of fundamental human rights, such as acts involving killing, enforced disappearance, or torture and ill-treatment, since the "prohibition on torture and the arbitrary deprivation of life are absolute and cannot be justified, even by reference to important law enforcement goals such as the investigation of terrorism."[215] Immunity must not lead to impunity where serious human rights violations are at stake.[216] It should also be stressed that the practice of the various international criminal tribunals has established the general principle under international criminal law that no one can

---

[214] United Nations Office on Drugs and Crime, *Counter-Terrorism Legal Training Curriculum: Module 4 Human Rights and Criminal Justice Responses to Terrorism*, Terrorism Prevention Branch, (2014), p. 93. See also UNODC Model Legislative Provisions against Organized Crime at Article 15, para 3.

[215] United Nations Office on Drugs and Crime, *Counter-Terrorism Legal Training Curriculum: Module 4 Human Rights and Criminal Justice Responses to Terrorism*, Terrorism Prevention Branch, (2014), p. 93.

[216] *Countering Terrorism, Protecting Human Rights: A Manual*, Organization for Security and Cooperation in Europe (2007), p. 144.

be granted immunity from prosecution for involvement in war crimes, crimes against humanity, genocide, or acts of torture.

Human intelligence assets have been a part of the struggle against terrorism from the earliest days of the emergence of the terrorist threat in the nineteenth century. The Third Section of the Russian Department of Police recruited Peter Rachkovsky to successfully infiltrate *Narodnaya Volya* and he later graduated to running networks of informers himself against the Russian anarchist diaspora from the Tsar's Embassy in Paris.[217] One Russian counter-terrorism official, Colonel Georgy Porfiryevich Sudeykin, was so successful at penetrating *Narodnaya Volya* that the post of Inspector of the Secret Police was created specially for him. Sudeykin recruited a former artillery officer called Sergei Degaev who had been placed in charge of *Narodnaya Volya*'s "military" operations by Vera Figner. Over the course of his relationship with Sudeykin, Degaev gave up most of the organization's senior leadership including Figner herself. Although Degaev eventually turned on Sudeykin as well, setting him up for assassination, *Narodnaya Volya* never recovered from his betrayal.[218] The British government recruited Henri le Caron, an American Civil War veteran of English origin, to infiltrate the Irish Fenian movement, and he was able to provide forewarning of a wildly ambitious plot led by John O'Neill to invade Canada.[219] Le Caron subsequently published a best-selling memoir entitled *Twenty-Five Years in the Secret Service*. Rachkovsky, Degaev, and Le Caron were merely the best known of the countless spies and informers deployed against aspirant terrorists by the European powers, some successful, some considerably less so.

An informant's motivation for cooperating with the authorities can be as simple or complex as the pathway that led him or her to

---

[217] Alex Butterworth, *The World That Never Was: A True Story of Dreamers, Schemers, Anarchists and Secret Agents* (Pantheon Books; 2010), pp. 138 and 180–181 and Frederic Zuckerman, *The Tsarist Secret Police Abroad: Policing Europe in a Modernising World* (Palgrave MacMillan; 2003), pp. 124–150.

[218] See Richard Pipes, *The Degaev Affair: Terror and Treason in Tsarist Russia* (Yale University Press; 2003).

[219] K. R. M. Short, *The Dynamite War: Irish-American Bombers in Victorian Britain* (Gill and Macmillan; 1979), pp. 21–24.

become involved in a terrorist group in the first place. Source handlers struggle to understand what motivates an asset just as social scientists struggle to understand what motivates a terrorist. During the Cold War, Western intelligence agencies often summarized the core motivations exploited by recruiters with the mnemonic MICE — Money, Ideology, Compromise and Ego — which remains an enduring trope of source recruitment literature.[220] A review of 104 cases in which US nationals had agreed to spy for a foreign power between 1947 and 1989 conducted by the US Department of Defense found that the majority cited money as their sole or primary motivation.[221] Further insights into the recruitment process can be gleaned from operational manuals such as the US Army Field Manual on Human Intelligence Collector Operations published in 2006, which explores potential source motivations in some detail noting: "Sources will cooperate with the HUMINT collector for various reasons ranging from patriotic duty to personal gain … They may also respond to emotion or logic."[222] A sense of guilt over past acts can be a powerful factor, as can be a desire to gain revenge for personal slights.

The US Army Field Manual also draws upon the celebrated research conducted by the psychologist Dr Robert Cialdini on what he termed "weapons of mass influence". In his seminal work, *Influence: The Psychology of Persuasion*, Cialdini identified six "fixed action patterns" that human beings tend to fall back on automatically when faced with making a difficult choice: reciprocation, authority, scarcity, commitment/consistency, liking, and social proof, collectively known by the acronym RASCLS. Cialdini argued that "compliance professionals" — such as salesmen, reporters or human source handlers — can exploit their knowledge of these

---

[220] Randy Burkett, An Alternative Framework for Agent Recruitment: From MICE to RASCLS, *Studies in Intelligence*, Vol. 57, No. 1 (March 2013), p. 7. See also Henry Crumpton, *The Art of Intelligence: Lessons from a life in the CIA's Clandestine Service* (Penguin Books; 2012), p. 58.

[221] Randy Burkett, An Alternative Framework for Agent Recruitment: From MICE to RASCLS, *Studies in Intelligence*, Vol. 57, No. 1 (March 2013), p. 9.

[222] *Field Manual 2-22.3: Human intelligence Collector Operations*, United States Army, 6 September 2006, pp. 8–2.

patterns to manipulate individuals into adopting the choice they are promoting, and many intelligence collection agencies around the globe would agree with his assessment. The bottom line is that there are a multitude of entirely lawful approaches that can result in a successful agent recruitment.

There is no shortage of modern examples of law enforcement and intelligence agencies successfully using techniques like these to recruit or turn members of terrorist groups and put them back to work in the service of the state. British intelligence enjoyed considerable success in penetrating the Provisional IRA despite the close-knit world of Irish republicanism. For example, in the mid-1980s, British military intelligence officers recruited a former Provisional IRA quartermaster called Frank Hegarty who was aggrieved about his dismissal from his clandestine post by the local PIRA commander in Londonderry, Martin McGuinness. The surprisingly moralistic McGuinness disapproved of Hegarty leaving his wife for his mistress. After Hegarty was able to worm his way back into PIRA's good graces under British direction, he provided crucial intelligence on a major arms shipment sent to the Provisional IRA by the Libyan leader Colonel Muammar Gadhafi.[223] Another notable success was the recruitment of Freddie Scappaticci (codenamed Steak Knife) by the British Army's Force Research Unit (FRU). Scappaticci was Deputy Head and then Head of the Provisional IRA's Security Department in the 1980s and was responsible for preventing British intelligence from penetrating PIRA's operations. It is hard to imagine a better placed asset. Scappaticci volunteered his services to the British after being badly beaten up by another republican in the late 1970s.[224]

British intelligence has also enjoyed some success infiltrating *al-Qaeda*. One case that has received considerable publicity is that of Aimen Dean, a young Saudi who fought in Bosnia as a *mujahedin* volunteer alongside Bosnian government forces before being drawn into the orbit of *al-Qaeda* where he became a religious counselor

---

[223] Stephen Grey, *The New Spymasters: Inside the Modern World of Espionage from the Cold War to Global Terror* (St. Martins Press; 2015), pp. 76–77.

[224] Ed Moloney, *Voices from the Grave: Two Men's War in Ireland* (Public Affairs, 2010), p. 278.

working with the organization's new recruits. Dean began to question the legitimacy of *al-Qaeda*'s use of terrorist violence in the aftermath of the 1998 attacks on the US embassies in Nairobi and Dar-es-Salaam, which killed many innocent local citizens in addition to US embassy staff. Seeking guidance from *al-Qaeda*'s senior religious adviser, Abu Abdullah al-Muhajir, he found the arguments the latter put forward justifying the collateral injury of innocent civilians, grounded as they were in a thirteenth century *fatwa* written in response to Mongol incursions into Muslim lands, completely unconvincing and began to turn away from the organization. He visited the Gulf for medical treatment at the end of 1998 privately determined to leave *al-Qaeda* and while he was there, he was approached by the Secret Intelligence Service (SIS) and ultimately recruited. After a number of months being debriefed by British intelligence officers, he was asked if he would be prepared to go back to *al-Qaeda* and act as an informer. Dean agreed to the plan and remained an active intelligence source for many years. In an interview with the BBC conducted in 2015, Dean was asked if he had had any moral qualms about betraying his former comrades: "Whatever moral misgivings I had, I have my ex-comrades to thank for driving those moral misgivings away because the more I see what they were planning — for example, I was there basically when *al-Qaeda* was constructing their first workable chemical device and talking about this with such glee and such deep psychopathic satisfaction ... that is when you say to yourself, 'Why do I have any moral misgivings about spying on you guys?' Whatever they are doing is justifying whatever you are doing."[225]

Morten Storm, also known as Murad Storm Al-Denmarki, is another interesting figure. After a troubled childhood, Storm joined the Bandidos motorcycle gang. He also became interested in Islam after coming across a biography of Mohammed in his local library. He was arrested in 1997, befriended a Danish convert to Islam in prison and began to become more serious about his faith,

---

[225] Peter Marshall, The spy who came in from Al-Qaeda, *BBC News Magazine*, 3 March 2105 at http://www.bbc.com/news/magazine-31700894. Viewed 21 October 2015.

which led him into extremist circles in both Denmark and the United Kingdom. Over time, he also became friendly with Anwar al-Awlaki, the US-born religious scholar, who would become the spiritual adviser to *al-Qaeda* in the Arabian Peninsula. In this period, he was approached by several Western intelligence agencies but rebuffed them all. However, after he found his path to joining the Islamic Courts Union in Somalia blocked by Ethiopian troops gaining control of Mogadishu airport, he began to question God's purpose for him. Storm eventually began to reject the extremist narrative promoted by his friends: "Now I thought of the Twin towers, Bali, Madrid in 2005, London in 2005 ... If they were part of *Allah's* predominated plan, I now wanted no part of it ... My loss of faith was as frightening as it was sudden ... I was the convert unconverted."[226] Storm sought out the Danish Security and Intelligence Service (PET) and offered to spy on his former comrades for them — in doing so, Storm became a distinct type of human intelligence asset known in the jargon of espionage as "a volunteer". The Danes were delighted to take him up on his offer, and Storm was also introduced to British and American intelligence officers. By Storm's own account, it was information he was able to obtain about the whereabouts of his friend Anwar al-Awlaki in Yemen that ultimately enabled the United States to eliminate al-Awlaki in a drone strike.

Of course, it is not always possible to identify a potential recruitment candidate inside a group under investigation, and timely and well-placed volunteers are rare. When there are no obvious well-placed potential recruitment targets, intelligence officers will often seek to maneuver an existing asset alongside the target group and then facilitate his or her infiltration of the organization. The Canadian Security and Intelligence Service (CSIS) and Royal Canadian Mountain Police (RCMP) were able to do precisely this in the 2006 case of the Toronto Eighteen terror cell — a disparate group of Canadian Muslims led by

---

[226] Morten Storm, *Agent Storm: My Life Inside Al-Qaeda and the CIA* (Atlantic Monthly Press; 2014), pp. 118 and 122.

Fahim Ahmad and Zakaria Amaraa who had been angered by
Canada's military involvement in Afghanistan and plotted to
storm Parliament Hill in Ottawa and detonate truck bombs in
downtown Toronto. The Canadian authorities were able to infiltrate two informers into the social circle of the plotters: Mubin
Shaikh and Shaher Elsohemy. A former army cadet, Shaikh
offered instruction on the use of firearms to the group. Elsohemy
helped the group acquire credit cards and explosives. Shaikh was
motivated partly by a desire for adventure and partly by a sincere
and deeply-held religious belief that jihadi terrorism was a profound perversion of Islam — he was also paid CDN$300,000 by
the Canadian authorities for his actions. Elsohemy's motivation
was predominantly financial in nature and he was given a compensation package reportedly worth about CDN$4,000,000 by the
Canadian government and a new identity within the witness
protection program.

Having an asset in place who holds the trust of terrorist group
members opens up further possibilities beyond just the acquisition
of intelligence, it can allow law enforcement and security agencies
to take proactive action to disrupt terrorist plots before they can
escalate to the point at which the public is put at risk. The tactic
that tends to be most favored by the authorities is the sting operation, in which aspirant terrorists are unwittingly given the space by
a person they trust to incriminate themselves in tightlycontrolled
circumstances, such as an arms deal or a planned attack. When the
British Security Service learned in 2001 that the Real IRA was looking for a "rogue state" to sponsor its operations,[227] MI5 officers
posing as representatives of the Iraqi Intelligence Service met with
members of the Real IRA in Dublin, Slovakia, Austria, and
Budapest before triggering an arms sting in Piešt'any, Slovakia,
that resulted in the arrest and subsequent conviction of three Real
IRA operatives: Fintan O'Farrell, Declan Rafferty, and Michael
McDonald. Operation Samnite was the first MI5 operation in

---

[227]Jason Bennetto, Irish terrorists captured in MI5 sting plead guilty, *The Independent*, 3 May
2002.

which evidence was gathered entirely overseas and it still stands out today as an exemplar of the power of international cooperation.[228]

In undercover operations and sting operations, any individual acting under the direction of the authorities — law enforcement officers, intelligence officials, police informants or intelligence assets — must be careful to avoid any situation in which they become the instigator or *agent provocateur* behind a crime — such action on the part of the authorities is known as entrapment. Entrapment occurs when a person who would not otherwise be predisposed to commit an offence is encouraged to do so by a government official who then instigates prosecution against the same individual. On 26 November 2010, accompanied by an undercover FBI Special Agent, Mohamed Osman Mohamud, a Somali-American student at Oregon State University, tried to detonate a car bomb near a public Christmas tree-lighting ceremony in Portland's Pioneer Courthouse Square attended by thousands of families. The bomb had been constructed with the FBI's help from inert material and did not explode. However, Mohamud did not know this and made a triggering call from his cellphone to the bomb's detonator. He was then arrested. Mohamud had first come to notice because he had made contact with a suspected *al-Qaeda* recruiter in the Middle East and had written an article on physical fitness for an English-language publication called *Jihad Recollections*. An Undercover FBI Special Agent made contact with Mohamud in June 2010 posing as a terrorist. In early November 2010, undercover FBI agents traveled to a remote location with Mohamud for a trial run of the bombing in which Mohamud actually detonated a functional backpack bomb.

In a pre-emptive strategy in the Pioneer Courthouse Square Case to rebut allegations of entrapment, the FBI agents deliberately offered Mohamud multiple less violent alternatives to take action in support of *al-Qaeda*'s cause, including prayer, but Mohamud insisted he wanted to play an "operational" role. In an affidavit, the FBI stated that Mohamud chose the venue for the attack and also

---

[228] Richard Norton-Taylor, 30 years in jail for Real IRA trio, *The Guardian*, 8 May 2002.

shrugged off attempts to interrupt the plot once it was under way. US Attorney General Eric Holder told reporters: "There were a number of opportunities the defendant was given to retreat and to take a different path and he chose at every step to continue."[229] Mohamud was reportedly told several times that his planned bomb could kill women and children, but he told agents: "Since I was 15 I thought about all this... It's gonna be a fireworks show... a spectacular show."[230]

The European Court of Human Rights has explored the question of entrapment in some detail. Two cases in particular, both relating to drug purchases, illustrate the basic principle at work quite clearly: *Francisco Teixeira de Castro v. Portugal* (ECtHR; 1998) and *Grigoriy Arkadyevich Vanyan v. Russia* (ECtHR; 2006). In the Portuguese case, a textile worker was offered money by two plain-clothes police officers to supply them with heroin. Although he had no previous criminal record, Teixeira de Castro did have the necessary contacts to obtain the drug. Tempted by the money, the applicant accepted the officers' request and was subsequently charged and convicted of a drug offence. In reviewing the case, the Court concluded that the officers "did not confine themselves to investigating Mr. Teixeira de Castro's criminal activity in an essentially passive manner, but exercised an influence such as to incite the commission of the offence."[231] The Russian case is very similar except that in this instance, it was a police informant, rather than a police officer, who encouraged the suspect to make a drug purchase.[232] The "passivity" standard set by the European Court essentially prohibits the authorities from playing any kind of active role in the commission of a criminal act as a pretext to

---

[229] Dina Temple-Raston, *Alleged Portland Bomber To Claim Entrapment*, National Public Radio, 30 November 2010 at http://www.npr.org/2010/11/30/131704930/alleged-portland-bomber-to-claim-entrapment.

[230] Liz Robbins and Edward Wyatt, Somali-Born Teenager Held in Oregon Bomb Sting, *New York Times*, 27 November 2010.

[231] European Court of Human Rights, *Francisco Teixeira de Castro v. Portugal*, Application no. 44/1997/828/1034, Judgment, 9 June 1998, pp. 37–38.

[232] European Court of Human Rights, *Grigoriy Arkadyevich Vanyan v. Russia*, Application no. 53203/99, 15 March 2006, pp. 45–50.

making an arrest. Any evidence obtained as a result of police incitement must be excluded from trial.[233]

One final tactic often used in human intelligence operations is the disruption — a concept as simple as it is efficient. Disruptions are non-judicial interventions designed simply to upset a terrorist group's plans. A disruption might be as simple a matter as increasing the security presence around a target or releasing advance warning of an attack to the media, so that a terrorist cell is panicked into aborting its operation. On occasion, the authorities might even approach suspects directly and warn them that the state is aware of their plans, knowing that this leaves them with little choice but to abandon the operation they have planned. In the spring of 1947, Ezer Wiezman (a future President of Israel) was recruited by *Irgun* to assassinate the former General Officer Commanding in Palestine, Sir Evelyn Barker, at his home in the United Kingdom. As the plan progressed, Wiezman received training from *Irgun* in France and then began to gather intelligence on Barker's residence. The British were tipped off but lacked the evidence to make an arrest, and so before Wiezman could execute the attack, a detective from the Metropolitan Police Special Branch appeared on his doorstep and suggested he "be so kind as to return to Palestine".[234] Wiezman took his advice and the threat was averted.

Almost fifty years later, the CIA was still using the same basic tactic. After the bombing of the Khobar Towers housing facility in Dhahran, Saudi Arabia, by the Saudi off-shoot of *Hezbollah*, which killed nineteen Americans in June 1996, the Clinton White House debated many military and non-military responses against Iran, whom it believed had sponsored the attack. One response that was implemented consisted of a large-scale covert operation that "outed" Iranian agents around the world, putting them on notice that their affiliation was known to US Intelligence, in order to deter Tehran from threatening

---

[233] European Court of Human Rights, *Ramanauskas v. Lithuania*, Application no. 74420/01, Judgment, 5 February 2008, para 60.

[234] Bruce Hoffman, *Anonymous Soldiers: The Struggle for Israel, 1917–1947* (Knopf; 2015), p. 405.

US facilities. Among the participants in this operation was the then CIA Station Chief in Saudi Arabia, John Brennan, who reportedly knocked on the car window of an Iranian intelligence officer and announced: "Hello, I'm from the US Embassy, and I've got something to tell you."[235] The Iranian was left knowing his cover was blown and wondering just how much the US knew about his activities and how badly his operational security had been compromised. For an operative in the field, such uncertainty can be crippling.

## Surveillance operations

The term "surveillance" covers a multitude of Special Investigation Techniques, including mobile and static visual surveillance by teams of investigators, the interception of communications, and remote monitoring using equipment such as eavesdropping devices, radio beacons or GPS trackers. Used in isolation, but more commonly in combination, surveillance techniques can enable investigators to build up a comprehensive picture of a target's contacts and activities, and ultimately guage his or her intentions. These techniques are extremely intrusive and have been specifically developed with the intent of violating an individual's privacy, but when used in accordance with the kind of established legal procedures outlined above in a manner that is both necessary and proportionate, they are entirely lawful.

Physical surveillance operations, in which law enforcement or intelligence personnel are deployed in the field to personally monitor the activities of a designated suspect, are both time- and labor-intensive and consume considerable resources to keep in place. While it is possible to conduct basic mobile vehicle or foot surveillance with just a handful of officers, this is unlikely to be of sufficient quality and sophistication to meet the needs of a counter-terrorism investigation in which the target is situationally aware and may have anti- or counter-surveillance training and thus the ability to evade or detect surveillance. In such cases, a professional mobile

---

[235] George Tenet, *At the Center of the Storm* (HarperCollins; 2009), p. 124.

surveillance team might employ 15–20 specially trained officers to follow one individual for an eight-hour shift, and if the target is highly active, this might require the assignment of more than one team to keep him or her under continuous surveillance for a twenty-four-hour period. A terror cell consisting of just four persons — the size of a typical Provisional IRA active service unit (ASU) — could conceivably require the allocation of more than 200 officers to ensure comprehensive coverage of its activities. It might also require the deployment of aerial assets such as light aircraft, helicopters, or more recently unmanned aerial vehicles (UAVs), commonly known as 'drones'.

One of the greatest challenges for law enforcement and security officials is deciding precisely where to concentrate a resource-intensive effort of this type. In 2006, the British Parliament's Intelligence and Security Committee noted: "An intensive operation, for example into imminent attack planning, can consume almost half of the Security Service's operational and investigative resources."[236] After the 7 July 2005 bombing of the London Transport system which claimed fifty-two lives and injured more than 700 people, it emerged that one of the bombers, Mohammad Siddique Khan, had come to notice in the course of surveillance operations conducted on other Islamist targets in 2003 and 2004 (on the second occasion along with another 7/7 bomber Shehzad Tanweer) but that no further action had been taken because of the need to prioritize other seemingly more pressing inquiries.[237] As the then Head of MI5, Dame Eliza Manningham-Buller, admitted in a rare public lecture: "We are faced by acute and very difficult choices of prioritization."[238] The Intelligence and Security Committee similarly acknowledged: "We have been struck by the sheer scale of the

---

[236] Intelligence and Security Committee, *Report into the London Terrorist Attacks on 7 July 2005,* May 2006, p. 7.

[237] Intelligence and Security Committee, *Could 7/7 Have Been Prevented? Review of the Intelligence on the London Terrorist Attacks on 7 July 2005,* HM Stationary Office, May 2009, paras 47 and 68–70.

[238] Eliza Manningham-Buller, *The International Terrorist Threat to the UK: Speech by the Director General of the Security Service,* Queen Mary's College, 9 November 2006.

problem that our intelligence and security agencies face and their comparatively small capacity to cover it."[239]

Static surveillance requires considerably fewer human resources but nevertheless presents its own challenges, principal of which is the successful acquisition of a suitable viewpoint — for example, a neighbor's house, or a rural or urban hide. A hide could be anything from a hole in the ground camouflaged with netting or branches to a parked vehicle. Hides are typically uncomfortable and difficult to service over long periods. Securing the right viewpoint may also involve the clandestine recruitment of a human intelligence asset, for example, the owner of the property from which the surveillance will take place.

Because of its great cost in both financial and human resources, most law enforcement and intelligence agencies tend to use physical surveillance sparingly, preferring where possible to monitor targets remotely using electronic surveillance assets that broadly speaking fall into four categories: visual surveillance (i.e. Closed Circuit Television or CCTV); audio surveillance (i.e. eavesdropping devices); tracking surveillance (i.e. GPS responders); and data surveillance (i.e. keystroke monitoring). The use of electronic surveillance techniques is most properly regulated by some form of warrant-based authorization system — typically, such a warrant is authorized by a judge in common law systems and by the public prosecutor in civil law systems. Warrant applications usually require of the requesting authority that the target of the surveillance be identified along with the nature and duration of the operation, as well as an outline of why traditional investigation techniques have proved inadequate to the task. Some forms of electronic surveillance (i.e. directional microphones) may be exempt from warranty requirements if (like traditional forms of surveillance) they take place in a public place where an individual cannot have a reasonable expectation of privacy.

---

[239] Intelligence and Security Committee, Intelligence and Security Committee, *Report into the London Terrorist Attacks on 7 July 2005*, May 2006, p. 16.

Comprehensive video surveillance systems are becoming commonplace in major cities and, when situated in public places where there would be no reasonable expectation of privacy, their use is typically governed by non-judicial codes of practice, if at all.[240] CCTV played an important role in the investigation of the 7 July 2005 London Transport Bombings — after the incident, police investigators were able to trace the movements of all four suicide bombers back to their shared point of departure in Luton Railway Station car park after reviewing thousands of hours of CCTV footage of the public transport system. The United Kingdom was an early adopter of public surveillance systems and by 2013 there were 5,900,000 operational CCTV cameras in Britain — one camera for every ten citizens.[241] Around the world, remote-controlled surveillance cameras are increasingly taking the place of static viewpoints in intelligence operations. The European Commission on Human Rights considered the general use of CCTV cameras in public spaces in the case of *Herbecq and the association "Ligue des droits de l'homme" v. Belgium* (ECHR; 1998) and found that systems deployed in public places, or on premises occupied by the operator, where the information collected was not recorded, posed no threat to the privacy rights of individuals since it is simply allowing the operator to observe public behavior that he or she would be able to see if he or she was present in person.[242]

However, such systems can also pose a significant challenge to privacy rights when allied to new technologies — for example, computerized pattern recognition systems. It is now possible to program smart CCTV systems to register individuals who are behaving abnormally, for example, by remaining in one place for long periods while surrounding crowds are moving, or alternatively by moving in a different direction to the rest of the crowd, which may in certain

---

[240] United Nations Office on Drugs and Crime, *Current practices in electronic surveillance in the investigation of serious and organized crime* (2009), p. 13.

[241] Janice Turner, CCTV Britain, the world's most paranoid nation, *The Times*, 13 July 2013, p. 23.

[242] *Herbecq and the association "Ligue des droits de l'homme" v. Belgium*, Applications nos. 32200/96 and 32201/96, Commission decision of 14 January 1998, DR 92-B, para 92.

circumstances be a potential indicator of criminal behavior. Automatic detection can then be used to alert human observers to the suspicious activity for follow up action. Such technology can easily be abused, for example, to stifle freedom of association and legitimate protest rights.

Technological innovation is already enabling the authorities to police public space in remarkably comprehensive but still discreet ways. The Automatic Number Plate Recognition Database (ANPR) developed by the United Kingdom was first introduced in static form as part of the series of vehicle checkpoints known as "The Ring of Steel" erected around the City of London in 1993 in an effort to prevent further attempts by the Provisional IRA to infiltrate truck bombs into the financial district. The ANPR Database can now be utilized in real time through both mobile cameras mounted in police vehicles and fixed cameras across the country to scan every vehicle license plate that passes in front of a camera linked to the network. If a camera records a license plate number that has been flagged in connection with criminal activity, this triggers an alert for the nearest police unit. The database can register 50,000,000 reads in a single day. In November 2005, Constable Sharon Beshenivsky was shot and killed during a robbery in Bradford. The CCTV network was linked to the ANPR system and was able to identify the getaway car and track its movements, leading to the arrest of six suspects. A number of other countries — including Belgium, Turkey and the United States — are now utilizing similar equipment to some degree.

Another emerging technology that is attracting both interest and alarm is the development of facial recognition software. There are still some limitations — the software requires high-resolution pictures and the subject's image needs to be recorded on an existing (and accessible) computer database — for example, a driving license register. At the time of writing, most current systems require multiple images of a person from different angles to create a composite match and can often be defeated by simple expedients such as wearing sunglasses. False positives are still common. Attempts by the FBI to use facial recognition software to identify the Boston Marathon bombing suspects failed in April 2013 even though bomber Dzhokhar Tsarnaev's photograph was in the Boston Department of Motor Vehicles database. However, facial recognition software continues to improve at a rapid pace. South Wales Police became the first force in the United Kingdom to use Automated Facial Recognition (AFR) to make an arrest in June 2017, and between 28 July and 18 December 2017 registered 191 positive matches, resulting in 50 charges, 12 arrests, and 8 convictions. The system is mobile and accesses a database of 500,000 custody images.[243] In December 2017, the Chinese government announced ambitious plans to install more than 400,000,000 new CCTV cameras by 2020, many of them linked to facial recognition software and pattern recognition technology.[244] It is not too fanciful to suggest that technology may soon theoretically be able to render anonymity in public spaces a redundant concept. At the time of writing, such automated systems have rarely if at all been subject to legislative action, but this is no doubt coming. From a human rights perspective, the same basic tests of lawfulness, necessity and proportionality apply to their use, as with any other surveillance tool.

Intercepting and clandestinely reading postal communications has been a staple of intelligence operations for as long as postal services have existed. Intercepting landline, internet, or mobile communications is equally straightforward from a technical standpoint and in the digital era can be done remotely so the concept of a telephone 'tap' is largely obsolete.[245] However, telecommunications intercepts can be resource-intensive because someone has to listen to all the recordings. Most terrorists are aware that states have the facility to monitor suspect communications and typically use rudimentary coded language while

---

[243] Philip Dewey, Facial recognition software is used by police to identify a dead body, Wales Online, 18 December 2017.

[244] John Sudworth, In Your Face: China's all-seeing state, BBC News, 10 December 2017.

[245] Human Rights Council, *Report of the Special Rapporteur on the promotion and protection of the right to freedom of opinion and expression, Frank La Rue*, A/HRC/23/40, 17 April 2013, para 34.

discussing sensitive operations on the telephone — *al-Qaeda* members often refer to attacks as "weddings" and the Provisional IRA sometimes referred to planned operations as "football matches". It still takes a human being to effectively identify and interpret coded or guarded speech.

The international human rights law standard is that communication interception requires due process authorization, as the European Court of Human Rights found in the case of *Malone v. United Kingdom* (ECtHR; 1984). In *Weber and Saravia v. Germany* (ECtHR; 2006), the Court articulated the following minimum safeguards that should be written into any statute law in order to avoid the potential abuse of surveillance powers: "The nature of the offences which may give rise to an interception order; a definition of the categories of people liable to have their telephones tapped; a limit on the duration of telephone tapping; the procedure to be followed for examining, using, and storing the data obtained; the precautions to be taken when communicating the data to other parties; and the circumstances in which recordings may or must be erased, or the tapes destroyed."[246]

The primary challenge with eavesdropping devices is placing them in a well-hidden location where they can pick up relevant conversations. This frequently requires the recruitment of an access agent and the covert interference with private property. For example, in the 1980s, the RUC Special Branch recruited a Belfast estate agent and petty crook on the fringes of the Provisional IRA called Joe Fenton and under its direction, he made himself invaluable to PIRA members by helping them to fraudulently obtain mortgages, find safe houses, and transport weapons — all of which provided the RUC with opportunities to plant eavesdropping devices, suborn PIRA volunteers, and neutralize weaponry. Brendan Hughes, Head of PIRA's Security Department at the time, estimated that at least eight PIRA houses were compromised in this way.[247]

---

[246] European Court of Human Rights, *Weber and Saravia v. Germany*, Application no. 54934/00, 29 June 2006, para 95.

[247] Ed Moloney, *Voices from the Grave: Two Men's War in Ireland* (Public Affairs, 2010), p. 284. Fenton was finally unmasked by the Provisional IRA in February 1989 and murdered.

As with interception techniques, the invasion of privacy involved is considerable and thus the use of eavesdropping devices requires a similar regime of due process protections. In 1977, the Royal Commission of Inquiry into Certain Activities of the Royal Canadian Mounted Police (RCMP), better known as the McDonald Commission, was established to investigate a series of abuses by the RCMP — most famously burning down a barn where the Black Panther Party and *Front de Libération du Québec* were thought to be planning a rendezvous with the intention of forcing them to meet instead in a location that would be easier to surveil — the Commission found that the RCMP had gone too far and admonished that it was necessary to "secure democracy against internal and external enemies without destroying democracy in the process."[248] The scandal also ultimately resulted in the RCMP losing its security intelligence role, and the creation of the Canadian Security Intelligence Service to take on this mission.

The growing use of new technologies, such as GPS devices on cell phones and smart passes for toll roads or building entry systems, has outstripped many national regulatory regimes creating a grey area for what is and is not permissible. Some guidance can be gleaned from the case of *Uzun v. Germany* (ECtHR; 2010).[249] In 1993, Bernhard Uzun was identified as a possible member of a violent extremist group known as the *Antiimperialistische Zelle.*[250] In 1995, this group was linked to a number of bombings targeting German politicians and Uzun was placed under investigation, which involved extensive use of surveillance tools including covert video cameras, phone intercepts, and wireless transmitters. When Uzun and an associate, Michael Steinau, found and destroyed the transmitters hidden in Steinau's car, the police covertly fitted a GPS beacon so that they could at least track the car's movements. The police were ultimately able to use the GPS data (in conjunction with other surveillance material) to tie Uzun to at least one crime scene, an arms cache, and

---

[248] SIRC (2005). Reflections, at http://www.sirc-csars.gc.ca/pdfs/rfcrfx_2005-eng.pdf.
[249] European Court of Human Rights, *Uzun v Germany*, Merits, Application no. 35623/05, Judgment, 2 September 2010.
[250] Anti-Imperialist Cell.

to several locations from which claims of responsibility for attacks had been mailed by the cell. Uzun was subsequently successfully convicted on one count of attempted murder and four counts of causing an explosion. He was sentenced to thirteen years in prison.

Uzun complained to the European Court of Human Rights that the German authorities' use of the GPS beacon had violated his right to privacy in that it had enabled them gain a comprehensive picture of his movements, and that the use of GPS had not been authorized by a court order. There was no requirement for court authorization to deploy a GPS beacon stipulated in the German criminal code. In its judgment, the Court found that the German authorities had actually applied extensive measures to prevent misuse of the power of surveillance in this case. The Court further observed that GPS surveillance could be distinguished from other methods of "visual or acoustical surveillance", which are significantly more instrusive "because they disclose more information on a person's conduct, opinions or feelings."[251] Finally, the Court also noted that the surveillance measures had been proportionate in that other investigative means had been tried, and had failed owing to the conduct of the applicant; that the investigation was into a serious matter, involving terrorist bombings; and that the measures had only been employed for a short period of time. Given the safeguards and proportionality of the measures applied, the Court concluded that Uzun's right to privacy had not been violated.

The use of metadata — descriptive, structural, or administrative data that provides information about other data — has become an increasingly important analytical tool for law enforcement and intelligence agencies alike.[252] For example, the Special Tribunal for Lebanon, established to investigate the bombing of the motorcade of former Lebanese Prime Minister Rafik Hariri, used call data records in the indictment of *Ayyash et al.* to tie four suspects to the

---

[251] European Court of Human Rights, *Uzun v Germany*, Merits, Application no. 35623/05, Judgment, 2 September 2010, para 52.

[252] See Laura Donohue, The Dawn of Social Intelligence (SOCINT), *Drake Law Review*, Vol. 63 (2015).

bombing.[253] By tracking calls made between different numbers and location data from cell towers pinpointing the position of each telephone, the Office of the Prosecutor was able to identify five inter-related telephone networks apparently associated with the operation to assassinate Hariri. There is little doubt that the collection of metadata is a powerful investigative tool, but again the use of such techniques is governed by the same human rights regime as any other SIT.

The UN General Assembly has strongly affirmed that the rights held by people offline must also be protected online.[254] Concerns have been raised about the impact that the mass collection and retention of communications metadata (such as telephone numbers called, call frequencies, call durations, or a cell phone's location) and other personal records (such as those held by public housing agencies, social service providers, libraries, or universities) may have on the enjoyment of human rights and fundamental freedoms.[255] In the case of *Digital Rights Ireland and Seitlinger and Others* (ECJ; 2014), the Court of Justice of the European Union found the European Union Data Retention Directive to communication service providers requiring them to retain traffic data so as to permit access by the competent national authorities for the purpose of preventing, investigating, detecting and prosecuting serious crime, including terrorism, to be incompatible with the right to respect for private life and the right to the protection of personal data.[256] The Court observed that the collection of metadata taken as a whole "may allow very precise conclusions to be drawn concerning the private lives of the persons whose data has been retained" and concluded that the

---

[253] Special Tribunal for Lebanon, *Prosecutor v. Ayyash et al.*, Indictment, STL-11-01/I/PTJ, 10 June 2011.

[254] See General Assembly resolution 68/167 on the "Right to privacy in the digital age". See also http://www.ohchr.org/EN/Issues/DigitalAge/Pages/DigitalAgeIndex.aspx accessed on 26 August 2014.

[255] Human Rights Council, Report of the Office of the United Nations High Commissioner for Human Rights, *The Right to Privacy in the Digital Age*, A/HRC/27/37, 30 June 2014, paras 19–20.

[256] Court of Justice of the European Union, *Digital Rights Ireland and Seitlinger and Others*, in Joined Cases C-293/12 and C-594/12, Judgment, 8 April 2014.

Directive constituted a "particularly serious interference" with both rights, and failed to satisfy the principle of proportionality.[257] The Court's point was well illustrated by a 2015 study conducted at Stanford University that analyzed the phone metadata provided by 500 volunteers over a three-month period, and in doing so discovered participants' medical conditions, gun purchases, the cultivation of illegal drugs, and at least one decision to have an abortion.[258]

The UN Special Rapporteur on the promotion and protection of human rights and fundamental freedoms while countering terrorism has warned that "in the absence of special safeguards, there is virtually no secret dimension of a person's private life that would withstand close metadata analysis" and that consequently "automated data-mining ... thus has a particularly corrosive effect on privacy."[259] This is not hyperbole, Stewart Baker, the former General Counsel of the US National Security Agency, perhaps the world's most sophisticated and voracious governmental consumer of metadata, has stated on record that "metadata absolutely tells you everything about somebody's life. If you have enough metadata you don't really need content."[260] Consequently, the UN High Commissioner on Human Rights has advised that "any capture of communications data is potentially an interference with privacy and, further, that the collection and retention of communications data amounts to an interference with privacy whether or not those data are subsequently consulted or used. Even the mere possibility of communications information being captured creates an interference with privacy, with a potential chilling effect on rights, including those to free expression and association. The very existence of a mass surveillance programme thus creates an interference with

---

[257] Court of Justice of the European Union, Judgment in Joined Cases C-293/12 and C-594/12, *Digital Rights Ireland and Seitlinger and Others,* Judgment, 8 April 2014, paras 26–27, and 37.

[258] Laura Donohue, The Dawn of Social Intelligence (SOCINT), *Drake Law Review,* Vol. 63 (2015) at 1091.

[259] Human Rights Council, *Report of the Special Rapporteur on the Promotion and Protection of Human Rights and Fundamental Freedoms while Countering Terrorism, Ben Emmerson,* A/69/397, 23 September 2014, para 53.

[260] Laura Donohue, The Dawn of Social Intelligence (SOCINT), *Drake Law Review,* Vol. 63 (2015), p. 1089.

privacy. The onus would be on the state to demonstrate that such interference is neither arbitrary nor unlawful."[261]

A growing number of legal systems are beginning to subject communications metadata to the same privacy protections as the content of individual communications.[262] In the aftermath of the September 11th attacks, the German police authorities obtained data sets from universities, colleges, immigration offices and other private and public entities that contained information on several hundred thousand individuals. This information was then processed to identify all individuals of male gender, aged 18–40, who professed a religious affiliation with Islam, and came from a country with a predominantly Islamic population. These names were then cross-referenced against the register of licensed pilots in an effort to identify potential terrorists. This operation did not result in any charges being brought against any individual. However, a complaint was filed with the German Federal Constitutional Court, which then subsequently considered the actions of the police. The Constitutional Court noted that each individual piece of information gathered had relatively limited relevance to the right to privacy and that a very specific heightened threat of a terrorist attack might justify such measures, but ultimately concluded that the situation in Germany at the time did not meet this threshold.[263] While this is a purely domestic case, it is perhaps illustrative of how courts might address the use of metadata in the future.

## Summary

The use of Special Investigation Techniques is limited for the most part only by the requirement that they are defined in law, that due

---

[261] Human Rights Council, Report of the Office of the United Nations High Commissioner for Human Rights, *The Right to Privacy in the Digital Age,* A/HRC/27/37, 30 June 2014, para 20.
[262] United Nations Office on Drugs and Crime, *Counter-Terrorism Legal Training Curriculum: Module 4 Human Rights and Criminal Justice Responses to Terrorism,* Terrorism Prevention Branch, (2014), p. 98.
[263] *Bundesverfassungsgericht* (BverfG — Federal Constitutional Court) of 4 April, 2006 (1 BvR 518/02).

process is observed in their application, and that they are used in a manner that is reasonable, necessary and proportionate to the threat posed by criminal activity. There is a growing body of international jurisprudence that delineates where the line between proportionate and disproportionate action should be drawn. However, it is important to acknowledge that international law recognizes that states may need to recruit informants, conduct sting operations, intercept communications, and deploy electronic surveillance measures to keep their citizens safe. Navi Pillay, the former UN High Commissioner for Human Rights, has acknowledged the vital role that intelligence collection plays in the prevention of terrorist violence: "The use of accurate intelligence is indispensible to preventing terrorist acts and bringing individuals suspected of terrorist activity to justice."[264] The Council of Europe's Committee of Experts on Special Investigation Techniques in relation to Acts of Terrorism similarly noted in a report published in 2005: "The objective of the European Convention on Human Rights is not to disarm the authorities responsible for prevention or prosecution in criminal matters. The Convention sets out criteria in order that the authorities' activities should constantly be guided by the rule of law and the pursuit of the democratic ideal."[265]

Not every terrorist attack is preventable, and the reality is that when opportunities to prevent attacks are missed, this typically reflects a failure of competency, imagination, or capacity on the part of the authorities, rather than an institutional shortfall in investigatory powers. Clues that might have enabled the US authorities to disrupt the planning of the September 11 attacks — most notably the presence of future hijackers Khalid al-Mihdhar and Nawaf al-Hazmi in the United States — were not acted upon in large part because of the "stovepiping" that characterized the American intelligence community at the time.[266] The chance sightings of the

---

[264] *Report of the United Nations High Commissioner for Human Rights on the protection of human rights and fundamental freedoms while countering terrorism,* UN General Assembly, A/HRC/16/50, 15 December 2010, para 33.

[265] Council of Europe, *Terrorism: Special Investigation Techniques,* April 2005, p. 27.

[266] *The 9/11 Commission Report: Final Report of the National Commission on Terrorist Attacks Upon the United States,* Authorized Edition (W. W. Norton and Company; 2004), pp. 266–272.

London Transport bombers Mohammed Siddique Khan and Shehzad Tanweer in the company of known Islamic extremists were not followed up because MI5 was overwhelmed by what seemed at the time like more important investigative leads.[267] Intelligence and security agencies are not infallible, and it is unrealistic to expect them to be so. More intrusive powers would not have prevented either attack and would likely have just generated additional intelligence clutter further obscuring the needle represented by *al-Qaeda*'s activities in a giant haystack of irrelevant data.[268] In the intelligence business, less is often more, intelligence-driven investigation is efficient, datadriven investigation for the most part is not.

The tests set by international human rights law for the use of Special Investigative Techniques go to the heart of the dilemma facing all national security actors operating within democratic systems — how does one protect the public while also protecting the rights and freedoms they enjoy. There is little point adopting policies that ultimately undermine the institutions they are supposed to protect. As a bumper sticker popular in the United States declaims: Freedom isn't free. Some risk is inevitably involved in living in a free society. The challenge is to get the balance right, to ensure, in the words of the current Director General of the British Security Service, Andrew Parker, that being on the authorities' radar is not the same as being under their microscope.[269]

## Investigative Interviewing

The apprehension of a terrorist suspect presents counter-terrorism investigators with a tremendous opportunity to learn intimate details

---

[267] Intelligence and Security Committee, *Could 7/7 Have Been Prevented? Review of the Intelligence on the London Terrorist Attacks on 7 July 2005*, HM Stationary Office, May 2009, paras 47 and 68–70.

[268] Rosa Brooks, The Threat Is Already Inside: And nine other truths about terrorism nobody wants to hear, *Foreign Policy*, 20 November 2015.

[269] *Address by the Director General of the Security Service, Andrew Parker, to the Royal United Services Institute (RUSI)*, Whitehall, 8 October 2013.

of the men and women they are seeking to frustrate, as well as to gain an understanding of the organizational structure and ethos of the terrorist group itself. In a criminal justice context, the opportunity to question the suspect represents an important evidence gathering opportunity. It is therefore unsurprising that many investigators, and perhaps even more importantly many policymakers above them, see investigative interviewing as a zero-sum game in which getting the suspect to talk is everything. There is unquestionably great value to a cooperating suspect who is prepared to provide answers to his interlocutors' questions openly, honestly, and to the best of his or her ability. However, the zero-sum mindset is greatly flawed and lies at the heart of one of the most common human rights abuses that occurs in the counter-terrorism context — the physical and mental abuse of detainees in custody by their interviewers.

Often described as 'the king of evidence', confession-based testimony can actually be profoundly unreliable. As a result, modern police work tends to place far less emphasis on the importance of gaining a confession from a potential perpetrator than investigators did in the past. Recent research in the United States has found that false confessions and admissions were present in 15–20% of all DNA exonerations; and of the 354 serious cases overturned by fresh DNA evidence obtained by the Innocence Project in the United States between 1992 and 2017, 28% involved false confessions.[270] Adolescence, intellectual disability, mental illness, intoxication, certain personality traits, aggressive interrogation tactics, and the phenomenology of innocence (a suspect waiving the right to silence because they believe that is how an innocent individual would behave) can all contribute to unsound confessions. Equally, an individual may conclude, as a consequence of the institutionalized bias they have experienced, that they will not receive a fair hearing and that taking a plea deal is the best route to the least severe punishment even though they did not commit the offence in question.

---

[270] Saul Kassin, Steven Drizin, Thomas Grisso, Gisli Gudjonsson, Richard Leo, and Allison Redlich, Police-Induced Confessions: Risk Factors and Recommendations, *Law and Human Behavior*, Vol. 34, No. 3 (February 2010) at 3, and www.innocenceproject.org/dna-exonerations-in-the-united-states/. Viewed 8 April 2018.

A prominent example of this latter scenario can currently be seen in the operation of the Military Commissions process underway in Guantanamo Bay, Cuba. The individuals tried before the Commissions are accused of committing war crimes but this is not the reason for which they were originally detained — they are detained primarily as prisoners of war (POW), not as criminal suspects. The US Department of Defense has made it clear in public statements that the outcome of a Military Commission trial has no bearing on the decision as to whether or not the defendant will continue to be held as a POW. This means that even if a defendant wins his case (there are no female detainees in Guantanamo), or completes his sentence, he may still be detained indefinitely. In fact, his only guaranteed path to freedom is to strike a plea deal with the Prosecuting Authority and plead guilty in return for a guarantee that after a finite period of custodial detention he will actually be released. At the time of writing, six detainees have taken this deal, of whom four have subsequently been repatriated.[271] One must therefore ask how accurate one can expect an individual's testimony to be in circumstances where only a version of events that the prosecution wants to hear can lead to the outcome the suspect is seeking.

The real goal of an investigative interview should be to gain the trust and cooperation of the suspect. It is clearly not going to be possible to do this in every case, but, as we shall see below, experienced and skilled interviewers are surprisingly successful at getting even hardened terrorists to cooperate, at least to some degree. In the cases in which a suspect simply clams up and refuses to speak, investigators still have many avenues of inquiry open to them. Witness interviews, physical searches, and forensic examination can reveal an enormous amount of information about a suspect's movements, contacts, and intentions. Not every state has the capability to exploit every potential line of inquiry, but most do, and those that don't could if they prioritized the development of basic detection techniques and forensic skills.

---

[271] Ibrahim al Qosi, Omar Khadr, Noor Utham Muhammed, Majid Khan, Ahmed al Darbi, and David Hicks. Khan and al Darbi still remain in custody serving out their sentences.

Two *al-Qaeda*-related case studies — one factual, one theoretical but fact-based — should be sufficient to illustrate this point. On 14 December 1999, Algerian national and *al-Qaeda* affiliate Ahmed Ressam panicked during a routine customs check at Port Angeles, Washington, as he tried to enter the United States from Canada and was detained. Customs agents discovered a range of explosive materials and IED components in the trunk of his car, including ten garbage bags containing 118 pounds of urea, two bottles filled with the primary explosives hexamethylene triperoxide diamine (HMTD) and cyclotrimethylenetrinitramine (RDX), and two 22-ounce jars of the secondary explosive ethylene glycol dinitrate (EGDN). Forensic scientists were able to recover latent fingerprints from four timing devices, a hair trapped under a piece of clear tape on one of the timing devices was associated with Ressam, and a road map of Los Angeles found in the car had three airports circled in blue pen.[272] A diary used by Ressam contained contact details for two other identified members of *al-Qaeda*.[273] Canadian investigators also traced credit card purchases at several electronics shops in Montreal thought to be the timing devices, and searched a hotel room in Vancouver and an apartment in Montreal used by Ressam.[274] The physical evidence retrieved was more than sufficient for the US authorities to secure a conviction.

In 2005, a briefing note prepared by the Assistant Commissioner (Specialist Operations) of the London Metropolitan Police Service, Andy Hayman, described the volume of material typically generated by a major post-terrorist incident operation, the case itself was fictional but it was based on recent Metropolitan Police operations. In Hayman's theoretical case study, police officers conducted 165 interviews in fourteen days, and carried out fifty-five forensic searches in four days, recovered approximately 4,000 individual exhibits, and seized 268 computers along with 591 floppy discs, 920 CD-ROMs, and forty-seven zip discs. Sixty personal cell phones were seized in

---

[272] https://www.fbi.gov/about-us/history/famous-cases/millennium-plot-ahmed-ressam. Viewed 17 November 2015.
[273] ibid.
[274] ibid.

the first two weeks, 25,000 man-hours were spent reviewing CCTV coverage, and 3,674 man-hours on reviewing eavesdropping material. 850 surveillance logs were compiled.[275] None of the techniques described here are particularly sophisticated, and both scenarios are pretty typical of modern counter-terrorism investigations. It should be readily apparent from both cases that law enforcement and security officials still have many options available to them to move an investigation forward, even when confronted by a suspect who refuses to cooperate at the time of arrest.

## The presumption of innocence

The commander of French forces in Algeria, General Jacques Massu, famously justified the physical abuse of suspected FLN members committed by the soldiers under his command during the Battle of Algiers with the remark: "The innocent deserve more protection than the guilty."[276] Of course, the fallacy at the heart of Massu's statement is the assumption that it is always easy to distinguish the innocent from the guilty, that the investigator's instinct for identifying wrongdoers is always infallible, that mistakes are never made, and that human prejudice, ignorance, or malice never play a part in the process. Investigators often believe that they have a 'gut instinct' for when a suspect is telling the truth or not. In fact, this is rarely the case. Across academic studies, people are, on average, 54% accurate in deception detection experiments, a success rate that is barely much better than random chance.[277] Studies involving police officers and military interrogators have demonstrated that professional investigators are typically no better at spotting deception than ordinary members of the public, but typically tend to think

---

[275] *Letter from Andy Hayman to the Home Secretary, Rt. Hon. Charles Clarke,* 6 October 2005, at http://www.publications.parliament.uk/pa/jt200506/jtselect/jtrights/75/75we02.htm. Viewed 17 November 2015.

[276] French General Jacques Massu speaking in Algiers in 1956, quoted in George Armstrong Kelly, *Lost Soldiers: The French Army and Empire in Crisis, 1947–1962* (The MIT Press; 1965), p. 201.

[277] Charles Bond and Bella DePaulo, Accuracy of deception judgments, *Review of Personality and Social Psychology,* Vol. 10, No. 3 (2006), p. 224.

they are much more perceptive.[278] In fact, professional training appears to have a negligible effect on detecting deception but increases confidence in the ability to do so, leading to a greater number of false positives. The problem is that many of the behaviors associated with lying by investigators — nervousness, fear, confusion, hostility, and inconsistency — are also attributes commonly displayed by human beings in conditions of high stress or anxiety.[279]

Technology does not fare much better. A number of investigative and intelligence agencies, most notably in the United States, place a great deal of faith in the ability of the polygraph, more popularly known as a lie detector, to tell truth from falsehood. The classic polygraph machine assesses three indicators of autonomic arousal in human beings: heart rate/blood pressure, respiration, and skin conductivity.[280] But there is a major flaw in this approach — these indications of arousal do not necessarily translate into evidence that someone is lying. As a British Psychological Society report on polygraphic detection techniques noted: "Although polygraph equipment does accurately measure a number of physiological activities, these activities do not reflect a single underlying process. Furthermore, these activities are not necessarily in concord either within or across individuals."[281] A report prepared by the US National Research Council (NRC) concluded: "Almost a century of research in scientific psychology and physiology provides little basis for the expectation that a polygraph test could have extremely high accuracy."[282] The American Psychological Association put it more baldly still: "Most psychologists agree that there is little evidence that polygraph tests can accurately detect lies."[283] Put simply, what a polygraph really

---

[278] Matthew Semel, Military Interrogations: Best Practices and Beliefs, *Perspectives on Terrorism*, Vol. 7, No. 2 (April 2013), pp. 45 and 52.

[279] Saul Kassin and Christina Fong, "I'm Innocent!": Effects of Training on Judgments of Truth and Deception in the Interrogation Room, *Law and Human Behavior*, Vol. 23, No. 5 (1999), p. 501.

[280] http://www.apa.org/research/action/polygraph.aspx. Viewed 27 November 2015.

[281] British Psychological Society Working Party, *A Review of the Current Scientific Status and Fields of Application of Polygraphic Deception Detection* (British Psychological Society; 2004), p. 29.

[282] Committee to Review the Scientific Evidence on the Polygraph, *The Polygraph and Lie Detection* (The National Academies Press; 2003), p. 2.

[283] http://www.apa.org/research/action/polygraph.aspx. Viewed 27 November 2015.

detects is stress — and stress can be triggered by honest nervousness, loss of face, or embarrassment, just as easily as by the fear of discovery. In the hands of a skilled interviewer, a polygraph can be a useful tool but it is not, and has never been, a lie detector. The only reliable method to determine the truth or accuracy of a statement is to compare it against the observable evidence.

Precisely because it is so difficult to determine with any confidence the likely guilt or innocence of a suspect at the outset of an investigation, international law has identified the operating principle that any individual held under suspicion should be presumed innocent until convicted by a court of law as one of the cornerstones of a fair and equitable judicial system. The presumption of innocence is enshrined in Article 14(2) of the International Covenant on Civil and Political Rights, which states: "Everyone charged with a criminal offence shall have the right to be presumed innocent until proven guilty according to law." In 2001, the UN Human Rights Committee commented that it considered the presumption of innocence to be a peremptory norm of international law and thus non-derogable in any circumstances.[284]

This presumption of innocence serves both a practical and a philosophical purpose. At the philosophical level, the presumption of innocence ensures that everyone is treated equally before the law and receives the same degree of protection during an investigation, even when public feeling is running high or there is great political pressure to obtain results.[285] At the practical level, the presumption of innocence protects individuals from prejudice and poor judgment. It also reminds officers of the state that they must approach each case in an open-minded, dispassionate, and professional manner regardless of the apparent facts at the outset

---

[284] Human Rights Committee, *General Comment 29, States of Emergency (Article 4)*, UN Doc. CCPR/C/21/Rev.1/Add.11 (2001), para 11.

[285] Bruce MacFarlane, *Wrongful Convictions: The Effect of Tunnel Vision and Predisposing Circumstances in the Criminal Justice System*, Prepared for the Inquiry into Pediatric Forensic Pathology in Ontario, The Honourable Stephen T. Goudge, Commissioner (2008), p. 7. See https://www.attorneygeneral.jus.gov.on.ca/inquiries/goudge/policy_research/pdf/ Macfarlane_Wrongful-Convictions.pdf. Viewed 13 January 2016.

of the case, which rarely remain unchanged as a case progresses. In the aftermath of a major crime, there is typically a great deal of confusion and contradictory information, mistakes are often made and false leads generated. It is incumbent on investigators to set aside any preconceived notions they may have and, rather than rush to judgment, to painstakingly build up an accurate account of what has happened, based on the evidence recovered from witnesses and the crime scene, and this takes time. The presumption of innocence exists in part to remind officers to adhere to this professional standard. As the distinguished American legal scholar Herbert Packer noted: "The presumption of innocence is a direction to officials about how they are to proceed, not a prediction of outcome."[286]

It is all too easy for investigators to become overly committed to a working hypothesis to the exclusion of other lines of inquiry, or to paraphrase President Franklin Delano Roosevelt's first Attorney-General, Homer Cummings, to find their suspect and then search for the facts to fit him.[287] This phenomenon has been well documented, most notably by a series of public inquires held into miscarriages of justice in Canada in the late 1990s and early 2000s. The descriptive term "tunnel vision" was first applied to such cases in the Morin Public Inquiry. Guy Morin was wrongfully convicted of the rape and murder of Christine Jessop and eventually exonerated by DNA evidence. A commission of inquiry was established, with Judge Fred Kaufman appointed as commissioner, to inquire into the conduct of the original police investigation. Amongst Judge Kaufman's recommendations in his concluding report was that "one component of educational programming for police and Crown Counsel should be the identification and avoidance of tunnel vision," which he described as "the single-minded and overly narrow focus on a particular investigative or prosecutorial theory, so as to

---

[286] Herbert Packer, *The Limits of the Criminal Sanction* (Stanford University Press; 1968), p. 161.

[287] Speaking in relation to the unsolved 1943 murder of Sir Harry Oakes. See Rupert Hughes, *The Complete Detective: The Life and Strange and Exciting Cases of Raymond Schindler, Master Detective* (The Rowman and Littlefield Publishing Group; 2014), p. 94.

unreasonably colour the evaluation of information received and one's conduct in response to that information."[288]

In the commission of inquiry established to investigate the wrongful conviction of Thomas Sophonow of the murder of Barbara Stoppel, former Canadian Supreme Court Justice Peter deCarteret Cory reported further evidence of a disturbing trend: "Tunnel vision is insidious. It can affect an officer or, indeed, anyone involved in the administration of justice with sometimes tragic results … Anyone, police officer, counsel or judge can become infected by this virus."[289] Across the border in the United States, the exoneration of thirteen men on death row led the Governor of Illinois to establish a Commission on Capital Punishment to review the mistakes made in these cases and suggest reforms. Reporting in 2002, the commissioners found "tunnel vision" or "confirmatory bias" to be a factor in a number of these cases and warned: "The problem of confirmatory bias is not a problem associated with any one group of police officers or any one department. It is a potential problem in all investigatory agencies."[290]

Perhaps, one of the most infamous examples of tunnel vision affecting a counter-terrorism investigation concerns the bombing of the Centennial Olympic Park during the 1996 Atlanta Olympic Games. The blast killed a woman and injured 111 others (a Turkish cameraman also died of a heart attack in the ensuing panic) — the death toll would have likely been far higher but for the actions of a park security guard, Richard Jewell, who discovered the device and

---

[288] The Honourable Fred Kaufman, C.M., Q.C., *Report of the Kaufman Commission on Proceedings Involving Guy Paul Morin, Recommendation 74: Education Respecting Tunnel Vision* (31 March 1998), p. 26.

[289] Bruce MacFarlane, Convicting the Innocent: A Triple Failure of the Justice System, *Manitoba Law Journal*, Vol. 31, No. 3 (2006), p. 429.

[290] Bruce MacFarlane, *Wrongful Convictions: The Effect of Tunnel Vision and Predisposing Circumstances in the Criminal Justice System*, Prepared for the Inquiry into Pediatric Forensic Pathology in Ontario, The Honourable Stephen T. Goudge, Commissioner (2008), p. 33. See https://www.attorneygeneral.jus.gov.on.ca/inquiries/goudge/policy_research/pdf/ Macfarlane_Wrongful-Convictions.pdf. Viewed 13 January 2016. See also *Report of the Governor's Commission on Capital Punishment, George H. Ryan Governor* (15 April 2002), p. 20.

was moving the public away from the area when it exploded.[291] The device consisted of three homemade pipe bombs packed with nails concealed in a military rucksack. The FBI investigation focused for several months on Richard Jewell, with investigators suspecting that he had staged the whole incident to make himself out to be a hero. Both his home and his mother's home were very publicly searched by the FBI, he was placed under twenty-four-hour surveillance, and he was vilified in the media.[292]

In fact, the device in Centennial Olympic Park had been planted by a right-wing extremist and anti-abortion activist called Eric Rudolf, who had targeted the games as part of a wider campaign "to confound, anger and embarrass the Washington government in the eyes of the world for its abominable sanctioning of abortion on demand", and because he believed the Games themselves celebrated "the ideals of global socialism".[293] Rudolf went on to stage three more bombings — of a gay nightclub and two abortion clinics — that killed a policeman and crippled a nurse.[294] If the investigation had not wasted time focused on Jewell, perhaps these subsequent attacks could have been prevented, which is one more reason why it is so important for investigators to keep an open mind. Rudolf was finally arrested in 2003 and was convicted of the Atlanta attack, among a number of other crimes, in 2005. He is currently serving four life terms in the United States Penitentiary, Administrative Maximum Facility (ADX) in Florence, Colorado. Richard Jewell received a formal apology from the Governor of Georgia in 2006 and substantial financial compensation from a range of media outlets, but it didn't do him much good — he died in 2007.[295]

---

[291] Kevin Sack, Bomb at the Olympics: The Overview; Olympics Park Blast Kills One, Hurts 111; Atlanta Games Go On, *The New York Times*, 28 July 1996.

[292] David Kohn, *FBI Fingers Richard Jewell As Bombing Suspect*, 60 Minutes, CBS News, 2 January 2002.

[293] Full Text of Eric Rudolf's Statement, Army of God website at http://www.armyofgod.com/EricRudolphStatement.html. Viewed 13 January 2016.

[294] Press Release *Eric Rudolph Charged in Centennial Olympic Park Bombing*, Department of Justice, 14 October 1998 at http://www.justice.gov/archive/opa/pr/1998/October/477crm.htm. Viewed 13 January 2016.

[295] Harry Weber, Former Olympic Park Guard Jewell Dies, *The Washington Post*, 30 August 2007.

Closely related to the presumption of innocence is the right not to be compelled to testify against oneself that is enshrined in Article 14(3)(g) of the ICCPR. Commonly described as the right to silence, a distinction is sometimes drawn between the clearly expressed legal prohibition on any attempt, direct or indirect, physical or psychological, to force an individual to testify against his or her wishes, and the potential conclusions that can be drawn from the exercise of his or her right to remain silence. Although the ICCPR does not address this point directly, in 1995, the UN Human Rights Committee noted with concern that the British decision to introduce legislation allowing both the judge and the jury in criminal cases to draw adverse inferences from an individual's exercise of his or her right to remain silence violated "various provisions" of Article 14 of the Covenant.[296] Furthermore, Article 67(1)(g) of the Rome Statute of the International Criminal Court extends to suspects the right to remain silent, and provides that silence cannot be used as "a consideration in the determination of guilt or innocence". Thus, the right to remain silent without adverse inference being drawn would also seem to be an established international standard. The decision to remain silent should therefore never be taken as an indication of guilt — it might reflect fear, caution, distrust of police, or simply sound legal advice. It is incumbent on any investigator preparing to interview a suspect to keep an open mind, to follow the evidence, and to respect the rights of the accused.

## Human rights compliant interviews

The fundamental purpose of interviewing a suspect, or indeed any witness, is to establish a truthful and accurate record of an event, or events, of interest. For intelligence officers, this is their overriding concern. Law enforcement officials also have two additional, but related, objectives to keep in mind as they prepare for, and then conduct, interviews. First and foremost, law enforcement investigators are collecting evidence to support a legal case that will

---

[296] *Concluding Observations of the Human Rights Committee: United Kingdom of Great Britain and Northern Ireland*, CCPR/C/79/Add 55, 27 July 1995, para 17.

ultimately be heard in a court of law, ensuring justice is done and that the public is protected from harm. Law enforcement investigators also have an obligation to the victims and survivors of crimes. Victims are often desperate for information even when the details of their experience, or that of their loved ones, may be difficult to relive. Getting the story right is important, those investigating terrorist incidents are creating the official record of what may become important historical events, imbued with deep meaning for a society as whole. Consider the impact of the National Commission on Terrorist Attacks Upon the United States, whose public hearings and subsequent report, played an important role in helping the American public process the events of 9/11.[297] An accurate accounting of events can contribute powerfully to future narratives of recovery, justice, and legitimacy. In contrast, getting the story wrong can lead to what the Canadian lawyer Bruce MacFarlane has termed "a triple failure of justice" — an innocent individual is wrongfully punished, a guilty individual remains at large to offend again, and victims have been robbed of the redress to which they are entitled, and may even be retraumatized when old wounds are reopened as a consequence of the miscarriage of justice being exposed.[298]

On 5 October 1974, the Provisional IRA planted two improvised explosive devices, each consisting of six pounds of high explosive detonated by a timer, in two pubs in Guildford, Surrey. The first bomb exploded without warning at 8.30 pm in the Horse and Groom Public House, killing five people and injuring many others. Four of the fatalities were off-duty British Army personnel. The second bomb went off half-an-hour later in the Seven Stars Public House but it had already been evacuated and there were no serious injuries. The Guildford bombings were the most serious and complex crime

---

[297] *The 9/11 Commission Report: Final Report of the National Commission on Terrorist Attacks Upon the United States,* Authorized Edition (W. W. Norton and Company; 2004).

[298] Bruce MacFarlane, *Wrongful Convictions: The Effect of Tunnel Vision and Predisposing Circumstances in the Criminal Justice System,* Prepared for the Inquiry into Pediatric Forensic Pathology in Ontario, The Honourable Stephen T. Goudge, Commissioner (2008), p. 3. See https://www.attorneygeneral.jus.gov.on.ca/inquiries/goudge/policy_research/pdf/Macfarlane_Wrongful-Convictions.pdf. Viewed 13 January 2016.

that had ever occurred in Surrey Constabulary's area of responsibility and the force came under great pressure to get a quick result.

Despite an intensive investigation in which the police recorded some 4,000 statements, took 600 photographs, and interviewed 6,000 people in an effort to determine who had planted the bombs, investigators made little progress beyond the identification of a "courting couple" — the only patrons in the Horse and Groom that evening who had not subsequently come forward to volunteer statements to the police — as the prime suspects in the case. Pressure on the police mounted after further attacks took place on pubs in Woolwich, London, and Birmingham. As the scope of the enquiry widened to encompass almost anyone with a potential connection to republican areas of Northern Ireland, police detained Belfast-born Paul Hill in his North London apartment. Hill was from the militantly pro-IRA Falls Road area of Belfast and had come to notice as being loosely connected to the Provisional IRA. In fact, Hill had actually fled Belfast after running afoul of the Provisionals, possibly for misusing a PIRA weapon or possibly because he was suspected of being an informer. Once in custody, Hill claimed he was stripped naked and physically abused by police officers, and that his pregnant girlfriend was also threatened. He confessed to the Guildford bombing naming two other former associates from the Falls Road area who were now also living in London as co-conspirators: Gerry Conlon and Patrick Armstrong. Police soon picked up both men, along with Armstrong's girlfriend Carole Richardson. Police immediately suspected Armstrong and Richardson were the courting couple seen at the Horse and Groom pub before the explosion.[299]

Conlon said he was beaten repeatedly in police custody, threatened with a gun, and deprived of sleep for seven days. Police also allegedly threatened to have his mother killed. Fearing for his life, he signed a confession. Armstrong and Richardson also quickly confessed to being the courting couple when police played them off against each other. As soon as the suspects were granted access to

---

[299] Grant McKee and Ros Franey, *Time Bomb: Irish Bombers, English Justice and the Guildford Four* (Bloomsbury; 1988).

defense counsel, the confessions stopped and thereafter all four consistently protested their innocence. Police were unable to find any eyewitness testimony or forensic evidence linking any of the four to the Guildford bombing. Years later, it also emerged that alibis placing Conlon and Richardson away from the crime scene at the time of the attack had been altered or hidden in police files. Nevertheless, in September 1974, they were put on trial, convicted, and sentenced to decades in prison. Because of her young age, Richardson received the lightest sentence — in his summing up, the presiding judge told the three male defendants that if hanging had still been an option, "you would have been executed."[300]

Despite the Guildford arrests, Provisional IRA attacks on the British mainland continued. In several incidences, the *modus operandi* was identical to the attacks that had gone before. Over a fourteen-month campaign on the mainland lasting from October 1974 to December 1975, long after the arrest of the Guildford Four, the Provisional IRA was responsible for nineteen murders, three kidnappings, nine shootings, thirty-two bombings and nearly $30,000,000 worth of damage. On 6 December 1975, a Provisional IRA active service unit shot up Scott's Oyster Bar in Central London — police gave chase and the team was cornered in a house on Balcombe Street. After a five five-day siege, the PIRA men finally gave themselves up. In police custody, the men claimed responsibility for both the Guildford and Woolwich attacks. One of the men, Joseph O'Connell, even refused to plead guilty to the charges brought against him at trial in January 1977 telling the judge: "I refuse to plead because the indictment does not include two charges concerning the Guildford and Woolwich pub bombings. I took part in both, for which innocent people have been convicted."[301] But, despite his testimony, the Guildford Four case was not reopened.

For fifteen years, supporters of the Guildford Four kept their case alive and in 1987 the British Home Secretary finally authorized

---

[300] Douglas Dalby, Gerry Conlon, 60, Imprisoned in I.R.A. Attack and Freed After 15 Years, Dies, *New York Times*, 22 June 2014.

[301] Grant McKee and Ros Franey, *Time Bomb: Irish Bombers, English Justice and the Guildford Four* (Bloomsbury; 1988), p. 372.

police investigators from a different constabulary to review the case. In the course of this investigation, it emerged that the police had falsified their notes from the suspect interviews, and altered statements — including, crucially, the testimony of forensic scientists. An emergency Court of Appeal hearing was scheduled and it concluded that if police had lied about the confessions (which had been immediately withdrawn by the defendants), then all the evidence they had submitted in the case was unreliable. The Guildford Four were released on 19 October 1989, after having their convictions quashed, and ultimately each received compensation from the British government in the region of £400,000–£500,000. In 1993, a film was made about their case based largely on Gerry Conlon's autobiography, *Proved Innocent.* This film, *In The Name of the Father*, was nominated for seven Oscars and was shown all round the world — for many people internationally, it was their first introduction to the Northern Ireland conflict and it was greatly damaging to the United Kingdom's reputation, and to the reputation of the British Police, around the world.

　The Guildford Four scandal was only one of a series of high-profile miscarriages of justice in the United Kingdom in the 1970s and 1980s, many of them related to counter-terrorism investigations, that revealed the extent to which manipulative and coercive practices had been used to extract confessions.[302] As a result, in 1992, the British Home Office, the government department responsible for policing in the United Kingdom, began to develop a new approach to investigative interviewing that would become known as the PEACE model — a mnemonic derived from the five stages of the model's approach: **P**lanning and preparation; **E**ngage and explain; **A**ccount and clarify; **C**losure; and **E**valuation. The PEACE model is based on psychological principles and theory, and encourages an open-minded approach to interviewing suspects.

---

[302] *UK: A long line of miscarriages of justices*, BBC News, 17 December 1998 at http://news.bbc. co.uk/2/hi/uk_news/237296.stm. Viewed 14 December 2015. Other terrorism-related miscarriages of justice in this period include Danny McNamee's conviction for the IRA's 1982 Hyde Park, the Birmingham Six, the Maguire Seven, and John Kinsella's conviction for the Warrington gasworks bombing.

PEACE deliberately moves the focus of an interview away from obtaining a confession and places the emphasis instead on gathering information in a fair, open, and honest fashion.[303] The model has since been adopted by a number of countries outside the UK as representing a best practice approach.[304]

The PEACE model is an example of what is often termed "ethical interviewing," an approach to interviewing suspects that can be traced back to developments in Swedish policing in the 1940s and the work of two pioneering Swedish researchers, Ernst Leche and Victor Hagelberg.[305] Leche and Hagelberg recommended police focus on gaining the trust of their interview subjects and stressed the importance of asking open-ended questions rather than trying to direct the suspect's answers.[306] They also suggested that Swedish police officers could benefit from understanding how human memory actually works. These were revolutionary concepts in a world which mostly put its faith in the coercive approach to interviewing often known as 'the third degree' — the approach that had failed so completely in the case of the Guilford Four — and it took decades, and a deepening body of research on miscarriages of justice, for such ideas to gain currency outside Scandinavia.[307]

The essence of the PEACE approach is the presumption of innocence — investigators are encouraged to approach each interview without preconceptions, or prejudging the guilt or innocence of the suspect. The focus is on establishing the truth, not gaining a

---

[303] Andrea Shawyer, Becky Milne, and Ray Bull, Investigative Interviewing in the UK, in Tom Williamson, Becky Milne and Stephen Savage (eds.), *International Developments in Investigative Interviewing* (Willan Publishing; 2009), p. 27.

[304] Including Norway, Sweden, Denmark and New Zealand.

[305] Eric Shepherd, Ethical Interviewing, *Policing*, Vol. 7 (1991), pp. 42–60 and Colin Clarke, Rebecca Milne and Ray Bull, Interviewing Suspects of Crime: The Impact of PEACE Training, Supervision and the Presence of a Legal Adviser, *Journal of Investigative Psychology and Offender Profiling*, Vol. 8 (2011), pp. 149–150.

[306] Karl Roberts, Police Interviewing of Criminal Suspects: A Historical Perspective, *Internet Journal of Criminology* (2012), p. 5.

[307] Saul Kassin, Steven Drizin, Thomas Grisso, Gisli Gudjonsson, Richard Leo and Allison Redlich, Police-Induced Confessions: Risk factors and Recommendations, *Law and Human Behavior*, Vol. 34, No. 1 (February 2010).

confession.[308] By adopting this mindset, investigators avoid the trap of confirmation bias — asking questions that serve only to advance the investigative theory they have constructed — and instead create a space in which a suspect or a witness can relay their own account of events. Even in circumstances in which a suspect seeks to mislead investigators, the challenge of inventing sufficient detail to populate the kind of convincing fraudulent narrative that can sustain an open accounting offers investigators numerous opportunities to test, and ultimately disprove, the suspect's story.

The first stage of the PEACE model stresses the importance of effective preparation before investigators sit down with the suspect. In the law enforcement context, investigators may only have a limited opportunity to put questions to the suspect and so it is important that they have a thorough understanding of all the pertinent issues that need to be addressed.[309] The interviewer's credibility with the interviewee will depend heavily on his or her command of the facts of the case. Effective preparation also requires that thought be given to the atmospherics in which the interview will be conducted. The goal of the PEACE model is to build rapport with the interview subject and so investigators eschew confrontational staging. Modern interview suites tend to be set up with two comfortable chairs placed at a 120 degree angle to each other, as studies have shown that this configuration is most conducive to positive conversation.[310] In high-profile cases, investigators will also typically give a great deal of consideration to who on the team would likely elicit the best response from the subject. For example, one might decide to use a father figure, a peer from the same age group, or a female officer as the lead interviewer to set the right tone. If one is dealing with a foreign subject, or someone from a

---

[308] Andrea Shawyer, Becky Milne and Ray Bull, Investigative Interviewing in the UK, in Tom Williamson, Becky Milne and Stephen Savage (eds.), *International Developments in Investigative Interviewing* (Willan Publishing; 2009), p. 27.

[309] Crown Prosecution Service, *Achieving Best Evidence in Criminal Proceedings: Guidance on interviewing victims and witnesses, and guidance on using special measures* (HM Ministry of Justice; March 2011), p. 2.1.

[310] ibid., p. H.3.4.3.

different ethnicity or faith, it is good practice to use someone sensitive to, and knowledgeable of, the subject's culture.

The second step of the PEACE model is to engage the interview subject and begin to build rapport, which has been appositely described as the closest thing interviewers have to a truth serum.[311] Behavioral science research suggests that the window of opportunity to make a good first impression on someone is at most about thirty seconds. Unless there is a compelling reason not to, interviewers are encouraged to shake hands with the subject, again because research suggests that it can take an average of three hours of continuous interaction to develop the same level of rapport that you can get with a single handshake. Maintaining eye contact is always important. Finally, officers are encouraged to manage the subject's expectations at the outset of the interview by explaining how the interview process works, and by outlining the subject's civil rights. The purpose is to put the subject at ease so that they are focused on the interview not their wider situation. This phase is all about metacommunication and building trust through openness.

The "account and clarify" phase of the PEACE model encompasses the bulk of the interview. The objective is to move away from a straightforward question and answer exchange, typical of the 'third degree' approach, by encouraging the interviewee to put forward his or her own version of events in an uninterrupted or 'free' account. During this portion of the interview, the interviewer engages in active or emphatic listening — a rapport-building technique that stresses the adoption of an attentive, open posture by the interviewer to encourage conversation.[312] The interviewer's focus should be entirely on what is being said in the interview, and he or she should make sure the subject is receiving the verbal and non-verbal cues that underscore that the interviewer is playing close attention to what is being said. The British Crown Prosecution

---

[311] Ian Leslie, The long read: The scientists persuading terrorists to spill their secrets, *The Guardian*, 13 October 2017.

[312] Crown Prosecution Service, *Achieving Best Evidence in Criminal Proceedings: Guidance on interviewing victims and witnesses, and guidance on using special measures* (HM Ministry of Justice; March 2011), p. 3.28.

Service guidance on interviewing witnesses also stresses the value of synchrony, noting that by adopting a calm and relaxed demeanor the interviewer can model positive behavior for the interview subject.[313] Active listening also encourages interviewers to make effective use of silence — as social animals, most humans find it difficult to sit in silence with another individual, and will often seek to fill the void with conversation. As the interview progresses, a pause may also give a subject time to consider his or her options, especially as a false narrative begins to unravel, and can lead him or her reevaluate his or her approach, and perhaps consider cooperation.

Once the subject has completed his or her account, the interviewer can begin to clarify aspects of this account by asking questions. In the PEACE model, interviewers are encouraged to use open-ended or 'tell' questions, such as "tell me what happened next", "explain that to me" or "describe that in more detail".[314] Interviewers are also cautioned to only use 'closed' questions — questions requiring simple one word "yes" or "no" answers — as a last resort. Closed questions inhibit rapport-building and prevent the subject from answering discursively and perhaps revealing more information. Interviewers should always avoid asking leading questions for fear of both tainting the subject's testimony, and of perhaps giving away too much about the investigation itself. Even the choice of words used by interviewers in their questions can have a distorting effect on testimony. Emotive language can provoke a powerful reaction, the information provided in a question can condition the response, and research has shown that even small changes in language, for example substituting "smash" for "bumped" or "hit", can influence testimony.[315]

It is also important for investigators to be aware that imprecise or inaccurate recall is not in itself reason to conclude that a subject is seeking to dissemble, fabricate testimony, or otherwise mislead the

---

[313] ibid., p. H.3.4.4.

[314] ibid., pp. 3.45 and 3.46.

[315] Elizabeth Loftus and John Palmer, Reconstruction of Automobile Destruction: An Example of the Interaction Between Language and Memory, *Journal of Verbal Learning and Verbal Behavior*, Vol. 13 (1974), p. 588.

interviewer. In its *Guidelines on Memory and the Law*, the British Psychological Society cautioned interviewers: "Memories are records of people's experiences of events and are not a record of the events themselves. In this respect, they are unlike other recording media such as videos or audio recordings, to which they should not be compared."[316] In other words, memory is a reconstructive process. Cognitive science has established that memories tend to exist of fragments of genuine recall with the mind often supplying missing details logically but unreliably — a process labeled "affective realism" by the psychologists Lisa Feldman Barrett and Kyle Simmons, which also appears closely tied to emotion.[317] Investigators should also be aware that when more than one person witnesses an incident or participates in an event a collective narrative can develop over time — often reinforced by media reporting and conversations between witnesses — that replaces individual memories and can lead to flawed recall.

However, if an interviewer comes to suspect that a subject is willfully fabricating a false narrative, he or she can begin to test this hypothesis by requesting greater detail or introducing new facts — such as eyewitness testimony or CCTV coverage — to force the subject to adjust this false narrative in such a way as to take these new data points into account. Giving the subject additional facts to assimilate adds to the mental stress or "cognitive load" that maintaining a false narrative requires and ultimately makes it increasingly difficult to sustain, thus exposing inconsistencies. Another powerful falsification technique is to revisit the narrative out of sequence or in reverse order. Fabricators typically create and rehearse a false narrative in a progressive temporal sequence — "first I did *x*, then I did *y*, after that I did *z*." Taking events out of sequence makes it harder to accurately recall false details. Psychologists Aldert Vrij and Ronald Fisher have reported a significant improvement in investigators' ability to detect deception in

---

[316] *Guidelines on Memory and the Law: Recommendations from the Scientific Study of Human Memory*, British Psychological Society Research Board (June 2008), p. 2.

[317] Lisa Feldman Barrett and Jolie Wormwood, When a Gun is Not a Gun, *The New York Times*, 17 April 2015.

reverse order accounts.[318] It should be stressed that no method for detecting deception is anywhere close to being foolproof — such methods simply amount to another tool in the investigator's tool-box. Finally, when deception is detected interviewers are best advised to leave direct challenges to the end of the interview because this can understandably (but not always) undermine rapport.

The final two phases of the PEACE model — Closure and Evaluation — are both fairly self-explanatory. Interviewers should aim to end each interview in such a manner that the subject wants to come back for further conversations. This can be done in part by summarizing what has been discussed at the end of the session so that there is a common agreement about what has happened and the subject feels he or she has been given a fair hearing. Evaluation should be a constant process in the course of an interview. If things are not going well an investigator needs to be honest about whether or not he or she is the best person for the job — it may be that another investigator would be a better fit for the subject. Once an interview is completed, the investigative team can benefit from taking the time to consider potential lessons learned from the approach taken in the interview. There is an important welfare aspect here as well. The stress on an interviewer in a major case can be immense and the unpleasantness of the subject matter under discussion can be difficult to process — creating the space for interviewers to seek support from their colleagues and to let off a little steam is vitally important. This also affords supervisors an opportunity to evaluate for themselves the wellbeing of the investigators on their staff, and to address potential problems before they become more serious.

Working with police officers and civilian and military intelligence officers from around the world, I am often met with incredulity when I introduce them to the PEACE model for the first time. It is not uncommon for experienced counter-terrorism investigators to challenge whether such an approach could possibly ever bear fruit when

---

[318] Aldert Vrij, Samantha Mann, Ronald Fisher, Sharon Leal, Rebecca Milne and Ray Bull, Increasing Cognitive Load to Facilitate Lie Detection: The Benefit of Recalling an Event in Reverse Order, *Law and Human Behavior*, Vol. 32 (2008), pp. 262–263.

deployed against a hardened terrorist in detention. While this might intuitively make sense to some, the available evidence does not actually support such skepticism. In the only scientific study of its kind that I have been able to identify, the forensic psychologists Laurence Alison and Emily Alison were granted access to review 878 tape recordings of 45-minute interview segments with 181 convicted terrorism-related suspects conducted by British police since 2004. They found that the majority of the subjects in their study were "mostly adaptive in their relating styles; contradicting the oft held view that suspects are *de facto* noncompliant and are all committed to frustrating the attempts of interrogators to interact positively", meaning that the subjects tended to respond in line with the approach adopted by their interviewer. Strategies that tended to work were empathy, focus on discrepancies between suspect behaviors and values, encouraging confidence, and acceptance. This led the Alisons to conclude that adaptive communication and rapport building approaches were more likely to elicit information than more aggressive approaches, although they also acknowledged that such approaches were by no means foolproof.[319] The *Educing Information* report on best practice interrogation methods produced by the US Intelligence Science Board in December 2006, while more discursive and historical in nature, reached a very similar conclusion.[320]

Human rights compliant rapport-building interview techniques have been employed with considerable success in the aftermath of very serious terrorist incidents. On 22 July 2011, the Norwegian right-wing extremist Andreas Behring Breivik detonated a 950 Kilogram nitrate fertilizer bomb concealed in a white Volkswagen van parked outside government buildings in Oslo, killing eight

---

[319] See Laurence Alison, Emily Alison, Geraldine Noone, Stamatis Elntib and Paul Christiansen, Why Tough Tactics Fail and Rapport Gets Results: Observing Rapport-Based Interpersonal Techniques (ORBIT) to Generate Useful Information From Terrorists, Psychology, *Public Policy and Law*, Vol. 19, No. 4 (2013), p. 427 and Laurence Alison and Emily Alison, Revenge versus Rapport: Interrogation, Terrorism, and Torture, *American Psychologist*, Vol. 72, No. 3 (2017), pp. 271–273.

[320] Intelligence Science Board, Educing Information — Interrogation: Science and Art, Foundations for the Future, Center for Strategic Intelligence Research, National Defense Intelligence College, December 2006.

people and injuring nine seriously. Luckily, the bomb was detonated at 3.25 pm on a Friday afternoon in mid-summer and many government workers had already left for home or were on holiday, which minimized casualties.[321] Two hours later, Breivik attacked a Labor Party youth camp on the island of Utøya killing sixty-nine and wounding thirty-three, shooting them all individually. Breivik later stated that one of the reasons he had specifically chosen the island as a target was that the former Norwegian Prime Minister Gro Harlem Brundtland had been scheduled to speak there, but she had already left Utøya by the time he arrived. Instead, Breivik, dressed as a police officer, first killed the camp security officer and the camp director, and then walked around the island for about an hour, armed with a Glock automatic pistol and semi-automatic Ruger carbine, methodically shooting campers. There were approximately 560 youths attending the camp. Breivik only intentionally spared two campers he encountered — the eleven-year-old son of the camp security officer and a twenty-two-year-old man who successfully begged for his life. Fifty-seven of the sixty-nine victims on the island were killed by a shot to the head. Breivik only fired 186 rounds in total.

Breivik surrendered to the first heavily armed police units that arrived on the island and was taken into custody. He immediately claimed that several further attacks were imminent, and that he would call these attacks off if his demands were met.[322] This was the worst deadly incident in Norway since the Second World War and commentators estimated that one in four Norwegians knew someone personally affected by the attacks — even the Norwegian royal family was touched, the step-brother of the Crown Princess was killed on Utøya island.[323] It is difficult to imagine an attack that could hit a community much harder than this one did.

---

[321] Åsne Seierstad, *One of Us: The Story of Anders Breivik and the Massacres in Norway* (Farrar, Straus and Giroux; 2013).

[322] ibid., pp. 366 and 390.

[323] *1 av 4 kjenner rammed*, Klassekampen, 19 August 2011, at www.klassekampen.no/59186/article/item/null/-av–kjenner-rammede, viewed 234 December 2015 and Raf Sanchez, Norway Killings: Princess's brother Trond Berntsen among dead, *The Daily Telegraph*, 25 July 2011.

Breivik was interviewed briefly at the scene and then taken to a secure police facility where he was placed in the care of specially trained police interviewers, supported by a forensic psychologist and a team of criminal analysts. Breivik was keen to explain his actions even consenting to be interviewed by a female police officer despite his misogynistic views. A 1,500 page manifesto entitled *2083: A European Declaration of Independence* written by "Andrew Berwick" was emailed to more than 1,000 email addresses ninety minutes before the bomb blast in Oslo — and this was quickly attributed to Breivik. He had a right-wing Islamophobic political agenda that he was keen to promote and he introduced himself to the police interviewer as representing a clandestine organization called the Knights Templar, named after the order of Medieval warrior monks.[324]

The Norwegian Police took the position from the outset that Breivik would be treated just like any other criminal, despite the enormity of the crimes of which he was accused. They used their standard PEACE interview approach and were able to establish a good working rapport with him to the extent that he cooperated pretty fully with the investigation. The ticking bomb threat evaporated as it became apparent that Breivik had been working alone, and that the Knights Templar were simply a figment of his imagination. Brievik ultimately participated in 220 hours of interviews and even walked the police through the crime scene at Utøya reconstructing his actions for investigators. On 24 August 2012, Breivik was convicted and sentenced to twenty-one years of preventive detention in prison, which can be repeatedly extended for five-year periods for as long as he is still considered to pose a threat to society.

In the immediate aftermath of the 9/11 attacks, FBI Special Agent Ali Soufan was still in Yemen as one of the lead investigators of the October 2000 bombing of the USS Cole in which seventeen US sailors had died. One of the suspects in the Cole investigation

---

[324] Åsne Seierstad, *One of Us: The Story of Anders Breivik and the Massacres in Norway* (Farrar, Straus and Giroux; 2013), p. 366 and Åsne Seierstad, *One of Us: The Story of Anders Breivik and the Massacres in Norway* (Farrar, Straus and Giroux; 2013), p. 366.

was Fahd al-Quso, an *al-Qaeda* operative, who had been tasked with filming the operation and who was being held in Yemeni custody. Al-Quso was able to identify one of the suspected 9/11 hijackers as Marwan al-Shehhi, and he recalled meeting al-Shehhi in a Kandahar guesthouse run by Osama bin Laden's former bodyguard Nasser al-Bahri, better known as Abu Jandal. By coincidence, Abu Jandal was also in Yemeni custody at that time and so Soufan asked to interview him.[325]

Abu Jandal was a hardened member of *al-Qaeda* who was well trained in counter-interrogation techniques, and when put in the same room as Soufan he initially turned his back on him and refused to speak. Soufan was able to coax Abu Jandal into turning round and soon he was haranguing Soufan about the failings of the United States. In his lengthy monologues, Abu Jandal portrayed himself as a good Muslim who had become disillusioned with *jihad* — he also saw himself not as a terrorist but as a revolutionary trying to rid the world of evil, which he mostly saw as coming from the United States — a country that it was soon apparent he actually knew very little about. This gave Soufan his way in.

Abu Jandal's weak spot was his sociability and Soufan was able to earn his respect by demonstrating an understanding of both Islam and the prisoner's personal world view — coupled to an encyclopedic knowledge of *al-Qaeda*'s key players and operational activity. Soufan built rapport by using arguments drawn from Abu Jandal's own moral landscape and through small acts of kindness. Soufan noticed that Abu Jandal had declined the cookies offered to him on the first day of the interview and discovered that he was diabetic. Soufan arrived at the next interview session with sugar-free cookies for Abu Jandal to snack on and later also gave him a biography of the American Revolutionary War leader George Washington, so that he could learn something of America's history and values. These small courtesies had a major impact.[326]

---

[325] Ali Soufan and Daniel Freedman, *The Black Banners: The Inside Story of 9/11 and the War against Al-Qaeda* (W. W. Norton & Co.; 2011), p. 295.

[326] ibid., pp. 311–312 and 330.

Abu Jandal was fascinated by the story of America's rebellion against the British Crown, and saw many parallels between this and the Arab struggle.[327] Soufan had been able to creatively call Abu Jandal's existing worldview into question. He built on this opening by engaging Abu Jandal in a detailed discussion about the injunctions contained in the *Koran* and *hadith* about the honorable conduct of warfare — especially concerning the treatment of innocents and non-combatants. Once he had successfully engaged Abu Jandal on the morality of terrorist violence, and had a good understanding of the latter's internal moral compass, Soufan finally confronted him about the 9/11 attacks of which, at that point, Abu Jandal still knew very little. The scale of the loss of life stunned Abu Jandal and when Soufan showed him a local Yemeni newspaper with the headline *Two Hundred Yemeni Souls Perish in New York Attack* Abu Jandal flatly refused to believe *al-Qaeda* was responsible for such a terrible atrocity.[328]

Soufan pounced, sensing his opportunity. He showed Abu Jandal mug shots of suspected members of *al-Qaeda*, including that of Marwan al-Shehhi, who had stayed in the Kandahar guesthouse he had run. Al-Quso had said that Abu Jandal even looked after al-Shehhi when the latter came down with a fever. When Abu Jandal initially failed to identify al-Shehhi, Soufan presented him with this titbit of information and, taken aback that Soufan should know such an intimate detail, Abu Jandal admitted he knew al-Shehhi. He also identified six other residents of the guesthouse. When Soufan revealed that all seven men had participated in the 9/11 attacks, Abu Jandal was stunned. He asked for a moment alone to think — Soufan left the room to allow him to collect himself and when he went back in Abu Jandal told him everything he knew about *al-Qaeda*.[329]

In his memoir, Soufan also described getting Osama bin Laden's former driver Salim Hamdan to cooperate in an interview at Guantanamo through the simple expedient of allowing him to

---

[327] ibid., p. 315.
[328] ibid., pp. 319–320.
[329] ibid., p. 321.

make a phone call to his wife on Soufan's satellite phone — the first and only time Hamdan had been able to communicate with the outside world since his arrest.[330] Soufan also brought Hamdan fish sandwiches from McDonalds and car magazines from the Navy Exchange to further consolidate their relationship. Hamdan cooperated fully with Soufan, although all previous US efforts to get him to talk had failed. Hamdan had been in the room when 9/11 mastermind Khalid Sheikh Mohammed briefed the leadership of *al-Qaeda* about the operation, so one can imagine just how significant a breakthrough this was at the time. Soufan told *The New York Times* in 2010: "Whether suspects cooperate depends on the skill of the interrogator and the mindset of the suspects — not whether they've been told they can remain silent. When legally required, I've read some top *Qaeda* terrorists their rights and they've still provided valuable intelligence."[331]

Soufan's success gaining the trust and cooperation of *al-Qaeda* members was replicated by other FBI investigators working on counter-terrorism cases across America. FBI Special Agents were able to cajole both the Millennium bomber Ahmed Ressam and the underwear bomber Umar Farouq Abdulmutallab to answer their questions. Ressam cooperated with the FBI for a period following his conviction in 2001 in the hopes of receiving a significantly reduced sentence. In Abdulmutallab's case, the FBI worked with his family to secure his cooperation.[332] FBI agents were also able to turn Bryant Neal Vinas, a US-born convert to Islam and former US Army soldier, who traveled to Pakistan to join *al-Qaeda* in 2007 and participated in two assaults on American troops in Afghanistan before being captured by Pakistani security forces. Vinas was transferred to US custody in January 2009 and subsequently pled guilty to the charges brought against him. He quickly began to volunteer "valuable information" to US officials including details of a plot to attack the

---

[330] ibid., pp. 453–454.

[331] Ali Soufan, Tribunal and Error, *The New York Times*, 11 February 2010.

[332] Ed Henry, *White House reveals secret cooperation with AbdulMutallab family*, CNN, 3 February 2010 at http://edition.cnn.com/2010/CRIME/02/02/plane.bomb.suspect/. Viewed 27 December 2015.

Long Island Light Railway and Pennsylvania Station in New York City. [333] He also cooperated as a key prosecution witness in French and Belgian trials of *al-Qaeda* members he had previously met in Pakistan. One of the most surprising aspects of the decision by the Bush administration to introduce so-called Enhanced Interrogation Techniques (of which more below) is just how unnecessary it seems to have been. The simple fact is that in the aftermath of the 9/11 attacks, the traditional law enforcement approach to countering terrorist threats worked again, and again, and again. It was when the US decided to depart from this path that things began to go spectacularly wrong.

There is no single approach to interviewing that guarantees the cooperation of an interview subject. There are subjects who will talk if the right circumstances are created, and there are those who, for one reason or another, will not cooperate at any price. The strength of the PEACE approach, and that of ethical interviewing in general, is that it maximizes the amount of information that can be gained from an interview, while at the same time minimizing the likelihood of the kind of abuses in the interview room that can undermine the integrity of the information gained, and the legitimacy of police investigations and the criminal justice system as a whole.[334] Evaluations of the PEACE model have noted an improvement in the quality of witness and suspect statements, and a significant reduction in the number of miscarriages of justice in which abusive interviewing practices were cited as a contributing factor.[335] In a conflict in which legitimacy is a key contested value, the abuse of suspects affords very little advantage to the abusers, and can deliver a substantial propaganda victory to their opponents, whereas ethical

---

[333] William Rashbaum and Souad Mekhennet, L.I. Man Helped Qaeda, Then Informed, *The New York Times*, 22 July 2009.

[334] Karl Roberts, Police Interviewing of Criminal Suspects: A Historical Perspective, *Internet Journal of Criminology* (2012), p. 12.

[335] ibid., p. 8 and See Eric Shepherd and Rebecca Milne, Have you told the management about this? Bringing witness interviewing into the 21st Century, in Anthony Heaton-Armstrong, Eric Shepherd, Gisli Gudjonsson, and David Wolchover (eds.), *Witness Testimony: Psychological, Investigative, and Evidential Perspectives* (Oxford University Press; 2006), pp. 131–151.

interviewing delivers stronger, more reliable, results with substantially less moral hazard.

## Torture

In 1961, the veteran French Special Forces officer Roger Trinquier published *La Guerre Moderne*, an influential treatise on counter-insurgency operations, in which he sought to pass on the lessons he had learned from fighting national liberation movements in both Indochina and Algeria, including his belief that the clinical application of torture to obtain specific intelligence could be an effective counter-terrorism tool: "Science can easily place at the army's disposal the means for obtaining what is sought."[336] The fact that France had not shrunk from using this tool in both Indochina and Algeria, and had still lost both conflicts, did not seem to give Trinquier any pause before recommending its use to his readers, nor despite his focus on the psychological and political dimensions of counter-insurgency, did he consider that this might have been a factor in alienating key segments of the local population in either country.[337] Trinquier was hardly the first national security hawk to embrace torture as a potential weapon in the fight against terrorism, and he was certainly not the last. Torture has been a feature of military-led counter-terrorism campaigns in theaters as diverse as, and certainly not limited to, Ireland, colonial Kenya, Uruguay, Peru, Egypt, Israel, Chechnya, French Algeria, and today's near global conflict with *al-Qaeda* and its various affiliates and successors. In the aftermath of the 9/11 attacks, one Harvard Law Professor, Alan Dershowitz, even went so far as to argue for the adoption of interrogational torture warrants that would empower investigators to use violent coercive measures to try to force information out of uncooperative suspects.[338]

---

[336] Roger Trinquier, *Modern Warfare: A French View of Counterinsurgency* (Praeger Security International; 1964), p. 19.

[337] ibid., pp. 6 and 29.

[338] See Alan Dershowitz, *Why Terrorism Works* (Yale University Press; 2002), pp. 140–141.

So what exactly constitutes torture? Article 1 of the Convention against Torture and Other Cruel, Inhuman or Degrading Treatment or Punishment (CAT) defines torture as "any act by which severe pain or suffering, whether physical or mental, is intentionally inflicted on a person for such purposes as obtaining from him or a third person information or a confession, punishing him for an act he or a third person has committed or is suspected of having committed, or intimidating or coercing him or a third person, or for any reason based on discrimination of any kind, when such pain or suffering is inflicted by or at the instigation of or with the consent or acquiescence of a public official or other person acting in an official capacity." Distilled to its essence, the key elements of the crime of torture are "severe" pain or suffering "intentionally" inflicted to elicit "information" or a "confession" by anyone acting in "an official capacity". The Convention entered into force on 26 June 1987 and is considered to amount to a peremptory norm of international law, which means that it applies universally whether an individual nation has signed the Convention or not. The Convention creates an international crime of torture and establishes universal jurisdiction for this offense that allows any state that wishes to assert such jurisdiction to bring torturers to justice.

What amounts to "severe" is a matter of considerable debate and different states have advanced different interpretations. Bush administration lawyers, for example, controversially described the threshold for severe pain as being "equivalent in intensity to the pain accompanying serious physical injury, such as organ failure, impairment of bodily function, or even death."[339] Yet, at the same time, diplomats in the US State Department were describing the kind of Enhanced Interrogation Techniques authorized by the Bush administration, such as the use of stress positions or sleep deprivation, as "torture" when they were being used by foreign powers.[340]

---

[339] Office of Legal Counsel US Department of Justice, *Memorandum for Alberto R. Gonzales Counsel to the President Re: Standards of Conduct for Interrogation under 18 USC §§ 2340-2340A,* 1 August 2002, at http://nsarchive.gwu.edu/NSAEBB/NSAEBB127/02.08.01.pdf.

[340] Tom Malinowski, *Banned State Department Practices,* in Kenneth Roth, Minky Worden and Amy Bernstein (eds.), *Torture* (Human Rights Watch; 2005).

However, there is a growing body of international jurisprudence generated by the UN Human Rights Council, international tribunals, and regional courts such as the European Court of Human Rights that designates a wide variety of acts as amounting to torture. For example, the international jurisprudence unambiguously designating waterboarding as an act of torture dates back to the International Military Tribunal for the Far East established by the Allies after World War II to try Japanese war crimes.[341]

Often overlooked in this debate is the second aspect of the Convention — the prohibition of Cruel, Inhuman or Degrading Treatment, which is also criminalized. These are acts that perhaps do not cross the notional threshold established by the term "severe" — such as forcing an individual to strip naked for the purposes of humiliation during an interview — but which would likely be considered degrading treatment and thus also amount to a breach of the Convention. Other acts described in international jurisprudence — most notably in the landmark case *Ireland v. The United Kingdom* (ECtHR; 1978) — as at least amounting to cruel, inhuman or degrading treatment include hooding, the use of stress positions, sleep deprivation, subjecting prisoners to white noise, and withholding food and water. Committing either an act of torture or an act that amounts to cruel, inhuman and degrading treatment is a serious international crime — the only difference ultimately comes down to the likely length of the perpetrator's sentence. As the former US Navy General Counsel, Alberto Mora, who took a principled stand against the use of the Enhanced Interrogation Techniques authorized by the Bush administration, told the Senate Armed Services Committee in June 2008: "There is little or no moral distinction between cruelty and torture, for cruelty can be effective as torture in savaging human flesh and spirit and in violating human dignity. Our efforts should be focused not merely on banning torture, but on banning cruelty."[342]

---

[341] See Evan Wallach, Drop by Drop: Forgetting the History of Water Torture in U.S. Courts, *Columbia Journal of Transnational Law*, Vol. 45 No. 2 (2007).

[342] Joshua Philips, *None of Us Were Like This Before: American Soldiers and Torture* (Verso; 2010), p. 155.

The Convention Against Torture applies in all circumstances, both in war and in peace, but it is also bolstered in times of conflict by Common Article 3 of the Geneva Conventions of 1949, which establishes a minimum level of protection for individuals taking no active part, or no longer taking any active part, in hostilities, including members of armed forces who have laid down their arms and those placed *hors de combat* by sickness, wounds, detention, or any other cause. Common Article 3 provides that any and all such individuals shall in all circumstances be treated humanely, without any adverse distinction founded on race, color, religion or faith, sex, birth or wealth, or any other similar criteria. Common Article 3 specifically prohibits the following acts: "(a) Violence to life and person, in particular murder of all kinds, mutilation, cruel treatment and torture; (b) Taking of hostages; (c) Outrages upon personal dignity, in particular humiliating and degrading treatment; (d) The passing of sentences and the carrying out of executions without previous judgment pronounced by a regularly constituted court, affording all the judicial guarantees which are recognized as indispensable by civilized peoples." We can therefore say with absolute certainty that the following acts are prohibited in the context of an investigative interview of any character by international law in any and all circumstances: physical violence; threat of violence; enforced humiliation; deliberate mental cruelty; threats to family; and rendition to torture.

Proponents of torture often contend that it gets results that can't be obtained using lawful techniques. The counterfactual is of course impossible to prove one way or another in any one individual case, but while undoubtedly some people do cooperate under duress, the historical record also clearly shows that others do not. Professor Darius Rejali noted in an extensive study of the *Gestapo*'s use of torture that this most brutal of organizations failed to break senior leaders of French, Danish, Polish and German resistance groups,[343] and that, compared to the information generated from public cooperation and informers, the leads gained from torture were, to quote

---

[343] Darius Rejali, *Torture and Democracy* (Princeton University Press; 2007), p. 496.

an internal *Gestapo* report, "pathetic".[344] There are many other well-documented examples of members of armed groups resisting coercive interrogation.

Tomás O'Maoileóin, the Vice-Commandant of the East Limerick Brigade of the IRA and a veteran of both the Easter Uprising of 1916 and Frongach internment camp, was captured near Cork by Royal Irish Constabulary Auxiliaries on Christmas Day, 1920. The Auxiliaries had a well-deserved reputation for brutality and O'Maoileoin was beaten badly in custody, losing most of his teeth. He was then interrogated by British officers looking for an elusive local IRA commander called Sean Forde. Sean Forde was actually O'Maoileoin's own *nom de guerre* and the Auxiliaries had no idea that they had actually caught their target. Despite being beaten, and tortured by having a red-hot pair of blacksmith's tongs applied to his back, O'Maoileoin held to his cover story. In fact, this abuse only strengthened his resolve to stay silent. He later recalled: "I felt that this was not playing the game. I felt that, as their prisoner, they were entitled to question me and I was answering as best I could, to give them as little information as possible and yet satisfy them, but now they had, by their actions, decided me to adopt an attitude of defiance."[345] O'Maoileoin stuck to his story even when threatened with summary execution and eventually his interrogators lost interest in him. He soon escaped from British custody and returned to the fight. As the historian of the Anglo-Irish War J. B. E. Hittle observed, O'Maoileoin's example was a powerful fillip to IRA resolve: "His story was evidence that a man could resist torture and survive to fight again."[346]

The LEHI gunman Yaacov Eliav described in his memoir, *Wanted*, being captured and tortured by the Criminal Investigation Department of the Palestinian Police Force in August 1939. At the

---

[344] Darius Rejali, 5 Myths About Torture and Truth, *The Washington Post*, 16 December 2007. See also Darius Rejali, *Torture and Democracy* (Princeton University Press; 2007).

[345] Statement by Witness Tomas O Maoileoin, Bureau of Military History, Document Number W.S. 845, at 72. See http://www.bureauofmilitaryhistory.ie/reels/bmh/BMH.WS0845.pdf.

[346] J. B. E. Hittle, *Michael Collins and the Anglo-Irish War: Britain's Counterinsurgency Failure* (Potomac Books; 2011), p. 203.

hands of a British police officer called Ralph Cairns, Eliav was sleep deprived, beaten, choked, whipped, suspended by his thumbs, subjected to water torture, burned with cigarettes, his genitals were crushed, and his jailers threatened to rape his girlfriend and sisters in front of him, but he didn't break.[347] In fact, Eliav was able to escape from British custody and just fifteen days after regaining his freedom he supervised a LEHI operation in which Cairns and another British officer, Ronald Barker, were killed in a bomb blast in the Jerusalem neighborhood of Rehavia. Cairns' fate is a cautionary tale for would-be torturers everywhere.

The use of torture during the Battle of Algiers in 1957 is often held up as an example of torture being used to good effect to counter terrorism but the historical record is rather more complicated than its advocates would have one believe. To be sure, some individuals tortured in French custody undoubtedly provided useful information. French interrogators focused on identifying FLN personnel. Roger Trinquier summarized the process in *La Guerre Moderne*: "Each man has a superior whom he knows; he will first have to give the name of this person, along with his address, so that it will be possible to proceed with the arrest without delay ... If the prisoner gives the information requested, the examination is quickly terminated; if not, specialists must force his secret from him."[348] However, as one French interrogator acknowledged, it was still difficult to separate the wheat from the chaff: "Just as the interrogation starts they speak abundantly, cite the names of the dead or militants on the lam, indicate the placement of an old arms cache in which we will find only a couple of documents without interest."[349] Furthermore, the FLN hierarchy knew that the men under its command faced torture if captured and moved to exploit the situation by instructing its fighters to give up the names and locations of their more moderate rivals in the *Mouvement national algérien* (MNA).

---

[347] Yaacov Eliav, *Wanted* (Shengold Publishers; 1984), pp. 85–94.

[348] Roger Trinquier, *Modern Warfare: A French View of Counterinsurgency* (Pall Mall Press; 1964), p. 21.

[349] Darius Rejali, *Torture and Democracy* (Princeton University Press; 2007), p. 481.

The French were thus goaded into torturing MNA activists, which only served to push its surviving members into the embrace of the FLN.[350]

One of Roger Trinquier's closest colleagues during the Battle of Algiers was Paul Aussaresses, the intelligence officer who was actually responsible for the torture program instituted by French paratroopers to gather intelligence on the FLN cells operating in the city. In 2001, Aussaresses provoked an outcry in France by publishing a memoir, entitled *Services Spéciaux*, in which he described the harsh treatment he had meted out to the FLN operatives who fell into his hands: "Beatings, electric shocks, and, in particular, water torture, which was the most dangerous technique for the prisoner."[351] This was the "science" Trinquier alluded to in *La Guerre Moderne*. Aussaresses recalled one instance in which a prisoner died while being waterboarded without revealing anything of value with a chilling lack of remorse: "I had no regrets over his death — if I had any regrets, it was because he did not talk."[352] It wasn't the only time he failed to make someone talk — he admitted somewhat grudgingly in his memoir that his victims "would talk either quickly or never."[353] There wasn't much that Aussaresses was not prepared to do to someone unlucky enough to be placed in his custody, so we can take it from a very accomplished torturer that a willingness to torture does not guarantee results. Indeed, one of those apprehended by Aussaresses and his men was the editor of the pro-independence communist newspaper *Alger Républicain*, Henri Alleg. Despite being subjected to electric shocks and water torture, burned, beaten, and drugged with sodium pentothal, Alleg famously did not give up the name of the individual who had hidden him

---

[350] Darius Rejali, *Torture and Democracy* (Princeton University Press; 2007), pp. 481–482.

[351] Paul Aussaresses, *The Battle of the Casbah: Terrorism and Counterterrorism in Algeria 1955–1957* (Enigma Books; 2002), p. 128. The original French title was *Services Spéciaux: Algérie 1955–1957.*

[352] Adam Shatz, The Battle of Algiers, *The Nation*, 18 June 2001, at http://www.thenation.com/article/battle-algiers-0/. Viewed on 30 December 2015.

[353] Paul Aussaresses, *The Battle of the Casbah: Terrorism and Counterterrorism in Algeria 1955–1957* (Enigma Books; 2002), p. 128.

from the authorities.[354] Henri Alleg's account of his treatment in French custody, *La Question*, published in 1958, became a international sensation.

Despite FLN's sly tactics and the bravery of individual captives, torture may have helped to briefly tip the tactical balance in France's favor during the Battle of Algiers, but it is important to note that it did so at a profound strategic cost. The FLN Commander Saadi Yacef later observed: "Actually torture helped the FLN enormously because what it did was expose the real face of the French military ... you could say that Aussaresses was one of the FLN's most important assets because the more he tortured, the more militants we recruited."[355] The use of torture further radicalized Algerian Arabs, it alienated the French public, it contributed to the political collapse of the Fourth Republic, and it eroded good order and discipline within the French army to the point that disgruntled military personnel led two abortive coup attempts in 1958 and 1961. French military veterans also established the nativist terrorist group, the *Organisation de l'armée secrète* (OAS), and later the *Conseil National de la Résistance* (CNR) which attempted to assassinate French President Charles de Gaulle on several occasions.[356] Algeria gained its independence in 1962, following a referendum in which 99.72% of those taking part (most European settlers had already left for France) voted in favor of independence.

Even in the modern era, one can find contemporary accounts of terrorism suspects either holding out against torture or managing to lie under duress. At least 119 detainees were held in so-called CIA 'black sites' — secret detention centers operating clandestinely on the territory of allied nations — in the years following the 9/11 attacks. The US Senate Select Intelligence Committee's *Study of the Central Intelligence Agency's Detention and Interrogation Program* released in 2014 identified thirty-nine detainees as having been subjected to

---

[354] See Henri Alleg, *The Question* (George Braziller Inc; 1958).

[355] Mike German, *Thinking Like a Terrorist: Insights of a Former FBI Undercover Agent* (Potomac Books; 2007), p. 119.

[356] Paul Henissart, *Wolves in the City: The Death of French Algeria* (Simon and Schuster; 1970), pp. 475–476.

Enhanced Interrogation Techniques.[357] Seven of these thirty-nine detainees produced absolutely no intelligence while in CIA custody.[358] Furthermore, the Select Committee's study reported that "while being subject to Enhanced Interrogation Techniques, multiple CIA detainees fabricated information, resulting in faulty intelligence, including terrorist threats the CIA identified as its highest priorities."[359]

Self-proclaimed 9/11 mastermind Khalid Sheikh Mohammed, who was subjected to waterboarding 183 times by the CIA, told delegates from the International Committee of the Red Cross (ICRC) who interviewed him in Guantanamo: "I gave a lot of false information in order to satisfy what I believed the interrogators wished to hear in order to make the ill-treatment stop ... I'm sure that the false information I was forced to invent ... wasted a lot of their time and led to several false red-alerts being placed in the US."[360] Similarly, the Mauritian Guantanamo detainee Mohamedou Ould Slahi has written that in US custody he was subjected to sleep deprivation, death threats, sexual humiliation, threats against his family, immersed in ice for three hours, beaten and forced to drink salt water. In the end, he admitted that he made up information, including a plot to bomb the CN Tower in Toronto, to get his captors to stop. When asked by one interrogator if he was telling the truth about the CN Tower plot he replied: "I don't care as long as you are pleased. So if you want to buy, I am selling."[361]

The fabrication of information by those in custody is always a concern for investigators, but the use of torture introduces an additional dynamic in which the victim is greatly incentivized to invent information to make the abuse stop, or at least secure temporary

---

[357] United States Senate Select Committee on Intelligence, *Findings and Conclusions, Committee Study of the Central Intelligence Agency's Detention and Interrogation Program*, released 9 December 2014, p. xxi.

[358] ibid., p. xi.

[359] ibid., p. xi.

[360] Mark Danner, *US Torture: Voices from the Black Sites*, The New York Review of Books, 9 April 2009.

[361] Spencer Ackerman and Ian Cobain, Guantánamo Diary exposes brutality of US rendition and torture, *The Guardian*, 16 January 2015.

reprieve from pain. Acting on such flawed intelligence can have devastating consequences. Perhaps, the most infamous contemporary example of this concerns the case of Ibn al-Shaykh al-Libi, the former *emir* of *al-Qaeda*'s al Khaldan training camp, who was captured in Afghanistan in November 2001 and rendered to Egypt by the United States in 2002, where, by his own account, "a long list of methods ... which were extreme" were used to make him talk.[362] To get his Egyptian interrogators to stop, al-Libi invented a story that three *al-Qaeda* operatives had visited Saddam Hussein's Iraq to learn about nuclear weapons.[363] This intelligence was passed back to the United States and formed one of the main planks of the case the Bush administration presented to the United Nations Security Council for intervening in Iraq.[364] In reality, no such link existed. Ironically, Ali Soufan reported (and additional sources concur) that al-Libi had begun to cooperate with forward-deployed FBI and NYPD interviewers employing traditional law enforcement techniques shortly after his capture in Afghanistan, providing timely intelligence on the shoe bomber Richard Reid and on several active *al-Qaeda* plots, including a plan to attack the US Embassy in Yemen, before he was turned over to the CIA.[365]

The apogee of the utilitarian argument in favor of torture is the ticking bomb thought-experiment.[366] The torturer Paul Aussaresses summarized the argument in *Services Spéciaux*: "Just think for a moment that you are personally opposed to torture as a matter of principle and that you have arrested a suspect who is clearly involved in preparing a violent attack. The suspect refuses to talk. You choose not to insist. Then the attack takes place and it's extremely bloody. What explanation will you give to the victim's

---

[362] *The Report of the Constitution Project's Task Force on Detainee Treatment* (The Constitution Project; 2013), p. 262.

[363] ibid.

[364] Alan Clarke, *Rendition to Torture* (Rutgers University Press; 2012), p. 154.

[365] *The Report of the Constitution Project's Task Force on Detainee Treatment* (The Constitution Project; 2013), p. 261.

[366] Rod Morgan and Tom Williamson, A critical analysis of the utilitarian case for torture and the situational factors that lead some people to become torturers, in Tom Williamson *et al.* (eds.), *International Developments in Investigative Interviewing* (Routledge; 2009), p. 131.

parents, the parents of a child, for instance, whose body was torn to pieces by the bomb, to justify the fact that you didn't use every method available to force the suspect into talking."[367] As a thought-experiment, the ticking bomb scenario dispenses with all the complications that make the real world so difficult to navigate, and as such it may provoke an interesting philosophical discussion but it has little value as a tool for analyzing public policy. In the fantasy constructed by Aussaresses and his modern peers, you always have the right suspect in custody, the bomb is always real, the suspect always has the information you need, the suspect always talks when tortured, and the information the suspect then provides is always sufficiently accurate and detailed to avert the looming catastrophe. This makes the utilitarian case for using torture difficult to rebut on all but moral grounds, allowing proponents like Roger Trinquier to retort: "It is deceitful to permit artillery or aviation to bomb villages and slaughter women and children, while the real enemy usually escapes, and to refuse interrogation specialists the right to seize the truly guilty and spare the innocent."[368] However, as Bob Brecher points out in *Torture and the Ticking Bomb*, in the real world, none of these variables are quite so certain.[369]

Torture is a very blunt tool. Interviewers rarely have all the facts at their disposal when conducting interviews and a discursive, rapport-based interview technique is much more likely to assist the interviewer successfully navigate complex narratives of which he or she often has limited prior knowledge because it allows the subject to introduce new information into the conversation, and correct misapprehensions and flawed intelligence. Physical abuse creates a very different dynamic. The torturer sets the boundaries of the interrogation and it is driven forward by the knowledge he or she already possesses, and the assumptions he or she has made. The torturer is mostly reduced to asking closed questions, which

---

[367] Paul Aussaresses, *The Battle of the Casbah: Terrorism and Counterterrorism in Algeria 1955–1957* (Enigma Books; 2002), p. 17.

[368] Roger Trinquier, *Modern Warfare: A French View of Counterinsurgency* (Pall Mall Press; 1964), p. 23.

[369] See Bob Brecher, *Torture and the Ticking Bomb* (Blackwell Publishing; 2007).

further confines and restricts his or her exchange with the prisoner. French paratroopers were able to use torture with some initial intelligence-gathering success in the Battle of Algiers because they were seeking very specific information — a name or a location — and closed questions can at least adequately support this objective if the information the interrogator has at the outset of the interrogation is accurate. Even Trinquier admitted: "A profound knowledge of the [terrorist] organization is required. It is useless to ask a funds collector about caches of weapons or bombs."[370] The constraints imposed by a coercive approach are simply not conducive to accurate, nimble, and comprehensive intelligence collection in a poorly understood, complex, and fast-changing environment.

Another question that proponents of torture rarely seem to consider is the point at which an interrogator should stop torturing someone. When does it become obvious, if at all, that the subject being tortured does not have the information the interrogator is seeking, and how badly damaged, both mentally and physically, is the subject likely to be when the abuse finally stops? During the Mau Mau uprising against British colonial rule in 1950s Kenya, Kikuyu internee Gacheche Gathambo was subjected to the brutal screening process developed by the British Army in an attempt to identify Mau Mau sympathizers. He recalled: "One thing I will never forget is screening. Those British were never satisfied; they just wanted more information from me but I didn't have any. They just beat me and beat me."[371] Indeed, much of the abuse that takes place in the context of police and intelligence interviews seems to be driven by the frustration of the investigators themselves — or in the immediate aftermath of an incident by anger at the perpetrators — rather than by any genuine calculation that abuse will result in getting the suspect in front of them to share the information they need. Laurence Alison and Emily Alison have described such interactions as

---

[370] Roger Trinquier, *Modern Warfare: A French View of Counterinsurgency* (Pall Mall Press; 1964), p. 23.

[371] Caroline Elkins, *Imperial Reckoning: The Untold Story of Britain's Gulag in Kenya* (Henry Holt & Co.; 2005), p. 62.

"revenge interrogations".[372] Perhaps, this issue is rarely discussed because, as we have seen, the underlying assumption underpinning the moral universe of most torturers is that the suspect in their custody is guilty of something, and thus on some level deserves what is happening to them, even if it proves to be unproductive. President Donald Trump's statement at a November 2015 campaign rally in Columbus, Ohio, that he would approve waterboarding in a heartbeat because "if it doesn't work, they deserve it anyway for what they do to us" was revealing in its honesty.[373]

Torture is rarely administered in the clinical, impersonal, almost regretful, manner that some of its proponents would have us believe. The authorization of special measures to make a suspect talk often creates an enabling environment for the kind of mindless abuse perpetrated by Charles Graner, Lynndie England, and other members of the 372nd Military Police Company in Abu Ghraib in order to soften prisoners up for interrogation.[374] The patina of legitimacy imparted by superior orders often liberates dark impulses leading to escalating abuse, often of a sexual nature. There is an attraction to acts of wanton cruelty that lurks inside many human beings which can be easily encouraged in permissive circumstances — the social psychologist Philip Zimbardo famously dubbed this phenomenon "the Lucifer Effect".[375] One US Army veteran implicated in detainee abuse in Iraq, Daniel Keller, told the reporter Joshua Philips: "Honestly, a lot of the things that were done to the detainees were ... just someone's idea of a good time ... We were doing things because we could. That's it. And the objective got less and less important."[376]

---

[372] See Laurence Alison and Emily Alison, Revenge versus Rapport: Interrogation, Terrorism, and Torture, *American Psychologist*, Vol. 72, No. 3 (2017).

[373] Ben Jacobs, Donald Trump on waterboarding: "Even if it doesn't work they deserve it", *The Guardian*, 24 November 2015.

[374] Scott Higham and Joe Stephens, Punishment and Amusement: Documents Indicate 3 Photos Were Not Staged for Interrogation, *Washington Post*, 22 May 2004.

[375] See Philip Zimbardo, *The Lucifer Effect: Understanding How Good People Turn Evil* (Random House; 2007).

[376] Joshua Philips, *None of Us Were Like This Before: American Soldiers and Torture* (Verso; 2010), pp. 64–65.

And what happens when the authorities have entirely the wrong person in custody? Counter-terrorism officials are only human and they do make mistakes, but clandestine organizations also tend to be averse to washing their dirty linen in public. In December 2003, German national Khaled el-Masri was plunged into a Hitchcockian nightmare of mistaken identity when he was detained in Macedonia at the CIA's request because the agency had confused him with a wanted *al-Qaeda* suspect with a similar name and wrongfully believed him to be traveling on a false passport. After a month in Macedonian custody, el-Masri was transferred to a CIA black site in Afghanistan known as the "The Salt Pit" where he was subjected to Enhanced Interrogation Techniques.[377] When the CIA realized their error they did not, as one might hope, dismiss the incompetent officials involved and immediately release el-Masri with a handsome apology and meaningful compensation for the profound distress they had caused him and his family. In fact, fearing the exposure of their secret detention program, the CIA initially resisted releasing Khaled el-Masri at all and, when finally instructed to do so in May 2004 by National Security Adviser Condeleezza Rice, they drugged and blindfolded him, and then flew him from Afghanistan and dumped him abandoned, confused and alone on a hilltop in Albania to explain his presence as best he could to the Albanian authorities.

In 2005, German Chancellor Angela Merkel told reporters that the United States had accepted that it had made an "error" in el-Masri's case, and in 2007 German prosecutors filed indictments against thirteen CIA officers allegedly involved in his mistreatment.[378]

---

[377] Human Rights Council, *Joint study on global practices in relation to secret detention in the context of countering terrorism of the Special Rapporteur on the promotion and protection of human rights and fundamental freedoms while countering terrorism, Martin Scheinin; the Special Rapporteur on torture and other cruel, inhuman or degrading treatment or punishment, Manfred Nowak; the Working Group on Arbitrary Detention represented by its Vice-Chair, Shaheen Sardar Ali; and the Working Group on Enforced and Involuntary Disappearances represented by its Chair, Jeremy Sarkin,* A/HRC/13/42, 19 February 2010, p. 62.

[378] Open Society Foundations, *Litigation: El-Masri v. Macedonia,* 23 January 2013 at https://www.opensocietyfoundations.org/litigation/el-masri-v-macedonia. Viewed 10 January 2016.

The Obama administration invoked the state secrets privilege found in US law to block el-Masri from seeking redress in US courts. However, el-Masri was successfully able to bring a case against the government of Macedonia at the European Court of Human Rights for the part it had played in his abduction. The Court ruled in his favor in December 2012 and instructed Macedonia to pay him €60,000 in compensation. If torture is employed, even with the best will in the world and with safeguards firmly in place, it is inevitable that mistakes will be made and some innocent individuals will be tortured. Indeed, the Senate Select Intelligence Committee reported that at least twenty-six of the detainees held in CIA black sites had been "wrongfully detained".[379] As Roger Trinquier acknowledged: "During a period of crisis, we complain of not being better informed. We accuse the people unjustly of concealing the truth or of not giving us the information they possess. And very often, because we have not prepared anything, we will be tempted to obtain by violence information which a well-organized service would have given us without difficulty."[380] Fear, ignorance, power, and lack of accountability make for a very dangerous combination.

Finally, there is the impact of torture on the torturer to consider. Reflecting on his treatment at the hands of Aussaresses' men, Henri Alleg described the *Centre de Tri* where he was held as "a school of perversion for young Frenchmen".[381] It was an accurate description. One of the young paratroopers, Pierre Leulliette, who worked in the detention center subsequently confirmed his insight: "All day, through the floor-boards, we heard their hoarse cries, like those of animals being slowly put to death. Sometimes I think I can still hear them ... I felt myself becoming contaminated. What was more serious, I felt that the horror of all these crimes, our everyday battle, was

---

[379] United States Senate Select Committee on Intelligence, *Findings and Conclusions, Committee Study of the Central Intelligence Agency's Detention and Interrogation Program*, released 9 December 2014, p. xxi.
[380] Roger Trinquier, *Modern Warfare: A French View of Counterinsurgency* (Pall Mall Press; 1964), pp. 35–36.
[381] Alistair Horne, *A Savage War of Peace: Algeria 1954–1962* (History Book Club; 2002), p. 201.

losing force daily in our minds."[382] The FLN commander Saadi Yacef, who was finally captured in September 1957 after a tense stand off with French paratroopers in the Casbah, witnessed a similar process at work with other French soldiers, and later observed: "When a balanced individual tortures someone who is very much like himself, it wounds him in the most sensitive place within a human being — the conscience — and this is a wound which doesn't heal ... Whoever orders torture, practices it, or plots it, becomes involved in a suicidal environment from which he will not escape without some form of atonement."[383]

Decades later, Tony Lagouranis, a US Army interrogator who also participated in detainee abuse in Abu Ghraib, described to the Washington Post the lasting toll it had taken on his psyche, mostly in the intangible daily form of a pervasive sense of dread: "It feels like fear. Of what? I'm not sure. You know what I think it is? You don't know if you'll ever regain a sense of self ... I used to have a strong sense of morals. I was on the side of good. I don't even understand the sides anymore."[384] In recent years, the term "moral injury" has gained increasing currency amongst mental health professionals as therapists seek to counsel troubled individuals like Leulliette and Lagouranis.[385] The pioneering clinicians who first identified this condition defined moral injury as resulting from "perpetrating, failing to prevent, bearing witness to, or learning about acts that transgress deeply held moral beliefs and expectations," and noted that it could have deleterious long-term emotional, psychological, behavioral, spiritual, and social effects.[386] Chilean

---

[382] ibid.

[383] Gary Crowdus, Terrorism and Torture in "The Battle of Algiers": An Interview with Saadi Yacef, *Cineaste Magazine*, Vol. 29, No. 3 (2004), pp. 33–34.

[384] Laura Blumenfeld, The Tortured Lives of Interrogators, *The Washington Post*, 4 June 2007.

[385] Shira Maguen and Brett Litz, Moral Injury in Veterans of War, *PTSD Research Quarterly*, Vol. 23, No. 1 (2012). See also Camillo Mac Bica, *The Invisible Wounds of War*, Truthout, 24 October 2011 at http://www.truth-out.org/opinion/item/3770:the-invisible-wounds-of-war. Viewed 10 January 2016.

[386] Brett Litz, Nathan Stein, Eileen Delaney, Leslie Lebowitz, William Nash, Caroline Silva, and Shira Maguen, Moral injury and moral repair in war Veterans: A preliminary model and intervention strategy, *Clinical Psychology Review*, Vol. 29 (2009), p. 695.

military veterans who served the right-wing dictatorship of Augusto Pinochet had an equally descriptive term for their comrades who had tortured leftist students and aspirant revolutionaries on behalf of the regime — *manchado* — which means stained.[387] Both terms capture an essential truth about torture — very few people leave a torture chamber unscathed regardless of their role inside it.

Darius Rejali's comprehensive study of the use of torture by democracies led him to conclude that "torture follows soldiers back from war", casting a long shadow that blights both the perpetrators themselves and the society they return to.[388] In two groundbreaking works, *Achilles in Vietnam* and *Odysseus in America,* Jonathan Shay has documented how abusive behavior in war can lead to domestic violence, post-combat criminal activity, and a legacy of crippling psychological burdens at home.[389] Joshua Philips in *None of Us Were Like This Before* recorded the struggles endured by members of Battalion 1–68 of the US Army's 4th Infantry Division, a tank unit assigned to detention duties, who were scarred by the memory of abuses they had inflicted on Iraqi detainees. It was an experience that led two members of the unit, Sergeant Adam Gray and Specialist Jonathan Millantz, to take their own lives.[390] Rejali further notes that many former military professionals gravitate naturally in civilian life towards employment in a similarly regimented and close-knit mission-driven profession — law enforcement.[391] He has found that torture sometimes follows in their wake eventually infecting domestic policing, a process he has labeled, borrowing a term from psychoanalysis, "transference".

---

[387] Beth Slovic, Darius Rejali: Reed College Professor and Torture Expert Talks About The Trauma To Interrogators, *Willamette Week*, 26 December 2014.

[388] ibid.

[389] Jonathan Shay, Foreword, in Joshua Philips (eds.), *None of Us Were Like This Before: American Soldiers and Torture* (Verso; 2010). See also Jonathan Shay, *Achilles in Vietnam: Combat Trauma and the Undoing of Character* (Atheneum; 1994) and Jonathan Shay, *Odysseus in America: Combat Trauma and the Trials of Homecoming* (Scribner; 2002).

[390] Joshua Philips, *None of Us Were Like This Before: American Soldiers and Torture* (Verso; 2010).

[391] Beth Slovic, Darius Rejali: Reed College Professor and Torture Expert Talks About The Trauma To Interrogators, *Willamette Week*, 26 December 2014.

Rejali contends that such transference occurred within French society twice in the twentieth century, and twice in America: "The technique we now call 'water boarding' was unknown in American policing until after American soldiers returned from the Philippines in 1905, and by the 1930s it was common throughout the country in police stations large and small."[392] Torture (often involving the application of electric shocks) was also introduced into the Chicago Police Department by veterans who joined the force in the early 1970s.[393] The city investigator, Michael Goldston, identified fifty cases between 1973 and 1986 involving more than thirty officers, many of whom were under the command of decorated Vietnam veteran Jon Burge.[394] The number of identified incidents has only increased with further investigation. Transference can also jump international boundaries, encouraging new abuses overseas. The Director of the Sawasya Center for Human Rights and Anti-Discrimination, Gamal Tajeldeen Hassan, reported the sudden addition of sexual humiliation to the repertoire of interrogators working for the Egyptian security services in the mid-2000s, a technique they themselves labeled "the Abu Ghraib": "Torturers here seem now to compare their methods to what happened in Iraq and say, 'Hey, there are more things that we need to try.'"[395]

For all these reasons and more, the utilitarian debate about torture is not a simple equation in which one guilty man's pain is the price paid to protect the wider population, rather, as the Georgetown Professor of Law and Philosophy David Luban has cogently observed, "it is the debate between the certainty of anguish and the mere possibility of learning something vital and

---

[392] ibid.

[393] Darius Rejali, *Torture and Democracy* (Princeton University Press; 2007) at 192 and Beth Slovic, Darius Rejali: Reed College Professor and Torture Expert Talks About The Trauma To Interrogators, *Willamette Week*, 26 December 2014. See also John Conroy, *Unspeakable Acts, Ordinary People: The Dynamics of Torture* (University of California Press; 2000).

[394] Darius Rejali, *Torture and Democracy* (Princeton University Press; 2007), p. 240.

[395] Joshua Philips, *None of Us Were Like This Before: American Soldiers and Torture* (Verso; 2010), p. 159.

saving lives."[396] The celebrated French author Albert Camus, who was born and raised in Algeria, and was deeply affected by the brutal conflict between the FLN and French settlers, further noted that an act of torture does not occur in a vacuum: "Torture has perhaps saved some, at the expense of honor, by uncovering thirty bombs, but at the same time it arouses fifty new terrorists who, operating in some other way and in some other place, will cause the death of even more innocent people."[397] As we saw in Part II, this is no mere literary flight of fancy, revenge is a well-documented driver of terrorism.

It is now a relatively uncontroversial observation that the US adoption of Enhanced Interrogation Techniques proved to be a profound misstep that generated little intelligence and provided *al-Qaeda* with a propaganda windfall — the US treatment of prisoners in Guantanamo was mentioned thirty-two times in *al-Qaeda* propaganda messages between 2003 and 2010, and by affiliate groups twenty-six times.[398] Abu Mus'ab al-Zarqawi was quick to take advantage of the publicized abuse of detainees in a communiqué entitled *Our Shari'i Stance with Regard to the Government of the Iraqi Karzai*, commenting: "I do not think that any intelligent person remains who believes in the monstrous lie of promised democracy after the revelations of Abu Ghraib and the joke of Guantanamo,"[399] and half a decade later *al-Qaeda* was still belaboring the point. The first issue of the online magazine *Inspire*, published by *al-Qaeda* in the Arabian Peninsula in the summer of 2010, featured an essay by Osama bin Laden in which he specifically referenced "the crimes at Abu Ghraib and Guantanamo, those ugly crimes which shook the conscience of humanity."[400]

---

[396] David Luban, Liberalism, Torture and the Ticking Bomb, in Karen Greenberg (ed.), *The Torture Debate in America* (Cambridge University Press, New York; 2006), pp. 46–47.

[397] Albert Camus, Preface to Algerian Reports, in Albert Camus (ed.), *Resistance, Rebellion and Death* (Modern Library; 1963), p. 84.

[398] James Gordon Meek, Gitmo Fades as "Recruiting Tool for Al-Qaeda", *New York Daily News*, 25 January 2010.

[399] David Cook, *Understanding Jihad* (University of California Press; 2015), p. 223.

[400] Thérèse Postel, How Guantanamo Bay's Existence Helps Al-Qaeda Recruit More Terrorists, *The Atlantic*, 12 April 2013.

Donald Rumsfeld, the US Secretary of Defense at the time of the Abu Ghraib scandal, later told the documentary filmmaker Errol Morris that when he learned about the abuses: "I knew that it would create an advantage for the terrorists, for *al-Qaeda*, and for the people in the insurgency who were out recruiting. They could show that the Americans were treating people badly. It worked against everything we were trying to do."[401] Mark Fallon, a US Naval Criminal Investigation (NCIS) Special Agent who led the task force investigating the 2000 bombing of USS Cole and was a close colleague of the FBI agent Ali Soufan, put it even more starkly, writing in 2014: "It enabled — and, in fact, is still enabling — *al-Qaeda* and its allies to attract more fighters, more sympathizers, and more money."[402]

The use of torture and other forms of cruel, inhuman and degrading treatment by the United States in this period also created significant ethical and legal dilemmas for some of its closest allies, and European support for US counter-terrorism measures was drastically impacted by policies that clearly violated the European Convention on Human Rights.[403] Perhaps, the most dramatic example of this was the *in absentia* conviction of twenty-three US intelligence agents in an Italian court for the role they played in the extraordinary rendition of radical *Imam* Hassan Mustafa Osama Nasr from Milan to Cairo in 2003.[404] Nine Italian officials, including two senior officers of the *Servizio per le Informazioni e la Sicurezza Militare* (SISMI), also faced prosecution in the case although none ultimately went to jail. In 2012, Polish prosecutors charged the former Head of Polish Intelligence, Zbigniew Siemiatkowski, with "unlawfully depriving prisoners of the their liberty" because of the alleged role he played in helping to establish a CIA black site in

---

[401] Errol Morris, *The Known Unknown*, Documentary film (History Films; 2013).

[402] Mark Fallon, Dick Cheney Was Lying About Torture, Politico Magazine, 8 December 2014 at http://www.politico.com/magazine/story/2014/12/torture-report-dick-cheney-110306. html#.VbvcDpNVikp. Viewed 8 January 2016.

[403] Intelligence and Security Committee, *Rendition*, July 2007, pp. 12–13.

[404] See Steve Hendricks, *A Kidnapping in Milan: The CIA on Trial* (W. W. Norton & Company; 2010).

Stare Klejkuty, north-eastern Poland, in 2002–2003.[405] The case is still unresolved at the time of writing. The Polish President at the time, Aleksander Kwasniewski, later ruefully admitted: "We had concerns, but they did not include that the Americans would break the law in a knowing and uncontrolled way."[406] The possibility of being held legally liable for the criminal acts of an allied power has inevitably had a chilling effect on the predisposition of some US allies to work so closely with their American counterparts. The British authorities were surprisingly open about the difficulties that policies such as rendition to torture and the operation of secret prisons have caused the transatlantic "special relationship". The Director General of MI5, Dame Eliza Manningham-Buller, acknowledged in testimony before the Parliamentary Intelligence and Security Committee in 2007: "We certainly now have inhibitions ... greater inhibitions than we once did."[407] Sir John Scarlett, Chief of the Secret Intelligence Service, similarly reported that his agency now sought "credible assurances" that any action taken by the US on the basis of intelligence provided by UK agencies would be "humane and lawful" and that when such assurances were lacking "we cannot provide the information."[408]

Darius Rejali has observed that there are essentially only three reasons for a state to employ torture: "to intimidate, to coerce false confessions, and to gather accurate security information."[409] Torturers may, through the exercise of brutality, successfully achieve the first two of these goals, but the record shows that as a means for collecting accurate information torture is unreliable, and its use comes at great personal, reputational, and moral costs that can have a profoundly detrimental impact on counter-terrorism efforts by undermining popular support for the state, antagonizing key

---

[405] Joanna Berendt and Nicholas Kulish, Polish Ex-Official Charged With Aiding CIA, *The New York Times*, 27 March 2012.

[406] Detention Site Blues: Poles are not happy about CIA torture, but they need America too much to start a row, *The Economist*, 11 December 2014.

[407] Intelligence and Security Committee, *Rendition*, July 2007, p. 47.

[408] ibid.

[409] Darius Rejali, *Torture and Democracy* (Princeton University Press; 2007), p. 23.

constituencies, and alienating much needed allies. This was certainly the experience of the United States, which paid a high price for what comprehensive bipartisan Congressional investigation has since established was an almost entirely an unproductive policy. When President Obama came into office in January 2009, one of his first actions was to issue *Executive Order 13491* to improve the effectiveness of human intelligence gathering and to promote the safe, lawful, and humane treatment of individuals in United States custody.[410] This executive order put a formal end to the use of Enhanced Interrogation Techniques and restricted the intelligence community to methods authorized and listed by the *US Army Field Manual on Human Intelligence Collector Operations* (FM 2-22.3). Speaking at Fordham University in March 2010, Michael Sulick, then Head of the CIA's National Clandestine Service, told his audience: "I don't think we've suffered at all from an intelligence standpoint [because of that decision]."[411]

## Summary

The capacity to effectively interview terrorism suspects is an important tool in any counter-terrorism campaign, but it is important to remember that it is not the only one available to investigators. The recovery of physical evidence, surveillance capabilities, human intelligence, signals intelligence, liaison partnerships, and witness testimony all offer profitable alternative lines of inquiry for both law enforcement and intelligence officers. The "Ticking Bomb" thought-experiment posits a binary challenge — success or failure hinges on whether or not a suspect can be persuaded to talk. In the real world, the challenge facing counter-terrorism officials is both more nuanced and multifaceted.

---

[410] Barack Obama, *Executive Order 13491 — Ensuring Lawful Interrogations*, The White House, 22 January 2009 at https://www.whitehouse.gov/the_press_office/EnsuringLawfulInterrogations. Viewed 9 January 2016.

[411] Jeff Stein, *CIA's top spy: No losses from waterboarding ban*, Washington Post Partner blog, 1 April 2010 at http://voices.washingtonpost.com/spy-talk/2010/04/cias_top_spy_no_losses_from_wa.html. Viewed 8 January 2016.

Torture and abuse more often than not result from a failure of competence and imagination, rather than any genuine necessity. In their influential critical analysis of the utilitarian case for torture, Rod Morgan and Tom Williamson highlighted the corrosive effect such tactics have on the institutions that embrace them: "What begins with tidy intellectual debates about the public interest and lesser evils ends with dirty, hole-in-the-corner contests of will waged in sordid environments by underground officials against demonized *others* whose assumed *evil* and *inhumanity* mean that they do not count in a calculus where, gradually, almost anything goes."[412] Laurence Alison and Emily Alison have warned of a "deskilling effect" that can result when "police and security forces adopt a default position of using coercion and intimidation rather than exploring more sophisticated and potentially productive tactics."[413] Darius Rejali has also emphasized the same point in his work.

Active terrorist threats and post-incident investigations place a tremendous amount of pressure on counter-terrorism officials to get results. Investigators are often working with incomplete information and have little alternative but to fall back on assumptions and speculation to fill the gaps in the initial stages of an investigation. In such circumstances, tunnel vision can take over and mistakes can be made. Upholding the presumption of innocence places a vital check on proceedings. In the aftermath of Andreas Behring Breivik's murderous rampage on the island of Utøya in July 2011, Norwegian Police also took into custody one of the survivors of the attack, Anzor Djoukaev, who was originally from Chechnya, and held him for seventeen hours before releasing him.[414] Djoukaev was held purportedly because police found his calm demeanor suspicious and

---

[412] Rod Morgan and Tom Williamson, A critical analysis of the utilitarian case for torture and the situational factors that lead some people to become torturers, in Tom Williamson *et al.*, (eds.), *International Developments in Investigative Interviewing* (Routledge; 2009), pp. 136–137.

[413] Laurence Alison, Emily Alison, Geraldine Noone, Stamatis Elntib and Paul Christiansen, Why Tough Tactics Fail and Rapport Gets Results: Observing Rapport-Based Interpersonal Techniques (ORBIT) to Generate Useful Information From Terrorists, Psychology, *Public Policy and Law*, Vol. 19, No. 4 (2013), p. 412.

[414] http://www.vg.no/nyheter/innenriks/terrorangrepet-22-juli-etterforskningen/utoeya-offer-17-kastet-paa-glattcelle/a/10097733/.

because he did not much resemble the picture on his Norwegian ID card. One can't help but speculate that his foreign name and the fact that he was born in a region so closely associated with terrorism also likely played a role in arousing their suspicions. Djoukaev's experience perfectly illustrates one of the main flaws with the "Ticking Bomb" thought-experiment. As discussed above, Norwegian police initially had good reason to think they were facing a "Ticking Bomb" scenario and it took seventeen hours to clear Djoukaev as a suspect. In such circumstances, advocates of coercive interrogation methods might easily have condemned a totally innocent man, himself the victim of a terrorist attack, to be tortured.

The PEACE model and other human rights compliant interview techniques have a proven track record of success at producing accurate, detailed, and timely information, and they significantly reduce the chances of a miscarriage of justice like that which befell the Guildford Four. There is ample evidence in the historical record to show that abusive interrogation tactics typically backfire on those who use them. The information gained is often unreliable. Even on the occasions that such techniques do elicit accurate information, the individuals that employ them have nonetheless committed an international offense for which there is no statute of limitations. Their mental health may suffer as a result of the moral injury they have sustained. States that condone torture and abuse, no matter how circuitously, lose considerable legitimacy in their struggle against terrorist threats, often alienating those on whose support they must rely to defeat terrorism. Dr. Karl Roberts has described the manner in which law enforcement interviews are conducted as "an acid test of the professionalism of the police".[415] The same might be said of any other state agency, covert or otherwise. International human rights law exists to protect the innocent and the guilty, but it also protects the integrity of information collected in the interview room, and the integrity of those who collect it.

---

[415] Karl Roberts, Police Interviewing of Criminal Suspects: A Historical Perspective, *Internet Journal of Criminology* (2012), p. 12.

## Detention Regimes

The avowed purpose of police counter-terrorism investigations is the arrest, conviction and subsequent incarceration of suspected terrorists, and the power to deprive an individual of his or her liberty is not one that should be taken lightly. To be cut off from the support of family and friends, to lose one's ability to earn income and advance one's career, to have one's freedom of movement severely restricted, to have even small pleasures denied and one's daily routine imposed from above, can be a devastating, humiliating, and dehumanizing experience. The impact can go far beyond the individual prisoner alone, throwing entire families into despair and destitution. Furthermore, detention also comes in a variety of forms only some of which are actually intended to be retributive in nature: administrative detention, pre-trial detention, punitive detention, and the confinement of prisoners of war. All of these forms are tightly circumscribed by international human rights law and international humanitarian law. A fifth form, arbitrary detention, is outlawed altogether. The manner in which prisoners can be treated and the circumstances in which they can be held are similarly well defined.

From a public policy perspective, incarcerating both suspected and convicted terrorists also presents the state with a number of practical dilemmas, not least that incarceration may not necessarily be the final stage in a militant's political journey. A jailed activist can remain just as influential in jail as at liberty. The leading female Irish republican, Constance Markievicz, who was widely suspected of having shot an unarmed policeman during the 1916 Easter Uprising and whose subsequent death sentence for the part she had played in the rebellion was commuted to life in prison, said of her incarceration by the British authorities: "Sending you to jail is like pulling out all the loud stops on all the speeches you ever made … our arrests carry so much further than speeches."[416] Indeed, many terrorist organizations just see prison as a new front in the struggle. The Provisional IRA produced a quarterly journal written by

---

[416] Charles Townshend, *The Republic: The Fight for Irish Independence* (Allen Lane; 2013), p. 17. Markievicz was released from prison as part of a general amnesty in 1917.

prisoners called *An Glor Gafa*,[417] the Muslim Brotherhood ideologue Sayyid Qutb wrote two of his most influential works — *Milestones*
and *In the Shade of the Qur'an* — while in prison, and incarcerated
members of the Greek anarchist terror group *Synomosía Pyrínon Tis
Fotiás* established the *Nucleus of the Imprisoned Members of the
Organization* to issue communiqués to show that "even in captivity
they have reversed the terms of a defeatist capitulation and have
proudly taken responsibility for their actions, defending the
positions and values of SPF."[418]

Furthermore, prison can have a radicalizing effect on the prisoners themselves and afford terrorist recruiters with an opportunity to
attract fresh blood into their ranks. Che Guevara's mother Celia,
who was incarcerated by the Argentine authorities in April 1963 after
visiting her son in Cuba, insightfully described the prison in which
she was held as "a marvelous deformatory", highlighting the energiz-
ing impact it seemed to have on her fellow political prisoners: "If you
are lukewarm, you become active; if you're active, you become
aggressive; and if you're aggressive, you become implacable."[419]
Sayyid Qutb made a point of meeting new arrivals in the exercise
yard of the Egyptian prison he was held in and engaging them in
discussion.[420] He estimated that he had recruited "perhaps 25" new
inmates to "an unambiguous understanding of the Islamic creed and
its correct application."[421] As we noted in Part II, Irish veterans of the
Easter Uprising held at the Frongoch internment camp in Wales
christened it the University of the Revolution because of the critical
role it played in facilitating the exchange of knowledge between
rebels from across Ireland, thus laying the foundation for the successful Irish War of Independence. Former inmate Joe Stanley
described Frognoch as "a national conference, representative of the
entire country [of Ireland]" and labeled it "one of Britain's biggest

---

[417] The Captive Voice.

[418] George Kassimeris, *Inside Greek Terrorism* (Oxford University Press; 2013), p. 106.

[419] Jon Lee Anderson, *Che Guevara: A Revolutionary Life* (Grove Press; 1997), p. 562.

[420] John Calvert, *Sayyid Qutb and the Origins of Radical Islamism* (Columbia University Press; 2010), p. 234.

[421] ibid.

blunders".[422] Almost a century later, General David Petraeus made a similar observation about the US-run Camp Bucca in Iraq where the nucleus of ISIL, including the group's future leader Abu Bakr al-Baghdadi, came together in the mid-2000s: "These extremists were basically running a terrorist training university, or at least a radicalization school, in our own detention facilities."[423]

Prisons can be hard to govern in the face of determined resistance from radicalized inmates. In the 1990s, Abu Muhammad al-Maqdisi and Abu Mus'ab al-Zarqawi ran a campaign of violence intimidating guards and prisoners alike in Jordan's Suwaya prison.[424] In 2000, Mamdouh Mahmud Salim, a founder member of *al-Qaeda* and a suspect in the 1998 US Embassy bombings, stabbed a prison guard in New York's Metropolitan Correction Center in the eye with a sharpened comb causing him permanent brain damage.[425] In 2007 and 2008, convicted Islamist terrorists in HM Prison Frankland in the north of England led other Muslim prisoners in a series of confrontations with white prison gangs that led to a number of serious injuries and a riot in which prison facilities were significantly damaged.[426] Similar violence has been reported in Australian, Belgian, French, and Italian prisons.[427] Of course, such forms of collective resistance are not limited to Islamist extremist groups. Provisional IRA prisoners exerted so much control over the space they were confined to in Northern Ireland's Maze Prison that they were able to drill with wooden replica weapons, paint political slogans on the walls, and hold both military and political lectures.[428]

---

[422] *Frongoch Internment Camp: University of the Revolution*, TG4, 2007 at https://www.youtube.com/watch?v=6d_Y1xvIiGA.

[423] Peter Taylor, *Comparing the evolution of IS and the IRA*, BBC News, 22 April 2015.

[424] James Brandon, The Danger of Prison: Radicalization in the West, *CTC Sentinel*, Vol. 2, No. 12 (December 2009), p. 2.

[425] Benjamin Weiser, Reputed bin Laden Adviser Gets Life Term in Stabbing, *New York Times*, 31 August 2010.

[426] James Brandon, The Danger of Prison: Radicalization in the West, *CTC Sentinel*, Vol. 2, No. 12 (December 2009), p. 3.

[427] ibid.

[428] Michael Keith and Steven Pile (Eds.), *Geographies of Resistance* (Routledge; 1997), p. 16 and S. Alexander Haslam and Stephen Reicher, When Prisoners Take Over the Prison: A Social Psychology of Resistance, *Personality and Social Psychology Review*, Vol. 16 No. 2 (2012), p. 162.

Although it seems obvious it still bears restating, terrorist prisoners can be extremely dangerous.

Not only do prison authorities have to contend with attempts by hostile inmates to organize and continue the fight, they also have to be vigilant regarding the potential for corruption and abuse on the part of custodial and correctional staff. Professor Philip Zimbardo's 1971 Stanford Prison Experiment into the psychology of imprisonment famously raised troubling questions about the patterns of behavior that can emerge in a correctional context. Zimbardo randomly assigned twenty-four male college students roles as guards or prisoners in a mock prison situated in the basement of Stanford's Psychology Department. Conditions in the 'prison' quickly began to deteriorate as the 'guard force' began to institute arbitrary and demeaning punishments in response to challenges to their authority and other perceived infractions of 'prison' discipline. Zimbardo was forced to abort the experiment only six days in to a planned two-week program.[429] The very nature of detention facilities, and the power differential that exists between custodian and prisoner, creates a permissive environment for abuse, and as we saw in the previous section, such abuses can have a degrading effect on the institutions of law and order, can alienate close allies, and can hand a major propaganda weapon to terrorist groups. Sayyid Qutb, for instance, spent nine years in jail, and the author Lawrence Wright has observed that "stories [of his] suffering in prison have formed a kind of Passion Play for Islamic fundamentalists."[430]

However, for sophisticated counter-terrorism programs, prisons also represent an opportunity to engage with individual terrorists, and even whole groups, while members are incarcerated. Engaging members of any clandestine organization in dialogue is a challenge and typically it is something that states seek to do either remotely — through such mediums as public service announcements, propaganda broadcasts, and more recently social media platforms — or

---

[429] *The Stanford Prison Experiment: A simulation study on the psychology of imprisonment* at http://www.prisonexp.org.

[430] Lawrence Wright, *The Looming Tower: Al-Qaeda and the Road to 9/11* (New York: Vintage Books, 2007), p. 33.

through gatekeepers — terrorist negotiators or political parties closely allied to their goals, such as the Irish republican party *Sinn Féin* or the former Basque nationalist party *Herri Batasuna*.[431] Both approaches are pretty unsatisfactory, either being too unfocused or too easily disrupted by potential spoilers. By way of contrast, as we will see in the section on deradicalization programs below, a captive prison population can be engaged directly. In short, detention facilities can present the authorities with significant challenges, and expose them to serious reputational risks, but they also play an indispensable role in counter-terrorism operations by removing dangerous individuals from public circulation, and in doing so can create opportunities for dialogue and intelligence gathering. A well run prison facility is a tremendous asset, a badly run one is a major liability.

## The right to liberty and due process

The right to liberty is well established in human rights law. It is enshrined in Article 3 of the Universal Declaration of Human Rights and in Article 9 of the International Covenant of Civil and Political Rights, which states: "Everyone has the right to liberty and security of person. No one shall be subjected to arbitrary arrest or detention. No one shall be deprived of his liberty except on such grounds and in accordance with such procedure as are established by law." The right to liberty is also protected by the principal regional human rights instruments, and the International Court of Justice found in the *Case Concerning United States Diplomatic and Consular Staff in Tehran* (ICJ; 1980) that it was even protected by the United Nations Charter itself.[432] However, it should also be noted that the right to liberty is not an absolute right — it is a limited right. An individual can be deprived of liberty in specific circumstances according to procedures established by law, but any

---

[431] *Herri Batasuna* (Popular Unity) was outlawed by the Spanish Supreme Court in 2003 and dissolved itself in January 2013.

[432] *Case Concerning United States Diplomatic and Consular Staff in Tehran (United States of America v. Iran)*, ICJ Reports 1980, p. 42, para 91.

arrest or detention must be carried out by a competent official authorized by law for that purpose.

Any individual deprived of his or her liberty without legal basis is considered under international human rights law to have been detained arbitrarily. The drafters of the ICCPR made it clear in their preparatory work that "arbitrariness" should not simply be equated with "unlawful" but should rather be interpreted more broadly "to include elements of inappropriateness, injustice, lack of predictability, and due process of law."[433] The prohibition on arbitrary detention can be found in every major international and regional human rights treaty, and the UN Working Group on Arbitrary Detention has found this prohibition to be a universally binding norm of customary international law.[434] The UN Working Group also identified a number scenarios in which detention could be considered arbitrary including where it is clearly impossible to invoke any legal basis for the deprivation of liberty, where the deprivation of liberty results from domestic legal provisions that are incompatible with fundamental rights and freedoms guaranteed under international human rights law,[435] where the failure to observe international fair trial norms is of sufficient gravity to give any sentence an arbitrary character, where prolonged administrative detention of asylum seekers, immigrants or refugees occurs without review of remedy,[436] and where deprivation of liberty is driven by discrimination on such grounds as race, religion, gender, sexual orientation, political opinion, or social status.[437] The UN Human Rights Committee has identified further "egregious" examples of

---

[433] Report of the Working Group on Arbitrary Detention (A/HRC/22/44), Part III, Deliberation No. 9 concerning the definition and scope of "arbitrary deprivation of liberty" under customary international law, 24 December 2012, para 61.

[434] ibid., para 51.

[435] Specifically: equality before the law, freedom of movement, the right to seek asylum, freedom of thought, conscience and religion, freedom of opinion and expression, freedom of peaceful assembly, and the right to take part in government.

[436] See Human Rights Committee, *General Comment No. 35 on Article 9 (Liberty and security of person)*, 2014, para 18.

[437] Arbitrary deprivation of liberty motivated by discrimination on grounds analogous to those found in Article 1(a)(2) of the 1951 Convention relating to the Status of Refugees may constitute the basis for a legitimate claim to refugee status and the extension of international protection.

arbitrary detention including the detention of family members of an alleged criminal who are not themselves accused of any wrong-doing, the holding of hostages, and arrests for the purpose of extorting bribes or other similar criminal purposes.[438] No derogation from the customary international law prohibition on arbitrary detention is possible.[439]

In the past fifteen years, one form of arbitrary detention has attracted more attention than any other: secret detention.[440] The United Nations *Joint Study on Global Practices in Relation to Secret Detention in the Context of Countering Terrorism* describes "secret detention" as being defined by three key elements: State authorities acting in their official capacity, or other persons acting with the authorization, consent, support or acquiescence of the state, deprive persons of their liberty; the person deprived of liberty is not permitted any contact with the outside world including, for example, with family, independent lawyers or non-governmental organizations; the detaining authority denies, refuses to confirm or deny, or actively conceals the fact that the person is deprived of his or her liberty hidden from the outside world, or refuses to provide or actively conceals information about the fate or whereabouts of the detainee.[441] Such practices have a long history — Adolf Hitler introduced the infamous *Nacht und Nebel*[442] Decree in 1941 authorizing his forces to combat resistance to German occupation (which

---

[438] See Human Rights Committee, *General Comment No. 35 on Article 9 (Liberty and security of person)*, 2014, para 16.

[439] Report of the Working Group on Arbitrary Detention (A/HRC/22/44), Part III, Deliberation No. 9 concerning the definition and scope of "arbitrary deprivation of liberty" under customary international law, 24 December 2012, para 50 and Human Rights Committee, General Comment No. 29 on Article 4 (States of Emergency), U.N. Doc. CCPR/C/21/Rev.1/Add.11 (2001), para 13(b).

[440] *Joint Study on Global Practices in Relation to Secret Detention in the Context of Countering Terrorism of the Special Rapporteur on the promotion and protection of human rights and fundamental freedoms while countering terrorism, Martin Scheinin; the Special Rapporteur on torture and other cruel, inhuman or degrading treatment or punishment, Manfred Nowak; the Working Group on Arbitrary Detention; and the Working Group on Enforced and Involuntary Disappearances*, A/HRC/13/42, 19 February 2010, p. 2.

[441] ibid., pp. 11–12.

[442] Night and Fog.

the Nazis often characterized as terrorism) using "measures by which the relatives of the criminal and the population do not know [the prisoner's] fate."[443] The Argentine National Commission on the Disappeared (CONADEP) reported the military *junta* that fought Marxist terrorism and revolutionary activity in the Dirty War of 1976–1983 operated at least 651 secret detention centers which held tens of thousands detainees over the duration of the conflict,[444] and at least six other Latin American regimes instituted similar policies during this period.[445] But it is the far flung network of secret prisons, black sites, operated by the US Central Intelligence Agency in its struggle against *al-Qaeda* that has attracted the most detailed international legal scrutiny.

President George W. Bush signed a covert action Memorandum of Notification on 17 September 2001 granting the CIA a number of "unprecedented" counter-terrorism authorities, including to covertly capture and detain individuals "posing a continuing, serious threat of violence or death to US persons and interests or planning terrorist activities."[446] The CIA slowly began to establish secret detention facilities in different countries around the globe in 2002, and in January 2003 the CIA Director George Tenet issued formal guidelines on their operation.[447] The US Senate Select Intelligence Committee has identified at least 119 detainees who

---

[443] The quote is from the implementation letter written by Field Marshall Wilhelm Keitel, Chief of the German Armed Forces High Command. See United States Holocaust Memorial Museum, *Holocaust Encyclopedia*, at http://www.ushmm.org/wlc/en/article.php?ModuleId=10007465. Viewed 20 February 2016.

[444] Antonius Robben, *Political Violence and Trauma in Argentina* (University of Pennsylvania Press; 2007), p. 404.

[445] Brazil, Chile, El Salvador, Paraguay, Peru and Uruguay. See Joint Study on Global Practices in Relation to Secret Detention in the Context of Countering Terrorism of the Special Rapporteur on the promotion and protection of human rights and fundamental freedoms while countering terrorism, Martin Scheinin; the Special Rapporteur on torture and other cruel, inhuman or degrading treatment or punishment, Manfred Nowak; the Working Group on Arbitrary Detention; and the Working Group on Enforced and Involuntary Disappearances, A/HRC/13/42, 19 February 2010, pp. 28–33.

[446] United States Senate Select Committee on Intelligence, *Findings and Conclusions, Committee Study of the Central Intelligence Agency's Detention and Interrogation Program*, released 9 December 2014, p. xviii.

[447] ibid., p. xviii.

were held in CIA black sites and, while the Senate Committee did not reveal the actual locations of any of the detention facilities, the Bureau of Investigative Journalism in the United Kingdom was able to match the codenames used by the Senate to physical sites in Afghanistan, Guantanamo, Lithuania, Morocco, Poland, Romania, and Thailand.[448] The largest black site — the Salt Pit in Afghanistan (codenamed Cobalt by the Senate Committee) — operated between September 2002 and April 2004 and consisted of twenty cells that housed at least sixty-four detainees over its operational lifetime.[449] The US did not formally acknowledge the existence of the black site program until September 2006, when the remaining detainees were transferred to the main US military-run detention facility in Guantanamo Bay.

The revelations surrounding the US black site program led directly to the UN's *Joint Study on Global Practices in Relation to Secret Detention*. In addition to putting the US program under the microscope, the UN experts found that secret detention in connection with counter-terrorism opertions was a "serious problem" in all regions of the world, identifying specific cases in Africa, Asia, Central Asia, the Middle East, and Europe.[450] The experts opined that a state could be considered complicit in an act of secret detention if it took place at its request, or if it participated at any stage in the clandestine apprehension, rendition, or transfer of an individual to such a facility. They also found that any country that seeks to take advantage of the secret detention of an individual by another state by submitting questions to that state, or otherwise soliciting or receiving information derived from this unlawful

---

[448] ibid., and https://www.thebureauinvestigates.com/2015/10/14/revealed-cia-torture-black-sites-history-boom-bust/. Viewed 20 February 2016.

[449] See https://www.thebureauinvestigates.com/2015/10/14/revealed-cia-torture-black-sites-history-boom-bust/. Viewed 20 February 2016.

[450] *Joint Study on Global Practices in Relation to Secret Detention in the Context of Countering Terrorism of the Special Rapporteur on the promotion and protection of human rights and fundamental freedoms while countering terrorism, Martin Scheinin; the Special Rapporteur on torture and other cruel, inhuman or degrading treatment or punishment, Manfred Nowak; the Working Group on Arbitrary Detention; and the Working Group on Enforced and Involuntary Disappearances*, A/HRC/13/42, 19 February 2010, p. 89.

activity, could be considered to be complicit in it.[451] The study concluded, "international law clearly prohibits secret detention, which violates a number of human rights and humanitarian law norms that may not be derogated from under any circumstances" and cautioned that "states of emergency, international wars and the fight against terrorism — often framed in vaguely defined legal provisions — constitute an 'enabling environment' for secret detention."[452]

The United States government has so far largely managed to avoid being held accountable for its black site program, but for several of the countries that provided material support to the program it has been a different story. In the cases of *Al Nashiri v. Poland* (ECtHR; 2014) and *Husayn (Abu Zubaydah) v. Poland* (ECtHR; 2014), the European Court of Human Rights considered the role played by the Polish government in enabling the CIA to establish the secret detention facility in Stare Kiejkuty where Abd al-Rahim al-Nashiri, the alleged *al-Qaeda* commander behind the October 2000 bombing of the USS Cole, and Zayn al-Abidin Muhammad Husayn, thought to have been a member of Osama bin Laden's inner circle, were secretly held for six months and ten months respectively without charge.[453] The Court found that the Polish government had violated the prohibition on torture, the right to liberty and security, the right to a fair trial, the right to privacy, and the right to an effective remedy. Poland was ordered to pay both men damages of €100,000. At the time of writing, further cases are pending before the European Court against both Lithuania (*Abu Zubaydah v. Lithuania*) and Romania (*Al Nashiri v. Romania*).[454]

Every instance of secret detention also amounts to enforced disappearance as defined by the International Convention for the Protection of All Persons from Enforced Disappearance: "The arrest, detention, abduction or any other form of deprivation of liberty ... followed by a refusal to acknowledge the deprivation of liberty or by

---

[451] ibid., p. 82.

[452] ibid., p. 129.

[453] European Court of Human Rights, *Al Nashiri v. Poland*, Application no. 28761/11, Judgment, 24 July 2014 and European Court of Human Rights, *Husayn (Abu Zubaydah) v. Poland*, Application no. 7511/13, Judgment, 24 July 2014.

[454] European Court of Human Rights, Press Unit, *Factsheet — Secret detention sites*, June 2015.

concealment of the fate or whereabouts of the disappeared person."[455] Any instance of secret detention would likely also amount to cruel, inhuman and degrading treatment, and thus could be considered an international crime. If resorted to in a widespread or systematic manner, secret detention may even reach the threshold of a crime against humanity.[456] Secret detention is also typically closely linked with the practice of torture.

The most problematic legitimate form of detention often used in the context of counter-terrorism operations is administrative detention — also known as security detention or internment — in which the incarceration of an individual or individuals is authorized by law in exceptional circumstances without trial or conviction, and with no intention of bringing a prosecution against the individual or individuals concerned. The UN Office of the High Commissioner for Human Rights has described this practice as "highly controversial" and the UN Working Group on Arbitrary Detention has expressed particular concern about the frequent use of such measures by states, often for very long periods of time and without any opportunity for detainees to challenge the legality of their detention or the factual grounds on which it has been authorized.[457]

However, despite such concerns, it is clear that international law nevertheless acknowledges that a need to impose administrative detention measures may exist in certain circumstances. In the case of *Cámpora Schweizer v. Uruguay* (HRC; 1982), the UN Human Rights Committee found that "administrative detention may not be

---

[455] Article 2, International Convention for the Protection of All Persons from Enforced Disappearance.

[456] *Joint Study on Global Practices in Relation to Secret Detention in the Context of Countering Terrorism of the Special Rapporteur on the promotion and protection of human rights and fundamental freedoms while countering terrorism, Martin Scheinin; the Special Rapporteur on torture and other cruel, inhuman or degrading treatment or punishment, Manfred Nowak; the Working Group on Arbitrary Detention; and the Working Group on Enforced and Involuntary Disappearances*, A/HRC/13/42, 19 February 2010, p. 2.

[457] Office of the High Commissioner for Human Rights in cooperation with the International Bar Association, Professional Training Series No. 9, *Human Rights in the Administration of Justice: A Manual on Human Rights for Judges, Prosecutors and Lawyers* (2003), Chap. 5, Sec. 4.7 and Human Rights Council, *Report of the Working Group on Arbitrary Detention*, A/HRC/27/47, 30 June 2014, para 28.

objectionable in circumstances where the person concerned constitutes a clear and serious threat to society which cannot be contained in any other manner."[458] In 1994, the Human Rights Committee offered specific guidance on the use of administrative detention for "reasons of public security" in its *General Comment No. 8* noting that it must not be applied in an arbitrary manner, and must rather be based on grounds and procedures established by law, information on the reason requiring detention must be given, judicial control of the detention must be available, and a mechanism for redress must exist should a breach of the ICCPR occur.[459]

The Human Rights Committee returned to this subject in 2014 in *General Comment No. 35* and, having noted the "severe risks" of abuse presented by the introduction of "security detention", refined its advice still further: "If under the most exceptional circumstances, a present, direct and imperative threat is invoked to justify detention of persons considered to present such a threat, the burden of proof lies on States Parties to show that the individual poses such a threat and that it cannot be addressed by alternative measures, and this burden increases with the length of the detention. States Parties also need to show that detention does not last longer than absolutely necessary, that the overall length of possible detention is limited, and that they fully respect the guarantees provided for by Article 9 in all cases. Prompt and regular review by a court or other tribunal possessing the same attributes of independence and impartiality as the judiciary is a necessary guarantee for these conditions, as is access to independent legal advice, preferably selected by the detainee, and disclosure to the detainee of, at least, the essence of the evidence on which the decision is taken."[460]

---

[458] Human Rights Committee, *D. A. Cámpora Schweizer v. Uruguay*, Communication No. 66/1980, in UN doc A/38/40, 12 October 1982, para 18(1).

[459] Human Rights Committee, *General Comment 8, Article 9 (right to liberty and security of persons)*, Compilation of General Comments and General Recommendations Adopted by Human Rights Treaty Bodies, U.N. Doc. HRI/GEN/1/Rev.1, 1994, p. 8.

[460] Human Rights Committee, *General Comment No. 35: Article 9 (Liberty and security of person)*, CCPR/C/GC/35, 16 December 2014, p. 15.

If we accept that the lawful authority exists in international law to order administrative detentions in the context of counter-terrorism operations, albeit carefully circumscribed by human rights protections, the question still remains as to whether or not the introduction of internment is likely to be a productive public policy decision, and on that point history certainly offers a number of cautionary examples. As the establishment of internment camps is typically a response to a major crisis, they are often created in conditions of confusion and uncertainty, and the absence of due process protections during the cycle of apprehension and incarceration means that mistakes are inevitably made in the identification of terrorist suspects. As a result, internment camps can quickly become symbols of injustice, breeding grounds for militancy, and, the record suggests, their introduction may only serve to exacerbate an already combustible situation.

On 29 June 1946, the British Army launched Operation Agatha in response to the murder of twenty-one British soldiers over the preceding six months with the intention of interning the leadership of the Jewish community in Palestine, both extremists associated with *Irgun* and LEHI, and more moderate Zionist figures. The event became known within the Jewish community as the Black Sabbath. By the time the operation wound up two days later, 2,718 leading Zionists had been taken into custody, but, as more active militants had already gone underground, these were mostly figures on the more moderate end of the political spectrum.[461] Although the operation was publicly hailed as a success, internally, local British commanders acknowledged that "the operation has temporarily lost us what friends amongst the Jews we still had."[462] The impact on the strained relationship between the Mandate government and the Jewish community was indeed dramatic, as the newspaper *Ha'aretz* reported: "This is the first time that the public cannot escape the feeling that the bridges between us and Britain have been blown up and that the action taken by the Government affected not only this

---

[461] Bruce Hoffman, *Anonymous Soldiers: The Struggle for Israel, 1917–1947* (Knopf; 2015), p. 280.
[462] ibid., p. 283.

or that political scheme but the very foundation of the idea of a National Home."[463] Jewish officials resigned *en masse* from thirty-seven of the thirty-nine government committees on which they served, and US President Harry Truman released a joint statement with the American members of the Jewish Agency's executive committee condemning the British action.[464] British Intelligence reported an upsurge in recruitment for *Irgun*, including some experienced partisans who had fought in Central and Eastern Europe.[465] US Intelligence reported a dramatic increase in financial donations to *Irgun* from American Jews.[466]

Furthermore, the introduction of internment led directly to the lifting of the veto on *Irgun*'s plan to attack the nerve center of British civil and military power in Jerusalem, the King David Hotel, which had been imposed on Menachem Begin by the *Haganah* in April 1946.[467] Begin recorded in his memoirs that following the detentions the Jewish underground had acknowledged the pressing need to address the intimidatory effect that Operation Agatha was having on the wider Jewish community, and to demonstrate that despite the expansive sweep of the operation the British Army was not an insurmountable foe: "Defeatism raised its deathly head. People had begun to question our ability to fight the British regime ... These questions were pregnant with danger ... We realized that Jewish self-confidence could be restored only by a successful counter attack."[468] So, on 22 July 1946, *Irgun* operatives planted 700 lbs of high explosive, concealed in seven milk churns, in the basement of the King David Hotel. Ninety-one people were killed in the ensuing blast, including forty-one Arabs, twenty-eight Britons, and seventeen Jews.[469] The vast majority were civilians, and twelve were women. This was the highest death toll of any terrorist attack to date

---

[463] ibid., p. 282.

[464] ibid., p. 284.

[465] ibid., p. 285.

[466] ibid., p. 284.

[467] ibid., pp. 291–292.

[468] Menachem Begin, *The Revolt: Story of the Irgun* (Steimatzky's Agency Ltd.; 1977), p. 217.

[469] Bruce Hoffman, *Anonymous Soldiers: The Struggle for Israel, 1917–1947* (Knopf; 2015), p. 298.

anywhere in the world, a grim marker that stood unchallenged for another thirty-seven years, until the US Marine Barracks bombing in Beirut.[470]

Over the course of the twentieth century, the British also introduced internment for suspected members of outlawed Irish terrorist organizations on four separate occasions. Twice, during the Second World War and the IRA's Cross-Border Campaign in the late 1950s and early 1960s, it was introduced with the full support of the Irish government against what on each occasion was a fringe element within Irish society that enjoyed little popular support on the island, and it was successful in helping to reduce terrorist violence. However, on the other two occasions, after the 1916 Easter Uprising and during early years of The Troubles, when the measure was employed against significantly more substantial threats, it was an unmitigated disaster, damaging the legitimacy of the British government and enabling aspirant terrorists to organize while radicalizing others. Internment was not a decisive factor in the successful defeat of terrorist campaigns in the first two examples, but its introduction played a key role in the failure of British counter-terrorism efforts in the other two periods. This was especially true during The Troubles.

In the fall of 1971, faced with escalating violence in the Province, the Unionist Prime Minister of Northern Ireland, Brian Faulkner, persuaded the British government that the introduction of internment might bring the situation under control. On 9 August 1971, British troops mounted a series of raids across Northern Ireland and detained 342 IRA suspects. The operation, codenamed Demetrius, was characterized by poor and out-of-date intelligence which resulted in many individuals being detained who had long since retired from active involvement with republican terrorist groups.[471] Other detainees were politically active but had no connection to terrorism whatsoever, as the Provisional IRA volunteer Maria McGuire recalled: "The British also picked up civil rights activists and other figures who were popular in the Catholic population,

---

[470] ibid.

[471] Peter Taylor, *Provos: The IRA and Sinn Fein* (Bloomsbury; 1997), p. 93 and Paul Wilkinson, *Terrorism and the Liberal State* (Macmillan; 1986).

even though they may have actively and publicly opposed the use of force. The anger that these arrests in particular caused was of great help to the Provisionals. The British could have thought of no more effective way of helping to recruit members of the republican movement if they had tried."[472] Joe Cahill, then Chief of Staff of the Provisional IRA and a prominent target of Operation Demetrius, taunted the authorities by surfacing to hold a press conference in Belfast at which he claimed only thirty of the men who had been detained were actually members of the Provisional IRA.[473] The government was increasingly embarrassed by revelations about the paucity of the intelligence underpinning internment — 105 of the initial 342 detainees were released immediately after questioning once it had been established that they posed no security threat.[474] This intelligence did not appear to improve over time, and by November 1971, 508 of the 980 suspects detained had been released.[475]

Nationalist anger at internment resulted in an immediate upsurge in violence against the security forces in Northern Ireland. Twenty-seven people had been killed in the first eight months of 1971, which prompted the introduction of internment, but in the four remaining months of the year 147 people were killed. 467 were killed in 1972 as a result of terrorist action.[476] The number of terrorist bombings in the Province increased dramatically from around 150 in 1970, to 1,382 in 1972.[477] In the words of a former British Intelligence officer, Frank Steele, who served in Northern Ireland as a secret liaison between the British government and the Provisional IRA during this period: "[Internment] barely damaged the

---

[472] Maria McGuire, *To Take Arms: A Year in the Provisional IRA* (MacMillan; 1973), p. 23.

[473] Conflict Archive on the Internet (CAIN), *Internment — A Chronology of the Main Events*, at http://cain.ulst.ac.uk/events/intern/chron.htm.

[474] Sir Edmund Compton, *Report of the Enquiry into Allegations against the Security Forces of Physical Brutality in Northern Ireland arising out of events on the 9th August 1971* (HMSO; November 1971).

[475] ibid.

[476] Philip Thomas, Emergency and Anti-Terrorism Power: 9/11: USA and UK, *Fordham International Law Journal*, Vol. 26 (April 2003), pp. 1223–1224.

[477] John Newsinger, *British Counter-insurgency from Palestine to Northern Ireland* (Palgrave; 2002), p. 167.

Provisional IRA's command structure and led to a flood of recruits, money and weapons."[478] It is hard to imagine anyone at the time who would have been better placed to know. Another side effect was that internment created an opportunity for a new, more radical, generation of republican activists to come to the fore, including the future Deputy First Minister of Northern Ireland, Martin McGuinness: "The day before internment I was a nobody. The day after internment I still regarded myself as a nobody. I did not know what to do. People credit you with this great military mind but it was a debacle, a mish-mash. A large number of young people who had joined the movement wanted to be organized. I wanted to be as organized as they did. Unfortunately for me many of them felt I could do a good job. So that is what I did."[479]

Internment was to continue in Northern Ireland until 5 December 1975 by which time a total of 1,981 people had been detained, the vast majority of them from the Catholic community.[480] The British Army estimated that up to 70% of the long-term internees became re-involved in terrorist acts after their release so the measure clearly did little to deter committed activists.[481] As Maria McGuire noted: "We soon discovered that men who have been held in prison without trial for six months do not forget the experience quickly. We also found that many of the men released were coming home with a far greater political consciousness than when they had been arrested. In [the British internment camp] Long Kesh, of course, there was nothing to do but talk."[482] The British government finally took the decision to discard the power of internment from the Northern Ireland (Emergency Provisions) Bill in January 1998. Announcing the decision, the Junior Northern Ireland Minister Lord Dubs told the House of Lords: "The Government

---

[478] Peter Taylor, *Provos: The IRA & Sinn Féin* (Bloomsbury; 1997), pp. 129–130.

[479] Kevin Toolis, *Rebel Hearts* (St. Martin's Griffin; 1997), p. 304.

[480] Conflict Archive on the Internet (CAIN), *Internment — A Chronology of the Main Events*, at http://cain.ulst.ac.uk/events/intern/chron.htm.

[481] Paul Wilkinson, *Terrorism and the Liberal State* (New York; New York University Press; 1986), p. 162.

[482] Maria McGuire, *To Take Arms: A Year in the Provisional IRA* (MacMillan; 1973), p. 106.

have [sic] long held the view that internment does not represent an effective counter-terrorism measure ... The power of internment has been shown to be counter-productive in terms of the tensions and divisions which it creates. Quite apart from any judgment about its appropriateness in principle, the fact is that internment has not worked in practice. Indeed many would say it was a disaster when last used in the 1970s."[483] In his groundbreaking study of micromobilization within the ranks of the Provisional IRA, Robert White wholeheartedly concurred with Lord Dubs' assessment, noting: "After internment, many peaceful protestors turned to political violence."[484] The cost–benefit analysis does not come down well in the power's favor.

Despite the understandable focus of human rights defenders on the threat of arbitrary detention and the kind of detention regimes outlined above, it must be acknowledged that by far the most common method by which a suspected terrorist has been subjected to detention over the past 150 years is within the criminal justice system, a process that in most terrorism cases consists of three distinct phases: arrest, pre-trial confinement, and post-conviction incarceration. An individual can only be lawfully detained when there is a reasonable suspicion that he or she has committed an offence. There are several elements to this standard: The offence must exist in national law; the objective in detaining the individual must be to bring him or her before a competent legal authority; and there must be objective grounds for suspecting the individual committed the offence in question — a prior history of related previous offences is not sufficient. The reasonableness of the suspicion on which an arrest must be based is an essential safeguard against arbitrary arrest and detention.[485] The European Court of Human Rights has used the following formula: "A 'reasonable suspicion' presupposes the existence of facts or information which would satisfy an

---

[483] House of Lords Debates, *Hansard*, Vol. 584 (12 January 1998), pp. 889–890.

[484] Robert White, From Peaceful Protest to Guerrilla War: Micromobilization of the Provisional Irish Republican Army, *American Journal of Sociology*, Vol. 94 No. 6 (May 1989), p. 1289.

[485] United Nations Office on Drugs and Crime, *Handbook on Criminal Justice Responses to Terrorism*, Criminal Justice Handbook Series (2009), p. 55.

objective observer that the person concerned may have committed the offence. What may be regarded as 'reasonable' will, however, depend upon all the circumstances."[486]

International human rights law also establishes clear standards for the proper execution of an arrest. Article 9(2) of the ICCPR states: "Anyone who is arrested shall be informed, at the time of arrest, of the reasons for his arrest and shall be promptly informed of any charges against him." The UN Body of Principles for the Protection of All Persons under Any Form of Detention or Imprisonment establishes the standard that any arrest should be carried out by the competent authorities, that details of the arrest should be recorded, and that the detainee must be promptly informed of the reasons and grounds for the arrest — that is to say, the cause of the accusation and the nature of the charge in question — in a language he or she understands.[487] This latter requirement can also be found in the ICCPR.[488] The UN Human Rights Committee has explained that citing "state security" (and by extension other such similar formulations) is not a sufficient explanation for detention.[489]

It is a fundamental tenet of international human rights law that no one should be detained without prompt judicial or administrative review of whether or not legitimate grounds exist for their detention. This includes detention for terrorism and national security related offenses, and even psychiatric referrals. The detainee must be given the opportunity to challenge the circumstance of his or her detention. Article 9(4) of the ICCPR states: "Anyone who is deprived of his liberty by arrest or detention shall be entitled to take proceedings before a court, in order that that court may decide without delay on the lawfulness of his detention and order his release if the detention is not lawful." The right to prompt and

---

[486] European Court of Human Rights, *Fox, Campbell and Hartley v. the United Kingdom*, 30 August 1990, paras 32 and 34.

[487] Human Rights Committee, General Comment No. 32, July 2007, p. 31.

[488] Article 14(3).

[489] *Ilombe and Shandwe v. Democratic Republic of the Congo*, Human Rights Committee Communication No. 1177/2003, UN Doc CCPR/C/86/D/1177/2003, 2006, p. 6.2.

effective access to legal counsel is protected in all major universal and regional human rights treaties. The ICCPR also guarantees a defendant the right to have legal assistance assigned to him or her by the court and that such assistance should be provided free if he or she does not have sufficient means to pay for it.[490]

In the highly charged atmosphere of a terrorism trial, it is extremely important that government officials continue to treat the defense counsel as professionally and dispassionately as they would in any other case. The *UN Basic Principles on the Role of Lawyers* note that "lawyers shall not be identified with their clients or their clients' causes as a result of discharging their functions."[491] Government authorities have an obligation to ensure that defense counsel are free to perform all of their professional functions without intimidation, harassment or improper interference, and that they do not suffer adverse consequences for any action taken in accordance with their professional obligations.[492] In the case of foreign nationals detained in connection with a terrorism offense, most international counter-terrorism instruments also enshrine a right to consular assistance, which is a general principle established by the Vienna Convention on Consular Relations (1963).[493] In the case of a stateless person, such an individual should have right to call upon the assistance of a consular official from the country in which he or she resides. This general principle encompasses both a right to communicate with a consular representative "without delay" when taken into custody, and a right to be visited in detention by such an official should this be requested.

International jurisprudence does not set a specific time limit within which states must inform an accused individual of the charges he or she faces beyond the injunction that it should be done "promptly". However, in *Brogan and Others v. United Kingdom* (ECtHR; 1998), the European Court of Human Rights provided

---

[490] Article 14(3)(d).

[491] *UN Basic Principles on the Role of Lawyers adopted by the Eighth United Nations Congress on the Prevention of Crime and the Treatment of Offenders* (1990), p. 18.

[492] ibid., p. 16.

[493] Article 36.

some guidance on what does not meet this standard finding that the detention without charge of four individuals suspected of links to terrorism for more than four days and six hours violated the promptness standard.[494] The Court revisited the issue in the case of *Shayan Baram Saadi v. United Kingdom* (ECtHR; 2008) finding on this occasion that a delay of only three days and four hours before the reason for detention was communicated to a detained person could not be considered prompt.[495]

In 2006, the United Kingdom introduced controversial legislation to extend the maximum period of detention without charge in connection with terrorism-related offenses from seven days to twenty-eight days.[496] The British government explained this decision in the following terms: "The principal usefulness of the power ... [is that] it allows arrests to be made at an earlier stage than if there was a requirement for suspicion of a specific offence."[497] Attempts by the government to extend this period of detention still further failed and in 2011 the maximum length of detention was reduced back down to fourteen days. Only six people were ever held for the maximum period of twenty-eight days and of these only three were ultimately charged with an offense. Under the current arrangement, a person can be detained in connection with a suspected terrorism offence for an initial period of forty-eight hours. Additional periods of detention, in increments of seven days, can be granted on application to a magistrate for up to a maximum of fourteen days in total. The United Kingdom lodged formal derogations from Article 5 of the ECHR and Article 9 of the ICCPR in response to the September 11th attacks and the ongoing threat from international terrorism in late 2001, after the events considered by the European

---

[494] European Court of Human Rights Judgment, *Brogan and Others v. United Kingdom*, Application no. 11209/84, 29 November 1988.

[495] European Court of Human Rights, *Saadi v. United Kingdom*, Application no. 13229/03, Judgment, 29 January 2008, p. 84.

[496] The Terrorism Act (2006).

[497] The Government Reply to the Fourth Report from the Home Affairs Committee Session 2005–2006, H.C. 910, Terrorism Detention Powers, 2006–2007, Cm. 6906, p. 9.

Court in both cases cited above, and so this new legislation has yet to be examined in a regional or international forum.

One particularly contentious practice in the immediate post-arrest period is incommunicado detention — holding a suspect in conditions in which they are unable to communicate with the outside world, even to inform someone that they have been detained. The UN Human Rights Committee has recommended that states establish provisions in law to guard against incommunicado detention. In its *General Comments*, the Committee has noted that incommunicado detention prevents prompt presentation of a detained person before a judge and "inherently violates" at least one article of the ICCPR (Article 9(3)), and may also violate several others.[498] However, many states see the issue somewhat differently. It is not uncommon for law enforcement officials to find themselves with an opportunity to exploit intelligence arising from an arrest before a suspect's confederates become aware that any information the suspect may have been privy to (such as names, locations, or targets associated with the conspiracy) has been compromised. For instance, the Spanish Criminal Procedure Code allows for the detention of a person arrested in connection with terrorist offenses to be detained for up to five days without the fact of his or her detention being disclosed to any third party, including defense counsel and family members.[499] As a safeguard, in such circumstances, the incommunicado detention of a terrorism suspect must be authorized by a judge.

The Council of Europe's Committee for the Prevention of Torture has accepted that there might sometimes be an operational need, and thus a legitimate public interest, to withholding the fact of a suspect's detention for a brief period of time. However, the Committee considered "several days" to be much too long a period to withhold such information, concluding that the Spanish authorities had failed to strike "a proper balance ... between the

---

[498] Articles 7, 9(4), and 10(1).

[499] United Nations Office on Drugs and Crime, *Counter-Terrorism Legal Training Curriculum Module 4: Human Rights and Criminal Justice Responses to Terrorism*, Terrorism Prevention Branch, p. 112 (Draft).

requirements of investigations and the interests of detained persons" and thus recommending that this period of incommunicado detention be shortened substantially.[500] Spanish practice also came in for further criticism from the UN Special Rapporteur on the promotion and protection of human rights and fundamental freedoms while countering terrorism who noted that "this regime is on its own highly problematic and both provides a possibility for the commission of prohibited treatment against the detainee and makes it difficult for Spain to defend itself against allegations of such treatment."[501]

The UN Special Rapporteur on torture has noted that torture is "most frequently practised during incommunicado detention" with the implication that such detention should therefore be outlawed. In *Egyptian Initiative for Personal Rights and Interights v. Egypt* (ACHPR; 2011), the African Commission on Human and Peoples' Rights ruled that any confession obtained during a period of incommunicado detention should be considered to have been obtained by coercion and must thus be excluded from evidence. This case was brought by Egyptian human rights organizations on behalf of three individuals who had been subjected to incommunicado detention in the aftermath of the October 2004 bombings of the tourist resorts of Taba and Nouweiba on Egypt's Red Sea coast, which claimed thirty-four lives.[502] All three men had confessed under torture during their incommunicado detention to being involved in the attacks and were subsequently sentenced to death on the basis of these confessions.

The customary international law principle of presumption of innocence should inform the circumstances of any pre-trial detention.[503] This includes both the conditions in which an individual is

---

[500] European Committee for the Prevention of Torture and Inhuman or Degrading Treatment or Punishment (CPT), Report to the Spanish Government on the visit to Spain carried out by the Committee from 1 to 12 April 1991, p. 47.

[501] Report of the Special Rapporteur on the promotion and protection of human rights and fundamental freedoms while countering terrorism, Martin Scheinin, *Mission to Spain*, A/HRC/10/3/Add.2, 16 December 2008, p. 15.

[502] Mohamed Gayez Sabbah, Osama Mohamed Abdel-Ghani Al-Nakhlawi and Younis Mohamed Abu-Gareer.

[503] ICCPR, Article 14(2).

held and the duration of the period in which he or she can be held before being brought to trial. The ICCPR states that accused persons and convicted prisoners should be housed separately, and that detainees are entitled "to be tried without undue delay" and within a "reasonable time", or, failing that, they should be released.[504] The European Convention on Human Rights, the American Convention on Human Rights, and the African Charter on Human and Peoples' Rights all contain similar language regarding bringing cases to trial within a reasonable time. The UN Human Rights Committee has further clarified that the reasonable time requirement applies not only to how soon the trial starts, but also to the time period within which it should end and judgment be rendered.[505] It also applies to any appeals process.

Terrorism investigations and related prosecutions can of course be immensely complex affairs — involving the collection of forensic evidence, expert testimony, witness statements, and the like. Obtaining cross-border assistance in international or trans-national terrorism cases can likewise be a time-consuming process, as can be the declassification of sensitive intelligence documents for use in court. Any resulting delay in bringing a suspect to trial must be reasonable in the context of circumstances involved. In a series of linked cases involving five suspected members of the Basque separatist group ETA detained on remand in French prisons pending trial for more than four years, the European Court of Human Rights found that the delay in bringing their cases to trial was unreasonable and thus a violation of their rights under the European Convention (and indeed the ICCPR).[506] The Court acknowledged the complexity of the investigation in this case had necessitated extended enquiries over a period of several years and that this was an appropriate reason to delay going to trial, however, it also noted that a two-year period of inactivity attributed to a

---

[504] ICCPR, Article 10(2), Article 14(2)(c) and Article 9(3).

[505] United National Human Rights Committee, General Comment 13, 13 April 1984, p. 10.

[506] European Court of Human Rights, *Berasategi v. France* (application no. 29095/09), *Esparza Luri v. France* (no. 29119/09), *Guimon Esparza v. France* (no. 29116/09), *Sagarzazu v. France* (no. 29109/09 and *Soria Valderrama v. France* (no. 29101/09), Judgment, 26 January 2012.

backlog of cases in the Assize Court contributed to the delay and that this was not acceptable.

Factors that therefore may help determine the reasonableness of any delay include the complexity of the case, and the conduct of investigative, prosecutorial and judicial authorities, as well as the conduct of the defendant. In the case of *Lubuto v. Zambia* (HRC; 1995), the Human Rights Committee also made it clear that a lack of resources is not a sufficient reason for delay — in such circumstances, the government has an obligation to allocate additional resources.[507] Inefficiencies in the effective administration of justice are common to many legal systems around the world and a substantial body of regional and international jurisprudence has grown up around this issue reinforcing the reasonable time standard.[508] The need to bring a case expeditiously to trial is especially important if an individual as been remanded in custody awaiting trial, which is often the norm in terrorism cases. Furthermore, delays in bringing a case to trial can result in the degradation of evidence — for example, eyewitness recollections — thus undermining the fairness of the trial.

The UN Human Rights Committee and the Inter-American Commission on Human Rights have both supported the notion that the presumption of innocence standard, and the protections that flow from it, can not be dispensed with in any circumstances.[509] This standard also logically creates a presumption against the practice of pre-trial custodial detention, which is reflected in the ICCPR.[510]

---

[507] Human Rights Committee, *Lubuto v. Zambia*, Communication no. 390/90, CCPR/C/55/D/390/1990/Rev.1, 31 October 1995.

[508] *Kudla v. Poland, Kalashnikov v. Russia*, Application no. 47095/99, Judgment of 15 July 2002; *Loffler v. Austria*, Application no. 72159/01, Judgment of 4 March 2004; HRC: *Fei v. Colombia*, Communication no. 514/192, Views of 4 April 1995 and *Muñoz Hermoza v. Peru*, Communication no. 203/86. Viewed 4 November 1988.

[509] International Committee of the Red Cross, *Customary International Humanitarian Law*, Rule 100: Fair Trial Guarantees at http://www.icrc.org/customary-ihl/eng/docs/v1_rul_rule100#Fn_10_40. UN Human Rights Committee, General Comment No. 29 (Article 4 of the International Covenant on Civil and Political Rights), p. 2998; Inter-American Commission on Human Rights, Report on Terrorism and Human Rights, p. 3019.

[510] Article 9(3).

Accordingly, government authorities are encouraged to make provision for suspects to be released on bail pending their appearance in court. However, human rights law recognizes that there may be some circumstances in which the granting of bail may not be appropriate. Reasons for refusing bail might include the existence of a flight risk, concerns about possible interference with evidence or testimony, the protection of the general public, the preservation of public order, and the protection of the defendant.

Finally, due process protections naturally also apply to the trial itself. Article 10 of the Universal Declaration of Human Rights and Article 14 of the ICCPR set out what the UN High Commissioner of Human Rights has described as "the bedrock norms applicable in all trials" including a fair hearing by a competent, independent (of the legislative and executive branches of government) and impartial tribunal established by law.[511] This is considered to be an absolute right.[512] However, the right to a public hearing is not; in exceptional circumstances, the ICCPR allows that the press and public can be excluded from all or part of a trial for reasons of "morals, public order ... or national security in a democratic society", or to protect the private lives of the parties involved, or where publicity would prejudice the interests of justice, although the judgment itself must be made public. It is not uncommon in terrorism cases for part of the evidence to presented *in camera*, that is without the press or public present, because of the sensitivity of the material involved. However, in such cases a strict necessity requirement should be applied.

The guiding principle underpinning the right to a fair trial is the concept of "equality of arms" — meaning that both the prosecution and the defense are treated in a manner that ensures that they have a procedurally equal position during the course of a trial and

---

[511] *Report of the United Nations High Commissioner for Human Rights on the protection of human rights and fundamental freedoms while countering terrorism*, A/HRC/16/50, 15 December 2010, para 29.

[512] Human Rights Committee, *General Comment 32: Article 14 (on the right to equality before courts and tribunals and to a fair trial)*, CCPR/C/GC/32, 23 August 2007, para 19.

are given the same opportunity to make their case.[513] Given the superior resources at the disposal of the state, it is critical that the defense not be placed at an unfair disadvantage as it prepares for trial. Government authorities have an obligation to ensure that defense counsel are free to perform all of their professional functions without intimidation, harassment, or improper interference, and that they do not suffer adverse consequences for any action taken in accordance with their professional obligations.[514] The key components of a fair trial are articulated best by the ICCPR and the UN Human Rights Committee's *General Comment No 32*.[515] These include the right to have adequate time and facilities for the preparation of a defense, and the right to examine prosecution witnesses and to obtain the attendance and examination of witnesses that could aid the defense. The critical importance of disclosure and the burdens it imposes on the state to ensure that all relevant material, especially that of an exculpatory nature, has been made available to the defense has been discussed above in relation to the use of Special Investigation Techniques. The Human Rights Committee has explicitly stated that the "fundamental principles of fair trial", including the presumption of innocence, must be respected during a state of emergency.[516] The High Commissioner for Human Rights has further warned that military tribunals and special courts established for the express purpose of trying terrorism suspects may not meet the independence and impartiality standard required by international human rights law.[517]

---

[513] ibid., para 13.

[514] *UN Basic Principles on the Role of Lawyers adopted by the Eighth United Nations Congress on the Prevention of Crime and the Treatment of Offenders*, 1990, p. 16.

[515] Human Rights Committee, *General Comment 32: Article 14 (on the right to equality before courts and tribunals and to a fair trial)*, CCPR/C/GC/32, 23 August 2007.

[516] Human Rights Committee, *General Comment 29: Article 4 (States of Emergency)*, CCPR/C/21/Rev.1/Add.11, 31 August 2001, paras 11 and 15 and Human Rights Committee, *General Comment 32: Article 14 (on the right to equality before courts and tribunals and to a fair trial)*, CCPR/C/GC/32, 23 August 2007, para 6.

[517] *Report of the United Nations High Commissioner for Human Rights on the protection of human rights and fundamental freedoms while countering terrorism*, A/HRC/16/50, 15 December 2010, para 31.

Another key right is that of the accused to speak in privacy and total confidence with his or her attorney. State authorities have been known to express concern that some defense attorneys, who may be actively sympathetic to the aims of a particular terrorist group, could overstep the bounds of their role by acting as a channel of communication between those confined in prison and their associates still at liberty. This does sometimes happen; in 2005, US attorney Lynne Stewart was jailed for ten years for passing messages on behalf of her client, the so-called "blind sheikh" Omar Abdel-Rahman, implicated in the first World Trade Center bombing in 1993 and an associate of Osama bin Laden and Ayman al-Zawahiri, to his followers in Egypt.[518] The German lawyer Horst Mahler was a key figure in the foundation of the *Rote Armee Fraktion* and, acting in his professional capacity as Andreas Baader's lawyer, helped to plan the operation that sprang Baader from custody in May 1970 before going underground himself as a fully fledged member of the group.[519] Ingrid Schubert, who was later jailed alongside Andreas Baader and Gudrun Ensslin in Stammheim prison, admitted that the group used "private visits, visits from lawyers" to smuggle items, including in one instance a Minox camera, in and out of prison.[520] Another RAF member, Volker Speitel, identified defense lawyer Arndt Müller as having been chosen to smuggle three small pistols into Stammheim in hollowed-out legal binders, along with five sticks of explosives, radios, and other small items requested by the prisoners. Andreas Baader and Jan-Carl Raspe would later use these pistols to take their own lives in October 1977, after a plot to secure their exchange for the passengers and crew of a hijacked Lufthansa airliner was foiled by the newly formed West German Special Forces unit *Grenzschutzgruppe 9* (GSG9).[521]

In exceptional and tightly controlled circumstances, it may be acceptable on a case-by-case basis to monitor attorney-client communication for potential security threats, but anything material to

---

[518] Benjamin Weiser, 10-Year Sentence for Lawyer in Terrorism Case Is Upheld, *New York Times*, 28 June 2012.

[519] Stefan Aust, *Baader-Meinhof: The Inside Story of the RAF* (Oxford University Press; 2009), p. 60.

[520] ibid., p. 272.

[521] ibid., pp. 277–278.

the detainee's defense must still be protected. In *Erdem v. Germany* (ECtHR; 2001), the European Court of Human Rights found that a provision in German criminal procedures relating solely to terrorism cases, that a suspect may only exchange documents with his or her lawyer if both parties agree to allow the documents to be monitored by a judge unconnected with the suspect's case who is required to keep the contents confidential, did not infringe the suspect's fair trial rights.[522] Selahattin Erdem, also known as Duran Klakan, was one of the founders of the *Partiya Karkerên Kurdistan* (PKK) who had been detained by German border police in 1988 and then subsequently sentenced to six years imprisonment for being a member of a terrorist organization. The *UN Body of Principles for the Protection of All Persons under Any Form of Detention or Imprisonment* also establishes that any communication between a detainee and his or her legal counsel should be considered inadmissible as evidence unless it is connected with an on-going or planned crime.[523]

One particular point of concern expressed by the UN High Commissioner for Human Rights has been the adoption and application in many countries of legislation containing "overly broad and vague definitions of terrorist offences", which fail to comply with the principle of legality outlined in the ICCPR in that "they do not provide for reasonable notice of what actions they cover, or are so broad that they cover actions which either should not reasonably be deemed terrorist in nature, or considered to be crimes at all."[524] The High Commissioner has also criticized the abuse of the state secrets privilege by states, including by Western nations like the United States and Germany, to evade disclosure and accountability, as in the case of Khaled el-Masri outlined in the previous section.[525] Both the inherent need for secrecy which governs the world of

---

[522] European Court of Human Rights, *Erdem v. Germany*, Application no. 38321/97, Judgment of 5 July 2001.

[523] Principle 18 of the *UN General Assembly Body of Principles for the Protection of All Persons under Any Form of Detention or Imprisonment*.

[524] *Report of the United Nations High Commissioner for Human Rights on the protection of human rights and fundamental freedoms while countering terrorism*, A/HRC/22/26, 17 December 2012, p. 21.

[525] *Report of the United Nations High Commissioner for Human Rights on the protection of human rights and fundamental freedoms while countering terrorism*, A/HRC/16/50, 15 December 2010, paras 37 and 46.

intelligence, and the fact that foreign intelligence is often obtained in a manner that would not meet legal scrutiny from sources of often dubious reliability, combine to make it typically unsuitable for use in court and necessitates that, if it is introduced as evidence into legal proceedings, the defense must have the opportunity to meaningfully challenge its reliability as such.[526]

Finally, the presumption of innocence principle places the burden on the prosecution in every trial to prove the charge at issue beyond reasonable doubt. It is also an obligation incumbent on all state officials not to prejudge the outcome of a trial by making public statements affirming the guilt of the accused. Even after the conclusion of a trial, the defendant must be accorded the opportunity to appeal that his or her conviction and sentence be reviewed by a higher tribunal, both on the basis of the sufficiency of the evidence presented and of the correct application of the law.[527] Such an appeal is not intended to be a retrial but rather a review of the facts of the case. The right of appeal is especially important in cases where the death penalty has been applied. Should an appeal determine that a miscarriage of justice has indeed occurred then the individual concerned must be entitled to financial compensation.[528] Miscarriages of justice are not unknown in terrorism cases, as the example of the Guildford Four, also outlined at length in the previous section, amply illustrates. A person cannot be tried twice for the same offence.[529]

In the years since 9/11, ordinary US courts (as distinct from the Military Commissions established in Guantanamo) have successfully prosecuted, amongst others, the Millennium bomber Ahmed Ressam, the underwear bomber Umar Farouq Abdulmutallab, the shoe bomber Richard Reid, the Times Square bomber Faisal Shahzad, and the Boston Marathon bomber Dzhokhar Tsarnaev.

---

[526] ibid., para 40 and Amnesty International, *USA: Blocked at every turn. The absence of effective remedy for counter-terrorism abuses*, AMR 51/120/2009, 30 November 2009.

[527] Human Rights Committee, *General Comment 32: Article 14 (on the right to equality before courts and tribunals and to a fair trial)*, CCPR/C/GC/32, 23 August 2007, para 45.

[528] ibid., para 52.

[529] ibid., para 54.

Indeed, US Federal Courts successfully prosecuted 523 terrorism-related defendants between 11 September 2001 and 11 September 2009, with a conviction rate of 88.2%.[530] Sentencing Ahmed Ressam in 2005, Judge John C. Coughenour noted in his summing up: "Our system works. We did not need to use a secret military tribunal, or detain the defendant indefinitely as an enemy combatant ... We can deal with the threats to our national security without denying the accused fundamental constitutional protections."[531] While human rights organizations like Human Rights Watch and Amnesty International have admittedly expressed concerns both about the over-broad application of the material support statute and the application of restrictive Special Administrative Measures in pre-trial confinement, it is fair to say that the US criminal justice system is essentially representative of the standards applied in most Western democracies and is, for the most part, compliant with international human rights law.[532] We can therefore conclude with some confidence that human rights norms which ensure the application of due process in the arrest and prosecution of terrorist suspects do not appear to present any meaningful practical impediment to the conduct of successful prosecutions in terrorism-related cases.

## The humane treatment of prisoners

Imprisonment is a term specifically applied to those detained following conviction of a criminal offense. The administration of justice

---

[530] These cases include all individuals prosecuted in association with terrorism but not all are charged with terrorism-related offenses — racketeering, drugs, fraud and immigration offenses also feature heavily. Only 244 cases deal directly with terrorism charges. Center on Law and Security, *Highlights from the Terrorist Trial Report Card 2001–2009: Lessons Learned*, New York University School of Law, January 2010, p. 2.

[531] Trying Terrorists in Our Courts, *Congressional Record*, Vol. 151, No. 106 (29 July 2005).

[532] Nicole Hong, "Material Support" Statute Is Front and Center in Antiterror Push, *Wall Street Journal*, 27 May 2015 and Amnesty International Press Release, *USA: Rights Groups Issue pen Letter on Hashmi Trial and SAMs*, 27 April 2010, at http://www.amnestyusa.org/news/press-releases/usa-rights-groups-issue-open-letter-on-hashmi-trial-and-sams. Viewed 7 March 2016.

has a range of purposes including to provide an element of retribution for victims, to signal societal intolerance for anti-social behavior, to deter other potential lawbreakers, to discourage recidivism, and to promote the reformation of criminals. The operation of custodial facilities in the criminal justice system serves all these ends but has one principal objective above all which is enshrined in the ICCPR — to promote the reformation and social rehabilitation of prisoners.[533] The deprivation of liberty is the punitive element of a custodial sentence, the conditions in which any incarceration is served should not be. International human rights law establishes a basic minimum standard with which all prisoners should be treated regardless of the circumstances of their detention. States have a fundamental obligation to treat prisoners with humanity and dignity regardless of the crimes of which they have been convicted.[534] Articles containing formulations to this effect can be found in the ICCPR, the American Convention on Human Rights, the African Charter on Human and Peoples' Rights, and the revised Arab Charter on Human Rights. The UN Human Rights Committee has described humane treatment and respect for the dignity of a detained person as a fundamental and universally applicable rule.[535]

The United Nations General Assembly has considered the question of how prisoners and detainees should be treated in detail, which led to the adoption of the *Body of Principles for the Protection of All Persons under Any Form of Detention or Imprisonment* in 1988, and their further reinforcement in 1990 with a set of 11 *Basic Principles for the Treatment of Prisoners.*[536] Basic Principle 5 states that "except for those limitations that are demonstrably necessitated by the fact of incarceration, all prisoners shall retain the human rights and

---

[533] ICCPR, Article 10(3).

[534] ibid. Article 10(1).

[535] Human Rights Committee, *General Comment 21: Article 10 (Humane Treatment of Persons Deprived of Their Liberty)*, 10 April 1992, para 4.

[536] United Nations General Assembly, Body of Principles for the Protection of All Persons under Any Form of Detention or Imprisonment, A/RES/43/173, 9 December 1988 and United Nations General Assembly, Basic Principles for the Treatment of Prisoners, A/RES/45/111, 14 December 1990.

fundamental freedoms set out in the Universal Declaration of Human Rights, and, where the state concerned is a party, the International Covenant on Economic, Social and Cultural Rights, and the ICCPR and the Optional Protocol thereto, as well as such other rights as are set out in other United Nations covenants."[537] While neither the *Body of Principles* nor the *Basic Principles* are intended by the General Assembly to be legally binding as such, they are intended to be authoritative and to assist states and other international bodies to interpret and apply existing international legal norms.

Furthermore, certain categories of prisoners are extended special protection under international human rights law. Specific guidelines for the protection of women prisoners are enumerated in the *United Nations Rules for the Treatment of Women Prisoners and Non-Custodial Measures for Women Offenders,* also known as the *Bangkok Rules.* Notable recommendations include that attention shall be paid to the admission procedures for women "due to their particular vulnerability at this time" and that women with caretaking responsibilities for children should be given sufficient opportunity to make arrangements for the care of those children that takes into account their best interests.[538] The *Bangkok Rules* make provision for gender specific healthcare arrangements and screening methods, as well as for mechanisms to be put in place to assist women who have experienced sexual abuse or other forms of violence before or during detention.[539] Article 10 of the ICCPR directs that children under the age of eighteen should be held separately from adult prisoners. Article 37 of the UN Convention on the Rights of the Child reinforces this standard, "unless it is in the child's best interests", and adds that the incarceration of minors should be a measure of last resort and as strictly limited in duration as possible. Whenever possible, detention pending trial should be replaced by

---

[537] Basic Principles for the Treatment of Prisoners, adopted under General Assembly resolution 45/111 (1990) (hereafter the UN Basic Principles) at Principle 5.

[538] *United Nations Rules for the Treatment of Women Prisoners and Non-custodial Measures for Women Offenders,* A/RES/65/229, 16 March 2011, at Rules 2(1) and 2(2).

[539] ibid. at Rules 7, 10 and 19–21.

alternative measures, such as close supervision, placement with a
foster family, or residence in an educational setting or home. Delays
in any criminal procedure should be minimized. Every child
deprived of liberty should be treated in a manner which takes into
account age appropriate needs and while detained they should
receive care, protection and all necessary individual assistance —
social, educational, vocational, psychological, medical and
physical — that might be required.[540]

For the most part, safety and security in modern prisons largely
depend on creating a positive climate that encourages the cooperation of prisoners. The most effective strategy for ensuring both
external security (preventing escapes) and internal safety (preventing disorder) is to build positive relationships between prisoners
and staff — an approach often described as "dynamic security".[541]
This concept rests on the notion that engaging with prisoners, and
getting to know them, enables staff to develop the situational
awareness to anticipate, and prepare for, potential security threats.
The core building blocks of "dynamic security" are developing
positive relationships with prisoners, diverting prisoners' energy
into constructive work and activity, providing a decent and balanced regime with individualized programs for prisoners, and
establishing an adequate ratio of staff to prisoners.[542] Another key
component in creating this positive climate is the recruitment and
retention of well-trained and well-remunerated prison staff.

However, in the context of counter-terrorism, it is likely that
prison officials will encounter significant hostility and opposition
from inmates who still consider themselves to be actively engaged
in an ongoing confrontation with the authorities. Jan-Carle Raspe,
one of the original members of the *Rote Armee Faktion*, who was

---

[540] Also relevant in this regard are the "Beijing Rules" (United Nations Standard Minimum
Rules for the Administration of Juvenile Justice, A/RES/40/33, 29 November 1985) and the
"Havana Rules" (United Nations Rules for the Protection of Juveniles Deprived of Their
Liberty, A/RES/45/113, 14 December 1990).

[541] UNODC, *Handbook for Prison Leaders: A basic training tool and curriculum for prison managers
based on international standards and norms, Criminal Justice Handbook Series* (2010), p. 106.

[542] ibid. and Otto Billig, The Lawyer Terrorist and His Comrades, *Political Psychology*, Vol. 6
No. 1 (March 1985), p. 34.

caught by the police along with Andreas Baader and Holger Meins visiting an explosives cache in June 1972, summed up the attitude of many such militants on their arrival in prison: "As I came here, I had only one thought in my head. Resistance whenever possible. Not only because I knew that it was politically right and necessary, but because I knew it in theory... that it is necessary to keep my identity, so I would not be made kaput."[543] During The Troubles in Northern Ireland there were more than 2,700 incidents of prison officers being threatened or attacked, twenty-nine were killed and six more committed suicide.[544] One former prison officer recalled: "The Maze was like any prison in that there were very few secrets. In no time, the prisoners knew I was an ex-soldier, what regiment I had been in and, more or less, what I wore in bed. The IRA prisoners would taunt me when they got a chance, saying that they knew where I lived and where my children went to school."[545] And perhaps the most high-profile example of prison unrest involving terrorist detainees involves the Maoist terrorist organization *Sendero Luminoso*, which organized simultaneous uprisings in three Peruvian prisons in June 1986. A number of guards and three visiting journalists were taken hostage, and the prisoners demanded the release of 500 inmates convicted of terrorism-related offenses before a major military operation was finally able to retake the prisons (of which more in the section on the use of armed force below). Monitoring the activities of prison inmates to ensure that they are not posing a threat to the security of the prison or are not involved in ongoing criminal activity is a legitimate concern for the authorities, and they are entitled to take reasonable, but not excessive, measures to protect prison staff and members of the general public from harm.

In taking protective measures, prison authorities must abide by certain norms of behavior. The principles of equality and non-discrimination apply equally in the context of corrections facilities.

---

[543] Otto Billig, The Lawyer Terrorist and His Comrades, *Political Psychology*, Vol. 6 No. 1 (March 1985), p. 34.

[544] Peter Foster, Inside story of the Maze, *The Telegraph*, 28 July 2000.

[545] ibid.

This does not exclude the possibility of different treatment for individuals held for terrorism offences, but any measures taken would need to have a legitimate objective, and be reasonable and proportional to the end sought. However, no distinction can be made on the basis of religion or ethnicity. The Special Rapporteur on the promotion and protection of human rights and fundamental freedoms while countering terrorism has expressed concern, for example, over the different treatment accorded to Muslim detainees in Spain and has recommended human rights education for penitentiary and law enforcement staff, as well as disciplinary measures against any official involved in discriminatory conduct.[546] Providing for the special needs of a minority, or at-risk, group is not regarded as discrimination. Indeed, the economic, social and cultural rights of detainees must be protected at all times. The Human Rights Committee has commented in relation to this issue that "persons already subject to certain legitimate constraints, such as prisoners, continue to enjoy their rights to manifest their religion or belief to the fullest extent compatible with the specific nature of the constraint."[547] In *Boodoo v Trinidad and Tobago* (HRC; 2002), the HRC found that the removal of Muslim prayer books from the prisoner Clement Boodoo, and the refusal to allow him to attend prayer services, amounted to a violation of the ICCPR.[548] It should be further stressed that prison authorities have a duty of care for the wellbeing of every detainee in their custody. Prisoners convicted of terrorist-related crimes may find themselves the target of hostility from other inmates and thus may inhabit a vulnerable category of their own. A failure by the authorities to put sufficient protections in place that leads to the death of a prisoner may amount to a violation of right to life protections.

Prison officers cannot take the law into their own hands when confronted with a hostile or recalcitrant inmate. Penal disciplinary

---

[546] *Report of the Special Rapporteur on the promotion and protection of human rights and fundamental freedoms while countering terrorism, Martin Scheinin* (A/HRC/10/3/Add.2), p. 61.
[547] Human Rights Committee, *General Comment 22 — Article 18 (Freedom of Thought, Conscience and Religion)*, CCPR/C/21/Rev.1/Add.4, 30 July 1993, p. 8.
[548] United Nations Human Rights Committee, *Clement Boodoo v. Trinidad and Tobago*, CCPR/C/74/D/721/1996, 15 April 2002.

codes must be established by law and clearly state what conduct constitutes an offence, the nature of the punishment incurred, and the legitimate authority to administer that punishment.[549] There must also be due process protections. Under no circumstances are corrections staff permitted to mete out informal punishments. Any punishment by the prison administration should be subject to appeal and/or judicial review, and there must be a formal complaint mechanism to address grievances.[550] International human rights law prohibits corporal punishment, collective punishment, forced labor, restriction of diet, the punitive use of restraints, or lengthy solitary confinement. No prisoner should be employed, in the service of the institution, in any disciplinary capacity.[551]

The Council of Europe's *Guidelines on Human Rights and the Fight Against Terrorism* acknowledges that "the imperatives of the fight against terrorism may ... require that a person deprived of his [or] her liberty for terrorist activities be submitted to more severe restrictions than those applied to other prisoners" and that this might include the restriction and surveillance of their communications, holding them in "specially secured quarters", and their separation from other prisoners.[552] However, the guidelines also add the important proviso that any special regime imposed must be proportional to the lawful objective sought. In 1994, Maxime Frérot, a former member of the French Marxist terrorist group *Action Directe* serving multiple life sentences in France for a litany of offenses

---

[549] See *The UN Body of Principles for the Protection of All Persons under Any Form of Detention or Imprisonment*, A/RES/43/173, 9 December 1988 and *The United Nations Standard Minimum Rules for the Treatment of Prisoners*, adopted by the First United Nations Congress on the Prevention of Crime and the Treatment of Offenders in 1955, and approved by the Economic and Social Council (resolutions 663 C (XXIV) of 31 July 1957 and 2076 (LXII) of 13 May 1977).

[550] Principle 30(2) of the UN General Assembly Body of Principles for the Protection of All Persons under Any Form of Detention or Imprisonment.

[551] UN Standard Minimum Rules for the Treatment of Prisoners at 28(1).

[552] Council of Europe, *Guidelines on Human Rights and the Fight Against Terrorism*, adopted by the Committee of Ministers on 11 July 2002 at the 804th meeting of the Ministers' Deputies. See Guideline XI.

including murder, attempted murder, armed robbery, possession of explosives and hostage-taking, lodged an administrative appeal against the frequent imposition — sometimes by force — of prison strip searches, which he claimed infringed his human dignity. The case made its way to the European Court of Human Rights which held in *Frérot v. France* (ECtHR; 2007) that while "body searches, including full body searches, might sometimes be necessary to maintain security inside a prison, to prevent disorder or prevent criminal offences" they should only be undertaken "when absolutely necessary in the light of the special circumstances and where there were serious reasons to suspect that the prisoner was hiding such an object or substance in that part of the body."[553] The Court also found that there had been a frequency and an apparently arbitrary quality to the application of this procedure in the French prison system that exceeded this standard and thus amounted to a violation of the European Convention.

Some states have responded to terrorist threats by constructing special prisons — or self-contained wings within prisons — to hold those convicted of terrorism offenses separate from the general prison population. For example, in 1975 the West German authorities opened a new maximum security court room and cell block in Stammheim Prison purposefully designed to try and subsequently incarcerate members of the Baader-Meinhof terrorist cell, including its eponymous members Andreas Baader and Ulrike Meinhof. The facility was guarded by military Special Forces supported by more than 400 police officers and was illuminated at night by fifty-four spotlights. Such measures are typically taken so that such individuals can be held securely and to prevent the political or social radicalization of other prisoners. International human rights law does not take a position on this practice. The United Nations Office on Drugs and Crime has offered the following advice on establishing a human rights compliant high security detention regime: "The greatest attention must be paid to a clear

---

[553] European Court of Human Rights *Frérot v. France*, Application no. 70204/01, Chamber Judgment, 12 June 2007.

legal framework, continuous monitoring of the detainee's wellbe-ing, [and] transparent procedures and avenues for the detainee to challenge the measures, including judicial review."[554]

The European Court of Human Rights also considered the imposition of high security regimes in the case of *Enea v. Italy* (ECtHR; 2009),[555] which dealt with measures introduced to control the activities of a convicted organized crime figure, Salvatore Enea, who was being held in a high supervision *Elevato Indice di Vigilanza* Unit run by the Italian prison service. The controls imposed on Enea included restrictions on visits by family members (a maximum of a single one-hour visit per month), no meetings with non-family members, no telephone access, no more than two parcels to be received per month, a ban on organizing cultural, recreational or sports activities, no right to vote in elections for prisoners' repre-sentatives or to be elected as a representative, and no more than two hours of outdoor exercise per day. The Court observed "the restrictions imposed as a result of the special prison regime were necessary to prevent the applicant, who posed a danger to society, from maintaining contacts with the criminal organization to which he belonged" and added that Enea had not submitted any evi-dence to suggest "the extension of those restrictions was patently unjustified."[556] The Court also noted approvingly that "each time the measure was extended the Minister of Justice took account of recent police reports stating that the applicant was still danger-ous", that the measures were progressively eased, and that the special regime was eventually discontinued by the court responsi-ble for the execution of sentences on the grounds that the security considerations which had justified it were no longer valid — all of which were positive factors that contributed to the Court rejecting

---

[554] United Nations Office on Drugs and Crime, *Counter-Terrorism Legal Training Curriculum Module 4: Human Rights and Criminal Justice Responses to Terrorism*, Terrorism Prevention Branch (Draft), Sec. 4.7.2.

[555] European Court of Human Rights, *Enea v. Italy*, Application no. 74912/01, Grand Chamber Judgment, 17 September 2009.

[556] ibid., p. 65.

Enea's contention that the circumstances of his detention amounted to cruel, inhuman or degrading treatment.

The most severe form of lawful incarceration is the imposition of solitary confinement — the practice of holding a prisoner in isolation from the rest of the prison population. Typically, this is done either as a disciplinary measure, for their own protection, or because they pose a threat to other inmates. The *Istanbul Statement on the Use and Effects of Solitary Confinement*, prepared by twenty-four international experts on solitary confinement, prisons, and torture convened under the auspices of the Human Rights Foundation of Turkey in 2007, defines solitary confinement as "the physical isolation of individuals who are confined to their cells for 22–24 hours a day."[557] Limited periods of solitary confinement may comply with Article 10 of the ICCPR, but longer periods may not. Both the *UN Basic Principles* and the Committee Against Torture recommend that the practice of solitary confinement be abolished, or at least restricted to the most serious cases and for strictly limited periods. At a minimum, a doctor should visit prisoners in solitary confinement daily to assess the state of their physical and mental health. In a report dedicated to the practice of solitary confinement, the UN Special Rapporteur on torture, Juan Méndez, took the view that "the longer the duration of solitary confinement or the greater the uncertainty regarding the length of time, the greater the risk of serious and irreparable harm to the inmate that may constitute cruel, inhuman or degrading treatment or punishment or even torture."[558] He further added that in his opinion the use of prolonged solitary confinement, which he defined as any period exceeding fifteen days, would be a violation of the prohibition on torture, inhuman or

---

[557] United Nations Office on Drugs and Crime, *Counter-Terrorism Legal Training Curriculum Module 4: Human Rights and Criminal Justice Responses to Terrorism*, Terrorism Prevention Branch (Draft), Sec. 4.7.2.

[558] *Interim report of the Special Rapporteur of the Human Rights Council on torture and other cruel, inhuman or degrading treatment or punishment*, United Nations General Assembly A/66/268, 5 August 2011, para 58.

degrading treatment.[559] Méndez was himself a survivor of torture meted out during Argentina's Dirty War.

In the case of *Ramirez Sanchez v. France* (ECtHR; 2006), the European Court of Human Rights found that solitary confinement coupled with sensory deprivation could amount to inhuman treatment, but that a prisoner's segregation from the prison community did not in itself amount to inhuman treatment. While Sánchez — better known by the *nom de guerre* Carlos the Jackal, which he used while fighting for the Popular Front for the Liberation of Palestine (PFLP) — was held in solitary confinement for eight years in total, the Court found his isolation was "relative" and not too severe.[560] The Court also noted that Sánchez had been seen twice a week by a medical doctor, received a monthly visit from a priest and very frequent visits from his entourage of fifty-eight lawyers, one of whom was now his wife. Sánchez had a varied terrorist career during which time he was responsible for multiple murders, failed assassination attempts, car bombings, a rocket attack on Orly Airport in Paris, and the takeover of an OPEC meeting in Vienna. In December 1997 he was sentenced to life in prison for the murder in Paris of two officers of the French Security Service, *Direction de la surveillance du territoire* (DST), and their informant in June 1975. By way of contrast, the leader of the PKK, Abdullah Öcalan, was held as the sole prisoner on the island of İmralı in the Sea of Marmara after his capture in Kenya in February 1999, with a garrison of more than 1,000 Turkish soldiers deployed on the island to oversee his detention. After the Council of Europe's Committee for the Prevention of Torture raised concerns about Öcalan's isolation in 2009, the Turkish government transferred a handful of other PKK prisoners to the island facility with whom he was allowed to interact for ten hours a week.[561]

All persons deprived of liberty have the right to be visited by and correspond with members of their family and to communicate

---

[559] ibid., para 61.

[560] European Court of Human Rights, *Ramirez Sanchez v France*, Application no. 59450/00, Grand Chamber Judgment, 4 July 2006, p. 123.

[561] PKK leader Ocalan gets company in prison, United Press International, 17 November 2009.

with the outside world, subject to reasonable conditions and restrictions specified by law or lawful regulations. If possible, to facilitate family visits, prisoners should be held close to their usual place of residence. These rights are laid out in the *UN Body of Principles for the Protection of All Persons under Any Form of Detention or Imprisonment.*[562] It is not uncommon for states — typically citing physical security concerns — to incarcerate convicted terrorists in prisons located a substantial distance from the area in which they were active. For example, from 1989 onwards, members of the Basque separatist group ETA apprehended by the Spanish authorities were often sent to serve out their sentences in prisons located outside the Basque country in more distant regions of Spain (including the Canary Islands) as part of a deliberate dispersal strategy.[563] This placed a considerable temporal and financial burden on their family members who then had to travel great distances to visit their incarcerated relative.[564] ETA propaganda even equated the deaths of thirteen family members of incarcerated ETA terrorists killed in road traffic accidents that occurred en route to prison visits to state murder.[565] In January 1996, ETA kidnapped and held hostage a Spanish prison official, José Antonio Ortega Lara, for 532 days in an effort to force the state to transfer ETA prisoners closer to the Basque region. Spanish police eventually located where Lara was being held and he was recovered alive. ETA responded to this reversal in July 1997 by kidnapping Miguel Ángel Blanco, and restating their demands, this time giving the government only forty-eight hours to comply. The government refused to give in and Blanco was

---

[562] See Principles 19, 20 and 28.

[563] Part of the logic of the dispersal strategy was to remove ETA prisoners from the peer pressure experienced in prison to remain loyal to the group's cause. The Basta Ya Citizens' Initiative Group has claimed that between 1989–1995 112 ETA prisoners broke with the organization partly because this dispersal strategy quite literally created the space for them to disengage form their former comrades.

[564] See Eileen MacDonald, *Shoot the Women First* (Random House; 1992).

[565] Basta Ya Citizens' Initiative Group, *Report on Torture Denunciations in Spain*, presented to the United Nations High Commissioner on Human Rights on 9 March 2004. See *Chapter 2: The Dispersal of ETA Prisoners* at http://www.bastaya.org/actualidad/Violencia/InformeTorturas/TheDispersalsofetaPrisoners.pdf.

murdered. Prisoner relocation would continue to be an important negotiating point in peace talks.

Another core principle is that all "prisoners shall have access to the health services available in the country without discrimination on the grounds of their legal situation."[566] The *UN Body of Principles* create further obligations for states in this regard including that a detainee should be offered a prompt medical exam on arrival in his or her place of detention or imprisonment; that medical treatment must be provided free of charge; that detainees have the right to request, or petition a judicial authority, for a second medical examination or opinion; and, finally, that a record should be kept of any medical examination of a detainee that takes place and access to these records should be ensured for all relevant parties.[567] Along with access to a lawyer and access to family members, medical access is considered by many human rights defenders as being one of the three key components of torture prevention.[568]

One significant and contentious area in which a state's medical obligations have been called into question in relation to the treatment of terrorism detainees is in responding to hunger strikers. Hunger strikes have been a passive resistance tool used by social activists going back centuries — there is a tradition of fasting against injustice that dates to pre-Christian times in Ireland where the practice was variously known as *Troscadh* or *Cealachan*. In the modern era, it is also associated with the British and American suffragette movement, and the struggle for Indian independence. Mahatma Gandhi embarked on several famous hunger strikes, as did the revolutionary socialist Bhagat Singh, jailed for murdering a colonial police officer and throwing two bombs onto the floor of India's Central Legislative Assembly.

---

[566] *Basic Principles for the Treatment of Prisoners*, adopted and proclaimed by UN General Assembly resolution 45/111 of 14 December 1990, Principle 9.

[567] Principles 24, 25 and 26.

[568] European Committee for the Prevention of Torture and Inhuman or Degrading Treatment or Punishment (CPT), *The CPT Standards: "Substantive" sections of the CPT's General Reports*, Council of Europe, CPT/Inf/E (2002) 1 — Rev. 2006.

This is a tactic frequently used by terrorist detainees and other political prisoners to put pressure on the state and mobilize supporters. In 1974, imprisoned members of the *Rote Armee Fraktion* launched a third hunger strike demanding to be allowed to associate with other political prisoners. Till Meyer, a member of *Bewegung 2. Juni,* explained the logic of the prisoners' protest: "Our demand — association of all prisoners — is the opposite of what the pigs offer us. Association means, above all, survival, collective political imprisonment, political identity, self-organization — while the dead wing [solitary confinement] means annihilation."[569] RAF member Holger Meins died on 9 November 1974 after six weeks on hunger strike and two weeks of forced feeding. News of Meins' death brought protestors on to the streets of Berlin, and clashes with police put five officers in hospital. On 10 November, *Bewegung 2. Juni* killed the President of the West Berlin Supreme Court, Günter von Drenkmann, in a botched kidnapping attempt carried out as a reprisal. Meins' lawyer, Siegfried Haag, who was one of the last people to see him alive was so moved by the experience that he too took up the armed struggle: "I was so intensely involved [with his situation] at the time and I felt that as a lawyer I could not defend him the way he needed to be defended."[570] Haag was not the only person on the German left to react this way. Stefan Wisniewski was another activist who attributed his decision to join the RAF to the manner of Meins' death, and he recalled the galvanizing effect this incident had on his comrades: "Some people who had been critical of the RAF up to that point immediately began to assemble Molotov cocktails and head to the Ku'damm."[571]

Perhaps the best known example of this kind of action were the Provisional IRA hunger strikes of 1981. The hunger strikes were called by republican prisoners in an effort to assert the status of

---

[569] J. Smith and André Moncourt, *The Red Army Faction A Documentary History: Volume 1 — Projectiles for the People* (PM Press; 2009), p. 254.

[570] ibid., p. 261.

[571] Stefan Wisniewski and André Moncourt, *We Were so Terribly Consistent ... A Conversation About the History of the Red Army Faction* (Kersplebedeb; 2009), pp. 7–8.

convicted Provisional IRA members as "political" rather than "criminal" detainees. The British government unsurprisingly refused to accept this distinction, and in all ten prisoners starved themselves to death before the strike was called off. The episode radicalized nationalist opinion and helped make *Sinn Féin* a mainstream political party. Sixty-one people were killed in the upsurge of sectarian violence that accompanied the hunger strikes, and the security forces fired a total of 29,695 plastic bullets in 1981 during public disturbances — almost twice the number fired in the following eight years combined.[572] Anthony McIntyre, a convicted Provisional IRA member who served in prison alongside the hunger strikers, recalled: "The hunger strike was the most intense moment in the history of the Provisional IRA. It has assumed the status of sacred. Those of us involved in the blanket protest still shake with emotion when the memory of the ten men visit our consciousness."[573]

A common state response to hunger strikers — from the era of the suffragettes onwards — has been forced feeding. The Israeli government, for example, introduced forced feeding after Palestinian detainees began using hunger strikes as form a protest in the late 1960s. The practice was suspended by the Israeli authorities after several Palestinian prisoners died during the procedure in the early 1980s. However, it was reintroduced by the *Knesset* in 2015. The forced feeding of detainees on hunger strike by medical personnel involves the use of restraints and invasive techniques such as liquid nutrient administered through a tube inserted in the nose or throat. In its 1991 *Declaration of Malta on Hunger Strikers*, the World Medical Association came to the conclusion that "forcible feeding is never ethically acceptable."[574]

---

[572] Peter Taylor, *Provos: The IRA and Sinn Féin* (Bloomsbury Publishing; 1997), p. 237 and Brendan O'Brien, *The Long War: The IRA and Sinn Féin 1985 to Today* (Syracuse University Press; 1995), p. 44.

[573] Jeffrey William Lewis, *The Business of Martyrdom: A History of Suicide Bombing* (Naval Institute Press; 2012), pp. 130–131.

[574] Björn Elberling, *The Defendant in International Criminal Proceedings: Between Law and Historiography, Studies in International and Comparative Criminal Law* (Hart Publishing; 2012), p. 27.

Palestinian detainee Moussa Sheikh, who participated in a mass hunger strike in 1970, described the procedure from the prisoner's perspective: "When it was done to me, I felt my lungs close as the tube reached my stomach ... I almost suffocated. They poured milk down the tube, which felt like fire to me. It was boiling. I could not stay still, I danced from the pain."[575] Before his death, the RAF veteran Holger Meins described undergoing a forced feeding in Wittlich Prison in similar terms: "A red stomach pipe (not a tube) is used, about the thickness of a middle finger ... The slightest irritation when the pipe is introduced causes gagging and nausea and the cramping of the chest and stomach muscles, setting off a chain reaction of extremely intense convulsions throughout the body, causing one to buck against the pipe ... The pipe is, regardless of circumstances, torture."[576] Another RAF hunger striker, Margrit Schiller, recalled: "I was force-fed every day for a month. Each time was like a rape. Each time, I felt totally humiliated and destroyed."[577]

At one point in 2013, 106 of the 166 detainees in the US detention facility in Guantanamo were participating in a hunger strike and the US authorities responded by forcibly feeding the strikers to keep their strength up.[578] The crisis in Guantanamo attracted the attention of the Inter-American Commission on Human Rights (IACHR), the United Nations Working Group on Arbitrary Detention, and several UN Special Rapporteurs who came together to issue a statement to the effect that it is "unjustifiable" to engage in forced feeding of individuals contrary to their informed and

---

[575] Addameer (Prisoner Support and Human Rights Association), *Factsheet: Force-feeding under International Law and Medical Standards,* 16 November 2015, at http://www.addameer.org/ publications/factsheet-force-feeding-under-international-law-and-medical-standards. Viewed 16 March 2016.

[576] J. Smith and André Moncourt, *The Red Army Faction A Documentary History: Volume 1 — Projectiles for the People* (PM Press; 2009), p. 259.

[577] ibid.

[578] Charlie Savage, Guantánamo Hunger Strike Is Largely Over, U.S. Says, *The New York Times,* 23 September 2013 at http://www.nytimes.com/2013/09/24/us/guantanamo-hunger-strike-largely-over-us-says.html?_r=0.

voluntary refusal of such a measure.[579] The UN Special Rapporteur on torture, Juan Méndez, went even further suggesting that forced feedings "induced by threats, coercion, force or use of physical restraints of individuals, who have opted for the extreme recourse of a hunger strike to protest against their detention, are, even if intended for their benefit, tantamount to cruel, inhuman and degrading treatment."[580]

Finally, any form of detention must be subject to effective oversight. The *UN Body of Principles for the Protection of All Persons under Any Form of Detention or Imprisonment* requires the provision of a complaint mechanism for detainees, and a detainee's family or legal representative, in relation to the detainee's treatment. The *Body of Principles* directs states to appoint "qualified and experienced persons" to conduct regular prison visits to ensure that prison authorities are adhering to the relevant laws and regulations.[581] These individuals should operate independently of the authority directly in charge of administering the prison and prisoners should be afforded access to speak with them confidentially. The UN Special Rapporteur on torture has described such visits as one of the most effective preventive measures against torture.[582] The *Body of Principles* commits states to hold a full inquiry into the cause of death or disappearance of any prisoner held in custody, which may also be warranted when a detainee's death or disappearance occurs shortly after release from detention,

---

[579] Office of the High Commissioner for Human Rights, Press Release, *IACHR, UN Working Group on Arbitrary Detention, UN Rapporteur on torture, UN Rapporteur on human rights while countering terrorism, and UN Rapporteur on health reiterate need to end the indefinite detention of individuals at Guantánamo Naval Base in light of current human rights crisis*, 1 May 2013, at www.ohchr.org/EN/NewsEvents/Pages/DisplayNews.aspx?NewsID=13278#sthash.8G3ofRBt.dpuf. Viewed 13 March 2016.

[580] Office the High Commissioner for Human Rights, Press Release, UN experts urge Israel to halt legalization of force-feeding of hunger-strikers in detention, 28 July 2015, at http://www.ohchr.org/RU/NewsEvents/Pages/DisplayNews.aspx?NewsID=16269&LangID=E. Viewed 16 March 2016.

[581] Principle 29.

[582] United Nations Economic and Social Council, *Report of the Special Rapporteur on torture, Nigel Rodley, submitted pursuant to Commission on Human Rights Resolution 1992/32*, E/CN.4/1995/34, 12 January 1995, para 926(c).

and to provide compensation for any injury caused by the act or omission of a public official that arises from a breach of the UN Principles.[583]

## Prisoners of war and enemy combatants

The Global War on Terror declared by the Bush administration saw the United States introduce a novel form of indefinite detention for terrorism suspects similar in most respects to internment, but introduced under an entirely different legal rubric: suspected members of *al-Qaeda* were detained and held by the US authorities as enemy combatants. Designating the events of September 11th as an "armed attack" within the meaning of both the UN Charter and the NATO treaty, and armed with an Authorization for the Use of Military Force (AUMF) passed in a joint resolution by the US Senate and Congress, the United States declared itself to be in a non-international armed conflict of a global character with members of *al-Qaeda*. William Haynes, the General Counsel of the Department of Defense, explained the logic of this decision in a memorandum written to the Council on Foreign Relations in December 2002: "War implicates legal powers and rules that are not available during peacetime. Among other things, the war context gives the President the authority to detain enemy combatants at least until hostilities cease."[584] However, in asserting this authority, the United States has found itself mired in a complex and confusing legal quagmire, which has resulted in the extended detention without trial in Guantanamo of a minority of genuinely (at least according to successive US administrations) dangerous members or associates of *al-Qaeda*, amounting to thirty-three individuals out of an original prison population of 780, alongside three convicted inmates and five detainees who have long been cleared for release but are still being held simply because there is no country wiling to accept them

---

[583] Principles 34 and 35.

[584] William Haynes, *Memorandum to Members of the ASIL-CFR Roundtable on Enemy Combatants*, 12 December 2002 at http://www.cfr.org/international-law/enemy-combatants/p5312. Viewed 29 February 2016.

to which they can safely be returned. At the time of writing, at least 730 detainees have been released from Guantanamo (all but five without being charged with any offense), and nine detainees have died in custody, some by their own hand, others of natural causes.[585]

The power to detain enemy combatants in an international armed conflict — a conflict fought between two or more states — for the duration of the conflict is closely regulated by the Third Geneva Convention of 1949. A lawful combatant in an international armed conflict has broken no laws by taking up arms or by using them on the battlefield, and for this reason the designation "Prisoner of War" confers a degree of a legitimacy on a belligerent's actions so long as they remain within the parameters established by the law of armed conflict. As such, there can be no criminal or punitive character to an individual's incarceration as a Prisoner of War — it is simply a mechanism for ensuring that a former belligerent plays no further part in hostilities for the remainder of the conflict, or until a prisoner exchange occurs. In centuries past, it was not uncommon for a Prisoner of War to even be repatriated on condition that he give his word of honor, or *parole*, that he would play no further part in the fighting. Only if a Prisoner of War is suspected of having perpetrated a war crime could his incarceration take on a judicial character. If convicted of such a crime, the prisoner could then be held like any other criminal until the completion or commutation of his sentence.

While Prisoners of War may lawfully be questioned by the detaining power, they are only obliged to provide their name, rank, date of birth and service number, and are protected against any act of violence or ill treatment, including physical or mental torture, and from acts of medical experimentation, humiliating labor (and in the case of officers any labor at all), intimidation, insults, and public curiosity.[586] The Geneva Conventions define minimum conditions

---

[585] Guantanamo: Facts and Figures, Human Rights Watch, 30 March 2017 at https://www.hrw. org/video-photos/interactive/2017/03/30/guantanamo-facts-and-figures. Viewed 17 August 2017. See also Fact Sheet: Guantanamo by the Numbers, Human Rights First, 14 February 2018.

[586] See Third Geneva Convention Relative to the Treatment of Prisoners of War, 12 August 1949, Articles 13, 15, 17, 49, and 52.

of detention covering issues as diverse as accommodation, food, clothing, hygiene, and medical care.[587] Every Prisoner of War must be treated alike by the detaining authority with no distinction made on the basis of race, nationality, religion, political belief, or similar criteria.[588] Provision by the detaining authority must be made for Prisoners of War to be able to worship, and detaining authorities are enjoined to encourage "the practice of intellectual, educational, and recreational pursuits, sports and games amongst prisoners" (even to the extent of providing suitable facilities) while respecting an individual prisoner's right not to participate if he so chooses.[589] Prisoners of War are also entitled to send and receive cards and letters from the outside world.[590] The 1949 Geneva Conventions are considered to be customary international law in their entirety.

The political legitimacy associated with the designation "Prisoner of War", and the duty of care it places on the detaining authority, has meant that this status is often coveted by terrorist groups, even when they are clearly acting outside of the context of an international armed conflict and do not themselves appear to be complying with international humanitarian law. Lawful combatants must comply with a set of criteria to qualify as such — they must carry their weapons openly, wear uniforms or some form of identifying insignia, act within a distinct command structure, and respect the laws and customs of war, including the prohibition on deliberately targeting civilians.[591] This is a standard few, if any, terrorist organizations would objectively meet, meaning the best that most terrorists could reasonably aspire to in an international armed conflict is the label of "unlawful combatant", which is applied to civilians directly participating in hostilities in certain circumstances.[592] Unlawful

---

[587] ibid., Articles 22, 25–28 and 29–32.

[588] Third Geneva Convention Relative to the Treatment of Prisoners of War, 12 August 1949, Article 16.

[589] ibid., Articles 34 and 38.

[590] ibid., Article 71.

[591] The Hague Convention (18 October 1907), Annex to the Convention, Section I "On Belligerents", Chapter I "The Qualifications of Belligerents", Article 1, and the Third Geneva Convention Relative to the Treatment of Prisoners of War, 12 August 1949, Article 4.

[592] Fourth Convention relative to the Protection of Civilian Persons in Time of War, 12 August 1949, Secs. III and IV.

combatants are not accorded Prisoner of War status, the regime governing their treatment is laid out in the Fourth Geneva Convention, and is the same as that applied to other civilians caught up in the conflict.[593] Nevertheless, as we have just seen above, this has not stopped some terrorist groups, such as the Provisional IRA and the *Rote Armee Fraktion,* seeking to lay claim to Prisoner of War status on behalf of their captured comrades.[594] In a letter written to her lawyer in December 1975, Ulrike Meinhof provided a useful insight into the perceived political value of doing so: "[The] struggle for Prisoner of War status ... is the operator for mobilizing international publicity for our struggle ... and indeed for the recognition under international law of revolutionary movement as parties to a conflict."[595]

The International Committee of the Red Cross, custodian of the Geneva Conventions, takes the view that combatant status does not exist in non-international armed conflicts and thus that the regimes outlined in the Third and Fourth Geneva Conventions do not apply in such circumstances.[596] Members of armed groups engaged in non-international armed conflicts therefore enjoy no special status and can be prosecuted under domestic law for the part they play in hostilities since taking up arms unlawfully is likely to be considered an illegal act. The UN Special Rapporteur on protection of human rights and fundamental freedoms while countering terrorism, Martin Scheinin, has similarly commented that "persons directly participating in hostilities during the course of a non-international armed conflict may arguably be detained for the duration of the hostilities, but can alternatively be treated as criminal suspects for

---

[593] International Committee of the Red Cross, *The relevance of IHL in the context of terrorism,* 01-01-2011 FAQ, para 4(a) at https://www.icrc.org/eng/resources/documents/misc/terrorism-ihl-210705.htm. Viewed 1 March 2016.

[594] 594 David Beresford, *Ten Men Dead: The Story of the 1981 Irish Hunger Strike* (Atlantic Monthly Press; 1997), p. 13.

[595] Leith Passmore, *Ulrike Meinhof and the Red Army Faction: Performing Terrorism* (Palgrave Macmillan; 2011), p. 101.

[596] International Committee of the Red Cross, *The relevance of IHL in the context of terrorism,* 01-01-2011 FAQ, para 4(b) at https://www.icrc.org/eng/resources/documents/misc/terrorism-ihl-210705.htm. Viewed 1 March 2016.

their use of violence."[597] However, Common Article 3 of the 1949 Geneva Conventions does establish a basic minimum standard for the treatment of detainees in the context of a non-international armed conflict, including that they must be treated "humanely", without discrimination, and that they should be protected from "violence to life and person", "murder", "torture", "cruel treatment", "outrages upon personal dignity" and "humiliating and degrading treatment". This is a standard that the United States consistently failed to meet in its treatment of individuals detained as enemy combatants in the course of the Global War on Terror. Indeed, the UN Special Rapporteur on torture, Juan Méndez, has declared on several occasions that the apparently indefinite detention of individuals at Guantanamo in and of itself, quite apart from the conditions of detention, "causes a state of suffering, stress, fear and anxiety, which ... constitutes a form of cruel, inhuman, and degrading treatment."[598] The United States has ultimately paid an enormous political price to detain just forty-one individuals without meeting the burden of proof imposed by the criminal justice system, and it has abused the rights of ten times as many civilians in the process. It is hard to imagine that in most cases the threat posed by these forty-one men could not have ultimately been negated by other lawful action. The challenge of converting intelligence into evidence while protecting the original source is one that intelligence and law enforcement officials are well used to. Once again, the cost–benefit analysis does not seem to support the value of the policy.

## Deradicalization programs

One of the earliest terrorism-related prison de-radicalization programs was introduced by the Italian government to encourage jailed members of the *Brigate Rosse* (and other left-wing extremist groups

[597] Note by the Secretary-General, *Protection of human rights and fundamental freedoms while countering terrorism*, A/63/223, 6 August 2008, para 21.

[598] *Statement of the United Nations Special Rapporteur on torture at the Expert Meeting on the situation of detainees held at the U.S. Naval Base at Guantanamo Bay*, Inter-American Commission on Human Rights, 3 October 2013.

like *Prima Linea*) to cut their ties with the movement. The tide was turning against the *Brigate Rosse* in the early 1980s as consequence of a variety of disparate but related factors. Policing methods undoubtedly improved over time restricting the activities of the terrorist group, but it was the shift in attitudes on the political left described in Part II, coupled with deft legislative steps to take advantage of this shift that made the crucial difference.[599]

In May 1982, the Italian authorities exploited the growing fragmentation of the far left by introducing a "collaboration" law that allowed for the proportional reduction of sentences passed for crimes committed prior to 1981 in return for the prisoner's active cooperation with the authorities. This might be no more than a full confession by the prisoner to his or her own crimes. Within 120 days of the law entering into force, 389 terrorist prisoners had taken advantage of it to cut a deal. Of these, seventy-eight were classified as *grandi pentiti* who had made an "exceptional contribution" to police investigations.[600] Providing information that led to "decisive proof" in a case against an active member of a terrorist organization could lead to the reduction by ⅓–½ of the *pentito*'s sentence.[601] In 200 hours of taped testimony, one *pentito*, the Turin-based Brigadist Patrizio Peci, shared information that led to the arrest of seventy members of the organization.[602] In 1986, the Italian government went still further extending sentence reductions to those who simply disassociated themselves from their former activities. In the words of the researcher Alison Jamieson: "Enlightened legislation and prison administration ... created the possibility for many ex-terrorists to re-examine the past critically, and to work through individual and collective responsibilities as a prelude to rehabilitation and

---

[599] Luciana Stortoni-Wortmann, The Police Response to Terrorism in Italy from 1969 to 1983, in Fernando Reinares (ed.), *European Democracies Against Terrorism* (Dartmouth; Ashgate 2000), pp. 159–161 and 163.

[600] Donatella Della Porta, Institutional Responses to Terrorism: The Italian Case, *Terrorism and Political Violence* (Winter 1992), p. 167.

[601] George Kassimeris, *Inside Greek Terrorism* (Oxford University Press; 2013), p. 38.

[602] Michael Burleigh, *Blood and Rage: A Cultural History of Terrorism* (Harper; 2009), p. 217.

release."[603] The collaboration law created a political exit for former members of the *Brigate Rosse* and within a year of its introduction outgoing Interior Minister Virginio Rognoni was able to leave office confident that terrorism had been "politically defeated".[604]

Several European governments followed Italy's lead. The Greek government introduced legislation modeled on the Italian approach to gain the cooperation of captured members of November 17 with some success.[605] One former November 17 member who took advantage of the Greek government's offer, Patroklos Tselentis, unconsciously echoed Jamieson's characterization of the *pentiti* program commenting that he gained from it "a sense of freedom, that comes from the possibility to recollect your life using the normal logic for which murder is murder, wounding is wounding, a ferocious comrade is a ferocious man, and not a vanguard with a higher level of class consciousness."[606] In 1992, German Justice Minister Klaus Kinkel announced that his government would explore "reconciliation" in appropriate cases, if the *Rote Armee Fraktion* abandoned its armed campaign. A brief public dialogue followed, at the end of which the RAF released a communiqué explicitly renouncing political murder, this in turn led to the release of nine RAF prisoners by September 1993.[607] There was no subsequent resurgence of RAF terrorism and in April 1998 the rump organization issued its final valedictory communiqué formally concluding hostilities with the observation that "the urban guerrilla, in the form of the RAF, is now history."[608]

However, one-sided amnesties have proved notably less successful. In May 1981, an incoming French socialist government, headed by François Mitterrand, granted a presidential amnesty to incarcerated members of the Maoist and anarchist inspired French terrorist

---

[603] Alison Jamieson, Entry, Discipline and Exit in the Italian Red Brigades, *Terrorism and Political Violence*, Vol. 2, No. 1 (1990), p. 19.

[604] Donatella Della Porta, Institutional Responses to Terrorism: The Italian Case, *Terrorism and Political Violence* (Winter 1992), p. 163.

[605] George Kassimeris, *Inside Greek Terrorism* (Oxford University Press; 2013), p. 38.

[606] ibid., p. 56.

[607] Michael Burleigh, *Blood and Rage: A Cultural History of Terrorism* (Harper; 2009), p. 264.

[608] ibid., p. 266.

group *Action Directe* — at least those not charged with murder — but without the provision of any reintegration services. While some former members did cut their ties with the organization after their release, others like Régis Schleicher, Jean-Marc Rouillan, and Nathalie Ménigon went underground and emerged more violent than before.[609] Following a similar trajectory to the *Tupamaros, Action Directe* cadres moved from whimsical stunts such as stealing the Socialist Party First Secretary Lionel Jospin's car and occupying the famous Parisian gourmet restaurant *La Tour d'Argent*, to bombing such targets as the headquarters of Interpol and the European Space Agency, and killing the Israeli diplomat Youri Barsimantov, the Director of International Affairs at the French Ministry of Defense, General René Audran, and the President of the car manufacturer Renault, Georges Besse.[610] In classic armed propaganda fashion, Besse's murder was accompanied by a twenty-six-page declaration from *Action Directe* justifying the action.[611] The French amnesty law was revised in July 1988.[612]

Disengagement and deradicalization initiatives have now become an integral part of many countries' counter-terrorism strategies, from Latin America to South East Asia. Such initiatives typically share a number of features, including a mix of vocational and ideological programming, risk assessments, an emphasis on creating commitments, after-care, the prominent role of credible interlocutors or mentors, and the use of material incentives and inducements.[613] In the late 1990s and early 2000s, Colombia passed laws allowing individuals who had belonged to terrorist groups like *Fuerzas Armadas Revolucionarias de Colombia — Ejército del Pueblo* (FARC) and *Ejército de Liberación Nacional* (ELN) to seek amnesty for their "political crimes" although involvement in acts of

---

[609] Michael Dartnell, France's Action Directe: Terrorists in Search of a Revolution, *Journal of Terrorism and Political Violence*, Vol. 2, No. 4, 1990, p. 460.

[610] ibid.

[611] ibid., p. 476.

[612] Gilbert Guillaume, France and the Fight Against Terrorism, in Ronald Crelinsten and Alex Schmid (eds.), *Western Responses to Terrorism* (Frank Cass & Co.; 1993), p. 132.

[613] John Amble, *Five Questions with Peter Neumann on his Trip to Mogadishu, War on the Rocks*, 6 January 2014 at http://warontherocks.com/2014/01/five-questions-with-peter-neumann/.

"ferocity or barbarity, terrorism, kidnapping ... [and] homicide committed outside of combat" disqualified potential applicants from consideration.[614] Successful applicants are eligible to receive a variety of vocational, educational, and economic benefits to aid their reintegration into mainstream Colombian society — so long as they remain in contact with government "reference centers" established to supervise their reintegration. The Colombian government has also deployed social workers to work individually or in small groups with former fighters to help them change their "violent ways" and take responsibility for their lives without direction from above.[615]

One component of the 1998 Good Friday Agreement that brought an end to The Troubles in Northern Ireland was an Early Release Scheme for convicted terrorists affiliated with groups that recognized the ceasefire. Early release was contingent on the individual not violating the terms of his or her release, and on the group he or she belonged to continuing to respect the ceasefire.[616] However, it soon became clear to the authorities in both London and Dublin that release alone was not sufficient and Prime Ministers Tony Blair and Bertie Ahern issued a joint letter to the political parties of Northern Ireland emphasizing their commitment to "facilitate the reintegration of prisoners into the community, and to address related issues."[617] As in Colombia, this mostly took the form of financial assistance, job placement, or vocational training. More than £9,200,000 in funding was provided to ninety different ex-prisoner-related groups and projects between 1995 and 2003 by the Community Foundation for Northern Ireland and the European Special Support Programme for Peace and Reconciliation.[618] One beneficiary was *Coiste na n-Iarchimí*, which helped set up a company

---

[614] John Horgan and Kurt Braddock, Rehabilitating the Terrorists?: Challenges in Assessing the Effectiveness of De-Radicalization Programs, *Journal of Terrorism and Political Violence*, Vol. 22 (2010), p. 271.

[615] ibid., p. 272.

[616] ibid., p. 269.

[617] ibid.

[618] Stephen White and Kieran McEvoy, *Countering Violent Extremism: Community Engagement Programmes in Europe*, Qatar International Academy for Security Studies (February 2012), p. 41.

specializing in "Irish Political Tours" of sites connected with The Troubles, like Milltown Cemetery or the Falls Road, for visiting tourists in order to create employment opportunities for former prisoners.[619] Of the 453 prisoners freed under the Early Release Scheme between April 1998 and May 2010, only twenty-three had their release licenses revoked, of which ten were rearrested for terrorist-related activity.[620] John Horgan and Kurt Braddock have reported that this was one-fifteenth the recidivism rate associated with ordinary criminals in Northern Ireland.[621]

In recent years, the United Kingdom has approached the rehabilitation of terrorist offenders in large part through the lens of therapy and psycho-social support, and this too has shown promise. In 2012, there were about 120 convicted terrorists in the UK prison system and all of them had been put through an intensive psychological assessment process run by the National Offender Management Service known as the Extreme Risk Guidance Programme (ERG22+).[622] About one-third of these offenders refused to engage with their interviewers, but Natasha Sargeant, Head Psychologist at Whitemoor Prison, was surprised at how much many of the others actually wanted to talk: "In some cases, there's been this huge sense of relief at having an opportunity to explain and understand how they got involved, and then to do something about it."[623] 'Karim', a prisoner who participated in the ERG22+ program, told a reporter: "Coming to your senses doesn't happen in a moment — it's not as if you just click your fingers. It takes a lot of time and courage. But I've come to the conclusion that I took a very wrong turning. It has been

---

[619] http://www.coiste.ie/.

[620] Stephen White and Kieran McEvoy, *Countering Violent Extremism: Community Engagement Programmes in Europe*, Qatar International Academy for Security Studies (February 2012), pp. 39–40.

[621] John Horgan and Kurt Braddock, Rehabilitating the Terrorists?: Challenges in Assessing the Effectiveness of De-Radicalization Programs, *Journal of Terrorism and Political Violence*, Vol. 22 (2010), p. 271.

[622] Richard Pickering, Terrorism, Extremism, Radicalization and the Offender Management System: The Story So Far, *Prison Service Journal*, No. 203, September 2012, pp. 9–14 and David Rose, Inside Britain's Terror Cells, *The Daily Mail*, 29 September 2012.

[623] David Rose, Inside Britain's Terror Cells, *The Daily Mail*, 29 September 2012.

traumatic, first coming into prison, and then coming to terms with what I've done, and finally to let all this out when I'm under constant pressure not to. But this course has given me the means to look at myself, and to gain perspective. It's been a massive burden off my shoulders, a breath of fresh air."[624]

Indonesia has enjoyed a degree of success with an *ad hoc* deradicalization program, built around a combination of religious and socio-economic engagement, which has succeeded persuading at least two-dozen members of *Jemaah Islamiyah* to cooperate with the police.[625] The Indonesian police counter-terrorism unit *Detasemen Khusus 88*[626] worked closely with a former *Jemaah Islamiyah* commander, Mohammed Nasir bin Abbas, who had fought against the Soviets in Afghanistan, and a former *Jemaah Islamiyah* cell member involved in the 2002 Bali bombings, Ali Imron, to engage with members of terror group held in custody, and, in the words of Abbas, help them to "return to the right path of Islamic teaching."[627] Abbas, who has impeccable Islamic credentials, would often spend up to a week with newly apprehended *Jemaah Islamiyah* members challenging the religious foundation of their embrace of indiscriminate violence and seeking to persuade them to cooperate with the authorities. A former Commissioner of the Australian Federal Police, Mick Keelty, who worked closely with *Detasemen Khusus 88*, observed it was the very fact that Abbas had held a senior position within *Jemaah Islamiyah* that ensured he was heard with respect by other detainees.[628] Another fundamental premise of the Indonesian approach was that police could change the militants' assumption that government officials were un-Islamic, and thus illegitimate, through acts of kindness. *Detasemen Khusus 88* commanders, like Brigadier General Surya Dharma, leveraged their shared Islamic faith by organizing

---

[624] ibid.

[625] International Crisis Group, *"Deradicalisation" and Indonesian Prisons*, Asia Report No. 142, 19 November 2007, p. i.

[626] Special Detachment 88.

[627] John Horgan and Kurt Braddock, Rehabilitating the Terrorists?: Challenges in Assessing the Effectiveness of De-Radicalization Programs, *Journal of Terrorism and Political Violence*, Vol. 22 (2010), p. 273.

[628] ibid., p. 274.

joint prayer sessions with *Jemaah Islamiyah* detainees.[629] When a new detainee was arrested, police interviewers would also probe their economic concerns and then find funds to address these concerns in a way that earned the detainee's gratitude and encouraged cooperation; this might extend to paying children' school fees, providing welfare support to family members, or facilitating prison visits. One Indonesian police officer told a researcher from the International Crisis Group that if he had to choose between religious and socio-economic approaches to deradicalization, he would always choose the latter, "because it worked".[630]

The Saudi Prevention, Rehabilitation and After Care (PRAC) program, established after the series of *al-Qaeda*-inspired attacks struck the Kingdom in 2003–2004, has also sought to fuse theological and welfare approaches to deradicalization, and the Saudi government has claimed significant success.[631] The PRAC program is aimed at terrorist detainees in the Saudi prison system — it seeks to expose them to alternate interpretations of Islam through sustained theological debate with a focus on civic responsibility.[632] The central principle of the program is that the detainees have been "misled" and thus require guidance rather than punishment.[633] The program is overseen by an Advice Committee which draws on the expertise of clerics, psychologists, and scientists, mostly drawn from the conservative *sahwaist* segment of Saudi society, committed proponents of stronger religious institutions many of whom have been through a deradicalization experience

---

[629] Tore Bjorgo and John Horgan, *Leaving Terrorism Behind: Individual and Collective Disengagement* (Routledge; 2009), p. 200.

[630] International Crisis Group, *"Deradicalisation" and Indonesian Prisons*, Asia Report No. 142, 19 November 2007, p. 13.

[631] Hamed El-Said, *De-Radicalisation Islamists: Programmes and their Impact in Muslim States*, International Centre for the Study of Radicalisation and Political Violence, January 2012, p. 37.

[632] William Sheridan Combs, Assessing Two Countering Violent Extremism Programmes: Saudi Arabia's PRAC and the United Kingdom's Prevent Strategy, *Small Wars Journal*, July 2013.

[633] Hamed El-Said, *De-Radicalisation Islamists: Programmes and their Impact in Muslim States*, International Centre for the Study of Radicalisation and Political Violence, January 2012, p. 38.

of their own in the 1990s, and thus could reportedly establish common ground with many of the detainees.

The first stage of the PRAC program is prison-based and is known as the *al-Munasah* (Advice) phase — prisoners are offered the opportunity to participate in either a two-week or six-week programme of individual and group sessions. Prisoners that demonstrate progress in these sessions begin to cooperate with the authorities, moderate their views, and renounce violence are moved to the Mohammed bin Nayef Centre for Counselling and Care. At the Centre, detainees take a variety of courses focusing on religion, social responsibility, art, and history. They undergo psychological counseling, and the program also places significant emphasis on sport, encouraging prisoners and staff to play together and thus further strengthen the social bond between instructor and student. If they successfully complete the deradicalization program, PRAC graduates can expect to receive extensive social welfare support once they are released from custody. The Saudi government pays graduates of the program a monthly stipend until they can make their own way without assistance; it helps them find employment, offers education funding, assists in their reintegration into their communities and even on occasion, controversially, acts as a matchmaker finding potential marriage partners. The PRAC program also seeks to involve family members closely in the rehabilitation process, offering counseling to family members and paying for them to visit their loved ones in detention, and maintaining close contact with them after the detainee's release. By 2008, only forty-five of the 1,400 individuals who had completed the program had been re-arrested[634] and in 2013 government officials claimed the program had a success rate of 80–90%.[635]

Family members are often as surprised and appalled by an individual's involvement in terrorism as anyone else, and so may prove to be an important asset to a police investigation — if they have

---

[634] Christopher Boucek, *"Saudi Arabia's 'Soft' Counterterrorism Strategy: Prevention, Rehabilitation, and Aftercare"*, Carnegie Paper Middle East Program, No. 97, September, 2008.

[635] William Sheridan, Assessing Two Countering Violent Extremism Programs: Saudi Arabia's PRAC and the United Kingdom's Prevent Strategy, *Small Wars Journal*, July 2013.

faith that police will deal with them and their accused relative fairly. Working with suspects' families in the aftermath of an arrest can thus be just as important as working with victims' families, and can potentially be extremely productive for investigators. A number of governments around the world have instituted practices to ensure the needs of suspects' families are not neglected by society. The Malaysian government provides financial support to the families of individuals detained in connection with terrorism investigations — they have found that detainees tend to be more cooperative after their wives visit them in prison and share with them details of what the government is doing for their families. In the United Kingdom, Counter-terrorism Contact Officers work with suspects' families post-arrest to provide them with information about the case, assisting in the return of confiscated property, escorting the family to court, and generally facilitating their participation in the judicial process. Australian Police have also adopted similar practices. One relatively recent example of a family member working closely with the authorities after the arrest of a relative is Umaru Abdulmutallab, the father of the underwear bomber Farouq Abdulmutallab. Not only did Umaru raise concerns about his son's intentions with US officials prior to his travel to the United States, after Umar's arrest Umaru also traveled to the United States at the request of the FBI to urge his son to cooperate with US Prosecutors.[636]

In addition to providing a potential venue for one-on-one engagement with individual terrorist actors and their families, prisons can provide a platform for the wider engagement of a terrorist group — especially if key members of the group's leadership can be found among those incarcerated, as occurred with Egypt's *al-Gama'a al-Islamiyya* in the late 1990s.[637] Between 1992 and 1996, 401 members of the Egyptian security forces, 306 Egyptian civilians, and ninety-seven foreign tourists were killed in incidents linked to the

---

[636] CBS News, *Abdulmutallab: Cleric Told Me to Bomb Jet*, 4 February 2010 at http://www.cbsnews.com/news/abdulmutallab-cleric-told-me-to-bomb-jet/.

[637] Hamed El-Said, *De-Radicalisation Islamists: Programmes and their Impact in Muslim States*, International Centre for the Study of Radicalisation and Political Violence, January 2012, p. 17.

group.[638] Egypt seemed to be locked in an escalating spiral of violence but in July 1997 an unexpected peace overture was made by jailed members of the original leadership of *al-Gama'a al-Islamiyya*, who released a statement calling for a unilateral ceasefire on the part of their followers. The Egyptian prison authorities were quick to take advantage of this evolution in the group's political and theological thinking by helping to facilitate internal dialogue and debate amongst the leadership cadre once the process of revision was underway. The Egyptian authorities also invited credible scholars from *Al-Azhar* University, one of the most respected institutions of Islamic scholarship in the world, to visit prisons to participate in theological discussions.[639] Eventually, the leaders of *al-Gama'a al-Islamiyya* instructed their followers that it was time to pursue a less violent path, publishing a series of books and pamphlets collectively known as *The Revisions* in which they explained their decisions in powerful theological terms, and, because of the credibility and respect which they commanded, their followers listened.[640] Counter-radicalization researchers like Omar Ashour have emphasized the important role that "message validators" — individuals whose opinion carries weight with the relevant target audience — can play in shifting entrenched mindsets. In the case of hardcore members of terrorist groups, it is usually the voices of former comrades that appear to register most powerfully. Mamduh Yusuf, a former commander of the armed wing of *al-Gama'a al-Islamiyya*, told Ashour: "Hearing the arguments directly from the *Sheikhs* was different ... we accepted them from the *Sheikhs* because we knew them and we knew their history."[641]

Sayyid Imam al-Sharif, better known as Dr. Fadl, had been a senior figure in *Tanzim al-Jihad* in the 1980s, and was the author of a

---

[638] Omar Ashour, *The Radicalization of Jihadists: Transforming Armed Islamist Movements* (Routledge; 2009), p. 50.

[639] Hamed El-Said, *De-Radicalisation Islamists: Programmes and their Impact in Muslim States*, International Centre for the Study of Radicalisation and Political Violence, January 2012, p. 18.

[640] ibid., p. 17 and Omar Ashour, *The Radicalization of Jihadists: Transforming Armed Islamist Movements* (Routledge; 2009), p. 92.

[641] Omar Ashour, *The Radicalization of Jihadists: Transforming Armed Islamist Movements* (Routledge; 2009).

seminal militant jihadist text, *The Essential Guide for Preparation.* He was detained without charge in Yemen after the 9/11 attacks and was transferred to Egypt's Tora Prison in 2004. From prison Dr. Fadl published *Advice Regarding the Conduct of Jihadist Action in Egypt and the World* in which he now denounced terrorism as unIslamic and recast the concept of *jihad* in tightly circumscribed defensive terms. The fact that Dr. Fadl had once been a close friend and colleague of *al-Qaeda* head Ayman al-Zawahiri made the former's change of heart, and the message contained in *Advice,* all the more remarkable — and all the more impactful. Egypt ended up releasing almost 12,500 repentant members of *al-Gama'a al-Islamiyya* and *Tanzim al-Jihad,* which explicitly followed *al-Gama'a al-Islamiyya*'s lead and renounced armed struggle in 2007.[642]

While incarcerated in the island prison of İmralı, the leader of the PKK, Abdullah Öcalan, remained politically active publishing several volumes of prison writings in which his ideological positions continued to evolve.[643] In September 2006, he issued a statement through his lawyer calling for a PKK ceasefire and declaring, in a marked change from his previous rhetoric, that "the PKK should not use weapons unless it is attacked with the aim of annihilation ... [it is] very important to build a democratic union between Turks and Kurds. With this process, the way to democratic dialogue will be also opened."[644] In 2011, the Turkish government tentatively entered into secret talks with Öcalan, ultimately recognizing him as

---

[642] Hamed El-Said, *De-Radicalisation Islamists: Programmes and their Impact in Muslim States,* International Centre for the Study of Radicalisation and Political Violence, January 2012, p. 19 and Omar Ashour, De-Radicalization of Jihad? The Impact of Egyptian Islamist Revisionists on Al-Qaeda, *Perspectives on Terrorism,* Vol. 2, No. 5 (2008).

[643] In *Abdullah Öcalan v Turkey* (2005) the European Court of Human Rights considered a complaint from Öcalan about the manner in which he had been returned to Turkey to face trial. The court found that, in the absence of a formal extradition treaty, and since there appeared to be cooperation between the Kenyan and Turkish authorities, there had been no violation of Kenyan sovereignty and the transfer was lawful within the meaning of the 5(1)(c) of the ECHR.

[644] BBC News, *Kurdish rebel boss in truce plea,* 28 September 2006 at http://news.bbc.co.uk/2/hi/europe/5389746.stm. Viewed 5 March 2016.

the chief negotiator representing the interests of Turkish Kurds.[645] Prime Minister Recep Erdoğan revealed the existence of these talks to the Turkish public in December 2012, and in March 2013 Öcalan called on his followers to end their conflict with the Turkish state, a conflict that had cost 40,000, mostly Kurdish, lives. Erdoğan's ruling Justice and Development Party found common ground by emphasizing the Islamic "brotherhood" shared by the two communities, which in turn led Öcalan to acknowledge that Turks and Kurds had "been marching under the banner of Islam for a thousand years."[646] While this rapprochement did not survive the deteriorating circumstances in neighboring Syria that gave rise to ISIL, it does further illustrate the potential value of prolonged engagement with a captive leader.

The Peruvian authorities similarly enjoyed some success engaging with the leader of *Sendero Luminoso*, Abimael Guzmán, after his apprehension and incarceration in September 1992. After little over a year of direct negotiations with the Peruvian presidential adviser and intelligence chief Vladimiro Montesinos, Guzmán called publicly from his prison cell for a temporary ceasefire and the commencement of peace talks.[647] However, in ironic contrast to the credibility that the leadership of *al-Gama'a al-Islamiyya* brought to the peace process in Egypt, Guzmán's *volte face* was so vastly at odds with his previously held public positions, this was after all a man who had once promised to put a noose around the necks of imperialists and reactionaries and garrot them, that his disciplined followers initially rejected his statement as a "baseless and ridiculous lie".[648] The disappointment and sense of betrayal in *Sendero Luminoso*'s ranks was so

---

[645] Kevin Matthees and Günter Seufert, *Erdoğan and Öcalan Begin Talks: A Paradigm Shift in Turkey's Kurdish Policy and a New Strategy of the PKK*, German Institute for International and Security Affairs, Comments no. 13, April 2013.

[646] Halil Karaveli, Turkey's Decline: Ankara Must Learn from Its Past to Secure Its Future, *Foreign Affairs*, 2 March 2016.

[647] David Marcus, Peru Leader Makes Use of Unusual Ally, *Chicago Tribune*, 25 November 1993.

[648] Orin Starn, Maoism in the Andes: The Communist Party of Peru–Shining Path and the Refusal of History, *Journal of Latin American Studies*, Vol. 27, No. 2 (May 1995), p. 404 and Carlos Iván Degregori, The Maturation of a Cosmocrat and the Building of a Discourse Community: The Case of Shining Path, in David Apter (ed.), *The Legitimization of Violence* (New York University Press; 1997), p. 74.

great that when it became clear that this was indeed Guzmán's genuine position, it led to cadres deserting the organization in droves.[649] Approximately 1,000 of his most militant former followers broke away to establish *Sendero Rojo* dedicated to keeping the "Popular War" alive.[650] However, the fact remains that the government of Alberto Fujimori was able to actively involve the captive leadership of *Sendero Luminoso* in peace talks, and this in turn split and undermined the movement significantly reducing the terrorist threat.

Finally, it is important to stress that rehabilitation programs also raise important, and sometimes difficult, questions about punishment and impunity. Victims of violent crimes have a right to seek justice and redress, which is enshrined in international human rights law. They are often understandably hostile to any government initiative that allows a convicted perpetrator to get out of prison early, or perhaps even escape punishment altogether. Some victim groups have expressed concern over programs that seem to 'reward' former militants by providing them with financial assistance and other social support. Matthew Waxman, a former Deputy Assistant Secretary of Defense for Detainee Affairs in the Bush administration, has likewise observed that when the public gets to hear the specifics of rehabilitation programs they often react with annoyance characterizing the support offered by such initiatives as "coddling terrorists".[651] Finding an acceptable balance between upholding the rights of victims, while also creating the political space for the rehabilitation of former terrorists is a complex challenge, but one with which any successful deradicalization or demobilization process must successfully grapple if it aspires to make a sustainable contribution to lasting peace.

---

[649] Carlos Iván Degregori, The Maturation of a Cosmocrat and the Building of a Discourse Community: The Case of Shining Path, in David Apter (ed.), *The Legitimization of Violence* (New York University Press; 1997), p. 74.

[650] Red Path. See Cyrus Zirakzadeh, From Revolutionary Dreams to Organizational Fragmentation: Disputes over Violence within ETA and Sendero Luminoso. *Terrorism and Political Violence*, Vol. 14, No. 4 (2002), p. 84.

[651] Jessica Stern, Deradicalization or Disengagement of Terrorists: Is It Possible? A Future Challenges Essay, Koret-Taube Task Force on National Security and Law, Hoover Institution, Stanford University (2010), p. 10.

## Summary

The Scottish comedian Frankie Boyle once observed: "I think the most effective place for [terrorists] to end up is not in a martyr video, but in a small but comfortable jail cell. Somewhere in Kent, perhaps. No paradise, no virgins, no meaning leant by us to their stupidity, no glory, no attention. Just a guard wishing them a bland good morning, and a regular change of towels. And if you think that's insufficient punishment, give them a television that only gets terrestrial, and all our newspapers everyday."[652] It is the banality and increasingly irrelevance of prison life that makes the deprivation of liberty such a profound and meaningful punishment.

International human rights law protects every individual from being detained arbitrarily and deprived of his or her liberty without due process. It requires that an individual accused of a crime has the opportunity and means to challenge this accusation promptly, that a suspect is presumed innocent until proven guilty in a court of law and should be treated appropriately in the pre-trial stage, and that any trial is conducted in fair and equitable circumstances with the burden of proof on the state to make its case. If convicted, international human rights law requires that a prisoner be treated with humanity and dignity, and that the overarching aim of a prisoner's incarceration should be to promote his or her reformation and social rehabilitation. However, it also acknowledges that some prisoners — for example, members of terrorist groups — may pose an ongoing threat while incarcerated, both to other prisoners and to prison staff, and that it might be necessary to take certain measures within the boundaries established by human rights protections to address and contain this threat. International human rights law simply requires that in doing prison authorities do not impose such measures arbitrarily or in a discriminatory fashion, and that they do so only to the extent that such measures are necessary, reasonable, and proportional to the legitimate end sought.

---

[652] Frankie Boyle, Isis want an insane, medieval race war — and we've decided to give them one, *The Guardian*, 4 December 2015.

None of the restrictions enumerated above seem to represent a meaningful impediment to successfully prosecuting and incarcerating terrorists, and once in prison the authorities have a real opportunity to engage, deradicalize, and, perhaps, even reform men and women formerly committed to political violence. This is a process that can certainly go either way, but there is considerable evidence that effective engagement from prison authorities can make a critical difference, sometimes even with the most recalcitrant prisoners. Ultimately, it is just a question of getting it right. Peter Neumann, Director of the International Centre for the Study of Radicalisation at King's College London, has put it most succinctly: "Prisons matter. They have played an enormous role in the narratives of every radical and militant movement in the modern period. They are 'places of vulnerability' in which radicalization takes place. Yet they have also served as incubators for peaceful change and transformation ... Prisons are not just a threat — they can play a positive role in tackling problems of radicalization and terrorism as a whole."[653]

## Using Force

Force is an extremely broad concept in international law, with lawful forms of compulsion extending from the verbal notice of arrest and minimal physical restraint at one end of the spectrum, to the use of potentially lethal weapons at the other. In this section, we will explore the wide range of circumstances in which law enforcement and security officials might be called upon to consider using force in the context of counter-terrorism operations, encompassing the kind of challenges that might be faced on a daily basis by police officers patrolling the streets of any city around the world, as well as much rarer incidents that might require the intervention of specialized police units, or even the support of military assets; we will consider two key human rights — the right to life, and the right to

---

[653] Peter Neumann, *Prisons and Terrorism: Radicalisation and De-radicalisation in 15 Countries*, The International Centre for the Study of Radicalisation and Political Violence, 2010, p. 1.

lawful and peaceful assembly — impacted by the use of force by agents of the state; we will examine the manner in which force can be used legitimately in the context of law enforcement operations, intelligence activities, and military deployments; and finally we will take a critical look at states' growing use of lethal force against terrorist targets operating outside the reach of traditional law enforcement mechanisms.

As with other areas of executive action, international human rights law imposes two core obligations on officials who are lawfully empowered to use force in performance of their duties — that force is used only when it is necessary to do so, and that, when it is used, it is used in a manner strictly proportionate to the seriousness of the offence and the legitimate objectives sought.[654] The requirement of necessity also imposes an obligation to minimize the level of force applied "regardless of the level of force that would be proportionate".[655] It is not the gravity of the threat that determines the level of force that can be used to contain it, but rather the manner of action that would be sufficient to neutralize the threat. The criterion that there should be a proportionate relationship between the degree of force used and the legitimate objective for which it is being used, requires that any escalation of force ceases when the consequences of applying additional force outweigh the value of the objective for which it is being employed.[656] For example, it would never be a proportionate act to use lethal force to prevent the escape of an individual who poses no threat to the public. In sum, international human rights law envisages the legitimate need for force to be used by the authorities on occasion, but also imposes limits to ensure that it is used as sparingly as possible.

Governments have a social and legal obligation to protect the lives and property of all those living under their jurisdiction, and, as

---

[654] Extrajudicial, summary or arbitrary executions, Note by the Secretary-General, A/61/311, 5 September 2006, para 42.

[655] *Note by the Secretary General: Extrajudicial, summary or arbitrary executions*, 5 September 2006, A/61/311, para 41.

[656] Extrajudicial, summary or arbitrary executions, Note by the Secretary-General, A/61/311, 5 September 2006, para 42.

the United Nations Security Council has acknowledged, terrorist violence "in all forms and manifestations" poses a serious threat to international peace and security, and leaves tragedy in its wake.[657] As much as we may wish it otherwise, the simple truth is that sometimes the only way to protect the public from acts of violence is to meet force with force. The ability to project and apply force — even on occasion lethal force — is thus a necessary tool in the arsenal of those involved in counter-terrorism, and in some circumstances may be indispensable. Accepting the Nobel Peace Prize in Oslo in 2009, President Barack Obama, soberly reminded the Nobel Committee of this unpalatable reality: "Evil does exist in the world ... To say that force may sometimes be necessary is not a call to cynicism — it is a recognition of history, the imperfections of man, and the limits of reason."[658]

## Maintaining public order

The classic Weberian definition of statehood is that a state has a monopoly on the legitimate use of physical force within a given territory, and this monopoly on the use of force is invested primarily in law enforcement personnel to ensure the safety of the general public, maintain public order and, when necessary, apprehend and detain suspects. Every five years since 1955 the United Nations has convened a Congress on the Prevention of Crime and the Treatment of Offenders to address pressing issues confronting the international law enforcement community, and in 1990 127 states came together in Havana, Cuba, at the eighth such congress to agree *Basic Principles on the Use of Force and Firearms by Law Enforcement Officials*. Although these *Basic Principles* do not have the same standing as a treaty or convention, the fact that they were developed through intensive dialogue between law enforcement experts and human rights experts, and that their development and adoption involved a substantial majority of UN Member States, is persuasive evidence, as

---

[657] S/RES/2178 (2014).

[658] Peter Bergen, *United States of Jihad: Investigating America's Homegrown Terrorists* (Crown; 2016), p. 200.

the UN Secretary-General has observed, that there is "near universal consensus on their content".[659]

The *Basic Principles* enjoin law enforcement officers to seek first to resolve conflicts through non-violent means — for instance, persuasion and negotiation — before resorting to force.[660] The drafters further agreed that should the use of force be unavoidable, law enforcement officials would, as a minimum, "exercise restraint in using force and act in proportion to the seriousness of the offence and the legitimate objective to be achieved," and "minimize damage and injury, and respect and preserve human life."[661] The dual principles of necessity and proportionality were thus recognized as the foundation upon which any decision to employ force should be based.[662] The *Basic Principles* dwell on the use of firearms in particular detail stating that law enforcement officials should not use firearms against persons except in self-defense or in defense of others against the imminent threat of death or serious injury, to prevent the perpetration of a particularly serious crime involving grave threat to life, to arrest a person presenting such a danger and resisting their authority, or to prevent his or her escape, and only when less extreme means are insufficient to achieve these objectives.[663] Or to put it more simply, officers can only take a life to save a life.

The decision to fire a weapon should always be a measure of last resort and is fraught with risk. A 2008 RAND Corporation *Evaluation of New York City Police Department Firearm Training and Firearm Discharge* found that "the best officers of the nation's biggest and arguably best-trained police department" only hit their intended target

---

[659] Extrajudicial, summary or arbitrary executions, Note by the Secretary-General, (A/61/311), para 35.

[660] Basic Principles on the Use of Force and Firearms by Law Enforcement Officials, Adopted by the Eighth United Nations Congress on the Prevention of Crime and the Treatment of Offenders, Havana, Cuba, 27 August to 7 September 1990, para 4.

[661] ibid., para 5.

[662] Extrajudicial, summary or arbitrary executions, Note by the Secretary-General, (A/61/311), para 34.

[663] See Basic Principles on the Use of Force and Firearms by Law Enforcement Officials, Adopted by the Eighth United Nations Congress on the Prevention of Crime and the Treatment of Offenders, Havana, Cuba, 27 August to 7 September 1990, para 9.

during gunfights 18% of the time when returning fire at an armed perpetrator.[664] This percentage increased to 30% in incidents in which a target was not firing back. With 70–80% of shots fired in dynamic situations missing their target, the potential for injury to other members of the public in the vicinity is obvious. The *Basic Principles* further require law enforcement officials to identify themselves as such and give a clear warning of their intent to use firearms, with sufficient time for the warning to be observed, unless to do so would unduly place the law enforcement officials at risk or would create a risk of death or serious harm to other persons, or would be clearly inappropriate or pointless in the circumstances of the incident.[665] In *Kallis and Androulla Panayi v. Turkey* (ECtHR; 2009) the European Court of Human Rights went even further finding that, if circumstances allow, officers should fire warning shots before engaging a target directly.[666]

The *Basic Principles* stress the importance of governments establishing clear rules and regulations to govern the use of force and the need to keep the "ethical issues" associated with the use of force under "constant review".[667] They also encourage governments to equip law enforcement officers with the broadest possible range of tools to allow for a "differentiated use of force" and to ensure that officers feel sufficiently protected so that the need to use weapons is reduced.[668] In modern policing, this might include issuing non-lethal tools such as tasers and pepper spray to officers on patrol, as well as body armor, helmets, riot shields, and other

---

[664] Bernard Rostker, Lawrence Hanser, William Hix, Carl Jensen, Andrew Morral, Greg Ridgeway and Terry Schell, *Evaluation of the New York City Police Department Firearm Training and Firearm-Discharge Review Process* (RAND Corporation; 2008).

[665] See Basic Principles on the Use of Force and Firearms by Law Enforcement Officials, Adopted by the Eighth United Nations Congress on the Prevention of Crime and the Treatment of Offenders, Havana, Cuba, 27 August to 7 September 1990, para 10.

[666] European Court of Human Rights, *Kallis and Androulla Panayi v. Turkey*, Application No. 45388/99, 27 October 2009, p. 62.

[667] Basic Principles on the Use of Force and Firearms by Law Enforcement Officials, Adopted by the Eighth United Nations Congress on the Prevention of Crime and the Treatment of Offenders, Havana, Cuba, 27 August to 7 September 1990, para 1.

[668] ibid., paras 2–3.

protective equipment in volatile situations, as well as providing an appropriate level of training in their use.[669] Finally, the *Basic Principles* committed governments to ensure that any arbitrary or abusive use of force by law enforcement officials was criminalized in law and offered clear direction that exceptional circumstances such as "internal political instability" could not justify any breach of these principles.[670]

Several of these issues had already been explored by the UN Human Rights Committee in the case of *Suarez de Guerrero v. Colombia* (HRC; 1982).[671] On 13 April 1978, Colombian police raided a house in the Contador district of Bogotá under the belief that the former Colombian Ambassador to France, Miguel de German Ribon, who had been kidnapped several days earlier by the M-19 terrorist group, was being held inside. The house was empty but the police officers decided to lie in wait for the persons they believed to be the kidnappers to return. All seven individuals who subsequently entered the house, including Mrs. Suarez de Guerrero, were accosted individually by the police and killed. It was initially alleged by the Colombian authorities that the deceased had all resisted arrest and had brandished or fired weapons. However, forensic reports indicated that the victims had died at intervals as they returned to the house; that none of them had fired a shot; and that all had been killed at point-blank range, some shot in the back or in the head. Witnesses indicated that the victims were not given the opportunity to surrender. The authorities were unable to present any evidence suggesting that any of the victims had been involved in Ambassador Ribon's abduction.[672] The Colombian government maintained that

---

[669] Office of the High Commissioner for Human Rights, *Human Rights Standards and Practice for the Police*, Expanded Pocket Book on Human Rights for the Police, Professional Training Series No. 5/Add.3 (2004), p. 23.

[670] Basic Principles on the Use of Force and Firearms by Law Enforcement Officials, Adopted by the Eighth United Nations Congress on the Prevention of Crime and the Treatment of Offenders, Havana, Cuba, 27 August to 7 September 1990, paras 7–8.

[671] *Suarez de Guerrero v. Colombia*, Communication no. R.11/45, U.N. Doc. Supp. No. 40 (A/37/40), p. 137 (1982).

[672] Ambassador Ribon was subsequently released by his actual kidnappers in September 1978 after 161 days in captivity and on the payment of a substantial ransom.

Legislative Decree No. 0070 of 20 January 1978 had amended the Penal Code "for so long as the public order remains disturbed and the national territory is in a state of siege" and had created special immunities for members of the police force if an otherwise punishable act was committed "in the course of operations planned with the object of preventing and curbing the offences of extortion and kidnapping, and the production and processing of and trafficking in narcotic drugs."[673] The police officers involved in the case had relied on this amendment to the Penal Code to secure acquittals when they were eventually prosecuted for their various roles in the killings.

The Human Rights Committee did not accept the Colombian government's interpretation and found: "The police action was apparently taken without warning to the victims and without giving them any opportunity to surrender to the police patrol or to offer any explanation of their presence or intentions. There is no evidence that the action of the police was necessary in their own defence or that of others, or that it was necessary to effect the arrest or prevent the escape of the persons concerned. Moreover, the victims were no more than suspects of the kidnapping which had occurred some days earlier and their killing by the police deprived them of all the protections of due process of law laid down by the Covenant."[674] In the circumstances, the Committee concluded that the police action that had led to the death of Mrs. Suarez de Guerrero was "disproportionate to the requirements of law enforcement". The Committee also found that the amendment to the penal code under which the police officers had justified their actions failed to adequately protect the victims' rights, and should therefore be amended.

In a further application of the logic that the calculation of how much force is proportionate or necessary in a given situation is contingent on the totality of the circumstances concerned, and not just the nature of the offence or threat at issue, the question of a

---

[673] *Suarez de Guerrero v. Colombia*, Communication no. R.11/45, U.N. Doc. Supp. No. 40 (A/37/40) 137 (1982), para 11.2.
[674] ibid., para 13.2.

measure's appropriateness cannot be made in advance. Such a judgment can only be made according to the given circumstances on case-by-case basis — for example, the degree of resistance exhibited by the suspect. The UN Special Rapporteur on extrajudicial, summary or arbitrary executions reported critically on a 2002 operation conducted by the Nigerian Police titled Operation Fire-for-Fire that authorized police officers to use firearms against criminals in "very difficult situations" and which, according to police statistics, in the first 100 days resulted in the deaths of 225 suspected criminals and forty-one innocent bystanders.[675] In its *Fact Sheet on Human Rights, Terrorism and Counter-Terrorism*, the Office of the UN High Commissioner for Human Rights has since further clarified that before any resort could be made to deadly force "all measures to arrest a person suspected of being in the process of committing acts of terror must be exhausted."[676]

Permissive and generic operational instructions not only fail to meet the requirements of proportionality and necessity, but they also have a tendency to remove the restraints on police behavior that can prevent the kind of tragedies associated with the insidious "tunnel vision" that Canadian judges Kaufman and Cory warned can sometimes prejudice police action — something that seems to be especially true in relation to counter-terrorism where the stakes are so high.[677] This was graphically illustrated in the immediate aftermath of the suicide bombings that struck the London Transport system in July 2005. Two years earlier the Metropolitan Police Service, following consultation with colleagues in Israel, Russia, and Sri Lanka, had adopted a standing response to the threat codenamed Operation Kratos which authorized armed officers to engage suspected suicide bombers without warning "to retain the element

---

[675] Note by the Secretary-General: Extrajudicial, summary or arbitrary executions, 5 September 2006, A/61/311, para 34.

[676] United Nations Office of the High Commissioner for Human Rights, *Fact Sheet No. 32: Human Rights, Terrorism and Counter-Terrorism* (2008), p. 30.

[677] The Honourable Fred Kaufman, C.M., Q.C., *Report of the Kaufman Commission on Proceedings Involving Guy Paul Morin, Recommendation 74: Education Respecting Tunnel Vision* (31 March 1998), p. 26 and Bruce MacFarlane, Convicting the Innocent: A Triple Failure of the Justice System, *Manitoba Law Journal*, Vol. 31, No. 3 (2006), p. 429.

of surprise" and with sufficient force as to ensure "immediate incapacitation".[678] This operational stance was subsequently adopted by other British police forces, and the stage was set for a tragedy of errors to unfold.

Exactly two weeks after the 7 July suicide bombings, four more devices were discovered on the London Transport system but on this occasion they had failed to detonate. A manhunt was immediately launched for the men responsible for this second attack. One of the suspects was identified as Hussain Osman — and a gym membership card found in a bag containing one of the devices linked him to an apartment block in Tulse Hill, South London. The building was immediately placed under surveillance. A Brazilian electrician called Jean Charles de Menezes lived in the block of flats under surveillance, although he had no connection whatsoever to the copycat bombers. On the morning of 22 July, de Menezes left his apartment to go to work and as he left the building surveillance officers thought he might be a possible match for the poor quality CCTV photograph the police had received of their suspect, Hussain Osman. De Menezes took a bus to Brixton Underground Station and, finding it closed because of a security alert, traveled on by bus to Stockwell Underground Station. The whole time he was being kept under mobile surveillance by the Metropolitan Police and they began to find his movements on public transport suspicious, as buses in the capital had twice been targeted by bombers in the past month. This growing concern in turn led them to have greater confidence in the erroneous identification of de Menezes as Osman — a textbook illustration of the "tunnel vision" effect in action. The officers relayed their suspicions to police commanders, who fearing another attack may be imminent, ordered them to prevent the suspect from boarding a train. A police firearms team was nearby to provide support.

Completely oblivious to police presence surrounding him, De Menezes entered Stockwell Underground Station and boarded a

---

[678] See Detective Superintendent Steve Swain, *Report 13: Suicide Terrorism*, Metropolitan Police Authority, 27 October 2005 at http://policeauthority.org/Metropolitan/committees/mpa/2005/051027/13/index.html#h2000.

train heading into the city. Three surveillance officers followed him into the carriage. One surveillance officer called out de Menezes' location to arriving firearms officers and seized hold of him. The firearms officers entered the carriage and then fired eleven shots. De Menezes was hit seven times in the head, killing him instantly. Under the standing instructions laid down by Operation Kratos, firearms officers tackling suspected suicide bombers had been instructed to fire at the target's head to avoid detonating a suicide vest. De Menezes was completely unarmed, was not wearing an explosive device of any kind, and had absolutely no links to terrorism. The Metropolitan Police ultimately agreed to pay an undisclosed sum in compensation to the de Menezes family in an out-of-court settlement. No police officers were prosecuted over the fatal shooting because the Crown Prosecution Service found that with the information available to them the officers concerned had "genuinely believed" de Menezes was a suicide bomber. However, the Office of Metropolitan Police Commissioner was successfully prosecuted in 2007 under sections three and thirty-three of the 1974 Health and Safety at Work Act for "failing to provide for the health, safety and welfare" of de Menezes and was fined £175,000. The UN Special Rapporteur on extrajudicial, summary or arbitrary executions has since warned that "the rhetoric of shoot-to-kill and its equivalents poses a deep and enduring threat to human rights-based law enforcement approaches."[679] That this tragedy could occur in Britain where police officers do not routinely carry firearms and the specialist units that do are highly trained and rarely use lethal force — in 2006–2007, across the country, officers only fired their weapons on nine occasions — further serves to underline the perils of adopting such an approach.[680]

In addition to interdictions and arrests, another common area in which police use of force can impact human rights protections is in seeking to control demonstrations or other public displays of

---

[679] Office of the United Nations High Commissioner for Human Rights, *Human Rights, Terrorism and Counter-Terrorism: Fact Sheet No. 32*, p. 30.

[680] See Peter Squires and Peter Kennison, *Shooting to Kill? Firearms and Armed Response* (Wiley-Blackwell; 2010).

protest or dissent. Article 21 of the ICCPR protects the right to participate in lawful and peaceful assemblies. The right to assemble is a limited right — no restrictions can be placed on this right except in conformity with the law and which are necessary in a democratic society to protect national security, public order, public safety, health or morals, and the protection of the rights of others, but, as the UN Special Rapporteur on extrajudicial, summary or arbitrary executions has acknowledged, "the state has wide discretion to impose content-neutral restrictions on demonstrations in order to minimize any disruptive effect, keeping in mind the importance of assemblies being held within 'sight and sound' of the target audience."[681] The purpose of peaceful assemblies is to express opinion and have a voice in public debate — to prevent or unnecessarily restrict participants from conveying their message effectively to their target audience undermines the fundamental nature of the right. This means that the state has the power to impose restrictions on where and when a demonstration can be held, but in exercising this power any such restriction must be both necessary and proportional to the legitimate objective sought. Forcing demonstrations to take place too far from the target of their protest, or even prohibiting the use of some form of sound amplification, might constitute interference with the right to assemble.[682]

In circumstances in which assemblies take place unlawfully — for example, by trespassing on private property — or become unlawful while in progress, the police may legitimately be called upon to disperse protestors. The *UN Basic Principles on the Use of Force and Firearms by Law Enforcement Officials* state that in the dispersal of assemblies, law enforcement officials shall avoid the use of force or,

---

[681] Basic Principles on the Use of Force and Firearms by Law Enforcement Officials, Adopted by the Eighth United Nations Congress on the Prevention of Crime and the Treatment of Offenders, Havana, Cuba, 27 August to 7 September 1990, paras 12–13 and Christof Heyns, *Report of the Special Rapporteur on extrajudicial, summary or arbitrary executions*, (A/HRC/17/28), para 89.

[682] Organization for Security and Cooperation in Europe, *Handbook on Monitoring Freedom of Peaceful Assembly* (Office for Democratic Institutions and Human Rights; 2011), p. 23. See also European Court of Human Rights, *Kasparov and Others v. Russia*, Application no. 21613/07, Judgment, 17 February 2015.

where that is not practicable, shall restrict such force "to the minimum extent necessary".[683] Many Western police forces have since developed crowd management tactics designed to contain unruly protestors rather than disperse them, until tensions begin to dissipate. The use of excessive force against protestors may conceivably constitute an international crime under the Rome Statute of the International Criminal Court. In 2011, the UN Security Council referred the "gross and systemic violation of human rights, including the repression of peaceful demonstrators" by Libyan security forces to the ICC for investigation.[684]

The European Court of Human Rights considered the question of both necessity and proportionality in the context of policing demonstrations in the case of *Andreou v. Turkey* (ECtHR; 2009), which revolved around an incident in August 1996 when Turkish troops fired on a protest taking place next to the United Nations Buffer Zone between the Republic of Cyprus and the Turkish Republic of Northern Cyprus. A Greek Cypriot man, Solomos Solomou, entered the Buffer Zone and climbed a flagpole in an apparent attempt to take down a Turkish flag. He was shot five times by Turkish soldiers, and subsequently died of his wounds. Greek Cypriot demonstrators armed with sticks and iron bars began throwing stones at the Turkish forces and the troops opened fire hitting two British UNFICYP soldiers and two civilians (one of whom was Georgia Andreou) on the Republic of Cyprus side of the Buffer Zone. The Court found that firing indiscriminately into the crowd constituted a disproportionate use of force in the circumstances and could not be justified by the argument, as suggested by the Turkish Government, that it had been necessary to quell "a riot or insurrection". Regarding Ms. Andreou, the Court noted she had not been armed, had not behaved in a violent manner, had not offered any resistance to the police or posed a threat to public order. Moreover, she had not crossed the

---

[683] Basic Principles on the Use of Force and Firearms by Law Enforcement Officials, Adopted by the Eighth United Nations Congress on the Prevention of Crime and the Treatment of Offenders, Havana, Cuba, 27 August to 7 September 1990, paras 12–13.

[684] S/RES/1970 (2011). See also Christof Heyns, *Report of the Special Rapporteur on extrajudicial, summary or arbitrary executions,* (A/HRC/17/28), p. 72.

ceasefire line, which might have made it necessary to effect a lawful arrest. In fact, she had been shot while standing outside the UN Buffer Zone and consequently the Court ruled that the use of potentially lethal force against the applicant had not been "absolutely necessary".[685]

One final area in which force has been used by agents of the state to effect arrests in controversial circumstances in pursuit of counter-terrorism goals is the practice known as extraordinary rendition, in which an individual is seized overseas in the absence of due process and then forcibly returned to face justice in a domestic court. Extraordinary rendition is often conflated with, but is distinct from, rendition to torture, which is both unlawful and an international crime. The jury is still out at the international level whether or not the legal doctrine of *male captus, bene detentus* (wrongly captured, properly detained) is an accepted — and acceptable — standard. At the national level, states are divided. Probably, the most famous such case is the rendition of the Nazi war criminal Adolf Eichmann from Argentina to Israel in May 1960 by the Israel Intelligence Service, *Mossad*. Eichmann was subsequently successfully prosecuted in an Israeli court, convicted of war crimes, crimes against humanity, and crimes against the Jewish People, and then executed.[686] Courts in the United States have also consistently upheld the principle of *male captus, bene detentus*, where it is better known as the Kerr-Frisbie doctrine after two foundational Supreme Court cases.[687] In the 1980s, the United States introduced a number of so-called long-arm statutes to empower US law enforcement officials to pursue individuals who are alleged to have committed crimes, including terrorism, against US citizens overseas.[688] In September 1987, the FBI used these new legal authorities to

---

[685] European Court of Human Rights, *Andreou v. Turkey*, Application no. 45653/99, Judgment, 27 October 2009. See also European Court of Human Rights, *Solomou and others v. Turkey*, Application no. 36832/97, Judgment, 24 June 2008.

[686] Hans Baade, The Eichmann Trial: Some Legal Aspects, *Duke Law Journal*, Vol. 10, No. 3 (1961).

[687] Jane Chong, Pre-Abu Khattala: Yunis, That 1987 Shipboard Terrorist Interrogation Case, *Lawfare*, 1 July 2014 at https://www.lawfareblog.com/pre-abu-khattala-yunis-1987-shipboard-terrorist-interrogation-case. Viewed by the author on 8 May 2016.

[688] Alan Clarke, *Rendition to Torture* (Rutgers University Press; 2012), p. 78.

apprehend Fawaz Younis, a member of the Lebanese *Amal* militia and subsequently *Hezbollah*, who had led the hijacking of Royal Jordanian Flight 402 two years earlier.[689] An FBI agent posing as an international drug dealer lured Younis from the island of Cyprus into international waters whereupon he was arrested, taken aboard a waiting American warship, the USS Butte, and then transferred to the United States.[690] He was subsequently convicted in federal court and served sixteen years of a thirty-year sentence before being repatriated to Lebanon. Although the Lebanese Justice Minister, Nabih Berri, described Younis' apprehension at sea as "an act close to piracy", there was little other adverse international reaction.[691]

The alternate legal view is *ex iniuria ius non oritur* (no right can be derived from wrong), and that Article 9 of the ICCPR protects individuals from unlawful arrest and detention.[692] This is the position that has been taken by the United Kingdom, New Zealand, and South Africa in unlawful rendition to justice cases.[693] In December 1986, Ebrahim Ismail Ebrahim, a long-term member of *Umkhonto we Sizwe*, was abducted in Swaziland by agents of the *apartheid* state and brought back to face trial in South Africa for high treason. Another member of *Umkhonto we Sizwe*, Msizeni Shadrack Mapamulo, was shot and killed during the abduction. Although he was convicted and sentenced to twenty-years imprisonment on Robben Island, Ebrahim successfully appealed the manner of his apprehension in a case that went to the Supreme Court of South Africa, and he was released in early 1991. The Court

---

[689] Associated Press, Convicted Terrorist Deported to Lebanon After Prison Term, *Washington Post*, 30 March 2005.

[690] Matthew Purdy, A Web of Intrigue, Betrayal Snared A Lebanese Hijacker, *Philadelphia Inquirer*, 4 December 1987.

[691] Robert Beck and Anthony Clark Arend, "Don't Tread On Us": International Law and Forcible State Responses to Terrorism, *Wisconsin International Law Journal*, Vol. 12 (Spring 1994) at footnote 100.

[692] Christophe Paulussen, *Male Captus Bene Detentus? Surrendering Suspects to the International Criminal Court* (Intersentia; 2010).

[693] South Africa, Supreme Court (Appellate Division), *State v. Ebrahim*, 26 February 1991; *R. v. Hartley*, Court of Appeal Wellington, 5 August 1977 and *Regina v Horseferry Road Magistrates' Court, Ex parte Bennett* — House of Lords (Lord Griffiths, Lord Bridge of Harwich, Lord Oliver of Aylmerton, Lord Lowry and Lord Slynn of Hadley), 24 June 1993.

explained its decision in *State v. Ebrahim* (1991) in the following terms: "The individual must be protected against illegal detention and abduction, the bounds of jurisdiction must not be exceeded, sovereignty must be respected, the legal process must be fair to those affected and abuse of law must be avoided in order to protect and promote the integrity of the administration of justice ... When the state is a party to a dispute ... it must come to court with 'clean hands'. When the state itself is involved in an abduction across international borders, as in the present case, its hands are not clean."[694] Ebrahim would go on to serve as a deputy minister in successive post-*apartheid* ANC governments.

There is one, albeit rather dated, terrorism-related case that offers some guidance on the direction in which international law is likely to lean. In 1996, the European Court of Human Rights was asked to consider the circumstances of the rendition of the notorious terrorist Carlos the Jackal, Ilich Ramírez Sánchez, from Sudan to stand trial in France.[695] Sánchez had long been sought by the French authorities in connection with a variety of serious criminal offences. In August 1994, Sánchez was sedated without his knowledge by his Sudanese bodyguards while he was recovering from a medical procedure in Khartoum. Sudanese police officers then handed the unconscious Sánchez over to representatives of the French government who flew him back to France where he was formally arrested. French Interior Minister Charles Pasqua briefed reporters that Sánchez was believed to be responsible for fifteen deaths in France alone, and, by his own admission, as many as eighty-three deaths worldwide.[696] Sánchez protested that his rendition to France had been unlawful and his complaint was ultimately heard by the European Court. In *Illich Sánchez Ramirez v. France* (ECtHR; 1996), the Court noted that, in the absence of an

---

[694] South Africa, Supreme Court (Appellate Division), *State v. Ebrahim*, 26 February 1991, in International Legal Materials, Vol. 31 (1992), p. 896.

[695] European Court of Human Rights, *Illich Sánchez Ramirez v. France*, Decision, Application No. 28780/95, 24 June 1996.

[696] Alan Riding, Carlos the Terrorist Arrested and Taken to France, *The New York Times*, 16 August 1994.

extradition treaty between France and Sudan, any decision to expel or deport Sánchez fell within the sovereign discretion of the state concerned. The Court further observed that the circumstances of his rendition "had not vitiated the search for and process of establishing the truth, nor made it impossible for the defense to exercise its rights before the investigating authorities and the trial courts."[697] It therefore seems likely that, at the international level at least, the courts will continue to take into account the totality of circumstances and accord states a degree of latitude when they pursue suspects outside the reach of conventional judicial mechanisms with the intention of rendering them to face justice in a properly constituted court of law.

In summary, international human rights law recognizes that law enforcement and other security officials may sometimes have no option but to resort to force in the performance of their duties — whether this be effecting an arrest, or maintaining public order. Not every criminal comes quietly, and not every demonstrator is peaceful. The constraint that international human rights law places on these agents of the state is that they do so in a lawful manner and in pursuit of a legitimate objective, using force only when it is necessary to do so and to the minimum extent that is necessary to achieve the end result sought. However, the law does recognize that in some circumstances the degree of force required to effect a lawful outcome may be considerable, and, in rare circumstances, might even necessitate the use of potentially lethal tools, such as firearms. Being invested with the lawful authority to employ force is a tremendous responsibility and it is a power that can be easily abused, both by individual officers and by the state. As we have seen in Parts I and II, heavy-handed policing tactics can quickly become a major social problem, generating powerful grievances and supporting the radicalizing narratives promoted by violent extremist groups. The *UN Basic Principles on the Use of Force and Firearms* therefore place significant emphasis on the importance of effective oversight to ensure such abuses are discouraged, and that

---

[697] European Court of Human Rights, *Illich Sánchez Ramirez v. France*, Decision, Application No. 28780/95, 24 June 1996.

when they occur they are swiftly addressed. Such oversight is vital to ensure that when states use force, they do so in a measured manner; and using force in a measured manner is an essential prerequisite of an effective counter-terrorism strategy.

## The right to life

The right to life has been characterized as "the supreme human right".[698] It is enshrined in the Universal Declaration of Human Rights, the ICCPR, and every major international and regional human rights convention. The Human Rights Committee has commented that the inherent right of life is non-derogable even in the context of a public emergency, and the International Court of Justice found in its *Advisory Opinion on the Legality of the Threat or Use of Nuclear Weapons* (ICJ; 1996) that "the right not arbitrarily to be deprived of one's life applies also in hostilities."[699] However, it should also be noted that the right to life is not absolute — the ICCPR states that "no one shall be arbitrarily deprived of his life", an acknowledgment that some signatories still apply the death penalty, and that international human rights law also recognizes that circumstances may arise in which it is lawful to take a life to protect a life.

The right to life creates both positive and negative obligations for states. States have a positive obligation to ensure the right to life of all individuals falling under their jurisdiction. This requires states to take proactive measures to secure individuals from potential risks, to create a legal and administrative framework to protect life, and to

---

[698] United Nations Human Rights Council, *Report of the Special Rapporteur on the promotion and protection of human rights and fundamental freedoms while countering terrorism, Ben Emmerson: Framework principles for securing the human rights of victims of terrorism*, A/HRC/20/14, 4 June 2012, para 17.

[699] Manfred Nowak, *UN Covenant on Civil and Political Rights*, CCPR Commentary (Rhein, Engel: 2005), p. 121; Human Rights Committee, *General Comment No. 6* (1982), para 1; and *Joint Study on Global Practices in Relation to Secret Detention in the Context of Countering Terrorism of the Special Rapporteur on the promotion and protection of human rights and fundamental freedoms while countering terrorism, Martin Scheinin; the Special Rapporteur on torture and other cruel, inhuman or degrading treatment or punishment, Manfred Nowak; the Working Group on Arbitrary Detention; and the Working Group on Enforced and Involuntary Disappearances*, A/HRC/13/42, 19 February 2010, para 52.

investigate suspicious deaths to ensure that no unlawful deprivation of life goes unpunished.[700] Where the state has knowledge of a specific threat, it has an obligation to take action. As acts of terrorism can infringe on the right to life — as well as many other rights states are obligated to protect, such as freedom of expression and freedom of association — in working to prevent terrorism, in a very real sense, law enforcement and security officials are themselves human rights defenders.

The European Court of Human Rights has explored a state's obligation to protect the lives of those living under its jurisdiction in two markedly different terrorism-related cases. In the case of *Kiliç v. Turkey* (ECtHR; 2000), the Court considered the failure of the Turkish government to provide adequate protection to Kemal Kiliç, a reporter working for the newspaper *Özgür Gündem* in southeast Turkey.[701] In December 1992, Kiliç sent a press release to the Turkish governor of Sanliurfa detailing death threats that had been made against some of *Özgür Gündem's* distributors. The newspaper had a difficult relationship with the local Turkish authorities who considered it to be sympathetic to the PKK, and they responded by formally charging Kiliç with insulting the governor because he had made details of the press release public. Kiliç was briefly detained at the Sanliurfa Security Directorate on 18 January 1993 but was released the same day. A month later, he was shot dead by four unidentified men who ambushed him on his way home from work.

An indictment brought before the Diyarbakir State Security Court identified a member of Turkish *Hezbollah* called Hüseyin Güney as a suspect in the murder but there was no real evidence tying him to the incident, and he had originally been arrested on unrelated charges. The investigation was closed within a month of the murder. Güney was eventually acquitted of Kiliç's murder in 1999 but the investigation was never reopened. Kiliç's family was convinced that he had been murdered by members of the security

---

[700] *Report of the Special Rapporteur on the promotion and protection of human rights and fundamental freedoms while countering terrorism, Ben Emmerson* (A/HRC/20/14), para 21.

[701] European Court of Human Rights, *Kiliç v. Turkey*, Application no. 22492/93, Judgment, 28 March 2000.

forces, and his brother brought a complaint to the European Court of Human Rights alleging that Kemal had been murdered by, or at least with the connivance of, the Turkish authorities because of his work as a reporter for *Özgür Gündem*. The complaint also stated that the Turkish authorities had not properly investigated the murder and had allowed the perpetrators to go unpunished. The Court found, *inter alia*, that there was insufficient evidence to support the contention that the Turkish authorities had been complicit in Kiliç's murder. However, the Court ruled that given the nature of Kiliç's position at *Özgür Gündem* and the tensions in south-east Turkey at the time, the government should have been aware that he may have been at particular risk — not least because he had brought death threats against individuals involved with the paper to the governor's attention — and should have taken "reasonable measures" to ensure his protection. Accordingly, the Court found that there had been a violation of Kiliç's right to life.[702]

In *Finogenov and others v. Russia* (ECtHR; 2012), the European Court examined a situation that often confronts governments beset by terrorism — a hostage crisis. Hostage-taking is a common terrorist tactic which has been utilized by groups as diverse as Black September, the *Rote Armee Fraktion*, *Movimiento Revolucionario Túpac Amaru*, ISIL, and *Euskadi Ta Askatasuna*. Determined hostage-takers can present the authorities with a stark binary choice: capitulate to their demands, often the release of jailed comrades, or attempt to storm the terrorist stronghold and rescue the hostages. Either course of action potentially puts members of the public, for whom the state has a duty of care, in harm's way. Although states have been known to accede to terrorist demands on occasion, and terrorists can sometimes be talked into surrendering their hostages unharmed

---

[702] The ECtHR also commented that the state should have been aware of the possibility that the threat to Kiliç's safety might have come from elements within the security forces, which could call into question the independence of local authorities to properly investigate the crime and thus undermine the effectiveness of criminal law protection. The Court noted the cursory and one dimensional nature of the official investigation into Kiliç's murder (the possibility that state officials might be involved was never explored) and thus found that there had not been an effective investigation into his death, and that this too was a violation of his right to life. The concept of an effective investigation will be addressed later in this section.

by specialist negotiators, the deployment of special forces units in such situations is not uncommon. Although military and police units like the Britain's Special Air Service (SAS), Germany's GSG9, France's *Groupe d'intervention de la Gendarmerie nationale* (GIGN), and Israel's *Sayeret Matkal* do have an impressive track record in resolving hostage crises successfully, a benign outcome is far from guaranteed. Even successful resolutions often involve some loss of innocent life, and some rescue attempts can go catastrophically wrong, as in the case of the Beslan school siege in September 2004. The domestic legal circumstances governing the deployment of such units varies from country to country, but the basic principles of necessity and proportionality still apply to any action. These principles were examined in some detail in the *Finogenov* case.

In October 2002, a group of at least forty Chechen separatist terrorists led by Movsar Barayev took over the House of Culture of State Ball-Bearing Plant Number 1 in Dubrovka, Moscow, in the middle of a sold-out performance of the play Nord-Ost, holding 850 people hostage for two-and-a-half days. The terrorists were heavily armed and some wore suicide vests, they also positioned a number of powerful improvised explosive devices around the auditorium.[703] The terrorists demanded that all Russian forces be immediately withdrawn from Chechnya. The audience contained approximately seventy-five foreign nationals from fourteen different countries including Australia, Germany, The Netherlands, Ukraine, and the United States, which placed a great deal of international pressure on the Russian government to resolve the siege without loss of life. On the fourth day of the standoff, the Russian authorities took desperate measures to resolve the crisis by deploying a fast- acting narcotic gas to incapacitate hostage-takers and hostages alike. As the gas began to take effect, Russian *Spetsnaz* stormed the building. Forty terrorists were killed, including Barayev, and most were reportedly shot while unconscious. While the majority of the 778 hostages still being held in the theater by

---

[703] It was later reported that an FSB asset had been able to sabotage many of the devices with drained batteries and insufficient accelerator or booster charges to inhibit detonation prior to their deployment in Moscow although the authorities could not be sure of this at the time.

this point in the siege survived, 129 died as a direct result of inhaling the gas. Russian officials were blamed for these deaths.

Sixty-four survivors and bereaved family members brought a case against the Russian authorities alleging that they had used excessive force in an inadequately planned operation to end the siege, and that as a result innocent civilians had been killed in violation of their right to life. When the case finally reached the European Court of Human Rights, it found that the use of the supposedly non-lethal gas to incapacitate the hostage-takers was not disproportionate to the "very alarming" threat faced, but that the planning of the rescue operation had been inadequate regarding the provision of medical treatment — health workers were given no information about the nature of the narcotic gas used so were unable to devise a suitable medical response, they were also overwhelmed by the number of casualties — and that this amounted to a violation of the right to life of the hostages killed.[704] The case effectively illustrates how international human rights law is flexible enough to take into account competing interests and complex circumstances, while still holding states liable for preventable errors. In *Finogenov*, the Court acknowledged that the authorities' actions had saved almost 650 lives, but still held them responsible for those lives perhaps lost unnecessarily. States are held to a high standard, but this simply reflects the tremendous responsibilities that go hand-in-hand with government.

In addition to their positive obligations to protect those under their care, states also have a negative obligation to refrain from taking life arbitrarily. In addition to the application of the death penalty in accordance with law for "the most serious crimes", international human rights law broadly recognizes three other categories of action in which the deprivation of life would not be considered arbitrary: When death results from the use of force, which is "no more than absolutely necessary", to defend a person from unlawful violence, to effect a lawful arrest or prevent the escape of someone lawfully

---

[704] European Court of Human Rights, *Finogenov and others v. Russia*, Application no. 18299/03 and 27311/03, 4 June 2012.

detained, or to take lawful action to quell a riot or insurrection.[705] It is important to emphasize that the disproportionate or unnecessary use of force in such circumstances would still amount to arbitrary deprivation of life — for example, opening fire on an escaping prisoner who posed no physical threat to the public would be unjustifiable.

If the death penalty is to be imposed in a jurisdiction where it still applies, there must be procedural safeguards, including measures to protect potentially vulnerable citizens. Anyone sentenced to death must have the right to appeal for clemency, and the manner of execution must not involve the infliction of any unnecessary suffering. The ICCPR prohibits the imposition of the death penalty on anyone either under the age of eighteen or pregnant.[706] One country in six still retains the death penalty, including three permanent members of the UN Security Council (China and the United States actively apply the death penalty, but Russia has upheld a moratorium on the use of the death penalty since 1996) and according to Amnesty International at least 1,634 people were executed by due process of law globally in 2015, a total which does not include the number of executions conducted in China for which no comprehensive figure exists.[707]

States are also required to put safeguards in place to prevent arbitrary killing by their own security forces, which has two major operational implications.[708] First, commanders have a responsibility to ensure that those under their command are properly trained and adhere to professional standards. They must further ensure that those under their command are properly briefed prior to the start of an operation, both in terms of the information provided about the nature of the threat that they are facing, and regarding the proper and lawful execution of the operational plan. The Special

---

[705] European Convention on Human Rights, Article 2.

[706] International Covenant of Civil and Political Rights, Article 6(5).

[707] Amnesty International, *Death penalty 2015: Alarming surge in recorded executions sees highest toll in more than 25 years*, 6 April 2016 at https://www.amnesty.org/en/latest/news/2016/04/Alarming-surge-in-recorded-executions-sees-highest-toll-in-more-than-25-years/. Viewed on 14 May 2016.

[708] *Klaus Dieter Baumgarten v. Germany*, Communication No. 960/2000, U.N. Doc. CCPR/C/78/D/960/2000 (2003), paras 9.4 and 9.5.

Rapporteur on extrajudicial, summary or arbitrary executions has commented that senior officers have particular responsibility to ensure that tactical intelligence is used effectively to inform operations and operational planning.[709] Second, following any incident in which lethal force is used in a civil context all reasonable steps must be taken to ensure that an effective, independent investigation is conducted to determine whether or not such action was taken lawfully. As the European Court of Human Rights has noted: "A general legal prohibition of arbitrary killing by the agents of the state would be ineffective, in practice, if there existed no procedure for reviewing the lawfulness of the use of lethal force by state authorities."[710]

These principles were put to the test in the case of *McCann and Others v. the United Kingdom* (ECtHR; 1995), which considered the use of force by British Special Forces to interdict a Provisional IRA operation in the British Overseas Territory of Gibraltar in March 1988. The British government had received partial intelligence concerning the activities of a Provisional IRA active service unit (ASU) composed of persons who had previously been convicted of bombing offences and a known explosives expert — Danny McCann, Seán Savage, and Mairéad Farrell — who were thought to be planning to detonate a vehicle-borne improvised explosive device (VBIED). As the intelligence information was incomplete the British authorities were obliged to formulate their response on the basis of a working hypothesis about the ASU's intentions. They also decided that the interests of a successful prosecution would best be served if the PIRA team was actually arrested in the act of the deploying the car bomb, and began to plan accordingly (Operation Flavius). The PIRA team was operating from a base in Spain and, with the assistance of the Spanish authorities, M15 kept them under close observation.[711] The ASU's target was believed to be the changing of the guard ceremony which took place outside

[709] Human Rights Commission, *Extrajudicial, summary or arbitrary executions: Report of the Special Rapporteur, Philip Alston*, E/CN.4/2006/53, paras 53–54.

[710] European Court of Human Rights, *McCann and Others v. the United Kingdom*, Application no. 18984/91, Judgment, 27 September 1995, para 161.

[711] IRA Gibraltar deaths "a mistake", BBC News, 6 October 2009.

the Governor's Residence, and it was thought that the team was planning to place a car bomb along the route used during the parade.

On 6 March 1988, McCann and his partners left their safe house on the Spanish Mainland and drove to Gibraltar. They parked their car along the route that would be taken by the Royal Anglian band, and then began to walk back towards the border crossing. Soldiers from Britain's elite Special Air Service regiment were standing by to assist the police in making the arrest. The soldiers were informed by their superiors that there was a car bomb in place which could be detonated by any of the three suspects by means of a radio-control device concealed on their persons; that the device could be activated by pressing a button; that the suspects would be likely to detonate the bomb if challenged, thereby causing heavy loss of life and serious injuries, and were also likely to be armed and to resist arrest. These assumptions all proved to be false. It subsequently turned out that all three suspects were unarmed, that they did not have a remote detonator on their persons, and that there was no bomb in their car, although the actual car bomb (with a conventional timer) was eventually located forty-six miles away in Marbella. The police found the keys to this car in Farrell's handbag.

The British soldiers confronted the three suspects. The soldiers later all gave evidence that McCann and Farrell made hostile movements when challenged and that, fearing they may be reaching for a weapon or trying to detonate the putative car bomb, they had had no choice but to open fire with the explicit intent to kill in order to neutralize this threat. McCann was shot five times, Farrell eight — both were killed instantly. Savage had been walking a little behind the others and he turned and fled back towards the city center. A soldier chased after Savage, caught him up and shot him between sixteen and eighteen times, killing him too. The European Court considered that the soldiers had acted reasonably given the intelligence briefing they had received, and also noted that "the use of force by agents of the state in pursuit of one of the aims delineated in paragraph two of Article 2 of the [European] Convention may be justified under this provision where it is based on an honest belief which is perceived, for good reasons, to be valid at the time but which subsequently turns out to be mistaken. To hold otherwise would be to impose an unrealistic burden on the state and its law-enforcement personnel in the execution of their duty, perhaps to the detriment of their lives and those of others."[712] This aspect of the judgment is often overlooked, but the Court clearly acknowledged that at the moment of interdiction, the severity of the threat to the general public could justify the action taken by the soldiers.

However, the Court then went on to question whether Operation Flavius as a whole had been organized in a manner which respected the requirements of Article 2 of the European Convention and whether the information given to the soldiers "which, in effect, rendered inevitable the use of lethal force," took adequately into consideration the right to life of the three suspects.[713] The Court noted that the British authorities could have chosen to make the arrests earlier, thus avoiding the threat of a potentially active explosive device. For example, the PIRA team could have been arrested at their safe house in Spain or at the border crossing. The Court also noted that in making assumptions about the PIRA team's objectives in Gibraltar on 6 March, the British authorities quickly discarded the possibility that they may have only been conducting a reconnaissance mission, rather than planting a bomb, even though the changing of the guard ceremony was not scheduled to take place until 8 March. The Court therefore commented critically that "insufficient allowances appear to have been made for other assumptions."[714] Finally, the Court was also critical of the speed and deliberate intent with which the British soldiers resorted to the use of lethal force, noting: "Their reflex action in this vital respect lacks the degree of caution in the use of firearms to be expected from law enforcement

---

[712] European Court of Human Rights, *McCann and Others v. the United Kingdom*, Application no. 18984/91, Judgment, 27 September 1995, para 200. Article 2 of the ECHR enshrines the Right to Life.
[713] European Court of Human Rights, *McCann and Others v. the United Kingdom*, Application no. 18984/91, Judgment, 27 September 1995, para 201.
[714] ibid., para 208.

personnel in a democratic society, even when dealing with dangerous terrorist suspects."[715]

The Court concluded that there had been a violation of the
right to life by the British authorities in relation to the planning of
the Gibraltar operation, finding: "The authorities were bound by
their obligation to respect the right to life of the suspects to exercise the greatest of care in evaluating the information at their
disposal before transmitting it to soldiers whose use of firearms
automatically involved shooting to kill."[716] Accordingly, it must be
emphasized that effective planning of operations where lethal force
is likely to be used is essential in order to minimize false assumptions being made, which may result in the unnecessary loss of life.
The Court also considered whether the inquest into the deaths of
the ASU members held on Gibraltar by the British authorities
amounted to a thorough and impartial investigation. The Court
noted that the inquest proceedings lasted nineteen days and heard
the testimony of seventy-nine witnesses, and that lawyers representing the families of the deceased were able to examine and
cross-examine key witnesses.[717] It concluded that the procedural
shortcomings highlighted by the complainants did not substantially
hamper the thorough examination of the circumstances surrounding the killing of the PIRA team.

In *Al-Skeini and Others v. The United Kingdom* (ECtHR; 2011), the
European Court further ruled that the requirement of effective
post-incident investigation even extends to situations that include
military occupation and martial law, where a state has effective
control of a given territory and has assumed the powers normally
exercised by a sovereign government. The *Al-Skeini* case concerned
the deaths of six men in Basrah, Iraq, in 2003 while the UK was the
occupying power: three of the victims were shot dead or shot and
fatally wounded by British soldiers on patrol; one was shot and
fatally wounded during an exchange of fire between a British patrol
and unknown gunmen; one was beaten by British soldiers and then

---

[715] ibid., para 212.

[716] ibid., para 211.

[717] ibid., para 162.

forced into a river, where he drowned; and one died while in custody on a British military base. The Court concluded that the United Kingdom had violated right to life protections by failing to perform an adequate investigation into the incidents identified in five of the six cases. An initial requirement to refer all shooting incidents to the Royal Military Police for evaluation and review had been downgraded to allow company commanders on the ground to conduct the investigation. The standard set by the Court was that "even in difficult security conditions, all reasonable steps must be taken to ensure that an effective, independent investigation is conducted."[718] The Court held that there was a jurisdictional link for all of the cases as the UK had effective control of the territory concerned having assumed "the exercise of some of the public powers normally exercised by a sovereign government", especially as regards security.[719]

If it should turn out that a senior officer has given an unlawful order they can of course be held criminally liable. The issue of command responsibility is enshrined, *inter alia*, in Article 28 of the Rome Statute of the International Criminal Court and Article 6(1)(b) of the International Convention for the Protection of All Persons from Enforced Disappearance. Command authority maybe established on a *de jure* or *de facto* basis. Willful ignorance is not a defense either — the ICC Statute creates the possibility of culpability where a superior officer should have been aware of the activities of individuals under his or her command. Commanders have both a duty to prevent, and a duty to punish, human rights abuses — especially in circumstances in which unlawful force is used. Equally, subordinate officers should also be aware that obedience to superior orders does not amount to a meaningful defense if lethal force is used unlawfully. Human rights instruments such as Article 2(3) of the Convention against Torture and Article 33 of the ICC Statute make it quite clear that an order from a superior officer or a public authority may not be invoked as a justification for committing unlawful acts. The *UN Basic Principles*

---

[718] European Court of Human Rights, *al-Skeini et al. v. United Kingdom*, Application no. 55721/07, Judgment, 7 July 2011, para 164.

[719] European Court of Human Rights, *al-Skeini et al. v. United Kingdom*, Application no. 55721/07, Judgment, 7 July 2011, para 149.

*on the Use of Force and Firearms by Law Enforcement Officials* further clarify that if a junior official is aware that an order is manifestly unlawful, and he or she has a reasonable opportunity to refuse to carry it out, then this is the course of action he or she must follow or be personally held criminally liable.[720] The ICC Statute notes that any order to commit an act of genocide or crimes against humanity would be manifestly unlawful.

These issues were put to the test in a series of cases brought in the aftermath of German Reunification. States naturally have a sovereign right to control access across their borders, indeed, in the context of counter-terrorism, Security Council Resolution 1373 actually requires states to "prevent the movement of terrorists or terrorist groups by effective border controls." However, this does not mean that it is either necessary or proportional for border guards to use lethal force to prevent illegal border crossings. In the period between the construction of the Berlin Wall in August 1961 and its fall in November 1989, at least 264 individuals were killed trying to cross to the West, and an attempt was made after reunification to bring those responsible — both individual border guards and senior East German officials — to account.[721] Successive German courts found that the use of lethal force to prevent illegal border crossings amounted to the arbitrary deprivation of life as no danger was posed to the public by the transgressors. Several of those convicted appealed to the European Court of Human Rights on the basis that their actions had been lawful under East German law and that they were being punished retrospectively for a crime that did not exist at the time these events occurred. The prohibition on retroactive punishment is an established principle of international law enshrined in both the ICCPR and European Convention. The European Court upheld the judgment of the

---

[720] See Basic Principles on the Use of Force and Firearms by Law Enforcement Officials, Adopted by the Eighth United Nations Congress on the Prevention of Crime and the Treatment of Offenders, Havana, Cuba, 27 August to 7 September 1990, para 26.

[721] European Court of Human Rights, *K.-H.W. v. Germany*, Application no. 37201/97, Judgment, 22 March 2001. Some sources put the number of persons killed crossing the East German border during the Cold War as high as 938.

domestic courts in *K.-H.W. v. Germany* (ECtHR; 2001) and *Streletz, Kessler and Krenz v. Germany* (ECtHR; 2001).[722] The Court observed that in the case of the eponymous border guard K.-H.W that "it should have been obvious that firing at an unarmed person infringed the duty of humanity" and that he had the option of firing wide of his target and allowing the victim, twenty-nine-year-old Manfred Weylandt, to escape.[723]

The UN Human Rights Committee received a similar application from a fourth senior East German official, Klaus Dieter Baumgarten, the former Deputy Minister of Defense and Head of Border Troops (*Chef der Grenztruppen*). Baumgarten had been convicted by the Berlin Regional Court of being responsible for the deaths or injuries inflicted on persons trying to cross the Berlin Wall before reunification, by virtue of the fact that the annual orders he issued in his official capacity set in motion a chain of subsequent orders that effectively incited the use of lethal force against unarmed fugitives by individual border guards. In *Baumgarten v. Germany* (HRC; 2003), the former Minister argued along similar lines to Streletz, Kessler and Krenz that his conviction was unsound, although in this case he alleged it was in breach of the ICCPR rather than the European Convention.[724] Following the same logic applied by the European Court, the HRC took the view that Germany had not violated the ICCPR in prosecuting Baumgarten, commenting: "The disproportionate use of lethal force was criminal according to the general principles of law recognized by the community of nations already at the time when the author committed his acts."[725]

---

[722] See Rudolf Geiger, The German Border Guard Cases and International Human Rights Law, *European Journal of International Law*, Vol. 9 (1998) and Magdalena Forowicz, *The Reception of International Law in the European Court of Human Rights* (Oxford University Press; 2010), pp. 175–179.

[723] European Court of Human Rights, *K.-H.W. v. Germany*, Application no. 37201/97, Judgment, 22 March 2001, at http://www.ucs.louisiana.edu/~ras2777/judpol/khw.htm. Viewed 26 May 2016.

[724] *Klaus Dieter Baumgarten v. Germany*, Communication no. 960/2000, U.N. Doc. CCPR/C/78/D/960/2000 (2003).

[725] ibid., paras 9.4 and 9.5.

The obligation to protect the right to life of every individual within their jurisdiction does not place an unreasonable burden on states as they seek to combat terrorist threats. Lethal force can be used legitimately in self-defense or to protect members of the public, so long as it is used only when absolutely necessary and strictly in proportion to the objective sought. States are enjoined from depriving any individual of life arbitrarily, which simply requires the application of due process in the judicial arena, and the responsible use of force in the field. Counter-terrorism operations must be well planned and executed lawfully — if a non-lethal outcome is possible it should always be the desired end result and this should be reflected in operational planning. Police and security force personnel should be well trained in both weapons and tactics, and on the legal constraints within which they operate. When a life is taken, states have an obligation to investigate the circumstances, and if an agent of the state has acted negligently or unlawfully he or she must be held to account. It is hard to imagine any individual who genuinely believes in democratic accountability and the rule of law objecting to a single one of these strictures. When they are ignored, the all too common result is that innocent lives are lost.

## Targeted killing

President Barack Obama authorized more lethal strikes against terrorist targets in more places than any other world leader in history. In February 2016, the Bureau of Investigative Journalism's Drone War Project reported that a minimum of 2,494 men, women and children had been killed by US drone strikes in Afghanistan, Pakistan, Somalia, and Yemen since 2004.[726] The true death toll in these countries is probably significantly higher, and this figure does not include US drone strikes that have taken place in Syria and Iraq. The United States is not the first nation to take covert action against

---

[726] Jack Serle, *Naming the dead: Only 10 of scores killed by US drones in Pakistan last year have been identified*, The Bureau of Investigative Journalism, 3 February 2016, at https://www.thebureauinvestigates.com/2016/02/03/naming-the-dead-only-10-of-scores-killed-by-us-drones-in-pakistan-last-year-have-been-identified/. Viewed 27 May 2016.

individuals associated with terrorist violence, but it is the first to do so on an almost industrial scale, and this is perhaps one of the lasting legacies of the conceptual framework underpinning the War on Terror. In a speech delivered at the National Defense University in May 2013, President Obama justified the policy in the following terms: "In some of these places — such as parts of Somalia and Yemen — the state has only the most tenuous reach into the territory. In other cases, the state lacks the capacity or will to take action. It is also not possible for America to simply deploy a team of Special Forces to capture every terrorist ... It is in this context that the United States has taken lethal, targeted action against *al-Qaeda* and its associated forces."[727]

The desire to take lethal covert or military action against terrorist targets is hardly a new phenomenon. As the UN Special Rapporteur on extrajudicial, summary or arbitrary executions, Philip Alston, pointed out in his 2010 *Study on Targeted Killings* the means and methods used by states over the years to kill men and women they have labeled as terrorists have varied considerably and include "sniper fire, shooting at close rage, missiles from helicopters, gunships, drones, the use of car bombs and poison."[728] After World War II the British established clandestine "Special Squads" within the Palestinian Police Force — consisting of former British Special Forces veterans — to hunt down members of the Jewish terrorist groups LEHI and *Irgun*. In January 1947, following a series of incidents that culminated in the detonation of a LEHI truck bomb outside the police headquarters in Haifa, which killed four and wounded sixty-three, the British Cabinet resolved that "more vigorous action" should be taken "against the terrorists" and a plan was set in motion to deploy a select number of officers "who have the technical and psychological knowledge of terrorism, having themselves been engaged in similar operations on what might have been termed the terrorists' side in countries occupied by the

---

[727] Remarks of President Barack Obama, National Defense University, 23 May 2013 at http://www.whitehouse.gov/the-press-office/2013/05/23/remarks-president-barack-obama.

[728] *Report of the Special Rapporteur on extrajudicial, summary or arbitrary executions, Philip Alston, Addendum: Study on targeted killings* (A/HRC/14/24/Add.6), para 8.

enemy in the late war" to kill or capture LEHI and *Irgun* cadres.[729] As one of the architects of this plan, Lt. Col. Bernard Fergusson, put it: "We planned to be unorthodox, but not illegal. The idea was to provoke contact, to look for confrontation, but not to fire the first shot."[730] The "counter-gang" experiment was not much of a success on its own terms, but was nevertheless replicated by British veterans of the Palestine Mandate in counterinsurgency and counter-terrorism operations in Malaya and Kenya, where, in the words of the historian David Cesarani, "its worst qualities tended to bulk large."[731]

Israel is probably the modern exemplar of the fight-fire-with-fire approach. In the aftermath of the Munich Olympics hostage crisis, Prime Minster Golda Meir's reported instruction to "send forth the boys" set in motion Operation Wrath of God to hunt down those responsible for planning and executing the attack.[732] *Mossad* set to work killing associates of the Black September Organization in Athens, Beirut, Nicosia, Paris, and Rome in 1972 and 1973. *Mossad* deliberately adopted an approach that was intended to intimidate and unbalance Palestinian militants. According to David Kimche, former deputy head of *Mossad*: "The aim was not so much revenge but mainly to make them frightened. We wanted to make them look over their shoulders and feel that we are upon them. And therefore we tried not to do things by just shooting a guy in the street — that's easy."[733] Sporadic clandestine killings continued into the 1980s and 1990s, but by the outbreak of the Second *Intifada* in September 2000 Israel's policy of targeted killing (rebranded "targeted preventions" by Attorney General Elyakim Rubinstein in 2011) had come to rely more heavily on air strikes delivered initially by helicopter gunships

---

[729] David Cesarani, *Major Farran's Hat: The Untold Story of the Struggle to Establish the Jewish State* (Da Capo Press, Cambridge, Massachusetts; 2009), p. 61.

[730] ibid., 63.

[731] ibid., 216.

[732] Simon Reeve. *One Day in September: The Full Story of the 1972 Munich Olympics Massacre and the Israeli Revenge Operation "Wrath of God"* (Arcade Publishing; 2006), p. 159.

[733] Jessica Elgot, Mossad spy and founding father David Kimche dies, *The Jewish Chronicle*, 9 March 2010.

and fast jets, but more recently by unmanned aerial vehicles.[734] The Israeli human rights organization *B'Tselem* reported that between September 2000 and May 2008, such strikes claimed the lives of at least 234 Palestinian militants.[735] Avi Dicter, Director of the Israeli General Security Service, *Shin Bet*, during the Second *Intifada*, reportedly described the philosophy underpinning these attacks in the following terms: "All the time we have to mow the grass — all the time — and the leaders with experience will die and the others will be without experience and finally the 'barrel of terror' will be drained."[736] While drone strikes have become the preferred method of attack, the Israeli intelligence services also continue to mount occasional lethal covert operations to the present day, mostly recently attracting attention for the January 2010 murder of Mahmoud al-Mabhouh, a founding member of *Hamas'* Izz ad-Din al-Qassam Brigades, who was smothered to death in a Dubai hotel.[737]

In 1983, the newly elected Spanish government of Prime Minister Felipe González, facing an upsurge of terrorist violence, authorized the creation of a secret paramilitary organization — known as the *Grupos Antiterroristas de Liberación* (GAL) — to take the fight to the Basque separatist group ETA, especially across the border in France. Spain did not yet have an extradition treaty with France (a legacy of Spain's fascist past) and the French Basque country had become something of a safe haven for ETA activists. Operating between 1983 and 1987, GAL carried out bomb attacks, kidnappings and shootings, and was responsible for the murders of twenty-seven people. One incident that came to typify the ruthlessness with which GAL operated was the September 1985 attack on the Monbar Hotel in Bayonne in which heavily armed hitmen opened fire on the bar of the hotel during an international football

---

[734] Andrew Cockburn, *Kill Chain: The Rise of the High-Tech Assassins* (Henry Holt and Co.; 2015), p. 116.

[735] *Report of the Special Rapporteur on extrajudicial, summary or arbitrary executions, Philip Alston, Addendum: Study on targeted killings* (A/HRC/14/24/Add.6), para 14.

[736] Andrew Cockburn, *Kill Chain: The Rise of the High-Tech Assassins* (Henry Holt and Co.; 2015), p. 117.

[737] *Report of the Special Rapporteur on extrajudicial, summary or arbitrary executions, Philip Alston, Addendum: Study on targeted killings* (A/HRC/14/24/Add.6), para 7.

match killing four members of ETA. Two of the hitmen, both French nationals, were subsequently arrested by the French police and confessed to having been recruited by a Spanish police sub-commissioner from Bilbao, José Amedo Fouce. Historically, French antipathy to the fascist regime of Generalissimo Francisco Franco and its consistent persecution of Basque nationalists had ensured that ETA activists enjoyed a degree of protection in France, and Spanish intelligence documents suggest that GAL's primary objective had been to force the French government to address the presence of ETA members on its soil.[738] González later obliquely defended his government's action, asserting: "The rule of law is defended in the courts, and in the salons, and in the sewers."[739]

Claiming to be inspired by the actions of both the United States and Israel, Russian lawmakers passed Federal Law No. 35-FZ in 2006 authorizing the Russian President to deploy the Armed Forces of the Russian Federation and special-purpose units "to suppress international terrorist activity outside the Russian Federation".[740] However, there are credible grounds to believe that the law simply sought to put on a legal basis a practice that was already well entrenched in the Russian intelligence community, of which, of course, President Vladimir Putin was once famously a member. The Soviet Union had a well-established history of extra-territorial assassinations of dissidents and political opponents, the most notorious of which is probably the murder of Leon Trotsky in Mexico City in August 1940, and there is much evidence to suggest such activities continued in the post-Soviet era. Russian security forces successfully targeted and killed a number of Chechen separatist leaders: Dzhokhar Dudaev was killed by a precision airstrike in April 1996, Thamir Saleh Abdullah (aka Ibn al-Khattab) by a letter coated in a fast-acting nerve agent in March 2002, and Shamil Basayev by an IED hidden in an arms shipment in July 2006. In February 2004, the former

---

[738] Paddy Woodworth, Why Do They Kill: The Basque Conflict in Spain, *World Policy Journal*, Vol. 18, No. 1 (Spring 2001), p. 7.

[739] Michael Burleigh, *Blood and Rage: A Cultural History of Terrorism* (Harper; 2009), p. 285.

[740] Steven Eke, *Russia law on killing "extremists"*, BBC News, 27 November 2006 at http://news.bbc.co.uk/2/hi/europe/6188658.stm. Viewed 4 June 2016.

Chechen separatist president Zelimkhan Yandariev was killed, along with two bodyguards, by a car bomb in Doha. The Qatari authorities subsequently detained, prosecuted and convicted two Russian military intelligence (GRU) officers based in Doha, Anatoly Yablochkov and Vasily Pugachyov, of the murders. The two Russians were transferred to Russia to serve out their sentence in December 2004 but within two months the Russian authorities admitted that they were no longer being held in detention.[741] President Putin has been quite explicit about his intentions: "We'll get them anywhere. If we find terrorists in the shithouse, then we'll waste them in the shithouse. That's all there is to it."[742]

Finally, I should note that the United States itself had also resorted to lethal strikes on specific targets in response to terrorist attacks on a number of occasions prior to the 9/11 attacks. In the aftermath of the April 1986 bombing of *La Belle Discothèque* in Berlin, which claimed the lives of two American servicemen and a Turkish woman, and injured more than seventy people, US signals intelligence quickly identified Libyan agents as having been behind the attack. President Ronald Reagan then authorized Operation El Dorado Canyon, a series of major air strikes on targets in the Libyan cities of Tripoli and Benghazi, including the Bab al-Azizia compound which was home to the Libyan leader, Colonel Muammar Gadhafi. Forewarned of the attack, Gadhafi survived but the strikes reportedly killed at least fifteen people, including (according to Libyan sources) one of his adopted daughters. Two US flight crew were also killed when their F-111 fighter-bomber was shot down by Libyan air defenses.

Following the foiled attempt by Saddam Hussein to assassinate former President George H. W. Bush during a visit to Kuwait, along with several members of his former cabinet, in April 1993 with a particularly sophisticated car bomb, the Clinton administration launched twenty-three Tomahawk cruise missiles at targets in Iraq believed to be associated with the attack, including the headquarters of the Iraqi *Jihaz Al-Mukhabarat Al-Amma* (Directorate of General

---

[741] Sarah Rainsford, *Convicted Russia agents "missing"*, BBC News, 17 February 2005.

[742] Michael Burleigh, *Blood and Rage: A Cultural History of Terrorism* (Harper; 2009), p. 408.

Intelligence).[743] In a public address, President Clinton said the strike had been intended to send three messages: "We will combat terrorism. We will deter aggression. We will protect our people."[744] Clinton authorized a further seventy-nine cruise missile strikes in August 1998 against targets associated with Osama bin Laden in Sudan and Afghanistan after *al-Qaeda* mounted its simultaneous truck bomb attacks on the US embassies in Nairobi and Dar es Salaam.[745]

The foregoing is not intended to be an exhaustive list of countries that have used such methods. One could equally look at the Islamic Republic of Iran's violent pursuit of the *Mojahedin-e-Khalq* (MEK) whose post-revolutionary campaign of terror claimed the lives of many prominent members of the newly installed clerical establishment, including the President of the Republic, the Prime Minister, and the President of the Supreme Court,[746] or the creation of *Operación Cóndor* by right-wing governments in Latin America in the 1970s to hunt down and assassinate leftist opponents.[747] However, it is intended to be an illustration of the lengths to which states have been prepared to go to hit back at terrorist groups operating outside their judicial reach, and to demonstrate that this is a more widespread and well-established practice than is commonly acknowledged. The UN Special Rapporteur, Philip Alston, has defined targeted killing as "the intentional, premeditated and deliberate use of lethal force, by states or their agents acting under color of law, or by an organized armed group in armed conflict, against a specific individual who is not in the

---

[743] David Von Drehle and R. Jeffrey Smith, U.S. Strikes Iraq for Plot to Kill Bush, *Washington Post*, 27 June 1993.

[744] ibid.

[745] W. Michael Reisman, International Legal Responses to Terrorism, *Houston Journal of International Law*, Vol. 22, No. 3 (1999), p. 47.

[746] Ervand Abrahamian, *Radical Islam: The Iranian Mojahedin* (I. B. Taurus; 1989), p. 198 and Dilip Hiro, *Iran Under the Ayatollahs* (Routledge Revivals; 2013), p. 190.

[747] See J. Patrice McSherry, *Predatory States: Operation Condor and Covert War in Latin America* (Rowman & Littlefield Publishers; 2005).

physical custody of the perpetrator."[748] Whether or not a specific targeted killing accords with the obligations of international human rights law and international humanitarian law depends on the context in which it is conducted — whether in armed conflict, outside armed conflict, or in relation to the inter-state use of force — and the manner in which it was carried out.[749] The UN Special Rapporteur on the Promotion and Protection of Human Rights and Fundamental Freedoms while Countering Terrorism, Ben Emmerson, summed up the applicable legal regimes in the following terms: "In a situation qualifying as an armed conflict, the adoption of a pre-identified list of individual military targets is not unlawful; if based upon reliable intelligence it is a paradigm application of the principle of distinction. Conversely, outside situations of armed conflict, international human rights law prohibits almost any counter-terrorism operation that has the infliction of deadly force as its sole or main purpose."[750]

On those occasions when deadly force is used extraterritorially and outside the parameters of armed conflict, the most common justification offered by a state is that it is acting in self-defense.[751] Article 2(4) of the United Nations Charter obliges all Member States to "refrain in their international relations from the threat or use of force against the territorial integrity or political independence of any state." Articles 42, 43, and 51 of the UN Charter recognize only two exceptions to this rule — action taken in self-defense against "armed attack" and collective action authorized by the Security Council to promote international peace and security. The UN General Assembly explored the contours of what might, and might not, constitute an "armed attack", and thus an act of aggression, in Resolution 3314 (XXIX), which was adopted in 1974 and is considered to amount to

---

[748] *Report of the Special Rapporteur on extrajudicial, summary or arbitrary executions, Philip Alston, Addendum: Study on targeted killings* (A/HRC/14/24/Add.6), para 1.

[749] ibid., para 28.

[750] Note by the Secretary-General, *Promotion and protection of human rights and fundamental freedoms while countering terrorism*, A/68/389, 18 September 2013.

[751] See *Letter dated 7 September 2015 from the Permanent Representative of the United Kingdom of Great Britain and Northern Ireland to the United Nations addressed to the President of the Security Council*, United Nations Security Council, S/2015/688, 8 September 2015.

customary international law.[752] This definition of aggression includes the "sending by or on behalf of a state of armed bands, groups, irregulars or mercenaries … [to] carry out acts of armed force against another state", but also implicitly recognized that some acts of force may not be of sufficient gravity to be considered acts of aggression.[753] The same phrasing was adopted by the Rome Statute of the International Criminal Court when its jurisdiction was expanded to include the crime of aggression with effect from July 2018 (for states that have ratified or accepted this amendment).[754] In *Nicaragua v. United States* (ICJ; 1986), the International Court of Justice further clarified that the concept of armed attack could not be stretched to include the provision of assistance to rebels or other armed groups in the form of weapons or logistical or other support.[755] In the *Case Concerning Oil Platforms* (ICJ; 2003), the Court also took the view that any violent incident must have been "aimed specifically" at the state effected to arise to the level of an armed attack.[756] So, whether or not a terrorist attack can amount to an armed attack in the sense meant by international law would ultimately seem to be a question of intent, degree, and implicit state support.

Prior to 9/11, the international community was, as a whole, very reluctant to recognize that any extra-territorial military response to a terrorist attack could be considered a legitimate act of self-defense. Israel's October 1985 raid on the PLO Headquarters outside Tunis — Operation Wooden Leg, launched in response to the murder of three Israeli tourists sailing on a yacht off the coast

---

[752] International Court of Justice, *Case Concerning Military and Paramilitary Activities in and against Nicaragua (Nicaragua v. United States)*, Judgment, 27 June 1986, para 195.

[753] *Definition of Aggression*, United Nations General Assembly Resolution 3314 (XXIX), 1974, at Article 3(g).

[754] The definition of aggression was agreed by ICC States Parties at a Review Conference of the Rome Statute in Kampala in 2010. A resolution activating the ICC's jurisdiction over the crime of aggression was adopted at the Sixteenth Annual Assembly of States Parties to the Rome Statute in New York in December 2017.

[755] International Court of Justice, *Case Concerning Military and Paramilitary Activities in and against Nicaragua (Nicaragua v. United States)*, Judgment, 27 June 1986, para 195.

[756] International Court of Justice, *Case Concerning Oil Platforms (Islamic Republic of Iran v. United States)*, Judgment, 6 November 2003, para 64.

of Cyprus by members of the PLO's Force 17 — was condemned by the Security Council as an "act of armed aggression ... in flagrant violation of the Charter of the United Nations".[757] The Security Council urged other states "to take measures to dissuade Israel from resorting to such acts against the sovereignty and territorial integrity of all states".[758] Similarly, the American air raids on Tripoli and Benghazi in response to the *La Belle Discothèque* bombing in April 1986 were roundly rejected by the General Assembly as "a violation of the Charter of the United Nations and of international law."[759]

Even Israel's successful July 1976 rescue of hostages being held by the Popular Front for the Liberation of Palestine — External Operations (and its German allies from *Revolutionäre Zellen*) in Entebbe Airport, with the manifest collusion of the Ugandan President Idi Amin, was condemned by the Organisation of African Unity (OAU) as an act of "unprecedented aggression" and "a danger not only to Uganda and Africa but to international peace and security."[760] The Secretary-General of the UN, Kurt Waldheim, condemned Operation Thunderbolt as "a serious violation of the national sovereignty of a United Nations member state."[761] The Soviet Union described the Israeli action as "an act of piracy", and Egypt labeled it "government terrorism".[762] Several dozen Ugandan soldiers had indeed been killed in the raid, but the fact that Amin subsequently took revenge for his humiliation by authorizing the murder of an elderly hostage, Dora Bloch,

---

[757] United Nations Security Council Resolution 573, 4 October 1985.

[758] ibid.

[759] *Declaration of the Assembly of Heads of State and Government of the Organization of African Unity on the aerial and naval military attack against the Socialist People's Libyan Arab Jamahiriya by the present United States Administration in April 1986*, United Nations General Assembly, A/RES/41/38, 20 November 1986.

[760] Saul David, *Operation Thunderbolt: Flight 139 and the Raid on Entebbe Airport, the Most Audacious Hostage Rescue in History* (Little, Brown and Company; 2015), p. 350.

[761] ibid., p. 351.

[762] ibid.

hospitalized prior to the rescue and thus left behind in Uganda, passed almost without comment.[763]

However, there is some evidence to suggest that this mindset has begun to change since the rise to prominence of *al-Qaeda*, ISIL, and their affiliates, or at least that these older attitudes are now substantially contested.[764] The Clinton administration justified its cruise missile strikes against targets associated with Osama bin Laden in the wake of the African embassy bombings as being "pursuant to the right of self-defense confirmed by Article 51 of the Charter of the United Nations".[765] The government of Israel argued before the International Court of Justice in *Legal Consequences of the Construction of a Wall in the Occupied Palestinian Territory* (ICJ; 2004) that the international response to the 9/11 attacks — most notably the passage of Security Council Resolutions 1368 and 1373, which explicitly acknowledged both the United States' inherent right to defend itself and the threat posed to international peace and security by international terrorism — "clearly recognized the right of states to use force in self-defense against terrorist attacks."[766] Although the ICJ ultimately rejected Israel's argument in its Advisory Opinion, it is clear that many states retain a degree of sympathy for this interpretation — the North Atlantic Treaty Organization (NATO), for instance, reacted to the 9/11 attacks by invoking Article 5 of its charter, pertaining to collective self-defense, for the first time in its history. The British government's notification to the UN Security Council that it would be joining the US invasion of Afghanistan stated that its armed forces were "employed in exercise of the inherent right of individual and collective self-defense, recognized in Article 51, following the terrorist outrage of 11 September, to avert the continuing threat of attacks

---

[763] ibid., pp. 345–346.

[764] See for example Jordan Paust, Use of Armed Force against Terrorists in Afghanistan, Iraq, and Beyond, *Cornell International Law Journal*, Vol. 35, No. 3 (2002).

[765] W. Michael Reisman, International Legal Responses to Terrorism, *Houston Journal of International Law*, Vol. 22, No. 3 (1999), pp. 48–49.

[766] International Court of Justice, *Legal Consequences of the Construction of a Wall in the Occupied Palestinian Territory*, Advisory Opinion, 9 July 2004, para 138.

from the same source."[767] Philip Alston has expressed concern that such an increasingly permissive response to terrorist attacks diminishes the "foundational prohibition" contained in Article 51 on the use of force, and has urged that UN Security Council support should continue to act as the basic arbiter of whether or not an armed response is appropriate and lawful. But such an essentially political solution, albeit well established, is heavily informed by the national prejudices of the members of the Council and so is unlikely to satisfy everyone in the current security climate.[768] As Alston also notes: "Many of the justifications for targeted killings offered by one or other of the relevant states in particular current contexts would in all likelihood not gain their endorsement if they were to be asserted by other states in the future."[769]

More problematic still is the issue of pre-emptive self-defense — a profoundly controversial concept in international law. The traditional tests for the legality of pre-emptive use of force revolve around concepts of imminence, necessity, and proportionality — as first articulated by the US Secretary of State Daniel Webster after the Caroline Incident of 1837, which took place during the Mackenzie Rebellion in Upper Canada.[770] British troops crossed the border into the United States to put a steamboat used to supply the rebels out of commission. The steamboat was called the Caroline and it was destroyed in the attack. A US national was also killed. The British had previously requested the US authorities to take action to interdict the Caroline without result. The US protested the violation of its sovereignty but the British invoked the principle of self-defense. Daniel Webster took the position that, for the British claim to be admitted, the British would have to "show a necessity of self-defense, instant, overwhelming, leaving no choice of means, and no moment

---

[767] *Letter from Stewart Eldon, Chargé d'Affaires, UK Mission to the UN in New York, to the President of the Security Council,* S/2001/947, 7 October 2001.

[768] *Report of the Special Rapporteur on extrajudicial, summary or arbitrary executions, Philip Alston, Addendum: Study on targeted killings* (A/HRC/14/24/Add.6), para 40–41.

[769] ibid., para 4.

[770] Yoram Dinstein, *War Aggression and Self-Defence* (Cambridge University Press; 2011), paras 218–219.

for deliberation."[771] The action taken must also involve "nothing unreasonable or excessive; since the act, justified by the necessity of self-defense, must be limited by that necessity, and kept clearly within it."[772] In essence, as Webster conceived it, the scope for the pre-emptive use of force was limited to a counterpunch delivered to forestall an impending blow.

The Obama administration, in particular, sought to stretch this concept well beyond Webster's original intention. Harold Koh, the former Dean of the Yale Law School who joined the administration as the Legal Adviser to the State Department in 2009, developed a theory that he termed "elongated imminence".[773] Koh posited a four-part test for using force in self-defense against *al-Qaeda*: the target had to be a member of *al-Qaeda*; the target had to play a unique role in the organization that was hard to replicate; the target must be externally focused not consumed with local conflicts; and the target must be plotting to carry out an attack.[774] He further argued that if an individual had manifested a consistent pattern of aggressive behavior it was not necessary to wait until his or her next plan was actually underway to take action in self-defense.[775] In February 2002, the Judge Advocate General of the Israeli Defense Forces (IDF), Menachem Finkelstein, had issued a similar set of instructions to govern the Israeli use of targeted killings in the context of the Second *Intifada*: the Palestinian Authority must ignore requests for the arrest of the target; the Israeli authorities must be unable to effect an arrest themselves; and the use of lethal force must be necessary to prevent imminent or future terrorist attacks.[776] Avi Dicter and Daniel Byman have further noted that Israel sought to restrict its targeted strikes to "arch terrorists" — leaders, senior

---

[771] Daniel Webster, *Letter to Mr. Fox, British Minister at Washington*, 24 April 1841, at http://avalon.law.yale.edu/19th_century/br-1842d.asp. Viewed on 28 November 2017.

[772] ibid.

[773] Daniel Klaidman, *Kill or Capture: The War on Terror and the Soul of the Obama Presidency* (Houghton Mifflin Harcourt; 2012), p. 219.

[774] ibid.

[775] ibid., pp. 219–220.

[776] Steven David, Israel's Policy of Targeted Killing, *Ethics and International Affairs*, Vol. 17, No. 1 (2003), p. 115.

planners and bomb-makers "whose removal would have a signifi-cant impact on the terrorist group's operations".[777] The Israeli Supreme Court upheld what it saw as the essential lawfulness of the IDF's approach in *The Public Committee against Torture in Israel v. The State of Israel* (ISC; 2006), but stressed that each instance in which lethal force is used must be examined on its own individual merits.[778]

Koh's philosophy played out, at least in part, in the targeting of the radical Islamist preacher Anwar al-Awlaki, who was killed by a US drone strike in Yemen in September 2011 along with the editor of *al-Qaeda*'s English-language *Inspire* Magazine, Samir Khan, and two other suspected members of *al-Qaeda* as they were driving by car to the Ma'rib Governorate. Al-Awlaki was a US citizen of Yemeni origin whose *Forty-Four Ways to Support Jihad* had been especially influential amongst anglophone Islamic extremists, and he was con-sidered by the US government to be the leader of *al-Qaeda* in the Arabian Peninsula's external operations and thus responsible for planning and directing terrorist attacks against the United States.[779] He had been associated with two 9/11 hijackers, helped the failed underwear bomber Umar Farouq Abdulmutallab film a martyrdom video and gave him operational instructions to target an interna-tional airliner, and he was in direct communication with Nidal Hasan who shot and killed thirteen US soldiers in Fort Hood, Texas, in November 2009. Indeed, no fewer than eighty Americans charged with links to Islamist terrorism since 9/11 have cited al-Awlaki as an influence, or have been found to have read or possessed a copy of one of his sermons — approximately one case in four.[780] Al-Awlaki's

---

[777] Daniel Byman and Avi Dicter, *Israel's Lessons for Fighting Terorirsts and their Implications for the United States*, Saban Center for Middle East Policy at the Brookings Institution, Analysis Paper, No. 8 (March 2006), p. 9.

[778] Israel Supreme Court, *The Public Committee against Torture in Israel v. The State of Israel*, HCJ 769/02, Judgment, 13 December 2006.

[779] John Brennan, Assistant to the President for Homeland Security and Counterterrorism, *The Ethics and Efficacy of the President's Counterterrorism Strategy*, Remarks to the Woodrow Wilson International Center for Scholars, 30 April 2012.

[780] Peter Bergen, *United States of Jihad: Investigating America's Homegrown Terrorists* (Crown; 2016), p. 43.

killing was hugely contentious both inside and outside America, not least because of his status as a US citizen, but it took place with the full backing of the US Department of Justice, which concluded he posed a "continued" and "imminent" threat to the United States,[781] and quoted with approval from a 1989 legal memorandum prepared by the International Affairs Division of the Department of the Army, which stated: "A national decision to employ military force in self-defense against a legitimate terrorist or related threat would not be unlike the employment of force in response to a threat by conventional forces; only the nature of the threat has changed, rather than the international legal right of self-defense."[782]

While the international legal regime surrounding the use of force by states in self-defense is currently the subject of considerable debate, what is not, and has never been, at issue is that any state wishing to lawfully employ armed force in self-defense outside the confines of armed conflict would still be bound by international human rights law and the degree of force used must therefore, as in the context of domestic law enforcement, be both proportional to the threat posed, and an absolutely necessary resort because no lesser alternative to meet the defensive need exists.[783] Furthermore, the invocation of the right to self-defense cannot be used to justify any violation of international human rights law.[784] However, in both the US and Israeli cases cited above self-defense is rarely the only, or even the most important ground, on which targeted killing has been justified. Both states have used lethal force in the context of what they consider to be armed conflicts and thus we must also consider the implications and prohibitions that may result from the application

---

[781] David Barron, Office of Legal Counsel, *Memorandum for the Attorney-General re. Applicability of Federal Criminal Laws and the Constitution to Contemplated Lethal Operations Against Shaykh Anwar al-Aulaqi*, US Department of Justice, 16 July 2010, p. 95.

[782] W. Hays Parks, Chief, International Law Branch, *Memorandum of Law: Executive Order 12333 and Assassination*, Department of the Army, Office of the Judge Advocate General, DAJA-IA (27-1A), 2 November 1989.

[783] *Report of the Special Rapporteur on extrajudicial, summary or arbitrary executions, Philip Alston, Addendum: Study on targeted killings* (A/HRC/14/24/Add.6), para 43.

[784] International Law Commission, *Articles on Responsibility of States for Internationally Wrongful Acts*, adopted by the Commission at its fifty-third session in 2001 at Article 21.

of international humanitarian law to this practice. In essence, there are three categories of international and civil conflict: international armed conflict fought between states; non-international, or internal, armed conflict typically fought between a government and a non-state armed group; and finally, in much the same way that there can be violent assaults that are not considered to be of sufficient gravity to amount to an "armed attack", there can be acts of violence and civil disturbance that do not amount to armed conflict. A civil disturbance that does not amount to either international or non-international armed conflict must be addressed entirely within the rubric of international human rights law.

Traditionally, as we have already touched upon, most states have been reluctant to accord terrorist organizations the perceived legitimacy of belligerent status preferring to treat them as criminal enterprises. For example, the United Kingdom refused to acknowledge the existence of an armed conflict in Northern Ireland with the Provisional IRA, and Russia took a similar stance regarding separatist violence in Chechnya.[785] British Prime Minister Margaret Thatcher famously summarized her government's position regarding the Provisional IRA's status in the following uncompromising terms: "crime is crime is crime. It is not political, it is crime."[786] The United States and Israel have taken a contrary view because of the far greater latitude they perceive is afforded to the use of force in an armed conflict. It is, of course, entirely permissible to kill enemy belligerents in an armed conflict — although there are still limits to how force can be employed. The degree of force employed must be proportional to the military objective sought. Any belligerent party taking part in an armed conflict has an obligation to distinguish between combatants and non-combatants, and it is unlawful to deliberately target civilians. This doctrine of distinction places an obligation on states to demonstrate due diligence in identifying appropriate targets

---

[785] *Report of the Special Rapporteur on extrajudicial, summary or arbitrary executions, Philip Alston, Addendum: Study on targeted killings* (A/HRC/14/24/Add.6), para 46.

[786] John Bingham, Margaret Thatcher: Seconds from death at the hands of an IRA bomber, *The Telegraph*, 8 April 2013. Footage of this statement can be viewed at https://www.youtube.com/watch?v=D7bTsRZh5bk.

to engage, and to ensure that civilian lives are not lost unnecessarily. The prohibition on taking civilian life is not absolute — international humanitarian law recognizes that civilian casualties are an unavoidable consequence of armed conflict — but the taking of civilian life can never be the objective of a military operation. If a party to an armed conflict uses force disproportionately, or deliberately targets civilians, this would be considered a war crime. Finally, the laws of armed conflict also forbid "treacherous killing" and "perfidy", as well as the use of certain prohibited weapons such as poison gas or dum-dum bullets.[787]

There are established legal criteria for determining whether or not a state of armed conflict exists. The simple definition of international armed conflict is set out in Common Article 2(1) of the Geneva Conventions: "Any difference arising between two states leading to the intervention of armed forces." An international armed conflict cannot occur between a state and a non-state actor. The test for the existence of a non-international armed conflict is rather more complex, and may also vary depending whether the state concerned is a party to either Additional Protocol I or Additional Protocol II to the Geneva Conventions.[788] However, at the very least, treaty and customary international law requires that the non-state actor involved must at least have an identifiable personality, have a command structure capable of applying the Geneva Conventions, and be engaged in collective, armed, anti-government action of sufficient intensity and duration to rise to the level of armed conflict.[789] Additional Protocol II clarifies that such violence must go "beyond the level of intensity of internal disturbances and tensions, such as riots, isolated and sporadic acts of violence."[790]

---

[787]Yoram Dinstein, *The Conduct of Hostilities under the Law of International Armed Conflict* (Cambridge University Press; 2004), p. 198.

[788]See Sylvain Vité, Typology of armed conflicts in international humanitarian law: legal concepts and actual situations, *International Review of the Red Cross*, Vol. 91, No. 873 (March 2009). Neither the United States nor Israel has ratified Protocol II.

[789]*Report of the Special Rapporteur on extrajudicial, summary or arbitrary executions, Philip Alston, Study on Targeted Killings* (A/HRC/14/24/Add.6, 28), para 52.

[790]Protocol Additional to the Geneva Conventions of 12 August 1949, and relating to the Protection of Victims of Non-International Armed Conflicts (Protocol II), of 8 June 1977, at Article 1(2).

However, in the case of *Juan Carlos Abella v. Argentina* (IACtHR; 1997), the Inter-American Court of Human Rights also suggested that an isolated incident of a sufficiently high degree of intensity, involving a high level of organization on the part of the non-state armed group responsible — in the case in question, an attack on La Tablada military base in January 1989 by forty-two members of the *Movimiento Todos por la Patria* — could meet the threshold of an armed conflict.[791] Thus, in sum, the critical factors come down to the intensity of the violence that occurs and the degree of organization demonstrated by the non-state actor involved, which must both be assessed on a case-by-case basis.[792]

The applicable legal framework in the case of Israel's conflict with Palestinian armed groups is especially complicated to unravel, with even the government of Israel admitting in legal argument that it has "characteristics that point in different directions".[793] The legal status of the Palestinian National Authority (PNA) has been contested during the period in which Israel has carried out targeted killings on its territory, and for long periods the Gaza Strip has been under the *de facto*, if not *de jure*, control of *Hamas* not the PNA. Both the International Court of Justice and the UN Special Rapporteur on the situation of human rights in the Palestinian territories occupied since 1967 have contended that Israel remains an occupying power in the West Bank, East Jerusalem, and (in the case of the Special Rapporteur) Gaza.[794] In *The Public Committee against Torture in Israel v. The State of Israel* (ISC; 2006), the government of Israel submitted that it ultimately didn't matter how the conflict was classified since, whether it was considered to be an international

---

[791] Inter-American Court of Human Rights, *Juan Carlos Abella v. Argentina*, Report No. 55/97, OEA/Ser.L./V./II.95, doc. 7 rev. 271, 18 November 1997, paras 154–156.

[792] Sylvain Vité, Typology of armed conflicts in international humanitarian law: legal concepts and actual situations, *International Review of the Red Cross*, Vol. 91, No. 873 (March 2009), p. 76.

[793] Israel Supreme Court, *The Public Committee against Torture in Israel v. The State of Israel*, HCJ 769/02, Judgment, 13 December 2006, para 11.

[794] Note by the Secretary-General, *Report of the Special Rapporteur on the situation of human rights in the Palestinian territories occupied since 1967, John Dugard, on the Situation of human rights in the Palestinian territories occupied since 1967*, A/62/275, 17 August 2007, and International Court of Justice, *Legal Consequences of the Construction of a Wall in the Occupied Palestinian Territory*, Advisory Opinion, 9 July 2004, para 78.

armed conflict, a non-international armed conflict, or "a new category of armed conflict which has been developing over the last decade in international law ... of armed conflicts between states and terrorist organizations", the rules of war would still permit the use of targeted lethal force against combatant parties.[795] The Israel Supreme Court itself has consistently maintained that a state of armed conflict exists between Israel and "the Palestinian terrorist organizations operating from Judea and Samaria and the Gaza Strip" and that "therefore, the normative framework applying to the armed conflict between Israel and the Palestinians is the international law governing armed conflicts of an international nature."[796]

The legal argument put forward by the United States to justify its use of lethal force against the *Taliban, al-Qaeda*, and their affiliates was similarly complex. On 14 September 2001, the US Congress authorized the president to "use all necessary and appropriate force against those nations, organizations, or persons he determines planned, authorized, committed or aided the terrorist attacks that occurred on September 11, 2001, or harbored such organizations or persons, in order to prevent any future acts of international terrorism against the United States by such nations, organizations, or persons."[797] At the domestic level, this provides the legal underpinning for the US government's program of targeted killing, but it does not in any way exempt the United States from its international legal obligations. The United States has informed the international community that it considers itself to be in a "transnational non-international armed conflict" with *al-Qaeda* and its affiliates and, on this basis, considers itself lawfully entitled to use lethal force against *al-Qaeda* operatives and their allies whenever and wherever they are encountered. This characterization has

---

[795] Israel Supreme Court, *The Public Committee against Torture in Israel v. The State of Israel*, HCJ 769/02, Judgment, 13 December 2006, para 11.

[796] ibid.

[797] Authorization for Use of Military Force ("AUMF"), Pub. L. No. 107-40, 115 Stat. 224, §2(a) (2001).

not received wide acceptance outside the US.[798] With the exception of its involvement in the armed conflict with US forces in Afghanistan, and previously in Iraq, the UN Special Rapporteur Philip Alston has questioned whether the violence currently practiced by *al-Qaeda* could even be said to meet the threshold required of an armed conflict.[799] He further noted that, unlike the United States, many of the countries in which much of this violence has actually occurred — such as the United Kingdom, Spain, Indonesia, Germany, and Saudi Arabia — do not consider themselves to be engaged in an armed conflict with *al-Qaeda*.[800] To the contrary, these states all regard *al-Qaeda*'s operatives, some little more than volunteers acting on their own initiative, as criminals to be confronted appropriately within a law enforcement framework. In February 2014, the European Parliament passed a resolution condemning the use of lethal force "outside a declared war by a state on the territory of another state without the consent of the latter or of the UN Security Council" as a violation of international law.[801]

There are, therefore, a number of very troubling aspects to the embrace of targeted killing by the United States. The preferred method used by the US — in more than 95% of reported cases since 9/11 — is a missile fired from a UAV, or, as they are more commonly known, a drone.[802] The use of US drones in the ongoing armed conflict in Afghanistan, if employed with due diligence and in a proportional manner to the military objective sought, is most likely to be lawful. The use of US drones in Syria, Iraq, Yemen, Somalia, and Pakistan may be lawful if carried out at the behest of a local

---

[798] *Report of the Special Rapporteur on extrajudicial, summary or arbitrary executions, Philip Alston, Study on Targeted Killings* (A/HRC/14/24/Add.6, 28), para 53.

[799] ibid.

[800] ibid., para 54.

[801] Morten Pihl, "There is overwhelming evidence against Denmark", *Jyllands-Posten*, 30 April 2014.

[802] Micah Zenko, *Reforming US Drone Strike Policies*, Council on Foreign Relations (2013), p. 8. Other methods include Special Forces raids, AC-130 gunships and cruise missile strikes. The term "drone" was first coined by the US Navy in 1936 and experiments with unmanned aircraft date back to the First World War.

government engaged in an armed conflict with local armed groups, again within the constraints of the laws of war. It is not always clear whether such an arrangement exists, since the governments in question rarely wish to publicize their cooperation with, or reliance on, the United States. For example, a State Department memorandum released by Wikileaks revealed that the Yemeni President Ali Abdullah Saleh deliberately concealed US involvement in strikes against *al-Qaeda* affiliates in his country, telling General David Petraeus: "We'll continue saying the bombs are ours, not yours."[803] One consequence of this reluctance is that such drone strikes have typically been conducted covertly by the Central Intelligence Agency (CIA), as opposed to the US military, with a concomitant lack of transparency making any measure of accountability almost impossible.[804] The UN Special Rapporteur has commented that, while it is not unlawful for intelligence officers to participate in armed conflict, unlike members of the armed forces they cannot be considered to be privileged combatants, meaning that they could bear a legal liability for their actions in any foreign country in which they carry out their operations.[805]

Finally, it is worth also taking a moment to address the use of the drones themselves in this context. Drones *per se* are just another, albeit sophisticated, weapons platform and are something of a red herring in the targeted killing debate. If anything, the arrival of drones on the battlefield should be a cause for cautious optimism since the surveillance equipment with which they are mounted, and the manner in which they are employed, allow for the most discriminating and proportional use of force in the history of armed conflict to date. The International Committee of the Red Cross (ICRC) has observed regarding drones that "any weapon that makes it possible to carry out more precise attacks, and helps avoid or minimize incidental loss of civilian life, injury to civilians, or damage to civilian objects, should be given preference over weapons that do

---

[803] Nick Allen, Wikileaks: Yemen covered up US drone strikes, *The Telegraph*, 28 November 2010.
[804] *Report of the Special Rapporteur on extrajudicial, summary or arbitrary executions, Philip Alston, Study on Targeted Killings* (A/HRC/14/24/Add.6, 28), para 26.
[805] ibid., para 71.

not."[806] The lawfulness of a drone strike can thus be determined in the same way as the lawfulness of the use of any other weapon of war. The Obama administration stated that it had undertaken two distinct types of lethal drone operations: personality strikes, in which a specific member of *al-Qaeda* is stalked and killed, and signature strikes, in which a pattern of suspicious behavior, such as trying to conceal an item by a roadside routinely used by Coalition troops, led drone operators to suspect a given individual was engaged in terrorist activity and thus, in the US view, a legitimate target. John Brennan, who as Deputy National Security Adviser for Homeland Security and Counterterrorism initially oversaw the drone program in the Obama administration, made extravagant claims about the near infallibility of drone operations saluting the "surgical precision" of US strikes and "the ability, with laser-like focus, to eliminate the cancerous tumor called an *al-Qaeda* terrorist while limiting damage to the tissue around it".[807] However, in November 2014, the UK-based human rights organization Reprieve released a study of US drone strikes in which it concluded that, since 2006, personality strikes aimed at forty-one specific individuals — including Baitullah Mehsud, Ayman al-Zawahiri, Sirajudin Haqqani, and Fahd al-Quso — had resulted in the deaths of an estimated 1,147 people. Baitullah Mehsud alone survived six drone strikes before he was killed by the seventh — 164 other people died in the process.[808] John Brennan had previously told the Senate Select Committee on Intelligence that "it is exceedingly rare" that civilians have been killed by drone strikes.[809] It is certainly possible, indeed probable, that some of the collateral casualties were also members of *al-Qaeda* or its affiliates — subordinates, bodyguards, or drivers — but it

---

[806] ICRC, *The use of armed drones must comply with laws*, 10 May 2013, available at www.icrc.org/eng/resources/documents/interview/2013/05-10-drone-weapons-ihl.htm.

[807] John Brennan, Assistant to the President for Homeland Security and Counterterrorism, *The Ethics and Efficacy of the President's Counterterrorism Strategy*, Remarks to the Woodrow Wilson International Center for Scholars, 30 April 2012.

[808] Spencer Ackerman, 41 men targeted but 1,147 people killed: US drone strikes — the facts on the ground, *The Guardian*, 24 November 2014.

[809] Chris McGreal, John Brennan defends drone attacks as he prepares for tough Senate hearing, *The Guardian*, 7 February 2013.

surely stretches credulity to claim that they all were. Either way, more than a thousand unintended deaths is hardly evidence of a surgical approach.

One of the most challenging aspects of non-international armed conflicts is that it can be extremely difficult to distinguish combatants from civilians — insurgent groups are often unable to dress their fighters in a uniform, and terrorists are, by their very nature, clandestine actors who seek to blend into the civilian population. Protocols I and II to the Genera Conventions provide that in armed conflicts, civilians are protected against direct attack "unless and for such time as they take a direct part in hostilities",[810] a rule that was introduced to reflect increased civilian participation in armed conflict on an individual, sporadic, or unorganized basis, a category that might include acts of terrorism in some circumstances.[811] This rule is now considered to be a norm of customary international law applicable in both international and non-international armed conflicts.[812] What constitutes "direct participation" beyond a "continuous combat function" is not defined and, as the International Committee of the Red Cross notes, "a clear and uniform definition of direct participation in hostilities has not been developed in state practice."[813] The interpretive guidance offered by the ICRC posits a cumulative three-part test: (1) The act must be likely to adversely affect the military operations or military capacity of a party to an armed conflict or, alternatively, to inflict death, injury, or destruction on persons or objects protected against direct attack; and (2) there must be a direct causal link — one step — between the act and the harm likely to result from that act, or from a coordinated military operation of which that act constitutes an integral part; and (3) the act must be specifically designed to directly cause the required harm in support of a party to the conflict and to the detriment of

---

[810] Article 51(3) of Additional Protocol I to the Geneva Conventions; Article 13(3) of Additional Protocol II to the Geneva Conventions.

[811] *Report of the Special Rapporteur on extrajudicial, summary or arbitrary executions, Philip Alston, Study on Targeted Killings* (A/HRC/14/24/Add.6, 28), para 64.

[812] https://www.icrc.org/customary-ihl/eng/docs/v1_cha_chapter1_rule6.

[813] https://www.icrc.org/customary-ihl/eng/docs/v1_rul_rule6#refFn_45_21.

another.[814] The ICRC guidance notes that just as there is "direct participation in hostilities", there must also be its corollary, "indirect participation in hostilities". Indirect activity would not meet the threshold that would allow the use of armed force under the rules governing the conduct of hostilities. The ICRC draws a distinction between acts that actually cause the required "military harm" and acts that merely create the capacity to cause that harm.[815] It should also be noted that whatever meaning is given to the term "direct participation", immunity from attack does not imply immunity from arrest and prosecution.

Direct participation in hostilities clearly encompasses aiming a weapon or planting a bomb, but it is less clear whether it also includes such activities as recruitment, fundraising, disseminating propaganda, or other forms of material support far removed from any battlefield. The key word is "direct" — establishing just how strong and immediate the causal link between the act and the outcome is. The UN Special Rapporteur Philip Alston has suggested that "attenuated acts" such as providing financial support, political advocacy, and non-combat aid do not constitute direct participation.[816] The ICRC guidance specifically considers both recruitment and training functions, and concludes that general recruitment or training activity would only amount to indirect participation, but that the recruitment or training of an individual to carry out a specific predetermined hostile act — for example, a suicide bombing — might amount to direct participation.[817] Because civilians enjoy protection "unless and for such time" as they take a direct part in hostilities, the ICRC guidance also states that the concept of direct participation in hostilities must be interpreted as being restricted "to specific hostile acts" and not acts in the past, nor on speculation that past behavior predicts such behavior again in the

---

[814] See ICRC, *Interpretive Guidance on the Notion of Direct Participation in Hostilities*, (May 2009), available at https://www.icrc.org/eng/assets/files/other/icrc-002-0990.pdf, p. 46.

[815] ICRC, *Interpretive Guidance on the Notion of Direct Participation in Hostilities*, (May 2009), p. 51.

[816] *Report of the Special Rapporteur on extrajudicial, summary or arbitrary executions, Philip Alston, Study on Targeted Killings* (A/HRC/14/24/Add.6, 28), para 60.

[817] ICRC, *Interpretive Guidance on the Notion of Direct Participation in Hostilities*, (May 2009), p. 53.

future — direct participation is a concept rooted in the present.[818] If we were to apply the ICRC guidance to the US drone strike that killed Anwar al-Awlaki and were to accept the US contention that he was member of an organization engaged in an armed conflict with United States, then his involvement in Umar Farouq Abdulmutallab's attempt to bring down Northwest Airlines Flight 253, and his active engagement with *al-Qaeda* in the Arabian Peninsula in planning further attacks, might arguably amount to direct participation in hostilities, although this would probably still hinge on the immediacy of any specific upcoming threat. However, with all that said, from an operational perspective, there is a second important question that also needs to be asked: Does killing someone like Anwar al-Awlaki actually save lives, and does it bring the defeat of *al-Qaeda*, ISIL, or their affiliates any closer?

The Obama administration certainly believed in the efficacy of drone strikes. In an address accompanying the launch of President Obama's *National Strategy for Counterterrorism* in June 2011, John Brennan claimed: "Over the past two-and-a-half years, virtually every major *al-Qaeda* affiliate has lost its key leader or operational commander, and more than half of *al-Qaeda*'s top leadership has been eliminated."[819] Osama bin Laden himself also admitted in an undated document recovered from Abbottabad that CIA drone attacks had "led to the killing of many jihadi cadres, leaders and others," and noted, "this is something that is concerning us and exhausting us."[820] But this is not the whole story — as the former British Prime Minister Winston Churchill once observed: "All things are always on the move simultaneously."[821] While *al-Qaeda*'s ability to conceive and execute terrorist attacks had undoubtedly been greatly degraded by 2011, it had already been surpassed in

---

[818] ibid., p. 44 and p. 70ff.

[819] Paul H. Nitze School of Advanced International Studies, *Remarks of John O. Brennan, Assistant to the President for Homeland Security and Counterterrorism, on Ensuring al-Qa'ida's Demise*, 29 June 2011.

[820] Peter Bergen, *Secrets of the bin Laden treasure-trove*, CNN, 21 May 2015, accessed at http://edition.cnn.com/2015/05/20/opinions/bergen-bin-laden-document-trove/ on 21 May 2015.

[821] Max Hastings, *The Secret War: Spies, Codes and Guerrillas 1939–1945* (William Collins; 2015), p. 484.

terms of the threat it posed to Western interests, first by its affiliates and emulators around the world, and then by ISIL. Oddly enough, this is something that the bellicose US Secretary of Defense Donald Rumsfeld seemed to grasp instinctively as early as October 2003 when he asked his core advisers in The Pentagon: "Are we capturing, killing or deterring and dissuading more terrorists every day than the *madrassas* and the radical clerics are recruiting, training and deploying against us?"[822] In the assassination business, this would seem to be the critical metric and the results do not appear to be very encouraging for the proponents of targeted killing.

Avi Dicter, the former Director of *Shin Bet* during the Second *Intifada*, has made it clear that the Israeli targeted killing program is predicated on the critical zero-sum assumption that "the number of effective terrorists is limited."[823] Furthermore, Israeli proponents have placed a great deal of store in the disruptive impact that targeted killings have on the operational effectiveness of Palestinian terrorist groups, arguing that over time this effectiveness has been significantly degraded even if such strikes alienated the wider Palestinian population and inspired fresh recruits to fill the terrorists' ranks.[824] Dicter explained the logic of this argument in a paper co-authored with the American academic Daniel Byman: "More recruits do not necessarily increase a terrorist organization's effectiveness. *Hamas*' problem historically has not been a shortage of recruits, but rather a lack of experienced personnel to fully exploit the potential of its recruits … [new recruits] are far more likely to make mistakes than experienced operatives and they often have little sense of how to attack a target … If the pace of arrests and killings is rapid enough, then the terrorist organization can lose the

---

[822] Donald Rumsfeld, *Global War on Terrorism*, Memorandum, 16 October 2003, at http://www.sourcewatch.org/index.php/Rumsfeld_Memo_16_October_2003. Viewed 29 May 2016.

[823] Andrew Cockburn, *Kill Chain: The Rise of the High-Tech Assassins* (Henry Holt and Co.; 2015), p. 117.

[824] Alex Wilner, Targeted Killings in Afghanistan: Measuring Coercion and Deterrence in Counterterrorism and Counterinsurgency, *Studies in Conflict and Terrorism*, Vol. 33, No. 4 (2010), p. 312.

critical mass of skills and capabilities that it requires to function."[825] To support their point, Dicter and Byman noted that as the tempo of Israeli operations, including targeted killings, accelerated in 2004, there was a commensurate decline in *Hamas'* operational effectiveness on the West Bank, which in turn resulted in fewer Israeli deaths.[826] However, in the decade since Dicter and Byman's paper was published, it has become quite clear that despite all its technological and military advantages, Israel has not been able to reach that culminating point of victory where a skill-strapped *Hamas* is forced into collapse. While a seasoned terrorist may be difficult to replace in the short term, the reality is that, unless the state is able to kill every new volunteer before their skills mature, targeted killing is only likely to be at best a temporary fix, something that even Dicter and Byman ultimately admit, acknowledging: "Arrests, targeted killings, and defensive measures are means of managing a conflict, not means of solving it."[827]

Avi Dicter's predecessor as Director of *Shin Bet*, Major General Ami Ayalon, a veteran of the *Shayetet 13* naval commando unit and a recipient of Israel's Medal of Valor, has spoken out against the perceived efficacy of targeted killing, describing such strikes as being ultimately counterproductive: "War against terrorism is part of a vicious cycle. The fight itself creates ... even more frustration and despair, more terrorism and increased violence."[828] Short-term tactical 'successes' can often prove to be strategic setbacks if insufficient thought is given to the second and third order effects of lethal action. On 16 February 1992, Israeli Prime Minister Yitzhak Shamir authorized a cross-border Apache helicopter strike on a convoy carrying the Secretary-General and co-founder of *Hezbollah*, Sheikh Abbas al-Musawi, killing him, his family, and his bodyguards. This was

---

[825] Daniel Byman and Avi Dicter, *Israel's Lessons for Fighting Terrorists and their Implications for the United States,* Saban Center for Middle East Policy at the Brookings Institution, Analysis Paper, No. 8 (March 2006), pp. 10–12.

[826] ibid., p. 10.

[827] ibid., p. 13.

[828] Daniel Byman, *A High Price: The Triumphs and Failures of Israeli Counterterrorism* (Oxford University Press; 2011), p. 365.

the first targeted killing operation to involve the use of a drone to identify and track the target. A month later, *Hezbollah*'s new leader, Hassan Nasrallah, supported by Iran's Ministry of Intelligence and Security (MOIS), struck back by detonating a truck packed with explosives outside the Israeli Embassy in Buenos Aires killing twenty-nine people and wounding 240. A second attack in July 1994 on the *Asociación Mutual Israelita Argentina* building, a Jewish community center located in the same city, killed 100 and wounded 250. In his exploration of the militarization of Israeli politics, *Fortress Israel,* the American journalist Patrick Tyler noted that he had seen no evidence of any subsequent reflection amongst Israeli policymakers on how or why this escalation of the conflict with *Hezbollah* had occurred: "No Israeli commander stood to point out that deterrence had failed, that the decision to decapitate *Hezbollah* had given rise to a more brazen and radicalized successor, willing to strike in any corner of the globe where Israelis may be vulnerable."[829]

Another compelling example of the unintended consequences of kinetic operations comes in the form of the sophisticated Israeli operation to eliminate Yahya Ayyash, *Hamas*' chief bomb-maker, who had learned his craft from *Hezbollah* trainers in Camp Ibn Taymiyyah, and whose devices were used in a number of suicide bombings, including attacks on Hadera central bus station and at least four other buses. An estimated ninety Israeli lives were taken by IEDs he constructed in 1993–1994.[830] Ayyash was initially only known to the Israeli security forces as "the Engineer" until his true name was revealed during the interrogation of three would-be car bombers arrested in Ramat Ef'al, and he quickly became one of Israel's most wanted targets. *Shin Bet* eventually located Ayyash in Gaza City and tied him to the home of childhood friend, Osama Hammad, which he occasionally used as a safe house. The Israelis were able to recruit Osama Hammad's uncle as an asset and tasked him with delivering a "bugged" cellphone to Osama, knowing that Ayyash often borrowed

---

[829] Patrick Tyler, *Fortress Israel: The Inside Story of the Military Elite Who Run the Country — and Why They Can't Make Peace* (Farrar, Straus and Giroux; 2012), pp. 346–348.

[830] Daniel Byman, *A High Price: The Triumphs and Failures of Israeli Counterterrorism* (Oxford University Press; 2011), p. 93.

Osama's phones. What the uncle did not know was that the Israelis had also secreted 15 grams of RDX explosive in the cellphone.[831] On 5 January 1996, Ayyash borrowed the cellphone to speak with his father. This was the opportunity the Israelis had been waiting for and, once Ayyash's voice had been identified, they detonated the explosive killing him instantly. *Hamas* waited forty days — the traditional Muslim mourning period — and then launched (along with Palestinian Islamic Jihad) a series of four violent suicide bombings in reprisal that claimed fifty-nine Israeli lives, and maimed scores more, which in turn influenced the outcome of the May 1996 general election so that incumbent Labour Prime Minister Shimon Peres, who had authorized the strike on Ayyash, was defeated by *Likud* leader Benjamin Netanyahu. The former US Ambassador to Israel, Martin Indyk, commented that Peres had "failed his government" by provoking a retaliation that had driven him out of office and derailed the spluttering peace process.[832] One of the cells that claimed responsibility for the attacks called itself the Disciples of the Martyr Yahya Ayyash.

Avi Dicter and Daniel Byman have argued that the key to successful targeted killing operations is "superb intelligence" that is "accurate, timely and actionable".[833] However, the reality is that such intelligence is often in short supply. Having assured their readers that in Israel "information is repeatedly cross-checked and only the most reliable sources are used" and that "the government prohibits targeted killings in crowded areas ... where many innocents may be present", Dicter and Byman then go on to describe the killing of the head of the military wing of *Hamas*, Salah Shehada, in July 2002, in which thirteen innocent bystanders — including eight children, the youngest of whom, Dina Rami Matar, was only two-months-old — were killed and around 150 injured.[834] Without apparent irony,

---

[831] ibid., 94.

[832] ibid., p. 95.

[833] Daniel Byman and Avi Dicter, *Israel's Lessons for Fighting Terorirsts and their Implications for the United States*, Saban Center for Middle East Policy at the Brookings Institution, Analysis Paper, No. 8 (March 2006), pp. 8–9.

[834] United States District Court, Southern District of New York, *Ra'ed Mohamed Ibrahim et al. v. Avraham Dichter*, Complaint, 7 December 2005.

Dicter and Byman note that "part of the problem [with the Shehada operation] was an intelligence gap."[835] The strike had been conducted under Dicter's supervision. To most observers, the primary problem was not the paucity of intelligence but the less than surgical decision to drop a 1,000 kg bomb on a target located in a residential neighborhood. Another of Dicter's predecessors at *Shin Bet*, Avraham Shalom, was profoundly critical of the decision to carry out the strike: "Overkill! It's security stupidity. It's military stupidity. I don't know what to call it, but it makes no sense that to kill the most important man in Gaza you have to drop a one-ton bomb on a house surrounded by homes with families and children. That can't be moral, it's ineffectively militarily and it is certainly inhumane. Is it just? Not that either."[836] *Hamas'* official response came from Abdel Aziz al-Rantisi, who would be killed in his turn in April 2004 by another Israeli air strike: "There will be no peace initiative after today, we will chase them in their houses and in their apartments, the same way they have destroyed our houses and our apartments."[837]

According to *B'Tselem*, in addition to the 234 militants actually targeted, lethal Israeli strikes between September 2000 and May 2008 also killed 153 innocent civilians.[838] Total situational awareness — the *chimera* of military and security officials — is unobtainable. Some sources, like the Jordanian double agent Humam al-Balawi, lie to their handlers. Intercepted communications are often opaque. Targets lay false trails and camouflage their movements. Mistakes are inevitable — even in the most heavily surveilled environments like Gaza and the West Bank — and these mistakes can have severe consequences. Asmaa al-Ghoul, a columnist with *Al-Monitor*'s Palestine Pulse wrote after the death of nine members of her family in an Israeli airstrike: "If it is *Hamas* that you hate, let me tell you that the people you are

---

[835] Daniel Byman and Avi Dicter, *Israel's Lessons for Fighting Terrorists and their Implications for the United States*, Saban Center for Middle East Policy at the Brookings Institution, Analysis Paper, No. 8 (March 2006), p. 9.

[836] Dror Moreh Productions, *The Gatekeepers*, Documentary (2012).

[837] Suzanne Goldenberg, 12 dead in attack on Hamas, *The Guardian*, 23 July 2002.

[838] *Report of the Special Rapporteur on extrajudicial, summary or arbitrary executions, Philip Alston, Addendum: Study on targeted killings* (A/HRC/14/24/Add.6), para 14.

killing have nothing to do with *Hamas* ... But let me assure you that you have now created thousands — no, millions — of *Hamas* loyalists, for we all become *Hamas* if *Hamas*, to you, is women, children and innocent families. If *Hamas*, in your eyes, is ordinary civilians and families, then I am *Hamas*, they are *Hamas* and we are all *Hamas*."[839]

Poor intelligence has also been a feature of US drone operations particularly in Afghanistan and Pakistan, sometimes with significantly adverse strategic consequences. In March 2011, a US drone strike on a bus depot in Datta Khel, in Pakistan's Waziristan border region killed an estimated forty-two people. This was a signature strike — an attack triggered by a pattern of behavior that looked suspicious or hostile to US drone operators and intelligence analysts. However, it subsequently emerged that the "suspicious" event in question was a *jirga* of tribal elders — a meeting that those involved had appraised the Pakistani authorities of about ten days beforehand. Rather than contributing to local counter-terrorism efforts, the US blunder actually eliminated some of the most stabilizing influences in the entire community. One survivor, Jalal Manzar Khail, told reporters: "Convey my message to the Americans — the CIA and America have to stop ... they're just creating more enemies and this will last for hundreds of years."[840] The political commentator Arianna Huffington posed a similarly pertinent set of questions about the strike on Datta Khel: "What do you suppose happened to the support of any moderate or pro-America or pro-democracy leaders [left] in the community? (I'm, speaking of the ones who weren't killed, of course.) Was their standing enhanced? Did the strike help them make their case?"[841]

Of course, Datta Khel is just one incident, but other examples of poorly chosen and counterproductive strikes abound. In October

---

[839] Asmaa al-Ghoul, Never ask me about peace again, *Al Monitor*, 4 August 2014 at http://www.al-monitor.com/pulse/originals/2014/08/rafah-gaza-war-hospitals-filled-bodies-palestinians.html#.

[840] Arianna Huffington, 'Signature Strikes' and the President's Empty Rhetoric on Drones, *Huffington Post*, 10 July 2013, at http://www.huffingtonpost.com/arianna-huffington/signature-strikes-and-the_b_3575351.html?utm_source=DailyBrief&utm_campaign=071113&utm_medium=email&utm_content=FeatureTitle.

[841] ibid.

2006, a CIA strike on a *madrassa* in Chenegai, Pakistan, reportedly killed sixty-nine children, the youngest seven-years-old, their headmaster, a well-known militant, had been the target.[842] In November 2008, a US airstrike killed as many as thirty-seven wedding guests, including twenty-three children, at a family celebration in the Shah Wali Kot district of Kandahar. This was only one of several incidents in which wedding parties were mistakenly targeted with dozens of innocent victims killed each time. In September 2010, US Joint Special Operations Command mistakenly confused a telephone number used by Zabet Amanullah, a former mujahedin fighter who had embraced electoral politics in post-war Afghanistan, with a number associated with an Uzbek *Taliban* commander called Mohammed Amin, with the end result that a convoy of election workers was erroneously attacked and at least ten innocent civilians slain.[843] US aircraft have even mistakenly engaged and killed NATO troops, which just underscores the confusion and intelligence shortcomings that often bedevil kinetic operations. In April 2002, four Canadian soldiers were killed and eight wounded, and in August 2007, three British soldiers were killed and two injured in similar "friendly fire" incidents in Helmand Province.

Successful counter-terrorism is mostly about nuance, and for all the impressive advances that have undoubtedly been made in surveillance technology, innocent quotidian activity on the ground can look very different when viewed through the socio-cultural filter of a Western-educated military observer predisposed, even conditioned, to see threats lurking around every corner. There is very little nuance in a world observed from 20,000 feet, and this has led the UN Special Rapporteur Philip Alston to warn that the remote, sanitized, and screen-driven nature of drone warfare raises the risk of a "Playstation" mentality developing in relation to lethal

---

[842] Chris Woods, *Drones strikes in Pakistan*, The Bureau of Investigative Journalism, 11 August 2011, and Chris Woods, The day 69 children died, *The Express Tribune*, 12 August 2011.

[843] Andrew Cockburn, *Kill Chain: The Rise of the High-Tech Assassins* (Henry Holt and Co.; 2015), pp. 193–200 and Kate Clark, *The Takhar Attack: Targeted killings and the parallel worlds of US intelligence and Afghanistan*, Afghan Analysts Network, Thematic Report 05/2011.

operations.[844] This fear seems to have been borne out in a US post-incident investigation undertaken after another ill-conceived drone strike on a civilian convoy in February 2010, which resulted in the deaths of twenty-three Afghan civilians, including two small children. The investigating officer, Major-General Timothy McHale, reported that the Predator crew responsible were "almost juvenile in their desire to engage targets" and out to employ their weapons no matter what.[845] One member of the Predator crew told McHale: "Well, to be honest sir, everyone around here, it's like [the movie] Top Gun."[846] The families of the dead received $5,000 each and a goat in compensation from the US military.

The specter of collateral damage is not restricted to aerial strikes. Nine of the victims killed by the Spanish government-backed *Grupos Antiterroristas de Liberación* (GAL) had no link with any terrorist organization and included French nationals, innocent members of the public, and a newspaper photojournalist. In addition to targeted assassinations, GAL carried out indiscriminate attacks on bars and hotels where Basque refugees gathered in French cities like Bayonne and Biarritz, shooting them up from the street or tossing bombs inside.[847] One attack, on the Trinkete tavern in Ciboure, resulted in the killing of two tourists with no known affiliation to ETA. In 1983, GAL operatives kidnapped and held a French furniture salesman, Segundo Marey, who they mistakenly believed to be a member of ETA, for ten days.[848] After his release, the deeply traumatized Marey sued the Spanish government for redress.[849] Several

---

[844] *Report of the Special Rapporteur on extrajudicial, summary or arbitrary executions, Philip Alston, Study on Targeted Killings* (A/HRC/14/24/Add.6, 28), para 84.

[845] Andrew Cockburn, *Kill Chain: The Rise of the High-Tech Assassins* (Henry Holt and Co.; 2015), pp. 13–14.

[846] ibid., p. 14.

[847] Paddy Woodworth, *Dirty War, Clean Hands: ETA, the GAL and Spanish Democracy* (Yale University Press; 2003), p. 119.

[848] Paddy Woodworth, "Dirty War" trial may show new democracy was a façade, *The Irish Times*, 23 May 1998.

[849] Cyrus Zirakzadeh, From Revolutionary Dreams to Organizational Fragmentation: Disputes over Violence within ETA and Sendero Luminoso. *Terrorism and Political Violence*, Vol. 14, No. 4 (2002), p. 82.

GAL operatives were eventually arrested in France and the organization began to unravel as these operatives were tied to the Spanish intelligence services. In 1987, police inspectors José Amedo Fouce and Michel Domínguez were found guilty of GAL-related crimes. In the course of their trial, they took responsibility for the creation of GAL and were sentenced to nine-year and two-year prison terms, respectively. However, seven years later, they changed their story going to the press with more detail on how GAL had been organized and how it had been funded from a secret budget of the Ministry of Interior reserved for intelligence operations. As a result, eventually the Interior Minister, José Barrionuevo, and the Secretary of State for Security, Rafael Vera, were among the senior Spanish officials convicted for their roles in the illegal activities carried out by GAL and were both sentenced to ten-year prison terms. They were pardoned in 2001.

The Spanish experience is far from unique. Perhaps, the best known example of this type of covert action going catastrophically wrong is the failed attempt by *Mossad* to kill the Black September Organization's operations chief, Ali Hassan Salameh, in the town of Lillehammer, Norway, in July 1973. *Mossad's* operatives simply got it horribly wrong, completely misidentifying their target. The man they gunned down as he walked home from the cinema with his pregnant wife was an innocent Moroccan waiter called Ahmed Bouchiki who had nothing to do with terrorism or Black September whatsoever. The *Mossad* hit team also botched their escape and several were detained by the Norwegian authorities to whom they confessed everything. The debacle would convince Prime Minister Golda Meir to put an end to Operation Wrath of God. One senior *Mossad* officer later excused the error with the telling admission: "Our blood was boiling. When there was information implicating someone, we didn't inspect it with a magnifying glass."[850] *Mossad* finally settled its score with Salameh in January 1979 killing him, along with his bodyguards, with a car bomb in Beirut in an

---

[850] Daniel Byman, *A High Price: The Triumphs and Failures of Israeli Counterterrorism* (Oxford University Press; 2011), p. 53.

operation authorized by Prime Minister Menachem Begin, the one-time leader of *Irgun*. Four innocent bystanders, including a German nun and an English student, were also killed by the blast.[851] Israel would not formally apologize to the Bouchiki family for its fatal error until 1996.

The belief that specifically targeting key leadership figures can cause terrorist organizations to collapse has proved particularly resilient.[852] The 2006 US National Intelligence Estimate, for instance, posits that the loss of key leaders like bin Laden and al-Zarqawi in rapid succession "probably would cause [*al-Qaeda*] to fracture into smaller groups" and that the loss of these key leaders "would exacerbate strains and disagreements".[853] It is therefore worth considering if there is any merit to the argument that successful decapitation strikes can be a silver bullet in the fight against terrorism. The argument certainly has its detractors. The political scientist Robert Pape has argued the converse on three principal grounds: It is actually quite hard to find individual leaders and kill them; the death of a leader often brings less policy change than one might expect, especially in more horizontal leadership structures; and in most organizations, leadership succession can be very unpredictable, meaning that the leader's replacement may not be an improvement on his predecessor.[854] It is not difficult to find examples in the historical record that appear to support Pape's argument. For instance, as we have seen above, *Tehrik-i-Taliban Pakistan* leader Baitullah Mehsud survived six decapitation strikes before he was finally eliminated, Osama bin Laden remained at large for almost ten years after the September 11 attacks, and the Afghan *Taliban* leader Mullah Muhammad Omar died of natural causes in 2013; the decimation of *al-Qaeda*'s leadership has had little apparent impact on the group's stated goals, and *Hamas* remains as

---

[851] ibid., p. 54 and Death of a Terrorist, *Time Magazine*, 5 February 1979.

[852] US National Strategy for Combating Terrorism (2003), p. 6.

[853] Alex Wilner, Targeted Killings in Afghanistan: Measuring Coercion and Deterrence in Counterterrorism and Counterinsurgency, *Studies in Conflict and Terrorism*, Vol. 33, No. 4 (2010), pp. 313–314.

[854] Robert Pape, *Bombing to Win* (Ithaca: Cornell University Press, 1996), p. 79.

committed to the dissolution of the State of Israel as when it was founded in 1987; Abbas al-Musawi was replaced as Secretary-General of *Hezbollah* by Hassan Nasrallah, and a former ISIL militant Abu Ahmed told *The Guardian* newspaper that after Abu Mus'ab al-Zarqawi was killed by US Special Forces in June 2006, "the people who liked killing even more than him became very important in the organization."[855] The number of *al-Qaeda*-linked attacks in Iraq increased in the months after al-Zarqawi's death.[856]

Opinion on the efficacy of decapitation strikes is divided amongst both practitioners and academic researchers, but an increasing number of studies seem to suggest a fairly consistent story. An internal US military report conducted for the commander of Multi-National Corps — Iraq, General Ray Odierno, looked at 200 cases in which High Value Targets had been killed or captured in Iraq between June–October 2007 and found that attacks on Coalition Forces within three kilometers of the target's base of operations increased 40% in the thirty days after his (they were all men) removal.[857] By way of explanation, the report's author, Rex Rivolo, noted that the target's replacement was typically eager to prove himself and was also often under pressure from his predecessor's relatives and comrades to exact revenge on the Coalition, hence the increase in hostile activity. The International Security Assistance Force (ISAF) in Afghanistan found that successful sustained kill or capture campaigns tended to bring down the average age of *Taliban* commanders — a twelve-month campaign in Helmand Province in 2010–2011 reduced the average age from thirty-five to twenty-three.[858] A young US Marine officer told the journalist Andrew Cockburn that in his two tours in Helmand Province: "I saw multiple *Taliban* commanders come in and out. The turnover rate was cyclic. So even if I kill one, it only took two weeks before the next guy came in. They didn't miss a beat.

---

[855] Martin Churlov, ISIS: The Inside Story, *The Guardian*, 11 December 2014.

[856] Keith Dear, Beheading the Hydra? Does Killing Terrorist or Insurgent Leaders Work? *Defence Studies*, Vol. 13, No. 3 (2013), p. 299.

[857] Andrew Cockburn, *Kill Chain: The Rise of the High-Tech Assassins* (Henry Holt and Co.; 2015), p. 166.

[858] ibid., p. 205.

You replace one guy, chances are the guy that's coming in is more lethal, has less restraint and is more apt to make a name for himself and go above and beyond than if you had just left the first guy in there."[859] Mullah Abdul Hakim Mujahid, former *Taliban* ambassador to the United Nations, also reported that drone strikes had removed more pragmatic commanders and "the fanatical ones have come in their place ... In that way we are losing a lot of politically-minded *Taliban*. The new ones have a more religious mentality. They are only fighters."[860]

There is also an emerging scholarly consensus that decapitation strikes are for the most part ineffective and counterproductive.[861] In probably the most influential academic study to date, based on a dataset of 298 leadership strikes carried out on armed groups between 1945 and 2004, Jenna Jordan concluded that decapitation strikes do not increase the likelihood that terrorist groups will collapse, and that in the case of well-established religious or separatist groups, it may even have a negative effect strengthening group resolve and cohesion.[862] Jordan defined defeat as an absence of operations for two years and, by this standard, leadership decapitation (including both targeted killing and arrests) was successful in just 17% of the 298 cases she surveyed.[863] She found that decapitation was less effective against larger groups and that the smallest organizations were most susceptible to collapse. Groups with fewer than twenty-five members fell apart 54% of the time, and those with between twenty-six and 100 members fell apart 41% of the time. Organizations in the middle range fell apart with a lower frequency, groups with between 5,000 and 10,000 members fell apart in 36% of cases. Finally, decapitation was successful against only 9% of groups with over 10,000 members. Jordan's study put the

---

[859] ibid., p. 206.

[860] Keith Dear, Beheading the Hydra? Does Killing Terrorist or Insurgent Leaders Work? *Defence Studies*, Vol. 13, No. 3 (2013), p. 312.

[861] Bryan Price, Targeting Top Terrorists: How Leadership Decapitation Contributes to Counterterrorism, *International Security*, Vol. 36, No. 4 (Spring 2012), p. 43.

[862] Jenna Jordan, When Heads Roll: Assessing the Effectiveness of Leadership Decapitation, *Security Studies*, Vol. 8, No. 4, (2009).

[863] ibid., p. 745.

mean size for religious organizations at 9,123 members, and the mean size for both ideological and separatist organizations at about 2,460 members, suggesting that religiously inspired terrorism may be more resistant to decapitation strikes than other terrorist strains.[864] The maturity of a particular group also proved to be highly significant in Jordan's study. The oldest organizations, those that had been active for over forty years, were always resistant to decapitation strikes, while decapitation was successful against 29% of groups that had been active for less than ten years.[865] Bryan Price's study of 207 terrorist groups from sixty-five countries active between 1970 and 2008 likewise found that a terrorist group's organizational capacity tended to increase with age, making it more durable over time, and that commensurately the impact of decapitation strikes steadily diminished to the point that after twenty years, "decapitation may have no effect at all."[866]

Jordan also noted that the level of terrorist violence is more likely than not to increase post strike, citing examples drawn from case studies of ETA, *Hamas*, and FARC-EP.[867] She concluded that her data indicated that "going after the leader may strengthen a group's resolve, result in retaliatory attacks, increase public sympathy for the organization, or produce more lethal attacks."[868] Research conducted by Aaron Mannes highlighted in particular "the propensity of decapitation strikes to cause religious organizations to become substantially more deadly", which taken together together with Jordan's findings suggests that targeted killing is an especially poor tactic to use against well-established religious terrorist groups like *Hamas*, *Hezbollah*, and *al-Qaeda*.[869] Alex Wilner's nuanced analysis of four high profile Afghan cases found

---

[864] ibid., pp. 743–745.

[865] ibid., p. 741.

[866] Bryan Price, Targeting Top Terrorists: How Leadership Decapitation Contributes to Counterterrorism, *International Security*, Vol. 36, No. 4 (Spring 2012), p. 43 and p. 38.

[867] Jenna Jordan, When Heads Roll: Assessing the Effectiveness of Leadership Decapitation, *Security Studies*, Vol. 8, No. 4, (2009), pp. 732 and 749–753.

[868] ibid., p. 755.

[869] Aaron Mannes, Testing The Snake Head Strategy: Does Killing or Capturing its Leaders Reduce a Terrorist Group's Activity? *Journal of International Policy Solutions*, Vol. 9 (Spring 2008), p. 44.

that while "overall violence increased" following successful decapitation strikes, the method of attack also changed, with suicide bombings
decreasing and the number of IED, small arms, and indirect fire
attacks increasing. This, he concluded, was an indication of decreased
sophistication and capability, as was a 15% increase in the failure rate
of IEDs and a noticeable switch from harder to softer targets.[870]
However, a New America Foundation study based on a far larger sample size found that between 2002 and 2009, targeted strikes on
identified bomb-makers in Southern Afghanistan and Western Pakistan
neither reduced *Taliban* use of IEDs nor decreased the lethality of each
subsequent device.[871] Mohammed Hafez and Joseph Hatfield studied
Israeli targeted killings from the outbreak of the Second *Intifada* to
June 2004 and concluded that they appeared to have no appreciable
impact on the rate of Palestinian attacks on Israeli targets.[872] Although
these studies all differ somewhat in the outcomes they identify, none
found any evidence of the dramatic decrease in terrorist attacks that
the advocates of decapitation strikes have claimed would result.

Squadron Leader Keith Dear, a British military intelligence
officer who would go on to command the Operational Intelligence
Support Group in Kabul, contributed a powerful article on
the impact of targeted killing to the British journal *Defence Studies*
in which he suggested that decapitation strikes had introduced an
unhelpful element of natural selection to the *Taliban* leadership:
"Those leaders unable to maintain a sufficiently clandestine profile ... [are] killed leaving only the competent alive."[873] Dear also
questioned the disruptive impact of such strikes, challenging the
assertion made by Dicter, Byman, and Wilner that the supposed level

---

[870] Alex Wilner, Targeted Killings in Afghanistan: Measuring Coercion and Deterrence in Counterterrorism and Counterinsurgency, *Studies in Conflict and Terrorism*, Vol. 33, No. 4 (2010) p. 318.

[871] See Alex Barker, *Improvised Explosive Devices in Southern Afghanistan and Western Pakistan, 2002–2009*, New America Foundation, April 2010.

[872] See Mohammed Hafez and Joseph Hatfield, Do Targeted Assassinations Work? A Multivariate Analysis of Israel's Controversial Tactic during Al-Aqsa Uprising, *Studies in Conflict and Terrorism*, Vol. 29, No. 4 (June 2006).

[873] Keith Dear, Beheading the Hydra? Does Killing Terrorist or Insurgent Leaders Work? *Defence Studies*, Vol. 13, No. 3 (2013), p. 299.

of expertise lost in targeted strikes was hard to replace by noting that Professor Ehud Keinan of the Israeli Institute of Technology had described the manufacture of suicide vests as "embarrassingly easy".[874] He further suggested that another second-order effect of decapitation strikes is that there are diminishing returns with each strike as organizations learn to decentralize, disperse responsibility, and build redundancy into their command and control structures.[875] One consequence of drone use in Afghanistan has been that terrorist leaders have dispensed with their cellphones for fear of the signal giving away their location, which has in turn reduced the ability of security forces to monitor terrorist communications and planning.[876] Dear also argued that targeted strikes directed against *al-Qaeda* had forced the organization to abandon centrally planned and controlled operations, as its leaders went deeper into hiding, in favor of seeking to inspire "lone-wolf" attacks, an approach it had previously rejected. This, he noted, made future attacks much harder to predict as "isolated cells are more innovative than hierarchical bureaucracies."[877] Dear's research led him to conclude: "The *Taliban* leadership in 2011 is younger, more radical, more violent and less discriminate than in 2001, because of targeted killing."[878]

There is nothing new about trying to conduct counter-terrorism — or at least counter-insurgency — from the skies. Field Marshal Lord French, who was sent to Ireland as Military Commissioner in the spring of 1918, advocated the establishment of "strongly entrenched 'Air Camps'" in the center of all four Irish Provinces from which military aircraft could "play about with either bombs or machine guns" if the locals got out of hand, which he believed would "put the fear of God into these playful young *Sinn Féiners*".[879] Lord French's proposal was rejected, but it would soon be adopted in modified form in Britain's colonial possessions. On Empire Day 1919, the Royal Air

---

[874] ibid., p. 301.
[875] ibid., p. 303.
[876] ibid., p. 299.
[877] ibid., pp. 298 and 300.
[878] ibid., p. 312.
[879] Charles Townshend, *The Republic: The Fight for Irish Independence* (Allen Lane; 2013), p. 11.

Force (RAF) conducted a punitive strike on Kabul in retaliation for border attacks by Afghan Islamists against British interests on the Northwest frontier of colonial India. Deemed a success, this action spawned a policy of "air control" seen as a cost-effective method for dealing with restive local populations across the wide expanse of the British Empire. In 1920, as Secretary of State for both War and Air, Winston Churchill deployed the RAF in British Somaliland against dervish tribesmen inspired to revolt against colonial rule by Sayid Maxamed Cabdille Xasan. By 1922, air control had been adopted across the British-administered League of Nations mandate territories in Mesopotamia, Transjordan, and Palestine. When the Kurdish leader Sheikh Mahmud Barzani tried to encourage Turkish troops to join an anti-British uprising in December 1923, the RAF carried out an air strike on his headquarters, and in 1928 air control was introduced in the Protectorate of Aden in response to raids and hostage-taking encouraged by the *Imam* of Yemen.[880]

The RAF laid out its air control doctrine in *Air Staff Memorandum No. 46* placing a heavy emphasis on minimal use of force, effective intelligence gathering, and close cooperation between the military and political spheres. One of the architects of this doctrine, Charles Portal, who would ultimately rise to be Marshal of the Royal Air Force in World War II, wrote in the Journal of the Royal United Services Institute: "We want a change of heart, and we want to get it by the use of the minimum amount of force."[881] He added: "Bombing the wrong people, even once, would ruin the Government's reputation, and would take years to live down."[882] Air Commodore Arthur Harris, who oversaw the use of air control in Palestine in the late 1930s, believed it could "emulate the efficiency of the fly swatter" when used in conjunction with effective police action.[883] However, the British government

---

[880] Wing Commander A. J. C. Walters, Air Control: Past, Present, Future? *Air Power Review,* Vol. 8, No. 4 (Winter 2005), p. 4.

[881] Charles Portal, Air Force Co-operation in Policing the Empire, *RUSI Journal,* Vol. 82 (1937), p. 355.

[882] ibid., p. 351.

[883] Charles Townshend, The Defence of Palestine: Insurrection and Public Security 1936–1939, *The English Historical Review,* Vol. 103, No. 409 (October 1988), p. 935.

soon discovered the limitations of the policy — it conspicuously failed to deter organized resistance to British rule by the Jewish and Arab populations of Palestine, it proved ineffective in urban areas, mountainous terrain and wooded regions, and Portal himself questioned if it could effectively deter religious extremists.[884] Its use also came with an increasing political cost as the deployment of air power against restive civilian populations began attracting adverse publicity from the 1930s onwards.[885] As a result, the doctrine of air control was ultimately abandoned by the British in the early 1960s.[886]

Now, the doctrine of air control is back in a new guise, but the evidence suggests that it is ultimately unlikely to be any more successful at putting an end to terrorism this time around than in its previous incarnation. Indeed, if anything, in our modern globalized world, it is likely to be even more damaging to the West's reputation. The American legal scholar Thomas McDonnell has argued that "compiling hit lists and using a machine remotely operated from a distant land, to take the life of listed suspected terrorists appears much more like murder than honorable combat and, thereby, undermines world public order."[887] A simple thought experiment in which one imagines how Ahmed Bouchiki's widow and orphaned child, the surviving family of little Dina Rami Matar, or the residents of Datta Khel would describe what happened to their loved ones is enough to bring home the sobering reality of that statement. The cases of *Sendero Luminoso*'s Abimael Guzmán, the PKK's Abdullah Öcalan, and Palestinian Islamic Jihad's Fathi Shaqaqi, are most often held up as examples of the potential game-changing impact of decapitation strikes. Both Guzmán and Öcalan were detained, not killed, and Fathi Shaqaqi was shot dead in the street by a *Mossad* hit

---

[884] Wing Commander A. J. C. Walters, Air Control: Past, Present, Future? *Air Power Review,* Vol. 8, No. 4 (Winter 2005), p. 7.

[885] Neville Parton, *Air Power and Insurgency: Early RAF Doctrine,* in Joel Hayward (ed.), *Air Power, Insurgency and the War on Terror* (Centre for Air Power Studies; 2009), p. 41.

[886] Wing Commander A. J. C. Walters, Air Control: Past, Present, Future? *Air Power Review,* Vol. 8, No. 4 (Winter 2005), p. 9.

[887] Thomas McDonnell, Sow What You Reap? Using Predator and Reaper Drones to Carry Out Assassinations or Targeted Killings of Suspected Islamic Terrorists, *George Washington International Law Review,* Vol. 44 (2012), p. 316.

team in Malta in October 1995. Yet, none of these cases have actually stood the test of time. As Keith Dear has noted, where the underlying causes of violence go unresolved, a resurgence is probably inevitable and today all three organizations are still actively engaged in terrorist activity despite the temporary disruption suffered after the removal of their well-established and charismatic leaders.[888] In the final analysis, it is difficult to disagree with Dear's assessment that in the long-term targeted killing "unites insurgents, and brings forward a younger, more radical leadership which makes the group more indiscriminately violent ... [It] can be tactically effective but it is strategically counterproductive."[889]

## Summary

The UN Special Rapporteur, Philip Alston, has emphasized that states have a duty to respect and ensure the right to life and this entails an obligation to exercise "due diligence" to protect the lives of individuals from attacks by criminals, including terrorists.[890] In a civil context, force can only be used in proportion to the seriousness of the offence concerned and the legitimate objective sought. This means that lethal force is only appropriate when officers or members of the public are at risk of death or serious injury, and no alternative method is available to contain or defuse the threat. Police commanders have an obligation to plan their operations accordingly. No police action can be lawfully undertaken in which the sole objective is the death of a suspect or wanted felon.[891] Any incident in which lethal force is used must be subject to independent post-incident investigation. Where force is used unlawfully, those responsible must be held to account. These rules exist to protect members of the

---

[888] Keith Dear, Beheading the Hydra? Does Killing Terrorist or Insurgent Leaders Work? *Defence Studies*, Vol. 13, No. 3 (2013), p. 320.

[889] ibid., p. 297.

[890] *Report of the Special Rapporteur on extrajudicial, summary or arbitrary executions, Philip Alston, Addendum: Study on targeted killings* (A/HRC/14/24/Add.6), para 33.

[891] Note by the Secretary-General, *Promotion and protection of human rights and fundamental freedoms while countering terrorism*, A/68/389, 18 September 2013.

public, like Jean Charles de Menezes, from harm and to ensure democratic life is not undermined by aggressive government action. None of these strictures prevent law enforcement officials from using force to protect members of the public from terrorist threats, they simply require force to be used in a restrained and lawful manner.

The use of force in the context of an international armed conflict is uncontentious as long as international humanitarian law is observed in the conduct of any hostilities. The use of force in non-international armed conflict is more complex, not least because what constitutes such a conflict is clearly now a matter of some dispute between nations. It is unquestionably lawful to use force in the context of a non-international armed conflict against any individual directly participating in hostilities for the duration he or she is engaged in such activity, so long as international humanitarian law is observed in the manner in which force is applied. What constitutes direct participation is also the subject of much debate, but a clear conceptual boundary exists between direct participation, which makes an individual a legitimate target, and indirect participation, which does not. Locating precisely where that boundary lies in law is somewhat harder — the burden falls on states who wish to use force in this context to prove that the target was directly participating in hostilities at the time force was deployed. The case of Anwar al-Awlaki illustrates just how difficult it can be to make such a precise determination. The pre-emptive use of force in self-defense to prevent terrorist attacks is also contentious, particularly as the United States has developed a doctrine of self-defense that stretches the traditionally limiting concept of imminence to the point of meaninglessness. However, the right to use force to prevent an attack in progress, or on the cusp of unfolding, would be broadly accepted by most states.

Philip Alston has warned the United States that by seeking to legitimize targeted killings as a counter-terrorism tool, it has paved the way for other states to do the same: "It is also salutary to recognize that whatever rules the US seeks to invoke or apply to *al-Qaeda* and any 'affiliates' could be invoked by other states to apply to other non-state armed groups. To expand the notion of non-international armed conflict to groups that are essentially drug cartels, criminal gangs, or other groups that should be dealt with under the law enforcement framework would be to do deep damage to the IHL and human rights frameworks."[892] In 2014, the RAND Corporation identified twenty-three countries that were actively developing weaponized UAVs and at the time of writing, at least seven countries have deployed them in some form of combat — Iraq, Iran, Israel, Nigeria, Pakistan, the United Kingdom, and the United States.[893] *Hamas,* ISIL, and *Hezbollah* have also fielded UAVs of varying sophistication. When one further considers how broadly some states are now defining terrorism in their domestic legislation, one can quickly get a sense of just what a Pandora's Box may have been opened. Russia's Federal Law No. 35-FZ (2006), authorizing external military action against terrorist targets, went far beyond any conventional interpretation of direct participation in hostilities listing amongst the types of terrorist activity that could provoke a military response under the new law both fundraising and publicly justifying terrorism. The UN Special Representative on human rights defenders, Hina Jilani, has reported that anti-terrorism laws have been exploited by unscrupulous governments to justify "the arrest and detention of, among others, trade unionists, student leaders, political activists, members of religious groups, academics, lawyers, journalists and non-governmental organization workers".[894] In a world where an accusation of terrorism can be used as a pretext to launch a military strike or covert action, the potential risks to democratic life and legitimate protest are very real indeed.

The decision to invoke the right to use force in the context of counter-terrorism operations could thus have potentially serious consequences. US General Michael Hayden, the only individual

---

[892] *Report of the Special Rapporteur on extrajudicial, summary or arbitrary executions, Philip Alston, Study on Targeted Killings* (A/HRC/14/24/Add.6, 28), para 56.

[893] Lynn Davis, Michael McNerney, James Chow, Thomas Hamilton, Sarah Harting, and Daniel Byman, Armed and Dangerous? UAVs and US Security, *RAND Corporation*, 2014.

[894] *Report of the Special Representative on human rights defenders*, UN Doc. A/58/380, p. 18 September 2003 at 31. See also María Martín, *Criminalization of Human Rights Defenders: Categorisation of the Problem and Measures in Response* (Protection International, 2015), p. 3.3.5.

ever to head both the Central Intelligence Agency and the National Security Agency, and a staunch supporter, and indeed prosecutor, of kinetic strikes against terrorist targets has nevertheless warned about the unforeseen consequences of covert action: "There are always second and third order effects. Now, that's not, on the surface a *prima facie* case for never doing this, but it is reason to pause and make sure whoever is making that final decision is buying into the inevitable second and third order effects."[895] In the context of targeted killing, the data suggest that the use of lethal force can provoke an escalation of violence, bring more extreme elements into positions of authority, and alienate civilian populations generating sympathy and support for terrorist organizations. As Mir Alam Ghamgen, a forty-five-year-old farmer from Afghanistan's Helmand Province who lost his two-year-old daughter and nine other relatives to a NATO airstrike in 2006, told a British reporter: "When foreigners kill civilians, it affects the local people in the opposite way to what they wish."[896] Leadership decapitation has proved an ineffective tool for ending terrorist campaigns waged by well-established terrorist groups, and it does nothing to address the underlying political and social contexts that fuel terrorist violence, if anything it is only likely to exacerbate divisions. The activist journalist Robert Taber summed up the essential dilemma of trying to put down a terrorism campaign by force alone: "To try to suppress popular resistance movements by force is futile. If inadequate force is applied, the resistance grows. If the overwhelming force necessary to accomplish the task is applied, its object is destroyed. It is a case of shooting the horse because he refuses to pull the cart."[897]

In a thoughtful interview published by The New Yorker Magazine in 2014, Philip Alston told the writer Steve Coll: "I think the greatest

---

[895] *Playing to the Edge: An interview with General Michael Hayden*, Spycast Podcast, The International Spy Museum, 3 May 2016.

[896] Anthony Loyd, Britain killed our children with its "precision" bombing, *The Times*, 2 December 2015.

[897] Robert Taber, *The War of the Flea: How Guerrilla Fighters Could Win the World* (Citadel Press; 1970), p. 152.

problem is the mentality that accompanies drone strikes, the identification of a list of targets, and if we can succeed in eliminating that list we will have achieved good things — that mentality is what drives it all — if only we can get enough of these bastards, we'll win the war."[898] His description encapsulates the "barrel of terror" theory proposed by the former *Shin Bet* Director, Avi Dicter. However, a terrorist campaign is a dynamic system, fighters join and depart the fight at different rates and at different times, and a group's popular support ebbs and flows in response to a wide variety of both internal and external factors. The culminating point of victory envisaged by Dicter, and others of like mind, is not a static target. We have seen in Part I how terrorist groups actively seek to turn states' strengths to their advantage by provoking draconian measures that will polarize communities and alienate potential allies. We have also seen in Part II how social and psychological processes like micromobilization, feuding, and feelings of marginalization and exclusion can be driven by coercive state action. The use of force has its place in the fight against terrorism — sometimes, it is the only measure sufficient to prevent a threat — but it can also be a major driver of violent extremism with second- and third-order effects that can exacerbate situations rather than resolve them. International human rights and humanitarian law place constraints on the use of force that help ensure that it performs the former role without contributing to the latter. The fact that Israel appears to be no closer to defeating Palestinian terrorism today than it was twenty, thirty, or even forty years ago would seem to suggest that it is Alston, rather than Dicter, who has demonstrated greater insight.

## Conclusion

In an official program published in 1964, the Basque separatist group ETA celebrated the success of Federico Krutwig's theory of action–repression–action, which it had put into practice by provoking the

---

[898] Steve Coll, The Unblinking Stare: The drone war in Pakistan, *The New Yorker*, 24 November 2014.

fascist regime of Generalissimo Franco to crack down on opposition in the Basque heartland and so boost support for the organization: "We have achieved one of our major objectives — to oblige the enemy to commit a thousand wrongs and atrocities. Most of his victims are innocent. Meanwhile, the people, more or less passive until now, become indignant against the colonial tyrant and, in reaction, come over entirely to our side. We could not have hoped for a better result."[899] The moral case for observing human rights has been made many times over elsewhere, and it resonates with some and not with others — ETA's statement is a key exhibit in a different, altogether more practical case: states would be wise to respect human rights precisely because terrorist groups want states to abuse them. As I have sought to demonstrate in this section, human rights are not a luxury, and international human rights law is not an obstacle to implementing effective counter-terrorism policies. In fact, international human right law codifies a set of principles that actually help counter-terrorism practitioners to perform their duties with greater precision and professionalism, and help states to counter terrorism more effectively while also avoiding the traps that terrorist organizations have consistently set for them. Quite apart from the importance of a state's legal obligation to observe international law — a decision to ignore these rights in the interests of security can have disastrous policy implications both for operational efficacy and international cooperation, which is vital in a confrontation with a transnational threat. To paraphrase Napoleon Bonaparte's Chief of Police, Joseph Fouché, ignoring these strictures is not simply just a crime, it is also a colossal blunder.

Getting the public policy response to emerging terrorist threats right is absolutely crucial. There is not a single example of a democratic state successfully employing unfettered force to defeat a terrorist organization and remaining a functioning liberal democracy in the process. The Sri Lankan government led by President Mahinda Rajapaksa managed to defeat the Liberation Tigers of

---

[899] Claire Sterling, *The Terror Network: The Secret War of International Terrorism* (Holt, Rinehart and Winston; 1981), p. 191.

Tamil Eelam (LTTE) and kill their leader Velupillai Prabhakaran in 2009. However, in the course this conflict, Rajapaksa became increasingly authoritarian, subverting Sri Lanka's fragile democracy by centralizing power in his own hands and those of his close family members. Critical human rights campaigners and opposition journalists disappeared from the streets of Colombo never to be seen again. When General Sarath Fonseka, who had led the military campaign against the LTTE, had the temerity to run unsuccessfully against Rajapaksa in the 2010 presidential election, he was subsequently arrested and convicted of "military offenses". When Rajapaksa was voted from office in a surprise electoral upset in 2015, he briefly contemplated declaring a state of emergency and retaining his position by force, but could not muster sufficient political support.[900] The use of torture may arguably have tipped the balance for the French in the Battle of Algiers, but it ultimately further radicalized Algerian Arabs, alienated the French public, and helped erode good order and discipline within the French army to the point that the Fourth French Republic collapsed following what amounted to a military *putsch* in May 1958. Disaffected French military officers later went on to establish their own terrorist group, the *organisation de l'armée secrète* (OAS), which was responsible for almost 2,000 deaths between April 1961 and April 1962, and plotted to assassinate President Charles de Gaulle. Algeria achieved its independence in July 1962. The journalist Pierre Vidal-Naquet famously concluded that rather than proving the salvation of French Algeria, the military's decision to adopt torture and extra-judicial killing had instead become the "cancer of democracy".[901] It can also be argued that it was only once the British government managed to bring its counter-terrorism strategy in Northern Ireland more or less within human rights norms, after a series of media scandals and reversals at the European Court of Human Rights, that it became possible for the British to build a partnership for peace

---

[900] Rathana Thera Reveals Last Minute Attempt to Stay in Power: "Gota Looked Extremely Worried And Pensive", *Asian Mirror*, 10 January 2015.

[901] Pierre Vidal-Naquet, *Torture: Cancer of democracy. France and Algeria 1954–1962* (Penguin; 1963).

with the Irish government, based in large part on shared values and mutual interests, which in turn ultimately persuaded the Provisional IRA to abandon the armed struggle.

The failure of democratic governments to live up to their values is an ever-present theme in terrorist propaganda. In an interview conducted to mark the fourth anniversary of the September 11 attacks, and released in December 2005 by *al-Qaeda*'s media arm *as-Sahab*, Ayman al-Zawahiri observed: "Western civilizations sing [the praises of] 'human rights' and 'liberties' — as long as such singing serves its interests and benefits it. And after the London Raid [the July 2005 London Transport bombings], the British government started legislating a number of new laws that reveal Britain's despicable imperialistic face. It also revealed that British freedom is, in fact, the freedom to be hostile to Islam. They began talking about secret trials, and brought to mind the issues of secret evidence, secret witnesses, and unlimited detention, which contradict the most basic principles of fair trial."[902] In the same interview, al-Zawahiri leveled similar criticism at the United States: "Isn't it America that's sending prisoners from Guantanamo and Bagram to Egypt and Jordan, where they are tortured by the very same regimes that America insists should respect human rights? Brother Ibn al-Shaykh al-Libi was placed in a coffin and shipped from Bagram to the National Security Department in Cairo, where he was severely tortured and held for one year."[903] He summarized the lesson for his audience: "There are lots of other examples of Britain's and the Crusading West's hypocrisy but time does not permit addressing them. Yet they all point to the contradiction arising out of the Crusader claims of protecting freedom and human rights. The only explanation for this contradiction is the Crusaders' hostility to Islam."[904] For millions across the Muslim world — the majority of whom are unsympathetic to *al-Qaeda*'s agenda — this is a critique that rings

---

[902] Raymond Ibrahim, *The Al Qaeda Reader, The Essential Texts of Osama Bin Laden's Terrorist Organization* (Broadway Books; 2007), p. 183.

[903] ibid., pp. 186–187.

[904] ibid., p. 184.

depressingly true, greatly undermining the legitimacy of Western counter-narratives that focus on the promotion of liberal and democratic values.

When a country adopts counter-terrorism policies that contravene human rights norms or accepted international legal practices — such as coercive interrogation or targeted killing — it also makes it increasingly difficult for allies to work as closely with that country as they did before. In the past decade, we have seen European support for US counter-terrorism measures drastically impacted by policies that would fall foul of the European Convention on Human Rights. European governments are increasingly loath to turn prisoners over to US custody, or to provide intelligence that could lead to lethal strikes in circumstances that the vast majority of Western states would consider to fall outside the realm of armed conflict.[905] And when a country as powerful as the United States displays so little respect for the rule of law and for human rights, it emboldens other countries to follow suit and provides both political and legal cover for them to do so. Yet, as I have sought to demonstrate above, human rights-compliant counter-terrorism measures have a long track record of success. Community outreach efforts have led to important intelligence leads from previously marginalized communities. Effective police officers applying ethical and rapport-based interview techniques have been able to secure the cooperation in custody of hardened terrorists from groups as diverse as the Italian *Brigate Rosse* and the Provisional IRA, and *al-Qaeda* and ISIL.[906] Even the most impactful (albeit not decisive) examples of leadership decapitation — *Sendero Luminoso's* Abimael Guzmán and the PKK's Abdullah Öcalan — involve arrests not killings. Perhaps, this is because, as Audrey Kurth Cronin has observed, the arrest rather than killing of a terrorist group's leader is "an implicit answer to the illegitimacy of terrorism, and demonstrates the authority of

---

[905] Jochen Bittner, Spies Unlike Us, *The New York Times*, 14 July 2014.

[906] Tom Harper, First Isis supergrass helps UK terror police, *The Sunday Times*, 26 June 2016.

the rule of law".[907] Researchers Steven Hutchinson and Pat O'Malley have argued along similar lines that "the demoralization that accompanies seeing a leader captive and under control of the enemy appears highly relevant to group perseverance."[908] What is certain is that human rights law affords a full spectrum of operational tools and tactics for counter-terrorism practitioners to surveil, penetrate, detain, and, where necessary, forcefully confront terrorist groups. Even the most cursory review of the historical record shows that unlawful methods, such as torture and assassination, rarely seem to generate much short-term advantage and invariably incur debilitating long-term costs.

A final concern for security practitioners to bear in mind is their own personal domestic and international criminal liability for human rights abuses. There is no statute of limitations on torture or crimes against humanity — an individual who commits, or enables to be committed, any such offense may be held to account until his or her dying day. In June 2016, a German court convicted ninety-four-year-old Reinhold Hanning, a former guard at the Auschwitz concentration camp, as an accessory in the murder of 170,000 people between 1942 and 1944.[909] He was sentenced to five years in jail more than seventy years after the crimes in question. No one is too junior or too senior to escape culpability, and no one is beyond the potential reach of national or international law. In April 2009, Alberto Fujimori, President of Peru from 1990 to 2000, was convicted of human rights violations and sentenced to twenty-five years in prison for his role in killings and kidnappings by the government-run *Grupo Colina* death squad during his administration's battle against *Sendero Luminoso* in the 1990s.[910] Former President

---

[907] Audrey Kurth Cronin, *Ending Terrorism: Lessons for Defeating al Qaeda* (Routledge; 2008), p. 30.

[908] Steven Hutchinson and Pat O'Malley, *How Terrorist Groups Decline, Trends in Terrorism Series*, Vol. 1 (Carleton University; 2007), p. 6.

[909] Kate Connolly, Auschwitz guard jailed for Holocaust murder trial, *The Guardian*, 17 June 2016.

[910] Alberto Fujimori was briefly pardoned in December 2017 by President Pedro Pablo Kuczynski, but this pardon was overturned by Peru's Supreme Court in October 2018. Fujimori was ordered to return to prison by the Supreme Court and at the time of writing is appealing this decision, largely on medical grounds.

Fujimori was not the first head of state to be charged with human rights violations, but his case marked the first time that an elected head of state had been extradited back to his home country, tried, and convicted for such offenses — all committed as part of his country's counter-terrorism campaign.

The state itself may also be subject to far-reaching liabilities for human rights abuses. In October 2006, Kenyan victims began legal action in the United Kingdom to gain compensation for the torture they endured at the hands of British officials during the Mau Mau uprising against colonial rule in the 1950s. The British government fought the lawsuit, but in July 2011, a British court ruled that the claimants had an "arguable case" and it would be "dishonorable" to block the action. In June 2013, the British government announced that 5,228 Kenyans tortured by the colonial authorities during the Mau Mau uprising would receive compensation collectively totaling $30,500,000.

In the aftermath of the 9/11 attacks, some commentators, most notably Conor Gearty and Michael Ignatieff, speculated that the world might be entering a period in which concern for human rights would be forced to take second place behind the demands of greater security.[911] Instead, we have seen the failure of the United States to uphold its human rights commitments playing into the hands of *al-Qaeda*, ISIL, and their affiliates, undermining the rule of law at both the domestic and international level, and alienating potential friends and allies. Furthermore, those responsible for committing human rights abuses in this context may yet be held to account years, even decades, after their offence. In October 2015, former CIA officer Sabrina De Sousa became the first US official to face prison in connection with post-9/11 counter-terrorism practices. She was detained while transiting Portugal in response to a European Arrest Warrant issued by the Italian authorities in relation to her involvement in the kidnap and rendition to torture of *Imam* Hassan Mustafa Osama Nasr from the streets of Milan in February

---

[911] Conor Gearty, *Can Human Rights Survive? The Hamlyn Lectures 2005* (Cambridge University Press 2006) and Michael Ignatieff, Is the Human Rights Era Ending? *New York Times*, 5 February 2002.

2003. De Sousa had been convicted *in absentia* by an Italian court in 2009 and was held under house arrest in Portugal pending extradition. The situation was only resolved in February 2017 when she received a partial pardon from Italian President Sergio Mattarella, and while her conviction was not vacated, she is not now expected to serve a custodial sentence.[912] De Sousa may have been the first US official to find herself in such a position, but it is quite possible, even probable, that she will not be the last.

Placing human rights at the center of the state's counter-terrorist response is not only the right thing to do, it is the smart thing to do as well. Launching the UN's *Preventing Violent Extremism Plan of Action* in January 2016, Secretary-General Ban Ki-Moon observed: "Many years of experience have proven that short-sighted policies, failed leadership, heavy-handed approaches, a single-minded focus only on security measures and an utter disregard for human rights have often made things worse. We all lose by responding to ruthless terror with mindless policy — policies that turn people against each other, alienate already marginalized groups, and play into the hands of the enemy. We need cool heads and common sense."[913] The old saw "err in haste, repent at leisure" has never proved more true than in the arena of counter-terrorism.

---

[912] Stephanie Kirchgaessner, Ex-CIA officer pardoned for role in 2003 kidnapping of terrorism suspect, *The Guardian*, 28 February 2017.

[913] AFP World News, *UN chief unveils plan to counter violent extremism*, 15 January 2016 at http://www.i24news.tv/en/news/international/99291-160115-un-chief-unveils-plan-to-counter-violent-extremism. Viewed 15 January 2016.

# Final Thoughts

"The revolution says: I was, I am, I will be again."[1]

Terrorism has been a consistent feature of national and international life for at least 150 years, and it is likely to remain so for the foreseeable future. Yet, what is so striking about even the most cursory review of the literature generated by terrorists, and the literature written about terrorism, is how the same patterns seem to repeat themselves over and over again. The social, political, and psychological motives for terrorist violence have not changed, the tactics and strategies employed by terrorists and counter-terrorist officials have also remained much the same. Protagonists on both sides of terrorist conflicts seem fated to repeat the same mistakes in credulous expectation of obtaining different results. Terrorists believe that violent action will force governments to capitulate to their demands although this rarely happens. Governments repeatedly embrace coercive or repressive measures in the belief that a tough and uncompromising response is the only solution capable of meeting the threat terrorists pose and because leaders are afraid that a more measured response might make them look weak.

The war of the flea metaphor popularized by Mao Tse-tung and Robert Taber to explain the asymmetrical challenge guerrilla warfare — and by extension terrorism — poses to government authority has endured because it works on several levels. A single

---

[1] German communist icon Rosa Luxemburg quoted in *The Urban Guerrilla Is History*, The Final Communiqué From The Red Army Faction, 1 March 1998 at http://germanguerrilla. com/1998/03/01/the-urban-guerrilla-is-history/.

flea, like a single terrorist, is itself relatively inconsequential, although acting in concert with other fleas, it can become a serious irritant for the host. However, the real damage is done not by the fleas' bites but by the host's response — the self-inflicted wounds caused by scratching at the bites, which may even become infected leading to serious illness. The uncomfortable reality is that the existential threat posed by terrorism is not posed by the attack itself — it is posed by how we respond. While a terrorist attack may have devastating implications at the individual level, in strategic terms, a terrorist event — even one of the unprecedented magnitude of the September 11th attacks — rarely poses a meaningful challenge to the survival of the state. However, by reacting as if it does, states often overturn established norms of behavior and longstanding social compacts, and erode hard-won human rights protections that shield their citizens from a far more ubiquitous set of social ills such as public corruption, miscarriages of justice, the abuse of power by government officials, and systemic discrimination. This can change a society far more dramatically than any terrorist attack. Terrorists understand this dynamic all too well and they calibrate their attacks to exacerbate this effect. In the immediate aftermath of the Bataclan nightclub attack in Paris, ISIL issued a claim of responsibility which opened with a verse from the *Koran*, which reads in part: "But *Allah* came upon them from where they had not expected, and he cast terror into their hearts. They were demolishing their houses with their own hands and the hands of the believers."[2] The key to effective counter-terrorism is to avoid falling into this trap.

Of course, this is more easily said than done. As we have seen in the preceding chapters, acts of terrorism are crafted with theatrical flair with the specific goal of eliciting a fear-based response in which unreason trumps reason. In democratic societies, politicians and policymakers have to listen to the voices of their frightened constituents or face being removed from office.[3] The politician who finds himself or herself out of step with majority public opinion is flirting

---

[2] *Koran* 59:2. See also Gilles Kepel, *Terror in France: The Rise of Jihad in the West* (Princeton University Press; 2017) at Preface.

[3] Benjamin Friedman, *Leap before You Look*, Breakthroughs, Vol. 3, No. 1 (Spring 2004), p. 30.

with unemployment, as US Senator and Democratic challenger John Kerry discovered during the 2004 US Presidential election campaign when he told *The New York Times Magazine*: "We have to get back to the place we were, where terrorists are not the focus of our lives, but they're a nuisance. As a former law enforcement person, I know we're never going to end prostitution. We're never going to end illegal gambling. But we're going to reduce it, organized crime, to a level where it isn't on the rise. It isn't threatening people's lives every day, and fundamentally, it's something that you continue to fight, but it's not threatening the fabric of your life."[4] It was one of the few measured, non-hyperbolic comments made about terrorism by a leading American politician in the five years after the 9/11 attacks, and Kerry's comments were quickly set upon by his opponents. The chairman of the rival Bush campaign, Marc Racicot, told CNN: "You know, quite frankly, I just don't think he has the right view of the world. It's a pre-9/11 view of the world." This was a consistent republican talking point and a new political attack ad was rushed out highlighting Kerry's comments with the tagline: "How can Kerry protect us when he doesn't understand the threat?"[5] The voters agreed with the Bush administration and Kerry quickly retreated from his nuanced position.[6] The sad reality is that political incentives can limit the willingness of policymakers to play down threats and can also encourage them to inflate them.[7] Another former US presidential candidate, Al Gore, appositely described such narratives in a 2004 essay as "the politics of fear".[8]

---

[4] Special Report, *Bush campaign to base ad on Kerry terror quote*, CNN.com, 11 October 2004 at http://www.cnn.com/2004/ALLPOLITICS/10/10/bush.kerry.terror/. Viewed on 21 July 2017.

[5] Bush camp in new attack on Kerry, BBC News, 11 October 2004 at http://news.bbc.co.uk/2/hi/americas/3733504.stm. Viewed on 21 July 2017.

[6] John Mueller, *Overblown: How Politicians and the Terrorism Industry Inflate National Security Threats, and Why We Believe Them* (Free Press; 2006), p. 35.

[7] Benjamin Friedman, Managing Fear: The Politics of Homeland Security, *Political Science Quarterly*, Vol. 126, No. 1 (2011), p. 104; Stephen M. Walt, Think Before You March, *Foreign Policy*, 18 January 2015; and Mike German, *Thinking Like a Terrorist: Insights of a Former FBI Undercover Agent* (Potomac Books; 2007), p. 55.

[8] Al Gore, The Politics of Fear, *Social Research*, Vol. 71, No. 4 (Winter 2004).

In a democracy, the blame lies as much with the electorate as it does with politicians. The novelist and objectivist philosopher Ayn Rand has rather a neat line about public opinion in her novel *The Fountainhead*, in which a character observes that newspapers may guide public opinion on a leash, but they must always remember that a leash is just a rope with a noose at both ends. The implication, which holds just as true for politicians as it does for newspaper editors, is that the public can only easily be led where it wants to go, and, unfortunately, human beings are extraordinarily bad at accurately assessing risk. Cognitive biases — triggered and exacerbated by the carefully crafted attention-grabbing nature of the terrorist threat itself — cause people to equate vulnerability (the possibility of harm) with risk (the probability of harm), which in turn results in an increased demand for protection.[9] Stating that terrorists can strike anywhere at anytime with virtually any weapon, as, incredibly, the Bush administration's 2002 *Homeland Security Strategy* informed the public, is neither accurate nor useful.[10] Western intelligence professionals typically assess potential hostile threats by assessing both the intent and capability of a potential perpetrator to carry out the act in question. For instance, both *al-Qaeda* and ISIL may harbor the intent to use a weapon of mass destruction against the mainland United States, but both have manifestly lacked the capability to do so, rendering the threat essentially moot. To argue otherwise is to greatly magnify the threat and thus also the demand for protection. The CATO Institute researcher Benjamin Friedman, who has written extensively about ineffective and counterproductive security measures, warns: "We have created a culture of fear that rewards even dead terrorists for their perseverance; that allows threats to echo endlessly, distracting relatively safe people from real concerns."[11] Andrew Liepman, the former Deputy Director of the US National Counterterrorism Center, and Philip Mudd, the former Deputy Director of the CIA's Counterterrorism Center, also share

---

[9] Benjamin Friedman, Managing Fear: The Politics of Homeland Security, *Political Science Quarterly*, Vol. 126, No. 1 (2011), pp. 77–79.

[10] Benjamin Friedman, Leap before You Look, *Breakthroughs*, Vol. 3, No. 1 (Spring 2004), p. 30.

[11] ibid., p. 34.

this assessment, describing America's unhealthy and illogical obsession with terrorist violence as a national failing: "Terrorists want attention; our hyper-sensitivity to their violence feeds that need."[12]

The leading causes of death in America are heart disease, cancer, lung disease, accidents, diabetes, influenza, pneumonia, and Alzheimer's.[13] According to the US Center for Disease Control (CDC), heart disease is the number one killer claiming some 614,348 lives in 2014.[14] A 2017 investigation by the well-respected New American Foundation into Islamist terrorist incidents committed on US soil in the sixteen years since the 9/11 attacks identified a total of ninety-five fatalities, including the forty-nine people killed in the September 2016 Pulse nightclub attack in Orlando, Florida, the motivation for which has been widely disputed.[15] This equates to an average of approximately six fatalities a year, or just three if we exclude the Pulse nightclub incident. Between 2005 and 2014, the CDC reported that the average number of Americans shot and killed each year by their fellow citizens, either by accident or design, was a staggering 11,737.[16] In 2015, there were 372 mass shootings in the United States — so many that President Obama noted after a gunman killed eight students and a professor at a Community College in Roseberg, Oregon, that such incidents had somehow become routine.[17] Yet, gun control legislation has been consistently and successfully opposed in both national and state legislatures, and

---

[12] Andrew Liepman and Philip Mudd, Lessons from the 15-Year Counterterrorism Campaign, *CTC Sentinel*, Vol. 9, No. 10 (October 2016), p. 14.

[13] Benjamin Friedman, Leap before You Look, *Breakthroughs*, Vol. 3, No. 1 (Spring 2004), p. 30.

[14] American Heart Association News, *CDC: US deaths from heart disease, cancer on the rise*, 24 August 2016 at http://news.heart.org/cdc-u-s-deaths-from-heart-disease-cancer-on-the-rise/, Viewed on 10 August 2017.

[15] https://www.newamerica.org/in-depth/terrorism-in-america/what-threat-united-states-today/. Viewed on 10 August 2017.

[16] *10-year average 2005–2014*, Center for Disease Control, Injury Prevention and Control: Data & Statistics (WISQARS) at www.cdc.gov/injury/wisqars/fatal_injury_reports.html.

[17] *Guns in the US: The statistics behind the violence*, BBC News, 5 January 2016 at http://www.bbc.com/news/world-us-canada-34996604 (viewed on 8 August 2017), and Timothy Williams and Monica Davey, US Murders Surged in 2015, FBI Finds, *The New York Times*, 26 September 2016. See also Juliet Eilperin, Obama on mass shooting: 'Somehow, this has become routine', *The Washington Post*, 1 October 2015.

even rolled back in some instances.[18] In December 2003, General Richard Myers, Chairman of the Joint Chiefs of Staff, suggested in a television interview with Fox News that if terrorists succeeded in using a weapon of mass destruction to kill 10,000 Americans, they would successfully "do away with our way of life".[19] In fact, his fellow citizens, and their political representatives, have demonstrated that they are perfectly willing to live with a greater degree of carnage every single year simply to uphold Americans' constitutional right to bear arms.

Despite the almost negligible threat in real terms — fireworks, cows, and elevators all kill more US citizens every year — terrorism still casts a powerful shadow over the lives of ordinary Americans.[20] A December 2015 Gallup poll found that 51% of Americans questioned were "very worried" or "somewhat worried" that either they or a family member could become a victim of terrorism.[21] This is really just another example of the socialization processes discussed in Part II at work. Terrorism sets out to socialize its victims to feel impacted even when they do not experience the immediate incident itself. Breathless domestic media coverage simply amplifies this framing, as does hyperbolic political rhetoric. Benjamin Friedman has described this process as "democratizing fear".[22] When such fears are indulged by policymakers, it results in the kind of wasteful

---

[18] Ali Vitali, *Trump Signs Bill Revoking Obama-era Gun Checks for People with Mental Illness*, NBC News, 28 February 2017.

[19] John Mueller, *Overblown: How Politicians and the Terrorism Industry Inflate National Security Threats, and Why We Believe Them* (Free Press; 2006), p. 6.

[20] See Yongling Tu and Demar Granados, 2014 Fireworks Annual Report: Fire-works-Related Deaths, Emergency Department-Treated Injuries and Enforcement Activities During 2014, US Consumer Product Safety Commission (CPSC), June 2015 (The CPSC reported a minimum of seven deaths in 2014 from "impact injuries" and 10,500 firework related injuries); Karen Kaplan, Are elevators really hazardous to your health? *Los Angeles Times*, 15 December 2011 (The US Bureau of Labor Statistics reported an average of 27 elevator related deaths each year); and Christopher Ingraham, Chart: The animals that are most likely to kill you this summer, *The Washington Post*, 16 June 2015 (The CDC reported in the mid-2000s that cows were killing an average of 20 people a year — mostly farm workers).

[21] Gallup, *Terrorism in the United States*, In Depth: Topics A-Z at http://www.gallup.com/poll/4909/terrorism-united-states.aspx. Viewed on 10 August 2017.

[22] Benjamin Friedman, Leap before You Look, *Breakthroughs*, Vol. 3, No. 1 (Spring 2004). p. 34.

planning and resource allocation that saw the US Department of Homeland Security prepare an exhaustive list of 80,000 potential terrorist targets, which included such vital points of national infrastructure as the Weeki Wachee Springs water park in Florida, which, while doubtless delightful, is unlikely to feature on either *al-Qaeda* or ISIL's radar.[23] Could something happen in Weeki Wachee Springs? Perhaps. As the ability of Islamist terrorist groups to project force overseas is further diminished, the prevalence of lone-wolf attacks conducted with little or no central direction may increase, resulting in occasional, highly localized, incidents directed against targets of opportunity rather than vital national assets — such as Mohammad Taheri-Azar's March 2006 attack on the campus of the University of North Carolina (UNC) in Chapel Hill, which injured nine people.[24] Is it likely? No. The problem, as the current Director-General of the British Security Service, Andrew Parker, has identified, is that "terrorism, because of its nature and consequences, is the one area of crime where the expectation sometimes seems to be that the stats should be zero."[25] It is this public expectation that lies at the heart of practically every misstep taken in the struggle against terrorism.

Ethan Bueno de Mesquita of the University of Chicago has noted that it is possible to divide counter-terrorism policy responses into those measures that are tactic-specific and visible to both voters and terrorists, such as hardening targets, and those measures which are neither tactic-specific nor visible, such as increased intelligence gathering. In a democracy, policymakers display a bias for visible responses to specific terrorist tactics because they gain the politically optimal response from voters, even though they represent a sub-optimal response from both a financial and a security

---

[23]John Mueller, *Overblown: How Politicians and the Terrorism Industry Inflate National Security Threats, and Why We Believe Them* (Free Press; 2006), p. 1.

[24]Charles Kurzman, *The Missing Martyrs: Why There Are So Few Muslim Terrorists* (Oxford University Press, 2011), pp. 3–6.

[25]Address by the Director-General of the Security Service, Andrew Parker, to the Royal United Services Institute (RUSI), Whitehall, 8 October 2013. See also Andrew Liepman and Philip Mudd, Lessons from the 15-Year Counterterrorism Campaign, *CTC Sentinel*, Vol. 9, No. 10 (October 2016), p. 14.

perspective.[26] Friedman has dismissed such measures as security theatre, while Harvard professors Cass Sunstein and Richard Zeckhauser describe them as being little better than a fear placebo.[27] Friedman notes that the "quintessential example" of such high visibility, low utility, strategies in the United States is the dispatch of National Guard soldiers to patrol airports, which makes the public feel safer regardless of the fact that they don't really have the training or the equipment to engage terrorists in a civilian setting. An M16 assault rifle, which fires a round designed to travel through several people causing traumatic wounds rather than instant fatalities, is hardly an ideal weapon to engage a fast-moving target in a crowded building. And such an approach is not unique to the United States, in March 1994 and February 2003, successive British governments authorized the deployment of soldiers supported by Scimitar armored reconnaissance vehicles to help secure London's Heathrow Airport in response to serious terrorist threats, posed by the Provisional IRA and *al-Qaeda*, respectively.[28] It is hard to imagine any scenario in which it would be necessary to utilize the Scimitar's 30 mm L21 Rarden cannon or its coaxial 7.62 mm L37A1 machine gun, or even, if such an inconceivable circumstance arose, how this could be done without resulting in catastrophic civilian loss of life in such a public space.

Protective security measures introduced in panic rarely fare well over the long term. In the weeks following the 9/11 attacks, letters containing anthrax spores were mailed to two Democratic US Senators and several media outlets — including three network news programs, the New York Post, and the National Enquirer — leading to the deaths of five people and the infection of seventeen others.

---

[26] See Ethan Bueno de Mesquita, Politics and the Suboptimal Provision of Counterterror, *International Organization*, Vol. 61, No. 1 (2007).

[27] Benjamin Friedman, Managing Fear: The Politics of Homeland Security, *Political Science Quarterly*, Vol. 126, No. 1 (2011), p. 104 and Cass Sunstein and Richard Zeckhauser, Overreaction to Fearsome Risks, *Environmental and Resource Economics*, Vol. 48, No. 3 (2011), p. 448. Sunstein served as a senior administrator in the Office of Management and Budget (OMB) during the Obama administration.

[28] Paul Peachey, Troops patrol Heathrow after terror warning of 'missile attack on aircraft', *The Independent*, 12 February 2003.

Several of the envelopes contained notes that referenced the 9/11 attacks and concluded: "Death to America, Death to Israel, *Allah* is great." In the febrile atmosphere of the time, the letters were not unreasonably treated as a sustained terrorist attack, as the perpetrator clearly intended, although subsequent investigations finally led the US Department of Justice to conclude that they were most likely the work of a mentally disturbed biodefense researcher called Dr. Bruce Ivans, who worked at a US government facility where he had access to the strain of anthrax used in the attack. Ivans committed suicide in 2008 without being indicted. The protective measures put in place by the United States Postal Service to protect against the further use of anthrax spores in this manner cost $5 billion — $1 billion for each fatality caused by the attack.[29] To date, there have been no further such incidents. Security officials have a marked tendency to focus their efforts on preventing attacks that have already happened, even when they are unlikely to be repeated, as in the case of the failed shoe bomb plot, rather than on anticipating how the threat might evolve.

A 2008 report by the US Office of Management and Budget estimated that major homeland security regulations cost the US economy $3.4–$6.9 billion a year in lost commercial income.[30] Even factoring in the anomalously high death toll from the 9/11 attacks, the average number of Americans killed annually in terrorist incidents between 1971 and 2001 is 104.[31] Using this figure as baseline from which to estimate the number of lives potentially saved by homeland security expenditure between 9/11 and the end of 2007, Mark Stewart and John Mueller (very) roughly estimated that the United States had spent somewhere between $63,000,000 and $630,000,000 million for every individual life saved.[32]

---

[29] John Mueller, *Overblown: How Politicians and the Terrorism Industry Inflate National Security Threats, and Why We Believe Them* (Free Press; 2006), p. 31.

[30] Benjamin Friedman, Managing Fear: The Politics of Homeland Security, *Political Science Quarterly*, Vol. 126, No. 1 (2011), p. 84.

[31] ibid.

[32] See Mark Stewart and John Mueller, *Cost-Benefit Assessment of United States Homeland Security Spending*, Research Report No. 273.01.2009, Centre for Infrastructure Performance and Reliability, University of Newcastle, Australia, January 2009.

And this estimate did not include the cost of US military operations in Afghanistan and Iraq.[33]

Of perhaps even greater concern than the needless waste of money and material is the fact that policies introduced in haste to reassure the public are difficult, and sometimes impossible, to roll back when the dust finally settles — as President Obama's failed attempts to close the detention facility established in Guantanamo Bay by his predecessor amply testify. The costs, both financial and political, associated with ill-conceived counter-terrorism initiatives can prove astronomical. In January 2017, Human Rights First reported that from its establishment in January 2002 to the end of 2015, the Guantanamo facility had cost the US taxpayer at least $5.687 billion and estimated that the average annual cost of holding the remaining forty-one detainees at more than $10 million per detainee.[34] By way of contrast, the US Penitentiary Administrative Maximum Facility in Florence, Colorado, better known as Supermax, costs the taxpayer approximately $78,000 per detainee and, at the time of writing, this facility housed, amongst others, the World Trade Center bomber Ramzi Yousef, the Shoe Bomber Richard Reid, and the Unabomber Ted Kaczynski.[35] No prisoner has ever escaped.

Likewise, the Military Commissions established in Guantanamo by the Bush administration to try *al-Qaeda* operatives captured by US forces overseas have successfully convicted just eight people (six after plea deals) at similarly vast public expense. So far, three of these eight convictions have been completely overturned on appeal by US courts.[36] A comprehensive estimate is difficult to come by, but according to the US Department of Defense between 2007 and 2013, the Commissions cost the US taxpayer approximately $600

---

[33] Benjamin Friedman, Managing Fear: The Politics of Homeland Security, *Political Science Quarterly*, Vol. 126, No. 1 (2011), p. 90.

[34] Human Rights First, *The Cost of Guantanamo Fact Sheet*, 20 January 2017 at http://www. humanrightsfirst.org/resource/cost-guantanamo. Viewed on 30 July 2017.

[35] ibid.

[36] Human Rights Watch, *Q&A: Guantanamo Bay, US Detentions and the Trump Administration*, May 2017 at www.hrw.org/news/2017/05/04/qa-guantanamo-bay-us-detentions-and-trump-administration#q4. Viewed on 1 August 2017.

million, or roughly $80 million per conviction.[37] As if that wasn't failure enough, the Military Commissions have proceeded at a glacial pace — the trial for the surviving alleged perpetrators of the 9/11 attacks has been tied up in pre-trial hearings since May 2012.[38] This has hardly proved to be the swift justice the victims' families were promised. By way of contrast, Osama bin Laden's son-in-law Sulaiman Abu Ghaith was processed through the New York federal court system and convicted of terrorism-related offenses just eighteen months after he was detained by the Jordanian authorities in March 2013 and extradited to the United States.[39] He was sentenced to life in prison. As of May 2017, US federal courts had convicted 620 individuals of terrorism offenses associated with *al-Qaeda* since the 9/11 attacks.[40] Finally, the damage to America's global standing, and to its own self-image as a "beacon of freedom for all the peoples of the earth", the strains placed on its operational relationships with vital allies, and the propaganda victory gifted to its enemies, represents perhaps the greatest self-inflicted wound of all.[41] As Laura Pitter, Senior National Security Counsel at Human Rights Watch, noted with magnificent understatement: "Creating an entirely new justice system from scratch was never a good idea."[42]

In addition to disproportionate public fear and unscrupulous political fear-mongering, the third domestic factor that plays an important role in amplifying terrorist threats is what some have labeled the

---

[37] Zak Newman, *$600 Million and Counting: GTMO's Military Commissions*, American Civil Liberties Union, 24 October 2013, at https://www.aclutx.org/en/news/600-million-and-counting-gtmos-military-commissions. Viewed on 8 August 2017.

[38] Human Rights First, *Fact Sheet: Myth v. Fact — Trying Terror Suspects in Federal Courts*, 30 May 2017 at www.humanrightsfirst.org/resource/myth-v-fact-trying-terror-suspects-federal-courts. Viewed on 1 August 2017.

[39] Benjamin Weiser, Abu Ghaith, a Bin Laden Adviser Is Sentenced to Life in Prison, *New York Times*, 23 September 2014.

[40] Human Rights First, *Fact Sheet: Myth v. Fact — Trying Terror Suspects in Federal Courts*, 30 May 2017 at http://www.humanrightsfirst.org/resource/myth-v-fact-trying-terror-suspects-federal-courts. Viewed on 1 August 2017.

[41] President Ronald Reagan, *Remarks at the White House Ceremony Opening the "Roads to Liberty" Exhibit*, 11 March 1987.

[42] Human Rights Watch, *Military Commission Conviction Overturned*, Press Release, 12 June 2015 at www.hrw.org/news/2015/06/12/us-military-commission-conviction-overturned. Viewed on 1 August 2017.

security-industrial complex, and the expanding national security government bureaucracy that it serves.[43] The commercial interest that companies working in the security field have in protecting and expanding their marketplace is self-evident, and Jerry Pournelle's much cited *Iron Law of Bureaucracy* predicts that every public sector institution is sooner or later captured and controlled by those who put the need to sustain and protect the institution above the explicit purposes for which it was created. Pournelle has himself pointed to the growth of the Transportation Security Administration (TSA) as a classic example of his Iron Law in operation.[44] Friedman concurs, noting that organizations like the Department of Homeland Security can promote threats by issuing reports and communiqués, by providing expert testimony to government committees, briefing reporters, cultivating political allies who also benefit from security spending in their districts and constituencies, and sponsoring academic research.[45] In 2010, the Department of Homeland Security awarded grants for preparedness-related research worth almost \$5 billion, creating new business opportunities in the process.[46] Fear of terrorism helped the US defense budget (adjusted for inflation) grow by roughly 40% from 2001 to 2010, and, again, this figure does not include direct spending on the conflicts in Afghanistan and Iraq.[47] Needless to say, government departments typically embrace budget cuts with much the same enthusiasm that turkeys embrace Thanksgiving.

And this is where international human rights law comes in — it puts in place clear legal limits that prevent politicians and counter-terrorism officials in a society that respects the rule of law from succumbing to their own baser instincts, or to pressure from

---

[43] Heather MacDonald, *Commentary: The Security-Industrial Complex*, Manhattan Institute for Public Policy Research, 7 September 2006 at https://www.manhattan-institute.org/html/security-industrial-complex-1539.html and David Rohde, The Security-Industrial Complex, *The Atlantic* Monthly, 15 June 2013.

[44] See www.jerrypournelle.com/archives2/archives2mail/mail408.html#Iron. Viewed 7 August 2017.

[45] Benjamin Friedman, Managing Fear: The Politics of Homeland Security, *Political Science Quarterly*, Vol. 126, No. 1 (2011), p. 93.

[46] ibid., p. 94.

[47] ibid., p. 95.

panicked constituents and established commercial interests, to introduce draconian measures and thus fall into the terrorist trap. The supranational nature of international human rights law, reinforced by states' international treaty commitments, can provide the political cover politicians need to stand up to political pressure from both within and without to adopt unwise and self-defeating policies. We have seen in the above paragraphs some of the financial and political costs that can arise from hasty, ill-thought-out responses to terrorist threats. I have focused thus far in this section on the United States, but a similar case could be made in reference to other Western nations that have faced, or are facing, similar challenges. The tactics derived from colonial counter-insurgency campaigns — such as coercive interrogation and internment — that were introduced to Northern Ireland by British Army commanders in the early 1970s had a significantly detrimental effect on the conflict, alienating Irish Catholics on both sides of the border, damaging Britain's relationships with key allies such as the United States, and provoking a considerable escalation in violent incidents. By forcing the United Kingdom to adhere to international human rights law and discontinue the abusive practice of "interrogation-in-depth", the European Court on Human Rights helped to lay the foundation for the Northern Ireland Peace Process, since a more restrained British approach to containing the terrorist threat made rapprochement with the Irish government possible and thus also the adoption of a united Anglo-Irish approach to negotiations with both nationalist and loyalist paramilitaries.[48] It is no exaggeration to note that proper adherence to international human rights law could have prevented some of the most disastrous and counterproductive counter-terrorism debacles of the post-War period.

In Part III, we examined the principle tools used by counter-terrorism professionals in their struggle against terrorist violence and we explored the limits that international human rights law

---

[48] See Tom Parker, The Fateful Triangle: Identity Politics, Security Policy and Anglo-Irish Relations, in R. Orttung and A. Makarychev (eds.), *National Counter-Terrorism Strategies: Legal, Institutional, and Public Policy Dimensions in the US, UK, France, Turkey and Russia* (IOS Press; 2006).

imposes upon them. It may come as a surprise to most readers that international human rights law is actually quite permissive. The law recognizes the severity of the threat that terrorism poses to human life and takes into account how it also threatens the enjoyment and realization of protected rights by members of the public. It also allows counter-terrorism professionals considerable latitude — to engage at-risk communities, to detain and interview suspects, to collect intelligence on potential threats, and where necessary to use even lethal force to protect human life. International human rights law allows the use of human sources and the full panoply of electronic and physical surveillance techniques, if used appropriately in accordance with due process protections. I have sought to demonstrate, I think persuasively, that it is perfectly possible to conduct effective counter-terrorism investigations within the constraints imposed by international human rights law. Indeed, it has been my experience that these constraints tend to discourage lazy thinking and half-baked plans, and force counter-terrorism officials to think more carefully, and sometimes more creatively, about how to approach a particular threat. In short, international human rights law helps to create more agile, more scrupulous, more detail-oriented government investigators — and this, in turn, ensures that the general public is better protected.

By way of contrast, heavy-handed 'tough' and coercive counter-terrorism measures have a poor track record of success, typically giving rise to as many problems as they solve. It is extremely difficult to measure progress in counter-terrorist campaigns because so many of the variables are in flux. As a former member of *Euskadi Ta Askatasuna* (ETA) explained to the researcher Robert Clark: "A clandestine organization is living and dying every day. There are people who quit. Tired people leave. New people join, and we train them, and then we do it all over again."[49] The culminating point of victory is hard to establish and short-term successes such as the elimination or detention of senior leadership figures are often little more than what Michael Mazarr has termed Potemkin victories: "lovely little

---

[49] Robert Clark, Patterns in the Lives of ETA Members, *Studies in Conflict and Terrorism*, Vol. 6, No. 3 (1983), p. 451.

facades to look at as we march past on the road to strategic disaster."[50] However, the evidence presented in Part II strongly suggests that the principal radicalization processes identified by social scientists who specialize in studying terrorist organizations are all more likely to be exacerbated by coercive government tactics than they are to be alleviated.

In the aftermath of a major terrorist incident, the authorities come under tremendous pressure to quickly restore public order, to reassure a panicked populous, and to apprehend the perpetrators. In some cases, it may be days, or even weeks, before it becomes clear who was behind a particular incident — especially on those comparatively rare occasions, like the 2001 anthrax attacks or the 1996 bombing of Centennial Olympic Park in Atlanta, where there is no clear claim of responsibility. Inevitably, with the confusion that almost always follows a major incident combining unhelpfully with the pressure placed on investigators to obtain quick results, mistakes are often made. In the immediate aftermath of the 2004 Madrid train bombings, the Spanish government of José María Aznar was quick to blame the attack on the Basque separatist group ETA, although it would soon emerge that Islamist extremists linked to *al-Qaeda* were to blame.[51] This misidentification, largely driven by internal political considerations, would cost Aznar the general election a few days later. In Part III, we considered some of the different miscarriages of justice that can result from this kind of rush to judgment: the hounding of Richard Jewell after the Atlanta bombing; the wrongful conviction of the Guildford Four; the mistaken shooting of Jean Charles de Menezes; the abduction and torture of Khaled el-Masri; the erroneous US drone strike on Datta Khel bus depot; and the arbitrary detention of 731 (out of 780) detainees in Guantanamo Bay, held for years before being

---

[50] Michael Mazarr, *Unmodern Men in the Modern World: Radical Islam, Terrorism and the War on Modernity* (Cambridge University Press; 2007), p. 210.

[51] *Spain blames ETA for deadly Madrid blasts*, ABC News, 11 March 2004 at http://www.abc. net.au/news/2004-03-12/spain-blames-eta-for-deadly-madrid-blasts/150052. Viewed 17 August 2017.

released without charge.[52] As we have also seen, governments usually pay a very heavy political price for their role in such episodes.

There are, of course, those in the global national security establishment who claim the problem is that coercive measures don't go far enough, that "repression-lite" is insufficient, and that the authorities must be given an even freer hand to do whatever they deem necessary to defeat the enemy, to truly embrace, in Vice-President Dick Cheney's vivid phrase, the "dark side". But if one examines case studies where emerging, or even somewhat established, democracies embraced unbridled coercion and repression to defeat terrorism — for example, Uruguay in the early 1970s, or Sri Lanka in the 2010s — success in the short-term battle against terrorism frequently came at the expense of the long-term health of democratic governance, and only appear to have served to postpone the inevitable reckoning with legitimate political grievances.[53] The UN Secretary-General's 2016 *Plan of Action to Prevent Violent Extremism* explicitly warns Member States against the "overly broad application of counter-terrorism measures" against forms of conduct that should not qualify as terrorist acts.[54] Authoritarian-minded politicians have a well-documented history of exploiting counter-terrorism legislation and related states of emergency to silence legitimate political opposition. In its 2017 *World Report*, Human Rights Watch particularly highlighted the extensive use of this practice by President Recep Tayyip Erdoğan's regime in Turkey to dismantle the rival Gülen movement and crack down on Kurdish activists following a failed military coup attempt in July 2016.[55]

Highly coercive measures often fail on their own terms too. A report published by the Center for a New American Security in 2010 that sought to learn lessons from both US and Soviet

---

[52] Human Rights Watch, *Guantanamo: Facts and Figures*, 30 March 2017 at https://www.hrw.org/video-photos/interactive/2017/03/30/guantanamo-facts-and-figures. Viewed on 17 August 2017.

[53] Michael Mazarr, *Unmodern Men in the Modern World: Radical Islam, Terrorism and the War on Modernity* (Cambridge University Press; 2007), p. 205.

[54] Report of the Secretary-General, *Plan of Action to Prevent Violent Extremism*, United Nations General Assembly, Seventieth Session, A/70/674, 24 December 2015, para. 4.

[55] Human Rights Watch, *World Report 2017: Events of 2016*, 2017, pp. 36–37.

engagements in Afghanistan noted: "[M]erely killing insurgents usually serves to multiply enemies rather than subtract them. This counterintuitive dynamic is common in many guerrilla conflicts and is especially relevant in the revenge-prone Pashtun communities whose cooperation military forces seek to earn and maintain. The Soviets experienced this reality in the 1980s, when, despite killing hundreds of thousands of Afghans, they faced a larger insurgency near the end of the war than they did at the beginning."[56] The historian of guerrilla warfare Max Boot has observed that those who think "scorched-earth" tactics would be more effective are ignoring the evidence of countless brutally ineffective counter-insurgency campaigns dating from "ancient Akkad in Mesopotamia to Nazi Germany in the Balkans and the Soviet Union in Afghanistan".[57] Political scientists Ursula Daxecker and Michael Hess, whose 2012 quantitative study of 539 terrorist groups from eighty-five countries active between 1976 to 2006 found that the use of repression by democratic states decreased the likelihood of a negotiated settlement and increased the chances of a terrorist group victory, similarly concluded that even in case studies where the repression of a terrorist group by an authoritarian regime appeared to have worked, such as the Russian intervention in Chechnya, violence was often partially displaced to neighboring regions rather than eliminated, and in some cases, may have even provided the fuel for a more widespread subsequent popular revolt.[58]

Terrorist campaigns are fought first and foremost in the hearts and minds of men and women, rather than in any physical space. Perceptions of strength and weakness, of efficiency and competency, and of commitment and resilience are all important variables in counter-terrorism campaigns, but the critical factor is the degree to

---

[56] Michael Flynn, Matt Pottinger and Paul Batchelor, *Fixing Intel: A Blueprint for Making Intelligence Relevant in Afghanistan,* Center for a New American Security (January 2010), p. 8.

[57] Max Boot, *Invisible Armies: An Epic History of Guerrilla Warfare from Ancient Times to the Present* (Liveright Publishing Corporation; 2013), p. 541.

[58] Ursula Daxecker and Michael Hess, Repression Hurts: Coercive Government Responses and the Demise of Terrorist Campaigns, *British Journal of Political Science*, Vol. 43, No. 3 (2012), pp. 18–19.

which each side's cause is considered to be legitimate. Perceptions of legitimacy impact recruitment, fundraising, community support, international backing, and collective resolve.[59] Legitimacy is a remarkably complex and situational concept. It is extremely hard to pin down and is constantly in flux. Conflicting parties all lay claim to it, but they may define it by completely different standards — for liberal democracies, legitimacy comes above all from the practice of free and fair elections and respect for the rule of law; for Islamist extremists, in Sayyid Qutb's famous phrase, the *Koran* is the constitution; for national liberation movements, patriotism is the animating virtue; for Marxists, it is typically ideological purity. Human empathy can often play both a fickle and a critical role — high-profile government human rights abuses or a particularly callous terrorist attack can provoke revulsion and change the political calculus of a conflict overnight, especially if the incident is at odds with the stated values of the perpetrator. Hypocrisy acts like kryptonite on legitimizing narratives.

It must be acknowledged that there is undoubtedly a double standard at work here too. Robert Taber's experiences with Fidel Castro's revolutionaries in Cuba led him to observe that "it is an irony of political warfare — and a political fact to be considered and understood — that the rules are not the same for both sides."[60] Governments are held to a higher standard — by their own people, by their opponents, and by the international community. Governments possess the greater power, and both international law and public opinion expect that they will exercise it with restraint. But that does not mean that terrorists get a free pass, they too are judged by their behavior — the bar may be lower, but it is there nonetheless. This too Robert Taber acknowledged: "To be successful, the guerrilla must be loved and admired. To attract followers, he must represent not merely success, but absolute virtue, so that his enemy will represent absolute evil."[61] One remarkable example of this adherence to "virtue" in action followed the assassination of US President James Garfield in July 1881 by Charles

---

[59] ibid., pp. 5–7.

[60] Robert Taber, *The War of the Flea: How Guerrilla Fighters Could Win the World* (The Citadel Press; 1970), p. 117.

[61] ibid., p. 133.

Guiteau, who was initially and erroneously attributed a political motive in some quarters. The Russian populist terrorist organization *Narodnaya Volya* published a letter to the American people expressing sympathy for their loss and admonishing the assassin: "In a country where citizens are free to express their ideas and where the will of the people does not only make the law but selects the individual who executes the law — in such a country political assassination is the manifestation of the spirit of despotism that we have attempted to destroy in Russia."[62] Both governments and terrorist organizations assiduously cultivate the perception that they are acting legitimately.

When one or other party to a conflict loses legitimacy in the eyes of both observers and participants, its strategic position is considerably weakened. The deployment of the British Army to Northern Ireland in August 1969 to support the civil power is a classic illustration of how quickly things can go wrong when commanders on the ground overestimate the ability of their forces to impose order, and underestimate the damage that can be done when the optics appear to suggest that they are acting in a coercive and partisan manner. The British army was sent onto the streets of Northern Ireland by the Labour government of Harold Wilson to act as a buffer between the Catholic and Protestant communities, and initially they were received by the Catholic community in that spirit.[63] However, the transition from a Labour to Conservative government in June 1970 heralded the adoption of a more robust and proactive approach to public order, such as the introduction of a curfew on the Falls Road in July 1970, which was largely rooted in the counter-insurgency theories popularized by Brigadier Frank Kitson, a veteran of colonial counter-insurgency campaigns in Malaya, Kenya, and Aden. Kitson himself arrived in Belfast in September 1970 fresh from a visiting fellowship at Oxford University where he had been working on the draft of his influential military

---

[62] Norman M. Naimark, Terrorism and the fall of Imperial Russia, *Terrorism and Political Violence*, Vol. 2, No. 2 (1990), p. 189.

[63] Prime Minister Harold Wilson quoted in Peter Neumann, *Britain's Long War: British Strategy in the Northern Ireland Conflict 1969–1998*, Palgrave; (2003), p. 52.

treatise *Low Intensity Operations*.[64] The Conservative MP Philip Goodhart memorably described Kitson as the right man in the right job at the right time.[65] Subsequent events would soon make it quite clear that Goodhart could not have been more wrong.

The counter-insurgency tactics introduced by Kitson, and other like-minded British Army commanders, had a major impact on the Catholic community at large — not just on the militant republican element. In *Low Intensity Operations*, Kitson stressed the importance of imposing control over the local population, commenting in regard to Mao's famous *dictum*: "If a fish has got to be destroyed it can be attacked directly by rod or net . . . But if rod and net cannot succeed by themselves it may be necessary to do something to the water."[66] To this end, he favored the cordoning and mass screening of the population, the internment of suspected members of the IRA, the use of hard-charging units like the Parachute Regiment to enforce public order, the use of CS riot control gas, and the collection of intelligence through aggressive interview techniques. Some British units expressed concern that an encounter with the Paras could undo "six weeks of community work in 10 minutes".[67] The greater Belfast area, for which Kitson was personally responsible, became the early focus of the escalating conflict in 1971–1972, and the unit responsible for the Bloody Sunday shootings, the 1st Battalion of the Parachute Regiment, fell under his command and had been known colloquially in the Province as "Kitson's Private Army".[68] Bloody Sunday undoubtedly represented the biggest setback that the British experienced in the opening stages of the conflict. Kitson was recalled from Northern Ireland in April 1972 by the Secretary of State for Northern Ireland

---

[64] James Hughes, Frank Kitson in Northern Ireland and the 'British way' of counterinsurgency, *History Ireland*, Vol. 22, No. 1 (January/February 2014).

[65] Human Rights First, *Fact Sheet: Myth v. Fact — Trying Terror Suspects in Federal Courts*, 30 May 2017 at http://www.humanrightsfirst.org/resource/myth-v-fact-trying-terror-suspects-federal-courts. Viewed on 1 August 2017.

[66] Frank Kitson, *Low Intensity Operations. Subversion, Insurgency and Peacekeeping* (Faber & Faber; 1971), p. 49.

[67] Thomas Harding, Bloody Sunday Paras Were a 'jolly good' Unit, Says General, *The Telegraph*, 25 September 2002.

[68] ibid.

Willie Whitelaw shortly after the imposition of direct rule from London and the adoption of a more nuanced political approach to the security situation, but by then the damage was done and the military was firmly wedded to the course he had charted.[69] In July 1972, the Army launched Operation Motorman to seize back the "no-go areas" established by the Provisional IRA and other republican militants in Londonderry and Belfast.[70] Army foot patrols became a regular feature of Catholic neighborhoods along with the random stopping and questioning of pedestrians. By the end of the year, the British Army had searched more than 36,000 homes, and in 1973, this number increased to 75,000 homes. Between April 1973 and April 1974, an astounding four million vehicles were stopped and searched at military checkpoints.[71] Both Gerry Adams and Martin McGuinness have stressed the role this heavy military presence played in radicalizing the Catholic community.[72]

The British crackdown also coincided with a wave of sectarian killings carried out by loyalist paramilitary groups which claimed 193 lives in 1972 alone.[73] Acting as it was, predominantly against Catholics, the British military could not escape guilt by association in the eyes of the Catholic community and the Irish government. Republicans on both sides of the border made little distinction between incidents like the bombing of McGurk's Bar in Belfast on 14 December 1971 by loyalist paramilitaries which claimed sixteen Catholic lives and the events of Bloody Sunday, in which thirteen lives were lost. Intentional or not, as John Newsinger noted in his history of British counter-insurgency operations, there was an undeniable degree of symmetry to the British and loyalist

---

[69] James Hughes, *State Violence in the Origins of Nationalism: The British Reinvention of Irish Nationalism 1969–1972*, Paper for the Nationalism and War Workshop McGill University, Montreal, 24–26 March 2011, p. 12.

[70] John Newsinger, *British Counter-insurgency from Palestine to Northern Ireland* (Palgrave, Basingstoke; 2002), p. 172.

[71] ibid., p. 168.

[72] ibid., p. 169 and Richard English, *Armed Struggle. The History of the IRA* (Oxford University Press; 2004), p. 142.

[73] John Newsinger, *British Counter-insurgency from Palestine to Northern Ireland* (Palgrave, Basingstoke; 2002), p. 177.

campaigns[74] and the British government was well aware of the damage done to its position by suspicions of collusion.[75] Worse still was the fact that this early period of aggressive military activity established grievance frames that would be exacerbated with every British miscarriage of justice, like the Guildford Four case, and every perceived instance of British callousness or brutality, such as the Thatcher government's intransigence during the hunger strikes, for the remainder of The Troubles.

A similar dynamic also operates on the terrorist side of the equation. When Abu Mus'ab al-Zarqawi's *al-Qaeda* in Iraq launched suicide attacks on three luxury hotels in Amman, Jordan, on 9 November 2005 killing sixty people, including thirty-eight members of a local wedding party, the backlash from the Jordanian public, appalled at the massacre of their fellow countrymen, was swift and far-reaching. Polling conducted by the Pew Research Center between 2002 and 2005 found Jordanian support for the use of violence against civilians in defense of Islam had risen from 43 to 57%, but six months after the Amman hotel bombings, a new Pew poll conducted in Jordan found that support for violence against civilians had fallen to 29% and that public confidence in *al-Qaeda* leader Osama bin Laden had dropped from 64% before the bombings to 24% afterwards.[76] The percentage of Indonesians expressing support for Islamic extremist violence similarly dropped down to 20% following the bombing of two nightclubs in the popular tourist destination of Bali on 12 October 2002 by another *al-Qaeda* affiliate, *Jemaah Islamiyah*, which killed 202 people, including thirty-eight Indonesian nationals.[77] Local support declined still further to just 11% following further attacks on tourist sites in Bali in October 2005, which killed twenty people, mostly local Indonesian

---

[74] ibid., p. 178.

[75] Adrian Guelke, Review article, *Journal of Terrorism and Political Violence*, Vol. 15 No. 3 (Autumn 2003), p. 178.

[76] Jason Burke, *The New Threat: The Past, Present and Future of Islamic Militancy* (The New Press; 2015), pp. 69–70.

[77] ibid., p. 70.

employees.[78] This pattern of public disgust and repudiation following major terrorist incidents is well established. After the 2013 Westgate Shopping Center attack, Al Amin Kimathi, the Chair of the Nairobi-based Muslim Human Rights Forum, told the BBC reporter Will Ross: "Right now there is so much sympathy for the authorities from even those people who have stood at the borderlines of extremism [who] will feel that they have a duty now to even assist. If they can see that the investigations, the operations, are being conducted within the bounds of some civil order, then there will be quite a lot of collaboration and cooperation."[79] It is precisely for this reason that Audrey Kurth Cronin, author of *How Terrorism Ends*, has argued that terrorism can be self-defeating, but note the importance Kimathi placed on the authorities themselves also acting in a lawful manner.[80]

Some of the most important potential allies that governments have in their struggle against terrorist groups are found amongst the constituents to whom the terrorists themselves seek to appeal, but for one reason or another have failed to win over. Tips from the local community or family members played a role in a quarter of the 360 cases of home-grown militant activity examined in Peter Bergen's *United States of Jihad*.[81] The 1993 World Trade Center bomber Ramzi Yousef was apprehended in February 1995 after an associate, a South African Muslim called Ishtiaque Parker, contacted the US Embassy in Islamabad to pass on information regarding whereabouts.[82] Parker had been studying at Islamabad Islamic University where, as a Western passport holder, he had been scouted as a potential recruit by Yousef's brother-in-law. Yousef had tried to ensnare Parker in several terrorist plots and the increasingly

---

[78] ibid.

[79] Will Ross, *Kenyan MPs investigate attack*, BBC Newshour, 30 September 2013.

[80] Audrey Kurth Cronin, *How Terrorism Ends: Understanding the Decline and Demise of Terrorist Campaigns* (Princeton University Press, 2009), p. 94.

[81] Peter Bergen, *United States of Jihad: Investigating America's Homegrown Terrorists* (Crown; 2016), pp. 101–102.

[82] Marc Sageman, *Understanding Terror Networks* (University of Pennsylvania Press; 2004), p. 109.

panicked student concluded that contacting the Americans was his only way out of the situation he found himself in.

Abdelhamid Abaaoud, the mastermind behind the November 2015 Paris attacks, was killed resisting arrest after he sought help from his cousin and one of her close friends found out where he was hiding and informed the police.[83] The woman later told reporters: "It's important the world knows that I am Muslim myself. It's important to me that people know what Abaaoud and the others did is not what Islam is teaching."[84] Alhaji Umaru Mutallab, the father of the underwear bomber, Umar Farouq Abdulmutallab, contacted the US Embassy in Abuja to warn them that his son had become radicalized and that he was a "security threat".[85] One of the key leads in the aftermath of the Brussels airport bombing in March 2016 came from the Moroccan taxi driver who took the bombers to the airport. These examples demonstrate why authorities cannot afford to needlessly alienate any element of the community.[86] If members of minority groups are discouraged from dealing with the authorities because they have experienced systemic discrimination and are concerned that their own rights might be violated if they come forward, a vital potential source of intelligence is lost.

In fact, although you wouldn't know it from Western media coverage, *al-Qaeda*, ISIL, and their affiliates, actually struggle to attract meaningful support from their core constituencies. In *The Missing Martyrs*, Charles Kurzman posed a much overlooked and very apposite question: "If there are more than a billion Muslims in the world, many of whom supposedly hate the West and desire martyrdom, why don't we see terrorist attacks everywhere, every day?"[87] This is certainly a question that occupies the terrorist leadership. Islamist

---

[83] Greg Miller and Souad Mekhennet, One woman helped the mastermind of the Paris attacks. The other turned him in, *Washington Post*, 10 April 2016.

[84] ibid.

[85] Peter Bergen, *United States of Jihad: Investigating America's Homegrown Terrorists* (Crown; 2016), pp. 108–109 and p. 217.

[86] Christopher Dickey, Brussels Taxi Hero Shows How We Stop Terror Attacks, *The Daily Beast*, 23 March 2016.

[87] Charles Kurzman, *The Missing Martyrs: Why There Are So Few Muslim Terrorists* (Oxford University Press, 2011), p. 7.

extremists of all stripes have expressed widespread frustration at the lack of support they receive from the vast majority of their co-religionists. The current leader of *al-Qaeda*, Ayman al-Zawahiri, complained in a 2007 video: "We continue to be prisoners restrained by the shackles of [mainstream] organizations and foundations from entering the field of battle. We must destroy every shackle which stands between us and our performing this personal duty."[88] It is rarely ever referenced that the 9/11 attacks were denounced by *Hamas*, the Muslim Brotherhood in Egypt, *Jamaat-e-Islami* in Pakistan, and forty other Islamist movements in a joint statement issued just three days after the attacks.[89] Muhammed Sayyid al-Tantawi, Imam of al-Azhar mosque in Cairo, the pre-eminent center of *Sunni* Islamic scholarship, harshly criticized the perpetrators saying: "Attacking innocent people is not courageous, it is stupid and will be punished on the Day of Judgment."[90] Grand Ayatollah Muhammad Hussein Fadlallah, a *Shia* religious leader close to *Hezbollah*, likewise professed himself horrified by what he called a barbaric crime, and commented: "Beside the fact that they are forbidden by Islam, these acts do not serve those who carried them out but their victims, who will reap the sympathy of the whole world ... Islamists who live according to the human values of Islam could not commit such crimes."[91] Again, Robert Taber's insights are instructive: "When we speak of the guerrilla fighter [or terrorist] we are speaking of the *political partisan*, an armed civilian whose principal weapon is not his rifle or his machete but his relationship to the community, the nation, in and for which he fights."[92]

Al-Zawahiri was far from being alone in his frustration at his community's relative indifference to the militant cause. The Pakistani group *Harkat ul-Mujahideen* (HuM) has lamented on its

---

[88] ibid., p. 8.

[89] ibid., pp. 43–44.

[90] ibid., p. 43.

[91] Charles Kurzman, *Islamic statements against terrorism*, University of North Carolina, at http://kurzman.unc.edu/. Viewed on 26 August 2017.

[92] Robert Taber, *The War of the Flea: How Guerrilla Fighters Could Win the World* (The Citadel Press; 1970), p. 21.

website: "What is wrong with the Muslim *Ummah* today? When the *Kuffar* lay their hands on their daughters, the Muslims do not raise even a finger to help them!"[93] The leading *al-Qaeda* propagandist Anwar al-Awlaki also harangued the uncommitted: "How can you dare say that you love the religion of *Allah* and you know well that the enemy has desecrated the book of *Allah* and you do nothing... Do you need a bomb to drop on your house to give you a reason to get up and fight? It will be too late by then."[94] While *al-Qaeda's* affiliate in the Arabian Peninsula declared: "We are most amazed that the community of Islam is still asleep and heedless while its children are being wiped out and killed everywhere and its land is being diminished every day, God help us."[95] It is this frustration that drives the strategy of polarization pursued by terrorist groups like *al-Qaeda* and ISIL, with its focus on eliminating the "grayzone" occupied by more moderate political actors. A counter-terrorism strategy that contributes further to this polarization is simply throwing marginalized militants a lifeline. In Taber's words, governments must be wooers as well as doers.[96] As we saw in Parts I and II, left to play out on its own, a lack of significant public support can be fatal to the terrorist cause, something that terrorists themselves keenly understand.

In July 2017, the newly established United Nations Office of Counter-Terrorism published an insightful study based on interviews conducted with forty-three foreign fighters who had made contact with Islamist groups fighting in Syria, including ISIL and the *al-Qaeda* affiliated *Jabhat al-Nusra li Ahl al-Sham*. The UN report found that identity politics had played a key role in their radicalization and highlighted the "significant policy implications" arising from perceived injustice and discrimination. The authors, who included a former Head of the British Secret Intelligence Service's

---

[93] Charles Kurzman, *The Missing Martyrs: Why There Are So Few Muslim Terrorists* (Oxford University Press; 2011), p. 8.

[94] ibid., p. 34.

[95] ibid., p. 8.

[96] Robert Taber, *The War of the Flea: How Guerrilla Fighters Could Win the World* (The Citadel Press; 1970), p. 26.

counter-terrorism branch, warned: "Bad governance, especially disregard for the rule of law, discriminatory social policies, political exclusion of certain communities ... harassment by the security authorities, and confiscation of passports or other identity documents, all contribute to feelings of despair, resentment, and animosity towards the government and provide fertile ground for the terrorist recruiter."[97]

I have argued in these pages that international human rights law provides an effective blueprint for counter-terrorism policies that allow the authorities considerable latitude to pursue and frustrate terrorist threats, while also providing a system of checks and balances that prevents human rights-compliant states from falling into patterns of behavior that only serve to make the situation worse. Benjamin Friedman has argued more broadly that the very existence of mature liberal institutions serves to reduce the appeal of terrorist violence.[98] A 2015 survey conducted by the Pew Research Center into global support for the basic tenets of democracy found that a majority of those surveyed in thirty-eight nations chosen from Latin America, Africa, Asia, Europe, and the Middle East believed that it was at least somewhat important to live in a country with religious freedom, a free press, free speech, and competitive elections.[99] The rights guaranteed by liberal democracies are envied by many of those living in less open societies. Indeed, one only has to consider the mass migration of recent years, and the enormous risks migrants from Asia, Africa, and Latin America are prepared to take to reach Europe, Australasia, and North America to appreciate the gravitational pull of these values. These migrants aren't heading for China or Russia.

Fighting from the moral, and lawful, high ground bolsters a state's legitimacy and thus also strengthens a state's ability to conduct

---

[97] Hamed el-Said and Richard Barrett, *Enhancing the Understanding of the Foreign Terrorist Fighters Phenomenon in Syria*, United Nations Office of Counter-Terrorism, July 2017, p. 46.

[98] Benjamin Friedman, Managing Fear: The Politics of Homeland Security, *Political Science Quarterly*, Vol. 126, No. 1 (2011), p. 79.

[99] http://www.pewglobal.org/2015/11/18/1-support-for-democratic-principles/. Viewed on 26 August 2017.

effective counter-terrorism operations. But it also requires considerable nerve and courage to stay the course when panicked voters, cynical commercial interests, and opportunistic politicians are all clamoring for more forceful, but counterproductive, action. What Western political leaders have mostly lacked in the past two decades is sufficient grace under pressure to resist these insistent impulses. Michael Mazarr has written that "one necessary task for any refashioned strategy in the 'war on terror' is a reclaimed calmness."[100] Before this can happen, politicians and policymakers must first possess a realistic appreciation of what can and cannot be done to contain, and ultimately defeat, terrorism. In the first year of the EOKA campaign on Cyprus, the British Governor, Field Marshall Sir John Harding, offered the following assessment to the Colonial Secretary in London, Alan Lennox-Boyd: "The most we can hope for is a slowly rising curve of success in the aggregate. The actual course of the graph is bound to be erratic."[101] The bomber will always get through somewhere, no matter how tight the defenses, as threat simply cascades from a hard target to a softer one. No matter how effectively security forces pursue terrorist networks, some terrorists will inevitably slip through the net, or, like the San Bernardino killers Syed Rizwan Farook and Tashfeen Malik, strike before ever coming to the notice of the authorities. No matter how effectively the various arms of government combine to engage at-risk youth in an attempt to reduce violent extremism, some youths will inevitably turn to violence. The English poet John Milton captured an essential truth when he wrote in *Paradise Lost* that "the mind is its own place, and in itself can make a Heaven of Hell, a Hell of Heaven." The fact that none of these strategies can be 100% successful is not a reason to lose faith in them. A reduced threat is simply that — a reduced threat. The best we could have ever hoped for in the 'war on terror' was a slowly rising curve of success in the aggregate.

---

[100] Michael Mazarr, *Unmodern Men in the Modern World: Radical Islam, Terrorism and the War on Modernity* (Cambridge University Press; 2007), pp. 212–213.

[101] David French, *Fighting EOKA: The British Counter-Insurgency Campaign on Cyprus, 1955–1959* (Oxford University Press; 2015), p. 139.

In February 1950, another British Colonial Secretary, Arthur Creech Jones, instructed all Britain's colonial governors to adhere "as far as possible ... to the normal principles of English law by which the rights and liberties of the individuals are maintained. Any derogation from these rights and liberties is quite properly the occasion of criticism in Parliament and in the press."[102] The British manual on *Imperial Policing and Duties in Aid of the Civil Power* issued in 1949 also stressed the importance of security force personnel not allowing themselves to be provoked by seeing friends and colleagues struck down by "terrorists who are to the soldier no more than despicable murderers" and thus play into their enemies' hands.[103] Instead, the manual advised: "firmness, politeness, thoroughness and good humor must be the key notes."[104] Governor Harding reiterated this doctrine to his troops at the height of the Cyprus Emergency, instructing: "In spite of increased provocation the keynote for the conduct of the Security Forces to the general public is to remain the same, namely firmness with courtesy."[105] Leave it to the British to produce counter-terrorism guidelines that reference both humor and politeness, but one of the major tragedies of Britain's colonial counter-insurgency experience was that all too often, the British did not follow their own advice, adopting abusive practices that would ultimately migrate back to British soil and help lay the foundation for thirty years of sustained conflict in Northern Ireland.

This perhaps is the ultimate lesson of the past century and half of terrorist activity: we are quite literally our own worst enemies. Terrorists are going to do what terrorists do, and effective government action can mitigate but not eliminate this threat, while draconian government action is most likely to just pour more fuel on the fire. International human rights law can play a critical role, just as it did in Northern Ireland, in saving us from ourselves. In November 2001, George W. Bush was roundly criticized by

---

[102] ibid., p. 202.
[103] ibid., p. 203.
[104] ibid.
[105] ibid.

newspaper columnists and opinion writers for a speech in which he praised Americans for not allowing the events of 9/11 to disrupt the rhythm of American life: "This great nation will never be intimidated. People are going about their daily lives, working and shopping and playing, worshiping at churches and synagogues and mosques, going to movies and to baseball games."[106] It was a theme Bush returned to on several occasions and it contained the seeds of a wise public policy that sadly did not bear fruit under his subsequent leadership. Keep calm and carry on was good advice during World War II, and it is good advice now. The true test of a resilient society is not how it protects critical infrastructure, but how it protects and nurtures critical values. In the final analysis, the war of the flea is actually all about the dog.

---

[106] Thomas Friedman, 9/11 and 4/11, *The New York Times*, 20 July 2008; Ronald Spiers, Confusion in America: Try clearer thinking about 'terrorists', *The New York Times*, 14 January 2003; and *President Bush's address in Atlanta, Ga., on homeland security and the ongoing war on terrorism*, 8 November 2001 at http://www.washingtonpost.com/wp-srv/nation/specials/attacked/transcripts/bushtext_110801.html. Viewed 14 January 2016.

# Bibliography

## Books

A. W. Brian Simpson, *Human Rights and the End of Empire: Britain and the Genesis of the European Convention* (Oxford University Press; 2004)

Abdel Bari Atwan, *Islamic State: The Digital Caliphate* (Saqi Books; 2015)

Abu Iyad and Eric Rouleau, *My Home, My Land: A Narrative of the Palestinian Struggle* (Times Books; 1981)

Adam Ulam, *In the Name of the People: Prophets and Conspirators in Prerevolutionary Russia* (The Viking Press; 1977)

Alain Labrousse (trans. Dinah Livingstone), *The Tupamaros: Urban Guerrillas in Uruguay* (Penguin Books; 1973)

Alan B. Krueger, *What Makes a Terrorist: Economics and the Roots of Terrorism* (Princeton University Press; 2008)

Alan Clarke, *Rendition to Torture* (Rutgers University Press; 2012)

Alan Dershowitz, *Why Terrorism Works* (Yale University Press; 2002)

Alan Elms, *Personality in Politics* (Harcourt, Brace Jovanovich; 1976)

Albert Bandura, *Social Learning Theory* (General Learning Press; 1977)

Albert Camus, *The Rebel* (Vintage; 1991)

Alessandro Orsini, *Anatomy of the Red Brigades: The Religious Mindset of Modern Terrorists* (Cornell University Press; 2011)

Alex Butterworth, *The World That Never Was: A True Story of Dreamers, Schemers, Anarchists and Secret Agents* (Pantheon Books; 2010)

Alex Schmid and Garry Hindle (eds.), *After the War on Terror: Regional and Multilateral Perspectives* (2009)

Alexander Harrison, *Challenging De Gaulle: The O.A.S. and the Counterrevolution in Algeria 1954–1962* (Praeger Publishers; 1989)

Ali Soufan and Daniel Freedman, *The Black Banners: The Inside Story of 9/11 and the War Against Al-Qaeda* (W. W. Norton and Company; 2011)

Alison Jamieson, *The Heart Attacked: Terrorism and Conflict in the Italian State* (Marion Boyers; 1989)

Alistair Horne, *A Savage War of Peace: Algeria 1954–1962* (New York Review Books Classics; 2006)

Allen Trelease, *White Terror: The Ku Klux Klan Conspiracy and Southern Reconstruction* (Louisiana State University Press; 1971)

Ami Pedahzur (ed.), *Root Causes of Suicide Terrorism: The Globalization of Martyrdom* (Routledge; 2006)

Ami Pedahzur, *The Israeli Secret Services and the Struggle Against Terrorism* (Columbia University Press; 2009)

André Moncourt and J. Smith, *We were so terribly consistent: A conversation about the history of the RAF*, Stefan Wisniewski interviewed by TAZ (Kersplebedeb; 2009)

Andrea Nüsse, *Muslim Palestine: The Ideology of Hamas* (Harwood Academic; 1998)

Andrew Clapham, *Human Rights Obligations of Non-State Actors* (Oxford University Press; 2006)

Andrew Cockburn, *Kill Chain: The Rise of the High-Tech Assassins* (Henry Holt and Co.; 2015)

Andrew Marr, *My Trade: A Short History of British Journalism* (Pan Books; 2005)

Anna Geifman, *Death Orders: The Vanguard of Modern Terrorism in Revolutionary Russia* (Praeger Security International; 2010)

Anna Geifman, *Thou Shalt Kill: Revolutionary Terrorism in Russia, 1894–1917* (Princeton University Press; 1995)

Anthony Giddens, *Runaway World: How Globalization is Reshaping Our Lives* (Routledge; 2000)

Anthony Heaton-Armstrong, Eric Shepherd, Gisli Gudjonsson, and David Wolchover (eds.), *Witness testimony: Psychological, Investigative, and evidential perspectives* (Oxford University Press; 2006)

Antonius Robben, *Political Violence and Trauma in Argentina* (University of Pennsylvania Press; 2007)

Artur Beifuss and Francesco Trivini Bellini, *Branding Terror: The Logotypes and Iconography of Insurgent Groups and Terrorist Organizations* (Merrell; 2013)

Ashley Montagu and Floyd Matson, *The Dehumanization of Man* (McGraw-Hill; 1984)

Åsne Seierstad, *One of Us: The Story of Anders Breivik and the Massacres in Norway* (Farrar, Straus and Giroux; 2013)

Audrey Kurth Cronin and James M. Ludes (eds.), *Attacking Terrorism: Elements of a Grand Strategy* (Georgetown University Press, 2004)

Audrey Kurth Cronin, *Ending Terrorism: Lessons for Defeating al Qaeda* (Routledge; 2008)

Audrey Kurth Cronin, *How Terrorism Ends: Understanding the Decline and Demise of Terrorist Campaigns* (Princeton University Press, 2009)

Barry Rubin and Judith Colp Rubin, *Yasir Arafat: A Political Biography* (Oxford University Press; 2005)

Ben Saul, *Defining Terrorism in International Law* (Oxford University Press; 2006)

Benedict Anderson, *Imagined Communities: Reflections on the Origin and Spread of Nationalism* (Verso; 1983)

Benjamin Friedman, Jim Harper, and Christopher Preble (eds.), *Terrorizing Ourselves: Why US Counterterrorism Policy is Failing and How to Fix It* (Cato Institute, 2010)

Benjamin Grob-Fitzgibbon, *Imperial Endgame: Britain's Dirty Wars and the End of Empire* (Palgrave Macmillan; 2011)

Benjamin Netanyahu, *Fighting Terrorism: How Democracies Can Defeat Domestic and International Terrorists* (Farrar, Straus and Giroux; 2001)

Bernard Lewis, *The Assassins* (Basic Books; 2002)

Beverley Milton-Edwards and Stephen Farrell, *Hamas* (Polity Press; 2010)

Bill Edmonds, *God is Not Here: A Soldier's Struggle with Torture, Trauma and the Moral Injuries of War* (Pegasus Books; 2015)

Bill Rolston (ed.), *The Media and Northern Ireland* (MacMillan; 1991)

Björn Elberling, *The Defendant in International Criminal Proceedings: Between Law and Historiography*, Studies in International and Comparative Criminal Law (Hart Publishing; 2012)

Blake Mobley, *Terrorism and Counter-Intelligence: How Terrorist groups Elude Detection* (Columbia University Press; 2012)

Bob Brecher, *Torture and the Ticking Bomb* (Blackwell Publishing; 2007)

Bob Rowthorn and Naomi Wayne, *Northern Ireland: The Political Economy of the Conflict* (Polity Press, 1988)

Boris Savinkov, *Memoirs of a Terrorist* (A. & C. Boni; 1931)

Brandon Garrett, *Convicting the Innocent: Where Criminal Prosecutions Go Wrong* (Harvard University Press; 2012)

Brendan Koerner, *The Skies Belong to Us: Love and Terror in the Golden Age of Hijacking* (Crown Publishers; 2013)

Brendan O'Brien, *The Long War: The IRA and Sinn Féin 1985 to Today* (The O'Brien Press; 1993)

Brendan O'Leary and John McGarry, *The Politics of Antagonism* (Athlone Press; 1993)

Brian Jenkins, *Will Terrorists Go Nuclear?* (Prometheus Books; 2008)

Bruce Hoffman, *Anonymous Soldiers: The Struggle for Israel, 1917–1947* (Knopf; 2015)

Bruce Hoffman, *Inside Terrorism* (Columbia University Press; 2006)

Bruce Jentleson, *Military Force Against Terrorism: Questions of Legitimacy, Dilemmas of Efficacy*, in Ivo Daalder, *Beyond Preemption: Force and Legitimacy in a Changing World* (Brookings Institution Press; 2007)

Bruce Lawrence (ed.), *Messages to the World: The Statements of Osama bin Laden* (Verso; 2005)

Brynjar Lia, *The Society of the Muslim Brothers in Egypt: The Rise of an Islamic Mass Movement 1928–1942* (Ithaca Press; 1998)

Calder Walton, *Empire of Secrets: British Intelligence, the Cold War and the Twilight of Empire* (Overlook Hardcover; 2013)

Carlos Marighela, *For the Liberation of Brazil* (Pelican Books; 1971)

Caroline Elkins, *Imperial Reckoning: The Untold Story of Britain's Gulag in Kenya* (Henry Holt & Co.; 2005)

Charles Kurzman, *The Missing Martyrs: Why There Are So Few Muslim Terrorists* (Oxford University Press; 2011)

Charles Ruud and Sergei Stepanov, *Fontanka 16: The Tsar's Secret Police* (Sutton Publishing; 1999)

Charles Tilly, *From Mobilization to Revolution* (Addison-Wesley; 1978)

Charles Tilly, *The Politics of Collective Violence* (Cambridge University Press; 2003)

Charles Townshend, *The Republic: The Fight for Irish Independence* (Allen Lane; 2013)

Charlotte Heath-Kelly, *Politics of Violence: Militancy, International Politics and Killing in the Name* (Routledge; 2016)

Chester Barnard, *The Functions of the Executive* (Harvard University Press; 1938)

Christopher Andrew and Simona Tobia, *Interrogation in War and Conflict: Comparative and Interdisciplinary Analysis* (Routledge; 2014)

Claire Sterling, *The Terror Network: The Secret War of International Terrorism* (Holt, Rinehart and Winston; 1981)

Clark McCauley and Sophia Moskalenko, *Friction: How Radicalization Happens to Them and Us* (Oxford University Press; 2011)

Claudia Verhoeven, *The Odd Man Karakozov: Imperial Russia, Modernity and the Birth of Terrorism* (Cornell University Press; 2009)

Clyde Hendrick (ed.), *Group Processes and Intergroup Relations* (Sage; 1987)

Colin Shindler, *The Land Beyond Promise: Israel, Likud and the Zionist Dream* (I. B. Tauris; 2001)

Conor Gearty, *Can Human Rights Survive? The Hamlyn Lectures 2005* (Cambridge University Press 2006)

Dan Breen, *My Fight for Irish Freedom* (Anvil Books; 1981)

Daniel Byman, *A High Price: The Triumphs and Failures of Israeli Counterterrorism* (Oxford University Press; 2011)

Daniel Kahneman, *Thinking Fast and Slow* (Farrar, Straus and Giroux; 2013)

Daniel Klaidman, *Kill or Capture: The War on Terror and the Soul of the Obama Presidency* (Houghton Mifflin Harcourt; 2012)

Daniele Conversi, *The Basques, the Catalans, and Spain: Alternative Routes to Nationalist Mobilisation* (University of Nevada Press; September 2000)

Darius Rejali, *Torture and Democracy* (Princeton University Press; 2009)

David Apter (ed.), *The Legitimization of Violence* (New York University Press; 1997)

David Apter and Tony Saich, *Revolutionary Discourse in Mao's Republic* (Harvard University Press; 1994)

David Bonner, *Executive Measures, Terrorism and National Security: Have the Rules of the Game changed?* (Ashgate Publishing; 2007)

David Cesarani, *Major Farran's Hat: The Untold Story of the Struggle to Establish the Jewish State* (Da Capo Press, Cambridge, Massachusetts; 2009)

David Cole and James X. Dempsey, *Terrorism and the Constitution: Sacrificing Civil Liberties In The Name Of National Security* (New Press, 2006)

David Cook, *Understanding Jihad* (University of California Press; 2005)

David Fitzpatrick (ed.), *Terror in Ireland 1916–1923* (The Lilliput Press; 2012)

David French, *Fighting EOKA: The British Counter-Insurgency Campaign on Cyprus, 1955–1959* (Oxford University Press; 2015)

David Galula, *Counterinsurgency Warfare: Theory and Practice* (Frederick A. Praeger; 2005)

David Goslin (ed.), *Handbook of Socialization Theory and Research* (Rand McNally and Co.; 1969)

David Kilcullen, *Blood Year: The Unraveling of Western Counterterrorism* (Oxford University Press; 2016)

David Kilcullen, *The Accidental Guerilla: Fighting Small Wars in the Midst of a Big One* (Hurst & Co.; 2009)

David Luban, *Torture, Power and the Law* (Cambridge University Press; 2014)

David Macey, *Frantz Fanon: A Biography* (Picador; 2001)

David Scott Palmer (ed.), *Shining Path of Peru* (St. Martin's Press; 1994)

Denis O'Hearn, *Nothing But An Unfinished Song: Bobby Sands, the Irish Hunger Striker Who Ignited a Generation* (Nation Book; 2006)

Diego Gambetta (ed.), *Making Sense of Suicide Missions* (Oxford University Press; 2005)

Diego Gambetta and Steffan Hertog, *Engineers of Jihad: The Curious Connection between Violent Extremism and Education* (Princeton University Press; 2016)

Dilip Hiro, *Iran Under the Ayatollahs* (Routledge Revivals; 2013)

Don DeLillo, *Mao II* (Penguin Books; 1992)

Donatella Della Porta, *Clandestine Political Violence* (Cambridge University Press; 2013)

Donatella Della Porta, *Social Movements and Violence: Participation in underground organizations* (JAI Press; 1992)

Donatella Della Porta, *Social Movements, Political Violence and the State: A Comparative Analysis of Italy and Germany* (Cambridge University Press; 1995)

Doug McAdam, Sidney Tarrow and Charles Tilly, *Dynamics of Contention* (Cambridge; Cambridge University Press 2001)

Douglas Hibbs, *Mass Political Violence* (Wiley; 1973)

Douglas McAdam, *Political Process and the Development of Black Insurgency 1930–1970* (University of Chicago Press; 1982)

Ed Moloney, *Voices from the Grave: Two Men's War in Ireland* (Public Affairs; 2010)

Edvard Radzinsky, *Alexander II: The Last Great Tsar* (Free Press; 2005)

Edward De Burgh, *Elizabeth, Empress of Austria: A memoir* (J.B. Lippencott Co., 1899)

Elaine Frantz Parsons, *Klu Klux: The Birth of the Klan during Reconstruction* (University of North Carolina Press; 2016)

Eliza Manningham-Buller, *Securing Freedom* (Profile Books; 2012)

Ellen Dahrendorf (ed.), *Russian Studies* (Elisabeth Sifton Books, Viking; 1987)

Emma Goldman, *Anarchism and Other Essays* (Mother Earth Publishing Association; 1911)

Eric Hoffer, *The True Believer: Thoughts on the Nature of Mass Movements* (Harper Perennial Modern Classics; 2010)

Eric Schmitt and Thom Shanker, *Counterstrike: The Untold Story of America's Secret Campaign Against Al Qaeda* (Times Books; 2011)

Eric Shepherd, *Investigative Interviewing: The Conversation Management Approach* (Oxford University Press; 2008)

Ernest Alfred Vizetelly, *The Anarchists: Their Faith and Their Record* (Turnbull and Spears; 1911)

Ervand Abrahamian, *Radical Islam: The Iranian Mojahedin* (I. B. Taurus; 1989)

Erving Goffman, *Frame Analysis: An Essay on the Organization of Experience* (Northeastern; 1986)

Euan Hague, Heidi Beirich, and Edward Sebesta (eds.), *Neo-Confederacy: A Critical Introduction* (University of Texas Press; 2010)

Faisal Devji, *Landscapes of the Jihad: Militancy, Morality, Modernity* (London: Hurst; 2005)

Faisal Devji, *The Terrorist in Search of Humanity: Militant Islam and Global Politics* (Columbia University Press; 2009)

Fawaz Gerges, *Journey of the Jihadist: Inside Muslim Militancy* (2006)

Fernando Reineres (ed.), *European Democracies Against Terrorism: Governmental Policies and Intergovernmental Cooperation* (Dartmouth Publishing; 2000)

Franco Venturi, *Roots of Revolution: A History of the Populist and Socialist Movements in Nineteenth Century Russia* (Weidenfeld and Nicolson; 1960)

Frank Harvey, *The Homeland Security Dilemma: Fear, failure and the Future of American Insecurity* (Routledge; 2008)

Frank Kitson, *Low Intensity Operations. Subversion, Insurgency and Peacekeeping* (Faber & Faber; 1971)

Franklin C. Spinney, *Defense Facts of Life: The Plans/Reality Mismatch* (Westview Press; 1985)

Frantz Fanon, *Black Skin, White Masks* (Grove Press; 1967)

Frantz Fanon, *The Wretched of the Earth* (Grove Press; 1963)

Fred Kaplan, *The Insurgents: David Petraeus and the Plot to Change the American War* (Simon and Schuster; 2013)

Frederic Zuckerman, *The Tsarist Secret Police Abroad: Policing Europe in a Modernising World* (Palgrave MacMillan; 2003)

Frederick Hacker, *Crusaders, Criminals, Crazies: Terror and Terrorism in Our Time* (W. W. Norton: 1976)

Geoffrey Hosking, *Russia: People and Empire, 1552–1917* (Harvard University Press; 1999)

George Armstrong Kelly, *Lost Soldiers: The French Army and Empire in Crisis, 1947–1962* (The MIT Press; 1965)

George Grivas-Dighenis and Charles Foley, *The Memoirs of General Grivas* (Longmans; 1964)

George Kassimeris (ed.), *Playing Politics with Terrorism: A User's Guide* (Columbia University Press; 2007)

George Kassimeris, *Inside Greek Terrorism* (Oxford University Press; 2013)

George Lepre, *Himmler's Bosnian Division: The Waffen-SS Handschar Division 1943–1945* (Schiffer Military History; 1997)

George Michael, *Confronting Right-Wing Extremism and Terrorism in the USA* (Routledge; 2003)

George Richard Esenwein, *Anarchist Ideology and the Working-Class Movement in Spain, 1868–1898* (University of California Press; 1990)

George W. Bush, *Decision Points* (Crown; 2010)

Gerard Chaliand and Arnaud Blin, *The History of Terrorism: From Antiquity to Al-Qaeda* (University of California Press; 2007)

Gerold Frank, *The Deed* (Simon and Schuster; 1963)

Gerry Adams, *Hope and History: Making Peace in Ireland* (Routledge; 2004)

Gerry Adams, *The Politics of Irish Freedom* (Brandon Book Publishers; 1986)

Gilles Kepel, *Jihad: The Trail of Political Islam* (Belknap Press; 2002)

Gilles Kepel, *Terror in France: The Rise of Jihad in the West* (Princeton University Press; 2017)

Graham Fuller, *The Future of Political Islam* (Palgrave MacMillan; 2003)

Grant McKee and Ros Franey, *Time Bomb: The Irish Bombers, English Justice and the Guildford Four* (Bloomsbury; 1989)

Grant Wardlaw, *Political Terrorism: Theory, Tactics and Counter-Measures* (Cambridge University Press; 1989)

Grigory Gershuni, *From My Recent Past: Memoirs of a Revolutionary Terrorist* (Lexington Books; 2015)

Harry Patterson, *The Politics of Illusion: A Political History of the IRA* (Serif, London; 1997)

Heather Hamill, *The Hoods: Crime and Punishment in Belfast* (Princeton University Press; 2011)

Helen Duffy, *The 'War on Terror' and the Framework of International Law* (Cambridge University Press; 2005)

Henry A. Crumpton, *The Art of Intelligence: Lessons from a Life in the CIA's Clandestine Service* (Penguin Press; 2013)

Henry Steiner and Philip Alston, *International Human Rights in Context: Law, Politics, Morals* (Oxford University Press; 2000)

Herbert Blumer, *Symbolic Interactionism: Perspective and Method* (University of California; 1969)

Hugh Barlow, *Dead for Good: Martyrdom and the Rise of the Suicide Bombers* (Paradigm Publishers; 2007)

Hugh Graham and Ted Gurr (eds.), *The History of Violence in America* (Praeger; 1969)

Ian Brownlie, *International Law and the Use of Force by States* (Clarendon Press; 1963)

Ishwar Dayal Gaur, *Martyr as Bridegroom: A Folk Representation of Bhagat Singh* (Anthem Press India; 2008)

Ivo Daalder, *Beyond Preemption: Force and Legitimacy in a Changing World* (Brookings Institution Press; 2007)

J. B. E. Hittle, *Michael Collins and the Anglo-Irish War: Britain's Counterinsurgency Failure* (Potomac Books; 2011)

J. B. Watson, *Psychological Care of Infant and Child* (W. W. Norton and Co.; 1928)

J. Bowyer Bell, *Terror out of Zion: Irgun Zvai Leumi, LEHI, and the Palestine Underground, 1929–1949* (Academy Press; 1977)

J. Bowyer Bell, *The Secret Army: The IRA 1916–1979* (Poolbeg Press, Dublin; 1990)

J. M. Berger, *Jihad Joe: Americans Who Go to War in the Name of Islam* (Potomac Books; 2011)

J. Michael Waller, *Fighting the War of Ideas like a Real War* (IWP Press; 2007)

J. Patrice McSherry, *Predatory States: Operation Condor and Covert War in Latin America* (Rowman & Littlefield Publishers; 2005)

J. Smith and André Moncourt, *The Red Army Faction A Documentary History: Volume 1 — Projectiles for the People* (PM Press; 2009)

Jacques Rougerie, *la Commune de 1871* (Presses Universitaires de France; 2014)

James Barr, *Setting the Desert on Fire: T. E. Lawrence and Britain's Secret War in Arabia 1916–1918* (W. W. Norton & Co., New York; 2008)

James Duesenberry, *Income, Saving and the Theory of Consumer Behavior* (Harvard University Press; 1949)

James Gilligan, *Violence: Our Deadly Epidemic and Its Causes* (Putnam Adult; 1996)

James Q. Wilson, *Political Organizations* (Princeton University Press; 1974)

Janet Cherry, *Spear of the Nation: South Africa's Liberation Army 1960s–1990s* (Ohio University Press; 2011)

Jason Burke, *The New Threat: The Past, Present and Future of Islamic Militancy* (The New Press; 2015)

Jean Rosenfeld (ed.), *Terrorism, Identity and Legitimacy: The Four Waves Theory and Political Violence* (Routledge; 2011)

Jeffery Richelson, *A Century of Spies: Intelligence in the Twentieth Century* (Oxford University Press; 1997)

Jeffrey D. Simon, *The Terrorist Trap: America's Experience with Terrorism* (Indiana University Press; 2001)

Jeffrey Toobin, *American Heiress: The Wild Saga of the Kidnapping, Crimes and Trial of Patty Hearst* (Doubleday; 2016)

Jeffrey William Lewis, *The Business of Martyrdom: A History of Suicide Bombing* (Naval Institute Press; 2012)

Jerome Frank, *Sanity and Survival in the Nuclear Age: Psychological Aspects of War and Peace* (Vintage Books; 1968)

Jerrold Post, *The Mind of the Terrorist* (Palgrave Macmillan; 2007)

Jessica Stern, *Terror in the Name of God: Why Religious Militants Kill* (Harper Collins; 2003)

Jillian Becker, *Hitler's Children: The Story of the Baader-Meinhof Gang* (Panther Publishing; 1978)

Joan Grusec and Paul Hastings, *Handbook of Socialization: Theory and Research* (Guilford Publications; 2006)

Joan McEwen, *Innocence on Trial: The Framing of Ivan Henry* (Heritage House; 2015)

Joanne Wright, *Terrorist Propaganda: The Red Army Faction and the Provisional IRA 1968–1986* (Palgrave MacMillan; 1991)

Joby Warrick, *The Triple Agent: The Al Qaeda Mole Who Infiltrated the CIA* (Doubleday; 2011)

Joby Warrick, *Black Flags: The Rise of ISIS* (Doubleday; 2015)

Joel Beinin and Zachary Lockman, *Workers on the Nile: Nationalism, Communism, Islam, and the Egyptian Working Class 1882–1954* (American University in Cairo Press; 1998)

Joel Hayward (ed.), *Air Power, Insurgency and the War on Terror* (Centre for Air Power Studies; 2009)

John Bew, Martyn Frampton, and Inigo Gurruchaga, *Talking to Terrorists: Making Peace in Northern Ireland and the Basque Country* (C. Hurst; 2009)

John Calvert, *Sayyid Qutb and the Origins of Radical Islamism* (Columbia University Press; 2010)

John Conroy, *Unspeakable Acts, Ordinary People: The Dynamics of Torture* (University of California Press; 2000)

John Darby and Roger MacGinty (eds.), *The Management of Peace Processes* (Palgrave; 2000)

John Dempsey and Linda Forst, *An Introduction to Policing* (Delmar Cengage Learning; 2015)

John Horgan, *The Psychology of Terrorism* (Routledge; 2014)

John Horgan, *Walking Away from Terrorism: Accounts of Disengagement from Radical and Extremist Movements* (Routledge; 2009)

John Merriman, *The Dynamite Club: How a Bombing in Fin-de-Siècle Paris Ignited the Modern Age of Terror* (Houghton Mifflin Harcourt; 2009)

John Mueller, *Overblown: How Politicians and the Terrorism Industry Inflate National Security Threats, and Why We Believe Them* (Free Press; 2006)

John Newsinger, *British Counter-insurgency from Palestine to Northern Ireland* (Palgrave; 2002)

Jon Lee Anderson, *Che Guevara: A Revolutionary Life* (Grove Press; 1997)

Jonathan Shay, *Achilles in Vietnam: Combat Trauma and the Undoing of Character* (Atheneum; 1994)

Jonathan Shay, *Odysseus in America: Combat Trauma and the Trials of Homecoming* (Scribner; 2002)

Joseph Heller, *The Stern Gang: Ideology, Politics and Terror 1940–1949* (Frank Cass; 1995)

Joseph Nye, *Soft Power: The Means to Succeed in World Politics* (Public Affairs; 2004)

Joshua Philips, *None of Us Were Like This Before: American Soldiers and Torture* (Verso; 2010)

Juan Linz, *The Breakdown of Democratic Regimes* (John Hopkins Press; 1978)

Judith Palmer Harik, *Hezbollah: The Changing Face of Terrorism* (I. B. Taurus; 2004)

K. R. M. Short, *The Dynamite War: Irish-American Bombers in Victorian Britain* (Gill and Macmillan; 1979)

Ken Heskin, *Northern Ireland: A Psychological Analysis* (Gill and Macmillan; 1980)

Kenneth Roth, Minky Worden and Amy Bernstein, *Torture* (Human Rights Watch; 2005)

Kevin Toolis, *Rebel Hearts* (St. Martin's Griffin; 1997)

Konrad Lorenz, *On Aggression* (Routledge Classics; 2002)

Kosta Todorov, *Balkan Firebrand: The Autobiography of a Rebel, Soldier and Statesman* (Ziff-Davis; 1943)

Laura Sjoberg and Caron Gentry (eds.), *Women, Gender, and Terrorism* (University of Georgia Press; 2011)

Lawrence Freedman, *Strategy: A History* (Oxford University Press; 2013)

Lawrence Wright, *The Looming Tower: A Qaeda and the Road to 9/11* (Knopf; 2006)

Lee Jarvis and Michael Lister (eds.), *Critical Perspectives on Counter-terrorism* (Routledge; 2014)

Leila Khaled and George Hajjar, *My People Shall Live: The Autobiography of a Revolutionary* (Hodder and Stoughton; 1973)

Leith Passmore, *Ulrike Meinhof and the Red Army Faction: Performing Terrorism* (Palgrave Macmillan; 2011)

Leon Trotsky, *The History of the Russian Revolution* (Haymarket Books; 2017)

Liesbeth Zegveld, *The Accountability of Armed Opposition Groups in International Law*, Cambridge Studies in International and Comparative Law (Cambridge University Press; 2002)

Linda Miller, Kären Hess, and Christine Orthmann, *Community Policing: Partnerships for Problem Solving* (Cengage Learning; 2013)

Lodewijk Gunther Moor, Tony Peters, Paul Ponsaers, Joanna Shapland, and Bas van Stokkom (eds.), *Restorative Policing* (Maklu Publishers; 2009)

Lou Michel and Dan Herbeck, *American Terrorist: Timothy McVeigh and the Oklahoma City Bombing* (Harper; 2001)

Louise Richardson (ed.), *The Roots of Terrorism* (Routledge; 2006)

Louise Richardson, *What Terrorists Want: Understanding the Enemy, Containing the Threat* (Random House, 2006)

Lt. Col. T. N. Greene (ed.), *The Guerrilla and How to Fight Him: Selections from the Marine Corps Gazette*, US Marine Corps, FMFRP-12-25 (1962)

Luigi Galleani, *The End of Anarchism?* (Elephant Editions; 2012)

Lynne Olson, *Troublesome Young Men: The Rebels who Brought Churchill to Power and Helped Save England* (Farrar Straus Giroux; 2007)

M. L. R. Smith, *Fighting for Ireland: The Military Strategy of the Irish Republican Movement* (Routledge; 1995)

Mancur Olson, *The Logic of Collective Action: Public Goods and the Theory of Groups* (Harvard University Press; 1965)

Manfred Hildermeier, *The Russian Socialist Revolutionary Party Before the First World War* (Palgrave Macmillan; 2000)

Mao Tse Tung, *On Guerrilla Warfare*, translated by Brigadier-General Samuel B. Griffith II (University of Illinois Press; 1961)

Marc Sageman, *Understanding Terror Networks* (University of Pennsylvania Press; 2004)

Margaret MacMillan, *Dangerous Games: The Uses and Abuses of History* (Modern Library 2009)

Maria McGuire, *To Take Arms: A Year in the Provisional IRA* (Macmillan; 1973)

Mark Bowden, *Killing Pablo: The Hunt for the World's Greatest Outlaw* (Atlantic Monthly Press; 2001)

Mark Hamm, *The Spectacular Few: Prisoner Radicalization and the Evolving Terrorist Threat* (New York University Press; 2013)

Mark Juergensmeyer, *Terror in the Mind of God: The Global Rise of Religious Violence* (University of California Press; 2003)

Mark Urban, *Big Boys' Rules: The SAS and the Secret Struggle Against the IRA* (Faber & Faber; 1992)

Martha Crenshaw (ed.), *Terrorism in Context* (Pennsylvania State University Press; 1995)

Martha Crenshaw, *Explaining Terrorism: Causes, Processes and Consequences* (Routledge; 2011)

Martin Baumann, *Terror or Love?* (Pulp Press; 1977)

Mats Berdal and David Malone (eds.), *Greed and Governance: Economic Agendas in Civil Wars* (Lynne Reinner; 2000)

Matthew Carr, *The Infernal Machine: A History of Terrorism* (The New Press; 2007)

Matthew Levitt, *Hamas: Politics, Charity, and Terrorism in the Service of Jihad* (Yale University Press; 2006)

Matthew Levitt, Hezbollah: *The Global Footprint of Lebanon's Party of God* (Georgetown University Press; 2013)

Max Boot, *Invisible Armies: An Epic History of Guerrilla Warfare from Ancient Times to the Present* (Liveright Publishing Corporation; 2013)

Max Hastings, *The Secret War: Spies, Codes and Guerrillas 1939–1945* (William Collins; 2015)

Max Nomad, *Apostles of Revolution* (Collier Books; 1961)

Maxwell Taylor and Ethel Quayle, *Terrorist lives* (Brassey's; 1994)

Menachem Begin, *The Revolt: Story of the Irgun* (Steimatzky's Agency Ltd.; 1977)

Mia Bloom, *Bombshell: Women and Terrorism* (University of Pennsylvania Press; 2011)

Mia Bloom, *Dying to Kill: The Allure of Suicide Terror* (Columbia University Press; 2005)

Michael A. Innes and William Banks (eds.), *Making Sense of Proxy Wars: States, Surrogates & the Use of Force* (Potomac Books; 2012)

Michael Arena and Bruce Arrigo, *The Terrorist Identity: Explaining The Terrorist Threat* (New York University; 2006)

Michael Barkun, *Disaster and the Millennium* (Yale University Press; 1974)

Michael Burleigh, *Blood and Rage: A Cultural History of Terrorism* (Harper; 2009)

Michael Burleigh, *Small Wars, Far Away Places: The Genesis of the Modern World 1945—65* (MacMillan; 2013)

Michael Mazarr, *Unmodern Men in the Modern World: Radical Islam, Terrorism and the War on Modernity* (Cambridge University Press; 2007)

Michael Ryan, *Decoding Al Qaeda's Strategy: The Deep Battle Against America* (Columbia University Press; 2013)

Michael Scheuer, *Osama Bin Laden* (Oxford University Press; 2011)

Michael Sheehan, *Crush the Cell: How to Defeat Terrorism Without Terrorizing Ourselves* (Crown; 2008)

Mike German, *Thinking Like a Terrorist: Insights of a Former FBI Undercover Agent* (Potomac Books; 2007)

Mitchell Silber, *The Al Qaeda Factor: Plots Against the West* (University of Pennsylvania Press; 2012)

Morten Storm, *Agent Storm: My Life Inside Al-Qaeda and the CIA* (Atlantic Monthly Press; 2014)

Naim Qassem, *Hizbullah: The Story from Within* (Saqi; 2005)

Nelson Mandela, *Long Walk to Freedom* (Back Bay Books; 1994)

Niall Whelehan, *The Dynamiters: Irish Nationalism and Political Violence in the Wider World 1867–1900* (Cambridge University Press; 2012)

Nicholas Blanford, *Warriors of God: Inside Hezbollah's Thirty-Year Struggle Against Israel* (Random House; 2011)

Nick Crossley and John Krinsky (eds.), *Social Networks and Social Movements: Contentious Connections* (Routledge; 2015)

Nigel Gibson (ed.), *Living Fanon: Global Perspectives* (Palgrave MacMillan; 2011)

Nils Melzer, *Interpretive Guidance on the Notion of Direct Participation in Hostilities*, International Committee of the Red Cross (May 2009)

Nils Melzer, *Targeted Killings in International Law* (2009)

Noam Lubell, *Extraterritorial Use of Force Against Non-State Actors* (Oxford University Press; 2011)

Noel Malcolm, *Bosnia: A Short History* (New York University Press; 1996)

Omar Ashour, *The Radicalization of Jihadists: Transforming Armed Islamist Movements* (Routledge; 2009)

P. W. Singer, *Wired for War: The Robotics Revolution and Conflict in the 21$^{st}$ Century* (Penguin Books; 2009)

Pablo Brum, *The Robin Hood Guerrillas: The Epic Journey of Uruguay's Tupamaros* (CreateSpace; 2014)

Paddy Hillyard, *Suspect Community: People's Experience of the Prevention of Terrorism Acts in Britain* (Pluto Press; 1993)

Paige Whaley Eager, *From Freedom Fighters to Terrorists: Women and Political Violence* (Routledge; 2016)

Patrick Bishop, *The Reckoning: How the Killing of One Man Changed the Fate of the Promised Land* (William Collins; 2014)

Patrick Tyler, *Fortress Israel: The Inside Story of the Military Elite Who Run the Country — and Why They Can't Make Peace* (Farrar, Straus and Giroux; 2012)

Paul Aussaresses, *The Battle of the Casbah: Terrorism and Counterterrorism in Algeria 1955–1957* (Enigma Books; 2002)

Paul Avrich, *The Haymarket Tragedy* (Princeton University Press; 1986)

Paul Gilbert, *Human Nature and Suffering* (Lawrence Erlbaum Associates; 1989)

Paul Henissart, *Wolves in the City: The Death of French Algeria* (Simon and Schuster; 1970)

Paul Kennedy, *Preparing for the Twenty-First Century* (Random House; 1993)

Paul Lewis, *Guerrillas and Generals: the "Dirty War" in Argentina* (Praeger; 2001)

Paul Wilkinson, *Terrorism and Democracy: The Liberal State Response* (Routledge; 2006)

Paul Wilkinson, *Terrorism and the Liberal State* (New York University Press; 1986)

Peter Bergen, *The Longest War: The Enduring Conflict between America and Al-Qaeda* (Free Press; 2011)

Peter Bergen, *United States of Jihad: Investigating America's Homegrown Terrorists* (Crown; 2016)

Peter Birks, *Criminal Justice and Human Rights: Reforming the Criminal Justice System* (Oxford University Press; 1995)

Peter Katzenstein (ed.), *The Culture of National Security* (Columbia University Press; 1996)

Peter Neumann, *Britain's Long War: British Strategy in the Northern Ireland Conflict 1969–1998* (Palgrave; 2003)

Peter Romaniuk, *Multilateral Counter-Terrorism: The Global Politics of Cooperation and Contestation* (Routledge; 2010)

Peter Taylor, *Brits* (Bloomsbury; 2001)

Peter Taylor, *Provos: The IRA & Sinn Féin* (Bloomsbury; 1997)

Philip Alston, *Non-State Actors and Human Rights* (Oxford University Press; 2005)

Philip Heymann and Juliette Kayyem, *Protecting Liberty in an Age of Terror* (MIT Press; 2005)

Philip Heymann, *Terrorism, Freedom, and Security: Winning Without War* (Belfer Center Studies in International Security; 2004)

Philip Keefer and Norman Loayza (eds.), *Terrorism, Economic Development, and Political Openness* (Cambridge University Press; 2008)

Philip Pomper, *Sergei Nechaev* (Rutgers; 1979)

Philip Willan, *Puppetmasters: The Political Use of Terrorism in Italy* (Constable; 1991)

Philip Zimbardo, *The Lucifer Effect: Understanding How Good People Turn Evil* (Random House; 2007)

Pierre Vidal-Naquet, *Torture: Cancer of democracy. France and Algeria 1954–1962* (Penguin; 1963)

Rachel Rudolf and Anisseh Van Engeland, *From Terrorism to Politics* (Ashgate Publishing; 2013)

Randall Law (ed.), *The Routledge History of Terrorism* (Routledge; 2015)

Rashid Khalidi, *Palestinian Identity: The Construction of Modern National Consciousness* (Columbia University Press; 1997)

Raul Caruso and Andrea Locatelli (eds.), *Understanding Terrorism: A Socio-Economics Perspective* (Emerald Group Publishing Ltd; 2014)

Raymond Gillespie Frey and Christopher Morris (eds.), *Violence, Terrorism, and Justice* (Cambridge University Press; 1991)

Raymond Ibrahim, *The Al-Qaeda Reader, The Essential Texts of Osama Bin Laden's Terrorist Organization* (Broadway Books; 2007)

Reg Carr, *Anarchism in France: The Case of Octave Mirabeau* (McGill — Queen's University Press; 1977)

Richard Bach Jensen, *The Battle against Anarchist Terrorism: An International History, 1878–1934* (Cambridge University Press; 2014)

Richard English, *Armed Struggle: The History of the IRA* (Oxford University Press, 2003)

Richard Jackson and Samuel Sinclair (eds.), *Contemporary Debates on Terrorism* (Routledge; 2012)

Richard Jenkins, *Social Identity* (Routledge; 1996)

Richard Mitchell, *The Society of the Muslim Brothers* (Oxford University Press; 1969)

Richard Pipes, *The Degaev Affair: Terror and Treason in Tsarist Russia* (Yale University Press; 2003)

Richard Rubenstein, *Alchemists of Revolution: Terrorism in the Modern World* (Basic Books; 1987)

Richard Schwing and Walter Albers (eds.), *Societal Risk Management: How Safe is Safe Enough?* (Plenum; 1980)

Robert Art and Louise Richardson (eds.), *Democracy and Counterterrorism: Lessons from the Past* (United States Institute of Peace; 2007)

Robert Clark, *The Basque Insurgents: ETA 1952–1980* (University of Wisconsin Press; 1984)

Robert Kee, *The Green Flag: A History of Irish Nationalism* (Penguin, London; 2000)

Robert Lambert, *Countering Al-Qaeda in London: Police and Muslims in Partnership* (Hurst and Company; 2011)

Robert Lee, *Overcoming Tradition and Modernity: The Search for Islamic Authenticity* (Westview Press; 1997)

Robert Meade, *Red Brigades: The Story of Italian Terrorism* (Palgrave Macmillan; 1990)

Robert Pape and James Feldman, *Cutting the Fuse: The Explosion of Global Suicide Terrorism and How to Stop it* (University of Chicago Press; 2010)

Robert Pape, *Dying to Win: The Strategic Logic of Suicide Terrorism* (Random House; 2005)

Robert Taber, *The War of the Flea: How Guerrilla Fighters Could Win the World!* (Citadel Press; 1970)

Robert Trojanowicz and Bonnie Bucqueroux, *Community Policing: A Contemporary Perspective* (Anderson Publishing; 1990)

Robin Wagner-Pacifici, *The Moro Morality Play: Terrorism as Social Drama* (University of Chicago; 1986)

Rodney Barker, *Political Legitimacy and the State* (Clarendon Press; 1990)

Roger Trinquier, *Modern Warfare: A French View of Counterinsurgency* (Praeger Security International; 2006)

Ronald Clark, *Lenin* (Harper & Row, 1988)

Ronald Crelinsten and Alex Schmid (eds.), *Western Responses to Terrorism* (Frank Cass & Co.; 1993)

Ronald Seth, *The Russian Terrorists* (Barrie and Rockliff; 1966)

Rosemarie Skaine, *Suicide Warfare: Culture, the Military, and the Individual as a Weapon* (Praeger; 2013)

Roxanne Euben and Muhammad Qasim Zaman (eds.), *Princeton Readings in Islamist Thought: Texts and Contexts from Al-Banna to Bin Laden* (Princeton University Press; 2009)

Roy C. Macridis and Bernard Brown, (eds.), *Comparative Politics: Notes and Readings* (Harcourt Brace College Publishers; 1996)

Ruhollah Khomeini, *Islam and Revolution: Writings and Declarations of Imam Khomeini* (Mizan Press; 1981)

Rupert Allason, *The Branch: History of the Metropolitan Police Special Branch, 1883–1983* (Secker and Warburg; 1983)

Rupert Brown and Sam Gaertner (eds.), *Blackwell Handbook of Social Psychology: Intergroup Processes* (Wiley-Blackwell; 2000)

Ruth Dudley Edwards, *The Seven: The Lives and Legacies of the Founding Fathers of the Irish Republic* (Oneworld Publications; 2016)

Sam Keen, *Faces of the Enemy: Reflections of the Hostile Imagination* (Harpercollins; 1991)

Samuel Huntington, *Political Order in Changing Societies* (Yale University Press; 1969)

Samuel Huntington, *The Clash of Civilizations and the Remaking of the World Order* (Simon and Schuster; 1996)

Saul David, *Operation Thunderbolt: Flight 139 and the raid on Entebbe Airport, the most audacious hostage rescue in history* (Little, Brown and Company; 2015)

Scott Atran, *Talking to the Enemy: Faith, Brotherhood and the (Un)making of Terrorists* (Ecco; 2010)

Scott Miller, *The President and the Assassin: McKinley, Terror, and Empire at the Dawn of the American Century* (Random House; 2011)

Sean MacStiofain, *Memoirs of a Revolutionary* (Gordon & Cremonesi; 1975)

Shaul Bartal, *Jihad in Palestine: Political Islam and the Israeli-Palestinian Conflict* (Routledge; 2015)

Shaul Mishal and Avraham Sela, *The Palestinian Hamas: Vision, Violence, and Coexistence* (Columbia University Press; 2006)

Siddik Ekici, Ahmet Ekici, David McEntire, Richard Ward, and Sudha Arlikatti (eds.), *Building Terrorism Resistant Communities: Together Against Terrorism* (IOS Press; 2009)

Simon Reeve, *One Day in September: The Full Story of the 1972 Munich Olympics Massacre and the Israeli Revenge Operation "Wrath of God"* (Arcade Publishing; 2000)

Simon Sebag Montefiore, *Young Stalin* (Weidenfeld and Nicolson; 2007)

Stanley Milgram, *Obedience to Authority* (Harper and Row; 1974)

Stefan Aust, *Baader-Meinhof: The Inside Story of the R.A.F.* (Oxford University Press; 2009)

Stephen Vertigans, *Terrorism and Societies* (Routledge; 2008)

Steve Coll, *The Bin Ladens: An Arabian Family in the American Century* (The Penguin Press; 2008)

Steve Hendricks, *A Kidnapping in Milan: The CIA on Trial* (W. W. Norton & Company; 2010)

Strobe Talbot, Nyan Chanda, and John Lewis Gaddis, *The Age of Terror: America and the World After September 11* (Basic Books; 202)

Stuart Gottlieb (ed.), *Debating Terrorism and Counterterrorism: Conflicting Perspectives on Causes, Contexts, and Responses* (CQ Press; 2010)

Takie Sugiyama Lebra, *Japanese Social Organization* (University of Hawaii Press; 1992)

Ted Gurr, *Why Men Rebel* (Princeton University Press; 1970)

Teresa Whitfield, *Endgame for ETA: Elusive Peace in the Basque Country* (Oxford University Press; 2014)

Terry Eagleton, *Ideology: An Introduction* (Verso; 1991)

Thomas Kiernan, *Arafat: The Man and the Myth* (W. W. Norton & Co.; 1976)

Tim Pat Coogan, *1916: The Easter Uprising* (Cassell; 2002)

Tom Tyler and Yuen Huo, *Trust in the Law: Encouraging Public Cooperation with the Police and Courts* (Russell Sage Foundation Series on Trust; 2002)

Tom Vague, *The Televisionaries: The Red Army Faction Story, 1963–1993* (AK Press; 2001)

Tom Williamson, Becky Milne and Stephen Savage, *International Developments in Investigative Interviewing* (Routledge; 2009)

Tony Walker and Andrew Gowers, *Arafat: The Biography* (Virgin Books; 2003)

Tore Bjørgo (ed.), *Root Causes of Terrorism: Myth, Reality and Ways Forward* (Routledge; 2005)

Tore Bjørgo and John Horgan, *Leaving Terrorism Behind: Individual and Collective Disengagement* (Routledge; 2008)

Travis Hirschi, *Causes of Delinquency* (University of California Press; 1969)

Ulick O'Connor, *Michael Collins and the Troubles: The Struggle for Irish Freedom 1912–1922* (W. W. Norton & Company; 1996)

Vera Figner, *Memoirs of a Revolutionist* (Northern Illinois University Press; 1991)

Virginia Comolli, *Boko Haram: Nigeria's Islamist Insurgency* (C. Hurst & Co.; 2015)

Wael Ghonim, *Revolution 2.0: The Power of the People is Greater Than the People in Power* (Houghton Mifflin; 2012)

Walter Garrison Runciman, *Relative Deprivation and Social Justice: A Study of Attitudes to Social Inequality in Twentieth-Century England* (Routledge and Kegan Paul; 1966)

Walter Laqueur, (ed.), *Voices of Terror: Manifestos, Writings, and Manuals of Al Qaeda, Hamas, and other Terrorists from around the World and Throughout the Ages* (Sourcebooks Inc.; 2004)

Walter Laqueur, *Terrorism* (Widenfeld and Nicholson; 1977)

William A. Tidwell, *April '65: Confederate Covert Action in the American Civil War* (Kent State University Press; 1995)

William E. Dyson, *Terrorism: An Investigator's Handbook* (Anderson; 2011)

Yaacov Eliav, *Wanted* (Shengold Publishers; 1984)

Yezid Sayigh, *Armed Struggle and the Search for State, the Palestinian National Movement 1949–1993* (Oxford University Press; 1997)

Yiannos Katsourides, *The Greek Cypriot Nationalist Right in the Era of British Colonialism: Emergence, Mobilisation and Transformations of Right-Wing Party Politics* (Springer; 2017)

Yigal Allon, *Shield of David: The Story of Israel's Armed Forces* (Weidenfield and Nicolson; 1970) at 235

Yitzhak Shamir, *Summing Up: An Autobiography* (Weidenfeld and Nicolson; 1994)

Yonah Alexander and Alan O'Day, *Terrorism in Ireland* (Palgrave Macmillan; 1984)

Yoram Dinstein, *The Conduct of Hostilities Under the Law of International Armed Conflict* (Cambridge University Press; 2004)

Yoram Dinstein, *War, Aggression and Self-Defence* (Cambridge University Press; 2011)

Yuen Foong Khong, *Analogies At War: Korea, Munich, Dien Bien Phu, and the Vietnam Decisions of 1965* (Princeton University Press; 1992)

Yuval Ginbar, *Why Not Torture Terrorists? Moral, Practical, and Legal Aspects of the 'Ticking Bomb' Justification for Torture* (Oxford University Press; 2010)

## Articles

Aaron Mannes, *Testing The Snake Head Strategy: Does Killing or Capturing its Leaders Reduce a Terrorist Group's Activity?*, Journal of International Policy Solutions, Vol. 9 (Spring 2008)

Adam Majid, *The Unabomber Revisited: Reexamining the Use of Mental Disorder Diagnoses as Evidence of the Mental Condition of Criminal Defendants*, Indiana Law Journal Supplement, Vol. 84, No. 1 (2009)

Al Gore, *The Politics of Fear*, Social Research, Vol. 71, No. 4 (Winter 2004)

Alan Elms, *From House to Haig: Private Life and Public Style in American Foreign Policy Advisers*, Journal of Social Issues, Vol. 42, No. 2 (Summer 1986)

Alan Krueger and Jitka Malečková, *Education, Poverty, Political Violence, and Terrorism: Is There a Causal Connection?*, Journal of Economic Perspectives, Vol. 17, No.4 (Fall 2003)

Alan Krueger, *What Makes a Homegrown Terrorist? Human Capital and Participation in Domestic Islamic Terrorist Groups in the USA*, Economics Letters, Vol. 101, No. 3 (December 2008)

Aldert Vrij, Samantha Mann, Ronald Fisher, Sharon Leal, Rebecca Milne and Ray Bull, *Increasing Cognitive Load to Facilitate Lie Detection: The Benefit of Recalling an Event in Reverse Order*, Law and Human Behavior, Vol. 32 (2008)

Alex Wilner, *Targeted Killings in Afghanistan: Measuring Coercion and Deterrence in Counterterrorism and Counterinsurgency*, Studies in Conflict and Terrorism, Vol. 33, No. 4 (2010)

Alexander Lee, *Who Becomes a Terrorist? Poverty, Education, and the Origins of Political Violence*, World Politics, Vol. 63, No. 2 (April 2011)

Alison Jamieson, *Entry, Discipline and Exit in the Italian Red Brigades*, Terrorism and Political Violence, Vol. 2, No. 1 (1990)

Alison Jamieson, *Identity and Morality in the Italian Red Brigades*, Terrorism and Political Violence, Vol. 2, No. 4 (1990)

Andrea Kohn Maikovich, *A New Understanding of Terrorism Using Cognitive Dissonance Principles*, Journal for the Theory of Social Behaviour, Vol. 35, No. 4 (2005)

Andrew Liepman and Philip Mudd, *Lessons from the Fifteen-Year Counterterrorism Campaign*, CTC Sentinel, Vol. 9, No. 10 (October 2016)

Andrew Silke, *Cheshire-cat Logic: The Recurring Theme of Terrorist Abnormality in Psychological Research*, Psychology, Crime and the Law, Vol. 4, No. 1 (January 1998)

Annette Linden and Bert Klandermans, *Stigmatization and Repression of Extreme-Right Activism in the Netherlands*, Mobilization: An International Journal, Vol. 11, No. 2 (June 2006)

Anthony Oberschall, *Explaining Terrorism: The Contribution of Collective Action Theory*, Sociological Theory, Vol. 22, No. 1 (March 2004)

Arie Kruglanski, Michele Gelfand, Jocelyn Bélanger, Anna Sheveland, Malkanthi Hetiarachchi, and Rohan Gunaratna, *The Psychology of Radicalization and Deradicalization: How Significance Quest Impacts Violent Extremism*, Advances in Political Psychology, Vol. 35, Suppl. 1 (2014)

Aristide Zolberg, *Moments of Madness*, Politics and Society, Vol. 2 (Winter 1972)

Assaf Moghadam, *Failure and Disengagement in the Red Army Faction*, Studies in Conflict and Terrorism, Vol. 35, No. 2 (2012)

Assem Nasr, *An Historical Perspective on Fundamentalist Media: The Case of Al-Manar Television*, Global Media Journal, Vol. 6, No. 11 (Fall 2007)

Audrey Kurth Cronin, *Behind the Curve: Globalization and International Terrorism*, International Security, Vol. 27, No. 3 (Winter 2002–2003)

Audrey Kurth Cronin, *Why Drones Fail: When Tactics Drive Strategy*, Foreign Affairs, July/August 2013

Austin Turk, *Social Dynamics of Terrorism*, Annals of the American Academy of Political and Social Science, Vol. 463, No. 1 (September 1982)

Bader Araj, *Harsh State Repression as a Cause of Suicide Bombing: The Case of the Palestinian-Israeli Conflict*, Studies in Conflict and Terrorism, Vol. 31 (2008)

Ben Saul, *The Legal Response of the League of Nations to Terrorism*, Symposium on Contributions to the History of the International Criminal Justice, Journal of International Criminal Justice, Vol. 4 (2006)

Benjamin Friedman, *Leap before You Look*, Breakthroughs, Vol. 3, No. 1 (Spring 2004)

Benjamin Friedman, *Managing Fear: The Politics of Homeland Security*, Political Science Quarterly, Vol. 126, No. 1 (2011)

Benjamin Grob-Fitzgibbon, *From the Dagger to the Bomb: Karl Heinzen and the Evolution of Political Terror*, Terrorism and Political Violence, Vol. 16, No. 1 (Spring 2004)

Brett Litz, Nathan Stein, Eileen Delaney, Leslie Lebowitz, William Nash, Caroline Silva, and Shira Maguen, *Moral Injury and Moral Repair in War Veterans: A Preliminary Model and Intervention Strategy*, Clinical Psychology Review, Vol. 29 (2009)

Brian Burgoon, *On Welfare and Terror: Social Welfare Policies and Political-Economic Roots of Terrorism*, Journal of Conflict Resolution, Vol. 50, No. 2 (April 2006)

Brian Burridge, *UAVs and the Dawn of Post-Modern Warfare: A Perspective on Recent Operations*, Royal United Services Institute Journal (October 2003)

Brigadier Dr S. P. Sinha, *Unmasking of Prabhakaran*, Indian Defence Review, Vol. 17, No. 2 (April–June 2002)

Bruce Berman, *Bureaucracy and Incumbent Violence: Colonial Administration and the Origins of the "Mau Mau" Emergency in Kenya*, British Journal of Political Science, Vol. 6, No. 2 (April 1976)

Bruce MacFarlane, *Convicting the Innocent: A Triple Failure of the Justice System*, Manitoba Law Journal, Vol. 31, No. 3 (2006)

Bryan Price, *Targeting Top Terrorists: How Leadership Decapitation Contributes to Counterterrorism*, International Security, Vol. 36, No. 4 (Spring 2012)

Charles Portal, *Air Force Co-operation in Policing the Empire*, RUSI Journal, Vol. 82 (1937)

Charles Ruby, *Are Terrorists Mentally Deranged?*, Analysis of Social Issues and Public Policy, Vol. 2, No. 1 (December 2002)

Charles Tilly, *Terror, Terrorism and Terrorists*, Sociological Theory, Vol. 22, No. 1 (March 2004)

Charles Townshend, *The Defence of Palestine: Insurrection and Public Security 1936–1939*, The English Historical Review, Vol. 103, No. 409 (October 1988)

Chris Jochnick, *Confronting the Impunity of Non-State Actors: New Fields for the Promotion of Human Rights*, Human Rights Quarterly, Vol. 21 (1999)

Christopher Angevine, *The Vanguard: The Genesis and Substance of al-Qaeda's. Conception of Itself and its Mission*, Yale Journal of International Affairs, Vol. 3, No. 1 (Winter 2008)

Christopher Cradock and M. L. R. Smith, *No Fixed Values: A Reinterpretation of the Influence of the Theory of Guerre Révolutionnaire and the Battle of Algiers 1956–1957*, Journal of Cold War Studies, Vol. 9, No. 4 (Fall 2007)

Christopher Harmon, *The Myth of the Invincible Terrorist*, Policy Review, Hoover Institution, (1 April 2007)

Cindy Jebb, *The Fight for Legitimacy: Liberal Democracy Versus Terrorism*, Journal of Conflict Studies, Vol. 23, No. 1 (2003)

Clark McCauley and Sophia Moskalenko, *Mechanisms of Political Radicalization: Pathways Toward Terrorism*, Journal of Terrorism and Political Violence, Vol. 20, No. 3 (July 2008)

Claude Berrebi, *Evidence About the Link Between Education, Poverty and Terrorism Among Palestinians*, Peace Economics, Peace Science and Public Policy, Vol. 13, No. 1 (2007)

Colin Clarke, Rebecca Milne and Ray Bull, *Interviewing Suspects of Crime: The Impact of PEACE Training, Supervision and the Presence of a Legal Adviser*, Journal of Investigative Psychology and Offender Profiling, Vol. 8 (2011)

Cyrus Zirakzadeh, *From Revolutionary Dreams to Organizational Fragmentation: Disputes over Violence within ETA and Sendero Luminoso*, Journal of Terrorism and Political Violence, Vol. 14, No. 4 (2002)

Daniel Bessner and Michael Stauch, *Karl Heinzen and the Intellectual Origins of Modern Terror*, Terrorism and Political Violence, Vol. 22 (2010)

Daniel Byman, *Taliban vs. Predator: Are Targeted Killings Inside Pakistan a Good Idea?*, Foreign Affairs (August 2009)

Daniel Egiegba Agbiboa, *Living in Fear: Religious Identity, Relative Deprivation and the Boko Haram Terrorism*, African Security, Vol. 6, No. 2 (May 2013)

David Fromkin, The Strategy of Terrorism, *Foreign Affairs*, Vol. 53, No. 4 (July 1975)

David George, *Distinguishing Classical Tyrannicide from Modern Terrorism*, The Review of Politics, Vol. 50, No. 3 (Summer 1988)

David Moss, *The Gift of Repentance: A Maussian Perspective on Twenty Years of Pentimento in Italy*, European Journal of Sociology, Vol. 42, No. 2 (2001)

David Snow, E. Burke Rochford, Steven Worden, and Robert Benford, *Frame Alignment Processes, Micromobilization, and Movement Participation*, American Sociological Review, Vol. 51, No.4 (August 1986)

David Snow, Louis Zurcher, and Sheldon Ekland-Olson, *Social Networks and Social Movements: A Microstructural Approach to Differential Recruitment*, American Sociological Review, Vol. 45, No. 5 (1980)

Denis O'Hearn, *Catholic Grievances, Catholic Nationalism: A Comment*, British Journal of Sociology, Vol. 34, No. 3 (September 1983)

Derek Birrel, *Relative Deprivation as a Factor in Conflict in Northern Ireland*, Sociological Review, Vol. 20, No. 3 (1972)

Diego Gambetta and Steffen Hertog, *Why are There so Many Engineers among Islamic Radicals?*, European Journal of Sociological, Vol. 50, No. 2 (August 2009)

Donald Jackson, *Prevention of Terrorism: The United Kingdom Confronts the European Convention on Human Rights*, Journal of Terrorism and Political Violence, Vol. 6, No. 4 (Winter 1994)

Donatella Della Porta, *Institutional Responses to Terrorism: The Italian Case*, Terrorism and Political Violence (Winter 1992) at 167

Donatella Della Porta, *Introduction: On Individual Motivations in Underground Political Organizations*, International Social Movement Research, Vol. 4 (1992)

Donatella Della Porta, *Political Socialization in Left-Wing Underground Organizations: Biographies of Italian and German Militants*, International Social Movement Research, Vol. 4 (1992)

Donatella Della Porta, *Recruitment Processes in Clandestine Political Organizations: Italian Left-Wing Terrorism*, International Social Movement Research, Vol. 1 (1988)

Doug McAdam, *Recruitment to High-Risk Activism: The Case of Freedom Summer*, American Journal of Sociology, Vol. 92, No. 1 (1986)

Douglas Burgess, *The Dread Pirate Bin Laden: How Thinking of Terrorists as Pirates Can Help Win the War on Terror*, Legal Affairs, 23 June 2005

Edward Muller, *Income Inequality, Regime Repressiveness, and Political Violence*, American Sociological Review, Vol. 50, No.1 (1985)

Ehud Sprinzak, *Rational Fanatics*, Foreign Affairs, 1 September 2000

Elizabeth Loftus and John Palmer, *Reconstruction of Automobile Destruction: An Example of the Interaction Between Language and Memory*, Journal of Verbal Learning and Verbal Behavior, Vol. 13 (1974)

Eric Neumayer, *Good Policy Can Lower Violent Crime: Evidence from a Cross-National Panel of Homicide Rates, 1980–97*, Journal of Peace Research, Vol. 40, No. 6 (2003)

Eric Shepherd, *Ethical Interviewing*, Policing, Vol. 7 (1991)

Erich Weede, *Some New Evidence on Correlates of Political Violence; Income Inequality, Regime Repressiveness, and Economic Development*, European Sociological Review, Vol. 3, No. 2 (September 1987)

Erin Steuter and Deborah Wills, *Discourses of Dehumanization: Enemy Construction and Canadian Media Complicity in the Framing of the War on Terror*, Global Media Journal (Canadian Edition), Vol. 2, No. 2 (2009)

Ethan Bueno de Mesquita and Eric Dickson, *The Propaganda of the Deed: Terrorism, Counterterrorism, and Mobilization*, American Journal of Political Science, Vol. 51, No. 2 (April 2007)

Ethan Bueno de Mesquita, *Politics and the Suboptimal Provision of Counterterror*, International Organization, Vol. 61, No. 1 (2007)

Ethan Bueno de Mesquita, *The Political Economy of Terrorism: A Selective Overview of Recent Work*, The Political Economist (March 2008)

Ethan Bueno de Mesquita, *The Quality of Terror*, American Journal of Political Science, Vol. 49, No. 3 (2005)

Evan Wallach, *Drop by Drop: Forgetting the History of Water Torture in U.S. Courts*, Columbia Journal of Transnational Law, Vol. 45, No.2 (2007)

Fathali Moghaddam, *The Staircase to Terrorism: A Psychological Exploration*, American Psychologist, Vol. 60, No. 2 (February–March 2005)

Fernando Reinares, *Exit from Terrorism: A Qualitative Empirical Study on Disengagement and Deradicalization Among Members of ETA*, Journal of Terrorism and Political Violence, Vol. 23, No. 5 (2011)

Floris Vermeulen, *Suspect Communities — Targeting Violent Extremism at the Local Level: Policies of Engagement in Amsterdam, Berlin, and London*, Terrorism and Political Violence, Vol. 26, No. 2 (2014)

G. Davidson Smith, *Canada's Counter-Terrorism Experience*, Terrorism and Political Violence, Vol. 5, No. 1 (Spring 1993)

Gary Becker, *Crime and Punishment: An Economic Approach*, Journal of Political Economy, Vol. 76, No. 2 (March/April 1968)

George Kelling and James Wilson, *Broken Windows: The Police and Neighborhood Safety*, The Atlantic, March 1982

George Kennan, *The Sources of Soviet Conduct*, Foreign Affairs, July 1947

Geraldine Downey, Scott Feldman, and Ozlem Ayduk, *Rejection sensitivity and male violence in romantic relationships*, Personal Relationships, Vol. 7 (2000)

Gilda Zwerman, Patricia Steinhoff, and Donatella Della Porta, *Disappearing Social Movements: Clandestinity in the Cycle of New Left Protest in the US, Japan, Germany, and Italy*, Mobilization: An International Journal, Vol. 5, No. 1 (2000)

Halil Karaveli, *Turkey's Decline: Ankara Must Learn from Its Past to Secure Its Future*, Foreign Affairs, 2 March 2016

Hans Baade, *The Eichmann Trial: Some Legal Aspects*, Duke Law Journal, Vol. 10, No. 3 (1961)

Heidi Ellis and Saida Abdi, Building Community Resilience to Violent Extremism through Genuine Partnerships, *American Psychologists*, Vol. 72, No. 3 (2017)

Helen Ware, *Demography, Migration and Conflict in the Pacific*, Journal of Peace Research, Vol. 42, No. 4 (July 2005)

Henrik Urdal, *A Clash of Generations? Youth Bulges and Political Violence*, International Studies Quarterly, Vol. 50, No. 3 (2006)

Henry Patterson, *Gerry Adams and the Modernisation of Republicanism*, Conflict Quarterly (Summer 1990)

Herbert Moeller, *Youth as a Force in the Modern World*, Comparative Studies in Society and History, Vol. 10, No. 3 (April 1968)

Herminia Ibarra, *Personal Networks of Women and Minorities in Management: A Conceptual Framework*, Academy of Management Review, Vol. 18, No. 1 (1993)

Ian Wood, The IRA's Border Campaign 1956–1962, in Malcolm Anderson and Eberhard Bort, *The Irish Border: History, Politics, Culture* (Liverpool University Press; 1999)

J. B. Bell, *Terrorist Scripts and Live-Action Spectaculars*, Columbia Journalism Review (May–June 1978)

Jac Weller, *Irregular But Effective: Partizan Weapons Tactics in the American Revolution, Southern Theatre*, Military Affairs, Vol. 21, No. 3 (Autumn 1957)

James Brandon, *The Danger of Prison: Radicalization in the West*, CTC Sentinel, Vol. 2, No. 12 (December 2009)

James Fearon and David Laitin, *Ethnicity, Insurgency and Civil War*, American Political Science Review, Vol. 97, No. 1 (2003)

James Hughes, *Frank Kitson in Northern Ireland and the 'British way' of counterinsurgency*, History Ireland, Vol. 22, No. 1 (January/February 2014)

James Hughes, *State Violence in the Origins of Nationalism: The British Reinvention of Irish Nationalism 1969–1972*, Paper for the Nationalism and War Workshop McGill University, Montreal, 24–26 March 2011

James Marcia, *Development and Validation of Ego Identity Status*, Journal of Personality and Social Psychology, Vol. 3, No. 5 (1966)

James Piazza, *Incubators of Terror: Do Failed and Failing States Promote Transnational Terrorism?*, International Studies Quarterly, Vol. 52, No. 3 (2008)

James Piazza, *Poverty, Minority Economic Discrimination, and Domestic Terrorism*, Journal of Peace Research, Vol. 48, No. 3 (March 2011)

James Piazza, *Rooted in Poverty? Terrorism, Poor Economic Development, and Social Cleavages*, Terrorism and Political Violence, Vol. 18, No. 1 (2006)

Jamie Bartlett and Carl Miller, *The Edge of Violence: Towards Telling the Difference Between Violent and Non-Violent Radicalization*, Terrorism and Political Violence, Vol. 24, No. 1 (2012)

János Béres, *The Birth of Modern Terrorism in Europe*, AARMS, Vol. 6, No. 3 (2007)

Janusz Zawodny, *Internal Organizational Problems and the Sources of Tensions of Terrorist Movements as Catalysts of Violence*, Terrorism, Vol. 1, No. 3 (1978)

Jarret Brachman and William McCants, *Stealing Al Qaeda's Playbook*, Studies in Conflict and Terrorism, Vol. 29, No. 4 (June 2006)

Jean-Paul Azam and Alexandra Delacroix, *Aid and the Delegated Fight Against Terrorism*, Review of Development Economics, Vol. 10, No. 2 (2006)

Jean-Paul Azam, *Suicide-Bombing as Inter-Generational Investment*, Public Choice, Vol. 122, No. 1 (2005)

Jeffrey Handler, *Socioeconomic Profile of an American Terrorist: 1960s and 1970s*, Terrorism, Vol. 13, No. 3 (1990)

Jeffrey Ross and Ted Gurr, *Why Terrorism Subsides: A Comparative Study of Canada and the United States*, Comparative Politics, Vol. 21, No. 4 (July 1989)

Jeffrey Ross, *Structural Causes of Oppositional Political Terrorism: Towards a causal model*, Journal of Peace Research, Vol. 30, No. 3 (1993)

Jeffrey Seul, *Ours is the Ways of God: Religion, Identity and Intergroup Conflict*, Journal of Peace Research, Vol. 36, No. 5 (1999)

Jenna Jordan, *When Heads Roll: Assessing the Leadership of Decapitation Strategies*, Security Studies, Vol. 18, No. 4 (2009)

Jennifer Bosson and Joseph Vandello, *Precarious Manhood and Its Links to Action and Aggression*, Current Directions in Psychological Science, Vol. 20, No. 2 (April 2011)

Jennifer Klinesmith, Tim Kasser, and Francis McAndrew, *Guns, Testosterone, and Aggression: An Experimental Test of a Mediational Hypothesis*, Psychological Science, Vol. 17, No. 7 (August 2006)

Jerrold Post, *Notes on a Psychodynamic Theory of Terrorist Behavior*, Terrorism, Vol. 7, No.3 (1984)

Jerrold Post, *The New Face of Terrorism: Socio-Cultural Foundations of Contemporary Terrorism*, Behavioral Sciences and the Law, Vol. 23, No. 4 (July/August 2005)

Jessica Stern, *Radicalization to Extremism and Mobilization to Violence: What Have We Learned and What Can We Do about It?*, The ANNALS of the American Academy of Political and Social Science, Vol. 668, No. 1 (November 2016)

Jessica Stern, *The Protean Enemy*, Foreign Affairs, July/August 2003

Joan Fitzpatrick, *Speaking Law to Power: The War against Terrorism and Human Rights*, European Journal of International Law, Vol. 14 (2003)

John Horgan and Kurt Braddock, *Rehabilitating the Terrorists?: Challenges in Assessing the Effectiveness of De-Radicalization Programs*, Journal of Terrorism and Political Violence, Vol. 22 (2010)

John Mueller, *The Truth about Al-Qaeda*, Foreign Affairs, 2 August 2011

John R. Galvin, *Uncomfortable Wars: Toward a New Paradigm*, Parameters (Winter 1986)

John Regan, *Looking at Mick Again; Demilitarising Michael Collins*, History Ireland, Vol. 3, No.3 (Autumn 1995)

Jordan Paust, *Use of Armed Force against Terrorists in Afghanistan, Iraq, and Beyond*, Cornell International Law Journal, Vol. 35, No.3 (2002)

Karima Bennoune, *Terror/Torture*, Berkeley Journal of International Law, Vol. 26, No. 1 (2008)

Karl Roberts, *Police Interviewing of Criminal Suspects: A Historical Perspective*, Internet Journal of Criminology (2012)

Karl-Dieter Opp and Wolfgang Roehl, *Repression, Micromobilization, and Political Protest*, Social Forces, Vol. 69, No. 2 (1990)

Karma Nabulsi, *Don't Go to the Doctor*, London Review of Books, Vol. 39, No. 10 (18 May 2017)

Kathleen Carley, *A Theory of Group Stability*, American Sociological Review, Vol. 56, No. 3 (1991)

Keith Brown, *The King is Dead, Long Live the Balkans! Watching the Marseilles Murders of 1934*, Delivered at the Sixth Annual World Convention of the Association for the Study of Nationalities, Columbia University, 5–7 April 2001

Keith Dear, *Beheading the Hydra? Does Killing Terrorist or Insurgent Leaders Work?*, Defence Studies, Vol. 13, No. 3 (2013)

Ken Heskin, *Terrorism in Ireland: The Past and Future*, Irish Journal of Psychology, Vol. 15, No. 2–3 (1994)

Ken Menkhaus, *Quasi-States, Nation-Building and Terrorist Safe Havens*, Journal of Conflict Studies, Vol. 23, No. 2 (2007)

Kenneth Rodman, *Think Globally, Punish Locally*, Ethics & International Affairs, Vol. 12 (1998)

Kipling Williams, *Ostracism*, Annual Review of Psychology, Vol. 58 (2007)

Laura Donohue, *The Dawn of Social Intelligence (SOCINT)*, Drake Law Review, Vol. 63 (2015)

Laurence Alison, Emily Alison, Geraldine Noone, Stamatis Elntib and Paul Christiansen, *Why Tough Tactics Fail and Rapport Gets Results: Observing Rapport-Based Interpersonal Techniques (ORBIT) to Generate Useful Information From Terrorists*, Psychology, Public Policy and Law, Vol. 19, No. 4 (2013)

Laurence Alison and Emily Alison, *Revenge Versus Rapport: Interrogation, Terrorism, and Torture*, American Psychologist, Vol. 72, No. 3 (2017)

Lindsay Clutterbuck, *The Progenitors of Terrorism: Russian Revolutionaries or Extreme Irish Republicans?*, Journal of Terrorism and Political Violence, Vol. 16, No. 1 (2004)

Lorne Dawson and Amarnath Amarasingam, *Talking to Foreign Fighters: Insights in to the Motivations for Hijrah to Syria and Iraq*, Studies in Conflict and Terrorism, Vol. 40, No. 3 (2017)

Lou DiMarco, *Losing the Moral Compass: Torture and Guerre Revolutionnaire in the Algerian War*, Parameters, Vol. 36, No. 2 (Summer 2006)

Manfred Frings, *Max Scheler and the Psychopathology of the Terrorist*, Modern Age, Vol. 47, No. 3 (Summer 2005)

Manus Midlarksy, *Rulers and Ruled: Patterned Inequality and the Onset of Mass Political Violence*, American Political Science Review, Vol. 82, No. 2 (June 1988)

Manus Midlarsky, Martha Crenshaw and Fumihiko Yoshida, *Why Violence Spreads: The Contagion of International Terrorism*, International Studies Quarterly, Vol. 24, No. 2 (June 1980)

Marco Pinfari, *Exploring the Terrorist Nature of Political Assassinations: A Reinterpretation of the Orsini Attentat*, Terrorism and Political Violence, Vol. 21, No. 4 (2009)

Margo Wilson and Martin Daly, *Competitiveness, Risk Taking, and Violence: The Young Male Syndrome*, Ethology and Sociobiology, Vol. 6, No. 1 (1985)

Marie Fleming, *Propaganda by the Deed: Terrorism and Anarchist Theory in Late Nineteenth-Century Europe*, Terrorism: An International Journal, Vol. 4 (1980)

Mark Granovetter, *Economic Action and Social Structure: The Problem of Embeddedness*, American Journal of Sociology, Vol. 91, No. 3 (November 1985)

Mark Granovetter, *Threshold Models of Collective Behavior*, The American Journal of Sociology, Vol. 83, No. 6 (May 1978)

Mark Lichbach, *An Evaluation of "Does Economic Inequality Breed Political Conflict?" Studies*, World Politics, Vol. 41, No. 4 (July 1989)

Mark Lichbach, *Deterrence of Escalation? The Puzzle of Aggregate Studies of Repression and Dissent*, The Journal of Conflict Resolution, Vol. 31, No. 2 (1987)

Martha Crenshaw, *The Causes of Terrorism*, Comparative Politics, Vol. 13, No. 4 (1981)

Martha Crenshaw, *The Psychology of Terrorism: An Agenda for the 21$^{st}$ Century*, Political Psychology, Vol. 21, No. 2 (June 2000)

Martha Crenshaw, *Theories of Terrorism: Instrumental and Organizational Approaches*, Journal of Strategic Studies, Vol. 10, No. 4 (1987)

Mary Beth Altier, John Horgan and Christian Thoroughgood, *In Their Own Words? Methodological Considerations in the Analysis of Terrorist Autobiographies*, Journal of Strategic Security, Vol. 5, No. 4 (2012)

Mauricio Florez-Morris, *Joining Guerrilla Groups in Colombia: Individual Motivations and Processes for Entering a Violent Organization*, Studies in Conflict and Terrorism, Vol. 30, No. 7 (2007) at 615–634

Max Abrahms, *Does Terrorism Really Work? Evolution in the Conventional Wisdom Since 9/11*, Defence and Peace Economics, Vol. 22, No. 6 (2011)

Max Abrahms, *What Terrorists Really Want: Terrorist Motives and Counterterrorism strategy*, International Security, Vol. 32, No.4 (Spring 2008)

Michael Barkun, *Appropriated Martyrs: The Branch Davidians and the Radical Right*, Terrorism and Political Violence, Vol. 19, No. 1 (2007)

Michaël Confino, *Bakunin et Nečaev*, Cahiers du Monde Russe et Soviétique, Vol. 7, No. 4 (1966)

Michael Connelly, *Rethinking the Cold War and Decoloanlization: The Grand Strategy of the Algerian War of Independence*, International Journal of Middle Eastern Studies, Vol. 33, No. 2 (2001)

Michael Dartnell, *France's Action Directe: Terrorists in Search of a Revolution*, Journal of Terrorism and Political Violence, Vol. 2, No. 4 (1990)

Michael Ignatieff, *Is the Human Rights Era Ending?*, New York Times, 5 February 2002

Michael Kenney, *Beyond the Internet: Metis, Techne, and the Limitations of Online artifacts for Islamic Terrorists,* Journal of Terrorism and Political Violence, Vol. 22, No. 2 (2010)

Michael Munoz, *Selling the Long War: Islamic State Propaganda after the Caliphate,* CTC Sentinel, November 2018

Michael Scharf, *Case Analysis: The Prosecutor v. Slavko Dokmanovic. Irregular Rendition and the ICTY,* Leiden Journal of International Law, Vol. 11, No. 2 (1998)

Miller McPherson, Lynn Smith-Lovin, and James M. Cook, *Birds of a Feather: Homophily in Social Networks,* Annual Review of Sociology, Vol. 27, No. 1 (2001)

Mohammed Hafez and Joseph Hatfield, *Do Targeted Assassinations Work? A Multivariate Analysis of Israel's Controversial Tactic during Al-Aqsa Uprising,* Studies in Conflict and Terrorism, Vol. 29, No. 4 (June 2006)

Mohammed Hafez, *Rationality, Culture, and Structure in the Making of Suicide Bombers: A Preliminary Theoretical Synthesis and Illustrative Case Study,* Studies in Conflict and Terrorism, Vol. 29, No. 2 (2006)

Muhsin Hassan, *Understanding Drivers of Violent Extremism: The Case of Al-Shabaab and Somali Youth,* CTC Sentinel, Vol. 5, No. 8 (August 2012)

Norman Naimark, *Terrorism and the Fall of Imperial Russia,* Terrorism and Political Violence, Vol. 2, No. 2 (1990)

Nunzio Pernicone, *Luigi Galleani and Italian Anarchist Terrorism in the United States,* Studi Emigrazione, Vol. 30 (September 1993)

Omar Ashour, *De-Radicalization of Jihad? The Impact of Egyptian Islamist Revisionists on Al-Qaeda,* Perspectives on Terrorism, Vol. 2, No. 5 (2008)

Orin Starn, *Maoism in the Andes: The Communist Party of Peru–Shining Path and the Refusal of History,* Journal of Latin American Studies, Vol. 27, No. 2 (May 1995)

Otto Billig, *The Lawyer Terrorist and His Comrades,* Political Psychology, Vol. 6, No.1 (March 1985)

Pablo Brum, *Revisiting Urban Guerrillas: Armed Propaganda and the Insurgency of Uruguay's MLN-Tupamaros, 1969–70,* Studies in Conflict & Terrorism, Vol. 37, No. 5 (2014)

Paddy Woodworth, *Why Do They Kill? The Basque Conflict in Spain,* World Policy Journal, Vol. 18, No. 1 (Spring 2001)

Paul Gill and John Horgan, *Who Were the Volunteers? The Shifting Sociological and Operational Profile of 1240 Provisional Irish Republican Army Members,* Terrorism and Political Violence, Vol. 25, No. 3 (2013)

Paul Gill, *Suicide Bomber Pathways among Islamic Militants*, Policing, Vol. 2, No. 4 (2008)

Peter Bergen and Katherine Tiedemann, *The Almanac of Al Qaeda*, Foreign Policy, May/June 2010

Peter Heehs, *Terrorism in India during the Freedom Struggle*, The Historian (Spring 1993)

Peter Rosendorff and Todd Sandler, *Too Much of a Good Thing? The Proactive Response Dilemma*, Journal of Conflict Resolution, Vol. 48, No. 4 (2004)

Philip Thomas, *Emergency and Anti-Terrorism Power: 9/11: USA and UK*, 26 Fordham International Law Journal, Vol. 26 (April 2003)

Randy Burkett, *An Alternative Framework for Agent Recruitment: From MICE to RASCLS*, Studies in Intelligence, Vol. 57, No. 1 (March 2013)

Raphael Cohen-Almagor, *The Terrorists' Best Ally: The Quebec Media Coverage of the FLQ Crisis in October 1970*, Canadian Journal of Communication, Vol. 25, No.2 (2000)

Reg Whitaker, *Keeping up with the Neighbours? Canadian Responses to 9/11 in Historical and Comparative Context*, Osgoode Hall Law Journal Vol. 41 (Summer/Fall 2003)

Régius Debray, *Latin America: The Long March*, New Left Review, No. 33 (September–October 1965)

Richard Bach Jensen, *Daggers, Rifles and Dynamite: Anarchist Terrorism in Nineteenth Century Europe*, Terrorism and Political Violence, Vol. 16, No. 1 (Spring 2004)

Richard Bach Jensen, *Nineteenth Century Anarchist Terrorism: How Comparable to the Terrorism of al-Qaeda?*, Journal of Terrorism and Political Violence, Vol. 20, No. 4 (2008)

Richard Bach Jensen, *The International Anti-Anarchist Conference of 1898 and the Origins of Interpol*, Journal of Contemporary History, Vol. 16, 1981 at 323–347

Richard Bach Jensen, *The Pre-1914 Anarchist "Lone Wolf" Terrorist and Government Responses*, Journal of Terrorism and Political Violence, Vol. 26, No. 1 (2014)

Richard Pickering, *Terrorism, Extremism, Radicalization and the Offender Management System: The Story So far*, Prison Service Journal, No. 203 (September 2012)

Robert Agnew, *Foundation for a General Strain Theory of Crime and Delinquency*, Criminology, Vol. 30, No. 1 (February 1992)

Robert Beck and Anthony Clark Arend, *"Don't Tread On Us": International Law and Forcible State Responses to Terrorism*, Wisconsin International Law Journal, Vol. 12 (Spring 1994)

Robert Clark, *Patterns in the Lives of ETA Members*, Studies in Conflict and Terrorism, Vol. 6, No. 3 (1983)

Robert Hager and David Lake, *Balancing Empires: Competitive Decolonization in International Politics*, Security Studies, Vol. 9, No. 3 (Spring 2000)

Robert Powell, *Defending Against Terrorist Attacks with Limited Resources*, American Political Science Review, Vol. 101, No. 3 (2007)

Robert Rotberg, *Failed States in a World of Terror*, Foreign Affairs (July/August 2002)

Robert Sampson, Stephen Raudenbush, Felton Earls, Neighborhoods and violent crime: A multilevel study of collective efficacy, *Science*, Vol. 277 (August 1997)

Robert White, *Commitment, Efficacy, and Personal Sacrifice Among Irish Republicans*, Journal of Political and Military Sociology, Vol. 16 (1988)

Robert White, *From Peaceful Protest to Guerrilla War: Micromobilization of the Provisional Irish Republican Army*, American Journal of Sociology, Vol. 94, No. 6 (May 1989)

Roberta Senechal de la Roche, *Toward a Scientific Theory of Terrorism*, Sociological Theory, Vol. 22, No. 1 (March 2004)

S. Alexander Haslam and Stephen Reicher, *When Prisoners Take Over the Prison: A Social Psychology of Resistance*, Personality and Social Psychology Review, Vol. 16, No. 2 (2012)

S. K. Mittal and Irfan Habib, *The Congress and the Revolutionaries in the 1920s*, Social Scientist, Vol. 10, No. 6 (June 1982)

Saad Eddin Ibrahim, *Anatomy of Egypt's Militant Groups: Methodological Note and Preliminary Findings*, International Journal of Middle East Studies, Vol. 12, No. 4 (1980)

Saul Kassin and Christina Fong, *"I'm Innocent!": Effects of Training on Judgments of Truth and Deception in the Interrogation Room*, Law and Human Behavior, Vol. 23, No. 5 (1999)

Saul Kassin, Steven Drizin, Thomas Grisso, Gisli Gudjonsson, Richard Leo and Allison Redlich, Police-Induced Confessions: Risk Factors and Recommendations, Law and Human Behavior, Vol. 34, No. 3 (February 2010)

Scott Atran, *The Moral Logic and Growth of Suicide Terrorism*, The Washington Quarterly, Vol. 29, No. 2 (2006)

Sean Maloney, *A Mere Rustle of Leaves: Canadian Strategy and the 1970 FLQ Crisis*, Canadian Military Journal (Summer 2000)

Seth Schwartz, Curtis Dunkel and Alan Waterman, *Terrorism: An Identity Theory Perspective*, Studies in Conflict and Terrorism, Vol. 32, No. 6 (2009)

Shandon Harris-Hogan, *The Importance of Family: The Key to Understanding the Evolution of Jihadism in Australia*, Security Challenges, Vol. 10, No. 1 (2014)

Shane Kenna, *'One skilled scientist is worth an army' — The Fenian Dynamite campaign 1881–85*, The Irish Story, 13 February 2012

Sheldon Himelfarb, *The Quiet Revolution*, Foreign Policy, 3 October 2013

Shira Maguen and Brett Litz, *Moral Injury in Veterans of War*, PTSD Research Quarterly, Vol. 23, No. 1 (2012)

Sidney Tarrow, *Cycles of Collective Action: Between Moments of Madness and the Repertoire of Contention*, Social Science History, Vol. 17, No. 2 (Summer 1993)

Steve Ratner, *Corporations and Human Rights: A Theory of Legal Responsibility*, Yale Law Journal, Vol. 111 (2001)

Steven David, *Israel's Policy of Targeted Killing*, Ethics and International Affairs, Vol. 17, No. 1 (2003)

Sulastri Osman, *Jemaah Islamiyah: Of Kin and Kind*, Journal of Current Southeast Asian Affairs, Vol. 29, No. 2 (2010)

Sylvain Vité, *Typology of Armed Conflicts in International Humanitarian Law: Legal Concepts and Actual Situations*, International Review of the Red Cross, Vol. 91, No. 873 (March 2009)

Thomas Hegghammer, *Should I stay or Should I Go? Explaining Variation in Western Jihadists' Choice between Domestic and Foreign Fighting*, American Political Science Review, Vol. 107, No. 1 (February 2013)

Thomas Hegghammer, *Terrorist Recruitment and Radicalization in Saudi Arabia*, Middle East Policy, Vol. 13, No. 4 (Winter 2006)

Thomas Hegghammer, *Why Terrorists Weep: The Socio-Cultural Practices of Jihadi Militants*, Paul Wilkinson Memorial Lecture, University of St. Andrews, 16 April 2015

Thomas McDonnell, *Sow What You Reap? Using Predator and Reaper Drones to Carry Out Assassinations or Targeted Killings of Suspected Islamic Terrorists*, George Washington International Law Review, Vol. 44 (2012)

Tim Krieger and Daniel Meierrieks, *What Causes Terrorism?*, Public Choice, Vol. 147, No. 1/2 (April 2011)

Tom Parker, *Redressing the Balance: How Human Rights Defenders Can Use Victim Narratives to Confront the Violence of Armed Groups*, Human Rights Quarterly, Vol. 33, No. 4 (November 2011)

Tom Parker and Nick Sitter, *Fighting Fire with Water: NGO and Counter-Terrorism Policy Tools*, Global Policy, Vol. 5, No. 2 (May 2014)

Tom Parker, *It's a Trap: Provoking an Overreaction is Terrorism 101*, Royal United Services Institute Journal, Vol. 160, No.3 (June/July 2015)

Tom Parker and Nick Sitter, *The Four Horsemen of Terrorism: It's Not Waves, It's Strains*, Journal of Terrorism and Political Violence, Vol. 28, No. 2 (2016)

Ursula Daxecker and Michael Hess, *Repression Hurts: Coercive Government Responses and the Demise of Terrorist Campaigns*, British Journal of Political Science, Vol. 43, No. 3 (2012)

Vamik Voltan, *Trauma, Identity, and Search for a Solution in Cyprus*, Insight Turkey, Vol. 10, No. 4 (2008)

Virginia Fortna, *Do Terrorists Win? Rebels' Use of Terrorism and Civil War Outcomes*, International Organization, Vol. 69, No. 03 (June 2015)

W. H. Nagel, *A Socio-legal View on the Suppression of Terrorists*, International Journal of the Society of Law, Vol. 8, 213–221 (1980)

W. Michael Reisman, *International Legal Responses to Terrorism*, Houston Journal of International Law, Vol. 22, No. 3 (1999)

Walter Enders and Todd Sandler, *The Effectiveness of Antiterrorism Policies: A Vector-autoregression-Intervention Analysis*, American Political Science Review, Vol. 87, No. 4 (December 1993)

Walter Laqueur, *The Futility of Terrorism*, Harper's Magazine, March 1976

Wesley Kilham and Leon Mann, *Level of Destructive Obedience as a Function of Transmitter and Executant Roles in the Milgram Obedience Paradigm*, Journal of Personality and Social Psychology, Vol. 29, No. 5 (1974)

Wilfried Rasch, *Psychological Dimensions of Political Terrorism in the Federal Republic of Germany*, International Journal of Law and Psychiatry, Vol. 2, No. 1 (1979)

William Eubank and Leonard Weinberg, *Does Democracy Encourage Terrorism?*, Terrorism and Political Violence, Vol. 6, No. 4 (1994)

William Eubank and Leonard Weinberg, *Terrorism and Democracy: What Recent Events Disclose?*, Terrorism and Political Violence, Vol. 10, No. 1 (1998)

William McCants, *The Foreign Policy Essay — Special Edition: First, Do No Harm*, Lawfare, 17 February 2015

William Rose and Rysia Murphy, *Does Terrorism Ever Work? The 2004 Madrid Train Bombings*, Correspondence, International Security, Vol. 32, No. 1 (Summer 2007)

Wing Commander A. J. C. Walters, *Air Control: Past, Present, Future?*, Air Power Review, Vol. 8, No. 4 (Winter 2005)

Yael Stein, *By Any Name Illegal and Immoral*, Ethics and International Affairs, Vol. 17, No.1 (Spring 2003)

Yoshikuni Igarashi, *Dead Bodies and Living Guns: The United Red Army and Its Deadly Pursuit of Revolution, 1971–1972,* Japanese Studies, Vol. 27, No. 2 (2007)

Ze'ev Iviansky, *Individual Terror: Concept and Typology*, Journal of Contemporary History, Vol. 12, No. (1977)

## Reports

Anneli Botha, *Radicalisation in Kenya: Recruitment to al-Shabaab and the Mobasa Republican Council,* Paper 265 (Institute for Security Studies; September 2014)

Arie Perliger, *Challengers from the Sidelines: Understanding America's Violent Far-Right* (Combating Terrorism Centre at West Point; November 2012)

Ashley Jackson, *Nowhere to Turn: The Failure to Protect Civilians in Afghanistan,* A Joint Briefing Paper by 29 Aid Organizations Working in Afghanistan for the NATO Heads of Government Summit. Lisbon, 19–20 November 2010

*Basic Human Rights Reference Guide: Security Infrastructure,* Working Group on protecting human rights while countering terrorism, United Nations Counter-Terrorism Implementation Task Force, September 2010

Basic Principles on the Use of Force and Firearms by Law Enforcement Officials, Adopted by the Eighth United Nations Congress on the Prevention of Crime and the Treatment of Offenders, Havana, Cuba, 27 August to 7 September 1990

Bernard Rostker, Lawrence Hanser, William Hix, Carl Jensen, Andrew Morral, Greg Ridgeway and Terry Schell, *Evaluation of the New York City Police Department Firearm Training and Firearm-Discharge Review Process* (RAND Corporation; 2008)

Bonnie Cordes, *When Terrorists do the Talking: Reflections on Terrorist Literature,* The Rand Corporation, August 1987

Brian Michael Jenkins, *Would-be Warriors: Incidents of Jihadist Terrorism Radicalization in the United States since September 11, 2001* (RAND Corporation; 2010)

Bruce MacFarlane, *Wrongful Convictions: The Effect of Tunnel Vision and Predisposing Circumstances in the Criminal Justice System,* Prepared for the Inquiry into Pediatric Forensic Pathology in Ontario, The Honourable Stephen T. Goudge, Commissioner (2008)

Cass Sunstein and Richard Zeckhauser, *Overreaction to Fearsome Risks*, Environmental and Resource Economics, Vol. 48, No. 3 (2011)

Center on Law and Security, *Highlights from the Terrorist Trial Report Card 2001–2009: Lessons Learned*, New York University School of Law (January 2010)

Charles Kurzman, *Muslim American Terrorism in 2013* (Triangle Center on Terrorism and Homeland Security; 2014)

Charlie Winter, *Media Jihad: The Islamic State's Doctrine for Information Warfare*, International Centre for the Study of Radicalisation and Terrorist Violence (2017)

Chris Toensing and Ian Urbina, *Israel, the US and "Targeted Killings"*, Middle East Research and Information Project, 17 February 2003

Col. John Venhaus, *Why Youth Join al-Qaeda*, United States Institute of Peace: Special Report No. 236 (May 2010)

Council of Europe, *Terrorism: Special Investigation Techniques* (April 2005)

Crown Prosecution Service, *Achieving Best Evidence in Criminal Proceedings: Guidance on interviewing victims and witnesses, and guidance on using special measures* (Ministry of Justice; March 2011)

Daniel Byman and Avi Dicter, *Israel's Lessons for Fighting Terrorists and Their Implications for the United States*, The Saban Center at the Brookings Institution, Analysis Paper No. 8, March 2006

David Jaeger, Esteban Klor, Sami Miaari and Daniele Paserman, *The Struggle for Palestinian Hearts and Minds: Violence and Public Opinion in the Second Intifada*, National Bureau of Economic Research, Working Paper No. 13956 (April 2008)

David Ronfeldt, *The Mitrione Kidnapping in Uruguay* (RAND Corporation; 1987)

Edwin Bakker and Peter Grol, *Motives and Considerations of Potential Foreign Fighters from The Netherlands* (International Centre for Counter-Terrorism Policy Brief; July 2015)

Eli Berman and David Laitin, *Religion, Terrorism and Public Goods: Testing the Club Model*, National Bureau of Economic Research, Working Paper No. 13725, January 2008

Eli Berman, *Hamas, Taliban and the Jewish Underground: An Economist's View of Radical Religious Militias*, National Bureau of Economic Research Working Paper, No. 10004 (2003)

European Court of Human Rights, *Fact Sheet: Terrorism and the ECHR*, Press Unit, January 2014

Executive Office of the President of the United States, *Strategic Implementation Plan for Empowering Local Partners to Prevent Violent Extremism in the United States*, 1 December 2011

Global Counterterrorism Forum, *Ankara Memorandum on Good Practices for a Multi-Sectoral Approach to Countering Violent Extremism* (March 2013)

Global Counterterrorism Forum, *Good Practices on Community Engagement and Community — Oriented Policing as Tools to Counter Violent Extremism* (March 2013)

*Guidebook: Understanding Intelligence Oversight*, Geneva Center for the Democratic Control of Armed Forces (DCAF) (2010)

*Guidelines on Memory and the Law: Recommendations from the Scientific Study of Human Memory*, British Psychological Society Research Board (June 2008)

Guilain Denoeux and Lynn Carter, *Guide to the Drivers of Violent Extremism* (United States Agency for International Development; February 2009)

Hamed el-Said and Richard Barrett, *Enhancing the Understanding of the Foreign Terrorist Fighters Phenomenon in Syria*, United Nations Office of Counter-Terrorism, July 2017

Hamed el-Said, *De-Radicalisation Islamists: Programmes and their Impact in Muslim States*, International Centre for the Study of Radicalisation and Political Violence, January 2012

*Handbook on Criminal Justice Responses to Terrorism*, United Nations Office on Drugs and Crime, 2009

HM Government, *Prevent Strategy* (HM Stationary Office; June 2011)

Human Rights Committee, *General Comment No. 6,*

Human Rights Committee, *General Comment No. 8,*

Human Rights Committee, *General Comment No. 13,*

Human Rights Committee, *General Comment No.16,*

Human Rights Committee, *General Comment No. 21,*

Human Rights Committee, *General Comment No. 22,*

Human Rights Committee, *General Comment No. 29,*

Human Rights Committee, *General Comment No. 32,*

Human Rights Committee, *General Comment No. 35 on article 9 (Liberty and security of person)*, 2014

Human Rights First, *Al Qaeda and ISIL Use of Guantanamo Bay Prison in Propaganda and Materials*, Issue Brief, May 2015

Human Rights Watch, *World Report 2017: Events of 2016*, 2017

Intelligence and Security Committee, *Report into the London Terrorist Attacks on 7 July 2005* (HM Stationary Office; May 2006)

Intelligence Science Board, *Educing Information — Interrogation: Science and Art, Foundations for the Future*, Center for Strategic Intelligence Research, National Defense Intelligence College, December 2006

International Committee of the Red Cross, *The Use of Force in Armed Conflicts: Interplay Between the Conduct of Hostilities and law Enforcement Paradigms*, Expert Meeting, 2012

International Crisis Group, *"Deradicalisation" and Indonesian Prisons*, Asia Report No. 142, 19 November 2007

James Khalil and Martine Zeuthen, *Countering Violent Extremism and Risk Reduction*, Royal United Services Institute Whitehall Report 2–16, June 2016

Jessica Stern, *Deradicalization or Disengagement of Terrorists: Is It Possible?*, A Future Challenges Essay, Koret-Taube Task Force on National Security and Law, Hoover Institution, Stanford University (2010)

*Joint Study on Global Practices in Relation to Secret Detention in the Context of Countering Terrorism of the Special Rapporteur on the promotion and protection of human rights and fundamental freedoms while countering terrorism, Martin Scheinin; the Special Rapporteur on torture and other cruel, inhuman or degrading treatment or punishment, Manfred Nowak; the Working Group on Arbitrary Detention; and the Working Group on Enforced and Involuntary Disappearances*, A/HRC/13/42, 19 February 2010

*Joint study on global practices in relation to secret detention in the context of countering terrorism of the Special Rapporteur on the promotion and protection of human rights and fundamental freedoms while countering terrorism, Martin Scheinin; the Special Rapporteur on torture and other cruel, inhuman or degrading treatment or punishment, Manfred Nowak; the Working Group on Arbitrary Detention represented by its Vice-Chair, Shaheen Sardar Ali; and the Working Group on Enforced and Involuntary Disappearances represented by its Chair, Jeremy Sarkin*, Human Rights Council, A/HRC/13/42, 19 February 2010

Jonathan Cooper, *Countering Terrorism, Protecting Human Rights: A Manual*, Office for Democratic Institutions and Human Rights, Organization for Security and Cooperation in Europe, 2007

Joseph Felter and Jarret Brachman, *An Assessment of 516 Combatant Status Review Tribunal Unclassified Summaries*, Combating Terrorism Center Report (15 July 2007)

*Journey to Extremism in Africa: Drivers, Incentives and The Tipping Point for Recruitment*, United Nations Development Programme (2017)

Kate Clark, *The Takhar Attack: Targeted killings and the parallel worlds of US intelligence and Afghanistan*, Afghan Analysts Network, Thematic Report 05/2011

Katya Leney-Hall, *The Evolution of Franchise Terrorism: Al-Qaeda*, Hellenic Foundation for European and Foreign Policy, Working Paper No. 1 (September 2008)

Kevin Matthees and Günter Seufert, *Erdoğan and Öcalan Begin Talks: A Paradigm Shift in Turkey's Kurdish Policy and a New Strategy of the PKK*, German Institute for International and Security Affairs, Comments No. 13, April 2013

Kris Christmann, *Preventing Religious Radicalisation and Violent Extremism: A Systematic Review of the Research Evidence*, Youth Justice Board for England and Wales (2012)

Luke Condra, Joseph Felter, Radha Iyengar, and Jacob Shapiro, *The Effect of Civilian Casualties in Afghanistan and Iraq*, Working Paper 16152, National Bureau of Economic Research, July 2010, DTIC Online (ADA524439)

Madeleine Shaw and Vaughne Miller, *Detention of Suspected International Terrorists — Part 4 of the Anti-Terrorism, Crime and Security Act 2001*, House of Commons Library, Research paper 02/52, 16 September 2002

María Martín, *Criminalization of Human Rights Defenders: Categorisation of the Problem and Measures in Response*, Protection International, December 2015

Mark Stewart and John Mueller, *Cost-Benefit Assessment of United States Homeland Security Spending*, Research Report No. 273.01.2009, Centre for Infrastructure Performance and Reliability, University of Newcastle, Australia, January 2009

Micah Zenko, *Reforming US Drone Strike Policies*, Council on Foreign Relations (2013)

Michael Flynn, Matt Pottinger and Paul Batchelor, *Fixing Intel: A Blueprint for Making Intelligence Relevant in Afghanistan*, Center for a New American Security (January 2010)

Minerva Nasser-Eddine, Bridget Garnham, Katerina Agostino and Gilbert Caluya, *Countering Violent Extremism (CVE) Literature Review* (Australian Government, Department of Defence; March 2011)

Mitchell Silber and Arvin Bhatt, *Radicalization in the West: The Homegrown Threat*, New York Police Department (Intelligence Division), 2007

Mohammed Ali Musawi, *Cheering for Osama: How Jihadists use Internet Discussion Forums*, Quilliam Foundation (London; August 2010)

Naomi Feldman and Bradley Ruffle, *Religious Terrorism: A Cross-Country Analysis*, Samuel Neaman Institute, Economics of National Security Working Paper Series (March 2008)

National Coordinator for Counter-Terrorism (NCTb), *Countering Radicalization: Perspectives and Strategies from Around the World* (Ministerie van Binnenlandse Zaken; March 2008)

Naureen Chowdhury Fink and Jack Barclay, *Mastering the Narrative: Counterterrorism Strategic Communication and the United Nations*, Center on Global Counterterrorism Cooperation (2013)

Naureen Chowdhury Fink and Rafia Barakat, *Strengthening Community Resilience against Violence and Extremism: The Roles of Women in South Asia*, Center on Global Counterterrorism Cooperation (2013)

Nick Adams, Ted Nordhaus and Michael Shellenberger, *Planes, Trains and Car Bombs: The Method Behind the Madness of Terrorism*, The Science of Security (Breakthrough Institute; January 2012)

Noman Benotman and Nikita Malik, *The Children of Islamic State*, Quilliam Foundation (March 2016)

Note by the Secretary General, *Promotion and Protection of the Rights to Freedom of Opinion and Expression*, A/66/290, 10 August 2011

Office for Democratic Institutions and Human Rights and the OSCE Secretariat Transnational Threats Department, *Preventing Terrorism and Countering Violent Extremism and Radicalization that Lead to Terrorism: A Community Policing Approach* (Organization for Security and Cooperation in Europe; 2014)

Office for Democratic Institutions and Human Rights, *Human Rights In Counter-Terrorism Investigations: A Practical Manual for Law Enforcement Officers* (Organization for Security and Cooperation in Europe; 2013)

Office of Legal Counsel US Department of Justice, *Memorandum for Alberto R. Gonzales Counsel to the President Re: Standards of Conduct for Interrogation under 18 USC §§ 2340–2340A*, 1 August 2002

Office of the High Commissioner for Human Rights, *Human Rights Standards and Practice for the Police*, Expanded Pocket Book on Human Rights for the Police, Professional Training Series No. 5/Add.3 (2004)

Open Source Center, *Special Report: Al Qaeda Master Narratives and Affiliate Case Studies* (September 2011)

Paul Collier and Anne Hoeffler, *Greed and Grievance in Civil War*, World Bank, Policy Research Working Paper No. 2355 (2000)

Paul Collier, *Economic Causes of Civil Conflict and Their Implications for Policy*, in Chester Crocker, Fen Osler Hampson and Pamela Aal (eds.), *Turbulent Peace: The Challenge of Managing International Conflict* (United States Institute of Peace; 2001)

Paul Davis and Kim Cragin (eds.), *Social Science for Counterterrorism: Putting the Pieces Together* (Rand; 2009)

Peter Bergen, Courtney Schuster and David Sterman, *ISIS in the West: The New Faces of Extremism* (New America Foundation; November 2015)

Peter Neumann, *Prisons and Terrorism: Radicalisation and De-radicalisation in 15 Countries,* The International Centre for the Study of Radicalisation and Political Violence, 2010

*Report of the Constitution Project's Task Force on Detainee Treatment* (The Constitution Project; 2013)

*Report of the Governor's Commission on Capital Punishment, George H. Ryan Governor* (15 April 2002)

*Report of the Kaufman Commission on Proceedings Involving Guy Paul Morin: The Honourable Fred Kaufman, C.M., Q.C.* (31 March 1998)

Report of the Secretary General, *Uniting against terrorism: recommendations for a global counter-terrorism strategy,* A/60/825, April 27, 2006

*Report of the Special Rapporteur on extrajudicial, summary or arbitrary executions, Philip Alston, Addendum: Study on targeted killings* (A/HRC/14/24/Add.6)

*Report of the Special Rapporteur on the promotion and protection of human rights and fundamental freedoms while countering terrorism: Ten areas of best practices in countering terrorism,* United Nations Human Rights Council, A/HRC/16/51, 22 December 2010

*Report of the Special Rapporteur on the Promotion and Protection of Human Rights and Fundamental Freedoms while Countering Terrorism,* A/68/389, 18 September 2013

*Report of the Special Rapporteur on the Promotion and Protection of the Right to the Freedom of Opinion and Expression, Frank La Rue,* Human Rights Council, A/HRC/23/40, 17 April 2013

Report of the Special Representative on human rights defenders, UN Doc. A/58/380, 18 September 2003

*Report of the Working Group on Arbitrary Detention* (A/HRC/22/44), Part III, Deliberation No. 9 concerning the definition and scope of 'arbitrary deprivation of liberty' under customary international law, 24 December 2012

Richard Barrett, *The Islamic State* (The Soufan Group; November 2014)

Rik Coolsaet, *Facing the Fourth Foreign Fighter Wave: What Drives Europeans to Syria, and to Islamic State? Insights from the Belgian Case,* Egmont-Royal Institute for International Relations, March 2016

Rui de Figueiredo Jnr and Barry Weingast, *Vicious Cycles: Endogenous Political Extremism and Political Violence,* Working Paper No. 9, Institute of Governmental Studies, University of California Berkeley, 2001

Saad Eddin Ibrahim, *Egypt's Islamic Militants,* Middle East Research and Information Project (MERIP) Reports 103 (February 1982)

Stephen Krasner, *A Grand Strategy Essay: Transnational Terrorism*, Working Group on Foreign Policy and Grand Strategy (Hoover Institution; 2014)

Stephen White and Kiernan McEvoy, *Countering Violent Extremism: Community Engagement Programmes in Europe*, Qatar International Academy for Security Studies (February 2012)

*Terrorism and Human Rights: Progress report prepared by Ms. Kalliopi K. Koufa, Special Rapporteur*, Economic and Social Council, E/CN.4/Sub.2/2001/31, 27 June 2001

*The 9/11 Commission Report: Final Report of the National Commission on Terrorist Attacks Upon the United States*, Authorized Edition (W. W. Norton and Company; 2004)

United Nations Development Programme, *Global Expert Consultation: Radicalization and Its Implications for Development, Violence Prevention and Conflict Resolution*, Summary Report, May 2014

United Nations General Assembly, *The United Nations Global Counter Terrorism Strategy*, A/RES/60/288, 20 September 2006

United Nations Office of the High Commissioner for Human Rights, *Fact Sheet No. 32: Human Rights, Terrorism and Counter-Terrorism* (2008)

United Nations Office on Drugs and Crime, *Current practices in electronic surveillance in the investigation of serious and organized crime* (2009)

United Nations Office on Drugs and Crime, *Handbook for Prison Leaders: A basic training tool and curriculum for prison managers based on international standards and norms*, Criminal Justice Handbook Series (2010)

United Nations Office on Drugs and Crime, *Handbook on Criminal Justice Responses to Terrorism* (2009)

United Nations Office on Drugs and Crime, *The Criminal Justice Response to Support Victims of Acts of Terrorism* (2011)

United Nations Office on Drugs and Crime, *The Use of the Internet for Terrorist Purposes* (2012)

United Nations Security Council, *Letter dated 19 May 2015 from the Chair of the Security Council Committee pursuant to resolutions 1267 (1999) and 1989 (2011) concerning Al-Qaida and associated individuals and entities addressed to the President of the Security Council*, S/2015/358, 19 May 2015

United Nations Special Rapporteur on the promotion and protection of human rights and fundamental freedoms while countering terrorism, Martin Scheinin, *Report to the UN Human Rights Council*, 17 May 2010, A/HRC/14/46

United Nations, *Symposium on Supporting Victims of Terrorism* (2008)

United States Agency for International Development, *Guide to the Drivers of Violent Extremism* (February 2009)

United States Senate Armed Services Committee, *Inquiry into the Treatment of Detainees in U.S. Custody*, 20 November 2008

United States Senate Select Committee on Intelligence, *Committee Study of the Central Intelligence Agency's Detention and Interrogation Program*, released 9 December 2014

USAID Policy, *The Development Response to Violent Extremism and Insurgency*, United States Agency for International Development (September 2011)

Vidhya Ramalingam, *On the Front Line: A guide to Countering far-right Extremism* (Institute for Strategic Dialogue; 2014)

# Index

# Insurgency and Terrorism Series

*(Continuation of series card page)*

CPSIA information can be obtained
at www.ICGtesting.com
Printed in the USA
BVHW040556190619
551261BV00003B/6/P